THE OXFORD HANDBOOK OF

EDUCATION AND GLOBALIZATION

OXFORD LIBRARY OF
INTERNATIONAL SOCIAL POLICY

EDITORS-IN-CHIEF
Douglas Besharov and Neil Gilbert
In collaboration with the International Network
for Social Policy Teaching and Research

Oxford Handbook Governance and Management for Social Policy
Edited by Karen J. Baehler

Oxford International Handbook of Family Policy: A Life-Course Perspective
Edited by Mary Daly, Birgit Pfau-Effinger, Neil Gilbert, and Douglas J. Besharov

Oxford International Handbook of Child Protection Systems
Edited by Jill Duerr Berrick, Neil Gilbert, and Marit Skivenes

Oxford Handbook of Education and Globalization
Edited by Paola Mattei, Xavier Dumay, Eric Mangez, and Jacqueline Behrend

Oxford Handbook of Program Design and Implementation Evaluation
Edited by Anu Rangarajan

THE OXFORD HANDBOOK OF
EDUCATION AND GLOBALIZATION

Edited by
PAOLA MATTEI, XAVIER DUMAY,
ERIC MANGEZ,
and
JACQUELINE BEHREND

Oxford University Press is a department of the University of Oxford. It furthers
the University's objective of excellence in research, scholarship, and education
by publishing worldwide. Oxford is a registered trade mark of Oxford University
Press in the UK and certain other countries.

Published in the United States of America by Oxford University Press
198 Madison Avenue, New York, NY 10016, United States of America.

© Oxford University Press 2023

All rights reserved. No part of this publication may be reproduced, stored in
a retrieval system, or transmitted, in any form or by any means, without the
prior permission in writing of Oxford University Press, or as expressly permitted
by law, by license, or under terms agreed with the appropriate reproduction
rights organization. Inquiries concerning reproduction outside the scope of the
above should be sent to the Rights Department, Oxford University Press, at the
address above.

You must not circulate this work in any other form
and you must impose this same condition on any acquirer.

Library of Congress Cataloging-in-Publication Data
Names: Mattei, Paola, 1974, author. | Dumay, Xavier, author. |
Mangez, Eric, author. | Behrend, Jacqueline, 1975, author.
Title: The Oxford handbook of education and globalization / Paola Mattei, Xavier Dumay,
Eric Mangez, Jacqueline Behrend.
Other titles: Handbook of education and globalization
Description: New York, NY : Oxford University Press, [2023] |
Series: Oxford library of international social policy |
Includes bibliographical references and index.
Identifiers: LCCN 2022054459 (print) | LCCN 2022054460 (ebook) |
ISBN 9780197570685 (hardback) | ISBN 9780197570715 |
ISBN 9780197570708 (epub)
Subjects: LCSH: Education and globalization. | Education and state. |
Education—Social aspects.
Classification: LCC LC191 .D747 2023 (print) | LCC LC191 (ebook) |
DDC 379—dc23/eng/20221216
LC record available at https://lccn.loc.gov/2022054459
LC ebook record available at https://lccn.loc.gov/2022054460

DOI: 10.1093/oxfordhb/9780197570685.001.0001

Printed by Integrated Books International, United States of America

CONTENTS

Preface xi
List of Contributors xix

PART I SOCIAL THEORY, GLOBALIZATION, AND EDUCATION

Introduction to Part I 3
Xavier Dumay and Eric Mangez

Section I: Culture, Globalization, and Education

1. Globalizing Nation States and National Education Projects 29
Francisco O. Ramirez and Seungah S. Lee

2. An Anthropological Perspective on Globalization and Schooling 51
Kathryn Anderson-Levitt

3. Historical Institutionalism in Education and Globalization 76
Lukas Graf

4. Education in a Postliberal World Society 96
Jared Furuta, John W. Meyer, and Patricia Bromley

5. World Culture, Education, and Organization 119
Minju Choi, Hannah K. D'Apice, Nadine Ann Skinner, and Patricia Bromley

6. Globalization, New Institutionalisms, and the Political Dimension 147
Christian Maroy and Xavier Pons

7. Globalization, Cultural Logics, and the Teaching Profession 170
Gerald K. LeTendre

8. Higher Education and Organizational Theory: Systems, Fields, Markets, and Populations in an Increasingly Global Context   191
JEROEN HUISMAN

Section II: Structural Approaches to Globalization in Education

9. The Globalization of Expertise?: Epistemic Governance, Quantification, and the Consultocracy   213
JENNY OZGA

10. Globalization, Personalization, and the Learning Apparatus   228
MAARTEN SIMONS

11. Field Theory Beyond the Nation State   248
JULIAN HAMANN

12. Inclusive Education, Globalization, and New Philosophical Perspectives on Social Justice   267
MARIE VERHOEVEN AND AMANDINE BERNAL GONZALEZ

13. Globalization, Uncertainty, and the Returns to Education Over the Life Course in Modern Societies   287
HANS-PETER BLOSSFELD AND GWENDOLIN J. BLOSSFELD

14. Globalization of Education and the Sociology of Elites   304
CAROLINE BERTRON AND AGNÈS VAN ZANTEN

15. Mobilizing Whiteness: Race, Futurity, and Globalization of Higher Education   328
RIYAD A. SHAHJAHAN AND KIRSTEN T. EDWARDS

Section III: Systems Theory, Globalization, and Education

16. Education in a Functionally Differentiated World Society   351
RAF VANDERSTRAETEN

17. Education Reform as a Global Phenomenon   367
GIANCARLO CORSI

18. The Rats Under the Rug: The Morphogenesis of Education in a Global Context   385
PIETER VANDEN BROECK

19. Redrawing What Counts as Education: The Impact of the Global
    Early Childhood Education Program on German Kindergarten   404
    CHRISTINE WEINBACH

20. The University as a World Organization   424
    RUDOLF STICHWEH

21. Small Worlds: Homeschooling and the Modern Family   443
    ERIC MANGEZ AND ALICE TILMAN

PART II POLICY CHALLENGES AND IMPLICATIONS OF GLOBAL PRESSURES ON NATIONAL EDUCATION SYSTEMS

Introduction to Part II   461
PAOLA MATTEI AND JACQUELINE BEHREND

Section IV: International Organizations and Education Policy

22. The Expansion of Education in and Across International
    Organizations   481
    KERSTIN MARTENS, DENNIS NIEMANN, AND DAVID KROGMANN

23. The OECD's Boundary Work in Education in the United States and
    Brazil: A Historical Comparative Analysis of Two Federal States   498
    CHRISTIAN YDESEN AND NANNA RAMSING ENEMARK

24. Playing God: Education Data Visualizations and the Art of
    World-Making   518
    SOTIRIA GREK

Section V: The Responses of National Education Systems to Global Pressures

25. The PISA Pendulum: Political Discourse and Education Reform in
    the Age of Global Reference Societies   539
    LOUIS VOLANTE

26. Why Globalization Hardly Affects Education Systems: A Historical
    Institutionalist View   554
    JULIAN L. GARRITZMANN AND SUSANNE GARRITZMANN

27. Policy Advice and Policy Advisory Systems in Education   576
    MARIA TULLIA GALANTI

viii   CONTENTS

28. The Formation and Development of a Norwegian Accountability
System   594
    ASTRID TOLO

Section VI: The Massification of Secondary Education

29. Diffusion of Mass Education: Pathways to Isomorphism   615
    FABIAN BESCHE-TRUTHE, HELEN SEITZER, AND MICHAEL WINDZIO

30. The Politics of Equality in Secondary Education Across Wealthy
Postwar Democracies   633
    JANE R. GINGRICH, ANJA GIUDICI, AND DANIEL MCARTHUR

31. Examining the Impact of Educational Reforms on Schooling and
Competences in PIAAC   657
    LORENZO CAPPELLARI, DANIELE CHECCHI, AND MARCO OVIDI

32. Educational Expansion and Inequality: School in Italy in the Second
Part of the 20th Century   672
    GABRIELE BALLARINO AND NAZARENO PANICHELLA

Section VII: Globalization of Higher Education and Science

33. Can Non-Western Countries Escape From Catch-Up Modernity?
The Troubling Case of Japan's Education Reforms in a Global Era   695
    TAKEHIKO KARIYA

34. The Global Scale in Higher Education and Research   711
    SIMON MARGINSON

35. The Globalization of Science: The Increasing Power of Individual
Scientists   728
    MAREK KWIEK

36. China's Responses to Globalization and Higher Education Reforms:
Challenges and Policy Implications   762
    KA HO MOK, GUO GUO KE, AND ZHEN TIAN

37. Reforming Higher Education in India in Pursuit of Excellence,
Expansion, and Equity   783
    JANDHYALA B. G. TILAK

CONTENTS ix

38. The Rehabilitation of the Concept of Public Good: Reappraising the Attacks From Liberalism and Neoliberalism From a Poststructuralist Perspective   824

MARK OLSSEN

Section VIII: Latin America

39. Educational Challenges in Latin America: An Outline From Conquest to COVID-19   869

LAURENCE WHITEHEAD

40. Technocrats and Unions in the Politics of Reforming Teacher Careers in Colombia and Peru   891

RICARDO CUENCA, SANDRA GARCÍA, AND BEN ROSS SCHNEIDER

41. Subnational Variations in Education and Policy Innovation in Argentina   911

JACQUELINE BEHREND

42. Economic Globalization and Evolution of Education Spending in the Brazilian Federation, 2013–2019   938

CRISTIANE BATISTA AND STEVEN DUTT-ROSS

43. Does Globalization Reward Education? Evidence for Mexico   956

INGRID BLEYNAT AND LUIS MONROY-GÓMEZ-FRANCO

44. Factious Education Politics in Chile, 1981–2021: Enduring Contention Over Privatization, Inequality, and Quality   985

ALEJANDRA MIZALA AND BEN ROSS SCHNEIDER

Index   1005

PREFACE

THE GLOBALIZATION-EDUCATION NEXUS: SOCIAL THEORY AND COMPARATIVE POLITICS

This Handbook deals with education and globalization. Building on two disciplinary approaches, social theory and comparative politics, it aims to contribute to the conceptual clarification and empirical discussion of how the processes of globalization and education interact. Bringing the two notions together in the analysis is far from evident. The categories commonly mobilized to think about education have long been associated with the notion of the nation state, but by themselves are insufficient for an understanding of how globalization plays out in this particular field. The historical development of school education is indeed closely linked to state building (Tilly, 1990). It operated as a symbol and an institution for the rejection of premodern hierarchies and the construction of what many have learned to understand as "national societies" and democratic political systems. The ordinary meaning of notions such as "state" and "society" tend to remain shaped by this historical and institutional process: Countries are conceived of as societies and political systems; societies as governed by states; and states as the ultimate locus of public authority governing complex "political conflicts" (Schattschneider, 1975) and policymaking arenas dealing with the needs and problems of their citizens. Each national "society" is assumed to develop a bundle of domains (law, economy, education, etc.) and to (re)produce its own culture, its own language(s), and its own traditions. Comparative politics deals with interactions within political systems and focuses specifically on internal political structures, actors, and processes. It analyzes these interactions empirically by describing and explaining their variation across national, regional and local political systems. The notions of sovereignty and the state are at the heart of comparative politics as a discipline (Caramani, 2020).

In contrast, some social scientists have criticized this mode of description and analysis for its "methodological nationalism" (Beck, 2000), that is, the well-anchored assumption that the nation state is the natural social and political unit of the modern world. Social theory responded to the critique. Some scholars started speaking of "world society" (Luhmann, 1997; Meyer et al., 1997) while others argued for dropping the concept of society altogether (Urry, 2000). The notion of the sovereign nation state capable of governing autonomously the key domains of society came to be regarded as insufficiently sophisticated and in need of refinement by some scholars in international relations. Notions that had long been treated as equivalents have increasingly been distinguished: not only "nation state" and "society" but also "nation state," "political authority," and even "sovereignty." Both social theory and comparative politics, the two key disciplines mobilized respectively in Part I and Part II of this Handbook, have grappled with these theoretical challenges in their own way. It could be argued that social theory concerned itself with the concept of society and its postnationalistic reconceptualization, while comparative politics rather focused on developing a more complex view on political authority and sovereignty by acknowledging new emerging policy arenas and self-organizing governance processes at work at multiple levels beyond and within the nation state (Hooghe & Marks, 2020). Nowadays, most scholars in the field of comparative politics support the idea that fundamental transformations in the form of governance have taken place and take diverging paths in different countries.

The critique of methodological nationalism proved particularly relevant for those scholars of social theory who, following Durkheim or Parsons, for example, still considered society as a normatively integrated national unit. Several social theorists have now broken away from this assumption. No one will deny that the economy constitutes a central domain of society, nor that it has become a global process, which states struggle to regulate. In the domains of education and education policy as well, it is not difficult to see that a number of structural and semantic evolutions have spread globally and tend to diffuse themselves across states. As historians and neoinstitutionalists had already shown in the 1970s, the expansion of (national) education itself is a global process: Within a few decades, education systems grew all over the world; all nations, rich or poor, from the north or the south, democratic or authoritarian, have somehow put in place an educational system. The observation of wide differences in the success, or even the shape, of such attempts and in the way school education is organized in different national or local contexts does not make it less of a global process. The opposite could actually be argued: Differences themselves can come to light and be observed only thanks to their being part of a global phenomenon. Through processes that remain debated (cultural isomorphism, capitalism, functional differentiation), education imposed itself upon all states across the globe. Observations of this kind have led social theory to dissociate the concept of society from the notion of the nation. A number of theories have been developed to describe a global society evolving across borders. Part I of this Handbook is dedicated to presenting, discussing, and comparing three such theories of globalization and their implications for our understanding of education and education policy.

In contrast, the state as an actor and institution (Skocpol, 2013) is at the very heart of comparative politics. Comparative politics concerns itself with discussing complexities and variations across countries, in order to illuminate the persistence of political contestation and analyze the impact of global norms and ideas on local institutions and national education systems. Providing an account of the many ways in which the field of comparative politics has evolved in the last few decades is beyond what is possible in the context of this brief preface. One key development consisted in elaborating a more complex, less unified, and "transformationalist" view of the state by acknowledging the fragmentation and distribution of its functions among distinct instances and levels (Caramani, 2020; Held et al. 1999). Multilevel governance is a key concept intended to describe and analyze this distribution of functions across various arenas. Decentralization, especially of education, and federalization redistributed power and resources between levels of government and empowered territorially based actors (Gibson, 2004). Comparative historical analysis and historical institutionalism show how domestic conflicts shape the institutional framework within which globalized public policy reforms are then produced. These theoretical advances proved particularly useful in the field of education, where resources (law, money) often stay tightly coupled to the national level, while policy formulation, implementation, and evaluation have become increasingly distributed among both international organizations and subnational and local decision-makers (Almond et al., 2004). This means that similar policies are adopted and implemented in diverse ways across countries and even within countries. Many chapters in Part II of this Handbook gravitate around this global constellation, whether they focus on global reforms and the ideas put forward by international organizations (Organization for Economic Cooperation and Development [OECD], World Bank, European Union), on evaluation processes (like Program for International Student Assessment [PISA], Trends in International Mathematics and Science Study [TIMSS], university rankings, etc.), or examine the ways in which nation states or local actors adopt, implement, or resist global ideas and reforms. Several chapters elaborate on the multilevel governance approach that presupposes a high level of variations across countries and regions of the world as far as the effects of globalization are concerned. Other chapters interrogate the globalization-education nexus from a perspective of international political economy.

STRUCTURE OF THE BOOK

The Handbook is divided into two main Parts that reflect two distinct disciplinary approaches to the relation between globalization and education: social theory and comparative politics. Together, these two approaches seek to provide a comprehensive overview of how globalization and education interact to result in distinct and varying outcomes across world regions.

Part I presents, discusses, and compares three major attempts to theorize the process of globalization and its relation to education: the neoinstitutionalist theorization of world culture (with John Meyer as an emblematic, though not unique, figure); the materialist and domination perspectives (well represented by Wallerstein's world system theory); and Luhmann's theory of world society. While highlighting their specific merits, key differences, and shared findings, we pay attention in particular to how each of these three branches of social theory accounts for the emergence, evolution, and problematic consequences of the globalization of education. The theoretical efforts involved in Part I of the Handbook are also intended to help gain some analytical distance from the often-emotional topic of globalization.

Section I draws on globalization understood as a cultural process (change) emphasizing culturally embedded ideational factors. Education and human activity more generally are considered as highly embedded in collective cultural patterns. In this paradigm, the dominant theory is the neoinstitutional approach typically associated with the theoretical work of John Meyer and his colleagues, as situated within new institutionalism in sociology, which defines modernity and globalization as a cultural rationalization relying on isomorphic processes. However, subsequent strands of research have developed that draw on anthropological studies of school and learning. These studies explore cultural variations in educational norms and practices, and employ distinctive theoretical constructs but draw heavily on research about cultural dynamics at the local, national, and global levels. This section also incorporates the contributions of historical new institutionalism, field theories, and new-institutionalist policy studies as a way to highlight the theoretical plurality involved in this field of study and to bring forth conceptions of globalization insisting on cultural complexity and fragmentation. Such a view of cultural globalization as plural, fragmented, and conflictual is also presented in the recent developments of the world culture theory looking at problematic consequences of globalization resulting from the crisis of the modern project of rationalization and the spread of illiberal contestations of the modern cultural order.

Section II builds on world system theory even if some of its chapters do not refer explicitly to Wallerstein's seminal work. What brings them together is the structuralist perspective they bring to the study of globalization in education, their focus on power relations and discursive and material domination, and their interest in democratic struggle and resistance in globalizing capitalist economies. They include post-Marxism and post-Fordism, Foucauldian socio-historical approaches to forms of power in modernity and late modernity, the Bourdieusian theory of social fields, and the political economy of education in advanced capitalist societies. This section looks in particular at how theories forged in the "structural" context of the nation state and its core institutions (representative democracy, capitalist economy, Fordist organization of work, and the knowledge regime of science) may be extended to capture the reconfiguration of education's structural embeddedness and its distributional effects and to renew the critical perspective on education and inequalities.

Section III focuses on sociological systems theory. Systems theory has a long interdisciplinary history. Its early developments in sociology, most notably with the work of Talcott Parsons, could not avoid the trap of methodological nationalism and have been widely criticized for their functionalist orientation. In the context of this Handbook, we therefore choose to focus on the most recent developments of sociological systems theory and its most important figure, Niklas Luhmann. Breaking away from the two pitfalls of methodological nationalism and functionalism, Luhmann's sociology develops a theory of world society that contrasts with neoinstitutionalist and structuralist approaches: It does not start with culture, or with power, but rather with functional differentiation. Moreover, in sharp contrast with most existing approaches of functional differentiation (Durkheim's division of labor; Weber's spheres; Parsons' systems, Bourdieu's fields, etc.), Luhmann considers modern society as a genuine heterarchy of coevolving, hardly coordinated, global systems. Education appears as a global function system next to others, endlessly dealing with its turbulent and changing environment.

Part II of the Handbook analyzes the political and institutional factors that shape the adoption of global reforms at the national and local level of governance, emphasizing the role of different contexts in shaping policy outcomes. The chapters engage with the existing debates of globalization mainly in the field of public policy and comparative politics by analyzing contemporary education reforms in a multilevel governance perspective. They explore the social, political, and economic implications of globalization for national systems of education, their organizations, and institutions. Global education policies promoted by international actors and organizations are filtered through local contexts that mediate global processes within countries, regions, and local communities. In Part II, we focus on advancing our understanding of the complex system of economic and political relationships between the local and the global (Almond et al., 2004) that have direct and indirect implications for the policy and politics of education. Education is a policy field dominated by a constant struggle for resources, and power among actors, which creates the institutional framework within which globalized public policy is designed and implemented locally. We therefore need to simultaneously capture national developments and globalized education policies and norms.

Section IV contributes to mapping the historical development of international organizations onto the field of education. Many organizations, such as the OECD, have become leading advocates of education accountability worldwide, and others have been key actors in the development of the educational rights of children in Africa. The scope of their actions varies, such as their focus, which ranges from economistic and evidence-based programs to more holistic and humanistic ones. The chapters interrogate the role of international organizations in setting the policy agenda, and how they are capable of informing education reforms worldwide. They also show the limitations of such process of shaping local agendas, by emphasizing variations in national and local responses.

Section V analyzes the national policy responses to reform agendas set by global actors. The institutions of the nation state are analyzed in order to understand how global policy convergence masks a high degree of differentiation of educational systems and processes at subnational levels of government. The nation state and domestic politics has been the predominant framework for analyzing education policy developments until recently. Does the concept of globalization undermine the analytical power of the state in education? This section focuses on the contemporary challenges to the relationship between education and domestic systems of policy advice and networks. How is the role of the state changing in the globalized policy community of education? Central to the chapters is an analysis of how globalization has transformed existing state power and institutions dealing with education. Instead of taking a benign view of the relationship between the global and the national, the chapters shed light on the complexity of the challenges posed to education by global scripts and ideologies, and their variations across countries.

Section VI zooms in on one specific dimension of globalization: the massification of education. The overall question is: Does convergence in conceptions of equality among secondary pupils, and more generally, of education policy globally eliminate national and local political contestation? The chapters investigate empirically with original data this question in a comparative perspective, with a special focus on secondary schooling and the reforms of massification and extension of access to secondary pupils. It emerges that no single model of access to mass education existed and that education inequality remains a highly diversified and contested notion and policy across countries. This section draws upon case studies mainly from European countries.

In Section VII, the focus shifts on the case of higher education policy, which is the most globalized of the education sectors. Although the chapters show that there has not been a fundamental destabilization of the nation state form, and that there is no reduction in the role of the state, normative globalization and cultural theories hold very strongly in this field of higher education reforms. We look not only at Europe but also at other emerging countries such as China and India which have been exposed to the influence of normative ideas.

In the final section, Section VIII, the book looks at the huge variations of the effects of globalized education policies in the Global South, with a focus on Latin America. Despite assertions that education policies are increasingly converging in a globalized world, Latin American countries vary widely in the resources they devote to education and the development of human capital, and in how global education policies are adopted and implemented. In addition, there is also important variation *within* countries in educational investment and policies. As in other developing regions, in Latin America the implications of globalization and integration into the world economy are diverse and mediated by local actors, structures, and processes.

REFERENCES

Almond, G. A., Powell, G. B., Strom, K., & Dalton, R. (2004). *Comparative politics today: A world view*. Pearson Longman.

Beck, U. (2000). The cosmopolitan perspective: Sociology in the second age of modernity. *British Journal of Sociology, 51*(1), 79–105.

Caporaso, J. A. (1996). The European Union and forms of state: Westphalian, regulatory or post-modern. *Journal of Common Market Studies, 34*(1), 29–52.

Caramani, D. (2020). *Comparative politics*. Oxford University Press.

Gibson, E. L. (2004). *Federalism and democracy in Latin America*. Johns Hopkins University Press.

Held, D., McGrew, A., Goldblatt, D., & Perraton, J. (1999). *Global transformations: Politics, economics and culture*. Polity and Stanford University Press.

Held, D., & McGrew A. (2007). *Globalization/anti-globalization*. Polity Press.

Hooghe L., & Marks G. (2020). A postfunctionalist theory of multilevel governance. *British Journal of Politics and International Relations, 22*(4), 820–826.

Luhmann, N. (1997). Globalization or world society: How to conceive of modern society? *International Review of Sociology, 7*(1), 67–79.

Meyer, J., Boli, J., Thomas, G. M., & Ramirez, F. O. (1997). World society and the nation-state. *American Journal of Sociology*, 103(1), 144–181.

Schattschneider, E. E. (1975). *The semisovereign people: A realist's view of democracy in America.* Harcourt Brace Jovanovich.

Skocpol, T. (2013). Bringing the state back in. In M.Hill (ed). The Policy Process. A Reader. Routledge, Abingdon, 126–139

Tilly, C. (1990). *Coercion, capital and European states: AD990–1990.* Blackwell.

Urry, J. (2000). *Sociology beyond societies: Mobilities for the twenty-first century.* Routledge.

Contributors

Kathryn Anderson-Levitt
University of Michigan, Dearborn

Gabriele Ballarino
University of Milan

Cristiane Batista
Universidade Federal do Estado do Rio de Janeiro

Jacqueline Behrend
Consejo Nacional de Investigaciones Científicas y Técnicas and Universidad Nacional de San Martín

Caroline Bertron
University of Paris 8

Fabian Besche-Truthe
University of Bremen

Ingrid Bleynat
King's College London

Gwendolin J. Blossfeld
Hans-Peter Blossfeld
University of Bamberg and European University Institute

Patricia Bromley
Stanford University

Lorenzo Cappellari
Catholic University of Milan

Daniele Checchi
University of Milan

Minju Choi
Stanford University

Giancarlo Corsi
University of Modena

Ricardo Cuenca
Instituto de Estudios Peruanos

Hannah K. D'Apice
Stanford University

Xavier Dumay
UCLouvain

Steven Dutt-Ross
Universidade Federal do Estado do Rio de Janeiro

Kirsten T. Edwards
University of Oklahoma

Nanna Ramsing Enemark
University of Aalborg

Jared Furuta
Stanford University

Maria Tullia Galanti
University of Milan

Sandra García
Universidad de los Andes

Julian L. Garritzmann
Goethe University Frankfurt

Susanne Garritzmann
Goethe University Frankfurt and University of Konstanz

Jane R. Gingrich
University of Oxford

Anja Giudici
University of Newcastle

Amandine Bernal Gonzalez
UCLouvain

Lukas Graf
Hertie School – The University of Governance in Berlin

Sotiria Grek
University of Edinburgh

Julian Hamann
Humboldt-Universität zu Berlin

Jeroen Huisman
Ghent University

Takehiko Kariya
University of Oxford

Guo Guo Ke
Lingnan University of Hong Kong

David Krogmann
University of Bremen

Marek Kwiek
AMU University of Poznan

Seungah S. Lee
NY University

Gerald K. LeTendre
Pennsylvania State University

Eric Mangez
UCLouvain

Simon Marginson
University of Oxford

Christian Maroy
UCLouvain

Kerstin Martens
University of Bremen

Paola Mattei
University of Milan

Daniel McArthur
University of York

John W. Meyer
Stanford University

Alejandra Mizala
Universidad de Chile

Ka Ho Mok
Lingnan University of Hong Kong

Luis Monroy-Gómez-Franco
City University of New York

Dennis Niemann
University of Bremen

Mark Olssen
University of Surrey

Marco Ovidi
Università Cattolica del Sacro Cuore di Milano

Jenny Ozga
University of Oxford

Nazareno Panichella
University of Milan

Xavier Pons
University Claude Bernard Lyon

Francisco O. Ramirez
Stanford University

Ben Ross Schneider
Massachusetts Institute of Technology

Helen Seitzer
University of Bremen

Riyad A. Shahjahan
Michigan State University

Maarten Simons
KU Leuven

Nadine Ann Skinner
Stanford University

Rudolf Stichweh
University of Bonn

Zhen Tian
Lingnan University of Hong Kong

Jandhyala B. G. Tilak
Council for Social Development

Alice Tilman
UCLouvain

Astrid Tolo
University of Bergen

Pieter Vanden Broeck
Columbia University

Raf Vanderstraeten
Ghent University

Agnès van Zanten
Sciences Po Paris

Marie Verhoeven
UCLouvain

Louis Volante
Brock University & UNU-MERIT

Christine Weinbach
University of Bonn

Laurence Whitehead
Nuffield College, University of Oxford

Michael Windzio
University of Bremen

Christian Ydesen
University of Aalborg

PART I

SOCIAL THEORY, GLOBALIZATION, AND EDUCATION

INTRODUCTION TO PART I

XAVIER DUMAY AND ERIC MANGEZ[*]

Setting the Stage

"Globalization" has become one of the most recurrent concepts in social sciences. More often than not, however, the concept is handled without much of a properly articulated theory capable of explaining its historical origin and expansion. For education researchers attempting to elucidate how global changes and processes affect their field of study, this situation is problematic. When mobilized in the field of education, the notion seems to suffer from a persistent lack of conceptual clarity. It is often taken to mean a number of different things. For some it refers to the emergence of supranational institutions; others view its effects essentially through the development of international comparison and accountability; others understand it as an outcome of capitalist expansion; yet others associate it with the rise of the new technologies of communication or conceive of it merely as a discursive ideological construction meant to legitimate change.

While a comprehensive convergence of views on how to theorize this important notion might not be possible, or even desirable, the field would nevertheless benefit from an effort to clarify the main lines of demarcation of the debate. For all intents and purposes, what emerges now is a somewhat confusing situation where more and more references are made to a still rather elusive concept. Seemingly simple problems are not solved: Should we speak of "the globalization of education," or is "globalization" a noneducational process that somehow affects education from the outside? Is "globalization" essentially an economic process? Is it a "cultural" process? The outcome of politics/policy? Or yet something else? How did it come about and evolve? Fundamentally, what theories of society do we have at our disposal to help make sense of it?

---

[*] Authors in alphabetical order.

The ambition of Part I of this Handbook is to develop a firmer and tighter iterative dialogue between social theory, long concerned with theories of globalization, and education research. To a certain extent, education research and social theory have remained worlds apart, each busy with its own, seemingly specific, problem of reference. Attempts to bridge the gap between fundamental theories of globalization and the study of educational problems are still rare and often insufficiently sophisticated. The way the two fields of research relate to the notion of the nation state sheds some light on the gap between them: While social theorists have not always managed to account sufficiently clearly for the role of the nation state in globalization, or have even merely overlooked it, education research has, for its part, often emphasized the national level, to the point of finding itself trapped in "methodological nationalism" and subsequently failing to see education and education policy as global phenomena from the start.

Globalization studies in education have come to the forefront of the research agenda rather recently, following patterns of evolution in the 1990s in other disciplines such as political science and international relations (Held, 1997), anthropology (Appadurai, 1996), and sociology (Guillen, 2001). The notion that modern society had acquired a global or worldwide character has, however, a much longer history in the social sciences. Karl Marx's work on capitalism was entirely dedicated to the study of the autonomization of "a system" capable of imposing and expanding its logic toward ever more objects and all over the world: "The need of a constantly expanding market for its products chases the bourgeoisie around over the whole surface of the globe. It must nestle everywhere, settle everywhere, establish connections everywhere" (Marx & Engels, 1848/1998, p. 243). Marx and Engels further emphasized that the "exploitation of the world market" had progressively "given a cosmopolitan character to production and consumption in every country." The notion of a world society that possesses not only a global economy (a world market) but also a number of other global systems (science, religion, politics, education, law . . .) is certainly not absent from the early days of sociology and the work of Weber, Simmel, or Tarde, for example.

From the 1970s, building on the foundational works of sociology, major theories of "world-level" culture (Meyer & Hannan, 1979), system (Wallerstein, 1974), or society (Luhmann, 1971) developed by analyzing globalization as the expansion of modern society's principles of organization (i.e., normative integration and isomorphism; class divisions and conflict; functional differentiation and self-referentiality). Globalization, in each of these analytical perspectives, is conceived of as a progressive process with its own history. In the "world culture" perspective, the Renaissance and the humanistic orientation of monotheist religions gave birth to a culturally rationalized humanistic project of creating progress and justice; in the world system theory, it is the (self-) expansion of capitalism observable from the 15th century and its demands on other, noneconomic, domains of social life which created a world system; and in Luhmann's systems theory, wars of religion and the invention of the printing press (which revealed the contingency of the world) triggered the gradual replacement of a stratified societal order by another order emphasizing functional differentiation. These three theories were chosen as entry points for this chapter because they offer, in our view, the most sophisticated accounts of modernity and globalization, and therefore allow an in-depth comparison between them. Of course, they do not cover the entire spectrum of existing theories of globalization. In order to nuance our main arguments, we therefore also refer, to some extent, to other complementary theoretical approaches.

These three theories have been variably influential in shaping the field of globalization studies in education. They are, however, rarely discussed comparatively from a paradigmatic perspective (with some exceptions; see, for instance, Burbules & Torres, 2000, or Popkewitz & Rivzi, 2009, for a discussion of globalization in education; or Holzer et al., 2015, for a broader comparison of world-culture theory with Luhmann's systems theory). Our goal in Part I of this Handbook is therefore to take up the challenge and discuss the nature, forms, and drivers of globalization in education from these three distinct theoretical perspectives. Part I is organized in three sections, each dedicated to one pivotal paradigm. While each section inevitably puts forward some specific topics and problems, a number of themes are also dealt with across the sections in order to facilitate comparison and transversal reflection. Section I deals with cultural approaches of globalization in education, Section II is concerned with how more structural frameworks and political economy approach the problem; and Section III focuses on systems theory's understanding of globalization and the globalization of education.

In this Introduction, we start by discussing comparatively the core principles underpinning the theories of (world) society involved in the three paradigms. Then, we present how each theoretical orientation assesses the temporal evolution of globalization and identifies and explains its (problematic) consequences in late modernity before looking more specifically at how each conceives the place or function of education in its worldwide perspective. Finally, we delve into the way each strand conceptualizes the relations between education and policy, and we conclude by pointing to emerging debates and research avenues.

Globalization Theories as Theories of (Modern) Society

World culture (Meyer), world system (Wallerstein), and world society (Luhmann) theories, to name the main protagonists,[1] situate globalization in a long-term historical perspective as a corollary of modernity, but bring forth different answers to the questions of what makes social order possible in modernity, and what demarcates the modern period from preceding ones.

The world culture theory (WCT) situates the institutional origins of globalization in the cultural transformation of Europe at the end of the Middle Ages. Institutions, in this perspective, are "cultural rules giving collective meaning and value to particular entities and activities, integrating them into the larger schemes" (Meyer et al., 1987, p. 2), and not merely formal institutions (e.g., political, economic, or educational institutions or fields). WCT nurtures the ambition of explaining the structuration of modern society as a whole, by considering that all societal sectors (education, economy, polity, etc.) are embedded in a single process of cultural rationalization. Drawing on Weber's analysis of Western rationalization, modernity and globalization are seen as historical processes through which society becomes progressively governed by culturally rationalized rules, and no longer by reference to the tradition (even if religions have strongly inspired the humanistic model of rationalization).[2] Both nature and the moral order (society) have become understandable, predictable, and thus manageable and governable. World society is filled with global models, transcendental principles devoted to defining possible collective and shared horizons. These models are education models (modern educational systems and the grammar of schooling, but not only), economic models defining how to govern a world-level economic exchange system, political ideals on the participation of actors in political decisions, but mainly cultural representations made possible by the rationalization and emergence of a shared model of rational actorhood. Rationalization operates as a grand cultural process producing institutionalized myths shaping the sectors of society. Even more importantly, the myth of actorhood assumes that the underlying social entities of the global world (individuals, organizations, and states) think of themselves as genuine actors with their own agency and a sense of identity. The cognitive structures of society are located within actors, which, being entitled to autonomy and protection, become agentic. This cultural transformation of society relies on mechanisms of isomorphism: Social entities identify with the same set of norms, which facilitates their diffusion, even in the absence of direct contact between the entities in question. In this way, no society and no human groups, in the world society, can escape the education question, the environmental question, the question of participation in democracy, the question of the expansion of science, or the issue of human rights. Institutionalized conceptions of the organizations provide recipes for successful management; states subscribe to similar purposes and possess similar structures that make the circulation of public policies and institutional structures possible.

Wallerstein's world system theory takes a different entry in the analysis of modernity and globalization. It builds on a historical analysis of the development of modern capitalism as a world-historic mode of production. The distinctive feature of this mode of production (compared with preceding forms of economy), which emerges in Europe in the 15th century, stems from its ability to fuel its own expansion (see also the distinction between embedded and disembedded economy in Polanyi, 1944), that is, the accumulation of capital. In previous economic systems, the long and complex process of accumulation of capital was usually blocked, for reasons linked to morality or to the nonavailability of one or more elements of the accumulation process (e.g., accumulated value in the form of money, labor power, network of distributors, and consumers) (Wallerstein, 1983). The unification of a world market and the concomitant division of labor at the world level relied on extended commodification and produced a "capitalist civilization" by the penetration of the capitalist mode of production into other domains of social life. In his historical account of the modern world system, Wallerstein insistently underlined that the capitalist economy came into existence in Europe *before* all other modern institutions (education included). He understands such precedence as evidence of the primacy of the economy over other modern dynamics (Wallerstein, 1984, p. 29). As a forerunner, capitalism, it is argued, explains and actually motivates, or even demands, the subsequent development of modern institutions orchestrated by nation states. Nation states, in turn, became the most essential building blocks of the capitalist world system. Only (strong and sovereign) states can create and maintain the conditions necessary for establishing a global capitalist interstate system.

World system theory understands (national) societies as class societies and analogously describes the modern world as a stratified order of nations, a power hierarchy among states and other transnational organizations, in which exploitative dynamics between core and (semi)peripheral zones are continually at work. With its Marxist inspiration, world system theory contends that these dynamics of exploitation rely on, as much as they generate, ideological supports. It should therefore not come as a surprise that, next to their analysis of the material aspects of the world economy (i.e., their focus on how surplus value is created and distributed), world system scholars have grown increasingly interested in the analysis of the discourses, ideas, and policies that support capitalism and its dominating structures. They find that modern education emerged in the 19th century as a component of a broader "liberal program" promoted by the core countries (strong states) of the modern world system, to consolidate the emerging world order and their own functioning and favorable position within it. Note that the notion of a "strong state" designates well-functioning liberal states, as opposed to (former) colonies or dictatorships for example, which are considered weaker states (even when they may, on the face of it, seem more violent). While Wallerstein's initial project does not aim to contribute to social theory per se,[3] he thus nonetheless ends up with a theory of society where the emerging capitalist economy structures and relies on other sectors of society to perpetuate and expand itself.

Like all social theories, Luhmann's theory of a global world society deals with the question of understanding how social order is possible. Its answer is: By means of differentiation. Order comes about by establishing and stabilizing differences, drawing lines, making distinctions, and in this way organizing communicative processes. Different societies differentiate themselves differently, distinguishing for example between "us" and "them," superior and inferior, center and periphery, religion and science, and so on. The societies of our traditions relied on segmentary differentiation and, eventually, on hierarchical differentiation (stratification). Stratified societies were grounded on an external point of reference (God, nature) on which they could build their internal order: There was then "only one position from which to develop and circulate self-descriptions: the position of the center or of the hierarchical leaders, i.e., the position of the city or of the aristocracy" (Luhmann, 1988, p. 27).

For systems theory, globalization, or rather the emergence of world society, begins when another mode of differentiation—functional differentiation—surfaces and gradually replaces stratification. Functional differentiation has developed since the late Middle Ages but "was recognized as disruptive only in the second half of the 18th century" (Luhmann, 1997, p. 70). Luhmann published studies dedicated to the differentiation of a series of function systems: law, education, art, politics, science, the mass media, and so on. Often symbolized by the French Revolution, the more profound historical causes of the break away from older societal forms are to be found in the printing press and religious wars: Both played the same role of revealing the contingency of the world. With the resulting dissolution of a fixed and extra-societal point of reference capable of univocally ordering society (Clam, 2004, p. 247; Luhmann, 2013, p. 225) comes the progressive structural primacy of cognitive expectations (doubts) over normative expectation (certainties). The shared norms, which ensured the integration of premodern society, were thus progressively replaced by a "precarious order based on the institutionalization of learning."

That society no longer depends on a hierarchical order (discriminating spaces and peoples) but on functional differences is a very foundational, and maybe the most important, statement that systems theory makes about modern society. Functional differentiation indeed comes with far-reaching consequences. One such consequence is the establishment of world society through multiple processes of globalization. Function systems know no physical boundaries: They do not contain a certain population, and they do not end at this or that spatial frontier (Luhmann 2008, p. 41). In their very principles (specificity and universality), they are therefore global from the start. Just as there is only one world economy (with all its internal and regional differences), there is today only one global scientific system (internally differentiated into disciplines, problems, theories, etc. and populated with many distinct organizations), one political system (differentiated into nation states most notably), one education system (with its own internal complexity and reliance on nation states), and so on. The (only) limit of such systems is the limit of their function. Function systems are, as a result of this limitation, not capable of grasping their environment comprehensively. All they can do—and this is how they form themselves—is to observe their environment very selectively, by relying on their own specific way of observing.

Each system produces its limited, reductive, focused, necessarily partial version of the world (and in this way it produces itself). Modern society is therefore not capable of observing and knowing the world unequivocally. Instead, it produces, within itself, a series of diverse, multiple, incompatible descriptions of the world and of itself.

Thus, while world culture and world system theories explain the origin and expansion of globalization in relation to the primacy of a preponderant logic (culture or the economy), Luhmann's sociological systems theory starts from a different, opposite, premise: Not the predominance but instead the lack of any predominant logic, and the ensuing "heterarchy" of—specific yet universal—systems, fuels globalization processes. In this way, systems theory develops a theory of world society which contrasts with neoinstitutionalist and structuralist approaches: It does not start with imitation and isomorphism, nor with conflict and power, but rather with contingency and functional differentiation.

World culture, world system, and world society theories, while providing different accounts of the global character of modern society, nonetheless share important landmarks that differentiate them from the recent literature on globalization. First, they conceive of globalization as a long historical development triggered by the turn to modernity itself, and not as a recent development of a global arena beyond the frontiers of the nation states. Second, they put forward an analysis of the state as a global phenomenon, which means that they reject the conceptual opposition between the national and the global. In Wallerstein's world system theory, states are among the key components of the interstate dynamic supporting the development of world-level capitalism. In WCT, states, like organizations or individuals, are culturally rationalized actors, both enacting global models and scripting other actors (inter alia other states) in the adoption of global models. In Luhmann's theory of a global world society, in which functional differentiation prevails, segmentation between nation states is but the internal mode of differentiation of the (global) political system. Thanks to this territorial anchorage, the political system could give rise to its most central organization, the nation state, and allow it to develop its function of making collectively binding decisions. Other differentiated systems, perhaps most notably the education system, profited from that national milieu (and from the state's organizing ability) to build their own global modus operandi (Mangez & Vanden Broeck, 2020).

The (Problematic) Consequences of Globalization

Globalization is apprehended, in the three theoretical paradigms, as an *expansion*: ever-increased cultural rationalization in WCT; accrued accumulation of capital in the world system approach; and exacerbation of the self-centeredness of function systems in Luhmann's world society. The expansive dynamics pervading modernity do not come about without creating or accentuating a number of problems, which are symptomatic of the current era (populism, illiberalism, excessive inequalities, terrorism, etc.). The theories under scrutiny in this Handbook have not always accorded the same importance to these problems, nor are they equally equipped to explain them. With its seminal focus on diffusion and isomorphic processes, WCT has perhaps been less inclined to put much emphasis on conflicts and tensions. Some recent developments, however, now aim to integrate in the neoinstitutional framework the structuring of counter-reactions in the face of the hyperdevelopment of rationalization and liberalization. Attention to the problems that come with globalization is arguably more evident in the world system perspective where the disputed accumulation of capital has always been analyzed in relation to social movements, power struggles, and inequalities. Luhmann's systems theory of world society has, for its part, also given much attention to the problematic consequences of modernity, the heterarchy of function systems leading to the excessive, invasive, and uncoordinated expansion of increasingly self-referential logics.

In WCT, the principle of cultural rationalization spreading through all sectors of society suggests a rather harmonious conception of society. Globalization in WCT seems less associated with (growing) violence, conflicts, or societal fragmentation than in world system or world society approaches. Nonetheless, WCT has ever since its early development involved ideas of growing complexity, with the expansion of the world society entailing both the expansion of societal sectors and modern actors. Over time, the cultural rationalization of society turned modern actors into more and more complex entities, equipped with many instruments for developing their agency and pressing others to develop theirs. Nation states have become more elaborate than they were a few decades ago: They have programs, ministries, and policies covering a much wider range of activities; organizations have built up more complex structures; individuals are also equipped with more elaborate self-knowledge instruments. Modern actors, organizations in particular, are also subject to multiple forms of decoupling (see Bromley & Powell, 2012): not only the (vertical) decoupling between institutional expectations and adaptation to local constraints (e.g., policy-practice gap) but also the (horizontal) decoupling between self-developing organizational equipment, and the core technology and objectives of the organization (e.g., means and ends gap). Societal sectors as well become more complex, crossed by multiple, often contradictory, institutional logics (see LeTendre, Chapter 7, this volume). The education sector, for instance, is growing without any real limitations, to instantiate modern principles of rationalization, freedom, and progress, with any domain being potentially subject to rationalization and teaching/learning (e.g., from entrepreneurship to environmental values) (see Lee & Ramirez, Chapter 1, this volume).

From the 1990s, the spread of organizations and increased individualization signaled a neoliberal turn (see Choi et al., Chapter 5, this volume), which also triggered new sorts of contestation opposing the very principle of cultural rationalization focused on the sacredness of individual choice, actorhood, and ideals of progress. Such "postliberal reactions" (see Furuta et al., Chapter 4, this volume) suggest a possible decline in the hegemony of the liberal order (or, in the language of institutionalism, the deinstitutionalization of the global liberal order). The decline of the liberal United States, the rising influence of the BRIC countries, the dramatic 2008 financial crisis, or the spread of liberal models into traditional arenas of social, communal, and family life together led to some contestations of the liberal/neoliberal order. These reactions involve challenges to some of the main cultural principles of modernity: the predominance of rationalization over tradition; the myth of actorhood; or the landmark values of progress, freedom, and human rights. They are mainly right-wing, but left-wing manifestations are observed as well. On the right, they involve a return to more traditional modes of integration and the reinforcement of collectives (e.g., religious, political-populist, familial), or the essentialization of individuals in friction with the myth of actorhood. And on the left, they bring forth contestations of the cultural, economic, and political institutions based on the tensions between ideals of progress and justice, and rising inequalities.

The world system approach has always associated capitalism with a number of problematic consequences, in particular its tendency to produce, and amplify, inequalities, both locally and globally. Depending on the period in history, these problems have been more or less contained, and legitimated. The world economy developed by drawing on the development of an interstate system of exchange and competition but also on political structures and administrations (involving welfare systems), and a geoculture (ideologies, science, social movements) transcending to a certain extent the conflictual interests of capitalists and proletarians. As noted by post-Marxist authors, "capitalism is an economic system that always requires extra-economic embedding; its fundamental character means that it is unable to provide the necessary conditions of its continued expansion" (Dale, 2005, p. 121). In other words, the world economy established itself by subordinating polity and culture to its requirements (see the infrastructure-superstructure dialectic in Marx and Engels, or the embeddedness of the economy in Polanyi). However, the recent neoliberalization—that is, the ever-expanding uncontained capitalist logic—brings forth a series of exacerbated consequences, resulting from a deterioration of several mechanisms of legitimization and redistribution. First, it aggravated social inequalities and the polarization of wealth distribution (Piketty, 2021), especially in some regions of the world. In some others, domestic institutions (among others, education) rather keep individuals—at least some categories of them—from becoming losers in the process of globalization (see Blossfeld & Blossfeld, Chapter 13, this volume). Second, and relatedly, it renewed ideological resistance and reshaped social movements (e.g., right-wing populism) triggered by the socioeconomic and cultural marginality of those left behind by these processes of neoliberal globalization (Robertson & Nestore, 2021). Third, it also affects modern political and cultural institutions on which the economy is now more loosely relying, or rather drawing on in new ways. In the words of Colin Crouch (2004) about political institutions, "democracy in many advanced societies was being hollowed out, its big events becoming empty rituals as power passed increasingly to circles of wealthy business elites and an ever more isolated political class," as a result of global financial deregulation and the weakening of class identities and struggles. Speaking of the institutions of industrial democracy, Baccaro and Howell (2017) describe a (neoliberal) dismantling of industrial relations[4] revolving around the expansion of employer discretion in several strategic domains (wage determination, personnel management, work organization, and hiring and firing procedures). In the same vein, Jenny Ozga's analysis (Chapter 9, this volume) of educational policy in the neoliberal age shows an usurpation of scientific expertise in the interest of international organizations creating international competition. In addition, many other authors (e.g., Giroux, 2018) link the development of the learner-centered approach or education focused on market-driven competitiveness to the neoliberalization of education and pedagogy (for other examples of critical analyses of neoliberalization in education, see Ball, 2003).

By emphasizing the heterarchical character of functional differentiation, Luhmann's systems theory rejects all views attributing modernity's specificity to any one ordering principle: To speak, for example, of modernity as neoliberal society, or alternatively to characterize it by an all-encompassing process of rationalization and standardization, is a claim whose flaw, according to Luhmann, is to oversimplify and thus misunderstand modernity by reducing it to only one of its facets (Luhmann, 1995, pp. 464–465). In contrast to most social theorists, Luhmann associates functional differentiation with the lack of any primary ordering principle and emphasizes the problematic consequences that ensue from such an absence. Among the many problematic consequences of functional differentiation, the best known "is certainly the failure of the world economic system to cope with the problem of the just distribution of wealth," but, Luhmann adds, "[s]imilar problems can be cited for other functional systems" (Luhmann 2013, p. 124). In the absence of any prevailing ordering principle, systems do not complement one another so as to establish a coherent whole (as Talcott Parsons would have it), nor do they converge to ensure the reproduction of capital (as Marxism might assume). Instead, each system recklessly assumes the primacy of its own function and tends to expand its reach and invade its surroundings.

Function systems exhibit a built-in expansive logic. When society renounced establishing its internal order on an external ground (nature and God), it condemned itself to self-reference. Whatever is, then, can no longer remain stable or solid for long; new possibilities can now constantly be thematized: Why this, why not that instead? "What (. . .) if we set out to observe the natural as artificial and the necessary as contingent?" (Luhmann, 2002, p. 90). The question operates as the leitmotiv of modernity. It can and will be applied to ever more aspects of modern life. Modernity thus presents us with a "cosmology of contingency" (Luhmann, 2005, p. 39): How can one know what to do, what to believe, what to think? Uncertainties proliferate as regards the future and the decisions to be made globally. Individuals, organizations, and systems all seem to experience an acceleration of the pace of time (Rosa, 2013). Faced with this specific mode of experiencing the future, which Luhmann (1976) refers to as the "futurization of the future," different functional systems (law, economy, politics, education, science, etc.) can react in different ways (on this topic, see also Mangez & Vanden Broeck, 2020). Understanding how such systems internalize "future emergencies" (Opitz & Tellman, 2015) has become a central concern for a number of systems theorists. One first possible answer to this question consists in considering future uncertainties as a resource (Esposito, 2015) for the expansion of each system, rather than as an obstacle to its operations: Uncertainties then lead to ever more policy, ever more science, ever more economic operations, ever more art, more laws, and so on, thus endlessly feeding a global process of systemic expansion. In the realm of education, too, questions have been asked which have contributed to expanding the system: Why only teach and learn between the ages of 5 or 6 and 16 or 18? Why not earlier, later, or even throughout life? Why only learn in schools and universities? Why not include nonformal, real-life situations within learning processes? Why not teach citizenship, entrepreneurship, or coding? Why not learn how to learn? A substantial acceleration of the evolution process is rendered possible by the thematization of possible variations (see Luhmann, 1990, p. 67). As argued elsewhere, it enables education's global expansion in all directions: in its temporal dimension, as lifelong learning; in its social dimension, as mass schooling; and in its material dimension, as the "educationalization" of all facets of life (Mangez & Vanden Broeck, 2021; Vanden Broeck, 2020). There seems no longer to be any legitimate limit to the list of possibilities with regard to who, what, or when to educate. Expansive dynamics are at work in various systems simultaneously (and this means: without coordination). The result of such multiple, uncoordinated, dynamics "will reinforce unpredictability (. . .) and bring about a higher degree of uncertainty with respect to the future" (Luhmann, 1990, p. 184). Systems theory portrays modern society's future as a series of imbalances among expansive, invasive, self-centered logics.

None of the three paradigms under examination considers the problematic consequences and reactions to hypermodernity or late modernity as obstructions to globalization. In WCT, modern myths of the liberal order indeed cohabit with postliberal reactions making the world culturally more complex. The world system theory, for its part, has always pointed to the adaptive capacities of capitalism in the face of social movements or restructured economic parameters (i.e., green capitalism as an adaptation to the consumer market and the scarcity of natural resources). Social movements, global or national, have hardly constrained capitalist development in history, but the recent economic and health crises suggest some possible resurgence of modern institutions (democracy, redistributive social policies, etc.) limiting the consequences of expanding capitalism (Crouch, 2020). Finally, Luhmann's system theory has from its early development integrated ideas of improbability, instability, and violence, and rather sees the global expansion of self-centered systems as a source of increased complexity giving rise to a society constantly on the edge of chaos.

Modern Forms of Education and Beyond

The three theories under discussion in this Handbook view education as part and parcel of the complex set of social and institutional domains that emerged along with (early modern) nation-state society and eventually evolved in relation to the ensuing (late modern) transformations of nation states themselves. Theories differ, however, in their analysis of the role or function of education in this increasingly global context. In the cultural approach, education seems to stand both as an outcome of, and a means for, the diffusion of rationalization. World system theory develops a more conflictual perspective on capitalism in which education seems to operate as an instrument supporting broader local and global processes of domination and legitimation. Systems theory, for its part, prefers to characterize education as an autopoietic system capable of adapting to its changing environment and also of parasitizing and coupling itself with strategic allies like the nation state. In this section, we look at the place given to modern education by each of the three core theories and we further reflect on how they interpret recent evolutions in education, notably the new global emphasis on learning.

The different strands of cultural or institutional theorizations have not all given the same importance to modern education and its school form. In WCT, modern education, even if mainly organized by nation states, is seen as a global product, universal and universalistic in aspiration (Meyer & Ramirez, 2000). Nation states are themselves a global construct embedded in world society. Education and schools more particularly operate as a vehicle for the rationalization of the world and the acculturation of individuals. The idea of a "schooled society" (Baker, 2014) indicates that society is increasingly created and defined by education. The dramatic expansion of education should be regarded as responding to the need for modern societies to incorporate and locate within actors the principle of the modern world society. Education is thus a core and causal part of the cultural model of the modern society or nation state.

With globalization, education models are increasingly diffused from international organizations. Nonetheless, the institutional dynamic of diffusion and standardization of modern education remains fundamentally linked to the spread of the world culture and isomorphism. The expansion and standardization of education cover educational structures (e.g., mandatory schooling and nonselective school structures), content (e.g., civics education) and instruction (e.g., active learner), and the organization of educational work and education organizations. The recent phase of educational expansion relies more strongly on the expansion of organizations (see Choi et al., Chapter 5, this volume), which profoundly alters education. The most dramatic worldwide changes in education, such as privatization, the rise of testing, and the emergence of multi-stakeholder governance regimes that run from local to global levels, are better understood as part of an organizational transformation of schooling and society than by any interpretations in terms of the (interest-based, economy-defined) neoliberalization of society. In other words, in the world culture perspective, the expansion of education and the growth of organizations have the same root, that is, cultural rationalization. In particular, curricula put increased emphasis on organizations (of different kinds, not only international organizations) and participation of individuals in the organizational society, which may explain the expansion of 21st-century skills (critical thinking, problem-solving, entrepreneurial thinking, etc.) and pedagogies such as project-based learning.

In addition to the spread of organizations, the decline in liberal hegemony outlined earlier weakens the centrality of common forms of education inspired by principles of universality. It then furthers the rise of alternative and oppositional models of society and redirects education toward less liberal-individualist forms, which is now a central concern for world culture theorists. This is how WCT, in its most recent developments, interprets the growing success of homeschooling (specifically in the United States, but not only) or the resurgence of identity-based, religious or politically oriented sorts of education. These are part of a broader movement of contestation of cultural institutions, precisely those in charge of reproducing and legitimating the global cultural order.

With the exception of these more recent developments, the cultural approaches to the role of education in our global, modern society do not put much emphasis on conflicts and inequalities in their analysis.[5] The opposite could be said of the second group of theories to which we now turn. For world system scholars and other structuralists or poststructuralists, the function of formal education, or that of the more diffused notion of "learning," can indeed not be detached from an analysis of power mechanisms and an examination of the economy and the state. Strong states (need to) protect and educate their citizens, first to make "dangerous classes" less dangerous but then also to establish a market of consumers and to have "those with 'merit' (. . .) play the key roles in political, economic, and social institutions" (Wallerstein, 2004, p. 52). Together with other social or health policies, education establishes the conditions for strong states to function and perform within a liberal modern stratified social order.

Not unlike class sociologists who view education as an indirect and subtle, even hidden, means for the reproduction and legitimation of class structure within national societies, those walking in Wallerstein's footsteps attribute a similar function to the programs of educational assistance that organizations (the World Bank, typically) and strong states from the core zone of the world system grant to those situated on the periphery. Such programs, whether or not they are perceived as instruments of domination by their addressees, are analyzed as direct or indirect means ensuring the maintenance and even the expansion of the capitalist world economy (Clayton, 1998). Almost half a century ago, Philip G. Altbach (1977) used the notion of "neocolonialism" to describe American foreign aid programs and spoke then of "a servitude of the mind" to characterize the educational effects of such programs. This line of analysis has been pursued and nuanced since then (Robertson, 2005). Research on policy transfer showed that pressure on weak states to adapt and adopt "international standards" in education does not lead to a global convergence of systems, but rather generates hybrid forms (Schriewer, 2016; Steiner-Khamsi, 2004). It is important to notice that the power dynamics at work at this global interstate level constantly interact with the more local or national class struggles. In the weak states in particular, fractions of local elites may benefit from allying with powerful interests outside the country.

Whether within nation states or at a more global interstate level, education, it is claimed, operates as an instrument of legitimation (next to and embedded with other such instruments) and as a condition for the dynamic reproduction of a constantly evolving global social order. In a somewhat similar vein, several scholars (see Ozga, Chapter 9, this volume) consider today's knowledge-based economy capable of shaping, or even instrumentalizing, a number of subordinated and interdependent (equally global) processes, whether they be educational, political, or even legal. Of all such subordinated systems, education often appears the least autonomous in the eyes of these analysts: It merely follows the economy and responds to its needs. And now that the new knowledge economy has turned knowledge itself into a key component, or even raw material, for its operations, education in a sense slavishly aligns with the demands of this economy for an accrued emphasis on learning, learning to learn, solving problems and other similar qualities expected from "knowledge workers." These analysts thus see education as responding to the needs of the economy in the same way as Wallerstein when he analyzed how science (by rationalizing the world and institutionalizing the principle of universality), the polity (by guaranteeing stability and developing the interstate system), or education (by generating ideational support) has been instrumental in the development of world-level capitalism.

The new emphasis on learning has also attracted the attention of a number of researchers inspired by the work of Michel Foucault (see Ball, 2013). Their perspective, it must be recognized, is different from that outlined earlier.[6] At the center of the Foucaldian tradition, one finds the notion of the "apparatus" (*dispositif*). An apparatus operates as a solution to a problem, that of conducting the conduct of individuals, but, and this is important, as a solution without an author. It designates the very diffuse, ubiquitous, unavoidable presence of power in the social world. It is less about power mechanisms at work between identifiable groups or logics than about society exercising power on itself. Maarten Simons (Chapter 10, this volume) links Europeanization and globalization with the progressive replacement of the "social apparatus" by the "learning apparatus." Lifelong learning is becoming an apparatus through which individuals learn to govern themselves and conduct their lives by constantly investing in their own learning.

Like the branches of social theory discussed earlier, systems theory acknowledges education as a latecomer among the various function systems that have differentiated themselves in the course of the long transition to modernity. The differentiation of a system for education indeed started after most other function systems had begun their own differentiation (see Vanderstraeten, Chapter 16, this volume). Only when the process of functional differentiation had rendered modern society more complex was the need for an education system deemed necessary. According to systems theory, however, no conclusion can be drawn from this delay with regard to the status of education, as compared with other systems. That it came after several other developments does not make it a product of, or a simple support system for, say, the economy or politics, or any other logics. Systems theory thus diverges both from neoinstitutionalism(s) and from the more power-centered approaches outlined earlier. Education is not merely a channel for a broader process of rationalization; nor is it a stratagem for establishing and legitimating power relations locally and globally.

Instead, systems theory understands education as a global system with a life of its own. It is a specific form of communication, which emerged in response to increased complexity and which became capable of perpetuating itself. In order to avoid any misunderstanding, the problem of the relationship between education and politics deserves some development. Perhaps surprisingly Luhmann argues that education has a life of its own but simultaneously acknowledges that it lacks the technology to achieve its task on its own. The contradiction is only apparent. In contrast with several other systems such as the economy or science, education does not possess a genuine generalized symbolic medium to increase the probability of its success. Luhmann and Schorr (1979, 2000) speak of a technological deficit to emphasize the insurmountable difference between education as a social system (communication) and the learners' psychic systems (consciousness) which it hopes to change. In an attempt to overcome its limit, education relies on the organization of lengthy interactions between teachers and students (on this topic, see Vanden Broeck, 2020). Their co-presence in the classroom during extended periods of time is supposed to help education reach its unattainable target. But, for these interactions to even take place, an organization is needed: There must be schools and teachers, a precise yearly calendar and daily timetable, a population of pupils and students actually attending schools on a regular basis and divided into distinct age groups, and so on. All such requirements do not and cannot result from an operation of the education system itself. For all this, education has had to rely on the political system and the decision-making ability of the state. Such dependence should not be equated with a lack of autonomy. Education needs the state to ensure its organization in schools and classrooms, but the interaction order thus rendered possible then acquires a life of its own. Education operates a bit like a parasite that uses another system's organizing ability as a support on which to perform its own operations. While his sociology thus describes education as a system which found in the state the perfect host to ensure its organization, Luhmann himself did not really explore much whether and how education could make use of other such supports. The task has hardly been taken up by other scholars with the exception of Pieter Vanden Broeck (2021), who has examined education's reliance on the European Union, a transnational organization that lacks the means of the nation state, and documented the resulting emergence of a new educational form that no longer resembles the school and its classrooms.

In their more detailed analysis of modern education, Luhmann and Schorr (2000, p. 70) distinguish stages in the evolution of the system. Education, they argue, organized itself successively around different "contingency formulas" (see Weinbach, Chapter 19, this volume). In the early 1980s already, they found that education increasingly relied on what they labeled the "learning to learn formula." With the notion of "learning," they argued, education achieves self-referentiality: It now possesses a specific formula, independent from (any other system in) its environment, and which can be applied universally to any item or topic in this environment. It is crucial to understand that, for systems theory, the turn to learning is an accomplishment of the education system itself. While Luhmann and Schorr (2000) acknowledge that "with the quickly increasing differentiation, specialization, and fluctuation of work requirements," the learning formula is probably more relevant for the economy, they maintain that its emergence cannot be attributed to demands from the economy but must be understood as the result of a reflective process of the education system itself. The contrast with the world system perspective could hardly be sharper.

Education and Policy

The three main lines of theorization under scrutiny in the first part of this Handbook hold different views on the relations between education and politics.

The policy dimension is arguably not predominant in WCT (see Maroy & Pons, Chapter 6, this volume). Cultural rationalization involves in the foreground institutions of rationalization (e.g., science) and acculturation (e.g., education);[7] or rather, education, science, and polity are all embedded in the world culture. In this perspective, the nation state itself is a product of globalization and a vehicle for diffusing models across the globe (Meyer, 1980). In addition to nation states, a constellation of international actors (not really conceptualized as a field in WCT) act as rationalized others while increasing the institutional value and the diffusion of global models. The recognition of several types of interdependencies (political with the issue of world conflict and peace; economic with the issue of the governability of the world-level economic exchange system; and cultural with the issue of migration for instance) has led to the creation and expansion of several types of international organizations (political nongovernmental associations, and professional and scientific organizations) forming a "world polity" (Meyer et al., 1997). In scriptwriting the world, these organizations are confronted with difficulties and problems that indicate the path through which they develop the global models. Due to the absence of a real possibility for authoritative resolutions, they have to diffuse their idealized models through soft law. And their narratives are anchored in the dominance of collective and nonconflictual ideas. These characteristics indicate the peculiar nature of the world polity: It involves limited power relations and competition among states given the actors' common identity; and in the same way, limited constraints or coercive power. Power is therefore not evacuated but limited by the injunction on states to behave according to shared norms and structures.

Consequently, states, like other actors (individuals, organizations), tend to grow more structured and elaborated with time. They develop ever more ministries, policies, programs, regulations, and instruments of every kind in search of legitimacy, thus expanding the policy sector in the same way as an expansion of education has been observed by WCT. However, polity is also decoupled in many ways. Global models are decoupled from the real activity of states because "nation states are modeled on an external culture that cannot simply be imported wholesale as a fully functioning system" (Meyer et al., 1997, p. 154), and policies on the national scene are most often decoupled from the real practices in societal sectors (i.e., education). If coherence or standardization is observed (among organizations in the same sector, or among sectors of society), it is not much due to policy structuration or coupling effects. Rather, it results from similar patterns of rationalization rooted in the world culture that make policy systems like education or science look similar from one place to another.

As outlined earlier, the world system literature also gives a central place to states. However, their role is of a different nature than in WCT. States put in place the necessary conditions for the development of capitalism (Dale, 2005). Strong states manage to implement a number of policies that strengthen their position (e.g., by educating their citizens or adapting the workforce). They may even manage to educate workers of weak states in a way that corresponds to their interests. The analysis is directed in parallel toward the unequal distribution of surplus value and toward the ideas, discourses, and policies that support its expansion. Education is seen as an instrument in the hands of politics and the economy that permits their reproduction and development. The more recent evolutions in the field have drawn attention to the elaboration of a neoliberal discourse and the implementation of neoliberal policies across the globe. In education, for instance, neoliberalism relies essentially on a simple rationale. First comes the critique of the system: Schools, teachers, and students do not perform well enough, inequalities are growing, and the system is not working. Next comes scapegoating: Public education is bureaucratic, personnel have linear and secure careers, and pedagogy is inefficient. One of the key, and most contested, arguments of neoliberalism consists in presenting social problems (poverty, inequality, and unemployment) as resulting from a lack or mismatch of skills and competencies. Neoliberalism (in education) then consists essentially in promoting a number of remedies variably developed from one context to another: school choice policy, privatization, intensive testing (assessing students, schools, and national systems), and rewards and incentives for schools and teachers.

In the same way, policy is often analyzed as subordinated to expanding economic interests (see Crouch, 2004). This subordination, it is argued, diverts democratic institutions from their task of representing and debating the common goods in favor of lobbies and business interests. Policy actors are then marginalized or suspected of acting in the service of capitalist development. Foucaldian analysts, as presented in this volume by Maarten Simons (Chapter 10), even if they make a very different argument on the nature of modern forms of power, join critical analyses of democracy (in the neoliberal age) by not locating power in the hands of policy actors. Power, then, is not the prerogative of formal policy circles. Instead, it is a diffuse process through which individuals are led to govern themselves by learning, made thus responsible for solving themselves different sets of individual problems (e.g., unemployment) and societal problems (e.g., social exclusion). Making individuals responsible for their own learning thus takes the place of social policies in bridging ideals of freedom and security.

According to systems theory, the very notion of reforming, or that of policymaking, only acquired its current meaning with the turn to modernity (see Corsi, Chapter 17, this volume). It relies on the modern and nowadays global assumptions that the future will differ from the past and that it is possible to act upon it in the present. That these assumptions are solidly anchored in today's world society does not make them unproblematic (Vanderstraeten, 1997). In Luhmann's recently translated book *Organization and Decision* (2019, pp. 273–298), one finds a chapter entitled "Structural Change: The Poetry of Reform and the Reality of Evolution." The opposition conveyed by the title of the chapter subsumes systems theory's view on the problem of reforming or policymaking: Reality never obeys even the best of intentions to reform it, but results instead from a nongovernable, nonpredictable process of becoming, which Luhmann refers to here under the notion of evolution. To grasp the argument, one must acknowledge that any reform, any political attempt to steer a system, necessarily involves two strands of operations: "one has to distinguish the operation of steering, which produces its own effects, from the operation of observing this operation, which produces for its own part its own effects" (Luhmann, 1997, p. 45). These intertwined interventions by the reforming system and by the system it addresses trigger "strange loops." The mere attempt to steer the world, simply by virtue of being visible to that world, tends to produce effects that cannot be steered: "steering always creates an additional effect by being observed and by the reactions of the observer in the one or the other way" (1997, p. 49). This should not be taken to mean that reforms are pointless and make no difference in the world. It rather implies that they lack control over their own effects. It is therefore unlikely that reforms merely meet their target: As is particularly obvious in the domain of education, reforms regularly fail, their effects are often moderate, uncertain, multiple, sometimes contradictory, regularly unexpected, and even counterproductive. Reforming then can never end; it constantly produces reasons to start reforming anew. But, as Luhmann warns, more steering will only lead to "more (and more rapid) unintentional evolution" (Luhmann, 1982, p. 134).

DISCUSSION AND CONCLUSION

The first part of this Handbook discusses three ways in which social theory attempts to describe and explain the emergence of a single worldwide social reality. The three theoretical orientations under scrutiny differ in many respects but converge on one fundamental idea: The world we live in has been global for quite some time. Pointing to the exact beginnings is not easy, but all agree that the turn toward a global society can be linked to the emergence of modernity itself. Many notions that too hasty analysts associate with the nation state and oppose to globalization are in fact global from the start. The very idea of a nation—and that of a nation state—are global ideas. The grammar of schooling is another typical example of a global form (which explains why we immediately recognize a school as a school no matter where we travel in the world, and no matter how different it may appear from the schools we are most familiar with at home). Even where schools are lacking, the notion of a grammar of schooling is present and imposes itself, making their absence noticeable and even problematic.

Curiously, however, this observation has not always been noticed. In the eyes of many, our modern global society has long taken the appearance of "a series of national societies." The concept of globalization itself only gained broad, and indeed global, attention in the 1980s and has since then often been associated with some sort of ubiquitous threat. Apparently, society became increasingly sensitive to its global character long after the turn to modernity. The fact that globalization is now met with much ambivalence cannot be overlooked: It needs itself to be understood as an evolution in the process of globalization.

While the ambivalence associated with the notion of globalization has become more intense in the last decades, it also resonates with concerns that had been expressed much earlier. Marx and Engels had long underlined the lack of a stable ground resulting from capitalism's constant orientation toward change. Weber was even more concerned than Marx with the global movement of modernity. For him, clearly, the uninterrupted preoccupation with the pursuit of order would inevitably come with a darker side filled with insecurities, unexpected consequences, and multiple alienations. The disappearance of shared norms haunted Durkheim's perspective on the future of modernity.

In view of the many global crises that we experience, one could argue that the problematic consequences that these founding figures had sensed long ago have remained with us and even worsened. The theoretical orientations that we have been discussing indeed all describe globalization as an ambivalent, double-edged, evolving process. Each perspective acknowledges, though with more or less emphasis, that globalization carries with it a series of problematic consequences. These take the form of an epistemological crisis of modern rationality, values, and institutions in the recent development of WCT; the form of aggravated inequalities feeding resentment and distrust in democratic institutions in the world system perspective; and the form of increased uncertainty and the social exclusion of persons by uncoordinated expansive systemic logics in Luhmann's systems theory.

Different lines of research have emerged as attempts to better grasp these changes. The evolving role of the state has notably attracted the attention of several authors. Is the state still capable of containing the consequences of capitalism and does it contribute to reinventing new sorts of solidarities (Thelen, 2014)? What roles should modern educational systems and other kinds of learning play? Is the historical model of political constitution (of the nation state) relevant for inspiring world-level civil constitutions, and renewed couplings of politics and law at multiple levels (Teubner, 2004)? Are there any other means than law to limit the expansive dynamic of differentiated systems? What theories of global justice can be proposed in a politically and economically ever more interconnected world, taking into account the rising importance of commons (Risse, 2012, p. x), specifically in the face of the climate change crisis? How can educational policies and systems contribute to renewed dynamics of citizenship and democracy (Torres, 2002)? Still others are looking at the increased role of organizations or between-organization dynamics in globalization (e.g., Choi et al., Chapter 5, this volume). Should these dynamics be seen as complements or competitors to modern institutions? More broadly, do they signal transformations in the fundamental characteristics of (global) organizations and institutions towards more reflexive but also more contested institutions (Zürn, 2018)?

Part I of this Handbook is intended as an invitation to amplify these emerging debates while simultaneously anchoring them in the evolution of social theories of modernity and globalization. At a time when globalization increasingly elicits emotional logics of fear and hope, in academia as well, this collection of chapters strongly encourages researchers to reinforce theoretical developments that capture fundamental mechanisms at work and so make sense of the seemingly troubled times of globalization.

NOTES

1. Cultural analyses of globalization represented in the first section of this Handbook, for instance, include a significant diversity of theoretical approaches ranging from cultural anthropology (see Anderson-Levitt, Chapter 2, this volume) to different strands of new-institutionalism, in particular the sociological and historical new institutionalisms (see Graf, Chapter 3, this volume). In this text, however, we mainly refer to the world culture theory (WCT) as an exemplification of the cultural analyses of globalization to avoid overcomplexity and allow for comparison of theoretical paradigms. In the same spirit, we mainly draw on Wallerstein's world system theory to cover analyses of globalization from a perspective of domination, materialism, and inequalities, but theoretical approaches of this kind are much broader, including post-Marxism, political economy, social philosophy, field theories, and comparative policy (see this Handbook, Section II). Section III, with its focus on Niklas Luhmann's systems theory and its recent developments, is more homogeneous.
2. For a critical discussion on the Weberian heritage of Meyer, see Carney et al. (2012), or a critical appraisal of the historical interpretation proposed by WCT, see Tröhler (2009).
3. The main field of study of Wallerstein is history or rather "socio-history" (see Braudel, 1958). His history of capitalism is inspired by Marx, but he does not embed his historical analysis in the broader sociological theory of historical materialism, class divisions, and infrastructure/superstructure dialectic, as Marx and Engels do, for example.
4. In the political-economy scholarship in historical institutionalism, the thesis of a neoliberalization of the economy and, beyond it, society, is disputed by alternative explanations focusing on the multiple trajectories of liberalization (Thelen, 2014).
5. One should note that in some strands of cultural anthropology, nevertheless, authors such as Jonathan Friedman (2007) precisely argue that analyses of globalization in terms of institutional arrangements or cultural meanings cannot be properly addressed without being integrated into the structural (Marxist) framework of reproduction.
6. Interestingly, Foucaldian analyses share some points with WCT. In WCT, the cultural rules of modernity involve the idea of a self-governing actor. In other words, the myth of actorhood implies self-governmentality. However, the two perspectives differ in the status given to power issues, much more central for Foucault than for WC theorists.
7. For David Kamens (1988), the development of political systems in nations, and the way popular participation in politics within democratic systems is organized, precisely results from educational expansion.

REFERENCES

Altbach, P. (1977). Servitude of the mind? Education, dependency, and neocolonialism. *Teachers College Record*, 79(2), 187–204.

Appadurai, A. (1996). *Modernity at large: Cultural dimensions of globalization*. University of Minnesota Press.

Baccaro, K., & Howell, C. (2017). *Trajectories of neoliberal transformation. European industrial relations since the 1970s*. Cambridge University Press.

Baker, D. (2014). *The schooled society: The educational transformation of global culture*. Stanford University Press.

Ball, S. (2003). The teacher' soul and the terrors of performativity. *Journal of Education Policy, 18*(2), 215–228.

Ball, S. (2013). *Foucault and education: Disciplines and knowledge*. Routledge.

Braudel, F. (1958). Histoire et sciences sociales: La longue durée. *Annales, 13*(4), 725–753.

Bromley, P., & Powell, W. W. (2012). From smoke and mirrors to walking the talk: Decoupling in the contemporary world. *The Academy of Management Annals, 6*(1), 483–530.

Burbules, N. C., & Torres, C. A. (Eds.) (2000). *Globalization and education: Critical perspectives*. Routledge.

Carney, S., Rappleye, J., & Silova, I. (2012). Between faith and science: World culture theory and comparative education. *Comparative Education Review, 56*(3), 366–393.

Clam, J. (2004). *Kontingenz, Paradox, Nur-Vollzug. Grundprobleme einer Theorie der Gesellschaft (Wissen und Studium)*. UVK.

Clayton, T. (1988). Beyond mystification: Reconnecting world-system theory for comparative education. *Comparative Education Review, 42*(4), 479–496.

Crouch, C. (2004). *Post-democracy*. Polity Press.

Crouch, C. (2020). *Post-democracy after the crises*. Polity Press.

Dale, R. (2005). Globalization, knowledge economy and comparative education. *Comparative Education, 41*(2), 117–149.

Esposito, E. (2015). Beyond the promise of security: Uncertainty as resource. *Telos, 170*, 89–107.

Friedman, J. (2007). Global systems, globalization, and anthropological theory. In I. Rossi (Ed.), *Frontiers of globalization research* (pp. 109–132). Springer.

Giroux, H. A. (1997/2018). *Pedagogy and the politics of hope*. Routledge.

Guillen, M. F. (2001). Is globalization civilizing, destructive or feeble? A critique of five key debates in the social science literature. *Annual Review of Sociology, 27*, 235–260.

Held, D. (1997). Globalization and cosmopolitan democracy. *Peace Review, 9*(3), 309–314.

Holzer, B., Kastner, F., & Werron, T. (Eds.) (2015). *From globalization to world society: neo-institutional and systems-theoretical perspectives*. Routledge (Routledge advances in sociology).

Kamens, D. (1988). Education and democracy: A comparative institutional analysis. *Sociology of Education, 61*(2), 114–127.

Luhmann, N. (1971). Die Weltgesellschaft. *Archiv für Rechts- und Sozialphilosophiei, 57*, 1–35.

Luhmann, N. (1976). The future cannot begin: Temporal structures in modern society. *Social Research, 43*(1), 130–152.

Luhmann, N. (1982). The world society as a social system. *International Journal of General Systems, 8*(3), 131–138.

Luhmann, N. (1988). Tautology and paradox in the self-descriptions of modern society. *Sociological Theory, 6*(1), 21–37.

Luhmann, N. (1990). *Essays on self-reference*. Columbia University Press.

Luhmann, N. (1995). *Social systems*. Stanford University Press.

Luhmann, N. (1997). Globalization or world society: How to conceive of modern society? *International Review of Sociology, 7*(1), 67–79.

Luhmann, N. (2002). *Theories of distinction*. Stanford University Press.

Luhmann, N. (2005). Entscheidungen in der "Informationsgesellschaft." In G. Corsi & E. Esposito (Eds.), *Reform und innovation in einer unstabilen Gesellschaft* (pp. 27–40). De Gruyter.

Luhmann, N. (2008). Beyond barbarism. *Soziale Systeme, 14*(1), 38–46.

Luhmann, N. (2013). *Theory of society* (Vol. 2). Stanford University Press.

Luhmann, N. (2019). *Organization and decision* (D. Baecker, Ed.). Cambridge University Press.

Luhmann, N., & Schorr, K. E. (1979). Das Technologiedefizit der Erziehung und die Pädagogik. *Zeitschrift für Pädagogik* Weinheim, *25*(3), 345–365.

Luhmann, N., & Schorr, K. E. (2000). Problems of reflection in the system of education. Waxmann.

Mangez, E., & Vanden Broeck, P. (2020). The history of the future and the shifting forms of education. *Educational Philosophy and Theory, 52*(6), 676–687.

Mangez, E., & Vanden Broeck, P. (2021). Worlds apart? On Niklas Luhmann and the sociology of education. *European Educational Research Journal, 20*(6), 705–718.

Marx, K., & Engels, F. (1848/1998). Manifesto of the Communist Party. Progress Publishers.

Meyer, J. W. (1980). The world polity and the authority of the nation-state. In A. Bergesen (Ed.), *Studies of the modern world-system* (pp. 139–158). Academic Press.

Meyer, J., Boli, J., & Thomas, G. M. (1987). Ontology and rationalization in the Western cultural account. In G. M. Thomas, J. W. Meyer, F. O. Ramirez, & J. Boli (Eds.), *Institutional structure: Constituting state, society, and the individual* (pp. 2–37). Sage.

Meyer, J. W., Boli, J., Thomas, G. M., & Ramirez, F. O. (1997). World society and the nation-state. *American Journal of Sociology, 103*(1), 144–181.

Meyer, J. W., & Hannan, M. (1979). *National development and the world system: educational, economic and political change, 1950–1970*. University of Chicago Press.

Meyer, J. W., & Ramirez, F. O. (2000). The world institutionalization of education. In J. Schriewer (Ed.), *Discourse formation in comparative education* (pp. 111–132). Peter Lang.

Opitz, S., & Tellmann, U. (2015). Future emergencies: Temporal politics in law and economy. *Theory, Culture & Society, 32*(2), 107–129.

Piketty, T. (2021). *Une brève histoire de l'égalité*. Ecole d'économie de Paris.

Polanyi, K. (1944). *The great transformation*. Farrar & Rinehart.

Popkewitz, T. & Rizvi, F. (Eds.) (2009). *Globalization and the study of education*. National Society for the Study of Education, 108th NSSE Yearbook.

Risse, M. (2012). *On global justice*. Princeton University Press.

Robertson, S. L. (2005). Re-imagining and rescripting the future of education: Global knowledge economy discourses and the challenge to education systems. *Comparative Education, 41*(2), 151–170.

Robertson, S. L., & Nestore, M. (2021). Education cleavages, or market society and the rise of authoritarian populism? *Globalisation, Societies and Education, 20*(2), 110–123.

Rosa, H. (2013). *Social acceleration: A new theory of modernity*. Columbia University Press.

Schriewer, J. (Ed.) (2016). *World culture re-contextualised: Meaning constellations and path-dependencies in comparative and international education research*. Routledge.

Steiner-Khamsi, G. (Ed.) (2004). *The global politics of educational borrowing and lending*. Teachers College Press, Columbia University.

Teubner, G. (2004). Societal constitutionalism: alternatives to state-centered constitutional theory? In C. Joerges, I-J. Sand, & G. Teubner (Eds.), *Constitutionalism and transnational governance* (pp. 3–28). Oxford University Press.

Thelen, K. (2014). *Varieties of liberalization and the new politics of social solidarity.* Cambridge University Press.

Torres, C. A. (2002). Globalization, education, and citizenship: Solidarity versus markets? *American Educational Research Journal, 39*(2), 363–378.

Tröhler, D. (2009). Globalizing globalization: The neo-institutional concept of world culture. In T. Popkewitz & F. Rizvi (Eds.), *Globalization and the study of education* (pp. 29–48). National Society for the Study of Education, 108th NSSE Yearbook.

Vanden Broeck, P. (2020). Beyond school: Transnational differentiation and the shifting form of education in world society. *Journal of Education Policy, 35*(6), 836–855.

Vanden Broeck, P. (2021). Education in world society: A matter of form. *European Educational Research Journal, 20*(6), 791–805.

Vanderstraeten, R. (1997). Circularity, complexity and educational policy planning: A systems approach to the planning of school provision. *Oxford Review of Education, 23*(3), 321–332.

Wallerstein, I. (1974). *The modern world system I: Capitalist agriculture and the origins of the European World-economy in the sixteenth century.* Academic Press.

Wallerstein, I. (1983). *Historical capitalism with capitalist civilization.* Verso.

Wallerstein, I. (1984). *The politics of the world economy: The states, the movements, and the civilizations.* Cambridge University Press and Maison des Sciences de l'Homme.

Wallerstein, I. (2004). *World-systems analysis.* Duke University Press.

Zürn, M. (2018). *A theory of global governance.* Oxford University Press.

SECTION I

Culture, Globalization, and Education

CHAPTER 1

GLOBALIZING NATION STATES AND NATIONAL EDUCATION PROJECTS

FRANCISCO O. RAMIREZ AND SEUNGAH S. LEE

INTRODUCTION

THE triumphant diffusion of the nation state as blueprint or model has impacted the world, generating the "age of nation-states" (Weitz, 2019). This is also the "world educational revolution" era, with both mass schooling and higher education globally expanding (Baker, 2014). At the center of these developments lie the reimagined individual person, entitled to education as a citizen, and now human rights, and expected to contribute to national development as a font of human capital (Ramirez et al., 2016). The empowered individual has also globalized as a key feature of what constitutes a legitimate nation state.

In what follows, this chapter first revisits some of the main conceptual building blocks of the world society perspective and how these facilitate our understanding of the global rise of mass schooling and higher education as nation state projects that enhanced their legitimacy. Next, we focus on cross-national studies of textbooks—the main technologies of the intended curricula—to ascertain what constitutes legitimate knowledge transmitted to future citizens. At issue here is whether there are global trends that can be accounted for by reflecting on the influence of world models of the legitimate nation state. We apply the same lens to higher education to gauge how much global models of excellence influence changes in the direction of more accessible and more flexible universities. We pay particular attention to the changing status of women in higher education, mindful of their historical exclusion. Lastly, in recognition of recent challenges to the dominant world models (see Furuta et al., Chapter 4, this volume), this chapter concludes by briefly reflecting on which educational developments are likely to persist and which are more vulnerable.

Globalization and the Nation State

Much of the recent literature on the impact of globalization on the nation state does not take into account the globalization of the nation state model itself, from its 17th-century Westphalian roots (Krasner, 1993) to its post–World War incarnation. The triumph of this model motivated imperial dynasties and former colonies (Chirot, 1986; Strang, 1990) to refashion themselves as territorially bounded "imagined communities" (Anderson, 1991) with scripted national constitutions and other similarly scripted symbols of a unified nation state (Meyer et al., 1997). In Anderson's words:

> The independence movements in the Americas became, as soon as they were printed about, "concepts," "models," and indeed "blueprints" [. . .] Out of the American welter, came these imagined realities: nation-states, republican institutions, common citizenships, popular sovereignty, national flags and anthems, etc. [. . .] In effect by the second decade of the nineteenth century, if not earlier, a "model" of the independent national society was available for pirating. (Anderson 1991, p. 81)

From a world society perspective, the enactment of the model is crucial to projecting a legitimate nation state identity. Epistemic communities emerge and generate scripts on how to become a legitimate nation state (Meyer, 1997; Schofer et al., 2012). These scripts vary over time on how much development should be state or market driven. But development as a national goal for all nation states is now taken for granted. Though there is variation on whether development is construed narrowly (economic growth) or broadly (sustainable development), it would be hard to imagine a contemporary nation state that simply eschewed development as a national goal—or, for that matter, one that proudly proclaimed military conquest of other nation states as its development strategy. Both national development goals and national strategies for attaining these goals are subjected to world inspection and international approval. "Getting it right" is what enactment of a legitimate nation state identity entails.

To get it right, the legitimate nation state must look like an organizational actor (see Choi et al., Chapter 5, this volume, for the importance of organizational actorhood). National development plans, for example, were an earlier manifestation of legitimate nation state actorhood, as these transform development aspirations into goal-oriented policy directions (Fägerlind & Saha, 1989). State planning became less fashionable in the neoliberal era (Hwang, 2006), though the focus on education for development continued. International conferences dedicated to national development issues reflected widespread interest in pursuing national development. Legitimate nation states are likely to show up. Neither plans nor participation in conferences may add up to development, but these are some ways of displaying proper nation state commitment and active engagement.

Beyond development goals, "getting it right" has increasingly emphasized state responsibility for the well-being of its citizens. While the Treaty of Westphalia (1648) was designed to promote peace via emphasizing state sovereignty with little regard to the rights of the people within these states, subsequent developments emphasized nation states consisting of rights-bearing citizens. In reaction to the horrors of World War II, often blamed on excessive state power fueling excessive nationalism, the United Nations sought to reaffirm citizen rights now reframed as human rights. The legitimate nation state was now expected to respect these rights and to attend to inequalities, increasingly seen as arising from past or continuing violations of these rights. The right to rights (Arendt, 1951; Somers, 2008) indeed led to an expanding set of rights claims often grounded on an expanding scope of recognized inequalities (see Tsutsui, 2018, for the case of Japan). The legitimate nation state was expected to pursue not only progress or development but also equity or justice for its citizens. Herein we also find epistemic communities at work, setting equity standards and processes for safeguarding rights. A proliferation of human rights treaties, organizations, and conferences now characterizes the global landscape (Elliott, 2007; Gordon, 1998; Lauren, 2003). To be sure, there are gaps between the talk and the walk, but the talk is widespread and to some extent consequential (Cole & Ramirez, 2013; Hafner-Burton & Tsutsui, 2005; Hathaway, 2002).

From a world society perspective, models, scripts, and identities are crucial conceptual building blocks, and these differ from other perspectives that emphasize the primacy of autonomous actors, local interests, and context-specific goals. A basic problem with some of these perspectives is that they struggle to account for why one finds common outcomes across different entities. Their country-specific interpretations abound at great costs to theoretical parsimony. A second issue is that when these perspectives more broadly address the impact of globalization, they often favor mechanisms such as coercion and learning (Dobbin et al., 2007). These are indeed sensible mechanisms for some outcomes, such as the role of the International Monetary Fund on the social programs of its borrowers (Vreeland, 2003). But as we shall see, there is less evidence of these mechanisms at work when it comes to a range of educational outcomes. We shall also see that the crucial mechanisms are often awareness of the educational decisions other countries have made and links to international organizations through which "expertise" on what constitutes "getting it right" is acquired. Furthermore, the zeitgeist of an era is consequential. Note that at the beginning of the 20th century one could muse about the danger of women in universities (see Mazon, 2003, for the case of Germany), but in the 21st century lack of women in science, technology, engineering, and mathematics (STEM) is the agreed-upon problem (European Technology Assessment Network, 2010).

Taken as a whole, these mechanisms emphasize the influence of a global environment on nation states and national educational institutions and dynamics. From a world society perspective, the environment consists in world models of progress and justice and the organizational carriers and epistemic communities that articulate and disseminate these models (Boli & Thomas 1999). This perspective is a special case of social constructivist theory often employed in diffusion studies (Dobbin et al., 2007). The key thesis is that nation states enact legitimate identity by adhering to world models of progress and justice. This leads to common outcomes that are both widespread (diffusion) and appropriate (institutionalization) (Colyvas & Jonsson, 2011). This also results in gaps between policies and practices (Meyer et al., 1997; Ramirez, 2012). Thus, we get both institutional isomorphism and loose coupling (DiMaggio & Powell, 1983).

Globalization and National Educational Developments

Throughout the 20th century and especially after World War II, mass schooling dramatically expanded throughout the world (Meyer et al., 1977, 1992). One might have anticipated the expansion in more democratic or more industrialized countries, with the local needs for better citizens in democratic regimes or more productive workers in industrialized countries shaping the outcomes. However, the commitment to schooling the masses transcended variations in societal conditions. Older fears about the educability of peasants or workers or girls dissipated. Optimistic assumptions about the transformative power of schooling emerged (Ramirez & Boli, 1987). Schooling for individual development and individual development as a key to national development became tenets in national agendas in the latter half of the 20th century (Fiala & Langford, 1987). What was dubbed the "world educational revolution" (Coombs, 1968; Meyer et al., 1977) led to the celebration of "Education for All" (Chabbott, 2003) and to uncontested aspirations to become "The Schooled Society" (Baker, 2014). The Global Campaign for Education brought together nongovernmental organizations and teacher unions in over 150 countries to advocate for the promotion of universal primary education (Mundy & Murphy, 2000). This advocacy network echoed and amplified the earlier message of N'Krumah, the Ghanian leader who famously declared that the people would abandon him as a responsible national leader if he did not build the primary school system. Indeed, a commitment to mass schooling was expected of responsible national leadership.

In the current milieu, it is hard to imagine that schooling the masses was ever a contested terrain. But there were indeed skeptics who questioned the value of compulsory schooling (see the papers in Mangan, 1994). There were certainly policies to limit time in school for children, policies such as high-stake tests that led to early exits for most children (Eckstein & Noah, 1992). There were also policies to differentiate the experiences of school children via their early assignment to different tracks. These policies did not reflect positive assumptions about the value of extended and less differentiated schooling for all. Quite the contrary, these policies were motivated by the premise that most children were destined to find work that required limited doses of literacy and numeracy, seasoned with respect for authority.

However, recent studies show a global decline in the use of high-stakes testing at the primary and lower secondary levels (Furuta, 2021) as well as less early track assignment (Furuta, 2020). In 1970, about 70% of countries worldwide tracked students at the junior secondary level. Forty years later, less than 20% continue to do so. A related study reveals the negative impact of tracking on educational expansion in more recent periods (Furuta et al., 2021). In another study, Chmielewski (2017), using Program for International Student Assessment (PISA) data from 2000 to 2015, finds that the share of enrollment in vocational tracks had declined in nearly every country (and conversely that the share in academic and general tracks has increased). These cross-national changes suggest an expanded and more universalistic understanding of what constitutes educability. All were increasingly imagined to be educable and not in sharply differentiated spheres. Not surprisingly, the right to an elementary education is now enshrined in most national constitutions, and national educational ministries have become commonplace national institutions (Ramirez & Ventresca, 1992). This right is now framed as a human right, as in Article 26 of the United Nations Charter. This expanded vision of educability itself presupposes an enhanced vision of human potential, one in which all individual persons have enormous capacities worth nurturing through schooling (Baker, 2014; Benavot & Resnik, 2006). This basically is both a human right and a human capital vision. Both visions are embedded in contemporary world models of progress and justice. Not surprisingly, the scope of compulsory schooling has expanded with greater numbers of students entering secondary schools.

There is no evidence of national resistance to the "education for all" agenda, especially at lower levels of education. This is not an instance of powerful actors, be they international organizations or hegemonic powers coercing commitments to expanding education. One can contend that some specific educational decisions, privatization, for instance, may be influenced by external educational aid carrots or sticks or more broadly by the diffuse authority of educational experts far removed from local scenes (Verger, 2009). However, the overall commitment to schooling the masses with individual and national development as intertwined goals is clearly derived from the pervasive sense that that this is what good nation states do. It is, of course, possible to argue that what is involved is learning from the experiences of other nation states, a form of rational adaptation. Many educational reform initiatives indeed refer to the superior educational policies and practices in other countries that supposedly led to higher levels of academic achievement or greater economic growth. The Japanese educational system was much admired in some educational circles in the United States, in the "A Nation at Risk" report for example (National Commission on Excellence in Education, 1983). But only some features of the system were theorized as crucial to success and framed as portable best practices. Having master teachers mentoring novices was deemed worthy of emulation. Setting national achievement standards was also valued (Smith & O'Day, 1991). Having high-stakes exams at the end of high school—examination hell—was ignored. Also ignored were school uniforms and the collective solidarity these symbolized (Rholen, 1989). What learning takes place is filtered by theorization, and the latter is much influenced by the dominant ideas or models in an era (Fourcade & Healy, 2017; Meyer & Rowan, 1977; Strang & Meyer, 1993).

Earlier rationales for schooling girls, for example, often centered on their future roles as mothers, not their own individual development. An 1879 plan for the secondary schooling of girls in France illustrates this point:

> The mother speaks the language of superstition, the father that of reason. When these contradictory ideas enter the mind so malleable and impressionable and begin to germinate, the child not knowing whether to believe his mother or his father, will commence to doubt. (Maynes, 1985, p. 88)

More recent rationales are much more likely to emphasize *her* human capital and *her* human rights. The earlier rationales reflect an era when women were mainly seen as mothers and wives, and the more contemporary ones are grounded in understanding women as agentic persons (Berkovitch, 1999).

More astonishing than the phenomenal growth of mass schooling is the more recent expansion of higher education across the world (Barro & Lee, 2015; Schofer & Meyer, 2005). What was a very limited enterprise at the beginning of the 20th century is now a globally expanded institution (Frank & Meyer, 2020). The expansion is not driven by a few outliers with very large populations. The earlier "American advantage" was often attributed to political and educational decentralization that facilitated competitive dynamics between different classes and status groups (Collins, 1979). But, in fact, educational expansion is now evident in centralized political and educational systems, for example, in South Korea (Douglass et al., 2009). As we pointed out earlier, gatekeeping high-stakes tests are declining and even milder test-based barriers to entry into higher education are challenged by the rise of test-optional policies in American higher education, for example (Furuta, 2017).

The challenges are motivated by the triumph of optimistic ideas framed with references to "late bloomers" and, more recently, to the importance of "grit" (Duckworth, 2016) and "growth mindsets" (Dweck, 2007). The early sorting function of high-stakes tests is increasingly regarded as a waste of human capital. Early sorting is also seen as unfair to the many who did not enjoy the home background (social and cultural capital) with which to better hone and display their actual or potential talent.

Also challenged are manpower planning perspectives that sought to limit higher educational growth via an analysis of labor markets that linked educational courses to job requirements. Critics of these perspectives argued that the highly educated would be entrepreneurial and innovative, creating new jobs and not simply fitting into pre-existing occupational slots, notwithstanding Boudon (1973). Higher educational expansion in the service of the knowledge society would gain worldwide currency (Frank & Meyer, 2020). Efforts to curb its growth failed even in communist countries (Baker et al., 2004). Ironically much of the accelerated growth is driven by women, a point we address later. The premise that there was "no salvation outside higher education" (Shills, 1971) initially proposed in an ironic vein was embraced in country after country.

The second world educational revolution has also intensified the authority of higher education in shaping what constitutes legitimate knowledge and fair personnel allocation (Meyer, 1977). All sorts of knowledge innovations would seek the imprimatur of university standing, from computer science to women's studies. Universities as sites of exclusive canonical knowledge eroded (Readings, 1996). And, indeed, a global explosion of university appropriate courses has become evident (Frank & Gabler, 2006). It is also clear that possession of a higher educational degree not only predicts positive occupational and related life course outcomes (Hout, 2012) but also is globally seen as a fair ticket for upward mobility. What gets derided as unfair are the obstacles some individuals face due to circumstances beyond their control, born and raised in poverty, for example, or because they are discriminated against on the basis of ascribed characteristics, race or gender, for instance. However, the authority of higher education and the ever more credential-based society has globalized.

To summarize, nation states gain external legitimacy standing by enacting models of the legitimate nation state. "Getting it right" is crucial, and there are consultants without borders to facilitate getting it right. In earlier eras, the expansion of mass schooling displayed proper commitment to the idea that a legitimate nation state needed territorially bounded loyal and productive citizens who were properly schooled. In more recent periods, this idea has been extended to the realm of higher education. The first- and second-world education revolutions reflect the profound centrality of education in enacting proper and agentic nation state identity. Earlier fears about schooling the masses are not in sight. Earlier concerns about "overeducation" are less convincing. What has triumphed instead is a model of the good nation state as one in which more people have the right to get more education and more educated people are seen as vital keys to national development. Mass schooling and higher education have been clearly institutionalized as nation state projects. What were once contested terrains have become taken for granted or institutionalized domains.

In what follows, we first explore the implications of this global model on what constitutes legitimate knowledge in schools by reviewing cross-national analyses of textbooks. Next, we focus on changes in universities, the main actors in the credential societies that dominate the world. Lastly, we reflect on recent challenges to the role and centrality of educational developments in world models of progress and justice.

What Counts as Knowledge? Expansion of Curricula as Reflected in Textbooks

Textbooks are important lenses through which models of society are formed and communicated. They represent not only institutional understandings about the nature of society but also are authoritative statements that communicate what society perceives as being important for its young people to know (Schissler, 1989). There are textbook controversies because all sorts of groups and organizations see textbook content as consequential, revealing what is real and who and what is important (Apple, 1989). Most textbook studies focus on single countries. These are important in their own right but cannot shed light on whether there are cross-national trends regarding who and what count. In what follows, we reflect on recent cross-country studies that examined a common set of textbooks, mostly housed at the Georg Eckert Institute for International Textbooks in Germany. These studies employed similar methods of analysis, depicting trends and identifying national and transnational variables that accounted for these trends. These studies utilized a large number of textbooks, typically over 400, and covered countries from every region of the world, typically about 70. However, these studies also recognized the limitations of working with nonrandom samples of textbooks and countries (for more information on the textbook data collection process and analysis strategy, see Meyer et al., 2010).

Figure 1.1 displays global trends reported in several cross-national textbook studies, i.e., trends regarding human rights, individual agency, global citizenship, and emphasis on the nation state and national institutions. The underlying question in these studies is whether what counts as legitimate knowledge varies over time and, if so, whether there are global predictors. Let us first consider each trend and what the studies identified as the main determinants of the changes in textbook emphasis. Next, we reflect on the overall pattern.

Figure 1.1 shows that the proportion of textbooks that explicitly mention human rights has increased globally over time. Data for Figure 1.1 draw upon a cross-national data set of over 500 textbooks from 1950 to 2011 (see Bromley & Cole 2017; Russell et al.,

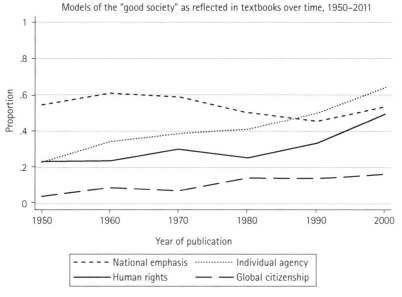

FIGURE 1.1 Legitimating models of the "good society" as reflected in textbooks over time.

2018; Terra & Bromley, 2012, for studies using the same data set), where textbooks were coded for discussions and emphasis of various topics such as human rights, diversity, citizenship, nationalism, and international coverage of social issues. We observed items from the coding document pertaining to human rights, individual agency, global citizenship, and emphasis on the nation state that are similar to those explored in studies examining textbooks from 1970 to 2011.

This finding is consistent with prior longitudinal textbook studies that there have been worldwide increases in valorized human rights (Bromley & Lerch, 2018; Meyer et al., 2010) and diversity (Jimenez & Lerch, 2019; Ramirez et al., 2009). There are two additional findings especially relevant to thinking about globalization and education. First, there is a surge in human rights emphases in the post-1990 era. This is a period characterized by the collapse of the Soviet Union and the increase in democracies around the world (Diamond, 1999). More person-centric understandings of progress and justice models overshadow more state-centric ones. Thus, a strong era zeitgeist impact is found, net of the positive influence of country-level democracy itself. Secondly, countries better connected to the world society via membership in international nongovernmental organizations are more likely to incorporate discussions of human rights and diversity into their textbooks (Bromley & Lerch, 2018; Jimenez & Lerch, 2019). This is consistent with the world society hypothesis that countries that are more embedded in the global environment would reflect the values and standards of world culture more prominently than their more isolated counterparts such as North Korea. In the latter, one can find textbooks that refer to "capitalist American" bastards (Lankov, 2013, p. 60).

Textbooks are increasingly more student centered, encouraging students to develop their own opinions and views on various issues and portraying active students involved and participating in society by volunteering to help the poor or joining a political party (Bromley et al., 2011). Other studies also find that textbooks increasingly portray individuals, including from traditionally marginalized groups such as women, children, and minorities, as having agency to make their own decisions and play a contributing role in society (Lerch et al., 2017). These studies also show post-1990 era surges as well as the positive influence of greater integration in the global environment.

This increased sense of agency and empowerment is not limited to the local and national contexts. Textbooks throughout the world increasingly mention globalization and even global citizenship (Buckner & Russell, 2013). Textbooks also further emphasize and encourage students to become more aware of the world, develop skills to function in an interconnected world, and suggest ways for students to be involved and take action at the global level (Lee, 2020). In other words, textbooks do not simply transmit knowledge that indicates that more individuals have rights and are empowered participants in the world. Rather, textbooks increasingly depict a world where individuals, including children and youth, are believed to have agency and encouraged to take positive action as contributing members of national and world society (Wotipka et al., 2020). The Education for All Conferences emphasized the benefits of expanded education not only for individuals and their countries but for the world itself (Chabbott, 2003). This worldview is reflected in the changing content of school textbooks, with its greater emphasis on individual agency addressing world problems, such as environmental issues.

These ideas of increased agency are further supported by pedagogy embedded in the textbooks. Examination of pedagogical emphases in textbooks finds that students are increasingly encouraged to be active learners who construct knowledge instead of being passive recipients of information (Bromley et al., 2011). Although these studies are not indicators of what actually happens in the classroom, the fact that textbooks increasingly promote student-centered pedagogical approaches suggests that educational ideas about how to deliver curricula have been changing to reflect the legitimated global model which emphasizes the empowered individual.

Although textbooks reflect a globalizing world where individuals are empowered to engage with and take action around issues outside their own immediate communities, the historic nationalizing purpose of schooling does not go away. Textbooks continue to celebrate a distinctive national state or society, even with the slight decline in the 1980s and 1990s (Figure 1.1). Nation-centered narratives in textbooks persist into the era of globalization and are not diminished in countries that are more economically, politically, or socially globalized (Lerch et al., 2017). In fact, as we see in Figure 1.1, more social studies textbooks emphasize the national narrative as compared to notions of human rights, individual agency, or global citizenship. What this suggests is that though the legitimating global models of human rights and empowered individualism are increasingly incorporated in textbooks, the celebration and emphasis of the national not only persist but remain important elements of what is included in social studies throughout the world. This is not a zero-sum game, as Moon and Koo (2011) demonstrate in their analysis of textbooks in South Korea.

In sum, cross-national studies of textbooks reveal how knowledge transmitted to students in mass schooling expands and changes over time to reflect legitimating global models of human rights and the empowered individual. It is not just that mass schooling expands as more groups of people (e.g., women, minorities, economically disadvantaged) are viewed as having the right to education. Curricular content changes to reaffirm these global models as the "right knowledge" to have. Furthermore, the young are encouraged to enact the models by emphasizing their individual agency to take action as participants and contributors to society, local or global—all the while continuing to celebrate the nation state as loyal and productive citizens.

WHO COUNTS AND WHAT COUNTS IN HIGHER EDUCATION: CELEBRATING ACCESSIBILITY AND FLEXIBILITY

Higher education predates nation states, though universities evolved to become national educational projects in the era of nation states (Ben-David, 1977). Though higher education continues to differ with respect to governance and funding issues (Clark, 2006), the legitimate nation state is now expected to embrace higher education as a more accessible and more flexible institution. Greater accessibility is evident in the worldwide expansion of higher education, fueled by the legitimacy of higher education credentials in allocating and determining the life course chances of greater numbers of people. Greater flexibility is evident in the worldwide expansion of educational innovations, as manifested in the proliferation of new courses and different degrees in higher education (Frank & Gabler, 2006). The globally legitimated credential society is one where more people pursue higher education and what is pursued is increasingly shaped by the tastes and interests of more people. Who counts and what counts change over time, and the changes transcend variations in the historical legacies of universities. These changes are widely construed as progressive and fair. There are critics, and we turn to these in a brief concluding reflection.

We address the greater accessibility issue by focusing on groups previously excluded from higher education, paying special attention to women and the scope of their inclusion. Next, we examine the growing flexibility of universities, shifts in the terms of inclusion that further valorized diversity and agentic empowerment.

The worldwide expansion of higher education also featured the global increase in women in higher education, as measured by gross tertiary enrollment ratio for women.[1] Figure 1.2a depicts this expansion, and it is clearly not a region-specific phenomenon. Here we also see surges across the world in the more recent decades. These are, of course, decades in which broader issues regarding and affirming women's equality gained global traction, the Ratification of the Convention to Eliminate All Forms of Discrimination Against Women, for example (Cole, 2005; Wotipka & Ramirez, 2008a). Not only were

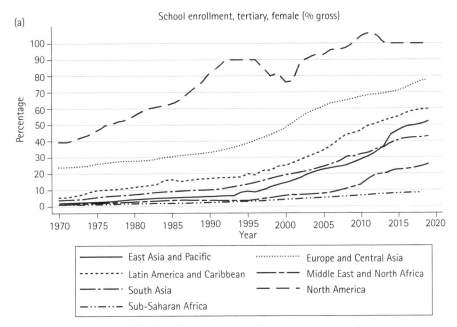

FIGURE 1.2A Expansion of higher education access for women across regions.

(*Source*: UNESCO)

there more women in higher education, but between 1970 and 2010 women's share of higher education increased worldwide (Ramirez & Kwak, 2015). One earlier reaction to this trend was to suggest that the growth was in areas of study other than STEM (Kelly, 1992). But in fact, women's share of STEM enrollments also increased in all regions except Eastern Europe (Kwak & Ramirez, 2018; Ramirez & Kwak, 2015; Wotipka & Ramirez, 2008b).

Another reaction was to call attention to the difference between enrollments and graduates. It is indeed reasonable to assume that graduating with a STEM degree is more difficult than merely being enrolled in this area. This may be especially the case for women as they face "chilly climates" and pressures to retreat to more culturally acceptable domains of study, education or the arts, for example (Charles & Bradley, 2009). But our preliminary studies of STEM graduation trends challenge even this reasonable assumption. To be sure, there are more STEM graduates who are men. However, between 1998 and 2018 women's share of STEM graduates has increased, albeit modestly (Lee et al., 2021). Figure 1.2b shows that women in STEM relative to the college age cohort have increased in all but sub-Saharan Africa.

Inequalities still persist, and groups of people such as the poor and minorities have a more difficult time accessing higher education than their privileged counterparts. However, the ascendancy of women in higher education worldwide undercuts the earlier and established idea that universities were naturally inhabited by men (White men in the Western world). More recent concerns shift from a focus on students to

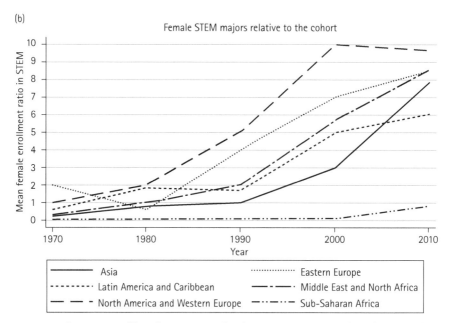

FIGURE 1.2B Percentage of female science, technology, engineering, and mathematics (STEM) majors out of the relevant age group, by region.

(*Source*: Kwak & Ramirez, 2018)

faculty. Even in this regard though, we find an increase in women faculty across the world (Wotipka et al., 2018), indicating expanded understanding of not only who gets to participate in education but also who gets to teach and contribute to what constitutes knowledge at the university level.

In retrospect, these worldwide changes should have been anticipated. The standardization and routinization of primary to secondary to tertiary education eased access for all people, including historically marginalized groups, to obtain university degrees (Frank & Meyer, 2020). Moreover, issues of barriers to access, quality, and equity became critical issues as higher education expanded, resulting in the creation of initiatives, taskforces, and offices at the university level to support efforts to diversify the student population and provide more equitable access to higher education. In America, an increasing number of universities established diversity offices and appointed senior-level diversity officers (Kwak et al., 2019). Similar university developments have been present in other countries such as Germany (Ortel, 2018). Programs, initiatives, and scholarships for women, minorities, and the economically disadvantaged multiplied over the 20th century and became institutionalized (Frank & Meyer, 2020).

Greater accessibility to higher education is both evident and much celebrated. Both human capital and human rights scripts favor greater accessibility. Reimagined as citizens and persons, women also count. The legitimate nation state is expected to utilize these scripts and, in tandem with international organizations and consultants without borders, favor a more accessible system of higher education.

One can imagine greater accessibility without greater flexibility in what counts as legitimate university knowledge. However, changes in the organization of universities are not limited to establishment of initiatives, activities, and offices to enact and reaffirm the global norm that all people have a right to pursue more higher education. The dominant notion that individuals are empowered actors who have freedom and agency to make their own choices has also influenced universities to widen their academic portfolio to cater to various kinds of perspectives and interests of individual persons (Frank & Gabler, 2006). Students and professors can break through old boundaries of sacred disciplines and canonical knowledge to claim and invoke new materials and repurpose existing materials and knowledge to their own tastes and interests (Frank & Meyer, 2002; Frickel & Gross, 2005).

Though extreme in the United States, students across the world are increasingly empowered to choose among a myriad of majors and can even create their own majors by piecing together knowledge from different disciplines and subdivisions. And since students are empowered to choose from an increasingly large pool of courses with flexibility (without extensive prerequisites or involved sequences), students can shape their own pathways to a degree (Robinson, 2011). Likewise, professors are also empowered to choose among endless research topics and influence course content in a way that speaks to their own interests and tastes (Frank & Meyer, 2020). They can move beyond the confines of their own disciplines to borrow, mix, and compound other disciplines to the point where disciplinary lines, though they do exist, are blurred and new disciplines emerge and gain traction.

In the era where the "good society" is one where individuals are empowered with rights, what emerges and constitutes knowledge to be transmitted expands to encompass what is of interest and meaningful to the individuals. What counts as "knowledge" under this global model of the "good society" is much influenced by empowered individuals who have the agency to pursue and create novel inquiries, research, and disciplines. Subsequently, universities change and adapt their organization to reflect global norms as legitimate institutions by allowing for self-designed majors, decreasing the number of required courses for all students, and establishing initiatives and programs to support interdisciplinary research for example. Thus, we find the rise of ethnic, women's, and environmental studies as well as management and computer science.

To be sure, there have always been curricular wars in universities. What is distinctive about the recent globalization era is the magnitude of the educational innovations and the rapidity of their diffusion. You can "read" feminist studies at Oxford and pursue ethnic studies at the Humboldt! The changes meet with some resistance but are not extensive enough for others. But it is clear that both greater accessibility and greater flexibility are now educational desiderata.

Concluding Thoughts

National educational projects were once contested terrain. Were the masses really educable? Should everyone really pursue higher education? Was the expansion and institutionalization of mass and higher education really indicative of a legitimate nation state? Did these national educational projects signal commitment to progress and justice?

Throughout the 20th century and especially after World War II, country after country answered these questions in the affirmative. International organizations and epistemic communities nudged laggards in the appropriate direction. What were once contested terrains became institutionalized or taken-for-granted domains. But, of course, these changes involved the erosion of earlier taken-for-granted realities—dynasties, colonies, the primacy of families and kin networks, unchangeable inequalities designed by "nature" and so forth. Within these earlier frameworks, education was limited and differentiated by class, race, and gender. Education for all and education for national development are recent, though very successful ideas much linked to the legitimacy of the nation state and the empowered individual.

Absent an "end of history" teleological perspective, one can recognize that the taken for granted can be challenged. Institutionalized domains can once again become contested terrains. In what follows, we briefly reflect on which educational developments are likely to persist and which are more vulnerable.

First, education for individual and for national development is likely to persist. The much-discussed ascendancy of China is not a return to the epoch of "Red over Expert" framing of progress. China is committed to expanding mass schooling and higher education as national educational projects. Its pursuit of "world class" universities illustrates the ongoing value of higher education to its educational and political leadership. Its framing of "world class" in favor of science and technology is attuned to contemporary global emphases on science and technology. Students from Shanghai participate in international testing regimes and command favorable global attention. Some Chinese universities are ascending in international rankings. Surprisingly some of China's universities also embrace progressive pedagogy, though in fact, much resistance from students ensues (Ouyang, 2003). Even more surprisingly, there are national educational guidelines that favor more progressive pedagogy, though these falter in rural schools with a lot of loose coupling between policy and practice taking place (Wang, 2013). The ascendancy of China may alter the balance between empowered individuals and national interests, with empowered individuals as human capital more emphasized. There may be a lot more state steering in the uses of education to develop human capital and corresponding less curricular innovations centered on the tastes and preferences of students and professors. This does not bode well for innovations such as women's studies and perhaps even environmental studies. Interest in progressive pedagogy may wane. Or, alternatively, these innovations may continue but "with Chinese characteristics."

The empirical issue is whether Chinese educational developments will be globalized as world models impacting both mass schooling and higher education. Will school textbooks in the coming decades be more nation state focused? Will there be a decline in references to human rights and global citizenship? Or will we see more significant between-region differences, implying an era of greater contestation as to what counts as knowledge and who counts in the pursuit of national development?

Secondly, it is doubtful that national policy will dramatically reverse course and return to an era where women were not much seen in higher education. There are indeed efforts to re-emphasize women's status as mothers and wives under the banner of saving families. Women's studies programs are likely vulnerable and especially so in authoritarian regimes in the recent climate of declining democracies. Whether we will continue to see a decline in democracies in the 21st century is unclear. However, educational participation rights earlier extended to men are more likely to be "sticky" rights for women. Newer rights claim specific to women are both more historically difficult to attain (Orloff, 1993) and more vulnerable to future challenges.

Lastly, what are we to make of challenges that target the authority of experts on climate change, human sexuality, or pandemics, to cite a few examples? The authority of experts presupposes a culture in which the educational credential is taken for granted as a sign of expertise. That culture requires logics of confidence (Meyer & Rowan, 1977) to be in place, in part because the experts at times disagree, change their assessments, and often opine on matters some steps removed from the specific domains of their credentialed authority. Much trust is required of nonexperts. However, that same culture empowers an ever-growing number of individuals. This can and has led to a proliferation of professions, with new entities seeking to become certified experts (Wilensky, 1964). Taken as a whole, the expansion of professionals strengthened the credential society.

However, more recently, the escalation of Internet-assisted virtual communities of empowered individuals challenges authority based on educational certification (Eyal, 2019). To be sure, the challengers often cite this medical doctor or that psychologist in support of their views. But these are not challengers that seek to be incorporated into the realm of experts, the rise and professionalization of economics, for example (Fourcade, 2006). Quite the contrary, these challenges directly confront the globally validated credential society. Some of these challenges are motivated by the view that all or most opinions have equal standing because we are all entitled to have opinions. None should be privileged by "listening to the science." This populist perspective challenges education as the institutional basis for determining what constitutes real knowledge. This challenge potentially undercuts efforts to further professionalize via educational certification with more people attuned to noneducational knowledge sites.

A different but also potent challenge questions the legitimacy of higher education as justification for allocating different people to different jobs associated with very unequal wages and life chances (Jackson, 2020). Here the critique goes beyond the importance of equalizing educational opportunities. Even where the latter is to be achieved, why is the credential a fair explanation for the growing income gap between the more and the less highly educated? This social democratic perspective challenges education as the institutional basis for determining who gets ahead and to what extent. This challenge potentially undercuts education-based efforts to rationalize inequalities.

These are both fundamental challenges to the authority of education to determine what counts and who counts. The degree to which these challenges upend education-based models of progress and justice remains to be seen.

To summarize and reiterate, the earlier expansion of mass schooling and the more recent growth of higher education were contested terrains that became institutionalized domains. What got institutionalized was a model of the good nation state as one committed to the first and second educational revolutions with education for individual and national development as overriding and interrelated goals. The world society perspective addressed these developments emphasizing their global character and the extent to which education was increasingly linked to progress (human capital) and justice (human rights). We explore what and who counts in a number of interrelated textbook analyses. These studies show an increased focus on empowered individuals but also of the persistence of the nation state. We also explored changes in who and what counts in higher education. Here we find that more categories of people (women, for example) count and what counts (fields of study) expands. More inclusive and more flexible higher education is valorized. Lastly, we reflected on different kinds of challenges to education to as an institution, suggesting which educational developments are likely to persist and which are more vulnerable.

NOTE

1. The gross enrollment ratio (GER) for tertiary school is calculated by dividing the number of students enrolled in tertiary education regardless of age by the population of the age

group which officially corresponds to tertiary education, and multiplying by 100 (UNESCO Institute of Statistics, 2020). The GER can be over 100% due to the inclusion of overaged and underaged students due to early or late entrants, and grade reputation.

REFERENCES

Anderson, B. R. O. G. (1991). *Imagined communities: Reflections on the origin and spread of nationalism*. Verso.

Apple, M. W. (1989). Textbook publishing: The political and economic influences. *Theory into Practice, 28*(4), 282–287.

Arendt, H. (1951). *The origins of totalitarianism*. Schocken Books.

Baker, D. (2014). *The schooled society: The educational transformation of global culture*. Stanford University Press.

Baker, D., Köhler, H., & Stock, M. (2004). *Socialist ideology and the contraction of higher education: Institutional consequences of state manpower and education planning in the former East Germany, 1949 to 1989*. Max Planck Institute for Human Development.

Barro, R. J., & Lee, J. (2015). *Education matters. Global schooling gains from the 19th to the 21st century*. Oxford University Press.

Benavot, A., & Resnik, J. (2006). Lessons in the past: A comparative socio-historical analysis of primary and secondary education. In J. E. Cohen, D. E. Bloom, & M. B. Malin (Eds.), *Educating all children: A global agenda* (pp. 123–229). MIT Press.

Ben-David, J. (Ed.). (1977). *Centers of learning: Britain, France, Germany, United States*. McGraw-Hill.

Berkovitch, N. (1999). The international women's movement: transformations of citizenship. In J. Boli & G. M. Thomas (Eds.), *Constructing world culture: International nongovernmental organizations since 1875* (pp. 100–126). Stanford University Press.

Boli, J., & Thomas, G. M. (1999). INGOs and the organization of world culture. In J. Boli & G. M. Thomas (Eds.), *Constructing world culture: International nongovernmental organizations since 1875* (pp. 100–126). Stanford University Press.

Boudon, R. (1973). Education and social mobility: A structural model. *Sociologie et Société, 5*(May), 111–124.

Bromley, P., & Cole, W. (2017). A tale of two worlds: The inter-state system and world society in social science textbooks. *Globalisation, Societies and Education, 15*(4), 425–447.

Bromley, P., & Lerch, J. C. (2018). Human rights as cultural globalization: The rise of human rights in textbooks, 1890–2013. In E. Fuchs (Ed.), *Palgrave handbook of textbook studies* (pp. 345–356). Palgrave Macmillan.

Bromley, P., Meyer, J. W., & Ramirez, F. O. (2011). Student centrism in social science textbooks: 1970–2005. *Social Forces, 90*(2), 547–570.

Buckner, E., & Russell, S. G. (2013). Portraying the global: Cross-national trends in textbooks' portrayal of globalization and global citizenship. *International Studies Quarterly, 57*(4), 738–750.

Chabbott, C. (2003). *Constructing education for development: International organizations and education for all*. Routledge.

Charles, M., & Bradley, K. (2009). Our gendered selves? Sex segregation by field of study in 44 countries. *American Journal of Sociology, 114*(4), 924–976.

Chirot, D. (1986). *Social change in the modern era*. Harcourt Brace Jovanovich.

Chmielewski, A. K. (2017). Social inequality in educational transitions under different types of secondary school curricular differentiation. In I. School & R. Silbereisen (Eds.), *Pathways to adulthood: Educational opportunities, motivation and attainment in times of social change* (pp. 51–72). UCL IoE Press.

Clark, W. (2006). *Academic charisma and the origins of the research university*. University of Chicago Press.

Cole, W. M. (2005). Sovereignty relinquished? Explaining commitment to the international human rights covenants, 1966–1999. *American Sociological Review, 70*(3), 472–495.

Cole, W. M., & Ramirez, F. O. (2013). Conditional decoupling: Assessing the impact of national human rights institutions, 1981 to 2004. *American Sociological Review, 78*(4), 702–725.

Collins, R. (1979). *The credential society: An historical sociology of education and stratification*. Columbia University Press.

Colyvas, J. A., & Jonsson, S. (2011). Ubiquity and legitimacy: Disentangling diffusion and institutionalization. *Sociological Theory, 29*(1), 27–52.

Coombs, P. H. (1968). *The world educational crisis: A systems analysis*. Oxford University Press.

Diamond, L. (1999). *Developing democracy: toward Consolidation*. Johns Hopkins University Press.

DiMaggio, P. J., & Powell, W. W. (1983). The iron cage revisited: Institutional isomorphism and collective rationality in organizational fields. *American Sociological Review, 48*(2), 147–160.

Dobbin, F., Simmons, B., & Garrett, G. (2007). The global diffusion of public policies: Social construction, coercion, competition, or learning? *Annual Review of Sociology, 33*, 449–472.

Douglass, J. A., King, C. J., & Feller, I. (Eds.) (2009). *Globalization's muse: Universities and higher education systems in a changing world*. Institute of Governmental Studies Press.

Duckworth, A. (2016). *Grit: The power of passion and perseverance*. Scribner.

Dweck, C. (2007). *Mindset: The new psychology of success*. Ballantine Books.

Eckstein, M., & Noah, H. (1992). *Examinations: Comparative and international studies*. Pergamon Press.

Elliott, M. A. (2007). Human rights and the triumph of the individual in world culture. *Cultural Sociology, 1*(3), 343–363.

European Technology Assessment Network. (2010). *Science policies in the European Union: promoting excellence through mainstreaming gender equality*. European Union.

Eyal, G. (2019). *The crisis of expertise*. Polity Press.

Fägerlind, I., & Saha, L. (1989). *Education and national development: A comparative perspective*. Butterworth-Heinemann.

Fiala, R., & Lanford, A. G. (1987). Educational ideology and the world educational revolution, 1950–1970. *Comparative Education Review, 31*(3), 315–332.

Fourcade, M. (2006). The construction of a global profession: The transnationalization of economics. *American Journal of Sociology, 112*(1), 145–194.

Fourcade, M., & Healy, K. (2017) Seeing like a market. *Socio-economic Review, 15*(1), 9–29.

Frank, D. J., & Gabler, J. (2006). *Reconstructing the university: Worldwide shifts in academia in the 20th century*. Stanford University Press.

Frank, D. J., & Meyer, J. W. (2002). The profusion of individual roles and identities in the postwar period. *Sociological Theory, 20*, 86–105.

Frank, D. J., & Meyer, J. W. (2020). *The university and the global knowledge society*. Princeton University Press.

Frickel, S., & Gross, N. (2005). A general theory of scientific/intellectual movements. *American Sociological Review, 70*, 204–232.

Furuta, J. (2017). Rationalization and student/school personhood in US college admissions: The rise of test-optional policies, 1987 to 2015. *Sociology of Education, 90*(3), 236–254.

Furuta, J. (2020). Liberal individualism and the globalization of education as a human right: The worldwide decline of early tracking, 1960–2010. *Sociology of Education, 93*(1), 1–19.

Furuta, J. (2021). Western colonialism and world society in national education systems: Global trends in the use of high-stakes exams at early ages, 1960 to 2020. *Sociology of Education, 94*(1), 84–101.

Furuta, J., Schofer, E., & Wick, S. (2021). The effects of high stakes educational testing on enrollments in an era of hyper-expansion: Cross-national evidence, 1960–2010. *Social Forces, 99*(4), 1631–1657.

Gordon, P. (1998). *The evolution of international human rights: Visions seen.* University of Pennsylvania Press.

Hafner-Burton, E. M., & Tsutsui, K. (2005). Human rights in a globalizing world: The paradox of empty promises. *American Journal of Sociology, 110*(5), 1373–1411.

Hathaway, O. A. (2002) Do human rights treaties make a difference? *The Yale Law Journal, 111*, 1935–2042.

Hout, M. (2012). Social and economic returns to college education in the United States. *Annual Review of Sociology, 38*, 379–400.

Hwang, H. (2006). Planning development: Globalization and the shifting locus on planning. In G. S. Drori, J. W. Meyer, & H. Hwang (Eds.), *Globalization and organization: World society and organizational change* (pp. 69–90). Oxford University Press.

Jackson, M. (2020). *Manifesto for a dream: Inequality, constraint, and radical reform.* Stanford University Press.

Jimenez, J., & Lerch, J. C. (2019). Waves of diversity: Depictions of marginalized groups and their rights in social science textbooks, 1900–2013. *Comparative Education Review, 63*, 167–188.

Kelly, G. (1992). Women and higher education reforms: expansion without equality. In P. Cookson, A. Sadovnik, & S. Semel (Eds.), *International handbook of educational reform* (pp. 545–559). Greenwood Press.

Krasner, S. D. (1993). Westphalia and all that. In J. Goldstein & R. O. Keohane (Eds.), *Ideas and foreign policy: Beliefs, institutions, and political change* (pp. 235–264). Cornell University Press.

Kwak, N., Gavrila, G. S., & Ramirez, F. O. (2019) Enacting diversity in American higher education. In T. Christense, A. Gornitzka Å., & F. O. Ramirez (Eds.), *Universities as agencies: Public sector organizations.* Palgrave Macmillan.

Kwak, N., & Ramirez, F. O. (2018). Is engineering harder to crack than science? A cross national analysis of women's participation in male-dominated fields of study in higher education. In A. Wiseman (Ed.), *Annual review of comparative and international education. International Perspectives on Education and Society* (Vol. 37, pp. 159–183). Emerald.

Lankov, A. (2013). *The real North Korea: Life and politics in the failed Stalinist utopia.* Oxford University Press.

Lauren, P. (2003). *The evolution of international human rights.* University of Pennsylvania Press.

Lee, S. S. (2020). Fostering "global citizens"? Trends in global awareness, agency, and competence in textbooks worldwide, 1950–2011. *Prospects, 48*, 215–236.

Lee, S. S., Wotipka, C. M., & Ramirez, F. O. (2021). A cross-national analysis of women graduates with tertiary degrees in science, technology, engineering, and math, 1998–2018: Commonalties and variations. In H. Ro, F. Fernandez, & B. House (Eds.), *Gender equity in STEM in higher education: International perspectives* (pp. 13–26). Routledge Research in STEM Education.

Lerch, J. C., Bromley, P., Ramirez, F. O., & Meyer, J. W. (2017). The rise of individual agency in conceptions of society: Textbooks worldwide, 1950–2011. *International Sociology*, 32(1), 38–60.

Lerch, J. C., Russell, S. G., & Ramirez, F. O. (2017). Wither the nation-state? A comparative analysis of nationalism in textbooks. *Social Forces*, 96(1), 153–180.

Mangan, J. A. (Ed.). (1994). *A significant social revolution: Cross-cultural aspects of the evolution of compulsory education*. Woburn Press.

Maynes, M. J. (1985). *Schooling in Western Europe: A social history*. State University of New York Press.

Mazon, P. (2003). *Gender and the modern research university: The Admission of women to German higher education, 1865–1914*. Stanford University Press.

Meyer, J., Boli, J., Thomas, Thomas, G. M., & Ramirez, F. O. (1997). World society and the nation-state. *American Journal of Sociology*, 103(1), 144–181.

Meyer, J., Ramirez, F., Rubinson, R., & Boli-Bennett, J. (1977). The world educational revolution, 1950–1970. *Sociology of Education*, 50(4), 242–258.

Meyer, J. W. (1977). The effects of education as an institution. *The American Journal of Sociology*, 83(1), 55–77.

Meyer, J. W., Bromley, P., & Ramirez, F. O. (2010). Human rights in social science textbooks, 1975–2006. *Sociology of Education*, 83, 111–134.

Meyer, J. W., Ramirez, F. O., & Soysal, Y. (1992). World expansion of mass education, 1870–1980. *Sociology of Education*, 65(2), 128–149.

Meyer, J. W., & Rowan, B. (1977). Institutional organizations: Formal structure as myth and ceremony. *American Journal of Sociology*, 83, 340–363.

Moon, R. J., & Koo, J. (2011). Global citizenship and human rights: A longitudinal analysis of social studies and ethics textbooks in the Republic of Korea. *Comparative Education Review*, 55(4), 574–599.

Mundy, K., & Murphy, L. (2000). Beyond the nation state: Educational contention in global civil society. In H. D. Meyer & B. Boyd (Eds.), *Education between state, markets and civil society—Comparative perspectives* (pp. 223–244). Lawrence Erlbaum Associates.

National Commission on Excellence in Education. (1983). *A nation at risk: The imperative for educational reform*. U.S. Department of Education.

Orloff, A. S. (1993). Gender and the social rights of citizenship: The comparative analysis of gender relations and welfare states. *American Sociological Review*, 58(3), 303–328.

Ortel, S. (2018). The role of imprinting on the adoption of diversity management in German universities. *Public Administration*, 96, 104–118.

Ouyang, H. (2003). Resistance to the communicative method of language instruction within a progressive Chinese university." In K. M. Anderson-Levitt (Ed.), *Local meanings, global schooling: Anthropology and world culture theory* (pp. 121–140). Palgrave Macmillan.

Ramirez, F. O. (2012). The world society perspective: Concepts, assumptions, and strategies. *Comparative Education Review*, 48(4), 423–439.

Ramirez, F. O., & Boli, J. (1987) The political construction of mass schooling: European origins and worldwide institutionalization. *Sociology of Education*, 60(1), 2–17.

Ramirez, F. O., Bromley, P., & Russell, S. G. (2009). The valorization of humanity and diversity. *Multicultural Education Review*, 1(1), 29–54.

Ramirez, F. O., & Kwak, N. (2015) Women's enrollments in STEM in higher education: Cross-national trends, 1970–2010. In W. Pearson, L. Frehill, & C. McNeely (Eds.), *Advancing women in science* (pp. 9–49). Springer.

Ramirez, F. O., Meyer, J. W., & Lerch, J. (2016). World society and the globalization of educational policy. In K. Mundy, A. Green, R. Lingard, & A. Verger (Eds.), *The handbook of global education policy* (pp. 43–63). Wiley-Blackwell.

Ramirez, F. O., & Ventresca, M. J. (1992). Building the institution of mass schooling: Isomorphism in the modern world. In B. Fuller & R. Rubinson (Eds.), *The political construction of education: The state, school expansion, and economic change* (pp. 47–59). Praeger.

Readings, B. (1996). *The university in ruins.* Harvard University Press.

Rholen, T. P. (1989). Order in Japanese society: Attachment, authority, and routine. *Journal of Japanese Studies, 15*(1), 5–40.

Robinson, K. J. (2011). The rise of choice in the U.S. university and college: 1910–2005. *Sociological Forum, 26,* 601–622.

Russell, S. G., Lerch, J. C., & Wotipka, C. M. (2018). The making of a human rights issue: A cross-national analysis of gender-based violence in textbooks, 1950–2011. *Gender & Society, 32*(5), 713–738.

Schissler, H. (1989). Limitations and priorities for international social studies textbook research. *The International Journal of Social Education, 4*(3), 81–89.

Schofer, E., Hironaka, A. Frank, D. J., & Longhofer, W. (2012). Sociological institutionalism and world society. In E. Amenta, K. Nash, & A. Scott (Eds.), *The Wiley-Blackwell companion to political sociology* (pp. 57–68). Blackwell.

Schofer, E., & Meyer, J. W. (2005). The worldwide expansion of higher education in the twentieth century. *American Sociological Review, 70*(6), 898–920.

Shills, E. (1971). No salvation outside higher education. *Minerva, 9*(3), 313–321.

Smith, M. S., & O'Day, J. (1991). Systemic school reform. In S. H. Fuhrman & B. Malen (Eds.), *The politics of curriculum and testing: The 1990 yearbook of the politics of education association* (pp. 233–267). Falmer Press.

Somers, M. R. (2008). *Genealogies of citizenship: Markets, statelessness, and the right to have rights.* Cambridge University Press.

Strang, D. (1990). From dependency to sovereignty: An event history analysis of decolonization, 1870–1987. *American Sociological Review, 55*(6), 846–860.

Strang, D., & Meyer, J. (1993). Institutional conditions for diffusion. *Theory and Society, 22*(4), 487–511.

Terra, L., & Bromley, P. (2012). The globalization of multicultural education in social science textbooks: Cross-national analyses, 1950–2010. *Multicultural Perspectives, 14*(3), 136–143.

Tsutsui, K. (2018). *Rights make might: Global human rights and minority social movements in Japan.* Oxford University Press.

UNESCO Institute of Statistics (2020). *Data for the sustainable development goals.* UNESCO.

Verger, A. (2009). The merchants of education: Global politics and the uneven education liberalization process within the WTO. *Comparative Education Review, 53*(3), 379–401.

Vreeland, J. R. (2003). Why do governments and the IMF enter into agreements? Statistically selected case studies. *International Political Science Review, 24*(3), 321–343.

Wang, D. (2013). *The demoralization of teachers: Crisis in a rural school in China.* Lexington Books.

Weitz, E. D. (2019). *A world divided: The global struggle for human rights in the age of nation-states.* Princeton University Press.

Wilensky, H. (1964). The professionalization of everyone? *American Journal of Sociology, 7,* 137–158.

Wotipka, C. M., Nakagawa, M., & Svec, J. (2018). Global linkages, the higher education pipeline, and national contexts: The worldwide growth of women faculty, 1970–2012. *International Journal of Comparative Sociology*, *59*, 212–238.

Wotipka, C. M., & Ramirez, F. O. (2008a). World society and human rights: An event history analysis of the Convention on the Elimination of All Forms of Discrimination Against Women. In B. A. Simmons, F. Dobbin, & G. Garrett (Eds.), *The global diffusion of markets and democracy* (pp. 303–343). Cambridge University Press.

Wotipka, C. M., & Ramirez, F. O. (2008b). Women's studies as a global innovation. In A. Wiseman (Ed.), *The worldwide transformation of higher education* (pp. 89–110). Emerald.

Wotipka, C. M., Yiu, L., Svec, J., & Ramirez, F. O. (2020). The status and agency of children in school textbooks, 1970–2012: A cross-national analysis. *Compare*.

CHAPTER 2

AN ANTHROPOLOGICAL PERSPECTIVE ON GLOBALIZATION AND SCHOOLING

KATHRYN ANDERSON-LEVITT

THIS chapter lays out an understanding of education around the world—particularly schooling—from the perspective of anthropologists. It will argue that anthropologists note and document the worldwide spread of Western-style schooling, highlighting the roles of coercion and "soft power" in its original dissemination and in the promotion of further convergence around "global education reforms." However, anthropologists also document the ways in which local actors translate into their own terms and sometimes resist Western schooling and global reforms, leading to the general consensus among anthropologists that, in this case as in others, "cultural differentiation tends to outpace homogenization" (Appadurai, 2015, p. 235).

The chapter begins with background information on anthropologies and aligned disciplines, our understanding of "education" and "schooling," and our approaches to studying schooling in global context. The second section discusses anthropological views on "globalization" in general. After noting anthropological interest in the global movement of *things* and especially of *people* as they impact schools, I then examine the global movement of two *ideas*, the original spread of a Western form of schooling, and the recent spread of "global" ideas for reforming it. The conclusion discusses some implications of continual cultural differentiation for attempts to improve schooling around the world.

Anthropologies and Anthropologies of Education

"Anthropology," glossed as the study of human beings, refers to a family of overlapping disciplines that study human populations around the world from the beginning of humanity through the present. The anthropology that focuses on living people is variously called social or cultural anthropology, *ethnographie* (Gingrich, 2005, p. 138), or ethnology (Bošković & Eriksen, 2008). In some nations, social/cultural anthropology emphasizes doing research "abroad," and that experience gave the discipline early familiarity with processes that draw diverse parts of the world into a tighter economic network, and with the two-way movement of things, people, and ideas.

Despite the disciplinary diversity, I believe many anthropologists would agree that we try to see through two different lenses simultaneously, on the one hand, seeking to understand human life across the whole earth yet, on the other, zooming in on everyday experiences in particular places. In addition, many anthropologists would accept three premises that guide this chapter: First, reality is socially constructed (a premise shared with neo-institutionalists per Schofer et al., 2012); indeed, anthropology's concept of "culture" can be understood as the process of making and remaking meaning in every social situation (Anderson-Levitt, 2012). Second, human beings nonetheless also live in a real physical world and therefore need resources such as food and the tools for making a living—resources that are often unequally distributed across families and across societies. Third, unequal distribution is created largely through the exercise of power by some people over others.

Anthropologies of Education

Anthropologists use the word *education* to refer to any intervention in learning, that is, any "deliberate and systematic attempt to transmit skills and understandings, habits of thought and deportment" (Hansen, 1979, p. 28). Humans use a wide variety of methods to educate one another (Henry, 1960), whether the goal is to prepare workers, to socialize community members, or to expand intellectual horizons (Biesta, 2009). Schooling is just one subset of educational methods. We define *schooling* as institutionalized education deliberately divorced from everyday life (Hansen, 1979; Lancy et al., 2010; cf. Danic, 2008). This definition includes many forms, such as initiation schools and Quranic, Sanskrit, and Buddhist institutions (Dasen & Akkari, 2008). However, like other articles in this volume, this chapter will focus on Western-style schooling, especially at the primary and early secondary levels.

When studying education with attention to globalization, anthropologists use ethnography, a philosophical approach to research using participant observation, interviews, and other methods to understand everyday life and how people make sense of it in particular settings (e.g., Sánchez, 2020). A study of "global" educational policy may require multisited ethnography, with coherence maintained by "studying through" (Wright & Reinhold, 2013), that is, by tracing a policy "through space, through time, and through the transformation of key words and discourses" (Wright, 2016, p. 60). Ethnographers often seek to amplify the voices of less powerful actors who otherwise may be ignored, but we also attempt to "study up" (Nader, 1969), conducting ethnography with the powerful originators of policy ideas.

"Anthropology of education" overlaps with other disciplines that use similar methods. Indeed, in some countries, the majority of ethnographic work on schooling has been conducted not by anthropologists but rather by sociologists (Delamont, 2011; Raveaud & Draelants, 2011; although see Filiod, 2007; Mills, 2012); psychologists (Minoura, 2011); or scholars of ethnic minorities (Eröss, 2011; Ouyang, 2011).

Anthropologists also use comparison, the discipline's oldest methodology. Particularly useful for studying globalization and education is the comparative case study approach (Bartlett & Vavrus, 2017), which compares across three dimensions: "vertically," tracing policies from macro to micro scales; "horizontally" across different local contexts; and "transversally" through time.

"Globalization" Seen From Anthropology

Scholars disagree on the meaning of "globalization," but a good starting point, simplifying from Appadurai (1996) and Trouillot (2001), is to focus on the global flow of things, of people, and of ideas. However, because "flow" can imply displacement without agency, struggle, or transformation of the terrain, I follow Anna Tsing in using the term "movement" (2000, pp. 349–351; see also Graeber, 2002, p. 1224).

For anthropologists, movements of things, ideas, and people—diffusion and migration—are hardly new. Indeed, during their 100,000 to 200,000 years on earth, "most human societies have *always* been in interactive relations with others, forming spheres of exchange and circulation" (Appadurai, 2015, p. 233, emphasis his; see also Bentley, 1993; Graeber & Wengrow 2021; McNeill & McNeill, 2003). However, one could say that "*massive* flow of goods, peoples, information, and capital," creating worldwide, unequal, economic interdependence, has occurred since the 16th century (Trouillot, 2001, p. 128, my emphasis). Granted, movements became even more massive during the 20th century, but that is partly because the human population itself has quadrupled since 1920 (Roser et al., 2019).

Power Matters

Most anthropologists studying global schooling pay attention to power (e.g., Stambach & Ngwane, 2011, p. 307). This is not surprising since, with few exceptions, Western-style schooling originally spread beyond Europe in the context of colonialism and economic pressure.

However, military force and economic force are not the only forms of power. Besides such "compulsory" power, Barnett and Duvall (2004, 2005) distinguish among the following:

- "institutional" power to set an agenda or rules such that all actors are subsequently constrained, as in struggles to define Sustainable Development Goals (Tikly, 2017);
- "structural" power that is built into the "underlying social structures," such as the global capitalist economy, "that advantage some and disadvantage others" (Barnett & Duvall 2005, pp. 42–43), such as the power of the donors who wield the funds or, more subtly, the power of English and French speakers in the Global Partnership for Education (Menashy, 2019); and
- "productive" power, referring to the production of "subjectivities" (Barnett & Duvall, 2004, p. 10), such as the ability to define "what constitutes legitimate knowledge" (2004, p. 3) as in the widespread agreement that Program for International Student Assessment (PISA) results and league tables matter (Tikly, 2017).

While institutional power implies deliberate action, structural and productive power can operate even unintentionally. Structural power can make reforms associated with the wealthiest states seem inevitable (Barnett & Duvall, 2005), while productive power operates in the background to enhance the "attractiveness" of policies, which Nye called "soft power" (2004, p. 256). None of this means that less advantaged actors are completely powerless, as I will note in the section on policy.

I refer first to states because states still matter to anthropologists (Appadurai, 2015, p. 234; Trouillot, 2001). They still function as "the supreme authorizer" of education policy within their boundaries (Levinson et al., 2009, p. 771; see also Miñana & Arango, 2011), while wealthy aid-giving states use economic rewards and the cachet accrued from structural and productive power to influence other states' policies. At the same time, some international organizations, founded and often funded by wealthy states, now also exercise power, including compulsory power (Barnett & Finnemore, 2005), as when the World Bank has conditioned desperately needed loans on acceptance of certain reforms. Anthropologists likewise acknowledge the growing use of power by corporations (Okongwu & Mencher, 2000, p. 108).

An emphasis on power does not exclude the possibility that actors borrow ideas about schooling simply because they are good ideas. Indeed, demand from families and communities has driven much of the expansion of schooling in Africa (Lange & Yaro, 2003) while states sometimes deliberately seek out good policies from other states (Phillips, 2006); thus, some scholars propose a continuum from voluntary to coerced borrowing (Portnoi, 2016, drawing on Ochs & Phillips, 2004). However, family demand often represents a strategy for economic survival in desperately unequal state and global economies, while states may borrow because they accept the ideology of cross-national economic competition legitimized by reports from the Organization for Economic Cooperation and Development (OECD) and the World Bank. Thus, it can be difficult to distinguish truly voluntary borrowing from the operation of subtler forms of power.

Action Is Local and Travel Means Translation

From an anthropological perspective, global ideas do not become real or have impact until they exert or encounter "friction" in specific encounters (Tsing, 2005). Encounters are local in the sense that real, specific people interact with one another (and I would apply the word "local" even when an encounter is mediated by telephone, Internet, or written text). "Local" as opposed to global is also a relative term used variously to refer to encounters at national ministries, subnational units, school districts, or individual schools (Anderson-Levitt, 2012). From this perspective encounters between real, specific people, even when labeled "global," happen locally. Referring to global and local "levels" can therefore be a misleading metaphor; "there is no global space floating above the local" (Friedman, 2007, p. 111; see also Latour 2005, p. 177).

What do anthropologists mean by "global," then? For Tsing, the global is what travels (2005, p. 213); it spreads through "translation" (2005, p. 224). I would add that what makes an organization "global" is official recognition as being "global" by states or other actors (recognition enjoyed by UNESCO and the World Bank as arms of the United Nations), or simply a little-challenged claim to speak for the world (as enjoyed by the OECD).

Anthropologists recognize movement toward homogenization as a result of widespread diffusion, as in, for example, the spread of the English, Spanish, and Portuguese languages. However, because we understand humans as engaged in ongoing processes of making meaning (e.g., Street, 1993), when an idea claimed to be global travels to a new locality, whether presented by officials as a new policy, offered on a website, or introduced by a colleague who has encountered it elsewhere, local actors necessarily interpret it within their own frame of reference and, if they seek to implement it, must make it fit within local practices. Thus, they cannot help but remake its meaning in local terms (Anderson-Levitt, 2012). The same form, whether television or schooling, quickly begins to be remade after traveling to a new place—and then is the same no more (e.g., Tobin, 1992). Indeed, even as travelers share policy ideas, they tend to share them "in bits and pieces" and the ideas thus travel as "policies already-in-transformation" (Peck & Theodore, 2010, p. 170).

Many metaphors for the remaking appear in anthropological texts: Local actors, again, "translate" the incoming idea (Shore, 2012), "appropriate" it to make it their own (Levinson et al., 2009), "indigenize" it (Appadurai, 1996, p. 32), or "creolize" it (Hannerz, 1987). These metaphors all point to the ongoing processes of cultural differentiation that happens as people remake ideas or objects, explaining why, ultimately, "globalisation is *not* the story of cultural homogenization" (Appadurai 1996, p. 11, my emphasis; cf. Comaroff & Comaroff, 2000, p. 305; Trouillot, 2001, p. 129).

Movement of Things

Here I shift from general theoretical background to anthropological studies of education in the context of globalization, commenting briefly on the movement of things and of people before examining the movement of ideas in more depth.

Because anthropologists work in real-world settings, we cannot help noticing the movement of things involved in the travel of schooling and its reforms. For example, publication and import of textbooks can involve a huge effort of physical distribution from, say, multinational companies to rural schools in the Global South. Schooling may also require the import of chalkboards, slates, and/or ballpoint pens from multinational companies. Thus, schooling implies the movement of money as well, in its various tangible forms as marks in a ledger, bits in a computer file, or physical cash paid as teachers' salaries in many parts of the Global South. Movement of things also accompanies traveling ideas; for example, a new curriculum inspired in part by the OECD's promotion of 21st-century skills leads to documents posted on computer networks and the publication of new teachers' guides.

Ironically, the unequal global movement of things contributes to diversity rather than homogenization on the ground by exacerbating economic inequalities within states and between states, producing inequalities in material resources and teachers' preparation across schools (e.g., Eisenhart, 2008; Weis & Dolby, 2012).

Movement of People

People on the move in the realm of schooling include educational consultants, aid officers, and Ministry personnel who have traveled to the Americas or Europe for advanced education. However, the global movement that preoccupies anthropologists of education is the massive movement of migrants and refugees and their children (Suárez-Orozco et al., 2011), which raises the question of how schools are educating millions of pupils moving into national school systems (Gibson & Koyama, 2011). For example, anthropologists ask whether and how schools serve migrant pupils' needs (García Castaño & Carrasco Pons, 2011), and they uncover the ways teachers "other" migrants' children and frame them as "culturally deprived" (Meo et al., 2019). In France, where the government prohibits recording people's self-identified ethnicities, ethnographers nonetheless document the salience of ethnicity for the children and grandchildren of immigrants in their interactions with schools (Ichou & van Zanten, 2019, p. 540).

A pertinent strand of this research examines schools as sites for creating national citizens (Chee & Jakubiak 2020) juxtaposed to the occasional countermoves by pupils to create identities as "sojourners" (Sarroub, 2005) or as "transnational" people with a foot in two or more countries (Lukose 2007; Vandeyar & Vandeyar, 2015). Ethnographers also record cases in which the "reanimation of xenophobic nationalism" undermines transnational identities (Solano-Campos, 2019, p. 63).

Movement of Ideas: Forms of Schooling

This section and the next examine the global movement of ideas about education, focusing here on the spread of the Western model of schooling and in the next section on the movement of "global" education reforms.

A New Universal

Western-style schooling has spread to the entire world, as mentioned, largely due to differential power. Colonization created easier access for missionary schooling, and it later led to decisions to "civilize" larger segments of the colonized populations through state-run schooling (e.g., Depaepe & Hulstaert, 2013; Swartz & Kallaway, 2018). Never-colonized states and empires like China and Japan imported Western forms of schooling "voluntarily" (Hayhoe 1992; Rappleye & Kariya, 2011), but in the context of Western military and economic expansion.

Although several forms of Western schooling were disseminated, including "individual" instruction in one-room schools, monitorial schooling, and mixed individual-monitorial structures, these were eventually displaced by a single form, namely, age-graded, self-contained classrooms (Caruso, 2015). In this model, the curriculum is divided into subjects (Tyack & Tobin, 1994), which are fairly uniform worldwide at the primary level (Meyer et al., 1992), with emphasis on numeracy and on literacy in a national language or world language (Cha, 1992). Teaching most often relies on lecture-recitation and seatwork (LeTendre et al., 2001), although the precise use of these pedagogies varies (Givvin et al., 2005). Also, since the late 20th century, boys and girls study together almost everywhere (Rogers, 2004; Tyack & Hansot, 1990).

Today, children in every society spend at least a few months if not years of their lives in schools that more or less fit this model, and it could be called a new cultural universal alongside mass media, mobile phones, and plastic containers. "Universals" are practices appearing in virtually all *societies*, not individuals (Antweiler, 2016). Individuals' experiences vary, and parents may give up on schooling when it does not keep its promise of leading to employment (Kendall & Silver, 2014). Even so, in 2020, an estimated 87.2% of the world's individuals over age 15 had experienced at least some Western-style schooling, and by 2100 that proportion is projected to be 99% (Roser & Ortiz-Ospina, 2016).

The spread of Western-style schooling, even when children learn little of the official curriculum, has had several consequences. Schooling provides new learning opportunities, exposing children (who might or might not have otherwise been so exposed) to literacy, often to a world language like Spanish or a national language like Indonesian, and to the idea of being citizens of a particular state. However, attending school also reduces or eliminates other learning opportunities (Rival, 1996). Western schooling has contributed to the loss of thousands of the world's languages and the knowledge systems embedded in their lexicons and grammars (Harrison, 2007). It has introduced instruction by strangers in places where learning used to take place only among kin or local community members. Because schools segregate children from adults and from everyday life, attendance reduces children's "opportunities to learn from observing and from becoming involved in the mature activities of their communities" (Rogoff et al., 2005, p. 227). In the case of Guatemalan Mayan children, schooling thereby reduced occasions to learn through keen observation and group collaboration (Rogoff et al., 2003). Schooling may also interfere with the widespread practice of sibling caretaking, thereby reducing opportunities for children to learn the perspective-taking and empathy that it develops (Maynard & Tovote, 2010, p. 198). In addition, schooling makes children less available to help the family economy through paid and unpaid labor (e.g., Lancy, 2022), a role some children have sought out even when staying in school would improve their later earning opportunities (Schlemmer, 2002). Western-style schooling has also become central to the process of stratifying members of society, supplanting direct inheritance of a parent's role (Baker, 2014; Vincent et al., 1994, p. 40).

The spread of Western schooling has also affected other forms of education. For example, initiation schools in West Africa now take place in condensed time frames during school vacations, and Quranic schools likewise may take place in the hours before or after the school day. Some madrasahs have modified their curricula to include the "scientific" curriculum of Western-style schools alongside advanced Islamic studies (Boyle, 2019). In informal education at home, Western-schooled mothers may interact in more "school-like" ways with their children than had been the prior norm in their society, as shown in studies of Guatemalan Mayan mothers (Rogoff et al., 2005).

Yet Divergent Pedagogies

At the same time, the spread of Western schooling illustrates how local actors—including national policymakers as well as educators in schools—have appropriated an incoming idea and made it their own, resulting in diverse local experiences. In richly documented comparisons of primary school classrooms in the United States, England, France, Russia, and India, Alexander (2000) demonstrated pedagogical differences rooted in history and culture across the five nations. He also identified transnational pedagogical traditions, namely, a continental European tradition of highly structured lessons traceable to 17th-century pedagogue Comenius (Alexander, 2001, p. 519) and an "Anglo-American nexus" focused on developmental readiness and democracy (2001, p. 520). From another part of the world, historian and anthropologist Elsie Rockwell described how teaching genres developed historically in Mexico, showing how contemporary teachers drew on practices rooted in national reforms of different eras as well as on more local cultures of teaching (2000, 2007).

The work of Joseph Tobin and his colleagues has particular importance for claims about globalization because it challenges the idea that pedagogies converge over time (Tobin et al., 1989, 2009; see also Hayashi, 2022). Although Tobin and colleagues studied early childhood education rather than compulsory schooling, they documented in detail teaching cultures in three countries (Japan, China, and the United States) at two different moments about 20 years apart. Comparing across both time and national cultures enabled them to demonstrate that:

> despite modernization and globalization, Chinese, Japanese, and American approaches to early childhood education are no more alike in their core practices and beliefs than they were a generation ago. Or rather we should say that over time they have become more alike in some ways and more different in others. (Tobin et al., 2009, p. 232)

Other comparative studies using methods similar to their "video-cued ethnography" have documented single-moment differences in pedagogical beliefs and practices between pairs of nations (Anderson-Levitt, 2002; Ben-Peretz & Halkes, 1987; Fujita & Sano, 1998; Spindler & Spindler, 1987). And many single-case ethnographies document the particularities of teaching and learning in other settings, such as Cameroon (Moore, 2010) and India (Clarke, 2001; Thapan, 2014). Anthropologists also document efforts by educators to create schooling that explicitly conforms to local community norms rather than to national or global models (e.g., Jordan, 1995; McCarty, 2001; Ladson-Billings, 2009; Sumida Huaman & Abeita, 2018).

In short, the Western form of schooling has spread throughout the globe, and its barebones structure has had an impact. Nonetheless, anthropologists like those cited here have documented the diversification that created different—sometimes radically different—experiences on the ground even where the outer form appears from a distance to be homogenous.

Movement of Ideas for Reforming Schooling

Global Reforms

Schooling as currently practiced is not serving pupils well in many places, as indicated by measures of learning and of equity (e.g., UNESCO, 2020), and hundreds of reformers have proposed to reform schooling—that is, to give it a new form as a more just, a more liberating, or a more efficient institution. This section examines anthropological studies of one particular set of reforms, policy ideas that have been promoted by global actors in recent decades. The global actors championing these reforms include international organizations—World Bank, UNESCO, and particularly the OECD—as well as large corporations and many educational consultants and academics.

The reforms in question include those listed in Table 2.1, updated from Anderson-Levitt (2003) in light of Pasi Sahlberg's discussion of Global Education Reform (2015, 2016) and insights from other analyses (e.g., Dale, 2000; Welmond, 2002). The label "global" refers to aspiration rather than fact, as Sahlberg listed many countries, including Germany and Japan, that "remained distant" to this "market-based reform ideology" (2016, p. 131). The first tier of the table notes the continued expansion of schooling, including the worldwide spread of early childhood education (Wotipka et al., 2013) and the expanding availability of higher education. In the second tier, "decentralization" refers to the idea of school autonomy, which is linked with neoliberalism's market competition and the supposed right of families to "choose" among government schools, reforms highlighted by Sahlberg (2016). The import of corporate models he noted also fits under decentralization in the sense that corporations tend to favor privatization of schools and experimentation in the interest of competition. I see "standardization" on the right side of the table as conceptually in tension with decentralization, although many observers see them as linked (Sahlberg 2016, p. 133; Verger & Curran, 2014, p. 256; Verger et al., 2019). For example, in Sweden in the 1990s, control over schooling shifted from the central government to municipalities, but at the same time a heavy burden of accountability fell on teachers (Nordin & Sundberg, 2021, p. 27). In another example of the tension, in the already decentralized United States of the late 1980s, the president argued for national standards to balance the autonomy exercised by districts and schools (Mehta, 2013, p. 194).

The third tier of the table focuses on pedagogy and curriculum or learning goals. Reformers continue to promote learner-centered pedagogies (Schweisfurth, 2013; Tabulawa, 2013). On the other hand, Sahlberg pointed out an increased focus on the disciplinary content of reading, mathematics, and, nowadays, science—in tension with learner-centered instruction, which in theory "is not based on learning a rigid content-centered curriculum" (Schweisfurth, 2013, p. 10). I add the notion of "competencies,"

Table 2.1 Proposed Global Reforms

Continued expansion of early childhood, secondary, and higher education		
Decentralization		Standardization
Market competition and "choice"	but also	Test-based accountability
Corporate models and privatization		Standards for learning outcomes
Learner-centered instruction	but also	Core disciplines: Literacy, numeracy, science
Competencies ("21st-century skills")		
Teacher professionalization	but also	Teacher accountability

also known as "21st-century skills," a set of interdisciplinary dispositions and skills like "critical thinking" and "creativity" and various "social and emotional" dispositions now promoted by international organisations as learning goals for the "knowledge economy" (e.g., OECD, 2018). Competencies are caught in the middle of the tension between decentralization and standardization; proponents often argue that they require learner-centered or "active" pedagogy, yet a number of nations have incorporated specific competencies into national standards (Anderson-Levitt & Gardinier, 2021). Finally, the fourth tier of the table, which shows teacher professionalization in tension with accountability for teachers, is an oversimplified reference to the many reforms focused on the quality of teachers and of teaching (e.g., Akiba, 2017).

Policy as the Practice of Power

Reform movements are efforts to change policy, and an anthropology of policy developed in part as a response to global reform efforts (e.g., Henze, 2020; Miñana & Arango, 2011). As one indicator of interest, in the past 15 years, the keyword "policy" was used for 11 articles in the US-based journal *Anthropology & Education Quarterly* and 18 articles in the Europe-based *Ethnography and Education*; "neoliberalism" for 10 and 2 articles respectively, and "reform" for 9 and 4.

Anthropologists see policy as not simply as text or discourse, but as "a kind of social practice, specifically, a practice of power" (Levinson et al., 2009, p. 767). As mentioned, reforms noted in Table 2.1 have been promoted through economic power as well as the "soft power" of authoritative web sites and comparative international assessment. However, anthropologists of policy also distinguish "authorized policy" from "unauthorized, or informal policy," arguing that local actors such as teachers and pupils on the receiving end of authorized policy also make policy themselves through the way they "appropriate" (or resist) what has been mandated (Levinson et al., 2009, p. 768). As a result, "a policy is a narrative in a continual process of translation and contestation" (Shore & Wright, 2013; see also Shore, 2012).

Making Authorized Policy

A few ethnographers have found ways to accomplish the daunting task of "studying up" (Nader, 1969), that is, conducting participant observation and interviews with powerful people making authorized policy. Peter Jones used his position as an insider to study workings of the European Union and its Commission, documenting contention between different units of the Commission over humanistic versus economic visions of education (2012, p. 98). Camilla Addey (2017, 2018) used interviews and participant observation to investigate the making of PISA for Development (PISA-D) in Ecuador and Paraguay. Strikingly, Elena Aydarova gained access as an outsider to observe and interview Russian experts who shaped major reforms of teacher education and learning goals in Russia (2019); the Russian experts, some of whom consulted on the side for the World Bank, modified a reform introducing "competencies" for all pupils as promoted by the Bank into a stratified system with distinct goals for elite pupils and the masses (Aydarova, 2021).

These studies suggest two lessons about homogenization and diversification. First, the international organizations that author proposals for global education policies are hardly monoliths; there is dispute and struggle within them over what such policies should be. On this point, see also the qualitative but nonanthropological studies on early struggles within OECD over whether it was right or even possible to design the assessments that would become PISA (Morgan, 2007), and on the early lack of transnational consensus about competencies needed for the "knowledge economy" (Morgan, 2016). The second lesson is that translation from international organizations to national reformers, even when national reformers have one foot in the international organizations as in the Russian case, can result in authorized policies completely refashioned to suit a (contested) national agenda. On this point, see also qualitative nonanthropological studies on the diverse translations of national standards within federated states (Hartong, 2014) and on the processes whereby policymakers in France constructed first one and then a different competency-based reform (Clément, 2021).

Remaking Policies in Schools and Communities

More often than "studying up," anthropologists have studied how local, less powerful educators and pupils experienced incoming policies or translated them locally. For example, regarding the continuing expansion of higher education, Aomar Boum (2008) showed how increasing university access in rural Morocco, combined with the government's effort to decolonize the education system, marginalized rural pupils even as they gained access to university.

Anthropologists have tracked reforms promoting market competition and "choice" in multiple localities, including universities (e.g., Shore, 2010; Wright & Rabo, 2012). In studies of primary and secondary settings from India to Chile, ethnographers demonstrated that "the vocabulary of 'choice' provides a loose and malleable language for a variety of actors to pursue widely ranging goals" (Forsey et al., 2008, p. 22; see also Forsey, 2006). In a rich case from southwest China, Jinting Wu shows how rural teachers engaged creatively with audit culture and neoliberal market mandates, arguing that their "creative tactics and hybrid subjectivities challenge the resistance–compliance dichotomy" (Wu, 2018). Nonetheless, forcing market competition can have the negative consequence of pushing school leaders to "sell" their schools when they could otherwise have been supporting teachers to improve instruction (Delvaux & van Zanten, 2006; van Zanten, 2012).

Meanwhile, test-based accountability has drawn close attention in US-based studies (e.g., Valli & Chambliss, 2007; Zoch, 2017). In a notable example, Jill Koyama (2009, 2010) traced the US policy No Child Left Behind (NCLB) as it was translated by New

York City's school district, and from there to the varied ways in which 42 different public schools in the city appropriated the policy, which mandated tutoring by for-profit tutoring companies in "failing" schools. Although not explicitly addressing the "global," Koyama's ethnography is a model of a critical comparative case as laid out by Bartlett and Vavrus (2017); it moves "vertically" from the state of New York to the city school district to particular schools, and also compares "horizontally" across the schools, demonstrating "the remarkable variation in responses to NCLB across contexts" (Koyama, 2010, p. 6).

Koyama's focus on private tutoring companies also highlights the growing role of corporations that Sahlberg (2016) included as part of the Global Education Reform Movement. In another ethnographic study of corporate intervention, Geoffrey Saxe and Kenton Kirby examined implementation of the "One Laptop per Child" program in a remote part of Papua New Guinea (2018). Their analysis demands attention for its nuanced theoretical conception of "context," which they describe as a dynamic process "inseparable from the activities of individuals" (2018, 407), "historically contingent," and therefore not predictable (409), with "the potential to give rise to multiple trajectories" rather than follow a single pathway (2018, p. 409).

In the domain of curricular reforms, anthropologists and other qualitative researchers have followed local reactions to efforts by the World Bank and OECD to get states to include "21st-century skills" or "competencies" among national standards (Anderson-Levitt et al., 2017; Fichtner, 2012). While interdisciplinary competencies such as "critical thinking" and "collaboration" are often promoted to develop "human capital" for the "knowledge economy," some competencies are also cast as important to develop citizenship in democracies (Gardinier & Worden, 2010), or even global citizenship (Gardinier, 2021). Particularly relevant to the issue of globalization is that several states—Sweden, England, and Poland—have backtracked from the 21st-century skills they had previously built into national learning goals, suggesting a swing of the pendulum rather than a pattern of convergence (Anderson-Levitt & Gardinier, 2021).

In the realm of pedagogy, learner-centered instruction, a complex spectrum of approaches (Schweisfurth, 2013), has attracted close attention from anthropologists. Arathi Sriprakash (2012) traced the historical development of two learner-centered instructional programs in India, documenting influence by the World Bank, the European Community, UNICEF, the United Kingdom, and the Netherlands but also by a Krishnamurti Foundation school in India. She then turned to interpretations of learner-centered instruction in two programs in the state of Karnataka, providing ethnographic details on how teachers reconfigured each program to adapt to their working conditions as well as to their own deficit models of rural children (cf. Sarangapani, 2003). In another case, US-based anthropologists studied their own effort to introduce learner-centered pedagogy among groups of teachers in Tanzania, likewise acknowledging not only European and US roots but also local precedent in the form of Nyere's Education for Self-Reliance (Vavrus & Bartlett, 2012, 2013). They followed secondary teachers whom they themselves had trained into their classrooms, showing how the teachers adapted the pedagogy to their own understanding of knowledge as something predetermined, not constructed.

CONCLUSION AND DISCUSSION

Ongoing Differentiation

This review of anthropological research on globalization and schooling teaches three lessons. First, in the case of schooling, as in many other human endeavors, "no anthropologist . . . argues that the global future will be culturally homogeneous" (Tsing 2000, p. 339). Anthropologists do indeed acknowledge processes of homogenization such as the spread of Western-style schooling to every society. We also document its impacts on languages spoken in communities, on familiarity with literacies, on what young people learn and no longer learn, and often on typical ways of learning— although the specific impact in any particular society depends on specific prior practices. However, anthropologists have also demonstrated that educators and pupils regularly translate Western-style schooling into distinctly different lived experiences in different nations and sometimes even in different neighborhoods within the same city (e.g., Eisenhart, 2008). Likewise, as globally minded reformers seek to reform the original form to introduce market competition, standardized testing and autonomy but also accountability, learner-centered pedagogies, and standardized learning goals, anthropologists and fellow ethnographers document how local actors translate and sometimes subvert traveling policies to make sense of them within their own intellectual frameworks, and to adapt them to local constraints. Ethnographic studies document ambivalence or outright resistance among many local actors to reforms such as market competition. Other reforms such as learner-centered instruction sometimes appeal philosophically to local educators but fit poorly with material conditions in their classrooms. The end result is that traveling policies, already contested within organizations that promote them, diversify further as hundreds of millions of educators and their billion pupils and students work to translate them in local encounters all over the world.

This lesson does not imply that local is always and automatically better. Aydarova's research in Russia (2021) illustrates how local actors can reinterpret a traveling policy to the detriment of working-class pupils. Some local logics and practices also maintain the exclusion of girls or of minoritized populations. Moreover, there may be multiple local perspectives in competition; just as there is contestation within international organizations over how to define global policies, there is often contestation over how to translate policies at the national and district levels (e.g., Aydarova, 2019).

Rather, the lesson simply means that attempts to bend local practices to a single arc, one defined by a relatively few decision-makers and scholars based in affluent countries, will not lead to convergence on homogenized practices because local actors will necessarily remake reforms. If momentary convergence seems to appear, it will not last for long. Also, what looks like convergence may turn out to be a swing of the pendulum, a shift from one side to the other in perennial cultural debates such the tension between learner-centered and content-centered pedagogy.

Power

A second lesson is that Western-style schooling and later reforms have spread in large part due to the exercise of power. In fact, some anthropologists of education policy state very simply that "policy formation is best conceived as a practice of wielding power" (Levinson et al., 2009, p. 771). Sometimes power has been exercised baldly in the form of colonial conquest or conditions placed on crucial loans; in other cases, states, international organizations, or corporations exercise "soft" power by supporting and reporting research and creating comparative assessments that enhance the legitimacy of selected reforms. Structural and productive power can enhance the perceived inevitability if not the legitimacy of reforms favored by advantaged actors without direct action by those actors. Thus, even when families and decision-makers willingly choose certain educational options, their choices may have been biased by economic need or desire for prestige in a system shaped by structural inequalities.

Ethnographers and other qualitative researchers make visible policy as a practice of power by describing struggles within bodies like the European Commission and the OECD over the creation of proposed reforms, standardized tests, and similar tools. They also make the exercise of power visible when exposing local actors' overt resistance to policies or efforts to manipulate waves of incoming reforms.

States

A third lesson—one with which many political scientists agree (Guillén, 2001)—is that even as the power of international organizations and corporations grows, the state matters. It is national ministries—or in federal systems, subnational ministries (Hartong, 2014)—that translate reform ideas into authorized policy. Thus, when local actors experience reform imposed "from above," they often experience it as coming from the state. Moreover, translations of a global idea such as "21st-century skills" by national ministries of education can vary markedly (Care et al., 2016). As described earlier, anthropologists have also documented the continuing role of the state, through its schools, in converting the children of migrants into national citizens, or in excluding them from full belonging.

Implications

The implication from this review is to avoid placing trust in a single form of schooling or a simple list of reforms. Advocates of global reforms should not expect them to translate uniformly in local contexts, and should beware of unintended negative consequences in new contexts, as amply documented in ethnographic work.

Making change to improve schooling is best done by school leaders and teachers themselves, provided with the time and support to work year after year (Erickson, 2014). In fact, this review implies that making change in schooling is work actually accomplished by no one other than educators in local schools, however much they are inspired or pushed by district, ministry, or global reformers. Local educators are the ones who, within the constraints of layers and layers of prior reforms, struggle over the purposes of education within their school (Biesta, 2009) and over the methods they use to try to achieve those purposes. Ideally, they do that in dialogue with the pupils and communities they serve.

As noted, local interpretations are not guaranteed to be just, and they may well be contested. Therefore, there can be roles for outsiders, who can gently and nonjudgmentally but persistently raise questions about justice, such as "Who benefits and who does not?" or "Are you remembering everyone?" (Ladson-Billings & Gomez [2001] offer one example of ethnographers doing such work). In the same vein, outsiders can use their research to amplify the voices of local actors who are not being heard, as ethnographers have often done. Importantly, actors beyond individual schools, ideally national or subnational governments, must supply the resources, including time, for educators to do the work over the years that improving schooling requires. Outsiders to a school, beginning with local pedagogical counselors or inspectors, can also facilitate the sharing of ideas not about global reforms or "what works" in general, but about "what worked at a particular moment in a particular school"—ideas that can inspire local educators to adapt them to their own circumstances.

Again, the lesson from the ongoing diversification of reforms imposed or borrowed from elsewhere is that it is and will be local educators who do the work of improving schooling. They need to be provided with the opportunities and support to make education both stimulating and useful for their pupils. Although the task is urgent in many places, real reforms require long-term—in fact, permanent—efforts at helping pupils learn better what they need to learn. Reformers will have to accept that there is probably more than one way to acquire literacy or to develop numeracy, and that educators and families will not always agree on the purpose of schooling. The educators and their allies will move toward the goal of all pupils learning, and learning better, by shaping schools or other educational settings that probably turn out to be at least as diverse as are present-day schools around the world.

Acknowledgments

Thanks to Xavier Dumay for thought-provoking questions, and to colleagues in anthropology and other disciplines whose work, cited and uncited, informed this chapter. Although the chapter refers to "we anthropologists," the interpretations are my own.

References

Addey, C. (2017). Golden relics and historical standards: How the OECD is expanding global education governance through PISA for Development. *Critical Studies in Education*, *58*(3), 311–325. doi:10.1080/17508487.2017.1352006

Addey, C. (2018). Researching inside the international testing machine: PISA parties, midnight emails and red shoes. In B. Maddox (Ed.), *International large-scale assessments in education: Insider research perspectives* (pp. 13–29). Bloomsbury.

Akiba, M. (2017). Understanding cross-national differences in globalized teacher reforms. *Educational Researcher*, *46*(4), 153–168. doi:10.3102/0013189X17711908

Alexander, R. J. (2000). *Culture and pedagogy: International comparisons in primary education*. Blackwell.

Alexander, R. J. (2001). Border crossings: Towards a comparative pedagogy. *Comparative Education*, *37*(4), 507–523. https://doi.org/10.1080/03050060120091292

Anderson-Levitt, K. M. (2002). *Teaching cultures: Knowledge for teaching first grade in France and the United States*. Hampton Press.

Anderson-Levitt, K. M. (2003). A world culture of schooling? In K. M. Anderson-Levitt (Ed.), *Local meanings, global schooling: Anthropology and world culture theory* (pp. 1–26). Palgrave Macmillan.

Anderson-Levitt, K. M. (2012). Complicating the concept of culture. *Comparative Education*, *48*(4), 441–454. doi:10.2307/23524668

Anderson-Levitt, K. M., Bonnéry, S., & Fichtner, S. (2017). Introduction to the dossier. "Competence-based" approaches as "traveling" reforms: Ideas, trajectories and practices in implementation. *Cahiers de la recherche sur l'éducation et les savoirs*, *16*(27–45). https://journals.openedition.org/cres/3009

Anderson-Levitt, K., & Gardinier, M. P. (2021). Contextualising global flows of competency-based education: Polysemy, hybridity and silences. *Comparative Education*, *57*(1), 1–18. https://doi.org/10.1080/03050068.2020.1852719

Antweiler, C. (2016). *Our common denominator: Human universals revisited*. Berghahn Books.

Appadurai, A. (1996). *Modernity at large: Cultural dimensions of globalization*. University of Minnesota Press.

Appadurai, A. (2015). Globalization, anthropology of. In J. D. Wright (Ed.), *International encyclopedia of the social & behavioral sciences* (2nd ed., pp. 233–238). Elsevier.

Aydarova, E. (2019). *Teacher education reform as political theater: Policy dramas in global contexts*. SUNY Press.

Aydarova, E. (2021). Knowledge for the elites, competencies for the masses: Political theater of educational reforms in the Russian Federation. *Comparative Education*, *57*(1), 51–66. https://doi.org/10.1080/03050068.2020.1845060

Baker, D. P. (2014). *The schooled society: The educational transformation of global culture*. Stanford University Press.

Barnett, M., & Duvall, R. (2004). Power in global governance. In M. Barnett & R. Duvall (Eds.), *Power in global governance* (pp. 1–32). Cambridge University Press.

Barnett, M., & Duvall, R. (2005). Power in international politics. *International Organization*, *59*(1), 39–75. doi:10.1017/S0020818305050010

Barnett, M., & Finnemore, M. (2005). The power of liberal international organizations. In M. Barnett & R. Duvall (Eds.), *Power in global governance* (pp. 161–184). Cambridge University Press.

Bartlett, L., & Vavrus, F. (2017). *Rethinking case study research: A comparative approach.* Routledge.

Ben-Peretz, M., & Halkes, R. (1987). How teachers know their classrooms: A cross-cultural study of teachers' understanding of classroom situations. *Anthropology & Education Quarterly, 18*(1), 17–32. https://doi.org/10.1525/aeq.1987.18.1.04x0759e

Bentley, J. H. (1993). *Old World encounters: Cross-cultural contacts and exchanges in pre-modern times.* Oxford.

Biesta, G. (2009). Good education in an age of measurement: On the need to reconnect with the question of purpose in education. *Educational Assessment, Evaluation and Accountability, 21*(1), 33–46. https://doi.org/10.1007/s11092-008-9064-9

Bošković, A., & Ericksen, T. H. (2008). Introduction: Other people's anthropologies. In A. Bošković (Ed.), *Other people's anthropologies: Ethnographic practice on the margins* (pp. 1–19). Berghahn Books.

Boum, A. (2008). The political coherence of educational incoherence: The consequences of educational specialization in a southern Moroccan community. *Anthropology & Education Quarterly, 39*(2), 205–223. https://doi.org/10.1111/j.1548-1492.2008.00016.x

Boyle, H. N. (2019). Registered medersas in Mali: Effectively integrating Islamic and Western educational epistemologies in practice. *Comparative Education Review, 63*(2), 145–165. https://doi.org/10.1086/702592

Care, E., Anderson, K., & Kim, H. (2016). *Visualizing the breadth of skills movement across education systems.* Brookings Institute. https://www.brookings.edu/research/visualizing-the-breadth-of-skills-movement-across-education-systems/

Caruso, M. (2015). Classroom struggle: Organizing elementary school teaching in the 19th century. In M. Caruso (Ed.), *Classroom struggle: Organizing elementary school teaching in the 19th century* (pp. 9–30). Peter Lang.

Cha, Y.-K. (1992). The origins and expansion of primary school curricula: 1800–1920. In J. W. Meyer, D. Kamens, & A. Benavot (Eds.), *School knowledge for the masses* (pp. 63–73). Falmer.

Chee, W.-C., & Jakubiak, C. (2020). The national as global, the global as national: Citizenship education in the context of migration and globalization. *Anthropology & Education Quarterly, 51*(2), 119–122. doi:10.1111/aeq.12337

Clarke, P. (2001). *Teaching and learning: The culture of pedagogy.* Sage.

Clément, P. (2021). The introduction of competence-based education into the compulsory school curriculum in France (2002–2017): A hybridizing process. *Comparative Education, 57*(1), 35–50. https://doi.org/10.1080/03050068.2020.1845062

Comaroff, J., & Comaroff, J. (2000). Millennial capitalism: First thoughts on a second coming. *Public Culture, 12*(2), 291–343.

Dale, R. (2000). Globalisation and education: Demonstrating a "common world education culture" or locating a "globally structured agenda for education"? *Educational Theory, 50*(4), 427–448. https://doi.org/10.1111/j.1741-5446.2000.00427.x

Danic, I. (2008). Socialisation scolaire. In A. van Zanten (Ed.), *Dictionnaire de l'éducation* (pp. 621–625). PUF.

Dasen, P. R., & Akkari, A. (Eds.). (2008). *Educational theories and practices from the majority world.* Sage.

Delamont, S. (2011). The parochial paradox: Anthropology of education in the Anglophone world. In K. Anderson-Levitt (Ed.), *Anthropologies of education* (pp. 49–69). Berghahn Books.

Delvaux, B., & van Zanten, A., guest editors. (2006). Les établissements scolaires et leur espace local d'interdépendance [dossier]. *Revue Française de Pédagogie, 2006*(156). https://doi.org/10.4000/rfp.260

Depaepe, M., & Hulstaert, K. (2013). Creating cultural hybridity by exporting metropolitan structures and cultures of schooling and educationalisation? The emergence of a Congolese "elite" in the 1950s as a starting point for further research. *European Educational Research Journal, 12*(2), 201–214. doi:10.2304/eerj.2013.12.2.201

Eisenhart, M. (2008). Globalization and science education in a community-based after-school program. *Cultural Studies of Science Education, 3*(1), 73–95.

Erickson, F. (2014). Scaling down: A modest proposal for practice-based policy research in teaching. *Education Policy Analysis Archives, 22*(9), 1–8. http://dx.doi.org/10.14507/epaa.v22n9.2014.

Eröss, G. (2011). Central Europe (Bulgaria, the Czech Republic, Hungary, Poland, Romania, Slovakia). In K. M. Anderson-Levitt (Ed.), *Anthropologies of education* (pp. 167–191). Berghahn Books.

Fichtner, S. (2012). *The NGOisation of education: Case studies from Benin* (Vol. 31). Rüdiger Köppe Verlag.

Filiod, J.-P. (2007). Anthropologie de l'école. Perspectives. *Ethnologie française, 2007/4*(37), 581–595. https://doi.org/10.3917/ethn.074.0581

Forsey, M. G. (2006). *Challenging the system? A dramatic tale of neoliberal reform in an Australian high school.* Information Age.

Forsey, M. G., Davies, S., & Walford, G. (Eds.). (2008). *The globalisation of school choice?* Symposium Books.

Friedman, J. (2007). Global systems, globalization, and anthropological theory. In I. Rossi (Ed.), *Frontiers of globalization research* (pp. 109–132). Springer.

Fujita, M., & Sano, T. (1988). Children in American and Japanese day-care centers. In H. Trueba & C. Delgado-Gaitán (Eds.), *School & society: Learning content through culture* (pp. 73–97). Praeger.

García Castaño, F. J., & Carrasco Pons, S. (Eds.). (2011). *Población inmigrante y escuela: conocimientos y saberes de investigación.* Gobierno de España, Ministerio de Educación.

Gardinier, M. P. (2021). Imagining globally competent learners: Experts and education policy-making beyond the nation-state. *Comparative Education, 57*(1), 130–146. doi:10.1080/03050068.2020.1845064

Gardinier, M. P., & Worden, E. A. (2010). The semblance of progress amidst the absence of change: Educating for an imagined Europe in Moldova and Albania. In I. Silova (Ed.), *Post-socialism is not dead: (Re)reading the global in comparative education* (Vol. 14, pp. 183–211). Emerald.

Gibson, M. A., & Koyama, J. P. (2011). Immigrants and education. In B. A. U. Levinson & M. Pollack (Eds.), *A companion to the anthropology of education* (pp. 389–407). Wiley-Blackwell.

Gingrich, A. (2005). The German-speaking countries. In F. Barth, A. Gingrich, R. Parkin, & S. Silverman (Eds.), *One discipline, four ways* (pp. 61–153). University of Chicago Press.

Givvin, K. B., Hiebert, J., Jacobs, J. K., Hollingsworth, H., & Gallimore, R. R. (2005). Are there national patterns of teaching? Evidence from the TIMSS 1999 video study. *Comparative Education Review, 40*(3), 311–343.

Graeber, D. (2002). The anthropology of globalization. *American Anthropologist, 104*(4), 1222–1227. https://doi.org/10.1525/aa.2002.104.4.1222

Graeber, D. & Wentgrow, D. (2021). *The dawn of everything: A new history of humanity*. Farrar, Strauss & Giroux.

Guillén, M. F. (2001). Is globalization civilizing, destructive or feeble? A critique of five key debates in the social science literature. *Annual Review of Sociology, 27*(1), 235–260. doi:10.1146/annurev.soc.27.1.235

Hannerz, U. (1987). The world in creolisation. *Africa, 57,* 546–559.

Hansen, J. F. (1979). *Sociocultural perspectives on human learning: An introduction to educational anthropology*. Prentice Hall.

Harrison, K. D. (2007). *When languages die: The extinction of the world's languages and the erosion of human knowledge*. Oxford University Press.

Hartong, S. (2014). Global policy convergence through "distributed governance"? The emergence of "national" education standards in the US and Germany. *Journal of International and Comparative Social Policy, 31*(1), 10–33. doi:10.1080/21699763.2014.977803

Hayashi, A. 2022. *Teaching expertise in three countries: Japan, China, and the United States*. University of Chicago Press.

Hayhoe, R. (1992). Modernization without westernization: Assessing the Chinese educational experience. In R. F. Arnove, P. G. Altbach, & G. P. Kelly (Eds.), *Emergent issues in education: Comparative perspectives* (pp. 75–91). State University of New York Press.

Henry, J. (1960). A cross-cultural outline of education. *Current Anthropology, 1*(4), 267–305. doi:10.1086/200114

Henze, R. (2020). Anthropology of education. In M. Aldenderfer (Ed.), *Oxford research encyclopedia of anthropology* (pp. 1–46). Oxford University Press.

Ichou, M., & van Zanten, A. (2019). France: The increasing recognition of migration and ethnicity as a source of educational inequalities. In P. A. J. Stevens & A. G. Dworkin (Eds.), *The Palgrave handbook of race and ethnic inequalities in education* (pp. 509–556). Springer.

Jones, P. D. (2012). *The European commission and education policy in the European Union: An ethnographic discourse analysis* [Unpublished doctoral dissertation]. University of Bristol.

Jordan, C. (1995). Creating cultures of schooling: Historical and conceptual background of the KEEP/Rough Rock collaboration. *Bilingual Research Journal, 19*(1), 83–100. doi:10.1080/15235882.1995.10668592

Kendall, N., & Silver, R. (2014). The consequences of global mass education: Schooling, work and well-being in EFA-era Malawi. In N. P. Stromquist & K. Monkman (Eds.), *Globalization and education: Integration and contestation across cultures* (2nd ed., pp. 239–257). Rowman & Littlefield.

Koyama, J. P. (2009). Localizing No Child Left Behind: Supplemental educational services (SES) in New York City. In F. K. Vavrus & L. Bartlett (Eds.), *Critical approaches to comparative education: Vertical case studies from Africa, Europe, the Middle East, and the Americas* (pp. 21–37). Palgrave Macmillan.

Koyama, J. P. (2010). *Making failure pay: For-profit tutoring, high-stakes testing, and public schools*. Chicago University Press.

Ladson-Billings, G. (2009). *The dreamkeepers: Successful teachers of African American children* (2nd ed.). Jossey-Bass.

Ladson-Billings, G., & Gomez, M. L. (2001). Just showing up: Supporting early literacy through teachers' professional communities. *Phi Delta Kappan, 82*(9), 675–680. https://journals.sage pub.com/doi/pdf/10.1177/003172170108200908

Lancy, D. F. (2022). *The anthropology of childhood: Cherubs, chattel, changelings* (3rd ed.). Cambridge University Press.

Lancy, D. F., Bock, J. C., & Gaskins, S. (Eds.). (2010). *The anthropology of learning in childhood*. AltaMira Press.

Lange, M.-F., & Yaro, Y. (2003). *L'évolution de l'offre et de la demande d'éducation depuis 20 ans en Afrique*. Paper presented at the Fourth African Population Conference UAPS/UEPA, Tunis, Tunisia. https://core.ac.uk/download/pdf/39844464.pdf

Latour, B. (2005). *Reassembling the social: An introduction to actor-network theory*. Oxford University Press.

LeTendre, G., Baker, D. P., Akiba, M., Goesling, B., & Wiseman, A. W. (2001). Teachers' work: Institutional isomorphism and cultural variation in the U.S., Germany and Japan. *Educational Researcher, 30*(6), 3–15. https://doi.org/10.3102/0013189X030006003

Levinson, B. A. U., Sutton, M., & Winstead, T. (2009). Education policy as a practice of power: Theoretical tools, ethnographic methods, democratic options. *Educational Policy, 23*(6), 767–795. https://doi.org/10.1177/0895904808320676

Lukose, R. A. (2007). The difference that diaspora makes: Thinking through the anthropology of immigrant education in the United States. *Anthropology & Education Quarterly, 38*(4), 405–418.

Maynard, A., & Tovote, K. E. (2010). Learning from other children. In D. F. Lancy, J. C. Bock, & S. Gaskins (Eds.), *The anthropology of learning in childhood* (pp. 181–205). AltaMira Press.

McCarty, T. L. (2001). *A place to be Navajo: Rough Rock and the struggle for self-determination in indigenous schooling*. Erlbaum.

McNeill, J. R., & McNeill, W. H. (2003). *The human web: A bird's-eye view of world history*. W.W. Norton.

Mehta, J. (2013). *The allure of order: High hopes, dashed expectations, and the troubled quest to remake American schooling*. Oxford University Press.

Menashy, F. (2019). *International aid to education: Power dynamics in an era of partnership*. Teachers College Press.

Meo, A. I., Cimolai, S., & Encinas, L. A. (2019). Argentina. Researching ethnic and educational inequalities in changing policy scenarios: From homogenization to the recognition of diversity. In P. A. J. Stevens & A. G. Dworkin (Eds.), *The Palgrave handbook of race and ethnic inequalities in education* (2nd ed., pp. 7–60). Springer.

Meyer, J. W., Kamens, D., & Benavot, A. ([1992] 2017). *School knowledge for the masses: World models and national primary curricular categories in the twentieth century*. Falmer.

Mills, D. (2012). Anthropology and education. In S. Delamont (Ed.), *Handbook of qualitative research in education* (pp. 33–47). Edward Elgar.

Miñana Blasco, C., & Arango Vargas, C. (2011). Educational policy, anthropology, and the state. In B. A. U. Levinson & M. Pollack (Eds.), *A companion to the anthropology of education* (pp. 368–387). Wiley-Blackwell.

Minoura, Y. (2011). The development of ethnographic studies of schooling in Japan. In K. Anderson-Levitt (Ed.), *Anthropologies of education* (pp. 213–234). Berghahn.

Moore, L. C. (2010). Learning in schools. In D. F. Lancy, J. Bock, & S. Gaskins (Eds.), *The anthropology of learning in childhood* (pp. 207–232). AltaMira Press.

Morgan, C. (2007). *The OECD Programme for International Student Assessment: Unravelling a knowledge network*. Carleton University, Ottawa.

Morgan, C. (2016). Testing students under cognitive capitalism: Knowledge production of twenty-first century skills. *Journal of Education Policy, 31*(6), 805–818. https://doi.org/10.1080/02680939.2016.1190465

Nader, L. (1969). Up the anthropologist—Perspectives gained from studying up. In D. Hymes (Ed.), *Reinventing anthropology* (pp. 285–311). Pantheon Books.

Nordin, A., & Sundberg, D. (2021). Transnational competence frameworks and national curriculum-making: The case of Sweden. *Comparative Education, 57*(1), 19–34. doi:10.1080/03050068.2020.1845065

Nye Jr, J. S. (2004). Soft power and American foreign policy. *Political Science Quarterly, 119*(2), 255–270. doi:10.2307/20202345

Ochs, K., & Phillips, D. (2004). Processes of educational borrowing in historical context. In D. Phillips & K. Ochs (Eds.), *Educational policy borrowing: Historical perspectives* (pp. 7–23). Symposium Books.

OECD (Organisation for Economic Co-Operation and Development). (2018). *The future of education and skills: Education 2030.* https://www.oecd.org/education/2030-project/

Okongwu, A. F., & Mencher, J. P. (2000). The anthropology of public policy: Shifting terrains. *Annual Review of Anthropology, 29*(1), 107–124. doi:10.1146/annurev.anthro.29.1.107

Ouyang, H. (2011). Bamboo shoots after rain: Educational anthropology and ethnography in mainland China. In K. Anderson-Levitt (Ed.), *Anthropologies of education* (pp. 235–255). Berghahn Books.

Peck, J., & Theodore, N. (2010). Mobilizing policy: Models, methods, and mutations. *Geoforum, 41*(2), 169–174. https://doi.org/10.1016/j.geoforum.2010.01.002

Phillips, D. C. (2006). Investigating policy attraction in education. *Oxford Review of Education, 32*(5), 551–559. https://doi.org/10.1080/03054980600976098

Portnoi, L. M. (2016). *Policy borrowing and reform in education: Globalized processes and local contexts.* Palgrave Macmillan.

Rappleye, J., & Kariya, T. (2011). Reimagining self/other: "Catch-up" across Japan's three great education reforms. In D. B. Willis & J. Rappleye (Eds.), *Reimagining Japanese education: Borders, transfers, circulations, and the comparative* (pp. 51–85). Symposium Books.

Raveaud, M., & Draelants, H. (2011). Ethnographies of education in the French-speaking world. In K. M. Anderson-Levitt (Ed.), *Anthropologies of education* (pp. 131–149). Berghahn Books.

Rival, L. (1996). Formal Schooling and the production of modern citizens in the Ecuadorian Amazon. In B. A. U. Levinson, D. Foley, & D. C. Holland (Eds.), *The cultural production of the educated person* (pp. 153–168). SUNY.

Rockwell, E. (2000). Teaching genres: A Bakhtinian approach. *Anthropology and Education Quarterly, 31*(3), 260–282.

Rockwell, E. (2007). Huellas del pasado en las culturas escolares: Hacia una antropología histórica de procesos educativos. *Revista de Antropología Social (Universidad Complutense de Madrid), 16*, 175–212. https://revistas.ucm.es/index.php/RASO/article/view/RASO0707110175A

Rogers, R. (Ed.) (2004). *La mixité dans l'éducation: Enjeux passés et présents.* ENS Éditions.

Rogoff, B., Correa-Chávez, M., & Navichoc Cotuc, M. (2005). A cultural-historical view of schooling in human development. In D. B. Pillemer & S. H. White (Eds.), *Developmental psychology and social change* (pp. 225–263). Cambridge University Press.

Rogoff, B., Paradise, R., Mejía Arauz, R., Correa-Chávez, M., & Angelillo, C. (2003). Firsthand learning through intent participation. *Annual Review of Psychology, 54*, 175–203. https://doi.org/10.1146/annurev.psych.54.101601.145118

Roser, M., & Ortiz-Ospina, E. (2016). Projected world population by level of education [1970–2100]. Global rise of education. *Our World in Data.* https://ourworldindata.org/grapher/projection-of-world-population-ssp2-iiasa?country=~OWID_WRL

Roser, M., Ritchie, H., & Ortiz-Ospina, E. (2019, May). World population growth. *Our World in Data.* https://ourworldindata.org/world-population-growth

Sahlberg, P. (2015). *Finnish lessons 2.0: What can the world learn from educational change in Finland?* (2nd ed.). Teachers College Press.

Sahlberg, P. (2016). The global educational reform movement and its impact on schooling. In K. Mundy, A. Green, B. Lingard, & A. Verger (Eds.), *Handbook of global policy and policy making in education* (pp. 128–144). John Wiley and Sons.

Sánchez, M. (2020). Methodologies for an anthropology of education. In M. R. M. Ward & S. Delamont (Eds.), *Handbook of qualitative research in education* (2nd ed., pp. 16–26). Edward Elgar.

Sarangapani, P. (2003). *Constructing school knowledge: An ethnography of learning in an Indian village.* Sage.

Sarroub, L. (2005). *All American Yemeni girls: Being Muslim in a public school.* University of Pennsylvania Press.

Saxe, G. B., & Kirby, K. (2018). Analyzing the evolution of a digital technology intervention: One Laptop per Child in a remote Papua New Guinea community. *Anthropology & Education Quarterly, 49*(4), 394–412. https://doi.org/10.1111/aeq.12263

Schlemmer, B. (2002). Paradigmes de l'enfance et de l'école, droit à l'éducation et droit au travail. *Communications, 2002*(72), 175–194. https://doi.org/10.3406/comm.2002.2104

Schofer, E., Hironaka, A., Frank, D. J., & Longhofer, W. (2012). Sociological institutionalism and world society. In E. Amenta, K. Nash, & A. Scott (Eds.), *The Wiley-Blackwell companion to political sociology* (pp. 57–68). John Wiley.

Schweisfurth, M. (2013). *Learner-centred education in international perspective: Whose pedagogy for whose development?* Routledge.

Shore, C. (2010). Beyond the multiversity: Neoliberalism and the rise of the schizophrenic university. *Social Anthropology, 18*(1), 15–29. https://doi.org/10.1111/j.1469-8676.2009.00094.x

Shore, C. (2012). Anthropology and public policy. In R. Fardon (Ed.), *The SAGE handbook of social anthropology* (pp. 89–105). Sage.

Shore, C., & Wright, S. (2013). Conceptualising policy: Technologies of governance and the politics of visibility. In C. Shore, S. Wright, & D. Però (Eds.), *Policy worlds: Anthropology and the analysis of contemporary power* (pp. 1–25). Berghahn Books.

Solano-Campos, A. (2019). The Nicaraguan diaspora in Costa Rica: Schools and the disruption of transnational social fields. *Anthropology & Education Quarterly, 50*(1), 48–65. https://doi.org/10.1111/aeq.12274

Spindler, G. D., & Spindler, L. S. (1987). Cultural dialogue and schooling in Schoenhausen and Roseville: A comparative analysis. *Anthropology & Education Quarterly, 18*(1), 3–16. https://doi.org/10.1525/aeq.1987.18.1.04x0758d

Sriprakash, A. (2012). *Pedagogies for development: The politics and practice of child-centred education in India.* Springer Netherlands.

Stambach, A., & Ngawane, Z. (2011). Development, post-colonialism, and global networks as frameworks for the study of education in Africa and beyond. In B. A. U. Levinson & M. Pollack (Eds.), *A companion to the anthropology of education* (pp. 299–315). Wiley-Blackwell.

Street, B. V. (1993). Culture is a verb: Anthropological aspects of language and cultural process. In D. Graddol, L. Thompson, & M. Byram (Eds.), *Language and culture* (pp. 23–43). BAAL and Multilingual Matters.

Suárez-Orozco, M. M., Darbes, T., Dias, S. I., & Sutin, M. (2011). Migrations and schooling. *Annual Review of Anthropology, 40*(1), 311–328. doi:10.1146/annurev-anthro-111009-115928

Sumida Huaman, E., & Abeita, S. (2018). Indigenous teachers and learners: Higher education and social justice. *Anthropology & Education Quarterly, 49*(2), 201–209. https://doi.org/10.1111/aeq.12239

Swartz, R., & Kallaway, P. (2018). Imperial, global and local in histories of colonial education. *History of Education, 47*(3), 362–367. https://doi.org/10.1080/0046760X.2018.1425742

Tabulawa, R. (2013). *Teaching and learning in context: Why pedagogical reforms fail in Sub-Saharan Africa.* CODESRIA.

Thapan, M. (Ed.) (2014). *Ethnographies of schooling in contemporary India.* Sage.

Tikly, L. (2017). The future of Education for All as a global regime of educational governance. *Comparative Education Review, 61*(1), 22–57. https://www.journals.uchicago.edu/doi/abs/10.1086/689700

Tobin, J. (Ed.) (1992). *Re-made in Japan: Everyday Life and consumer taste in a changing society.* Yale University Press.

Tobin, J., Hsueh, Y., & Karasawa, M. (2009). *Preschool in three cultures revisited: China, Japan, and the United States.* University of Chicago Press.

Tobin, J., Wu, D., & Davidson, D. (1989). *Preschool in three cultures.* Yale University Press.

Trouillot, M.-R. (2001). The anthropology of the state in the age of globalization: Close encounters of the deceptive kind. *Current Anthropology, 42*(1), 125–138. https://doi.org/10.1086/318437

Tsing, A. L. (2000). The global situation. *Cultural Anthropology, 15*(3), 327–360. https://doi.org/10.1525/can.2000.15.3.327

Tsing, A. L. (2005). *Friction: An ethnography of global connection.* Princeton University Press.

Tyack, D., & Hansot, E. (1990). *Learning together: A history of coeducation in American public schools.* Yale University Press/Russell Sage Foundation.

Tyack, D., & Tobin, W. (1994). The "grammar" of schooling: Why has it been so hard to change? *American Educational Research Journal, 31*(3), 453–479. https://doi.org/10.3102/00028312031003453

UNESCO. (2020). *EFA global education monitoring report, 2020: Inclusion and education: all means all.* https://unesdoc.unesco.org/ark:/48223/pf0000373718

Valli, L., & Chambliss, M. (2007). Creating classroom cultures: One teacher, two lessons, and a high-stakes test. *Anthropology & Education Quarterly, 38*(1), 57–75. doi:10.1525/aeq.2007.38.1.57

van Zanten, A. (2012). *L'école de la périphérie: Scolarité et ségrégation en banlieue.* Presses Universitaires de France.

Vandeyar, S., & Vandeyar, T. (2015). *The construction, negotiation, and representation of immigrant student identities in South African schools.* Information Age.

Vavrus, F. K., & Bartlett, L. (2012). Comparative pedagogies and epistemological diversity: Social and materials contexts of teaching in Tanzania. *Comparative Education Review, 56*(4), 634–658. https://doi.org/10.1086/667395

Vavrus, F. K., & Bartlett, L. (Eds.). (2013). *Teaching in tension: International pedagogies, national policies, and teachers' practices in Tanzania.* Sense Publishers.

Verger, A., & Curran, M. (2014). New public management as a global education policy: Its adoption and re-contextualization in a Southern European setting. *Critical Studies in Education, 55*(3), 253–271. https://doi.org/10.1080/17508487.2014.913531

Verger, A., Fontdevila, C., & Parcerisa, L. (2019). Constructing school autonomy with accountability as a global policy model: A focus on OECD's governance mechanisms. In C. Ydesen (Ed.), *The OECD's historical rise in education* (pp. 219–243). Springer.

Vincent, G., Lahire, B., & Thin, D. (1994). Sur l'histoire et la théorie de la forme scolaire. In G. Vincent (Ed.), *L'éducation prisonnière de la forme scolaire* (pp. 11–48). Presses Universitaires de Lyon.

Weis, L., & Dolby, N. (Eds.). (2012). *Social class and education: Global perspectives*. Routledge.

Welmond, M. (2002). Globalization viewed from the periphery: The dynamics of teacher identity in the Republic of Benin. *Comparative Education Review*, 46(1), 37–65. https://doi.org/10.1086/324049

Wotipka, C. M., Rabling, B. J., Sugawara, M., & Tongliemnak, P. (2017). The worldwide expansion of early childhood care and education, 1985–2010. *American Journal of Education*, 123(2), 307–339. https://doi.org/10.1086/689931

Wright, S. (2016). Universities in a knowledge economy or ecology? Policy, contestation and abjection. *Critical Policy Studies*, 10(1), 59–78. https://doi.org/10.1080/19460171.2016.1142457

Wright, S., & Rabo, A. (2010). Introduction: Anthropologies of university reform. *Social Anthropology*, 18(1), 1–14. https://doi.org/10.1111/j.1469-8676.2009.00096.x

Wright, S., & Reinhold, S. (2013). "Studying through": A strategy for studying political transformations. Or sex, lies and British politics. In C. Shore, S. Wright, & D. Però (Eds.), *Policy worlds* (pp. 86–104). Berghahn.

Wu, J. (2018). Performing the nation, performing the market: Hybrid practices and negotiated meanings of Chinese rural teachers. *Anthropology & Education Quarterly*, 49(4), 428–443. https://doi.org/10.1111/aeq.12267

Zoch, M. (2017). A school divided: One elementary school's response to education policy. *Anthropology & Education Quarterly*, 48(1), 23–41. https://doi.org/10.1111/aeq.12181

CHAPTER 3

HISTORICAL INSTITUTIONALISM IN EDUCATION AND GLOBALIZATION

LUKAS GRAF

INTRODUCTION

HISTORICAL new institutionalism (HI) is one of the major schools of thought used to analyze how globalization leads to institutional changes in educational systems. HI emphasizes the relevance of temporal sequences, path dependencies, and critical junctures in the study of education and institutional change. Due to long-standing historical legacies and complex actor constellations, education systems are often considered to be strongly path dependent and resistant to reforms (Busemeyer & Trampusch, 2012). Early versions of HI offered one main explanation for the occurrence of institutional change in strongly path-dependent contexts. This explanation referred to exogenous shocks to institutional systems, for instance, related to technological change or major political conflicts, that would create a critical juncture and, in turn, a moment of contingency allowing change agents to alter the prior institutional trajectory (Baumgartner & Jones, 1993; North, 1990). Newer versions of HI offer tools to analyze institutional changes also in the absence of exogenous shocks, focusing on endogenous change and the possibility of gradual changes to path-dependent institutions, which, however, may nevertheless add up to transformative change over time (Streeck & Thelen, 2005). Through this lens, globalization—or the "transformation in the spatial organization of social relations and transactions" (Held et al., 1999, p. 16)—is typically captured as globalization pressures related to, for instance, increasing cross-border activities in production or trade (Campbell, 2004). In HI, such globalization pressures are usually not so much framed as exogenous shocks—the focus is rather on how domestic actors translate them into endogenous change processes, leading to distinct trajectories of institutional development, which depend on specific national-institutional contexts.

This chapter first reviews recent contributions to HI linked to the study of education and globalization, illustrating how this approach can help scholars grasp how change agents—that is, the actors that actively seek to change a given status quo—may achieve educational reforms in the context of globalization despite obstacles to change (e.g., path dependencies or veto players). From this perspective, globalization is not seen as isomorphic pressure that leads to convergence across countries (Baker, 2014; Meyer et al., 1997). Rather, it is captured as globalization pressures—for instance, to deregulate the economy (Baccaro & Howell, 2011) or to upskill workers in the rising global knowledge economy (Brown et al., 2012)—that may apply "globally" but are dealt with in specific ways by actors on the ground.[1] This implies that the outcome is shaped by the institutional context in a specific country or policy field. Here, key factors include the position and strength of the veto players to an institutional reform and the discretion given to relevant actors to reinterpret a given institutional configuration (Mahoney & Thelen, 2010).

After introducing the aforementioned debates and concepts in general terms, the chapter theorizes the link between globalization and modes of gradual institutional change in education, with special reference to the case of vocational education and training (VET).[2] While the literature review shows that HI is beginning to have a significant impact in research on all sectors of education—from early childhood education to higher education (HE)—its contribution is most advanced in VET (Thelen, 2004). VET represents a policy field situated at the nexus of education and the economy in which multiple public and private actors tend to cooperate in a decentralized manner (Emmenegger et al., 2019). Therefore, the VET sector can be regarded as an ideal example to demonstrate the analytical strength of HI which, like other political economy approaches (e.g., Hall & Soskice, 2001), has a pronounced interest in the interaction of multiple actors and socioeconomic spheres in the economy.

Globalization presents the policy field of VET with a major challenge. In the case of VET, one of the most profound influences of globalization is related to academization—that is, the rising salience of academic forms of knowledge production and academic qualifications (Severing & Teichler, 2013)—and, specifically, the rapid growth of HE enrolments worldwide (Schofer & Meyer, 2005). Globalization is associated with structural shifts that have led to an expansion of HE relative to VET. This is visible in the general increase in the participation in academic relative to vocational programs in the past decades (Benavot, 1983; Powell & Solga, 2010). The growing demand for academic skills on the sides of both employers and individuals results from a more or less global transition from manufacturing to a service and knowledge economy (Andersen & Hassel, 2013; Mayer & Solga, 2008), the digitalization of education and the world of work (Schmidt & Tang, 2020), the growing influence of large export-oriented firms (Thelen & Busemeyer, 2012), and an influential world polity, represented by international organizations like the United Nations (UN) and the Organization for Economic Cooperation and Development (OECD) (Martens et al., 2007), who have long promoted the expansion of HE.[3] All these challenges are inseparable from globalization, which is why they are here understood as globalization pressures, pushing for educational expansion and academization.

In recent years, this academization challenge has prompted a range of reforms to strengthen VET (Graf, 2018; Wolter & Kerst 2015). These reforms have the goal to promote changes that help to maintain the societal and economic function that VET ideally fulfils, for instance, in terms of providing youth with practice-oriented polyvalent skills (Bosch & Charest, 2008) and a stable pathway into the labor market (Protsch & Solga, 2016), while allowing employers to screen and train their future workforce (Culpepper 2003), as well as supporting a diversified production strategy (Streeck, 1991). HI is well fitted to explore the institutional trajectories that derive from the aforementioned pressures on national VET systems—starting with the premise that in a changing environment, an institution can only be maintained if it constantly evolves (Streeck & Thelen, 2005). Adopting a sectoral HI perspective, this chapter argues that in view of globalization pressures on VET promoting increasing academization and educational expansion, the dominant pattern of institutional change on which the respective policy responses rely is *layering*. This mode of change implies that new institutions or rules are added on top of existing ones, instead of replacing them. To illustrate the argument, the chapter presents case studies of recent institutional reforms in the German skill formation system, representing one of the world's largest VET systems.

The following section reviews the state of the literature on HI and education, with a special focus on globalization. Next, the chapter presents main theoretical tools of the HI framework and how it can be operationalized for the study of institutional change in education in the context of globalization pressures. This is followed by the case study on globalization, academization, and gradual change in German VET. The conclusion discusses the generalizability of the proposed sectoral HI perspective as well as prospects for further research linking HI and education in a globalizing world.

Historical New Institutionalism in Education: A Review

HI has been applied to various educational sectors, from early childhood education to HE. While this body of literature overall is still rather small, it is growing rapidly. Most of the contributions originate from the last few years, indicating that HI is increasingly being picked up by scholars studying education. This section provides an overview on applications of HI in the domain of education, providing examples for different educational sectors. The review suggests that most of these HI studies have looked at European countries (e.g., German-language regions, France, Scandinavia, Benelux, and the United Kingdom), the European Union (European Higher Education Area, Bologna process), Anglophone countries (Australia, Canada, and the United States), and Asia (China, India, Korea, and Japan).

There are some few studies that apply HI to *early childhood education and childcare*. For instance, Lewis and West (2017) analyze continuity and change in early childhood education and care in England under austerity. Offering a case study of Japan, Nishioka (2018) studies gradual policy changes in the privatization of childcare service. Wang and Lee (2020) trace institutional changes in quality assurance of early childhood education, focusing on the case of China. In the sector of *secondary education*, HI studies look, for instance, at the case of federalist systems (especially Germany) and how different states embark on distinctive reform trajectories. Edelstein and Nikolai (2013) focus on structural change at the secondary school level focusing on the determinants for school reform policies in Saxony and Hamburg. Powell et al. (2016) explore the impact of path dependence on the effects of the UN Convention on the Rights of Persons with Disabilities on education systems comparing German states. Contrasting two federal systems (that of Germany and the United States), Niemann et al. (2018) show how institutional path dependencies shape the outcome of international, large-scale student assessments on education. Maroy et al. (2016) speak to the theme of globalization by analyzing policy trajectories in France and Quebec, considering historical legacies related to earlier educational policy choices. There are also some HI studies looking at the *training of teachers and educators*. Thus, Lu (2019) studies the historical thread of teacher education policy in China, while Geiss and Westberg (2020) compare the emergence of training regimes for early childhood professionals in Sweden and Switzerland. In the sector of *HE*, prime examples of HI studies explore the impact of European educational policies. For example, Dobbins and Knill (2014) consider historical legacies in university governance related to "soft" Europeanization. Barret (2017) shows that the Bologna process is part of a path-dependent trajectory of integration in Europe. Feeney and Hogan (2017) adopt a path-dependent approach exploring policy harmonization in relation to qualification frameworks in the European Higher Education Area. At the national level, Schmidt (2017) examines different path developments resulting from quality assurance policies in Scandinavian HE systems.

However, while HI is beginning to have a significant impact in research on HE and other educational sectors, its contribution is still most pronounced in the sector of VET. Studies of VET have been instrumental to theory development in HI. The most prominent example of this is the work by Thelen (2004) in which she explores the evolution of institutions at the example of vocational skill formation and incremental change. Her book represents a steppingstone for the present-day understanding of gradual institutional change in HI. There have since been a range of studies that apply HI to VET. For example, Trampusch (2010) carves out transformative and self-preserving change in the Swiss VET system. Graf et al. (2012) identify gradual change in the changing relationship between apprenticeship training and school-based VET in Austria. Analyzing the Swedish case, Persson and Hermelin (2018) trace incremental institutional changes to explain an "anomaly" within a statist VET system, namely the technical college scheme. Schneider and Pilz (2019) apply HI to analyze the institutional embeddedness of polytechnics in the Indian education system. Fortwengel et al. (2019) carve out distinct trajectories of institutional renewal of apprenticeship training in Australia, England, and the United States. Building on the varieties of capitalism approach and HI, Busemeyer and Vossiek (2016) show that common structural pressures are not leading to a full-scale convergence in the German and British skill formation systems.

Overall, this review shows that only in a few cases do analyses of HI and education work explicitly with the concept of globalization (Busemeyer & Vossiek, 2016; Maroy et al., 2017). One likely reason for this is that the theoretical enterprise of HI has developed in tandem with institutional approaches in comparative political economy that emphasize the nation level as the main unit of analysis (Hall & Soskice, 2001). Yet in several HI studies, specific international influences on national or subnational education systems are studied, as in the case of international large-scale student assessments (Niemann et al., 2018), UN conventions and agencies (Powell et al., 2016), or European educational policy (Barret, 2017; Feeney & Hogan, 2017). The review also indicates that HI studies have only recently been extended more broadly beyond the sector of VET. Due to the close link between HI and VET, this educational sector is given special attention in this chapter. This is not least due to VET representing a policy field deeply embedded in national labor markets and respective systems of industrial relations, both being fields extensively studied by HI scholars (Streeck & Thelen, 2005), making it a particularly interesting case for the analysis of the impact of globalization pressures on skill formation. In other words, as HI studies of globalization tend to focus on economic aspects of globalization, and because VET is closely related to the economy and labor markets, the VET sector represents a good starting point for a discussion of the relationship between globalization and education from a HI perspective.[4]

Next, the chapter presents the HI framework with a focus on its contribution to the analysis of institutional change.

Theoretical Framework: Analyzing Globalization and Academization Through HI

The HI Toolbox: Path Dependency and Modes of Gradual Change

This section introduces HI with a focus on the concepts of path dependence, critical junctures, and the gradual modes of change. As Pierson (2004, p. 179) observes, "[. . .] policymakers operate in an environment fundamentally shaped by policies inherited from the past." For instance, in the case of many established institutional systems of VET, there are powerful constraints built into the system that prevent an outright defection from the nationally standardized regulative VET framework. These constraints include institutional complementarities between VET and the industrial relations system, such as collective bargaining, and labor-market security regulations (e.g., Estévez-Abe et al., 2001) that link the VET system to such related fields, and the overall institutional configuration of the national political economy. These linkages also make it difficult to achieve change in one field unless there is corresponding change in the other ones (Amable, 2003). In such a context, newer HI approaches are suitable means for identifying institutional changes for which no critical juncture is necessarily required.

Broadly speaking, definitions of institutions usually refer to some sort of regulative, normative, or cultural-cognitive social ordering that "provide stability and meaning to social life" (Scott, 2008, p. 48). HI is mainly referring to the regulative dimension of institutions or the formal and informal rules and procedures, for instance, codified in the law or deployed by states or firms (Thelen & Steinmo, 1992). Institutional theory has long tended to explain path dependency and institutional stability rather than institutional change. The basic idea of path dependence is that established institutions, or the "interdependent web of an institutional matrix" (North, 1990, p. 95), typically generate conditions that strengthen patterns of institutional stability (Pierson, 2000, p. 255). In this context, classical institutional theory has usually accounted for change processes "merely" via exogenous shocks that unsettle a given social institutional ordering and lead to critical junctures. As a result, change could mostly be envisaged only as a form of radical change presupposing an exogenous shock that creates a moment of contingency opening a window for change (Djelic & Quack, 2007). This earlier emphasis on long phases of institutional stability punctuated by periods of exogenous shocks and subsequent episodes of path departures (Baumgartner & Jones, 1993) largely neglected the role of agency in creating more endogenous forms of change that can but need not be exogenously induced.

In recent years, institutionalists have developed fine-grained concepts to analyze endogenous forms of gradual change that may, for instance, be influenced by globalization pressures. This transition builds on a more dynamic understanding of institutions not mainly as constraining but also as enabling agency. This allows HI to focus on processes of endogenous change influenced by globalization pressures in a more grounded way than, for instance, in the case of studies highlighting globalization in the form of exogenous shocks or global isomorphism and convergence. Thus, Streeck and Thelen (2005, p. 16) emphasize that "What an institution is defined by [is] continuous interaction between rule makers and rule takers during which ever new interpretations of the rule will be discovered, invented, suggested, rejected, or for the time being, adopted." Similarly, Campbell (2004, p. viiii) sees institutional change as "constrained innovation," stressing that next to constraining the range of options available to actors, institutions can enable actors to strive for institutional innovation. In other words, "institutions also provide principles, practices, and opportunities that actors use creatively as they innovate within these constraints." In line with these definitions, HI scholars began to develop typologies for different modes of such change based on constrained innovation. For instance, Ebbinghaus (2005) discusses several "branching pathways" (path cessation, path switch, path departure, and path stabilization). The present chapter mainly refers to the four *modes of gradual institutional change* that are today most frequently applied by HI scholars studying endogenous forms of change. Streeck and Thelen (2005), similar to Hacker (2004), identify the following four modes: (a) displacement, (b) layering, (c) drift, and (d) conversion. In all four modes, incremental changes over time can add up to transformative change, and substantial institutional change may be masked by relative stability on the surface: (a) when existing rules are removed and new ones are introduced, this is *displacement*; (b) when, instead of replacing existing institutions, new institutions are added on top of existing institutions, this is *layering* (see also Schickler, 2001); (c) *drift* refers to shifts occurring in the external conditions of a rule, implying that the rule formally stays the same but that its impact changes (Hacker, 2005); (d) when rules are interpreted and implemented in new ways but formally stay the same, this redirection or redeployment is called *conversion*.

Recent work by Mahoney and Thelen (2010, pp. 18–22) is instructive in this regard, as it links each of these modes of gradual institutional change to a typical combination of (1) key characteristics of the *political context* and (2) the *targeted institution* (Table 3.1).[5] The political context is defined in terms of the veto possibilities (strong or weak), whereas the characteristics of the targeted institution refer to the level of discretion in the interpretation or enforcement of a particular institution (low or high). Where the *political context* gives the defenders of the status quo strong veto possibilities, potential change agents will find strategies of displacement and conversion less feasible. This is because—unlike layering and drift—they require direct changes to the targeted institution. However, where the *targeted institution* offers potential change agents a low level of discretion in interpreting or enforcing that institution, drift and conversion strategies are less likely to be successful, as both these modes rely on significant leeway in how the institutions are implemented. Drift often builds on a gap between institutions and how

Table 3.1 Modes of Change in Relation to Characteristics of Political Context and Targeted Institution

		Characteristics of Targeted Institution (A)	
		Low Level of Discretion in Interpretation/Enforcement (A.1)	High Level of Discretion in Interpretation/Enforcement (A.2)
Characteristics of the political context (B)	Strong veto possibilities (B.1)	Layering	Drift
	Weak veto possibilities (B.2)	Displacement	Conversion

Source: Mahoney and Thelen (2010, p. 19); annotations added by author.

they are enforced. Such gaps usually occur when a specific institution is not strongly enforced. Conversion builds on the ambiguities related to a specific institution, which allow it to be reinterpreted for a different purpose.

Globalization Pressures and Gradual Institutional Change

In HI, globalization is often used to refer to significant increases in cross-border flows of economic and social activities, including production, capital, and trade (Campbell, 2004) but also growing global competition leading to swift changes in skills demands (Di Maio et al., 2020) that in turn induce educational expansion and academization processes (Durazzi, 2019; Graf, 2018). Linking HI to globalization, the strength of HI is that it allows us to analyze how specific globalization pressures get translated in view of different domestic institutional configurations. A classic example of this would be how pressures to liberalize and deregulate markets linked to global production chains are taken up in specific national political economies (Thelen & Wijnbergen, 2003). Thus, while globalization theorists and organizational institutionalist often have maintained that globalization leads to more homogenous institutions across countries (Meyer et al., 1997), from a HI perspective, we would expect different trajectories of change rather than convergence, given the robustness of domestic institutions (Campbell, 2004) and political coalitions that mediate external globalization pressures (Sancak & Özel, 2018). Furthermore, HI scholars are interested in the interrelation between different socioeconomic spheres. When studying the impact of global trends within national skill formation systems, HI often considers the interactions and complementarities with developments and actors in the closely related realm of industrial relations (Strebel et al., 2020). Given gradual changes but persistent differences in industrial relations systems (Thelen, 2014), this further explains why HI studies highlight national differences in the adjustment of education and training systems to globalization pressures.

For HI scholars, the arena of domestic reform politics is usually the main unit of analysis (Trampusch, 2009). That is, they study how globalization pressures are playing out in the domestic arena, in which endogenous change dynamics play a crucial role. In this context, the modes of gradual change can help us understand how pressure for change that derives from the outside (here: globalization) activates actors in the relevant field in the domestic arena, especially if this field is characterized by path dependency but provides some room for endogenous strategies of gradual change, depending on the targeted institution and the political context (Mahoney & Thelen, 2010). Thus, the HI perspective and in particular the modes of gradual change make it possible to capture how globalization—understood as concrete globalization pressures (here related to academization and educational expansion)—play out in specific domestic cases characterized by path dependence (here: the German VET system).

It is interesting to observe that we still lack an understanding of whether specific policy fields are more likely associated with a specific mode of change. Against this backdrop, this chapter explores whether one can observe a dominant mode of change in terms of how VET adjusts to global academization. In view of ongoing globalization and academization pressures, the core argument of this chapter is that in the case of VET, institutional change in the form of layering is likely to represent the dominant pattern. This is argued to be, first, due to VET often being strongly institutionalized through national VET legislation regulating multiactor cooperation, leaving limited room for discretion or creative reinterpretations in terms of the interpretation of rules (A.1). The second main reason is vested interests and strong veto powers of key private and public stakeholders in the VET system (often including business, unions, and state agencies) (B.1). Beyond this, VET is usually deeply embedded in national legacies related to distinct occupational traditions, national labor markets, and respective systems of industrial relations (Amable, 2003; Busemeyer & Trampusch, 2012; Hall & Soskice, 2001), which render radical forms of change rather unlikely.

Case Selection, Methods, and Data

In the case of VET, the most profound influence of globalization is manifest in the increase of academic relative to vocational educational programs (Benavot, 1983; Powell & Solga, 2010), driven by a growing demand for academic skills, both on the side of employers and individuals. A key consequence is that actors who want to prevent VET from losing its significance are seeking reforms that maintain the societal role of VET—which includes but is not limited to generating smooth transitions from education to work also for disadvantaged youth (Bonoli & Wilson, 2019). In this context, HI is well fitted to analyze institutional patterns through which globalization plays out on the ground at the national and subnational levels. For this purpose, this chapter presents case studies of recent institutional reforms in the German skill formation system, which is well known for its tradition of apprenticeship training and full-time vocational schooling. As it represents one of the world's largest multiactor VET systems (Busemeyer & Trampusch, 2012; Culpepper, 2003), here the effect of the global trend of academization should be particularly sizeable. However, the findings for Germany should to some extent be transferable to other countries that feature a tradition of multiactor VET systems and, beyond VET, to other educational sectors characterized by strong path dependence, the presence of public and private actors with vested interests in the status quo, and an institutional context offering limited discretion to change agents.

This chapter focusses on two major areas of activity to maintain VET in the era of academization. In each of these, globalization pressures can be expected to play out through endogenous institutional change as change agents work to translate an incrementally growing globalization pressure into concrete reforms. The first area of activity is the *reconfiguration of the relationship between VET and HE*. This area of activity is further broken down into two major change processes. The first one is the *development of hybrid study programs at the nexus of VET and HE* that transpose the principle of work-based training characteristic for VET to HE (Graf, 2018). In Germany, the core example of this is dual study programs that have been rapidly growing in recent years (Ertl, 2020). The second major change process relates to *reforms that increase the permeability between VET and HE*. This process is about enhancing HE access options for VET graduates (Bernhard, 2017; Powell & Solga, 2010). In this way, the attractiveness of VET is increased as it does not represent a "dead end." Here, the key example is a policy promoted by the Standing Conference of the Ministers of Education and Cultural Affairs of the Länder (KMK) that regulates HE access for VET graduates in Germany.

The second area of activity to maintain VET in the era of academization relates to *reforms in the VET governance system* that aim to create innovation in VET, strengthen the commitment of key stakeholders—on the part of both training firms and apprentices—and, more generally, improve the coordination among all involved actors. Again, this area of activity is broken down into two major change processes. The first major change process refers to the creation of additional *governance platforms at the national and state levels*, steered by the responsible state agents at the respective governance levels, that allow the relevant public and private stakeholders to develop new policy responses to strengthen VET. The prime example in Germany is the Alliance for Initial and Further Education and Training (*Allianz für Aus- und Weiterbildung*, AfAW) (AfAW, 2019). The second change process relates to the creation of *European governance platforms* and derives from European educational policy aimed at improving the conditions for apprenticeship training in Europe. The main instance of this is the European Alliance for Apprenticeship (EAfA) (EC, 2017).

The study analyzes institutional changes mainly during the two decades from 2000 to 2020—a time when massive educational expansion of higher levels of education started to exert significant pressure on VET systems. Regarding the comparative method, it applies the method of parallel demonstration of theory (Skocpol & Somers, 1980). More specifically, the two areas of activity and the two respective change processes are analyzed to examine whether the argument about layering in the context of VET adjusting to globalization pressures is supported or not. To uncover and explore pertinent developments in VET and understand contemporary change processes, the case studies rely on process analysis, which has special value for historical-institutionalist analyses and the examination of theory-oriented explanations in the context of small-n case studies (see Mahoney, 2004). The process tracing is carried out on the basis of available secondary sources, document analysis, and numerous expert interviews (Gläser & Laudel, 2009) with key stakeholders in the field.

Next, the case studies are presented. For each main area of activity, a description of the outcome of the respective change process is presented before tracing their historical evolution.

Case Studies: Globalization, the Knowledge Economy, and Academization—Strengthening VET in Times of Global Academization

Reconfiguration of the Relationship of VET to HE

Hybrid Study Programs

Academization implies that firms face a shrinking pool of talented youth interested in entering dual VET at the upper-secondary level (Powell & Solga, 2010). As more and more young talent gets diverted into HE, this poses a threat for the traditional German model of diversified quality production that builds significantly on workers with industry-specific skills (Streeck, 1991). Some German employers fear that the growing number of HE graduates are receiving a predominantly academically oriented education and, hence, are more removed from the actual world of work (Hillmert & Kröhnert, 2003). The emergence of dual study programs is a response to this concern. Dual studies transpose the work-based training principle characteristic for VET to the HE level. As hybrid organizations, they mix selected elements of the traditional VET system and the HE system—especially in terms of curricula, teaching staff, and funding (Graf, 2018). Dual studies combine training in a firm with courses in a HE institution rather than a vocational school as in traditional apprenticeship training. Thus, the learning environments of the firm and the university are integrated in one curriculum. Dual study programs most often lead to a bachelor's degree and sometimes additionally an official VET certificate.

This transposition of work-based training to HE is motivated by the obstacles to carrying out direct reforms in the VET system. In the latter, veto players have more power due to the consensus principle and the institutionalized balance of power between unions and employers, on the one hand, and within the employer camps, on the other hand (Di Maio et al., 2019). At the same time, the level of discretion for reinterpretations of the existing regulative framework is low due to the detailed and strongly institutionalized national VET regulation (Emmenegger et al., 2020). As a result, already starting in the 1970s, large industrial German firms—who represent the key change agents in this case—set up the first vocational academies to offer dual studies in cooperation with local chambers and in a bottom-up process. As these were placed in a "niche" on top of VET, key opponents, consisting mainly of small firms and unions, had limited influence on this reform process. Many small firms are less in favor of an academization of VET, partly as they rely on apprentices as a productive workforce already during the training phase (Thelen & Busemeyer, 2012). For unions, traditional VET serves as a key channel to recruit new members and influence education policy, while they play a very small role in the HE sector where dual studies are located (Graf, 2018). Since their creation, dual study programs have massively grown in Germany and are increasingly being taken up by universities of applied sciences as well (Ertl, 2020), adding up to around 110,000 dual students at the bachelor level alone (BIBB, 2020). Overall, the creation and expansion of dual studies on top of VET represents a layering process through which the work-based training principle was introduced at the HE level.

The KMK Reform of 2009

The 2009 KMK resolution on "Higher Education Access for Vocationally Qualified Applicants Without a School Entrance Qualification" is a major response to the academization challenge for VET in Germany. It provides extended pathways from VET to HE and enables the expansion of VET graduates' HE participation (Banscherus et al., 2016). This reform implies that holders of numerous higher VET qualifications have a study authorization equivalent to a general university entrance qualification (Ulbricht, 2012). It also means that, with some exceptions, graduates of initial VET programs— after a period of employment—receive a subject specific HE entrance qualification. That is, they can take up a course of study that corresponds to the subject of the learned profession.

Like in the case of dual study programs, from the point of the VET system, this KMK reform represents a rather indirect response to the academization challenge. As mentioned before, the collectively governed VET system is strongly path dependent, granting strong veto powers to its key stakeholders, whose interests are strongly institutionalized, for instance, in national-, state-, and local-level VET governance boards (Emmenegger et al., 2020). The national VET law also implies that there is limited room for discretion within the regulative setting. Thus, while state agents and especially large, export-oriented large firms (Thelen & Busemeyer, 2012) are interested in adjusting VET to their rising skills demands, this is difficult to achieve by way of a direct reform of VET. Especially small firms are often not very keen to see a significant increase of the general education proportion in VET programs because this can increase the time spent in the school and, hence, decrease the economic utility they can derive from the apprentice during the training period. Due to such opposition, the reform pressure deriving from globalization and academization was playing out at the margins of the VET system in the form of the reconfiguration of the rules of access to HE. These are rules defined by the HE sector, not the VET actors. That is, the KMK as the main state actor in German HE system (Ulbricht, 2012) was in the driver seat and could advance the reform without having to give too much consideration to the interests of private actors in VET. In sum, the changes leading up to the eventual KMK 2009 resolution represent a layering process, not requiring direct changes leading to an academization of the core VET system.

Governance Reforms in VET

Alliance for Initial and Further Education and Training

Academization and the rise of the knowledge economy bring with them the challenge that there are often either too few firms offering apprenticeships or too few students applying for apprenticeships—with both predicaments often being related to the relative rise of attractiveness of HE. This policy problem was one of the reasons why the AfAW was signed in 2014 by the German federal government, businesses, unions, states, and the Federal Employment Agency to provide an additional coordination platform for the various public and private stakeholders in the collective governance of VET. Furthermore, at the German state level, 16 complementary state alliances for apprenticeships (*Länderbündnisse*) have been created, some of which came into existence even a few years before the launch of the national alliance. Both the national- and the state-level alliances aim to increase the attractiveness and quality of initial and further VET for both students and employers through the exchange of best practices and deepened cooperation between all stakeholders, including social partners and civil society organizations (Rohde-Liebenau & Graf, 2023).

The origin of the preceding National Pacts and the subsequent AfAW was the failed attempt by the federal government to introduce a training levy in the early 2000s. This training levy would have implied a direct and transformative change in the governance structure of traditional VET, forcing firms that do not train to pay a special tax to support apprenticeship training (Busemeyer, 2009). However, this reform was blocked by the employers, who feared that this would lead to excessive state intrusion in the decentralized system of governance in VET and, in turn, limit employer influence. The state, as the key change agent in this case, therefore opted for the introduction of an additional governance platform that would be placed on top of the traditional governance structure. The AfAW can therefore be seen as the result of the strong veto powers of employers and the limited room for the state to reform VET within the preexisting governance framework. In a nutshell, the AfAW is a new alliance that brings together a variety of relevant actors to foster collective governance and provide novel policy insights. It represents a layer on top of the traditional VET governance structure in the form of strongly institutionalized governance boards at the national, state, and local levels.

European Alliance for Apprenticeships

The EAfA aims to strengthen and revive the historical legacy of VET by improving its prestige and enhancing its European dimension. This involves fostering participation by VET stakeholders at the European, national, and local levels, but especially employers and youth. The European alliance was launched in 2013 by social partners, the European Commission (EC) and the EU Council Presidency, to increase VET quality, supply, and attractiveness in the EU member states through linking relevant stakeholders, VET providers, and think tanks (EC, 2017). It relies on national commitments and stakeholder pledges in its pursuit of enhancing both economic competitiveness and social cohesion. Engaging governments, social partners, and other key stakeholders, it also organizes bench learning and supports collective activities for governments and stakeholders (Graf & Marques, 2022).

The origin of the EAfA lies in the 2008 financial crisis and the huge increase in youth unemployment this crisis has caused in many European states. Apprenticeships were then framed as an important tool to combat youth unemployment and improve the resilience of European youth labor markets (Rohde-Liebenau & Graf, 2023). However, the EC's influence on the governance of education and training at the national level is limited. Education is a policy field still mainly under the authority of national governments, which hesitate to give up their regulative powers over skill formation, given its economic and cultural significance for the nation state (Martens et al., 2007). At the same time, it is very difficult for the EC, which represents the key change agent regarding the EAfA, to develop a policy that would be differentiated and sophisticated enough to achieve change through a strategy related to the reinterpretation of the highly distinct national legislation for VET. Hence, the EC, in cooperation with other stakeholders, devised the EAfA as a new layer of VET governance placed at the European level. It is designed to inspire policy innovation in VET without interfering too deeply with national-level VET governance, "merely" building on national commitments from member states but also pledges from individual actors at the local level (EC, 2017). Overall, the EAfA can be understood as a layer on top of respective national VET governance systems. In the German case, this implies that the EAfA, next to the AfAW, represents another layer on top of the traditional collective governance system.

CONCLUSION

This chapter first offered a review of the literature on HI and education, highlighting how HI relates to the study of globalization in the sector of education. We saw that the HI studies that address globalization mainly treat it in terms of how it plays out in and is translated by different national institutional systems. That is, in HI studies, globalization is typically analyzed in how it is related to distinct national trajectories of institutional development. Next, the chapter presented the theoretical framework of HI with a special focus on the four main modes of gradual institutional change. This was followed by four representative case studies on globalization, academization, and gradual change in VET as the pivotal educational sector studied by HI. Here, the starting point for a sectoral HI perspective was that globalization pressures have promoted the expansion of HE relative to VET. In recent years, this has prompted a range of reforms to strengthen VET in times of ongoing academization. Focusing on the case of such institutional reforms in Germany, the chapter found that due to the presence of strong veto players and limited discretion in the interpretation of rules, layering represents the main pattern of gradual institutional change on which these reforms rely—implying that new rules are added on top of existing ones, instead of replacing the latter. This enables incremental changes despite the strong degree of path dependence typical for the VET sector. We observed this pattern both in activities related to the reconfiguration of the relationship of VET to HE and the reform of VET governance structures. However, it remains a question for future research to what extent such layering is sufficient to fully adjust VET to the challenges related to increasing globalization and academization or whether, in the long run, the institutional core of VET will deteriorate, given that much of the institutional innovation is taking place "merely" at its margins, while the institutional core of traditional apprenticeship training remains more or less unchanged.

This chapter has identified patterns of change observable in many other countries beyond Germany. For example, new rules reconfiguring the access for VET graduates to HE have been added in other countries with established VET systems, including Austria and Switzerland and beyond (Ebner et al., 2013). Also, one can observe the expansion of hybrid work-based study programs—which transpose the VET principle to the HE sector but without implying direct changes to traditional VET systems—in countries such as France and the United States and as a broad trend in several world regions (Graf et al., 2014). Furthermore, both the AfAW and the EAfA can be seen as illustrations of more general strategies by educational public policymakers to promote new layers of governance in political contexts where their capacity to carry out policies in a top-down way is limited.

Thus, this chapter showed that the HI perspective and the modes of gradual change make it possible to capture how globalization understood as concrete globalization pressures (here: academization and educational expansion) plays out in specific domestic arenas characterized by path dependence (here: the German VET system). A core strength of HI is that it allows us to analyze how such globalization pressures get translated in view of distinct institutional configurations on the ground, often leading to divergent trajectories of change. HI builds on a dynamic understanding of institutions, which are framed not only as constraining but also enabling change agents. Thus, HI is well adapted to studying how globalization pressures get taken up in domestic arenas where endogenous change dynamics play a crucial role. From the HI perspective, the way this unfolds most crucially depends on characteristics of the targeted institution and the political context—as well as the interrelation of education and training to other socioeconomic spheres.

An obvious prospect for future research in the domain of HI, education, and globalization is to further extend the insights from the application of the modes of gradual institutional change to VET to other educational sectors. This could lead to a more general theory of how education may "globalize" in different ways in different sectors. For instance, the HE sector, as the other major sector that prepares students for labor market entry, represents a nice point of comparison. It can be argued that—in view of globalization pressures—universities are likely to be more open toward processes of *conversion* than is typically the case in VET. Due to the relatively high level of autonomy granted to universities, there tend to be fewer veto players (B.2) but more scope for the creative reinterpretation of institutions (A.2)—at least if the university as the central organizational actor agrees to or even promotes the envisaged changes. In addition, HE is more directly connected to the world polity (Zapp & Ramirez 2019), meaning that there are likely to be fewer opponents to the implementation of related global trends (B.2). In contrast, the VET sector is often more strongly embedded in national labor markets and respective systems of industrial relations. An indication for this is that the Bologna process for the Europeanization of HE more immediately converted European HE systems than did the Copenhagen process for European VET systems. For instance, the Bologna degree structure was rapidly implemented also in countries that did not have a tradition of dividing study programs into BA and MA degrees (Powell et al., 2012), while the uptake of the Copenhagen process on VET was more ambivalent and selective (Bieber, 2010). In line with this, the present analysis of the EAfA found that it represents layering rather than conversion, not least due to the obstacles to more direct changes in strongly institutionalized national VET systems. Similar patterns unfold in other Europeanization initiatives for VET, such as the European Qualification framework, which was initially intended to strengthen the standing of VET in Europe, but, like the KMK 2009 resolution in Germany, was eventually introduced on top of the national qualification system rather than fully integrated (Graf, 2015).

Overall, with its focus on path dependence and change, HI carries great potential when it comes to the analysis of education and globalization in given institutional contexts. While a key strength of sociological institutionalism is the analysis of processes of global isomorphism and convergence, the HI toolbox is especially useful for researchers aiming to trace in detail how globalization pressures play out in national and local contexts, while taking special note of the respective institutional conditions and actor constellations in specific sectors. By focusing on institutional trajectories of change, HI can contribute to our understanding of how present-day globalization is influencing education in different societal, political, and economic arenas.

Notes

1. HI studies typically focus less on developing a complex theory of globalization but rather on specific pressures—such as the one to deregulate national markets (Thelen & Wijnbergen, 2003)—deriving from globalization and affecting specific policy fields.
2. See the conclusion for an extension of the argument to HE.
3. In sociological institutionalism, the structuration of the world polity is seen as key factor for the expansion of HE as a worldwide phenomenon (Zapp & Ramirez, 2019). While sharing the perspective that globalization is associated with educational expansion and academization, this chapter applies an HI approach to uncover the divergent impact of this development on the ground.
4. This is also the reason why in the outlook section of this chapter the discussion is extended to HE, that is, another education sector close to the labor market and economy. Further research is needed to explore the extent to which the HI perspective on globalization presented here is applicable also to education sectors further removed from the economy and economic aspects of globalization.
5. These two characteristics capture key aspects of HI-oriented analyses that are often interested in agency (here: focus on change agents and veto players) and the respective institutional context (here: level of discretion available in a specific case). In principle, further complexity could be introduced, for instance, by integrating additional factors such as interaction effects with developments in related socioeconomic spheres (Graf, 2018; Mettler & Sorelle, 2018).

REFERENCES

AfAW. (2019). *Allianz für Aus- und Weiterbildung 2019–2021*. Allianz für Aus- und Weiterbildung (AfAW).

Amable, B. (2003). *The diversity of modern capitalism*. Oxford University Press.

Andersen, K. M., & Hassel, A. (2013). Pathways of change in CMEs. In A. Wren (Ed.), *The political economy of the service transition* (pp. 171–194). Oxford University Press.

Baccaro, L. & Howell, C. (2011). A common neoliberal trajectory. *Politics & Society, 39*, 521–563

Baker, D. P. (2014). *The schooled society*. Stanford University Press.

Banscherus, U., Bernhard, N., & Graf, L. (2016). *Durchlässigkeit als mehrdimensionale Aufgabe. Bedingungen für flexible Bildungsübergänge*. Friedrich-Ebert-Stiftung.

Barret, B. (2017) *Globalization and change in higher education*. Palgrave Macmillan.

Baumgartner, F., & Jones, B. D. (1993). *Agendas and instability in American politics*. University of Chicago Press.

Benavot, A. (1983). The rise and decline of vocational education. *Sociology of Education, 56*(2), 63–76.

Bernhard, N. (2017). *Durch Europäisierung zu mehr Durchlässigkeit?* Budrich UniPress.

BIBB. (2020). *AusbildungPlus-Datenbank des Bundesinstituts für Berufsbildung (Stand 2019)*. Bundesinstitut für Berufsbildung (BIBB).

Bieber, T. (2010). Europe à la carte? Swiss convergence towards European policy models in higher education and vocational education and training. *Swiss Political Science Review, 16*(4), 773–800.

Bonoli, G., & Wilson, A. (2019). Bringing firms on board. Inclusiveness of the dual apprenticeship systems in Germany, Switzerland and Denmark. *International Journal of Social Welfare, 28*(4), 369–379.

Bosch, G., & Charest, J. (2008). Vocational training and labour market in liberal and coordinated economies. *Industrial Relations Journal, 39*(5), 428–447.

Brown, P., Lauder, H., & Ashton, D. (2012). *The global auction: The broken promises of education, jobs, and incomes*. Oxford University Press.

Busemeyer, M. R. (2009). *Wandel trotz Reformstau*. Campus.

Busemeyer, M. R., & Trampusch, C. (2012). *The political economy of collective skill formation*. Oxford University Press.

Busemeyer, M. R., & Vossiek, J. (2016). Global convergence or path dependency? In K. Mundy, A. Green, B. Lindgard, & A. Verger (Eds.), *The handbook of global education policy* (pp. 145–161). Wiley-Blackwell.

Campbell, J. L. (2004). *Institutional change and globalization*. Princeton University Press.

Culpepper, P. D. (2003). *Creating cooperation: How states develop human capital in Europe*. Cornell University Press.

Di Maio, G., Graf, L., & Wilson, A. (2019). Torn between economic efficiency and social equality? Short-track apprenticeships in Denmark, Germany and Switzerland. *European Educational Research Journal, 18*(6), 699–723.

Di Maio, G., Graf, L. & Wilson, A. (2020). Embedded flexibilization and polite employer domination: the case of short-track apprenticeships in Switzerland. *Empirical Research in Vocational Education and Training, 12*(2), 1–21.

Djelic, M.-L., & Quack, S. (2007). Overcoming path dependency. *Theory and Society, 36*, 161–186.

Dobbins, M., & Knill, C. (2014). *Higher education governance and policy change in Western Europe*. Palgrave.

Durazzi, N. (2019). The political economy of high skills: Higher education in knowledge-based labour markets. *Journal of European Public Policy, 26*(12), 1799–1817.

Ebbinghaus, B. (2005). *Can path dependence explain institutional change?* In MPIfG Discussion Paper 05/2. Max Planck Institute for the Study of Societies (MPIfG).

Ebner, C., Graf, L., & Nikolai, R. (2013). New institutional linkages between dual vocational training and higher education. In M. Windzio (Ed.), *Integration and inequality in educational institutions* (pp. 281–298). Springer.

EC. (2017). *European alliance for apprenticeships*. European Commission.

Edelstein, B., & Nikolai, R. (2013). Strukturwandel im Sekundarbereich. *Zeitschrift für Pädagogik, 59*(4), 482–495.

Emmenegger, P., Graf, L., & Strebel, A. (2020). Social versus liberal collective skill formation systems? A comparative-historical analysis of the role of trade unions in German and Swiss VET. *European Journal of Industrial Relations, 26*(3), 263–278.

Emmenegger, P., Graf, L., & Trampusch, C. (2019). The governance of decentralised cooperation in collective training systems. *Journal of Vocational Education & Training, 71*(1), 21–45.

Ertl, H. (2020). Dual study programmes in Germany. *Oxford Review of Education, 46*(1), 79–95.

Estevez-Abe, M., Iversen, T., & Soskice, D. (2001). Social protection and the formation of skills. In P. A. Hall & D. Soskice (Eds.), *Varieties of capitalism* (pp. 145–183). Oxford University Press.

Feeney, S., & Hogan, J. (2017). A path dependence approach to understanding educational policy harmonisation. *Higher Education Policy, 30*(3), 279–298.

Geiss, M., & Westberg, J. (2020). Why do training regimes for early childhood professionals differ? *European Educational Research Journal, 19*(6), 544–563.

Gläser, J., & Laudel, G. (2009). *Experteninterviews und qualitative Inhaltsanalyse als Instrumente rekonstruierender Untersuchungen*. VS Verlag für Sozialwissenschaften.

Fortwengel, J., Gospel, H., & Toner, P. (2019). Varieties of institutional renewal. *Journal of Vocational Education & Training, 73*(1), 1–24.

Graf, L. (2015). The European educational model and its paradoxical impact at the national level. In D. Tröhler & T. Lenz (Eds.), *Trajectories in the development of modern school systems: Between the national and the global* (pp. 227–240). Routledge.

Graf, L. (2018). Combined modes of gradual change: The case of academic upgrading and declining collectivism in German skill formation. *Socio-Economic Review, 16*(1), 185–205.

Graf, L., Lassnigg, L., & Powell, J. J. W. (2012). Austrian corporatism and gradual institutional change in the relationship between apprenticeship training and school-based VET. In M. R. Busemeyer & C. Trampusch (Eds.), *The political economy of collective skill formation* (pp. 150–178). Oxford University Press.

Graf, L., & Marques, M. (2022). Towards a European model of collective skill formation? Analysing the European Alliance for Apprenticeships. *Journal of Education Policy, 38*(4), 665–685.

Graf, L., Powell, J. J. W., Fortwengel, J., & Bernhard, N. (2014). *Dual study programmes in global context: Internationalisation in Germany and transfer to Brazil, France, Qatar, Mexico and the US*. German Academic Exchange Service (DAAD).

Hacker, J. (2005). Policy drift. In W. Streeck & K. Thelen (Eds.), *Beyond continuity* (pp. 40–82). Oxford University Press.

Hacker, J. S. (2004). Privatizing risk without privatizing the welfare state. *The American Political Science Review, 98*(2), 243–260.

Hall, P. A., & Soskice, D. (2001). *Varieties of capitalism.* Oxford University Press.

Held, D., McGrew, A., Goldblatt, D., & Perraton, T. (1999). *Global transformations.* Polity Press.

Hillmert, S., & Kröhnert, S. (2003). Differenzierung und Erfolg tertiärer Ausbildungen. *Zeitschrift Fur Personalforschung, 17*(2), 195–214.

Lewis, J., & West, A. (2017). Early childhood education and care in England under austerity. *Journal of Social Policy, 46*(2), 331–348.

Lu, X. (2019). The historical thread and analysis of teacher education policy in the past 70 years of New China. *Canadian Social Science, 15*(4), 62–70

Mahoney, J. (2004). Comparative-historical methodology. *Annual Review of Sociology, 30,* 81–101.

Mahoney, J., & Thelen, K. (2010). A theory of gradual institutional change. In J. Mahoney & K. Thelen (Eds.), *Explaining institutional change* (pp. 1–37). Cambridge University Press.

Maroy, C., Pons, X., & Dupuy, C. (2017). Vernacular globalisations. *Journal of Education Policy, 32*(1), 100–122.

Martens, K., Rusconi, A., & Leuze, K. (Eds.) (2007). *New arenas of education governance.* Palgrave.

Mayer, K. U., & Solga, H. (2008). *Skill formation.* Cambridge University Press.

Mettler, S. & Sorelle, M. (2018). Policy feedback theory. In C. W. Weible & P. A Sabatier (Eds.), *Theories of the policy process* (pp. 103–134). Routledge.

Meyer, J. W., Boli, J., Thomas, G. M., & Ramirez, F. O. (1997). World society and the nation-state. *American Journal of Sociology, 103*(1), 144–181.

Niemann, D., Hartong, S., & Martens, K. (2018). Observing local dynamics of ILSA projections in federal systems. *Globalisation, Societies and Education, 16*(5), 596–608.

Nishioka, S. (2018). Privatization of childcare service in Japan. *Journal of Asian Public Policy, 11*(3), 285–298.

North, D. C. (1990). *Institutions, institutional change and economic performance.* Cambridge University Press.

Persson, B., & Hermelin, B. (2018). Mobilising for change in vocational education and training in Sweden. *Journal of Vocational Education & Training, 70*(3), 476–496.

Pierson, P. (2000). Increasing returns, path dependence, and the study of politics. *American Political Science Review, 94*(2), 251–267.

Pierson, P. (2004). *Politics in time.* Princeton University Press.

Powell, J. J. W., Bernhard, N., & Graf, L. (2012). The emerging European model in skill formation: Comparing higher education and vocational training in the Bologna and Copenhagen processes. *Sociology of Education, 85*(3), 240–258.

Powell, J. J. W., Edelstein, B., & Blanck, J. M. (2016). Awareness-raising, legitimation or backlash? *Globalisation, Societies and Education, 14*(2), 227–250.

Powell, J. J. W., & Solga, H. (2010). Analyzing the nexus of higher education and vocational training in Europe. *Studies in Higher Education, 35*(6), 705–721.

Protsch, P., & Solga, H. (2016). The social stratification of the German VET system. *Journal of Education and Work, 29*(6), 637–661.

Rohde-Liebenau, J., & Graf, L. (2023). Two instruments, one melody: The parallel evolvement of European and German alliances for apprenticeships. *European Educational Research Journal,* Advance access: https://doi.org/10.1177/14749041221148282.

Sancak, M., & Özel, I. D. (2018). When politics gets in the way: Domestic coalitions and the making of skill systems. *Review of International Political Economy, 25*(3), 340–363.

Schickler, E. (2001). *Disjointed pluralism.* Princeton University Press.

Schmidt, J. T., & Tang, M. (2020). Digitalization in education. In *Führen und Managen in der digitalen Transformation* (pp. 287–312). Springer.

Schmidt, K. E. (2017). Quality assurance policies and practices in Scandinavian higher education systems. *Journal of Higher Education Policy and Management, 39*(3), 247–265.

Schneider, S., & Pilz, M. (2019). The function and institutional embeddedness of polytechnics in the Indian education system. *International Journal for Research in Vocational Education and Training, 6*(3), 284–308.

Schofer, E., & Meyer, J. W. (2005). The worldwide expansion of higher education in the twentieth century. *American Sociological Review, 70*(6), 898–920.

Scott, W. R. (2008). *Institutions and organizations.* Sage.

Severing, E., & Teichler, U. (Eds.) (2013). *Akademisierung der Berufswelt?* W. Bertelsmann.

Skocpol, T., & Somers, M. (1980). The uses of comparative history for macrosocial inquiry. *Comparative Studies in Society and History, 22*(2), 174–197.

Strebel, A., Emmenegger, P. & Graf, L. (2020). New interest associations in a neo-corporatist system: Adapting the Swiss training system to the service economy. *British Journal of Industrial Relations, 59*(3), 848–873.

Streeck, W. (1991). On the institutional conditions of diversified quality production. In E. Matzner & W. Streeck (Eds.), *Beyond Keynesianism* (pp. 21–61). Edward Elgar.

Streeck, W., & Thelen, K. (2005). *Beyond continuity.* Oxford University Press.

Thelen, K. (2004). *How institutions evolve.* Cambridge University Press.

Thelen, K. (2014). *Varieties of liberalization and the new politics of social solidarity.* Cambridge University Press.

Thelen, K., & Busemeyer, M. R. (2012). Institutional change in German vocational training. In M. R. Busemeyer & C. Trampusch (Eds.), *The political economy of collective skill formation* (pp. 68–100). Oxford University Press.

Thelen, K., & Steinmo, S. (1992). Historical institutionalism in comparative politics. In S. Steinmo, K. Thelen, & F. Longstreth (Eds.), *Structuring politics: Historical institutionalism in comparative analysis* (pp. 1–32). Cambridge University Press.

Thelen, K., & Wijnbergen, C. V. (2003). The paradox of globalization. *Comparative Political Studies, 36*(8), 859–880.

Trampusch, C. (2009). Europeanization and institutional change in vocational education and training in Germany and Austria. *Governance, 22*(3), 371–397.

Trampusch, C. (2010). Transformative and self-preserving change in the vocational education and training system in Switzerland. *Comparative Politics, 41*(2), 187–206.

Ulbricht, L. (2012). Öffnen die Länder ihre Hochschulen? *Die Hochschule, 21*(1), 154–168.

Wang, J., & Lee, S.-M. (2020). Study on the institutional change of early childhood education quality assurance in China. *Family and Environment Research, 58*(1), 87–103.

Wolter, A., & Kerst, C. (2015). The "academization" of the German qualification system. *Research in Comparative and International Education, 10*(4), 510–524.

Zapp, M., & Ramirez, F. O. (2019). Beyond internationalisation and isomorphism. *Comparative Education, 55*(4), 473–493.

CHAPTER 4

··

EDUCATION IN A POSTLIBERAL WORLD SOCIETY

··

JARED FURUTA, JOHN W. MEYER, AND PATRICIA BROMLEY

THE global liberal order of the postwar period celebrated empowered individuals as the central source of progress in all institutional arenas (Meyer, 2010). These models entailed that individuals required education to actively contribute to society; they also projected broader visions of progress as rooted in individual actors in a rationalized world. Education was seen as a panacea for a widened array of problems, and it expanded dramatically around the world. This process intensified in the "neoliberal" period that began in the 1990s, celebrating the centrality of individual and organizational (rather than state) action in all arenas of global society and marketplaces. This worldwide movement followed the fall of communism as an alternative model and led to notions of a global "knowledge society" rooted in education (Lerch et al., 2022a). Thus, in 1950 the average person over 15 years in age in the world had just 3.2 years of schooling. By 1980, this had increased to 5.3 years, and by 2010 individuals were schooled for an average of 7.8 years (Barro & Lee, 2015). The worldwide character of these changes suggests the relevance of neoinstitutional theories that attend to the force of worldwide cultural models in shaping educational change (Meyer, 2010), rather than functional and conflict theories that attribute change to local circumstances or more realist global forces. Neoinstitutional theories emphasize cultural models as underlying educational change; in the postwar liberal period—and even more the neoliberal period—these models have been elaborated at the global level and have treated educational expansion as central to both national and global society.

In recent years, the global authority of this institutionalized liberal order has weakened, and widespread critical economic, political, and cultural perspectives on it—from the left, right, and center—have grown stronger, in a period we see as fragmented and "postliberal." Global levels of democracy are in decline, restrictions on civil society are on the rise, and populism is increasingly taking hold around the world (Diamond, 2019). Criticisms of, and sometimes direct attacks on, liberal world culture weaken or at least revise emphases on education that are central to its vision and that in neoinstitutional perspectives drive educational change (Lerch et al., 2022b). Instead, education comes more often to be seen as elitist, or as reflecting arbitrary or Western (or Christian, or American) values. Possible outcomes of these attacks are restrictions on education or educational expansion, or on the long-term worldwide increase in educational organization all the way to the global level (see Choi et al., Chapter 5, this volume, for a review). Other likely outcomes involve constraints on (or redirection of) education, away from schooled empowerment and toward the celebration of popular autonomy rooted in uncontrolled individualism or embedded in political, religious, familial, or cultural collectives.

In this chapter, we review ideas and evidence on recent trends that oppose or provide alternatives to liberal world society. From a neoinstitutional point of view, we see the sweeping modern educational expansion as directly rooted in the cultural frames of this society. And we similarly use this point of view to explore the dimensions on which education is limited or reconstructed with the weakening of global cultural support. We begin by discussing the expansion of education and the empowerment of individual actors that emerged as part of the postwar liberal order, and then depict more recent contestations of this international model. Then, we present two general themes on the effects of these contestations on education: We suggest that the decline in liberal hegemony weakens the centrality of education in models of society, and further that the rise of alternative and oppositional models of society redirects education toward less liberal-individualist forms. To elaborate on this argument, we then outline the implications of these speculative hypotheses for dependent variables such as school enrollments, educational stratification, curricular content, pedagogy, and educational organization.

BACKGROUND

The period since World War II has been marked by a dominant liberal global culture shaped by rationalized markets and polities, where economic freedoms are emphasized on the political right and political and social freedoms on the left (Ruggie, 1982). The first half of the 20th century had demonstrated the evils of statism and European corporatism, with two world wars, a depression, and extreme violations of human rights (Judt, 2005). As a result, the authority of corporate society over the rights of the individual (seen in free polities and markets) was delegitimated in world discourse and organization (Djelic, 1998). A liberal United States was dominant during the period: It was seen as a formal exemplar, and it also shaped the construction of international institutions

(Ikenberry, 2011). Liberal models were intensified in competition with a conspicuously illiberal communism (Westad, 2017).

The imagined alternative to delegitimated collectivisms was a dramatic assertion of the standing of the human individual (Frank & Meyer, 2002). The constructed individual was entitled but also (a) seen as responsible and empowered in a free and rationalized society and (b) theorized as the source of social, political, and economic progress. These claims cut across multiple institutional arenas: The theorized individual could make economic choices in markets, political choices in democracies, cultural choices of religion and language, and social choices in familial and associational life. These choices would, according to liberal faith, add up to collective social goods. A global explosion of formal assertions of individual human rights, empowerment, and responsibilities followed (Elliott, 2007, 2011, 2014; Lauren, 2011; Moyn, 2010; Stacy, 2009). These trends intensified with neoliberalism in the 1980s, emphasizing and globalizing liberal foci on the actors within society rather than the collective states representing society itself (Mudge, 2008; Ruggie, 1998). The end of the Cold War generated a triumphalist assertion of the standing of the individual, now in a stateless global society rather than a bounded national state.

These changes supported explosive educational expansion: As a central component of liberal theories of progress, education was essential for both empowering individuals and incorporating and controlling them in rationalized environments. Compulsory education had long been a feature of the nation state model, and now enrollments expanded everywhere (Chapter 1, Lee & Ramirez, this volume). Preschool educational enrollments grew (Wotipka et al., 2017), primary school became universal in "Education for All" global norms and practices (Chabbott, 2003; Meyer, Ramirez, & Soysal, 1992), mass secondary education became common (Barro & Lee, 2015), higher education enrollments grew exponentially in all regions (Schofer & Meyer, 2005), and postschooling lifelong learning became a world ideal (Jakobi, 2011). Beyond national schooling systems, education for the disabled, the refugee, the marginal, the immigrant, or the inhabitant of a conflict society received global support (Lerch & Buckner, 2018).

These changes reflected the influence of global models, more than local or national functional forces. They were enacted in liberal countries but also illiberal ones: Rapid educational expansion, for instance, characterized the communist world (although efforts were made in the 1970s to constrain higher educational expansion in preference for more collective control; Baker et al., 2007). The culture of global liberal society was structured in world discourse and organization (Meyer et al., 1997). It was also asserted in professional communications and by international organizations (Boli & Thomas, 1999).

The neoliberal culture, with its mythic emphasis on the individual and organizational actor as central in social, political, and economic life, rose in the 1980s. Despite its financial pressures, it carried emphases on education beyond functional justifications (e.g., older "human capital" ideas). During this period, conceptions of socioeconomic progress valued a "knowledge society" (Nowotny et al., 2001; Stehr, 1994); even in peripheral countries, it became an aspirational target. Education was seen as an economically valuable investment, and the professions produced and legitimated by education were redefined and accounted as economically productive (Schofer et al., 2021).

POSTLIBERALISM

The dramatic changes reviewed earlier (and in Chapter 1, Ramirez & Lee, this volume) occurred against a range of oppositions. Despite the hegemony of the liberal model and cultural frame, criticisms came in several varieties, all with legitimated interests and actors, and all with discursive cultural support. (a) There were those who saw overeducation as a problem: On the right, it would produce unfulfilled aspirations and destructive status claims; on the left, it would undercut class consciousness and proletarian power; and for the centrists, it was inefficient (e.g., Berg, 1970; Boudon, 1973; Shils, 1971). (b) Others mourned the decline of the traditional family and religion and culture with the rise of female and child autonomy. (c) Still others saw political democracy as mass society filled with demagogues and uncontrolled individualism (Ziblatt, 2017). (d) Many saw rationalized markets and culture as exploiting or destroying local economies and communities (Manza & McCarthy, 2011).

These oppositional alternatives have gained strength in the last decade (e.g., Guillen, 2018). Liberal models continued to retain force and, indeed, expand. But liberalisms of all sorts have weakened, relatively, in the face of populist mobilization from below and authoritarian elitism from above. As part of this process, attacks on economic free trade and support for economic forms of nationalism have become pressing political issues (Colantone & Stanig, 2019). Democracy has faced setbacks around the world as it encountered global criticism (Diamond, 2019; Przeworski, 2019). Nongovernmental civil society organizations, conceived as threats to government authority, have faced restrictions in a growing number of countries (Bromley et al., 2020). On one hand, the suppression of individual choice in the name of collectives has gained force as liberal ideologies weaken: Resurgent nationalisms, assertions of religious solidarities, ethnic status claims, and ideas about the putatively natural base of familial, sexual, and gender identities have gained traction in the global society (Bonikowski, 2017; Velasco, 2018). On the other hand, populist libertarianism also celebrates the freedom of individuals to escape the social control of the rationalized society and knowledge system.

Several factors explain why these sea changes in global society have taken place. Some are external to the liberal order, such as shifts in power and centrality in world society. Others reflect the failures of the liberal model, and dramatic decoupling between the myths embodied in the model and realities on the ground. We can, thus, list some factors involved:

(a) The decline in the world standing of the liberal United States, with its conspicuous domestic and foreign policy failures, has led liberal internationalism to look like neocolonialism (e.g., Mann, 2003). (b) The rising influence of the BRIC countries—particularly China—with aggressively illiberal models has created visible alternatives

(Orban, 2014). (c) The dramatic failure of the 2008 financial crisis produced local disasters, but more importantly delegitimated global capitalism as exploitive (Tooze, 2018). The associated attention to dramatic intranational and international inequalities created legitimation crises even in developed countries. (d) The overreach of liberal models penetrated traditional arenas of social, communal, and family life: The forceful restructuring of these domains created active resistance (Bourguignon, 2015; Mearsheimer, 2019). (e) The extremes of neoliberalism supported libertarianisms that attack the social structures of liberal individualism: These attacks gained standing after the end of the Cold War, weakening justifications for state power (which came to look arbitrary and coercive). (f) And most recently, a viral pandemic now creates attention to the threats of globalization, the failures of global control, and the need to bound, reassert, and defend the local (Kahl & Berengaut, 2020).

IMPACT ON EDUCATION

The global decline in liberal hegemony and the rise of alternative societal models entails the decline or modification of educational arrangements celebrating notions of empowered individuals in rationalized societies. The education of people as individual "actors" is central to liberal models of society, as these actors are understood to create and recreate society; indeed, the term "education" comes, around the world, to mean the construction of individual persons as global or national citizens and economic actors— more than the creation of corporate national, sociocultural, occupational, or class groups (Lerch et al., 2022a). Global and cultural shifts away from liberalism in more recent years have weakened these universalized pictures of education as a Durkheimian religion (Meyer, 2000). We approach the issue with two very general interpretive themes:

> *Theme 1:* The decline in liberal hegemony weakens the centrality of education in models of the individual in society. As a result: (a) Commitments to and resources for education decline. (b) Growth rates in enrollments and educational resources tend to decline.

> *1.1:* The effects of the declining centrality of education in models of society are worldwide.
> *1.2:* The effects of the declining centrality of education are concentrated in countries with illiberal structures and linkages.

> *Theme 2:* With the decline of liberal models of society, education is redirected away from disciplined individual choice toward the reinforcement of alternatives. Some reassert collective identities (religious, political, economic, sociocultural, or familial). Others may assert uncontrolled individual expression. Thus, some reactions

can be called anti-liberal, while others enact fragmented versions of liberalism. We use a general term—postliberal—to include the variations.

2.1: The effects of postliberal models on the educational celebration of the disciplined liberal individual are worldwide.
2.2: The effects of postliberal models are concentrated in countries with illiberal structures.

These themes are only partly consistent with each other: The matter depends on whether we consider (a) the effects of a global decline in liberal hegemony or (b) the impact of the rise of a variety of postliberal alternatives. Both are plausible implications of the declining relative authority of the liberal order. In the sections that follow, we consider evidence, often speculative or illustrative, for these ideas.

Educational Expansion and Structure

Education was a most central social institution in liberal global society (circa 1950 to the 1980s) and even more in the neoliberal period (1990–2010), as depicted generally in Ramirez and Lee (Chapter 1, this volume) and organizationally in Choi et al. (Chapter 5, this volume). With the rise of oppositions to liberal models, and the rise of alternatives, education may become less central, producing absolute or relative declines in enrollment, lowered political centrality, and structural peripheralization.

Enrollments

Theme 1 suggests that in the postliberal period since 2008, the pell-mell expansion of educational enrollments has slowed or stopped. Education becomes less central as a collective good, and it is increasingly seen as a constraint on individuals, families, and corporate groups. Social incentives for participation thus decline.

In the case of tertiary education, detailed analyses have been carried out by Schofer et al. (2022). They show the average annual growth rates in higher educational enrollments for countries for which data are available (1980 to 2015), using data from the World Development Indicators (World Bank, 2019). Growth rates, worldwide, were very high in early postwar period. But in the recent decade, average growth rates for higher education decline (but remain positive). Declines turn out to be especially concentrated in countries with illiberal polities and linkages, as Theme 1.2 would suggest.

Available studies also address whether female enrollments are especially constrained in the postliberal period, which carries some elements of the reassertion of traditional familial arrangements, with their special controls over women. The findings of Lerch et al. (2022b) support a version of Theme 2—growth in enrollment rates of women slowed more than those of men, though expansion continued through the period.

Themes 1.1 and 2 suggest that enrollment slowdowns—particularly those of women—might especially characterize countries with illiberal structures and linkages. The studies cited earlier find supportive evidence for this this by classifying countries on membership in one of several illiberal organizations (see Bromley et al., 2020; Schofer et al., 2022).

Political Support

We also expect to find weakening political support for education. In a postliberal institutional environment, negative sentiments about education may increase: From the left, or center, education spending may come to be seen as wasteful, inefficient, or elitist (e.g., Caplan, 2018); from the right, schooling may be denigrated for undercutting primordial collectivities—or as an imposition on putatively free individuals and families. For example, a speech by US Secretary of Education Betsy DeVos in October 2020 sharply criticizes the public education system for undermining the family as a sovereign institution: "Let me suggest we could fix education for so many children in America if we . . . embrace the family as the sovereign sphere that it is. A sphere that predates government altogether. It's been said, after all, that the family is not only an institution; it's also the foundation for all other institutions" (Strauss, 2020).

To explore this issue, we draw on data from the Manifesto Project (Volkens et al., 2020), which tracks political party platforms for many countries over time, coding them on a variety of topics (e.g., discussions of education) and by whether the party is left, center, or right. We focus on the depiction of trends in mentions of limiting state expenditures on education in the party platforms. These trends extend the analyses described in greater detail by Jakobi (2011). They rely on a set of 56 Organization for Economic Cooperation and Development (OECD) and Central/Eastern European countries from 1960 to 2018. Each data point at the start of a given decade reflects the percentage of platforms for the entire decade; for example, the data point for 1980 reflects the data from 1980 to 1989. We consider parties sorted out on a left-right scale, as parties on the left are generally more supportive of education.

The results from Figure 4.1 present a clear recent trend: On the left, right, and center, the percentage of political parties that mention limiting state expenditures increases during the recent decade, compared with the neoliberal period of the 1990s (though not earlier periods).

Structure

The postwar liberal expansion of education took place with a strong emphasis on equality among individual persons. The idea of distinctive educations for special social groups (by race, class, ethnicity, or gender) was in disrepute as a violation of liberal egalitarian principles. As a result, distinct categories of institutions of postsecondary education declined (Frank & Meyer, 2020), and a linear and universalistic hierarchy of education cycles grew stronger. Similarly, in primary and secondary school, extreme versions of school tracking declined, and simpler models of a universalistic schooling process at early ages grew stronger (Furuta, 2020). These shifts produced a long-term decline in differentiated systems of vocational education, disconnected as "training" from broad conceptions of education (Benavot, 1983). Even in the Germanic

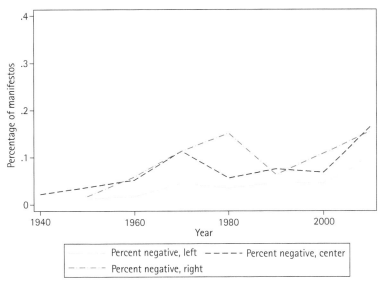

FIGURE 4.1 Percentage of political party platforms that mention limiting state expenditures on education, 1960–2018.

(*Source:* Political Manifesto Project; Volkens et al., 2020)

countries, in which vocational training had developed highly, linkages to the general educational stream moved forward with the development of institutions like the German *Gesamtschule*.

A question for research is whether postliberal educational arrangements bring more differentiated forms of school tracking. Theme 1 suggests they do: Education may be less structured around individuals integrated in an equalitarian public, and more built around differences of individual choice and/or past or future social roles. This suggests that the overall liberal focus on education for everyone in the public would weaken, in preference for more and earlier specialization. Theme 2.2 suggests that this might occur more strongly in countries with histories of strong statist or corporatist polities: Notions of the nation as an organic community lead in this direction. Systematic data are not yet available, but suggestive examples are common. In Hungary, for example, Viktor Orban advocates education tied to occupational needs and away from producing graduates with "useless knowledge," as does Recep Erdogan in Turkey (Schofer et al., 2022). In the United Kingdom, Boris Johnson advanced a self-proclaimed "radical" plan to promote vocational education in September 2020, calling for an end to the "pointless nonsensical gulf that's been fixed for more than 100 years between the so-called academic and so-called practical side of education" (quoted from Stewart, 2020). Further research might find an expansion in separate educational streams for male and female students: Principled coeducation increased sharply in the long liberal period. In the same way, the long-term trend against differentiation by religious, ethnic, or national characteristics may be slowed or even reversed under some illiberal conditions (Cakmakli et al., 2017). It seems likely that postliberal regimes might, for example, create exclusions for nonnationals.

Finally, declines in the global model of education for liberal society make education a less central public good (Theme 1), even as it remains a private good in social stratification. Beyond the neoliberal increases in private education (Buckner, 2017) that are often linked to funding arrangements, private alternatives arise as a cultural and ideological matter in oppositions to the values of public education (e.g., in homeschooling, see Chapter 21, Mangez & Tilman, this volume). In all of these cases, private and perhaps idiosyncratic choices of individuals—and/or demands of corporate groups—take preference over liberal notions of nationally and globally responsible individual citizenship. The overall result, we speculate, might be increased educational differentiation around matters of individual or familial taste or group memberships.

Education as Central in Social Stratification

The liberal institutional order, with its focus on the rights and capacities of the individual in rationalized society, puts education at the center of the stratification system. Occupational, income, and organizational status have all been constructed as products of educational attainment. Collins's (1979) title "The Credential Society" captures the idea, as does Dore's (1976) more explicit formulation of "The Diploma Disease." Further developments during the neoliberal period created an expanded service sector and led to the construction of the "knowledge society" as a global model: As part of this process, much professional and organizational expansion was explicitly created by, and to be achieved through, education (Schofer et al., 2021).

These developments moved away from older conceptions of stratification that (a) valued achievement in economic, political, and social markets, and (b) denigrated the shift to educational conceptions of merit (Kett, 2013). But schooling became increasingly important, and students of social stratification everywhere incorporated educational attainment (of individuals and of roles) as mainstays of hierarchies. While older conceptions of stratification lived on with terms like "socioeconomic status," actual measurement increasingly employed education as the core property of both individuals and occupations. Correspondingly, students and parents devoted themselves more intensely to strategies for educational success (Baker & LeTendre, 2005).

Ideologies of the current postliberal period increasingly emphasize the negative consequences of existing educational arrangements for student overwork, overstress, and suicide (e.g., Pope, 2001), and for the class and status biases in resultant student attainments. For example, a recent article on education in the *American Sociological Review* begins from a stated assumption that schools are "privilege-dependent organizations" (Calarco, 2020). Such ideologies attack the credentialist society as elitist and arbitrary, rather than functional (Sandel, 2020). Of course, from a libertarian perspective, compulsory education itself can be seen as a violation of due process rights (Payne, 2014). Much of the criticism involved has a populist flavor, denigrating the putative expertise of the schooled professionals (as with anti-vaccination movements [Hussain et al., 2018]), or homeschooling advocacy [Chapter 21, Mangez & Tilman, this volume]).

As Theme 1 suggests, efforts are advanced to limit the assignment of social value to educational credentials. As a result, there are waves of attacks on the schools themselves, or on elite schools, or on the power of the professionals legitimated by them. Most of the attacks come from the political right, but left-wing attacks on educational elitism or selective institutions occur, too (e.g., the obvious inequalities involved in liberal foci on "school choice"). From either side, teachers are criticized for placing their own job security ahead of students' learning and for resistance to innovation and improvement (Moe, 2011). In higher education, professors are criticized as irrelevant and out of touch, preferring "rigor over relevance" (Desch, 2019). There are claims that the current pandemic exacerbates the failures of education and learning, especially for lower status groups (Allen, 2020). Many of the critical themes here have long been available: Under changed conditions the relevant movements seem to acquire more centrality in national and global discourses.

In a postliberal world, educational certificates may lose centrality in the allocation of social positions (e.g., appointments and promotions), in favor of such other measures of qualification as relevant experience, assessments of skill and performance capabilities, qualities of character, or interview performance. For example, in 2018, Google launched a certificate program that is intended to serve as a replacement for a four-year degree; it will qualify those who complete it for highly paid technology industry jobs, such as data analysis and project management (Google Website, 2020). A management advice column reviewing the trend notes, "more and more employers have signaled that they no longer view them [degrees] as a must-have—Apple, IBM, and Google, just to name a few. So, if you're an employer or hiring manager, ask yourself: Is it time to rewrite our own job descriptions, to eliminate the requirement of a four-year degree? . . . Remember: Nowadays, it's all about skills. Not degrees" (Bariso, 2020). As another example, an op-ed in the *New York Times* in December 2020 complains that US Congress members are "credentialed out the wazoo" (Senior, 2020); the editorial postulates that increasing representation from the noneducated could make the political process more effectual.

Within educational systems, Theme 2 suggests an expanded focus on the relevance of dimensions of social stratification linked to practice more than an educational core. Professional schools may become more central—engineering, business and public administration, education, medicine, law, public policy, and social work. They organize education in applied formats appropriate to social needs. Frank and Meyer (2020) refer to them as the "socio-sciences," as they organize knowledge around the purposes of human action. Theoretical knowledge may be marginalized in favor of hands-on training in the real world, with internships and apprenticeships becoming the foci of education (Illich, 1970). Tests administered through hands-on experience or simulated (or actual) occupational settings may become more frequently used in place of reliance on traditional academic exams, or courses and degrees related directly to practice may expand more rapidly than other areas.

Beyond concrete attacks on educational credentialism, rhetorical changes also occur. Educational status and authority depend heavily on culturally constructed respect and deference, and the status-denigrating discourse of postliberal society has diffuse effects over and above immediate social-organizational ones. If the empowered professionals of neoliberal society are reduced to technical specialists and consultants, then their role in broad social change will also be undercut. It seems clear that the exalted role of "think tanks" comes under increased criticism; and nongovernmental organizations are expected to demonstrate concrete impacts. With the decline in the authority of liberal society and the rise of a postliberal libertarian conceptions of freedom outside formal structures, young people themselves might envision more desirable futures outside the educational system.

Curricula

In the liberal world, people are to be educationally constructed as empowered and responsible *actors* across social arenas from economy to family life (Hwang & Colyvas, 2020). To do this, they are to learn about rationalized society and nature, through the natural and social sciences. The educational process also cultivates capabilities for purposive action. Thus, curricula emphasize the capacities of students, who are to be proactive researchers and critical thinkers, and who possess active skills in art, social behavior, and technical analysis. They are to do this, as rational and responsible actors, in a world that is tamed by scientific and social scientific knowledge. Courses in methods proliferate, and student projects become as central as passive learning (Frank & Meyer, 2020).

Actorhood and its entitled choices make sense if the wider environment is a rationalized enterprise, and it became an important business of education to do this. Thus, curricula expanded dramatically: Education replicated standard knowledge but also created new scientized fields, from astrobiology to ethnic studies to the micropolitics of sexual behavior (Frank & Meyer, 2020). Mass education replaced traditional history with more rationalized and scientized civics and social studies, adding foreign languages, and incorporating broadened and often participatory and empowered notions of the arts and literature (Benavot et al., 1992). Curricular strategies that emphasize "design thinking" in higher education also became increasingly popular, with the development of global consulting firms. In all areas, globalization proceeded apace, with international flows of students and teachers, international conferences, and consultancies.

In a postliberal world less focused on the responsible individual actor in rationalized environments, Theme 1 suggests that these forms of curricular expansion may weaken and be supplemented by highly variable new foci. (a) The liberal individual may be suppressed—or alternatively freed from responsibilities to a given society and knowledge system. (b) The liberal model of society can return to be an ultimate locus of identity, or a variable focus of political, religious, or cultural entities. (c) Knowledge can have traditional foci on known market arenas for social and economic action, or highly debatable pictures of socially constructed realities.

So one can envision a return from emphases on student empowerment to more passive notions of education for competence and conformity: more history and less social studies, and less abstract science and more practice. On the other hand, one can also imagine the decline of any kind of canon, and a focus on identities and expression detached from the rationalized elements of liberalism. Both responses are likely, and an obvious result would be increases in curricular variation across schools and educational systems. If the educationally disciplining effect of global liberal models declines, fragmented and diverse educational models grow, some supporting expanded individual taste and idiosyncrasy, but others a variety of group identities or distinctive knowledge systems.

For instance, the social sciences, which develop abstract and universalistic principles to explain societal processes and empower individuals, are to be marginalized in Turkey and Hungary (Schofer et al., 2022). Similarly, the basic and abstract sciences may decline in relative dominance. Both may decline more generally in the world, to be replaced by the rapidly expanding professional schools, and by new arenas for individual action such as data science (Frank & Meyer, 2020). Curricular attention is on problems to be solved, more than on abstractions. Thus, there are foci on issues of gender and race relations. But women's studies and ethnic studies, which reflect recognition of an expanding set of individual identities in liberal society, are attacked in multiple places (Lerch et al., 2022b). There are more calls for local relevance, in reaction to foci on national and global orientations: In the extreme, these could lead to decreased international flows of students, teachers, conferences, and collaborations, and increased linkages of the schools to local political and economic contexts, perhaps with local rather than cosmopolitan internships and related foci. But the emphasis on local relevance can also support idiosyncratic curricular variations reflecting individual or familial or subgroup foci.

Theme 2 suggests that we should look for assertions of a wide range of postliberal identities and knowledge systems in the curriculum. Some may dramatize individual subjectivity or distinctive cultural frames. Other, and more common, models may increasingly emphasize corporate structures (e.g., family, community, ethnicity, religion) that are seen as having primordial properties; the empowered individual may thus give some ground to a more obedient and knowledgeable one. A first place to look for support for Theme 2 would therefore be to find indicators of resurgent nationalisms, perhaps replacing emphasis on the rationalized state (Guadiano, 2020). Curricular developments in less liberal contexts may increasingly emphasize nationalist history, culture, language, family structures, and religion—and curricular support for diversity on these dimensions may decline. For instance, civics courses might emphasize conformity more than proaction (Bromley et al., 2011; Lerch et al., 2017).

Cultural nationalism would probably produce a greater emphasis on war in school textbooks (Lachmann & Mitchell, 2014). Or there might be growing resistance to liberal cultural assertions of sex education curricula built around ideas of choice and autonomy, as seen in a recent political campaign by Poland's Law and Justice Party (Davies, 2020). Conservative movements might promote sex only within marriage for the purposes (and duties) of procreation, heterosexuality, and pro-life stances (Zimmerman, 2016). Such movements are increasingly organized at the global level (Velasco, 2018, 2020). In Romania, for example, the Orthodox Church criticizes sex education and promotes creationism, in opposition to the work of many nongovernmental organizations (Stan & Turcescu, 2005). But the weakening of the general liberal model might also produce a continuation of less controlled individualistic sexual and gender expression. Again, this leads to the idea that postliberal curricula should show expanded variation across programs and countries.

The changes considered here might be best evidenced in countries with illiberal polities. On the other hand, we can also expect changes in the historically liberal polities—perhaps toward further developments of a less liberal individualism, with more idiosyncratic variation among individuals and groups.

Pedagogy

The rise of the empowered individual in the postwar period was characterized by a global shift in pedagogical theory (and sometimes in practice). In textbooks, the development of the student as a participatory person was increasingly emphasized (Bromley et al., 2011), rather than the passive acquirer of top-down knowledge. Student choice was also empowered in both mass and higher education (Frank & Meyer, 2020; Robinson, 2011): Long chains of required courses and curricular steps tended to disappear, and optional alternatives expanded. Student-centered forms of education were valued by worldwide and national policies and professionals (Rosenmund, 2006), and rigid systems of evaluation criticized in preference for conceptions of students with multiple intelligences (Gardner, 1983).

With the rise of alternatives to liberal models of society, Theme 2 suggests we will find cases of increased emphases on the student as subordinated to traditional (and emergent) authority—but also the legitimation of the free student/child outside of schooled controls.

On one hand, there may be increases in educational discipline across the board—emphasizing the collective authority of the teacher, the school, or larger powers (Arum, 2005). For example, perhaps the long-term decline in policies and practices of corporal punishment is slowed or reversed: In Samoa and Cameroon, there have been recent movements to reinstate legislation that allows teachers to use corporal punishment in schools (Godfrey, 2018; Kindzeka, 2020). In the United States, many states have continually allowed corporal punishment, and several jurisdictions that had previously restricted the practice are now resurrecting it (Human Rights Watch, 2008; Marilisaraccoglobal, 2018; Saxena, 2020). In Brazil, furthermore, Jair Bolsonaro initiated a plan to expand the "civic military" model of schooling by establishing 108 such schools in the country by 2023 (Tokarnia, 2019). As part of the weakening empowerment of students as actors, it is also possible that behavioral requirements will be reasserted, as seen in some schools in India (Bénéï, 2008). School uniforms and stricter dress codes may also make a comeback. As the intrinsic authority of education weakens, traditional arbitrary authority may gain.

On the other hand, postliberal ideologies also expand on the imagined individual of liberal theory, emphasizing free or variable expression against controls of schooled knowledge and responsibility. Programs specialized in terms of religious, cultural, or artistic knowledge frames or technical skills might be more common, whether controlled by individual choice or group norms.

These ideas suggest a rise in oppositional relations between teacher and student. Theme 1 suggests increases in student resistance as legitimated by illiberal identities, and by postliberal notions of freedom, autonomy, and empowerment without the rationalized responsibilities of the liberal system. Teacher and school may thus be weaker but more authoritarian in response. Without the framework of the liberal system, a much wider variety of educational—or marginally educational—structures may develop, around variations in student and family tastes, or variations in definitions of core knowledge, or variations in social identities. Thus, we could imagine increases in both extremely "progressive" educational models and very conservative ones. Perhaps in liberal national contexts, libertarian models gain strength with the weakening of the authority of the global liberal model: So we might anticipate declines in the power and standardization of compulsory education. In parallel, assertions of national and religious authority, in other contexts, might produce narrowing and rigidity of individual-centered education, perhaps in preference for collective power and authority.

Organization and the Universalized Education Regime

The postwar liberal society dramatically expanded formal organization in social life and education around the world (Bromley & Meyer, 2015; Choi et al., Chapter 5, this volume). Sleepy universities became "organized actors," with expanded and differentiated organizational structures (Kruecken & Meier, 2006; Ramirez, 2020), and school systems acquired expanded formal structures. Education became increasingly organized and rationalized at every level—local units, national ministries, and a huge array of international organizational structures proliferated (Bromley, 2010). Teachers were organized at the international level, and educational credentials became increasingly standardized worldwide.

As a result, students and schools could be ranked on worldwide scales (Kijima & Lipscy, 2020). Mass educational systems were evaluated on rationalized measures—TIMSS, PISA, or other assessments administered by the International Association for the Evaluation of Educational Achievement (Baker & LeTendre, 2005; Kamens & McNeely, 2010). Universities were evaluated on globally standardized criteria through the Times Higher Education or Shanghai rankings systems.

These changes reflected a cascade of organizational structuration under the global cultural canopy of liberal models. Great international governmental and nongovernmental structures could arise—UNESCO and the World Bank and USAID on one side, and professional and service organizations on the other. World regions could mobilize, as with the European Union and the Bologna Process. National ministries of education expanded in mission and structure, as did nongovernmental associations. At local levels, administrative machineries expanded.

Theme 1 suggests a weakening of this formalized system, with a weakened global cultural canopy, and thus declines in the centrality and legitimacy of supranational organization. There could also be declines in national-level organization, as education becomes less central to world-certified notions of progress. It seems likely that even local educational institutions would have less organizational formalization—and the world of educational administration might lose its forward motion. For example, there are demands for universities to focus on local relevance rather than global rankings: a recent call for Australian institutions to give up their efforts at "bogus" global rankings and strive for greater local impact (van Onselen, 2020). And at the student level, there are clear American and perhaps global rejections of the once-dominant national selective tests (e.g., Furuta, 2017).

Theme 2 suggests not only the breakdown of a global liberal educational order, with its standards and rankings, but the partial replacement of this order by less universalistic alternatives. Religion may be one alternative basis of organization. One can foresee universities as ranked in terms of their Islamic or Christian proprieties—recent mobilization against a prestigious university in India has this character (Bhatty & Sundar, 2020). Or one could imagine universities evaluated by their support for gender-distinct and cisgender curricula, admissions, and pedagogy; or their loyalty to (or functionality for) the nation and national solidarity. Perhaps student and teacher character will be assessed in less academic terms (Karabel, 2005).

As an example of an emphasis on more collective identities in educational structuring, education organizations from around the world have participated in international conferences aimed at strengthening family values and control over children, such as the World Congress of Families (Velasco, 2018, 2020). Figure 4.2 lists the country location of education organizations that have participated in the World Congress of Families' events from 1997 to 2018. These organizations include many religiously affiliated entities and advocates of homeschooling, such as "Take Back Our Schools" (Canada), "Taiwan Homeschool Advocates," "Homeschooling Catolico" (Mexico), "African Christian Church & Schools" (Kenya), "Islamic Waqf Society for Education and Guidance" (Nigeria), and "Student Christian Movement of India." The United States is heavily represented (hosting 46 organizations), but other countries are well-represented, too (such as Russia with 10 organizations, India with 7, and Canada and Kenya with 6 each). An additional 51 countries have fewer than 6 organizations. The number of domestic entities is far higher, but we are focused here on an international system that counters the current liberal world order. Some of these structures can reflect a generalized objection to this order (as with sweeping religious claims), while others may support global doctrines of legitimate and proper localism, as with Robertson's (1992) notion of "glocalization."

Beyond the participation of these national organizations in an international congress, a handful of explicitly supranational education organizations participate in pro-family

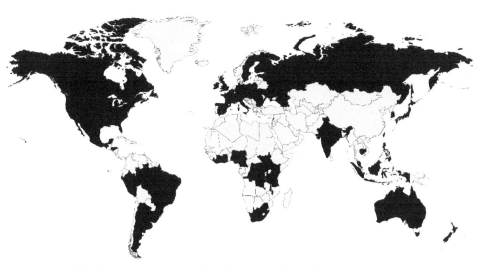

FIGURE 4.2 World map of countries with at least one of education organization participating in the World Congress of Families, 1997–2018.

(*Source:* Adapted from Velasco, 2020)

conferences (Velasco, 2020). In particular, the International Federation for Parents Education; the European Institute for Family Education; the International Association of Science, Ethics, and Integrated Education; and the International Council for Evangelical Theological Education span multiple countries. Structures of this sort, often linked to religious commitments, have long histories. The recent wave of expansion, in some cases extending earlier transnational communities, may indicate the growth of a globally linked system in opposition to parts of liberal educational culture.

Conclusion

The success of neoinstitutional theories of education, including their "world society" variants, has been empirical. These theories responded to the failures of functionalist assumptions, which see education as a creature of local economic or political dominance. Institutionalists call attention to global cultural structures: These theories can thus explain isomorphic postwar global expansion. They are also useful for explaining reactions to global liberalism in more recent years. If such reactions were concentrated in national locales with specific economic problems (e.g., local unemployment), more realist and functionalist models might make more sense, but there is little evidence that this is true. Populist criticisms of education arise in economically successful contexts as well or more than in those crushed by the global economy (Schofer et al., 2022).

Most functional theories emphasize economic challenges to liberalism, while overlapping realist arguments emphasize political ones (e.g., Colantone & Stanig,

2019, Mearsheimer, 2019). Neither of these perspectives explains why so much reaction is to the status and authority of educational institutions and the sciences they legitimate, rather than to much more conspicuous inequalities of wealth and power. It seems that in the current context, Harvard University is criticized more than Goldman Sachs.

A near parallel to sociological institutionalism's discussion of world society can be found in systems theory derived from the work of Niklas Luhmann (1982). Comparisons between these lines of argument, some directly related to education, can be found in a recent collection edited by Holzer and his colleagues (2014; see also Chapter 21, Mangaz & Tilman, this volume).

In such formulations, the global liberal system can be seen as involving the shift of functional differentiation from the contained nation state level to the global (and stateless) level. This formulation directly parallels neoinstitutional thinking, though (as noted later) the causal structures of the arguments differ. Systems theory arguments would then see the reactions we focus on in this chapter as responses to the stresses for individuals and groups of global differentiation. Neoinstitutional theories see these reactions as reflecting the weakening of the legitimated ontologies of liberal world society, and the rise of stronger alternatives. It is not clear how the predictions produced by systems theories would differ from the institutionalist arguments put forward here. Both lines of thought emphasize variations in the "system-ness" of global society against, for example, nationalist alternatives. A difference might be in conceptions of the strength of global society: Systems theorists might emphasize the continuing high levels of differentiation at the global level, while neoinstitutionalists would emphasize its lower legitimation and the rise of alternatives.

Thus, institutional analyses (and indeed most functional or conflict approaches—and systems theories as well) see the world expansion of education as occurring under the pressures or opportunities of a liberal global regime. Neoinstitutional ideas stress the individual person as the ontological base of liberal modernity, and the weakness of global entitivity. In these frames, the constructed "interests" of almost all its participants lie with educational expansion: The child and family gain success, the community gains capacity, the nation gains progress, and the world economy gains peace and development. Systems theories see the mobilizations of individualism—possibly including both populist movements and popular aspects of educational expansion—as a reaction to the social differentiation of modernity, and to the stresses involved. Thus, these lines of theory employ different and partly opposing causal imageries. Systems theories see differentiation as central, and individualisms as reactions; neoinstitutional theories, by contrast, see Western and now world individualism as driving much nominally functional differentiation.

In any case, the liberal world is a cultural construction at odds with much of reality—extreme economic and political inequalities at individual, societal, and global levels, and extreme variations in a wide range of cultural and religious matters. It is easy to see why and how the constructed world of liberal/neoliberal society can come under attack. At present, however, there is no consolidated alternative global model similar in strength to the fascist and communist challenges to of the 20th century. But the internal tensions of the liberal order contribute to its limitations as a global model (Friedland & Alford, 1991), and alternative visions of emerge in transnational formulations (Mearsheimer, 2019). Going forward, it is difficult to imagine that education in its liberal form will be as central as in the earlier postwar period.

ACKNOWLEDGMENTS

Work on this chapter was aided by comments from David Frank, Julia Lerch, Evan Schofer, Simona Szakacs-Behling, Kris Velasco, the editors of this Handbook, and participants in Stanford's Comparative Workshop, including Kiyoteru Tsutsui, Francisco Ramirez, and Mitchell Stevens. Funding was provided by the National Research Foundation (Korea): NRF-2017S1A3A2067636.

REFERENCES

Allen, J. (2020). Teachers union's actions exacerbate learning losses caused by coronavirus impact. *Forbes*. https://www.forbes.com/sites/jeanneallen/2020/07/28/teachers-unions-acti ons-exacerbate-learning-losses-caused-by-coronavirus-impact/#14402ad979d4.

Arum, R. (2005). *Judging school discipline: The crisis of moral authority*. Harvard University Press.

Baker, D., Kohler, H., & Stock, M. (2007). Socialist ideology and the contraction of higher education: Institutional consequences of state manpower and education planning in the former East Germany. *Comparative Education Review, 51*(3), 353–377.

Baker, D., & LeTendre, G. (2005). *National differences, global similarities: World culture and the future of schooling*. Stanford University Press.

Bariso, J. (2020). Google has a plan to disrupt the college degree. *Inc.* https://www.inc.com/ justin-bariso/google-plan-disrupt-college-degree-university-higher-education-certificate- project-management-data-analyst.html

Barro, R., & Lee, J. (2015). *Education matters: Global schooling gains from the 19th to the 21st century*. Oxford University Press.

Benavot, A. (1983). The rise and decline of vocational education. *Sociology of Education, 56*(2), 63–76.

Benavot, A., Cha, Y. K., Kamens, D., Meyer, J. W., & Wong, S. Y. (1992). Knowledge for the masses: World models and national curricula, 1920–1986. *American Sociological Review, 56*(1), 85–100.

Bénéï, V. (2008). Serving the nation: Gender and family values in military schools. In R. Chopra & P. Jeffery (Eds.), *Educational regimes in contemporary India* (pp. 141–159). Sage.

Berg, I. (1970). *Education and jobs: The great training robbery*. Praeger.

Bhatty, K., & Sundar, N. (2020). Sliding from majoritarianism toward fascism: Educating India under the Modi regime. *International Sociology, 35*(6), 632–650.

Boli, J., & Thomas, G. (Eds.) (1999). *Constructing world culture: International nongovernmental organizations since 1875*. Stanford University Press.

Bonikowski, B. (2017). Ethno-nationalist populism and the mobilization of collective resentment. *The British Journal of Sociology, 68*(S1), S181–S213.

Boudon, R. (1973). *Education, opportunity and social inequality*. John Wiley.

Bourguignon, F. (2015). Globalization and the forces behind the rise in inequality. In *The globalization of inequality* (pp. 74–91). Princeton University Press.

Bromley, P. (2010). The rationalization of educational development: Scientific activity among international nongovernmental organizations. *Comparative Education Review, 54*(4), 577–601.

Bromley, P., & Meyer, J. (2015). *Hyper-organization: Global organizational expansion*. Oxford University Press.

Bromley, P., Meyer, J., & Ramirez, F. (2011). Student-centeredness in social science textbooks, 1970–2008: A cross-national study. *Social Forces, 90*(2), 547–570.

Bromley, P., Schofer, E., & Longhofer, W. (2020). Contentions over world culture: The rise of legal restrictions on foreign funding to NGOs, 1994–2015. *Social Forces, 99*(1), 281–304.

Buckner, E. (2017). The worldwide growth of private higher education. *Sociology of Education 90*(4), 296–314.

Cakmakli, A., Boone, C., & Witteloostuijn, A. V. (2017). When does globalization lead to local adaptation? The emergence of hybrid Islamic schools in Turkey, 1985–2007. *American Journal of Sociology, 122*(6), 1822–1868.

Calarco, J. C. (2020). Avoiding us versus them: How schools' dependence on privileged "helicopter" parents influences enforcement of rules. *American Sociological Review 85*(2), 223–246.

Caplan, B. (2018). *The case against education*. Princeton University Press.

Chabbott, C. (2003). *Constructing education for development: International organizations and education for all*. Routledge-Falmer.

Colantone, I., & Stanig, P. (2019). The surge of economic nationalism in Western Europe. *Journal of Economic Perspectives, 33*(4), 128–151.

Collins, R. (1979). *The credential society: An historical sociology of education and stratification*. Academic Press.

Davies, C. (2020). Poland's law and justice party targeting sex education. *The Lancet, 395*(10217), 17–18.

Desch, M. (2019). How political science became irrelevant. *The Chronicle of Higher Education.* https://www.chronicle.com/article/how-political-science-became-irrelevant/

Diamond, L. (2019). *Ill winds: Saving democracy from Russian rage, Chinese ambition, and American complacency*. Penguin.

Djelic, M. L. (1998). *Exporting the American model*. Oxford University Press.

Dore, R. P. (1976). *The diploma disease: Education, qualification, and development*. University of California Press.

Elliott, M. (2007). Human rights and the triumph of the individual in world culture. *Cultural Sociology, 1*(3), 343–363.

Elliott, M. (2011). The institutional expansion of human rights, 1863–2003: A comprehensive dataset of international instruments. *Journal of Peace Research, 48*(4), 537–546.

Elliott, M. (2014). The institutionalization of human rights and its discontents: A world cultural perspective. *Cultural Sociology, 8*(4), 407–425.

Frank, D. J., & Meyer, J. (2002). The profusion of individual roles and identities in the postwar period. *Sociological Theory, 20*(1), 86–105.

Frank, D. J., & Meyer, J. W. (2020). *The university and global knowledge society*. Princeton University Press.

Friedland, R., & Alford, R. (1991). Bringing society back in: Symbols, practices, and institutional contradictions. In W. Powell & P. DiMaggio (Eds.), *The new institutionalism in organizational analysis* (pp. 232–263). University of Chicago Press.

Furuta, J. (2017). Rationalization and student/school personhood in U.S. college admissions: The rise of test-optional policies, 1987 to 2015. *Sociology of Education, 90*(3), 236–254.

Furuta, J. (2020). Liberal individualism and the globalization of education as a human right: The worldwide decline of early tracking, 1960–2010. *Sociology of Education, 93*(1), 1–19.

Gardner, H. (1983). *Frames of mind: The theory of multiple intelligences.* Basic Books.

Gaudiano, N. (2020). Trump appoints 1776 commission members in last-minute attempts to advance "patriotic education." *Politico.* https://www.politico.com/news/2020/12/18/trump-1776-commission-appointments-448229

Godfrey, D. (2018). Opposition to reinstating corporal punishment in Samoa. *Radio New Zealand.* https://www.rnz.co.nz/international/programmes/datelinepacific/audio/2018661581/opposition-to-reinstating-corporal-punishment-in-samoa

Google Website. (2020). Google career certificates. https://grow.google/certificates/

Guillen, M. (2018). *Rude awakening: Threats to the global liberal order.* University of Pennsylvania Press.

Holzer, B., Kastner, F., & Werron, T. (Eds.). (2014). *From globalization to world society: Neo-institutional and systems-theoretical perspectives.* Routledge.

Human Rights Watch. (2008). Do not reinstate corporal punishment in schools: Letter to the Jackson, MS public school district board of trustees. https://www.hrw.org/news/2008/03/26/do-not-reinstate-corporal-punishment-schools

Hussain, A., Ali, S., Ahmed, M., & Hussain, S. (2018). The anti-vaccination movement: A regression in modern medicine. *Cureus, 10*(7), e2919. doi:10.7759/cureus.2919

Hwang, H., & Colyvas, J. (2020). Ontology, levels of society, and degrees of generality: Theorizing actors as abstractions in institutional theory. *Academy of Management Review, 45*(3), 570–595.

Ikenberry, G. J. (2011). *Liberal leviathan: The origins, crisis, and transformation of the American world order.* Princeton University Press.

Illich, I. (1970). *Deschooling society.* Marion Boyars.

Jakobi, A. (2011). Political parties and the institutionalization of education: A comparative analysis of party manifestos. *Comparative Education Review, 55*(2), 189–209.

Judt, T. (2005). *Postwar.* Penguin.

Kahl, C., & Berengaut, A. (2020). Aftershocks: The coronavirus pandemic and the new world disorder. *War on the Rocks.* https://warontherocks.com/2020/04/aftershocks-the-coronavirus-pandemic-and-the-new-world-disorder/

Kamens, D., & McNeely, C. (2010). Globalization and the growth of international educational testing and national assessment. *Comparative Education Review, 54*(1), 5–25.

Karabel, J. (2005). *The chosen: The hidden history of admission and exclusion at Harvard, Princeton, and Yale.* Houghton Mifflin.

Kett, J. (2013). *Merit: The history of a founding ideal from the American Revolution to the 21st century.* Cornell University Press.

Kijima, R., & Lipscy, P. Y. (2020). International assessments and education policy. In J. Kelley & B. Simmons (Eds.), *The power of global performance indicators* (pp. 174–202). Cambridge University Press.

Kindzeka, M. E. (2020). Cameroon teachers protest, seek reinstatement of corporal punishment amid rising violence. *VOA News.* https://www.voanews.com/africa/cameroon-teachers-protest-seek-reinstatement-corporal-punishment-amid-rising-violence

Krucken, G., & Meier, F. (2006). Turning the university into an organizational actor. In G. Drori, J. Meyer, & H. Hwang (Eds.), *Globalization and organization: World society and organizational change* (pp. 241–257). Oxford University Press.

Lachmann, R., & Mitchell, L. (2014). The changing face of war in textbooks: Depictions of World War II and Vietnam, 1970–2009. *Sociology of Education, 87*(3), 188–203.

Lauren, P. G. (2011). *The evolution of human rights: Visions seen.* University of Pennsylvania Press.

Lerch, J., Bromley, P., & Meyer, J. W. (2022a). The expansive educational consequences of global neoliberalism. *International Journal of Sociology, 52*(2), 97–127.

Lerch, J., Bromley, P., Ramirez, F., & Meyer, J. (2017). The rise of individual agency in conceptions of society: Textbooks worldwide, 1950–2011. *International Sociology, 32*(1), 38–60.

Lerch, J. C., & Buckner, E. (2018). From education for peace to education in conflict: Changes in UNESCO discourse, 1945–2015. *Globalisation, Societies, and Education, 16*(1), 27–48.

Lerch, J. C., Schofer, E., Frank, D. J., Longhofer, W., Ramirez, F. O., Wotipka, C. M., & Velasco, K. (2022b). Women's participation in the post-liberal era. *International Sociology, 37*(3), 305–329.

Luhmann, N. (1982). The world society as a social system. *International Journal of General Systems, 8*(3), 131–138.

Mann, M. (2003). *Incoherent empire.* Verso.

Manza, J., & McCarthy, M. (2011). The neo-Marxist legacy in American sociology. *Annual Review of Sociology, 37,* 155–183.

Marilisaraccoglobal. (2018). U.S. school reinstates corporal punishment with paddling. *Global News Canada.* https://globalnews.ca/news/4441097/school-paddling-georgia/

Mearsheimer, J. (2019). Bound to fail: The rise and fall of the liberal international order. *International Security, 43*(4), 7–50.

Meyer, J. (2000). Reflections on education as transcendence. In L. Cuban & D. Shipps (Eds.), *Reconstructing the common good in education* (pp. 206–222). Stanford University Press.

Meyer, J. (2010). World society, institutional theories, and the actor. *Annual Review of Sociology, 36,* 1–20.

Meyer, J., Boli, J., Thomas, G., & Ramirez, F. (1997). World society and the nation-state. *American Journal of Sociology, 103*(1), 144–181.

Meyer, J., Ramirez, F., & Soysal, Y. (1992). World expansion of mass education, 1870–1980. *Sociology of Education, 65*(2), 128–149.

Moe, T. M. (2011). *Special interest: Teachers unions and America's public schools.* Brookings Institution Press.

Moyn, S. (2010). *The last utopia: Human rights in history.* Harvard University Press.

Mudge, S. (2008). What is neo-liberalism? *Socio-economic Review, 6*(4), 703–731.

Nowotny, H., Gibbons, M., & Scott, P. (2001). *Rethinking science: Knowledge and the public in an age of uncertainty.* Polity Press.

Orban, V. (2014). Full text of Viktor Orban's speech at Baile Tusnad. *The Budapest Beacon,* July 26, 2014. https://budapestbeacon.com/full-text-of-viktor-orbans-speech-at-baile-tusnad-tusnadfurdo-of-26-july-2014/

Payne, D. (2014). Abolish compulsory education. *The Federalist.* https://thefederalist.com/2014/02/04/abolish-compulsory-education/

Pope, D. (2001). *"Doing school": How we are creating a generation of stressed out, materialistic, and miseducated students.* Yale University Press.

Przeworski, A. (2019). *Crises of democracy.* Cambridge University Press.

Ramirez, F. (2020). The socially embedded American university: Intensification and globalization. In L Engwall (Ed.), *Missions of universities* (pp. 131–161). Springer.

Robertson, R. (1992). *Globalization: Social theory and global culture.* Sage.

Robinson, K. (2011). The rise of choice in the U.S. university and college: 1910–2005. *Sociological Forum, 26*(3), 601–622.

Rosenmund, M. (2006). The current discourse on curriculum change: A comprehensive analysis of national reports on education. In A. Benavot & C. Braslavsky (Eds.), *School knowledge in comparative and historical perspective* (pp. 173–194). Springer.

Ruggie, J. G. (1982). International regimes, transactions, and change: Embedded liberalism in the post-war economic order. *International Organization, 36*(2), 379–415.

Ruggie, J. G. (1998). Globalization and the embedded liberalism compromise: The end of an era? In W. Streeck (Ed.), *Internationale Wirtschaft, Nationale Demokratie* (pp. 79–97). Campus Verlag.

Sandel, M. (2020). *The tyranny of merit.* Farrar, Straus, and Giroux.

Saxena, V. (2020). Texas school district is bringing back corporal punishment—Legal in 19 states. *BPR Business & Politics.* https://www.bizpacreview.com/2020/03/08/texas-school-district-is-bringing-back-corporal-punishment-legal-in-19-states-895185

Schofer, E., Lerch, J., & Meyer, J. W. (2022). Illiberal reactions to the university in the 21st century. *Minerva, 60*(4), 508–534.

Schofer, E., & Meyer, J. (2005). The worldwide expansion of higher education in the twentieth century. *American Sociological Review, 70*(6), 898–920.

Schofer, E., Ramirez, F. O., & Meyer, J. W. (2021). The societal consequences of higher education: 1960–2012. *Sociology of Education, 94*(1), 1–19.

Senior, J. (2020). 95 percent of representatives have a degree. Look where that's got us. *New York Times.* https://www.nytimes.com/2020/12/21/opinion/politicians-college-degrees.html

Shils, E. (1971). No salvation outside higher education. *Minerva, 6,* 313–321.

Stacy, H. (2009). *Human rights for the 21st century: Sovereignty, civil society, culture.* Stanford University Press.

Stan, L., & Turcescu, L. (2005). Religious education in Romania. *Communist and Post-Communist Studies, 38*(3), 381–401.

Stehr, N. (1994). *Knowledge societies.* Sage.

Stewart, H. (2020). Boris Johnson announces "radical" plan to boost vocational training. https://www.theguardian.com/politics/2020/sep/29/boris-johnson-announces-radical-plan-to-boost-vocational-training

Strauss, V. (2020). In a steely anti-government polemic, Betsy DeVos says America's public schools are designed to replace home and family. *Washington Post,* October 21, 2020. https://www.washingtonpost.com/education/2020/10/21/steely-anti-government-polemic-betsy-devos-says-americas-public-schools-are-designed-replace-home-family/

Tokarnia, M. (2019). Brazil to have 108 civic-military schools implemented by 2023. *AgenciaBrasil.* https://agenciabrasil.ebc.com.br/en/educacao/noticia/2019-07/brazil-have-108-civic-military-schools-implemented-2023

Tooze, A. (2018). *Crashed: How a decade of financial crises changed the world*. Penguin Books.

Van Onselen, L. (2020). Australia's universities must abandon the bogus rankings game. *Macrobusiness*. https://www.macrobusiness.com.au/2020/06/australias-universities-must-abandon-the-bogus-rankings-game/

Velasco, K. (2018). Human rights INGOs, LBGT INGOs, and LGBT policy diffusion, 1991–2015. *Social Forces, 97*(1), 377–404.

Velasco, K. (2020). Queering the world society: Global norms, rival transnational networks, and the contested case of LGBT rights. doi:10.31235/osf.io/3rtje

Volkens, A., Burst, T., Krause, W., Lehmann, P., Matthieß, T., Merz, N., Regel, S., Weßels, B., & Zehnter, L. (2020). *The manifesto data collection*. Manifesto Project: Version 2020a. Wissenschaftszentrum Berlin für Sozialforschung (WZB). https://doi.org/10.25522/manifesto.mpds.2020a

Westad, O. A. (2017). *The cold war: A world history*. Basic Books.

World Bank. (2019). *World development indicators (dataset)*. World Bank Group. http://data.worldbank.org/data-catalog/world-development-indicators

Wotipka, C. M., Jarillo Rabling, B., Sugawara, M., & Tongliemnak, P. (2017). The worldwide expansion of early childhood care and education, 1985–2010. *American Journal of Education, 123*(2), 307–339.

Ziblatt, D. (2017). *Conservative parties and the birth of democracy*. Cambridge University Press.

Zimmerman, J. (2016). *Too hot to handle: A global history of sex education*. Princeton University Press.

CHAPTER 5

WORLD CULTURE, EDUCATION, AND ORGANIZATION

MINJU CHOI, HANNAH K. D'APICE, NADINE ANN SKINNER, AND PATRICIA BROMLEY[1]

INTRODUCTION

AN "organizational revolution" has reshaped societies, polities, and economies around the world—including producing fundamental changes to education. At the turn of the 20th century, there were relatively few formal organizations in most countries; instead, religious institutions and government were the dominant social structures. But in the contemporary world it is hard to imagine an arena of life, including education, that is organization-free, and their reach extends into the most remote parts of the globe. Today, nonprofit organizations do everything from providing sex education programs in the Middle East to providing digital health education about COVID-19 to promoting higher education in the Arctic. Massive global firms produce curricular materials. And small education start-ups are founded at a rapid rate. Together, these diverse organizations make up a vibrant institutional field across the globe (DiMaggio & Powell, 1983). Although what counts as an "education organization" today is extremely varied, what unites these entities is their cultural construction as autonomous social actors (Bromley & Meyer, 2015; King et al., 2010). The global expansion of organizational actorhood profoundly alters education. Indeed, the most dramatic worldwide changes in education, such as privatization, the rise of testing, and the emergence of multi-stakeholder governance regimes that run from local to global levels, are best understood as part of an organizational transformation of schooling and society. Furthermore, for better or worse, education plays a role in deepening the reach of organizations into contemporary life.

We call attention to widespread organizational changes in education, which occur in countries with highly varied contexts (rich and poor, autocracy and democracy), at multiple levels of education (from local to global, from early childhood to higher education), and across sectors (including public and private). Drawing on a neoinstitutional lens in organization theory, we argue that a globalizing world culture, characterized by the valorization of the intertwined principles of scientized rationalization and individual empowerment, is at the root of these changes (Meyer et al., 1997; Meyer, 2010). First, empirical research has documented that the hegemonic rise of a world culture has spurred the expansion of education at all levels (Meyer et al., 1992; Ramirez & Boli, 1987; Schofer & Meyer, 2005; Wotipka et al., 2017). Second, a related set of studies has shown that world culture also generates the global expansion of organizational actors (Drori et al., 2006). Bringing these two lines of research together, we consider how the expansion and growing dominance of organization fundamentally transforms the structure and content of education. Moreover, the expanded education systems serve to normalize and legitimate the dominance of organizations throughout contemporary society. We thus note a recursive relationship between the expansion of education and organization.

In what follows we provide background on the rise of world culture that emerged after World War II, which emphasized both progress (e.g., economic development, improved health) and justice (e.g., individual human rights, civic and political rights, equality) (Meyer et al., 1997). Our focus is on its core principles of scientized rationalization and individual empowerment. We briefly review the research documenting how world culture generates both organizational and educational expansion. Next, we shift to our core argument; namely, that the structure and content of education around the world has undergone an organizational transformation driven by the expansion of liberal world culture.

We define liberal world culture as a system that enshrines the sacredness of individual choice, actorhood, and ideals of progress, most substantially reflected in principles of free markets and democracy. The foundations of liberal world culture were amplified during the neoliberal era. In the 1990s, the collapse of the Soviet Union and subsequent dominance of American authority changed the world order that emerged after World War II. With the end of the Cold War, boundaries between nation states no longer limited the spread of liberal models of society. Importantly, the neoliberal era is not just about profit or capitalism; it is about the globalization of a core cultural belief in the value of individual choice and action that crosses sectors, including celebrations of civil society, democracy, and human rights of all kinds. We understand the rise of both organizational and educational society as closely linked to the dominance of a liberal and neoliberal cultural system. To spur future research, we provide empirical illustrations of our arguments that could be valuably extended to test the assertions in this chapter.

In a final discussion we consider the implications of the organizational transformation of education. In contrast to functional views that celebrate the rise of organizations in education as effective and efficient, and in contrast to critical views that point to the evils of privatization, our cultural arguments suggest that organizational changes in education are neither inherently positive nor negative. We can observe both harmful and beneficial consequences, as well as a great deal of decoupling between discourse and practice. A key message of our arguments is that as culture changes, education is again likely to be fundamentally transformed: The rise of populism, nationalism, and other illiberal trends worldwide suggests such a shift may already be underway and is expected to have substantial consequences for contemporary education (see Furuta et al., Chapter 4, this volume, for more discussion).

BACKGROUND

The 20th century witnessed the rise and globalization of a liberal and neoliberal world culture built on the principles of scientific rationalization and individual empowerment (see Meyer et al., 1997, for the canonical statement). These cultural principles underpin the core institutions of modernity, including education systems and formal organizations. Modern liberal culture and its institutions emerged earlier in Western countries, especially following the Enlightenment and Industrial Revolution (see Lechner & Boli, 2005, for a detailed historical account). But World War II was a turning point that legitimated and globalized the liberal cultural model, accelerating its diffusion to diverse countries (Drori et al., 2003; Thomas et al., 1987).[2] Ultranationalist notions were denounced as contributing to the atrocities of war, weakening state authority relative to the standing of science and the individual, and international cooperation gained status. During the postwar period of American dominance, scientific rationalization and individual empowerment became hegemonic principles at the world level. The collapse of the Soviet Union and end of the Cold War accelerated the globalization process further. Naturally, cross-sectional variation between countries remains with very different cultural, economic, and political contexts, but in the period since World War II most took on more features of liberal and neoliberal world culture than in prior eras.

The intertwined cultural principles of scientific rationalization and individual empowerment are complex, and a full discussion goes beyond our purposes here (see Meyer, 2010, for a more detailed discussion). Briefly, scientific rationalization is defined as systematically developed knowledge by trained experts, who follow the standards of their professions (Drori et al., 2003; Weber, 1978). Scientific rationality is tied to individual empowerment because it relies on and valorizes the knowledge gained by those individuals who are empowered to practice professional expertise, in "contrast to alternative bases of authority such as charisma, tradition, or tacit and implicit forms of knowledge" (Bromley & Meyer, 2017, p. 948). Progress, rather than salvation, takes center stage; and scientists and professionals are the new priests. Over time, more and more people can gain the skills and knowledge needed. Individual empowerment goes beyond just taming knowledge, however; it is linked to the belief in justice: Individuals have inalienable rights. These rights specify basic equality on many fronts and allow individuals to become empowered through their agency and opportunity to gain expertise (in principle, not always in practice). Individual empowerment is thus composed of the ability to make purposeful choices, and equality in an opportunity structure (Bromley, 2016). Therefore, any disenfranchisement of an individual's human rights is in conflict with the ideals of individualism and rationality. Scientific rationality demands that the critically rational individual have autonomy of reason and a right of free inquiry, ensuring the connection between the two concepts (Durkheim, 1961, 1973; Elliott, 2007).

The rise of world culture has expanded education and transformed the ways in which we understand and carry out education (see Lee & Ramirez, Chapter 1, this volume, for a more detailed account). Systems of mass schooling have expanded to the point where they are ubiquitous, but they are also marked by growing similarities in content, structure, and curricula that conform to the liberal cultural model (Meyer et al., 1992; Ramirez & Boli, 1987). Higher education also expands, especially in countries more linked to world culture (Schofer & Meyer, 2005). The goal is now "Education for All," establishing education as a universal human right (Chabbott, 2003). Curricular content has also expanded and transformed to include new topics and degrees in fields such as women's studies, Black studies, and Indigenous studies (Ramirez et al., 2009; Rojas, 2010; Wotipka & Ramirez, 2008).

Under the cultural tenets of individual empowerment and scientific rationalization, organizations have also undergone a transformation that distinguishes them from traditional collectivities. Modern organizations are different from older communal associations in that they assume a greater sense of "actorhood" in which they are attributed with expanded sets of rights and responsibilities (Drori et al., 2006).[3] As a cultural model, organizational actors are expected to display autonomy (largely linked to the cultural principle of empowerment) and purposiveness (largely linked to the principle of scientific rationalization), and they have a responsibility to recognize the autonomy and purposiveness of other actors. Older collectives drew their authority from sources such as the state or the church and did not operate within a cultural framework of an expanded sense of rights and autonomy (King et al., 2010; Lamoreaux & Wallis, 2017). How modern organizations form their identity is debated among scholars, with some emphasizing fundamental attributes or static roles of the organizations and others focusing more on the socially constructed and dynamic characteristic of organizational identity (Albert & Whetten, 1985; Glynn, 2008). Our argument here understands modern organizations themselves as representative of a new form of authority in society. Through their "actorhood," organizations are no longer simple congregations of individuals or the tool of a sovereign but are unique entities that take purposeful and legitimate actions to carry out their goals and responsibilities (Brunsson & Sahlin-Andersson, 2000). In practice, actual entities may vary greatly from this ideal type; that is, their goals and actions are highly decoupled (Bromley & Powell, 2012; Meyer & Rowan, 1977).

Rooted in a rapidly globalizing liberal culture, the type, number, size, purposes, and status of organizations have multiplied, and increasingly organizations are constructed as independent social actors (Bromley & Sharkey, 2017; Coleman, 1982; Drori et al., 2006). For instance, the number of multinational corporate organizations increased from 3,000 in 1900 to more than 63,000 by the early 2000s (Bromley & Meyer, 2015). The growth of international nongovernmental organizations (INGOs) in a variety of fields has also far outpaced either population or economic growth in countries worldwide (Bromley & Meyer, 2017): The number of INGOs has grown from approximately 0.1 organization per million people in 1909 to 8 organizations per million people in 2009 (Bromley, 2020; see also Boli & Thomas, 1999). And since the 1990s, the fastest growth for domestic associations is occurring in developing countries (Schofer & Longhofer, 2011). These organizations are not only increasing in types, numbers, and sizes, but also as rationalized actors drawing on scientized practices to legitimate their goals and purposes. For example, many contemporary international organizations rely on their scientific knowledge as the basis for their expertise and the reasoning for their actions (Zapp, 2020), which gives them their own expanded purpose and status.

Overall, existing literature shows that the rise of scientific rationalization and individual empowerment drives the expansion of education and organization. We elaborate on the interconnectedness of these expansions. That is, the structure and content of education systems are reshaped by the rise of organizations in society. In turn, education normalizes and legitimates the dominance of organizations in contemporary society. Figure 5.1 outlines our conceptualization of the relationship between world culture, education, and organization. Given this volume's focus on education, we mainly examine the ways in which schooling is changed, though we provide some additional reflections on how education shapes organization.

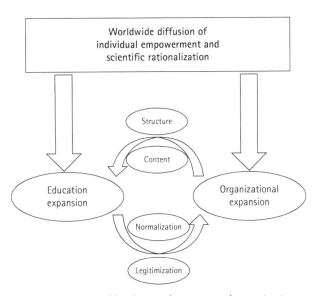

FIGURE 5.1 Relationship among world culture, education, and organization.

Arguments

Proposition 1. Transformed Structure: Expansion of Organizational Actors in Education

We argue that the worldwide rise of scientific rationalization and individual empowerment provides a globalized cultural framework that promotes the expansion of organizational actors as central units in education systems. Government, with its traditional features of bureaucratic hierarchy and centralized control, persists as a main provider of education, but private education organizations, characterized by autonomy and rationalized purposiveness, expand in number and status. At the same time, even government agencies are transformed to become more like contemporary organizational actors (Brunsson & Sahlin-Andersson, 2000). Furthermore, organizing fragments built on the same world cultural principles exist even outside the boundaries of any given entity (Ahrne & Brunsson, 2011, 2019). There is a proliferation of organizations and organizing in all kinds of roles in education, as well as changes to the internal structures of education institutions as they take on the trappings of contemporary organized actors.

Empirical data as well as extant literature suggest that the organizational transformation of education occurs in several ways. First, the education landscape becomes increasingly littered with organizations of all types, as for-profit, nonprofit, and nongovernmental organizational actors increase in number at local and global levels. Second, existing education activities and providers become more organizational in character, acquiring rationalized features of organizational actorhood (i.e., autonomy, purposiveness, and responsibility to recognize other actors). Across these dimensions of change, we expect greater shifts in contexts more closely linked to world culture. Stated formally, we propose the following changes to the structure of education systems and provide some illustrative empirical material:

1. *Increased Numbers.* The number of education organizations will expand over time in both domestic and international contexts, beginning in the liberal period of post–World War II and accelerating under the neoliberal world society starting in the 1990s. This will occur most in contexts tied more closely to liberal world culture (e.g., over time with cultural globalization or in countries most linked to global cultural shifts), beyond the material interests of elites and beyond demonstrable function.[4]

2. *Increased Actorhood.* Education will be characterized by increasing displays of organizational actorhood over time in both domestic and international contexts, beginning in the liberal period of post–World War II, and accelerating under neoliberal world society starting in the 1990s. This will occur in contexts tied more closely to liberal world culture (e.g., over time with cultural globalization or in

countries most linked to global cultural shifts), beyond the material interests of elites and beyond demonstrable function.

Increased Numbers

Our arguments predict growing numbers of education organizations of all sorts (e.g., for-profit and nonprofit), across a wide array of levels (e.g., local and global, early childhood through higher education). Prior research further suggests this will occur in a range of settings, representing both elite and grassroots interests, and beyond functional needs, including expressive and instrumental entities (Bromley et al., 2018). Given data availability, empirical trends in the United States serve as a useful starting point, though our arguments and preliminary data can be extended globally.

In the case of the United States, the elaboration of the organizational environment for education occurs at both the basic and higher education levels. We use data from the National Center for Charitable Statistics (NCCS), published by the Urban Institute (2015), to document these trends. The NCCS offers the most comprehensive and up-to-date source of information on nonprofit member organizations in the United States based on tax filings with the Internal Revenue Service, covering charities, foundations, and other types of tax-exempt education nongovernmental organizations. Note that, in the United States, these types of organizations frequently receive a mixture of both private and public funding; hence funding source has very little to do with governance (Davies, 2013; Willetts, 2002). Figure 5.2 illustrates the total number of education

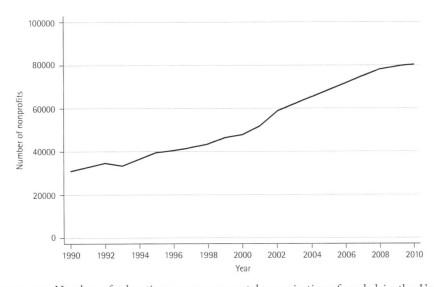

FIGURE 5.2 Number of education nongovernmental organizations founded in the United States, 1990–2010.

(*Source*: Urban Institute, National Center for Charitable Statistics, 2015)

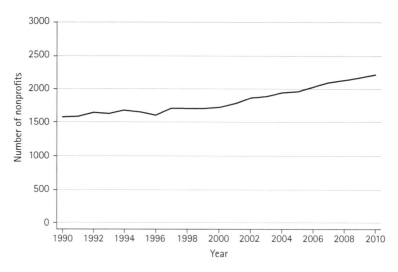

FIGURE 5.3 Number of higher education nongovernmental organizations founded in the United States, 1990–2010.

(*Source*: Urban Institute, National Center for Charitable Statistics, 2015)

organizations between 1990 and 2010, which has more than doubled, while Figure 5.3 illustrates increasing trends for education organizations specific to higher education.

Cross-national data—and data going back in time prior to the 1990s—are far less complete, but even partial data suggest an increase in the number of domestic education organizations founded throughout the world. The best data we could find come from the Gale Group's Associations Unlimited database, which contains information on more than 30,000 domestic civil society organizations (CSOs) around the world (Gale Group Website, 2017).[5] The database provides keywords to identify groups with an education focus, and we exclude organizations that were branches of INGOs. Bromley et al. (2018) used this data to analyze the global expansion of domestic education organizations over the period from 1990 to 2018, finding the number of organizations increasing beyond functional explanations such as country wealth: Countries more linked to world culture have a particular increase, net of other factors. Furthermore, expansion occurs not only in North America and Western Europe but across non-Western regions such as sub-Saharan Africa, East Asia, and Southeast Asia. Figures 5.4 and 5.5 illustrate the change in numbers of domestic education associations reported in countries around the world in 1970 and 2018, respectively. The figures show that diverse sets of countries are generating their own domestic education organizations, as opposed to this activity being solely located in the West.

Taken together, these trends suggest that the organizational environment in education within countries around the world became more elaborate over time, with greater numbers of organizations participating in education services and provision. Importantly, nongovernmental organizations do not necessarily replace the state in terms of education provision, but rather may be engaged by the state itself. Sending and Neumann

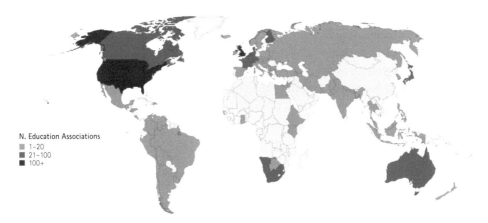

FIGURE 5.4 Number of domestic education associations by country, 1970.
(*Source*: Data adapted from Bromley et al., 2018)

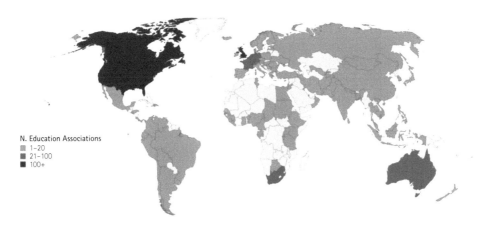

FIGURE 5.5 Number of domestic education associations by country, 2018.
(*Source*: Data adapted from Bromley et al., 2018)

(2006) describe this relationship between the state and non-state actors as "an expression of a changing logic or rationality of government" (p. 652), by which the state may fund organizations as complementary actors in the process of governance, as opposed to competing with them in an imagined zero-sum game. This perspective is consistent with studies on public administration which find that government agencies increasingly engage multiple interdependent actors in the delivery of public services (Osborne, 2010, as cited in Bromley & Meyer, 2017). A cross-national study of domestic CSOs also finds that the domestic CSO sector is highly associated with an expanded state and an expanded education system (Bromley, et al., 2018).

Such expansion also likely occurs at the global level. To document global trends, we draw on data from the Yearbook of International Organizations (YBIO), published by the Union of International Associations, which includes detailed information on over

73,000 international organizations across 300 countries and territories (Yearbook of International Organizations, 2020). Figure 5.6 leverages the YBIO data to chart trends in the foundings of international nongovernmental education organizations worldwide.

This figure reveals an acceleration of education INGO foundings through the 1990s. While the rates of foundings may decrease thereafter, the cumulative number of INGOs continues to increase. Some suggest this decline in the founding rate indicates that the landscape reaches a saturation of organizations (Bush & Hadden 2019), but a detailed analysis of the YBIO data collection procedures suggests an extended data collection lag of over a decade may account for some or all of the apparent drop (Boli & Thomas 1997).

An implication of this transformation is that globally, authority is increasingly diffused such that it is no longer concentrated solely within government. Sassen (1996, 2003) asserts that governance is diffused internationally among international governmental organizations, beyond the provenance of the nation state. Simultaneously, the logic of government shifts to create space for organizations as complementary actors in governance (Sending & Neumann, 2006), and organizations themselves proliferate. In addition to these trends, we argue that authority becomes shared with the private sector, in the form of both nonprofit and for-profit organizations. These shifts from the national to the international, and from the public to the private, are both part of the increasing organizational elaboration of governance.

The trends we observe in Figure 5.6 begin with the liberal regimes of the immediate post–World War II period, but reach their peak in acceleration during the neoliberal period of the 1990s. Under the neoliberal rhetoric of post-1990s world culture, private actors are seen as more flexible in their ability to effectively provide both academic and nonacademic services, including food provision and infrastructure. In practice, evidence of effectiveness is mixed, and features of privatization or quasi-market regulations, such as increased school autonomy or school competition for student recruitment, may even exacerbate inequality (Dumay & Dupriez, 2014; Patrinos et al.,

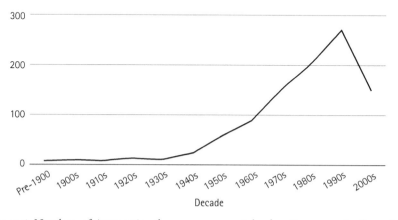

FIGURE 5.6 Number of international nongovernmental education organizations founded cross-nationally by decade, 1886–2009.

(*Source*: Yearbook of International Organizations, 2020)

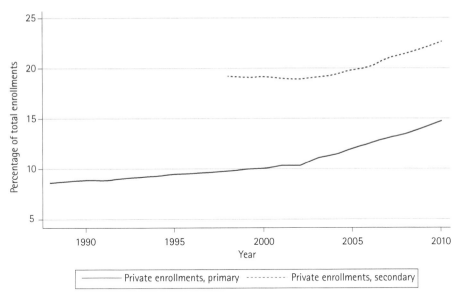

FIGURE 5.7 Global average percentages in private enrollment by level of schooling, 1987–2010.
(*Source*: World Bank, 2020)

2009). This decoupling of the dominant theory of progress from known outcomes, combined with its wide embrace by an array of actors, indicates deep beliefs in such cultural underpinnings.

The expanded role of private actors in education can be seen in both increased enrollments in private schools cross-nationally, as well as increases in the number of private organizations in higher education. Figure 5.7 visualizes data from the UNESCO Institute for Statistics, accessed via the World Bank, which show that the percentage of private school enrollment as a percentage of primary and secondary schooling has increased over time. Based on available data, private primary school enrollments have increased from just under 9% in 1990 to 14.9% by 2010, whereas secondary school enrollments have increased from about 19.2% in 1998 to 22.7% in 2010.

Meanwhile, at the tertiary level, the number of private higher education institutions has increased over time to the point of exceeding those of public institutions globally. Replicating analyses from Buckner (2017) with data from Pearce (2016), Figure 5.8 outlines the cumulative number of private versus public universities between 1800 and 2013. Though the number of private universities trails that of public universities through the mid-20th century, this trend is reversed around the late 1980s, when private university numbers begin to increase dramatically.

These increases are not merely occurring in countries with existing private or semi-private education markets. Rather, the number of different countries with private higher education institutions is increasing as well. The expansion can even be seen in countries where private higher education was previously considered controversial and contested (Buckner, 2017). The percentage of countries with private higher education institutions

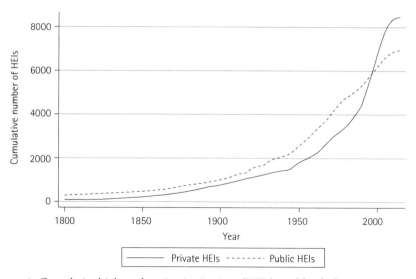

FIGURE 5.8 Cumulative higher education institutions (HEIs) worldwide, by sector.

(*Source*: Data from Pearce, 2016; adapted from Buckner, 2017)

increased from around 55% in 1960 to over 80% in the 2000s, with this rate of increase exceeding that of countries with public higher education institutions in the same period (Buckner, 2017).

Many studies focus on the privatization of education, and certainly the evidence of this is strong. But mainstream explanations tend to focus on the political economy of the neoliberal era (Ball, 2012; Verger, 2016) and overlook that these trends are in part cultural. We see increasing privatization and organizational elaboration as distinct but related phenomena. All aspects of society become increasingly organizationally elaborated under the rise of scientific rationalization and individual empowerment (Bromley & Meyer, 2017), and increasing privatization is, in part, motivated by these trends. Taking a broader cultural lens which focuses on the organizational transformation of society in general, we can see that there is a massive growth in nonprofit organizing beyond private business interests. Moreover, this organizing represents grassroots interests and growth in all sorts of organizations beyond those involved in the privatization of service provision. At the global level there has been an explosion of transnational activism and prosocial activity around the goal of "Education for All," leading to the creation of a dense network of organizations (Mundy, 2007; Tikly, 2017).

Moreover, the organizational expansion in education is characterized by a general blurring of the lines between for-profit and nonprofit sectors, which is hard to account for using views that pit private and public goals against one another (Dees & Anderson, 2003). "Hybrid" organizations, social enterprises, and social entrepreneurship are increasingly common (Mair, 2020). Social institutions that previously had distinct structures, such as charities and schools, begin to act as organizational actors, gaining similar structures and features (Bromley & Meyer, 2017). Instead of viewing themselves as unique entities, with distinct contexts and needs, modern organizational actors consider themselves as "organizations, having typical organizational problems and being in need for efficient organizational solutions" (Krücken & Meier, 2006, p. 242).

Increasing Actorhood

In addition to an increase in the density of education organizations, the nature of education as an institution changes to reflect the principles of organizational actorhood. Extant literature on the transformation of universities offers an illustration of these trends. Krücken and Meier (2006) argue that four features in particular document the transformation of universities into organizational actors: the creation of accountability systems; adoption of organizationally defined (as opposed to imposed) goals; the elaboration and expansion of formal organizational structures centered on these goals; and finally, the rise of managerialism among professors, who are increasingly involved in rationalized administrative tasks beyond teaching and research. Universities also establish various offices of development, diversity, legal affairs, and so on, as formalized managerial structures that institutionalize and rationalize activities which may have previously been informal (Furuta & Ramirez, 2019; Kwak et al., 2019; Skinner & Ramirez, 2019). The emergence of such offices occurs, in part, in response to the rise of empowered individuals in colleges and universities (Furuta & Ramirez, 2019).

More broadly, there is a growing cultural celebration of actorhood in all sorts of education entities, even leading government agencies to become more like contemporary organizations (Brunsson & Sahlin-Andersson, 2000). From the turn of the 20th century, a focus on the achievement of administrative efficiency in schools expanded in the image of Frederick Taylor's conceptions of scientific management (1911). The pursuit of finding an imagined "one best system" of schooling became a central focus (Tyack, 1974). Measurement of inputs and outputs are central to processes of scientized managerial control, and in education all sorts of data and measurement activities expand. Early efforts included more localized counting of pupils, teachers, and materials, with expansion over time into more complex concepts—such as learning and school quality—now to be measured globally. Quantified assessment in its current form is largely a product of organization and management theory, and increasingly independent organizations are the entities used to administer and monitor a great deal of testing. International tests such as the Program for International Student Assessment (PISA) are explicitly conceived of as instruments for scientific, external evaluation of education systems, as part of knowledge production for evidence-based policymaking (Mangez & Hilgers, 2012). In line with our arguments here, several studies document the central role of world culture in driving the expansion of testing worldwide, alongside factors such as colonial legacy, wealth, and level of democracy (Furuta, 2020; Kamens & Benavot, 2011; Kamens & McNeely, 2010; Ramirez et al., 2018). Moreover, within education INGOs there is an increase over time of world cultural emphases, as mission statements increasingly emphasize scientific, expert, and knowledge-based activities (Bromley, 2010).

Very much related, there is now a large body of literature looking at the effect of ideas of the "world class university" and global university rankings systems (Deem et al., 2008;

Sadlak & Liu, 2007; Shin & Khem, 2012). Some of these entities are for-profit organizations, such as the US News & World Report, which administers a powerful ranking of American universities. Others are nonprofit, such as the International Association for the Evaluation of Educational Achievement (IEA), or intergovernmental organizations such as the Organization for Economic Cooperation and Development (OECD), which operates PISA. The scientization behind this transformation to education is direct. For example, the organization that carries out what is known as the "Shanghai Ranking" of universities states:

> Academic Ranking of World Universities (ARWU) uses six objective indicators to rank world universities, including the number of alumni and staff winning Nobel Prizes and Fields Medals, number of highly cited researchers selected by Clarivate Analytics, number of articles published in journals of Nature and Science, number of articles indexed in Science Citation Index-Expanded and Social Sciences Citation Index, and per capita performance of a university. More than 1800 universities are actually ranked by ARWU every year and the best 1000 are published. One of the factors for the significant influence of ARWU is that its methodology is scientifically sound, stable and transparent. (ARWU Website, 2020)

Importantly, the expansion of principles of scientific management as a means to govern educational outcomes is not a neutral act. It represents a power structure, including the rise of a cadre of autonomous organizations producing assessments, ratings, and rankings. There are dramatic consequences for institutions of education. As one example, sociologists Wendy Espeland and Michael Sauder have produced a series of outstanding studies documenting the ways in which universities respond to rankings (Espeland & Sauder, 2007, 2016). They describe a process akin to Foucault's concepts of governmentality and self-discipline, whereby the principles of scientific rationalization embedded in the rankings possess a power and authority unto themselves (Sauder & Espeland, 2009). It is an ironic twist that actors, in the liberal model, are imagined to be both highly empowered and great conformists (Meyer, 2010).

Proposition 2. Rise of Emphases on Organization in Content of Education

A second expected change is that the content of education shifts to place more emphasis on formal organization. We argue that this increased emphasis on organization in the content of education normalizes and legitimates the expansion of organizations and participation in an organizational society. This normalization and legitimation process reinforces the recursive relationship between education and organization. An increasingly central, but often implicit, goal of contemporary schooling is to prepare students for participation in a globalized organizational society. Earlier goals continue, such as providing national citizenship training, preparation for a domestic economy, or religious and cultural socialization, but organizational emphases are on the rise. We expect parts of this change to be very direct, such as growing emphasis on organizations of all sorts in curricular content at both lower and higher levels of education. But changes could also be indirect, with more nuanced changes in the nature of schooling toward preparing students to participate in a world of modern, formal organization, rather than one of, say, religious institutions or bureaucracy. For instance, students may informally receive guidance from teachers on "being professional" in how they send emails, with the implication being they are preparing for proper participation in a contemporary organizational workplace. We can think of this as "organizational socialization" for participation in an organizational society, akin to the processes of political socialization for which schooling is well known (Van Maanen & Schein, 1977). In the institutional arguments put forth here, we expect curricular changes to occur as a cultural matter beyond functional demands; educational changes may outpace actual organizational expansion in some areas, and educational changes are unlikely to create objectively functional organizations.

More specifically, we expect:

1. *Increased Curricular Emphases on Organizations.* Curricular content will expand to discuss organizations in both domestic and international contexts. This will occur most in contexts more closely to liberal and neoliberal world culture (e.g., over time with cultural globalization or in countries most linked to global shifts), beyond the material interests of elites and beyond demonstrable function.
2. *Increased Emphases on Participation in an Organizational Society.* Schooling will increasingly aim to prepare students to participate in an organizational society in both domestic and international contexts. This will occur most in contexts tied more closely to liberal and neoliberal world culture (e.g., over time with cultural globalization or in countries most linked to global shifts), beyond the material interests of elites and beyond demonstrable function.

Increased Curricular Emphases on Organizations

As preliminary evidence of our arguments in mass schooling, we draw on two data sets that track changes in high school textbook content over time for history, civics, social studies, and geography. The first data set is a sample of 527 Canadian and US textbooks published between 1836 and 2011, which were coded for whether different types of organizations are discussed as positively contributing to society. We observe Canada and the United States as "early adopters" of these norms (DiMaggio & Powell, 1983). The empirical study observes the overall trends of proportions of textbooks that discuss domestic for-profit, nonprofit organizations, and international governmental, nongovernmental organizations. While the empirical examples below demonstrate how textbooks positively discuss organizations, one could also examine how organizations are perceived negatively in textbooks.

As observed in Figure 5.9, textbooks increasingly discuss both for-profit and nonprofit forms of organizations over time. Business actors are discussed at greater frequencies than nonprofit organizations at all time periods, and they are also discussed earlier on in textbooks. Legalization and codification of for-profits mark the beginning of the legitimization process for business organizations in Canada and the United States. Discussions of nonprofits appear around the 1870s, as they became formalized as organizational actors separate from their for-profit counterparts (Kaufman, 2008; Levy, 2016). For both groups, there is a fairly steady increase over time, with the increase in discussions of nonprofits most noticeable in the 20th century. Organizations are perceived as social actors, as evidenced by this example from a Canadian textbook published in the 1980s. The textbook portrays the Canadian Pacific Railway as a powerful actor that solves social problems and contributes to society's development:

> The completion of the Canadian Pacific Railway made large-scale settlement of the West possible. The potential for wheat farming on the fertile Prairie lands had been recognised for some time` .. The CPR owned vast areas of the Prairies. It started immediately to sell many of these lands, making them available to settlers. (Bowers & Garrod, 1987, p. 212)

In comparison to domestic organizations, international organizations are relatively new forms of organizations that gained authority and legitimacy in the early 20th century and particularly after World War II. For example, a Canadian textbook

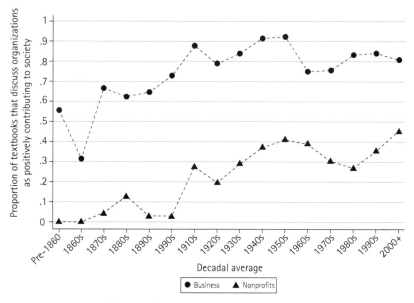

FIGURE 5.9 Discussions of for-profit and nonprofit organizational actors in Canadian and US textbooks, 1836–2011.

(*Source*: Data adapted from Choi et al., 2020)

from the 2000s describes Amnesty International as a legitimate actor that resolves social problems. The textbook describes an instance during which the organization successfully addressed a domestic challenge: "in 1986, the Canadian branch of Amnesty International played a leading role in opposing the campaign to reinstate the death penalty in Canada" (Fielding & Evans, 2001, p. 439). The textbook also legitimizes Amnesty International's actions in the global sphere, stating that "Amnesty's work was recognized when it received the Nobel Peace Prize in 1977" (Fielding & Evans, 2001, p. 439). As demonstrated in Figure 5.10, discussions of international governmental organizations (IGOs) and international nongovernmental organizations (INGOs) in Canadian and US social science textbooks start to emerge in the 1920s. In earlier decades of the 20th century, a greater proportion of textbooks mention IGOs as actors positively contributing to society. INGOs rise at a slower rate than IGOs but steadily increase, with a notable rise in the 1990s.

Similarly, preliminary evidence suggests a growing emphasis on international organizations in textbooks as occurring worldwide. Our second data set presents a cross-national sample of 643 social science textbooks from 80 countries around the world, which shows similarly increasing discussions of IGOs and INGOs in middle and high school textbooks published between 1950 and 2011. These textbooks cover subjects including social studies, civics or government, history, religion, geography, and moral education. The proportions of textbooks that mention IGOs and INGOs both increase

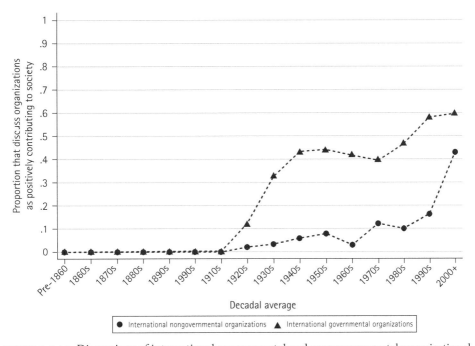

FIGURE 5.10 Discussions of international governmental and nongovernmental organizational actors in Canadian and US textbooks, 1836–2011.

(*Source*: Data adapted from Choi et al., 2020)

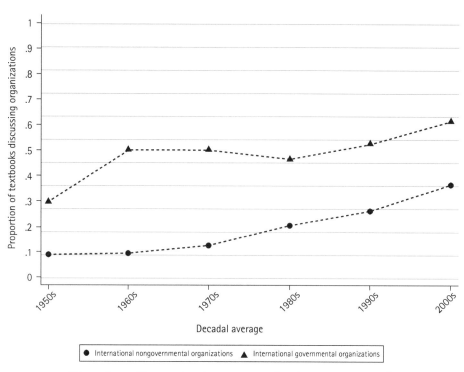

FIGURE 5.11 Discussions of international governmental and nongovernmental organizational actors in cross-national textbooks, 1950–2011.

over time, although INGOs are discussed at lower rates than IGOs (Figure 5.11).[6] This finding is consistent with what was observed in the Canadian and US textbooks, demonstrating that the rising emphasis on organizations in educational content is not unique to Canada and the United States. While country and regional variations certainly exist, the empirical study sheds light on the worldwide diffusion of the "organizational society."

Illustratively, we also observe changes in higher education and its curricular content. Professional management education diffuses worldwide, with an increasing number of countries adopting Masters of Business Administration (MBA) programs and establishing business schools in universities (Moon & Wotipka, 2006). Similarly, nonprofit management programs and studies have rapidly expanded in the last several decades. In the late 1970s and 1980s, few US and UK universities started establishing master's degree programs in nonprofit management, which has grown exponentially in the 1990s (Mirabella & Young, 2012). As demonstrated in Table 5.1, the number of US universities offering nonprofit management education continues to grow. Notably, these programs are spread throughout academic disciplines, including arts and sciences, business, public administration, and social work, among others (Mirabella, 2007). These programs can be found worldwide, offered by universities as well as nonprofit sector-based organizations themselves in Africa, Asia, Europe, and Latin America (Mirabella et al., 2007).

With a growing number of nonprofit programs and courses offered, the number of doctoral dissertations and theses that focus on nonprofit organizations steadily

Table 5.1 Growth of Nonprofit Management Education (NME) by Program Type in the United States

Year	1996	2002	2006	2020
Universities offering NME undergraduate courses	66	86	117	145
Universities offering NME graduate courses	128	155	161	252
Universities offering NME noncredit courses	51	72	75	86
Universities offering NME continuing education courses	39	57	56	78
Universities offering NME online courses	N/A	10	17	82
Number of institutions	179	253	238	342

Source: Adapted from Mirabella (2007) and Mirabella (2020).

increases. The proportion of theses and dissertations relating to nonprofit studies, out of the total number of theses and dissertations published between 1986 and 2010, increased five times from 0.1% in 1986 to 0.5% in 2010 (Shier & Handy, 2014). Reflecting this growing attention to nonprofit organizations and their management in higher education content, the number of peer-reviewed articles that focus on nonprofit and/or philanthropic topics, themes, or organizations also proliferated from 8,037 published articles in the 2000–2005 time period to 13,290 articles in the 2006–2011 time period (Jackson et al., 2014). As evidenced by these expansionary trends, nonprofit and philanthropic organizations increasingly become recognized as a legitimate academic field.

Relatedly, a cursory search of a university catalog would likely reveal dozens of courses about organizations in many fields. Looking just at the 2020–2021 course offerings at Stanford University shows dozens of courses that span multiple departments—education, business, engineering, and others—and they address a wide range of issues. Some focus on capitalist agendas of profit growth and marketing, but many others address social issues and seemingly look for ways to tame unfettered capitalism by focusing on ameliorating gender and racial discrimination, emphasizing corporate social responsibility, or considering issues of the nonprofit sector and inequality. Although a more detailed empirical study is needed, our argument is that broad organizational offerings like these are not unique to one university but rather emerge in many universities in a wide array of settings over time (e.g., public and private universities, wealthy and poor universities, universities in all kinds of countries). This expansiveness occurs, in our view, because of the globalized cultural principles underpinning educational and organizational expansion.

Increased Emphases on Participation in an Organizational Society

A long-standing assertion in the sociology of education is that schooling reflects wider influences. Most literatures have focused on the ways in which schooling reflects goals of socializing national citizens (Dreeben, 1968; Marshall, 1950), provides skills that produce more productive workers (Becker, 1964; Schultz, 1961), or serves the interests of the elite (Bourdieu, 1977). In contrast, we propose that education reflects a broader cultural context that is not reducible to self-interest or function (Meyer, 1977). With the rise of an organizational society as a cultural ideal, old purposes are not enough and a new agenda emerges in education: Education should now also teach students to participate in a world of organizations where they should be part of these entities for work, to promote social change, and for well-being. The question of whether such a shift occurs, and if it is in part culturally driven, can be answered empirically.

For example, studies could examine the possible expansion and effects of 21st-century skills that encourage students to develop skills such as critical thinking, problem solving, entrepreneurial thinking, communication, and use of technology (Kay & Greenhill, 2011). Pedagogies such as project-based learning indicate a transformed vision of the ways in which students acquire knowledge and skills. Rather than solely assessing students' ability to retain information, project-based learning is thought to promote students' ability to use knowledge to carry out a successful project. The introduction of such pedagogical practice emphasizes the skills such as collaboration, negotiation, and planning, all of which are viewed as essential for success in the modern organizational workplace (Bell, 2010). In an alternative world where organizations are not the dominant form of social structure, schooling might be imagined as preparing students for obedience to God or to follow the rules of factory work.

At the extreme, students are even supported to participate and establish their own organizations—a reflection of the valorization of organizations in society. For example, establishing an organization in high school becomes a useful signal for university applications. The Princeton Review, a company that offers test preparation and college admissions resources, lists a number of tips for participating in high school clubs. One piece of advice encourages students to "try to gain professional experience," preparing students for a smooth transition into not only college clubs but also the professional world (The Princeton Review, n.d.). Another tip advises students to start their own clubs if they cannot find ones they want to join. Taking such initiatives demonstrates students' leadership skills and empowers individual students to achieve goals through organizations. Accordingly, increased emphasis on participation in an organizational society through educational content normalizes and legitimizes the role of organizations as active and purposeful social actors. We view these trends as in part culturally driven, likely to diffuse far beyond elite self-interest or known effectiveness or need in settings linked to world culture. Future research could test our propositions, particularly considering the various types of organizational actors that are represented in and are shaping education.

Conclusion

One core implication of our arguments is that the organizational transformation of education, arising as part of world culture, marks a fundamental shift in the nature of authority that underpins education systems. As the number and type of organizational actors expand and their status and legitimacy grow, decision-making processes are transformed. Nonprofit and community organizations, alongside other private actors, become increasingly active in political processes by advocating policy solutions to governments (Ball, 2012; Reckhow, 2016; Tompkins-Stange, 2020). Unilateral directives from the top of a hierarchy become less acceptable, and instead it becomes an imperative to consult with an array of stakeholder groups (typically organizations). Relatedly, partnerships and collaborations, especially across sectors (e.g., public–private partnerships), become more celebrated.

Public administration scholars have described a shift from "government" to "governance" to capture the changed nature of control occurring across all public sectors (Rhodes, 2007). The concept is intended to convey horizontal relations where decisions are negotiated across multiple stakeholders and levels (e.g., Bache & Flinders 2005; Fransen, 2012; Vidal, 2014), in contrast to top-down government regulation (Osborne, 2006). Education remains largely in the hands of national governments, yet independent organizational actors play increasing roles not only in service provision but also in policy and decision-making, and in monitoring and evaluation activities. For example, during the COVID-19 global pandemic San Francisco Unified School District (SFUSD), like many other school systems, needed to decide on policies for school reopening in the wake of closures. To come to a decision, SFUSD coordinated not only with health authorities but also with local nonprofit organizations, universities, parent–teacher associations (PTAs), the teachers' union, and looked to countries like South Korea and Denmark for guidance (Stanford-SFUSD Partnership, 2019). In the midst of a medical public health crisis, it was taken for granted that the inclusion of different types of actors was not only legitimate but necessary. Inclusive decision-making processes make sense in a context where all sorts of entities are imagined as actors sharing the basic principles of world culture.

A second key implication is that education plays a central role in shaping, normalizing, and legitimizing the "organizational society" (Thompson, 1980). Formal organizations emerged as a distinctive feature of modernity, and the structures of these organizations have been heavily influenced by modern schooling (Duke, 2019). Education links the empowerment of individuals with greater control over a rationalized knowledge system in the world (Bromley & Meyer, 2015). Education shapes individuals' participation in organizational society by influencing and supporting a rationalized knowledge system. Through educational content, practices, and structures, education also normalizes and legitimizes organizational society.

In some views, expanded organization is a key solution to pressing global problems, although historically this has not always been the case. When a social, political, or economic need or problem emerges in the globalized liberal cultural context, a common response is to create new organizations and organizational practices to "solve" the problem. And all kinds of organizations, including for-profit, nonprofit, and nongovernmental organizations, are increasingly led by managerial professionals with degrees in business administration (Hwang & Powell, 2009). In other views, organizations represent a central source of inequality and oppression in society (Coleman, 1982; Perrow,

1991). Business organizations are frequently accused of the pursuit of self-interest at the expense of social good (Alcadipani & de Oliveira Medeiros, 2019; Washburn, 2004). But nonprofit and philanthropic organizations are also pointed to as sources of corruption and inequality in need of ethical oversight (Archambeault et al., 2015; Bromley & Orchard, 2016; Burger & Owens, 2010). Regardless of one's position on organizations, to fully participate in global organizational society—and especially to excel in it—requires a great deal of formal education. Thus, these two spheres—education and organizations—are at the heart of national and global stratification systems. In the contemporary world broadly, and in education systems specifically, organizations serve as a core source of both problems and solutions, placing greater authority in organizations as actors. As decoupling occurs between signaled commitments and actual enactments of proposed organizational solutions, organizations themselves are called upon as the solutions to the very problems they create.

NOTES

1. The three first authors contributed equally.
2. We focus on an institutional explanation for the diffusion of Western cultural principles (Meyer et al., 1997), but multiple factors are likely at play and empirical research can help to disentangle the explanations. For instance, some scholars focus on the exploitative power dynamics that benefit Western countries (Tabulawa, 2003; Wallerstein, 1984), and others argue a functional modernization process is at work (classically, see Lipset, 1959).
3. For detailed discussions of the concept of actorhood, see also Hwang et al., 2019; Hwang & Colyvas, 2020; Patriotta, 2020.
4. Paxton et al. (2015) operationalize country-connectedness to the world polity using country scores that measure centrality in the global country-INGO network. Other measures that are often used in measuring embeddedness in world polity include the KOF cultural globalization index, Polity IV data set, and World Development Indicators, among others.
5. See Schofer and Longhofer (2011) for a detailed discussion of the strengths and weaknesses of these data, and an analysis of their representativeness.
6. Preliminary analysis from a cross-national data set that covers 1900 to 2011, encompassing the sample of 643 textbooks discussed here, shows that discussions of IGOs in textbooks appear since the 1910s and reach a peak in the 1930s. Approximately half of the textbooks published in the 1930s mention IGOs, but this proportion declines in the following two decades, perhaps reflecting a weakening role of IGOs and international cooperation associated with the World War II period.

REFERENCES

Academic Ranking of World Universities. (n.d.). *About academic ranking of world universities.* http://www.shanghairanking.com/aboutarwu.html
Ahrne, G., & Brunsson, N. (2011). Organization outside organizations: The significance of partial organization. *Organization, 18*(1), 83–104.

Ahrne, G., & Brunsson, N. (Eds.). (2019). *Organization outside organizations: The abundance of partial organization in social life*. Cambridge University Press.

Albert, S., & Whetten, D. A. (1985). Organizational identity. *Research in Organizational Behavior, 7*, 263–295.

Alcadipani, R., & de Oliveira Medeiros, C. R. (2019). When corporations cause harm: A critical view of corporate social irresponsibility and corporate crimes. *Journal of Business Ethics, 167*, 285–297.

Archambeault, D. S., Webber, S., & Greenlee, J. (2015). Fraud and corruption in U.S. nonprofit entities: A summary of press reports 2008–2011. *Nonprofit and Voluntary Sector Quarterly, 44*(6), 1194–1224.

Bache, I., & Flinders, M. V. (2005). *Multi-level governance*. Oxford University Press.

Ball, S. J. (2012). *Global Education Inc.: New policy networks and the neoliberal imaginary*. Routledge.

Becker, G. S. (1964). *Human capital: A theoretical and empirical analysis, with special reference to education* (1st ed.). National Bureau of Economic Research.

Bell, S. (2010). Project-based learning for the 21st century: Skills for the future. *The Clearing House, 83*(2), 39–43.

Boli, J., & Thomas, G. M. (1997). World culture in the world polity: A century of international non-governmental organization. *American Sociological Review, 62*(2), 171–190.

Boli, J., & Thomas, G. M. (1999). INGOs and the organization of world culture. In *Constructing world culture: International nongovernmental organizations since 1975* (pp. 13–49). Stanford University Press.

Bourdieu, P. (1977). Cultural reproduction and social reproduction. In J. Karabel & A. H. Halsey (Eds.), *Power and ideology in education* (pp. 487–511). Oxford University Press.

Bowers, V., & Garrod, S. (1987). The Western frontier, 1871–1905. In *Our land: Building the West* (pp. 186–221). Gage Educational.

Bromley, P. (2010). The rationalization of educational development: Scientific activity among international nongovernmental organizations. *Comparative Education Review, 54*(4), 577–601.

Bromley, P. (2016). Empowered individualism in world culture: Agency and equality in Canadian textbooks, 1871–2006. *European Journal of Cultural and Political Sociology, 3*(2–3), 177–200.

Bromley, P. (2020). The organizational transformation of civil society. In P. Bromley & W. W. Powell (Eds.), *The nonprofit sector: A research handbook* (3rd ed.) (pp. 123–143). Stanford University Press.

Bromley, P., & Meyer, J. W. (2015). *Hyper-organization: Global organizational expansion*. Oxford University Press.

Bromley, P., & Meyer, J. W. (2017). "They are all organizations": The cultural roots of blurring between the nonprofit, business, and government sectors. *Administration & Society, 49*(7), 939–966. https://doi.org/10.1177/0095399714548268

Bromley, P., & Orchard, C. O. (2016). Managed morality: The rise of professional codes of conduct in the U.S. nonprofit sector. *Nonprofit and Voluntary Sector Quarterly, 45*(2), 351–374.

Bromley, P., & Powell, W. W. (2012). From smoke and mirrors to walking the talk: The causes and consequences of decoupling in the contemporary world. *Academy of Management Annals, 6*(1), 483–530.

Bromley, P., Schofer, E., & Longhofer, W. (2018). Organizing for education: A cross-national, longitudinal study of civil society organizations and education outcomes. *VOLUNTAS: International Journal of Voluntary and Nonprofit Organizations, 29*(3), 526–540.

Bromley, P., & Sharkey, A. J. (2017). Casting call: The expanding nature of actorhood in U.S. firms, 1960–2010. *Accounting, Organizations and Society, 59*, 3–20.

Brunsson, N., & Sahlin-Andersson, K. (2000). Constructing organizations: The example of public sector reform. *Organization Studies, 21*(4), 721–746.

Buckner, E. (2017). The worldwide growth of private higher education: Cross-national patterns of higher education institution foundings by sector. *Sociology of Education, 90*(4), 296–314.

Burger, R., & Owens, T. (2010). Promoting transparency in the NGO sector: Examining the availability and reliability of self-reported data. *World Development, 38*(9), 1263–1277.

Bush, S. S., & Hadden, J. (2019). Density and decline in the founding of international NGOs in the United States. *International Studies Quarterly, 63*(4), 1133–1146.

Chabbott, C. (2003). *Constructing education for development: International organizations and education for all.* Routledge-Falmer.

Choi, M., D'Apice, H. K., & Skinner, N. (2020). The rise of the organisational society in Canadian and U.S. textbooks: 1836–2011. *Globalisation, Societies and Education, 19*(1), 7–22.

Coleman, J. (1982). *The asymmetric society.* Syracuse University Press.

Davies, T. (2013). NGOs: A long and turbulent history. *The Global Journal, 15*, 28–34.

Deem, R., Mok, K. H., & Lucas, L. (2008). Transforming higher education in whose image? Exploring the concept of the "world-class" university in Europe and Asia. *Higher Education Policy, 21*, 83–97.

Dees, J. G., & Anderson, B. B. (2003). Sector-bending: Blurring lines between nonprofit and for-profit. *Society, 40*(4), 16–27.

DiMaggio, P., & Powell, W. (1983). The iron cage revisited: Institutional isomorphism and collective rationality in organizational fields. *American Sociological Review, 48*, 147–160.

Dreeben, R. (1968). Schooling and citizenship. In *On what is learned in school* (pp. 63–111). Addison-Wesley.

Drori, G. S., Meyer, J. W., & Hwang, H. (Eds.). (2006). *Globalization and organization: World society and organizational change.* Oxford University Press.

Drori, G. S., Meyer, J. W., Ramirez, F. O., & Schofer, E. (Eds.). (2003). *Science in the modern world polity: Institutionalization and globalization.* Stanford University Press.

Duke, D. L. (2019). Historical perspectives on schools as organizations. In M. Connolly, D. H. Eddy-Spicer, C. James, & S. D. Kruse (Eds.), *The SAGE handbook of school organization* (pp. 29–48). Sage.

Dumay, X., & Dupriez, V. (2014). Educational quasi-markets, school effectiveness and social inequalities. *Journal of Education Policy, 29*(4), 510–531.

Durkheim, E. (1961). *Moral education: A study in the theory and application of the sociology of education* (E. K. Wilson, Ed.; E. K. Wilson & H. Schnurer, Trans.). Free Press of Glencoe.

Durkheim, E. (1973). Individualism and the intellectuals. In R. N. Bellah (Ed.), *Emile Durkheim on morality and society* (pp. 43–57). University of Chicago Press.

Elliott, M. A. (2007). Human rights and the triumph of the individual in world culture. *Cultural Sociology, 1*(3), 343–363.

Espeland, W. N., & Sauder, M. (2007). Rankings and reactivity: How public measures recreate social worlds. *American Journal of Sociology, 113*(1), 1–40.

Espeland, W. N., & Sauder, M. (2016). *Engines of anxiety: Academic rankings, reputation, and accountability.* Russell Sage Foundation.

Fielding, J., & Evans, R. (2001). Global forces. In *Canada: Our century, our story* (pp. 422–451). Nelson Thomson Learning.

Fransen, L. (2012). Multi-stakeholder governance and voluntary programme interactions: Legitimation politics in the institutional design of corporate social responsibility. *Socio-Economic Review*, *10*(1), 163–192.

Furuta, J. (2020). Western colonialism and world society in national education systems: Global trends in the use of high-stakes exams at early ages, 1960 to 2010. *Sociology of Education*, 1–18.

Furuta, J., & Ramirez, F. O. (2019). The legal rationalization of American higher education. In T. Christensen, Å. Gornitzka, & F. O. Ramirez (Eds.), *Universities as agencies: Reputation and professionalization* (pp. 229–247). Palgrave Macmillan.

Gale Group. (2017). *Encyclopedia of associations: International organizations.* Gale Cengage Learning.

Glynn, M. A. (2008). Beyond constraint: How institutions enable identities. In R. Greenwood, C. Oliver, R. Suddaby, & K. Sahlin, *The SAGE handbook of organizational institutionalism* (pp. 413–430). SAGE Publications Ltd. https://doi.org/10.4135/9781849200387.n17

Hwang, H., & Colyvas, J. A. (2020). Ontology, levels of society, and degrees of generality: Theorizing actors as abstractions in institutional theory. *Academy of Management Review*, *45*(3), 570–595.

Hwang, H., Colyvas, J. A., & Drori, G. S. (Eds.). (2019). *Agents, actors, actorhood: Institutional perspectives on the nature of agency, action, and authority.* Emerald Group.

Hwang, H., & Powell, W. W. (2009). The rationalization of charity: The influences of professionalism in the nonprofit sector. *Administrative Science Quarterly*, *54*, 268–298.

Jackson, S. K., Guerrero, S., & Appe, S. (2014). The state of nonprofit and philanthropic studies doctoral education. *Nonprofit and Voluntary Sector Quarterly*, *43*(5), 795–811.

Kamens, D. H., & Benavot, A. (2011). National, regional and international learning assessments: Trends among developing countries, 1960–2009. *Globalisation, Societies and Education*, *9*(2), 285–300.

Kamens, D. H., & McNeely, C. L. (2010). Globalization and the growth of international educational testing and national assessment. *Comparative Education Review*, *54*(1), 5–25.

Kaufman, J. (2008). Corporate law and the sovereignty of states. *American Sociological Review*, *73*(3), 402–425. https://doi.org/10.1177/000312240807300303

Kay, K., & Greenhill, V. (2011). Twenty-first century students need 21st century skills. In G. Wan & D. M. Gut (Eds.), *Bringing schools into the 21st century* (Vol. 13, pp. 41–65). Springer.

King, B., Fellin, T., & Whetten, D. (2010). Finding the organization in organizational theory: A meta-theory of the organization as a social actor. *Organization Science*, *21*(1), 290–305.

Krücken, G., & Meier, F. (2006). Turning the university into an organizational actor. In G. S. Drori, J. W. Meyer, & H. Hwang (Eds.), *Globalization and organization: World society and organizational change* (pp. 241–257). Oxford University Press.

Kwak, N., Gavrila, S. G., & Ramirez, F. O. (2019). Enacting diversity in American higher education. In T. Christensen, Å. Gornitzka, & F. O. Ramirez (Eds.), *Universities as agencies: Reputation and professionalization* (pp. 209–228). Palgrave Macmillan.

Lamoreaux, N. R., & Wallis, J. J. (2017). Introduction. In *Organizations, civil society, and the roots of development* (pp. 1–21). University of Chicago Press. http://www.nber.org/chapters/c13503

Lechner, F. J., & Boli, J. (2005). *World culture: Origins and consequences.* John Wiley & Sons.

Levy, J. (2016). Altruism and the origins of nonprofit philanthropy. In R. Reich, C. Cordelli, & L. Bernholz (Eds.), *Philanthropy in democratic societies: History, institutions, values* (pp. 19–43). University of Chicago Press.

Lipset, S. M. (1959). Some social requisites of democracy: Economic development and political legitimacy. *The American Political Science Review*, 53(1), 69–105.

Mair, J. (2020). Social entrepreneurship: Research as disciplined exploration. In W. W. Powell & P. Bromley (Eds.), *The nonprofit sector: A research handbook* (3rd ed., pp. 333–357). Stanford University Press.

Mangez, E., & Hilgers, M. (2012). The field of knowledge and the policy field in education: PISA and the production of knowledge for policy. *European Educational Research Journal*, 11(2), 189–205.

Marshall, T. H. (1950). *Citizenship and social class and other essays*. Cambridge University Press.

Meyer, J. W. (1977). The effects of education as an institution. *American Journal of Sociology*, 83(1), 55–77.

Meyer, J. W. (2010). World society, institutional theories, and the actor. *Annual Review of Sociology*, 36, 1–20.

Meyer, J. W., Boli, J., Thomas, G. M., & Ramirez, F. O. (1997). World society and the nation-state. *American Journal of Sociology*, 103(1), 144–181.

Meyer, J. W., Ramirez, F. O., & Soysal, Y. N. (1992). World expansion of mass education, 1870–1980. *Sociology of Education*, 65(2), 128–149.

Meyer, J. W., & Rowan, B. (1977). Institutionalized organizations: Formal structure as myth and ceremony. *American Journal of Sociology*, 83(2), 340–363.

Mirabella, R. M. (2007). University-based educational programs in nonprofit management and philanthropic studies: A 10-year review and projections of future trends. *Nonprofit and Voluntary Sector Quarterly, Supplement* 36(4), 11S–27S.

Mirabella, R. M. (2020, October 16). *Nonprofit management education: Current offerings in university-based programs*. http://academic.shu.edu/npo/

Mirabella, R. M., Gemelli, G., Malcolm, M.-J., & Berger, G. (2007). Nonprofit and philanthropic studies: International overview of the field in Africa, Canada, Latin America, Asia, the Pacific, and Europe. *Nonprofit and Voluntary Sector Quarterly, Supplement* 36(4), 110S–135S.

Mirabella, R. M., & Young, D. R. (2012). The development of education for social entrepreneurship and nonprofit management: Diverging or converging paths? *Nonprofit Management & Leadership*, 23(1), 43–57.

Moon, H., & Wotipka, C. M. (2006). The worldwide diffusion of business education, 1881–1999: Historical trajectory and mechanisms of expansion. In G. S. Drori, J. W. Meyer, & H. Hwang (Eds.), *Globalization and organization: World society and organizational change* (pp. 121–136). Oxford University Press.

Mundy, K. (2007). Global governance, educational change. *Comparative Education*, 43(3), 339–357.

Osborne, S. P. (2006). The New Public Governance? *Public Management Review*, 8(3), 377–387.

Patrinos, H. A., Barrera-Osorio, F., & Guáqueta, J. (2009). *The role and impact of public-private partnerships in education*. The World Bank.

Patriotta, G. (2020). Actors and actorhood in institutional theory. *Journal of Management Studies*, 57(4), 867–872.

Paxton, P., Hughes, M., & Reith, N. (2015). Extending the INGO Network Country Score 1950–2008. *Sociological Science*, 2(4), 287–307. https://doi.org/10.15195/v2.a14

Pearce, M. (2016). *Macro-macro emergence: The internet as a cultural institution* [Unpublished dissertation]. University of California-Irvine.

Perrow, C. (1991). A society of organizations. *Theory and Society*, 20(6), 725–762.

The Princeton Review. (n.d.). How important are high school clubs? https://www.princetonrev
iew.com/college-advice/joining-high-school-clubs

Ramirez, F. O., & Boli, J. (1987). The political construction of mass schooling: European origins and worldwide institutionalization. *Sociology of Education*, *60*(1), 2–17.

Ramirez, F. O., Bromley, P., & Russell, S. G. (2009). The valorization of humanity and diversity. *Multicultural Education Review*, *1*(1), 29–54.

Ramirez, F. O., Schofer, E., & Meyer, J. W. (2018). International tests, national assessments, and educational development (1970–2012). *Comparative Education Review*, *62*(3), 344–364.

Reckhow, S. (2016). More than patrons: How foundations fuel policy change and backlash. *PS: Political Science & Politics*, *49*(3), 449–454.

Rhodes, R. A. W. (2007). Understanding governance: Ten years on. *Organization Studies*, *28*(8), 1243–1464.

Rojas, F. (2010). *From Black power to Black studies: How a radical social movement became an academic discipline*. Johns Hopkins University Press.

Sadlak, J., & Liu, N. C. (Eds.). (2007). *The world-class university and ranking aiming beyond status*. UNESCO-CEPES.

Sassen, S. (1996). *Losing control? Sovereignty in the age of globalization*. Columbia University Press.

Sassen, S. (2003). The participation of states and citizens in global governance. *Indiana Journal of Global Legal Studies*, *10*(1), 5–28.

Sauder, M., & Espeland, W. N. (2009). The discipline of rankings: Tight coupling and organizational change. *American Sociological Review*, *74*(1), 63–82.

Schofer, E., & Longhofer, W. (2011). The structural sources of association. *American Journal of Sociology*, *117*(2), 539–585.

Schofer, E., & Meyer, J. W. (2005). The worldwide expansion of higher education in the twentieth century. *American Sociological Review*, *70*, 898–920.

Schultz, T. W. (1961). Investment in human capital. *The American Economic Review*, *51*(1), 1–17.

Sending, O. J., & Neumann, I. B. (2006). Governance to governmentality: Analyzing NGOs, states, and power. *International Studies Quarterly*, *50*(3), 651–672.

Shier, M. L., & Handy, F. (2014). Research trends in nonprofit graduate studies: A growing interdisciplinary field. *Nonprofit and Voluntary Sector Quarterly*, *43*(5), 812–831.

Shin, J. C., & Kehm, B. M. (Eds.). (2012). *Institutionalization of world-class university in global competition* (Vol. 6). Springer Science & Business Media.

Skinner, N. A., & Ramirez, F. O. (2019). Marketing the American university: Professionalization of development in entrepreneurial universities. In T. Christensen, Å. Gornitzka, & F. O. Ramirez (Eds.), *Universities as agencies: Reputation and professionalization* (pp. 185–207). Palgrave Macmillan.

Stanford-SFUSD Partnership. (2019). *International Covid-19 Database Brief* (November Issue) [Stanford-SFUSD Partnership Newsletter]. California Education Partners.

Tabulawa, R. (2003). International aid agencies, learner-centred pedagogy and political democratisation: A critique. *Comparative Education*, *39*(1), 7–26.

Taylor, F. W. (1911). *The principles of scientific management*. Harper & Brothers.

Thomas, G. M., Meyer, J. W., Ramirez, F. O., & Boli, J. (Eds.). (1987). *Institutional structure: Constituting state, society, and the individual* (1st ed.). Sage.

Thompson, K. (1980). The organizational society. In G. Salaman & K. Thompson (Eds.), *Control and ideology in organizations* (pp. 3–23). Open University Press/MIT Press.

Tikly, L. (2017). The future of education for all as a global regime of educational governance. *Comparative Education Review, 61*(1), 22–57.

Tompkins-Stange, M. E. (2020). *Policy patrons: Philanthropy, education reform, and the politics of influence*. Harvard Education Press.

Tyack, D. B. (1974). *The one best system: A history of American urban education* (Vol. 95). Harvard University Press.

Union of International Associations. (2020). *Yearbook of international organizations*. https://uia.org/yearbook

Urban Institute, National Center for Charitable Statistics. (2015). *Core file fiscal year trends for public charities, private foundations, and other exempt organizations*. Data Files: Coreco. CoreCoFyTrend201509, Nccs.CorePcFyTrend201508, Nccs.CorePfFyTrend201509. http://nccs-data.urban.org

Van Maanen, J. E., & Schein, E. H. (1977). *Toward a theory of organizational socialization*. MIT Alfred P. Sloan School of Management.

Verger, A. (2016). The global diffusion of education privatization: Unpacking and theorizing policy adoption. In K. Mundy, B. Lingard, & A. Verger (Eds.), *The handbook of global education policy* (1st ed., pp. 64–80). John Wiley & Sons.

Vidal, I. (2014). Multi-stakeholder governance in social enterprise. In J. Defourny, L. Hulgård, & V. Pestoff (Eds.), *Social enterprise and the third sector: Changing European landscapes in a comparative perspective* (1st ed., pp. 176–186). Routledge.

Wallerstein, I. (1984). *The politics of the world-economy: The states, the movements, and the civilizations*. Cambridge University Press.

Washburn, J. (2004). *University, Inc.: The corporate corruption of higher education*. Basic Books.

Weber, M. (1978). *Economy and society: An outline of interpretive sociology* (G. Roth & C. Wittich, Eds.; Vol. 1). University of California Press.

Willetts, P. (2002). What is a non-governmental organization? City University, London. http://www.staff.city.ac.uk/p.willetts/CS-NTWKS/NGO-ART.HTM

World Bank. (2020). *World development indicators*. World Bank.

Wotipka, C. M., Rabling, B. J., Sugawara, M., & Tongliemnak, P. (2017). The worldwide expansion of early childhood care and education, 1985–2010. *American Journal of Education, 123*, 307–339.

Wotipka, C. M., & Ramirez, F. O. (2008). Women's studies as a global innovation. In A. W. Wiseman & D. P. Baker (Eds.), *The worldwide transformation of higher education* (pp. 89–110). Emerald Group.

Zapp, M. (2020). The authority of science and the legitimacy of international organisations: OECD, UNESCO and World Bank in global education governance. *Compare: A Journal of Comparative and International Education, 51*(7), 1–20.

CHAPTER 6

....

GLOBALIZATION, NEW INSTITUTIONALISMS, AND THE POLITICAL DIMENSION

....

CHRISTIAN MAROY AND XAVIER PONS

INTRODUCTION

....

THE aim of this chapter is to examine the different conceptions of globalization in education proposed by authors who have drawn inspiration from one or other of the neoinstitutionalist approaches and to analyze the status of the political dimension involved in the changes studied. At first glance, one might think that much of this work has already been done. The neoinstitutionalist perspective on world culture theory (WCT), developed as early as the 1970s by John Meyer and his colleagues, has been massively taken up but also repeatedly criticized (e.g., Carney et al., 2012; Hartley, 2003; Schriewer, 2012). Partly in response to these criticisms, literature reviews of the neoinstitutionalist theories used in the field of comparative education have already clarified the different approaches (e.g., Wiseman et al., 2014). Nevertheless, three considerations call for a careful reexamination of this subject. First, neoinstitutionalist approaches are much more diverse than these initial debates suggest. The work on WCT and the mechanisms of isomorphism is indeed far from exhausting the different conceptions of institutions, institutional change, and institutionalist theories proposed in the international literature. It is even far from exhausting the sociological neoinstitutionalism (NI) itself in which they are sometimes classified. For example, recent work is more based on the multidimensional conceptualizations of institutions proposed by Richard Scott (1995) or places greater emphasis on change and the institutional work of actors (Campbell, 2004; Lawrence et al., 2009). The opening of WCT proposed by Alexander Wiseman, Fernanda Astiz, and David Baker (2014) in their review proves in this respect to be still very timid and limited to a NI qualified as "political."

Second, reflections on NI beyond the field of educational research, for example in political science, sociology, or economics, have evolved considerably in recent years and strong criticism has sometimes been leveled at the institutionalist work involved. Vivien Schmidt (2008), for example, argued that NIs do not take sufficient account of the importance of discourses in analyzing institutional change. This, she maintains, undermined the political dimension of institutional change. It does not give sufficient weight to ideas, deliberative processes, the persuasive power of political actors, and more generally to the ongoing reshaping of the interests of actors in the battle of ideas. All these dimensions are considered much more, in her view, by discursive NI. Are these new reflections and criticisms then taken into account in neoinstitutionalist work when thinking about the globalization of education (policies), and how?

Third, a significant part of the work on globalization, understood, for example, through questions of policy transfers, the circulation of influential transnational doctrines, or the performative power of new measurement instruments, proposes hybrid theoretical frameworks in which the institutionalist perspective is nourished and enriched by numerous and varied theoretical contributions from, for example, policy analysis or governance theories (e.g., Steiner-Khamsi & Waldow, 2012).

For these reasons, we argue for the importance not to approach the articulation among NI, globalization, and educational policies primarily through an abstract dialogue of major theoretical approaches. Indeed, this dialogue, already partly debated in the literature, often depends on the privileged, but in fact partial, observation posts of the field of research to which the authors concerned, however eminent they may be, have access. There would then be a great risk of perpetuating a form of "neoinstitutionalist parochialism," to paraphrase Roger Dale (2005), according to which this articulation would only be thought out from a particular point of view on what "real" NI would or should be.

Our approach, on the contrary, is more empirical and based on a literature review of a corpus of 61 English- and French-language articles. The modalities of constitution and exploitation of this corpus are detailed in the first section. The analysis of the selected contributions consisted in studying precisely, for each of them, the visions proposed by the authors of globalization, NI, and politics in the broad sense. This analysis led us to distinguish three major research strands. The first is largely structured around the debate on WCT and isomorphism of education systems under the effect of a world culture and world polity. The second strand consists in analyzing the importance of the institutional mediations of globalization at work in different educational contexts under the effect of various mechanisms, not only mimetic, the agency of certain actors, and/or the instrumentation of education policies. The last strand is more heterogeneous and brings together works that have in common the emphasis on institutional change and institutional emergence as it weakens or recomposes preexisting institutional arrangements. These strands are not impermeable to each other. Rather, they sediment as authors cross-reference their work at some point. However, as we shall see, they convey often contrasting visions of globalization and, most important for our purpose, of the policy dimension. We thus present, in conclusion, some complementary lines of analysis offering relevant avenues for theoretical developments.

METHODOLOGY

Our literature review can be defined as a scoping review. Focusing on theoretical aspects, its objective is to "map rapidly the key concepts underpinning a research area and the main sources and types of evidence available" (Mays et al., 2001, p. 194) in order to "examine the extent, range and nature of research activity" and to "identify [possible] research gaps in the existing literature" (Arksey & O'Malley, 2005, p. 21). This review is based on the intensive analysis of a corpus of 61 research articles, in both English (n = 51) and French (n = 10). Several stages of research were necessary to constitute this corpus. First, we queried two types of online databases known for the richness of their documentary holdings—commonly used documentary portals giving access to numerous journals (Eric, Sociological abstracts, Worldwide political science abstracts for the English-speaking works; Cairn, Erudit, Openeditions, and Persée for the French-speaking part) and the online search engines of the publishers of large international journals particularly relevant to our object, such as Sage (*European Educational Research Journal*), JSTOR (*Comparative Education Review*), and Taylor & Francis (*Comparative Education*; *Compare*; *Discourse*; *Journal of Education Policy*; and *Globalisation, Societies and Education*).

In each of these databases, we carried out a keyword search for the period 2000–2020, primarily in the abstract field, using the following series of keywords: "global" (use of truncation as systematically as possible), "policy/politics/polity/reform," "institutionalism," and "education." After a first reading of the results, we add "theory" to the keyword "institutionalism," to get access to articles with a strong theoretical dimension.

We went through or read the 1,245 abstracts of articles obtained in this way, and in the end, we selected 103 of them (75 in English, 28 in French). The main reasons for nonselection at this stage were the general lack of relevance of the article to our research object (no reflection on globalization or institutionalist theories, for example), the existence of duplicates, or coverage of a field other than education.

We went through all these articles in a double-blind fashion, excluding those that made no or little explicit mention of institutions in the broad sense and to institutional processes (reason 1) and those that proposed an essentially descriptive (meaning not theorized or conceptualized) approach to institutionalization (reason 2). The comparison of our individual selections led us to retain only 61 articles. They are cited in the References section with an asterisk, to distinguish them from other references that we mobilize for the needs of the analysis. These additional references are of two types: (1) important references to account for WCT that escape our review either because they are prior to 2000 or because they are extracted from Handbooks that our sources do not allow to be considered, (2) various references on one or other forms of NI or relating to our perspective of analysis, questioning globalization, politics, and institutions (e.g., Schmidt, 2008).

We then coded these articles in three dimensions. The first was about globalization: Is it conceptualized, or even just defined? Is it understood by related objects or by some of its manifestations (measurement instruments or transnational doctrines, for example) or is it left implicit? The second dimension concerned neoinstitutionalist theories themselves. What type of NI is favored by the authors: rational, historical, sociological, discursive . . . or implicit when some authors propose an institutionalist reasoning without referring to these main types distinguished in the literature? What vision of institutional change do these articles present? What factors of institutional change or convergence/divergence are envisaged (role of mechanisms, ideas, actors, instruments, discourses, etc.)? The last dimension referred to the importance of the political question in these articles. At this stage, we relied on a classic distinction in political science between polity, politics, and policy. This led us to interrogate this political dimension by studying how the articles analyzed the design and implementation of educational policies, reforms, measures (policy), the struggles among constituted political actors to define their common political project (politics), and finally what general political model or higher and encompassing symbolic and institutional entity these public policies and these struggles drew (polity) (Leca, 2012).

RESEARCH STRAND 1: "WORLD CULTURE" AND WORLD POLITY

The theory of "world culture" developed by John Meyer and his colleagues is important for our purposes for two reasons. It has a central scientific status in the field of comparative education and the globalization of education. And it transposes and deepens concepts of sociological NI initially applied to the field of organizations (Meyer & Scott, 1983; Scott & Meyer, 1994). This is the case for the notions of isomorphism, decoupling, or the constitution of actors' identities and interests by institutions, considered as "cultural accounts" internalized in the cognitive and normative visions of the actors but also objectified in structures, perceived as external and reified (in the wake of the constructivist sociology of Berger & Luckmann, 1967).

The Centrality and Dual Status of Globalization in WCT

Globalization appears in two forms in WCT: The first derives from the theoretical assumptions of sociological NI and the other from a set of empirical studies that have developed notably in the field of education, from the 1980s until today. Neoinstitutionalists recognize that globalization at the turn of the 21st century has several dimensions (political, economic, expansion of a global expressive culture) (Drori, 2008; Meyer, 2000). However, what is central to their theoretical concerns is the reality of an "expanded flow of instrumental culture around the world. Put simply: Common models of social order become authoritative in many different social settings" (Meyer, 2000, pp. 233–234). This "world order" is linked to the existence of a global sociological level (world society, world culture, world polity), the extent and mechanisms of which must be taken into account in order to understand the institutional transformations taking place in national and local contexts: "in many areas of social life, common models organized in world discourse arise and penetrate social life worldwide" (Meyer, 2000, p. 234).

Thus, there would be a set of "rationalized myths," conceptions of the world and of humans constructed in the course of Western history but which have subsequently acquired a global status (Meyer et al., 1997). This global culture—the content of which is in line with a Weberian reading of Western rationalization (Carney et al., 2012)—carries values (progress, human rights, democracy, rationality) and defines principles that ontologically circumscribe the identity of conceivable and legitimate actors in the modern world (nation states, organizations, individuals). These "taken-for-granted" identities go hand in hand with normative expectations of them (e.g., autonomy, instrumental rationality).[1] Rather than mechanically applying these "scripts" or models, actors actively take them into account and "enact" them creatively (Boli & Thomas, 1999), to (secure) the legitimacy of their status and identity (Ramirez, 2012). It should also be noted that the components (values, scripts, norms, standards) of this global culture are presented in increasingly universalist (but not universal), highly rationalized forms, such as the abstract definition of human rights, health, or development.

This global culture is a key explanatory variable for the empirical form of globalization in the education sector (Ramirez & Meyer, 1980). On the one hand, education is becoming increasingly valuable to individuals and nation states, as it is seen as a driver of economic and social development, but also as a guarantor of the development of individual citizens. This belief, which is at the heart of world culture, is reflected in the expansion of mass schooling, which has grown decisively worldwide since World War II (Boli et al., 1985; Meyer et al., 1992). On the other hand, educational globalization is manifested in the isomorphism of educational structures (school curriculum, ministries of education, qualification structures) (Benavot et al., 1991). In the recent period, educational policies have also tended to converge globally (Ramirez et al., 2016): for example, inclusion policies (Powell et al., 2016), standards for crisis education (Bromley & Andina, 2010), international standardized assessments (Kamens & McNeely, 2010), the "research university" model (Powell et al., 2017), lifelong learning (Jakobi & Rusconi, 2009), or educational policy goals (Jakobi, 2011).

The formalization and dissemination of the principles and scripts of this rationalized and universalist world culture is promoted mainly by two types of organizations, which form the "world polity," the second organizational component which, together with world culture, constitutes the diptych of world society. It is made up of international nongovernmental organizations (INGOs, such as Amnesty, etc.) or intergovernmental organizations (IGOs, such as UNESCO, the OECD, and so on) which experienced remarkable growth and extension of their fields of action throughout the 20th century (Boli & Thomas, 1999). In addition, professional associations play a key role in the adaptation and dissemination of streamlined models or standards in national or subnational entities (Meyer, 2000).

These processes of convergence and isomorphism do not mean, however, that these proclaimed ideals, stated policies, or similar educational structures and programs are translated into actual practices that conform to them. Indeed, taking up a concept they had already used in their earlier studies on organizations (Meyer & Rowan, 1977), this theory argue that the highly abstract character, the tensions inherent in the rationalizing myths of world culture, and the contradictions between the different institutional scripts that make it up (between freedom and equality, between the individual or collective goals of education) favor a "decoupling" between formal models, categories, and structures and their actual practices. Such a decoupling explains why very divergent practices can be observed from one country or organization to another.

Finally, educational globalization is doubly important for WCT. First, it is an important empirical variable to explain the increasing convergence and isomorphism of structures and policies at the international level. It is also a sociological and conceptual reality (world culture and its organizational forms—world polity—constitutive of "world society") which is distinguished as much by its scale of analysis (global) as by its more abstract level of complexity and its effect of structuring and orienting entities of lesser abstraction such as individuals, organizations, or nation states (Jepperson & Meyer, 2011). The concepts of "world society" and "world polity" will be used above all to show that globalization is neither reducible to a network of interdependencies between local or national actors nor to "supranational" actors (dominant states, multinationals) orchestrating globalization from above (Thomas, 2009).

The Political Dimension

In the vast body of research developed by WCT, the place given to the political dimension is relatively modest. There is an empirical emphasis on the emergence and reinforcement of a "world polity" without the notion being really elaborated in reference to political theory (Leca, 2012). Many authors use it interchangeably with the notion of world society (Thomas, 2009), even if the latter notion is often preferred (as in the canonical text by Meyer et al., 1997). Moreover, the role of political struggles and domination (politics), like that of "policies," is minor or secondary in the explanations of the emergence of world culture/polity, as well as in the mechanisms of its global extension or its manifestations in different fields of social life.

What then are the contours of this world polity? It is made up of multilateral international organizations—often nongovernmental organizations—which do not have the power to impose themselves on actors at other levels of analysis, nation states, companies, nonprofit organizations, or individual citizens. Indeed, "the world society is a stateless polity. It has no central, controlling political organizations in it—no state organization with legitimate sovereignty over or responsibility for the whole" (Meyer, 2000, p. 236).

The diffusion of the common principles of world culture therefore operates through osmosis and the cognitive and normative influence of the international organizations that promote them. The networks of influential organizations are perceived as "disinterested third parties" by the subunits of world society (Meyer et al., 1997) who refer to them according to the authority (of science or technical or moral expertise) of which they are the carriers. For example, the convergence of educational goals, structures, and policies in the world is essentially linked to the quest for legitimacy of nation states (emerging or old) which tend, in order to ensure their credibility and the legitimacy of their status as modern states, to align their school structures and practices with the principles and models of world culture, particularly with regard to education. The authority of the world polity is therefore not the same as (legal or traditional) domination in the sense of Max Weber (Boli & Thomas, 1999).

Moreover, the dynamics of this polity do not equate it with those of canonical types (nation state or empire). In fact, the existence and expansion of world society derive, according to Drori, from a dynamic "between polity and culture," where "the current world polity is a reflection of world cultural trends as much as it is a codification of such norms into formal structures of action and policy making" (Drori, 2008, p. 457). The form of the world polity thus has four characteristics: It is "expansive," "heterogeneous," "dynamic," and "loosely organized and highly decentralized" (Drori, 2008). In turn, the world polity tends to influence the development of world culture in two ways: (1) growth of issues defined as global (from human rights to environmentalism to inequality); (2) treatment of these issues by a double logic of "rationalization" (systematization, standardization, scientization of social life) and "actorhood" (i.e., "the sense of empowered agency attributed to social actors," which goes hand in hand with the idea of a "manageable" world) (Drori, 2008, p. 461).

Finally, the world polity as understood by WCT does not have the classic attributes associated with a polity by political theory (Leca, 2012). It implies neither an obligatory and nonchosen membership of this political entity nor the prohibition of the use of violence by its members, whose legitimate monopoly is the prerogative of the polity itself, empire, or nation state. On the other hand, the world polity is said to share another feature of a polity, which "is the symbolic assertion of an all-embracing collective identity" (Leca, 2012, p. 63), since, on the basis of the different facets of human rights, the world polity promotes the model of a global citizenship (Boli & Thomas, 1999), without all states or individuals claiming it. It contributes to consolidating "a global imagined community" (Drori, 2008, p. 456).

Unlike the concept of polity, the active exercise of power (*politics*), whether at the level of international organizations, the state, or other spheres, is given very little consideration in WCT's theorization of globalization. First, the genesis of the world polity cannot be reduced, from their point of view, "to states, transnational corporations, or national forces and interest groups" as claimed by critical theories, which tend to reduce them to power relations, reducing culture to a "set of values" and to an ideology linked to interests (Boli & Thomas, 1999, p. 13; see also Meyer, 2000). Nor can it be reduced to controversial responses to functional coordination needs related to increasing global interdependencies among nation states or multinational firms (Ramirez, 2012). The emergence of the world polity seems rather to be the international organizational counterpart and vector of the global culture. It proceeds from an endogenous cultural trend of modern and now global society. We are far from the explanations of "polities" by political sociology, several of whose theories have, for example, emphasized the crucial role of conflicts and struggles in the socio-historical construction of the nation state, which is seen as a polity monopolizing various key "capitals" and resources of power (Weber, Elias, Bourdieu, for example). WCT's analysis of the socio-historical genesis of world society and world polity thus clearly tends to underplay struggles and relations of domination.

Similarly, the mechanism of "coercion" (DiMaggio & Powell, 1983) is downplayed (if not eliminated) as a mechanism for the diffusion of global culture, in favor of a cognitive mechanism, since the diffusion of norms is achieved through the enactment of institutionalized cultural models or scripts. However, some authors argue that the structuring role of world culture does not mean that the models and standards disseminated by world society do not imply political conflicts or struggles (Boli & Thomas, 1999). Indeed, global cultural frameworks can be ambiguous, contradictory, or only ceremonially and symbolically applied, thus generating conflict and dissent. Moreover, some works consider the conflict issues and struggles of (subnational) social movements as structured by legitimate transnational cultural models, which these movements thereby contribute to symbolically reinforcing (Astiz et al., 2002). Zapp and Ramirez (2019) analyze the diverse mechanisms (cognitive/discursive, normative, regulatory, and coercive) through which the trend toward the construction of a "global regime of higher education" operates. Finally, educational *policies* are considered by WCT, but as dependent rather than independent variables. Policies are various enactments of the principles and frameworks of global culture, rather than the result of national or local political struggles. For example, the parallel development of standardized assessment of students is explained by the influence of cultural principles on government action, the influence of global educational ideology, the hegemony of science as a way of interpreting the world, and the conception of society as a "managed society" (Kamens & McNeely, 2010).

Thus, for WCT the focus is primarily on the cognitive and normative constructs that constitute political interests and issues, rather than on political power plays and relations. Moreover, although modern rationalized and universalist culture circulates globally, it is not the result of a political structure or a globalized political entity, but rather of the uncoordinated action of different networks of international organizations (governmental or associative) that adhere to it and are its vectors. The result is the existence of a "world society," the product of a "world culture," crossed with a "world polity" of a non-state nature (Drori, 2008; Thomas, 2009).

Research Strand 2: Analyzing the Logics of Institutional Mediation of Globalization in Different Contexts

In the second research strand, framework and theoretical tools of NI, most often in its historical and/or sociological variations, are used to think about the logics of mediation of educational globalization at work in different contexts (often between the global and national levels, but not only). Published from 2010 onward (with three exceptions), articles represent half of our sample (31 articles). French-language works ($n = 8$) and those on higher education ($n = 13$) are particularly represented.

Some of these articles are clearly an extension of the previous perspective. The aim is to use NI to shed light on the two sides of the globalization process. On the one hand, globalization is characterized by the dissemination of a global culture, a dissemination that takes place through various channels that are institutional pressures for change, whether these pressures are normative or cognitive, as WCT initially suggests, or of another nature. The diffusion of global scripts, such as the new imperative to implement "excellence" policies in higher education and research (Antonowicz et al., 2017), or that of various rankings with strong performative power (Buckner, 2020), are two examples. On the other hand, this diffusion can be "contingent" and give rise to strong local empirical variations depending on the weight of historical legacies. Some authors even argue that holding together these two aspects of the analysis—both a global convergence of discourses on educational governance and strong local divergences in implementation according to the weight of institutional legacies—constitutes a particularly fertile avenue of research for comparative education (Takayama, 2012).

Nevertheless, this rather cumulative vision, which attempts to couple the proposals from WCT and historical NI, is clearly in the minority in this second group. On the contrary, the main analytical perspective remains to criticize the homogenizing vision of globalization present in their eyes in the work of WCT. They thus stress the centrality of domestic institutional arrangements which are at the origin of different forms of adaptation, sometimes of resistance, more often of translation, recontextualization, or accommodation to international or global institutional pressures.

Mediation Mechanisms, Actors, and Instruments

Several theoretical approaches are proposed for the factors at the origin of these institutional arrangements. The first emphasizes the role of powerful institutional mechanisms such as path dependency in order to highlight the prevalence of local governance models that involve contrasting forms of globalization depending on the context (Hajisoteriou, 2010; Mincu, 2015; Powell et al., 2016). From a list of "indicators of change" such as the decision-making process or patterns of control and quality evaluation, Michael Dobbins distinguishes, for example, three ideal types of university governance in Europe: the state-centered model, the model of self-governing academic communities, and the market-oriented model. These models then allow him to study the trajectory of certain higher education systems in Eastern Europe to show that these trajectories are far from being reduced in all cases to an automatic alignment with a transnational model (even if this type of alignment may exist) (Dobbins, 2011, 2017). In line with developments in historical NI, which form the theoretical framework of much of this literature, these trajectories are envisaged as the result of multiple path dependencies combined with the mechanisms of gradual change highlighted by Paul Pierson or Kathleen Thelen (Corbett, 2011; Maurer, 2012).

The second approach aims to revalue in the analysis the role of actors and their room for maneuver in the adaptation of these institutional arrangements in the context of public policy change. This revaluation takes several forms and is more or less strong depending on the authors. Some point to the considerable scope for interpretation of institutional parameters by individuals when implementing education policies or producing discourses on them (Alexiadou & Bunt-Kokhuis, 2013). Others understand these actors as fundamentally embedded in "policy networks" (Holland, 2010), "political settlements" (Rosser, 2016), or "institutional configurations" that strongly predefine their interests and possibilities for action (Luova, 2020). Others mobilize John Campbell's multidimensional approach to institutions and emphasize the bricolage and translation operations of new public policy imperatives carried out by actors to evolve existing institutional arrangements while being constrained by them (Hsieh, 2016; Hsieh & Huisman, 2017).

The latter approach is particularly developed in French-language articles, where it ultimately constitutes the main analytical perspective, particularly as a result of the field of research on the instrumentation of public policies opened up in France by Pierre Lascoumes and Patrick Le Galès (2007). It emphasizes the importance of instruments and tools of "public action" in the analysis of policy change and the interest of taking into account the processes of instrumentation of these policies in order to understand the institutionalization of new modes of regulation or governance of education systems, as in the case of accountability policies (Verger et al., 2019). Some authors emphasize, for example, the performative effect of these instruments. This performative power is based both on their power to label the practices of actors, as in the case of international league tables, and on the anxious internalization of the stakes of this labeling by the actors (Buckner, 2020; Erkkilä & Kauppi, 2013; Mignot-Gérard, 2012). Others use these tools methodologically as tracers of institutional change to study the processes of microinstitutionalization of new modes of regulation, such as the introduction of a new management of pedagogy under the effect of accountability policies in certain school systems (Maroy et al., 2012; Maroy & Vaillancourt, 2019). This approach often leads authors to qualify and complicate both the analysis of the reception of international measurement instruments and their power to influence the making of education policies, by stressing, for example, the structuring role of local institutional dynamics (Niemann et al., 2018).

Surrounding Globalization

With a few exceptions that theorize globalization as a process of convergence toward a market-oriented model (Dobbins, 2011, 2017) that is fundamentally neoliberal (Rosser, 2016), particularly in higher education, the majority of these works on institutional mediations do not theorize the notion of globalization itself. Globalization is mainly considered as an institutional environment that is the source of new institutional pressures, the effects of which are studied in context, in the education systems themselves.

Globalization is thus studied mainly through the concrete forms taken by these pressures. The latter are often considered in the analysis as exogenous to the education systems studied and may be conceptualized differently from one author to another: "transnational discourses" (Alexiadou & Bunt-Kokhuis, 2013), "travelling myths" (Mincu, 2015), and "global scripts" (Antonowicz et al., 2017). Several works also address globalization through the contextually differentiated reception of transnational doctrines, which often overlap in practice, such as New Public Management, accountability, or quality assurance (Csizmadia et al., 2008; Hsieh, 2016; Hsieh & Huisman, 2017; Maroy & Vaillancourt, 2019; Verger et al., 2019).

Nevertheless, the theoretical tools of NI are not primarily used to conceptualize these institutional pressures as such. Symbolically, the aforementioned notions of scripts, discourses, or myths are most often evoked as contextual elements at the beginning of the analysis, and little taken up afterward, and it is generally assumed that their mere dissemination and adoption in formal policy programs are sufficient to illustrate their institutionalization.

The tools of NI, particularly those of historical NI, are used instead to feed theoretical models that make it possible to think about the filtering, framing, and sometimes resisting role played by local institutional arrangements. According to an analytical movement common in the analysis of policy transfers, borrowings, and lendings, it is then a question of highlighting the differentiated political "responses" according to the predominant organizational logics (Csizmadia et al, 2008), the maintenance of a key role played by certain still dominant institutional actors such as the governments in power (Hsieh, 2016), or the concrete forms of political changes initiated from one system to another under the effect of various bricolage or translation operations (Hsieh & Huisman, 2017). Consequently, this work rarely leads to a reconceptualization of globalization as such from the theoretical tools of NI. The main horizon of the analysis remains the institutional mediations themselves and the highlighting of their deployment logics through detailed and often comparative empirical analyses.

Politics of Situated Institutionalizations

While such kind of interrogation does not immediately allow for a reconceptualization of globalization in education, it does have the merit of placing the political question at the heart of the analysis, by taking into account the political struggles that characterize policy change. One of the transversal characteristics of many works on the institutional mediations to which globalization gives rise is in fact that they are in strong dialogue with the results of international research on education policies, in particular with certain theoretical frameworks of policy analysis in political science. In this sense, these works clearly place policies (policy matters) at the center of the analysis. The aim may be to analyze the recomposition of policy spaces (Alexiadou & Bunt-Kokhuis, 2013), to question the extent and concrete modalities of policy change (Hsieh, 2016; Hsieh & Huisman, 2017), or to study policy practices themselves, their institutionalization, and the translation operations at their foundation (Massouti, 2018).

Depending on the authors, however, this approach can give rise to two different (but not incompatible) analytical perspectives on the political dimension. The first is more of a polity perspective and consists in mobilizing the theoretical frameworks of (historical) NI and policy implementation to question the evolution of major policy models in the face of transformations in the regulative dimension of institutions. This may involve questioning the reconfiguration of institutional arrangements characteristic of an initial public policy model, such as the welfare state at the origin of investment in children policies in Great Britain and Canada (Saint-Martin, 2002); using the notion of institutional learning to highlight the Europeanization logics of educational policies at work in the field of lifelong learning (Lee et al, 2008); or, on the contrary, pointing out, on the basis of an analysis of long historical trajectories, the resistance of national models to international injunctions in certain developing countries, such as Sri Lanka and Bangladesh in the field of technical and vocational education and training (Maurer, 2012).

Nevertheless, this perspective seems less developed in our sample than the second, which is closer to a politics perspective insofar as it pays close attention to the interests of the actors in the policy process and the struggles that characterize them. Institutions are then seen as "rolling agreements among powerful actors that are constantly subject to renegotiation and contestation," to use T. Parks and W. Cole's expression (quoted by Rosser, 2016, p. 112). This perspective is particularly developed in articles on the new regulatory instruments emblematic of globalization, such as league tables or accountability tools. Indeed, these tools are often considered by the authors as interesting tracers of institutional change to be considered in the analysis. The latter then focuses on the instrumentation process as such, the forms and dynamics of which also depend on the outcome of the struggles among the institutional actors concerned. In all cases, the articles in this second group have in common that they put back actors, albeit embedded in preexisting institutional orders, struggling to define the constitutive rules of the policies that govern them. This aspect is, however, even more emphasized in the following research strand.

RESEARCH STRAND 3: THE INSTITUTIONAL CONSTRUCTION OF NEW FORMS OF GLOBALIZATION

The research pieces that we grouped under this third strand are the most recent in our sample, published between 2009 and 2019, mainly in English-language journals (11 texts out of 61, including two French-language ones).[2] While this research strand seems less stabilized and homogeneous than the previous ones, it nevertheless presents three remarkable features which form its specificity. First, these texts clearly emphasize institutional change. Rather than analyzing the diffusion of established global cognitive and normative constructs (strand 1) or focusing on contextually differentiated institutional mediations (strand 2), this third research strand analyzes the processes of change and the elaboration of new institutional constructs, which entangle, weaken, or recompose preexisting institutional arrangements. Second, the articles emphasize one or more sources (notably political) of institutional change, which tend to be minimized by classical (historical or sociological) NI: the role of actors and entrepreneurs of change; of ideas or discursive formations; or of policy tools in the orientation or effectiveness of institutional change. The impact of the three policy dimensions is thus highlighted. Third, this research is based on complex theoretical frameworks, which articulate notions from different branches of NI with one another or with more or less general theories from other streams. Finally, the empirical objects studied are renewed and vary in their nature and their scales of analysis (consideration of subnational or local levels).

Policies and Institutional Change: The Role of Discourses and Ideas

A central feature of these issues is to mobilize NI (in its different versions) to think about institutional change and to understand its origins and singular orientations. It is a question of analyzing the very movement of changes linked to globalization through analysis of the genesis of various institutional constructs, of tracing the work of various entrepreneurs of change (political or organizational) who promote them "from above" and "from below," or from outside the nation states. This problematic is thus in line with new theorizations of institutions that place greater emphasis on the issue of change, a less deterministic view of actors, and a more political and open conception of institutionalization processes (Boxenbaum & Pedersen, 2009; Demailly et al., 2019; Meyer &

Rowan, 2006). In other words, the institutional canopy is less concentrated on long cultural movements (Western modernity, cultural globalization) and is subject to shorter temporal changes, hence the focus on institutionalization/deinstitutionalization, especially of political origin.

Within this logic, the impact of policy ideas and discourses on the change of educational institutions is thematized in a particularly visible way. For example, Ninni Wahlström and Daniel Sundberg (2018) invoke discursive NI to analyze curricular changes in Sweden. Swedish policies are seen as discursive productions, whose contours must be traced in several "arenas" (transnational, national, local), where ideas of diverse nature (cognitive or normative, background and foreground) are articulated and transformed through discursive activities, either "communicative" or "coordinative." They point to the differences in ideas conveyed by different "discursive coalitions" that will generate the particularity of Swedish curriculum policy, combining an emphasis on subject-based knowledge and the preparation of students for global competition. A political paradigm shift is also invoked by Metha to explain the changes in institutional governance arrangements in the United States between 1980 and 2001, notably the introduction of federal control over schooling and accountability for performance (Mehta, 2013).

Ideas, embedded in policies or more diffuse in institutional fields, do not, however, remain inert in their appropriation by local actors, at the school and classroom level. Wahlström and Sundberg (2018) emphasize the notion of "recontextualization" of ideas from one arena to another, a notion taken from Bernstein and "curriculum theory." Other works identify dynamics between several scales of analysis, in terms either of "sensemaking" or of "translations" of ideas and institutional arrangements. Thus, Burch et al. (2018) seek to build "a stronger conceptual bridge between macro level theories of new institutionalism (e.g., organizational fields, isomorphism) and more micro theories such as sensemaking" (Burch & Miglani, 2018, p. 3). They discuss the role of actors (companies, government) in the "Ed Tech movement" in India and thematize the tensions and influences of a private company on the "sensemaking" of educational technology uses, at the level of schools and teachers in the classroom. Similarly, drawing on the sociology of translation (Callon, 1986) and micro-institutionalist theories of sensemaking, Maroy et al. (2012) seek to understand the processes of translation and differentiated appropriation of the discourses and tools associated with policies promoting standardized external evaluations in primary schools in French-speaking Belgium.

Entrepreneurs and Mechanisms of Institutional Change in the Policy Process

In this strand, the processes of change and institutional construction (associated with or constitutive of educational globalization) are analyzed through the discursive formation or implementation of policies. The constructs proceed from ideas and discourses, carriers of transformation, thematized in terms either of "recontextualization," "sense-making," or "translation." The notions of "bricolage" and "translation" formalized by John Campbell (Campbell, 2004) are thus taken up by several works to underline the mechanisms of transformation/diffusion of institutions, whether they are thematized as "ideas" (paradigms or programmes) or as regulatory and technical devices (Hsieh, 2016; Hsieh & Huisman, 2017). Maroy and Vaillancourt thus question the regulatory tools and devices that results-based management policy puts in place in Quebec schools. Based on pragmatic sociology (Boltanski, 2008), they show that instrumental devices accentuate control over teaching work through reality tests, while the theatrical staging of statistical results and improvement plans works on organizational myths and the definition of the organization's identity, during rituals that are so many truth tests (Maroy & Vaillancourt, 2019).

Alongside these mechanisms of change, the place and status given to actors in these processes of institutional construction and change in relation to globalization must also be emphasized. Far from being reduced to mere agents, enacting scripts, or "carrier" organizations of these scripts, actors are seen as simultaneously constrained by institutions and capable of creating and changing them (Schmidt, 2008). They can be direct promoters of public policies (governments, local authorities) (Hsieh, 2016), members of "discursive coalitions" generating ideas structuring policies (politicians, transnational actors, private firms) (Hsieh & Huisman, 2017), or actors accompanying the (cognitive or practical) implementation of reforms or policy tools (inspectorate and intermediary school authorities) (Maroy et al., 2012; Wahlström & Sundberg, 2018). In addition, it is important to point out the presence of organizational actors from the private sector (Burch & Miglani, 2018). In the field of university education, McClure highlights the role of "managing consulting firms" that influence the reforms carried out by American universities through the "frames" and "ideas" they circulate in their interventions (McClure, 2017). In the Francophone context, Dahan et al. (2016) show symmetrically, within the communication services of universities, the difficulty of their identity work and their dependence on externally imposed identity categories.

A Theoretical Plurality

In this third strand, the theoretical frameworks articulate concepts of plural origins, either by combining different NIs with one another, or by combining NI concepts with other theoretical framings: actor-structure theory (Schwinn, 2012), theory of academic capitalism (McClure, 2017), curriculum theory (Wahlström & Sundberg, 2018), actor-network theory (Maroy et al., 2012), and pragmatic sociology, among others. This contrasts with the more linear and hypodeductive development of the WCT research program.

The analyses of the links among institutions, policies, and globalization developed in this stream certainly highlight an empirical globalization of the education sector, in the sense that interdependencies between national and regional systems are increasing, or that supranational private or public logics, standards, or actors are becoming more important. Moreover, the various empirical paths and forms of globalization are apparent in these works.

However, this polymorphic globalization is not theorized as such, and these middle-range theorizations lack a structured and integrative theoretical framework. The scope of these works is mainly to show the insufficiencies or the limits of the available theorizations, notably in the neoinstitutionalist galaxy. Their originality lies in showing the impact of the configurations of national, transnational, and often subnational actors that influence the meaning and direction of the theory. It is also to point out the heuristic fruitfulness of attending to the political processes of creation or of institutional changes, constitutive of these plural globalizations. In other words, globalization in its phenomenal diversity cannot be explained solely by macro-sociological theories, whether they be neoinstitutionalist (WCT), neo-Marxist (Dale, 2000; Dale & Robertson, 2002), or more broadly critical (Carney et al., 2012; Silova & Brehm, 2015; Sobe, 2015). In contrast, the diversity of globalization is not subsumed by the sole factors of inertia or resistance to global cultural or political trends thematized by historical NI (cf. the second research strand).

Conclusion

This literature review clearly invites us not to overhomogenize neoinstitutionalist work on the globalization of educational policies. It shows that there are three ways to consider the role of the political dimension in the nature of institutions and institutional change involved in the globalization of education. The WCT perspective highlights the emergence of a world polity/society, emphasizes institutional diffusion mechanisms, and assigns a minor role to politics. The second one focuses on institutional mediations. Often (but not only) anchored in historical NI, it gives a central role to the policy dimension, but mainly from a "reception" paradigm. The last way, more hybrid (because it often relies on middle-range theories), has as its common point stress on the institutionalization dynamics and institutional work at the intersection of multilevel/multiscalar dimensions. If we were to model these three approaches, we would present them in three conceptual pairs: convergence and isomorphisms (strand 1), divergence and mediations (strand 2), and emergence and reconfigurations (strand 3). These three research strands all involve different visions of globalization, its political dimension, and institutions. These strands are synthesized in Table 6.1.

They show that the landscape of approaches labeled as neoinstitutionalist has become progressively more complex. A constructivist theory of globalization, leaving little room for the political question, has been increasingly challenged empirically by a current of analysis that emphasizes much more the importance of domestic policy processes and their local institutional or cultural anchors, but does so by making globalization a general institutional environment that is not really conceptualized. Finally, the third

Table 6.1 Research Strands

		Strand 1: Convergence/Isomorphisms	Strand 2: Divergence/Mediations	Strand 3: Emergence/Reconfigurations
Dimension 1: Globalization	Conceptualization of globalization	Cultural globalization (set of rationalized myths, scripts, and worldviews)	General environment as a source of institutional pressure	No real conceptualization
		Existence/influence of a world society, between world culture and world polity		
	Related concepts	Isomorphism, enactment (of identities, scripts), decoupling	Transnational doctrines, rankings	Transnational doctrines, rankings
	Role of NI in thinking about globalization	Major	Minor	Minor
Dimension 2: Institutions	Preferred type of NI	Sociological	Sociological and historical	Pluralist approaches to institutionalization
	Vision of institutional change	Mimetic, osmosis	Path dependency plus gradual changes plus instrumentation	Permanent (de-)institutionalizations
	Temporality of change	Long term	Medium term	Short term
	Main factors of change	Cognitive and normative mechanisms	Mechanisms, actors, instruments	Discourses and ideas, linked to actors (entrepreneurs) and instruments
Dimension 3: Political Question	Polity	Strong presence in analysis	Unevenly present in the analysis	Weak presence in the analysis
		Stateless world polity composed of international organizations and professional organizations	Recomposition of education policy models	
	Politics	Little present	Unevenly present. Struggles between institutional actors located	Strong presence. Importance of translation and deliberation processes
	Policy	Little present	Strong presence. Policy matters. (Instruments, bricolage, translation)	Strong presence (sensemaking, paradigms, discursive coalitions, arenas)

NI, neoinstitutionalism.

strand also strongly emphasizes the political struggles at work on several scales but that have difficulty in thinking about globalization in a theoretical and integrated way, in the diversity of its empirical paths and in the articulation of the processes and scales involved.

Therefore, we wish to stress in conclusion the need to develop this last point further. We argue it would be important in future theoretical developments to engage in a stronger dialogue with other theories of cultural globalization than WCT, whether this globalization is understood as a compression of time and space or through specific notions such as those of hybridization or creolization. Among these theories, the theory of vernacular globalizations developed by Arjun Appadurai (1996) and then introduced into the field of education by Bob Lingard (2006) seems to be a particularly fruitful perspective. By insisting on the role of cultural contexts that are more or less generative of specific globalized practices, it can be articulated particularly well with works from strands 2 and 3. Our research on accountability policies has indeed shown the interest of NI not only in thinking about long institutional trajectories (whether they be of policies, organizations, or school systems as a whole), and conceptually equipping the multiple inflection or translation modalities of these trajectories, but also in theoretically grasping contexts that are more or less generative of specific practices (Maroy et al., 2017). Tools of NI that have currently minor status, such as institutional orders or institutional configurations, could be very relevant for capturing the weight of these contexts and determining whether they give rise to vernacular globalizations, and the forms they take.

NOTES

1. "The claims of actorhood are rewarding, exorbitant and utterly unrealistic. Under elaborate, standardized and very general rules, actors are thought to have clear purposes, means-ends technologies and analysed resources. They are to have unified decision sovereignty, effective control of their internal activities and clearly defined boundaries. They are to have complete and accurate analyses of their environments. They are, in short, to be little gods" (Meyer, 2000, p. 237).
2. Some references ($n = 4$) have been classified under both strands 2 and 3.

REFERENCES

Note: References with asterisks are part of our corpus.

*Alexiadou, N., & van de Bunt-Kokhuis, S. (2013). Policy space and the governance of education: Transnational influences on institutions and identities in the Netherlands and the UK. *Comparative Education, 49*(3), 344–360. doi:10.1080/03050068.2013.803750

*Antonowicz, D., Kohoutek, J., Pinheiro, R., & Hladchenko, M. (2017). The roads of "excellence" in Central and Eastern Europe. *European Educational Research Journal, 16*(5), 547–567. doi:10.1177/1474904116683186

Appadurai, A. (1996). *Modernity at large: Cultural dimensions of globalization.* The University of Minnesota Press.

Arksey, H., & O'Malley, L. (2005). Scoping studies: Towards a methodological framework. *International Journal of Social Research Methodology, 8*(1), 19–32. doi:10.1080/1364557032000119616

*Astiz, M. F., Wiseman, Alexander W., & Baker, David P. (2002). Slouching towards decentralization: Consequences of globalization for curricular control in national education systems. *Comparative Education Review, 46*(1), 66–88. doi:10.1086/324050

Benavot, A., Cha, Y., Kamens, D., Meyer, J., & Wong, S. (1991). Knowledge for the masses: World models and national curricula, 1920–1986. [http://www.jstor.org/stable/2095675]. *American Sociological Review, 56* (1), 85–100.

Berger, P., & Luckmann, T. (1967). *The social construction of reality.* Doubleday.

Boli, J., Ramirez, F. O., & Meyer, J. W. (1985). Explaining the origins and expansion of mass education. *Comparative Education Review, 29*(2), 145–170. http://www.jstor.org/stable/1188401

Boli, J., & Thomas, G. M. (1999). INGOs and the organization of world culture. In J. Boli & G. M. Thomas (Eds.), *Constructing world culture: International nongovernmental organizations since 1875.* (pp. 13–49). Stanford University Press.

Boltanski, L. (2008). Institutions et critique sociale. Une approche pragmatique de la domination. *Tracés. Revue des Sciences Humaines, 08* (Hors-série 2008 Présents et futurs de la critique), 17–43.

Boxenbaum, E., & Pedersen, J. S. (2009). Scandinavian institutionalism—A case of institutional work. In T. B. Lawrence, R. Suddaby, & B. Leca (Eds.), *Institutional work: Actors and agency in institutional studies of organizations* (pp. 178–204). Cambridge University Press.

*Bromley, P., & Andina, M. (2010). Standardizing chaos: A neo-institutional analysis of the INEE minimum standards for education in emergencies, chronic crises and early reconstruction. *Compare: A Journal of Comparative and International Education, 40*(5), 575–588. https://search.proquest.com/docview/757168187?accountid=12543

*Buckner, E. (2020). Embracing the global: The role of ranking, research mandate, and sector in the internationalisation of higher education. *Compare: A Journal of Comparative and International Education,* 1–18. doi:10.1080/03057925.2020.1753499

*Burch, P., & Miglani, N. (2018). Technocentrism and social fields in the Indian EdTech movement: Formation, reproduction and resistance. *Journal of Education Policy, 33*(5), 590–616. doi:10.1080/02680939.2018.1435909

Callon, M. (1986). Some elements of a sociology of translation: domestication of the scallops and the fisherman in St Brieuc Bay. In K. Knorr-Cetina & A. V. Cicourel (Eds.), *Advances in social theory and methodology: Toward an integration of micro and macro-sociologies* (pp. 196–223.). Routledge & Kegan Paul.

Campbell, J. L. (2004). *Institutional change and globalization.* Princeton University Press.

*Carney, S., Rappleye, J., & Silova, I. (2012). Between faith and science: World culture theory and comparative education. *Comparative Education Review, 56*(3), 366–393. doi:10.1086/665708

*Corbett, A. (2011). Ping pong: Competing leadership for reform in EU higher education 1998–2006. *European Journal of Education, 46*(1), 36–53. http://dx.doi.org/10.1111/j.1465-3435.2010.01466.x

*Csizmadia, T., Enders, J., & Westerheijden, D. F. (2008). Quality management in Hungarian higher education: Organisational responses to governmental policy. *Higher Education: The*

International Journal of Higher Education and Educational Planning, 56(4), 439–455. http://dx.doi.org/10.1007/s10734-007-9103-3

*Dahan, A., Draelants, H., & Dumay, X. (2016). Quand être soi ne suffit plus. Les nouvelles modalités du travail identitaire des universités belges francophones. *Recherches Sociologiques et anthropologiques, 47*(1), 111–131. doi:10.4000/rsa.1626

*Dale, R. (2000). Globalization and Education: Demonstrating a "Common World Educational Culture" or Locating a "Globally Structured Educational Agenda"? *Educational Theory, 50*(4), 427–448.

*Dale, R. (2005). Globalisation, knowledge economy and comparative education. *Comparative Education, 41*(2), 117–149. http://www.informaworld.com/10.1080/03050060500150906

*Dale, R., & Robertson, S. L. (2002). The varying effects of regional organizations as subjects of globalization of education. *Comparative Education Review, 46*(1), 10–36. http://ovidsp.ovid.com/ovidweb.cgi?T=JS&CSC=Y&NEWS=N&PAGE=fulltext&D=eric3&AN=EJ645961

*Demailly, L., Giuliani, F., & Maroy, C. (2019). "Le changement institutionnel: processus et acteurs" [En ligne]. *Sociologies*. http://journals.openedition.org/sociologies/9999

DiMaggio, P. J., & Powell, W. W. (1983). The iron cage revisited: Institutional isomorphism and collective rationality in organisational fields *American Sociological Review, 48*(2), 147–160.

*Dobbins, M. (2011). Explaining different pathways in higher education policy in Romania and the Czech Republic. *Comparative Education, 47*(2), 223–245. doi:10.1080/03050068.2011.555116

*Dobbins, M. (2017). Exploring higher education governance in Poland and Romania: Re-convergence after divergence? *European Educational Research Journal, 16*(5), 684–704. doi:10.1177/1474904116684138

Drori, G. S. (2008). Institutionalism and globalization studies. In R. Greenwood, C. Oliver, K. Sahlin, & R. Suddaby (Eds.), *The SAGE handbook of organizational institutionalism* (pp. 449–472). Sage.

*Erkkilä, T., & Kauppi, N. (2013). Définir l'université mondiale. Les logiques de compétition et l'internationalisation de l'enseignement supérieur. In *Services sans frontières* (pp. 317–336). Presses de Sciences Po.

*Hajisoteriou, C. (2010). Europeanising intercultural education: Politics and policy making in Cyprus. *European Educational Research Journal, 9*(4), 471–483. doi:10.2304/eerj.2010.9.4.471

*Hartley, D. (2003). Education as a global positioning device: Some theoretical considerations. *Comparative Education, 39*(4), 439–450. doi:10.1080/0305006032000162011

*Holland, Dana G. (2010). Waves of educational model production: The case of higher education institutionalization in Malawi, 1964–2004. *Comparative Education Review, 54*(2), 199–222. doi:10.1086/651139

*Hsieh, C.-C. (2016). A way of policy bricolage or translation: The case of Taiwan's higher education reform of quality assurance. *Policy Futures in Education, 14*(7), 873–888. http://dx.doi.org/10.1177/1478210316645250

*Hsieh, C.-C., & Huisman, J. (2017). Higher education policy change in the European higher education area: Divergence of quality assurance systems in England and the Netherlands. *Research Papers in Education, 32*(1), 71–83. http://dx.doi.org/10.1080/02671522.2015.1129645

*Jakobi, A. P. (2011). Political parties and the institutionalization of education: A comparative analysis of party manifestos. *Comparative Education Review, 55*(2), 189–209. doi:10.1086/657931

*Jakobi, A. P., & Rusconi, A. (2009). Lifelong learning in the Bologna process: European developments in higher education. *Compare: A Journal of Comparative and International Education, 39*(1), 51–65. doi:10.1080/03057920801936977

Jepperson, R., & Meyer, J. W. (2011). Multiple levels of analysis and the limitations of methodological individualisms. *Sociological Theory, 29*(1), 54–73. doi:10.1111/j.1467-9558.2010.01387.x

*Kamens, D. H., & McNeely, C. L. (2010). Globalization and the growth of international educational testing and national assessment. *Comparative Education Review, 54*(1), 5–25. doi:10.1086/648471

Lascoumes, P., & Le Gales, P. (2007). Introduction: Understanding public policy through its instruments? From the nature of instruments to the sociology of public policy instrumentation. *Governance, 20*(1), 1–21. doi:10.1111/j.1468-0491.2007.00342.x

Lawrence, T. B., Suddaby, R., & Leca, B. (2009). Introduction: theorizing and studying institutional work In T. B. Lawrence, R. Suddaby, & B. Leca (Eds.), *Institutional work: Actors and agency in institutional studies of organizations* (pp. 1–27). Cambridge University Press.

Leca, J. (2012). L'État entre politics, policies et polity ou peut-on sortir du triangle des Bermudes? *Gouvernement et action publique, 1*(1), 59–82.

*Lee, M., Thayer, T., & Madyun, N. i. (2008). The evolution of the European Union's lifelong learning policies: An institutional learning perspective. *Comparative Education, 44*(4), 445–463. doi:10.1080/03050060802481496

Lingard, B. (2006). Globalisation, the research imagination and deparochialising the study of education. *Globalisation, Societies and Education, 4*(2), 287–302.

*Luova, O. (2020). Local environmental governance and policy implementation: Variegated environmental education in three districts in Tianjin, China. *Urban Studies, 57*(3), 490–507. http://dx.doi.org/10.1177/0042098019862230

*Maroy, C., Mangez, C., Dumay, X., & Cattonar, B. (2012). Processus de traduction et institutionnalisation d'outils de régulation basés sur les connaissances dans l'enseignement primaire en Belgique. *Recherches sociologiques et anthropologiques, 43*(2), 95–119. doi:10.4000/rsa.795

Maroy, C., Pons, X., & Dupuy, C. (2017). Vernacular globalisations: Neo-statist accountability policies in France and Quebec education. *Journal of Education Policy, 32*(1), 100–122. doi:10.1080/02680939.2016.1239841

*Maroy, C., & Vaillancourt, S. (2019). L'instrumentation de la nouvelle gestion publique dans les écoles québécoises: Dispositifs et travail de changement institutionnel. *SociologieS [En ligne]* (Dossiers, Le changement institutionnel, mis en ligne le 27 février 2019). http://journ als.openedition.org/sociologies/10075

*Massouti, A. (2018). (Re)thinking the adoption of inclusive education policy in Ontario schools. *Canadian Journal of Educational Administration and Policy, 185*, 32–44. https://sea rch.proquest.com/docview/2101378093?accountid=12543

*Maurer, M. (2012). Structural elaboration of technical and vocational education and training systems in developing countries: The cases of Sri Lanka and Bangladesh. *Comparative Education, 48*(4), 487–503. doi:10.1080/03050068.2012.702011

Mays, N., Roberts, E., & Popay, J. (2001). Synthesising research evidence. In N. Fulop, P. Allen, A. Clarke, & N. Black (Eds.), *Studying the organisation and delivery of health services: Research methods* (pp. 188–220). Routledge.

*McClure, K. R. (2017). Arbiters of effectiveness and efficiency: The frames and strategies of management consulting firms in US higher education reform. *Journal of Higher Education Policy and Management, 39*(5), 575–589. http://dx.doi.org/10.1080/1360080X.2017.1354753

*Mehta, J. (2013). How paradigms create politics: The transformation of American educational policy, 1980–2001. *American Educational Research Journal, 50*(2), 285–324. http://dx.doi. org/10.3102/0002831212471417

Meyer, H.-D., & Rowan, B. (2006). *The new institutionalism in education*. SUNY Press.

Meyer, J. W. (2000). Globalization: Sources and effects on national states and societies. *International Sociology, 15*(2), 233–248. doi:10.1177/0268580900015002006

Meyer, J. W., Boli, J., Thomas, G. M., & Ramirez, F. O. (1997). World society and the nation-state. *The American Journal of Sociology, 103*(1), 144–181. http://www.jstor.org/stable/2782801

Meyer, J. W., & Rowan, B. (1977). Institutionalized organizations: Formal structure as myth and ceremony. *American Journal of Sociology, 83*(2), 340–363. doi:10.2307/2778293

Meyer, J. W., & Scott, W. R. (Eds.). (1983). *Organisationnal environments: Ritual and rationality*. Sage.

*Mignot-Gérard, S. (2012). Le gouvernement d'une université face aux "Initiatives d'Excellence": Réactivité et micro-résistances. *Politiques et Management Public, 29*(3), 519–539.

*Mincu, M. E. (2015). The Italian middle school in a deregulation era: Modernity through path-dependency and global models. *Comparative Education, 51*(3), 446–462. doi:10.1080/03050068.2015.1033249

*Niemann, D., Hartong, S., & Martens, K. (2018). Observing local dynamics of ILSA projections in federal systems: A comparison between Germany and the United States. *Globalisation, Societies and Education, 16*(5), 596–608. doi:10.1080/14767724.2018.1531237

*Powell, J. J. W., Edelstein, B., & Blanck, J. M. (2016). Awareness-raising, legitimation or backlash? Effects of the UN Convention on the Rights of Persons with Disabilities on education systems in Germany. *Globalisation, Societies and Education, 14*(2), 227–250. doi:10.1080/14767724.2014.982076

Powell, J. J. W., Fernandez, F., Crist, J. T., Dusdal, J., Zhang, L., & Baker, D. P. (2017). Introduction: The worldwide triumph of the research university and globalizing science. *International Perspectives on Education and Society, 33*, 1–36. http://dx.doi.org/10.1108/S1479-367920170000033003

*Ramirez, F. O. (2012). The world society perspective: Concepts, assumptions, and strategies. *Comparative Education, 48*(4), 423–439. doi:10.1080/03050068.2012.693374

Ramirez, F. O., & Meyer, J. W. (1980). Comparative education: The social construction of the modern world system. *Annual Review of Sociology, 6*, 369–399.

Ramirez, F. O., Meyer, J. W., & Lerch, J. C. (2016). World society and the globalization of educational policy. In K. Mundy, A. Green, R. Lingard, & A. Verger (Eds.), *The handbook of global education policy* (pp. 43–63). Wiley-Blackwell.

*Rosser, A. (2016). Neo-liberalism and the politics of higher education policy in Indonesia. *Comparative Education, 52*(2), 109–135. doi:10.1080/03050068.2015.1112566

*Saint-Martin, D. (2002). Apprentissage social et changement institutionnel: La politique de "l'investissement dans l'enfance" au Canada et en Grande-Bretagne. *Politique et sociétés, 21*(3), 41–67. https://id.erudit.org/iderudit/000496ar

Schmidt, V. A. (2008). Discursive institutionalism: The explanatory power of ideas and discourse. *Annual Review of Political Science, 11*(1), 303–326. doi:10.1146/annurev.polisci.11.060606.135342

*Schriewer, J. (2012). Editorial: Meaning constellations in the world society. *Comparative Education, 48*(4), 411–422. doi:10.1080/03050068.2012.737233

*Schwinn, T. (2012). Globalisation and regional variety: Problems of theorisation. *Comparative Education, 48*(4), 525–543. doi:10.1080/03050068.2012.728048

Scott, W. R. (1995). *Institutions and organizations: Toward a theoretical synthesis*: Sage.

Scott, W. R., & Meyer, J. W. (1994). *Institutional environments and organizations: Structural complexity and individualism.* Sage.

*Silova, I., & Brehm, W. C. (2015). From myths to models: The (re)production of world culture in comparative education. *Globalisation, Societies and Education, 13*(1), 8–33. doi:10.1080/14767724.2014.967483

*Sobe, N. W. (2015). All that is global is not world culture: Accountability systems and educational apparatuses. *Globalisation, Societies and Education, 13*(1), 135–148. doi:10.1080/14767724.2014.967501

Steiner-Khamsi, G., & Waldow, F. (Eds.). (2012). *World yearbook of education 2012. Policy borrowing and lending in education.* Routledge.

*Takayama, K. (2012). Exploring the interweaving of contrary currents: Transnational policy enactment and path-dependent policy implementation in Australia and Japan. *Comparative Education, 48*(4), 505–523. doi:10.1080/03050068.2012.721631

Thomas, G. M. (2009). World polity, world culture, world society. *International Political Sociology, 3*(1), 115–119.

*Verger, A., Fontdevila, C., & Parcerisa, L. (2019). Reforming governance through policy instruments: How and to what extent standards, tests and accountability in education spread worldwide. *Discourse: Studies in the Cultural Politics of Education, 40*(2), 248–270. doi:10.1080/01596306.2019.1569882

*Wahlström, N., & Sundberg, D. (2018). Discursive institutionalism: Towards a framework for analysing the relation between policy and curriculum. *Journal of Education Policy, 33*(1), 163–183. doi:10.1080/02680939.2017.1344879

*Wiseman, A. W., Astiz, M. F., & Baker, D. P. (2014). Comparative education research framed by neo-institutional theory: A review of diverse approaches and conflicting assumptions. *Compare: A Journal of Comparative and International Education, 44*(5), 688–709. doi:10.1080/03057925.2013.800783

*Zapp, M., & Ramirez, F. O. (2019). Beyond internationalisation and isomorphism—The construction of a global higher education regime. *Comparative Education, 55*(4), 473–493. doi:10.1080/03050068.2019.1638103

CHAPTER 7

GLOBALIZATION, CULTURAL LOGICS, AND THE TEACHING PROFESSION

GERALD K. LETENDRE

INTRODUCTION

CONCERNS about the teacher's role—what should the teacher do and how critical is that work—have come to occupy the attention of transnational organizations (OECD, 2005; UNESCO, 2006), national governments (Akiba, 2013), and academics (Paine & Zeichner, 2012; Robertson, 2000). While neoinstitutionalist theory offered a powerful explanatory framework for understanding the genesis and relationship of mass schooling to the rise of modern nation state (Boli et al., 1985), it offered little analysis of the role that teachers played in the rise of mass schooling. In order to understand the ongoing patterns of national differences and global similarities in teachers' work (Kim, 2019; LeTendre et al., 2001) theorists needed to account for micro- and meso-levels of interaction. Subsequent theoretical traditions (world society and world polity) emerged and emphasized the mimetic and normative diffusion of universalistic cultural scripts (Buhari-Gulmez, 2010), but unraveling how globalization has affected the role of teachers within mass schooling and the nation state requires theoretical mechanisms that can account for the role that teachers play in institutional change (Niemi et al., 2018).

World culture theorists (e.g., Baker & LeTendre, 2005) accepted the neoinstitutional perspective that "institutions constrain human action; scripts, norms, and rules concatenate to form cultural logics" (Rao & Giorgi, 2006, pp. 269–270), but they sought to better understand the processes that create persistent national differences in classroom practices and school routines. The idea that teachers (as individuals or groups) might resist or modify the institutional rules or "rational myths" that undergird the organization of mass schooling aligned world culture theorists with scholars who took an anthropological or culturalist perspective on globalization (Anderson-Levitt, 2003). Understanding how teachers are affected by globalization, and what role they play in the process of institutional change required theoretical elaboration of (a) the relationship between culture and institutions; (b) the "institutional work" (Suddaby, 2010) teachers do to transmit or disrupt institutional patterns (Thornton et al., 2012); and (c) how "institutional logics" may conflict or align with broader cultural systems of meaning, that is, "cultural logics."

Elaborating these three points is made difficult because theorists have often used the terms "culture" and "institution" almost interchangeably (see arguments in Alesina & Giuliano, 2015). Many, like Guiso et al. (2015), follow North (1991) in differentiating between "informal institutions" (taboos, customs) and "formal institutions" (those with some legal standing). The problem with such a dichotomy is that our thinking is structured by both cultural and institutional logics as Douglas (1986) discussed. Furthermore, as Colyvas and Jonsson (2011) demonstrate, sociologists have defined institutionalization both as a process of "integration . . . into a social order without substantial recurrent mobilization" (e.g., "taken-for-grantedness") as well as the ability to "sanction or enforce it, such as law or government policy" (e.g., "legitimization"). This adds to the difficulty in separating out "cultural" from "institutional" effects. Finally, the culture of most national societies has been shaped by the profusion of organizational forms (Scott, 1995) and thus imbued with the "packets of meaning" that organizational forms transmit (Berger et al., 1974).

In the subsequent sections of this chapter, I will work to further define cultural and institutional logics and clarify how they interact by first reviewing how research on teacher work roles raised awareness of the fact that both nation-specific cultural logics and the institutional logics of mass schooling appear to define these roles. Such work also identified the need for a theory of teachers themselves as agents of institutional change. In the second section, I propose that further theoretical mechanisms (resonance and elaboration) are required to explain how actors on the local and national levels incorporate both institutional and cultural logics into their sense-making (see Akiba, 2017, for a discussion of sense-making and national reform). In the third section, I demonstrate that clearly differentiating between the concepts of "legitimacy" and "taken-for-grantedness" highlights how teachers (as individuals or groups) or other actors utilize dissonance between cultural and institutional logics to create change. In the conclusion, I note that the dramatic expansion of information and communication technologies will generate more diverse and highly elaborated cultural logics that can be rapidly disseminated in an increasingly interconnected world.

Teachers as Agents of Institutional Change or Stability

There has been little research on the role that teachers played in either the institutionalization of mass schooling, its persistence, or the deinstitutionalization of specific forms of schooling (e.g., segregated schools in the United States). Historical research on the earliest stages of globalization suggests that the diffusion of the "new" institution of mass schooling involved considerable borrowing and adaptation consistent with a process of pervasive cultural adaption of organizational forms (Lincicome, 1995) as well as a far greater role for coercive (e.g., military) force (Tsurumi, 1977). Thus, by the end of World War II, there was more cross-national variation in the status of teachers as a mass profession than was later identified in classic works on semi-professions (Etzioni, 1969; Lortie, 1975) that focused only on the United States.

Mass Education, Teachers, and the Nation State

The lack of theorizing about teachers in various neoinstitutional strands reflects the mindset of the times, particularly within sociological circles. Like Etzioni (1969) or Lortie (1969), theorists understood globalization as a supranational process and teachers as essentially hired workers within national institutions. In Meyer's seminal essay on the effects of education as an institution (Meyer, 1977), he did not define a role for teachers (or administrators) in either altering or elaborating the "taken-for-granted" rationales of schooling. Rather, he located agentic force at the institutional level (e.g., the transnational institutions of mass schooling and the nation state legitimate the status of teachers and other professionals). Further expansion of this theory moved beyond the idea of mass schooling as an exogenous global model, to positing "education as a primary, culture constructing institution" (Baker, 2014, p. 13). In other words, school as its own "self-referencing" (Mangez et al., 2017) system is given a more dynamic role in the ongoing process of cultural production in world culture theory.

Because teachers were largely ignored in early neoinstitutional work, their relationship to the state was also ignored, and the status or actorhood of teachers was not fully articulated. As national systems of education developed, particularly in the late 1800s and early 1900s, the institutional logic of mass schooling in many states was founded on the idea of enculturation of future citizens. The focus on human rights (Meyer et al., 2010) arose later and is most clearly seen in nations with post–World War II constitutions. Even later, the idea of national citizens who participate in a global world as "global citizens" emerged (Kamens, 2012), but never effectively disseminated and continues to be most prevalent in unstable national states. In Japan, the teacher's status as a civil servant carrying out the state's authority to assure the enculturation of future citizens was established early in the modern era, and Japanese teachers have exhibited an ability to alter school reforms not seen in nations that weakly developed these institutional logics (Lincicome, 1995; Schoppa, 1991; Thurston, 1973).

National Differences as Variation in Cultural Logics

This gives us our first key insight: National differences are not simply localized accommodations legitimated by an external world society as seen in world society theory; that is, "locals of the modern world become relatively standardized variants of

locals everywhere else" (Drori & Krucken, 2009, p. 267). This can be seen in Japan—
"The rapid implementation of a national school system not only eliminated many . . .
traditional forms of learning and teaching but also subordinated those that survived"
(Rohlen & LeTendre 1995, p. 12). Although subordinated to the dominant institutional
logic of mass schooling within Japan (and likely other nations, see the case of Amish
schooling in the United States; Hostetler & Huntington, 1992), multiple alternative
"logics" continued to exist. Institutions like the family are also differently constructed
in different national contexts, raising the issue of conflict between cultural and institutional logics of child-rearing and teaching in the early years of the child's life (Tobin et
al., 1989). This "cultural pluralization of the world" (Friedman, 1988) is part of a global
cultural dynamic where national school systems become sites of cultural production,
enjoining us to understand what role teachers play in that process.

The subsequent debates about the effects of national, regional, or local cultures ("national culture") and transnational or globally shared cultures ("world culture") increasingly came to focus on what teachers do in their classrooms, not on national curriculum
guidelines or plans. This has raised many points of disagreement about how transnational organizational actors affect what goes on in classrooms around the world.
Attempts to understand how national differences persist in the face of global transformation processes have increasingly used data about teachers (Baker & LeTendre, 2005;
LeTendre, Baker et al., 2001) or classroom instruction (Desimone, Smith et al., 2005) to
assess the presence or absence of change. But, to account for teachers and their impact in
the transnational flows of information and reform, scholars in world culture traditions
have had to contend directly with how global and local forces might simultaneously affect instructional practice.

National Cultures of Teaching

Part of what drove an increasing awareness of national cultures that defied transnational
isomorphism were influential cross-national studies from culturalist and anthropological traditions. Tobin et al. (1989) showed profound differences in teachers' work as well
as in general attitudes toward child development in nations which had already seen significant isomorphic convergence in terms of school organization, curriculum, and other
aspects. This work was supported by studies that showed profound differences in individual identity development in nations like Japan (Shimizu & Levine, 2001). Finally, the
influential TIMSS video studies (Hiebert et al., 2005; Stigler et al., 2000) demonstrated
that even when teaching the exact same mathematics lesson, teachers in different nations approached the task in radically different ways that were easily recognizable as
consistent with national patterns.

Cross-national studies in the anthropological tradition had long posited that national
cultures of schooling are sustained by the day-to-day actions of teachers (Anderson-
Levitt, 1987; Spindler, 1987; Stevenson et al., 1978; Tobin et al., 1989). These anthropological theories adopted a "bottom-up" approach to institutionalization in which national

patterns of instruction are constantly being shaped by the actions of students and teachers in school. Such theories emphasized the cultural stability of institutions over long periods of time but gave significant emphasis to interactions between micro- and meso-levels on influencing national cultures of teaching. A full-fledged theory of how national cultures of teaching and learning created national differences in cognitive and academic outcomes among students (Stevenson & Stigler, 1992) was later extended to theories of effective teaching (Stigler & Hiebert, 1998, 1999). Stigler explicitly connected cultural patterns to efficacious teaching (Stigler & Stevenson, 1991). In their eponymous work, Stigler and Hiebert state not only that "teaching is a cultural activity" but one that has significant, lasting effects on students in a globalized world.

Actors, Levels, and Institutional Logics

Understanding the role that teachers play in the global diffusion of educational reforms requires a theory of cultural change at multiple levels. However, while conceptually useful, theories of macro- versus micro-levels oversimplify how the process of change occurs. As Thorton et al. (2012) noted, "individuals and organizations, if only subliminally, are aware of the differences in the cultural norms, symbols, and practices of different institutional orders and incorporate this diversity into their thoughts, beliefs, and decision making" (p. 4). Individuals interact at the micro-level, but their organizational frame of action may range from the local to the transnational. Individuals carry the cultural accounts and explanation of what the institution does and why (Spindler, 1977), and their frames of experience affect the account of the rationality that actors may use to interpret experiences within the frame of prevailing institutional logics at the level at which the organization has effects.

Drawing on Cuban's theory of the situationally constrained choices that teachers make, Gardiner (2011) emphasizes that teachers are "situated actors whose particular knowledge and expertise enable them to serve as both agents of change and stakeholders of continuity," at least in terms of local schools. Cultural change often occurs when new logics are introduced. Swidler (1986) noted that in times of social upheaval, cultural symbols become open to reuse and reinterpretation. The presentation of new institutional logics, in the form of globally diffusing reforms, may initiate such scenarios for teachers in some nations. To address adequately how some routines are learned by some organizations and not by others requires a theory about how actors within organizations organize meaning by adapting or modifying institutional logics. This means that institutional logics may be shaped, over time, by the frames of experience of individual actors, but the actions of teachers will likely be limited to the organization of the local school they work in.

Individual frames of experience are structured by institutional roles, but actors have the potential to play many roles and experience many frames of experience. Every individual engages in some process of sense-making, and it follows that the greater number of frames an individual experiences, the wider the range of interpretations that individual is open to, and the greater their capacity to interpret or imagine new scenarios. Teachers who have experienced a range of different cultural logics in their local environment may then be motivated, as actors within the institution of mass schooling, to ignore, revise, or even reject the dominant institutional logics of mass schooling: "glocalization is indeed a multilayered process that involves the discussion, adoption, and adaptation processes between global and local levels" (Astiz & Akiba, 2016, p. 3).

Cultural Logics and Institutional Change

Both neoinstitutional and national cultural models rely on static notions of culture that fail to capture the complexity of how culture and institutional logics affect teachers. Drori et al. (2006) noted that "cultural materials accumulate and are institutionalized at the global level over time" (p. 259). Stigler and Hiebert (1999) suggested that teachers are following "national scripts" for teaching which are part of "national cultures." An alternative, and more dynamic model, has been proposed by Anderson-Levitt (2003, pp. 12–13; see Chapter 2 in this volume), who borrowed the Spindler's concept of "cultural dialog" (Spindler & Spindler, 1990). The concept of a "dialog" emphasizes ongoing interaction and change. It can account for the fact that individuals may often have experience with multiple cultural or institutional logics of education and learning.

As Akiba indicates, the idea of interaction between levels needs to be conceived as a "multilayered process" which recognizes the heterogeneity that exists within each level. At the local level, teachers must reconcile the cultural logics (the values, norms, and expectations for teachers and students) of their local communities with the institutional logic of mass schooling. Indeed, there is strong evidence that there are multiple cultural logics at play at the transnational level (Fraser & Ikoma, 2015). The institutional logic of mass schooling has itself grown more complex over time, allowing new patterns of actorhood for teachers to be institutionalized. Modernity brings complexity to every "level," and this affects the level of institutionalization of organizational forms at multiple "levels."

Institutional Change Is Cultural Change

Neoinstitutional theory, in the 1990s, had reached a point of "theoretical gridlock" with regard to hypotheses about how institutional change occurs. Virtually all the important conceptual work on institutional change focused on the process of institutionalization—how things come to be institutions. Zucker (1977) correctly identified this as a theory of cultural persistence. Both Zucker (1983) and Jepperson (1991) conceptualized institutionalization as one way that social patterns of behavior remain stable across time. Implicit in this formulation is that everyday actions are reenactments of cognitively normative forces which would result in no possibility of change. But as we have seen, culturalist studies indicate that individuals negotiate these logics on a daily basis. Swidler's work (1986) on publicly available meanings showed that there is the possibility for individuals to question, contest, or reinterpret these meanings. Studies of teachers in the Global South suggest persistent, ongoing change perhaps because these teachers have indigenous "publicly available meanings" to draw on (Anderson-Levitt, 2004; Gardiner, 2011; Shinn, 2012).

The difference between "institutional logics" and "cultural logics" is not bounded by a clear line. As organizational forms, institutions like the school have highly codified dimensions, for example, "classifications often controlled by the state and enforced in daily life by rules about credentials written into law" (Meyer, 1977, p. 65). Organizations exist within the larger sphere of cultural interactions and expectations which includes "institutions" like "childhood," "individual," "lifecourse," or even "adolescence" (Aries, 1962; LeTendre, 2000; Mintz, 2004; Shanahan, 2000). Such institutions may vary in the degree they are codified in policies, laws, court decisions, and so on, but all have "taken-for-granted" meanings widely recognized within the population. Neoinstitutionalist studies (e.g., Boli & Meyer, 1978) focused on the codification of childhood in legal, policy, or treaty agreements while culturalist studies like Tobin et al. (1989) looked at the publicly shared meanings of childhood exemplified in everyday life. We can theoretically disaggregate legitimacy and taken-for-grantedness, but both aspects play a significant role in the cultural persistence of childhood and hence national differences in how schooling for children is constructed.

One form of institutional change results when cultural logics become codified into the existing universe of publicly available meanings within a given society. This process is different from change produced by exogenous shocks or long-term "institutional drift" that occurs when core institutional rationales and processes are kept intact, but significant change occurs in non-core processes (see Graf, Chapter 3, this volume). The reorganization of meaning over time occurs as individuals have experienced conflict among the institutional and cultural logics they encounter in daily life. A major way that globalization induces institutional change "is by interrupting 'thinking as usual'—the taken-for granted understandings and worldviews that shape cognitive and metacognitive styles and practices" (Suarez-Orozco & Qin-Hilliard, 2004, p. 4).

As transglobal educational reforms—based on rationalized beliefs about human capital development and individual rights rooted in Western European Christianity and capitalism—spread over the globe, they did indeed supplant premodern national school systems (Rohlen & LeTendre, 1995) creating significant uniformity in basic school processes and school structures. But at the same time older logics did not disappear completely. Religious systems of education—*Madrassah*, *Yeshiva*, and Buddhist monastic systems—still play a major role in many nations. Baker (2014) has speculated that one effect of mass schooling is that it may actually stimulate a revival of religiosity, a potential source of new logics for schooling (e.g., homeschooling).

The remnants or premodern educational institutions are not the only source of alternative cultural logics. Stein (2004) showed that with each new policy that governments implement comes the potential for the generation of new public meanings: "through the myriad interpretations of policy makers, policy implementers, policy target populations and policy analysts" (p. 6). Actors at local and regional levels within nations interpret policies in various ways, with substantial variation in how policies get enacted in the day-to-day operation of the school. Enactment and adaptations of new policies can even create new classes of actors that must then be accommodated within the institutional logic of the school (see Stein, 2004, for a discussion of "paraprofessionals").

Globalization has also allowed new models to be developed and spread. For example, Maguire (2002), Bartlett (2003), and Tarlau (2019) examined the conflict between national policies and alternative models of teacher practice and education informed by Freirean philosophy. Political parties may also engage in active "borrowing" of cultural logics to promote national reforms (Takayama & Apple, 2008). This highlights the fact that multiple logics are available at each level. It is not simply that "at the local level, teachers . . . adopt, mediate, resist or reject reforms" based on local cultural logics (Napier, 2003, p. 64). At the national level, reformers and policymakers may be dealing with conflicting institutional logics of educational reform that are globally diffusing. The overall isomorphic process observed during the rise and growth of mass schooling has evolved into a world cultural dynamic where multiple models of schooling and educational reform compete for attention. In such a dynamic environment, actors must make sense of logics that may conflict with, or resonant well with, one another.

Key Mechanism: Resonance

Globally diffusing models may not resonate with local cultural logics. In my work on the diffusion of adolescence, I used the metaphor of competing "storylines" to show how teachers adopted different rationalized myths about adolescence in Japan compared to the United States (LeTendre, 2000). Stark and Spreen (2020) use the concept of "global resonance" to account for how the GERM model is globally diffusing. This suggests that original theories of diffusion of change in organizational fields (Dimaggio & Powell, 1983) missed a key facet of institutional change: whether or not there is resonance with existing cultural logics or whether there may be different institutional logics at play. Early formulations of institutional isomorphism were developed at a time when the concept of institutional fields was underdeveloped. As institutional fields become more elaborated—more populated with multiple logics—it is more likely for new forms to emerge.

A similar concept emerges in the work of Bridwell-Mitchell (2020) on the micro-level processes of US school reform. She advances the theory of "institutional interstitiality" "defined as the cognitive state in which two alternative possible realities are juxtaposed in ways that disrupt institutionalized beliefs and practices" (p. 432). What occurs then is the opposite of resonance. The discordance between institutional logics works to make "accepted reality less durable," thus opening up the way to replacing or altering existing institutional logics.

In his paper on global convergence and national variation, Kim (2019) found long-term evidence of cross-national convergence in teaching practice, but in some respects within-nation variation actually increased over time. He shows that an increase in within-nation variation may be characteristic in the early stages of adoption, but he then goes on to speculate that future studies should "examine why the globally preferred pedagogical model does not resonate well in countries with centralized curriculum" (p. 371). This raises the interesting point that as a new educational reform enters a nation, it may undergo elaboration, but those key rational myths or storylines must find some resonance or similarity with existing cultural logics. Teacher and policymaker engagement in a sense-making process is likely to drive adaptation (Akiba, 2017) in ways similar to the "creolization" theory proposed in Anderson-Levitt (2003).

Key Mechanism: Power to Communicate and Define

Actors are provided with opportunities to change institutional logics when the institutional logics are in conflict with prevailing widespread cultural beliefs (in the case of adolescence mentioned earlier, see LeTendre, 2000) or when they can create new logics (Aurini, 2012). Institutions exist in a larger milieu of cultural beliefs or "social rationales or accounts" to use Jepperson's terms, but individuals vary enormously in their power to emphasize certain rationales (Suddaby & Greenwood, 2005). "There is a growing awareness that the manipulation of institutional logics is a fundamental mechanism of institutional change" (Green, 2004, p. 62). That is, to understand how the institution of school changes (or stays the same) as globalization progresses requires a theory of power to disseminate new visions or undercut old ones.

To adequately account for how institutional logics diffuse in a time of intense globalization requires a theoretical mechanism that accounts for differential power in disseminating beliefs. As Koyama (2013) showed, individuals exhibit different capabilities to marshal resources to communicate their beliefs. In the case of national policy debates, we see that sustained and coordinated communication (largely through the mass media) have indeed shaped public perception of the taken-for-granted functioning of public schooling (Berliner, 1992; Berliner & Biddle, 1995; Takayama, 2007). And, as Takayama (2007) further shows, this can result in formal policy changes (e.g., delegitimizing the institutional or actorhood within institutions). There is a clear element of power involved, and that power is defined by an organization or individual's ability to continually disseminate accounts that question the taken-for-granted assumptions we have about schooling.

The power of communication is ultimately tied to historically conditioned factors that affect teachers' ability to mobilize as national collectives. For example, Kim (2019, p. 357) found that "countries with centralised control of curriculum tended to buffer the global drift toward student-centered instruction, instead maintaining lecture-oriented classrooms and teacher control over instructional activities." National ministries, then, can affect the ability of teachers as individuals, or as collectives, to mobilize for change. Schoppa (1991) showed how Japan's national educational ministry engaged in "immobilist policies" subsequent to decades of remarkable collective activism by teachers (see also Duke, 1973). The delegation of educational powers to the states in the United States has resulted in a de facto system of 50 independent systems, and this focuses union attention on state-level policies (Earley et al., 2011) and exemplifies how extreme decentralization can also work to inhibit the efficacy of teacher collective action for institutional change.

Global Diffusion of Institutional Logics Across Multiple Levels

The concept of a "world society," first articulated in the 1980s (see Hufner, Meyer et al., 1987), is actually a theory of globalization which was subsequently elaborated (Drori et al., 2006; Meyer, 2007) to emphasize the "embeddedness" of local organizations and actors in the world society. This perspective, in some ways, conflates the cognitive and normative aspects of how institutions are sustained. In a world where actors have increasing access to multiple cultural logics, it is critical to distinguish between legitimacy as normative pressure residing in laws, treaties, and court decisions and the "taken-for-granted" status that allows certain logics to be routinely enacted by teachers in classrooms around the world.

But, in focusing on differences between levels (e.g., micro, meso, and macro), both theories of a world culture, on one hand, and culturalist theories, on the other, artificially reify the difference between global, national, regional, and local levels. All of these "levels" are interrelated and probably better conceptualized as continua or at least interpenetrating spheres (see Appadurai, 2010). Regarding teachers, Akiba (2017) states that "global dynamics" are actually constituted by an ongoing "collective sense-making" that involves contestation and negation with and across levels. Cultural and institutional logics are being reproduced or altered at all levels. Individuals, from teachers at a local level to ministers of education at a national or transnational level, are all engaged in the cultural "work" of collective sense-making and bring to it their individual frames of experience.

Micro-Processes Across Levels: Frames of Experience

Jepperson (1991) emphasizes that institutions are reproduced in distinct ways from other social phenomena, and that we have cultural accounts for certain organizations or behaviors, ranging from handshakes to hospitals. Douglas, in her seminal work, argued that institutions organize the categories of our thinking. For Douglas (1986), institutions are used in basic analogies to identify the pertinent features of the world and to set up the rules of rationality and causality. How then are these accounts of the world changed?

To understand how institutions change, one must have a theory of the everyday experience of actors within the institution, what Aurini (2012) calls the "inhabited institution," and how individual sense-making and action affect the broader organization and thus the institutional form of the organization. Early insight into how individual frames of experience within organizations resulted in organizational learning can offer some key insights. While institutions cannot learn in an intentional sense, individual frames of experience act as filters for institutions limiting what information gets interpreted, how it is interpreted, and how it is finally institutionalized. Here is where individuals and their frames of experience come into play. Rao and Giorgi (2006) wrote about "institutional entrepreneurs," certain individuals whose frames of experience allow them both the "ability to imagine an alternative" and the "latitude to get away with a framing of a problem and its attendant solution." (p. 273). These entrepreneurs do more than just "break" or subvert the rules of the institution; they use the cultural logics within and without the institution to shift others' frames of experience and begin to institutionalize new patterns or logics.

But, as Powell and Colyvas (2012) point out, too much emphasis may be placed on these change agents. Following Hedberg (1981), one can conceptualize organizational learning (e.g., organizational change) as a process of integrating new information based on the frames of experience of individual members, like teachers. "These local influences may bubble up and threaten or replace macro-level coherence" (Powell & Colyvas, 2012, p. 278). Similarly, Levitt and March (1988) postulates a slow model of instructional change wherein organizations learn as individuals code inferences from history into routines that guide their behavior.

Teachers or administrators in any given school come with their individual frames of experience and can exert influence over the individual organization of school, including what new procedures or rules become integrated into the existing logics of the organization. However, as Dimaggio and Powell (1983) pointed out, globalization has created significant isomorphism within many organizational fields. Large sectors of the economy (e.g., banking, retail, or automotive manufacturing) have come to resemble each other transnationally (Storey et al., 1997), and this indicates a homogenization of the meanings associated with internal roles and functions of the individuals who work in these institutions. This means that it is increasingly difficult for teachers or individual schools to make swift and dramatic changes in the institutional logics that prevail.

Globalization also brought repeated exogenous shocks to the institution of schooling (e.g., "PISA shock"; see Meyer & Benavot, 2013). What has been undertheorized is what happens when myriad individuals, across multiple organizations, reinterpret or subvert the logics of a new reform in similar ways. We have witnessed such widespread and direct challenges to the "taken-for-granted" status of schooling forms in the wake of a direct challenge to legitimacy (e.g., the rapid demise of legally segregated school following the *Brown vs. Board of Education* decision in the United States). What happens when the logics of a globally diffusing reform are fundamentally at odds with broader cultural logics held by the mass of teachers (and parents or students for that matter)? In such a case, how do the new cultural logics both gain legitimacy and ultimately become taken for granted?

Depth of Institutionalization: Legitimacy and "Taken for Granted"

The early modern phase of globalization saw the rapid diffusion of the institution of the individual, the nation state, and mass schooling, which were predicated on core beliefs that modern individuals have a unique sense of self, certain universal rights, and must give a rational account of their life history and trajectory. Such beliefs formed the core of institutional logics that informed the modern nation state and mass schooling. These logics clearly conflicted with older cultural logics, for example in Japan, where beliefs that the self exists partly in the individual and partly in the natural and social environment around the individual are still widespread (Hamaguchi, 1985; Hsu, 1985; Lebra, 1992). This deemphasis of the individual is consistent with Japanese beliefs in the fluidity or permeability of the self. These constructs are highly institutionalized within Japan and are often cited as critical to understanding the cultural differences between Japanese and Western society (Shimizu, 2000; Shimizu & Levine, 2001). How then to reconcile such conflicting logics without resorting to "decoupling" mechanisms as a means of explanation?

Deephouse and Suchman (2008) suggest that "taken for granted" and "cognitive legitimacy" are often conflated. Legitimacy, in world society studies, is often measured by the presence of logics in formal documents (e.g., constitutions; see Boli & Meyer, 1978). Legal status provides a powerful legitimacy but does not necessitate "taken-for-granted" status. The key point is that "taken-for-granted" is a cultural marker (Deephouse & Suchman, 2008) for things that fade into the background—patterns of action that we are so habituated to that we engage in them without active cognition. Exposure to a given organizational setting such as a school shifts individual expectations to what is taken for granted, or "just the way things are done," but some individuals appear to have more power to challenge the assumed norms.

In terms of actors and concepts of legitimacy, Meyer et al. (1983) noted that some professionals (e.g., lawyers) have a widespread perceived authority over "cultural theory." However, Deephouse and Suchman (2008, pp. 54–55) encouraged the use of more precise definitions in explaining "who has collective authority over legitimation in any given setting." Here, we see that teachers in different nations, or at different points in national history, have markedly different legitimacy over the cultural theory of schooling. For example, within Japan, teacher organizations exhibited considerable influence on the legal structures of mass schooling (Duke, 1973), resulting in stalemates and blocking reforms (Schoppa, 1991). However, it is clear that this authority over cultural theory—to redefine the cultural logics or provide legitimacy to specific logics—is not static. In the case of teachers it can ebb and flow (Takayama, 2007). Power to defy educational reforms is not the same as power to shape what is "taken for granted."

Institutionalization and diffusion are distinct processes (Colyvas & Jonsson, 2011). Even though patterns of schooling diffuse globally, adaptation of the institutional logics may well occur without those logics becoming highly taken for granted. "The depth of institutionalization depends on the extent to which objects and subjects become embedded in both higher- and lower-order frames, rules, and routines in a social setting. Links to only higher-order modes of reproduction will result in thin or shallow forms of institutionalization because local patterns may persist independently from higher-order structures" (p. 44). That is, they have not yet faded into the background as something assumed to be normal or expected in terms of teachers' day-to-day interactions with students, peers, and administrators. The "higher-order structures" of globally diffusing reforms may not affect "local patterns" of schooling, or perhaps even some national patterns of schooling.

Of course, the disconnection between global or even national logics and individual organizational idiosyncrasies has been typically explained in terms of "loose coupling" (Weick, 1976). But as Dimmock and colleagues show, coupling is a complex phenomenon, and traditional formulations of tight and loose coupling fail to capture the complexity of school systems as well as a theoretical change mechanism (Dimmock et al., 2021). They emphasize the importance of actors within local organizations (e.g., "internal enablers") in ways similar to (Rao & Giorgi, 2006) "institutional entrepreneurs." Suddaby and Greenwood (2005) also note the importance of such actors, who play a critical role in determining what external practices and patterns become established, but also in whether or not these practices or patterns become widely established.

Elaboration of Institutional Logics

Returning to a macro-level perspective, globalization produces a profusion of cultural logics available to actors. These logics are not simply globally "sanctioned" local variations as in Ramirez et al. (2016), but rather nascent institutions that may undergo increasing elaboration of core rational myths as more policy, research, and implementation provide actors with multiple opportunities to elaborate new rational myths. In my own work, I documented how the institutionalized life-course stage of adolescence in the United States and western Europe underwent extensive elaboration in the 1900s that did not occur in other nations (LeTendre, 2000). This process of elaboration appears linked to the ongoing adaptation, subversion, and other activities of local actors, policymakers, and academics. This process provided an increasingly diverse milieu of cultural logics that become available and could affect the process of institutional change.

What is missing in many theoretical accounts of institutional logics is the mechanism of elaboration—that institutional fields do not remain static over time but appear to become populated with increasingly elaborated narratives about the institution. Both neoinstitutional and world society perspectives undertheorized the dynamic aspect of culture and the fact that, as Aurini (2012, p. 375) noted, "the organizational field of education is becoming more diverse." That is, internal enablers or institutional entrepreneurs increasingly have wider and more diverse sets of cultural logics to draw upon over time.

Globalization, then, is not an external process that influences culture, but part of the cultural dynamic produced and sustained by the myriad interpretations of individuals. The rise of powerful communication technologies and networks is required to sustain this process (Castells, 2004), allowing individuals the potential to become influential producers of cultural variation. However, individuals rarely rise to the status of heroic "entrepreneurs" of institutional change (Rao & Giorgi, 2006).

This is the essential cultural dynamic of globalization in our age. We see the continual emergence and diffusion of new rationalized myths that both create common points of attention and elaboration as well as spur the creation of alternative interpretations and rational myths. The rationalized myth of education as essential to national economic survival in a globalized world is one example. National policymakers in the United States readily adopted the "logic" that better education equaled stronger economic performance (LeTendre, 1999) as it resonates with dominant logics of individualism, democracy, and private enterprise that are integrated into many globally diffusing reforms (Adamson et al., 2016). The "logic" of competition rationalizes narratives of "crisis" (Berliner & Biddle, 1995) and even becomes a mechanism of global governance (Robertson, 2012).

Yet this elaboration also produces conflicts and counternarratives. Lack of empirical evidence to justify the view that education drives economic competitive strength (Ramirez et al., 2018) undermines the legitimacy of this logic. Alternative, critical formulations may advance new cultural logics (Ball, 2012) which create new institutional interstitialities (Bridwell-Mitchell, 2020). In other words, the process of elaboration is self-sustaining. The endless production of variants on cultural logics creates further possibilities for individual actors like teachers to see resonance or dissonance within their individual frames of experience and assures the continued production of new rational formulations in order to resolve dissonance between visions of what teachers should or should not do.

Conclusion: The Impact of Information and Communication Technologies on the Global Diffusion of Cultural Logics

It is undeniable that both homogenization and elaboration are critical processes in "modernity" or "globalization." Benedict Anderson (1983) linked innovations in communications and media (the printed word) with the development of new national identities that both created a sense of homogenization (e.g., shared identity) and rapidly elaborated those identities. Globalization, as a process of dynamic cultural exchange via media, has made possible the rapid and continuous diffusion of cultural logics around the world. The expansion of information and communication technologies (ICT) has indeed created a "networked society" at the global level (Castells, 2004) and allowed teachers new ways of communicating and mobilizing (Baker-Doyle, 2015). ICT allows individuals dramatically increased access to a storehouse of imagined possibilities and requires us, then, to reconsider the role of individuals in the process of institutional change. We need to incorporate our knowledge of individuals as agents of institutional change into a theory of institutional change that recognize the forces of elaboration and resonance of cultural logics and can differentiate between superficial and deep institutionalization of these logics.

Micro-Processes, Sense-Making, and Institutional Change

We must account for the fact that actors "play" with the logics that are available to them in the world around them, "fighting over the very definition of reality" (Anderson-Levitt, 2003, p. 95). These actors are not simply peripheral to global diffusion; "they improvise, they perform, and they (re)make policy locally" (Koyama, 2013). And one tool at their disposal is their ability to "exploit the pre-existing logic within the social system, or import a logic from a different domain" (Rao & Giorgi, 2006). For these actors—teachers, principals, or even engaged parents—mismatches in the cultural logics (the elements of the rational myth) expose gaps or inconsistencies in what actions, behaviors and even what category of actors is consistent with the norms for the day-to-day operation of the organization. As actors engage in this *bricolage* of their cognitive worlds, they are informed by "preexisting beliefs, perceptions, and knowledge of the teaching and policy environments" (Akiba, 2017).

Bricolage of Meaning Conditioned by Power to Mobilize and Communicate

National cultural models and world culture cannot be merged without understanding the mechanisms of hybridization (Anderson-Levitt, 2003). "A truly hybrid theory would require that we recognize the local within the transnational. This means, first, acknowledging that local educators reshape global innovations as fast as they import them" (Anderson-Levitt, 2003, p. 20). But this mechanism also needs to account for power—the power to communicate but also the normative and cognitive dimensions of power. That is, a coherent, highly elaborated institutional logic of mass schooling did indeed rapidly reshape cultural logics in national societies around the world in the post–World War II era. As time has progressed, the ability of transnational organizations to diffuse large-scale educational reforms has increased, and thus resistance to, or *bricolage* of, diffusing institutional logics becomes highly difficult for teachers in many national societies (Gardiner, 2011; Shinn, 2012).

We must consider then, under what conditions do teachers, individually and collectively, have the means to effectively advocate for a new "logic" of how things are to run? Suddaby and Greenwood (2005) suggest that use of language can be a powerful tool in shifting organizational logics. This requires the incorporation of power to communicate or to control the focus and frequency of messages being broadcast in the environment. On a national level, teacher organizations can mount media campaigns that highlight specific institutional logics (e.g., the demand for pay consistent with a professional status), but other groups may mobilize competing logics. In the sphere of public media, these rhetorical challenges to institutional logics often make use of contrast to or resonance with existing cultural logics.

When or how teachers can actually change dominant cultural logics is limited by their access to communicative strategies that can deinstitutionalize certain norms and reinstitutionalize others. The ongoing development of new information and communication technologies can link hundreds of thousands of teachers across dozens of nations (e.g., eTwinning; see Blazic & Verswijvel, 2017). However, while such technologies allow the creation of dense, transnational networks of exchange between teachers, they also provide the nation state with manifold ways to enact surveillance of teachers (e.g., via classroom cameras and AI-supported monitoring software). The pertinent question is whether teachers can, via collective action, assert control over how these technologies are to be used.

At present, it seems unlikely that teachers will be able to achieve the national organizational capacity or professional status to act as agents of institutional change like other professions. But, as actors supported by broader social movements (e.g., the US civil rights movement), teachers may indeed play a significant role in reshaping educational systems through daily contestation of dominant logics and affirmation of new, alternative logics. On a day-to-day basis, the aggregate effect of teachers' sense-making will constitute a significant source of variation and dissonance in terms of the institutional logics of schooling but rarely become diffuse enough to alter the ongoing world cultural dynamic.

References

Adamson, F., Astrand, B., & Darling-Hammond, L. (2016). *Global education reform.* Routledge.

Akiba, M. (2013). *Teacher reforms around the world: Implementations and outcomes.* Emerald.

Akiba, M. (2017). Editor's introduction: Understanding cross-national differences in globalilzed teacher reforms. *Educational Researcher, 46*(4), 153–168.

Alesina, A., & Giuliano, P. (2015). Culture and institutions. *Journal of Economic Literature, 53,* 898–944.

Anderson, B. (1983). *Imagined communities*. Verso.

Anderson-Levitt, K. (1987). National culture and teaching culture. *Anthropology and Education Quarterly, 18*, 33–38.

Anderson-Levitt, K. (Ed.) (2003). *Local meanings, global schooling: Anthropology and world culture theory*. Palgrave Macmillan.

Anderson-Levitt, K. (2004). Reading lessons in Guinea, France, and the US: Local meanings or global culture? *Comparative Education Review, 48*(3), 229–252.

Appadurai, A. (2010). *Modernity at large*. University of Minnesota.

Aries, P. (1962). *Centuries of childhood*. Vintage.

Astiz, M. F., & Akiba, M. (Eds.). (2016). *The global and the local: Diverse perspectives in comparative Education*: Sense Publishers.

Aurini, J. D. (2012). Patterns of tight and loose coupling in a competitive marketplace: The case of learning center franchises. *Sociology of Education, 85*(4), 373–387. doi:10.1177/0038040712441375

Baker, D. (2014). *The schooled society*. Stanford University Press.

Baker, D., & LeTendre, G. (2005). *National differences, global similarities: World culture and the future of schooling*. Stanford University Press.

Baker-Doyle, K. (2015). No teacher is an island: How social networks shape teacher quality. In G. LeTendre & A. Wiseman (Eds.), *Promoting and sustaining a quality teacher workforce worldwide* (pp. 367–383). Emerald.

Ball, S. (2012). *Global Education Inc.: New policy networks and the neo-liberal imaginary*. Routledge.

Bartlett, L. (2003). World culture or transnational project? Competing educational projects in Brazil. In K. Anderson-Levitt (Ed.), *Local meanings, global schooling* (pp. 183–200). Palgrave Macmillan.

Berger, P., Berger, B., & Kellner, H. (1974). *The homeless mind*. Random House.

Berliner, D. (1992). *Educational reform in an era of disinformation*. Paper presented at the American Association of Colleges for Teacher Education, San Antonio, TX.

Berliner, D., & Biddle, B. (1995). *The manufactured crisis*. Addison-Wesley.

Blazic, A., & Verswijvel, B. (2017). eTwinning—A teacher network in Europe. In M. Akiba & G. LeTendre (Eds.), *Routledge international handbook of teacher quality and policy* (pp. 173–184). Routledge.

Boli, J., & Meyer, J. (1978). The ideology of childhood and the state: Rules distinguishing children in national constitutions, 1870–1970. *American Sociological Review, 43*(6), 797–812.

Boli, J., Ramirez, F., & Meyer, J. (1985). Explaining the origins and expansion of mass education. *Comparative Education Review, 29*, 145–170.

Bridwell-Mitchell, E. (2020). Between what is and what is possible: Theorizing the role of institutional interstitially in state-led school turnaround. *Peabody Journal of Education, 95*(4), 423–438.

Buhari-Gulmez, D. (2010). Stanford school on sociological institutionalism: A global cultural approach. *International Political Sociology, 4*, 253–270.

Castells, M. (2004). Informationalism, networks, and the network society: A theoretical blueprint. In M. Castells (Ed.), *The network society: A crosscultural perspective* (pp. 3–48). Edward Elgar.

Colyvas, J., & Jonsson, S. (2011). Ubiquity and legitimacy: Disentangling diffusion and institutionalization. *Sociological Theory, 29*(1), 27–53.

Deephouse, D., & Suchman, M. (2008). Legitimacy in organizational institutionalism. In R. Greenwood, C. Oliver, R. Suddaby, & K. Sahlin (Eds.), *Sage handbook of organizational institutionalism* (pp. 49–77). Sage Publications.

Desimone, L., Smith, T., Baker, D., & Ueno, K. (2005). Assessing barriers to the reform of U.S. mathematics instruction from an international perspective. *American Educational Research Journal, 42*(3), 501–535.

Dimaggio, P., & Powell, W. (1983). The iron cage revisited: Institutional isomorphism and collective rationality in organizational fields. *American Sociological Review, 48*(2), 147–160.

Dimmock, C., Tan, C. Y., Nguyen, D., Tran, T. A., & Dinh, T. T. (2021). Implementing education system reform: Local adaptation in school reform of teaching and learning. *International Journal of Educational Development, 80*, 1–43. https://doi.org/10.1016/j.ijedudev.2020.102302

Douglas, M. (1986). *How institutions think*. Syracuse University Press.

Drori, G., & Krucken, G. (2009). World society: A theory and a research program in context. In G. Krucken & G. Drori (Eds.), *World society: The writings of John W. Meyer* (pp. 3–35). Oxford University Press.

Drori, G., Meyer, J., & Hwang, H. (Eds.). (2006). *Globalization and organization: World society and organizational change*. Oxford University Press.

Duke, B. (1973). *Japan's militant teachers*. The University of Hawaii Press.

Earley, P., Imig, D., & Michelli, N. (Eds.). (2011). *Teacher education policy in the United States*. Routledge.

Etzioni, A. (Ed.) (1969). *The semi-professions and their organization: Teachers, nurses, social workers*. Free Press.

Fraser, P., & Ikoma, S. (2015). Regimes of teacher beliefs from a comparative and international perspective. In G. LeTendre & A. Wiseman (Eds.), *Promoting and sustaining a quality teacher workforce* (Vol. 27, pp. 111–144). Emerald.

Friedman, J. (1988). Cultural logics of the global system: A sketch. *Theory, Culture & Society, 5*, 447–460.

Gardiner, M. (2011). Agents of change and continuity: The pivotal role of teachers in Albanian educational reform and democratization. *Comparative Education Review, 56*(4), 659–683.

Green, S. E. (2004). A rhetorical theory of diffusion. *Academy of Management Review, 29*, 653–669.

Guiso, L., Sapienza, P., & Zingales, L. (2015). Corporate culture, societal culture, and institutions. *American Economic Review, 105*(5), 336–339.

Hamaguchi, E. (1985). A contextual model of the Japanese: Toward a methodological innovation in Japanese studies. *Journal of Japanese Studies, 11*(2), 289–321.

Hedberg, B. (1981). How organizations learn and unlearn. In P. C. N. W. H. Starbuck (Ed.), *Handbook of organizational design* (Vol. 1, pp. 3–27). Oxford University Press.

Hiebert, J., Stigler, J. W., Jacobs, J. K., Givvin, K. B., Garnier, H., Smith, M., Hollingsworth, H., Manaster, A., Wearne, D., &Gallimore, R. (2005). Mathematics teaching in the United States today (and tomorrow): Results from the TIMSS 1999 Video Study. *Educational Evaluation and Policy Analysis, 27*(2), 111–132. doi:10.3102/01623737027002111

Hostetler, J., & Huntington, G. (1992). *Amish children: Education in the family, school, and community*. Harcourt Brace Jovanovich.

Hsu, F. (1985). The self in cross-cultural perspective. In A. Marsella, G. De Vos, & F. Hsu (Eds.), *Culture and self*. Tavistock.

Hufner, K., Meyer, J., & Naumann, J. (1987). Comparative education policy research: A world society perspective. In M. Dierkes, H. Weikert, & A. Antal (Eds.), *Comparative policy research* (pp. 188–243). Aldershot.

Jepperson, R. (1991). Institutions, institutional effects, and institutionalism. In W. Powell & P. Dimaggio (Eds.), *The new institutionalism in organizational analysis* (pp. 143–163). University of Chicago Press.

Kamens, D. (2012). *Beyond the nation-state: The reconstruction of nationhood and citizenship.* Emerald.

Kim, Y. (2019). Global convergence or national variation: Examining national patterns of classroom instructional practices. *Globalisation, Societies and Education, 17*(3), 353–377.

Koyama, J. (2013). Global scare tactics and the call for US schools to be held accountable. *American Journal of Education, 120*(1), 77–99.

Lebra, T. (1992). Self in Japanese culture. In N. Rosenburger (Ed.), *Japanese sense of self* (pp. 105–120). Cambridge University Press.

LeTendre, G. (Ed.) (1999). *Competitor or ally: Japan's role in American educational debates.* Falmer.

LeTendre, G. (2000). *Learning to be adolescent: Growing up in U.S. and Japanese middle schools.* Yale University Press.

LeTendre, G., Baker, D., Akiba, M., Goesling, B., & Wiseman, A. (2001). Teacher's work: Institutional isomorphism and cultural variation in the U.S., Germany and Japan. *Educational Researcher, 30*(6), 3–16.

Levitt, B., & March, James G. (1988). Organizational learning. *Annual Review of Sociology, 14,* 319–340.

Lincicome, M. (1995). *Principles, praxis, and the politics of educational reform in Meiji Japan.* University of Hawai'i Press.

Lortie, D. (1969). The balance of control and autonomy in elementary school teaching. In A. Etzioni (Ed.), *The semi-professions and their organization* (pp. 1–53). Free Press.

Lortie, D. C. (1975). *Schoolteacher: A sociological study.* University of Chicago Press.

Maguire, M. (2002). Globalisation, education policy and the teacher. *International Studies in Sociology of Education, 12*(3), 261–276. https://doi.org/https://doi.org/10.1080/0962021020 0200093

Mangez, E., Bouhon, M., Cattonar, B., Delvaux, B., Draelants, H., Dumay, X., Dupriez, V., & Verhoeven, M. (2017). *Living together in an uncertain world. What role for the school?*

Meyer, H.-D., & Benavot, A. (2013). *PISA, power, and policy.* Symposium Books.

Meyer, J. W. (1977). The effects of education as an institution. *American Journal of Sociology, 83*(1), 55–77. http://www.jstor.org/stable/2777763

Meyer, J. W. (2007). Globalization: Theory and trends. *International Journal of Comparative Sociology, 48*(4), 261–273. doi:10.1177/0020715207079529

Meyer, J. W., Bromley, P., & Ramirez, F. O. (2010). Human rights in social science textbooks: Cross-national analyses, 1970–2008. *Sociology of Education, 83*(2), 111–134. doi:10.1177/ 0038040710367936

Meyer, J. W., Scott, R., & Deal, T. (1983). Institutional and technical sources of organizational structure: Explaining the structure of educational organizations. In W. R. S. J. W. Meyer, B. Rowan, & T. E. Deal (Ed.), *Organizational environments ritual and rationality* (pp. 45–70). Sage Publications.

Mintz, S. (2004). *Huck's raft: A history of American childhood.* Belknap Press.

Napier, D. B. (2003). Transformations in South Africa: Policies and practices from ministry to classroom. In K. Anderson-Levitt (Ed.), *Local meanings, global schooling: Anthropology and world culture today* (pp. 52–74). Palgrave.

Niemi, H., Toom, A., Kallioniemi, A., & Lavonen, J. (Eds.). (2018). *The teacher's role in the changing globalizing world*. Brill Sense.

North, D. (1991). Institutions. *Journal of Economic Perspectives, 5*(1), 97–112.

OECD. (2005). *Teachers matter*. Organisation for Economic Co-Operation and Development.

Paine, L., & Zeichner, K. (2012). The local and global in reforming teaching and teacher education. *Comparative Education Review, 56*(4), 569–586.

Powell, W., & Colyvas, J. (2012). Microfoundations of institutional theory. In R. Greenwood (Ed.), *The SAGE handbook of organizational institutionalism* (pp. 276–298). Sage.

Ramirez, F., Meyer, J., & Lerch, J. (2016). World society and the globalization of educational policy. In K. Mundy, A. Green, B. Lindgard, & A. Verger (Eds.), *The handbook of global education policy* (pp. 43–63). John Wiley & Sons.

Ramirez, F., Schofer, E., & Meyer, J. W. (2018). International tests, national assessments, and educational development (1970–2012). *Comparative Education Review, 62*(3), 344–364.

Rao, H., & Giorgi, S. (2006). Code breaking: How entrepreneurs exploit cultural logics to generate institutional change. *Research in Organizational Behavior, 27*, 269–304.

Robertson, S. (2000). *A class act: Changing teachers' work, globalisation and the state*. Falmer Press.

Robertson, S. L. (2012). Placing teachers in global governance agendas. *Comparative Education Review, 56*(4), 584–607. doi:10.1086/667414

Rohlen, T., & LeTendre, G. (1995). *Teaching and learning in Japan*. Cambridge University Press.

Schoppa, L. (1991). *Education reform in Japan: A case of immobilist policies*. Routledge.

Scott, R. (1995). *Institutions and organizations*. Sage.

Shanahan, M. J. (2000). Pathways to adulthood in changing societies: Variability and mechanisms in life course perspective. *Annual Review of Sociology, 26*, 667–692.

Shimizu, H. (2000). Japanese cultural psychology and empathic understanding: Implications for academic and cultural psychology. *Ethos, 28*(2), 224–247.

Shimizu, H., & Levine, R. (2001). *Japanese frames of mind*. Cambridge University Press.

Shinn, C. (2012). Teacher education reform in Palestine: Policy challenges amid donor expectations. *Comparative Education Review, 56*(4), 608–633. doi:10.1086/667434

Spindler, G. (1987). Cultural dialogue and schooling in Schoenhausen and Roseville: A comparative analysis. *Anthropology and Education Quarterly, 18*(1), 3–16.

Spindler, G., & Spindler, L. (1990). *The American cultural dialogue and its transmission*. Falmer Press.

Spindler, L. (1977). *Culture change and modernization: mini-models and case studies*. Waveland Press.

Stark, L. W., & Spreen, C. A. (2020). Teacher struggles against neoliberalism and for democracy and justice. In R. Kolins Givan & A. S. Lang (Eds.), *Strike for the common good: Fighting for the future of public education* (pp. 234–252). University of Michigan Press.

Stein, S. (2004). *The culture of educational policy*. Teachers College Press.

Stevenson, H., Parker, T., Wilkinson, A., Bonnevaux, B., & Gonzalez, M. (1978). *Schooling, environment, and cognitive development: A cross-cultural study* (Vol. 43, 3, #175, pp. 1–92). Monographs of the Society for Research in Child Development.

Stevenson, H., & Stigler, J. (1992). *The learning gap*. Summit Books.

Stigler, J., Gallimore, R., & Hiebert, J. (2000). Using video surveys to compare classrooms and teaching across cultures: Examples and lessons from the TIMSS video studies. *Educational Psychologist, 35*(2), 87–100.

Stigler, J., & Hiebert, J. (1998). Teaching is a cultural activity. *American Educator* (Winter), 4–11.

Stigler, J., & Hiebert, J. (1999). *The teaching gap: Best ideas from the world's teachers for improving education in the classroom.* Free Press.

Stigler, J., & Stevenson, H. (1991). How Asian teachers polish each lesson to perfection. *American Educator, 15*(1), 12–20.

Storey, J., Edwards, P., & Sisson, K. (1997). *Managers in the making: Careers, development and control in corporate Britain and Japan.* Sage.

Suarez-Orozco, M., & Qin-Hilliard, D. B. (Eds.). (2004). *Globalization: Culture and education in the new millennium.* UC Press.

Suddaby, R. (2010). Challenges for institutional theory. *Journal of Management Inquiry, 19*(1), 14–20.

Suddaby, R., & Greenwood, R. (2005). Rhetorical strategies of legitimacy. *Administrative Science Quarterly, 50,* 35–67.

Swidler, A. (1986). Culture in action: Symbols and strategies. *American Sociological Review, 51*(April), 273–286.

Takayama, K. (2007). A *Nation at Risk* crosses the Pacific: Transnational borrowing of the U.S. crisis discourse in the debate on education reform in Japan. *Comparative Education Review, 51*(4), 423–446.

Takayama, K., & Apple, M. (2008). The cultural politics of borrowing: Japan, Britain, and the narrative of educational crisis. *British Journal of Sociology of Education, 29*(3), 289–301.

Tarlau, R. (2019). *Occupying schools, occupying land: How the landless workers movement transformed Brazilian education.* Oxford University Press.

Thornton, P., Ocasio, W., & Lounsbury, M. (2012). Introduction to the institutional logics perspective. In P. Thornton, W. Ocasio, & M. Lounsbury (Eds.), *The institutional logics perspective: A new approach to culture, structure and process* (pp. 1–18). Oxford University Press.

Thurston, D. (1973). *Teachers and politics in Japan.* Princeton University Press.

Tobin, J., Wu, D. Y., & Davidson, D. H. (1989). *Preschools in three cultures: Japan, China and the United States.* Yale University Press.

Tsurumi, E. P. (1977). *Japanese colonial education in Taiwan, 1895–1945.* Harvard University Press.

UNESCO. (2006). *Teachers and educational quality: Monitoring global needs for 2015.* Institute for Statistics, UNESCO.

Weick, K. E. (1976). Educational organizations as loosely coupled systems. *Administrative Science Quarterly, 21,* 1–19.

Zucker, L. (1977). The role of institutionalization in cultural persistence. *American Sociological Review, 42*(October), 726–743.

Zucker, L. (1983). Organizations as institutions. In S. Bachrach (Ed.), *Research in the sociology of organizations* (pp. 1–47). JAI Press.

CHAPTER 8

HIGHER EDUCATION AND ORGANIZATIONAL THEORY

Systems, Fields, Markets, and Populations in an Increasingly Global Context

JEROEN HUISMAN

INTRODUCTION

THIS chapter focuses on how developments in organizational theory (revolving around key concepts such as organizational fields, systems, populations, isomorphism, and institutional logics) have affected the study of higher education. It is tempting to assume that theoretical ideas and concepts travel from the disciplines to the field of higher education. There is a compelling argument for this perspective. It is rooted in the idea that higher education is not a discipline in itself; it is "just" an object of study, in many respects comparable to police studies, sports studies, or urban studies. Tight has extensively explored the idea of higher education as a field of study versus a discipline. His early work on this theme argues that higher education researchers have—for a long time—constituted an a-theorical community of scholars (Tight, 2004). More recently, he argued that there are arguments to see higher education developing into a discipline of its own (Tight, 2014, 2020). A further specification of the argument is that not only higher education is an object of study, but that the aims of scholars in this field are significantly geared toward problem-solving. That is, real-life problems in policy or practice are key motivators for higher education researchers to investigate higher education (Teichler, 2000). In embarking on these studies, researchers may use the methodological and theoretical toolkit of the social sciences, but not necessarily.

Hence, this perspective argues that higher education researchers may be hesitant or slow to use theory.[1] Hesitance may stem from the view that they think they can do without to reach their aim, that is, to solve a problem in practice, although—following Lewin's adage—there is nothing as practical as a good theory. But hesitance (or uncertainty) may also be related to the multidisciplinary nature of higher education research, which implies that a researcher is not necessarily abreast of all the potentially useful theories/concepts. Such considerations have led analysts to argue that higher education scholars have been slow to pick up insights from organizational studies (Cai & Mehari, 2015; see also Lepori, 2016, although more implicitly) or emphasized that organizational studies in higher education are problem-oriented (Fumasoli & Stensaker, 2013). Paradeise and Thoenig (2013, p. 189) argued that "higher education and research institutions as organizations have remained for many years a rather unexplored topic" in organizational studies.

Interestingly, some organizational scholars would argue the other way around. For instance, Washington and Ventresca (2004, p. 93) claim that "[t]he study of higher education organizations was central in the development of macro theories of organizations," although they do not offer support for this claim. Also higher education scholars Elken and Vukasovic (2019) point at important organizational concepts being developed through the study of (higher) education, like loose coupling, myths and ceremonies, and garbage can decision-making. It would take a separate in-depth analysis to fully disentangle the influences of organizational theory on higher education research and vice-versa. This contribution therefore focuses on one side of that story: early (or even *avant la lettre*, as will be shown later) or late adoption of organizational thinking—around notions of fields, markets, and populations—by higher education scholars.

Another expectation might be that higher education researchers would closely follow the globalization literature because the two key activities in higher education (and possibly research more than teaching and learning) easily cross-national boundaries. In other words, higher education would be a prime example of the opening of international borders and increasingly fast flows of services, people, and ideas, two elements that figure largely in definitions and theories of globalization. Remarkably, the debate on globalization and higher education only emerged in the second half of the 1990s and gained more ground in the new millennium.

The structure of the contribution is as follows. First, I will address some characteristics of the community of higher education researchers. I then continue to organize my arguments around four key concepts in organizational theory: systems, fields, populations, and markets. I realize there are different ways to present the analysis, for example, chronologically, but I think centering the discussions around the notions of systems, fields, populations, and markets—and, importantly, their conceptual and theoretical connotations and denotations—serves the purpose. Moreover, by focusing particularly on fields and markets, I stay close to institutional strands in organizational theory. It also allows me to easily weave in the discourse on globalization and higher education. I then present a conclusion and reflection.

Higher Education Scholarship

As in any other field studying social objects (e.g., health or social work), researchers have studied quite diverse elements of that object. Studies in higher education pay attention to teaching, learning, and assessment; to curriculum development; to the teaching and research profession(s); to higher education institutions (as organizations) and its management; and to systems of higher education. Cross-cutting these themes are enduring challenges related to access, participation, equality, funding, quality, internationalization, and so on. An important corollary of this observation is that those focusing on micro-level issues like student assessment are often hardly aware—and it could be argued that they do not necessarily need to be aware—of the work of those studying macro-level national policy reforms. Even though social science disciplines also differ in terms of their theoretical and methodological coherence, what connects (sub)disciplinary scholars is that they—by and large—speak the same disciplinary language and build their work on that of its founding fathers and mothers. Instead, the large variety of subthemes has led higher education researchers to label their field as diverse (Macfarlane, 2012) or as highly specialized and fragmented (Daenekindt & Huisman, 2020). Within this highly diversified field, a substantial part of scholarly output focuses on teaching, learning, and assessment and to the student experience and student well-being (Tight, 2013), with much of this work being carried out by scholars in education studies, pedagogy, and psychology. A much smaller community focuses on the meso-level (higher education institutions as organizations) and macro-level (higher education systems).

The study of higher education is "special" in that researchers investigate their own world. In the early days of higher education research, this meant that basically anyone with some experience in higher education could write about the topic. It would not be uncommon for practitioners and leaders of higher education institutions to contribute to journals (less so in contemporary times, according to Macfarlane, 2012). Whether their insights were based on robust methodologies and solid theories or on limited personal (and biased) observations is a moot point. Clark (1984, pp. 4–5) wryly comments that "[l]earned professors, studious and rigorous in their own fields, often discuss higher education without much preparation." The fact that higher education researchers study their own field is often connected to an observation by many scholars that higher education research is of an a-theoretical nature and geared toward practice and problem-solving (Teichler, 2005; Tight, 2014).

It is therefore key to realize, first, that the share of higher education researchers that would potentially engage with organizational theories is relatively small. Obviously, those studying micro-level teaching and learning processes can do without organizational theory. Second, scholars may not have been trained in disciplines that make much use of those theories (sociology, political science, business and management studies, economics), so it is also a matter of being acquainted with potentially relevant theories. Third, even if there is an interest among higher education scholars in organizational theory, their attentiveness may be quickly superseded by prioritizing the practical relevance of higher education research, even though much of organizational theory emerged exactly to deal with practical organizational problems.

HIGHER EDUCATION: THE PREVALENCE FOR A SYSTEM APPROACH

In scholarly contributions focusing on higher education, the overwhelming majority of researchers would write about higher education as a system (or sometimes sector, although the latter term is often used for specific subsystems, e.g., the college sector). The term "field" is used much less frequently. A quick search on "higher education field" versus "higher education system" in titles of publications in the Web of Science database reveals 277 mentions for the former and 1,753 for the latter. The three key explanations for the very frequent use of "system" are pragmatics, the primacy of policy, and conceptual-theoretical considerations. The pragmatic use stems from the fact that the seemingly neutral term "system" denotes a group of related things, *in casu* a set of higher education institutions that are in one way or another connected to each other (geographically, politically, culturally). The pragmatic stance is often connected to policy considerations, an approach particularly visible in comparative higher education policy studies (Goedegebuure & Van Vught, 1994). Given that most policies stem from national governments (since the rise of the nation state; Neave, 2001), arguably the most important actor setting the direction for higher education, it is understandable—and largely unproblematic—to define the higher education system as the set of higher education organizations that are targeted and affected by national policies. "Unproblematic" needs to be qualified, in that a perception of systems defined by nationally determined boundaries may be less tenable in a context of highly internationalized and globalized higher education: Policies may be bound by national perimeters, but students, staff, and ideas (Czarniawksi & Sevón, 2005) travel across national borders (e.g., student mobility, international branch campuses, joint degrees, cross-border accreditation). I will return to this theme in the next section.

The choice for the use of the term "system" may, third, also be inspired by theory. Different theories spring to mind, such as Luhmann's theory of self-reproducing systems. Applying these theoretical notions to higher education means that units of the system (higher education institutions as organizations) are connected through communication (see, e.g., Pfeffer & Stichweh, 2015). Other system approaches in higher education are based on other strands of structural functionalism, such as Parsons and Platt's (1973) conceptual reflection on patterns of structural differentiation of the functions of the American university. Although critically received (see, e.g., Vanderstraeten, 2015), we still can find a fair amount of references to this book in the higher education literature. A final strand of system-inspired conceptual approaches can be found in work that is based on engineering and natural sciences notions of a system. Examples are studies on system dynamics (see e.g., Galbraith, 2013, using system dynamics for enrolment planning).

What About Globalization?

Before delving into conceptualizations of higher education organizations in fields, markets, or populations, the focus on systems—addressed in the previous section—offers a stepping stone for discussing globalization. It could be argued that the perspective on higher education systems demarcated by country borders as "natural," with reference to both legal and cultural arguments went hand in hand with an apparent neglect of globalization. The fact that higher education scholars "only" started addressing globalization by the end of the 1990s (e.g., Jarvis, 1999) and numbers of papers (in Web of Science) on the theme only passed the mark of 100 per year in 2010 may be seen as support for this claim, but there is a more nuanced story to tell, that goes beyond the "when" question and focuses on the how and why.

Higher education has always been an international endeavor, and the many manifestations of it (student mobility, staff mobility, and research collaboration, but also internationalization at home and international branch campuses) have been topics of much higher education research (see Kehm & Teichler, 2007, for taking stock at the beginning of a new millennium), even though it is important to note that not all higher education institutions participate extensively in internationalization strategies and activities. But exactly this focus (on internationalization policies and activities and their outcomes) possibly kept researchers from paying too much attention to an important driver of internationalization: globalization. Somewhat overstated, globalization was merely seen as context, important to mention, but challenging in terms of unpacking it. Only when scholars commenced to extensively address globalization itself (Beerkens, 2003; Marginson & Van der Wende, 2007), other higher education scholars started to see the value of investigating the topic in more detail.

A key theme in that emerging literature was national sovereignty, more specifically the potential loss of it (Beerkens, 2003), with various connotations of globalization being equated with increased competition and higher education markets offering tradeable commodities. This resulted in many higher education scholars taking a quite critical stance toward globalization. Most importantly, I argue, is that scholars positioned their work around notions of the political economy, hence particularly addressing the *agency* of globalization in combination with national and local forces (Marginson & Rhoades, 2002). At the same time, scholars acknowledged the *dynamics* of globalization: Whereas globalization affects higher education, the latter—being very international—can also be seen as a major contributor to processes of globalization. Instead of being perceived as context (quite often depicted in vague or abstract terms, even though higher education scholars relied on important theoretical and conceptual insights with reference to work of, e.g., Ulrich Beck, Manuel Castells, and Anthony Giddens), it gained prominence with visible agency in higher education. At the same time, the literature stressed the continued power and influence of the nation state and—importantly—emphasized that not all higher education systems and institutions equally participate in the global competition (Marginson & Van der Wende, 2007). Obviously, relatively concrete supranational developments, like GATS, the European Commission's increasing involvement in higher education affairs, and the Bologna Process helped giving globalization a face.

In that context, research also embarked on analyzing how globalization affects organizations. As said, not all higher education institutions are significantly engaged in internationalization and globalization dynamics. There is particular interest in investigating world-class universities and/or research universities in the top ranks of various global rankings. From the organizational scholar's perspective, one might expect a (renewed) engagement of higher education scholars with world society theory. Surely, these scholars (see Meyer et al., 1997, for an overview) have paved the way for seeing organizations being globally embedded institutions. But limited use has been made of these important theoretical insights (but see Ramirez, 2006; Ramirez & Tiplic, 2014).[2]

In more recent times, higher education scholars have embraced globalization as an important phenomenon. There is now a common understanding that higher education institutions (but not all of them) are under the influence of globalization, with also specific attention to themes like regional and supranational powers and policies (Chou & Ravinet, 2015) and global rankings, competition, and world-class universities (Hazelkorn, 2015). In this body of literature, there is relatively little reliance on organizational theories, but I will offer some important exceptions in the subsequent sections.

From System to Field . . . or Somewhere in Between

Interestingly, the author of one of the most quoted sources on higher education systems (Clark, 1983, p. 4) shows some uneasiness with the system concept. In the introduction of the book, he describes the higher education system "in a narrow, conventional sense to refer to an aggregate of formal entities," which clearly resonates with the neutral and the structural-functional sociological approach to systems. However, he also—purposively—uses a broader definition that "includes any of the population when engaged in postsecondary educational activities, either as controllers, organizers, workers, or consumers." This notion clearly reflects field thinking. DiMaggio and Powell (1983, p. 148) offer—in the same year, and very likely the authors are unaware of each other's writings—the following description of organizational field in their seminal work: "those organizations that, in the aggregate, constitute a recognized area of institutional life: key suppliers, resource and product consumers, regulatory agencies, and other organizations that produce similar services or products."

Clark (1983) acknowledges that the broader definition raises questions about the boundaries of systems, expanding and contracting across time and space, but accepts this ambiguity in light of the boundary-crossing nature of academic workers. They are (Clark, 1983, p. 5) "loosely bounded," being connected to colleagues in other universities but also often being legitimately employed elsewhere. The flexibility in approaches allows Clark to comfortably speak about government-system relationships in his chapter on authority (who rules?) and integration (how is organizational action coordinated?) in the narrow sense of the system concept. At the same time, he leans toward the broader field perspective in the chapters on beliefs, values, and knowledge (higher education being a social structure for the control of advanced knowledge).

Clark's struggle is not a wrestle that solely pertains to the study of higher education. Even the core proponents of the field approach in organizational theory sometimes lean toward a functionalist or pragmatic approach. Two examples are offered from seminal texts on organizational fields. In the second part of their 1983 paper, DiMaggio and Powell offer a set of hypotheses on organizational fields "to predict empirically which organizational fields will be most homogeneous in structure, process and behavior" (p. 154). It is clear from their predictions that they actually use a rather narrow definition of the field, focusing on key suppliers. Also subsequent field studies (see Mizruchi & Fein, 1999 for a review) focus on behavior of firms and businesses. Mezias's (1990, p. 443) study is a good example of how pragmatics and functional arguments play out in the determination of the field: "Data . . . were constrained by the availability of empirical measures . . . Because of this data-missing problem, the sample . . . consists of the 200 largest nonfinancial corporations in the United States in 1969." The second example stems from Scott's (2004) work. Here actually the word "functional" is explicitly used to denote a set of "similar and dissimilar interdependent organizations operating in a functionally specific arena together with their exchange partners, funding sources and regulators" (Scott, 2004, p. 9).

Isomorphism in Higher Education

In the 1980s, higher education policy scholars continued to rely on the systems concept, but higher education scholars interested in organizations and organizational change increasingly became interested in fields. It took, however, six years before DiMaggio and Powell's idea of institutional isomorphism is formally recognized in higher education studies. Checking citation patterns in the field of (higher) education (using Web of Science), the concept is first used by Levinson (1989) to illustrate developments in American higher education. The first European application can be found in Maassen and Potman (1990), questioning whether the intended governmental policies to create more distinctiveness across Dutch universities will be successful.

The former suggests a pattern of diffusion of DiMaggio and Powell's ideas. This notion of diffusion can also be found in Cai and Mehari (2015). They tracked when and how institutional theory has been applied in higher education journal articles. The authors conclude that "it took 10–15 years for higher education researchers to adopt the ideas and concepts of new institutionalism." This is a fair assessment, but a fundamental issue is the implicit assumption that the development of institutional concepts and thinking would *precede* the use in higher education studies. Could it actually be that institutional thinking—but possibly authors were using different concepts to denote the same phenomena—was already present in higher education research?

Particularly regarding isomorphism, this case can be made. For sure, DiMaggio and Powell's ideas are also built on earlier insights (e.g., Hawley, 1968, on human ecology approach that also features the concept of structural isomorphism), but the notion of organizational similarity can also be found in early writings on higher education. Next two concepts from higher education research are discussed that are—I argue—largely similar to DiMaggio and Powell's notion and mechanisms of isomorphism: institutional homogenization and academic drift.

Riesman (1958, p. 21) speaks to "institutional homogenization" as a process in which colleges tend to follow national models instead of following the quite often path-breaking ideas of their founding leaders. Whereas in early days international models may have guided these leaders, Riesman argues that in the 1950s, colleges model themselves upon each other. He uses the metaphor of the "snakelike procession" in which the avant-garde form the head and the middle part "seeks to catch up with where the head once was" (p. 35). Seeking prestige and legitimacy in the hierarchy of institutions (by college and university leaders but also by academic staff) is an important mechanism of homogenization. These mechanisms clearly resonate with DiMaggio and Powell's normative isomorphism stemming from professionalization, with reference to universities being important training grounds for the development of organizational norms that are disseminated and confirmed—with professors moving from college to college. Similarly, the notion of mimicry also resonates with the mechanism of organizations modeling themselves after similar organizations that are considered legitimate or successful. Admittedly, Riesman does not point at uncertainty being an important motive for copying behavior; he argues that college and university motives may vary considerably, depending—among others—on whether an institution is at the head, middle, or tail of the snake.

Readers may think the reference to this particular work of Riesman is somewhat obscure (the book is a collection of lectures), but Jencks and Riesman (1968) further explore the idea of the snakelike procession, now under the label "academic revolution." Also other authors in the 1960s referred to homogenization/isomorphism. Schultz and Stickler (1965) discuss vertical extension, alluding to the fact that colleges started to broaden their profile—read: tried to gain prestige—by offering four-year programs. Berelson (1960), in a similar vein, discusses the expansion of graduate programs at US universities.

The idea of the snakelike procession possibly did not catch a lot of attention beyond the United States, but the concept of academic drift did. Tight (2015) traces the first use of the concept of academic drift in higher education studies back to the 1960s, but he argues that the work of Pratt and Burgess (1974) on the developments in the UK polytechnic sector has been most influential in popularizing the concept. Academic drift denotes the historical process of aspiration to achieve university status and to resemble universities. The concept emerged from empirical observations of the authors while studying the developments in the polytechnic sector. Perhaps, academic drift was a more relevant anchor point for European higher education researchers and policymakers than Riesman's snakelike procession. This is due to the different configuration of higher education systems in Europe. European governments—in the main—chose the establish binary systems in the 1960s and 1970s to deal with the increasing demand for higher education. They created "alternative" sectors of higher education (Teichler, 1988), based on an equal-but-different philosophy. Stratification, a distinctive characteristic of the US system, was more an exception (United Kingdom, France) than a widespread phenomenon in Europe. Tight (2015) confirms—reporting 1,500 papers having used the concept of academic drift—the widespread use vis-à-vis less often used concepts like vertical extension or mission drift or creep. Despite the popularity of the concept, one cannot escape the observation that whereas conceptually rich and convincing, only few higher education researchers have studied the mechanisms of academic drift empirically. That is, many studies note—quite often based on personal observations or interpretations—increasing homogenization in higher education systems. Who (aspiring higher education leaders, academics, policymakers?) and why (esteem, legitimacy, uncertainty?), however, drove drift is quite often not sufficiently clear. Some studies clearly distinguish an important role of policy. Lepori and Kyvik (2010) saw important roles of governments that stimulated a research function in non-university sectors. Neave (1979) also points at imprecise policies that may have left higher education institutions of new sectors clueless regarding their position in the higher education system, particularly on how to position themselves vis-à-vis the dominant university sector. That said, most studies—implicitly or explicitly—seem to point at the organizations themselves (especially their leaders and academic staff) as drivers of the processes of drift.

Connecting these insights from studies on academic drift to the concept of isomorphism reveals striking similarities. The mechanisms portrayed by DiMaggio and Powell (1983) have been addressed by higher education scholars at least a decade before their seminal paper appeared. Uncertainty about their specific mission may have invited non-university institutions to mimic the traditional university. And normative-cognitive processes may have led staff and managers to achieve a similar status and level of legitimacy as the universities. There are differences as well. Higher education scholars were relatively slow to empirically detail the specific mechanisms of isomorphism, and—granted—DiMaggio and Powell (1983) were the first to holistically address isomorphism. Importantly, the latter may have been straightforward regarding the constraining roles of structures. Higher education scholars agreed that indeed regulation may be stifling innovative behavior, but argued at the same time that normative-cognitive pressures for academic drift may be so strong that governmental regulation—in this case, setting clear boundaries for sectors of higher education and clear mandates for specific institutions—is needed to counter isomorphic behavior (Huisman & Morphew, 1998).

FIELDS AND GLOBALIZATION

Returning to the use of the concept "field" and use thereof in higher education studies, it would be too simplistic to assume that higher education scholars—when referring to fields—only used DiMaggio and Powell's new institutional insights. Taking Kluttz and Fligstein's (2016) paper, who—next to new institutional theory, refer to strategic action fields (SAFs) and Bourdieu's field theory, we see that higher education scholars do use the latter approaches in their analyses. For instance, Naidoo (2010) analyses South African higher education through a Bourdieusian lens and also Marginson (2008) clearly situates his reflection on global higher education around Bourdieu's notions of power, agency, and position. The SAF theory has to a limited extent been applied to higher education (but see Taylor, 2015). Whereas it could be argued that both Bourdieu's field theory and SAF are quite flexible when it comes to the demarcation of fields—that is, they could be national, but not necessarily—and especially SAF's notion of emerging fields—it is interesting to see that most higher education scholars stay in the "comfort zone" of analyzing fields in "natural" contexts, that is, enclosed by national borders.

There are noteworthy exceptions of authors who use insights from field theories *and* address the global dimension. For instance, Paradeise and Thoenig (2013) discuss how universities in different geographical settings can be seen to grapple with paying attention to (global) notions of excellence and/or reputation as dimensions of quality. Importantly, they analytically debate the organizational consequences (organizational structure, role of management, social regulation of work) of the different emphases universities may put on excellence and/or reputation. Another example is Hüther and Krücken's (2016) argument to see universities as being embedded in fields at different levels: global, European, national, and regional. Universities actually are, it is argued, positioning themselves or are positioned in (nested) fields, and this may explain both processes of isomorphism and diversification in different fields. Also the literature on the phenomenon of so-called world-class universities increasingly starts to rely on the perspective of universities operating in a global field (Ramirez & Tiplic, 2014; Shin & Kehm, 2013).

FIELDS, SYSTEMS . . . AND WHAT ABOUT POPULATIONS?

I briefly address populations and population ecology, given the considerable interest of higher education researchers and policymakers in preserving organizational diversity.

Just before DiMaggio and Powell's (1983) ideas around field isomorphism found their way into higher education, a few scholars made use of insights from population ecology (Hannan & Freeman, 1977; see Baum & Shipilov, 2006, for an overview). But, despite the popularity of population ecology, especially in the 1970s and 1980s, it has hardly been applied to higher education. There are two explanations for scholars' hesitance to use these insights.

First, some pragmatic considerations. One would need sizeable populations to do relevant research. Even the largest European countries in Europe (United Kingdom, Germany, Italy) would have relatively small populations of higher education institutions suitable for sophisticated analyses. Apart from this, due to its primarily public nature and concomitant governmental (financial) support accompanied by considerable levels of bureaucracy, population dynamics are plausibly primarily dependent on one environmental factor: governmental regulation. A corollary is that death rates in many populations across the world have been close to zero for a long time, leaving limited scope for analyzing population dynamics. At most, population ecology would be helpful in explaining growth patterns.

Second, insofar that population ecology could possibly have shed new light on population growth in higher education, the theory needed to compete with a well-established literature in the sociology of higher education (particularly the work of Trow, 1974, 1979, 1999) to explain growth patterns. Trow analyzes the impressive transformation of US higher education from elite to mass (and later almost universal) participation. Because of his work with and for the Organization for Economic Cooperation and Development (OECD; Trow, 1974, 1979), these ideas gained attention beyond the United States, first in Europe, later in other regions (see Tight, 2019, for an analysis of the reception and use of the concept of massification). In studying the transformation of higher education, much attention was paid to student demographics, to a lesser extent to organizational demographics, and arguably scholars did not immediately link organizational growth to population dynamics (as central feature of population ecology). In short, institutional diversity was sidetracked given a high(er) interest in issues revolving around participation and access.

That said, analyses of US higher education (e.g., Birnbaum, 1983; Morphew, 2009; Zammuto, 1984) all build on population ecology thinking and offer interesting insights in the limited growth in institutional diversity, despite a vast increase of student enrolments. And there is continued interest in the theme, given recent contributions to the debate on institutional diversity (Harris, 2020) as well as a focus on quantitative studies on organizational diversity in higher education (Huisman et al., 2008, 2015).

As will be clear from both the theoretical underpinnings and the applications, in population ecology studies, there is limited conceptual space for addressing globalization. That is, almost by default domestic boundaries are used to indicate the "natural" boundaries of populations under study. In that sense, organizational population studies in higher education adhere to the same principles as the "higher education as a system" scholars. In case globalization is addressed, it merely features as a contextual incident. There is, however, an emerging literature that studies populations at a global level (e.g., Abbott et al., 2016), although not yet—as far as I could detect—on higher education institutions.

Variants of Institutionalism and Alternative Approaches: Institutional Logics and Markets

As in the case of isomorphism, an argument can be offered regarding the dissemination of the concept of institutional logics. Here the storyline would start with pointing at the early references to logics, with most scholars acknowledging that the roots can be found in the work of Friedland and Alford (1991); but see also Thornton et al. (2012). Logics are defined as "a set of material practices and symbolic constructions [that] constitute organizing principles" (Friedland & Alford, 1991, p. 24), examples being the state, the family, religion, and capitalism. Presented as a macro-theory, scholars quickly applied it to organizations, finding it a helpful tool to address issues of agency, change, and historical variance. Exchanging the fairly homogeneous idea of organizations as actors, organizations are viewed as being populated by human agents with different norms and value sets (based on different logics). I follow Cai and Liu (2020, p. 137), noting that in institutional logics the notion of organizational field is extended to institutional fields, which may consist of various organizational fields. Partly as a consequence, structuration (DiMaggio & Powell, 1983) is not the sole driving force of isomorphism. Institutional logics opens the door for influences from outside strictly defined organizational fields, enabling change.

Lepori (2016) shows that higher education scholars have made extensive use of the conceptual tools offered by institutional logics. One explanation is that many higher education researchers would argue that higher education institutions are prime examples of (complex) organizations characterized by different logics. In fact, the standard view in higher education research stresses goal ambiguity, disciplinary subcultures (Becher & Trowler, 2001), and social structures (Whitley, 1978) and—on top of that—inherent struggles between academic professionals, administrators, and management on the basis of different value sets (see, e.g., universities as republics of scholars versus stakeholder organizations, Bleiklie & Kogan, 2007).

It would be fair, therefore, to argue that the interest in potential value and culture clashes within higher education not only emerged after institutional logics gained ground. Lepori (2016)—almost in passing—notes a striking similarity between institutional logics and what Clark (1983) termed the "triangle of coordination." Clark's depiction of the market, state, and academic oligarchy as key coordinating forces in academia, with a keen eye for historical and cross-national differences, can certainly be seen as institutional logics *avant la lettre*, especially if one were to compare his coordination forces with Thornton's (2004) logics state, markets, and professions. Moreover, debates on the market and the state in higher education date back to the 1970s (Leslie & Johnson, 1974). Also at the organizational level, there has been a lively debate on shifts in higher education from being a public service to a public-private hybrid or to an entrepreneurial university (see especially Clark, 1998; Etzkowitz, 2003). Finally, at the individual level, we see major contributions from scholars analyzing how academics themselves deal with the shift from state to market. Slaughter and Leslie's (1997) much-cited work on academic capitalism particularly comes to mind but also Gumport (2000)—actually using the term "institutional logics," without explicit references to the works of Alford, Friedland, Thornton, and so on—and Slaughter and Leslie (1997) argue that increasingly US academics start to act as "capitalists from within the public sector: they are state-subsidized entrepreneurs" in "public research universities, an environment full of contradictions, in which faculty and professional staff expend their human capital stocks increasingly in competitive situations" (Slaughter & Leslie, 1997, p. 9). They note that the extent to which academics engage with academic capitalism will likely differ by discipline, some of these fields being closer to the market (see also Lam, 2011). Interestingly, this rich literature foreshadows discussions in the institutional logics literature focusing on the question of whether logics are compatible or not and under what circumstances (Battilana & Dorado, 2010; Besharov & Smith, 2014; Greenwood et al., 2010). Through deeming eyes, it looks like much of the higher education literature of the 1980s and 1990s speaks of gradual transitions to the market logic or the integration of market elements in the public/state bureaucracy domain. But there is also a considerable literature that talks about the incompatibility of the different value sets of markets and the state or that shows that the shift toward the market does not yield the expected outcomes (Münch, 2014).

Higher education scholars may have "discovered" logics before it became *en vogue* in institutional theory, but—even more than in the case of isomorphism—they were using quite distinctive concepts and built on different disciplinary insights (economics, public administration, political sociology). Although authors in different countries did address the same theme, a cumulative and integrated perspective did not emerge. Lepori (2016) contends that also with respect to the use of institutional logics in higher education studies, scholars have not yet made use of all elements of the theory's toolbox, and he offers an interesting agenda for research. In that agenda, there is attention to unravelling institutional complexity in higher education institutions, but limited attention to connecting institutional logics very explicitly to globalization. The latter observation is echoed by sparse attention from other scholars on this theme (but see Buckner and Zapp, 2021, analyzing the global higher education landscape through the lens of institutional logics).

Conclusion and Reflection

The analysis in this chapter leads me to the following conclusions. First, the claim that higher education scholars have been slow to pick up insights from organizational theory needs qualification. In some areas, higher education scholars offered important insights, particularly on the topics of academic drift (isomorphism) and coordination (logics) that could be labeled as institutionalism *avant la lettre*. Interestingly, conceptual thinking of higher education scholars on these themes, by, for example, Riesman (1958), Pratt and Burgess (1974), and Clark (1983), has hardly been noticed by institutional organizational scholars, with a few notable exceptions, such as Clark's (1972) work on organizational saga. Why this is the case is mere speculation, but the explanation that each group of researchers lives and works in their own subdisciplinary/theme-based field makes sense. How and why exactly ideas travel from the disciplines to the field of higher education and vice-versa is, however, an exciting question for further investigation, especially in light of creating more synergy between different branches.

Second, developments in higher education research have largely been driven by specific features of their organizational configurations and contexts. This explains why the system approach is much applied, certainly in the period until the 1980s, and also explains why globalization did not feature largely in higher education studies (until the 2000s): It fitted with the then existing consensus that national boundaries are natural demarcations of collectives of organizations worthy of investigation. The same argument goes for the use of markets and market-inspired theories, which were only considered as "useful" approaches and concepts, once market mechanisms were introduced in higher education (with the exception of early applications in the United States; Leslie & Johnson, 1974). The argument can be extended to the lack of early engagement of higher education scholars with themes like organizational identity and image: In a context in which governments largely dictated the missions of their higher education institutions and these institutions were not yet "complete organizations" (Brunsson & Sahlin-Andersson, 2000), higher education did not seem a priority area for studying identity, image, and related themes like branding (but see Clark, 1972, for an exception; see also Dumay et al., 2017, for an overview). These points support the overall idea that much of higher education researchers' curiosity continued to be driven by real-time challenges in higher education, and to a lesser extent by theoretical puzzles.

Third, as a corollary, higher education scholars have struggled—and likely continue to struggle—with concepts like market, fields, populations, and systems in that the community of higher education researchers continues to see fields, systems, and so on as empirical phenomena, not as theoretical or conceptual constructs. Likewise, important drivers of organizational change in fields and systems, such as globalization, are primarily presented as "neutral" facts and/or context, whereas there is a clear need to conceptualize and unpack the notion of globalization and pay specific attention to organizational and field ramifications of globalization. In case individual researchers are aware of the theoretical underpinnings of some of these concepts, they may pick and mix from the organizational studies toolbox as they see fit (but see, e.g., Hüther and Krücken, 2016; Marginson, 2008, for important exceptions). The pick-and-mix approach in many higher education studies certainly has the potential to lead to innovative insights, but at the same time it sustains the fragility and fragmentation of higher education research (see also Daenekindt & Huisman, 2020).

To end on a positive note, the important insights offered by field theories and the organizational scholars that make use of these, especially in relation to globalization, should be taken to heart by higher education scholars. That is not to say that institutional approaches are flawless (see e.g., the critical reflection on institutional logics by Johansen & Waldorf, 2017, and the many unsolved puzzles in institutional theory in general by Greenwood et al., 2017). Neither is it argued that all institutional theories have fully embraced globalization and incorporated mechanisms to explain how and why globalization affects organizational fields. But the various theoretical strands within institutional theory offer many opportunities for application in the context of higher education. With globalization now really becoming visible in that field (think of phenomena like world-class universities, the strive for excellence, global rankings, increasing international collaboration, the rise of the knowledge society, and shifting power balances between nation states and their higher education systems), it is impossible to ignore globalization or to present it as "just" context. This recommendation is backed with an invitation to organizational scholars to (continue to) investigate higher education and its institutions. As shines through in the higher education literature addressed in this chapter, various puzzles—especially the one on divergence and/or homogenization in higher education fields—have not yet been solved. It might be particularly fruitful if organizational scholars and higher education scholars would join hands and tackle these issues. A particular research agenda I deem worthwhile would be to continue to analytically and empirically bridge the macro- and meso-levels. The relatively robust expectations and findings of world society scholars at the macro-levels of the higher education fabric should be complemented with in-depth investigations of meso-level (and where appropriate, micro-level) developments. That is, the impact of global educational frames and standards and possibly the increased impact thereof is not denied, but they do not sit comfortably with the many studies that highlight the diversity across and within higher education organizational fields (e.g., Buckner & Zapp, 2021; Huisman et al., 2002; Hüther & Krücken, 2016). World society scholars are aware of variations of the globalized model, but they are somewhat hesitant in proposing how to investigate and explain variations and deviations (but see Schofer et al., 2022). Whereas some authors call for a further theoretical sophistication, for example, by proposing to combine world society theory with institutional logics (Lounsbury & Wang, 2020), my plea would be to particularly enrich our understanding through empirical elaboration at the field level. Our scholarly preoccupation with rankings, the knowledge society, excellence, and high-reputation universities should be balanced with investigating organizational dynamics at "average," "ordinary," and "unique" institutions and to research field dynamics in less obvious (i.e., non-Anglo-Saxon) higher education systems.

ACKNOWLEDGMENTS

I would like to thank the following colleagues for helpful comments on a draft version of the chapter: Jelena Brankovic (Bielefeld University, Germany), Yuzhuo Cai (Tampere University, Finland), Marco Seeber (University of Agder, Norway), and Malcolm Tight (Lancaster University, UK).

Notes

1. I am aware that—on the basis of a particular article—it is not always easy to decide whether the author is a higher education researcher or a discipline-based scholar. Generally, looking at a researcher's CV, one is probably able to decide whether s/he belongs to either camp, but arguably there is a significant gray area with higher education researchers unremittingly using disciplinary theories/concepts and disciplinary scholars spending much of their time researching higher education. The same applies to the use of the term "higher education literature" (some if it being applied, but some also discipline based) and higher education journals.

2. Here it is worthwhile to note that Ramirez actually is a key representative of the Stanford School with a keen interest in higher education. In that sense it is difficult to label him strictly as a higher education scholar (he pays a lot of attention to higher education and publishes in typical higher education journals) or a disciplinary scholar (educational sociologist in the Stanford tradition).

References

Abbott, K. W., Green, J. F., & Keohane, R. O. (2016). Organizational ecology and institutional change in global governance. *International Organization, 70*(2), 247–277.

Battilana, J., & Dorado, S. (2010). Building sustainable hybrid organizations: The case of commercial microfinance organizations. *Academy of Management Journal, 53*(6), 1419–1440.

Baum, J. A. C., & Shipilov, A. V. (2006). Ecological approaches to organizations. In S. R. Clegg, C. Hardy, T. B. Lawrence, & W.R. Nord (Eds.), *Sage handbook for organization studies* (pp. 55–110). Sage.

Becher, T. and Trowler, P. (2001), *Academic tribes and territories: Intellectual enquiry and the cultures of disciplines* (2nd ed.). Open University Press/SRHE.

Beerkens, E. (2003). Globalisation and higher education research. *Journal of Studies in International Education, 7*(2), 128–148.

Berelson, B. (1960). *Graduate education in the United States*. McGraw-Hill.

Besharov, M. L., & Smith, W. K. (2014). Multiple institutional logics in organizations: Explaining their varied nature and implications. *Academy of Management Review, 39*(3), 364–381.

Birnbaum, R. (1983). *Maintaining diversity in higher education*. Jossey-Bass.

Bleiklie, I., & Kogan, M. (2007). Organization and governance of universities. *Higher Education Policy, 20*, 477–493.

Brunsson, N., & Sahlin-Andersson, K. (2000). Constructing organizations: The example of public sector reform. *Organization Studies, 21*(4), 721–746.

Buckner, E., & Zapp, M. (2021). Institutional logics in the global higher education landscape: Differences in organizational characteristics by sector and founding era. *Minerva, 59*(1), 27–51.

Cai, Y., & Liu, C. (2020). The role of university as institutional entrepreneur in regional innovation system: Towards an analytical framework. In M. T. Preto, A. Daniel, & A. Teixeira (Eds.), *Examining the role of entrepreneurial universities in regional development* (pp. 133–155). IGI Global.

Cai, Y., & Mehari, J. (2015). The use of institutional theory in higher education research. In J. Huisman & M. Tight (Eds.), *Theory and method in higher education research, volume III* (pp. 1–25). Emerald,.

Chou, M.-S., & Ravinet, P. (2015). The rise of "higher education regionalism": An agenda for higher education research. In J. Huisman, H. de Boer, D. D. Dill & M. Souto-Otero (Eds.), *The Palgrave international handbook of higher education policy and governance* (pp 361–378). Palgrave.

Clark, B. R. (1972). The organizational saga in higher education. *Administrative Science Quarterly, 14,* 178–184.

Clark, B. R. (1983). *The higher education system. Academic organization in cross-national perspective.* University of California Press.

Clark, B. R. (1984). Introduction. In B. R. Clark (Ed.), *Perspectives on higher education. Eight disciplinary and comparative views* (pp. 1–16). University of California Press.

Clark, B. R. (1998). *Creating entrepreneurial universities. Organizational pathways of transformation.* Pergamon Press.

Czarniawska, B., & Sevón, G. (2005). *Global ideas: How ideas, objects and practices travel in a global economy.* Liber & Copenhagen Business School Press.

Daenekindt, S., & Huisman, J. (2020). Mapping the scattered field of research on higher education: A correlated topic model of 17,000 articles, 1991–2018. *Higher Education, 80*(3), 571–587.

DiMaggio, P. J., & Powell, W. W. (1983). The iron cage revisited: Institutional isomorphism and collective rationality in organizational fields. *American Sociological Review, 48*(2), 147–160.

Dumay, X., Draelants, H., & Dahan, A. (2017). Organizational identity of universities: A Review of the literature from 1972 to 2014. In J. Huisman & M. Tight (Eds.), *Theory and method in higher education research, volume 3* (pp. 99–118). Emerald.

Elken, M., & Vukasovic, M. (2019). The looseness of loose coupling: The use and misuse of "loose coupling" in higher education research. In J. Huisman and M. Tight (Eds.), *Theory and method in higher education research, volume V* (pp. 53–71). Emerald.

Etzkowitz, H. (2003). Research groups as "quasi-firms": The invention of the entrepreneurial university. *Research Policy, 32,* 109–121.

Friedland, R., & Alford, R.R. (1991). Bringing society back in: Symbols, practices, and institutional contradictions. In W.W. Powell & P.J. DiMaggio (Eds.), *The new institutionalism in organizational analysis* (pp. 232–263). University of Chicago Press.

Fumasoli, T., & Stensaker, B. (2013). Organizational studies in higher education: A reflection on historical themes and prospective trends. *Higher Education Policy, 26*(4), 479–496.

Galbraith, P. (2013). Out of the frying pan: Into the fire of post-global financial crisis (GFC) university management. *Higher Education Policy, 26*(4), 523–550.

Goedegebuure, L., & van Vught, F. (1994). *Comparative policy studies in higher education.* Lemma.

Greenwood, R., Magán Díaz, A., Xiao Li, S., & Céspedes Lorente, J. (2010). The multiplicity of institutional logics and the heterogeneity of organizational responses. *Organization Science, 21*(2), 521–539.

Greenwood, R., Oliver, C., Lawrence, T. B., & Meyer, R. E. (Eds.) (2017). *The SAGE handbook of organizational institutionalism.* Sage.

Gumport, P. J. (2000). Academic restructuring: Organizational change and institutional imperatives. *Higher Education, 39*(1), 67–91.

Hannan, M. T., & Freeman, J. (1977). The population ecology of organizations. *American Journal of Sociology, 82*(5), 929–964.

Harris, M. S. (2020). An empirical typology of the institutional diversity of U.S. colleges and universities. *Innovative Higher Education, 45*, 183–199.

Hawley, A. (1968). Human ecology. In D. L. Sills (Ed.), *International encyclopedia of the social sciences* (pp. 328–337). Macmillan.

Hazelkorn, E. (2015). *Rankings and the reshaping of higher education: The battle for world-class excellence*. Palgrave Macmillan.

Huisman, J., Lepori, B., Seeber, M., Frølich, N., & Scordato, L. (2015). Measuring institutional diversity across higher education systems. *Research Evaluation, 24*(4), 369–379.

Huisman, J., Meek, L., & Wood, F. (2008). Institutional diversity in higher education: A cross-national and longitudinal analysis. *Higher Education Quarterly, 61*(4), 563–577.

Huisman, J., & Morphew, C.C. (1998). Centralization and diversity. Evaluating the effects of government policies in U.S.A. and Dutch higher education. *Higher Education Policy, 11*(1), 1–13.

Huisman, J., Norgard, J., Gulddahl-Rasmussen, J., & Stensaker, B. (2002). Alternative universities revisited: A study of the distinctiveness of universities established in the spirit of 1968. *Tertiary Education and Management, 8*(3), 316–332.

Hüther, O. & Krücken, G. (2016). Nested organizational fields: Isomorphism and differentiation among European universities. *Research in the Sociology of Organizations, 46*, 53–83.

Jarvis, P. (1999). Global trends in lifelong learning and the response of the universities, *Comparative Education, 35*(2), 249–257.

Jencks, C., & Riesman, D. (1968). *The academic revolution*. Doubleday.

Johansen, C. B., & Waldorff, S. B. (2017). What are institutional logics—And where is the perspective taking us? In G. Krücken, C. Mazza, R. E. Meyer, & P. Walgenbach (Eds.), *New themes in institutional analysis. Topics and issues from European research* (pp. 51–76). Edward Elgar.

Kehm, B., & Teichler, U. (2007). Research on internationalization of higher education. *Journal of Studies in International Education, 11*(3–4), 260–273.

Kluttz, D. N., & Fligstein, N. (2016). Varieties of sociological field theory. In S. Abrutyn (Ed.), *Handbook of contemporary sociological theory* (pp. 185–204). Springer.

Lam, A. (2011). What motivates academic scientists to engage in research commercialization: "Gold," "ribbon" or "puzzle"? *Research Policy, 40*, 1354–1368.

Lepori, B. (2016). Universities as hybrids: Applications of institutional logics theory to higher education. In J. Huisman & M. Tight (Eds.), *Theory and method in higher education research, volume II* (pp. 245–264). Emerald.

Lepori, B., & Kyvik, S. (2010). *The research mission of higher education institutions outside the university sector*. Springer.

Leslie, L. L., & Johnson, G. P. (1974). The market model and higher education. *Journal of Higher Education, 45*(1), 1–20.

Levinson, R. M. (1989). The faculty and institutional isomorphism. *Academe, 75*(1), 23–27.

Lounsbury, M., & Wang, M. S. (2020). Into the clearing: Back to the future of constitutive institutional analysis. *Organization Theory, 1*(1), 1–27.

Maassen, P. A. M., & Potman, H. P. (1990). Strategic decision making in higher education. An analysis of the new planning system in Dutch higher education. *Higher Education, 20*, 393–410.

Macfarlane, B. (2012). The higher education research archipelago. *Higher Education Research & Development, 31*(1), 129–131.

Marginson, S. (2008). Global field and global imagining: Bourdieu and worldwide higher education. *British Journal of Sociology of Education, 29*(3), 303–315.

Marginson, S., & Rhoades, G. (2002). Beyond national states, markets, and systems of higher education: A glonacal agency heuristic. *Higher Education, 43*, 281–309.

Marginson, S., & Wende, M. van der (2007). *Globalisation and higher education*. OECD.

Meyer, J. W., Boli, J., Thomas, G. M., & Ramirez, F. O. (1997). World society and the nation-state. *American Journal of Sociology, 103*(1), 144–181.

Mezias, S. J. (1990). An institutional model of organizational practice: Financial reporting at the Fortune 200. *Administrative Science Quarterly, 35*(3), 431–457.

Mizruchi, M. S., & Fein, L. C. (1999). The social construction of organizational knowledge: A study of the uses of coercive, mimetic, and normative isomorphism. *Administrative Science Quarterly, 44*(4), 653–683.

Morphew, C. C. (2009). Conceptualizing change in the institutional diversity of US colleges and universities. *Journal of Higher Education, 80*(3), 243–269.

Münch, R. (2014). *Academic capitalism. Universities in the global struggle for excellence.* Routledge.

Naidoo, R. (2010). Fields and institutional strategy: Bourdieu on the relationship between higher education, inequality and society. *British Journal of Sociology of Education, 25*(4), 457–471.

Neave, G. (1979). Academic drift: Some views from Europe. *Studies in Higher Education, 4*(2), 143–159.

Neave, G. (2001). The European dimension in higher education: An excursion into the modern use of historical analogues. In J. Huisman, P. A. M. Maassen, & G. Neave (Eds.), *Higher education and the nation state. The international dimension of higher education* (pp. 13–73). Pergamon.

Paradeise, C., & Thoenig, J.-C. (2013). Academic institutions in search of quality: Local orders and global standards. *Organization Studies, 34*(2), 189–218.

Parsons, T., & Platt, G. M. (1973). *The American university*. Cambridge, MA: Harvard University Press.

Pfeffer, T., & Stichweh, R. (2015). Systems theoretical perspectives on higher education policy and governance. In J. Huisman, H. de Boer, D. D. Dill, & M. Souto-Otero (Eds.). *The Palgrave international handbook of higher education policy and governance* (pp. 152–175). Palgrave.

Pratt, J., & Burgess, T. (1974). *Polytechnics: A report.* Pitman.

Ramirez, F. O. (2006). The rationalization of universities. In M. L. Djelic & K. Sahlin-Andersson (Eds.), *Transnational governance: Institutional dynamics of regulation* (pp. 224–245). Cambridge University Press.

Ramirez, F. O., & Tiplic, D. (2014). In pursuit of excellence? Discursive patterns in European higher education research. *Higher Education, 67*, 439–455.

Riesman, D. (1958). *Constraint and variety in American education.* Doubleday.

Schofer, E., Lerch, J. C., & Meyer, J. W. (2022). Illiberal reactions to higher education. *Minerva, 60*(4), 509–534.

Schultz, R. E., & Stickler, W. H. (1965). Vertical extension of academic programs in institutions of higher education. *Educational Record, 46*(Summer), 231–241.

Scott, W. R. (2004). Reflections on a half-century of organizational sociology. *Annual Review of Sociology, 30*(1), 1–21.

Shin, J. C., & Kehm, B. (Eds. (2013). *Institutionalization of world-class university in global competition.* Kluwer.

Slaughter, S., & Leslie, L. L. (1997). *Academic capitalism: Politics, policies, and the entrepreneurial university.* Johns Hopkins University Press.

Taylor, B. J. (2015). Strategic action fields in US higher education: The 1939 Mercer University heresy trial. *Journal of Historical Sociology, 29*(3), 359–384.

Teichler, U. (1988). *Changing patterns of higher education systems.* Jessica Kingsley.

Teichler, U. (2000). Higher education research and its institutional basis. In S. Schwarz & U. Teichler (Eds.), *The institutional basis of higher education research. Experiences and perspectives* (pp. 13–24). Kluwer Academic.

Teichler, U. (2005). Research on higher education in Europe. *European Journal of Education, 40*(4), 447–469.

Thornton, P. (2004). *Markets from culture: Institutional logics and organizational decisions in higher education publishing.* Stanford University Press.

Thornton, P. H., Ocasio, W., & Lounsbury, M. (2012). *The institutional logics perspective: A new approach to culture, structure and process.* Oxford University Press.

Tight, M. (2004). Higher education research: An atheoretical community of practice? *Higher Education Research and Development, 23*(4), 395–411.

Tight, M. (2013). Discipline and methodology in higher education research. *Higher Education Research & Development, 32*(1), 136–151.

Tight, M. (2014). Discipline and theory in higher education research. *Research Papers in Education, 29*(1), 93–110.

Tight, M. (2015). Theory development and application in higher education research: The case of academic drift. *Journal of Educational Administration and History, 47*(1), 84–99.

Tight, M. (2019). Mass higher education and massification. *Higher Education Policy, 32*(1), 93–108.

Tight, M. (2020). Higher education: discipline or field of study? *Tertiary Education and Management.*

Trow, M. (1974). Problems in the transition from elite to mass higher education. In OECD (Ed.), *General report on the conference on future structures of post-secondary education* (pp. 55–101). Organisation for Economic Cooperation and Development.

Trow, M. (1979). Elite and mass higher education: American models and European realities. In NBUC (Ed.), *Research into higher education: Processes and structures* (pp. 44–53). National Board of Universities and Colleges.

Trow, M. (1999). From mass higher education to universal access: The American advantage. *Minerva, 37*(4), 303–328.

Vanderstraeten, R. (2015). The making of Parsons's The American University. *Minerva, 53*(4), 307–325.

Washington, M., & Ventresca, M. J. (2004). How organizations change: The role of institutional support mechanisms in the incorporation of higher education visibility strategies, 1874–1995. *Organization Science, 15*(1), 82–97.

Whitley, R. (1978). Types of science, organizational strategies and patterns of work in research laboratories in different scientific fields. *Social Science Information, 17*(3), 427–447.

Zammuto, R. F. (1984). Are the liberal arts an endangered species? *Journal of Higher Education, 55*(2), 184–211.

SECTION II

Structural Approaches to Globalization in Education

CHAPTER 9

THE GLOBALIZATION OF EXPERTISE?

Epistemic Governance, Quantification, and the Consultocracy

JENNY OZGA

INTRODUCTION

THIS discussion draws on research on education primarily, but not exclusively, focusing on Europe, which explores knowledge-governing relations and highlights the knowledge-based resources available to transnational governing elites, including regulatory instruments and performance data (see, e.g., Fenwick et al., 2014; Grek et al., 2021; Lawn & Grek, 2012; Ozga et al., 2011). It shows how those instruments make possible the shift toward governing through networks of new actors, who define education in global terms, and look to the benchmarking and competitive performance regimes of transnational organizations for solutions to be applied across nation states (Gorur, 2017, 2019). The discussion highlights the interconnection of changes in knowledge and change in governing, including the rapid dissemination of knowledge as data, its increased availability and complexity, along with change in the actors producing knowledge, especially the growth of private actors, brokers, consultants, and specialists who move knowledge into policy (Ball, 2016, 2018a, 2018b), and the politicization of knowledge production and its shaping by policy requirements into "actionable" knowledge (Grundmann & Stehr, 2012). The consequences of this development may be summarized as the simultaneous *externalization* of policy advice, especially from scientific and technical sources, and the *politicization* of the knowledge production processes through which scientific and technical knowledge is produced (Fourcade 2010; Stone 2013, 2019).

Globalization is understood here primarily as neoliberal globalization, that is, as the global reconstruction of production relations, as a neoliberal "project" driving the global integration of markets (Bishop & Payne, 2021; Robinson, 2017). The dominance of economic logic in this project reduces the capacity of nation states and prioritizes their activity in the economic sphere, including in the policy field of education. Neoliberal globalization drives the restructuring of education provision and encourages the entry of new, often commercial actors into the field. The changes that follow from neoliberal globalization of education illustrate an often overlooked feature of education, that is, the extent to which it is embedded in wider economic relations, and reveals that it is not an autonomous field. Even within its traditional location in the nation state, it was subject to three distinct, sometimes competing demands—serving and sustaining the economy, enabling political stability, and building social and cultural cohesion. Globalization, and the pursuit of the knowledge economy, prioritizes the economic, at the expense of the social/cultural and political, and with consequences for these spheres of activity.

It was within the nation state in Western Europe that most education and training systems developed in the 19th and 20th centuries as negotiated settlements between nation-building states and education workforces, to advance agendas driven by projects of national identification, industrialization, and by Enlightenment commitments to individual equality and collective progress. These agendas were framed by nation-building activities and by a modernist scientific rationality that sought evidence about populations, and which relied upon and built a professional workforce of state employees to deal with social problems. The "problem-solving" functions of education included preparation of the workforce, shaping and disciplining identities to ensure social order and cohesion, and legitimating social selection and ordering that often mirror social and economic inequalities. Education policy and national education systems, with different emphases and different traditions, mediated these contradictory imperatives in different ways, for example through a professionalized teaching workforce, and assessment and examinations systems that were accepted as objective measures of merit, but without solving the problems they create, or eliminating the tensions that they generate. Education was (and is) contested terrain, historically sedimented in distinctive national systems, and functioning as a repository and agency of—sometimes disputed—national traditions and sometimes shifting—identities (Ozga, 2017). The contradictory functions demanded of it were pursued with varying levels of intensity, depending on largely exogenous factors.

The knowledge economy agenda combines with globalization to disrupt those nationally embedded and institutionalized practices and norms in education/learning, as in other spheres. Education systems are tightly coupled to the knowledge economy (Jessop et al., 2008), in which knowledge—its production and application—is seen as essential in securing long-term economic growth, and which therefore requires restructuring of education provision at all scales. Knowledge economy-driven change from the 1980s onward includes the increasingly technocratic rationalization of work in the context of globalized production and the introduction of new work cultures and the relationships that accompany them, creating increased employee dependency, encouraging limited and punitive contractual relations that advantage transnational employers, fueling demand for intensified productive efforts from workers, resulting in their heightened risk and insecurity, as well as the de-collectivization of their interests and alienation from historically embedded values. These alterations in working conditions do little to sustain the idea that workers and workplaces are generating resources for the Knowledge Economy in knowledge-rich continuously learning environments. All forms of education, from early childhood provision, through schools, vocational education and training, and higher education, are now interconnected through the attitudes and dispositions encouraged by new knowledge practices, which are consistent and coherent across the range of institutions and beyond and outside them. Schooling and postschool education develops learners' capacity to learn, while learners also learn to constantly evaluate their learning through self-evaluation, and embodied human capital, codified through qualifications, is differentially valorized in labor markets that are ordered by knowledge.

Changes wrought by neoliberal globalization include changes in the architecture of power globally and within nation states, so that the market is treated as "a kind of constitutional order, with its own rules, procedures and institutions" (Jayasuriya, 2001, p. 452), placing economic institutions, such as multinationals, and other international organizations (IOs) beyond politics. Its key characteristics are the flexibilization of labor, commodification of goods and services, privatization, deregulation and reregulation, outsourcing, subcontracting, worldwide production chains, and a global regulatory structure—the World Trade Organization (Robinson, 2011). The consequences are truly global, as from the 1990s onward, unstoppable neoliberal globalization of markets spread beyond the Anglosphere and is evident in post-communist Central and Eastern Europe, and in the acceleration of China's Western-style economic development. These features combine to deepen inequalities, within and between nation states, including in educational opportunities. There is evidence of reduced social mobility and increasing economic inequality in countries as politically and economically diverse as Singapore, the United States, Israel, Australia, Sweden, Denmark, Japan, and Germany (Williamson, 2013). The neoliberal state is reduced to a facilitator of globalization, and thus can no longer be attentive to the function of maintaining a degree of social harmony or inclusion in order to reduce internal conflict, nor can it sustain and promote a coherent account of national identity, and thus maintain legitimacy. As a consequence, inequalities become more evident and deeper, conflicts between groups increase, and vulnerable social groups feel—and indeed are—abandoned. Put bluntly, "the transnational model of accumulation does not require an inclusionary social base and is inherently polarizing" (Robinson, 2011, p. 363).

As the nation state declines, so global governance is facilitated through multilayered networks of collaboration linking national and local actors to worldwide networks and structures, with the capacity for global political action. These networks are populated by a transnational global elite, engaged in epistemic governance that reflects the contemporary interdependency of governing and knowledge (Alasuutari, 2016; Normand, 2016). This interdependency is made possible by the work of experts, and the discussion now focuses on their role in governing education; on knowledge production and use by international organizations; on the construction, diffusion, and use of knowledge expressed as performance data, and the relationship of knowledge to politics. It highlights the ways in which transnational economic and political organizations pursue the global knowledge economy, enrolling nation states in this project so that the growing economization of education globally is both "colonising the cultural and transforming the nature of the political, at all scales" (Robertson & Dale, 2017, p. 857). The concluding section offers a preliminary assessment of the impact of COVID-19 on globalization, expertise, and transnational education policy.

EPISTEMIC GOVERNANCE, EXPERTS, AND INTERNATIONAL ORGANIZATIONS

Epistemic governance foregrounds the importance of knowledge as a resource for governing, knowledge that is available in mobile, global forms, produced and translated into "actionable knowledge" (Grundmann & Stehr, 2012) by experts and collected and distributed through knowledge-based technologies. Epistemic governance works through networks of experts who claim to possess objective policy-relevant knowledge, but who often share a set of normative beliefs about competition, performance measurement, and the applicability of business methods to public services that guide their knowledge production activities (Shiroma, 2014). The influence of global education reform programs, promoted by IOs, and networks of experts and the technologies associated with them (Grek, 2017; Sahlberg, 2016) is a key feature of neoliberal globalization in education. Hierarchical organization and formal regulation are increasingly displaced by networks of new actors, especially policy entrepreneurs (Ball, 2012; Ball et al., 2016), public/private hybrids, and nonformal actors (consumers, third-sector members, media organizations), working with standards and benchmarks and guided in action by data. Political actors appeal to the authority of science and expert knowledge (Alasuutari, 2016; Normand, 2012; Ozga, 2019) most visibly in the policy field of education in the Organization for Economic Cooperation and Development's (OECD) Program for International Student Assessment (PISA) for schools and its publication of comparative performance data, enabling IOs to establish themselves as authoritative sources of epistemic capital and capacity-building knowledge, as sources of information about the performance of competitors, and as offering evidence to justify the pursuit of particular domestic agendas. Supra/transnational organizations, including the OECD and the European Union, pursue a "structured agenda" for education (Robertson & Dale, 2017). That structured agenda contains prescriptions for effective education governance, prescriptions which include performance measurement, decentralization, and the involvement of private actors, and which works through coordination alongside a more direct regulating role. There is an increasingly complex landscape requiring coordination: public-private hybrids offer education services, provision is shaped by parental choice and other new public management methods, and this calls up different local, national, and international networks seeking to influence education policy, and has seen the emergence of new "knowledge actors" engaged in transnational governance (Stone, 2013, 2019). These knowledge actors operate to "translate" the increasing amount of information available, often in the form of performance data, as the massive expansion of information requires networks of experts with skills in synthesizing and brokering who reduce possibilities and make knowledge actionable:

> The rapid growth of experts, advisers and consultants in education arises from the rapid expansion of knowledge/information, this provides opportunities for simplification of the problem of endless competing interpretation in order to provide a basis for action. (Grundmann & Stehr, 2012, 20–21)

This network of experts operates to produce and disseminate a "cognitive consensus," that is, a system of standardized policy agendas and their repertoire of benchmarks, indicators, and competitive testing regimes. The homogeneity of programs of whole system structural education reform (Ball, 2016; Sahlberg, 2016) is striking, and this consensus is promoted through appeals to its "evidence-based" nature, or its "common sense" about "what works" which conceals the political nature of translation, because, as Shiroma (2014) points out, the label "expert" confers scientific status and authority. This is a limited, truncated version of science that does not acknowledge its often-contested nature, nor is it attentive to the political conditions in which scientific knowledge is produced, accepted, or contested. The growth of this form of expertise is recognized as a transnational phenomenon, with experts increasingly working between national and transnational arenas, and identified as a "new governing elite" (Stone, 2013, p. 41).

The OECD provides a good case study of the increasing transnational influence of IOs, and their changing production of knowledge and expertise from the 1960s to contemporary times, reflecting a shift from independent research activity to the advocacy of standardized policies in education globally. The OECD is able to promote itself as an expert knowledge-based organization, "above" national politics, and sufficiently distanced from the context to be dispassionate and objective. Through a longitudinal study over five countries and six decades, Rautalin et al. (2021) show how OECD's Economic Surveys have shifted in tone and content, from concentration in the 1960s on amassing information through background research, to the prioritization of policy recommendations, presented with a sharper focus, claiming ontological authority and designed to inform not only policymakers but also wider publics. Over time, the importance of the independent research activity of the organization and its basis in academic literature has declined, so that it becomes a background to the increasing use of "persuasive talk" that foregrounds more directive advice and policy steering. A further, parallel development is the growing disconnection between evidence collected in the reviews and the policy advice offered. Indeed, Rautalin and her colleagues conclude (2021, p. 15) that the OECD has moved, in this period, from being "a multi-centred organization for cooperation and development" to operating as a global policy consultancy.

The capacity of IOs to shape a global education policy field is also apparent in the influence of experts working with OECD in defining and promoting global competency, an idea directly connected to the knowledge economy. Global competency assumes the possibility of a measurable and shared level of capacity and orientation to learning worldwide, assessable through OECD's PISA for Global Competence (OECD, 2017). As Gardinier (2021, pp. 8–9) demonstrates, the measurement of global competence promotes an idea of global learners as "autonomous individuals who can separate themselves from their social identities"; the imagined ideal learner is "future oriented, socially-mature, goal oriented, and extremely self-aware" (pp. 9–10). This instrument was developed, through the meeting of a group of international experts in 2015 who worked to construct a system of assessment designed to "help education systems identify what is working and what needs to be implemented more intentionally and systematically to ensure all students develop global competence" (Asia Society/OECD, 2018, p. 4 quoted in Gardinier, 2021, p. 13).

The influence of global networks of experts is further apparent in the growing use and impact of Country Reviews (see, e.g., Browes & Verger, 2020; Grek, 2017, 2019, 2020; Hunter, 2013). The OECD's PISA publishes data on performance that ranks nations competitively and thus identifies "problems" that need to be addressed. Those problems may then be further investigated and remedies proposed through OECD's process of Country Review, in which international teams of experts are invited by national governments to work with "local" experts to gather and analyze data to highlight issues at the national level. This process culminates in the provision of advice and tools judged necessary to put things right. For example, Scotland has engaged substantially with OECD, following poor performance in PISA for schools in 2015, where schools recorded their worst-ever performance, and scores for math, reading, and science all declined. This put pressure on the Scottish government (TSG), as the ruling Scottish National Party (SNP) had been in power for a decade, and the attainment gap between less affluent pupils and their more privileged peers sat uncomfortably with their claim of combining excellence in education with equity and fairness (Ozga, 2019). TSG commissioned OECD expert reviews (OECD, 2015, 2021) as well as appointing an International Council of Education Advisers, which together called for intensive reform processes that signaled disruptions and departures from established relationships among expertise, knowledge, and policy. These required substantial system restructuring, increased concentration on attainment measures, and stronger assessment and testing regimes. TSG also initiated a full-scale review of curriculum design and delivery, later extended to include examinations and assessment policy. Before these interventions, Scotland's policy knowledge and expertise was located within a national "policy community" of central government, the local authorities, and educational institutions, including the organized teaching profession, operating relatively consensually, against a background of fairly widespread support for public comprehensive education. Media reporting of the PISA "crisis" fueled criticism of the narrowness and interdependence of that community, and of the conservatism and complacency of the teaching profession, and encouraged an attempted policy shift toward the closer alignment of Scottish education with OECD's norms. This instance also illustrates the importance of performance data as a key element in the repertoire of IOs, and, indeed, as a central feature of neoliberal globalization of education.

Datafication, Digitization, and Quantification

Data enter the frame because the transmission of information is necessary to hold together the diverse and networked governing forms that accompany globalization. Data enable this complex education arena to be calculated, for example through the Bologna Accord, that harmonizes different European higher education systems by creating a single degree system, and the Lisbon Process or Open Method of Coordination (OMC), in which benchmarking and comparison are core governing processes across a learning society shaped by economic reform, citizenship obligations, employability, and international comparison and performance testing in education (Grek et al., 2021). Data production and management are essential to the new governing practices; constant comparison is its symbolic feature, as well as a distinctive mode of operation. Adherence to the market principle of competition drives the engagement with comparison, and comparison establishes three key principles (1) that regular and systematic assessments are truthful practices for the improvement of national education systems; (2) that such improvement has to be analyzed in relation to the pace of change of other countries; (3) that international comparison of student performances develops the quality of national education systems while capturing educational complexity and diversity (Carvalho, 2012). What counts as knowledge work—and especially knowledge work for policy—is now highly dependent on data patterning and its interpretation. New networked data-rich governing forms promote the idea of transparency and accountability so that knowledge is drawn in to supporting the authority of these social and political processes: potentially disruptive elements are harnessed to promote a discourse of continuous scientific and technical advance (Fenwick et al., 2014; Gorur, 2019).

The construction of indicators and the collection and processing of performance data install comparison as a basic principle in building policy consensus and also, importantly, in embedding self-regulation (Ozga et al., 2011; Verger et al., 2018) as data systems not only monitor the activity of teachers and learners, but also shape individual conduct while apparently enabling autonomous, choice-making activity supported by information (e.g., in parental choice of school, student choices in higher education, and, more broadly, life choices about individual health, investments, and so on; Piattoeva, 2014). The "popular" work that data do is to make connections to individual citizens/learners/pupils in such a way as to steer or mediate their decisions and actions in relation to economic demands, to family relationships, and to all other aspects of everyday life. As Piattoeva points out, this development is not confined to "official" data:

> social media has grown into an efficient tool for the government of individuals and masses. The Internet sites that promote the neoliberal evaluation culture are motivated by and deeply embedded in contemporary social and political reforms, and rely on a new mode of regulation—governing at a distance through the regulated choices of individual citizens, and through specifying subjects of responsibility, autonomy and choice. (Piattoeva, 2014, p. 8)

Digital data enable schools and entire sectors of society such as education to be seen as "computational" projects (Molstad & Pettersson, 2019). The "modeling" of education through digital data creates algorithmically driven "systems thinking" where complex social problems are converted into complex but solvable statistical problems. Thus, digital data encourage "solutionism." Data analysis thus begins to produce education settings, to the same degree as education settings produce data (Selwyn, 2018). Put differently, data and data practices are not neutral representations or measurements of educational activities, but bring these activities and results into being (Decuypere, 2021).

Digital data work within education/schooling is now normalized—it is understood universally as the basis of improvement, and it is increasing in scope: for example, there is software to support classroom management; to guide school inspection (Ozga, 2016) to perform assessment (Hartong, 2021); and to monitor school performance across all sectors and stages, including in higher education, where multinationals see market opportunities (Williamson, 2021). The generation, accumulation, processing, and analysis of digital data are understood transnationally, nationally, and institutionally as a solution to problems of schooling. Government administrative systems have always kept records and monitored conduct and behavior; however, the capacity to track transactions in real time and to connect transactional data across sites is new. New forms of data thus enable a shift from collectivized governing strategies—applied to the "school populations" or to "ethnic minority pupils"—to individualized, targeted practices that recognize how people move and change and "keep up" with them: it enables individualization, personalization, and differential treatment (Kitchin & Dodge, 2011).

From this perspective, the very significant development of data resources in education from the early 2000s is not only a story of increased technical capacity but connects directly to the prioritization of attainment (often measured by national or international test results at fixed intervals in the school career, the results of which are published) and to a determined effort to shift school cultures so that data monitoring and active data use became the driving force of school activity. This real-time tracking of activity has greatly increased pressure on schools to be actively engaged with their data and to be able to demonstrate their engagement through constant attention to maintaining and updating their various data systems. This state of permanent engagement creates what Thrift and French call an "automagical" system of regulation in which pupil and teacher values, eligibility, and rewards are constantly calculated and recalculated (Thrift & French, 2002).

ELITES AND EXPERTISE

Globalization is characterized increasingly through reference to its horizontal, culturally based forms of power and control, and distributed social relations, reflecting its networked nature (Ball, 2018a; Ball et al., 2016). There is considerable potential, however, in revisiting conceptualizations of elites, including through the lens of expertise and the production of policy knowledge, in order to highlight elite strategies of knowledge production and to illustrate how they intersect with emergent and established governing forms. One effect of the current controversies and the hostility expressed toward elites in populist discourse has been to revive theoretical and empirical work in this area, as political scientists and sociologists of policy seek to understand the intersection between the possession of economic, cultural, and political capital and the growth of consultancy, technology, and new governing networks (Normand, 2016). Productive approaches to elites recognize their capacity to adjust to change in the structures of domination (Scott, 2008) and their ability to function as dynamic institutional formations, while continuing to store, hold, and combine this with the "exercise and mobilization of power" (Reed, 2012, p. 210).

In neoliberal globalization there is an interrelationship among networks, data, and the emergence of elites who mobilize knowledge resources in order to form rather than simply inform policy. These elites influence through what Eric Bonds, in his study of climate and environment policy (Bonds, 2010), calls "knowledge administration"—that is, by selecting what counts as knowledge and what does not. Indeed, Bonds draws attention to four distinct ways in which power is exercised by elites that combine to shape knowledge processes: *Information suppression*, that is, the purposive suppression of knowledge damaging to their interests; *contesting knowledge*, in which elites fund experts to attack knowledge that poses a threat to their power base; *knowledge production*, in which elites fund think tanks or otherwise promote the production of particular knowledges; and *knowledge administration*, in which elites influence the selection of what information counts as knowledge and what information does not. Elites organize themselves in networks that connect business interests with scientific consultancies, public relations firms, university researchers, and government decision-makers to mobilize resources in order to shape what is known about a subject of concern. Elites fund think tanks, or private foundations that channel money to researchers who produce knowledge useful to them. Elite-funded think tanks also channel money to experts who discredit or raise doubts about scientific research that may damage or challenge elite interests. This may be accomplished through lobbyists or through the personal and business relationships of elites. This focus on elites and experts reinforces the importance of attention to structures of domination and their continuity and power in the analysis of neoliberal globalization and education.

Those structures of domination can then be placed *in relation with* the contingent, fluid, and multiple centers of authority or "horizontal" coalitions that preoccupy much contemporary scholarship, which may underplay the enduring, "vertical" structures of domination within which they are embedded. Attention to those structures also foregrounds the capacity of expert elites to adjust and learn strategies through which they continue to pursue their material and social interests. As Scott suggests, "authoritative" and "expert" elites have the political and cultural capacity to develop "moral vocabularies of discourse" (Scott, 1996, p. 44) through which they are able to legitimate their dominance and to organize the governance regimes through which they maintain their authority.

The cognitive consensus in education referred to earlier is such a "moral vocabulary" that appeals to science and evidence as a way to support the claim that the politics has been taken out of education—the argument is that we are now "getting it right" educationally (Ramirez & Meyer, 2002, p. 94), leaving ideologically driven conflicts behind, identifying best practice, learning from it, and using data to guide policymaking that is effective, efficient, and equitable. This is a technocratic narrative that has established a space "cleansed" of debate: it is a narrative that is designed to silence progressive articulations of educational principles and priorities, and it creates a space hostile to debate, and from which the social is excluded. Ideas that privilege elite assumptions about knowledge and capacity as differentially distributed and objectively "real" become orthodoxy; segregated institutional provision and curriculum content operationalize these assumptions and enable the shift to "learning." The knowledge work of think tanks, who take on some of the appearance of research institutes, defines the horizon of what is politically possible by blurring the distinction between scientific knowledge and ideologically driven knowledge production.

Conclusion: COVID-19, Globalization, and Education

The previous discussion has stressed the importance of a structural approach to neoliberal globalization and highlighted the interdependency of elite experts and data systems in pursuit of a globally convergent "structured agenda" in education. However, the impact of the global pandemic that started in 2020 may have a significant effect on that agenda, as responses to economic crisis involve—to a greater or lesser degree—a revival of national governments and some interest in broadening the scope of education policy to include attention to the social functions of education. The impact of COVID-19 on the globalized economy was and is massive: it is claimed that the pandemic triggered the sharpest and deepest economic contraction in the history of capitalism (Roubini, 2020). The consequences have been summarized by Saad-Fihlo (2020, p. 477) as follows:

> To paraphrase *The Communist Manifesto*, all that was solid melted into air: "globalization" went into reverse; long supply chains, that were previously the only "rational" way to organize production, collapsed and hard borders returned; trade declined drastically; and international travel was severely constrained. In a matter of days, tens of millions of workers became unemployed and millions of businesses lost their employees, customers, suppliers and credit lines.

At the time of writing, it is difficult to know how enduring the turn away from neoliberal globalization and the return of the strong state will be, but in a situation of intense economic crisis the doctrine of competition and free markets is difficult to uphold, and the need for large-scale programs of public spending and state planning is apparent. The defense of neoliberalism is also muted, given the growing evidence that the impact of COVID-19 is selectively deepened because of the deliberate and cumulative impact of the destruction of state capacities in the name of the market. In the United Kingdom and elsewhere, the association of high death rates with economically deprived inner-city areas and, in some cases, with Black and Asian minority populations makes it difficult to conceal the effects of neoliberal globalization. In some contexts, those effects had created vulnerability among certain sectors of the population to loss of work and earnings along with vulnerability to severe illness because of poor housing and inadequate nutrition, especially where decades of austerity policies had removed their basic social security and left health and social service provision severely under-resourced.

Education has experienced disruption globally: UNESCO estimates that over 1.5 billion children missed schooling in 2020 because of school closures and lockdowns, while the World Bank has drawn attention to the particularly devastating consequences of the pandemic where education provision is already weak. The OECD, among others, highlights ways in which COVID-19 deepens existing inequalities in provision, from scarce technological equipment and support to lack of quality in teaching (Reimers & Schleicher, 2020). Indeed, the extent of the disruption of "normal" provision of education, across all sectors, globally, has prompted some discussion of responses that go beyond crisis management, to embrace radical thinking about the shape of future provision (Sahlberg, 2020), including reducing the emphasis on performance measurement, and prioritizing support for mental health, resilience, and well-being:

> the pandemic has highlighted how economic growth alone is not enough to sustain economies and societies. In the absence of a more comprehensive approach, which supports societies' health and well-being in addition to growth, we will remain very vulnerable to the next pandemic, as well as future waves of this one. (Graham, 2020, pp. 79–85)

Tensions arising from competing economic and social priorities in the policy field of education are illustrated in emerging debates about more inclusive pedagogies, in the demand for attention to more vulnerable learners, and for broader definitions of learning, while issues of purpose and fairness lie beneath the surface of controversies such as those around policy for national examinations or what should constitute the experience of higher education. Adjustments in the balance among the social, political, and economic functions of education may be pursued at the national level, as nation states reengage with debates about the knowledge to be prioritized in response to the pandemic, and about purposes and priorities in education, including the extent to which local, national, contextualized needs and priorities are identified and pursued.

The pandemic also reveals some fault lines in the globalized narrative of evidence-based policy in education, supporting cognitive consensus and informed by objective expertise. The crisis has demanded rapid and clear movement from scientific understanding into public direction (Weible et al., 2020), both in the general response to the pandemic and in the policy field of education. However, the difficulty of translating complex scientific knowledge and practice into action has become more and more apparent as the crisis unfolds, as the public and politicians have had to recognize that scientific knowledge is often emergent, disputatious, contingent, and slow (Stone, 2019; Van Doren & Noordegraaf, 2020) and that it does not necessarily provide a clear guide to action. As indicated earlier, COVID-19 has entered a policy space in education characterized, to a greater or lesser degree, by a proliferation of sources of expertise, accompanied by a narrowing of the kinds of expertise that count. Data had increasingly guided practice, and there has also been a turn toward hard(er) disciplinary sources of educational knowledge, such as neuroscience, and toward technological solutions for learning problems.

There are some indications that overreliance on technical expertise to address issues in education highlighted by the pandemic may create political problems, for example where algorithms have been used to calculate examination grades, with results perceived as unfair by public and learners, and impacting especially on pupils in poor areas. Whether this will lead to a fundamental change in the "structured agenda" for education, and a dilution of economically driven learning and data-driven performance measurement, is uncertain, especially given the opportunities now presented for the promotion of even greater dependence on educational technologies (Williamson, 2021) so that technological "solutionism" may yet continue to underpin a narrowly instrumental view of education (Teras et al., 2020), despite the inequalities revealed by COVID-19, and despite the huge social cost of the neoliberal globalizing project.

References

Alasuutari, P. (2016). *The synchronization of national policies*. Routledge.

Ball, S. (2012). *Global Education Inc.: New policy networks and the neoliberal imaginary*. Routledge.

Ball, S. J. (2016). Following policy: Networks, network ethnography and education policy mobilities. *Journal of Education Policy, 31*(5), 549–566. doi:10.1080/02680939.2015.1122232

Ball, S. J. (2018a). Commercialising education: Profiting from reform. *Journal of Education Policy, 33*(5), 587–589. doi:10.1080/02680939.2018.1467599

Ball, S. J. (2018b). Corporate elites and the reform of public education. *Educational Review, 70*(3), 383–384. doi:10.1080/00131911.2017.1375808

Ball, S. J., Junemann, C., & Santori, D. (2016). Joined-up policy: Network connectivity and global education. In K. Mundy, A. Green, B. Lingard, & A. Verger (Eds.), *The handbook of global education policy* (pp. 535–553). Wiley Blackwell.

Bishop, M. L., & Payne, A. (2021). The political economies of different globalizations: Theorizing reglobalization. *Globalizations, 18*(1), 1–21.

Bonds, E. (2010). The knowledge-shaping process: Elite mobilization and environmental policy. *Critical Sociology, 37*(4), 429–446.

Browes, N., & Verger, A. (2020). Global governance through peer review the Dutch experience of OECD reviews of national policies. *Critical Policy Studies, 15*(4), 405–424.

Carvalho, L. M. (2012). The fabrications and travels of a knowledge-policy instrument. *European Educational Research Journal*, *11*(2), 172–188. doi:10.2304/eerj.2012.11.2.172

Decuypere, M. (2021). The topologies of data practices: A methodological introduction. *Journal of New Approaches in Educational Research*, *10*(1), 67–84. http://dx.doi.org/10.7821/naer.2021.1.650.

Fenwick, T., Mangez, E., & Ozga, J. (Eds.). *Governing knowledge: Comparison, knowledge-based technologies and expertise in the regulation of education* (World Yearbook of Education 2014). Routledge.

Fourcade, M. (2010). The problem of embodiment in the sociology of knowledge: Afterword to the special issue on knowledge in practice. *Qualitative Sociology*, *33*, 569–574. https://doi.org/10.1007/s11133-010-9173-x

Gardinier, M. P. (2021). Imagining globally competent learners: Experts and education policy making beyond the nation state. *Comparative Education*, *57*(1), 130–146.

Gorur, R. (2017). Statistics and statecraft: Exploring the potentials politics and practices of international educational assessment. *Critical Studies in Education*, *58*(3), 261–265.

Gorur, R. (2019). Old power, new power and ontological flattening: The global data revolution in education. In C. E. Molstad & D. Pettersson (Eds.), *New practices of comparison, quantification and expertise in education* (pp. 66–83). Routledge.

Graham, C. (2020). The human costs of the pandemic: Is it time to prioritize well-being? Brookings. https://www.brookings.edu/research/the-human-costs-of-the-pandemic-is-it-time-to-prioritize-well-being/

Grek, S. (2013). Expert moves: International comparative testing and the rise of expertocracy. *Journal of Education Policy*, *28*(5), 695–709.

Grek, S. (2017). Socialisation, learning and the OECD's reviews of national policies for education: The case of Sweden. *Critical Studies in Education*, *58*(3), 295–310.

Grek, S. (2019). Global monitoring reports and the role of socialisation and learning: The case of the OECD impact on Sweden. NORRAG Special Issue 03 Global monitoring of national educational development: Coercive or constructive?

Grek, S. (2020). Facing "a tipping point"? The role of the OECD as a boundary organisation in governing education in Sweden, education inquiry. doi:10.1080/20004508.2019.1701838

Grek, S., Maroy, C., & Verger, A. (Eds). (2021). *Accountability and datafication in the governance of education*. World Yearbook of Education 2021. Routledge.

Grek, S., & Ozga, J. (2010). Re-inventing public education: The new role of knowledge in education policy making. *Public Policy and Administration*, *25*(3), 271–288.

Grundmann R., & Stehr, N. (2012). *The power of scientific knowledge*. Cambridge University Press.

Hartong, S. (2021). The power of relation-making: Insights into the production and operation of digital school performance platforms in the US. *Critical Studies in Education*, *62*(1), 34–49. doi:10.1080/17508487.2020.1749861

Hunter, C. P. (2013). Shifting themes in OECD country reviews of higher education. *Higher Education*, *66*, 707–723.

Jayasuriya, K. (2001). Globalisation, sovereignty and the rule of law. *Constellations*, *84*(4), 442–459.

Jessop, B., Fairclough, N., & Wodak, R. (2008). *The knowledge-based economy and higher education in Europe*. Sense Publications.

Kitchin, R., & Dodge, M. (2011). *Code/space: Software and everyday life*. The MIT Press.

Lawn, M., & Grek, S. (2012). *Europeanizing education: Governing an emerging policy space.* Symposium Books.

Means, A., & Slater, G. B. (2019). The dark mirror of capital: On post-neoliberal formations and the future of education. *Discourse, 40*(2), 162–175.

Molstad, C. E., & Pettersson, D. (2019). (Eds.). *New practices of comparison, quantification and expertise in education.* Routledge.

Normand, R. (2016). *The changing epistemic governance of European education.* Springer.

OECD. (2015). *Improving schools in Scotland.* OECD.

OECD. (2017). PISA 2015 results (Volume V): Collaborative problem solving. doi: 10.1787/19963777

OECD. (2021). *Scotland's curriculum for excellence: Into the future, implementing education policies.* OECD Publishing. https://doi.org/10.1787/bf624417-en

Olsen, M. (2004). Neo-liberalism, globalization, democracy, challenges for education. *Globalization, Societies and Education, 2*(2), 231–275.

Ozga, J. (2016). Trust in numbers? Digital education governance and the inspection process. *European Educational Research Journal, 15*(1), 69–81.

Ozga, J. (2017). Education and nationalism in Scotland: Nationalism as a governing resource. In K. Kantasalmi & G. Holm (Eds.), *The state, schooling and identity Singapore* (pp. 25–41). Palgrave Macmillan/Springer.

Ozga, J. (2019). Governing and knowledge: Theorising the relationship. In R. Langer & T. Brusemeister (Eds.), *Handbuch Educational Governance Theorien* (pp. 729–751). Springer.

Ozga, J., Dahler-Larsen, P., Segerholm, C., & Simola, H. (Eds.). (2011). *Fabricating quality in education: Data and governance in Europe.* Routledge.

Piattoeva, N. (2014). Elastic numbers: National examinations data as a technology of government. *Journal of Education Policy, 30*(3), 316–334.

Pigott, J. (2021). Less is more: Education for uncertain times. *Globalisation, Societies and Education,* 251–261. doi:10.1080/14767724.2021.1882956

Ramirez, F., & Meyer, J. (2002). *Expansion and impact of the world human rights regimes.* Stanford University.

Rautalin, M., Syvatera, J., & Vento, E. (2021). International organisations establishing their scientific authority: Periodizing the legitimation of policy advice by the OECD. *International Sociology, 36*(1), 3–24.

Reed, M. (2012). Masters of the universe: Power and elites in organization studies. *Organization Studies, 33*(2), 203–221.

Reimers, F. M., & Schleicher, A. (2020). *A framework to guide the education response to the Covid-19 pandemic.* OECD.

Robertson, S., & Dale, R. (2017). Comparing policies in a globalizing world. *Educacao e Realidade, 42*(3), 859–875.

Robertson, S. L., & Verger, A. (2012). Governing education through public private partnerships. In S. L. Robertson, K. Mundy, A. Verger, & F. Menashy (Eds.), *Public private partnerships in education: New actors and modes of governance in a globalizing world* (pp. 21–43). Edward Elgar.

Robinson, W. (2011). Global capitalism and the emergence of transnational elites. *Critical Sociology, 38*(3), 349–363.

Robinson, W. I. (2017). Debate on the new global capitalism: Transnational capitalist class, transnational state apparatuses, and global crisis. *International Critical Thought, 7*(2), 171–189. doi:10.1080/21598282.2017.1316512

Roubini, N. (2020). Coronavirus pandemic has delivered the fastest, deepest economic shock in history. *The Guardian*, March 25. https://www.theguardian.com/business/2020/mar/25/coronavirus-pandemic-has-delivered-the-fastest-deepest-economic-shock-in-history

Rowe, E. (2019). Capitalism without capital: The intangible economy of education reform *Discourse, 40*(2), 271–279.

Saad-Fihlo, A. (2020). From COVID-19 to the end of neoliberalism. *Critical Sociology, 4–5*, 477–485.

Sahlberg, P. (2016). The global educational reform movement and its impact on schooling. In K. Mundy, A. Green, B. Lingard, & A. Verger (Eds.), *The handbook of global education policy* (pp. 128–144). Wiley-Blackwell.

Sahlberg, P. (2020). Will the pandemic change schools?. *Journal of Professional Capital and Community, 5*(3/4), 359–365. https://doi.org/10.1108/JPCC-05-2020-00

Scott, J. (1996). *Stratification and power.* Cambridge University Press.

Scott, J. (2008). Modes of power and the reconceptualisation of elites. In M. Savage & K. Williams (Eds.), *Remembering elites* (pp. 27–43). Blackwell.

Selwyn, N. (2018). Technology as a focus of education policy. In R. Papa & S. W. J. Armfield (Eds.), *The Wiley handbook of educational policy* (pp. 459–477). John Wiley & Sons.

Shiroma, E. O. (2014). Expert consultants and knowledge production. In T. Fenwick, E. Mangez, & J. Ozga (Eds.), *Governing knowledge: Comparison, knowledge-based technologies and expertise in the regulation of education* (World Yearbook of Education 2014, pp. 101–113). Routledge.

Stone, D. (2013). *Knowledge actors and transnational governance: The private-public policy nexus in the global agora.* Palgrave Macmillan.

Stone, D. (2019). *Making global policy* (Elements in Public Policy). Cambridge University Press. doi:10.1017/9781108661690

Teras, M., Suoranta, J., Teras, H., & Curcher, M. (2020). Post-Covid 19 education and education technology "solutionism." *Post Digital Science and Education, 2*, 863–878.

Thrift, N., & French, S. (2002). The automatic production of space. *Transactions of the Institute of British Geographers, 27*, 309–335. https://doi.org/10.1111/1475-5661.00057

Van Dooren, W., & Noordegraaf, M. (2020). Staging science: Authoritativeness and fragility of models and measurement in the Covid-19. *Crisis Public Administration Review, 80*(4), 525–707.

Verger, A., Parcerisa, L., & Fontdevila, C. (2018). The growth and spread of large-scale assessments and test-based accountabilities: A political sociology of global education reforms. *Educational Review, 71*(1), 1–26.

Weible, C. M., Nohrstedt, D., Cairney, P., Carter, D. P., Crow, D. A., Durnová, A. P., Heikkila, T., Ingold, K., McConnell, A., & Stone, D. (2020). COVID-19 and the policy sciences: Initial reactions and perspectives. *Policy Sciences, 53*, 225–241.

Williamson, J. G. (2013). Demographic dividends revisited. *Asian Development Review, 30*(2), 1–25.

Williamson, B. (2016). Digital methodologies of education governance: Pearson plc and the re-mediation of methods. *European Educational Research Journal, 15*(1), 34–54.

Williamson, B. (2021). Making markets through digital platforms: Pearson, edu-business, and the (e)valuation of higher education. *Critical Studies in Education, 62*(1), 50–66. doi:10.1080/17508487.2020.173755

World Bank. (2020). The COVID-19 pandemic: Shocks to education and policy responses. http://worldbank.org

CHAPTER 10

GLOBALIZATION, PERSONALIZATION, AND THE LEARNING APPARATUS

MAARTEN SIMONS

INTRODUCTION

THE expression "lifelong learning" is now commonplace. To some, it sounds like a condemnation, to others a necessity, and to others still an ideal of freedom. However different these reactions to lifelong learning may be, they demonstrate that lifelong learning has become a reality, or at least a part of our shared world of experience, and consequently something we must relate to in one way or another. Regarding the pervasiveness of learning today, two approaches dominate our explanations. The recourse to learning can be understood as an expression of the logic of capital in late modern society, where the capitalization of learning is an attempt to reconcile social and cultural life with the necessity of (re)producing capital. In another approach, the organization of lifelong learning can be explained as a deliberate political project in which states or transnational entities—such as the European Union—seek renewed stability and legitimacy. Without questioning the value of previous approaches, a third and different one is developed in this chapter.[1]

Michel Foucault's work indicates that the functioning and impact of politics and the economy can only be clarified if we examine both how people are governed and how they come to govern themselves. This is formulated very precisely by Maurizio Lazzarato:

> The remarkable novelty introduced by Foucault in the history of capitalism since its origins, is the following: the problem that arises from the relation between politics

and the economy is resolved by techniques and dispositifs that come from neither. This "outside," this "other" must be interrogated. The functioning, the efficacy and the force of politics and the economy, as we all know today, are not derived from forms of rationality that are internal to these logics, but from a rationality that is exterior and that Foucault names "the government of men." (Lazzarato, 2006, p. 1)

In other words, the governing of people is characterized by its own rationality, or at least a rationality that cannot be derived from the logic of capital or the logic of political power alone. The field of governmentalization therefore becomes intelligible only when we focus on the technologies, instruments, and procedures, as well as the implied modes of reasoning and the resulting assemblage of apparatuses with their own operating logic. Foucault clarifies the key term *dispositif* (apparatus) as:

> a resolutely heterogeneous grouping comprising discourses, institutions, architectural arrangements, policy decisions, laws, administrative measures, scientific statements, philosophic, moral and philanthropic propositions; in sum, the said and the not-said, these are elements of the apparatus. The apparatus itself is the network that can be established between these elements. (Foucault, 1977a, p. 299)

An apparatus, thus, is a kind of strategic assemblage or a "dominating strategic response" to a "historical problem" and, hence, "apparatuses are the forms composed of heterogeneous elements that have been stabilised and set to work in multiple domains" (Rabinow, 2003, p. 54). The term "apparatus" defines a kind of self-regulating order that cannot be reduced to a single strategist or an underlying cause or actor, but nevertheless has an intelligibility at the strategic level, which emerges from an "assemblage" of heterogeneous components and local tactics (Rose, 1999, p. 53). Hence, as Rabinow puts it, the aim of the approach is "to identify apparatuses, to trace their genealogy, to show their emergence, and thereby to make them available for thought and change" (Rabinow, 2003, p. 55).

This chapter develops the thesis that a learning apparatus has taken shape in recent decades, and that understanding the constituents, assemblage, and operation of this strategic complex is essential to understanding the ubiquity of learning. As a consequence, we argue that the social apparatus—and the resulting governmentalization of the modern state in the name of the social—is gradually being replaced (or at least reassembled) by a learning apparatus and new forms of governmentalization of the European Union and its member states, the geographical focus of this chapter. This is a process through which lifelong learning is inscribed both as a reality that is susceptible to governmental intervention and as the ethical substance of governing oneself as a (European) citizen. Finally, we elaborate on two operational effects that play an important role in the steady expansion and stabilization of the (digital) learning apparatus: personalization (as a form of self-governing) and different sorts of globalization effects.

From the Social Question to the Learning Question

It has been discussed in great detail how security and freedom appeared as two interrelated objectives of the government of men and have allowed for the birth of modern, liberal states in Europe, as well as modern capitalist societies (Foucault, 2004a, 2004b). This is not a history of a growing *étatisation* ("statification") of society, but of a governmentalization of the state: The state—and the centralization of power acting upon a population in a defined territory—finds its (new) justification by governing men in the name of freedom and security. From the second half of the 19th century onward, the act of governing men gradually took on a social dimension that led to the birth of the social state, which attempted to align individual freedom and collective security through a "governing 'in the name of the social'" (Rose, 1999). Issues regarding individual freedom and collective well-being consequently became problematized in social terms, as well as those related to abnormality and deviance, which gradually came to be understood as social risks. Casting threats and dangers in terms of risks to the social order correlated with the appearance of "the social question," which found a governmental translation in strategies of risk prevention and social regulation. From there on, society became something that had to be defended (Foucault, 2003). One can observe the governmental translation of the social question in the way that the classic idea of solidarity was recast and made operational though centralized technologies of social security (e.g., health insurance, retirement benefits, as well as social rights and public services), which in turn grounded the authority and legitimacy of the state as a governing body (Ewald, 1986). The social therefore emerged as the strategic relay between freedom and security in what is now more commonly referred to as the welfare state. Without going into too much detail, three issues related to education should nonetheless be stressed regarding this governmentalization in the name of the social.

First, the social became a strategic medium for governments to translate societal problems into educational solutions: Schools were gradually turned into controlled locations of socialization, and society could thus be governed through school and curriculum reform. An example of this is how educational equality—previously framed in universal terms—gradually became problematized in social terms and was thereby reformulated into a governing issue: to promote equal opportunity and free access to education (as well as [extending] compulsory education) so as to ensure individual freedom and simultaneously safeguard social order and progress (Hunter, 1994, pp. 111–112). Second, the development of (scientific) knowledge was not separated from the social apparatus and new forms of governing. The most obvious expression of this can be found in the social sciences, with Durkheim's work (on education) in the early 20th century as a striking illustration. For Durkheim (1922)—who claimed, "we are who we are only because we live in society"—the role of education was to develop the "social being" of human beings: "[t]here is no school which can claim the right to give an anti-social education." He also explicitly argued that the "view of the disinterested bystander state makes little sense," since the state's responsibility is precisely "to guarantee that education be exercised in a social way." This is not meant to picture sociology as a kind of administrative science, but to indicate a shared problematization in social terms that allowed this knowledge to play a tactical role in the social apparatus. Third, governing in the name of the social also shaped specific experiences of time and space (Simons, 2014a, 2014b). Typical examples might be the images of progress and modernization and the dreams of social emancipation, upward social mobility, and economic growth. These images and dreams conveyed a specific conception of time that was linear and chronological: The present was seen as the moment of change in between past and future, and hence, the occasion to break with the past in making the future through social planning (Popkewitz, 2008, pp. 24–27). Foucault underlined "the discovery of an evolution in terms of 'progress'" (1977b, p. 160), where the experience of progress itself—both at an individual and social level—guided and legitimized governing in the name of the social, which in turn further stabilized the social apparatus. This conception of time was linked to a conception and organization of space as a set of spatially and socially defined activities (e.g., family life, education, work, leisure, etc.). These activities were located, coordinated, relatively stable, and worked together. More importantly, they were always already part of the ongoing process of modernization and progress.

Toward the end of the second half of the 20th century, a new question emerged that started to have a powerful impact on society, and would come to replace the social in terms of a different governmental problematization. A clear articulation of this new question can be read in The European Commission's white paper *Teaching and Learning: Towards the Learning Society* (1995):

> The individual's place in relation to their fellow citizens will increasingly be determined by their capacity to learn and master fundamental knowledge. The position *of everyone in relation to their fellow citizens in the context of knowledge and skills* therefore will be decisive. This relative position which could be called the "*learning relationship*" will become an increasingly dominant feature in the structure of our societies. (European Commission, 1995, p. 17; emphasis added)

Challenges are now addressed in terms of what could be called "the learning question": how to bring individual freedom in line with the new necessities of the knowledge society. Evidence that the learning question started replacing the social question can be found in the way the European Commission's report *Making the European Area of Lifelong Learning a Reality* (2001) articulates the double aim of freedom and security:

> both to empower citizens to move freely between learning settings, jobs, regions and countries, making the most of their knowledge and competences, and to meet the goals and ambitions of the European Union and the candidate countries to be more prosperous, inclusive, tolerant and democratic. (European Commission, 2001, p. 3)

The thesis developed in the next sections is that freedom and security remain the twin objectives of European governments today; however, learning is replacing the social as the strategic relay between a new form of freedom and security.

THE ASSEMBLAGE OF THE LEARNING APPARATUS

Forms of Problematization

In order to understand how lifelong learning became a reality in governing ourselves, we first draw attention to the way in which learning is problematized as an important issue for reflection and thought. Four related forms of problematization shaped in the previous century can be distinguished (see also Simons & Masschelein, 2008).

At the end of the 1960s, challenges started to be posed in terms of the development of a "knowledge society" and "knowledge economy." In this economy, knowledge functions as a "central capital," the "crucial means of production," and the "energy of a modern society" (Bell, 1973; Drucker, 1969, p. xi). Part of this line of thought claims that when professional activities begin to imply a "knowledge base," workers become "knowledge workers." In other words, it starts to make sense to address learning and continuing education as that which links these workers to the process of production, and, consequently, as something that requires adequate investment. What is at stake, then, in this first field of problematization is the *capitalization of learning*. For a second form of problematization, one may consider the notion of lifelong learning (*éducation permanente*), closely related to a broader concern for self-realization that appeared at the end of the 1960s. The basic idea is that education should not be limited to the school and to a particular time in one's life. Instead, education should allow all adults to face changes autonomously: that is, to "prepare mankind to adapt to change, the predominant characteristic of our time" (Faure et al., 1972, p. 2009). Part of this problematization of learning is the way adult education is reflected upon. Drawing on humanistic psychology, adult education becomes a defined challenge and is approached in terms of learning processes that require self-direction from the adult learners themselves (Knowles, 1975). In short, learning is objectified as a condition for individual freedom, and people are addressed as being responsible for their learning. In other words, a *responsabilization toward learning* begins to take shape. Although related to the previous forms of problematization, the new educational and psychological expertise concerning learning processes offers a third one. Expertise based on cognitive psychology starts to reflect upon learning as processes of cognition, transforming information into knowledge. Shuell's well-known definition articulates these ideas very well: "[l]earning is an active, constructive and social process where the learner strategically manages available cognitive, physical, and social resources to create new knowledge by interacting with information in the environment and integrating it with information already stored in memory" (Shuell, 1988). This suggests a kind of *managementalization of learning*: Learning appears as a process of construction that can and should be managed by learners themselves. Finally, in the early 1990s, the issue of learning goals starts to be discussed in terms of employability. Instead of lifetime employment of trained workers, the critical issue becomes the future potential of employees with a focus on their employability (Pochet & Paternotre, 1998). In this context, the notion of "competency management" emerges: Management and policy are no longer about performing functions (and finding workers that fit), but about developing competencies (and having workers that want to learn). In parallel to this line of thinking, the goal and method of education and training are being recoded in terms of competencies. In fact, competencies now refer to the intersection between (the organizations that provide) learning and (the requirements of) employability—that is, they represent employable learning results. In this form of problematization, *employability* appears as a permanent concern that learners require in order to live a successful life.

Of course, the term "learning" has a much longer history. What is new is that the term, now disconnected from issues of education and schooling, refers to a reality that is intelligible as a productive force which creates capital. From the learners' point of view, it implies something for which they are and may be held responsible, something that can and should be managed, and something that produces competencies and self-employability as a permanent concern. These forms of problematization have been combined and have found their material articulation in specific techniques, instruments, and procedures.

Material Inscriptions

The most telling examples of material instances through which the governmentalization of learning takes shape can be seen by developments at the European Union level. In fact, we prefer to speak of the governmentalization of the European Union through the deployment of multiple technologies, rather than a growing *étatisation* of the European Union. This governmentalization does not start from the key social role of "institutions of modernity," but begins explicitly from the strategic role of learners: "people, their knowledge and competencies, are the key to Europe's future" (European Commission, 2001, p. 3). The main objectives are no longer to reinforce the *social state* through institutional reform and increase social mobility, but to enable learning mobility, enhance the range of learning opportunities, and reduce obstructions in a *flexible state*. The problematization of obstructions to learning has a subjective and objective side: It is approached both in terms of governing the self and others.

On the one hand, lifelong learning is increasingly framed as a matter of motivation, while lack of motivation to learn becomes a governmental issue that must be resolved, for it poses a risk to both individual freedom and collective security (Ahl, 2008). Here, we notice a tactical alliance of governing with the new experts of learning that support people but also organizations, in their striving to remain employable and to embrace this required mobility, flexibility, and responsibility. Social work is no longer needed; instead, the excluded—ranging from the unemployed, new migrants, underperforming workers, to troubled families and weak schools—all now have to pass through learning support that acts upon their "will to learn." However, all sorts of objective limitations to the ideal of a mobile life afforded by the right competencies is problematized, along with the learners as the producers and carriers of these competencies. Limitations imposed by national borders (in terms of national territories and national populations), as well as institutional limitations of confined and stable spaces (such as schools, universities, and factories) are all seen as obvious challenges. The focus is no longer on institutional change through modernization and planned progress. Instead, innovation and creativity become the main drivers of change. Achieving freedom and security requires an innovation-friendly environment that disposes of all institutional barriers and, crucially, directly addresses the creative learning potential of citizens with their sense of initiative, entrepreneurship, and their ability to innovate (Council of the European Union, 2009, p. 4).

A key challenge once learning has been (temporarily) completed is to develop and offer equipment that "objectifies" this learning: "identification, assessment and recognition of non-formal and informal learning as well as on the transfer and mutual recognition of formal certificates and diplomas" (European Commission, 2001, p. 9). This is articulated very clearly in the different reference frameworks that Europe has developed. A case in point is the European Qualifications Framework (EQF) for lifelong learning:

> The EQF is a common European reference framework which links countries' qualifications systems together, acting as a translation device to make qualifications more readable and understandable across different countries and systems in Europe. It has two principal aims: to promote citizens' mobility between countries and to facilitate their lifelong learning. (European Commission, 2008, p. 3)

Whatever the length or the context of learning—be it formal, informal, or nonformal—the learner should be able to prove to the demand side the value of the accumulated human capital. And the demand side—that is, companies and higher education institutions all over Europe—should have a validation frame at its disposal or should be able to translate its needs for human resources according to a common reference framework. A key feature of the EQF, therefore, is its focus on learning outcomes: "a statement of what a learner knows, understands and is able to do on completion of a learning process" (European Commission, 2008, p. 3). This emphasis on learning outcomes implies that institutionally based qualifications related to official diplomas—previously developed and used in the social state—are no longer relevant for they mainly objectify length, domain, and aims of study. The focus now is on what is learned—all the rest is unimportant. In line with this logic, we see the emergence of various kinds of assessment centers, where learning outcomes can be determined and graded, as well as a market of open badges, which guarantee that acquired outcomes are visible and certified, all in view of helping learners to profile themselves (European Commission, 2013, p. 6). It is through these types of frameworks and practices that learning is inscribed as a reality, both for the individual that learns and for the outside world.

The result of these material inscriptions is that the learning reality is from the outset calculable and results in new centers of calculation as well as centers of validation (see also Miller & Rose, 1997). Learning can become calculated in terms of required time, packaged and labeled in view of recognition and transfer, framed in view of qualification and certification, and articulated in a common language to increase mutual understanding. Through operations such as these, learning turns into an object of investment, a domain to be regulated, and a value to claim freedoms. As a consequence, learners are increasingly looking out for new (centralized) forms of authority to have the outcomes of their learning lives validated. The Europass program is an interesting example of a device that makes lifelong learning a reality and furthermore articulates the governmentalization and new authorization of Europe. In using the portfolio, citizens objectify themselves in terms of accumulated competencies and become involved in a permanent process of "self-documentation" and "self-marketization" in a new European realm (Tuschling & Engemann, 2006, pp. 462–463). In contrast, the *curriculum vitae* (CV) offers a chronological overview of someone's individuality by drawing upon the transitions of their social biography, which is an adequate device for a society of institutions with rather stable routes and locations. When lifelong learning becomes a reality, however, what learners need instead is a portfolio, which is not biographical, but serves as a profile that can acknowledge and define one's permanent mobility and unique characteristics by capturing an intermediate learning balance.

What supports the inscription of learning as a reality, besides these *centers of calculation and validation* and *profiling tools*, are *centers of monitoring* and *feedback tools*. A portfolio alone does not suffice to act as a lifelong learner. In addition, permanent feedback loops must be created to constantly monitor one's learning balance and keep one's profile up to date, as part of the self-centered act of self-regulation. The same holds true for learning member states. Comparing and ranking member states according to several performance indicators functions, on the one hand, to provide European agencies with feedback information on the total mobilization of Europe's human resources (in comparisons to, for instance, the United States or Japan), and, on the other hand, to serve as a feedback instrument to mobilize member states and citizens and to make them responsible to improve their performance (Simons, 2014c). It should be stressed that benchmarking, like monitoring, functions as a strategy to fulfill the need for permanent feedback: "Where do I stand in relation to others?" (Larner & Le Heron, 2004, p. 227). Dashboards appear here as the appropriate tools to direct someone or something that is and should remain in constant motion. As far as these dashboards render intelligible the processes of lifelong learning, they can start to become "an obligatory passage point" in order for the European Union, the member states, and individual learners to come to know and regulate themselves. Self-knowledge and self-regulated learning therefore imply that one has to consider oneself as engaged in a permanent process of self-mobilization or "competitive self-improvement," where each moment represents an opportunity to be creative and innovate (Haahr, 2004).

Strategic Response

This short exploration of the governmentalization of learning can be concluded by mentioning two new "twin figures" that articulate and simultaneously stabilize the governmental concern with freedom and security through learning: *entrepreneurship* and *flexicurity*. These notions are not used as (theoretical) concepts or phenomena (to be observed), but as epistemological and strategical figures, for they both paradigmatically suggest the solutions or responses that are required, as well as summarize the set problems at hand. In addition, *freelance* can be added as a third figure to better demonstrate how the link between the entrepreneurial self and the securing of flexibility is strategically articulated.

As far as self-governing is concerned, the figure of the entrepreneurial self (and the entrepreneur of the self) best captures the way one is driven to capitalize the self and held responsible to manage one's life in view of employability. This is nicely summarized by Gordon:

> The idea of one's life as the enterprise of oneself implies that there is a sense in which one remains always continuously employed in (at least) that one enterprise, and that is part of the continuous business of living to make adequate provision for the preservation, reproduction and reconstruction of one's own human capital. (Gordon, 1991, p. 44)

Entrepreneurship is not just a mechanical process of allocation and production. It also involves an "element of alertness"; that is to say, a speculative, creative, or innovative attitude to see opportunities in a competitive environment (Kirzner, 1973, p. 33). Entrepreneurship is a creative and risky business. But risk is no longer, as in the social state, something to be prevented or secured against; instead, it becomes the condition for success—a kind of "stimulating principle" (Giddens, 1998). This entrepreneurship, which turns the self into a resource and asset, looks at risk as an opportunity and commits to creative and competitive self-improvement in all spheres of life, thereby also becoming a new kind of civic virtue. Furthermore, this implies that the absence of entrepreneurship is not only seen as the root of numerous problems, but increasingly regarded as well as a lack of true citizenship.

The figure of flexicurity plays a similar role at the governing of society level. The European Commission, along with several member states, adopted an "integrated flexicurity approach" in order to develop policies that support both flexibility and security—to create "a situation in which security and flexibility can reinforce each other" (European Commission, 2007, p. 4). Whereas the *social state* was a paradigmatic articulation of full and stable employment, free and compulsory education, social protection, and permanent tenured employment, the key components of the *flexicurity state* are permanent employability, lifelong learning and investment, incentives for activation, and reliable, flexitime contractual arrangements. The objective is to create a condition of both flexible security and secure flexibility. *Freelance work* appears in this configuration of governing as a strategic, paradigmatic figure that both includes entrepreneurial freedoms and the concerns with flexible employment. Freelancers or self-employed persons are the ones taking care of their own business and self-investment through learning and representation, and permanently look for opportunities to sell their expertise, products, or services. The freelancers' liberty—etymologically speaking, the ones whose "lance" is not sworn to a single king—is what secures in various ways the required flexible labor market: They provide always up-to-date expertise, represent a highly flexible pool of competitive workers, and allow for dynamic human resource management.

The figures of entrepreneurship, flexicurity, and freelance integrate the current forms of problematization concerning learning, as well as the tools and procedures previously discussed, and articulate the new dominating strategic response (or apparatus) implemented to face challenges today. The learning apparatus's overall strategy is to promote individual freedom and collective security by inscribing learning as the relay between freedom and security. When the learning apparatus comes to replace the social apparatus as the dominating response, what occurs is a shift from thinking in terms of social mobility to learning mobility, from social (in)equality to inclusion/exclusion, from strategies of socialization with social norms as the key substance to strategies of lifelong learning with (capitalized) competencies as the key entities, and from set work protected by social rights and risks avoidance to a mobile life of opportunistic freelancing characterized by social recognition and risk-taking. In Foucauldian terms, we could say that the learning apparatus is installed from the moment that learning—and learned competencies—start to function as both "unique signifier" and "universal signified" (Foucault, 1978, p. 154). This condition simultaneously implies that everything valuable can be expressed in terms of learning, while learning expresses all that is valuable. It is important to stress once again that by developing and providing these frameworks, measurements, and tools, the European Union, as well as its agencies and member states, all gain new forms of authority, and hence become "powerful." To conclude this section, we would like to highlight three elements in the operation of the learning apparatus.

First, analogous to the social apparatus, scientific knowledge development does not occur outside the learning apparatus. Giddens's work illustrates how inclusion and exclusion as well as empowerment, rather than social (in)equality and social mobility, form the starting point. Risk is no longer uniquely framed in social terms, where it might denote something against which society, and specific social groups especially, need to be protected. Risk is now also an opportunity that calls for creativity and innovation, and therefore requires entrepreneurship and investment in human capital: "[t]he guideline is that, when possible, investment in human capital should have priority over offering immediate economic support" (Giddens, 1998, p. 130). Poverty, and many other forms of exclusion, are now approached in research and policy as a lack of adequate human capital; consequently, they convey a sense of irresponsibility toward or inability to manage/regulate one's learning. Therefore, according to Giddens, the point of departure is no longer social (in)equality and "post-factum redistribution," but inclusion and exclusion, and hence having adequate learned competencies (Giddens, 1998, p. 114). In all these cases, investment in human capital is fundamental.

Second, the learning apparatus should not be viewed as an expansion of the school system that arose in the 18th century. Instead, what we notice today is school education gradually being transformed in response to the learning apparatus's growing dominance (Simons & Olssen, 2010). Numerous examples point in this direction. A notable case is that formal education increasingly subscribes to qualifications frameworks and favors the assessment of individually acquired competencies over examinations in view of obtaining diplomas. In addition, educational institutions must now assume that students never enter education as a blank sheet, and they must guarantee that competencies (or qualifications) acquired elsewhere be recognized. These examples clarify how the forms of problematization and related techniques and tools concerning learning are also entering schools and universities. But this does not mean that school education is gradually being absorbed into the learning apparatus. That this is not the case can be seen, among other things, in the way in which learning to learn (but also entrepreneurship education) is becoming one of the school's core objectives; in other words, education is called upon "to shape" the new *learning* citizen. With this alliance, the least one can say is that school education is being forced to reinvent itself in line with constraints from the learning apparatus.

Third, governing in the name of learning also results in a particular experience of time and space (Simons & Masschelein, 2008). The present moment, envisioned within the social apparatus, is an occasion to bring about profound changes as part of social planning; it refers to a break with the past in view of a planned future. On the other hand, with its focus on innovation, the learning apparatus no longer assumes a linear conception of time but a momentary one: resources available today for creative use. This approach sees the past as currently available, the present as momentarily opportune, and the future as virtually present. In addition, governing in the name of learning characterizes space as motion in environments, rather than merely as confined or located places. This ecological understanding, instead of a "locational" understanding, implies an experience of being (not fully) part of an environment, of being (more or less) mobile, of having (more or less) resources (i.e., rich or poor environments), and of facing openness (or obstructions). It is no longer about social mobility (and the experience of moving up or forward), but about flexibility (and the condition of being mobile). In order to navigate different environments, feedback loops and permanent ecological positioning become vital for the learner. In contrast, the social citizen is regarded as positioned in enclosed locations, moving between these places throughout her lifetime, and in need of *orientation* tools (such as institutionally based degrees and social norms and standards) to navigate her life. What the learning citizen needs instead when navigating through different environments are tools for permanent *positioning*—that is, global positioning systems and dashboards, to know where she stands and to assess permanently her available competencies.

The (Digital) Learning Apparatus in Action

This final section looks more closely at two effects of the learning apparatus: globalization or, more specifically, different globalization effects of governing in the name of learning, and personalization, or how the learner is turned into a person.

When considering the components that make up the learning apparatus, we see globalization playing a role in at least four different ways. First, "globalization" is a term that plays a specific role in the political discourse on learning. For example, there is constant reference to a so-called global competitiveness that calls for countries, and the European Union as a whole, to invest in the learning of their populations. Related to this reasoning is the recurring reference to the importance of allowing the free movement of capital, goods, and ideas, as well as humans and their human capital, on a global scale. These continual references to globalization evoke a reality which lends a sense of direction, legitimacy, and urgency to this new governmental rationality. Besides this *epistemological* role, the term "globalization" plays a *strategic* role as well. As already indicated, the governmentalization of learning cannot be dissociated from old and new actors, who become governmentally relevant as a result of new centers (of monitoring, validation, and calculation). The European Union is a good example of this, as well as the member states that now start to redefine, reprofile, and relegitimize themselves in the name of learning. The new role of Europe—or better: the European Union as a governmental entity—is an example of a more globalized, or a new regional, form of central governing. Third, globalization includes an *ethical* dimension. Namely, it plays a role in the form of self-government, and in the relation of the self to the self, promoted throughout the learning apparatus. For the figures of the lifelong learner or the entrepreneur of the self, who continually invests in their own competencies, globalization refers to an operation of scaling up and expressing "spatial opportunities" (or distances) in view of mobility (Simons, 2018). The increase in scale is about the expansion of space—or rather, the environment—within which mobile life takes place. The ideal for the lifelong learner is to live a global life, which means no longer being bound by borders or other obstacles of localities, no longer being embedded in one place but embodying a state of permanent mobility or flexibility. As a global learner, part of this ideal is to be able to use uniform and direct assessment and global communication systems, and to be free from the delaying effect of translations due to cultural or other local(ized) particularities. Being global means for the learning citizen what being modern—and breaking free from tradition and other temporal constraints—means for the progressive, socialized citizen. Fourth, globalization within the learning apparatus can also be observed at the *technological* level. Globalization here reveals itself primarily through the technologies that enable the governmentalization of learning to be rolled out. Techniques, procedures, and tools are increasingly digitalized and conducive to online and distance learning. Two dimensions of this governmentalization can be distinguished: the governmentalization of digital devices, on the one hand, and the governmentalization of online (learning) environments, on the other.

The governmentalization of devices becomes visible when, for example, the accessibility and openness of digital technologies and learning tools are problematized: "open technologies allow *All individuals to learn, Anywhere, Anytime, through Any device, with the support of Anyone*" (European Commission, 2013, p. 3, emphasis in original). The basic premise is that physical or localized learning and educational resources are always exclusive in terms of who can learn, in terms of the place and time of learning, but also in terms of resources and support. Digital learning technology, it is argued, can in principle be inclusive, but efforts must be made to ensure openness and accessibility to promote the learning freedom of all. The rationale behind this problematization that understands learning freedom in terms of openness and accessibility is not about equal opportunities or social mobility, but foremost about fine-tuning the learning apparatus's strategy to further "liberate" the mobilization of competencies. At this point, the availability of (online) platforms becomes of strategic importance (see also Poell et al., 2019). In a digital world, the platform can be understood as providing a sense of online stability, and for that reason supplies the learner with a solid online basis for further action (i.e., it "links" the learner with what is provided). Creating, protecting, and updating these (learning) platforms becomes a governmental concern to secure online learning freedom. Complementary to this "platformization" and liberation of learning is an immediate governmental urge to look after authorized forms of assessment, certification, and validation that ensure learning outcomes/competencies are unambiguously determined and allow for global communication. The free learner requires "qualifying authorities" (European Commission, 2013, p. 6) to assure that what is learned is determined and validated in such a way that the recognition and acknowledgment of competencies is assured as globally as possible. The need for new nonlocal (learning) authorities gives an additional impetus to the further deployment of the learning apparatus. Global, here, connotes foremost an absence of restrictions in terms of openness, accessibility, and authorization.

The second dimension of the governmentalization of learning technologies can be apprehended by noticing the governing mechanisms built into the online learning environments themselves. These environments are (at least partly) automated, based on algorithms and learning analytics, in order to create adaptive and customized learning trajectories and increase learning efficiency for the learner: "collecting traces that learners leave behind and using those traces to improve learning" (Duval, 2012). What takes shape is an "algorithmic governmentality" (Rouvray & Berns, 2013) that operates by creating new profiles; it is not only about profiling learners to act upon them in an adapted and differentiated way but also about making new profiles out of big data from online behavior (disregarding any subjects or subjectivity), and using these profiles with probabilistic reasoning to modify environments and change behavior in a predicted way. This results in a kind of digital behaviorism that does not govern by directly acting upon individuals, but instead steers their actions and choices through anticipation by manipulating the online environment within which these actions occur. An example of this is using "nudges"—and other insights from behavioral economics—in learning environments to make learners do certain things (Knox et al., 2019). This subtle stimulation through environmental modification is not about forbidding certain behaviors or providing financial incentives but adding something to the environment to make a preferred behavior or choice more probable (assuming, of course, more or less automated processes and reactions from the one who acts and chooses). Even nudging itself can be automated ("algorithmic nudging") and become part of an "algorithmic management" system that uses individual worker data to influence—even in real time—their behavior and choices through personalized strategies (Möhlmann, 2021). Uber's rewarding system, as well as Deliveroo's smartphone messaging management system, works along these lines.

We want to stress two aspects of the governmentalization of learning related to digitalization and onlinization. First, when governing mechanisms are built directly into online learning environments and become partly automated based on algorithms, this suggests that these mechanisms might also start to learn. This form of learning carried out by governing mechanisms themselves—as specific types of machine learning—is an example of how learning is built into digital modes of governing. The governmentalization of learning is complemented with the "learnification" of governing (Biesta, 2010). Second, globalization in modes of digital governing moves beyond the profiling of predefined (statistical) populations and given social categories, to a large and borderless field of big data, with techniques of data mining and inductive statistics. The globalization of data, profiles, and techniques foremost indicates that a (localized) world of fixed entities, given substances, and defined movements is left behind.

Besides the learning apparatus's operational effects resulting in multiple dynamics of globalization, we have to point at another effect: personalization, understood here as a novel way to shape human subjectivity and act as subject (Simons, 2021; Simons & Masschelein, 2021). The operation of personalization starts with the assumption that we are all individuals but differ as persons, and it insists that these differences be taken into account. Here, the focus is on the process through which someone is turned into a unique or singular person; how someone comes to understand the self as a (unique) person and starts to act or govern the self accordingly. Personalization is not only about focusing on the differences among individuals, but about making and remaking these differences. It relies therefore on a profiling that makes personal differences visible in order to act upon them. A profile shows a social identity by using differential or determining features. Everything is in principle eligible for profiling, as long as it is possible to express certain distinctive or determining features. In the learning portfolio that is gradually replacing the diploma, someone is not shown "frontally" but "in profile" by listing all obtained competencies. The specific set of acquired competencies is what personalizes the learner and creates her (learning) identity. It is of vital importance for social recognition that there exists a stage or platform on which visibility can be created. Social media are exemplary here. Your profile only has meaning or any reality when it has viewers (which can include yourself) that—through likes, emojis, and shares—recognize and acknowledge you. The habitat of the personalized subject is clearly no longer a normalized society, but, drawing on Tiana Bucher, a "programmed sociality" (Bucher 2018).

The profiling ideal, and this is a constant pursuit, is to profile yourself in such a way to ensure that how you see yourself corresponds with how others perceive you. The term "person" and its derivatives, such as uniqueness, identity, and authenticity, refer exactly to this ideal. It is worth recalling here the original Latin word *persona*, which referred to a mask, and more specifically, to the character or role of the actor on stage. It is precisely here that feedback appears as the reigning technique of power. In order to know who you are and how you continue to profile yourself, you constantly need a reaction to your profile. What is required is a conscious mobilization of others in order to confirm your existence. Instead of a need for rules and order (sovereign power) or a need for normality (disciplinary power), the need for recognition (feedback power) determines the process of personalization. While the norm asks for discipline and the law for submission, the profile requires constant feedback (Simons & Masschelein, 2021). With personalization, the learning apparatus further stabilizes its strategy and installs a logic that questions or even replaces other apparatuses. As soon as learners start to understand themselves as unique persons, they probably will start to criticize the rules (of juridical and administrative power) and the norms (of disciplinary power) for not taking into account their individual uniqueness. In the world of the personalized learner, norms and rules indeed pose a personal injustice (for the implied moralization: Pykett, 2009). The personalized learner does not ask to be treated equally, based on norms or rules, but wants to be treated differently. In addition, this explains a certain tension that confronts personalized learners: The expressions of freedom, discourses of independency, and acts of liberation in the name of personal differences all tend to forget the dependency on profiles, platforms, and feedback loops as well as the preprogrammed social life in which these differences are produced (see also Feuz et al., 2011).

In addition to the different globalizing effects already described, the digital learning apparatus therefore simultaneously produces and stresses interindividual differences. These profiled differences in turn become new pathways to self-knowledge and understanding, instilling in us a sense of uniqueness and need for recognition. Personalized learners are not modern, but global; they are not involved in the difficult struggle to emancipate themselves from the regressive effects of tradition, but in an equally challenging fight to empower themselves from the immobilizing effects of locality or embeddedness.

Concluding Thoughts

In describing the learning apparatus, we have tried to explain the omnipresence of learning by pointing at the assemblage of several material and discursive components, along with the resulting changes in how we are now both governed and governing ourselves. In this concluding section, we will focus on emerging tensions in the operation of the learning apparatus.

In Europe, states as well as the European Union have started to problematize themselves in terms of learning; they now mainly see themselves as situated in a changing environment and focus on its available resources (and no longer predominantly relate to their own history), are engaged in innovation and competitive self-improvement (and no longer follow the track of modernizing a national tradition), have started to understand and represent themselves through profiling (for which nearly everything can be used, as long as it is differentiating), and are welcoming international frameworks, comparative studies, and global platforms (in order to find recognition and an impetus for new investments). This self-problematization might give rise to new kinds of nationalism, but these are less about protecting given birth rights, territory, and population than about assembling identities as part of constructing and reconstructing new (national) profiles. We could think of populism as the political version of personalization.

As discussed earlier, there is also evidence that school and higher education become reassembled both in terms of their internal organization as well as their aims and role. Yet in addition to that, there is a growing governmental concern toward education as being regional, or national, strategic "sites of learning." This is less a matter of realizing an agenda of modernization and social equality through (public) education, but of involving these sites in an opportunistic agenda of innovation; the concern is less with marking them as key forces of progress and social adaptation, but reaching out to them as strategic sites of productive learning embodying openness and mobility. The new European Union's ambition to "build a European Education Area by 2025"—which no longer only focuses on learning but reintroduces education as a whole—evidences this governmental concern (European Commission, 2020). These developments clarify that, while the learning apparatus and its globalizing effects become dominant, "formal education" is not disappearing but—similar to states—being reassembled.

The world of the learning apparatus, of course, is not a world without conflicts and tensions. An obvious example is what has been problematized as brain drain (and brain gain), and which has resulted in national or regional strategies to reduce the mobility of the learner, to nudge the global mindset of the learner, and to develop legislation and funding schemes that in one way or another frame learning in legal or binding terms in order to protect human capital investments. Another example already mentioned is the tension between governing through rules and laws, which per definition make abstraction of interindividual differences, and personalized learners, who want their unique needs taken into account and may perceive any regulation or other impositions as personal injustice. Personalization may help to understand the increased focus on sensitivity toward the other, the use of trigger warnings to prevent personal harm, and the concern with the safety of spaces. Along similar lines, the learning apparatus and its personalization effects can result in social categories of class, ethnicity, and gender—concepts that play a key role in the social state—becoming part of profiling activities and the focus of a person's need for recognition. At such a point, socioeconomic status, ethnicity, but also race and gender no longer belong to an individual's *background* (a background being what is given and can be shared), but become part of the person's *foreground* (what makes them different if they are recognized). If this is the case, social struggles and structural conflict may become reinscribed in the ethical-political register of personal (in)justice and recognition, profiled identities, and all sorts of appropriation. It all becomes personal for the reason that it has been made personal. In the same way that when history becomes heritage, and the present is no longer conceived as a break but an opportunity, questions can arise about the origin and previous ownership or appropriation of the inherited material and immaterial goods, and about how or even to what extent they can remain resources to be used today (or should be cancelled out). In a similar way, with social media "the social" seems to be more present than ever today. But the social in these media most of the time does not represent an issue that necessitates governmental intervention, nor is it (already) treated as a medium itself through which to govern. The digital, (pre-)programmed or algorithmic logic of the social media and the mechanisms of recognition are to a large extent (still) perceived as a natural domain that requires laissez faire. A last example of a possible tension is that cognitive work and learning, being to a large extent online work and learning, may result in different sorts of immobility. Cognitive work can be done (from) anywhere, which often means it is homework. Paradigmatic is the freelancer staying at home, working from home, and having to stay home because of work. To a certain extent, this is telework or working and learning at a distance, although there is no longer a distance when all other parties involved work and learn online and at home. The least one could say is that the home becomes a strategic site in the digital learning apparatus, with homework and home delivery being crucial, and with leaving the house and home becoming more and more of a challenge.

Despite her global mindset and a new sense and enjoyment of learning freedom, the personal learner is dependent on all sorts of governing technologies and instruments. Foucault would probably argue that the tendency to forget these dependencies is precisely what all apparatuses share in common and have as consequence—"having us believe that our 'liberation' is in the balance" (Foucault 1978, p. 159). It is as if the liberation from normalizing institutions, confined places, and strategies of social planning unleashes an overwhelming sense of "personal freedom to learn" that makes the operations of new mechanisms and strategies go unnoticed, if not self-evident. After all, who can be against learning, against being a person, and against living a global life? We hope, nevertheless, to have made this question sound less rhetorical than it might appear.

Notes

1. For the elaboration of this approach, and part of the analysis presented in this chapter, we rely on Simons and Masschelein (2008), Simons and Olssen (2010), Simons (2014a).

References

Ahl, H. (2008). Motivation theory as power in disguise. In A. Fejes & K. Nicoll (Eds.), *Foucault and lifelong learning: Governing the subject* (pp. 151–163). Routledge.

Bell, D. (1973). *The coming of the post-industrial society: A venture in social forecasting.* Basis Books.

Biesta, G. J. J. (2010). *Good education in an age of measurement: Ethics, politics, democracy.* Routledge.

Bucher, T. (2018). *If . . . then. Algorithmic power and politics.* Oxford University Press.

Drucker, P. (1969). *The age of discontinuity: Guidelines to our changing society.* Harper & Row.

Durkheim, E. (1922). *Education and sociology* (Trans. Sherwood T. Fox). Education and Sociology (1922)—Classical Sociological Theory and Foundations of American Sociology (oregonstate.education). Oregon State University.

Duval, E. (2012). Learning analytics and educational data mining. https://erikduval.wordpress.com/2012/01/30/learning-analytics-and-educational-data-mining/

European Commission. (1995). *Teaching and learning: Towards the learning society.* European Commission.

European Commission. (2001). *Making a European area of lifelong learning a reality.* European Commission.

European Commission. (2007). *Towards common principles of flexicurity: More and better jobs through flexibility and security.* European Commission.

European Commission. (2008). *The European Qualifications Framework for lifelong learning (EQF).* European Commission.

European Commission. (2009). *Voorstel voor een beschikking van het Europees Parlement en de Raad betreffende het Europees jaar van de creativiteit en innovatie (2009).* (28.3.2008 COM (2008) 159). European Commission.

European Commission. (2013). *Opening up education.* Communication from the Commission (COM (2013) 654 final). European Commission.

European Commission (2020). *On achieving the European Education Area by 2025.* Communication from the Commission (COM (2020) 625 final). European Commission.

Ewald, F. (1986). *Histoire de l'état providence.* Grasset.

Faure, E., Herrera, F., Kaddoura, A.-R., Lopes, H., Petrovsky, A.-V., Rahnema, M., & Champion Ward, F. (1972). *Learning to be: The world of education today and tomorrow.* UNESCO.

Feuz, M., Fuller, M., & Stalder, F. (2011). Personal Web searching in the age of semantic capitalism: Diagnosing the mechanisms of personalization. *First Monday, 16*(2).

Foucault, M. (1977a). Le jeu de Michel Foucault. In D. Defert, F. Ewald, & J. Lagrange (Eds.), *Dits et écrits III 1975–1979* (pp. 298–329). Gallimard.

Foucault, M. (1977b). *Discipline and punish: The birth of the prison* (Trans. Alan Sheridan). Pantheon.

Foucault, M. (1978). *The history of sexuality.* Pantheon Books.

Foucault, M. (2003). *Society must be defended: Lectures at the College de France (1976–1977).* Picador.

Foucault, M. (2004a). *Naissance de la biopolitique, Cours au Collège de France (1978–1979).* Gallimard/Le seuil.

Foucault, M. (2004b). *Sécurité, territoire, population, Cours au Collège de France (1977–1978).* Gallimard/Le seuil.

Gordon, C. (1991). Governmental rationality: An introduction. In G. Burchell, C. Gordon, & P. Miller (Eds.), *The Foucault effect: studies in governmentality* (pp. 1–52). Harvester Wheatsheaf.

Giddens, A. (1998). *The third way: The renewal of social democracy.* Polity Press.

Haahr, J. H. (2004). Open co-ordination as advanced liberal government. *Journal of European Public Policy, 11*, 209–230.

Hunter, I. (1994). *Rethinking the school: Subjectivity, bureaucracy, criticism.* Allen and Unwin.

Kirzner, I. (1973). *Competition and entrepreneurship*. University of Chicago Press.

Knowles, M. (1975). *Self-directed learning: A guide for learners and teachers*. Association Press.

Knox, J., Williamson, B., & Bayne, S. (2019). Machine behaviourism: Future visions of "learnification" and "datafication" across humans and digital technologies. *Learning, Media and Technology, 45*(1), 31–45.

Larner, W., & Le Heron, R. (2004). Global benchmarking: Participating "at a distance" in the globalizing economy. In W. Larner & W. Walters (Eds.), *Global governmentality: Governing international spaces* (pp. 212–232). Routledge.

Lazzarato, M. (2006). Biopolitics/bioeconomics: A politics of multiplicity. *Multitudes*. http://multitudes.samizdat.net/Biopolitics-Bioeconomics-a

Miller, P., & Rose, N. (1997). Mobilizing the consumer: Assembling the subject of consumption. *Theory, Culture & Society, 14*(1), 1–36.

Möhlmann, M. (2021). Algorithmic nudges don't have to be unethical. *Harvard Business Review, 22*, April 11, 2021.

Pochet, Ph., & Paternotre, M. (1998). "Inzetbaarheid/employability" in de context van de werkgelegenheidsrichtsnoeren van de Europese Unie [Employability in the context of directions for employment of the European Union]. Observatoir Social Européen. http://www.ose.be:files:employa-nl.pdf]

Poell, T., & Nieborg, D., & van Dijck, J. (2019). Platformisation. *Internet Policy Review, 8*(4).

Popkewitz, T. S. (2008). *Cosmopolitanism and the age of school reform: Science, education and making society by making the child*. Routledge.

Pykett, J. (2009). Personalisation and de-schooling: Uncommon trajectories in contemporary education policy. *Critical Social Policy, 29*(3), 374–397.

Rabinow, P. (2003). *Antropos today: Reflections on modern equipment*. Princeton University Press.

Rose, N. (1999). *Powers of freedom: Reframing political thought*. Cambridge University Press.

Rouvroy, A., & Berns, T. (2013). Algorithmic governmentality and prospects of emancipation: Disparateness as a precondition for individuation through relationships? *Réseaux, 177*, 163–196.

Simons, M. (2014a). The learning question: Monitoring, feedback, and performance spectacles. In M. Pereyra & B. Franklin (Eds.), *Systems of reason and the politics of schooling: School reform and sciences of education in the tradition of Thomas S. Popkewitz* (pp. 145–162). Routledge.

Simons, M. (2014b). Governing education without reform: The power of the example. *Discourse Studies in Cultural Politics of Education, 36*(5), 712–731.

Simons, M. (2014c). Governing through feedback: From national orientation towards global positioning. In T. Fenwick, E. Mangez, & J. Ozga (Eds.), *World yearbook of education 2014: Governing knowledge: Comparison, knowledge-based technologies and expertise in the regulation of education* (pp. 155–171). Routledge.

Simons, M. (2018). Refiguring the European student: Mixed transnational feelings. In E. Hultqvist, S. Lindblad, & T. Popkewitz (Eds.), *Critical analyses of educational reforms in an era of transnational governance* (pp. 169–184). Springer.

Simons, M. (2021). The figure of the independent learner: on governing by personalization and debt. *Discourse: Studies in the Cultural Politics of Education, 42*(6), 813–827. doi: 10.1080/01596306.2020.1732302

Simons, M., & Masschelein, J. (2008). The governmentalization of learning and the assemblage of a learning apparatus. *Educational Theory, 58*(4), 391–415.

Simons, M., & Masschelein, J. (2021). *Looking after school: A critical analysis of personalisation in education.* Education, Culture & Society.

Simons, M., & Olssen, M. (2010). The school and learning apparatus. In D. Osberg & G. Biesta (Eds.), *Complexity theory and the politics of education* (pp. 79–92). Sense Publishers.

Shuell, T. J. (1988). The role of the student in learning from instruction. *Contemporary Educational Psychology, 13,* 276–295.

Tuschling, A., & Engemann, C. (2006). From education to lifelong learning: The emerging regime of learning in the European Union. *Educational Philosophy and Theory, 38*(4), 451–469.

CHAPTER 11

FIELD THEORY BEYOND THE NATION STATE

JULIAN HAMANN

How National Is Bourdieusian Field Theory?

PIERRE Bourdieu developed his sociology mostly on domestic issues of European societies. He had a particular focus on French society, and within France on education and higher education (Bourdieu, 1988, 1996b; Bourdieu & Passeron, 1977, 1979), but his research also attended to the French class society (Bourdieu, 1984, 1999) and to literature and the arts (Bourdieu, 1996a, 2017), to name just a few other examples. Although foundations of Bourdieu's theoretical work were laid by his early empirical studies of Kabyl life in Algeria (Bourdieu, 1962, 1995), and he occasionally discussed processes of field internationalization (cf. Bourdieu, 2005, pp. 223–232), it is probably fair to say that large parts of his research—and, importantly, his theorizing—have been informed by phenomena within national orders. Fields, for Bourdieu, were primarily national fields.

Because the empirical point of reference for Bourdieu's research was usually national and often Francocentric, several "nationalist" assumptions are engraved into his theory (cf. Schmitz & Witte, 2020). For example, he conceptualizes societies as national societies (Bennett et al., 2009, pp. 234–250). In addition, the two principles of social differentiation, classes and fields, are both situated within the national field of power and the national social space, respectively (Schmitz & Witte, 2017; Vandenberghe, 1999). Not least, Bourdieu sees the mechanisms and institutions responsible for the legitimation and reproduction of social order as granted, organized, and controlled by the nation state (Bourdieu, 2014). Despite such "nationalist" assumptions in Bourdieu's own theorizing, a diagnosis of methodological or, indeed, *epistemic* nationalism would be misguided if it was aimed at the field-theoretical research program per se. By principle, the research program of field theory goes beyond the work of Bourdieu himself

(Wacquant, 1992a). It does not exhaust itself in the mechanical application of the same theoretical concepts to ever-new empirical phenomena. In the following I will join other scholars who have rejected the claim that field theory is impeded by epistemic nationalism and who have argued that such a claim neglects the very epistemological foundations of the field-theoretical research program (cf. Go & Krause, 2016b; Krause, 2020; Schmitz & Witte, 2020).

A core principle of the field-theoretical research program is the relational co-constitution of theory, methodology, and epistemology (Bourdieu & Wacquant, 1992). According to this principle, theory is always deeply engrained in methodological and epistemological considerations and vice-versa. Thus, theoretical concepts like "field" do not come ready-made with definitions, waiting to be mechanically applied and filled with empirical content. Rather, field-theoretical concepts convey a particular way of studying social phenomena. The scope of such phenomena is an empirical question. Indeed, any a priori commitment to "the national" and "the global" is overcome by field theory's relational approach to start not from entities, but to establish relevant research objects through relations between units of analysis (Bourdieu, 1998; cf. Vandenberghe, 1999). According to the relational approach, the local, regional, national, transnational, or global character of empirical phenomena is not determined by their very essence, but with reference to the phenomena's relations to other phenomena (cf. Krause, 2020). Rather than starting from actors, the field-theoretical research program invites us to start from relationships between actors and to investigate the common orientations or stakes that define the relationships between them. A field, then, is the structured realm that emerges from relations between actors. Because both the construction of relevant stakes and actors' relations may be located on and between different geospatial scales, the concept of "field" is neither theoretically nor empirically committed to a specific scale.

What is more, the very claim to a specific geospatial scale is often enough part and parcel of actors' struggles and stakes. Higher education provides ample evidence for this: The national orientation of higher education systems has to be perceived as a historical specificity. For instance, in Germany, a field of higher education that is oriented toward the national scale emerged a mere 200 years ago. Before that, large parts of the German-speaking world were fragmented according to territorial principalities and ecclesiastical confessions. What was at stake for universities was the favor—both in symbolic and material terms—of princes and municipalities (cf. Rüegg, 1996). The very notion that the geospatial realm toward which universities are oriented is actually a "national state" was itself a matter of symbolic struggles. Those struggles were resolved with the proclamation of a German national state in 1871, a political project to which universities contributed the national narratives that were needed for imperial Germany (Gengnagel & Hamann, 2014; Ringer, 1990). Hence, if universities today compete for funding and status in national fields of higher education (Hicks, 2012), their orientation toward the national scale has to be historicized as a result of symbolic struggles. Other actors contest this national orientation. For example, the European Union claims that the definition of good research and the distribution of resources can also be organized at the European level (Baier & Gengnagel, 2018; König, 2017). Ranking agencies and media corporations even go beyond the European scale and try to engage universities in a global competition for status and visibility (Brankovic et al., 2018, 2023; Kauppi, 2016; Wedlin, 2010).

The example of higher education conveys, first, that the geospatial range of fields is a historical specificity and, second, that the very question which scales a field is oriented toward is often a contested issue in the field itself. The earlier example also illustrates a crucial third point: Different scales can matter at the same time (Krause, 2017; Witte & Schmitz, 2021). Not only can national higher education systems remain relevant if a relatively autonomous European field of higher education emerges. What is more, a strong national sphere can actually be a vital feature of a European field (cf. Schwarz & Westerheijden, 2007). Fields can be oriented toward different geospatial scales at the same time, and different scales can be of varying significance for a field. Indeed, it is likely that a field's orientation toward one scale affects its orientation toward other scales (Sapiro, 2018).

The field-theoretical research program allows us to see that local, regional, national, transnational, and global orders are produced according to the same principles, that is, as a social space that is structured by relations between actors and defined by their common orientation toward specific stakes. Just as national fields emerge when stakes are constructed on the national scale (cf. Bourdieu, 1994), processes of transnationalization are propelled by consecrating authorities that encourage actors to orient themselves toward stakes on the transnational level. More specifically, such processes of transnationalization imply, first, a (gradual) change of consecrating authorities and institutions; second, a change of the level on which actors orient their struggles; and third, a change in the constellation of agents involved (Sapiro, 2018).

Such changes throughout processes of transnationalization are illustrated by current developments in fields of education. In many regards, fields of education remain deeply embedded on the national scale. Education has a reproductive function for the class structure of national societies; it is anchored in national education systems, institutions, and policies; career paths for teachers are national; and, at least in some countries, education is funded by the state. Not least, education is indispensable for maintaining the symbolic power of the nation state, for example, because it issues certificates, and cultivates national languages and cultures (Bourdieu, 2014). Yet the national orientation of fields of education is currently challenged.

These challenges can be observed in education policy, where institutions and authorities of consecration on the national level now compete with other actors on regional, international, and transnational scales. What is at stake in these competitions is the definition of standards for good education, standards that are, for example, also claimed by the Program for International Student Assessment (PISA) tests of the Organization for Economic Cooperation and Development (OECD) (cf. Lawn & Lingard, 2002). Accrediting agencies and political authorities like the OECD and the European Union exert forces of transnationalization on fields of education (Dugonjic-Rodwin, 2021; King, 2007). Through the lens of field theory, such forces of transnationalization do not necessarily contradict the national orientation of educational fields: As I have argued earlier, fields can be oriented simultaneously toward the national, the transnational, and other scales. For example, PISA integrates fields of education on a transnational scale (Grek, 2012); at the same time, PISA results are widely deployed to shape national education policies (Rautalin & Alasuutari, 2009; Takayama, 2010; Waldow et al., 2014); and not least, PISA results are recontextualized on the local level according to specific constellations of actors and institutions (Hartong & Nikolai, 2017). Thus, processes of localization, nationalization, and transnationalization play out at the same time. The examples illustrate that there is neither a zero-sum relationship between the national and the global nor are these processes necessarily unidirectional (cf. Sassen, 2006).

The recent developments in higher education and education explain why research on these very fields has played an important role in pushing field theory beyond the nation state and dismissing the national as an a priori analytical category. Yet the move beyond the national scale has not been limited to studies on higher education and education. It has been a major concern in field analysis in general. In the last 20 years, a vibrant literature has formed to investigate phenomena beyond the national scale (cf. Go & Krause, 2016a; Schmidt-Wellenburg & Bernhard, 2020a). This research perspective, for which I adopt the label "post-national analysis of fields" (introduced by Krause, 2020), does not take the national for granted as a self-evident scale of social life, and it does not ascribe to it any inherent ontological or epistemological qualities. For the literature concerned with the postnational analysis of fields, the national is not irrelevant per se, but the empirical focus is on contexts that go beyond the national scope. While the nation state played a central role, indeed, for Bourdieu's own research, the postnational take on the field-theoretical research program assumes an agnostic stance toward the national. The following sections attend to this literature, focusing first on its empirical foci and analytical priorities, and then providing an overview over theoretical contributions to the postnational analysis of fields.

The Field of Postnational Field Analysis: Empirical Foci and Analytical Priorities

Empirical contributions to the postnational analysis of fields cover a wide range of research objects. They attend to the transnational diffusion and reproduction of religious or humanitarian virtues and values (Dromi, 2016; Krause, 2014; Petzke, 2016), to the transnational orientation of professions like journalism (Christin, 2016; Hussain, 2017) or law (Dezalay & Garth, 1996; Vauchez, 2008; Vauchez & de Witte, 2013), or to supranational relations in societal spheres like economy (Lebaron, 2010; Maeße, 2018; Mudge & Vauchez, 2016) and culture (Buchholz, 2016; Casanova, 2004; Kuipers, 2011).

Two empirical foci are of particular importance in postnational field analysis. First, contributions are often concerned with political entities, among them nation states and their transnational colonial pasts (Go, 2008; Steinmetz, 2008; Wilson, 2016), relations between nation states (Adler-Nissen, 2013; Schmitz et al., 2015), or the emergence of political entities on the supranational scale (Adler-Nissen, 2011; Büttner & Mau, 2014; Cohen, 2011; Kauppi, 2018). Second, perhaps the most prevalent empirical focus for postnational field analysis are fields of education and higher education. Contributions are concerned with transnational education policy instruments like PISA (Mangez & Hilgers, 2012; Rawolle & Lingard, 2008; Stray & Wood, 2020) and highlight how transnational developments and fields affect educational fields on the national scale (Hartong, 2020; Marttila, 2020; cf. Dugonjic-Rodwin, 2021). With a view on higher education, scholars have noted how universities are oriented toward global struggles for reputation (Münch, 2014); how global, transnational, and national orientations overlap in academic fields and disciplines (Heilbron et al., 2008; Heilbron, 2014; Krause, 2016); and how devices like rankings enforce fields to orient toward transnational stakes (Hamann & Schmidt-Wellenburg, 2020; Marginson, 2008).

Such an overview of empirical research objects across individual contributions provides valuable insights. It suggests that the empirical foci of postnational field analyses are similar to the foci of field analyses that are primarily concerned with fields on the national scale. In particular, the overview illustrates that political fields and fields of (higher) education are a core theme in both literatures. Yet, despite these insights, it is more rewarding to distinguish contributions to postnational field analysis not according to empirical foci but regarding analytical priorities, that is, with a view on the different attempts to transcend the national as the ex-ante geospatial unit of analysis. Although such distinctions are often gradual, they convey an analytical topology of the field of postnational field analysis. In the following, I will propose four levels of distinction.

One level of distinction concerns different approaches to geospatial scales. A large part of postnational field analyses focuses on the unilateral impact that transnational fields have on national fields, illustrating, for example, how national fields are structured by transnational influences (Hussain, 2017), how national policy fields respond to transnational assessments (Stray & Wood, 2020), how transnational fields intrude national fields (Petzke, 2016), how transnational field effects realign fields and professions that have hitherto been oriented toward the national scale (Schmidt-Wellenburg, 2017), and how national fields open up (Kuipers, 2011) or even dissolve in the face of transnational influences (Mangez & Hilgers, 2012). These studies are complemented by a second body of literature in which relations between transnational and national scales are conceptualized not as unilateral, but as bilateral. Scholars have noted, for example, how transnational and national fields affect each other and overlap (Krause, 2016), how national fields draw from transnational fields and simultaneously affect their emergence (Dromi, 2016), or how transnational fields have an impact on national fields, but the latter act back on the former (Stampnitzky, 2016). A third strand of literature pursues a slightly different approach to geospatial scales. Here, contributions focus less on relations between different scales and more on relations between positions within transnational or global fields. This is the case in studies that examine how transnational or global fields structure relations between universities (Münch, 2014), central bankers (Lebaron, 2008), bureaucratic professionals (Büttner & Mau, 2014), national literatures (Casanova, 2004), nation states (Go, 2008), countries as sites of cultural production (Buchholz, 2018), or how positions and fractions in the fields of economics or the social sciences develop global orientations (Heilbron, 2014; Maeße, 2018). It is worth pointing out that at least two other possible approaches to geospatial scales are much less frequently pursued: Few studies are concerned with "upward" unilateral relations according to which a national scale predominantly impacts a transnational sphere (but see Bigo, 2007; Cohen, 2011; Go, 2020). Even less prevalent are postnational field analyses that abandon the national scale altogether and focus on relations between, for example, transnational and regional fields (but see Krause, 2014).

In addition to different approaches to geospatial scales, a second level of distinction can contribute to an analytical topology of postnational field analysis. The field-theoretical research program rests on the assumption that different field-theoretical concepts relate to and build on each other (Wacquant, 1992b). Just like a study of habitus has to be complemented by the concept of capital because habitus are structured by capital endowment, comprehensive analyses of fields can be expected to rely on a number of theoretical concepts that are not only neighboring but indeed analytically related to the concept of field. Yet postnational field analyses seem to draw on a rather limited arsenal of theoretical concepts.[1] The most prominent additional concept mobilized to construct transnational fields is capital, understood as common stakes that orient struggles in a specific field. Some contributions draw on established forms of capital, revealing, for example, how cultural and economic capital structure the transnational field of education policy (Mangez & Hilgers, 2012), how transnational fields translate professional expertise into political capital (Schmidt-Wellenburg, 2017), or how central bankers' positions in the global field of power are structured by political and economic capital (Lebaron, 2008). Other studies identify new forms of capital, for example, ethnographic capital in the transnational field of colonial states (Steinmetz, 2008), informational capital structuring the European field of security agencies (Bigo, 2007), macro capital structuring the positions of countries, regions, or cities in a global field of cultural production (Buchholz, 2018), literary capital in the global field of literature (Casanova, 2004), and meta-capital structuring the relation among nation states in a global field of power (Schmitz et al., 2015).

Another theoretical concept regularly mobilized to complement the concept of field in postnational analyses is the concept of autonomy, which describes the degree to which fields have a logic of their own and the capacity to organize field-specific practices (cf. Krause, 2017). Contributions concerned with the relative autonomy and heteronomy of transnational or global fields examine, for example, the porous internal and external borders of the European legal field (Vauchez, 2008), the heteronomizing effects of globalization on fields of national educational policy (Lingard et al., 2005), how the relative autonomy of different national TV fields structures their incorporation into a transnational TV field (Kuipers, 2011), and how researchers in the social sciences and humanities mobilize the academic autonomy of their own field as a discursive strategy to gain advantages in the transnational field of European research funding (Baier & Gengnagel, 2018). While the concepts of capital and, to a lesser degree, autonomy are regularly mobilized in postnational field analyses, only very few contributions go beyond this conceptual basic equipment. For example, Bourdieu's key concept of habitus rarely complements the concept of field (but see Adler-Nissen, 2008; Büttner & Mau, 2014; Vaara & Faÿ, 2012; see also Carlson & Schneickert, 2021 on the concept of habitus on transnational contexts). Other field-theoretical concepts are even less prevalent. Illusio and doxa, describing the belief in field-specific values and orientations and the unquestioned acceptance of field-specific principles of order due to an alignment of mental and social structures, are mostly neglected or only mentioned in passing (but see Petzke, 2016; Schmitz & Witte, 2017).

Beyond different approaches to geospatial scales and the use of complementary field-theoretical concepts, two additional levels of distinction can contribute to an analytical topology of the field of postnational field analysis: A third level of distinction concerns the methodological design of the respective studies. Many postnational field analyses are conceptualized as single case studies concentrating on one transnational or global field, for example, the transnational field of higher education (Marginson, 2008; Münch, 2014), the transnational field of European social law and social policy (Feritkh, 2020), or the global field of power (Lebaron, 2008; Schmitz et al., 2015). Few contributions are conceptualized as multiple case studies with a focus on different fields and the relations between them. Exceptions are studies on how relations between transnational, national, and regional fields in the social sciences structure actors' positions and the prestige of research objects (Krause, 2016), how gatekeepers regulate access to established positions in the academic field compared to the field of stand-up comedy (Hamann & Beljean, 2021), or how different national TV fields are structured and relate to a transnational TV field (Kuipers, 2011).

A fourth and last level of distinction that can convey a topology of postnational field analyses sheds light on the methods mobilized in the literature. A large share of contributions draws on qualitative, text-based methods, the majority being interview transcripts (Adler-Nissen, 2008; Mudge & Vauchez, 2016; Stray & Wood, 2020) but also discourse analyses of documents (Baier & Gengnagel, 2018; Maesse, 2020), as well as interpretative analyses of archived records (Dromi, 2016; Wilson, 2016) and memoirs (Stampnitzky, 2016). Only few other qualitative methods are mobilized. For instance, ethnographic approaches are rather uncommon (but see Krause, 2014). In comparison to qualitative methods, quantitative or quantifying methods are less prevalent in postnational field analyses. Exceptions are occasional applications of descriptive statistics (Buchholz, 2018; Marginson, 2008; Münch, 2014) and methods of geometric data analysis (Baier & Gengnagel, 2018; Dugonjic-Rodwin, 2021; Lebaron, 2008; Schmitz et al., 2015). In sum, the methodological topology of postnational field analysis seems somewhat similar to analyses of primarily national fields.

This tentative topology suggests some lessons to learn for the study of education and higher education. The most obvious lesson is that the field-theoretical research program is by no means limited to the national scale. The overview illustrates a rich diversity of empirical studies of transnational and global fields. Yet the topology also highlights some issues and orientations that have thus far been neglected. Postnational field analyses of (higher) education could attend to these issues in the future. First, research should pay more attention to fields "below" the national scale, a perspective that promises valuable insights particularly into systems in which (higher) education policy is also located at the state level. Research should also consider multilateral relations between fields oriented toward the local, the state, the national, and the transnational scale. Second, the overview conveys what I coin "conceptual isolationism," according to which postnational field analyses rarely make use of field theory's full conceptual arsenal. Approaches that are more comprehensive in conceptual terms promise a more saturated and profound field-theoretical account. To increase their theoretical saturation, postnational field analyses of (higher) education should therefore take into account concepts related to the concept of field. Third, the topology suggests some rather untrodden methodological paths to follow. Both multiple case studies, in which fields are compared or examined according to their relation to each other, and quantitative and quantifying methods are less prevalent and could be mobilized more often in postnational field analyses of (higher) education.

Postnational field analyses in general and analyses of fields of (higher) education in particular cannot only draw from the existing literature reviewed in this section and attend to the issues that have been neglected thus far. Future research can also build on several theoretical and conceptual innovations that have been developed in postnational analyses of fields. Because the literature on postnational field analysis does not always explicitly leverage these innovations, the theoretical and conceptual contributions will be highlighted in the following section.

Theoretical and Conceptual Innovations in the Postnational Analysis of Fields

Attempts to move field theory beyond the national scale have yielded a number of theoretical and conceptual innovations. These innovations proceed from two gradually different strategies of theorizing: One strategy is to rescale existing field-theoretical concepts to make them suitable for postnational analyses. This strategy modifies said concepts but leaves their fundamental analytical architecture more or less unchanged. A second strategy of theorizing proceeds from the insight that field-theoretical concepts have to be revised more fundamentally to study transnational and global phenomena. The distinction between the two strategies is gradual because some contributions rescale certain field-theoretical concepts while revising other concepts more fundamentally. Both strategies share the insight that field-theoretical concepts are not only generative for analyzing transnational relations and phenomena but indeed for transcending ex-ante oppositions between different geospatial scales (cf. Go & Krause, 2016b; Schmitz & Witte, 2020).

Contributions to postnational field theory that pursue the first strategy of theorizing rescale theoretical concepts to be adequate to study transnational or global phenomena but leave the fundamental analytical architecture of said concepts unchanged. Rescaled for transnational or global fields, field-theoretical concepts facilitate insights, for example, into the emergence of fields in terms of a differentiation of a social space from existing spaces (Buchholz, 2016; Wilson, 2016); into struggles, competition, and power relations within transnational fields (Krause, 2016; Petzke, 2016); into internal struggle or external disruption as sources for change in transnational fields (Go, 2008); and into the effects transnational fields exert on different geospatial scales (Mudge & Vauchez, 2016; Stampnitzky, 2016). It is telling to review these innovations in light of my previous diagnosis of the conceptual isolationism of postnational field analysis. While the overview in the previous section has revealed that empirical research rarely makes use of the full theoretical arsenal of field theory, the examples here illustrate successful attempts to rescale some more general conceptual approaches of field theory—for example, the focus on field effects, on the emergence of fields, or on struggles and power relations.

The strategy of rescaling has not only been applied to theoretical concepts but also to methodological principles. Scholars have pointed out that the field-theoretical research program provides researchers with "a style of research with a distinct epistemology and methodology" (Schmidt-Wellenburg & Bernhard, 2020b, p. 2) For example, one methodological principle that has been fruitfully rescaled to be applicable to fields beyond the national scale is the principle to actively construct empirical phenomena as objects of investigation, instead of taking them for granted. With a view on transnational or global phenomena, this requires asking whether and how transnational or global practices differ from national practices, and how such practices relate to one another (cf. Bigo, 2020; Hartong, 2020). Another methodological principle of field theory is to attend to the generative characteristics of social phenomena. Rescaled for phenomena beyond the national scale, a focus on the notion of time and processes of becoming facilitates questions on the historical development of transnational or global practices and categories (cf. Go, 2020; Maesse, 2020). In sum, the strategy of rescaling both methodological principles and theoretical concepts has demonstrated a remarkable potential for illuminating phenomena and processes at transnational and global scales.

Gradually distinct from the first strategy of rescaling is a second strategy of theorizing that sees the need for more general conceptual revisions. Attempting to avoid a "deductive reification" (Buchholz, 2016, p. 31) of a one-sided perspective from the Global North, this strategy aims to move beyond the national scale by introducing not gradual, but more or less fundamental innovations that significantly extend the field-theoretical research program. In the following, I will review four such innovations that emerge from this strategy of revising.

A first significant extension of the field-theoretical research program introduces the scale across which fields extend as a hitherto neglected property of fields alongside which fields can be distinguished (Krause, 2017). According to this analytical proposition, it is an empirical question whether fields are initially located on one scale and then expand ("below" or "above" the initial scale) or whether they are located across different scales from the outset (see also Benson, 2005; Schmitz & Witte, 2020). As a case in point, the higher education field illustrates that fields can be historically located simultaneously on a transnational and on a subnational scale before being nationalized. Treating their scale as a variable property of fields has analytical benefits because it facilitates several systematic questions (cf. Krause, 2017). These questions concern, first, relations between different fields on the same scale (e.g., relations between national fields of education and national political fields); second, relations between fields of the same kind and on the same scale in different contexts (e.g., relations between national fields of education in different countries); and third, relations between fields of the same kind on different scales (e.g., relations between fields of education on the local, national, and transnational scale). Although the overview in the second section has conveyed that postnational field analyses attend to a variety of different relations on different geospatial scales, this approach allows for a more systematic take on such relations.

Treating the scale of fields as a variable property facilitates a second important innovation for the field-theoretical research program. An examination of the scale of fields comprises a systematic distinction between intranational, cross-national, and transnational relations between fields. Such a distinction of field relations has considerable analytical leverage. Not least, it allows for a differentiation of the central field-theoretical concept of autonomy: Questions about the relation between fields on the same geospatial scale (e.g., the field of education and the political field in the United Kingdom, or the fields of education in the United Kingdom and Romania) attend to what has been coined "horizontal autonomy" (Krause, 2017). Questions about the relation between fields of the same kind on different scales (e.g., the fields of education in the United Kingdom and the European Union) focus on what has been described as "vertical autonomy" (Buchholz, 2016). Distinguishing vertical and horizontal autonomy facilitates, first, a more differentiated view on the relative autonomy of fields. For example, the UK field of education may be *less* autonomous from the UK political field than some of its national counterparts are from the political fields in their contexts (horizontal autonomy), but it may be *more* autonomous from the European scale compared to other national fields of education (vertical autonomy) (cf. Grek, 2009; Grek & Ozga, 2010). Second, a differentiation of the concept of autonomy facilitates insights into transnational and global phenomena. For example, global fields can emerge not by constituting their independence from other global fields, but by becoming relatively autonomous from the logics of various national fields of the same kind (cf. Buchholz, 2013).

A different approach to the autonomy of transnational or global fields introduces the notion of "weak fields." Compared to the concepts of vertical and horizontal autonomy, the notion of weak fields is less distinct from the original field-theoretical concept of relative autonomy. It describes a type of transnational field that entails elements of both settled and emerging fields. Like settled fields, weak fields are characterized by densely institutionalized settings in which established professionals compete upon commonly valued stakes, and like emerging fields, weak fields are interwoven with neighboring fields and characterized by a low degree of internal differentiation (Vauchez, 2011). The "weakness" of transnational fields thus refers both to their interstitial position as they are merged into other fields that are constituted more firmly and to the blurriness of their internal boundaries (cf. Vauchez, 2008). Although the overview in the previous section has conveyed that some postnational field analyses mobilize the concept of autonomy, differentiations of the concept allow for a more fine-grained approach to relative autonomy. The full analytical potential of these theoretical innovations has yet to be tapped by empirical analyses.

A third innovation that emerges from the strategy of revising theoretical concepts can be seen in attempts to employ the analytical category of a global field of power which relates, for example, financial elites (Lebaron, 2008, 2010), hegemonic empires of the past (Go, 2008), or current nation states and cultures according to their similarities and differences (Schmitz et al., 2015). A concept to relate fields to each other—that is, a field of fields—and thus a key component of field theory, Bourdieu has used the field of power mostly as a theoretical reference in studies on individual fields, but not explicated it in a dedicated study. What is more, he located the field of power exclusively on the national scale where it is framed by the nation state (cf. Bourdieu, 1996b; see also Schmitz et al., 2016). Attempts to revise this concept for postnational analyses unfold considerable analytical potential. A revised concept of a field of power is particularly important for an approach coined generalized field theory (Schmitz & Witte, 2020). Instead of rescaling theoretical concepts, this approach attempts to release field theory from any ex ante assumptions on geospatial scales. Consequently, the key concept of the approach is a generalized field of power that discards not only epistemic nationalism, but any epistemology that takes geospatial scales for granted (e.g., internationalization, globalization, or cosmopolitanism). A field of power that has been revised accordingly suggests "the global" as the widest possible empirical and most general analytical frame of reference for research on social phenomena (Schmitz & Witte, 2020; Schneickert et al., 2020; Witte & Schmitz, 2021). Although some studies have put the concept of a global field of power to empirical use, the previous section has shown that most empirical contributions focus on transnational fields that span only selected parts of the world (i.e., the Global North).

Postcolonial strands in the field-theoretical research program also pursue the strategy of revising field-theoretical concepts. From their efforts emerges a fourth substantial attempt to release the field-theoretical research program from the specific geospatial context it has been developed in. Generally, postcolonial approaches challenge us to rethink hegemonic Western knowledges and to reconsider an epistemic unconscious from an alternative standpoint (Go, 2017). Although Bourdieu himself did offer a theory of colonialism and a systematic understanding of its effects and logics (Go, 2013), the field-theoretical research program reveals imprints of hegemonic Western epistemology. Such imprints are illustrated, for example, by a distinct analytical focus on transnational constellations in the Global North. Another example of the imprints of Western epistemology is field theory's taken-for-granted distinction between differentiated and nondifferentiated societies. This distinction, symbolized by Bourdieu's work on the precapitalist, agrarian society of Kabylia, on the one hand, and by his work on the strongly differentiated French society, on the other hand, organizes a number of oppositions—between Western and non-Western, heterogeneous and homogeneous, complex and simple, modern and archaic (Hilgers & Mangez, 2014). Postcolonial approaches attempt not only to replace the distinction between differentiated and nondifferentiated societies with a continuum of more or less differentiated societies. They also show that the type of differentiation that field theory is concerned with is, in fact, a particular form of functional differentiation that has been developed from Western societies. Postcolonial approaches thus draw attention to alternative types of differentiation that concern language, ethnicity, or territory (cf. Steinmetz, 2016). In sum, postcolonial perspectives are a powerful tool for reflexive postnational field analyses and a critique of the illusions of scholastic and epistemic universalism.

CONCLUSION: SOME OPEN QUESTIONS FOR THE POSTNATIONAL ANALYSIS OF FIELDS

Bourdieu's own research was mostly focused on fields oriented within the national scale. Yet the field-theoretical research program per se does not suffer from epistemological nationalism. Indeed, any a priori commitment to specific geospatial scales is overcome by field theory's relational approach to start not from entities, but to establish relevant research objects through relations between units of analysis. According to this methodological core principle, empirical phenomena are not local, regional, national, transnational, or global in essence. Rather, their geospatial range is to be determined empirically with reference to the phenomena's relations to other phenomena. Taking this principle seriously, the postnational analysis of fields has developed into a vast body of literature over the last two decades. It attends to various empirical foci, has pursued a number of analytical priorities, and brought about important theoretical and conceptual innovations. Research on education and higher education has played an important role in pushing field theory beyond the nation state because recent developments in (higher) education have made it necessary to dismiss the national as an a priori analytical category.

My contribution has demonstrated that the postnational analysis of fields has realized remarkable analytical leverage. Yet a few open questions remain. I will conclude with an empirical, a methodological, and a theoretical question that should be addressed by future research.

An empirical question that remains to be answered by postnational analyses of fields concerns functional equivalents of the state on the transnational or global scale (cf. Schmitz & Witte, 2020). On the national scale, the state has a central role in the (re-)production of the material and symbolic order of societies. The "grip of the state"

(Bourdieu, 1994, p. 2) lies in its ability to impose universal symbolic forms and principles of vision and division. The state's ability to impose principles of social order ranges from the structure of time (i.e., the school calendar, secular and religious holidays, etc.) over the distinction between public and private space to the definition of social problems (Bourdieu, 2014). Not least, there is a close complicity between the state and educational institutions in the (re-)production of social order (Bourdieu, 1996b). In its attempts to abandon "the national," the postnational analysis of fields has successfully moved beyond the nation state as an a priori geospatial scale. Yet the focus on geospatial entities has not corresponded with similar attention to the second meaning of the state as a site of material and symbolic power. Future research should therefore systematically inquire functional equivalents to state power on transnational or global scales. It should also examine the extent to which these functional equivalents can impose symbolic visions and divisions that might be as universal as those imposed by the nation state. With its focus on the symbolic power of entities like the European Union, the OECD, or media corporations like Bertelsmann or Times Higher Education, the study of transnational educational and political fields has thus far delivered the most promising insights in this regard.

A methodological question for postnational analyses of fields are geospatial scales "below" the national. Recapitulating the literature reviewed in this contribution, it is obvious that most attempts of postnational field analysis either go "above" or "across" the national scale. In other words, postnational field analysis thus far focuses either on transnational or on global fields. Less attention has been paid to local or regional fields, and existing work on the matter has not been incorporated into the body of literature. This bias is remarkable if we call to mind that, according to the relational principle, empirical phenomena do not have a geospatial essence. Assuming that the current scholarship takes this principle seriously, there can only be two reasons for the prevalence of transnational and global fields in the existing literature: Either fields "above" the national have a greater appeal to scholars, if only because transnational and global objects of research promise greater dividends in the academic field (Bourdieu, 1969). Or fields are indeed geospatially extensive rather than contractive; that is, they tend to extend to spaces equal to or "above" the national scale but less commonly contract "below" the national. Such fundamental issues of the spatial expansion and contraction of fields should be addressed more systematically by postnational field analysis. More systematic research on local and regional fields would be a first step toward addressing this question.

A theoretical question future research should attend to concerns the geospatial scope of class (cf. Bennett et al., 2009). Bourdieu's theory is one of the few modern sociological theories that integrates two principles of social differentiation: the structure of fields and the structure of classes. Crucially, both principles are linked on a theoretical level through the concept of structural homology, which designates the parallels between the oppositions within fields and the oppositions in social space (i.e., the structure of class society). The degree to which these parallels manifest is an empirical question and concerns the relative autonomy of the field in question. Bourdieu's studies of the French fields of (higher) education give examples for a rather pronounced structural homology between the structures of social space and specific fields: In the academic field, differences separating the academic faculties are structurally homologous to the economic and social differences that form the opposition between the subordinate and dominant classes in French society (Bourdieu, 1988, p. 41). The field of the Grandes Ecoles is structured to contribute to the reproduction of French class society (Bourdieu, 1996b, p. 285). A postnational analysis of fields that concentrates only on fields runs the danger of dissolving the theoretical link between fields and social space as two related principles of social differentiation. What is at stake here is not only theoretical comprehensiveness. An empirical approach to possible homologies between transnational or global fields and the—national or transnational—social space is also much better equipped to understand the positions and oppositions within the fields in question. Future research should therefore attempt to avoid the decoupling of field and social space.

NOTE

1. This observation also holds true for field analyses primarily concerned with fields on the national scale. Thus, the kind of conceptual isolationism diagnosed here is no peculiarity of the postnational analysis of fields.

REFERENCES

Adler-Nissen, R. (2008). The diplomacy of opting out: A Bourdieudian approach to national integration strategies. *Journal of Common Market Studies*, 46(3), 663–684.

Adler-Nissen, R. (2011). On a field trip with Bourdieu. *International Political Sociology*, 5(3), 327–330.

Adler-Nissen, R. (Ed.) (2013). *Bourdieu in international relations: Rethinking key-concepts in IR.* Routledge.

Baier, C., & Gengnagel, V. (2018). Academic autonomy beyond the nation-state: The social sciences and humanities in the European Research Council. *Österreichische Zeitschrift für Soziologie*, 43(1), 65–92.

Bennett, T., Savage, M., Silva, E., Warde, A., Gayo-Cal, M., & Wright, D. (2009). *Culture, class, distinction.* Routledge.

Benson, R. (2005). Mapping field variation: Journalism in France and the United States. In R. Benson & E. Neveu (Eds.), *Bourdieu and the journalistic field* (pp. 85–112). Polity Press.

Bigo, D. (Ed.) (2007). *The field of the EU internal security agencies.* Centre d'études sur les conflits/l'Harmattan.

Bigo, D. (2020). Adjusting a Bourdieusian approach to the study of transnational fields: Transversal practices and state (trans)formations related to intelligence and surveillance. In C. Schmidt-Wellenburg & S. Bernhard (Eds.), *Charting transnational fields. Methodology for a political sociology of knowledge* (pp. 55–78). Routledge.

Bourdieu, P. (1962). *The Algerians.* Beacon Press.

Bourdieu, P. (1969). Intellectual field and creative project. *Social Science Information*, 8(2), 89–119.

Bourdieu, P. (1984). *Distinction: A social critique of the judgement of taste.* Cambridge University Press.

Bourdieu, P. (1988). *Homo academicus.* Polity Press.

Bourdieu, P. (1994). Rethinking the state: Genesis and structure of the bureaucratic field. *Sociological Theory, 12*(1), 1–18.

Bourdieu, P. (1995). *Outline of a theory of practice.* Cambridge University Press.

Bourdieu, P. (1996a). *The rules of art: Genesis and structure of the literary field.* Stanford University Press.

Bourdieu, P. (1996b). *The state nobility. Elite schools in the field of power.* Polity Press.

Bourdieu, P. (1998). *Practical reason. On the theory of action.* Stanford University Press.

Bourdieu, P. (1999). *The weight of the world. Social suffering in contemporary society.* Stanford University Press.

Bourdieu, P. (2005). *The social structures of the economy.* Polity Press.

Bourdieu, P. (2014). *On the state. Lectures at the Collège de France, 1989–1992.* Polity Press.

Bourdieu, P. (2017). *Manet: A symbolic revolution.* Polity Press.

Bourdieu, P., & Passeron, J.-C. (1977). *Reproduction in education, society, and culture.* Sage.

Bourdieu, P., & Passeron, J.-C. (1979). *The inheritors. French students and their relation to culture.* University of Chicago Press.

Bourdieu, P., & Wacquant, L. D. (1992). *An invitation to reflexive sociology.* Polity Press.

Brankovic, J., Hamann, J., & Ringel, L. (2023). The institutionalization of rankings in higher education: continuities, interdependencies, engagement. *Higher Education,* online first.

Brankovic, J., Ringel, L., & Werron, T. (2018). How rankings produce competition: The case of global university rankings. *Zeitschrift für Soziologie, 47*(4), 270–288.

Buchholz, L. (2013). *The global rules of art* [PhD dissertation, Columbia University].

Buchholz, L. (2016). What is a global field? Theorizing fields beyond the nation-state. *The Sociological Review, 64*(2), 31–60.

Buchholz, L. (2018). Rethinking the center-periphery model: Dimensions and temporalities of macro-structure in a global field of cultural production. *Poetics, 71*(2018), 18–32.

Büttner, S., & Mau, S. (2014). EU-Professionalismus als transnationales Feld. *Berliner Journal für Soziologie, 24*(2), 141–167.

Carlson, S., & Schneickert, C. (2021). Habitus in the context of transnationalization: From "transnational habitus" to a configuration of dispositions and fields. *The Sociological Review, 69,* 1124–1140.

Casanova, P. (2004). *The world republic of letters.* Harvard University Press.

Christin, A. (2016). Is journalism a transnational field? Asymmetrical relations and symbolic domination in online news. *The Sociological Review, 64*(2), 212–234.

Cohen, A. (2011). Bourdieu hits Brussels: The genesis and structure of the European field of power. *International Political Sociology, 5*(3), 335–339.

Dezalay, Y., &Garth, B. G. (1996). *Dealing in virtue: International commercial arbitration and the construction of a transnational legal order.* Chicago University Press.

Dromi, S. M. (2016). For good and country: Nationalism and the diffusion of humanitarianism in the late nineteenth century. *The Sociological Review, 64*(2), 79–97.

Dugonjic-Rodwin, L. (2021). Field theory and education: A case study of the international baccalaureate. *International Studies in Sociology of Education, 30*(3), 325–348.

Feritkh, F. (2020). A weak field of social policy? A transnational perspective on the EEC's social policymaking (from the 1940s to the 1970s). In C. Schmidt-Wellenburg & S. Bernhard (Eds.), *Charting transnational fields: Methodology for a political sociology of knowledge* (pp. 178–195). Routledge.

Gengnagel, V., & Hamann, J. (2014). The making and persisting of modern German humanities: Balancing acts between autonomy and social relevance. In R. Bod, J. Maat, & T. Weststeijn (Eds.), *The making of the humanities III. The modern humanities* (pp. 641–654). Amsterdam University Press.

Go, J. (2008). Global fields and imperial forms: Field theory and the British and American empires. *Sociological Theory, 26*(3), 201–229.

Go, J. (2013). Decolonizing Bourdieu: Colonial and postcolonial theory in Pierre Bourdieu's early work. *Sociological Theory, 31*(1), 49–74.

Go, J. (2017). Decolonizing sociology: Epistemic inequality and sociological thought. *Social Problems, 64*(2), 194–199.

Go, J. (2020). Global change: A field theory perspective on the end of empire. In C. Schmidt-Wellenburg & S. Bernhard (Eds.), *Charting transnational fields. Methodology for a political sociology of knowledge* (pp. 141–159). Routledge.

Go, J., & Krause, M. (Eds.) (2016a). *Fielding transnationalism*. Wiley Blackwell.

Go, J., & Krause, M. (2016b). Fielding transnationalism: An introduction. *The Sociological Review, 64*(2), 6–30.

Grek, S. (2009). Governing by numbers: The PISA "effect" in Europe. *Journal of Education Policy, 24*(1), 23–37.

Grek, S. (2012). What PISA knows and can do: Studying the role of national actors in the making of PISA. *European Educational Research Journal, 11*(2), 243–254.

Grek, S., & Ozga, J. (2010). Governing education through data: Scotland, England and the European education policy space. *British Educational Research Journal, 36*(6), 937–952.

Hamann, J., & Beljean. S. (2021). Career gatekeeping in cultural fields. *American Journal of Cultural Sociology, 9*(1), 43–69.

Hamann, J., & Schmidt-Wellenburg, C. (2020). The double function of rankings. Consecration and dispositif in transnational academic fields. In S. Bernhard & C. Schmidt-Wellenburg (Eds.), *Charting transnational fields. Methodology for a political sociology of knowledge* (pp. 160–177). Routledge.

Hartong, S. (2020). Tracing "the transnational" in the nationalization of school policy: The transformation of standards-based reform in the United States. In C. Schmidt-Wellenburg & S. Bernhard (Eds.), *Charting transnational fields. Methodology for a political sociology of knowledge* (pp. 240–256). Routledge.

Hartong, S., & Nikolai, R. (2017). Observing the "local globalness" of policy transfer in education. *Comparative Education Review, 61*(3), 519–537.

Heilbron, J. (2014). The social sciences as an emerging global field. *Current Sociology, 62*(5), 685–703.

Heilbron, J., Guilhot, N., & Jeanpierre, L. (2008). Toward a transnational history of the social sciences. *Journal of the History of the Behavioral Sciences, 44*(2), 146–160.

Hicks, D. (2012). Performance-based university research funding systems. *Research Policy, 41*(2), 251–261.

Hilgers, M., & Mangez, E. (2014). Theory of fields in the postcolonial age. In M. Hilgers & E. Mangez (Eds.), *Bourdieu's theory of social fields. Concepts and applications* (pp. 257–273). Routledge.

Hussain, N. (2017). Bourdieu in Greenland: Elaborating the field dependencies of post-colonial journalism. In S. Tosoni et al. (Eds.), *Present scenarios of media production and engagement* (pp. 123–135). Edition Lumière.

Kauppi, N. (2016). Ranking and the structuration of a transnational field of higher education. In R. Normand & J.-L. Derouet (Eds.), *A European politics of education: Perspectives from sociology, policy studies and politics* (pp. 92–103). Routledge.

Kauppi, N. (2018). *Toward a reflexive political sociology of the European Union. Fields, intellectuals and politicians*. Palgrave Macmillan.

King, K. (2007). Multilateral agencies in the construction of the global agenda on education. *Comparative Education, 43*(3), 377–391.

König, T. (2017). *The European Research Council*. Polity Press.

Krause, M. (2014). *The Good Project: Humanitarian NGOs and the fragmentation of reason*. University of Chicago Press.

Krause, M. (2016). "Western hegemony" in the social sciences: Fields and model systems. *The Sociological Review, 64*(2), 194–211.

Krause, M. (2017). How fields vary. *British Journal of Sociology, 69*(1), 3–22.

Krause, M. (2020). The post-national analysis of fields. In C. Schmidt-Wellenburg & S. Bernhard (Eds.), *Charting transnational fields. Methodology for a political sociology of knowledge* (pp. 98–112). Routledge.

Kuipers, G. (2011). Cultural globalization as the emergence of a transnational cultural field: Transnational television and national media landscapes in four European countries. *American Behavioral Scientist, 55*(5), 541–557.

Lawn, M., & Lingard, B. (2002). Constructing a European policy space in educational governance: The role of transnational policy actors. *European Educational Research Journal, 1*(2), 290–307.

Lebaron, F. (2008). Central bankers in the contemporary global field of power: A "social space" approach. *The Sociological Review, 56*(1), 121–144.

Lebaron, F. (2010). European Central Bank leaders in the global space of central ankers: A geometric data analysis approach. *French Politics, 8*(3), 294–320.

Lingard, B., Rawolle, S., & Taylor, S. (2005). Globalizing policy sociology in education: Working with Bourdieu. *Journal of Education Policy, 20*(6), 759–777.

Maeße, J. (2018). Globalization strategies and the economics dispositive: Insights from Germany and the UK. *Historical Social Research, 43*(3), 120–146.

Maesse, J. (2020). The Euro crisis dispositif: Heterogeneous positioning strategies in polycentric fields. In C. Schmidt-Wellenburg & S. Bernhard (Eds.), *Charting transnational fields. Methodology for a political sociology of knowledge* (pp. 219–239). Routledge.

Mangez, E., & Hilgers, M. (2012). The field of knowledge and the policy field in education: PISA and the production of knowledge for policy. *European Educational Research Journal, 11*(2), 189–205.

Marginson, S. (2008). Global field and global imagining: Bourdieu and worldwide higher education. *British Journal of Sociology of Education, 29*(3), 303–315.

Marttila, T. (2020). The rise of a European field of evidence-based education. In C. Schmidt-Wellenburg & S. Bernhard (Eds.), *Charting transnational fields. Methodology of a political sociology of knowledge* (pp. 196–218). Routledge.

Mudge, S. L., & Vauchez, A. (2016). Fielding supranationalism: The European Central Bank as a field effect. *The Sociological Review, 64*(2), 146–169.

Münch, R. (2014). *Academic capitalism: Universities in the global struggle for excellence*. Routledge.

Petzke, M. (2016). Taken in by the numbers game: The globalization of a religious "illusion" and "doxa" in nineteenth-century evangelical missions to India. *The Sociological Review, 64*(2), 124–145.

Rautalin, M., & Alasuutari, P. (2009). The uses of the national PISA results by Finnish officials in central government. *Journal of Education Policy, 24*(5), 539–556.

Rawolle, S., & Lingard, B. (2008). The sociology of Pierre Bourdieu and researching education policy. *Journal of Education Policy, 23*(6), 729–741.

Ringer, F. K. (1990). *The decline of the German mandarins: The German academic community, 1890–1933.* University Press of New England.

Rüegg, W. (1996). *A history of the university in Europe, Vol. II Universities in early modern Europe (1500–1800).* Cambridge University Press.

Sapiro, G. (2018). Field theory from a transnational perspective. In T. Medvetz & J. J. Sallaz (Eds.), *The Oxford handbook of Pierre Bourdieu* (pp. 161–182). Oxford University Press.

Sassen, S. (2006). *Territory, authority, rights: From medieval to global assemblages.* Princeton University Press.

Schmidt-Wellenburg, C. (2017). Europeanisation, stateness, and professions: What role do economic expertise and economic experts play in European political integration? *European Journal of Cultural and Political Sociology, 4*(4), 430–456.

Schmidt-Wellenburg, C., & Bernhard, S. (Eds.) (2020a). *Charting transnational fields. Methodology for a political sociology of knowledge.* Routledge.

Schmidt-Wellenburg, C., & Bernhard, S. (2020b). How to chart transnational fields. Introduction to a methodology for a political sociology of knowledge. In C. Schmidt-Wellenburg & S. Bernhard (Eds.), *Charting transnational fields. Methodology for a political sociology of knowledge* (pp. 1–33). Routledge.

Schmitz, A., Heiberger, R. H., & Blasius, J. (2015). Das globale Feld der Macht als "Tertium Comparationis." *Österreichische Zeitschrift für Soziologie, 40*(3), 247–263.

Schmitz, A., & Witte, D. (2017). Der Nationalstaat und das globale Feld der Macht, oder: Wie sich die Feldtheorie von ihrem methodologischen Nationalismus befreien lässt. *Zeitschrift für theoretische Soziologie, 6*(2), 156–188.

Schmitz, A., & Witte, D. (2020). National, international, transnational, and global fields. Theoretical clarifications and methodological implications. In C. Schmidt-Wellenburg & S. Bernhard (Eds.), *Charting transnational fields. Methodology for a political sociology of knowledge* (pp. 79–97). Routledge.

Schmitz, A., Witte, D., & Gengnagel, V. (2016). Pluralizing field analysis: Toward a relational understanding of the field of power. *Social Science Information/Information sur les sciences sociales, 56*(1), 49–73.

Schneickert, C., Schmitz, A., & Witte, D. (2020). *Das Feld der Macht. Eliten—Differenzierung—Globalisierung.* VS Verlag.

Schwarz, S., & Westerheijden, D. F. (Eds.) (2007). *Accreditation and evaluation in the European higher education area.* Springer.

Stampnitzky, L. (2016). The lawyers' war: States and human rights in a transnational field. *The Sociological Review, 64*(2), 170–193.

Steinmetz, G. (2008). The colonial state as a social field: Ethnographic capital and native policy in the German overseas empire before 1914. *American Sociological Review, 73*(2), 589–612.

Steinmetz, G. (2016). Social fields, subfields and social spaces at the scale of empires: Explaining the colonial state and colonial sociology. *The Sociological Review, 64*(2), 98–123.

Stray, J. H., & Wood, B. (2020). Global-local education policy dynamics: A case study of New Zealand and Norway. *Scandinavian Journal of Educational Research, 64*(2), 256–269.

Takayama, K. (2010). Politics of externalization in reflexive times: Reinventing Japanese education reform discourses through "Finnish PISA success." *Comparative Education Review, 54*(1), 51–75.

Vaara, E., & Faÿ, E. (2012). Reproduction and change on the global scale: A Bourdieusian perspective on management education. *Journal of Management Studies, 49*(6), 1023–1051.

Vandenberghe, F. (1999). "The real is relational": An epistemological analysis of Pierre Bourdieu's generative structuralism." *Sociological Theory, 17*(1), 32–67.

Vauchez, A. (2008). The force of a weak field: Law and lawyers in the government of the European Union. *International Political Sociology, 2*(2), 128–144.

Vauchez, A. (2011). Interstitial power in fields of limited statehood: Introducing a "weak field" approach to the study of transnational settings. *International Political Sociology, 5*(3), 340–345.

Vauchez, A., & de Witte, B. (Eds.) (2013). *Lawyering Europe. European law as a transnational social field.* Hart.

Wacquant, L. D. (1992a). Preface. In P. Bourdieu & L. D. Wacquant (Eds.), *An invitation to reflexive sociology* (pp. ix–xiv). Polity Press.

Wacquant, L. D. (1992b). Toward a social praxeology: The structure and logic of Bourdieu's sociology. In P. Bourdieu& L. D. Wacquant (Eds.), *An invitation to reflexive sociology* (pp. 1–59). Polity Press.

Waldow, F., Takayama, K., & Sung, Y.-K. (2014). Rethinking the pattern of external policy referencing: Media discourses over the "Asian Tigers" PISA success in Australia, Germany and South Korea. *Comparative Education, 50*(3), 302–321.

Wedlin, L. (2010). Going global: Rankings as rhetorical devices to construct an international field of management education. *Organization, 42*(2), 199–218.

Wilson, N. H. (2016). Moral accounting as field foundation in an early modern empire: The English East India Company in the late eighteenth century. *The Sociological Review, 64*(2), 61–78.

Witte, D. & Schmitz, A. (2021). Relational sociology on a global scale: Field-theoretical perspectives on cross-cultural comparison and the re-figuration of space(s). *Forum Qualitative Sozialforschung/Forum: Qualitative Social Research, 22*, Art. 5.

CHAPTER 12

INCLUSIVE EDUCATION, GLOBALIZATION, AND NEW PHILOSOPHICAL PERSPECTIVES ON SOCIAL JUSTICE

MARIE VERHOEVEN AND
AMANDINE BERNAL GONZALEZ

INTRODUCTION

THIS chapter aims to uncover the theoretical and normative assumptions underpinning the overall inclusive education framework, currently promoted by a series of international organizations, such as the United Nations Educational, Scientific, and Cultural Organization (UNESCO) and the Organization for Economic Cooperation and Development (OECD). Our objective is twofold: first, to show how much, as a system of ideas (Hall & Taylor, 1993) or a normative and cognitive framework, this "référentiel" (Muller & Surel, 1998) bears the mark of the new social grammar; one that is specific to the reflexive societies of globalized modernity (Beck, 2003, 2006; Beck et al., 1997; Dubet, 2009a). Second, we offer critical elucidation of the new expectations of justice that are emerging in this new configuration.

Given that inclusive education now occupies a central place in the orientations proposed by the international institutions intending to outline a horizon for education, such as UNESCO (2015) and the OECD (2018), we felt that the subject demanded reflection. Over the past decade, the semantics of inclusion have progressively shaped most international conventions and declarations on education (Husson & Pérez, 2016;

Norwich, 2014), and now they seem to redefine the frames of meaning in which educational justice issues are formulated.

The main reforms enacted alongside the post–World War II democratization of education have been based on the normative principle of equality of opportunity. This principle combined a recognition of merit and talent (as opposed to inherited privilege) with the goal of universal access to a common schooling, via the equitable distribution of resources (Baluteau et al., 2018; Dupriez & Verhoeven, 2006). At the turn of the 21st century, new criteria emerged for evaluation in terms of justice, reflecting a growing interest in what education produces (Dupriez & Verhoeven, 2006). Initially focused on learning outcomes, this consequentialist perspective was, however, soon extended to other aspects of human life—such as citizenship, participation, and employability. In the course of the past decade, these developments seem to have coalesced into a coherent model: the inclusive education framework. It seems to us that this model updates the language used to express desirable perspectives for education.

Beyond its significance for the educational sciences, the inclusive education framework has been subject to a range of sociological interpretations, sometimes seen as a process of educationalization of social policies (De Paepe & Smeyers, 2016), other times as a new normativity serving New Public Management logics of performativity (Maroy, 2018), or neoliberalism (Laval et al., 2011). Other works analyze the varied policy translations this global framework is subject to (Hardy & Woodcock, 2015).

This chapter intends to offer an alternative reading. We argue that this new framework is in line with the new social grammar emerging from the transition from first modernity's national societies to the reflexive society of globalized second modernity (Beck, 2003, 2006; Beck et al., 1997; Giddens, 1994). This interpretation conceptualizes globalization as a profound transformation of the spatial and temporal coordinates of social exchanges. Because of the broadening of the scales of interdependence and the acceleration and uncertainty that mark the relationship to temporality, there is a reconfiguration of both the social bases of the construction of identities and the process of production of society (Touraine, 1995), generating increasing demand for reflexivity. In this sense, globalization demands a new metatheory of the social that departs from the parameters of first modernity (Beck, 2006; Dubet, 2009a). These transformations inevitably affect both socialization processes and representations of the role attributed to education in the social contract—of which the inclusive framework bears the marks.

As a corollary to this first hypothesis, we argue that these transformations raise new problems and expectations in terms of justice (Bernal Gonzalez et al., 2021), so that the conceptual tools available to problematize educational justice are in need of refreshing. To contribute to this endeavor, this chapter will draw on three conceptions of social justice—redistributive, recognitive, and capability-based—that are central to the contemporary debate in social philosophy. This allows us to identify their respective abilities to equip both researchers, and actors in the public debate, to address the normative issues at stake in education, in the context of second modernity.

The chapter is divided into three sections. The first briefly introduces the parameters of the inclusive school framework, as it emerges from international guidelines and scientific literature. The second returns to the constitutive elements of the social grammar of globalized reflexive modernity, highlighting its ongoing links to this framework. The third examines the heuristic potential of each of the three main approaches to social justice (redistributive, recognitive, and capability-based) for thinking about educational justice in a globalization context.

Inclusive Education: A Global Framework for Education

While the now-dominant inclusive education model emerged out of a concern for special needs educational provision, its reach now extends well beyond the field in which it was conceived. Originating in a denunciation of the negative side-effects (in terms of segregation and inequity) brought about by the existence of separate schools dedicated to special needs education, and the consequent recommendation to integrate children with special needs to mainstream establishments (Thomazet, 2009), the inclusive education model has quickly become an important landmark. Its focus has been considerably expanded, so that it now designates any pupil permanently or temporarily deviating from school norms and expectations—regardless of whether this is because of a health problem, learning disability, or difference in social or cultural background (Reverdy, 2019). In recent interpretations, the inclusive framework becomes more universal still, since all pupils, considered in their singularity, are targeted (Ebersold, 2014).

Against the backdrop of a fresh appreciation of learner diversity, now seen as an asset rather than a deficit (Rose & Meyer, 2022; Rouse 2008), the stated aim is to ensure that every pupil, regardless of individual characteristics (physical, cognitive, emotional, etc.), has the right to participate and succeed at school, by providing optimal development conditions for their own unique potential (European Agency for Special Needs and Inclusive Education, 2015; Plaisance 2013). In this sense, the inclusive education project proposes a reformulation of the right to education—one that is rooted more in recognition of human diversity. In this perspective, the well-being, dignity, and success of all (OECD, 2018; UNESCO, 2015) establish themselves as a new normative horizon. Correlated to this, the inclusive framework is very often associated with that of global citizenship education (UNESCO, 2015), which both encourages the development of intercultural competences and stresses the school's role in building a positive relationship with other cultures.

This objective is accompanied by an exhortation to change educational systems and organizations. Rather than pupils with disabilities being asked to fit in with school norms and expectations, schools are now asked to make themselves accessible and inclusive; they are invited not only to become more sensitive to learners' cognitive, physical, or emotional variability but also to constantly improve their ability to respond to this variability appropriately and effectively (European Agency for Special Needs and Inclusive Education, 2015). UNESCO advocates, for example, for adequately and equitably resourced, non-discriminatory, and "learning conductive" educational environments for every learner (UNESCO, 2015, p. 8). This sensitivity to diversity includes a pedagogical component, recommending the differentiation (and even personalization) of teaching practices (Ebersold, 2010), as well as an organizational component encapsulated in the notion of the learning organization (Ebersold, 2012), which refers to a stance of constant reflective evaluation of educational practices.

This attention to learner diversity is also supported by extrinsic concerns regarding economic and social participation (Ebersold, 2017; Maroy, 2018). The aim is to ensure that, through education, everyone has an "equal" right to participate in human development, considered in all its economic and social dimensions (OECD, 2018). UNESCO (2015) emphasizes education's decisive role as a central lever for human development, the expansion of rights and sustainable development; inclusive education is also presented as a safety net against forms of social vulnerability and future risk of exclusion. The OECD further associates inclusive education with the development of human capital (Robeyns, 2006); this is identifiable in the terms "skills and employability." It promotes numerous mechanisms for evaluating the performance of education systems, in terms of equity and citizenship as well as economic impact (Centeno, 2019; OECD, 2018). In both cases, there has been a shift toward "extrinsic" criteria in the focus of evaluation in terms of justice, with a fundamental insistence on what education produces for individuals and communities.

INCLUSION AND THE NEW GRAMMAR OF GLOBALIZED REFLEXIVE SOCIETIES

This section aims to situate this inclusive education framework within the social conditions of its emergence. The main milestones of the social grammar of globalized reflexive societies are introduced succinctly and linked to the theoretical presuppositions underpinning this framework.

A New Relationship to Space and Time

Many sociologists characterize globalization as the disruption of the spatial and temporal parameters within which social life takes place. First modernity is associated with a "national perspective" (Beck, 2006, p. 11) crystallized by the figure of the nation state and posited as both the container, and the horizon, of social life (Beck, 2006; Dubet, 2009a). The concept of social integration embodies this representation of social order and solidarity, which unfolds within a bounded national space (Dubet, 2002, 2009a). With globalization, this spatial framework is transformed through both an extension of the scales of cultural and symbolic exchange (Appadurai, 2015) and the economic exchanges linked to capitalist globalization (Amin, 1992; Wallerstein, 1990).

At the same time, the temporal markers of first modernity (built around notions of progress and planning) are also undergoing transformation driven by the acceleration of circulation (Appadurai, 2015). This context is also characterized by rising uncertainty in the face of global risks (Beck, 2003), unpredictability of the future, and a questioning of the idea of progress. Rosa (2014) conceptualizes this change of temporal regime using the concept of acceleration—which he argues is intrinsic to the very dynamics of modernity. Acceleration impacts every sphere of life, driving new moral imperatives connecting speed, performance, and recognition. In this way, first modernity optimism turns into an anxious relationship with the uncertainty of the future, generating an imperative for individuals to constantly keep up.

The inclusive education framework is clearly based on this new grammar of space and time. Its spatial horizon is the world society, and it seeks to open pupils up to the diversity of cultures, preparing them to exercise world citizenship. In terms of temporality, it is more a matter of enabling each individual to develop their potential throughout life than of providing individual pupils with once-and-for-all resources that will enable them to find their place in the social structure. It is all about equipping the individual with the knowledge, skills, and attitudes that will enable them to cope with novel situations and develop their agency, in a changing world (OECD, 2018). Evidence of this new temporal grammar can be found in the semantics of skills, particularly in the term "transformative competencies" (OECD, 2018)—which can be defined as dispositions demanding enactment (Genard, 2015)—as well as in the new emphasis on "learning to learn" as a reflexive and incremental view of learning.

Culture, Otherness, and Construction of Identities

Culture, hitherto perceived as national and territorialized, is now seen as being in a constant state of flux, an endlessly evolving configuration that results from encounters with other worldviews. Beck sees in it a new cosmopolitical horizon based on a principle of additive inclusion of differences (Beck, 2006, p. 116) that allows for the construction of a contextual universalism (Beck, 2006, p. 120) in which differences are situated, rather than denied or hypostasized. This is the representation conveyed by the international institutions responsible for disseminating the inclusion framework (UNESCO, 2020).

Similarly, identities are increasingly thought of in terms of hybridization; the intensification of exchanges leads them to disengage from assigned spatial contexts and integrate the plurality of others' perspectives into their own construction. This "dialogical imaginary of the internalised other" (Beck, 2006, p. 56) calls for particular dispositions, including empathy, the ability to put oneself in the place of the other, the semiotic skill to be able to interpret the culture of the other, the dialogical ability to both draw a global map of the diversity of cultures, and to situate one's own society and culture within it (Beck, 2006).

At the same time, the socialization process is undergoing change. Where first modernity organized it as early programming aimed at the integration of social roles linked to stable social positions (Beck, 2003; Dubet 2002), globalization-reflexive societies must develop the ability to manage multiple (potentially contradictory) normativities (Beck, 2003, 2006). Socializing an individual therefore means teaching one to build bridges between the plural universes of meaning encountered, and working on oneself in order to construct a biographical unity; this demands both reflexive and postconventional skills (Dubet, 1995, 2002, 2009a; Verhoeven, 1997).

The inclusion framework bears the mark of these parameters, as much in the positive relationship it aims to instill toward diversity, and in the development of the intercultural, deliberative, and critical skills associated with global and active citizenship.

Vulnerability and Empowerment

These mutations are part of a more fundamental transformation of the representation of the human being, conceptualized by Genard (2013) as a capacitating anthropology. Where first modernity drew a clear legal line between capable and incapable citizens, second modernity tends to conceive of the human being as at once both capable and vulnerable. The care paradigm (Tronto, 2009) expresses the imperative of acknowledging vulnerability as well as the need to accommodate it through care mechanisms. Mirroring this, the capacity of each human being is seen as a potentiality, capable of "expanding" or "shrinking" (Genard, 2013, p. 46), depending on the social and institutional contexts in which it is deployed. The inclusive framework is shot through with these semantics of vulnerability, potentialities, and empowerment (OECD, 2018). This mutation also brings with it a new relationship with institutions (especially educational ones), which are increasingly thought of in terms of affordance (Genard, 2015)—that is, their capacity to support the development of individual potential.

Inequalities and Domination

While contemporary sociology has not exactly abandoned the modern project of analyzing inequalities, it no longer indexes them exclusively to position occupied in the social structure. Instead, inequalities seem "diffracted" into a range of dimensions (social position, gender, ethnicity, race, etc.) and indicators (Dubet, 2009a), and these are constantly evaluated in order to measure the distance of each person from the norms that define inclusion. As a result, public power now focuses less on inequality of places and more on obstacles to participation. This shift explains the salience of the concept of discrimination in the denunciation of injustices (Dubet, 2010). The inclusive education framework reflects this attention to inequalities of participation (rather than of condition) as well as to the struggle against all forms of discrimination (Dubet, 2010; Ebersold, 2010).

At the same time, new forms of social domination are emerging (Martuccelli, 2004). These are formulated in terms of identity assignment, stigmatization, or alienation, and conceived as deprivation of access to rights, or an inability to construct oneself as an autonomous and responsible subject. Mirroring this, inclusive education advocates access to rights, respect, and dignity for all, and positive subjectivation conditions.

From Integration to Social Cohesion

Lastly, second modernity involves a transformation of society's modes of production. Dubet (2009a) highlights the decline of the modern representation of social integration, which is giving way to one of social cohesion. Beyond the neoliberal interpretations to which it is subject, this concept refers to a new way of thinking about social order, as a "process coming from below, as an effect of social practices" (Dubet, 2009a, p. 134). Conversely, the notion of integration evokes a stable structure in which social cohesion is the open-ended result of actors' involvement in the production of social arrangements. This grammar of social cohesion is strongly present in the inclusive framework, which considers the social contract a system of dynamic and generalized cooperation demanding each person's participation in building economic and social well-being (Dubet, 2009a; Ebersold, 2010; Maroy, 2018).

***

The inclusive school framework is thus fully in line with the parameters of the new social grammar of reflexive globalization societies. Inseparable from the discourse on lifelong learning, this framework places individual training into a new temporality: rather than being represented as a stage delimited in time, education becomes a continuous incremental process of learning and self-development—thanks to educational environments that are responsive to learner diversity. Inclusive education is aimed at an individual whose singularities must be recognized. This individual is considered in terms of personal vulnerability and personal potential, and must be offered support and guidance toward self-fulfillment. The individual is also, undeniably, a singularized person (de Singly, 2004), called upon to interact with multiple spaces of socialization. The inclusive school sets out to guide each individual toward autonomy and develop their agency, equipping them to become decision-makers and action-takers in a pluralistic and changing world. It is no surprise, then, that inclusive pedagogical models emphasize critical, dialogical, and reflexive skills (Beck, 2006). Lastly, inclusive education is thought of as a lever for human development and social cohesion—notions that symbolize an unstable social order to be constructed, in perpetual development.

INCLUSIVE EDUCATION THROUGH THE PRISM OF THREE THEORIES OF JUSTICE

In addition to leaving plentiful room for autonomy and self-fulfillment in a social world seen as open and bearing the mark of the inclusive education framework, this new social grammar also calls for a renewal of social justice conceptions. Having focused on equalizing both places, and the resources to access them, theories of justice are turning toward issues of recognition, self-fulfillment, and development of the capacity to act. The two most convincing theoretical tools for understanding these shifts are recognition theory (Honneth, 1999, 2000, 2002), which focuses on the social conditions of self-fulfillment, and the capability approach (CA), which focuses on real freedom to carry out the life courses that are personally valued (Sen, 1992, 1993, 1999). As we shall see, these two ways of redefining the horizon of justice undeniably reflect the individualized and capacitating grammar of the second modern era. That said, the concern for equality and the redistributive dimensions of justice (as thematized, in particular, by Rawls, 1971) has deserted neither the education field as a whole, nor that of inclusive education; it has, however, shifted in ways that may be connected to this new social grammar.

In what follows, we explain how these three approaches conceptualize the social justice question, and then examine their heuristic and critical potential for considering questions of educational justice (particularly as posed by the inclusive education framework).

The Redistributive Approach to Justice and Reformulations of the Principle of Equal Opportunities

In his "Theory of Justice," John Rawls (1971) sets out to clarify the conditions for a just society, that is, to specify the equitable terms of social cooperation. The Rawlsian model is a compromise between the principles of equality and freedom. Described as distributive, his approach aims to formulate rules to guarantee fair distribution of social goods. It essentially targets fair allocation of primary goods: "rights and freedoms, power and opportunity, income and health, self-respect" (Rawls, 1971, p. 62) to the broadest possible range of individuals, yet taking care to never harm those who have least. It seeks to use this equitable distribution to guarantee equal opportunities of access to different socioeconomic positions, on the basis of merit and talent (Arnsperger & Van Parijs, 2003; Rawls, 1971).

Though Rawls never produced a theory of educational justice, his general principles offer a pertinent evaluation grid for the examination of educational institutions (Michiels, 2017; Pourtois, 2008). Incidentally, this conception underpinned most educational reforms of the second half of the 20th century, upholding both the principle of de jure equality (against the supposedly natural hierarchies of the "Ancien Régime") and that of meritocratic equality of opportunity, while aiming to guarantee equal access to schooling for all, irrespective of background, and success at school based on individual merit rather than social conditioning. During the 20th century, this ideal translated into a set of policy principles (Dupriez & Verhoeven, 2006): equal access (equal right to education, considered a fundamental right); equal treatment (equal schooling conditions for all); and, later on, compensatory policies (corrective distribution of resources with the aim of restoring equity).

Though this distributive perspective remains present in dominant ideas about the aims of education (including the inclusive school framework), it is currently undergoing a number of shifts in meaning.

First, legal equality clearly persists, as a normative principle. The inclusive school framework is loud and clear in stating that it aims to make the universal right to education a reality, by eliminating all barriers to it (UNESCO, 1994). This time around, though, the translation of the normative principle into one of action takes on a more differentialist tone. Equal access is thus reformulated as the right of everyone, as a singular being, to school participation (Ebersold, 2010; Maroy; 2018). The "no-one left behind" leitmotiv associated with the inclusive framework translates this accessibility imperative to all singularities. The principle of equal treatment becomes one of equity of treatment, demanding both recognition and differentiation of each learner's specific needs, and expecting educational organizations to adapt in order to lead everyone to some form of success (Ebersold, 2017).

The principle of equality of resources also remains, though it moves toward equality of achievement at the end of a training period (Dupriez & Verhoeven, 2006). By emphasizing the role played by a common core of competences in subsequent development of the life course, the egalitarian resourcing perspective incorporates an extrinsic, consequentialist perspective that is also discernible in its insistence on the "right to participation in economic and social welfare" (UNESCO, 2015). This consequentialist shift is also notable in its emphasis on the contribution made by education to participation in economic and social well-being (UNESCO, 2015). The search for a more egalitarian society (in terms of equality of places) thus seems to be giving way to a principle of equal opportunities for everyone to participate in society to their fullest potential (Ebersold, 2017; Maroy 2018).

The principle of meritocratic equality of opportunity is also very much still with us, insofar as the idea of merit remains a powerful fiction (Allouch, 2020; Dubet, 2004). More than ever, this is now formulated as an individual right to participate, from the earliest age, in a fair competition (free from any social or circumstantial influence) for access to the best places. It also translates into a kind of moral imperative that education should contribute to optimal development of each individual's capacities. It is as though this principle of justice were internalizing both the open-ended temporality and the capacitating and incremental representation of identity construction that are specific to reflexive globalization societies. This dynamic redefinition of the equalization of opportunity can also be found in texts promoting positive guidance (OECD, 2018) throughout life. Meritocratic equality of opportunity is deployed in an extended biographical temporality, presented as the right to benefit, at each stage of training, from social conditions that guarantee the best possible match between real opportunities and talents.

Lastly, it is as though the logic of performativity, specific to the new governance (Maroy, 2018), were placed at the service of an ideal of equity. This is one reading of the development of new accountability mechanisms that call on educational organizations to become reflexive as to their ability to achieve objectives, particularly equity objectives.

Recognitive Justice and Education

The theory of recognition developed by Axel Honneth (2002) is presented as a counterpoint to Rawls's liberal egalitarianism. Instead of the desocialized individualism of liberalism, he proposes a contextualized anthropology that stresses both human rootedness in networks of interlocution and human vulnerability (Michiels, 2017). And, rather than proposing a "substantive conception of the good life," he reflects on the "indispensable conditions for its free realisation" (Michiels, 2017, p. 74). According to Honneth, these conditions concern the complex social recognition processes that are essential to the production and maintenance of a positive self-image (psychological integrity) and social integration. Conversely, the experience of (social and institutionalized) contempt hinders self-realization and the exercise of real freedom (Honneth, 2002). As a critic of Rawlsian resourcism, Honneth (2002) argues that a society's justice is measured not so much by its ability to eradicate inequality as by its "ability to guarantee conditions of recognition in which the formation of personal identity, and thus individual fulfilment, can take place under good enough conditions" (Honneth, 2002; translation mine). In centering self-respect and the social conditions necessary to the achievement of integrity and freedom, this approach thus echoes the individualized grammar of reflexive societies.

Recognition theory presents as a normative reconstruction method, aiming to detect expectations of justice as they are expressed in social institutions and struggles. Demands for recognition are always indexed to a given social and historical context (Honneth, 2002); the recognitive approach thus proposes a contextualized ethics (Michiels, 2017).

Honneth identifies three basic dimensions of recognition. The first is the sphere of family, friendship, and love, where recognition of the primary needs is at stake: protection, security, and love (preconditions for self-confidence). The second is the sphere of law and the respect it confers. This is about the expectation of being recognized as a subject of law, capable of participating freely and equally in the public sphere. The third dimension relates to social utility in the socio-professional sphere. Through the possibility of finding a recognized place within social exchanges, it develops self-esteem by recognizing the value of each person's particular contribution to society. For Honneth, all three dimensions of recognition are "indispensable to self-fulfilment" (Honneth, 2000, p. 208).

Once the existence of these different forms (or registers) of recognition is acknowledged, recognition theory provides a pertinent grid for interpretation of the normative principles at work in the educational space (Michiels, 2017). Indeed, as an institution of socialization, it is inevitably intersected by stabilized social interaction patterns, representations of the law and its exercise, conceptions of social utility, and the conditions of social integration.

Let us begin by considering the first register of recognition. The school institution cannot be assimilated to a sphere of intimate relations, yet it is increasingly both called upon to guarantee the dignity of its users and denounced when incidences of contempt, humiliation, or harassment take place. The question of developing self-confidence, or a sense of self-efficacy, is discussed at length by social psychologists (Bandura, 1997; Pekrun et al., 2017; Usher & Pajares, 2008). Similarly, sociologists are interested in the experience of contempt and humiliation, which have become ordinary categories of school experience (Dubet, 2004; Merle, 2012). Regardless of its effects on a person's place in social cooperation, failure at school can thus be interpreted as a relational experience of contempt (Michiels, 2017). In the same way, various forms of humiliation are denounced when the relationship between teachers and pupils leads to personal judgments of the student, exposing and publicly denigrating his or her intellectual, physical, or personal characteristics (Merle, 2012). The wealth of work on school bullying (Olweus, 1994; Volk et al. 2017), which can, incidentally, be analyzed in terms of moral disengagement (Bandura, 2002, 2016; Tolmatcheff, 2021), attests in turn to the centrality of relational and moral expectations in the school environment.

Insofar as it seeks to respect and value each individual in his or her singularity, this moral "interpersonal recognition" requirement clearly permeates the inclusive school project. It is important to bear in mind that the semantics of inclusion arose out of a demand for recognition of the value of each child, and an opposition to deficient readings of difference. Similarly, inclusion is often associated with caring and well-being (OECD, 2018).

The second register (rights) refers to the moral imperative to be recognized as a subject capable of expressing and acting freely and equally in the public sphere. However, though (as an institution responsible for the education of legally incompetent minors) the school has long functioned as a space governed by its own rules and exempt from democratic norms, it is currently being colonized by the rights register. This is evidenced by the emergence of democratic and communicative justice in school relations—as illustrated, for example, by the development of school mediation (Faget, 2010; Verhoeven, 1997). A second factor of this register is the rise of the theme of school democracy, observable through the co-construction of regulations or school participation (student councils). International injunctions to provide democratic citizenship education are also part of this movement; they seek to turn school into somewhere democracy must be learned, lived, and experienced. The denial of these rights, or the concrete experience of their limitations, may lead pupils to feel ashamed (unworthy of being listened to), yet also gives rise to criticism formulated as a denial of recognition as a subject of law. The inclusive school framework explicitly affirms this objective of "preparing young people to exercise their active, responsible and engaged citizenship" (OECD, 2018, p. 5) and promotes the learning of specific competences in this regard.

Lastly, the social utility register, understood as recognition of the value of each individual's contribution to society, is also visible in the education sphere. This register appears the moment there is an evaluation of education's ability to lead to social and professional integration. This expectation of recognition can be identified via denunciation of the (symbolic or instrumental) devaluation of certain sectors. In this respect, certain inauspicious pupil pathway decisions can be read as moral wounds linked to the principle of social utility, since they signify to pupils concerned that their skills (or potential contribution to society) carry little social value. The inclusive education framework largely echoes this perspective, both by validating each individual's participation in socioeconomic development, and in its concern for educational structures that confer value upon all pathways.

The inclusive school framework is intersected by all three types of expectations of recognition. The central importance of anti-discrimination can, moreover, be mapped onto these three registers systematically—as interpersonal prejudice, infringements of the law, and obstacles to social and economic participation.

Capacitating Justice and Education

The CA, initiated by Amartya Sen (1993) and Martha Nussbaum (2000), makes a major contribution to contemporary thinking on social justice. Making no claim to propose a substantive theory of the good life, it presents as a basis for criterion-referenced evaluation of social arrangements, with real freedom as its ultimate criterion of justice. The key concept of capability refers to real freedom to achieve the "functionings" (concrete ways of being and acting) to which everyone is entitled to attribute value (Sen, 1993). The capability space represents "the alternative combination of things a person is able to do or be" (Sen, 1993, p. 30). In Sen's view, the evaluation of individuals' "functionings" is certainly important, since these embody the concrete becoming of freedom. However, in terms of justice, they come into their own only with regard to the capabilities space in which they are embedded.

Sen aims to move beyond the Rawlsian approaches focused on equality of rights and resources. According to him, they focus "on means to freedom, rather than on the extent of the freedom that a person actually has" (Sen, 1992, p. 81). In so doing, Rawlsian approaches neglect human diversity—because given identical resources, different individuals will not necessarily attain the same set of capabilities or the same achievements (Verhoeven et al., 2007).

Sen departs from the desocialized individualism of liberalism to consider the social genesis of capabilities, as well as the social and institutional contexts in which freedom can unfold (De Munck, 2009; Gasper, 2002; Robeyns, 2006). He stresses the need to "recognise both the centrality of individual freedom and the strength of social influences on the scope and extension of that individual freedom" (Sen, 1999, p. xii). This is evidenced by his attention to the (social or environmental) conversion factors that can facilitate, or hinder, the conversion of resources into concrete achievements (Bonvin & Farvaque, 2007; Robeyns, 2006).

Although little explored by Sen himself, the application of this approach to issues of educational justice has been the subject of a growing body of work over the past 20 years (Farvaque, 2008; Hart, 2009; Robeyns, 2006; Saito, 2003; Terzi, 2004; Verhoeven et al., 2009; Walker, 2003, 2006; Wilson-Strydom & Walker, 2016). In terms of how relevant this approach is to our purposes, five key points are worth highlighting.

First, CA evaluates educational justice—not just as a right, but above all in terms of its many contributions to the concrete future of learners' freedom (Saito, 2003; Terzi, 2004). Education can, then, be understood as a conversion factor allowing the expansion of other skills (literacy, thinking skills, logical reasoning, understanding complex problems, etc.)—all of which are important, both for the continuation of schooling itself and for the development of future skills. More fundamentally, education can potentially contribute to the development of an ability to "formulate exactly the valued beings and doings that the individual has reason to value" (Terzi, 2004, p. 10).

Second, the CA provides a broad and normatively open basis for evaluation in terms of justice; it allows us to consider both the intrinsic value of education and its effects in terms of achievements, regardless of their nature (Robeyns, 2006). It can thus serve as a critical foundation for revealing the instrumental orientations of the human capital framework. Because of its insistence on participation in human development, it may resonate more readily with the inclusion framework—yet also offers an important normative support against the functionalist drift of social cohesion (which would equate it with the maintenance of social order). Lastly, as a result of its emphasis on individual valuation of life courses and its refusal to reduce normative pluralism (De Munck, 2008), the CA is embedded in the plural grammar of globalization societies.

Third, the CA invites questions regarding the specific temporality of education. Though Sen does recognize a certain level of agency in children, it is above all their education that raises the question of their real future freedoms (Saito, 2003). Educational processes should, then, be evaluated "according to their impact on people's present and future capabilities" (Otto & Ziegler 2006, p. 7). Empowerment in and through education can therefore only be seen in terms of lifespan, and this recalls the temporal grammar of globalization. Taking such biographical temporality into account, we are invited to further complexify our analysis, since at each key stage of schooling, achievements take on the status of conversion factors, unlocking access to new achievements and impacting the set of capabilities perceived as accessible. At each stage, educational contexts must therefore be evaluated in terms of real freedom. Because educational pathways are linked to decision mechanisms and the phenomena of asymmetric pupil pathways within hierarchical education systems, their irreversibility is problematic, from the capability justice perspective (Verhoeven et al., 2009). In this sense, by focusing attention on the complex articulations between educational opportunities and real freedom, rather than on instrumental criteria, the CA can be relevant to criticism of how lifelong learning pathways are envisaged within the inclusive framework.

A fourth benefit of using the CA is that it pays attention to the social and institutional conditions of capabilities deployment (Verhoeven et al., 2009). The achievements of the sociology of education can then be called upon, better taking into account what we know about the social construction of the relationship to knowledge (Rochex, 2004) and study aspirations (Unterhalter & Walker, 2007; Walker, 2003). These elements can be considered social conversion factors—likely to broaden or narrow the ability of pupils from different backgrounds to convert identical resources (access to schooling, certain pedagogical resources, etc.) into both effective learning and life projects that are attractive to them. The inclusion framework's emphasis on differentiated and socially adapted pedagogies is, in this respect, an interesting response.

Finally, the CA opens up a fifth important avenue for thinking about the contribution made by education to the deployment of real freedom. This reflection emerges from a paradox underlined by Vaughan and Walker (2012): While education does contribute to the social construction of values and aspirations, it is also likely to contribute to the expansion of real freedom. The problem (easily identifiable for sociology) is that of the social genesis of values, preferences, and aspirations (Bourdieu, 1979, 1994). Social position thus plays a decisive role in perception of the field of possibilities, with individuals adapting their aspirations to the social conditions of their existence, in line with adaptive preferences (Nussbaum, 2000). How can education contribute to the expansion of real freedom, even as it forges situated values and aspirations? For Vaughan and Walker (2012) the answer lies in an educational model that seeks to lead each individual to reflexively form their own conception of the good life, on the basis of a critical and dialogical examination of a wide range of perspectives. This implies the acquisition of a metacapability to develop critical and reflexive forms of consciousness, alongside two other capabilities: practical reasoning and a capacity for affiliation (which, in turn, demands capacities for empathy and decentering) (Nussbaum, 2006). Such a proposal seems to fit perfectly into the postconventional social grammar of globalized reflexive societies, where notions such as reflexivity and dialogical imagination are central.

FINAL DISCUSSION

In this chapter, we have examined the inclusive education framework from two distinct complementary perspectives: social theory and social philosophy.

We began by showing how the semantics of inclusion is embedded in the social grammar of second modernity reflexive societies. This framework conveys the image of a learner in constant development, called upon to develop their reflexivity and agency in order to cope with normative pluralism and uncertainty. Inclusive education systems are also charged with responding to the unique needs of each individual, taking account of both their vulnerabilities and their potential. Lastly, the notion of social cohesion (closely associated with this framework) both expresses an unstable and emerging representation of the social order and assigns the task of contributing to it to education, via the hoped-for encounter between individual fulfilment and global development.

This framework also raises important questions of social justice. How should contemporary expectations of recognition, and freedom to lead life according to your own values, be accommodated in the educational sphere? And how can they be linked to distributive equality concerns? In a bid to address these questions, this chapter has successively explored the tools developed by three social justice perspectives: the distributive, recognitive, and capability approaches.

Both the recognitive and the capability approaches are very much in tune with second modern social grammar. By acknowledging human diversity and reflecting on the social conditions in which the recognition of identities and real freedom are deployed, these approaches reflect the individualizing grammar of reflexive societies. They share the postulates of the contemporary anthropology of vulnerability and capacity, insisting on both the need to protect individuals from the moral wounds that can arise from relationships with others, and the importance of the social and institutional conditions of freedom. Neither approach accepts any reduction of the pluralism of values that constitutes second modernity. The CA is particularly emblematic of this new grammar. It promotes an open-ended temporal perspective and path reversibility over the linearity of social conditioning. Moreover, its most innovative proposals emphasize postconventional metacapabilities (reflexive, critical, and dialogical capacities), allowing individuals to construct their own agency and stand as moral subjects in a normatively plural world (Galliott & Graham 2014).

Distributive concerns, while not absent from the debate, are undergoing certain shifts—partly attributable to this new social grammar. The right to education thus incorporates differentialist connotations, articulating universality of access and respect for singularities. Meanwhile, the problem of inequality is less and less commonly framed in terms of the equalization of places or resources. New elements of the distributive register found in the inclusion framework include unequal opportunities to participate and the fight against discrimination of all kinds. Here, the pursuit of a more substantial ideal of equality is largely discarded, though we do see two promising ways of integrating an egalitarian concern to an inclusive frame of reference. On the one hand, the notion of equality of baseline skills, which aims to guarantee an equal supply of the basic skills essential for inclusion in the social exchange, deserves to be defended. It should be noted, however, that the inclusive education framework sees this baseline more as a safety net against exclusion, or a conversion factor opening the way to the future exercise of freedom, than as the foundation of social life. On the other hand, the issue of school choice and pathway guidance (often reduced to its neoliberal connotations) is also worthy of consideration in terms of distributive equality. If we are to reintroduce an egalitarian and emancipatory concern, then everyone must be equitably informed about the pathways open to them, so that possibilities other than those for which their initial socialization has prepared them become both perceptible and accessible. Moreover, to take account of the temporal grammar of second modernity, these steps should be repeated at each level of school options, and even throughout life—not to ensure that the logic of competition comes into play from the earliest age, but rather to avoid the irreversibility of educational and social destinies attributable to an inequitable distribution of resources.

While the redistributive dimension of justice therefore remains significant, this chapter has focused on showing the relevance of the recognitive approach to examining the inclusive education framework, which articulates expectations of recognition in terms of relationships, rights, and social utility. Furthermore, this perspective provides useful conceptual tools for normative assessment of the various ideological versions of inclusion (e.g., those advocated by OECD and UNESCO). By insisting on the social conditions in which identities are developed, it provides critical points of support for the most liberal and desocialized versions of freedom of choice and exploration of "talents" being promoted.

Third, the semantics of capability are central to the inclusive education framework discussed in this chapter; indeed, this last has stood its ground against the deficit view of difference. It aims to articulate an ideal of developing talents and potentialities, from a perspective of active participation in society, thus echoing both the individual and the collective facets of capabilities (De Munck, 2008). This framework also attaches central importance to the concrete destiny of real freedom. Beyond this shared language, the CA offers a useful critical apparatus with which to examine the dominant frames of reference. Thus, by insisting on both the social genesis of capabilities and the decisive role played by the institutional facilities in which freedom can be deployed, this approach makes it possible to criticize the desocialized conceptions of freedom found in certain international perspectives. While it shares with the human capital framework an interest in an extrinsic and consequentialist evaluation of education, its conceptual apparatus makes it possible to distinguish between educational devices oriented toward instrumental efficiency and those integrating the dimension of real freedom to their reflective processes. This is precisely where the distinction between learning organizations and enabling organizations comes in (Caillaud & Zimmerman, 2011), allowing movement toward a more emancipatory model of the reflexivity of educational organizations.

Each of the three approaches to social justice explored here provides certain critical tools for thinking about educational justice. Each allows us to identify certain points in which extra care must be taken regarding the concrete deployment of the inclusion paradigm—particularly in its most instrumental translations. We hope to have also shown that none can lay claim to self-sufficiency. It is undoubtedly through practical combinations of all three, and readiness to reinvent when facing complex situations, that educational justice can be pursued in our reflexive, plural societies as they reach out to an uncertain future.

References

Allouch, A. (2020). *Mérite*. Anamosa.

Amin, S. (1992). Capitalisme et système-monde. *Sociologie et sociétés, 24*(2), 181–202.

Appadurai, A. (2015). *Après le colonialisme. Les conséquences culturelles de la globalization*. Payot.

Arnsperger, C., & Van Parijs P. (2003). *Ethique économique et sociale*. La Découverte.

Baluteau, F., Dupriez V. & Verhoeven M. (2018). *Entre tronc commun et filières, quelle école moyenne? Etude comparative*. L'Harmattan.

Bandura, A. (1997). *Self-efficacy: The exercise of control*. W.H. Freeman.

Bandura, A. (2002). Selective moral disengagement in the exercise of moral agency. *Journal of Moral Education, 31*(2), 101–119.

Bandura, A. (2016). *Moral disengagement: How people do harm and live with themselves*. Macmillan Higher Education.

Beck, U. (2003). *Pouvoir et contre-pouvoir à l'heure de la mondialisation* (A. Duthoo, trans.) Flammarion.

Beck, U. (2006). *Qu'est-ce que le cosmopolitisme* (A. Duthoo, trans.). Aubier.

Beck, U., Giddens, A., & Lash, S. (1997). *Reflexive modernization: Politics, tradition and aesthetics in the modern social order*. Stanford University Press.

Bernal Gonzalez, A., Dumay, X., Dupriez, V. & März, V. (2021). Inclure en divisant: élucidation théorique autour du paradigme de l'école inclusive. In M. Jacobs, X. Conus, & J. Pelhate (Eds.), *Penser l'inclusion à travers la division du travail éducatif* [symposium]. L'école primaire au 21e siècle. Cergy. https://colloque-lp21.sciencesconf.org

Bonvin, J. M., & Farvaque, N. (2007). L'accès à l'emploi au prisme des capabilités, enjeux théoriques et méthodologiques. *Formation emploi. Revue française de sciences sociales, 98*, 9–22.

Bourdieu, P. (1979). *La distinction: critique sociale du jugement*. Minuit.

Bourdieu, P. (1994). *Raisons pratiques: sur la théorie de l'action*. Seuil.

Caillaud, P., & Zimmerman, B. (2011). Sécurisation des parcours et liberté professionnelle: de la "flexicurité" aux capacités. *Formation emploi. Revue française de sciences sociales, 113*, 33–48.

Centeno, V. G. (2019). The birth of the OECD's education policy area. In C. Ydesen (Ed.), The OECD's *historical rise in education*: The *formation of a global governing complex* (pp. 63–82). Springer International Publishing.

Cino Pagliarello, M. (2020). Aligning policy ideas and power: The roots of the competitiveness frame in European education policy. *Comparative Education, 56*(4), 441–458.

Damasio, A. R. (2008). *Spinoza avait raison: joie et tristesse, le cerveau des émotions*. Odile Jacob.

De Munck, J. (2008). Qu'est-ce qu'une capacité? In J. De Munck & B. Zimmermann (Eds.), *La liberté au prisme des capacités. Amartya Sen au-delà du libéralism* Editions de l'EHESS.

Depaepe, M., & Smeyers, P. (2016). Educacionalizaŋγo como um processo de modernizaŋγo em curso. *Perspectiva, 34*(3), 753–768.

Derouet, J. L. (2005). Repenser la justice educative. *Education et Sociétés, 2*(16), 29–40.

De Singly, F. (2004). *Les uns avec les autres. Quand l'individualisme crée du lien*. Armand Colin.

Dubet, F. (1995). *Sociologie de l'expérience*. Seuil.

Dubet, F. (2002). *Le déclin du programme institutionnel*. Seuil.

Dubet, F. (2004). *L'école des chances. Qu'est-ce qu'une école juste?* Seuil.

Dubet, F. (2009a). *Le travail des sociétés*. Seuil.

Dubet, F. (2009b). Les dilemmes de la justice. In J. L. Derouet & M. C. Derouet-Bresson (Eds.), *Repenser la justice dans le domaine de l'éducation et de la formation* (pp. 29–46). Peter Lang.

Dubet, F. (2010). *Les places et les chances. Repenser la justice sociale*. Seuil.

Dupriez, V., & Verhoeven, M. (2006). Débat sur l'égalité à l'école. *Les Temps Modernes, 3*, 479–501.

Ébersold, S. (2010). Idéologie de la réussite, réinvention des institutions et reconfiguration du handicap. *Alter-European Journal of Disability Research/Journal Européen de Recherche sur le Handicap, 4*(4), 318.

Ébersold, S. (2012). École inclusive. In A. van Zanten & P. Rayou (Eds.), *Dictionnaire de l'éducation* (pp. 237–239). Presses universitaires de France.

Ébersold, S. (2014). Les savoirs de la comparaison internationale. In C. Gardou (Ed.), *Handicap, une encyclopédie des savoirs* (pp. 79–94). Érès.

Ébersold, S. (2017). L'École inclusive, face à l'impératif d'accessibilité. *Éducation et sociétés, 2,* 89–103.

European Agency for Special Needs and Inclusive Education. (2015). *Agency position on inclusive education systems.* Odense, European Agency for Special Needs and Inclusive Education. https://www.europeanagency.org/resources/publications/agency-position-inclusive-education-systems-flyer

Faget, J. (2010). *Médiations. Les ateliers silencieux de la démocratie.* Érès.

Farvaque, N. (2008). Les apports de l'approche par les capacités de Sen pour penser l'action publique en éducation. In V. Dupriez, J.-F. Orianne, & M. Verhoeven (Eds.), *De l'école au marché du travail. L'égalité des chances en question* (pp. 65–88). Peter Lang.

Galliott, N., & Graham, L. J. (2014). A question of agency: Applying Sen's theory of human capability to the concept of secondary school student career "choice." *International Journal of Research & Method in Education, 37*(3), 270–284.

Gasper, D. (2002). Is Sen's capability approach an adequate basis for considering human development? *Review of Political Economy, 14*(4), 435–461.

Genard, J. L. (2013). De la capacité, de la compétence, de l'empowerment, repenser l'anthropologie de la participation. *Politique et sociétés, 32*(1), 43–62.

Genard, J. L. (2015). L'humain sous l'horizon de l'incapacité. *Recherches sociologiques et anthropologiques, 46*(1), 129–146.

Giddens, A. (1994). *Les conséquences de la modernité.* L'Harmattan.

Hall, P. A., & Taylor, R. (1993). Policy, paradigms, social learning and the state: The case of economic policy-making in Britain. *Comparative Politics, 25*(3), 275–296.

Hardy, I., & Woodcock, S. (2015). Inclusive education policies: Discourses of difference, diversity and deficit. *International Journal of Inclusive Education, 19*(2), 141–164.

Hart, C. S. (2009). Quo vadis? The capability space and new directions for the philosophy of educational research. *Studies in Philosophy and Education, 28*(5), 391–402.

Hart, C. S. (2016). How do aspirations matter? *Journal of Human Development and Capabilities, 17*(3), 324–341.

Honneth, A. (1999). Intégrité et mépris. *Recherches sociologiques, 2,* 11–22.

Honneth, A. (2000). *La lutte pour la reconnaissance.* Éditions du Cerf.

Honneth, A. (2002). Reconnaissance et justice. *Le passant ordinaire, 38.* http://www.passant-ordinaire.org/revue/38-349.asp#

Husson, L., & Perez, J. M. (2016). Handicap et inclusion à l'école: Entre mondialisation des droits et agir éducatif. *Carrefours de l'éducation, 2,* 187–200.

Laval, C., Vergne, F., Clément, P., & Dreux, G. (2011). *La nouvelle école capitaliste.* La Découverte.

Maroy, C. (2018). Nouvelles figures du social et reconfigurations de la normativité scolaire. *Raisons éducatives, 1*(22), 277–294.

Martuccelli, D. (2004). Figures de la domination. *Revue française de sociologie, 3*(45), 469–497.

Merle, P. (2012). *L'élève humilié: l'école un espace de non droit?* Presses Universitaires de France.

Michiels, T. (2017). *Justice scolaire: de la redistribution à la reconnaissance. Eléments pour une approche relationnelle de l'école* [Doctoral dissertation, Université de Louvain].

Muller, P., & Surel, Y. (1998). *L'analyse des politiques publiques.* Montchrestien.

Norwich, B. (2014). Recognising value tensions that underlie problems in inclusive education. *Cambridge Journal of Education, 44*(4), 495–510.

Nussbaum, M. (2000). *Women and human development.* Cambridge University Press.

Nussbaum, M. (2006). Education and democratic citizenship: Capabilities and quality education. *Journal of Human Development, 7*(3), 385–395.

OECD. (2018). The future of education and skills: Education 2030. *OECD Education Working Papers.* https://www.oecd.org/education/2030/E2030%20Position%20Paper%20(05.04.2018).pdf

Olweus, D. (1994). Bullying at school. In *Aggressive behavior* (pp. 97–130). Springer.

Otto, H.-U., & Ziegler, H. (2006). Capabilities and education. *Social Work & Society, 4,* 269–287.

Pekrun, R., Lichtenfeld, S., Marsh, H. W., Murayama, K., & Goetz, T. (2017). Achievement emotions and academic performance: Longitudinal models of reciprocal effects. *Child Development, 88*(5), 1653–1670.

Plaisance, E. (2013). Inclusion scolaire: Surmonter les nouvelles ambiguïtés. L'exemple du Québec. *La nouvelle revue de l'adaptation et de la scolarisation, 1,* 239–242.

Pourtois, H. (2008). Pertinence et limites du principe d'égalité des chances en matière d'éducation scolaire. In V. Dupriez, J.-F. Orianne, & M. Verhoeven (Eds.), *De l'école au marché du travail. L'égalité des chances en question* (pp. 49–64). Peter Lang.

Rawls, J. (1971). *A theory of justice.* Oxford University Press.

Reverdy, C. (2019). The origins of inclusive education. *Edubref.* Université de Lyon. http://veille-et-analyses.ens-lyon.fr/EB-Veille/Edubref-february-2019_EN.pdf

Robeyns, I. (2006). Three models of education: Rights, capabilities and human capital. *Theory and Research in Education, 4*(1), 69–84.

Rochex, J.-Y. (2004). La notion de rapport au savoir: Convergences et débats théoriques. *Pratiques psychologiques, 10,* 93–106.

Rosa, H. (2014). *Aliénation et accélération. Vers une théorie critique de la modernité tardive.* La Découverte.

Rose, D., & Meyers S. A. (2002) *Teaching every student in the digital age: Universal design for learning.* ASCD.

Rouse, M. (2008). Developing inclusive practice: A role for teachers and teacher education? *Education in the North, 16*(1), 6–13.

Saito, M. (2003). Amartya Sen's capability approach to education: A critical exploration. *Journal of Philosophy of Education, 37*(1), 17–33.

Sen, A. (1992). *Inequality reexamined.* Cambridge, MA: Harvard University Press.

Sen, A. (1993). Capability and well-being. In M. Nussbaum & A. Sen (Eds.), *The quality of life* (pp. 30–53). Clarendon Press.

Sen, A. (1999). *Development as freedom.* Oxford University Press.

Terzi, L. (2004). The social model of disability: A philosophical critique. *Journal of Applied Philosophy, 21*(2), 141–157.

Thomazet, S. (2009). From integration to inclusive education: Does changing the terms improve practice? *International Journal of Inclusive Education, 13*(6), 553–563.

Tolmatcheff, C. (2021). *Opening the black box of anti-bullying programs: An investigation of the effects, mediating roles, and implementation of moral disengagement and class norms as anti-bullying program components* [Doctoral dissertation, Université catholique de Louvain].

Touraine, A. (1995). *Critique de la modernité*. Fayard.

Tronto, J. (2009). *Un monde vulnérable. Pour une politique du care*. La Découverte.

Unterhalter, E., & Walker, M. (2007). *Amartya Sen's capability approach and social justice in education*. Palgrave.

Usher, E. L., & Pajares, F. (2008). Self-efficacy for self-regulated learning: A validation study. *Educational and Psychological Measurement, 68*(3), 443–463.

Vaughan, R., & Walker, M. (2012). Capabilities, values and education policy. *Journal of Human Development and Capabilities, 13*(3), 495–512.

Verhoeven, M. (1997). *Les mutations de l'ordre scolaire. Régulation et socialisation dans quatre établissements contrastés*. Bruylant-Academia.

Verhoeven, M., Dupriez, V., & Orianne, J.-F. (2009). Politiques éducatives et approche par les capacités. *Ethique publique, 11*(1), 44–53.

Verhoeven, M., Orianne, J.-F., & Dupriez, V. (2007). Vers des politiques d'éducation capacitantes? *Formation-Emploi, 98*, 93–108.

Volk, A. A., Veenstra, R., & Espelage, D. L. (2017). So you want to study bullying? Recommendations to enhance the validity, transparency, and compatibility of bullying research. *Aggression and Violent Behavior, 36*, 34–43.

Walker, M. (2003). Framing social justice in education: What does the "capabilities" approach offer? *British Journal of Educational Studies, 51*(2), 168–187.

Walker, M. (2006). Towards a capability-based theory of social justice for education policy-making. *Journal of Education Policy, 21*(2), 163–185.

Wallerstein, E. (1990). Culture is the ideological battleground of the modern world system. In M. Featherstone (Ed.), *Global culture: Nationalism, globalization and modernity* (pp. 31–55). Sage.

Wilson-Strydom, M., & Walker, M. (2015). A capabilities-friendly conceptualization of flourishing in and through education. *Journal of Moral Education, 44*(3), 310–324.

UNESCO. (1994) *Salamanca statement and framework for action on special needs education*. https://unesdoc.unesco.org/ark:/48223/pf0000098427

UNESCO. (2015). *Education 2030: Incheon Declaration and Framework for Action for the implementation of Sustainable Development Goal 4: Ensure inclusive and equitable quality education and promote lifelong learning opportunities for all*. ED-2016/WS/28.

UNESCO. (2020). *The future we want: The role of culture in sustainable development*. https://sustainabledevelopment.un.org/content/documents/733FutureWeWant.pdf

CHAPTER 13

GLOBALIZATION, UNCERTAINTY, AND THE RETURNS TO EDUCATION OVER THE LIFE COURSE IN MODERN SOCIETIES

HANS-PETER BLOSSFELD AND GWENDOLIN J. BLOSSFELD

INTRODUCTION

SINCE the early 1990s, globalization has increased the pace of social and economic change in modern societies. Globalization is an inherently complex concept (Guillén, 2001). It has become a central point of reference for media, politicians, academics, and policymakers to understand the accelerating social and economic changes in modern societies. The theoretical approach to globalization proposed in this chapter can be summarized under four interrelated structural shifts: (1) the swift internationalization of markets after the fall of the Iron Curtain and the breakdown of the East-West Divide (economic globalization); (2) the rapid intensification of competition based on deregulation, privatization, and liberalization within welfare states (political globalization); (3) the accelerated diffusion of knowledge and the spread of global networks that are connecting all kinds of actors on the globe via modern information and communication technologies (ICTs) (informational globalization); and (4) the rising importance of markets and their dependence on random shocks occurring somewhere on the globe (network globalization). Together, these global forces have generated an unprecedented level of structural uncertainties in modern societies over recent decades. They are filtered by various domestic institutions such as educational systems, labor market structures, welfare regimes, as well as family traditions and channeled toward specific social groups.

This chapter focuses on the role of education institutions in the process of globalization and describes how educational outcomes affect individual life courses in 17 different countries. Based on selected theoretical and empirical results of the international comparative *Globalife* project (Blossfeld, Buchholz, et al., 2006; Blossfeld & Hofmeister, 2008; Blossfeld et al., 2005; Blossfeld, Mills, et al., 2006), this chapter describes the interaction of global forces and country-specific educational institutions and shows how these changes produce path dependencies in educational systems and affect the outcomes of education over the life course in different countries. On the *Globalife* project, about 70 researchers from different educational systems (stratified vs. unstratified, occupation-specific vs. general vocational training), labor market structures (open vs. closed labor markets), welfare regimes (liberal, conservative, social-democratic, familistic, and postsocialistic), and family traditions (strong vs. weak family support) collaborated. The following 17 countries were studied in the *Globalife* project: Canada, the United States of America, United Kingdom, Germany, the Netherlands, France, Denmark, Norway, Sweden, Italy, Spain, Mexico, Ireland, the Czech Republic, Estonia, Poland, and Hungary. The empirical analyses of the *Globalife* project covered the historical period from the 1980s to the mid-2000s. The cross-national comparison of countries that are structurally different allows to gain an empirically grounded theoretical understanding of how globalization, and the apparent uncertainty that it generates at the individual level, leads to changes in the role of education at entry into the labor market as well as men's and women's midlife experiences.

The Process of Globalization Since the Early 1990s

Four Structural Shifts of Globalization

Since the early 1990s, four interrelated globalization shifts can be observed in modern societies. The first structural shift of globalization refers to the internationalization of markets and subsequent decline of national borders (see Figure 13.1). It is connected with political changes in laws, institutions, or practices which make various transactions (in terms of commodities, labor, services, and capital) easier or less expensive across national borders. The decline of national borders often relates to the modification of trade regulations, political discourse, and treaties. In the period of globalization, one can witness intensified interactions among nation states or social groups from various countries supported by international institutions. Some have argued that the decline of national borders undermines the authority or even heralds the fall of the nation state (Beck, 2000). The empirical results from the *Globalife* project show, however, that the

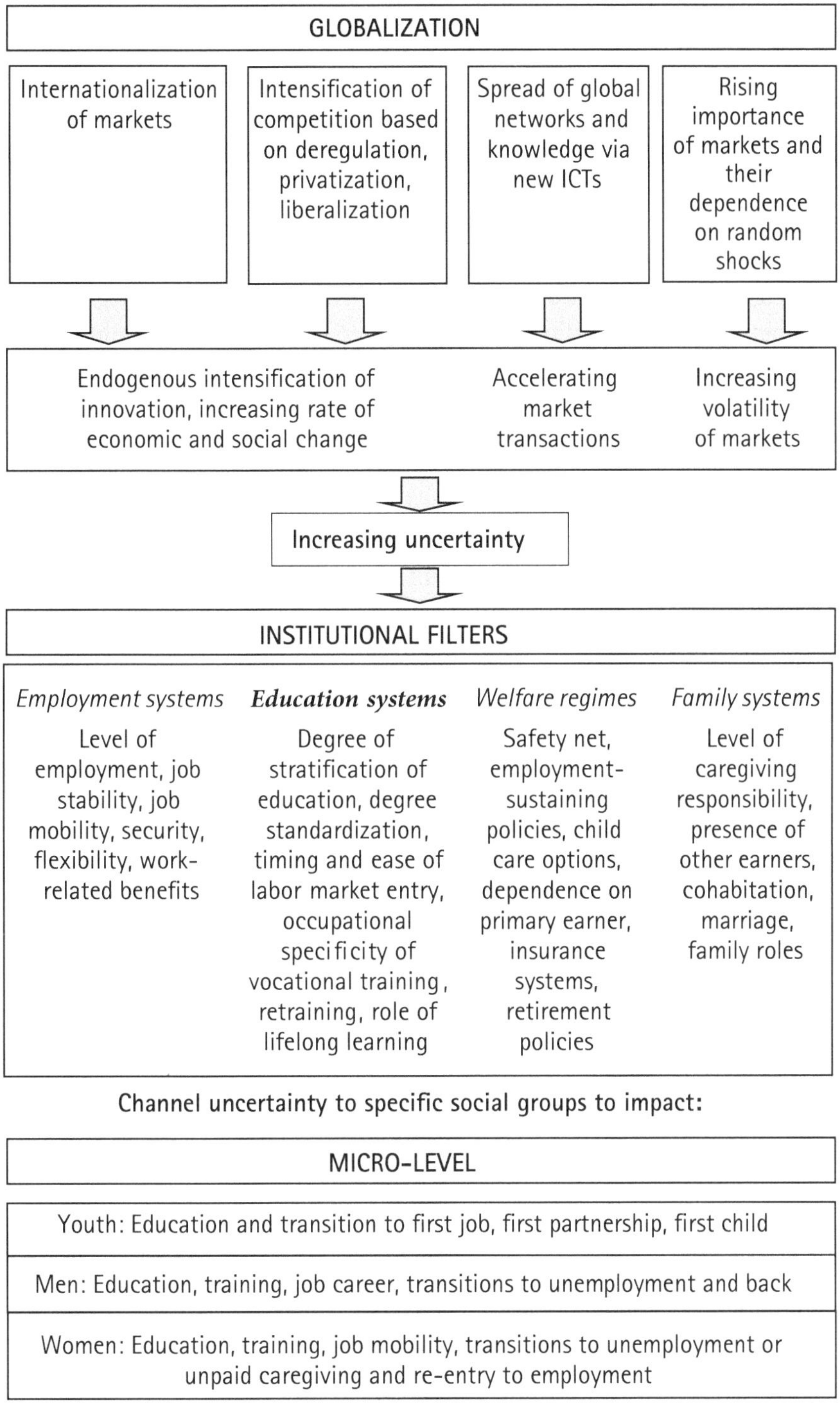

GLOBALIZATION			
Internationalization of markets	Intensification of competition based on deregulation, privatization, liberalization	Spread of global networks and knowledge via new ICTs	Rising importance of markets and their dependence on random shocks

Endogenous intensification of innovation, increasing rate of economic and social change	Accelerating market transactions	Increasing volatility of markets

Increasing uncertainty

INSTITUTIONAL FILTERS			
Employment systems	**Education systems**	*Welfare regimes*	*Family systems*
Level of employment, job stability, job mobility, security, flexibility, work-related benefits	Degree of stratification of education, degree standardization, timing and ease of labor market entry, occupational specificity of vocational training, retraining, role of lifelong learning	Safety net, employment-sustaining policies, child care options, dependence on primary earner, insurance systems, retirement policies	Level of caregiving responsibility, presence of other earners, cohabitation, marriage, family roles

Channel uncertainty to specific social groups to impact:

MICRO-LEVEL
Youth: Education and transition to first job, first partnership, first child
Men: Education, training, job career, transitions to unemployment and back
Women: Education, training, job mobility, transitions to unemployment or unpaid caregiving and re-entry to employment

FIGURE 13.1 How globalization creates increasing uncertainty and impacts life course transitions.

nation state and in particular their institutions that shape life courses across all age groups do not really lose their significance but generate country-specific problems that call for different solutions and transformations.

Internationalization of markets also means the integration of previously "isolated" nations into the world economy. For example, several countries in the *Globalife* study experienced closure to outside global forces such as the former communist East Germany, the Czech Republic, Poland, Estonia, or Hungary. After the fall of the Iron Curtain, these countries have been quickly integrated into the worldwide competition.

The second structural shift of globalization relates to the intensification of exchange and competition between nation states (see Figure 13.1), that is, the notion that capital and labor are increasingly mobile and forcing national economies to continuously adjust. For nation states this means an increased importance of governments to make their national economies internationally competitive. These policy measures include the improvement of the functioning of markets through the removal or relaxation of government regulation of economic activities (deregulation). It also suggests a shift toward relying more on the price mechanism to coordinate economic activities (liberalization), and a transfer to private ownership and control of assets or enterprises that were previously under public ownership (privatization). This neoliberal shift often means a push to adjust prices, products, technologies, and human resources more rapidly and extensively (Montanari, 2001; Regini, 2000a, 2000b).

A third feature of globalization is the spread of global networks of people and firms linked by ICTs such as computers, smartphones, and the Internet (see Figure 13.1) (Castells, 2000). These ICTs, together with modern social media, transmit messages and images instantaneously and permit a faster diffusion of information and knowledge over long distances and across countries. They increasingly allow for the creation of an instant common worldwide standard of comparison. Thus, recent ICTs have fundamentally altered the scope (widening reach of networks of social activity and power), intensity (regularized connections), velocity (speeding up of interactions and social processes), and impact (local impacts global) of societal transformations (Held et al., 1999).

The fourth structural shift of globalization is inherently related to the increasing interconnectedness of people and markets on the globe (see Figure 13.1). It increases the relevance of distant events for local decision makers in all modern societies. These developments inherently strengthen the worldwide interdependence of decision-making.

The Globalization Trend Empirically Examined

The development of worldwide globalization between 1970 and 2018 can be described by the KOF Globalization Index (Gygli et al., 2019). This measure is based on the same conceptual frame of globalization that has been used in the *Globalife* project and utilizes 42 yearly indicators (covering the economic, social, political, and ICT dimensions of

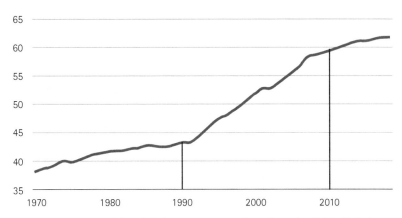

FIGURE 13.2 Description of the globalization process based on the KOF Globalization Index 1970–2018.

(*Source:* Gygli et al., 2019)

globalization) from 185 nations. Missing values of indicators within some country-specific time series are imputed using linear interpolation. Although globalization is not a new phenomenon, the KOF Index clearly shows that the slope of change of the globalization process increased steeply after the early 1990s and leveled off at a much higher degree of globalization at around 2010 (see Figure 13.2). Thus, there was a huge acceleration of globalization after the end of the Cold War.

Globalization and Increasing Uncertainty

Globalization does not only mean that actors are increasingly in the hands of anonymous global markets. What is equally important is that the changes on these markets are becoming more dynamic and less predictable. Thus, globalization is a catalyst of uncertainty in modern societies: First, the globalization of markets endogenously intensifies competition between firms, forcing them to be more flexible and innovative, to use the latest technologies, or to invent new products. This, in turn, increases the volatility of markets (Streeck, 1987). Second, modern ICTs, deregulation, privatization, and liberalization measures allow individuals, firms, and governments to react faster to observed market changes and simultaneously accelerate market transactions (Castells, 2000). This, in turn, makes long-term developments of globalizing societies inherently harder to predict. Third, global prices tend to become exogenously more liable to fluctuations because worldwide supply, demand, or both are getting increasingly dependent on random shocks caused somewhere on the globe (e.g., based on major scientific discoveries, technical inventions, new consumer fashions, and major political upsets such as wars and revolutions). The accelerated market dynamics and the rising dependence of prices on random events happening somewhere on the globe produce a higher frequency of surprises and lead to market prices which are different to an important extent from what people reasonably could have expected given the restricted information available to them. In other words, the increasing dynamics and volatility of outcomes of globalizing markets make it more difficult for individuals, firms, and governments to predict the future of the market and to make choices between different alternatives and strategies. Increasing uncertainty about economic and social developments is therefore a definitive feature of globalization in advanced economies. At the individual level, rising uncertainty for actors has several consequences: (1) rational decision-making is increasingly difficult because future outcomes of choices are harder to predict, (2) additional decision mechanisms (e.g., traditions, local social norms, local framing, habits, rules of thumb) are gaining in importance to compensate declining rational decision making, (3) there is a shift toward short-term time horizons and decision-making, (4) long-term self-binding individual decisions (in the spheres of education, training, careers, family, and children) are becoming more problematic, and (5) contexts of social reciprocity and trust (in partnerships, family, welfare state, etc.) are undermined by increasing uncertainty. In the *Globalife* project, uncertainty was operationalized by the precariousness of employment (type of job, occupational standing), by the quality of employment contracts (e.g., fixed term contracts, part-time work), and by the returns to education in terms of benefits as well as earnings over the life course.

Globalization and Institutional Filters

It is not essentially increasing uncertainty per se that is important if the consequences of globalization are studied. Rather, it is how rising uncertainty is "institutionally filtered" and channeled toward specific social groups in various countries (see Figure 13.1). Therefore, increasing uncertainty does not impact all regions, states, organizations, or individuals in the same way. There are institutional settings and social structures (historically grown and country-specific) that determine the degree to which people are affected by rising global uncertainty (DiPrete et al., 1997). These institutions have a strong inertial tendency to persist and act as a sort of intervening variable between global macro forces and the responses at the micro level (see Figure 13.1) (Esping-Andersen, 1993; Nelson, 1995). Thus, rising uncertainty does not lead to a simple convergence of life course institutions in all modern societies, as claimed, for example, by neoinstitutionalists (Meyer et al., 1992) or the proponents of the modernization hypothesis (Treiman, 1970). Rather, the results of the *Globalife* project suggest that there are path-dependent developments within each of the countries (Mayer, 2001; Nelson, 1995). The institutions that most impact life courses are educational systems, employment relations, national welfare state regimes, and the family traditions (see Figure 13.1). These institutional filters are described in detail in Blossfeld, Klijzing, Mills, and Kurz (2005). The following section focuses on hypotheses on the roles of education and educational institutions in globalized societies.

Hypotheses on the Interaction Between Globalization and Country-Specific Educational Institutions and Its Impact on the Returns to Education

In a globalized, knowledge-based society, education and labor force experience become the most important types of human capital. Educational attainment and occupational standing measure human capital, which may increase with education, labor force experience, and age.

There are great differences in educational institutions among nations in the way they (1) differentiate the maximum number of school years attended by all and tracking (stratification) (Blossfeld et al., 2016), (2) value certificates or ability-based learning, (3) standardize the quality of education and training (standardization), (4) link education with entry into the labor market and job careers, (5) offer nonformal and formal retaining, and (6) support lifelong learning (adult education). In the following, we discuss three hypotheses of how differences in educational institutions (that are also closely linked to structures in the labor market, welfare regimes, and retirement schemes) influence the returns to qualification over the life course in times of accelerated globalization.

First, one can think of differences in educational systems in terms of "qualificational" versus "organizational" space (Maurice & Sellier, 1979). "Qualificational" space means that education is closely tied to job requirements in the vocational system with a strong focus on diploma requirements and certificates, whereas "organizational" space means that education is academic or general in character with specific occupational skills learned on the job. Following Allmendinger (1989), educational systems can also be distinguished by their degree of educational "stratification" or "standardization" (see also Blossfeld, 1992; Shavit & Müller, 1998). In unstratified systems, all children have the opportunity to attend school, which may lead to postsecondary education until the age of 18, with the same range of options (theoretically) open to all students. In these countries (e.g., the United States of America, Canada, United Kingdom, or Sweden), a larger proportion of a cohort attains a higher number of school years provided by the general educational system. Whereas in the "stratified" educational systems (e.g., in the German-speaking countries, the Netherlands, Denmark, or Hungary), educational opportunities of youth are stratified as they are streamed into specific educational tracks at a younger age.

Second, the manner that countries combine theoretical learning with practical work experience in vocational training has direct implications for labor market entry and job mobility (Blossfeld, 1992). Examples of countries with systems of "organizational" space are the United States of America or France. Countries that focus on "qualificational" space value nationwide standardized certificates that are easily understood by employers (e.g., Germany or Denmark). Another important differentiation of educational systems is whether countries organize vocational training mainly through (1) "theoretical" training in vocational schools (e.g., France, the Netherlands, Hungary, Ireland, Estonia, or Mexico), (2) "practical" on-the-job training (e.g., the United States of America, United Kingdom, Canada, Italy, Spain, Sweden, or Norway), or (3) the so-called dual vocational training system, a pragmatic combination of theoretical learning at school and job experience at the workplace (e.g., Germany or Denmark).

Based on these institutional differences of the educational systems, the *Globalife* project proposed an educational system hypothesis, specifying the impact of the type of educational system on labor market entry and subsequent job careers in the periods shortly before (1980–1990) and during rapid globalization (1990 to mid-2000s): First, theoretical training in vocational schools promotes a broader understanding of occupational activities, but it does not confront youths with real work situations. Since practical experience is shifted to the period after theoretical vocational training, the hypothesis of the *Globalife* project was that youth engaged in training from these systems will have a relatively more difficult transition from school to work (higher unemployment rates and longer job search durations) in the period of accelerated globalization. Second, in the organizational system of practical on-the-job training (often unstratified and unstandardized), workers will be less restricted to narrowly defined occupational fields, have fewer structural barriers in terms of recognized certificates, and have a weaker link between the type of qualification they possess and the type of job they obtain. However, due to the heterogeneous quality of on-the-job training, the *Globalife* project assumed that this lack of shared definitions and standards with respect to skills, income, and job requirements will increase the risk of workers to move between firms in times of rising economic restructuring. Although the transition from school to work will be relatively easy in these systems, intense mobility and a protracted duration for workers to find a suitable and permanent job match is very likely in the period of accelerated globalization. Finally, in the dual system (often qualificational, highly standardized, and stratified), we expect workers to have less turbulent (early) labor market experiences (low youth unemployment rates and short job search durations). This is due to the fact that the dual system provides a smooth transition from the general educational school system to the employment system because the vocational training system feeds directly into jobs in the labor market (Blossfeld, 1992). The disadvantage of such a training system in a global era of rapidly shifting occupational structures is, however, that it leads to a too close coupling of vocational certificates and educational opportunities, and thus to a high degree of rigidity, a low level of job mobility, and often long-term unemployment.

Third, a related point is the degree of educational expansion in each country (Blossfeld et al., 2016). When the *Globalife* project examined the cohort-specific attendance rates across various levels of education for the countries under study, there has been a prolonged extension of school participation across birth cohorts in all countries. However, the *Globalife* project expected that, in some countries, this prolonged educational participation is also related to high unemployment rates in times of globalization.

For example, in Italy and Spain, there is a tendency among young adults to opt for the role of a student instead of leaving the educational system and becoming unemployed. In other words, the educational system then serves as a reservoir for otherwise unemployed youths with a tendency of overqualification (in particular in Spain) in times of accelerated globalization.

For young people entering the labor market, the *Globalife* project assumed that the global increase of uncertainty is experienced more directly. They are unprotected by seniority and experience, and they do not yet have strong ties to work organizations and work environments. Thus, one can expect that youth leaving the educational system and entering the labor market are more exposed to global uncertainty in all countries than qualified workers who are established in their job career or have gained several years of labor force experience (life course hypothesis).

In addition, the *Globalife* project expected that those lacking human capital (such as people with low education, weak occupational standing, or lacking work experience) will feel the impact of globalized labor markets more immensely in all modern societies. These individuals should be at a higher risk to enter into the increasingly created precarious, flexible, and uncertain employment situations (e.g., fixed-term contracts, part-time work, irregular working hours) in the course of globalization in many countries. Conversely, those with higher education or the "knowledge workers" should be more protected against the impact of globalization and should have more favorable career experiences because they are more competitive.

However, labor market theory suggests that better educated workers are not entirely immune to the consequences of globalization in different labor market structures. In countries with open employment relationships (such as the United States of America, Canada, Ireland, or United Kingdom), the labor market is characterized as decentralized, dualistic, and based on free market forces and competition. It is a system where employment relations are open in the sense that protective factors such as labor unions, legislation related to job security, and stability are weak. In these labor markets, shielding of even qualified workers is therefore smaller, market mechanisms are central, and individuals' human capital is crucial for finding a new job (DiPrete et al., 1997; Esping-Andersen, 1999; Sørensen, 1983).

Countries with labor markets with relatively closed employment relationships (such as Sweden, Norway, Germany, France, or Italy) (Sørensen, 1983) have centralized procedures for negotiating wages and, in extreme cases, can even be characterized as "insider-outsider" labor markets (e.g., Italy and Spain; Regini, 2000a). In these "insider-outsider" labor markets qualified workers, who have jobs (the "insiders"), are typically highly protected and the global uncertainty is largely channeled toward individuals who are searching for a first job, are unemployed, or have interrupted their career due to family reasons (the "outsiders").

Based on these labor market differences, the *Globalife* project proposed a qualification-employment-relationship hypothesis regarding the labor market experiences of qualified workers in various countries (Soskice, 1993, 1999). The main consequences of globalization in open employment relationship systems for qualified workers are predicted as follows: (1) a lower economic security (e.g., wages, benefits) for most jobs compared to closed employment relationships; (2) an environment that fosters flexible employment to the extent that it becomes more widespread among various, even qualified, social groups; (3) an increased importance of individual human capital resources for job success; (4) relatively easy (re-)entry into the labor market after unemployment or family-related job interruptions; (5) unemployment of a shorter duration; and (6) a relatively high rate of job mobility (which follows from the more flexible hire-and-fire principle). In contrast, the consequences of globalization on qualified workers in closed employment relationship systems are expected to be that (1) they are less affected by precarious employment forms (e.g., fixed-term contracts, part-time work), because these employment relationships are highly concentrated among unqualified workers; (2) first entry into the labor force is problematic, particularly under conditions of high general unemployment (Blossfeld, 1992); (3) unemployment is usually of a longer duration than in systems with open employment relationships; and (4) the rate of job mobility is relatively low. Within these closed labor markets most of the already employed qualified workers, the so-called insiders, will therefore be relatively shielded against the growing uncertainty and flexibility demands of the world market. Globalization in these countries tends to create a new kind of underclass of the low qualified workers, while the qualified employed have high levels of job security with relatively high wages. To test these hypotheses, the *Globalife* project examined the entry into the labor market and the subsequent job mobility by educational level and labor force experience.

There is still a debate over the "upgrading" or "deskilling" effects of accelerated change of modern technology induced by globalization and the change of the importance of competencies and qualification certificates in modern job careers. First, Standing (1997) claims that in the era of accelerated technological change, craft skills learned via apprenticeships and prolonged on-the-job training have declined. Second, there is the "skill polarization" hypothesis that claims that globalization produces only a small elite of technically skilled, high-status specialist workers possessing higher-level institutional qualifications, coupled with a larger mass of technically semi-skilled production and subsidiary workers requiring only minor training. This accelerated polarization in times of globalization places greater reliance on external than on internal labor markets, since workers are increasingly in jobs involving little or no prospect of upward mobility or firm-specific returns to on-the-job continuity. This, of course, means less benefits from on-the-job training and experience in times of globalization (Standing, 1997).

Finally, educational systems also influence the labor market opportunities of men and women by steering them into gender-specific vocational training and different fields of higher education. In vocational training, men are more often assigned into the fields of manufacturing, trade, and administration, while women focus on jobs in social, health, administration, and care. In higher education, men are steered into so-called STEM (science, technology, engineering, and mathematics) occupations, while women are predominantly channeled into so-called non-STEM occupations (e.g., humanities, arts, literature, social sciences, and teaching occupations). This not only leads to high levels of occupational segregation but also affects their careers (Blossfeld et al., 2015) and earnings trajectories (Hannan et al., 1990). Labor market participation and career success of midlife women also depend strongly on whether educational systems allow women to obtain further training or retraining after family interruptions so that they can compete in the labor market with often continuously employed men. The *Globalife* project therefore compared the careers of men in midcareer and women in midlife in different countries (Blossfeld et al. 2008; Blossfeld, Mills, et al. 2006).

Empirical Results on the Interdependence of Globalization, Uncertainty, and the Role of Education Over the Life Course in Modern Societies

The aim of the *Globalife* project was to empirically examine the consequences of rising global, social, and economic uncertainties on the role of education. By exploring cross-national patterns of education institutions and the returns to education in terms of precariousness of employment, the quality of employment contracts (e.g., fixed term contracts, part-time work, lower occupational standing), and earnings as well as job benefits over the life course. The research design included 17 highly standardized country case studies (from Canada, the United States of America, United Kingdom, Germany, the Netherlands, France, Denmark, Norway, Sweden, Italy, Spain, Mexico, Ireland, the Czech Republic, Estonia, Poland, and Hungary) that were based on the best available (longitudinal) individual-level data in these countries. The country case studies were carried out by national experts who were familiar with the data sets available within each country and were able to analyze them to the fullest advantage. The empirical analyses were guided by the same theoretical ideas and the same statistical models so that the results are highly comparable. The *Globalife* project studied life course transitions (leaving the educational system and entry into the labor market as well as career and midlife transitions) comparing successive birth cohorts in the historical period between 1980 and mid-2000s. In the following, we present selective empirical results from the *Globalife* project.

Youth

All countries of the *Globalife* project showed an increase in the amount of social and economic uncertainty in the course of accelerated globalization, confirming the

Globalife project's expectation that individuals in globalized societies experience more uncertainty in the employment sphere. However, it also demonstrated that the young generation entering the labor market was confronted with a particularly high level of uncertainty. This materialized in increasingly more precarious and lower-quality employment such as fixed-term contracts, part-time or irregular working hours, or lower occupational standing at entry into the labor market. This, in turn, bestowed the youngest labor market entrants with a more uncertain future. Youth, who have less labor market experience and who are not yet shielded by internal labor markets, are more greatly exposed to the forces of globalization, which makes them the "losers" of globalization.

The Globalife project also provided empirical evidence that the country-specific institutions are not converging worldwide in the course of globalization. Rather, the national institutions have a strong inertial tendency and interact with global forces. Because the globalization process leads to different problems within various institutional settings, nation states and individual actors react in varying ways toward global changes. This leads to path dependencies in educational and labor market institutions in different modern societies. Nation-specific educational institutions in combination with different types of labor market structures were quite persistent and clearly funneled uncertainty in unique ways and to particular qualification groups. For example, the youngest cohorts in Italy and Spain needed increasingly more time to find their first job and were less likely to convert the growing number of temporary contracts into permanent ones. Thus, in these two countries, younger cohorts were confronted with rising youth unemployment and, as a consequence, decided to participate longer in education. In other words, young adults from Spain and Italy opted increasingly for the role of student rather than leaving the educational system and becoming unemployed. To some extent, the educational system has become a "parking lot" for otherwise unemployed youth. In Spain, where the share of college graduates has risen particularly sharply, this expansion of educational participation has also been associated with a trend toward overqualification. In Italy and Spain, highly educated youth must find an appropriate job matching their educational qualification when entering the labor market. Because of the importance of a good job match in these closed employment systems, higher-educated youth are very selective and therefore have a longer search time. If they got a job below their skill level, it was much more difficult for them to resume a normal career. So, in these two countries, it is the highly skilled young people who are most affected by globalization.

In Germany, in contrast, there was a clear and significant stratification of the type of youth that experienced unemployment due to the tripartite school and dual vocational training system. The dual system, which combines theoretical learning with practical experience at the workplace, clearly served as a kind of bridge between the general educational system and the labor market, so that the unemployment rate was particularly low among young people with vocational training. The unemployment rate was also very low for German graduates of higher education because in the German qualificational space job opportunities are strongly tied to diploma requirements and certificates. In Germany, therefore, it is usually the unskilled who experienced particularly high youth unemployment, and it is very hard for them to move out of secondary labor market positions. This German pattern of transition from the educational system to the labor market stands in stark contrast to the "stop-gap" pattern generated by the system of in-company, on-the-job training combined with the open employment labor market in the United States of America. There, for many young (highly) qualified entrants, lower entry-level jobs have comparatively less harmful consequences on their later careers. This means that even if the first job is a precarious one, they can easily move on to a normal career sooner or later because the job careers are based on the logic of on-the-job training in the organizational space.

In summary, the *Globalife* project demonstrated that globalization accentuated the inequality in terms of returns to education for youth. Not only has uncertainty intensified but also a clear segmentation process comes about among youth with different qualifications. Certain groups of youth are disproportionately impacted, with the risks of globalization mainly accumulated at the bottom. In support of the employment-relationship hypothesis, the "insider-outsider" split was even more evident in societies with a closed employment system where uncertainty was clearly channeled to the un-skilled and even to qualified labor market outsiders much more intensively. The results of the *Globalife* project regarding open employment systems (such as in the United States of America, United Kingdom, or Canada) were also confirmed. Here the relative shielding of qualified workers was much less prevalent, with globalization risks spread over a wider base, leaving youth to rely much more on their own human capital. Yet in support of the human capital hypothesis, even though uncertainty was more perva-sive, inequality still accumulated disproportionately in groups with low human capital. Particularly in the closed employment systems (such as in Germany, Italy, or Spain), uncertainty took the form of employment relation or temporal uncertainty (the reduced attractiveness of long-term contracts). In these countries, qualified insiders were espe-cially protected. The only way to introduce flexibility into this system was by shifting it to outsiders who have not yet secured employment protection. The youngest and least qualified workers were increasingly in precarious, fixed-term contracts in Germany, Spain, and Italy. The use of fixed-term contracts has skyrocketed in many countries. In the Netherlands, for instance, there has been a clear drop in the number of youths who hold a permanent contract and a rise in those with temporary, part-time, or training contracts.

Midcareer Men

The *Globalife* project also showed that there are indeed some groups such as midcareer men, who generally surface as "winners" in the globalization process. With regard to the midcareer experiences, a central finding was that, in general, there has been employ-ment stability for qualified men in social-democratic (Denmark, Norway, and Sweden), familistic (Italy, Spain, Mexico, and Ireland), and, to a lesser extent, the conservative welfare regimes (Germany, the Netherlands, and France) in times of accelerated globalization. Employment patterns remained relatively constant particularly for qualified men in countries such as Denmark and Sweden, where they are largely shielded from globalization by the welfare regime. Midcareer men in the familistic regimes of Italy and Spain were the clear "insiders." As insiders, qualified midcareer men are to a large extent shielded by labor force experience, internal labor markets, and existing power structures in the "insider-outsider" countries. The forces of globalization are therefore shifted strongly to the labor market outsiders such as youth, the unemployed, or women who interrupted careers for family reasons. However, there were also some few examples of increased employment instability for men. For example, Mexico's orientation on economic integration, exports, and privatization reduced qualified men's possibilities of upward mobility and increased their representation in the informal sector. Men in the highly flexible, deregulated labor markets in the United Kingdom and the United States of America were more likely to experience increased employment instability. Finally, the collapse of socialism opened the gates for globalization in postsocialistic countries (the Czech Republic, Estonia, Poland, and Hungary), accompanied by rapid and deep political and economic changes. This resulted in a significant increase in employment instability even for established qualified men. In general, educational investments heightened the odds of occupational success and lowered the risk of employment failure of midcareer (mostly male) employees.

Women's Careers

Country-specific institutions are also strongly impacting qualified women's careers and mediate specific aspects of their employment trajectory such as the employment stability, duration of caregiving, and reentry after unemployment or caregiving. The *Globalife* project found that globalization appears to be passing uncertainty to qualified women, who have interrupted their careers due to family reasons (e.g., rearing children or caring for the elderly) in countries such as Germany, Italy, Spain, or Ireland. Based on their family roles, they have become "outsiders" in the globalized labor market. The pathways qualified women took to respond to this rising uncertainty were diverse. Some of them responded by decreasing their labor market attachment voluntarily by turning to caregiving options, while others more firmly committed to any sort of paid work to support their families financially. The exceptions were where qualified women are getting a strong state support in terms of further education (such as in the Netherlands, Sweden, or Denmark). In general, education heightened the odds of occupational success and lowered the risk of employment failure for qualified midlife women, but there were notable exceptions, including Germany and the postsocialistic countries, where high education failed to protect women from labor market vulnerability (in terms of unemployment or downward mobility) after family-connected employment interruptions.

Summary

The approach of the *Globalife* project deviated in several crucial ways from existing research in the field of globalization. First, it took an empirical approach. Among the vast amount of globalization literature in the social sciences, there have been only few attempts at constructing testable hypotheses or systematic empirical examinations of how the overarching global changes impact the life courses of individuals. A second related difference has been that the *Globalife* project focused on the individual in globalization research and used longitudinal data covering longer historical periods (from 1980 to mid-2000s). Third, rather than heralding the fall of the nation state, the empirical analyses of the *Globalife* project demonstrated that the institutions of nation states do not largely lose their significance but are facing a more general path-dependent transformation. Finally, the *Globalife* project empirically studied whether globalization results in changing returns to education and leads to new social and economic inequalities within industrialized nations.

The main results of the *Globalife* project with regard to returns to education can be summarized as follows. The most vulnerable group with regard to rising social and economic uncertainties are the low-qualified and unskilled workers in all countries. In other words, qualification and skills protect against the risks and uncertainties of globalization. However, there are remarkable differences of how qualified workers are affected by globalization over the life course. In most countries, the uncertainties are channeled toward the young generation, leaving the educational system and entering the labor market. Depending on the nation-specific institutional framework, young qualified people are confronted with higher unemployment rates, lower wages, precariousness of employment, or lower quality of employment contracts (e.g., fixed term contracts, part-time work). In particular in "insider-outsider" labor markets, it takes much longer until young adults establish themselves in the labor market and peruse a stable job career. While youth can therefore be called the "losers" of globalization, established qualified midcareer men are clearly the "winners" of globalization. They are able to enjoy both lower prices of goods which lead to higher standards of living in times of globalization and a high employment protection through the institutions of internal labor markets. Particularly, in conservative and familistic welfare regimes, where mainly women are interrupting their employment careers (e.g., for family-related care work) and thus become "outsiders," qualified midlife women are exposed to rising global uncertainties and have difficulties reentering the labor market in positions that fit their educational qualifications.

References

Allmendinger, J. (1989). Educational system and labor market outcomes. *European Sociological Review, 3,* 231–250. https://doi.org/10.1093/oxfordjournals.esr.a036524

Beck, U. (2000). *What is globalization?* (2nd ed.). Polity Press.

Blossfeld, H.-P. (1992). Is the German dual system a model for a modern vocational training system? *International Journal of Comparative Sociology, 33*, 168–181. https://doi.org/10.1163/002071592X00220

Blossfeld, H.-P., Buchholz, S., & Hofäcker, D. (Eds.) (2006). *Globalization, uncertainty and late careers in society: The losers in a globalizing world.* Routledge.

Blossfeld, H.-P., Buchholz, S., Skopek, J., & Triventi, M. (Eds.) (2016). *Models of secondary education and social inequality: An international comparison* (2nd ed.). Edward Elgar.

Blossfeld, H.-P., & Hofmeister, H. (Eds.) (2008). *Globalization, uncertainty and women's careers: An international comparison.* Edward Elgar.

Blossfeld, H.-P., Klijzing, E., Mills, M., & Kurz, K. (Eds.) (2005). *Globalization, uncertainty and youth in society: The losers in a globalizing world.* Routledge.

Blossfeld, H.-P., Mills, M., & Bernardi, F. (Eds.) (2006). *Globalization, uncertainty and men's careers: An international comparison.* Edward Elgar.

Blossfeld, H.-P., Skopek, J., Triventi, M., & Buchholz, S. (Eds.) (2015). *Gender, education and employment: An international comparison of school-to-work transitions.* Edward Elgar.

Blossfeld, P. N., Blossfeld, G. J., & Blossfeld H.-P. (2016). Changes in educational inequality in cross-national perspective. In M. Shanahan, J. Mortimer, & M. Kirkpatrick Johnson (Eds.), *Handbook of the life course* (pp. 223–247). Springer. https://doi.org/10.1007/978-3-319-20880-0_10

Castells, M. (2000). *The rise of the network society, the Information Age: Economy, society and culture* (Vol. 1). Blackwell.

DiPrete, T., de Graaf, P. M., Luijkx, R., Tåhlin, M., & Blossfeld, H.-P. (1997). Collectivist versus individualist mobility regimes? Structural change and job mobility in four countries. *American Journal of Sociology, 103*(2), 318–358. https://doi.org/10.1086/231210

Esping-Andersen, G. (1993). Post-industrial class structures: An analytical framework. In G. Esping-Andersen (Ed.), *Changing classes* (pp. 7–31). Sage.

Esping-Andersen, G. (1999). *Social foundations of postindustrial economies.* Oxford University Press.

Guillén, M. (2001). Is globalization civilizing, destructive or feeble? A critique of five key debates in the social science literature. *American Review of Sociology, 27*, 235–260. https://doi.org/10.1146/annurev.soc.27.1.235

Gygli, S., Haelg, F., Potrafke, N., & Sturm, J.-E. (2019). The KOF Globalisation Index—Revisited. *Review of International Organizations, 14*(3), 543–574. https://doi.org/10.1007/s11558-019-09344-2

Hannan, M. T., Schömann, K., & Blossfeld, H.-P. (1990). Sex and sector differences in the dynamics of wage growth in the FRG. *American Sociological Review, 55*, 694–713. https://doi.org/10.2307/2095865

Held, D., McGrew, A., Goldblatt, D., & Perraton, J. (1999). *Global transformations. Politics, economics and culture.* Polity Press.

Maurice, M., & Sellier, F. (1979). A societal analysis of industrial relations: A comparison between France and West Germany. *British Journal of Industrial Relations, 17*, 322–336. https://doi.org/10.1111/j.1467-8543.1979.tb00958.x

Mayer, K.-U. (2001). The paradox of global social change and national path dependencies: Life course patterns in advanced societies. In A. Woodward & M. Kohli (Eds.), *Inclusions and exclusions in European societies* (pp. 89–110). Routledge.

Meyer, J. W., Ramirez, F. O., & Soysal, Y. (1992). World expansion of mass education, 1970–1980. *Sociology of Education, 65*, 128–149. https://doi.org/10.2307/2112679

Montanari, I. (2001). Modernization, globalization and the welfare state: A comparative analysis of old and new convergence of social insurance since 1930. *British Journal of Sociology, 52*(3), 469–494. https://doi.org/10.1080/00071310120071142

Nelson, R. R. (1995). Recent evolutionary theorizing about economic change. *Journal of Economic Literature, 33*, 48–90.

Regini, M. (2000a). Between deregulation and social pacts: The responses of European economies to globalization. *Politics and Society, 28*(1), 5–33.

Regini, M. (2000b). The dilemmas of labor market regulation. In G. Esping-Andersen & M. Regini (Eds.), *Why deregulate labor markets?* (pp. 11–18). Oxford University Press.

Shavit, Y., & Müller, W. (1998). *From school to work: A comparative study of educational qualifications and occupational destinations.* Clarendon Press.

Sørensen, A. B. (1983). The structure of allocation to open and closed positions in social structure. *Zeitschrift für Soziologie, 12*, 203–224. https://doi.org/10.1515/zfsoz-1983-0302

Soskice, D. (1993). The institutional infrastructure for international competitiveness: a comparative analysis of the UK and Germany. In A. B. Atkinson & R. Brunetta (Eds.), *The economics of the new Europe* (pp. 45–66). MacMillan.

Soskice, D. (1999). Divergent production regimes: Coordinated and uncoordinated market economies in the 1980s and 1990s. In H. Kitschelt, P. Lange, G. Marks, & J. Stephens (Eds.), *Continuity and change in contemporary capitalism* (pp. 101–134). Cambridge University Press.

Standing, G. (1997). Globalization, labor flexibility and insecurity: The era of market regulation. *European Journal of Industrial Relations, 1*, 7–37. https://doi.org/10.1177/095968019731002

Streeck, A. (1987). The uncertainties of management in the management of uncertainties: Employees, labor relations and industrial adjustment in the 1980s. *Work, Employment and Society, 1*, 281–308. https://doi.org/10.1177/0950017087001003002

Treiman, D. J. (1970). Industrialization and social stratification. *Sociological Inquiry, 40*(2), 207–234.

CHAPTER 14

GLOBALIZATION OF EDUCATION AND THE SOCIOLOGY OF ELITES

CAROLINE BERTRON AND AGNÈS VAN ZANTEN

INTRODUCTION

BETWEEN the 1960s and the late 1990s, research on elite education focused on elite institutions' acculturation of children and youths to the values characterizing national elites, as well as preparing them for social and professional positions in national social structures (Bourdieu, 1989; Levine, 1980; Wakeford, 1969; Walford, 1986). This was also the case for the scarce comparative research on this topic conducted during the same period (Cookson & Persell, 1985). Over the last 20 years, new studies have emerged exploring the influence of international financial flux, of the global circulation of ideas and cultural forms, and of transnational individual mobility on elite education, establishing a fruitful dialogue with theoretical writings and empirical studies on globalization and its effects. These new strands of research have been fueled by studies on the emergence of a "transnational" upper class of top managers having in common an intense professional international mobility and associated lifestyles (Carroll, 2010; Sklair, 2001), and by numerous studies documenting and commenting the rise of global "superrich" and the unparalleled level of economic concentration and interconnectedness among the elites (Cousin & Chauvin, 2021). Another influence on the literature on elite education can be found in research on intraclass distinctions, exploring the national and international orientations of old and new bourgeoisies and economic, political, and cultural elites (Wagner, 2020). These strands of research have complicated the definition of "global educational elites" and even more so as some of the studies also take into account the transnational and cosmopolitan aspirations of a heterogeneous "global middle class" (Ball & Nikita, 2014; Koo, 2016).

These analyses are also modifying traditional definitions of elite schools. While established elite schools are still very much places for the reproduction of traditional elites and upper classes, they now face stronger pressures from new-moneyed groups investing economic capital in them in the hope of converting it into cultural and social capital valuable in both their home country and international social circles (Beech et al., 2021; Windle & Maire, 2019). The "usurpatory" strategies developed by newcomers (Elias & Scotson, 1965; Parkin, 1974) have created dilemmas for elite schools enrolling large numbers of international students, especially between promoting soft versions of multiculturalist ideals to appear inclusive of these students or inculcating the cultural norms of their established clientele (Kenway & Lazarus, 2017). These dilemmas are also the result of the expansionist strategies of some elite schools whose efforts to conquer new markets are likely to endanger a symbolic status based on the cultivation of exclusiveness (Bunnell et al., 2020). The dominant position of these schools and the definition of elite education are also being challenged by the growing popularity of *international* tracks and schools and the large diffusion of models of *global education* such as the international baccalaureate (IB) and global citizenship education (GCE).

The chapter is organized into two sections. Taking account of a variety of countries and geographical areas, the first section focuses on elite families and their cosmopolitan educational perspectives and practices. More broadly, it addresses the effects of transnational perspectives in education on social stratification, by examining the expanding cosmopolitan reach of the educational choices of upper-class and aspiring middle-class parents. The second section turns to educational offer to look into the globalizing practices of elite schools around the world, with a specific focus on secondary schooling.[1] It examines the meanings and forms that international curricula, tracks, and schools can take in various national and local contexts and in relation to different class fractions as well as the impact of these processes on the redefinition of what constitutes an elite education.

WHAT'S IN A COSMOPOLITAN EDUCATION?

The transnational circulation of children has historically been a central feature in elite training. In European aristocratic families, practices such as the "Grand" and "Petit Tour," visits to relatives in foreign countries, and family leisure trips or diplomatic sojourns abroad have been considered the foundations of a specific cosmopolitan *ethos* acquired from an early age. However, the academic debate on the emergence of a transnational class, distinct from national class structures and comprising global policy actors, as well as financial, professional, and media elites, only fully emerged in the late 1990s. The rise of this new group was sustained by the globalization of the economy and the emergence of global policy arenas and structured by class interests and lifestyles promoting geographical mobility, including attendance at the same international schools (Sklair, 2001; van der Pijl, 1998). Yet most empirical work using this framework has focused less on the global elite per se than on national contexts, studying either their practices in specific settings—mostly through the lens of expatriate communities (Beaverstock, 2002, 2005; Le Renard, 2019; Wagner, 1998)—or different national elites' pathways of internationalization or lack thereof (Bühlmann et al., 2013; Denord et al., 2018; Hartmann, 2011).

Bourdieu's theoretical writings have been instrumental in theorizing the role of education in the making of a transnational class, especially regarding the definition and the modus operandi of cosmopolitan and/or transnational capital, as a component of cultural capital or a capital in itself (Bühlmann & al., 2013; Igarashi & Saito, 2014; Weenink, 2008). Although "cosmopolitan(ism)" and "transnational(ism)" are two terms frequently used interchangeably (Bühlmann, 2020) when related to analyses in terms of cultural capital, they tend to refer to different dimensions. The term "cosmopolitanism" has widely been associated with worldviews, lifestyles, and identifications, and sometimes criticized for its historical and Eurocentric implicit ideology, as its genealogy traces back to a more idealist perspective related to openness to other places, cultures, and people (Oxley & Morris, 2013). Transnationalism, on the other hand, most often designates social practices of migration and mobility that allow individuals to build economic, social, cultural, and political strategies in order to benefit from resources from different nation state regimes. We have decided to distinguish both terms analytically here, with a first subsection focusing on the uneasy relation between cosmopolitan aspirations as revealed in educational choices and their qualification as "elite" strategies, and a second subsection focusing on the growing attention given by various social groups to international mobility as a way of enhancing their children's educational trajectories and career paths.

Socially Stratified Cosmopolitan Educational Practices

A New Neoliberal Type of Elite Cosmopolitanism?

The notion of cosmopolitanism has been historically associated in the literature with the *ethos* and *habitus* that the aristocracy and bourgeoisie traditionally transmit to their children. This cultural heritage is organized around a model of family and social life simultaneously aiming at the intergenerational production of future leaders and elite members and at the reproduction, over time, of traditional values and structures (Holmqvist, 2017; Mension-Rigau, 1997; Pinçon & Pinçon-Charlot, 2000). The norms, representations, and practices that define this model are both strongly embedded in national contexts and dependent on modes of transmission among elite groups that extend beyond national boundaries, relying on an inherited familiarity with similar social groups and cultural models in other countries, and on transnational connections and mobility patterns, professional and leisure-wise (Poupeau, 2004; Wagner, 2007).

For obvious reasons, families play a central role in instilling this cosmopolitan *habitus* in their children. However, to varying degrees across countries, parents have also partly delegated its transmission to, until recently predominantly single-sex, private boarding schools (Bertron, 2019; O'Neill, 2014). Historically, first-generation members of the economic upper class have also been driven toward these schools or private day schools, in order to favor the cultural and social integration of their children into the established national upper classes (Baltzell, 1958). Many of these schools also attracted foreign established and new elites or members of the upper classes from former colonized states and developing countries that complied with dominant norms of European and North American elites (Pinçon & Pinçon-Charlot, 2006).

If their role in the national and international diffusion of an aristocratic and bourgeois cosmopolitan ethos among new elite fractions is therefore not new, the content of this ethos has tilted toward a new neoliberal model of education centered on the development of individuality and the making of "global citizens" and "global leaders." This is partly the result of globalization discourses and trends that, as discussed in the second section of this chapter, have influenced schools' curricula and partly the consequence of ideological changes among the national and international families that these schools aim to attract.

Elite schools for girls in particular have recently started "grooming girls for the global" (Kenway et al., 2015, p. 155), and they arguably seem to be promoting and constructing femininity as the paragon of the accomplished neoliberal subject who should be flexible, mobile, responsible, self-sufficient, and productive (Allan & Charles, 2014; Harris, 2004). According to Kenway et al. (2015), these "faux-feminist" discourses in all-girls schools, which are also "bubbles of privilege" (Maxwell & Aggleton, 2010), do not, however, effectively prepare girls for the highly masculine worlds of global elites. Only a minority move on and out into competitive global environments (Maxwell & Aggleton, 2014) while a growing proportion, despite having assimilated discourses explicitly encouraging them to be ambitious (Forbes & Lingard, 2015), in fact remain within national elite higher education (HE) systems and graduate job markets (Maxwell & Aggleton, 2016a). This suggests that while these women may self-present as belonging to the "global elite," the actual impact of their elite schooling on their international mobility paths remains limited.

A Variety of Cosmopolitan Views and Practices Across Social Groups

Upper-class families' educational views and practices aim, to some extent, to imitate those of the aristocracy and bourgeoisie but are also strongly dependent on values, representations, and resources derived from their position in the social structure and the professional worlds in which they move. Lareau (2003) described upper- and middle-class (managers, college-educated professionals) families' dominant model through the concept of "concerted cultivation." While her main purpose was to contrast this outlook with the "natural growth" model prevalent among the working class, our comparison between the concerted cultivation practices of the middle and upper classes and the cosmopolitan child-rearing and educational models of the higher-status social elites just described highlights one main difference. While the latter rely on a long-term, osmotic transmission of dispositions, Lareau's subjects of study were involved instead in a more deliberate and systematic modeling of their children's attitudes and behavior and in providing them with various assets to secure their professional futures and social positions (Coulangeon, 2018; van Zanten, 2009; Vincent & Ball, 2007).

Owing to the growing globalization of the environments in which they live and work, these parents' educational perspectives and choices now frequently include an international dimension. As shown by Weenink (2008), in the Netherlands, upper-class parents and middle-class families engaged on an upward social mobility path are very much aware of the need to prepare children for globalized futures, and they increasingly opt for newly established bilingual and IB tracks. While the more traditional bourgeoisie, attached to classical culture, continues to value the content and social rewards associated with a *gymnasium* education, differences can be observed between the cultural and economic fractions of the new upper classes. The first are more likely to be, in Weenink's terms, "dedicated" cosmopolitans. These parents, who spoke at least two languages and had lived abroad, were keen to pass on to their children a mental disposition in which the world was viewed as a horizon, through conversations and activities both at home and at school, as well as through travel. "Pragmatic" cosmopolitans, on the other hand, were primarily managers with international work experience who valued the mastery of English mostly because of its expected advantages for HE and job markets.

Analyzing the Brazilian case, Windle and Nogueira (2015) found an even clearer contrast between these economic and cultural fractions of the upper class. Instrumental or pragmatic cosmopolitan perspectives and strategies were far more common among owners of medium and large companies, while "dedicated" outlooks and practices were more frequent among highly qualified university professors and researchers. The first used their economic capital to pay for North American and European holidays for their families without any specific educational purposes but also for their children's home tuition in English, short language courses abroad, or in national US-oriented bilingual schools for purposes of distinction and advantages in the national social system and job market (Windle & Marie, 2019). The second favored extended experiences in high-quality overseas education systems and an international education in European-oriented national schools, both to advantage their children in the selective Brazilian HE system and as a way of developing skills and values for purposes of personal enrichment and the pursuit of cultural ideals.

Studies in the United States underline a more complex interplay between commitment to diversity and to cosmopolitanism among the national upper classes. In a research in the wealthy Silicon Valley area, Horst (2015) found that at the elementary school level, many parents viewed sending their children to local public schools with a large immigrant community as a commitment to inclusiveness and diversity. However, as children grew older, these parents were more likely to turn to charter and private schools and to revert to extracurricular activities and international travel to ensure their children's acquisition of cosmopolitan skills valuable for their future professional and social lives.

To varying degrees according to national configurations, middle-class and sometimes working-class "aspirant" parents also aim at preparing their children to evolve in globalized contexts. Their practices, however, are not the same as those of the upper classes not only because they have fewer economic resources at their disposal but also because they are more locally oriented and often turn to opportunities offered by state institutions. While having their children learn a foreign language, particularly English, is a central concern for many of them, especially in countries where English is considered an important instrumental and symbolic component of white-collar jobs (Song, 2013), these parents mainly resort to language options and school trips to other countries, linguistic exchanges offered by local schools, or language classes offered by community centers. Moreover, because their practices are embedded in family and school contexts where elitist visions compete with other views, they lead to contrasting forms of cosmopolitanism among their children. While some turn to careers embracing neoliberal ideals of self-responsibility and maximization of educational opportunities associated to economic globalization, others see globalization as an ideal implying openness to others and become interested in global careers oriented toward social change (Engel & Wilson, 2020).

Can Cosmopolitan Habitus Become Cosmopolitan Capital?

Aside from showing that cosmopolitan practices are not homogeneous but socially stratified and differentiated (Maxwell, 2018), comparison across social groups also increases our theoretical understanding of how educational practices associated with internationalization are transformed into "cosmopolitan capital." In the case of established elites, cosmopolitanism is both a disposition and a way of life, and cosmopolitan attributes are easily (and often unconsciously) transformed into cosmopolitan capital in different social fields such as education, work, or marriage. Although new upper classes that owe their position to professional and economic success have to deploy more conscious efforts to acquire cosmopolitan dispositions, their strategies of internationalization are quite effective because, contrary to those of lower social groups, they are strongly rooted in parental perspectives and early education practices. These lead children to view an international education, whether at home or abroad, as a natural extension of their family education (Carlson et al., 2017).

On the basis of a recent multisited ethnography research conducted in five elite schools located in different areas of the Global North and South, Howard and Maxwell (2021) contend that they all put a strong emphasis, in discursive and practical forms adapted to each context, on a kind of cosmopolitanism combining a soft commitment to its ideological foundations and a strong focus on students' acquisition of a cosmopolitan status. However, the long-term effects that parents' cosmopolitan investments have on their children's HE trajectories and employment careers remain understudied (Bühlmann, 2020). Addressing these issues seems yet particularly important since existing studies have tended to reassert the major role played by inherited elite status when it comes to accessing transnational elite positions. Relying on her work on international schools attended by expatriate managers, Wagner (2020) has contended that international credentials do not lead to top positions if they are not accompanied by other types of capital (economic, cultural, and/or social) and that they are most efficient when they are supported by prior family international dispositions. While some researchers have argued that this is so because cosmopolitanism can only act as capital if it brings together specific forms of cultural and social capital (Bühlmann et al., 2013; Cousin & Chauvin, 2014), Wagner (2020) views cosmopolitan capital not as a form of capital per se but rather as a multiplier of economic, cultural, and social capital whose value can vary according to characteristics of social fields and national spaces.

The process of transforming a cosmopolitan *habitus* into a cosmopolitan capital is further complicated in the case of students from the Global South who move to US or UK elite schools and universities with the expectation that studying in these establishments and places will confer them a global elite status. Many of them find on the contrary that race trumps wealth as their national background and racial characteristics work against their being perceived as privileged. Lillie's research (2021a) shows nevertheless that students learn to navigate into these complex environments by relying on globally experienced members of their diasporas to get inside knowledge on how their identities are viewed in different places as well as which international degrees are recognized in their home country.

Transnational Educational Mobility Practices

From Travel to Long-Lasting Mobility Practices

In some countries, and for some social groups, transnational mobility patterns are a central component of globalizing educational strategies. This mobility might merely consist in family travel, which is considered by the most ambitious, internationally oriented, and educated upper-class parents as a way of fostering their children's aspirations, broadening their horizons, and preparing them for globalized environments (Yemini & Maxwell, 2020). It might also consist in more extended travel by students pursuing a gap year abroad before entering university or during their HE studies. This type of geographical mobility may not be perceived as a conscious strategy and might, on the contrary, be presented as "disinterested" by upper-class students, especially when they engage in humanitarian activities in less-advantaged countries. These experiences abroad are nevertheless very likely to act as signals of their "elite cosmopolitanism" in HE and job markets (Brooks et al., 2012).

Different fractions of the "global middle class" (Ball & Nikita, 2014) are also now frequently involved in more long-lasting mobility practices. Managers and professionals, freelance experts, and employees in multinational companies—who frequently move with their families—make complex decisions concerning their children's education. They might opt for private international schools and remain in an expatriate "bubble," or, on the contrary, favor more mixed local schools in order to become "global citizens" by integrating in different national contexts (Forsey et al., 2015). These educational decisions also depend on parents' long-term plans and their relationship with their home country. As shown by Yemini and Maxwell (2018) for Israeli families living in London, parents—and especially mothers—involved in a process of "decoupling" from their former nation state choose schools that help their children integrate into their temporary host country. On the contrary, those wanting to preserve their children's sense of belonging to their country of origin opt for schools whose language, religion, or pedagogy will facilitate their return.

"Study Mothers" and "Parachute Kids"

More radical mobility strategies from "aspiring" parents from the economic fractions of the upper and middle classes have been documented in the Pacific area in association with economic and educational processes and with the diffusion of ideologies promoting the "global worker." The case of Korean and Chinese "study mothers" accompanying their children to countries such as Singapore, the United States, or Canada (Huang & Yeoh, 2005), as well as the emergence of "parachute kids" (Zhou, 1998) and the "Pacific shuttle" of Hong Kong entrepreneurs relocating their children to schools in North America while also initiating transpacific economic investments (Ong, 1999), have been analyzed as part of broader transnational family economic strategies. Studying the international mobility patterns of Hong Kong families, Waters (2005) underlines, however, the importance of educational factors as well. For many Asian families, schooling children abroad is a way of circumventing the meritocratic selectiveness of their own educational systems and the fierce grade-based competition for access to the best local schools and universities (Waters & Leung, 2014). Young people are not, however, passive recipients of their parents' strategies. Many of them actively engage in their overseas education, claiming responsibility for choices promising high returns but implying strong sacrifices as well (Choi, 2021).

Many of overseas-educated nationals who return home become part of a national upper-class enjoying particular privilege because of their cosmopolitan social and cultural capital, and then act to reproduce this specific class position by sending their children to international schools (Waters, 2007). Others, however, can become disconnected from their home country. Tse and Waters (2013) found that once they had become young adults, Hong Kong students sent at a young age to Canadian elite schools had no intention of achieving their parents' initial goals of seeing their children return home. As Bourgouin (2007) showed in another study, children of East African political elites sent to London schools in the 1980s and 1990s, in order to get qualifications to achieve Pan-African ideals, returned home disillusioned and disconnected from their families' political strategies. They tended instead to identify with a cosmopolitan ethos of mobility that they enacted by living and working in the global city of Johannesburg.

ELITE SCHOOLS' GLOBAL OUTREACH AND COSMOPOLITAN IDENTITIES

Elite schools have traditionally been characterized by the "eliteness" of their students' backgrounds (mostly defined by wealth) as well as by their role as instruments for the social reproduction of different elite fractions and as channels for access to power positions (Baltzell, 1958; Bourdieu, [1989] 1996; Giddens, 1974; Mills, 1956). In the United States and the United Kingdom, these schools, especially boarding schools, have also been defined by the distinctiveness of their all-round educational model emphasizing certain academic subjects (such as Latin and the humanities), specific games and sports (sometimes only practiced in these schools), and educational settings characterized by physical closure and by their "enveloping" hold on children's lives for considerable periods of time (Cookson & Persell, 1985; Wakeford, 1969; Walford, 2005). Subsequent studies have shown that, due to the growing symbolic value of meritocracy, these schools are now more academically selective and more likely to highlight their academic results and the proportion of their students gaining entry to selective higher education institutions (HEIs) (Kenway et al., 2017).

In the United States, Khan (2011) pointed out changes in elite boarding schools' academic curriculum, which now values breadth rather than depth, as well as in their underlying social model in which instilling formal respect for social hierarchies has been replaced by the importance ascribed to social ease. Gaztambide-Fernandez (2009, p. 26) has, in turn, identified five major criteria defining the perimeter of elite schools—being typologically elite ("their identification as independent schools"), scholastically elite (a "sophisticated curriculum"), historically elite (the "role of elite social networks in their historical development"), demographically elite ("the population that attends schools"), and geographically elite (schools' physical character and location)—although this leaves open the debate of the status of schools that share only some of these characteristics.

Cosmopolitanism and globalization are additional dimensions that complexify the definition and dynamics of elite schools (Kenway & Fahey, 2014; van Zanten, 2018a) and raise novel questions. If the eliteness of schools depends on the web of relations in which they are embedded (Khan, 2016), are these relations fundamentally changed when elite schools systematically reach out to students beyond national borders, especially considering that international students' social status can be less certain or not as well recognized in the host country? To what extent can the internationalization of elite schools' intake be linked to deliberate changes in these establishments' curricular offer, internal dynamics, and public image? In order to answer these questions, we first focus on the changes generated by internationalization in the offer of traditional elite schools and on the transnational connections between these schools. We then examine whether new international curricular tracks are contributing to the expansion of elite schools or whether they constitute a different set of educational institutions catering to pretenders to elite status rather than to established elites.

A Global Turn Among Elite Schools?

The Colonial Heritage

Although elite schools were connected from the outset to national spheres of power—either through their contribution to unifying a national elite, as in the United States after the Civil War (Baltzell, 1958), or through their "incestuous" ties with key national institutions (Giddens, 1974) or state corps (Bourdieu, 1989; van Zanten & Maxwell,

2015)—they also played a central role in developing and legitimating imperial overseas colonies. Research conducted in the 1960s highlighted the role of elite English and colonial schools in constructing the British imperial elite by mixing English and local elite members and fostering a sense of camaraderie among them (Bamford, 1967; Wakeford, 1969). These studies focused more on characterizing the colonial elites themselves than on analyzing how these schools exported the "public school" model to colonial contexts (Mangan, 2013; Sandgren, 2017). An ambitious multisited global ethnography led by Jane Kenway and colleagues (2017) has nevertheless provided new data and interpretations on elite schools founded under the British Empire in Australia, Barbados, Hong Kong, India, Singapore, and South Africa. These schools still present many features related to their past as British colonial schools but now aim to globalize their institutional image, curricula, and ties with institutions and social groups in other countries (Kenway & Fahey, 2014).

The hybridization of older and new influences is apparent in their selective and strategic use of history and traditions to reposition themselves both in the national context (where they now frequently face competition from newly established schools), and in the emerging global market of elite schools where they aim to attract rising elites from various countries (Kenway & Fahey, 2014; Rizvi, 2014). It is also apparent in the values they promote, which mix loyalty to the postcolonial nation state and the inculcation of the supremacy of Western White culture with more liberal versions of cosmopolitanism (Ayling, 2019). For these schools, remaining attractive also implies maintaining old connections and establishing new ones with HEIs. Regular flows of students to Oxbridge and other highly regarded British HEIs are supported by host institutions (scholarships, financial support, etc.) and still bring considerable material and symbolic returns to schools, as well as to the nation states where they are located that sometimes directly sponsor this transnational mobility (Ye & Nylander, 2015). These schools are, however, also developing connections with other prestigious HEIs, especially in the United States, in response to pressures from students and parents keen to optimize HE careers by accessing world-ranked universities (Tarc & Tarc, 2015).

Lycées français à l'étranger, which also developed as part of France's colonial policy, especially in North Africa and in several African countries, now constitute one of the largest state-based networks of international schools. Some of these *lycées* were originally created for the French colonial elite and only started to accept local elite students in the 1950s. Although, unfortunately, they have not been the focus of the same degree of attention as the British colonial elite schools, it is well-known that many of them, having remained highly academically selective and providing an advanced French official curriculum, serve as pathways to elite HE tracks in France (Vermeren, 2011).

The situation in Latin American countries such as Argentina, colonized by the Spanish but where elite schools were also founded by Irish Catholic congregations or imitated the English public school model, is particularly interesting to observe. In these contexts, the elites' most brilliant children, especially boys, are sometimes sent to academically selective state schools that also traditionally trained future elites with middle-class or lower-class backgrounds (Gessaghi & Mendez, 2015; Mendez, 2018). However, the established elites, as in nearby Chile (Ilabaca, 2021), massively continue to send their children to elite private schools, less because of their alleged superior academic level than of the moral education and the social networks they provide. The distinctiveness and attractiveness of these schools are also related to their renewed ties with powerful countries, which are now visible in their provision of bilingual curricula for students planning to continue their studies abroad and to live and work in internationalized environments (Ziegler et al., 2018).

Elite Schools' Strategies of Internationalization and International Elite Schools

Strategies of internationalization are not specific to elite schools located in former colonized states. As attracting foreign students gradually came to the forefront of national educational policy agendas (Ball et al., 2007; Ball, 2012), many elite schools started to internationalize their intake, programs, networks, and public image as a way to "stay ahead in the game" (Kenway & Fahey, 2014) and preserve their elite status. A key move in order to distinguish themselves internationally has been for elite schools to cultivate cross-national networks with similar schools that boost their students' mobility and increase their international social capital. In some cases, this has been done with the financial and organizational support of elite nonprofit organizations, such as Round Square and the Duke of Edinburgh Award, which connect elite secondary schools worldwide through conferences, cultural and humanitarian trips, and student exchanges, and provide a space for elite schools to talk about their practices (Kenway et al., 2017).

English as well as Irish secondary schools have taken marked initiatives to internationalize their intake because the fees paid by foreign students are strongly sought after (Courtois, 2015; Maxwell & Aggleton, 2016a). These initiatives have been successful owing to the attractiveness of their educational model and of their connections with Oxbridge and other prestigious English HEIs. The aura of the public school ideal that they represent for various international audiences is so pervasive that they tend to underplay their role in preparing students for cosmopolitan ways of life and global HE and job markets (Maxwell & Aggleton, 2016a, 2016b), capitalizing instead on their "Britishness" in brochures, websites, and other tools of self-promotion and self-presentation (Brooks & Waters, 2014). Similarly, boarding prep schools in the United States are not encouraged to adapt an educational model that, together with the fact that they channel the great majority of their students to elite North American universities (Mullen, 2009), makes them particularly attractive to established and aspiring elites around the globe.

The situation of French elite schools is quite different. These schools have not massively internationalized their intake partly due to a language barrier but also owing to their attachment to a specific educational model strongly associated with French language and history. French secondary schools are also much less attractive internationally due to the characteristics of the French tertiary elite system, which rewards close connections with French secondary schools and with French high culture, even in scientific curricula (Darmon, 2013; François & Berkouk, 2018; van Zanten, 2018b). Moreover, although the landscape of French elite HEIs has undergone profound changes, with some institutions now widely internationalized with respect to their intake, faculty, curricula, and connections with job markets, the most prestigious of them still reflect the fact that they were designed as prerecruitment tracks to French state corps open only to French citizens (van Zanten & Maxwell, 2015).

Alongside these national elite schools, other types of schools, especially in Switzerland, promote themselves as being the only truly international elite schools in their conception and general orientation. These schools started to develop at the turn of the 20th century in a country with a highly globalized economy where schools played an integral role in the international strategies of firms and local actors alike. They share many of the attributes that Terwillinger (1972) used to define international schools: welcoming a substantial number of students who are not citizens of the host country; being ruled by a board of directors of diverse nationalities; having a teaching staff that has experienced cultural diversity and champion it as an ideal; and implementing a curriculum combining pedagogical methods and content from different national models.

New kinds of international schools are also being developed by new for-profit actors in global cities around the world. They have been identified as education multinationals, responsible for expanding "edu-business" (Ball, 2012) internationally. Two examples are Nord Anglia, founded in England in 1972 and operating 81 international schools in 32 countries (mainly in global cities) as of 2023; and GEMS Education, founded in Dubai and running international schools mainly in the Middle East (Ridge et al., 2016). With their promise of training "future global leaders," these schools, which mainly offer IB tracks or international versions of British and American curricula, aim to attract new moneyed upper-class and middle-class families.

Creating a Close-Knit Global Elite?

If some elite schools have strongly internationalized their intake, the extent to which they are creating a close-knit global elite needs to be further explored. Existing studies show that they do not seem systematically to foster friendships and long-term networks between young people from across the globe. In former colonial elite schools, the co-presence of students with national class backgrounds and global class routes generates processes of segregation and conflict, although, in the longer run, these schools do seem to be reconfiguring the class/race/nation nexus (Kenway et al., 2017). In English elite schools, local families seem worried about overseas students diluting the "Englishness" of their children's education (Maxwell & Aggleton, 2016a). Drewski et al. (2018) have in turn shown that "symbolic boundaries of nationality" persist in a European school in Brussels where status hierarchies and prejudice based on language skills, youth lifestyles, and effortless academic achievement associated with country of birth create strong intraschool status divisions, especially between Northwestern and Eastern European students.

In Swiss international schools, Lillie (2021b) has shown that geopolitical tensions tend to structure the relationships between students from diverse national backgrounds, with Ukrainian and Tatar students, for instance, "navigating an uneasy line" with

Russian students between a common identity and language, on the one hand, and national belongings, on the other. Lillie also hints that students are aware of their geopolitical vulnerability or status when it comes to actually being able to become "citizens of the world," just as they are aware of their exclusion from certain transnational spheres of power and contestation. Furthermore, social integration can be hindered across racial and national lines. This is the case for Chinese- and Russian-speaking students who perceive themselves as second-rate and feel stigmatized either owing to their racial or national assignation or because other students view them as "new rich."

New International Curricula and Schools

The Emergence of a New Model of International Education

A complementary way of exploring the links between globalization and elites in the field of education is to analyze the relationship between the expansion of international curricula and schools and the rise of a transnational elite. The emergence of a new model of international education can historically be traced back to the turn of the 20th century, with the foundation by transnational agencies and corporations of schools specifically designed for upper-class expatriates. Two of the most well-known of these schools—the Geneva International School and the United Nations International School—were respectively created by and for members of the League of Nations and the United Nations, that, in 1968, designed what remains the most sophisticated and popular international curriculum: the IB (Dugonjic-Rodwin, 2020).

The requirements for obtaining an IB diploma include mastery of six compulsory subjects (literature, languages, social sciences, sciences, mathematics, and the arts), three of which must be taken at an advanced level. The program, however, also includes an "international" subject ("world literature in translation") and a meta-subject, the "theory of knowledge." In terms of pedagogy, it favors a student-centered approach and an ethics of cultural openness and service. Using Basil Bernstein's (1971) categories, this curriculum can be described as an original combination of a classic European "collected code" (with high-status contents clearly separated from each other and an emphasis on the mastery of specialized knowledge certified by external examinations) and of an "Anglo-American" integrated code (where contents stand in relation to each other and the focus is on ways of knowing and on creating connections with everyday knowledge and activities).

Focusing on the promotion of internationalist values and training (Matthews, 1989), the Creativity Action Service (CAS) program of the International Baccalaureate Diploma Program (IBDP) promotes global engagement with world-scale issues (world hunger, poverty, climate change, refugee crises, access to education) through shared events, humanitarian trips, volunteering abroad, community service programs, and international charity. While claiming to educate "compassionate" and "courageous" leaders, these activities also help students stand out in university admissions (Jones, 2014; Khan, 2011; Persell & Cookson, 1985). Renewing an old elite tradition of charity and "privileged benefaction" (Kenway & Fahey, 2014), they also arguably lend new global meaning to *privilege*, by embedding it in a global imaginary of inequality and by inculcating and reproducing racialized hierarchies (Gaztambide-Fernandez & Angod, 2019).

Another model of international education increasingly popular among elite schools is GCE defined by the Global Citizenship Foundation as "a transformative, lifelong pursuit that involves both curricular learning and practical experience to shape a mindset to care for humanity and the planet, and to equip individuals with global competence to undertake responsible actions aimed at forging more just, peaceful, secure, sustainable, tolerant and inclusive societies." In practice, however, this "global consciousness" approach coexists with the acquisition of "global competencies" believed to be necessary to achieve prosperity in a highly competitive global marketplace (Oxley & Morris, 2013). In elite schools, both approaches coexist, the first serving less to encourage a critical and responsible response to social inequality and diversity than to instill in students a sense of moral superiority, reinforced by the second approach (Howard & Freeman, 2020; Kenway & Lazarus, 2017).

Is International Education Appealing for National Elites?

While GCE and some elements of the IBDP are clearly attractive to elite parents, the massive worldwide expansion of the IB (from 100 schools in 1982 [Bunnell, 2008] to 5,400 schools offering at least one IB program in 148 countries in late 2020) shows that this model of international education and its local adaptations appeal to many audiences around the world (Resnik, 2012; Steiner-Khamsi & Dugonjic-Rodwin, 2018). The IB curriculum is attractive for some upper- and middle-class parents because it is socially but also intellectually distinctive. This is the case in Canada and the United States but also in Australia. In this latter context, Doherty and colleagues (Doherty, Mu, & Shield, 2009; Doherty et al., 2012) have shown that parents of students in IB tracks are attracted to its cosmopolitan aura but also to its "collected code" dimension: they value the compulsory study of a broad set of subjects, the focus on the best of "Western cultural heritage" and traditions, and the emphasis given to external examinations, that is, a set of educational features that are not well-represented in the more "integrated code" national curriculum.

In European countries with a long tradition of elite schooling, IB and other types of international tracks and schools face stronger competition from more established schools and tracks offering curricula closer to the collected code and viewed by elite groups as more apt for social reproduction. However, national situations also vary. In England, the elite is still trained in traditional "public schools" whose curricula epitomize a mix of these two codes (Walford, 1986) and that are now more open to international culture and practices (Maxwell & Aggleton, 2016a). Frequently located in privileged neighborhoods, the number of schools offering the IBDP has, however, grown considerably as upper-class parents consider it a prestigious and well-rounded alternative to the system of A-Levels (Resnik, 2011).

In the Netherlands, international classes are attractive to upper-class families, but less so to the traditional elite who view national gymnasium curricula as the best preparation for both national and international HE and professional futures. France is a more extreme case, with very few IB-accredited schools (20 in 2021), generally private and mainly welcoming children of expatriate and binational couples.

The attractiveness of the IBDP is also largely due to the fact that it is growingly recognized by well-ranked universities. In the United States and Canada, numerous prestigious universities grant credits or advanced placement equivalents for students in IB advanced courses. In other national systems, however, the IBDP and other types of international tracks do not give any additional advantages and can even impede access to elite HE settings. This is the case, for instance, in Sweden and France where scientific tracks remain "the royal road" (Lidegran, 2017) to the most selective and renowned HEIs. In France, moreover, the chances of accessing these institutions and tracks is highly dependent on having attended a prestigious public or private *lycée* possessing its own *classes préparatoires* or well connected to those in other similar *lycées* (van Zanten, 2018b), in the same way that access to the *grandes écoles* is highly dependent on the type of *classes préparatoires* attended (François & Berkouk, 2018). For these reasons, as well as the language barrier, their attractiveness to international students and their access remain limited, even though some *grandes écoles* have developed specific admission procedures for international students and are well connected to HEIs abroad (Darchy-Koechlin, 2012; Delespierre, 2019).

International Tracks as Competitive Assets in School Markets

While IB programs and other international tracks were originally set up in selective schools willing to reaffirm their status and respond to demands from upper-class parents (Aguiar & Nogueira, 2012), they have since been adopted by other types of schools, sometimes in lighter versions, in order to improve their image and limit pupil flight. In the United States, IB tracks have become a key element of the marketing of state magnet schools to attract middle-class parents who would otherwise avoid local schools in racially mixed neighborhoods (Resnik, 2015, 2020).

In France, "European classes" constitute a "light" form of internationalization. These classes are present in many elite schools, where a small number of students follow them to enhance their academic CVs, especially if they plan to apply to French HEIs that have taken a "global turn" or to prestigious universities abroad. School managers and local educational authorities also use European classes to attract gifted students from the upper and middle classes and to enhance the reputation of schools in mixed urban areas. These softer versions of internationalization offer a striking contrast with the schools that promote themselves as "truly" international, showing that the definition and perimeter of what constitutes an international school remain subject to debate (Wagner, 2020).

CONCLUSION

In line with sociological studies on postcolonial schools (Kenway et al., 2017) and with historical accounts of elite education (Duval, 2009; O'Neill, 2014; O'Neill & Sandgren,

2019), we have suggested in this chapter that owing to their ethos—largely infused with European cosmopolitan ideals—but also to their intake—reflecting existing power relations and cultural influences across countries—many well-established elite schools may have always been cosmopolitan without necessarily presenting themselves as such. It nevertheless seems necessary to distinguish this model of education, which we might call "conservative" in terms of its role in the intergenerational transmission of status by established elites around the globe, from new neoliberal versions of cosmopolitanism that focus less on reproducing social order through traditions, and more on producing the responsible, flexible, and mobile subjects required by the prevailing economic and social context. However, rather than one supplanting the other, what we see instead is the hybridization of these educational models and the emergence of more subtle boundaries separating established elites from aspiring ones between—but also within—elite schools.

A subsidiary question relates to the specific kind of cosmopolitanism being encouraged in new international tracks and schools. Some of them, especially IB schools and GCE-accredited schools, have defined what constitutes a good international education through a set of curricular choices. They are also clearly involved in students' moral education through the renewal of existing charitable practices among elites and elite schools that create new ties between privileged and underprivileged groups while, at the same time, symbolically reinforcing the social distance between them. These schools and tracks have not, however, replaced traditional elite schools but coexist with them, providing an alternative type of education to some fractions of the elite and upper classes for whom they provide "navigation skills" for future HE and professional careers. Other schools, generally catering for middle-class groups, offer a lighter version of international education that cannot easily be transformed into cosmopolitan capital. They nevertheless help diffuse new neoliberal forms of cosmopolitanism across the social and institutional spectrum, while contributing to families' and schools' strategies of distinction.

Another issue lies in the degree to which established, but also recent, elites are embracing the new opportunities associated with educational globalization by constructing international pathways for their children either at home or through experiences of study abroad. The answer to this question is not as clear-cut as it might seem. National schools and tracks are still very much sought after by both groups in countries such as France, the United Kingdom, the Netherlands, or the United States that have a clear set of elite schools and tracks leading to prestigious HEIs and HE fields of study. Opting for internationally oriented schools and tracks might represent new opportunities either for new-moneyed upper-class fractions to consolidate their social position or for aspiring middle-class groups to move up the social scale. These choices are risky, however, not only because they are costly but because they presuppose strong adaptation skills among young people and because it is not easy to determine in advance what the market and social value of international educational trajectories will be, as this varies strongly across social fields and national contexts (Garza & Wagner, 2015; Wagner, 2020).

The fact that not all established and aspiring elites are adopting international pathways for their children and that considerable variation exists across countries and social groups should not, however, lead us to conclude that these processes are not significant. Rather, they should be seen as one of several alternative ways through which, on the one hand, dominant groups and dominant countries reassert their power and reinforce structural inequalities (Alvaredo et al., 2018; Cousin et al., 2018; Heemskerk & Takes, 2016; Piketty, 2014) and, on the other hand, certain groups and individuals, as well as certain countries, legitimate and conquer new social positions on the global scene. Future research should explore the precise content of cosmopolitan and transnational experiences across social groups with a view to examine the extent to which these can still be used by elites and upper-class groups to reproduce their advantage given that these experiences can only be transformed into capital if associated to other types of cultural, economic, and social capital, and the extent to which they contribute to further divisions among elite fractions (Bühlmann et al., 2013; Prieur & Savage, 2013) or constitute pathways for social mobility.

NOTE

1. Both secondary schools and higher education institutions contribute to the education and training of elites. Nevertheless, we have chosen to focus solely on secondary and pre-university schools and tracks because they have enduringly been the primary focus of the sociology of elite education in most national spaces and because, owing both to higher levels of social exclusivity and to their small size, common curriculum, and "well-rounded" socialization of students, they play a more important role as pipelines to the elite than elite universities themselves (Bond, 2012; Reeves et al., 2017). An additional reason is that although globalization is one of the major topics in the vast literature on higher education today, it is seldom analyzed with the specific aim of enhancing the study of global elites (for a comprehensive collection of works on global elite education, from early education to university, see Maxwell et al., 2018).

REFERENCES

Aguiar, A., & Nogueira, M. A. (2012). Internationalization strategies of Brazilian private schools. *International Studies in Sociology of Education*, 22(4), 353–368.

Allan, A., & Charles, C. (2014). Cosmo girls: Configurations of class and femininity in elite educational settings. *British Journal of Sociology of Education*, 35(3), 333–352.

Alvaredo, F., Chancel, L., Piketty, T., Saez, E., & Zucman, G. (2018). *World Inequality Report 2018*. Harvard University Press.

Ayling, P. (2019). *Distinction, exclusivity and whiteness: Elite Nigerian parents and the international education market*. Springer.

Ball, S. J. (2012). *Global Education Inc.: New policy networks and the neo-liberal imaginary*. Routledge.

Ball, S. J., Goodson, I. F., & Maguire, M. (2007). *Education, globalisation and new times: 21 years of the Journal of Education Policy*. Routledge.

Ball, S. J., & Nikita. D. V. (2014). The global middle class and school choice: A cosmopolitan sociology. *Zeitschrift Für Erziehungswissenschaft, 17*(3), 81–93.

Baltzell, E. D. (1958). *Philadelphia gentlemen: The making of a national upper class*. Free Press.

Bamford, T. W. (1967). *Rise of the public schools: A study of boys' public boarding schools in England and Wales from 1837 to the present day*. Nelson.

Beaverstock, J. V. (2002). Transnational elites in global cities: British expatriates in Singapore's financial district. *Geoforum, 33*(4), 525–538.

Beaverstock, J. V. (2005). Transnational elites in the city: British highly-skilled inter-company transferees in New York City's Financial District. *Journal of Ethnic and Migration Studies, 31*(2), 245–268.

Beech, J., Koh, A., Maxwell, C., Yemini, M., Tucker, K., & Barrenechea, I. (2021). "Cosmopolitan start-up" capital: Mobility and school choices of global middle class parents. *Cambridge Journal of Education, 51*(4), 527–541.

Bernstein, B. (1971). *Class, codes and control: Volume 1–Theoretical studies towards a sociology of language*. Routledge.

Bertron, C. (2019). Finishing schools: Le déclin des pensionnats internationaux de jeunes filles en Suisse (1950–1970). *Le Mouvement Social, 266*(1), 67–86.

Bond, M. (2012). The bases of elite social behaviour: Patterns of club affiliation among members of the House of Lords. *Sociology, 46*(4), 613–632.

Bourdieu, P. (1989/1996). *The state nobility: Elite schools in the field of power*. Stanford University Press.

Bourgouin, F. (2007). *The young, the wealthy, and the restless: Trans-national capitalist elite formation in post-apartheid Johannesburg*. Lund Monographs in Social Anthropology.

Brooks, R., & Waters, J. (2014). The hidden internationalism of elite English schools. *Sociology, 38*(2), 281–298.

Brooks, R., Waters, J., & Pimlott-Wilson, H. (2012). International education and the employability of UK students. *British Educational Research Journal, 38*(2), 281–298.

Bühlmann, F. (2020). How to study elites' "international capital"? Some methodological reflections. In F. Denord, M. Palme, & B. Réau (Eds.), *Researching elites and power* (pp. 241–251). Springer.

Bühlmann, F., David, T., & Mach, A. (2013). Cosmopolitan capital and the internationalization of the field of business elites: Evidence from the Swiss case. *Cultural Sociology, 7*(2), 211–229.

Bunnell, T. (2008). The global growth of the international baccalaureate diploma programme over the first 40 years: A critical assessment. *Comparative Education, 44*(4), 409.

Bunnell, T., Donnelly, M., Lauder, H., & Whewall, S. (2022). International mindedness as a platform for class solidarity. *Compare: A Journal of Comparative and International Education 52*(5), 712–728.

Carlson, S., Gerhards, J., & Hans, S. (2017). Educating children in times of globalisation: Class-specific child-rearing practices and the acquisition of transnational cultural capital. *Sociology, 51*(4), 749–765.

Carroll, W. K. (2010). *The making of a transnational capitalist class*. Zed Books.

Choi, L. J. (2021). The student as an enterprising self: Neoliberalism, English and early study abroad. *British Journal of Sociology of Education, 42*(3), 374–387.

Cookson, P. W., & Persell, C. H. (1985). *Preparing for power: America's elite boarding schools*. Basic Books.

Coulangeon, P. (2018). The impact of participation in extracurricular activities on school achievement of French middle school students: Human capital and cultural capital revisited. *Social Forces*, *97*(1), 55–90.

Courtois, A. (2015). "Thousands waiting at our gates": Moral character, legitimacy and social justice in Irish elite schools. *British Journal of Sociology of Education*, *36*(1), 53–70.

Cousin, B., & Chauvin, S. (2014). Globalizing forms of elite sociability: Varieties of cosmopolitanism in Paris social clubs. *Ethnic and Racial Studies*, *37*(12), 2209–2225.

Cousin, B., & Chauvin, S. (2021). Is there a global super-bourgeoisie? *Sociology Compass*, *15*(6), 1–15.

Cousin, B., Khan, S., & Mears, A. (2018). Theoretical and methodological pathways for research on elites. *Socio-Economic Review*, *16*(2), 225–249.

Darchy-Koechlin, B. (2012). Les Élites Étudiantes Internationales Face Au Modèle d'excellence Des Grandes Ecoles Françaises [PhD Dissertation, Institut d'études politiques].

Darmon, M. (2013). *Classes Préparatoires: La Fabrique d'une Jeunesse Dominante*. La Découverte.

Delespierre, A. (2019). L'usage du monde: Hiérarchie nationale et stratégies d'internationalisation des grandes écoles d'ingénieurs. *Actes de la recherche en sciences sociales*, *228*, 42–55.

Denord, F., Lagneau-Ymonet, P., & Thine, S. (2018). Primus inter Pares? The French field of power and its power elite. *Socio-Economic Review*, *16*(2), 277–306.

Doherty, C., Luke, A., Shield, P., & Hincksman, C. (2012). Choosing your niche: The social ecology of the international baccalaureate diploma in Australia. *International Studies in Sociology of Education*, *22*(4), 311–332.

Doherty, C., Mu, L., & Shield, P. (2009). Planning mobile futures: The border artistry of international baccalaureate diploma choosers. *British Journal of Sociology of Education*, *30*(6), 757–771.

Drewski, D., Gerhards, J., & Hans, S. (2018). National symbolic capital in a multinational environment: An exploratory study of symbolic boundaries at a European school in Brussels. *Innovation: The European Journal of Social Science Research*, *31*(4), 429–448.

Dugonjic-Rodwin, L. (2020). De la Concurrence Locale au Conflit Indirect Global: L'économie Symbolique du Baccalauréat International. *Education comparée*, *23*(1), 227–251.

Duval, N. (2009). *L'École des Roches*. Belin.

Elias, N., & Scotson, J. (1965). *The established and the outsiders*. Sage.

Engel, L. C., & Gibson, H. (2022). Elite making and increasing access to cosmopolitan capital: DC youth experiences in education abroad. *Compare: A Journal of Comparative and International Education*, *52*(3), 362–379.

Forbes, J., & Lingard, B. (2015). Assured optimism in a Scottish girls' school: Habitus and the (re)production of global privilege. *British Journal of Sociology of Education*, *36*(1), 116–136.

Forsey, M., Breidenstein, G., Krüger, O., & Roch, A. (2015). Ethnography at a distance: Globally mobile parents choosing international schools. *International Journal of Qualitative Studies in Education*, *28*(9), 1112–1128.

François, P., & Berkouk, N. (2018). Les Concours sont-ils Neutres? Concurrence et Parrainage dans l'Accès à l'École Polytechnique. *Sociologie*, *9*(2), 169–196.

Garza, D. G., & Wagner, A-C. (2015). L'Internationalisation des "Savoirs" des Affaires. Les Business Schols Françaises comme Voies d'Accès aux Élites Mexicaines (French). Cahiers *de la recherche sur l'éducation et les savoirs*, *14*, 141–162.

Gaztambide-Fernandez, R. (2009). *The best of the best: Becoming elite at an American boarding school*. Harvard University Press.

Gaztambide-Fernández, R., & Angod, L. (2019). Approximating whiteness: Race, class, and empire in the making of modern elite/white subjects. *Educational Theory, 69*(6), 719–743.

Gessaghi, V., & Méndez, A. (2015). Elite schools in Buenos Aires: The role of tradition and school social networks in the production and reproduction of privilege. In A. van Zanten, S. J. Ball, & B. Darchy-Koechlin (Eds.), *Elites, privilege and excellence: The national and global redefinition of educational advantage* (pp. 272). World Yearbook of Education, Routledge.

Giddens, A. (1974). Elites in the British class structure. In P. Stanworth & A. Gidden (Eds.), *Elites and power in British society* (pp. 261). Cambridge University Press.

Harris, A. (2004). *Future girl: Young women in the twenty-first century*. Psychology Press.

Hartmann, M. (2011). Internationalisation et spécificités nationales des élites économiques. *Actes de la recherche en sciences sociales, 190*(5), 10–23.

Heemskerk, E. M., & Takes, F. W. (2016). The corporate elite community structure of global capitalism. *New Political Economy, 21*(1), 90–118.

Holmqvist, M. (2017). *Leader communities: The consecration of elites in Djursholm*. Columbia University Press.

Horst, H. A. (2015). Cultivating the cosmopolitan child in Silicon Valley. *Identities, 22*(5), 619–634.

Howard, A., & Freeman, K. (2020). Teaching difference: Global citizenship education within an elite single-sex context. *International Studies in Sociology of Education, 29*(3), 204–223.

Howard, A., & Maxwell, C. (2021). Conferred cosmopolitanism: Class-making strategies of elite schools across the world. *British Journal of Sociology of Education, 42*(2), 164–178.

Huang, S., & Yeoh, B. S. A. (2005). Transnational families and their children's education: China's "Study Mothers" in Singapore. *Global Networks, 5*(4), 379–400.

Igarashi, H., & Saito, H. (2014). Cosmopolitanism as cultural capital: Exploring the intersection of globalization, education and stratification. *Cultural Sociology, 8*(3), 222–239.

Ilabaca, T. (2021). Projets éducatifs et stratégies de legitimation au sein des écoles d'élite chiliennes. L'éducation des élites face aux transformations de la société chilienne [PhD dissertation, UCLouvain].

Jones, S. (2014). "Ensure that you stand out from the crowd": A corpus-based analysis of personal statements according to applicants school type. In A. Mountford-Zimdars & D. Sabbagh (Eds.), *Fair access to higher education: Global perspectives* (pp. 39–65). University of Chicago Press.

Kenway, J., & Fahey, J. (2014). Staying ahead of the game: The globalising practices of elite schools. *Globalisation, Societies and Education, 12*(2), 177–195.

Kenway, J., Fahey, J., Epstein, D., Koh, A., McCarthy, C., & Rizvi, F. (2017). *Class choreographies: Elite schools and globalization*. Springer.

Kenway, J., Langmead, D., & Epstein, D. (2015). Globalizing femininity in elite schools for girls: Some paradoxical failures of success. In A. van Zanten, S. J. Ball, & B. Darchy-Koechlin (Eds.), *Elites, privilege and excellence: The national and global redefinition of educational advantage* (pp. 272). World Yearbook of Education, Routledge.

Kenway, J., & Lazarus, M. (2017). Elite schools, class disavowal and the mystification of virtues. *Social Semiotics, 27*(3), 265–275.

Khan, S. (2011). *Privilege: The making of an adolescent elite at St. Paul's school*. Princeton University Press.

Khan, S. (2016). The education of elites in the United States. *L'Année sociologique, 66*(1), 171–192.

Koo, H. (2016). The global middle class: How is it made, what does it represent? *Globalizations, 13*(4), 440–453.

Lareau, A. (2003). *Unequal childhoods: Class, race, and family life.* University of California Press.

Le Renard, A. (2019). *Le Privilège Occidental. Travail, Intimité et Hiérarchies Postcoloniales à Dubaï.* Presses de Sciences Po.

Levine, S. B. (1980). The rise of American boarding schools and the development of a national upper class. *Social Problems, 28*(1), 63–94.

Lidegran, I. (2017). The royal road of schooling in Sweden: The relationship between the natural science programme in upper secondary school and higher education. *Rassegna Italiana Di Sociologia, 2,* 419–448.

Lillie, K. (2021a). Mobile and elite: Diaspora as a strategy for status maintenance in transitions to higher education. *British Journal of Educational Studies, 69*(5), 641–656.

Lillie, K. (2021b). Multi-sited understandings: Complicating the role of elite schools in transnational class formation. *British Journal of Sociology of Education, 42*(1), 82–96.

Mangan, J. A. (2013). *The games ethic and imperialism: Aspects of the diffusion of an ideal.* Routledge.

Matthews, M. (1989). The scale of international education. *International Schools Journal, 17*(7), 7–17.

Maxwell, C. (2018). Changing spaces—The reshaping of (elite) education through internationalisation. In C. Maxwell, U. Deppe, H. H. Krüger, & W. Helsper (Eds.), *Elite education and internationalisation: From the early years to higher education* (pp. 347–367). Cham: Springer.

Maxwell, C., & Aggleton, P. (2010). The bubble of privilege: Young, privately educated women talk about social class. *British Journal of Sociology of Education, 31*(1), 3–15.

Maxwell, C., & Aggleton, P. (2014). The reproduction of privilege: Young women, the family and private education. *International Studies in Sociology of Education, 24*(2), 189–209.

Maxwell, C., & Aggleton, P. (2016a). Creating cosmopolitan subjects: The role of families and private schools in England. *Sociology, 50*(4), 780–795.

Maxwell, C., & Aggleton, P. (2016b). Schools, schooling and elite status in English education— Changing configurations? *L'Annee sociologique, 66*(1), 147–170.

Maxwell, C., Deppe, U., Krüger, H. H., & Helsper, W. (Eds.) (2018). *Elite education and internationalisation: From the early years to higher education.* Palgrave Macmillan.

Mendez, A. (2018). Socialisation into meritocracy at the *Colegio Nacional de Buenos Aires.* In Agnès van Zanten (Ed.), *Elites in education* (Vol. 3, pp. 235–249). Routledge.

Mension-Rigau, É. (1997). *Aristocrates et Grands Bourgeois: Éducation, Traditions, Valeurs.* Perrin.

Mills, C. W. (1956). *The power elite.* Oxford University Press.

Mullen, A. L. (2009). Elite destinations: Pathways to attending an Ivy League university. *British Journal of Sociology of Education, 30*(1), 15–27.

O'Neill, C. (2014). *Catholics of consequence: Transnational education, social mobility, and the Irish Catholic elite 1850–1900.* Oxford University Press.

O'Neill, C., & Sandgren, P. (2019). Education and elites. In T. Fitzgerald (Ed.), *Handbook of historical studies in education: Debates, tensions, and directions* (pp. 1–13). Springer.

Ong, A. (1999). *Flexible citizenship: The cultural logics of transnationality.* Duke University Press.

Oxley, L., & Morris, P. (2013). Global citizenship: A typology for distinguishing its multiple conceptions. *British Journal of Educational Studies, 61*(3), 301–325.

Parkin, F. (1974). *The social analysis of class structure*. Tavistock Press.

Persell, C. H., & Cookson, P. W. (1985). Chartering and bartering: Elite education and social reproduction. *Social Problems, 33*(2), 114–129.

Piketty, T. (2014). *Capital in the twenty-first century*. Harvard University Press.

Pinçon, M., & Pinççon-Charlot, M. (2000). *Sociologie de la Bourgeoisie*. La Découverte.

Pinçon, M., & Pinççon-Charlot, M. (2006). *Grandes fortunes: Dynasties Familiales et Formes de Richesse en France*. Payot.

Poupeau, F. (2004). Sur Deux Formes de Capital International. *Actes de La Recherche En Sciences Sociales, 151–152*(1), 126.

Prieur, A., & Savage, M. (2013). Emerging forms of cultural capital. *European Societies, 15*(2), 246–267.

Reeves, A., Friedman, S., Rahal, C., & Flemmen, M. (2017). The decline and persistence of the old boy: Private schools and elite recruitment 1897 to 2016. *American Sociological Review, 82*(6), 1139–1166.

Resnik, J. (2011). Internationalisation du Privé ou Privatisation de l'International? L'Expansion du Baccalauréat International dans le Monde. In Y. Dutercq (Ed.), *Où va l'éducation entre public et privé?* (pp. 202). de Boeck Supérieur.

Resnik, J. (2012). The denationalization of education and the expansion of the international baccalaureate. *Comparative Education Review, 56*(2), 248–269.

Resnik, J. (2015). The incorporation of the international baccalaureate in magnet schools in the United States: Survival strategies of low performing schools. *Educational Practice and Theory, 37*(2), 79–106.

Resnik, J. (2020). All against all competition: The incorporation of the international baccalaureate in public high schools in Canada. *Journal of Education Policy, 35*(3), 315–336.

Ridge, N., Kippels, S., & Shami, S. (2016). Economy, business, and first class: The implications of for-profit education provision in the UAE. In A. Verger, C. Lubienski, & G. Steiner-Khamsi (Eds.), *World yearbook of education 2016: The global education industry* (pp. 284–307). Routledge.

Rizvi, F. (2014). Old elite schools, history and the construction of a new imaginary. *Globalisation, Societies and Education, 12*(2), 290–308.

Sandgren, P. (2017). Globalising Eton: A transnational history of elite boarding schools since 1799 [PhD dissertation, European University Institute].

Sklair, L. (2001). *The transnational capitalist class*. Wiley Blackwell.

Song, J. J. (2013). For whom the bell tolls: Globalization, social class and South Korea's international schools. *Globalisation, Societies and Education, 11*(1), 136–159.

Steiner-Khamsi, G., & Dugonjić-Rodwin, L. (2018). Transnational accreditation for public schools: IB, PISA and other public–private partnerships. *Journal of Curriculum Studies, 50*(5), 595–607.

Tarc, P., & Tarc, A. M. (2015). Elite international schools in the Global South: Transnational space, class relationalities and the "middling" international schoolteacher. *British Journal of Sociology of Education, 36*(1), 34–52.

Terwilliger, R. I. (1972). International schools—Cultural crossroads. *The Educational Forum, 36*(3), 359–363.

Tse, J. K. H., & Waters, J. L. (2013). Transnational youth transitions: Becoming adults between Vancouver and Hong Kong. *Global Networks, 13*(4), 535–550.

van der Pijl, K. (1998). *Transnational classes and international relations*. RIPE Studies in Global Political Economy.

van Zanten, A. (2009). *Choisir son École. Stratégies Familiales et Médiations Locales*. Presses Universitaires de France.

van Zanten, A. (2018a). Elite education: Reconstructing a key field of social research. In Agnès van Zanten (Ed.), *Elites in education* (Vol. 1, pp. 1–42). Routledge.

van Zanten, A. (2018b). How families and schools produce an elite: Paths of upward mobility in France. In Agnès van Zanten (Ed.), *Elites in education* (Vol. 4, 195–221). Routledge.

van Zanten, A., & Maxwell, C. (2015). Elite education and the state in France: Durable ties and new challenges. *British Journal of Sociology of Education, 36*(1), 71–94.

Vermeren, P. (2011). La formation des élites marocaines, miroir de la mondialisation? *Le Télémaque, 39*(1), 53–66.

Vincent, C., & Ball, S. J. (2007). "Making up" the middle-class child: Families, activities and class dispositions. *Sociology, 41*(6), 1061–1077.

Wagner, A.-C. (1998). *Les Nouvelles Élites de la Mondialisation: une Immigration Dorée en France*. Presses Universitaires de France.

Wagner, A.-C. (2007). La Place du Voyage dans la Formation des Élites. *Actes de la recherche en sciences sociales, 170*(5), 58–65.

Wagner, A.-C. (2020). The internationalization of elite education: Merging angles of analysis and building a research object. In F. Denord, M. Palme, & B. Réau (Eds.), *Researching elites and power: Theory, methods, analyses* (pp. 193–200). Springer.

Wakeford, J. (1969). *The cloistered elite: A sociological analysis of the English public boarding school*. Praeger.

Walford, G. (1986). Ruling class classification and framing. *British Educational Research Journal, 12*(2), 183–195.

Walford, G. (2005). *Private education: Tradition and continuity*. Continuum.

Waters, J. L. (2005). Transnational family strategies and education in the contemporary Chinese diaspora. *Global Networks, 5*(4), 359–377.

Waters, J. L. (2007). "Roundabout routes and sanctuary schools": The role of situated educational practices and habitus in the creation of transnational professionals. *Global Networks, 7*(4), 477–497.

Waters, J., & Leung, M. (2014). "These are not the best students": Continuing education, transnationalisation and Hong Kong's young adult "educational non-elite." *Children's Geographies, 12*(1), 56–69.

Weenink, D. (2008). Cosmopolitanism as a form of capital: Parents preparing their children for a globalizing world. *Sociology, 42*(6), 1089–1106.

Windle, J., & Maire, Q. (2019). Beyond the global city: A comparative analysis of cosmopolitanism in middle-class educational strategies in Australia and Brazil. *Discourse: Studies in the Cultural Politics of Education, 40*(5), 717–733.

Windle, J., & Nogueira, M. A. (2015). The role of internationalisation in the schooling of Brazilian elites: Distinctions between two class fractions. *British Journal of Sociology of Education, 36*(1), 174–192.

Ye, R., & Nylander, E. (2015). The transnational track: State sponsorship and Singapore's Oxbridge elite. *British Journal of Sociology of Education, 36*(1), 11–33.

Yemini, M., & Maxwell, C. (2018). De-coupling or remaining closely coupled to "home": Educational strategies around identity-making and advantage of Israeli global middle-class families in London. *British Journal of Sociology of Education, 39*(7), 1030–1044.

Yemini, M., & Maxwell, C. (2020). The purpose of travel in the cultivation practices of differently positioned parental groups in Israel. *British Journal of Sociology of Education*, *41*(1), 18–31.

Zhou, M. (1998). "Parachute kids" in Southern California: The educational experience of Chinese children in transnational families. *Educational Policy*, *12*(6), 682.

Ziegler, S., Gessaghi, V., & Fuentes, S. (2018). Elite schools and institutional *ethos*: Differential options and profiles in the education on privileged sectors in Argentina. In A. van Zanten (Ed.), *Elites in education* (Vol. 2, pp. 180–200). Routledge.

CHAPTER 15

MOBILIZING WHITENESS

Race, Futurity, and Globalization of Higher Education

RIYAD A. SHAHJAHAN AND KIRSTEN T. EDWARDS

INTRODUCTION

DESPITE the ubiquity of global mass movements for racial justice, race and racism as a transnational force has received negligible attention in the globalization of higher education (HE) literature. Over the past two decades, the HE globalization literature has emphasized the drastic effects of globalization on HE's core objects of study—through technological changes, increased academic mobility, the global knowledge economy, transnational actors, and internationalization of curricula, students, and partnerships—and reshaping the functions, borders, and landscape of HE institutions and those who work and learn in them (see Brown et al., 2011; Cantwell & Kauppinen, 2014; King et al., 2012; Shahjahan & Kezar, 2013; Sidhu, 2006). However, remaining undertheorized are the ways in which race, and specifically Whiteness, as a cultural and social paradigm, and as a structural force underpins this transnational phenomenon (a recent exception is Shahjahan & Edwards, 2021).

The terms "globalization" and "internationalization" are used interchangeably in the HE field, particularly in practice. However, several scholars have offered meaningful distinctions (Altbach & Knight, 2007; Cantwell & Maldonando, 2009; King et al., 2012; Tight, 2021). Drawing on these scholars, we also differentiate the two. Derivative of a nation state ontological standpoint, we interpret internationalization as focusing on the relations and/or connections between nations (i.e., mobility of people, culture, and knowledge, and/or involvement of HE institutions across national borders). Meanwhile, our understanding of globalization encompasses the manifestations of internationalization but also includes relations or agency that spans, flows over, and/or ignores nation states. Such relations or agency include flows and disjunctures of culture, capital, technology, media, and the growing role of non-HE transnational actors (e.g., commercial rankers, publishing companies, and/or global media) transcending and reconstituting national borders mitigated locally with/in HE sectors and institutions globally (see Marginson, 2011; Shahjahan, 2019; Sidhu, 2006). In short, we understand globalization as involving flows, agency, and disjunctures tied to asymmetrical movements, networks, and untethered economies furthering colonial power relations and cultural imperialism (Sidhu, 2006; Shahjahan, 2019).

While racialized politics of global HE have been discussed in relation to race, these accounts tend to be about racism toward groups (e.g., international students or faculty) within institutions or countries (see Ahmed, 2016; Lee, 2020; Lee & Rice, 2007; Suspitsyna, 2021; Yao, et al., 2019). Such accounts tend to be trapped within national container accounts of society (Shahjahan & Kezar, 2013) (recent exceptions include Chatterjee & Barber, 2021; Ress, 2019; Stein & Andreotti, 2017) and/or are concerned with mapping and documenting contemporary racisms in or between specific geographies (Christian, 2019, p. 171). We suggest that our understanding of globalization of HE would benefit from an intersectional understanding of critical Whiteness studies and temporal studies to help racialize and further temporalize this phenomenon. Such an integrated approach would also illuminate the interconnections and complexities between the affective, political, sociocultural, and economic relations that remain unexplored in the HE globalization literature (Lee & Stensaker, 2021).

Our point of departure for this chapter stems from Marginson's (2012) suggestion that globalization of HE "fashions mentalities, and is fashioned by those mentalities in return" (p. 22). Extending our earlier work on Whiteness as futurity in the globalization of HE (Shahjahan & Edwards, 2022), we aim to demonstrate the racial asymmetries underpinning globalization of HE by drawing on contemporary mobility trends of people and resources in HE. We suggest that a critical race temporal account of contemporary mobility trends would help further complicate and unpack how a particular *Whiteness as futurity* orients movements we perceive spatially in globalization of HE. Whiteness as futurity uncovers the ways in which local subjects[1] (nation states, universities, and individuals) do not autonomously direct local HE processes, but instead are influenced by the global pressures of Whiteness.

By "Whiteness," we refer to a set of "narrative structural positions, rhetorical tropes and habits of perception" (Dyer, 1997, p. 12) standing for the normal. Whiteness, as a state of knowing and being, creates a superstructure (i.e., racial capitalism) that privileges White people, institutions, and cultural norms and *orients* social and political environments toward the benefit and protection of White life (Ahmed, 2007). In other words, Whiteness is as an unfinished process that reproduces itself through (a) structural (contemporary practices tied to historical global wealth accumulation and political economic power), and (b) symbolic (normative/lifestyle, imaginaries, cultural narrative oriented) dimensions (Christian, 2019). As the foundation of all racial hierarchies since modernity, Whiteness helps reproduce social inequalities stemming from race and racism in various ways in various contexts (Christian, 2019). While Whiteness is the centrifugal force organizing global racial hierarchies, we also suggest that race and racism are not uniform across the globe but continue as a transnational phenomenon. Lack of uniformity—malleability—supports the ability of Whiteness to become (re)centered in various contexts.

By futurity, we are referring to a state of being tied to an imagined time that is yet-to-come, and/or how this yet-to-come is invoked (Baldwin, 2012). Futurity can also be understood as a form of "absent presence." As Baldwin put it: "From tropes of uncertainty, Utopia, apocalypse, prophesy, hope, fear, possibility and potentiality, the future shapes the present in all manner of ways" (Baldwin, 2012, p. 172).

In the present chapter we first briefly delineate our Whiteness as futurity framework. We next demonstrate how Whiteness as futurity informs mobility of (a) imaginaries (via popular culture), (b) people (students and academics), and (c) resources (e.g., internationalization initiatives, cross-border HE, and education hubs). We conclude that globalization discussions need to consider its complicity, tensions, and complexity with modern onto-epistemic grammar[2] and desires for quick fixes.

WHITENESS AS FUTURITY

In a previous publication, we articulated the conceptual framework "Whiteness as futurity" (Shahjahan & Edwards, 2022). Drawing on two domains of knowledge—Whiteness and temporal studies (see Ahmed, 2007; Baldwin, 2012; Christian, 2019; Lipsitz, 2006; Mills, 2020)[3]—we delineate through the framework how the globalization of Whiteness governs futurity through three distinct pathways. First, Whiteness influences future aspirations of HE subjects, such as individuals, governments, institutions, and/or transnational actors. Contemporary sociopolitical asymmetries reinforce the power of Whiteness globally and shape invocations of the future. Individuals and institutions seeking global subjectivity must aspire to standards produced by/for Whiteness. Second, Whiteness as futurity creates conditions that make it harmful to not invest or continue the investment in Whiteness. Said differently, Whiteness produces global parameters that compel particular resource investments.

Finally, Whiteness maintains global supremacy by remaining malleable enough to disguise or superimpose and, therefore, (re)center itself in multiple contexts. Unlike the previous tenets which function as actions and responses to a global landscape of Whiteness, malleability is an inherent characteristic of Whiteness that makes its futurity possible. Whiteness as malleable suggests understanding White supremacy beyond corporeal bodies, but as "a process, not a "thing" (Christian, 2019, p. 179). Thus, a malleable understanding of Whiteness recognizes that non-White bodies and spaces can symbolically and materially project and gain advantages of Whiteness. As Christian (2019) noted, Whiteness offers global gradations. While the United States and United Kingdom may be the "whitest white," China, Japan, and South Korea offer an accessible Whiteness to the Eurasian region. Relatedly, although sub-Saharan Africa exists globally as the "Blackest Black," South Asia occupies geopolitical "Blackness" in the Asian region. These racialized containers also include internal malleability. For instance, although

Han Chinese may benefit from the privileges of accessible Whiteness, this benefit is not "within reach" for other Chinese ethnic groups (Ahmed, 2007, p. 152). The same could be said about high-caste Indians, White Brazilians, or Habeshas in Eastern Africa (see Christian, 2019). However, this presumed flexibility belies the ways in which Whiteness shapes periphery locales conformity toward a Whiteness orientation. By malleability, we are acknowledging the persistence of White domination globally, even in those regions that are absent of White bodies and/or institutions.

Through these three pathways, Whiteness constrains pasts and presents while producing White futures. Furthermore, the three characteristics detailed earlier do not emerge in a linear or hierarchical manner, but instead symbiotically, existing independently while also catalyzing the potency of one another. In the following sections, we explore "Whiteness as futurity" through global mobilities. Specifically, we excavate how Whiteness animates particular global flows, entrenching White futurity through various modes of movement. We provide a critical race temporal account of societies, institutions, and people deciding on mobility based on aspirations, investments, and malleability shaped by Whiteness. Our analysis focuses on mobility of imaginaries, people, and resources.

Mobility of Imaginaries

Global "mediascapes" feed the aspirations for Whiteness in global HE (Appadurai, 1996). Popular culture plays a public pedagogic role in constituting social imaginaries tied to Whiteness, serving as the catalyst for mobility. Such imaginaries are "image-centered, narrative-based accounts of strips of reality" that help form one's "imagined lives" or of others living elsewhere (Appadurai, 1996, p. 35). In the context of global HE, popular culture, such as movies, TV shows, music, social media, and so on, provide ongoing opportunities for imagined selves within particular spaces, prompting desires and action in the form of movement and mobility (i.e., students). As Kölbe (2020) noted, imaginaries of "other places, people, and cultures have always been a part of social life in the form of songs, paintings, myths, and stories" (p. 89), but amid modern techno and mediascapes, students who have not traveled abroad come to know about other cultures before they even engage in mobility through popular culture representations. In an era where more people than ever imagine the possibility of studying or working in other parts of the globe, the social imaginary holds growing White power.

The grammar of success embedded in Whiteness is evident in global media as media attach positive feelings or aspirations to certain regions, creating a global narrative that precarity is solved through accessing White regions. As Islam (2019) noted, global media circulates "images of wellbeing, happiness, freedom and success available in the developed countries" (p. 5) among students in the Global South. For example, the global circulation of White media "global consumerist imaginations" are interpreted as "individual imaginations" and "imagined dreams and desires" compelling Bangladeshi students' movement toward Australian HE (Islam, 2019, p. 3). Furthermore, in a recent study on Nepalese university students, Kölbe (2020) noted that "stories about and images of Nepalis studying in North America, Europe and Australia enter young people's daily routines through a host of information channels, including local newspapers, educational marketing campaigns and online social media" (p. 99). Given the malleability of Whiteness and how it manifests in non-White regions (e.g., Asia, Africa, etc.), global media constitutes the desired value of an international degree (i.e., White HEI credential) in the job market.

Popular culture also mediates cultural familiarity among students in non-White regions, shaping the desires for choosing certain Asian study destinations to get closer to the icons and symbols of popular culture. K-Pop (Korean pop), K-dramas (Korean drama), Chinese movie idols, and Japanese cultural symbols, such as anime, manga, and J-Pop (Japanese pop), are examples of popular culture through which the Asian audiences desire to move eastward (Sidhu & Ishikawa 2022, p. 408). In the last decade, for instance, due to *hallyu* (the Korean wave) in Asia, South Korea has emerged as an increasingly popular study abroad destination among Asian students, in part by their consumption of Korean popular culture in the form of movies, television dramas, and music (Takeda, 2020). Amid a global mediascape, students transform from consumers of particular popular culture (e.g., *hallyu*) into cosmopolitan global outlooking individuals, thus desiring certain study destinations (Takeda, 2020). As we noted elsewhere (Shahjahan & Edwards, 2022), malleable Whiteness constitutes Japan, China, and South Korea higher in the Whiteness spectrum than other regions, such as South Asia or Southeast Asia. In short, global media via popular culture plays an important role in controlling imagined selves and aspirations and evoking particular investments in moving toward certain destinations for studying. Such aspirations and investment reinforce White dominant nations' and institutions' occupation of the center.

Such global HE social imaginaries are products of "global cultural flows" meant for consumption (Appadurai, 1996, p. 30). As a form of public pedagogy, popular culture shapes the desires for Whiteness and mobility toward White regions. In recent analyses of Global North popular culture, Reynolds (2014) suggests that limited student representations in American popular culture "bear huge potential for (mis)education particularly for answers to questions about who belongs; it could seem that only white men [and women] truly belong in HE" (p. 96). However, the notion of Whiteness is also projected by the local popular culture industry. For instance, Balabantaray (2020) illuminated how local media including Bollywood normalizes Whiteness as desirable among Indian university students, such as fairer skin, Western outfits, and speaking English as reflecting higher intelligence. In other words, Whiteness is made malleable and reachable, which in turn shapes aspirations to go to certain study abroad destinations. As Kölbe (2020) argued, "images and stories circulated by the various actors involved in international education can further manifest historically rooted imaginative geographies in which the 'West' is seen to be more sophisticated and advanced than the 'East,' as these global connections are always underpinned by local status hierarchies" (p. 96). In short, while mediating cultural curiosity and associating Whiteness with better quality, status, and economic outcomes, popular culture circulates aspirations for Whiteness among audiences, thus catalyzing mobility toward certain destinations.

Finally, the grammar of success embedded in Whiteness is evident in institutional branding efforts (e.g., university websites, social media, and/or brochures) tied to their global status (Stack, 2016, 2020). For instance, marketing departments in the Global North construct the Global South as a population whose aspirations are to "do well," "be Western," to acquire the status of "a good English speaker" (Robertson & Komljenovic, 2016, p. 598). Such branding efforts are not simply about representing one's current content, but rather highlight the aspirational realities of regions or institutions. Many non-White regions will use White regions as reference societies to brand their HE locations. For instance, Singapore sought to establish itself as the "Boston" of Asia, borrowing from the Global North. To this end, Sidhu, Ho, and Yeoh noted, "Singapore was branded as 'the Boston of the East' and much was made of its networks with Anglophone knowledge centers including the presence of international staff from leading Anglophone universities" (cited in Sidhu & Ishikawa, 2022, p. 411). In a recent analysis of websites of four universities in China and South Korea seeking to become world-class universities, Bae et al. (2021) found that imagery depicting foreign students and scholars on their campuses, or specific events held for international cooperation, across the four universities featured White-skinned people. Given all four institutions highlighted their interactions with Whiteness as a means to show their capacity for catching global talents and emphasizing their internationalization, this highlights how Whiteness is an investment but also aspirational. Similarly, Estera and Shahjahan's (2019) critical analysis of commercial university rankers' websites' visual imagery of students found that Whiteness is normalized through imagery leading to the naturalization of Whiteness and alienation of other racial groups. As they asserted, in/visible Whiteness informs the various signifying practices positioning the White student as the HE default student. These interactive meanings thus construct who belongs and is desirable in global HE. All of these institutional, national, and rankers' efforts highlight the malleable nature of Whiteness as its uptake manifests in different forms (i.e., internationalization efforts, English language, and/or branding) and are taken for granted.

However, resource distribution informs global media circulating and forming non-White imaginaries. Resource precarity produces aspirations for security, and media communicates the message that the Global North can provide access to the resources needed to protect from poverty through a future subjectivity in the global marketplace. This has implications not only for individual pursuits but also local advancement. Intellectual resources and talent—not just bodies and ideas—move from periphery to the White core (Schopf, 2020).

MOBILITY OF PEOPLE

Whiteness as futurity mobilizes bodies in particular ways. Global flows attract and repel particular bodies to particular locations. As such, human movements not only map

Whiteness geographically but also entrench White aspirations, investments, and malleability. The mobilization of bodies for White futures emerges through various pathways and for a variety of reasons, such as pursuit of global subjectivity, contextual privileges, personal desires made possible by White national affiliations, and affective attachments.

Access to global resources or global subjectivity animates one of the most obvious movements. Whiteness as futurity compels many students in the Global South to aspire toward opportunities in the Global North. The number of internationally mobile students has doubled since 2005 to 5.6 million in 2018 (OECD, 2020), and it is expected to grow to 8 million by 2025 (Cheng, 2021). According to a report published by the Organization for Economic Cooperation and Development (OECD, 2020), Asian students are the largest group of internationally mobile students across all levels of HE. China is the largest country of origin for international students in the world (i.e., 622,100 international students). Both China and India are responsible for 30% of the pool of international students in OECD countries, and more than two-thirds of this pool is concentrated in only five countries: Australia, Canada, Japan, the United Kingdom, and the United States (OECD, 2020, p. 231). The United States is the top destination for international students, holding 18% of the global education market share. English-speaking countries are the most attractive destinations overall (Institute of International Education [IIE], 2018), with the United States, United Kingdom, Australia, and Canada receiving more than 40% of internationally mobile students studying in OECD and partner nations (OECD, 2020). Although Anglophone countries host the great majority of all internationally mobile students, Asian countries, such as China, South Korea, Malaysia, Singapore, and Japan, are experiencing faster growth among internationally mobile students. As of 2018, China has become the world's third largest receiving destination with 492,185 international students (Cheng, 2021). East Asian worldwide student mobility consists of 23%, of which 36% choose to stay within the East Asian region, with China as the number-one destination followed by Japan and South Korea (IIE, 2018). Student mobility is expected to continue to unfold in a multidirectional trend beyond the West through regional policy efforts, such as East Asia's CAMPUS initiative and the East Africa Higher Education Area mobility initiative, which seek to bolster enrollment of international students through immigration and labor market policies (Cheng, 2021; IIE, 2018). Student mobility trends to and within Asia exemplify empirically how China, Japan, and South Korea are achieving proximity to Whiteness, through their recent internationalization efforts and/or branding (e.g., English language instructions, international partnerships, recruitment, and/or improvements in their global university rankings) (Shahjahan & Edwards, 2022). Considering Christian's (2019) "Global Field of Whiteness," academic flows toward these three countries, in particular, entrench Whiteness in Asia, instead of disrupting malleability of Whiteness as futurity.

Students in the Global South "hoping" to access geopolitical centers to improve employment opportunities find future security particularly relevant (Foumunyam, 2017; Islam 2019; Winberg & Winberg, 2017). Preparing for one's future value and desires to quell fear shape students seeking study abroad in White (and White-approaching) locations. Xiang and Shen (2009) highlight the urgency and anxiety of students and families as tantamount to the risk of "missing the last bus" in their bid to acquire anticipated cultural and symbolic capital. Pursuing HE overseas became common in China even for those without much knowledge of international study destinations or financial capacity (Sidhu & Ishikawa, 2022, p. 406). Similar to the Chinese, Bangladeshi students and their parents invest in such study abroad to secure future market signals of intelligence (Islam, 2019). Additionally, Asian students invest in degrees from White nations because these degrees offer more mobility in their home countries (Chatterjee & Barber, 2021). Because Asian countries aspire to White prominence, they hire Asian students educated in White nations, which creates opportunities for social mobility (Chatterjee & Barber, 2021). To this end, some Bangladeshi students noted in Islam's (2019) study that one faces cultural challenges in securing a job if one doesn't have an overseas degree, and as mentioned in the previous section, "if you study from abroad, you like considered more smart or intelligent" (p. 5). Whiteness as investment situates mobility outside of Bangladesh and into global HE as a form of intelligence. Similarly, Kim (2016) noted that Koreans with US degrees are understood to have global capital, which separates them into elite categories over those who remained in Korea for their study. Koreans engage in mobility for the rewards (employment/social) they receive when they come back to South Korea, producing social elite Asians.

Since Whiteness is malleable, students also move to "within reach" (Ahmed, 2007, p. 152) non-White locations to access geopolitical privilege tied to global economies. Increasingly elite Asian HE offers an affordable Whiteness, an affordable investment (Sidhu & Ishikawa, 2022, p. 410). Many students speak to the changing global order, shifts toward China, as a reason for why they study in China instead of the White Global North. For instance, some Southeast Asian students cited China's emerging economic prowess as a reason to travel there instead of the Global North (Sidhu & Ishikawa, 2022). A student from Vietnam explained that prohibitive costs of studying in the Global North made China seem economically accessible (Sidhu & Ishikawa, 2022). Similarly, African students engage in mobility to China because of its rising global political power and foreign investments/trades with African nations, which made China a foreign job creator in African nations (Mulvey, 2021). According to Mulvey (2021), "China's relative position within the global political economy acts as a pull factor for African students, just as the West's relative position to East Asia has" (p. 443). Furthermore, China's recent *One Belt, One Road (BRI)* initiative is another example whereby students in Eurasia are drawn by Chinese scholarships and pour into China, reshaping regional education and affecting global HE (Peters, 2020). Others decided to move to peripheral players such as Sri Lanka because of the global presence of Korean multinational firms in the country (Sidhu & Ishikawa, 2022, p. 408), or even Pakistan/India where Nepalese students have traveled previously but now experience a rise in antiethnic sentiments. While non-White nations invest in the Global South, this "creates a demand for credentials in business, information technology, and competency in the respective language of the investor" (Mulvey 2021, p. 444). As Pfaff-Czarnecka (2020) put it: "While engaging in positional competition, institutions as well as students have engaged in self modelling driven by Western standards of academic excellence" (p. 1408). Morphing core-periphery relationships, evinced through varying degrees of Whiteness, shape student mobilities.

Movement is not isolated to those in the Global South or students. Global North White subjects also move for different but related reasons. Since the desire for access to Whiteness and global subjectivity is not isolated to individuals, many elite institutions in the global periphery—recognizing the relationship between Whiteness and aspiration—invest in aggressively recruiting White faculty or faculty with White national credentials. Universities in the Middle East, Southeast Asia, and East Asia are recruiting large numbers of English-speaking academics from the White world, both to their universities and to satellite campuses of White higher education institutions (HEIs) (Kim et al, 2021; Koshino, 2019; Tight, 2021). Institutional desire for proximity to Whiteness provides White faculty with privileged professional atmospheres. The experiences of White faculty in the periphery are telling. As one White woman faculty teaching at a Korean university said about her experience living in Korea, "I feel like I'm treated like a princess" (Kim et al. 2021, p. 10).

White bodies experiencing privilege in global contexts highlight Whiteness's malleability. For instance, Koshino (2019) noted in the Japanese HE context, "White instructors were routinely hired with lesser credentials than their Asian colleagues" (p. 54). As reflected in student examples, within such a context, Whiteness signals superior intellect, particularly when it comes to English-speaking ability (Koshino, 2019). Malleable Whiteness allows White bodies to access local resources and valuable information to advance one's social status. Given the dominance of Whiteness in knowledge production, through English, many faculty from White metropolitan centers can access non-Western regions for academic work. For instance, Western faculty teaching in Turkey cite being able to teach in English as a motivation for going to Turkey (Seggie & Calikoglu, 2021). Such linguistic capital allows White faculty to "enjoy . . . high living standards," allowing for more satisfaction (Seggie & Calikoglu, 2021, p. 10), and opportunities to consult (because Western knowledge is desirable by the wider society and networks). This same privilege was experienced by European faculty in Mexico (see Mendoza et al., 2019). Global asymmetries also impact temporary mobility investments. For example, academics from the Global North are hired or invited for research stays in the academic periphery because of their pedigree/prestige. As Schopf (2020) noted, due to their know-how on getting published in core journals and their (presumed) connections, Global North academics often find locals eager to work with them, doing translations and providing local knowledge. Thus, without having to invest time in studying the local language and culture, Global North academics can publish on Global South phenomena.

Ultimately, periphery resources are used to benefit core academics. However, faculty from the Global South moving to the Global North struggle to be seen as experts. The malleability here is that the presence of a faculty from the academic core seemingly benefits the periphery locales; however, the greatest beneficiary is the academic core faculty whose work furthers the maintenance of Whiteness.

Given that White credentials travel easily around the world, well-resourced Global North faculty also experience a privileged chronopolitical landscape. Since the global HE marketplace understands Global North faculty as leading scholars, employed by highly ranked universities, top conferences take place in their locations, saving them time from having to leave the academic core. Comparatively, those in the academic periphery trying to build their careers invest in frequent visits to the core for global conferences, spending time/resources in a way that faculty in the academic core do not. Those in the academic core benefit from their time being already protected by notions of expertise, allowing for continued productivity standards set by the Global North. Further, faculty in the Global South endure humiliating visa processes/delays which further infringe on their time and resources (Schöpf, 2020).

Global North White faculty also possess the privilege to globe trot, not necessarily for job or economic survival, but rather to pursue their intellectual or cultural curiosities. For instance, in China, motivations of such faculty included intellectual curiosity, engaging in novel projects, and taking on leadership positions, as well as personal reasons such as feeling bored with the previous job or life and seeking adventure (Cai & Hall, 2016). In Japan, motivations for international faculty included academic or personal reasons (e.g., fondness for Japanese culture, family conditions, etc.) (Huang, 2017). In Kazakhstan, international faculty were attracted by the salary, sense of adventure, and research and institutional building opportunities (Lee & Kuzhabekova, 2017).

However, as mentioned previously, Whiteness allows White bodies to avoid partaking in local socialization experiences. For instance, in Kim et al. (2021) study in South Korea, they noted that "Even though the interviewed participants confronted everyday difficulties related to language, most of them did not engage in learning Korean" (p. 11). Furthermore, "Due to the language difficulties and lack of support the university offers, however, nearly all interview participants (except those who are Korean descendants) did not attend department meetings or participate actively in local, institutional service" (p. 14). In short, when researchers from White regions move to non-White regions, they are not expected to make the same investments in socialization preparation as their contra-movement peers (Burford et al., 2021).

These examples also reveal how emotions move with global aspirations. For Global South subjects, movement toward the White global core provides positive emotions. Conversely, while some Global North subjects enjoy elevated treatment in the periphery, for those who move to the Global South under less than elite conditions or move to "less White" peripheral locales, the experience elicits negative emotions such as "'weird', 'backward' . . . 'stuckness' or regression" (Burford et al. 2021, p. 733). For instance, scholars from White nations who moved to Southeast Asia to teach displayed the following affective responses: "for me I guess it's pretty much all, all negatives in terms of uh, my academic development" (Burford et al., 2021, p. 738). Later the same faculty stated,

> I feel a bit ashamed to be working here. Whenever I send off a paper, I don't really like the fact that it says . . . [South Asian institution] on the paper, that the first response

> to anyone looking at it is gonna . . . make them wary . . . Yeah. I mean I'm kind of ashamed to work here. . . . I did my PhD at [prestigious European institution], which was pretty famous, and then I do kind of think, how did I end up . . . what am I doing? (Burford et al., 2021, p. 739)

Relatedly, researchers who move from the Global North to the Global South describe feeling "underdeveloped" and lacking opportunities for "advancement" (Burford et al., 2021; Kim et al, 2021). Comments suggest that faculty experience movement away from the core, away from the aspiration as penalty. While movement to the Global South represents stuckness, aspiring to move to the White core for Global South subjects, conversely, elicits feelings of freedom.

Charting the various movements of student and faculty bodies illuminates Whiteness as futurity. White aspirations, investments, and malleability shape mobilities. As such, Whiteness becomes the compass directing such movements.

MOBILITY OF RESOURCES

Tied to the mobility of imaginaries and people is also mobility of resources, driven by Whiteness as futurity. Futurity informed by anticipatory logics (precaution or preparedness) intervenes in the present (Baldwin, 2012). As such, local subjects fearing the "yet to come" or hoping for better things to come (Baldwin, 2012) increasingly turn into global subjects by adopting a global White eye, through initiatives such as internationalization efforts, international branch campuses (IBCs), and education hubs.

The mobility of resources oriented toward Whiteness is evident as many nations and institutions heavily invest in internationalization efforts to carve their place in the global market, hoping to attract future student consumers. Such investments include recruitment of academic stars, international collaboration efforts, and introducing more coursework in English. Such internationalization efforts range all the way in East Asia (i.e., China, Japan, and South Korea), South Asia (e.g., India), or Central Asia (Kazakhstan) to Mexico. In many locations to be global is to offer White canons of knowledge (e.g., English, liberal arts curriculum), or those perceived to have such knowledge (Shahjahan & Edwards, 2022). For instance, Japan's education ministry has invested in the Top Global University Project as a way to invest in its internationalization and HE competitiveness (Morely et al., 2020; Rose & McKinley, 2017). Japan is using HE internationalization efforts to increase funding to their institutions from international student recruitment. Similarly, the Chinese government is largely fueling the internationalization efforts in China's HE campuses via Ministry of Education funding and goals/assessment. Currently, Chinese universities compete with each other using English courses and offering curriculum in English to draw international students (Zha et al., 2019). Differently, in 2010, Kazakhstan, a peripheral HE nation, invested substantially in an international university by creating the Nazarbayev University (NU) as the flagship university of the country. NU touts close partnerships with University of Wisconsin-Madison, Cambridge, and the National University of Singapore. Faculty members at NU are largely expatriates who come from approximately 40 different countries (Lee & Kuzhabekova, 2017). Finally, Indian government's National Education Policy (NEP) 2020 seeks to promote internationalization in many different ways, including, to name a few, Indian HEIs offering internationally relevant curricula, global standards education at a relatively low cost, and permitting foreign universities to operate in India (Deb, 2020). In other words, academic mobility is racialized in that some parts of the world are trying to curb flow out of their national borders and draw more people in. Whiteness thus colonizes the aspirations and investments of HE stakeholders as all these actors aspire toward White norms, such as adopting English/liberal arts coursework, recruitment of White bodies, and/or international partnerships. Internationalization initiatives thus "orientates bodies [governments] in specific directions, affecting how they 'take up' space, and what they 'can do'" (Ahmed, 2007, p. 149).

Malleable Whiteness confers White bodies (i.e., institutions) with global privilege to be mobile around the world. As Ahmed (2007) reminds us, Whiteness informing a global arena can be discerned by the "repetition of the passing by of some bodies and not others" (p. 159). As we will demonstrate next, Whiteness shapes the mobility of material resources such as programs or institutions that cut across borders to deliver education and training. Cross-border HE initiatives exemplify Whiteness as aspirations, investments, and malleability in global HE. Over 300 IBCs operate around the world (Cross-Border Education Research Team [C-BERT], 2020). While IBCs are mainly hosted in Asian countries, the home campuses themselves are situated predominantly in White regions. Approximately 74% of IBCs were administered from institutions based in White countries, with English-speaking countries predominating (C-BERT, 2020). Comparatively, China (14%), United Arab Emirates (11%), Singapore (5%), Malaysia (4.5%), and Qatar (3.6%) are the top five host countries for IBCs. The top two exporting countries—the United States and the United Kingdom (the Whitest of Whiteness)—are the source for nearly 43% of the world's total IBCs while only hosting 1.6% and 3% of the world's international campuses respectively. France, Russia, and Australia round out the top five, exporting 38, 29, and 20 international campuses respectively. IBCs are located in host countries where English is not the official language. Most of the branch campuses situated in non-White regions are mostly from Anglophone world, that is, the United States and United Kingdom (though it has somewhat changed recently), highlighting how IBCs represent Whiteness as aspirations with local flavors. In short, White HEIs can easily expand to nations on the periphery through IBCs, as the latter, given the barriers they face, seek to integrate their HE systems more fully into the global education community (Mackie, 2019), by investing in Whiteness and making Whiteness reachable through IBCs.

IBCs help expand Whiteness's outreach. For instance, White nations, such as Britain, invest in emerging major powers, such as China, through branch campuses to ensure future markets (Feng, 2013, p. 472). Furthermore, the UAE expanded its private HE options in the last decade with the American University of Sharjah (AUS), the American

University of Dubai (AUD), the University of Wollongong, and more recently the opening of the Harvard-affiliated Dubai School of Government and NYU Abu Dhabi (Vora, 2015, p. 22). Such IBCs help White HEIs and their partners to increase brand recognition, global rankings, and provide more cosmopolitan educational experiences for their students (Wilkins & Juusola, 2018; Vora, 2015). Through IBCs, Whiteness's dominance into the future is protected, as White institutions provide global currency to locales.

IBCs, indeed, are investments in Whiteness because IBCs require paying hefty set-up costs and consultation fees, and importing non-native expert labor (as we discussed earlier). Governments such as China, Qatar, UAE, Kazakhstan, Turkey, and Singapore invest in international branch campuses, while a local university or a city usually becomes the IBC sponsor (Deb, 2020; Feng, 2013; Lee & Kuzhabekova, 2017; Mackie, 2019; Seggie & Calikoglu, 2021; Vora, 2015). For instance, NYU Shanghai was set up in 2012 as a collaboration between NYU and East China Normal University, with funding from the city of Shanghai and the district of Pudong. Yale-NUS, a liberal arts college, was set up through collaboration between Yale University and the National University of Singapore (Deb, 2020). Many new initiatives are taking place to erect branch campuses within domestic circles to help curb outward mobility. For instance, India's recent Internationalization at Home policy, seeks to center foreign HE providers within the HE sector (Deb, 2020). Such non-White regions seek to or have invested in Whiteness because they see the power of Whiteness to attract future student customers.

Why do local subjects invest in IBCs? Tied to internationalization initiatives, IBCs offer non-White actors seeking global aspirations the most convenient way to access and fulfill Whiteness aspirations in global HE. Non-White subjects pursue Whiteness through IBCs as precautionary practices to help prepare for the global economy, such as remedying the increased demand for HE, or boost their own knowledge economies with a skilled labor force. As such, in the Middle East, IBCs are part of state incentives to diversify away from finite oil wealth into knowledge-based economies (Vora, 2015). Many countries find it more attractive to host branch campuses of foreign public and private universities than to invest in the physical and human infrastructure needed for an expanded domestic HE sector (Knight, 2018). Furthermore, IBCs are seen as an entry point to quality education, English and other skills needed to be globally competitive, and national capacity building (Vora, 2015, 21). In short, Whiteness becomes the convenient means to remedy domestic issues, and as such, Whiteness becomes malleable and fits into such diverse contexts.

Tied to mobility of resources is the recent resurgence of education hubs that help make Whiteness reachable, given its malleability. An education hub is a concerted effort by a country, zone, or city to assemble a critical mass of local and international actors to support its efforts to build the HE sector, expand the talent pool, or contribute to the knowledge economy (Knight, 2018; Lee, 2014, 2015). C-BERT (2020) lists the following major global education hubs: United Arab Emirates (including Dubai Knowledge Park—Dubai International Academic City), Bahrain, Malaysia (Kuala Lumpur Education City, Iskandar), Singapore (Global Schoolhouse), Qatar (Education City), Republic of

Panama (City of Knowledge), and South Korea (Jeju Global Education City). All these education hubs have opened up in non-White regions, such as in the Arabian Gulf (UAE, Qatar), Africa (Botswana), and Asia (Hong Kong, Malaysia, Singapore, Korea) (Knight, 2018; Lee, 2014, 2015), which we would argue allows Whiteness to be reachable in geopolitical centers of the world. Furthermore, cities around the world are branding themselves as education or knowledge cities, such as Panama City, Bangalore in India, and Monterey in Mexico (Knight, 2018). For instance, over the last 10 or 15 years, Panama's City of Knowledge—an academic–economic free zone located in the former Panama Canal Zone—has undertaken several bold initiatives, including the establishment of a "Techno Park" that provides infrastructure and services to research and technology companies, houses many regional offices of international government organizations, and hosts foreign universities' international programs and one branch campus (i.e., Florida State University) (Altbach & Svenson, 2019; Knight, 2018). Hence, education hubs become the new imperial frontiers of Whiteness, whereby non-White actors partake in geopolitics of knowledge by mobilizing resources from elsewhere to establish knowledge centers privileging Whiteness. Education hubs help non-White actors to create concentrated areas of Whiteness to be consumed, in terms of knowledge, institutions, and gateways to the global economy.

CONCLUDING REMARKS

Our chapter highlights the complex interplay of race and racism informing globalization of HE, namely Whiteness. While we acknowledge that the geopolitical configurations of global HE are changing (e.g., Asia rising in global university rankings or mobility influxes), nevertheless we do not see Whiteness as futurity as something that can be quickly fixed. Such complexity also raises certain tensions in academic scholarship, namely tied to a modern onto-epistemic grammar, such as providing alternatives, accounting for agency, and/or future research directions.

By deliberately engaging the superstructure, we forgo the comfort that analyses of progress provide and instead invite the reader to sit with the complexity of now. And while an analysis of global subjects' agency can be a worthwhile scholarly endeavor, this is not our aim. Furthermore, agency doesn't necessarily entail resistance or subversion, but more often than not, conformity to large cultural scripts (Flaherty, 2012), in our case, Whiteness. We also recognize how admonitions toward agency reinscribe Enlightenment values.

While any deep analysis of race and racism invites complex intellectual projects, we will briefly share three directions. First, our analysis suggests examining the racialization process to go beyond national containers and examine the interplay between race and racism across scales, and their heterogeneous relations. For instance, it involves looking at the way subjects are jockeying for global positioning in a field of Whiteness (e.g., China's Belt and Road initiative). Second, we need to critically examine "future-facing" policies and practices in HE to see how they reproduce Whiteness. As such, we would recommend drawing on Black radical thought and/or anticolonial and antiracist social theory to imagine new analytics and methodologies for studying future-facing policies and practices. We also need to understand globalization of HE from the question of social difference, and how such social difference acts as transnational forces. Finally, we can examine the question of resistance to Whiteness but understand how they can also be forms of complicity to Whiteness as malleable. Empirical researchers could examine their own Whiteness assumptions (e.g., deficit notions of the Other and/or linear progress) as they research current HE practices and policies and so on.

However, we need to be wary of critical intellectual endeavors as they are fraught with tensions and contradictions within academia. Ultimately, we need to change our relationship with the contents and frames themselves, tied to a modern onto-epistemic grammar, in ways that they no longer define our existence or allocate our aspirations and investments. We need to move beyond changing our ways of knowing and embrace changing our ways of being (Shahjahan et al., 2017). The globalization of education field needs to challenge its own complicity in its underlying modern onto-epistemic grammar (see Shahjahan, 2019; Stein, 2017), by not only unpacking the geo/body politics of its own canonical thought but also when speaking of and using alternative and "Southern" perspectives. This amplification of possibilities requires, as Santos (2007) and Andreotti et al. (2018) state, an alternative way to *think about* and *be with* alternatives, in the field of globalization of education, that welcomes us first to the edge and then invites us beyond the abyss.

NOTES

1. By subjects, we are referring to actors (individual or collective entities) who are not self-contained entities driving their own agency or sense of self, but embody agency in relation to larger discursive and material forces. In other words, a subject is a form of personhood that is made in relation to others. Consequently, subjectivity refers to a state of being, or a subject's way of being that is fluid and relational, rather than something that is fixed or something one possesses (Nealon & Giroux, 2012).
2. By onto-epistemic grammar, we mean a dominant set of rules or assumptions structuring ways of knowing/being, derivative of coloniality/modernity, that defines what is real, ideal, desirable, and knowable. Such a grammar entails anthropocentrism, rationality, naïve realism, logocentrism, linearity, and singular notions of progress (material accumulation, social mobility, economic growth, and/or self-determination) (see Shahjahan, 2019; Shahjahan et al., 2017; Stein, 2017).
3. It is beyond the scope of this chapter for us to provide a theoretical genealogy of our Whiteness as Futurity framework. However, briefly, our framework derives concepts/vocabulary from various disciplines, and theoretical approaches ranging from more sociological structuralist accounts (such as world systems theory, decolonial thought, sociology of race studies, Black Marxism), to temporal accounts (concepts such as futurity and anticipation logics), and cultural studies accounts (from communication and media studies to feminist theories). As such, given the interdisciplinary root of our framework, we use a

variety of concepts in this chapter to highlight the manifestation of Whiteness as futurity, using terms such as subjectivity, imaginaries, fields, capital, and/or bodies, to name a few, to illuminate the ways in which Whiteness informs globalization of HE.

REFERENCES

Ahmed, S. (2007). A phenomenology of whiteness. *Feminist Theory*, 8(2), 149–168. doi:10.1177/1464700107078139

Ahmed, S. (2016). *On being included: Racism and diversity in institutional life*. Duke University Press.

Altbach, P., & Knight, J. (2007). The internationalization of higher education: Motivations and realities. *Journal of Studies in International Education*, 11(3–4), 290–305.

Altbach, P., & Svenson. N. (2019). Panama: Higher education is key. *International Higher Education*, 97, 23–25. doi:10.6017/ihe.2019.97.10789

Andreotti, V., Stein, S., Sutherland, A., Pashby, K., Susa, R., & Amsler, S. (2018). Mobilising different conversations about global justice in education: Toward alternative futures in uncertain times. *Policy & Practice: A Development Education Review*, 26, 9–41.

Appadurai, A. (1996). *Modernity at large: Cultural dimensions of globalisation* (Vol. 1). University of Minnesota Press.

Bae, S., Grimm, A., & Kim, D. (2021). Only one way to be a world-class university? Comparative analysis on the texts and visual images on websites of universities in China and South Korea. *Asia Pacific Journal of Education*, 43(1), 144–159. doi:10.1080/02188791.2021.1904832

Balabantaray, S. (2020). Impact of Indian cinema on culture and creation of world view among youth: A sociological analysis of Bollywood movies. *Journal of Public Affairs*, 22(2), e2405. doi:10.1002/pa.2405

Baldwin, A. (2012). Whiteness and futurity: Towards a research agenda. *Progress in Human Geography*, 36(2), 172–187. https://doi.org/10.1177/0309132511414603

Brown, P., Lauder, H., & Ashton, D. (2011). *The global auction*. Oxford University Press.

Burford, J., Eppolite, M., Koompraphant, G., & Uerpairojkit, T. (2021). Narratives of "stuckness" among north–south academic migrants in Thailand: Interrogating normative logics and global power asymmetries of transnational academic migration. *Higher Education*, 82(4), 731–774. doi:10.1007/s10734-020-00672-6

Cai, L., & Hall, C. (2016). Motivations, expectations, and experiences of expatriate academic staff on an international branch campus in China. *Journal of Studies in International Education*, 20(3), 207–222. doi:10.1177/1028315315623055

Cantwell, B., & Kauppinen, I. (Eds). (2014). *Academic capitalism in the age of globalization*. Johns Hopkins University Press.

Cantwell, B., & Maldonado-Maldonado, A. (2009). Four stories: Confronting contemporary ideas about globalisation and internationalisation in higher education. *Globalisation, Societies and Education*, 7(3), 289–306.

Chatterjee, S., & Barber, K. (2021). Between "here-now" and "there-then": The West and Asia's colonial entanglements in international higher education. *Higher Education*, 81(2), 221–239. doi:10.1007/s10734-020-00538-x

Cross-Border Education Research Team (C-BERT). (2020). *C-BERT international campus listing* [Data originally collected by Kevin Kinser and Jason E. Lane]. C-BERT. http://cbert.org/resources-data/intl-campus/

Cheng, M. (2021, February 22). Shifting trends in international student mobility: Embracing diversity and responding to change. *Trends & Insights.* https://www.nafsa.org/professional-resources/research-and-trends/shifting-trends-international-student-mobility-embracing

Christian, M. (2019). A global critical race and racism framework: Racial entanglements and deep and malleable whiteness. *Sociology of Race and Ethnicity, 5*(2), 169–185.

Deb, P. (2020). Vision for foreign universities in the National Education Policy 2020: A critique (Report). *Rajiv Gandhi Institute for Contemporary Studies.* https://www.rgics.org/wp-content/uploads/Foreign-Universities-in-India-Palash-Deb.pdf

Dyer, R. (1997). *White.* Routledge.

Estera, A., & Shahjahan, R. A. (2019). Globalizing whiteness? Visually re/presenting students in global university rankings websites. *Discourse: Studies in the Cultural Politics of Education, 40*(6), 930–945. https://doi.org/10.1080/01596306.2018.14537 81

Feng, Y. (2013). University of Nottingham Ningbo China and Xi'an Jiaotong-Liverpool University: Globalization of higher education in China. *Higher Education, 65*(4), 471–485. doi:10.1007/s10734-012-9558-8

Flaherty, M. (2012). Age and agency: Time work across the life course. *Time & Society, 22*(2), 237–253. doi:10.1177/0961463X12455598

Fomunyan, K. G. (2017). Decolonising the engineering curriculum in a South African university of technology. *International Journal of Applied Engineering Research, 12*(7), 6797–6805.

Huang, F. (2017). Who are they and why did they move to Japan? An analysis of international faculty at universities. Center for Global Higher Education working paper, 27. https://www.researchcghe.org/publications/working-paper/who-are-they-and-why-did-they-move-to-japan-an-analysis-of-international-faculty-at-universities/

Institute of International Education (IIE). (2018). A world on the move: Trends in global student mobility. IIE Center for Academic Mobility Research and Impact, no. 2, 1–18.

Islam, M. (2019). Bangladeshi young students' mobility for higher education and their relations to (un)employment and (un)employability. Paper presented at the Fourth Annual Conference on Social Research, Bangladesh, November 2, 2019, 1–6.

Kim, D., Yoo, S., Sohn, H., & Sonneveldt, E. (2021). The segmented mobility of globally mobile academics: A case study of foreign professors at a Korean university. *Compare: A Journal of Comparative and International Education, 52*(8), 1–18. doi:10.1080/03057925.2020.1860737

Kim, S. (2016). Western faculty "flight risk" at a Korean university and the complexities of internationalisation in Asian higher education. *Comparative Education, 52*(1), 78–90. doi:10.1080/03050068.2015.1125620

King, R., Marginson, S., & Naidoo, R. (Eds.). (2012). *Handbook on globalization and higher education.* Edward Elgar.

Knight, J. (2018). International education hubs. In P. Meusburger, M. Heffernan, & L. Suarsana (Eds.), *Geographies of the University* (pp. 637–655). Springer. doi:10.1007/978-3-319-75593-9_21

Koshino, K (2019). Tempted by Whiteness?: Linguistic capital and higher education in Japan. *The Journal of Educational Foundations, 32*(1–4), 49–71.

Lee, J. (2014). Education hubs and talent development: Policymaking and implementation challenges. *Higher Education, 68*(6), 807–823.

Lee, J. (2015). The regional dimension of education hubs: Leading and brokering geopolitics. *Higher Education Policy, 28,* 69–89. doi.org/10.1057/hep.2014.32

Lee, J. (2020). Neo-racism and the criminalization of China. *Journal of International Students, 10*(4), i–vi. https://doi.org/10.32674/jis.v10i4.2929

Lee, J., & Kuzhabekova, A. (2017). Reverse flow in academic mobility from core to periphery: Motivations of international faculty working in Kazakhstan. *Higher Education, 76*(2), 369–386. doi:10.1007/s10734-017-0213-2

Lee, J., & Rice, C. (2007) Welcome to America? Perceptions of neo-racism and discrimination among international students. *Higher Education, 53*, 381–409. https://doi.org/10.1007/s10734-005-4508-3

Lee, J., & Stensaker, B. (2021). Research on internationalisation and globalisation in higher education—Reflections on historical paths, current perspectives and future possibilities. *European Journal of Education, 56*(2), 157–168. doi.org/10.1111/ejed.12448

Lipsitz, G. (2006). *The possessive investment in Whiteness: How White people profit from identity politics.* Temple University Press.

Mackie, C. (2019). Transnational education and globalization: A look into the complex environment of international branch campuses. *World Education News and Reviews.* https://wenr.wes.org/2019/05/the-complex-environment-of-international-branch-campuses

Marginson, S. (2012). Imagining the global. In R. King, S. Marginson, & R. Naidoo (Eds.), *Handbook on globalization and higher education* (pp. 10–39). Edward Elgar.

Mendoza, C., Staniscia, B., & Ortiz, A. (2019). "Knowledge migrants" or "economic migrants"? Patterns of academic mobility and migration from Southern Europe to Mexico. *Population, Space and Place, 26*(2), e2282. doi:10.1002/psp.2282

Miao, S. (2020). Internationalization of African Higher education from a critical lens: A literature review. Unpublished manuscript, Michigan State University.

Mills, C. W. (2020). The chronopolitics of racial time. *Time & Society, 29*(2), 297–317. https://doi.org/10.1177/0961463x20903650

Mulvey, B. (2021). Conceptualizing the discourse of student mobility between "periphery" and "semi-periphery": The case of Africa and China. *Higher Education, 81*(3), 437–451. doi:10.1007/s10734-020-00549-8

Nealon, J., & Giroux, S. (2012). Theory toolbox. In *Critical concepts for the humanities, arts, and social sciences* (2nd ed.). Rowman & Littlefield.

OECD. (2020). *Education at a glance 2020: OECD indicators.* OECD. doi:10.1787/69096873-en

Peters, M. (2020) China's belt and road initiative: Reshaping global higher education *Educational Philosophy and Theory, 52*(6), 586–592. doi:10.1080/00131857.2019.1615174

Pfaff-Czarnecka, J. (2020). Shaping Asia through student mobilities. *American Behavioral Scientist, 64*(10), 1400–1414. doi:10.1177/0002764220947753

Ress, S. (2019). *Internationalization of higher education for development: Blackness and postcolonial solidarity in Africa-Brazil relations.* Bloomsbury.

Reynolds, P. (2014). Representing "U": Popular culture, media, and higher education. *ASHE Higher Education Report, 40*(4), 1–145. doi:10.1002/aehe.20016

Robertson, S., & Komljenovic, J. (2016). Non-state actors and the advance of frontier higher education markets in the Global South. *Oxford Review of Education, 42*(5), 594–611. doi:10.1080/03054985.2016.1224302

Rose, H., & McKinley, J. (2017). Japan's English-medium instruction initiatives and the globalization of higher education. *Higher Education, 75*(1), 111–129. doi:10.1007/s10734-017-0125-1

Schöpf, C. (2020). The coloniality of global knowledge production: Theorizing the mechanisms of academic dependency. *Social Transformations: Journal of the Global South, 8*(2), 5. doi:10.13185/3372

Seggie, N., & Calikoglu, A. (2021). Changing patterns of international academic mobility: The experiences of Western-origin faculty members in Turkey. *Compare: A Journal of Comparative and International Education, 53*(1), 1–18. doi:10.1080/03057925.2020.1868975

Shahjahan, R. A. (2019). From "geopolitics of being" towards inter-being: Envisioning the "in/visibles" in the globalization of higher education. *Youth and Globalization*, *1*(2), 282–306. https://doi.org/10.1163/25895745-00102005

Shahjahan, R. A., Blanco, G., & Andreotti, V. (2017). Attempting to imagine the unimaginable: A decolonial reading of global university rankings. *Comparative Education Review*, *61*(S1), S51–S73. https://doi.org/10.1086/ 690457

Shahjahan, R, A., & Edwards, K. T. (2022). Whiteness as futurity and globalization of higher education. *Higher Education*, *83*(4), 747–764. doi:10.1007/s10734-021-00702-x

Shahjahan, R. A., & Kezar, A. (2013). Beyond the "national container": Methodological nationalism and higher education research. *Educational Researcher*, *42*(1), 20–29. https:// doi.org/ 10.3102/0013189x12 463050

Sidhu, R. (2006). *Universities and globalization: to market, to market.* Lawrence Erlbaum Associates.

Sidhu, R., & Ishikawa, M. (2020). Destined for Asia: Hospitality and emotions in international student mobilities. *Compare: A Journal of Comparative and International Education*, *52*(3), 399–417. doi:10.1080/03057925.2020.1771544

Sousa Santos, B. (2007). Beyond abyssal thinking: From global lines to ecologies of knowledges. *Revista Critica de Ciencias Sociais*, *80*(June 29). http://www.eurozine.com/articles/2007-06-29-santos-en.html

Stack, M. (2016). *Global university rankings and the mediatization of higher education.* Palgrave MacMillan. doi:10.1057/9781137475954

Stack, M. (2020). Academic stars and university rankings in higher education: Impacts on policy and practice. *Policy Reviews in Higher Education*, *4*(1), 4–24.

Stein, S. (2017). Internationalization for an uncertain future: Tensions, paradoxes, and possibilities. *The Review of Higher Education*, *41*(1), 3–32. https://doi.org/10.1353/rhe.2017.0031

Stein, S., & Andreotti, V. (2017). Higher education and the modern/colonial global imaginary. *Cultural Studies↔Critical Methodologies*, *17*(3), 173–181. https:// doi.org/ 10. 1177/ 15327 08616 672673

Suspitsyna, T. (2021). Internationalization, whiteness, and biopolitics of higher education. *Journal of International Students*, *11*(S1), 50–67.

Takeda, A. (2020). Transnational mobility to South Korea among Japanese students: When popular culture meets international education. *Asian Anthropology*, *19*(4), 273–290. doi:10.1080/1683478X.2020.1730029

Tight, M. (2021). Globalization and internationalization as frameworks for higher education research. *Research Papers in Education*, *36*(1), 52–74.

Vora, N. (2015). Is the university universal? Mobile (re)constitutions of American academia in the Gulf Arab states. *Anthropology & Education Quarterly*, *46*(1), 19–36. doi:10.1111/aeq.12085

Wilkins, S., & Juusola, K. (2018). The benefits and drawbacks of transnational higher education: Myths and realities. *Australian Universities' Review*, *60*(2), 68–76.

Winberg, S., & Winberg, C. (2017). Using a social justice approach to decolonize an engineering curriculum. *2017 IEEE Global Engineering Education Conference* (EDUCON). doi:10.1109/educon.2017.7942855

Xiang, B., & Shen, W. (2009). International student migration and social stratification in China. *International Journal of Educational Development*, *29*(5), 513–522.

Yao, C. W., Mwangi, C. A., & Brown, V. K. (2019). Exploring the intersection of transnationalism and critical race theory: A critical race analysis of international student experiences in

the United States. *Race Ethnicity and Education*, 22(1), 38–58. https://doi.org/10.1080/13613
324. 2018 14979 68

Zha, Q., Wu, H., & Hayhoe, R. (2019). Why Chinese universities embrace internationalization: An exploration with two case studies. *Higher Education*, 78(4), 669–686. doi:10.1007/
s10734-019-00364-w

SECTION III

Systems Theory, Globalization, and Education

CHAPTER 16

EDUCATION IN A FUNCTIONALLY DIFFERENTIATED WORLD SOCIETY

RAF VANDERSTRAETEN

Introduction

This chapter will provide a reflection on the function of education in world society. It will build upon a sociological line of reasoning for which labels such as functionalism and systems theory are often used. As any other important sociological tradition, functionalism and systems theory have in the past attracted much criticism. At the same time, much has also been accomplished within this line of sociological thinking. The aim of this chapter is to build upon the accomplishments and indicate ways in which the position and the function of education within society can be approached critically, both historically and contemporary. The following analyses and reflections particularly rely on the work of the German sociologist Niklas Luhmann, who, arguably, has made the most important contributions to sociological systems theory and related traditions in recent history.

Our point of departure is an "un-functional" account of education that Luhmann provided. On the one hand, Luhmann argued that modern society comprises a variety of function systems. He put education on his list of important function systems, next to several other systems: politics, law, the military, the economy, science, the family (and intimate relations), art, medicine, religion, and so on (Luhmann, 2017, pp. 793–798). On the other hand, however, Luhmann also questioned whether this arrangement "worked" or "works." Historically, he once argued, education expanded at a relatively late moment in history. It is only after the differentiation of function systems for politics, economics, religion, and, in part, also for science that the prospects for education began to change.

With his typical irony, however, he also expressed his doubts about the "systemness" or functionality of this arrangement: "As with the completion of a puzzle, the pieces that have already been differentiated (from the others) have a suggestive influence on what can possibly and must necessarily be connected to them. But, unlike with a puzzle, it is not certain from the outset that a complete picture will be produced or that it will be understandable as a whole" (Luhmann & Schorr, 1988, p. 24).

Perhaps it might be said that modern society imagines itself as a system—well regulated, carefully planned, and responsibly engineered. But Luhmann did not think of systems as entities that (try to) control everything inside themselves. He rather used the notion of system as an epistemological device to look at the distinctions between systems and their environments. In this sense, his systems theory can be used to think against the "system," to look at issues and questions, which typically fall outside the scope of the dominant framework in functionalist sociology. Luhmann's contributions on the system of education, which were published in a period of about 20 years, from the mid-1970s until the mid-1990s, can also be understood from this point of view. These contributions draw attention to difference instead of unity, to "heterarchy" instead of hierarchy, to messiness instead of orderliness. They are here taken as a point of departure for analyses of both the rise of the education system in modern society and the position it has acquired in contemporary world society.

Apart from an introduction and conclusion, this chapter consists of six steps. To outline the basic characteristics of a functionalist perspective on education, I hereafter first present an overview of Talcott Parsons's classic (but also habitually rejected) functionalist perspective on society and its system of education. Next, I focus on some of the foundations of Luhmann's theoretical framework, especially the distinction between system and environment. Afterward, I turn to analyses of the system of education. In historical perspective, I look both at the institutionalization of inclusion imperatives and the "upgrading" of the public (children, students) in the education system, and at the relatively low social status of teaching and the claims that teaching constitutes a "semi-profession." I then discuss the recent rapid growth of participation in higher education and the appropriateness of present-day characterizations of world society as "schooled society" (e.g., Baker, 2014; Schofer et al., 2021). I conclude with more general reflections on the social function of education and also indicate how the rapid expansion of higher education changes the "puzzle" of world society.

System and Structure

Talcott Parsons was a towering figure in the social sciences in the period after World War II. He explicitly built upon a variety of sources, including the works of Emile Durkheim and Max Weber. But his frame of reference became itself also very influential; several concepts, including those of system, structure, and function, would not have the sociological currency they now possess without the distinctiveness of their employment by Parsons. It is therefore useful to start our reflection on the function of education in world society with a discussion of the ways in which Parsons conceived of functional differentiation and the societal function of education.

To grasp the particularities of this frame of reference, it is important to note that Parsons defined his viewpoint as "analytical realism." Already in his early work, he stressed that "facts" are never simply "observations," but statements about experiences in the terms of a specific conceptual scheme that provides a meaningful ordering of these experiences (1937, p. 730).[1] In Parsons's own view, his task consisted in building conceptual schemes that researchers could reliably use. The frame of reference, which he tried to articulate, was in his view the most general framework of concepts or categories in terms of which empirical scientific work could "make sense." It had to serve as a point of departure that was grounded in reality and that could be continuously tested against reality. For Parsons, this frame of reference could best be articulated in terms of systems theory. In the preface to *The Social System*, Parsons specified that this frame had to bring together "the main outlines of a conceptual scheme for the analysis of the structure and processes of social systems" (1951, p. vii).

On this basis, Parsons aimed to develop a general systems theory applicable within all of the social and behavioral sciences. He considered his general analytic model suitable for the analysis of all types of social units, from small, primary groups to entire societies. Within this theoretical model, the idea of "system needs" played a central role. His theory detailed the needs that had to be met if a social system were to survive. In his later work, this model was identified by the acronym AGIL, from the first initial of each of the four basic needs. Parsons distinguished between the system needs of Adaptation (the problem of adapting to the environment and acquiring sufficient resources), Goal attainment (the problem of setting and implementing goals), Integration (the problem of maintaining solidarity or coordination among the subunits of the system), and Latency (the problem of creating, preserving, and transmitting the system's distinctive culture and values). According to Parsons, all types of social systems had to satisfy these four basic needs. Complex systems, however, tend to differentiate along the lines of this frame; the functional imperatives (or "system needs") generate the fault lines along which system differentiation occurs (e.g., Parsons & Platt, 1973).

More details of this model of "system needs" can be found in his analyses of single subsystems. In *Economy and Society*, for example, which is the first of a series of publications devoted to major societal subsystems, the economy is defined as "a special type of social system. It is a functional sub-system of the more inclusive society, differentiated from other sub-systems by specialisation in the society's adaptive function" (Parsons & Smelser, 1956, p. 306). As part of the larger society, its primary function is the solution of the adaptive problems of society (as opposed to the problems related to other "system needs"). At the same time, it has to be bound by other system needs. As a differentiated subsystem within the larger system, Parsons and Smelser added, "the economy, like any social system, exchanges inputs and outputs over its boundaries with its situation. The most important part of the situation for the economy consists of the other cognate functional sub-systems of the same society and the institutionalised value system of the society" (1956, p. 307). Parsons's model thus put stress on the compatibility of the different subsystems of society and the ways in which the interchanges between all units are regulated and controlled. As a social system, society was in the first place characterized by relatively stable internal structures and subunits.

In later publications on other societal subsystems, including education, Parsons likewise tended to stress the function of the parts for the whole and the interchanges among the different parts of the system (e.g., Parsons & Platt, 1973). With regard to socialization and education, Parsons pointed, more particularly, to two types of social systems: families and schools. By and large, these two types of systems had to correspond with two phases in the entire process: primary socialization takes in this view place in the family, where newcomers learn in the first place the "particular" values of their family and community, while secondary socialization through the school should acquaint them more strongly with society's "universalistic" value orientations (e.g., Parsons, 1959). Parsons did not expect stark tensions between both systems; he rather stated that the family and the school system "have similar functions" (Parsons & Bales, 1955, p. 399). In modern society, he also maintained, "the school class may be regarded as the focal socializing agency," although "probably the most fundamental condition underlying this process is the sharing of common values by the two adult agencies involved—the family and the school" (Parsons, 1959, p. 298, p. 309).[2] The modern family had to be an important "support system" for the modern school organizations.

Moreover, Parsons also used advances in the fulfilment of specific "system needs" to characterize the evolution of modern society. *The American University*, for example, which is the last monograph he saw into print, starts with the statement that the "development of modern society included three processes of revolutionary structural change: the Industrial Revolution, the Democratic Revolution, and the Educational Revolution" (Parsons & Platt, 1973, p. 1). Parsons here linked the transformation of modern society with successes at the level of different function systems—first the economy (A), then the political system (G), and, finally, starting in the 20th century in the United States, the expansion of higher education and the value complex supported by it (L). "Compared to previous stages in the development of Western society, the educational revolution upgrades cultural interests relative to economic and political interests" (Parsons & Platt, 1973, p. 224). For Parsons, this development not only meant that "higher" system needs had been able to take the lead but also that the functional differentiation of society had been consolidated and its "systemness" improved.

As already indicated, Parsons's frame of reference triggered much resistance, especially during the "critical" 1960s and 1970s. His ideas of "systemness" were close to ideas of order, control, hierarchy, and regulated interchanges between the different subunits of society. His theory came to stand for an ideological commitment to the "system" (and especially to that of the American society of his time). It became a placeholder for the kind of perspective that was not to be pursued in the social sciences. In this "critical" era, his monograph on *The American University* did almost never receive serious attention (Vanderstraeten, 2014). Many of the references to this and other work of Parsons rather became ritualistic ones, intended to dismiss systems theory altogether. With Parsons's work, the concept of system also fell into disrepute in the social sciences.

It seems fair to say that the relative lack of response to the writings of Luhmann is an echo of the strong reactions against Parsons's frame of reference as well as against some of the applied forms of "systems engineering" that took shape in this period. In the following sections, I will, however, try to illustrate why Niklas Luhmann had good reasons to return to systems theory and why it today may still make sense to recur to systems theory in analyses of education.

SYSTEM AND LOOSE COUPLING

To situate Luhmann's approach, and distinguish it from the approaches of his predecessors, including Parsons, it is helpful to start with his view on the meaning and reality of (social) systems. Luhmann, who was in the 1960s a student of Parsons at Harvard University, took a stance to Parsons's analytical realism. The oft-cited first sentence of the first chapter of Luhmann's *Social Systems* says: "The following considerations assume that there are systems" (1995, p. 12). But in the introduction to this monograph, Luhmann also maintained something slightly different. "Thus the statement 'there are systems' says only that there are objects of research that exhibit features justifying the use of the concept of system, just as, conversely, this concept serves to abstract facts that from this viewpoint can be compared with each other and with other kinds of facts within the perspective of same/different" (1995, p. 2). The claim that systems exist relates to "objects of research," but these objects come into view only when the claim is made, because the concept system gives one the means to make the systems visible. Rather than an exercise in analytical realism, Luhmann conceived of systems theory as a mode of second-order observation, which had to undergo detailed empirical tests (Rasch, 2000, pp. 72–73; Vanderstraeten, 2001; von Foerster, 1984).

How did Luhmann describe the reality that emerges with the reality of systems? In a relatively early, programmatic article, which sketches the outlines of a theory of modern society, Luhmann started by stating that significant gains can be made by applying new paradigms of systems theory: "The most important contribution of systems theory has been a change in the conceptual framework in terms of which systems are conceived and analysed. General systems theory, as well as cybernetics, replaced the classical conceptual model of a whole that consists of parts and relations between parts by a model that focused on the difference between system and environment" (1977, p. 30). My intention (in this text), he added, "is to use the distinction of system and environment to work out a theory of system differentiation for the social system of the society" (1977, p. 30). For Luhmann, the concept of system presupposed the concept of environment and vice versa. He consequently did not use the notion of system as a methodological device to look at various manifestations of the "systemness" of modern society: structure and function, hierarchy and order, predictability and control. He was rather interested in forms of loose coupling, noise, and incomprehensibility.

A very similar argument is presented in his late work. In *Theory of Society*, the last book publication he saw into print, Luhmann writes that he intends to understand society "as a system; and the form of the system ... is nothing other than the distinction between system and environment" (2012, p. 40). In the chapter on the differentiation of society, he added: "System differentiation does not mean that the whole is divided into parts and, seen on this level, then consist only of the parts and the 'relations' between the parts. It is rather that every subsystem reconstructs the comprehensive system ... through its own (subsystem-specific) difference between system and environment" (2013, p. 3). In this version, systems theory does away with the traditional (Parsonian) connotations of the concept system. Society is not depicted as an organized social system, which possesses the qualities typically connected with "systemness." Not surprisingly, Luhmann also frequently referred to the cybernetic idea that the whole is less (not more) than the sum of the different parts, and even that any part of the whole is more intelligent than the whole (see Wiener, 1948, p. 162).

Luhmann thus did not depart from a catalogue of system needs, of functions that have to be fulfilled. Function systems crystallize around particular problems. Societal problems, such as the socialization of newcomers, may create opportunities for system formation, and function systems may therefore be defined by the historical conditions of their formation, but, as we will see, these systems may also develop their own dynamics and make their environments dependent on the ways they operate. In this sense, Luhmann also did not depict modern society as a tightly coupled, well-organized system. Social integration depends in his perspective on the way in which the different subsystems are able to regulate their mutual relationships—by developing both specific sensibilities and insensibilities toward their respective environments. Loosely coupled or decoupled systems might thus be dealt with as well-integrated systems, while loose coupling minimizes the problems which the different function systems create for one another (e.g., Luhmann, 2013, pp. 87–108). For Luhmann, functional differentiation gives precedence to horizontal or "heterarchical" relations.

Social changes may hence elicit a variety of consequences in our functionally differentiated society. The introduction of compulsory school attendance in the course of the long 19th century, for example, was a different environmental problem for the economic system, the political system, the religious system, the families, and so on (Vanderstraeten, 2006). As we will see, the rapid expansion of higher education in more recent decades also brings about a range of unforeseen and unexpected consequences, both at the level of society and at that of other subsystems. To address these issues, we now turn to the differentiation of the system of education and the ways in which education has been able to establish itself as function system.

DIFFERENTIATION AND INCLUSION

Luhmann described modern society as functionally differentiated, but he abandoned Parsons's analytical approach and the four-function scheme (AGIL), to which it led, and instead relied on an inductive approach to analyze functional differentiation. Next to several other ones, education appeared on his list of function systems. But how did education constitute itself as a function system? What have been decisive "moments" in this process of system formation? And how does this system make a difference in our functionally differentiated world society?

According to Luhmann, functional differentiation began quite early as a differentiation of social roles. "It gains momentum only when at least two distinct roles organise their complementary expectations around a specific function—for example, clerics and laymen, politicians and the public, or teachers and pupils. This requires the emergence of special roles for receiving services" (1977, p. 35). Next to the emergence of specific professional roles, Luhmann focused attention on the formation of client or public roles, which are complementary to the professional roles. His focus was less on forms of specialization and professionalization as such, but rather on the consequences of the transformation of the client or public roles.[3] Throughout his work on functional differentiation, he placed emphasis on the institutionalization of complementary roles or role expectations for the professionals and their public: roles for politicians and voters in the political system, for doctors and patients in the medical system, for priests and laypeople in the case of religion, and so on.

Luhmann argued, in addition, that functional differentiation was dependent on the differentiation of the rules for inclusion and exclusion in the client or public roles in different function systems. "If the society introduces compulsory school education for everyone, if every person regardless of his being nobleman or commoner, being Christian, Jewish, or Moslem, being infant or adult, is subject to the same legal status, if 'the public' is provided with a political function as electorate, if every individual is acknowledged as choosing or not choosing a religious commitment; and if everybody can buy everything and pursue every occupation, given the necessary resources, then the whole system shifts in the direction of functional differentiation" (1977, p. 40; see also Luhmann, 2013, pp. 16–27). From this point of view, Luhmann was thus interested in the social mechanisms used to regulate inclusion and participation in different function systems. His take on functional differentiation built upon the idea that different modes of inclusion (and exclusion) would allow these systems to elaborate their own *eigenvalues*—often without coordination with other systems.[4]

For education, such opportunities emerged at a relatively late moment in history, viz. at a moment that social mobility and social complexity had already become high (Luhmann & Schorr, 1988, p. 24). In the 18th and 19th centuries, during which the ideal of "schooling for all" was strongly put forward (as the introduction of compulsory education at many places in the world illustrates), education acquired a new meaning. This "redescription" is probably best known under the title of the invention or discovery of the child (Ariès, 1960). This redescription refers to a social construction process at the completion of which the child is no longer viewed as an incomplete adult who lives in the same world as adults do, who grows into this world and who therefore can be educated (i.e., completed) by adults, but who does not necessarily need education in order to become a human. Instead, the child is held to be a particular type of human being who lives in a particular type of world, who is naturally responsive to education (e.g., by being curious and sensitive), but who also makes education particularly difficult because it lacks good reason and is at the mercy of its own whims and weaknesses. The inclusion of the whole population into the process of education thus became explainable and justifiable, as everyone comes into the world being helpless and everybody is somehow—the question is: how well?—educated by one's environment.

In theoretical terms, the requirement of inclusion allowed for the rise of a generalized conception of the public, viz. a conception that abstracts from the (given) rank characteristics of the family to which the pupils belong, whereas the functional setting and orientation of school organizations allowed for a respecification of this "generalized other." As Luhmann suggested, the education system gradually became able to develop its own distinctions to observe and treat its public. By incorporating and articulating notions, such as "merit," "talent," or "IQ," for example, it increasingly secured its own space for meaningful educational action and decision-making. Such notions were able to fuel the expansion of a broad range of organizational arrangements (see Luhmann, 2002, pp. 111–141; Stichweh, 2016).[5] In this sense, the inclusion regulations also made it possible to underline the need for an appropriate and stimulating educational milieu, for the professionalization of teaching.

These structural changes point to the central importance of school organizations in the system of education. The differentiation of education is fueled by the expansion of school education—and has modified the role expectations with regard to parents and parenting within family contexts. Teachers are currently not just acting *in loco parentis*. Consider, for example, the wide-ranging impact on the family of the temporal organization of the school day and the school year. Consider the impact of homework or (re)marks on report cards. Or consider possible confrontations between the "natural" authority of parents and the "professional" authority of teachers, for example, during parent-teacher consultations in primary and secondary schools. Many other examples can be added (see Tyrell & Vanderstraeten, 2007; Vanderstraeten, 2007). Various processes of "schooling the family" have been triggered by the expansion of school education. While, for Parsons, the family and the school system had to fulfil similar functions for society at large, Luhmann's approach clearly points to the internal differentiation of, and the ensuing tensions within, the education system. The particularities of this system seem more and more defined by school organizations and the kinds of expectations and realities created by these organizations (Vanderstraeten, 2002, 2021).

DIFFERENTIATION AND PROFESSIONALISM

The organization setting also defines professionalization processes in the education system. School teachers are the main actors in this professionalization process—not parents and family education. This focus on teaching and its professionalization has to do with the fact that (almost) everyone can become parent, but that entry into school teaching can be regulated and controlled. Educational credentials are required of anyone who teaches in schools. It should be added, however, that it is often also doubted that teaching possesses the features of a full-fledged profession. Discussions about the social status or prestige of teaching also show that professionalism in teaching is perceived as a desideratum, as something that needs to be accomplished. Compared with doctors or lawyers, for example, teaching is time and again described as a "semi-profession" (e.g., Ingersoll & Collins, 2018; Lortie, 1969, 1975). It is useful to reflect upon this condition, as critical appraisals of teaching often go along with negative assessments of the position of education in society.

In line with much other sociological literature, Luhmann saw the professions as a specific, distinctive group of occupations (Luhmann & Schorr, 1976). They specialize in "people work." They deal with personal problems and risks: health or sickness (medicine), dispute resolution and law-based social order (law), consolation and salvation (religion). As education can also be defined as a form of people work, the status of its practitioners can be compared with that of other professionals.

It should be added that the professions do not simply find their work laid out for them. They rather "co-construct" the problems they deal with in their daily work. As the social psychologist Karl E. Weick argued, for example, physicians "often implant maladies that weren't there when the examination began. Their procedures consolidate numerous free-floating symptoms into the felt presence of a single, more specific, more serious problem" (1979, p. 153). Physicians and other professionals specify "vague" problems as tasks for which they can (and have to) assume responsibility. They make "something" of their clients' problems; they transform these problems into "manageable" tasks and "bearable" obligations, such as the obligation to do what "reasonably" can be done. The professions thus also redefine the boundaries of their territory (Abbott, 1988; Dingwall, 2017).

Seen in this light, several problems connected with people work in education are quite unlike those other professionals are accustomed to. Perhaps most obvious is the fact that most clients are minors. They are not perceived as clients who seek professional help for their personal problems; they are rather perceived as immature people in need of guidance and control. The social prestige of teachers is probably negatively affected by the low social status of children.

Moreover, students mostly exercise no choice about attending school until the age of 16 or 18 and have practically no say about what teacher they will have. They are legally required to attend school; they must be taught by whatever staff member is assigned by the school officials (Dreeben, 1970; Woods, 1990). The obligatory nature of the arrangement means that the students' interest (or lack thereof) plays no part in their disposition: any class will include at least some students who would rather be elsewhere. At the same time, there is considerable compulsion on the other side of the relation, too. Teachers have no formal right to choose or select their students. This arrangement might give teachers a sense of security. Lack of success in their work does not have to result in unemployment or loss of income; poor teachers normally have as many students as good teachers. Under these conditions, however, one also cannot count on the kind of commitment, which can be expected when partners voluntary engage in a (professional) relation.

It can be added that the need for education almost never becomes as urgent as the need for other forms of professional help: in the case of illnesses and injuries, conflicts and controversies, spiritual anguish and remorse. Teachers normally are not confronted with acute needs or risks; they cannot presume that they work with clients who "really" need their services. " 'No one ever died of a split infinitive' is a quip which throws the less-than-vital nature of teaching knowledge into relief" (Lortie, 1969, p. 24). People rather "need" education to the extent that school results determine future career paths. When what has been reached is a necessary condition for going further, pressure to perform well will be put on the starting phase of the career—especially during the early years in schools and at universities. Youngsters are pushed to take control of what is yet to come through what has already been achieved; for example, improving their chances at taking A-levels by choosing "good" schools, or improving their chances on the labor market by obtaining "good" credentials from "good" institutions at an early point in their career.

One might thus conclude that schools produce their own personal problems or crises to motivate their clients: decision moments, like tests and examinations, with consequences for later career transitions. Schools use these crises to motivate students to cooperate and work hard. But the "people work" in school organizations also creates opportunities for professionalization processes. It leads to the need to recruit well-trained teachers, viz. professionals able to handle the demands of people work (Vanderstraeten, 2007; see also Wermke & Salokangas, 2021). Altogether, however, the profession remains tied to the organization—and the social position and prestige of professional work in the education system might therefore be somewhat vulnerable. One might also conclude that the position or status of this system within our contemporary world society is likely to benefit more from an "upgrading" of the role of students, of the inclusion of large publics.

Schooled World Society?

Using a term coined by Lewis Coser (1974), schools can be described as "greedy institutions," while they seem able to extend their grasp on other institutions (Baker, 2014). In line with Luhmann's take on functional differentiation, it might be added that the system of education has become able to export its standards to its social environment. A broad variety of role structures are now coupled with educational outputs and credentials. Because, more particularly, people's career planning has come to rely heavily on education, participation in (higher) education has expanded rapidly and in unprecedented ways. Although school careers certainly do not neatly link up with occupational careers, dominant social structures now stimulate individuals to "go for it" (Labraña & Vanderstraeten, 2020; Vanderstraeten, 1999; Vanderstraeten & Van der Gucht, 2023).

A clear indication of this shift is the fact that expenses for education are now commonly perceived as investments in human capital. From an economic perspective, the "impact" of educational credentials and degrees on the labor market is nowadays unquestionable. Although it can be questioned what students really learn at school, there is little doubt that the labor market has become increasingly organized around educational credentials and that educational credentials now constitute formal requirements for entry into a broad range of occupations (Bills, 2004; Caplan, 2018).

Relevant, too, is the fact that the distinction between high- and low-schooled individuals has acquired special importance. Early school leaving has become a "social problem" precisely at the time when school participation was on the ascent. At the moment when it became more or less self-evident to participate in higher education, it also became problematic *not* to finish school and graduate. In this sense, the "school dropout" became the inverse of the university graduate (Dorn, 1996).[6] This dropout problem is another indication of the growing social belief in education and educational credentials. Early school dropout has increasingly become a *social issue*—and not just an educational one. Individuals who fail to meet the rising educational expectations have come to face severe disadvantages in different social settings, perhaps first of all when they apply for jobs. Formulated somewhat differently: the increasing expectations with regard to "full" inclusion in secondary and higher education have brought about new exclusion problems.

The distinction between the high- and the low-schooled nowadays gains relevance in socio-geographical regard. The shifting expectations regarding education are leading to new forms of geographical segregation and clustering at both ends of the human capital distribution. On the one hand, social and economic geographers now point to the geographically uneven rise of the so-called knowledge economy. It is the "skilled city," which currently flourishes (e.g., Glaeser & Saiz, 2004; Moretti, 2013). The geographical clustering of university graduates has increased markedly; "hubs" or "hot spots," characterized by high concentrations of university graduates, are emerging at the global level. On the other hand, additional analyses also point to the geographical segregation of early school leavers or school dropouts (Vanderstraeten & Van der Gucht, 2023). Geographical segregation and clustering now thus appear at both ends of the human capital distribution. And just as some places and local labor markets have become attractive because of the presence of many high-schooled individuals, other labor markets suffer from the presence of comparatively high shares of "unschooled" individuals. Geographical inequality and educational inequality can now be used as indices of social inequality.[7]

As the preceding comments suggest, participation in education has thus become "a difference which makes a difference" (to use Gregory Bateson's famous dictum). But is it useful to return to the idea of "the educational revolution" and characterize our world society as a "schooled society" (Baker, 2014; Parsons & Platt, 1973)? For sure, never before have so many individuals dedicated so much time, energy, and resources to becoming educated. In just a few generations, school education has, moreover, changed from a special experience for the few into an ordinary one for almost all. At the same time, however, many distinctions produced in the education system remain socially irrelevant, or only gain relevance under conditions that cannot be controlled by the education system itself. The economic value of education, for example, depends very much on specific forms of production and their organization. In other function systems, other distinctions are used to make sense of the world. We are familiar with definitions of society, which highlight the (un-)importance of particular function systems, including "secular society" (religion), "capitalist society" (economy), "democratic society" (politics), and "knowledge society" (science). In various ways, all major function systems leave their mark on world society. Education can now surely be added to this list. Seen from this perspective, however, it also seems clear that educational distinctions have not come to replace or overwrite most other social distinctions. Whether we like it or not, our functionally differentiated world society remains a loosely integrated social system (Luhmann, 2012, 2013).

CONCLUSION

We started this chapter with a brief overview of Parsons's analyses of "system needs" in relation to social differentiation. Parsons built various models of the system of modern societies—with a clear focus on internal aspects of the system: structure and function, hierarchy and control, integration and order. He imagined modern society as a (particular kind of) system—well regulated, carefully planned, and responsibly engineered. The resistance to Parsons's work in much of the sociological literature is certainly part of a broader reaction to these underlying ideas. In the latter decades of the 20th century, it became commonplace to argue that social systems theory was favored by scholars and decision-makers, who shared a belief in the "system."

Despite such a critical climate, Luhmann continued to work within this sociological tradition. But he also distanced himself from Parsons's work and explicitly tried to overcome some of the difficulties associated with Parsons's approach (Vanderstraeten, 2022). Altogether, Luhmann put less emphasis on "systemness," but instead directed attention to the distinction between system and environment and the autonomy of the function systems in the system of modern society.

Building upon Luhmann's approach, we have discussed three different aspects of the differentiation of the education system: inclusion imperatives, professionalization problems, and the rapid global expansion of higher education. As a consequence of the introduction of mandatory schooling and the expansion of school education, people have become able to experience the effects of education in two ways: (Almost) everyone is raised and educated in schools, and (almost) everyone can assume in their contacts with everyone else, that they, too, were raised and educated in schools. Most people are now not only themselves for several years of their life included in school education, but they have also become "consumers" of educational "outputs" (Luhmann & Schorr, 1988, p. 28). They are thus in the position to choose social contacts on the basis of educationally defined (and certified) bits of knowledge, which they can assume to be acquired by themselves and by the others.

Education "functions," one might say, when it includes large populations. It "functions," when it creates a basis for the expectations and actions of others, when people are able to assume that others, with whom they may engage, are educated, too. It now also makes sense to direct attention to specific types of "output": not just (well) educated individuals, but individuals with particular qualifications. Educational credentials and degrees may make it easier to meet "on common ground," while they provide individuals with "signposts" of the kinds of knowledge, skills, and expertise that people possess.[8] In this sense, the differentiation of the education system has transformed the foundations of the functionally differentiated world society in which we now live.

The rapid expansion of participation in higher education in recent decades has once more changed the social position and relevance of education. Following this expansion, forms of socio-geographical segregation have emerged. In recent decades, people are increasingly choosing social contacts on the basis of educational background and degree. They apparently seek the company of like-minded and like-educated others; they cluster together in rapidly changing and expanding "smart cities." Less-schooled people now also increasingly find themselves in each other's company. Birds of a feather indeed flock together (Vanderstraeten & Van der Gucht, 2023). The way education functions in our contemporary society may thus also be criticized. While the education system has been successful in hypostatizing its own "system need," the question indeed is whether this expansion process is "functional" for our contemporary world society at large.

NOTES

1. One can here see the roots of Parsons's approach in a neo-Kantian (and Weberian) vision of the ideal type, which is a purposively fictitious construction for the analysis of an infinite array of "facts." In Parsons's words: "in terms of the given conceptual scheme there is no such thing as action except as effort to conform with norms just as there is no such thing as motion except as change of location in space" (1937, p. 77).
2. Such expectations also feature in a number of "Parsonian" studies, which deal in more detail with the relation between the family and the school. Robert Dreeben, for example, sketched in *On What Is Learned in School* (1968) the unique role of the school in preparing children for adulthood. What children learn in school, via both the official and the hidden curriculum, serves in this perspective as a bridge from the limitations of family-centered behavior to the behavior of adults in society. Even the limitations and "uneducational" effects of schools, such as those that follow from the fact that "student crowds" limit the activities that can be pursued in classrooms and the roles that teachers can assume (sergeant, gatekeeper, privilege granter, participation signaler, etc.), do still seem to fulfil a function for modern society. With hindsight, it is not difficult to see that an altogether optimistic view on school education dominated in the 1950s and 1960s.
3. Typically, however, functionalist approaches direct attention to such forms of specialization. Neil Smelser, for example, who was a student and a close collaborator of Parsons, linked in his analyses of the genesis of "working-class education" in Great Britain increasing functional autonomy with increasing specialization at the level of organizations (schools) and roles (teachers, inspectors, curriculum developers) (Smelser, 1991).

4. The term "eigenvalue" is derived from the German word *Eigenwert*, that is, intrinsic value. By referring to the eigenvalue of function systems, one does not put emphasis on the function that these systems fulfil for society, but on the ways in which they define and sacralize their own raison d'être. Related terms, such as "closure" and "self-reference" (or "autopoiesis"), similarly point to the fact that Luhmann rejects expectations that systems might make specific "functional" contributions to some greater good as naïve (von Foerster, 1984).

5. In some of his later work, Luhmann also focused on the binary codes that divide the world into two values (e.g., true/false, legal/illegal, have/have-not), and their connection with functional specification. The most important function systems attain wide-ranging relevance, he argued, "because they are specialised according to the operations of a determinate code" (1989, p. 39). These codes enable systems to institute their own procedures for channeling information, for creating differences through differences. Each system can develop its own criteria to define what is relevant—and thus safeguard its autonomy (Vanderstraeten, 2004).

6. Dropping out came onto the public scene in the latter part of the 20th century, exactly at the time when school participation was on the ascent. It thus became a problem at precisely the time when the number of people dropping out of school was declining sharply. In other words, dropping out is not really a problem of numbers; it is an identification of deviant behavior, of not living up to the changing norms. The perceived problem is a consequence of the growing pressure to finish school and graduate.

7. It should also be seen that these forms of sociogeographical segregation, like other forms of segregation, tend to reinforce themselves. Parents who live in the same neighborhood often send their children to the same schools, while people who live at different places may diverge in the ways they are inclined to stimulate their own children (or those from family members or neighbors) to invest in education.

8. A comment might be added: Whether these social signposts do or do not reflect "real" psychic or bodily competences is not the issue; it suffices that they "function" within society. Bourdieu similarly speaks of *illusio*, that is, the belief that the fictions we create constitute reality (e.g., Bourdieu & Wacquant, 1992, p. 98).

REFERENCES

Abbott, A. (1988). *The system of professions: An essay on the division of expert labor*. University of Chicago Press.

Ariès, P. (1960). *L'enfant et la vie familiale sous l'Ancien Régime*. Plon.

Baker, D. P. (2014). *The schooled society: The educational transformation of global culture*. Stanford University Press.

Bills, D. B. (2004). *The sociology of education and work*. Blackwell.

Bourdieu, P., & Wacquant, L. J. D. (1992). *An invitation to reflexive sociology*. Polity.

Caplan, B. (2018). *The case against education: Why the education system is a waste of time and money*. Princeton University Press.

Coser, L. A. (1974). *Greedy institutions: Patterns of undivided commitment*. Free Press.

Dingwall, R. (2017). *Essays on professions*. Routledge.

Dorn, S. (1996). *Creating the dropout: An institutional and social history of school failure*. Praeger.

Dreeben, R. (1968). *On what is learned in school*. Addison-Wesley.

Dreeben, R. (1970). *The nature of teaching: Schools and the work of teachers*. Scott Foresman.

Glaeser, E. L., & Saiz, A. (2004). The rise of the skilled city. *Brookings-Wharton Papers on Urban Affairs*, 5, 47–94.

Ingersoll, R. M., & Collins, G. J. (2018). The status of teaching as a profession. In J. Ballantine, J. Spade, & J. Stuber (Eds.), *Schools and society: A sociological approach to education* (6th ed., pp. 199–213). Sage.

Labraña, J., & Vanderstraeten, R. (2020). Functional differentiation and university expansion in Chile. *Social and Education History*, 9(3), 252–277.

Lortie, D. (1969). The balance of control and autonomy in elementary school teaching. In A. Etzioni (Ed.), *The semi-professions and their organizations: Teachers, nurses and social workers* (pp. 1–53). Free Press.

Lortie, D. (1975). *Schoolteacher: A sociological study*. University of Chicago Press.

Luhmann, N. (1977). Differentiation of society. *Canadian Journal of Sociology*, 2(1), 29–53.

Luhmann, N. (1989). *Ecological communication*. Polity Press.

Luhmann, N. (1995). *Social systems*. Stanford University Press.

Luhmann, N. (2002). *Das Erziehungssystem der Gesellschaft*. Suhrkamp.

Luhmann, N. (2012). *Theory of society, Vol 1*. Stanford University Press.

Luhmann, N. (2013). *Theory of society, Vol 2*. Stanford University Press.

Luhmann, N. (2017). *Systemtheorie der Gesellschaft*. Suhrkamp.

Luhmann, N., & Schorr, K. E. (1976). Ausbildung für Professionen—Überlegungen zum Curriculum für Lehrerausbildung. In H. D. Haller & D. Lenzen (Eds.), *Jahrbuch für Erziehungswissenschaft* (pp. 247–277). Klett.

Luhmann, N., & Schorr, K. E. (1988). *Reflexionsprobleme im Erziehungssystem*. Suhrkamp.

Moretti, E. (2013). *The new geography of jobs*. Mariner Books.

Parsons, T. (1937/1968). *The structure of social action*. Free Press.

Parsons, T. (1951). *The social system*. Free Press.

Parsons, T. (1959). The school class as a social system: Some of its functions in American society. *Harvard Educational Review*, 29, 297–318.

Parsons, T., & Bales, R. F. (1955). *Family, socialization and interaction process*. Free Press.

Parsons, T., & Platt, G. M. (1973). *The American university*. Harvard University Press.

Parsons, T., & Smelser, N. J. (1956). *Economy and society*. Routledge & Kegan Paul.

Rasch, W. (2000). *Niklas Luhmann's modernity: The paradoxes of differentiation*. Stanford University Press.

Schofer, E., Ramirez, F. O., & Meyer, J. W. (2021). The societal consequences of higher education. *Sociology of Education*, 94(1), 1–19.

Smelser, N. J. (1991). *Social paralysis and social change: British working-class education in the nineteenth century*. University of California Press.

Stichweh, R. (2016). *Inklusion und Exklusion: Studien zur Gesellschaftstheorie*. Transcript.

Tyrell, H. & Vanderstraeten, R. (2007). Familie und Schule: zwei Orte der Erziehung. In J. Aderhold & O. Kranz (Eds.), *Intention und Funktion: Probleme der Vermittlung psychischer und sozialer Systeme* (pp. 159–174). VS Verlag für Sozialwissenschaften.

Vanderstraeten, R. (1999). Educational expansion in Belgium: A sociological analysis using systems theory. *Journal of Education Policy*, 14(5), 507–522.

Vanderstraeten, R. (2001). Observing systems: A cybernetic perspective on system/environment relations. *Journal for the Theory of Social Behaviour*, 31(3), 297–311.

Vanderstraeten, R. (2002). The autopoiesis of educational organizations: The impact of the organizational setting on educational interaction. *Systems Research & Behavioral Science*, *19*(3), 243–253.

Vanderstraeten, R. (2004). The social differentiation of the educational system. *Sociology*, *38*(2), 255–272.

Vanderstraeten, R. (2006). The historical triangulation of education, politics and economy. *Sociology, 40*(1), 125–142.

Vanderstraeten, R. (2007). Professions in organizations, professional work in education. *British Journal of Sociology of Education, 28*(5), 621–635.

Vanderstraeten, R. (2015). The making of Parsons's "The American University." *Minerva, 53*(4), 307–325.

Vanderstraeten, R. (2021). How does education function? *European Educational Research Journal, 20*(6), 729–739.

Vanderstraeten, R. (2022). Niklas Luhmann and Talcott Parsons. In J. Trevino & H. Staubmann (Eds.), *Routledge international handbook of Talcott Parsons studies* (pp. 271–280). Routledge.

Vanderstraeten, R., & Van der Gucht, F. (2023). Educational expansion and socio-geographical inequality (Belgium, 1961–2011). *Paedagogica Historica, 59*(3), 466–497.

von Foerster, H. (1984). *Observing systems*. Intersystems.

Weick, K. E. (1979). *The social psychology of organizing*. Addison-Wesley.

Wermke, W., & Salokangas, M. (2021). *Teacher autonomy unpacked and compared: Swedish, Finnish, German and Irish teachers' perceptions of decision-making and control*. Palgrave Macmillan.

Wiener, N. (1948). *Cybernetics: Or control and communication in the animal and the machine*. John Wiley.

Woods, P. (1990). *The happiest days? How pupils cope with school*. Falmer.

CHAPTER 17

EDUCATION REFORM AS A GLOBAL PHENOMENON

GIANCARLO CORSI

INTRODUCTION

NOWADAYS reforms and innovations are considered indispensable and are on the agenda of any subsystem of modern society globally. The education system, in particular, stands out in proposing continuous reforms to improve schools and universities, even though the experience of recent decades no longer justifies such insistence.

This chapter is not intended to give suggestions or recipes on the "best" way to plan and implement reforms. Instead, by following the approach of systems theory, we will try to understand what the socio-structural conditions are that have led to this centrality of reforms in the educational system.

A framework will therefore be offered to analyze the spread of reforms on a global scale in modern society and in particular in education. To this end, the first section seeks to expose the origins and development of the idea of reform, from the ancient meaning of condemning the corruption of creation to the modern one of planned change of social structures.

This development is linked to the modernisation process, in particular to the centrality that the future assumes, compared to traditional societies oriented to the past. The second section highlights the key features of reforms from a systems theoretical point of view. These include the central importance of formal organizations, the only type of social system that can be reformed, the peculiar way in which the objectives of reforms are defined, and the difficulties in evaluating their effects. Moving on to a more abstract theoretical level, the relationship between intentional changes due to reforms and changes due to the evolution of society—therefore unintentional—will be analyzed, focusing in particular on the education system and its peculiarities with respect to other societal subsystems. In conclusion, some theoretical questions will be raised that contemporary research leaves open.

Reforms in Ancient Tradition

In ancient tradition and almost up to the early modern period, the word *reform* meant the opposite of what it means today. As suggested by the iterative prefix "re," *reformatio* meant an intervention aimed at restoring a state that had been lost or corrupted over time.[1]

The distinction that defined the concept of reform was the distinction between *reformatio* and *deformatio*. The significance of this distinction derives from how time was conceptualized throughout this long historical period. Time was the time of creation, against the backdrop of divine eternity (*tempus/aeternitas*). Because of this, the past was the reference point for the present: Exposed to corruption and deformation, creation had gradually drifted away from perfection since the dawn of time. This gave rise to the idea that reforming meant restoring—as far as possible—a better state than the present one.

The various reform movements active not only in the ecclesiastical arena but also among guilds aimed not at a clean break with the past, but at reforming something that had been lost, at correcting errors and at protecting whatever was endangered by human imperfection and by the unpredictability of the future. When the Church spoke of itself as something that must be capable of renewal, it always meant knowing how to understand the Christian message in a richer and clearer manner. For this reason: *nihil innovetur, nisi quod traditum est.*[2] For its part, the future was not yet the future of plans, projects, and decisions, but was instead an outlook based on "fortune" and randomness, which could only be counteracted by virtue and the innate qualities of the high-born. Therefore, the present, including the intentions of its actors, was legitimized by the past.

Things changed with the approach of modernity and in particular with the invention of printing, which made it unnecessary not only to copy texts but also to repeat them, often mnemonically (Eisenstein, 1979, p. 66). "Instead of *repeating* reading, it seemed more useful to compare different, now easily accessible texts. Texts now had to be 'interesting'" (Luhmann, 2012, p. 175). The purpose of comparison is in fact to open up possibilities to modify the available knowledge without having to worry about protecting old knowledge from being forgotten or destroyed. The constraints of the past (customs, traditions, dogmas, mores, and so on) were progressively loosened and the future gradually became the time horizon of reference, to which semantics also had to adapt.

This also happened with words such as *reform* and *innovation* (cf. Slack, 1999). Here reference to Luther's Reformation, the historical case par excellence, is unavoidable. Printing was fundamental to the spread of Luther's ideas, as historiography has confirmed.[3] Luther had written his Theses basing himself on the traditional idea of reform and continuing a custom in theological studies, that of dispute in the interpretation of Scripture. The novelty of the Reformation is, therefore, independent of Luther's intentions: it was the printing press that forced hierarchies—and Luther himself—to confront what we might call the first signs of an active and demanding public sphere. The question we must ask ourselves, however, is, What becomes of the concept of reform in such a situation? Is it still about the need to correct deformations, to renew what has been handed down since the dawn of time, or are we already looking at a notion of reform that refers to radical change, to a break with the past?

However this question is answered, it is not too early to see the first cracks in the ancient meaning of the term in this historical case. It would take a long time for a future-oriented approach (meaning planning and programming based on decision-making processes) to become definitive. It was, in fact, the 18th century that completed this process and understood the concept of reform as change that sought not to restore the past, but to establish something new.[4] Legitimization of action, previously provided by the past, is now sought in the future: no longer in tradition, but in the goals that the reforms set themselves.

REFORM AS A GENERALIZED GLOBAL PHENOMENON

With modernity, a society was established that, thanks also to means of mass communication, became a world society, a globalized society (Luhmann, 2012, p. 83ff.; Luhmann, 2013, p. 127ff.). This involved, among other things, the rapid spread of innovation, resulting in highly accentuated interest in planned change. Terms such as *progress, revolution, innovation,* and *reform* entered the standard lexicon of the mass media and of every form of reflection and analysis. Thanks also to the development of technology, the impression that everything can be constantly improved through innovation and, therefore, that there are no limits to change became established and has dominated the global societal imagination up to the present.

But there was also another protagonist that became a center of attention for reformists and revolutionaries: formal organizations, which took the place of traditional corporations and spread rapidly throughout all subsystems of society, again on a global scale. Unlike corporations, organizations base work on the motivation of workers and no longer on their social origin. They also differentiate roles by orienting themselves to skills and decisional programs and can freely set purposes, without any teleology defined on the level of society as a whole. The rise of organizations is therefore correlated with the openness to the future that characterizes modernity. Only through them, in fact, is it possible to manage the enormous potential generated by this openness, reducing complexity to a format suitable for decision-making processes.

Businesses, courts, universities, religious denominations, museums and galleries, hospitals, information networks, sports associations, schools—organizations are everywhere and all of them focus on innovation and reform, each in their own way. As we will see in detail, the role of organizations is central for several reasons: It is no coincidence that the first discipline to take an interest in reform as a generalized ambition was organizational studies.[5]

What caught the attention of these researchers was first and foremost the ubiquity of reform. There is no subsystem of society or type of organization that does not consider itself as an object of possible reform. Education is undoubtedly a special case, but we should also consider the centrality of the concept of innovation (in technology, processes, etc.) for businesses, the continually reasserted need to reform public administration or the many work organization models that guide the management of any organization. Moreover, for decades now, the aims of organizational reforms have tended to become confused with broader aims that seek to improve society as a whole, as in the case of issues related not only to caring for the environment and reducing pollution but also to gender, ethnic minorities, and corporate social responsibility, which are very fashionable today (see Brunsson, 2009, p. 4), and certainly also to issues of equality, dissemination of knowledge, and the ability to apply it, issues particularly cherished by the educational system.

Furthermore, this widespread and pervasive tendency is based on the assumption that reform is something positive and that it can be achieved, especially if rational criteria are followed that ensure consistency between ideal principles, aims, and the means available[6]: "the guiding principle [of reforms] is that preferences are superior to alternatives and consequences. Preferences determine which consequences are relevant, and how they are assessed"; but this is already a problem, "because it requires that decision-makers evaluate the future about which, as we know, the only thing we can know for certain is that we know nothing" (Brunsson & Olsen, 1993, p. 65). The role of time, that is, the relationship between past and future, is also central to systems theory, as we shall see. This is a particularly complex issue, which is not limited to the unpredictability of the future. Indeed, many disciplines emphasize the fact that this uncertainty is actually the precondition that makes it possible, indeed necessary, to decide.[7]

However, the manner in which the past is processed is also important for reform. One of the most frequently cited topics in Brunsson and Olsen's book concerns the past: "reforms are facilitated not by learning but by forgetfulness, by mechanisms that cause the organization to forget previous reforms or at least those of a similar content. Reformers need a high degree of forgetfulness to avoid uncertainty as to whether their proposed reform is a good one . . . Forgetfulness ensures that experience will not interfere with reform: it prevents the past from disturbing the future" (Brunsson & Olsen, 1993, p. 41). In this way, reforms become routine and tend to be self-referential: Reforms generate reforms, making the reform process a stable state (Brunsson & Olsen, 1993, 44; cf. also Brunsson, 2009, pp. 91–104).

Other peculiarities of reforms will be explored in the sections that follow. The problem, at least from the perspective of social sciences, is evident: In today's global society, reform is considered necessary, normal, routine, and obvious. This goes beyond the effectiveness of the reforms, their outcomes and their assumptions, which are anything but obvious. The question that arises at this point is, Why? What is the function of reforms? More generally, one should also ask why a society such as the current one focuses so explicitly and unthinkingly on the planned change to its structures, despite being a system that has already demonstrated repeatedly that it cannot be planned and is simultaneously both highly stable and completely unstable.[8]

Central Importance of Organizations

What can be changed through reform? What can be decided by those who plan and implement a reform?

In the educational system, reforms have historically been directed toward the two values of equality and quality. Equality refers to equality of opportunity, that is, a common starting point for everyone, and then allowing quality (or excellence as it is called in America) to be expressed through talent and commitment. When pedagogy speaks of equality and quality, it is thinking of its own contribution to society at large: Only if education manages to implement both values through reforms can society count on competent and active human beings. The aim is to improve education in order to improve society[9]—otherwise why reform?

However, this apparent axiom hides some problems, which, from a sociological perspective, cannot be overlooked. The most important of these is posed by the initial question: On what can reform intervene to change education and improve society? What variables does it have at its disposal, on which to base its decisions? In other words, how does one engineer a reform when it comes to planning the interventions deemed necessary?

To answer this, we have to move up a few levels of conceptual abstraction and define as clearly as possible what the "object" of the reforms might be. According to Luhmann, a clear distinction between various types of social systems is needed. We have already mentioned societies and organizations and how reforms always refer to both, often giving the impression of confusing them and without ever clarifying what they mean by these concepts. Systems theory has insisted on this point since its inception and proposes distinguishing different types of social systems on the basis of the criterion that determines their boundaries (cf. Baraldi et al., 2021, entry "Social System").

The least complex social system is interaction, that is, communication based on the physical presence of participants; the boundaries of interaction are therefore set by the mutual perception of those who are present at the same time. The simultaneous presence of the participants is also the limiting factor on interaction, since one cannot produce many communications simultaneously without generating confusion and therefore incomprehensibility. But less complex does not mean less important: interaction, in fact, is a social system that emerges almost free of assumptions, simply through the presence of the participants. It was also the only way to produce communication before means of communication such as writing were invented, which allow people to communicate at a distance. In addition, interaction can be found everywhere, even in modern society.

Interaction includes bar conversations, company meetings, religious services celebrated in churches, sports competitions, and, of course, also lessons in school classrooms.

Regarding education, in particular, interaction is an indispensable point of reference.

Luhmann's argument in this regard is rather complex and has to do with the improbability of particularly sophisticated communications being accepted and taken as a starting point for further communications, for example in the case of scientific assertions, of arbitrary provisions by the political power or of access to scarce resources through money. The solution consists in symbolically generalized media of communication, such as scientific truth, power, or money (Luhmann, 2012, p. 190ff.), which motivate acceptance instead of rejection. Educational communication is also highly improbable, and it is so from at least two points of view: pupils can refuse the knowledge that is conveyed by the teachers and even more so their intention to educate them. But the function of education is to change the psychic dispositions of human beings, therefore the psychic environment of society, not in connecting communication to other communication—and for this reason it does not have its own symbolically generalized communication medium. It must rely on its functional equivalent, namely interaction in the classroom (Luhmann, 2012, pp. 246–247), where the resistance to, and refusal of educational communication can at least be kept under control. For this reason, education can be autonomous only in the classroom.

Nevertheless, some recent developments suggest that this constraint is loosening. The growing importance of transnational student mobility programs (such as Erasmus + in the European Union), for example, as well as the increasingly massive spread of distance learning platforms are signs of a trend toward education that transcends classroom boundaries (Vanden Broeck, 2020).

A second type of social system is the formal organization. As Luhmann points out, here the boundaries of the system are established by the criterion of membership, that is, the difference between those who are members of the organization and all others who are not. This is why organizations are different from interactions: They do not finish when employees go back home after working hours. The decisions taken by members of organizations are not simply part of the web of interactive communications, for example of a meeting, but are part of the much larger and more complex network that includes all the decisions of the organization. This is why organizational structures are of a completely different nature and are much more than the simultaneous presence of participants. We need to be precise about this point because it is of fundamental importance to our theme (Luhmann, 2018, p. 181ff.). There are at least three organizational structures:

- The personnel, which includes the characteristics of the organization's members. Typically, these are skills, training, experience, individual characteristics—that is, everything about the individual person that may be relevant to decision-making processes.
- Routes of communication, which shape the skills and responsibilities needed by the organization. Broken down into offices, for example, as well as hierarchy, technical skills, and management skills.

- Decision programs, which can be divided into conditional programs and purposive programs (Luhmann, 2018, p. 213ff). Conditional programs include all the conditions that decisions must take into account regardless of the actual future circumstances that might trigger the program (rules, organizational norms, and hierarchical constraints but also instructions for maintaining or repairing machinery, and so on). While conditional programs look to the past, purposive programs look to the future and include the goals and objectives that one seeks to achieve.

The more general resources of any organization, especially money, revolve in turn around these structures: Any reform project costs money and organizations are the place where the amount of money required, the purpose, and when it is needed are planned.

The third and final type of social system is society, which includes within itself all the communication that is produced, and only communication (Luhmann, 2012, p. 40ff.). Its boundaries are the boundaries of the social sphere; its environment therefore encompasses everything that is not communication—from matter to biological life, down to the consciousness of individuals. How society is differentiated internally is important. Systems theory speaks of functional differentiation, which is the primary structure of modern society. This concept indicates the fact that subsystems are distinguished from each other based on the function they fulfil, and today they are as follows: economics, law, politics, science, families, art, religion, mass media, medicine, and education. Unlike in ancient times, each subsystem has a de facto monopoly over its own function: Only education, for example, can set communicative processes in motion that force learning, in order to allow individual consciousness to participate adequately in the many social contexts in which they will find themselves. Only education as a subsystem can develop knowledge and pedagogical tools of all kinds in order to make something requiring huge expenditure of resources—namely, educating—normal and routine. This also means that no subsystem can intervene directly in other subsystems; as much as educational reforms may also place ideologies and political programs at the center of attention, it would make no sense to think that politics can educate. Politics can only set limits for education (or other subsystems) through the decisions it makes, but what happens afterward in school classrooms depends solely on education.[10]

Having clarified the difference between interactions, organizations, and society as a whole, now the following questions arise: What can be addressed by reform? What are the variables on which reforms intervene?

Since interactions are very limited, both temporally and in terms of the complexity they can reach, they cannot be the object of reforms. It is certainly possible to establish the conditions under which they can take place: In the case of education, classroom lessons have a certain duration, follow certain programs and certain teaching methodologies, and communication is regulated in quite a rigid manner (the teacher speaks, while the pupils listen). But such conditions can be set only at the organizational level, to which interactions will then adapt. In a school classroom, innovations that can be introduced at the interactive level have a chance of being registered and subsequently consolidated only if they are accepted by the organization, for example, through lesson planning. There is no possibility of amplifying variations in interactive communication to the orders of magnitude to which reforms usually aspire, unless they are extended to the level of school organizations.

Society, for its part, offers no foothold for reformers (or "revolutionaries"). The ambitions of reformers to change society can only be expressed as values or hopes; one certainly cannot imagine, for example, improving education and therefore society simply by deciding it. "Improvement" is not an option for any decision maker. A reform can certainly aim at increasing equality of opportunity and improving the quality of education, but then it must also state what it intends to change in order to achieve this result. And with that, we come to the central issue: The variables that can be made the object of decision-making and reform planning are not values or even "improvement" but only organizational structures.

Organizations are fundamental to modern society, not only because they make it possible to concentrate resources, motivate highly improbable behaviors ("working"), or guarantee a certain social order, but also because they are the only plane of social reality on which one can intervene in a programmed manner and in the medium and long term.[11] Whether and how an improvement can be achieved can be deduced retrospectively by analyzing data and interpreting differences and variations, which are, however, always related to the organizational dimension. Among other things, as we shall see, verifying whether there have been any improvements is not an easy task either.

If we consider how reforms are planned, it is actually always a question of rules and regulations (conditional programs), objectives to be achieved, deadlines and time limits (purposive programs), responsibilities and competencies (routes of communication), personnel to be recruited or involved and then funding, organizations to be entrusted with the work, checks and monitoring, and possibly technological apparatus.

For an outside observer of educational reforms (such as sociology or organizational studies), there is an obvious and significant problem here: How can one think of improving education and therefore society by intervening in organizations? Reformers take this possibility for granted, but the gap between ambitions and what can actually be accomplished remains evident and can already be seen by considering how reform projects are drawn up. There is usually a first part, which illustrates the ideals and values underlying the reform, followed by a second part, where it is specified what will be done in practice, above all the interventions at the level of programs and routes of communication, including, of course, the costs.[12] "Mechanisms of hope" (Brunsson, 2006) are combined with decision-making possibilities limited to the organizational level.

This is not all, however. There are other peculiarities that have to be taken into account.

Contradictions in Purpose

Since they are a form of planning, reforms are also characterized by their declared goals. This is what should give meaning to the intentions of the reformers. But here, too, things are far from simple.

The goals underlying reforms are often set and stated in a twofold manner. Education is a good example, as we have already outlined earlier: School reforms always start from the two traditional ideals of quality of education (or, to use American hyperbole, "excellence") and equality, today understood primarily as equality of opportunity. Regardless of how these two values are interpreted, it is nevertheless clear that they are incompatible with each other. "Quality" becomes visible only if it produces differences in performance, while equality can be observed only if no differences are found. Even when it comes to differences that may be attributed to students' performance, that is, to their talent and commitment, doubts may always remain about the possible negative role of extracurricular socializing factors that cannot be eliminated (family, social origin, the local environment in which the pupil grows up, and so on).

This incompatibility cannot be eliminated: precisely because they are formulated as distinguishing features, the ideal purposes of the reforms cannot be proposed separately. No one would support an initiative that aimed at achieving only quality of education without also demanding equality, or vice versa. The function of these ideal goals is probably to legitimize the reforms, since nobody could object to the "value of the values." The implementation of the reform is therefore left with the arduous task of concealing the contradiction, in fact, the constitutive paradox of the reforms.[13] Lastly, order and meaning must be restored to whatever is established as an actual consequence of the reforms—while waiting to plan the next one.

This issue can be analyzed from another perspective, distinguishing between values and programs (Luhmann, 2013, p. 105). Values are positive symbolic preferences, in regard to which no resistance, opposition, or dissent is expected: "the validity of values is *assumed*. Values are treated as *tacit knowledge*" (Luhmann, 1996, p. 65, italics in the original). In principle, in fact, no one denies the central importance of equality of opportunity or of the quality of education. Programs, on the other hand, correspond to what we previously said about organizations: They establish the criteria for the correctness of the decisions to be taken and therefore the conditions to be met and the objectives to be achieved. At this level of programs, opposition and disagreement are always and inevitably generated, since deciding means choosing one alternative while discarding others that are equally possible. Equality of opportunity can be expressed through various organizational and interactive approaches in the classroom: for example, how to manage the presence of disabled students, or how to introduce new teaching technologies, taking into account problems such as the digital divide or the financial difficulties of some families.

Values and programs are, therefore, loosely coupled: Values do not indicate unambiguously which programs should implement them, while programs can always be associated with different values without losing their purpose. This allows a certain freedom in the concrete planning of reforms, but, above all, it constructs the frame within which different positions and opinions can be articulated. The frame is the reform associated with the values that legitimize it, and in this way no one can question its necessity. Discussions start at the level of the programs, without going outside the frame. This is also probably one of the reasons why reforms are so widespread and considered indispensable. But this is also why they pose a further problem: how to evaluate their consequences.

ASSESSMENT

"Judging an innovation's success or failure is no easy task" (Cuban, 1998, p. 455). The failure/success perspective is rarely a true representation of the consequences of reforms. One usually finds oneself in a situation that can be viewed either way.

In times of open skepticism and pessimism, observers of the consequences of reforms are more likely to lean toward a negative assessment. But this, too, is part of planning: The time between the inception of a reform, based on principles, and its assessment, based on the results, means that "for all reforms, explanations for failure are thus built in from the outset" (Luhmann, 2018, p. 278).

Explaining apparent successes is also difficult, if not impossible. Indeed, just when it seems that the goals have been achieved, one does not know how to determine whether a given change (judged positively) can be attributed to the reform, as one of its effects. To give just one example, in the late 1960s and early 1970s, a reformist wave was set in motion on a global scale. Educational reforms were implemented in many countries, not only in Europe, and one of the goals was to eliminate gender inequalities in access to higher education (Corsi, 2013). After a while, it was found that such differences were no longer so conspicuous, and the question was, of course, whether it was thanks to the reform. But not even the reformers themselves arrived at a definite conclusion: Was it due to the reform or to the zeitgeist, which made certain differences (in this case, gender) progressively less relevant, replacing them with more "current" ones (today, e.g., religious or ethnic differences)? In any case, it is clear that cause/effect schemes are totally inadequate to describe, let alone explain, the consequences of reforms.[14]

At this point one must inevitably ask why reform is pursued continuously, intensively, and globally. It is very hard to give a clear answer to this question. Systems theory attempts to analyze this phenomenon from the perspective of the theory of evolution. The connection between reform and evolution is quite immediate, since reforming means changing structures, and structural change is the object of evolutionary theories. But this immediacy is lost as soon as one asks what role reforms may play in the evolution of society.

EVOLUTION

In his book *Organization and Decision*, Luhmann titles the chapter devoted to reforms "The Poetry of Reforms and the Reality of Evolution." The distinction between poetry and reality indicates the fact that reforms are based on projections of the future that coincide with desires and aspirations, more or less realistic, and a good dose of rhetoric that legitimizes them. Evolution, on the other hand, describes structural change as observed, whatever it may be. Furthermore, reforms appear as intentional and inherently positive changes, whereas evolution encompasses all structural changes, intentional or not, positive and negative. Extinction and destruction also contribute to evolution. For this reason, "evolution . . . is not a method for solving problems. It provides no answer to urgent questions that arise when an organisation seeks to improve things or react to deterioration. Reform can therefore not be abandoned in favour of evolution" (Luhmann, 2018, pp. 283–284).

For Luhmann, it is important to move beyond contrasting theories of planning and evolution as though they were alternatives or contradictory to each other. The planning of reforms is also a stage of evolution, even if its contribution cannot be predicted or kept under control. Besides, the problem is not only the unintended consequences of decisions or the many external factors that can interfere with planning. The problem is also, if not primarily, the fact that "as soon as the intention to reform becomes known, the situation becomes complicated. Opinions for and against reform are advanced, along with the wide-ranging modifications, stipulations, and anticipations. Delays occur, as well as oscillation between old and new ideas, and the intentions to reform have to be described over and over again in adaptation to changing situations" (Luhmann, 2018, p. 275). This is an extremely important point, which not only organizations but also theories of organization tend to underestimate or even ignore. The public visibility of reformers' intentions creates the possibility to react to them with acceptance or rejection and this will "oblige the affected parties to state their views. . . . The focus on the future that is now to be decided always intensifies conflicts" (Luhmann, 2018, p. 283). In this sense, "the function of reforms could then be to bring differences between interests to light that would otherwise have remained latent, thus contributing to controversial self-descriptions of the system; and hence to produce resistance by the system to the system, enabling a better understanding of reality than the problem/solution schema can offer" (Luhmann, 2018, p. 277).[15]

In other words, reforms generate an uncertainty produced by the organization itself, an uncertainty to which the organization must react—without being able to predict how. In this sense, Luhmann also attributes this function to reforms: "reforms are accordingly nothing other than an expression of a structural dynamic, and they serve not to attain their goals but to maintain this dynamic" (Luhmann, 2018, p. 278). And again: "This also creates a high degree of sensitivity to the changes that take place in society. The endogenously restless system can seize chance and opportunities and adopt the willingness to reform according to changing trends and needs. Thus, it cannot be planned, but it can evolve" (Luhmann & Schorr, 1988, p. 471).

The reforms of the 1960s and 1970s, for example, were oriented toward values such as the democratization of schools and the cooperation of all those involved. On the organizational level, the new models were the German comprehensive school (Gesamtschule) and the non-graded school in the United States. The watchwords were permeability, multiage grouping, team teaching, individual working, and mastering. Today few remember the enthusiasm of the time and what reformers wanted to achieve (Cuban, 2019). No one would say those ideals have come true—but no one would want to go back. Things have also changed thanks to the structural instability caused by those reforms.

In more recent times, some of those ideas have been taken up, naturally in new forms. Many scholars speak of a shift "from teaching to learning," focusing on what is being learned by pupils, that is, key skills or transferable skills for a future that remains unknown (Mangez & Vanden Broeck, 2020). Learning is understood as the students' ability to build the knowledge and skills that will become necessary or useful in the course of their life. We will see if and to what extent ideas like these and the consequent reforms will be able to "destabilize" the school system to allow it to adapt to a rapidly changing society. From a sociological point of view, an important question is how to manage such changes on an organizational level. If the boundaries of the school become less clear-cut, if—as we have seen above—the interaction in the classroom loses its centrality and if the political control of education shifts from the classic governing to forms of governance that no longer claim to impose themselves only through collectively binding decisions: Will it still be possible to recognize what students learn as educational outcome?

Be that as it may, thanks to developments like these, organizations create new possibilities for self-observation and "empower" their reality, in the sense that they activate possibilities that are not envisaged and are in fact excluded by the reforms, but which could be exploited. However, this potential, precisely because it is unplanned, can be exploited only on occasion, only incidentally, and only if the opportunity is seen and seized. That is, only evolutionarily. The calls for flexibility, creativity, or hypocrisy, widespread and welcome also in organizational studies,[16] seem to go in this direction of excluding and at the same time preserving possibilities—but they can do so only in paradoxical form, that is, with injunctions that can be followed only by contradicting them (Luhmann, 2018, p. 291). In the end, recommendations such as creativity or flexibility serve to hide the underlying problem: That things are changed through decision and reform, but we do not know exactly how.

All of this does not mean that systems theory in any way suggests that reforming is useless or even harmful. The basis for decision-making, that is, organizational structures, can be changed, and refraining from doing so simply because one fears disappointment or because one knows that the results will be different from those hoped for would make no sense—as little, in fact, as thinking about actually achieving the values deemed desirable. If one adopts the perspective offered by evolutionary theory, the problem must be approached quite differently, namely by asking under which conditions a divergent communication that changes structures can succeed (or not) and this despite, indeed precisely because it remains uncertain and unknown what future communication will make of it (Luhmann, 2018, p. 285). One of the cornerstones of the theory of evolution, in fact, is the idea that structural changes (variations), however they are induced, do not allow us to predict their outcomes. No social system can take into account every possible causal relationship nor control the consequences of a novelty that changes existing structures. In the language of systems theory, complexity must be reduced. In other words, certain connections, certain causal relationships can be observed and sometimes even kept under control, while many others are left to chance. This is all the more true in the case of reforms, since reactions are triggered not only by planned changes but also by the intentions of the reformers. In this sense, variations "are always embedded in an evolutionary process that takes them up, we may say, in a deformed state" (Luhmann, 2018, p. 286).[17]

Such a theoretical framework is very complex, but it allows us to understand more clearly the purpose of reforms and their peculiar characteristics. At the same time, however, it leaves many questions open, which we do not claim to resolve here. We have limited ourselves to highlighting two of them.

OPEN QUESTIONS

The first question concerns the evolution of education as a subsystem of society as a whole. As mentioned previously, according to systems theory, not only does the overall society evolve but also its subsystems. Education is one of these. However, Luhmann himself has some doubts. In his monograph on education, referring to the birth of modern education, he writes: "special demands on education presuppose a societal complexity that has already arisen, for which training must then be given. [Education] is a consequence of social differentiations that have already occurred; it is not a pacemaker of socio-cultural evolution" (Luhmann, 2000, p. 111). And then, at the end, regarding the connection between reforms and evolution and in contrast to what he himself had stated in previous writings: "Reforms are a kind of substitute for evolution, an evolution that, given the administrative centralisation of the system and the political responsibility for its top levels, is in fact excluded" (Luhmann, 2000, p. 166). Actually excluded! The text does not explain in detail what is meant.

So we must try to reconstruct the argument, starting with these two rather surprising statements. The first says that education follows societal evolution but does not stimulate it, as other subsystems do—think of the decisive role played by law and religion in tribal societies or by economics and politics in early modernity. The second adds that the educational system does not evolve and that to change its structures it relies on reforms. This would explain the centrality they have in the history of education, as well as their obsessive repetition, but it remains to be seen why education is such a glaring exception.

The answer could lie in its societal function, which consists in changing not the social structures, but the psychic dispositions of individuals, that is, the psychic environment of society. Educational communication makes sense only from this perspective, from didactics to pedagogy, to schools, up to major reforms. For this, education depends very strongly on interaction, and in turn interaction needs an organization to take place regularly. Then it can be assumed that state administrative control is necessary to guarantee a minimum of homogeneity and coherence of educational practices—in other words, to avoid chaos.

Moreover, this applies not only to education; it also applies to medicine, which intervenes on the environment of society (disease treatment) and for this reason requires interactions and organizations as well as strong state administrative control. Not surprisingly, even in medicine, reforms always have a political, as well as a medical, value.[18]

The second question that remains open concerns the relationship among evolution, society (with its subsystems), and formal organizations. There is no doubt that society is a system that evolves: One only needs to compare the tribal societies, studied by anthropology and ethnology, late medieval European society, and modern world society, to realize that the theoretical framework that started with Darwin can also be applied in the social sciences.

What about organizations? So far, no one has provided an answer. Organizational studies talk about evolution in regard to populations of organizations, especially in the field of economics. According to this theory, the evolving entity is the population, not the individual organization.[19] Whether the individual organization evolves or gradually adapts to changing conditions it encounters in its social environment, however, is unclear. It is obvious that organizations are constantly changing, but we know that structural change is also evolutionary change only if it can be observed on the basis of the distinction between variation and selection. Is this the case for organizations? It is, in fact, hard to say.

Furthermore, one should ask what role organizations play in the evolution of society. In the meantime, we know that social systems such as formal organizations exist only in modernity, and therefore in what systems theory calls functional differentiation. At a first glance, one might say that in modernity, significant innovations for the evolution of society are, if not produced, at least "channeled" by organizations. This is the case of communication technologies, from the printing press onward; even the phenomenon we call globalization has become visible thanks to organizations. This does not mean that the evolutionary achievements of modernity are to be attributed to one organization or another. However, the ability to generate structural changes today depends on decisions. Individual subsystems then select whatever has communicative connectivity and is therefore worth transforming into operational structure. This is where reforms come in, reforms understood as "self-generating programs for the variation of system structures" (Luhmann, 2000, p. 166)—in other words, reforms are not able to know whether there will be a positive outcome for evolution, but they "lead to more (and more rapid) unintentional evolution" (Luhmann, 1982, p. 134). This is just the start of the discussion. It is up to future research to develop these insights further.

NOTES

1. Typical and recurring expressions from this era are very clear: in the ecclesiastical sphere, for example, when writing: "omnia reformanda quae deformata sunt" or "ecclesia reformanda tam in capite quam in membris," in the sense of returning the institution "in pristinum statum." With many sources and historical material, see especially Ritter and Gründer (1992) and Brunner et al. (1972–1997).

2. On this maxim and on the difference between old and new in ancient tradition, see Stockmeier (1980).
3. Cf. the most widely known and seminal test: Eisenstein (1983/2005), Chapter 6.
4. See, for example, Condillac (1760): "pour corriger il suffit de faire quelques changements en mieux; pour réformer il faut tout changer," Synonymes, 481, entry "réformer," quoted in Reichardt et al. (1985–1988), entry "réform." In the Encyclopédie of 1751, tome 13: 890, this semantic shift seems to cause some embarrassment, as can be seen from the completely tautological definition of the concept of reform: "la réformation est l'action de reformer; la réforme en est l'effect."
5. The reference author is Nils Brunsson. See Brunsson and Olsen (1993) and Brunsson (2009).
6. In addition to rationality, the use of experts and participation also enables compensatory legitimation (Weiler, 1983).
7. See Luhmann (2018, p. 104). That a paradox is hidden here is clear in a famous sentence of Heinz von Foerster: "Only those questions which are in principle undecidable, *we* can decide" (Von Foerster, 2003, p. 293).
8. "Ultrastable" in the sense of Ashby (1952, pp. 80–99).
9. Education treats itself as though it needs educating (Luhmann & Schorr, 1988, p. 468).
10. This does not mean that one can only educate in schools—one can also educate in the family. In fact, subsystems do not coincide with the organizations that arise within them, even though without organizations they could not fulfil their function.
11. Of course, this does not apply only to education: for example, one can hope for a "fairer" economy, with a redistribution of income that avoids excessive concentrations of capital in a few hands, with work organization that respects workers' rights and so on. However, none of this can be achieved without changing the rules on financial transactions, forms of taxation or working conditions in companies, and in any case only by changing organizational parameters. Another example could be scientific research: Scientists cannot be forced by decree to discover or invent what one would like. However, one can (and can only) establish criteria to reward results deemed worthy, to encourage promising careers, or, in a negative direction, to avoid abuses of power in universities and so on. Again, these are organizational variables.
12. A parallel with a type of text coming from a completely different context—law and politics—springs to mind, namely the constitution: when constitutions are written, the first part establishes fundamental rights, and the second part specifies remits, powers and delegations. Here again, the ideal plane precedes the organizational one.
13. To maintain a broad outlook over the phenomenon we are studying, it is worth noting that this peculiarity is not limited to education. In public administrations, for example, reforms are often inspired by the twin ideals of flexibility and transparency. If one wants to promote flexibility, and therefore also a certain ability to adapt to local, concrete, or exceptional situations, thus delegating varying degrees of decision-making autonomy to peripheral administrations, one will certainly find it easier to meet needs that would otherwise become tangled up in bureaucracy; but then one cannot expect decision-making processes to be transparent, that is, that it will be easy and straightforward to trace the purpose of and responsibility for decisions taken or procedures implemented. In the same way, translating transparency into decisional programs can only mean: bureaucratic controls on what is decided (or not decided), more or less strict regulation of what is possible or excluded from the decision-making power of officials, easier access to documents,

records and protocols of the offices, and so on—in other words, the opposite of flexibility. Similar examples can be provided for all subsystems.

14. Similar considerations referring to reforms in the United Kingdom can be found in Hoyle and Wallace (2007, p. 10): the quality of education has improved, but it cannot be unequivocally demonstrated.

15. See also Van de Ven (2017), which defines innovation as a nonlinear cycle of divergent and convergent activities.

16. In the sense of Brunsson (2002).

17. It is interesting to note that while in the ancient tradition it was the nature of things, including human beings, to deform the state of creation in the course of finite time, now it is evolution, in the course of time without beginning or end. We could say that the concept of evolution has taken the place of nature in describing unpredictable change that goes beyond intentionality.

18. In both cases, however, the autonomy of the system is not threatened by the political value of the reforms: reforms, in fact, "are imposed or avoided by organizational means and therefore cannot go beyond the limits of this type of system. Furthermore, reforms refer to existing organizations and remain confined to the subsystem in which those organizations exist. Even here they cannot succeed in disrupting school interactions" (Luhmann, 2000, p. 166). Jesse Goodman (1995) also comes to the same conclusion: reforms cannot succeed in changing teaching and learning.

19. See Luhmann (2018, p. 284). For the "population ecology" of organizations, see Hannan and Freeman (1977) and Hannan (2005). An advantage of this population concept could be the following: "A population consists of individuals, and this means of differing individuals. It is thus a polymorphous unity. The source of variation is not seen . . . as the occasional occurrence of particularly creative, innovative, assertive individuals, but as the diversity of individuals in the collectivity of the population. . . . The possibility of variation lies in variety and not in the sufficiently probable chance of there being exemplars among a large number of individuals that distinguish themselves as being particularly innovative" (Luhmann, 2012, p. 263).

References

Ashby, W. R. (1952). *Design for a brain*. Chapman & Hall.

Baraldi, C., Corsi, G., & Esposito, E. (2021). *Luhmann unlocked*. Transcript Verlag.

Baratto, S. (1982). L'odierno stato dell'esperimento pedagogico. *Rassegna di pedagogia, 40*, 117–129.

Brunner, O., Conze, W., & Koselleck, R. (Eds.) (1972–1997). *Geschichtliche Grundbegriffe: historisches Lexikon zur politisch-sozialen Sprache in Deutschland*. Klett.

Brunsson, N. (2002). *The organization of hypocrisy: Talk, decisions and actions in organizations*. Copenhagen Business School Press.

Brunsson, N. (2006). *Mechanisms of hope*. Copenhagen Business School Press.

Brunsson, N. (2009). *Reform as routine: Organizational change and stability in the modern world*. Oxford University Press.

Brunsson, N., & Olsen, J. P. (1993). *The reforming organization*. Routledge.

Corsi, G. (2013). Negative Identität. Evolutionstheoretische Probleme mit Reformen im Erziehungssystem. In J. Müller & V. von Groddeck (Eds.), *(Un)Bestimmtheit: Praktische Problemkonstellationen* (pp. 133–145). Wilhelm Fink Verlag.

Cuban, L. (1990). Reforming again, again, and again. *Educational Researcher*, 19(1), 3–13.

Cuban, L. (1995). The hidden variable: How organizations influence teacher responses to secondary science curriculum reform. *Theory into Practice*, 34(1), 4–11.

Cuban, L. (1998). How schools change reforms: Redefining reform success and failure. *Teachers College Record*, 99(3), 453–477.

Cuban, L. (2019). Whatever happened to the non graded school? https://larrycuban.wordpress.com/2019/01/18/whatever-happened-to-the-non-graded-school/.

Eisenstein, E. (1979). *The printing press as an agent of change: Communications and cultural transformations in early-modern Europe*. Cambridge University Press.

Eisenstein, E. (1983/2005). *The printing revolution in early modern Europe*. Cambridge University Press.

Goodman, J. (1995). Change without difference: School restructuring in historical perspective. *Harvard Educational Review*, 65(1), 1–29.

Griewank, K. (1969). *Der neuzeitliche Revolutionsbegriff. Entstehung und Entwicklung*. Europäische Verlagsanstalt.

Hannan, M. T. (2005). Ecologies of organizations: Diversity and identity. *Journal of Economic Perspectives*, 19(1), 51–70.

Hannan, M. T., & Freeman, J. (1977). The population ecology of organizations. *American Journal of Sociology*, 82(5), 929–964.

Hoyle, E., & Wallace, M. (2007). Educational reform: An ironic perspective. *Educational Management Administration & Leadership*, 35(1), 9–25.

Luhmann, N. (1982). The world society as a social system. *International Journal of General Systems*, 8, 131–138.

Luhmann, N. (1996). Complexity, structural contingencies and value conflicts. In P. Heelas, S. Lash, & P. Morris (Eds.), *Detraditionalization: Critical reflections on authority and identity* (pp. 59–71). Blackwell.

Luhmann, N. (2000). *Das Erziehungssystem der Gesellschaft*. Suhrkamp.

Luhmann, N. (2012). *Theory of society* (Vol. 1). Stanford University Press.

Luhmann, N. (2013). *Theory of society* (Vol. 2). Stanford University Press.

Luhmann, N. (2018). *Organization and decision* (D. Baecker & R. Barrett, Eds.). Cambridge University Press.

Luhmann, N., & Schorr. K.-E. (1988). Strukturelle Bedingungen von Reformpädagogik: Soziologische Analysen zur Pädagogik der Moderne. *Zeitschrift für Pädagogik, 34*, 463–488.

Mangez, E., & Vanden Broeck, P. (2020). The history of the future and the shifting forms of education. *Educational Philosophy and Theory*, 52, 676–687.

Peters, B. G. (2001). From change to change: Patterns of continuing administrative reform in Europe. *Public Organization Review: A Global Journal*, 1(1), 37–50.

Rachum, I. (1995). The meaning of "revolution" in the English Revolution (1648–1660). *Journal of the History of Ideas*, 56, 195–215.

Reichardt, R., Schmitt, E., Lüsebrink, H.-J. (1985–1988). *Handbuch politisch-sozialer Grundbegriffe in Frankreich, 1680–1820*. Oldenbourg.

Ritter, J., & Gründer, K. (1992). *Historisches Wörterbuch der Philosophie*. Schwabe & Co. AG.

Slack, P. (1999). *From reformation to improvement: Public welfare in early modern England*. Clarendon Press.

Stockmeier, P. (1980). Alt und Neu als Prinzipien der frühchristlichen Theologie. In R. Bäumer (Ed.), *Reformatio Ecclesiae. Beiträge zu kirchlichen Reformbemühungen von der Alter Kirche bis zur Neuzeit. Festgabe für Erwin Iserloh* (pp. 15–22). Ferdinand Schöningh.

Van de Ven, A. H. (2017). The innovation journey: You can't control it, but you can learn to maneuver it. *Innovation*, *19*(1), 39–42.

Vanden Broeck, P. (2020). Beyond school: Transnational differentiation and the shifting form of education in world society. *Journal of Education Policy*, *35*(20), 836–855.

Von Foerster, H. (2003). *Understanding understanding: Essays on cybernetics and cognition.* Springer Verlag.

Weiler, H. N. (1983). Legalization, expertise, and participation: Strategies of compensatory legitimation in educational policy. *Comparative Education Review*, *27*(2), 259–277.

CHAPTER 18

....

THE RATS UNDER THE RUG

The Morphogenesis of Education in a Global Context

....

PIETER VANDEN BROECK

INTRODUCTION: EDUCATION, RATIONALITY, AND ITS OTHER SIDE

....

FEW themes are rooted as firmly in sociological tradition as the study of rationality. It forms the leitmotif of how sociologists examine a wide range of phenomena, stretching from the everyday practices by which we create social order up to the construction of scientific discovery. In large measure we owe this centrality to Max Weber, for whom rational action was the hallmark of modernity. As is well known, he pointed to rationality as the force that drove gods and unruly fate from our lives, along with unthoughtful traditions and the all too capricious realm of feelings, with its overpowering outbursts of passion or spontaneity. Instead, a calculating attitude is since said to prevail, intent on making the world more controllable and hence predictable. In Weber's account of our becoming modern, human action increasingly favored such an instrumental orientation to the world, where the conditions for goal attainment are carefully weighed in terms of risks and resources. This rational outlook shrinks the world to a tool, or an impediment, for our purposes. When grasped in these terms, rationality obtains the shape of a script for actors, a program to follow so as to optimize a course of action and maximize its hoped-for benefits. Weber thus laid the foundation for any sociology that refers to rationality as a matter of acting *individuals*, either when modeling their singular behavior as the utilitarian pursuit of self-interest (rational choice theory), when theorizing such voluntaristic effort as normatively organized (the early Talcott Parsons) or when labeling as rational the outcome of their intersubjective agreement (Jürgen Habermas).

Against such a view, or perhaps rather in an effort to venture beyond it, this chapter wagers that it might be more fruitful to consider rationality as a trait of *systems* instead of calculating actors. With this substitution, swapping the focus from purposeful humans to faceless systems, I wish to depict how education can be viewed as developing a rationale of its own, regardless of the human beings involved. As such, my contribution not only departs from the Weberian conception of rationality as a world orientation guiding the action of individuals. It also steps beyond his understanding of education as being subject to this instrumental orientation to the world. What follows will not portray an exogenous "rationalization of education." By the latter expression, Weber (1946, pp. 240–244) sought to summarize how education participates in the spread of bureaucracy and is ultimately transformed by this "irresistibly expanding bureaucratization of all public and private relations of authority," a process he saw intruding into all questions of intimately cultural character. For Weber, the problem at hand was to describe the role education plays in the establishment of a society-spanning bureaucratic structure. My interest in rationality, on the other hand, is to describe how *a reason proper and specific to education* comes into being. In particular, I wish to address how such a *ratio* makes itself apparent when education is organized on a global scale, beyond the borders of nation states and classrooms. What is at stake in this chapter is to uncover how new educational practices, taking place on a global scale from their outset, develop and how they relate to the school classroom. In Europe, European Union governance has since years contributed to the "projectification" of education via funding programs with a global outreach. The ongoing pandemic has spurned face-to-face instruction to move from the classroom toward globally operating platforms. With the current chapter, I wish to place these two present-day developments, projectification and platformization, in an historical overview to highlight a dynamic that shapes their evolutionary path.

Taking cues from Niklas Luhmann's theoretical framework, I shall attribute such an educational rationality neither to knowledge nor to knowing subjects or to other *idées fixes* stemming from Europe's philosophical tradition. Instead, with a recourse to second wave cybernetics, rationality will be redefined *as the ability of a system to observe and then orient itself by means of the difference between its own doing and that which such doing designates as foreign to its own operativity* (Luhmann, 1977, 1998). In Luhmann's work, rationality refers to this particular probing capacity, the ability of *systems* to organize and reorganize their own operativity in light of the effects thereby brought about in the *environment*. His notion of rationality means to capture the strange feedback loops drawn by a system that seeks to control the effects it has on its environment, but that can only do so by means of the repercussions these effects have for its own working, as Elena Esposito (2021, pp. 191–193) summarizes. Being rational, to sum it up, has more to do with a game of blind man's bluff than with the self-actualized certainty we commonly associate with the term: One gropes in the dark chasing the disorienting, often contradictory indications stemming from the outside world and alters course according to perceived changes, hoping not to break a leg.

What is gained from such a tottering, tentative rationality is never a steady foothold, not even a temporary one. Luhmann's redefinition of rationality in terms of the difference between a system and its environment does not bring us back to a unitary world on which Reason can report with authority. Instead of such self-assurance come always adjustable distinctions, differences which are open to change and hence provide detachment from what initially appeared necessary and hence unalterable. I omit, for reasons of clarity and conciseness, much of the proto-mathematical technicalities that usually adorn the literature once arrived at this stage. The keyword "re-entry" can suffice here to guide interested readers towards more exhaustive theoretical discussions and explorations of its formal calculus (cf. Baecker, 2007, 7394). Instead, I wish to draw attention to the conceptual merits of such an abstract redefinition of rationality as the tentative boundary management that systems engage in vis-à-vis their environment.

A first, very evident advantage of approaching rationality as the aptitude of systems to handle purposefully the relationship between themselves and their environment, is that new, unsuspected sites of *ratio* appear in sight. Rationality is no longer a privilege of humans and their actions but becomes central to portray how the social world, including education, organizes and reorganizes itself. Transposing the general and indeed overly abstract characterization to the topic of education, the question of rationality becomes one of maintaining and crossing the distinction between education and the rest of society—of *how education manages its boundaries*, in short. Education can then be observed as rational, whenever it attunes its own highly specific operativity of instruction (*system*) to the perceived demands or hoped-for outcomes occurring beyond its borders (*environment*). When education fashions itself as preparing the future professional life of its students, for example, by fine-tuning its pedagogical offer (*system*) to the estimated needs of the labor market (*environment*), such an attempt at self-rationalization becomes apparent. The same holds true whenever instruction (*system*) tries to attenuate the differences in upbringing (*environment*) among its pupils in order to guarantee them all an equally open future outside of school, unconditioned by their unequal starting position. Perhaps nowhere clearer than in its most elementary of intentions, namely the ambition to teach (*system*) so as to guide or to affect the learning processes pertaining to its addressees' invisible world of thought (*environment*), education can be described as the effort of establishing a sui generis rationality.

Secondly, redefining rationality as a characterization of how systems internally account for and respond to their outside environment has the benefit of pointing almost effortlessly toward the all too apparent difficulties to align one with the other. As the sociology of education likes to underline, school does not at all eliminate inequalities (one example standing for all: Bourdieu & Passeron, 1970), nor does school success safeguard future professional success (their canonical opposite: Boudon, 1974). Speaking of rationality should indeed not be taken to imply that society is thought to evolve or to be steerable toward preferable, more worthwhile outcomes. Luhmann's redefinition of rationality should not be mistaken as the recipe for such aspirations. On the contrary, his understanding of system rationality draws attention above all to the *deficits* of reason and the problems that arise whenever social activity develops in either willful or forced disregard of its constitutive environment. As the endless strings of ecological catastrophes illustrate, society as a whole can hardly be described in terms of reason. Our shifting climate exposes the evident difficulties modern society faces taking account of the natural world. "The undeniable, serious, future-threatening changes in the natural environment triggered by society itself are gradually becoming the rationality problem of this century." Luhmann (1988, p. 12) had hence already noted at the end of the eighties, spelling out the impasse which contemporary society is grappling with: modernity "depends on a high indifference to its environment for its own operations, but can no longer afford precisely this."

Making rationality distinction-dependent, contingent upon how the distinction between a system and its environment are drawn, Luhmann reformulates and silently upturns the Weberian notion of rationality. His abstraction uncouples it from acting individuals and from the prospect of a society-wide bureaucratic structure. The result is not a lazy postmodern compromise, where everybody and everything enjoys its own rationality, but an attempt to articulate the resulting pluralism as the core of the modern experience. In modernity, runs Luhmann's analysis (1998, pp. 25, 38), rationality increasingly "shifts to high-energy rationalities that only cover partial phenomena, only orient society's functions systems." With the summary label of functional differentiation, he sought to spell out how the various spheres of social activity—such as education, politics, economy, law, or science, next to, and perhaps surprisingly, love or art—become the true "operative dischargers of rationality in contemporary society." This reformulation or rather abstraction of goal rationality into system rationality does not necessarily lead to a rosier diagnosis than Weber's evocation of bureaucratic capitalism as an iron cage.[1] Luhmann's variation on this well-known theme lets it erupt into a multitude of domains, each with its own totalizing aspirations and without a common paradigm to reassemble them (Luhmann, 1991). The result, Luhmann notes, falling for a slight moment out of his typically subdued tone, is a society marked by "an excessively close connection between the rationality of the functional systems on the one hand and their fatal consequences on the other" (Luhmann, 1996, p. 197). Much, if not all of Luhmann's work can be read through this prism, as a research program that charts out these functional rationalities and their lack of integration.

But especially in his later years, his attention shifted increasingly to rationality's other side, zooming in on that which slips away through the cracks of reason. The intent or hope is not at all to thus come toward a tribunal of Reason, able to separate the wheat from the chaff, the reasonable from the unreasonable. Rather, the ambition is to portray rationality in more detail by including its always co-present opposite, acknowledging (rather than resolving) its inherent doubleness. What Luhmann aspires to is hence to gain

> a more precise understanding of the "other side of rationality," one that could be characterized by the semantics of paradox, imaginary space, the blind spot of all observations, the self-parasitizing parasite, chance or chaos, reentry or necessity, externalizing toward an "unmarked state." These are ideas that would gain their contours exclusively from precision, fixed by rationality, and that would finally lead to an indirect self-characterization of the rational. (Luhmann 1998, p. 40)

The following pages will seek to build on this ambition to explore the Dionysian unruliness that is always tied in with the Apollonian search for order and logic. By focusing on how Luhmann depicts the relation between school education and its environment, they wish to elucidate how he understood the birth of modern education as accompanied by an exclusionary movement that sought to expel part of the environment, as if it were a pest or a parasite, and so to get rid of the rats hiding under the rug, so to speak. Speaking of educational rationality and its other side, to rephrase it slightly differently, is hence above all a matter of looking at how education constructs the difference between its own reality and the outside world—and thus of highlighting what such a construction shuts out, what it treats as unwanted. The underlying suspicion is that the movement of expulsion Luhmann observed in school education proves to be instructive for better grasping the *ratio* that currently shapes the globalization of education.

School Education and Its Context

Georg Simmel (1950, p. 21) once compared sociology to geometry, noting how they share a primary interest in the formal traits of phenomena, often leaving the analysis of their content to other scientific disciplines. Either when observing interaction or inquiring into organizations, sociology indeed usually displays little interest in *what* is actually said among participants or *what* organizations precisely decide on. Rather, the stress falls on the *form* of these phenomena—on their role-taking procedures, for example, or the structure of their conflicts—and the thus emerging geometry of the social world. It should hence not surprise that systems theory, too, shows a particular interest in abstract forms, even if it operates along different conceptual oppositions. In what follows, I propose to explore how Luhmann's understanding of *context* can be brought into this equation. Both notions, form and context, will act as stand-ins for the more general terms already introduced, system and environment, respectively. The goal is to transpose the dynamic between the two sides of this opposition to the historical emergence of school education and its context, thus laying bare how an educational rationality develops and at what cost. To that end, I shall first briefly overview how form has been understood by Luhmann in the domain of education, so as to underline subsequently how his varying use of the notion of context offers useful hints on how to grasp the relationship between education and its form of school.

In Luhmann's account, the uniquely modern emergence of multiple distinction-dependent rationalities is closely related to their reference to a highly specific problem for which they claim universal authority—a reification process Luhmann (1995, pp. 464–465) also abridged as *hypostatization*. In contemporary society, finding solutions to the quandary of how to organize the scarcity of natural or human resources, for example, is thought of as the exclusive prerogative of the economy. Education, much like the economy and other major domains of social activity, similarly claims a monopoly for its own, highly specific reference problem. Many sociological accounts of what education does or aspires to do formulate education's problem in terms of individuals (the transmission of knowledge and skills) or their relationships (establishing normative consensus). The classical notion of socialization, then, serves to make such answers more probable. Luhmann made the infamous move to relocate humans outside of society, so as to highlight how the inner world of our individual thoughts strictly differs from the distinct logic of communication processes. As a result, his theory cannot be content with the answers commonly given by sociology to the question what education sets out to do. Luhmann painstakingly attempts to avoid the catch-all formulae, the "magic spells" (2002, p. 48) provided by classical sociology. Education, so goes his tiptoeing around the all too human-centric formulations of mainstream sociology, deals with the predicament of how to increase the odds of mutual understanding (2002, p. 81). Such a problem description starts from the hardly polemical given that what happens in our heads is fully untransparent to others and vice versa. How then to successfully imagine—imagine, *not* know or share: no philosophical (or any other sort of) mentalism is implied here—what others think when using words, representations, and other cultural schemes, becomes highly improbable in such a constellation.

School education can be described as the delegation of this problem of reference toward a different system type, an organization, which by its decision-making ability specifies, in always selective and hence contingent ways, what the pedagogical intention will amount to in the daily hustle and bustle of school life. Described in this way, school (as an organization) and education (as a function) do indeed *not* coincide. Luhmann's systems theory maintains a sharp distinction between function systems and organizations and considers such a difference characteristic for the complexity of modern society, preventing organizations from representing a function *in toto* or functions from being fully organized.

> In highly complex societies, none of the central functions of the societal system can be assumed by a unified organization—and today even less so than before. [. . .] The converse side of this impossibility of delegating major societal functions en bloc to single organizations is that such broad functions cannot be adequately mirrored or understood within the narrow limits of organizations. Neither the leeway for varying societal functions nor the conditions for the compatibility of their divergent ways of being fulfilled can be adequately expressed at the level of organizational goals and criteria. (Luhmann, 1982, p. 81)

The school organization hence neither represents education's function exclusively or exhaustively, nor does education become "organizable" as a whole. In this precise sense, it would be wrong, or at least short-sighted, to think of the relationship that Luhmann draws between education and school as a simple equation. For his systems theory unites the two in a functionalist manner, where the latter (school) is only a possible *solution* that emerged over the course of history in order to tackle the problem raised by the former: how to educate, when such a question no longer finds a legitimate answer in the nature of its addressee but turns into a matter of decision-making, that is: of organizations?

School education can hence be theoretically reframed as this act of delegation, lending its instruction a very recognizable shape or form, as I have elaborated elsewhere

(Vanden Broeck, 2021). When speaking of the form of school education, the question is not a matter of its essential substance or identity, but of a horizon of possibilities that emerge with this delegation to an organization and the difference that is thus established with all other social activity. The question I wish to raise now is how the distinction thus surfacing between school education and society can be understood in terms of their interrelationships.

In order to answer that question, I sketch next an exegetical summary that rereads Luhmann's writing and stages it as if it were a classical drama (cf. Freytag, 1900), in an effort to thus unearth the tragedy played out by the two protagonists: school and its context.

1. *Exposition.* As in every play, first one needs to set the scene and properly introduce the characters. While the form of school has been characterized already, the notion of context is still largely a stranger. *Context* is a word Luhmann uses sporadically when it comes to education and almost exclusively to indicate a specific and situated world. Never does the word develop into a self-standing concept with its own definition. But it is rather easy to notice how the notion implicitly functions as a complement to his much more frequently used concept of environment (*Umwelt*). Environment is by definition a residual but constitutive category. In Luhmann's systems theory, it acts as the undefined counterpart necessary to define the identity of systems. It is part of the conceptual dyad—system *and* environment—through which definitions in search of a system's essence or ultimate substance can be avoided and rephrased in terms of relationships: "the system is neither ontologically nor analytically more important than the environment; both are what they are only in reference to each other" (Luhmann, 1995, p. 177). Context, in turn, is used to identify specific parts of the relevant environment. Where environment is by definition a residual (but constitutive) category, the undefined counterpart necessary to define the identity of systems, context is used to identify specific parts of the relevant environment. Frequently returning to the expression of education "in the context of," for example, Luhmann uses the word to highlight how either a specific pedagogical practice, the evolving formulas by which education describes itself or the changing societal conception of time, all frame, enclose, and thus specify education by virtue of being its socio-historical context (Luhmann & Schorr, 2000, pp. 69–96, 106, 165–180). The career of pupils, similarly, is described as stretching out over a variety of discontinuous contexts provided by the school system (2000, p. 303), indicating again how *context* is a term used in reference to a specific, always determined part of the world surrounding the actual phenomenon put under attention.

Next to this largely familiar use of the term as the stage or setting for other phenomena, Luhmann also uses context to describe the close link between socialization and its immediate setting. Differing from the classical view that understands socialization as conducive to the internalization of values (Emile Durkheim) or normative consensus (Parsons again), Luhmann does not define the concept with reference to its capacity to successfully establish social conformity; quite to the contrary.[2] What is said to define socialization is its inevitable *context dependence*. Being socialized always implies learning in a specific context; it is restricted to the immediate setting wherein it occurs. When in Rome, one learns to do as the Romans do. But that is of little use elsewhere. What is learned through the accidental and largely implicit learning processes of socialization does not travel well beyond its context of origin. Precisely therein lies its main difference from (formal) education. What education achieves through its formal institutions is setting standards for life outside of school or university. And hence, Luhmann (1987, p. 178) notes, not without irony, that despite all the advertising for lifelong learning, "education does not have itself as its ultimate purpose. It creates conditions for participation in other systems, and since the 18th century this has been thought of primarily, almost exclusively, in terms of professional careers."[3] It is nothing short of utopian to expect that learning, whether formal or informal, leads us toward the normative consensus Parsons and Durkheim spoke of, in the sense of an agreement between our states of consciousness.

> But feigned consensus (if one may put it that way) is indispensable if the autopoiesis of social systems is to continue. And through education (we can now also say: training) it can be achieved that this is also possible in non-standardized situations, whereas socialization remains very strongly bound to its original context. (Luhmann, 2002, p. 81)

When such socialization occurs within the settings of the family, context becomes shorthand for the household, usable to indicate one's descent (*Herkunftskontext*). It indicates the limited perimeter family life offers for education as a distinctly formed activity (Luhmann, 2002, pp. 60–61). Here the story suddenly gains interest, because even if family education admittedly does not crystallize into a distinguishable (sub)system of education itself, its undeniable relevance means that school might very well obtain a primacy, but never an exclusivity on education. The two main characters not only require and evoke each other; the suspicion grows they also live at odds with one another. Not least because in modern family life, the possibilities for instruction are heavily confined by the redefinition of education in the household as preparation or support for school (cf. Tyrell & Vanderstraeten 2007). The household is expected to play second fiddle, as it were, without making too much of a scene.[4]

2. *Rise.* The play has begun, the protagonists have shown who they are, and the playwright hopes some interest has been aroused. Let us now pan across to show how the relationship between school and its context is further complicated. This is a good moment to point out that Luhmann uses context as well to indicate the historical change by which modern education became a specific setting in its own right. What is at stake in his writings could easily be summarized as an account of how education itself gradually became a "system context" (2000, p. 124), that is, a context of its own, emancipating itself from all other spheres of social activity.

Central to this development is the creation of a space or setting where, owing to its spatial layout, instruction unfolds under the condition of mutual perception. Pointing out how interaction in classrooms always develops under the condition of a shared situatedness—a physical co-presence of pupils and their teacher in a shared space—Luhmann remarks how this context enforces self-restriction onto all participants. All involved parties, teachers included, know they are perceived while they perceive each other. The classroom, in short, fences off a space for *reflexive perception*, a context (for the perception) of perception. Precisely this perceptual context, where "perceiving" always equates "being perceived," creates and ensures, so Luhmann emphasizes, the "peculiar and peculiarly evidential kind of sociality that makes it possible to focus the explicit communication on teaching" (2002, p. 57). Since all references to the shared context require no further explication, because their meaning is evident and visible to everybody present, the interaction is relieved from this communicative burden and can concentrate on instruction. The teacher only has to point to a pupil and say "you," for all the others to breathe a sigh of relief as the class continues. Such indexical expressions (like "you" or "we," "this" or "that") and other situation markers that would undoubtedly require further explication in a written text like the current chapter can be left implicit in class since its narrow perimeter limits their possible meaning sufficiently. The resulting complexity reduction, Luhmann notes, is what makes instruction possible in the first place.

3. *Climax.* What thus comes to the fore is a specific world of instruction, a world of school with its own autonomy. Behind the closed door of the classroom, education develops and implements its society-wide competence for conveying the knowledge considered necessary to lead our lives and codes (with the help of grades, tests, and assignments) the outcome of the resulting interaction as either successful or not. Any educational rationality, any attempt to attune the instruction to the perceived demands or changes of its environment starts from here. Only with the technical invention of the classroom could instruction emancipate itself from the surrounding social activity and begin the impossible task of bridging the thus created distance between education and society. Classroom interaction denotes, in other words, how school education creates the therefore necessary, secluded space. Classrooms provide a space where professional teachers can give expression to what education is and entails, freed from direct external interference. That holds true for religion and politics, historically the two ambits of society most closely involved with education, but also for the science that helped propel this move towards autonomy.

> The world of schools: it no longer only represents a Pedagogy that has been emancipated from "religion" and "state"; instead, it is a special world of specific experiences that neither the scientific Pedagogy nor the political system can ignore. (Luhmann & Schorr, 2000, p. 124)

Once instruction moved into the classroom, the necessary leeway—regarding who to teach what and when or how—emerged for school education to shape into its own distinctive form. From homework to salaries via school buildings, teaching material, professional qualifications, or curricular principles and much more: Apart from the good intentions shared by parental and scholastic education, "everything else needs to be rebuilt from there" (Luhmann, 2002, p. 61).

But while the modern school system thus (re)built education almost from scratch, it is certainly true that the resulting autonomy depended and today still depends on state involvement for many of its administrative and regulative needs. That makes it, even nowadays, hard to recognize the functional autonomy of the education system. Instead of insisting on educational autonomy, it might seem more appropriate to consider school as a cog in the machinery of the state administration, steered by its responsible ministry. The bulk of studies on education policy certainly seem to contend as much. Education's dependence on its political administration should, however, not be confused with a lack of educational autonomy, Luhmann (2002, p. 116) warns us. "The state can introduce school obligation and carry the costs of schools and higher education"; nevertheless "it can as an organization of the political system not teach itself." For teaching, schools with teachers, pupils, and curricula occur and one does not get very far explaining what happens in schools, if the resulting amalgam is understood as a mere matter of state governance or political decision-making, Luhmann (2002, p. 147) underlines. One can, in that regard, note a slight parallel with certain branches of the Anglo-Saxon literature. When speaking of a so-called grammar of schooling, David Tyack and Larry Cuban (1995) reached a very similar conclusion, stressing how only very "few reforms aimed at the classroom make it past the door permanently" (Cuban, 1990, p. 11). For Luhmann, too, the withdrawn space of the classroom generates an educational sovereignty within its limited perimeter. But curiously enough, the autonomy thus gained is observed as hinging on a very specific act of *exclusion*.

4. *Fall*. The latent conflict between the school and its context, which has been palpable from the outset, starts to gain clearer contours. Elaborating on the conditions necessary for the crystallization of education into a world sui generis, Luhmann indicates classrooms as the "technical invention" to keep the encompassing environment from seeping in, thus spurring the differentiation of education as a system, different from other societal spheres (Luhmann, 2002, p. 119). Understood as such, the environment comes to stand for an *obstacle* to overcome, something that must be kept at bay for instruction to become possible. That holds in particular for the context of one's upbringing, for the household. "The function of education is transferred from homes to schools and from fathers to teachers" (Luhmann, 2002, p. 176) and since then, any interference from pupils' households in the teaching amounts to an unwanted intrusion. With a variant on Ernst Gellner's (1983) transition to exo-education, moving education outside of the family household, Luhmann indeed labels school as the evolutionary achievement that expels the context established by pupils' family background, so as to organize inclusion universally, without distinction (Luhmann, 1990; 2002, p. 61). School is expected to be the place where one stops being a daughter or a son, at least temporarily. Without this expulsion of the family background—or emancipation from it, as pedagogy undoubtedly prefers—there can be neither pupils nor students.

The expression Luhmann (1990) favors to portray this state of affairs is the *homogenization* of education's point of departure on which all school interaction is said to rest. By addressing all pupils as equal at the beginning, by exorcising their differences in upbringing, as if they were all starting from a blank slate, their diverging previous experiences can be ignored and all differences among them that come to light afterward, during their school career, can be attributed to the thus developing education system itself.[5]

> In this way, the differentiated system of education reacts to a society in which, in general, origin is not a useful indicator of the future, but everything depends on what happens "in between." Accordingly, pedagogy shifts from the care (of fathers) for their offspring to the care (of educators) for the becoming-human (idea) and career (end dates) of the children. And it is no longer a matter of securing the well-born against the constantly lurking dangers of corruption and depravity (and especially in the weak and seducible youth). Rather, it is a matter of making the children into something other than what they are and would become on their own.

Precisely on this point Luhmann's position differs from Pierre Bourdieu's (1966) otherwise closely related expression that school is indifferent to the pupils' differences. Where Bourdieu only sees social conservatism, Luhmann points out the semantics and technology that made autonomous education possible in the first place. But for both authors, school's urge to homogenize pupils as equals by disregarding their differences inescapably involves harm—whether one dubs it symbolic violence (Bourdieu) or speaks, with Luhmann, of the cutting lines that a system traces in order to exclude the interference of any third party.

5. *Catastrophe.* The main character is not only a hero. Like all tragic heroes, it turns out to be deeply flawed. Similar to the establishment of any system rationality, the birth of school is strongly entwined with that which it actively seeks to exclude as foreign to its own doing. At this stage, the exegetical trajectory takes a surprising turn. Regardless, or rather exactly because of the disregard for disparities in upbringing that school education needs to profess, these class differences have a curious way of returning into the classroom. As sociological research over the past half century has repeatedly shown, the expulsion of the household has never been entirely successful. It might very well be that social descent is no longer the organizing principle of education. Children from better-off families nonetheless still have better chances of succeeding in the school system. The excluded household comes to haunt the classroom's lofty pedagogical ideals of equality, much like the parasite's inevitable return, which without exception comes to disturb any hope for harmony or pure order, as Michel Serres warned us.

> The rats climb onto the rug when the guests are not looking, when the lights are out, when the party's over. It's nighttime, black. What happens would be the obscure opposite of conscious and clear organization, happening behind everyone's back, the dark side of the system. But what do we call these nocturnal processes? Are they destructive or constructive? What happens at night on the rug covered with crumbs? Is it a still active trace of (an) origin? Or is it only a remainder of failed suppressions? We can, undoubtedly, decide the matter: the battle against rats is already lost; there is no house, ship, or palace that does not have its share. There is no system without parasites. (1982, p. 12)

Similarly, differences of social descent indeed return to torment the classroom, although the instruction desperately seeks to remain impartial to them and must do so to even begin teaching. Whether it is at the beginning of the pupil's school career or at the beginning of class, Luhmann (1990, p. 86) echoes Serres, each moment of instruction first requires an exclusion of its constitutive context, an expulsion which then ultimately and tragically defeats itself.

> The beginning is not eradication, it is exclusion of the third to establish a systemic logic. It ensures the unequal growth of what is equal and a more or less good harvest. But exclusion, inherent logic, equality and more or less are artificial institutions like geometry. They exclude what Pascal called "coeur" and what today is sometimes treated under the (less appropriate) title of "lifeworld." No wonder that what is excluded tries to return—be it as the Other, be it as a parasite, in any case as "noise" that disturbs the lesson.

With his reference to Serres's parasite, next to Hartmut and Gernot Böhme's (1982) seminal work on the other side of (Kantian) reason, Luhmann spells out the tragedy that lurks beneath the development of systemic rationality and the ensuing geometry of educational forms.[6] For each form of education that appears, an unwanted and expelled part of the environment silently returns to unsettle the thus emerging ratio. While school education cannot but embrace ideals of equality to become a workable reality, the rampant inequalities it generates always carry the distinctive mark of the exclusion that was therefore necessary (Corsi, 1992). The household welcomes itself back uninvited to the classroom in the guise of stubborn class differences that the teaching is unable to acknowledge. The rats return, inevitably, and the question is now how this applies to those forms of education that venture outside the classroom.

School Is Out

As I have elaborated in this chapter, Luhmann's oeuvre can be read as an account of how modern education obtained its precise form of school and allows one to highlight how this morphogenesis corresponded with the emergence of a precarious, always imperfect boundary management. Educational rationality, to summarize, covers then precisely this attempt to purposefully manage the borders between education and society—an attempt that always carries its own failure, so to speak. There is no building without rats, no Apollo without Dionysus, no system without an excluded environment ready to seep back in. Central to the historical evolution leading to the birth of school education has been the novel prominence of loosely coexisting societal functions and the delegation of that function, in the case of education, to the organizational level of schools. Education, when understood as such, hence stands for nothing more than a form-less function. It establishes merely a problem of reference that asks how to change people intentionally into persons able to participate in society (Luhmann, 2002, p. 38)—that is, capable of playing the serious game of feigned consensus. The distinctive form of school then appears as a variable and historically varying answer set out to solve that problem.

Such a perspective leaves the door open for other forms that address the same problem, and, by way of conclusion, I would like to indicate how two such alternative "formalizations," in turn, reenact the tragedy sketched herein. Perhaps not surprisingly, each of them relates closely to forms of supranational statehood that increasingly differ and are even said to oppose the nation state. Hence we come to the subject of global education. Because even if the education system functions on a worldwide scale, as I have recently addressed together with Eric Mangez and Vanden Broeck (2021), it is a rather straightforward conclusion that school education constitutes a form of instruction with limited geographical reach. Schools, although undoubtedly a globally present institution (cf. Meyer et al. 1992), do not organize education beyond national borders. To conclude, let me enumerate two contemporary organizational examples that on the contrary seek to precisely do that.

1. *Transnational projectification.* In recent decades, the European Commission has undertaken several reforms designed to harmonize its widening range of funding programs in the field of education. The various funding programs (Erasmus, Comenius, Grundtvig, da Vinci) previously overcrowding the Euro-pantheon were gradually streamlined into a single comprehensive program providing financial support for learning activities both inside and outside formal education. The resulting global funding instrument of the European Union, branded *Erasmus+* in 2014 and renewed for seven more years in 2021, breaks down education's sectoral boundaries while extending its reach to youth work, travel, and even sport. The program today funds a wide range of educational activities that go far beyond the institutional boundaries of school education and organize mobility projects, either virtually (online) or in the physical world (offline). Somewhat parallel to its funding efforts in the field of research, the program thus provides financial support for the projects of transnational networks that group together for a limited duration a multitude of organizations from around the globe, both educational and noneducational, for a one-off objective that is not expected to be repeated. These networks of organizations are not limited to education's formal institutions, but regularly include parties that would normally engage in very different social functions, whether private or public. In this way, funded projects assemble extremely heterogeneous networks, which can span almost anything imaginable between nurseries and Fortune 500 companies.

2. *Global platformization.* The current pandemic, with its widespread closure of schools and universities, has thrown into sharp relief how the introduction of digital technology fundamentally reshapes the organization of education. Within a few months, it became evident that schooling without school or studying without campus prompts the influx of new, private actors on an unprecedented scale, further expanding the global education industry (cf. Verger et al., 2016).

Private-run platforms are now a fixture in education, whether in higher education or kindergartens, and a number of so-called *mega-platforms* stretch out effectively over the entire globe. As Benjamin Bratton (2015) has theorized upon, such platforms establish a novel architecture for dividing up the world into new sovereign spaces that increasingly overlap, compete with and even perforate the borders of state sovereignty. As the burgeoning model of hybrid instruction has made tangible over the past year, by attempting to straddle both online and offline audiences, education finds itself in a strikingly similar predicament, caught in the uneasy balance between the norms of (national) school instruction and (global) platforms coming with their own rules of use.

What unites the two developments, next to their ability to organize education beyond national borders, is a profusely professed discontent with school.

For decades now, the European Union has made no secret of its disgruntlement with the national school systems of its member states. Resorting to the new(ish) vocabulary of *learning*—such as lifelong learning of course, next to learning outcomes, learning environments and other permutations—European Union policy openly disavows education that remains fenced within its formal institutions (cf. Mangez & Vanden Broeck, 2020). "Education and training can only contribute to growth and job-creation if learning is focused on the knowledge, skills and competences to be acquired by students (learning outcomes) through the learning process, rather than on completing a specific stage or on time spent in school," communicated the Commission to its member states already in 2012. Such disapproval echoed a statement from 1995, where it was made clear that while "reliance on a single institution to build up employability is an increasingly unsatisfactory option, people cannot be left to fend for themselves either. The indications are that it is by being positioned in a co-operative network that people will be best served in educational terms." The network-run projectification that Europe funds and thus promotes under its Erasmus+ banner is nothing if not the globe-spanning implementation of its openly asserted frustration with education's formal institutions.

The same dissatisfaction pervades the recent history of educational technology. Ever since the widespread diffusion of mass media, every technological aid has been touted as a new solution to bridge the gap between the school class and society at large. Whether it was radio or TV, computers or the Internet, the promise has always been to bring back the outside world into the classroom, with the often not even implicit ambition of thus revolutionizing an instruction mode declared broken and obsolete (cf. Cuban, 1986). As Audrey Watters (2021, p. 11) has recently hinted, each of these promises carried teleological assumptions about where education is inevitably heading: a future that is "more technological, more 'data-fied', more computerized, more automated." Implied in these lofty prognoses is the same dissatisfaction with school already pictured earlier: The classroom is too secluded from the world to allow for learning skills that really matter, and its heavily institutionalized character lacks the flexibility necessary for life in contemporary society. Much like the edu-projects funded by the European Union, the advent of educational platforms takes such unhappiness with school even a step further, by effectively offering a distinct organizational modus (cf. Stark & Pais, 2021), capable of bypassing the requirement of physical co-presence within a classroom. With the help of online video instruction, perhaps aided by artificially intelligent personalization algorithms and the like, they openly **aim to break** down the classroom's walls, **if not** to substitute for school all together. As a Californian *ed tech* start-up, egregiously named *Outschool*, has been promising: School's out.

By now this refrain should sound eerily familiar. The old is pushed out and expected to make room for new and brighter futures. It should not surprise, then, that much of the tragedy we have outlined in this chapter—school's expulsion of the family context and the subsequent, uninvited return of the household dressed up as class differences that disturb the classroom—can be expected to repeat itself within education's more novel organizational forms. The unwanted, exorcised school always returns. How that happens is a fully unexplored terrain, waiting for further sociological research. Some contours are easily visible: the differences that characterize schools' highly specific mode of instruction seem to linger on, despite (if indeed not because of) all organizational and pedagogical novelty. Even when reducing instruction to interaction with a faceless, glowing screen, platforms cannot but perpetuate the role distribution between teacher and pupil institutionalized by schools. Even in projects that let the boundaries between education and society implode, somebody or something is expected to take the teacher's role toward others who are expected to learn. Similarly, the distinction between instruction and evaluation, this most basic difference structuring all that is taught in school, always returns. Maybe in an unexpected, reversed order, as in the transnational projects funded by Europe, where an ex-ante evaluation always precedes the actual instruction (Vanden Broeck, 2020); maybe in the shape of automated correction systems or byzantine learning analytics. Either way, escaping the unity of this distinction, first established by modern school education (Luhmann, 1992), between education *stricto sensu* and the accompanying selection (who did better, who did worse), seems impossible.

One wonders if the Serresian metaphor of a parasite covers this phenomenon entirely. Without a doubt, the notion highlights brilliantly the incredible tenacity of that which the desire for system(at)ic order treats as unwanted and hence seeks to banish. But who is whose parasite in this educational symbiosis? Who is leeching off whom? Is the difference as asymmetrical as the notion seems to evoke? Is there not something more at play in this account of the crystallization of distinctly shaped contexts for instruction occurring within the global education system? What the metaphor offers in visceral spectacle, it seems to lack in evolutionary perspective. It appears less suitable to draw how education's past and recent history is as much the birth tale of new organization types and their societal trajectory, as it is a return of the repressed.

Perhaps then the uncanny reappearance is less a parasite, but an atavism, a return of traits we thought (or hoped) to be lost along society's long evolutionary path? Alas, that, too, only covers part of the phenomena. A snake suddenly has legs again, a horse's toes grow back, and somebody might grow an extra row of nipples. But the perdurance of differences in upbringing throughout school education is not a one-off throwback, an odd curiosity that strikes unpredictably. Nor should it be expected that scholastic differences will rear their heads only once in a while to shake up newer forms of education. The past's presence seems as durable as it is unasked for. Even switching from Serres's parasitology to Jacques Derrida's (1994) hauntology, the evolutionary mechanism envisaged here is not fully fathomed. Some pasts may very well haunt the present from beyond their grave. But in order to resurrect as a ghost, one first needs to die—and the household never really disappeared as a site for education. Nor did school for that matter. Johann Wolfgang Goethe, in turn, purportedly spoke of ducks to portray how some enduring pasts refuse to die (Eckermann 1852, p. 325). Like a diving duck, the past might disappear for a while below the surface. But it always turns up again, alive and kicking, and typically not where expected. This bucolic imagery of waterplay, however, fails to fully satisfy, too. For it lacks the bewilderment and tension inherent in the process of change discussed in this chapter.

The Italian *imbarazzo* might offer a final solace. Its double meaning, largely absent in English, covers both the sense of being an obstacle or hinder (*essere d'imbarazzo*) and the more familiar state of perplexity or uneasiness (*essere in imbarazzo*). The word identifies as much the source of nuisance that impedes a normal course of events, as the state of shame we might wish to bestow on it. When dealing with the boisterous novelty of learning platforms and the like, one might feel tempted to speak of *embarrassing* novelties, so as to highlight how the new seldom lives up to its promises to outdo the past. But perhaps it makes more sense to speak of pasts that get in the way of the new, that indeed embarrass. By refusing to disappear, the past is obstructing the novelty of the present to fully assert itself and thus always embarrassing it, as it were. Such talk of *embarrassed* novelty should not be taken as a negation or unwillingness to acknowledge the newness of the organizational changes I have outlined earlier. Transnational projects are not simple perpetuations of what Guy Vincent (1982) once dubbed the *forme scolaire* and neither are digital learning platforms. The specificity of these new educational forms cannot be fully grasped, however, if one does not observe how they always incorporate and are unsettled by the past they fervently seek to dismiss.

Acknowledgments

This work was supported by the European Commission under the Marie Skłodowska-Curie Action (MSCA) Morphogenesis (Grant ID 101032759). For their valuable remarks and suggestions, I am most grateful to Giancarlo Corsi, Eric Mangez, David Stark, and Gita Steiner-Khamsi.

Notes

1. Or perhaps more accurate: a shell hard as steel (cf. Baehr, 2001). Luhmann's (1996, p. 196) assessment of this Weberian imagery shows the direct lineage between the two oeuvres: "Max Weber had started this in a certain way when he spoke of value conflicts, life orders and tragic problems or of bureaucracy acting like a steel casing. Weber was himself involved in

a pessimist assessment of rationality with the assumption that bureaucracy was also everywhere, in the press, in the parties, in all organisations. But this must of course be formulated differently at the end of this century than at the end of the previous century and hung on a much broader and also more abstract theoretical framework, that is the only possibility."

2. Cf. Luhmann (1987, p. 177): Socialisation "is not simply a transfer of conformity patterns, but the constantly through communication reproduced alternative of conformity or deviation, adaptation or resistance."

3. On the end(lessness) of education and its relationship with career formation, see also Giancarlo Corsi (1999, 2020).

4. On the growing discontent this role distribution creates and the resulting surge in home-schooling, see Alice Tilman and Eric Mangez (2021). About the often paradox attribution of responsibility that comes along with the uneven role distribution between school and parents, see Hanne Knudsen and Niels Åkerstrøm Andersen (2014). As to the competition that school education increasingly faces from other societal spheres—in addition to family life, that is—see Corsi (2021): Because the labor market and mass media increasingly project career paths entirely foreign to the trajectories set out by formal education, the question arises how schooling should navigate this uneasy coexistence.

5. Note that speaking of equal opportunity, rather than of equality, or the more recent talk of "inclusive education" does not discredit Luhmann's assertion in any way, since what is at stake in these practices is not at all the acknowledgement of difference as such, but again rather its neutralization.

6. For an elaborate and knowledgeable comparison between the oeuvre of Serres and Luhmann, see Benedikt Melters (2016). As the repeated mention of parasites in Luhmann's writings already suggests, Serres's desire to roam the indeterminate non-place "in front of" difference, rather than to resolve its ambiguity, need not necessarily be at odds with a Luhmannian interest in the various processes of "necessification" populating our social world, as Melters also concludes, but may very well complement it.

REFERENCES

Baecker, D. (2007). *Form und Formen der Kommunikation*. Suhrkamp.

Baehr, P. (2001). The "iron cage" and the "shell as hard as steel": Parsons, Weber, and the Stahlhartes Gehäuse metaphor in the Protestant ethic and the spirit of capitalism. *History and Theory, 40*(2), 153–169.

Böhme, H., & G. Böhme (1982/1996). *Das Andere der Vernunft*. Suhrkamp.

Boudon, R. (1974). *Education, opportunity, and social inequality*. Wiley.

Bourdieu, P. (1966). L'école conservatrice: Les inégalités devant l'école et devant la culture. *Revue française de sociologie, 7*(3), 325–347.

Bourdieu, P., & Passeron, J.-C. (1970). *La reproduction*. Minuit.

Bratton, B. H. (2015). The stack. *Log, 35*, 128–159.

Corsi, G. (1992). Libertà, uguaglianza, eccellenza. I paradossi pedagogici. In R. Genovese (Ed.), *Figure del paradosso* (pp. 275–304). Liguori.

Corsi, G. (1999). The dark side of a career. In D. Baecker (Ed.), *Problems of form* (pp. 171–179). Stanford University Press.

Corsi, G. (2020). "Education has no end": Reconciling past and future through reforms in the education system. *Educational Philosophy and Theory, 52*(6), 688–697.

Corsi, G. (2021). Whose life is it anyway? The life course as an observational medium in the education system. *European Educational Research Journal, 20*(6), 740–757.

Cuban, L. (1990). Reforming again, again, and again. *Educational Researcher, 19*(1), 3–13.

Cuban, L. (1986). *Teachers and machines.* Teachers College Press.

Derrida, J. (1994). *Specters of Marx.* London.

Eckerman, J. P. (1852). *Conversations with Goethe.* James Munroe and Co.

Esposito, E. (2021). Rationality. In C. Baraldi, G. Corsi, & E. Esposito (Eds.), *Unlocking Luhmann* (pp. 191–193). Bielefeld University Press.

European Commission. (1995). *Teaching and learning: Towards the learning society (White Paper)* (COM [95] 590). Bruxelles.

European Commission. (2012). *Rethinking education: Investing in skills for better socio-economic outcomes* (COM [2012] 669). Bruxelles.

Freytag, G. (1990). *Technique of the drama.* Scott, Foresman and Co.

Gellner, E. (1983). *Nations and nationalism.* Blackwell.

Knudsen, H., & Åkerstrøm Andersen, N. (2014). Playful hyper-responsibility: Toward a dislocation of parents' responsibility? *Journal of Education Policy, 29*(1), 105–121.

Luhmann, N. (1977). *Zweckbegriff und Systemrationalität. Über die Funktion von Zwecken in sozialen Systemen.* Suhrkamp.

Luhmann, N. (1982). *The differentiation of society.* Columbia University Press.

Luhmann, N. (1987). *Soziologische Aufklärung 4.* VS Verlag.

Luhmann, N. (1988, August 4). Njet-Set und Terror-Desperados. In Die Tageszeitung (pp. 11–12).

Luhmann, N. (1990). Die Homogenisierung des Anfangs: zur Ausdifferenzierung der Schulerziehung. In N. Luhmann & K.-E. Schorr (Eds.), *Zwischen Anfang und Ende* (pp. 73–111). Suhrkamp.

Luhmann, N. (1991). Paradigm lost: On the ethical reflection of morality. *Thesis Eleven, 29*(1), 82.

Luhmann, N. (1992). System und Absicht der Erziehung. In N. Luhmann & K.-E. Schorr (Eds.), *Zwischen Absicht und Person* (pp. 102–124). Suhrkamp.

Luhmann, N. (1995). *Social systems.* Stanford University Press.

Luhmann, N. (1996). *Protest.* Suhrkamp.

Luhmann, N. (1998). *Observations on modernity.* Stanford University Press.

Luhmann, N. (2002). *Das Erziehungssystem der Gesellschaft* (D. Lenzen, Ed.). Suhrkamp.

Luhmann, N., & Schorr, K. E. (2000). *Problems of reflection in the system of education* (R. A. Neuwirth, Trans.). Waxmann.

Mangez, E., & Vanden Broeck, P. (2020). The history of the future and the shifting forms of education. *Educational Philosophy and Theory, 52*(6), 676–687.

Mangez, E., & Vanden Broeck, P. (2021). Worlds apart? On Niklas Luhmann and the sociology of education. *European Educational Research Journal, 20*(6), 705–718.

Melters, B. (2016). Vor der Differenz. Anmerkungen zum Verhältnis von allgemeiner Systemtheorie und der Philosophie Michel Serres. *Soziale Systeme, 21*(2), 390–418.

Meyer, J. W., Ramirez, F. O., & Soysal, Y. N. (1992). World expansion of mass education, 1870–1980. *Sociology of Education, 65*(2), 128–149.

Serres, M. (1982). *The parasite.* John Hopkins University Press.

Simmel, G. (1950). *The sociology of Georg Simmel* (K. H. Wolff, Ed.). Free Press.

Stark, D., & Pais, I. (2021). Algorithmic management in the platform economy. *Sociologica, 14*(3), 47–72.

Tilman, A., & Mangez, E. (2021). L'instruction à domicile comme phénomène global. *Éducation et sociétés*, 45(1), 123–141.

Tyack, D., & Cuban, L. (1995). *Tinkering toward Utopia*. Harvard University Press.

Tyrell, H., & Vanderstraeten, R. (2007). Familie und Schule: Zwei Orte der Erziehung. In J. Aderhold & O. Kranz (Eds.), *Intention und Funktion* (pp. 159–174). VS Verlag.

Vanden Broeck, P. (2020). Beyond school: Transnational differentiation and the shifting form of education in world society. *Journal of Education Policy*, 35(6), 836–855.

Vanden Broeck, P. (2021). Education in world society: A matter of form. *European Educational Research Journal*, 20(6), 791–805.

Verger, A., Lubienski, C., & Steiner-Khamsi, G. (Eds.). (2016). *The global education industry*. Routledge.

Vincent, G. (1982). *L'école primaire française*. Université de Lille.

Watters, A. (2021). *Teaching machines*. MIT Press.

Weber, M. (1946). *From Max Weber: Essays in sociology*. Oxford University Press.

CHAPTER 19

....

REDRAWING WHAT COUNTS AS EDUCATION

The Impact of the Global Early Childhood Education Program on German Kindergarten

....

CHRISTINE WEINBACH

INTRODUCTION

THIS chapter is interested in the long-term historical transformations in institutionalized early childhood education in Germany. These institutions, which operated for centuries at the margins of the formal education system, were gradually, and only relatively recently, incorporated into the core of the German education system. In the course of this development, the global program of early childhood education (ECE) replaced a system that privileged the simulation of familial environments over pedagogical achievement, and it was designed from the start as a learning process that brings together pedagogical and social objectives.

This chapter reconstructs this development from the perspective of Luhmann's systems theory. In contrast to conventional understandings of his work, Luhmann's conception of autopoietic and self-referential systems does not assume a world of self-sufficient, indivisible units. Rather, Luhmann urges a correction of "that obliquity of social theory that arises when one considers only the autopoietic dynamics of function systems" (Luhmann, 1997c, p. 778). Thus, the "differentiation of operatively closed function systems" remains incomprehensible without systematic consideration of the "establishment of their environmental relations within society" (Luhmann, 1997c, p. 779; Schimank, 2015; Schimank & Volkmann, 1999, p. 31). This essay focuses on the constitutive dependence of the self-referential education system on the political. Accordingly, the latter goes beyond providing educational organizations with the necessary resources of money, personnel, and sufficient clientele. Generally binding political decisions also provide them with educational goals deemed socially relevant. The autonomy of the education system becomes apparent through the pedagogical implementation of these educational goals.

My analysis of the reconstruction of institutional early childhood education necessitates a historical approach. To accomplish this, I draw on "Problems of Reflection in the System of Education" by Niklas Luhmann and Karl-Eberhard Schorr (Luhmann & Schorr, 2000), which asserts three phases of differentiation in a self-referential education system. Each phase is characterized by its own contingency formula: human perfection (typical of premodernity), all-around education (late 18th century), and the ability to learn (second half of the 20th century). ECE, as I will show, was from the beginning the program of an educational process that not only refers to an individual with the ability to learn but has the ability to learn itself.

DIFFERENTIATION THROUGH SELF-REFERENTIALITY: THE EDUCATION SYSTEM OF THE FUNCTIONALLY DIFFERENTIATED SOCIETY

Conversion of the Educational Setting to Self-Reference

According to Luhmann, self-referential function systems are being developed with the conversion of society to a functionally differentiated form. This also applies to the education system. Premodern education understood its task as an extension of the family and therefore defined its subject matter in relation to the position and activities of the household. Functional differentiation turns education into a self-referential system: educational institutions discard elements of "politically overdetermined estate-related education" (Stichweh, 1991, p. 82), which references societal areas outside of education, and replace them in a self-referential process of environmental adjustment by its "own systemic imperatives" (Stichweh, 1991, p. 80).

An essential building block in this process is the reinvention of the idea of the child (Aries) as a medium on which pedagogically intended forms can be imposed. The task of the educator to therefore "denature the human being" (Luhmann, 2002, p. 87) is related to the natural self-guided learning (*Selbsttätigkeit*) within the subject (Luhmann & Schorr, 2000, p. 87) and no longer pertains to the child's family background. A second essential building block here is the demand for the "education of the educator" (Luhmann & Schorr, 2000, p. 97). Only a trained educator can achieve the necessary autonomy from a stratified society's expectations, thereby focusing exclusively on the encouragement of the self-guided subject's natural urge to become educated (Roessler, 1978, p. 631). Education is thus founded on a relationship between the educated teacher and the self-guided subject to be taught. This active "reshaping of 'means' taken from the environment" by adapting the means "to the needs of the system" (Stichweh, 1991, p. 79) leads teachers to develop their own "self-specification" (Stichweh, 1991, p. 80) of a teaching environment less affected by interference from external societal conditions. In other words, educated teachers, as they develop their methodology and content, refer to their intention to educate their pupils.

Pedagogical Goals of the Education System

The education system removes the teaching setting from its social and political context and places it firmly in the pedagogical sphere. In the interaction between the educated teacher and the self-guided pupil, education seeks to produce a personal environment that works for the new society (Luhmann, 2017, p. 805). It is about the realignment of educational goals. For this to succeed, the education system had to detach itself from its outward orientation toward family households and develop a self-referential attitude toward a functionally differentiated society. To do this, it developed three environmental relations, or more precisely, "system references" (Luhmann, 1997a, p. 757) that it had to bring into agreement for its own sake. In the first system reference, "function," the education system relates to society as a whole and strives to produce members who meet society's requirements. For the second system reference, "performance," the education system identifies other social systems and forms relationships of performance with them; for example, it hopes to supply the economic system with employable labor. The nonidentity of function and performance exerts pressure on the system to adapt in response, which becomes the third system reference of "reflection" (Luhmann & Schorr, 2000, p. 60): The education system thus develops its own perspective on the world and distinguishes itself as a (total) system from the (total) environment. This leads to the emergence of the reflection theory called pedagogy.

However, pedagogy can only cope with the higher degrees of complexity that emerged from the education system's new position if it deploys a contingency formula. Contingency formulas reduce a function system's excess of possibilities by integrating its various environmental relationships into an overall concept. They are "performances of reflection that refer to the function and that, in order to do so, must control the relationship between function, performance, and reflection, and that, therefore, require reflection on the reflection, or two-step reflection" (Luhmann & Schorr, 2000, pp. 67–68). With the help of a contingency formula, the system "formulates . . . an articulated view of itself" (Luhmann & Schorr, 2000, p. 367). In pedagogy, therefore, a contingency formula functions as an ordering point of reference that is itself withdrawn from reflection, but that allows the education system to form a theory of reflection through which it can situate itself within a functionally differentiated society. The "microdiversity of classroom interactions" (Luhmann, 2002, p. 202) becomes the locus to which this self-understanding refers: Classroom interactions form the object around which the reflective work of pedagogy revolves. From this point, the education system locates itself within the functionally differentiated society through a pedagogical definition of the complementary roles of teacher and pupil, as well as a pedagogical definition of the educational goal that a teacher should pursue.

All-Around Education (*Bildung*): Pedagogy Diverges From *Social* Aims

Luhmann and Schorr find that premodern education was already in possession of a contingency formula: perfection in the sense of a "*moral* completion of *human* nature" (Luhmann & Schorr, 2000, p. 80). This formula welded together the system references of "function (completeness), performance (usefulness) and reflection (blissfulness)" by connecting them to the family household within a broader stratified society (Luhmann & Schorr, 2000, pp. 79–80). They began to come apart as family, politics, and economy functionally separated, and their divergence in terms of differentiated "orientations towards *function* and *performance*" of the education system (Luhmann & Schorr, 2000, p. 77) "necessitates in theory and in practice a new formulation of pedagogy" (Luhmann & Schorr, 2000, p. 80). However, the pedagogical discourses within the German-speaking world of 1800 did "not seek a solution of the problem in a different balancing of the system references of function, performance and reflection, but rather" in the new contingency formula of "all-around education (*Bildung*)" (Luhmann & Schorr, 2000, p. 81). The problem was that by orienting itself toward the contingency formula of all-around education, pedagogy systematically ignored the system reference of performance (usefulness). Consequently, within the education system, it remained unclear for which society education had to be provided.

A major cause of this deficit was the new pedagogy's radical orientation toward the subject. The contingency formula of all-around education perpetuated the figure of the self-guided human being and the idea of "education as the fashioning of 'inner form,'" which was already embedded within the contingency formula of human perfection (Luhmann & Schorr, 2000, p. 82). However, pedagogy no longer considered the goal of education to be the moral perfection of an estate-related subject. Instead, pedagogy imagined the self-guided subject's relationship to the world as one structured primarily along cognitive lines. This meant that the subject would require the structuring precepts of an educational process that shaped the mind through both instruction and self-guided engagement with scientific knowledge. The assumption that man has a natural instinct for self-guided learning (*Selbstbildung*) (Roessler, 1978, p. 631) set at least two suppositions in motion: first, that the self-guided subject seeks to know the world and to move freely on the basis of his own power of judgement; and second, that a science-oriented education would enable him to engage with true knowledge on a self-guided basis. This "learning process that was entirely determined by doctrine (at the universities)" (Luhmann & Schorr, 2000, p. 86) was "identified with the route to self-reliance" (Luhmann & Schorr, 2000, p. 90). By this means, the educated (*gebildete*) subject was supposed to acquire the ability to make independent judgements in situations requiring complex decision-making (Luhmann & Schorr, 2000, p. 85).

From a sociological perspective it is evident that this educational program amounted to an academically oriented grammar school for future holders of professional roles within differentiating function systems. Admittedly, the introduction of compulsory schooling for girls and boys in the principality of Palatinate-Zweibrücken had begun by the end of the 16th century and had reached the German states by 1835 when Saxony adopted a mandatory schooling scheme. Nevertheless, such programs never envisaged a single-track, comprehensive primary school education as a way to produce educated (*gebildete*) subjects.

However, pedagogy ignored the fact that its concept of all-around education (*Bildung*) was restricted to a narrow scope of educational interactions tied to schools. Instead, it conceived of its pedagogical program as the "elevation of humanity in the individual" (Luhmann, 2002, p. 187). In this "new distance to the problem of the usefulness of education" (Luhmann & Schorr, 2000, p. 86), education gained new independence from family-centered education and succeeded in asserting its own identity as a self-referential education system in the circle of function systems. However, its focus on "the subjectivity of the human being" did not indicate "for which society people are to be educated" (Luhmann, 2002, p. 18), because pedagogy teleologically derived its educational program from the self-guided nature of the individual subject (Treml, 2002, p. 654). This development superimposed the societal function of the education system upon the performance relationships that it had long maintained with other function systems (Luhmann & Schorr, 2000, p. 92). Pedagogy did not recognize that the performance relationships of the education system to other function systems were based on educational goals set by means of *generally binding decisions* of the state (Luhmann & Schorr, 2000, p. 120). State-mandated educational goals, which had to be managed and implemented by the schools, remained *pedagogically indeterminate*.

Dependence and Autonomy: State Performances for the Education System

Organizational Formation and Full Inclusion Through State Performances

The state of school education in the German states was thus contradictory. On one hand, with the introduction of compulsory schooling that occurred between the late 17th and early 19th centuries, a large part of the population was gradually included into instruction. On the other hand, only a fraction of this group was ultimately included in an all-around education program. This had to do with the education system's fundamental dependence on state services.

Unlike the political and the economic system, processing symbolically generalized communication media as power respective money, the self-demarcation of the education system against other social systems took place at an organizational level: The differentiation (*Ausdifferenzierung*) of the education system into an independently functional sector of society was "organizationally carried by schools" (Luhmann & Schorr, 2000, p. 69). Only those educational interactions that took place within this particular institutional setting were localized within the functionally specified education system. The resulting break with "the immediacy of family life" (Luhmann & Schorr, 2000, p. 89) facilitated education's self-referential approach and its demarcation from external systems (Luhmann, 2002, p. 128), and this permeated the entire school system.

The internal differentiation of the education system, on the other hand, functioned by means of "the possibility of differentiating participating systems" in universities, namely, school types, school classes, and school careers "from lower to higher classes or schools" (Luhmann, 2002, p. 161). Some schools in the emergent system followed pedagogically based all-around education programs, while most others sought to educate their students to become obedient and industrious subjects under the influence of external references such as religion and rule.

One reason for this was that the differentiation of the education system was based on prerequisites that it could not itself provide. Only the state could provide "effective organization potential" (Luhmann & Schorr, 2000, p. 82), but it was unable to do so without an egoistic interest in the education system's performance. As early as the 16th century, the early modern state was oriented toward the common good formula and saw itself as an interventionist and productive state (Stichweh, 1991, pp. 154–231). Motivated by a mercantilist state model, it set its sights on improving the working capacity and obedience of its subjects (Kaufmann, 2003, p. 152). In the 18th century, the Prussian state promoted a differentiated school system, wherein the *Gymnasium* (grammar school) was expected to develop loyal civil servants, and the *Volksschule* (one-class primary school) was to create pious and industrious subjects. The varying conditions of the institutional frameworks of the different types of schools, with their universally binding mandates, exercised an influence on classroom education.

Relevance of Educational Goals to Society Through State Target Setting

Diligence and Piety Through One-Class Primary School Education (*Volksschule*)

When the Prussian state was establishing compulsory schooling in 1717 for children who could not be educated privately, institutionalized education was still oriented toward the contingency formula of perfection. The Prussian state grounded its primary schools in the formats of classroom interaction used in the confessional sexton schools and placed them under the control of the municipalities (Titze, 1973, p. 16). Instruction in the catechism, Bible reading and singing religious songs served the religious legitimization of its authority (Geißler, 2013, pp. 94–101). To improve the work skills of Prussian subjects, basic knowledge of arithmetic and useful handicrafts such as knitting were taught. Teaching responsibilities that were usually the domain of local priests were gradually granted to former soldiers or full-time craftsmen, who often had only rudimentary knowledge. Instruction mostly consisted of having students memorize and recite learning content without understanding it.

This program of instruction, which persisted throughout the early 18th century, continued through to late 19th-century Prussia, under the consistent aim of stratifying education by class (Titze, 1973, p. 193). The proletariat was taught in primary schools "to willingly submit to predetermined relations of rule" (Titze, 1973, p. 174). Thus, well into the 19th century, the state continued to keep primary schools trapped in "style prescriptions" (Luhmann, 2000, p. 120), shaped by the earlier contingency formula of perfection: The pedagogy of the mid-19th century education, at least of the lower classes, was still, "in the last analysis, an issue of religion" (Luhmann & Schorr, 2000, p. 75). Primary school teachers such as Adolf Diesterweg, however, protested against the state's educational policy, and in keeping with the spirit of the modern concept of education, demanded that the lower classes be educated for "self-guided learning, self-determination and self-government" (Titze, 1973, p. 155). The fact that Diesterweg also perceived all-around education for the lower classes as a reliable means of containing social unrest illustrates the helplessness of a pedagogy whose educational program lacked a social educational goal. By contrast, the education prescribed by the Prussian state for its prospective primary school teachers was based on real conditions of social differentiation, and consistently on Romans 13:1, "Let every soul be subject unto the higher powers. For there is no power but of God: the powers that be are ordained of God" (quoted in Titze, 1973, p. 192).

All-Around Education in Grammar School Education (Gymnasium)

Pedagogical and state views also diverged with regard to grammar school education. The Prussian state intended the Gymnasium to prepare the sons of the nobility and the higher bourgeoisie for later university attendance through intellectual and scientific instruction, ultimately to launch their careers as civil servants (van Ackeren et al., 2015, p. 18). Accordingly, "the standardisation of educational qualifications and the creation of conditions for professional usability in the higher civil service" began to be regulated by the state in 1788 and were enforced across the board by 1834 (Thiel, 2008, p. 212). By contrast, pedagogy aimed to promote "the intellectual development of its pupils with the means of science" in grammar school education (Roessler, 1961, p. 292). According to the pedagogical perspective, the educator "does not have to inquire about what the adult human being is going to do with these powers" (Roessler, 1961, p. 279).

The various domains of instruction did not constitute separate subjects, which only happened later (Roessler, 1961, p. 316), and the teacher at grammar school saw himself as a "member of the academic profession" who "participate[d] in the learned discourse of the time with his scholarly publications" (Thiel, 2008, p. 216). However, over the course of the 19th century, the state began to force performance-based recruitment of its civil service by means of year-based classes, subject-related grades and certificates. Pedagogy experienced these targets as external to its concept of all-around education (Luhmann, 2002, p. 282). When school reform throughout the German Empire of the late 19th century systematized the national school system in such a way as to explicitly tie schooling to the needs of the highly industrialized German economy for the first time (Ringer, 1987, p. 2), educational intention (in the sense of all-around education) and selection requirements (in the sense of meaningful certificates for careers) began to drift even further apart within the classroom. Within the classroom, career-relevant performance goals came to the fore, displacing the goal of general education and leading to an "emptying" of the concept of all-around education (Luhmann & Schorr, 2000, p. 93).

System Autonomy: Dealing With Constraints

Luhmann writes that the "continuing administrative state dependence of schools" makes it difficult to "recognise the functional autonomy of the education system" (Luhmann, 2002, p. 146). Admittedly, the pedagogy of the self-referentially constructed education system relied on self-generated building blocks: the educated educator, the self-referential subject, pedagogy, and a contingency formula with "style regulations for the system's determinative performances" (Luhmann, 2000, p. 120). However, the education system's self-referential architecture only became possible by means of state power.

The state expresses this power by providing the education system with necessary organizational resources through generally binding decisions and by ensuring a sufficient number of pupils. These decisions set societal educational goals for educational organizations, resulting in a close interdependency between politics and education. In the early 19th century, the political system used the educational performance of classroom interactions to further its own objectives and, therefore, created framework conditions that partly enabled (grammar school) and partly inhibited (primary school) the rearrangement of the education system to self-referential foundations.

However, this newly emergent pedagogy reflected exclusively on the self-referentiality of the education system. Luhmann and Schorr identify profound deficits in this reflection, which had important consequences for the system's autonomy and its self-control as a function system within a functionally differentiated society. They understand system autonomy here not "as the absence of constraints, but rather as a form of dealing with constraints" (Luhmann & Schorr, 2000, p. 60). Autonomy, therefore, is possible in an education system that takes on and integrates state goals for instruction in its pedagogical methodologies, not one that has absolute freedom from state targets. On the contrary, institutions in whose services the state has no further interest occupied a marginal position within the educational system because they lack society's mandate.

INSTITUTIONALISED EARLY CHILDHOOD EDUCATION

The State's Lack of Interest in Early Childhood Education

Institutionalized early childhood education did not attract the interest of state institutions in Germany until the second half of the 20th century and therefore was located at the fringe of the education system. The German states of the 19th century explicitly rejected the break with family life represented by the institutional education of young children; indeed, the General Land Law for the Prussian States of 1794 vested mothers with the responsibility for taking care of their children until the age of 4 (Reyer, 1987b, p. 257). Progressive associations of primary school teachers in the mid-19th century unsuccessfully demanded the establishment of early childhood schools as a preparatory stage for a reformed school system (Franke-Meyer, 2011, p. 90). The German states, however, beginning in the 1820s, came to see the institutionalized education of young children merely as an effective means of combating the threat of revolution (Erning, 1987, p. 27). The ruling powers were more interested in the educational program of the Englishman Samuel Wilderspin (1824) and his "objective of an unreserved recognition and respect for the given conditions" (Erning, 1987, p. 26). Accordingly, the German states encouraged private initiatives to create such institutions by founding "associations of private charity" (Wasmuth, 2010, pp. 35–36). Thus, a type of voluntary early childhood education emerged in which classroom interactions resembled those of one-class primary schools and implemented the taxonomy of the contingency formula of perfection. An alternative vision of kindergarten, which was founded at the same time but was largely rejected by the state, promoted, like grammar school, a program of all-around education. However, the kindergarten model remained a minor phenomenon in the landscape of institutionalised early childhood education (3.3.2).

Early Childhood School and Kindergarten in the 19th Century

Education Leading to Moral Perfection

In 1835, the Protestant pastor Georg Heinrich Theodor Fliedner applied Wilderspin's model to found the first German school for young children (Erning, 1987, p. 33). Fliedner identified the neglect of young children as a sin, as a violation of the divine order. He saw strict religious education as the most appropriate means for the moral improvement of these children and their families (Erning, 1987, p. 34). By adhering to the outdated contingency formula of perfection, namely, moral "perfection according to the stipulations of the estate" (Luhmann & Schorr, 2000, p. 104), the "consciousness of belonging to the class of the poor . . . should be consolidated" (Reyer, 1987b, p. 254). Fliedner's method for training the mistresses for his early childhood school was thus based on the "form of the spiritual office of deaconess" (Erning, 1987, p. 36). The lessons taught at such schools resembled those seen in one-class primary school: religious instruction, rote "memorisation of prayers, religious songs and sayings" (Erning, 1987, p. 34), and instruction in discipline, cleanliness, order, and industriousness (Wasmuth, 2010, p. 71). Play was imbued with a moral component, for example, the "exercise-like movement of the body," which strengthened the limbs, made them limber, and accustomed "the children to attention, order and obedience" (Wasmuth, 2010, p. 73).

Education Leading to General Human Formation

At nearly the same time, Friedrich Froebel's alternative vision of kindergarten argued that "the task and goal of the kindergarten . . . is solely to promote and educate the child's natural talents" (Reyer, 2015, p. 42): the child's independent play and inner striving for a coherent life could express its cognitive relationship to the world, in which the "inner and outer" spheres came into contact (Wasmuth, 2010, p. 90). Science-based gifts, meant to shape and support play between the pedagogically enlightened mother and the self-referential child, were intended to support the child's efforts in an educational way (Erning, 1987, p. 37). Froebel called this educational setting the kindergarten. The institution of "kindergarten" was actually a school for mothers that intended to bring the educational setting of the kindergarten into families: trained kindergarten teachers, with a high level of general education, led play circles attended by bourgeois or aristocratic mothers and their children for a few hours a week (Wasmuth, 2010, pp. 35, 38).

The kindergarten gathered all of the self-referential building blocks of the education system: the educated educators (the kindergarten teacher and the mother), the self-guiding child, and a pedagogy oriented toward the contingency formula of all-around education. Unlike the early childhood schools informed by Wilderspin's theories, Froebel's kindergarten concept was either ignored by the state or became the object of its hostile attentions; after the failed revolution of 1848, for example, the kindergarten was denigrated as a socialist system and correspondingly banned (Franke-Meyer, 2011, p. 116). Consequently, its institutions found comparatively limited purchase in Germany at this time.

Family Childhood for All

As the national welfare state emerged in the German Empire in the late 19th century, this institutional landscape—which was differentiated according to the contingency formulas of perfection and all-around education—underwent a dramatic transformation toward standardization. In the process, institutionalized early childhood education was finally pushed to the margins.

Otto von Bismarck, chancellor of the new German Empire, reformulated the social question as the workers' question (Kaufmann, 2003, p. 260). Bismarck conceived of "the workers as a uniform 'status' or 'class' and made "the improvement of their overall situation the goal of state action" (Kaufmann, 2003, p. 272). Child labor and women's work became restricted, and the male family breadwinner became the norm, even for the lower social classes (Gottschall & Schröder, 2013). The notion of a private childhood for all social classes came within reach, and this idea began to be expressed by teachers, doctors, and psychologists in parenting guides (Hoffer-Mehlmer, 2003). Wherever the realization of this family model appeared to be endangered in spite of the employment-based social security system, the public benefits system intervened on a case-by-case basis.

The passage of the Reich Law on Youth Welfare in 1922 and its implementation in 1924 facilitated a systematic focus on early childhood education (Konrad, 2004, pp. 113, 127). Building on the new idea of a private childhood for all, kindergarten came to be seen as a "real nursery" where the child could "live and act entirely according to its own laws" (Weiß, member of the Reich School Conference 1921, quoted by Wasmuth, 2010, p. 245). Due to the kindergarten's function as a surrogate for the family, the state began to renounce specific educational objectives and granted pedagogical discretion to the kindergartens. In spite of the new legislative framework for youth welfare, the training of kindergarten teachers remained pedagogically modest (Wasmuth, 2010, p. 138).

In the context of these developments, the *Volkskindergarten*, which had existed since 1874, served as a prototype for denominational early childhood schools. Developed by Fröbel's student Henriette Schrader-Breymann, the Volkskindergarten dispensed with Fröbel's ideas in favor of the Swiss pedagogue and educational reformer Johann Heinrich Pestalozzi's idea of the family living room as a model for bringing together the various elements essential to human education. The Volkskindergarten attempted "to 'de-institutionalise' public child education by incorporating family and domestic elements" (Reyer, 1987b, p. 280), and its all-day opening hours catered to the lower social classes (Reyer, 1987a, p. 52). A Volkskindergarten schedule incorporated games, gymnastics, music and singing, gardening and domestic activities, each grouped around an item emblematic of the month (Wasmuth, 2010, p. 142). Soon after, denominational providers of early childhood schools adopted the Volkskindergarten as a model for their own activities, and educational programs that simulated the family home became widespread. Long rows of benches were replaced by a "loosened arrangement of individual tables," and the "toy cupboards" became "more and more accessible to the children," with "functional corners," and the "floor became 'a play area'" (Reyer, 1987a, p. 70). This coincided with the gradual diminution of religious influence on education (Wasmuth, 2010, p. 239).

After the ravages of World War II and the subjugation of all levels of society to National Socialist imperatives, the Federal Republic of Germany, formed in 1949, returned to the moral and institutional imperatives established by the Weimar Republic more than two decades earlier. Unlike the German Democratic Republic, where the government directed the entire education system, child and youth welfare institutions in the Federal Republic of Germany resumed responsibility for kindergarten education, which was regarded as a substitute for the family (Neumann, 1987, pp. 102–103). The after-effects of the authoritarian education imposed by the National Socialist system remained perceptible (Neumann, 1987, p. 96). Yet, as had long been the case previously, the "leading contemporary pedagogy, the humanities," had "little enriching effect on institutionalised early childhood education" (Wasmuth, 2010, p. 240). The family-like kindergarten was intended to "closely follow the protective and sheltering family up-bringing and to create a 'pedagogical resistance' to the 'hothouse climate of the modern world' . . . 'which presses the child to prematurely differentiate their holistic response to the impression of the environment'" (Neumann, 1987, p. 102). This program, which remained family-oriented, was only called into question when the West German state began to take an interest in the educational achievements of young children for reasons of economic policy. Since then, kindergartens have gradually been incorporated into the (West) German education system. The driving force behind this development originates in the political system of a global society.

REDRAWING WHAT COUNTS AS EDUCATION: GLOBALIZATION AND EDUCATION

Political Imperative: Education for a Rapidly Changing Society

Global political interest in the performance of the education system arose due to a par-adigm shift in economic policy initiated by the late-20th-century collapse of interna-tional regimes, such as the Bretton Woods system, which had been under US leadership. These regimes had provided a protective bulwark for Western European nation states, which after World War II had operated within a liberal framework that allowed them to "take advantage of the international division of labour while protecting their citizens from the consequences of the 'creative destruction' of an unleashed capitalism" (Scharpf, 1999, p. 112). The collapse of these regimes, however, led, among other things, to higher volatility in labor markets. In the 1970s, the Organization for Economic Cooperation and Development (OECD) therefore began proposing an agenda to its member states to improve the responsiveness of companies as well as the labor force to the new demands of the dynamic global economy. To this end, the OECD adopted the concept of "life-long learning," developed by the eponymous UNESCO Institute for Lifelong Learning, and integrated it in the context of employment policy. Since then, lifelong learning has been used as an instrument to improve the adaptability of the labor force with respect to the varying demands of the dynamic labor market. The "national school systems . . . throughout the world were declared to be one of the most important potentials for so-cial development" (Adick, 1992, p. 348). They were tasked with educating the individuals of the OECD member states for a "rapidly changing society" (CERI, 1973, p. 18). When the Iron Curtain fell at the end of the 1980s, and the world economy shifted into gear, the OECD boosted its economic and employment policy orientation and started initiating a second implementation phase of its education policy reform proposals (Papadopoulos, 1994, p. 202).

Once the concept of recurrent education became a component of lifelong learning, this meant that the entire population were to be educated as members of a rapidly and permanently changing society. Socially homogeneous educational careers were prised open, and institutionalized education was meant to begin at an early age. Over the course of this development, the education system formed its new contingency formula "ability to learn," and now "every process of the system exists under this condition of self-reference" (Luhmann & Schorr, 2000, p. 97): Now both the individual and the educational process were supposed to become capable of learning. The global ECE program, therefore, is designed from the start as an educational process that incorporates the ability to learn. It constantly reassesses its educational goals, its institutions, and its educational activities, with the help of modern monitoring instruments.

Reconfiguring What Counts as Early Childhood Education

The Young Child in the Context of Recurrent Education

Education policy in the late 20th century was long able to rely on forms of institutionalised performance linkage between the educational and political systems. At the level of society worldwide (Stichweh, 2007), global organizations such as UNESCO or the OECD function as one mechanism of structural coupling between politics and education. These organizations' programs tend to be a product of the systematic involvement of expert scholars and professionals. Abstract yet specialized approaches enrich political objectives, anticipating the inherent logic of the addressed social systems and increasing their connectivity within the national contexts of reception (Walgenbach, 2000, p. 181).

This interconnectedness also helps to understand why policy reform proposals for early childhood education from UNESCO or the OECD are predicated on a redefinition of the self-referential child as a fundamental building block of the education system. In the 1970s, the OECD's Centre for Educational Research and Innovation (CERI), for example, emphasized the "crucial role played by the events and the environment which affect the child in this period," which has been undisputed since the work of the psychologists Jean Piaget and Benjamin Bloom (CERI, 1975, p. 10). Many years later, the OECD noted that modern neuroscience corroborated this perspective: "These reciprocal learning interactions afford children ways to define who they are, what they can become and how and why they are important to other people" (OECD, 2006, p. 193).

In the mid-1970s, the OECD based its educational policy recommendations on this new image of a subject who was both self-guided and susceptible to environmental influences, according to which *recurrent education*, in the sense of an "educational service available to all, at every age, wherever and whenever required" (CERI, 1973, p. 6), should begin in early childhood (CERI, 1975, p. 5). Recurrent education presupposed the dismantling of social segmentation in schools and an emphasis on more equality of opportunity, more flexibility in personal, vocational, and professional development, and a closer alignment with the labor market. Early childhood education was given a social mandate related to the subsequent stages of the child's life, beginning with school. To do justice to the child's natural capacity for self-guided learning (*Selbsttätigkeit*), two established traditions in early childhood education were put into productive dialogue: While preschool (as found in, for example, France, the United Kingdom, and the Netherlands) primarily promoted the child's intellectual and cognitive development (CERI, 1975, p. 10), the holistic-social pedagogical tradition (as found in Germany and Scandinavia) focused on the social and emotional development of the child and its ability to cultivate self-guided learning (CERI, 1975, p. 10). CERI proposed an educational program with a "twofold orientation: that of adaptation and that of emancipation" to enable individuals to cope with their open future in a rapidly changing society (CERI, 1973, p. 47).

The Adaptive Educational Process: Shifting to Reflexivity

The implementation of an educational program related to a rapidly changing society necessitates the constant review of whether these measures are appropriate. For this to succeed, the educational process must itself develop the ability to learn. It must abandon any form of a priori anchoring that traps it within a first-order level of observation.[1] In the German context, all-around education in grammar schools, grounded in an ineluctable reference to science (Luhmann & Schorr, 2000, p. 97), culminated in university education as the ultimate form of human self-reliance. With the shift to recurrent education, the educational process detached itself from this objective and abandoned the notion that education ever reaches a terminal point; in other words, the educational process was no longer based on accessing an external system of science (in the sense of impartial, empirical knowledge of the world); from now on, education is supposed to focus on cognitive learning models entwined with the expectations of performance-related function systems.

Structurally, the reflexive nature of the educational process means that the disparity between the organizational and interactional levels has grown: Educational organization gains major independence from educational interaction. Education now deals with the expectations of performance-related function systems in a learning manner by taking up these expectations and incorporating them according to its own logic. To this end, the performance requests of the other function systems are translated at the organizational level into pedagogically based educational goals, and classroom interaction becomes subject to control mechanisms, such as the contingent curriculum, instruction-bound personnel, and variable quality and performance requirements (Luhmann & Schorr, 2000, p. 108). These control mechanisms are intended to ensure adherence to currently valid educational goals.[2] Thus, according to Luhmann and Schorr, the ability to learn does not mean "an unrestrained willingness to conform"; instead, it integrates constraints that provide direction to the educational process (Luhmann & Schorr, 2000, p. 101). The education system articulates this direction, within the context of global programs, as the "[smooth] transition to a career," an objective that holds relevance across all school forms (Luhmann & Schorr, 2000, p. 104).

The institutionalization of the education process also affects the perception of the self-guided subject. Thanks to a new *medium of education*, the *life course* (Luhmann, 1997b), the subject is observed, in terms of his or her past and future, without the assumption of "a teleological structure" (Luhmann, 1997b, p. 18). The contingent life course is left open for manifold future possibilities (Luhmann, 1997b, p. 26) for which the learning subject is to be prepared educationally. In the classroom, therefore, teachers focus less on imparting factual knowledge, favoring instead approaches "that lead more to learning how to learn than to learning information" (Luhmann & Schorr, 2000, p. 99).

Following the integration of early childhood education into the lifelong learning model, which is organized as a self-guided and self-referential process, the structural conditions of adaptive education also prevail: the global ECE program is designed as a process that anticipates the preschooler's next career stage.

On the Learning Ability of the Educational Processes of Early Childhood Education

Early Childhood Education: School-Oriented Educational Program, with the Ability to Learn

Global political interest in ECE has led to the initiation of its implementation in various nation states, which is still ongoing (Garvis et al., 2018; Phillipson & Garvis, 2019). Global organizations act as the designers of standards and are also involved in their diffusion through the creation of reciprocal observation contexts (Schäfer, 2005, p. 83). UNESCO's International Standard Classification of Education (ISCED) of 2011 laid the groundwork for institutionalized ECE. ISCED places ECE at the lowest level (Level 0) out of 10 consecutive education program, followed by primary education, ASO (UNESCO, 2012, p. 21). All 10 are realized in targeted educational interactions between teacher and student, whereby a "providing agency . . . facilitates a learning environment, and a method of instruction through which communication is organised" (UNESCO, 2012, p. 7). Limitations on what is to be learned are set through interlinked certificates (UNESCO, 2012, p. 8). Accordingly, the ECE program explicitly excludes institutions that "provide only childcare (supervision, nutrition and health)" and sees the essential difference in the pedagogical qualifications of staff (UNESCO, 2012, p. 27). Going beyond basic childcare, ECE aims "to develop socio-emotional skills necessary for participation in school and society" (UNESCO, 2012, p. 26).

Global Guidelines for the Adaptive Education Process: Observation as a Pedagogical Instrument

The OECD has followed up on ISCED with its Starting Strong policy series (2001–2021). To enable different national systems to implement the ECE program as an adaptive and purposeful education process, the OECD encourages governments to use monitoring tools (OECD, 2015, pp. 172–189). These tools are meant to force a constant reexamination of educational interactions, enabling the alignment of both school expectations and children's needs; in other words, such interactions should become adaptive.

Essentially, there are two types of such tools: the first type of monitoring tool is intended to ensure organizational learning capacity and goal orientation through the test-based examination of structural quality (spatial equipment, safety standards, staffing ratios, etc.) and process quality (qualification of staff, organization of work processes, implementation of the curriculum, quality of specialist-child interaction, etc.). The second type of monitoring tool assesses the learning ability and goal orientation of the professionals' educational activities, such as through observation methods, tests, or screenings, which can help assess the development of learning in the individual child to encourage its development according to his or her needs. The OECD has presented a comparison of different monitoring tools and countries' experiences with them (OECD, 2015, pp. 172–189).

Person Categories of the Adaptive Educational Interaction in Early Childhood Education

The institutionalization of adaptive educational interactions, which was done with the aid of monitoring instruments, creates specific person-related expectations. Many German institutions of early childhood education use observation, portfolios, and learning stories as monitoring instruments to ensure an educator's learning attitude. These instruments have different sources (Allmann, 2014; Carr & Lee, 2001; Gelfer & Perkins, 1996) and are, in practice, combined in specific ways to complete the ECE program. Along these lines, the German Twelfth Report on Children and Youth of 2005 prescribes a method for systematically documenting children's activities (Schulz & Cloos, 2013, p. 787), using observation sheets, checklists, or assessment scales for all ECE institutions (Schulz & Cloos, 2013, p. 790). The child's activities and educational support are assessed in the context of the competences related to later enrolment in school (Schulz & Cloos, 2013, p. 795).

In many cases, the educator capable of learning is supposed to translate his or her observation notes into learning stories for the child (Schulz & Cloos, 2013, p. 790), read them to the child, and include them in the child's portfolio. Portfolios are systematic collections of documents that the child usually populates him- or herself by means of artifacts that document his or her learning progress, such as pictures they have drawn or painted, or photos that show them in learning contexts. In a given situation, children know that they are being observed; their learning stories provide feedback on their developmental progress; the portfolio is usually kept within the child's reach so that it can be reviewed frequently, whether by the child alone, together with an educator, the child's own parents, or other children, which motivates the child to independently develop the portfolio by creating suitable documents. The active involvement of the child is meant to raise self-awareness of "learning processes and progress as well as learning strategies" (Schulz & Cloos, 2013, p. 791). *Educators who are capable of learning*, as well as *children who are capable of learning,* should regularly and systematically reflect on the consequences of their educational actions and adjust their future educational actions accordingly. In this way, they embody the expectations (Hirschauer, 2004) of an educational process capable of learning with a capacity for constant reflection and goal-oriented readjustment (Luhmann, 1992a, p. 103).

CONCLUSION

This text focused on the constitutive dependence of the self-referential education system on the performance of the political system to show that the recent redrawing of what counts as institutionalized early childhood education in Germany largely originates in the impulses of global organizations in the political system of world society. In Germany, the political system has imposed socially relevant educational goals on organizations working in the education system for centuries. However, it is only since its reorientation toward the contingency formula of the ability to learn and the accompanying institutionalization of an educational process with the ability to learn that the German education system has developed an inner-systemic resonance capacity that allows it to take up politically defined educational goals in pedagogical terms and incorporate them into the architecture of its educational designs. This applies to institutions of early childhood education as well: The global education program ECE is designed as a learning education process that features an objective deemed socially relevant: preparing young children with the ability to learn so that they can attend school in a rapidly changing society. Within this education process that has the ability to learn, the pedagogical goal, implemented with the accompaniment of monitoring instruments, forms a control mechanism through which educational interactions are guided and formed in a processual manner. As the educational field of institutionalised early childhood education is also influenced by the contingency formula of the ability to learn, it eventually moves into the core area of the self-referential educational system.

ACKNOWLEDGMENTS

The present work was completed in the context of my research project, "The Nursery as a Gender Political Module of the Workfare State of Functionally Differentiated Society: Assignment of Tasks and Its Implementation" at the University of Bonn, which is funded by the Deutsche Forschungsgemeinschaft (DFG). For this I am grateful to the DFG.

NOTES

1. On the distinction between first- and second-order observation, see Luhmann (1992a, p. 112).
2. On reflexivity as a process, see Luhmann (1992b, pp. 68–121).

REFERENCES

Adick, C. (1992). Transnationale Merkmale moderner Schulentwicklung. In D. Brenner, D. Lenzen, & H.-U. Otto (Eds.), *Erziehungswissenschaft zwischen Modernisierung und Modernitätskrise. Beiträge zum 13. Kongress der Deutschen Gesellschaft für Erziehungswissenschaften vom 16.–18. März 1992 an der FU Berlin* (pp. 345–351). Beltz.

Allmann, S. (2014). *Beobachtung in der Montessori-Pädagogik.* Herder.

Carr, M., & Lee, W. (2001). *Learning stories: Construction learner identities in early education.* Sage.

CERI. (1973). *Recurrent education: A strategy for lifelong learning.* Organisation for Economic Co-Operation and Development.

CERI. (1975). *Developments in early childhood education* (pp. 8–23). Organisation for Economic Co-Operation and Development.

Erning, G. (1987). Geschichte der öffentlichen Kleinkindererziehung von den Anfängen bis zum Kaiserreich. In G. Erning, K. Neumann, & J. Reyer (Eds.), *Geschichte des Kindergartens. Band I: Entstehung und Entwicklung der öffentlichen Kleinkinderziehung in Deutschland von den Anfängen bis zur Gegenwart* (pp. 13–41). Lambertus.

Franke-Meyer, D. (2011). *Kleinkindererziehung und Kindergarten im historischen Prozess. Ihre Rolle im Spannungsfeld zwischen Bildungspolitik, Familie und Schule.* Julius Klinkhardt.

Garvis, S., Phillipson, S., & Harju-Luukkainen, H. (Eds.). (2018). *International perspectives on early childhood education and care: Early childhood education in the 21st century* (Vol. I.). Routledge.

Geißler, G. (2013). *Schulgeschichte in Deutschland. Von den Anfängen bis in die Gegenwart* (2. aktualisierte und erweiterte Auflage). Peter Lang.

Gelfer, J. I., & Perkins, P. G. (1996). A model for portfolio assessment in early childhood education programs. *Early Childhood Education Journal, 24*(1), 5–10.

Gottschall, K., & Schröder, T. (2013). "Familienlohn"—Zur Entwicklung einer wirkmächtigen Normierung geschlechtsspezifischer Arbeitsteilung. *WSI Mitteilungen, 3,* 161–170.

Hirschauer, S. (2004). Praktiken und ihre Körper. Über materielle Partizipanden des Tuns. In K. H. Hörning & J. Reuter (Eds.), *Doing Culture: Zum Begriff der Praxis in der gegenwärtigen soziologischen Theorie* (pp. 73–91). Transkript.

Hoffer-Mehlmer, M. (2003). *Elternratgeber: Zur Geschichte eines Genres.* Schneider Verlag Hohengehren.

Kaufmann, F.-X. (2003). *Varianten des Wohlfahrtsstaats: Der deutsche Sozialstaat im internationalen Vergleich.* Suhrkamp.

Konrad, F.-M. (2004). *Der Kindergarten. Seine Geschichte von den Anfängen bis in die Gegenwart.* Lambertus.

Luhmann, N. (1992a). System und Absicht der Erziehung. In N. Luhmann & K. E. Schorr (Eds.), *Zwischen Absicht und Person. Fragen an die Pädagogik* (pp. 102–124). Suhrkamp.

Luhmann, N. (1992b). *Wissenschaft der Gesellschaft.* Suhrkamp.

Luhmann, N. (1997a). *Die Gesellschaft der Gesellschaft.* Suhrkamp.

Luhmann, N. (1997b). Erziehung als Formung des Lebenslaufs. In D. Lenzen & N. Luhmann (Eds.), *Bildung und Weiterbildung im Erziehungssystem. Lebenslauf und Humanontogenese als Medium und Form* (pp. 11–29). Suhrkamp.

Luhmann, N. (1997c). Organisation und Gesellschaft. In N. Luhmann (Ed.), *Die Gesellschaft der Gesellschaft* (pp. 826–847). Suhrkamp.

Luhmann, N. (2000). *Die Politik der Gesellschaft.* Suhrkamp.

Luhmann, N. (2002). *Das Erziehungssystem der Gesellschaft.* Suhrkamp.

Luhmann, N. (2017). *Systemtheorie der Gesellschaft.* Suhrkamp.

Luhmann, N., & Schorr, K. E. (2000). *Problems of reflection in the system of education* (Vol. 13). Waxmann.

Neumann, E. (1987). Geschichte der öffentlichen Kleinkindererziehung von 1945 bis in die Gegenwart. In G. Erning, K. Neumann, & J. Reyer (Eds.), *Geschichte des Kindergartens. Band I: Entstehung und Entwicklung der öffentlichen Kleinkinderziehung in Deutschland von den Anfängen bis zur Gegenwart* (pp. 83–115). Lambertus.

OECD. (2006). *Starting strong II: Early childhood education and care*. OECD.

OECD. (2015). *Starting strong IV: Monitoring quality in early childhood education and care*. OECD.

Papadopoulos, G. S. (1994). *Education 1960–1990: The OECD Perspective*. OECD.

Phillipson, S., & Garvis, S. (Eds.). (2019). *Teachers' and families' perspectives in early childhood education and care: Early childhood education in the 21st century* (Vol. II). Routledge.

Reyer, J. (1987a). Geschichte der öffentlichen Kleinkinderziehung im Deutschen Kaiserreich, in der Weimarer Republik und in der Zeit des Nationalsozialismus. In G. Erning, K. Neumann, & J. Reyer (Eds.), *Geschichte des Kindergartens. Band I: Entstehung und Entwicklung der öffentlichen Kleinkinderziehung in Deutschland von den Anfängen bis zur Gegenwart* (pp. 43–81). Lambertus.

Reyer, J. (1987b). Kindheit zwischen privat-familialer Lebenswelt und öffentlich veranstalteter Kleinkindererziehung. In G. Erning, K. Neumann, & J. Reyer (Eds.), *Geschichte des Kindergartens. Band II: Institutionelle Aspekte, systematische Perspektiven, Entwicklungsverläufe* (pp. 232–284). Lambertus.

Reyer, J. (2015). *Die Bildungsaufträge des Kindergartens. Geschichte und aktueller Status*. Beltz Juventa.

Ringer, R. (1987). Introduction. In D. K. Müller, F. Ringer, & B. Simon (Eds.), *The rise of the modern educational eystem* (pp. 1–12). Cambridge University Press.

Roessler, W. (1961). *Die Entstehung des modernen Erziehungswesens in Deutschland*. W. Kohlhammer.

Roessler, W. (1978). Pädagogik. In O. Brunner, W. Conze, & R. Koselleck (Eds.), *Geschichtliche Grundbegriffe: Historisches Lexikon zur politisch-sozialen Sprache in Deutschland* (pp. 623–647). Klett-Cotta.

Schäfer, A. (2005). *Die neue Unverbindlichkeit: Wirtschaftspolitische Koordinierung in Europa*. Campus.

Scharpf, F. (1999). *Regieren in Europa. Effektiv und demokratisch?* Campus.

Schimank, U. (2015). Modernity as a functionally differentiated capitalist society: A general theoretical model. *European Journal of Social Theory, 18*(4), 413–430.

Schimank, U., & Volkmann, U. (1999). *Gesellschaftliche Differenzierung*. Transcript.

Schulz, M., & Cloos, P. (2013). Beobachtung und Dokumentation von Bildungsprozessen. In M. Stamm & D. Edelmann (Eds.), *Handbuch frühkindliche Bildungsforschung* (pp. 787–800). Springer.

Stichweh, R. (1991). *Der frühmoderne Staat und die europäische Universität. Zur Interaktion von Politik und Erziehungssystem im Prozeß ihrer Ausdifferenzierung (16.–18. Jahrhundert)*. Suhrkamp.

Stichweh, R. (2007). The eigenstructures of world society and the regional cultures of the world. In I. Rossi (Ed.), *Frontiers of globalization research: Theoretical and methodological approaches* (pp. 133–149). Springer.

Thiel, F. (2008). Die Organisation der Bildung—eine Zumutung für die Profession? In Y. Ehrenspeck, G. de Haan, & F. Thiel (Eds.), *Bildung: Angebot oder Zumutung?* (pp. 211–228). Springer.

Titze, H. (1973). *Die Politisierung der Erziehung. Untersuchungen über die soziale und politische Funktion der Erziehung von der Aufklärung bis zum Hochkapitalismus.* Athenäum Fischer.

Treml, A. K. (2002). Evolutionäre Pädagogik—Umrisse eines Paradigmenwechsels. *Zeitschrift für Pädagogik, 48*(5), 652–669.

UNESCO. (2012). *International Standard Classification of Education (ISCED) 2011.* Montreal.

van Ackeren, I., Klemm, K., & Kühn, S. M. (2015). *Entstehung, Struktur und Steuerung des deutschen Schulsystems: Eine Einführung* (3rd ed.). Springer.

Walgenbach, P. (2000). *Die normgerechte Organisation.* Schäffer-Poeschel.

Wasmuth, H. (2010). Kindertageseinrichtungen als Bildungseinrichtungen—Zur Bedeutung von Bildung und Erziehung in der Geschichte der öffentlichen Kleinkinderziehung in Deutschland bis 1945. https://publikationen.uni-tuebingen.de/xmlui/bitstream/handle/10900/47814/pdf/kindertageseinrichtungen_als_bildungseinrichtungen.pdf?sequence=1

CHAPTER 20

THE UNIVERSITY AS A WORLD ORGANIZATION

RUDOLF STICHWEH

INTRODUCTION

SINCE its beginnings around 1200, the university has never been a local or regional school; nor has it been a local or regional knowledge organization. From its start in late medieval Europe, there were authors such as the Cologne scholar and canon Alexander von Roes (ca. 1225–1300) who defined the university as the third universal power in Christianity, standing beside the empire and the papacy (Stichweh, 1991a). Therefore, the knowledge it produced, taught, and examined, and the degrees it conferred, were of European relevance. After 1500, accompanying the rise of world empires and the migration of European colonizers and settlers with their monastic orders and churches,[1] the university became a world organization. It was soon present on several continents (North America, South America, several parts of Asia). In some relevant respects, the universities were part of one global network of scholars, and the knowledge systems they built were perceived as universal knowledge systems.

This chapter takes these historical circumstances as its point of departure. It focuses on the university from a sociological perspective, concentrating on its most distinguishing characteristics that explain the enormous relevance of universities in the genesis of world society. The university seems to be the best and most instructive case of a societal institution that combines a precise localization at a specific place and a belongingness and local impact in the cities where universities are established with an invariable global reach and relevance. The university is as much local as it is global,[2] and the goal of the chapter is to explore and to explain how universities work on the basis of a productive use of this distinction and the tensions built into it.

THE LOCALIZATION OF THE UNIVERSITY: THE UNIVERSITY AND THE CITY

The university is typically located either on a campus that has been specifically created for this purpose, in a characteristic quarter of a city that is then defined as the university quarter (e.g., the "Quartier Latin" in Paris), or in a third possibility—especially in smaller European cities—its buildings are to be found everywhere in the city. This third pattern is often to be found, when there are only few university buildings and most of the teaching takes place in the houses built or rented by the professors. By establishing a university in one of these three ways, it becomes strongly related to one and only one city—very often adopting the name of the city as its name. Adopting the name of the city where it resides ties the university even more closely to it. A migration to another city is, however, possible in principle, a rare event in the history of universities.[3]

This spatial concentration of the university and its persistence over decades and centuries is an exceptional structure if one compares universities to organizations in other societal spheres. There are similarities in team sports, for example, where one observes strong identifications that unite cities and sports teams. But in the case of sports teams, it is unlikely that a whole city quarter will be shaped by these teams, whereas for the universities, the link to the city is usually based on more complex connections, with more visible transformations of the city space. It is not only that the university is invariably tied to the city where it was founded: parallel to it, these cities often become "university cities." A significant part of the population of the cities are the members (students, university teachers, and many other employees) of the university. And even those citizens not tied to the university via membership often look to the university as a defining part of the identity of the city and may derive their income from activities related to it.

The university localized in one of the three ways mentioned is nearly always a global institution. Over centuries, the university tradition has acted as a selective force operating against alternative interpretations that were content with local relevance. University cities are occasionally global cities by their own sociocultural centrality; in other cases, however, the university functions as the driving force for the globality of the city. This is especially true for the small or medium-size university cities. They are mostly chosen as places for a university because they allow for a sufficient distance to the political, religious, economic, and military centers of the respective territories. This spatial separation of higher education from other societal functions by creating a city type defined by higher education is an important feature of late medieval and early modern university history.

Some continuities of the functional specificity of the university city as a functional city type of its own exist even today. However, from the enormous growth of the number of universities in the 20th and 21st centuries, at some point nearly every city and every region will have a university of its own. This strengthens and sometimes weakens the link from the city to the university. In some respects it can now be said that every "complete" city claims to build a university of its own. In other cases the regional placement of the university prevails over the claim of the biggest cities for "their" university. Then—and this could well be observed in the erection of new universities in England in the last 60 years—there is a search for a good place for a campus in a regional landscape and space, and the connection to a city becomes secondary.[4]

THE PERSISTENCE OF THE UNIVERSITY

It is a remarkable fact that universities, once they have been established, are nearly never closed again. In the economy most new firms only survive for a few years. The dynamics of economic systems are very much produced by this incessant circulation of new firms. It is wholly different with universities. They do not only exist for years or decades but often for hundreds of years. And there are no other institutions or organizations with which they share this remarkable quality.

Clark Kerr, in his book *Higher Education Cannot Escape History*, published in 1994 (Kerr, 1994), presents an extraordinary statistic: He claims that in the Western world, by the end of the 20th century, there were around 75 institutions that already existed in 1520 operating "with similar functions and with unbroken histories" (Kerr, 1994, p. 45). These institutions comprise the Catholic Church, the Parliaments of the Isle of Man, of Iceland and of Great Britain, the governance structures of several Swiss cantons, the Banca Monte dei Paschi di Siena[5]—and 61 universities (Kerr, 1994, Table 1, p. 46).

Comparison with a more recent situation reveals similar findings. In the United States, in 2019/2020, there were 3,982 colleges and universities (degree-granting postsecondary institutions) (Moody, 2021). These numbers actually represent a decline compared to the years 2012–2013, especially in the for-profit sector. Besides these for-profit institutions—which probably present the lifecycle of economic enterprises and not of typical higher educational organizations—the 800 small private colleges with student numbers below 1,000 are structurally endangered, as for them student fees are often the only source of income. Therefore, the long-term stability of institutions is not guaranteed for this basic level of small academic institutions.

The situation differs considerably if one looks for the most elite institutions. In the case of the United States, this elite segment is best defined by membership in the "Association of American Universities" (AAU), which was founded in 1900 by 14 universities.[6] In 2021, 66 universities were members of the AAU (64 in the United States and 2 Canadian universities), of which 57 already operated as universities in 1900—a good indicator of the stability of the core of the American university system. That is, in the 120 years between 1900 and 2021, only 9 new universities were founded that at a later point in time succeeded to become a part of the research core of the American university system. Among them, 6 belong to the campuses of the University of California (Davis, Los Angeles, Santa Barbara, San Diego, Irvine, Santa Cruz). The other three newcomers with founding dates after 1900 are Rice (1912), Brandeis (1948), and Stony Brook (1957).[7] This shows how rare it is for new universities to become significant addresses in the American university system, and how dominated the system is by institutions that have been around for a very long time. The contrast to the rapidity of organizational innovations in other sectors of American life (such as economy and religion) is, once again, enormous.

One difference between European and North American Universities must be emphasized. European Universities were universal or global institutions from the start. This was clearly not the case with American universities and colleges. Although derived from European institutions, with their universal aspirations, American universities themselves were regional institutions, recruiting most of their students from regional feeder schools and regional elites.[8] They always looked to the European institutions and the science and scholarship produced there. But they did not yet contribute to the production of science. Since the second half of the 19th century, great numbers of American students spent years studying in European institutions—in fact, the best colleges and universities recruited, after 1850, their presidents and professors among those teachers and researchers that had been to Europe. Nonetheless, American institutions mostly confined themselves to a regional reach, and this was even true for the "Big Three," Harvard, Yale, and Princeton (Karabel, 2006), which clearly had a national reputation but not a nationwide recruitment of students. Only after World War I, the best American universities slowly became national institutions. This did not happen by adding new institutions. Instead, it was the elite segment of universities that now extended its reach toward the whole nation. There arose the idea of "geographic diversity" of student recruitment, and there came about the creation of "national scholarships" (in the beginning only applying to few states as recipients) and, finally, the institution of need-blind admission was established. This is a model of admission in which the students' financial conditions are only examined after his or her admission, implying that the university becomes responsible for finding financial aid for those students who have no means of their own. This model was extended to international students by some of the leading universities at the end of the 20th century (Karabel, 2006).

In 1993, the incoming president of Yale, Rick Levin, was probably the first American university president to call his university a "world university" (Branch, 2001), and Levin meant this as a programmatic statement that still had to be realized. The concept of a "World University" here means the worldwide recruitment of students and—as a probable consequence—the education of leaders for many countries.

Why are universities so persistent? There is a first explanation that is nearly an obvious one, based on the analysis presented up to this point. If the university is closely tied to a city, it can age and survive and coexist with the city over decades and even over hundreds of years. The connections are symbolic, financial, territorial, and inscribed into buildings, and they accumulate over time. All these are reasons why, in most cases, there is only one (significant) university in a city. For very big cities it may be different. But even then, if there is more than one university in a city, there is often a characteristic functional differentiation between them (Harvard and MIT in Boston/Cambridge are good examples).

There is a second causal context that is often responsible for the persistence of universities. This is based on the link from the university to its alumni. For the alumni a successful academic track record and the achievement of a degree valid for national university systems become a permanent part of their biographical profile, from which may follow a motivation to invest money into "their" university to contribute to the permanent standing of their university. The accumulation of these investments builds endowments and donations, and finances territorial extensions of the university, which are strong factors for their persistence (Hansmann, 1990).

This second factor immediately leads us to a third argument for persistence. Universities are either public or private institutions. But even if they are private institutions, they are nearly always "not-for-profit" organizations. That is decisive for longevity or persistence. Profits are a very effective mechanism for the control of organizations. If these are less profitable than other organizations, investors, after some time, will lose their patience and redirect their investments to other, more profitable institutions, limiting in this way the life span of for-profit organizations. Not-for-profit organizations, on the other hand, will be able to survive for long times even under critical financial conditions. The comparisons they have to stand are mainly independent from financial criteria, and this contributes in a significant way to the longevity of universities.

THE INCLUSION INTO THE UNIVERSITY

From its beginnings, the university was an inclusive organization. In the late medieval and early modern period, it was never the institution of the most privileged strata of society. For this inclusivity, it was important that the university was closely coupled to religion and the organizations of the Christian Church, especially the monastic orders. Religion (Christianity) was the first socially inclusive function system in late medieval/early modern Europe (Stichweh, 2020). Therefore, the university as an organization, near to theology as science and to the life forms practiced in church organizations, in one key perspective did participate in the openness of religion to persons coming from all quarters of life. "Paupertas"/poverty was not only a monastic ideal; it was central to the self-description of late medieval universities. And in Europe, there was the institution of sponsorship of young men from humble or poor family backgrounds that supported them over years and sent them to university study. "Poverty" was not only a personal circumstance that in many individual cases did not prevent the access to the university. In other respects, "poverty" was a general symbol that pointed to a kind of purity near to the forms of intellectual absorption seen as a presupposition for intellectual passions and scholarship.

Besides being near to the church and religion, the university was nearly nowhere a place that was attractive to the nobility. The highest stratum of European society was not known for studying at universities. Of course, a certain number of nobles opted for the study of law, and there were always some European universities—Padova, Leiden, Göttingen, Edinburgh—who functioned as transnational attractors for these noble students. A second option was the possibility to visit universities as part of the "Grand Tour," as many nobles did. Those who did this spent short stays of 2–3 months at individual universities. Then, in the 17th and 18th centuries, a new institution arose, the "academy of nobles" (Ritterakademien, académie des nobles, seminaria nobilium) that taught to members of the nobility a mix of some learned knowledge and the major practical exercises (riding, dancing, fencing) that were part of the lifestyle of nobles (Brizzi, 1976; Conrads, 1982; Stichweh, 1991b).

To this double-faced position of the university in its European development—its openness toward the inclusion of everyone who showed some signs of being a gifted individual and the relatively weak links that connect the university to the dominant stratum of European society—a third feature should be added. The tripartite order of the three professional faculties, which in early modern Europe came about in the medieval institution that could still be seen as part of the church, functioned as the basis of a hierarchy of three professional estates. These professional estates were thought as controlling organs of society taking care of souls and beliefs (theology), social conflicts (law), and individual and collective physical health (medicine). The university became a part of "Polizey" (the early modern policies of building social order), based on relevant knowledge systems seen as representing aspects of "Polizey." It was not until the late 18th, early 19th-century scientific transformation of the university into an institution dominated by the knowledge systems of the philosophical faculty that its separation from the social hierarchies of the society of estates and the tasks of social control connected to it took place.[9]

The new university built on the basis of the disciplines of the philosophical faculty—which over time even institutionalized the disciplinary model for organizing knowledge production as a paradigm for the genesis and organization of research in the professional faculties (Stichweh, 1992)—is completely decoupled from the order of estates and strata in its societal environment. It can become inclusive in a new understanding that implies, in principle, openness for everyone who is able to fulfil intellectual demands defined by the disciplines originating in the philosophical faculty or is able to fulfil the (intellectual and practical) demands given by the professional faculties for law, medicine, theology, and other professions.

It is on this basis that the modern university arose as a world organization defined again by the inclusion of ever-growing segments of the population. The university around 1800 was inclusive in the understanding defined earlier, a potential openness to individuals coming from all stations in life. Nevertheless, during this period, it was still a very small societal institution, rarely including more than 1%–2% of the male population of European countries for relative short stays (1–2 years). Therefore, it might be said that the university was inclusive and exclusive at the same time. In the 200 years since then, incessant growth has become the most obvious characteristic of the university in a worldwide sense. This can be illustrated with some figures for the case of Germany. Already in 1750, the country had probably the highest number of university visitors in Europe (at this time 150,000 of 8 million males had some university experience). In 1830, the student population present in German universities numbered 16,049 (Müller-Benedict, 2015, p. 69). There was stagnation until 1865 when the number slightly dropped to 15,500 (Müller-Benedict, 2015, p. 65). From there on until 1931, the numbers show a rapid growth up to 129,200 students. National Socialism and World War II brought a significant decline of the student population. The growth resumed with similar rates in the FRG and the GDR from 1945 until 1970 when the combined number of students rose to 570.000 (3.5× in the 20 years from 1950 to 1970). In the next 20 years growth was by a factor of 4 in the FRG, whereas numbers declined by 10% in the GDR. In the reunited Germany of 2000, there were 1.8 million students (3× in the 30 years from 1970 to 2000). As a resumé, it can be said that the years from 1865 to 2000 brought about the rise of mass higher education in Germany: a growth by a factor of 120 in only 135 years, only half of which can be explained by population growth (39.5 million in 1865; 82.2 million in 2000). Of the remaining growth, nearly half can be explained by the rise of new institutions of higher education: technical universities, arts universities, applied sciences, and institutions for the education of public administrators. Similar stories can be told about many and perhaps most countries in the world. The rapidly rising inclusivity of higher education clearly is a world phenomenon. In 1900, the number of all students in the world amounted to 500,000, whereas in 2000 it sums up to 100 million. That is a worldwide growth over 100 years by a factor of 200 (Meyer & Schofer, 2007, p. 48). And this growth is going on: In 2021, there were 220 million university students.

Another perspective on the same phenomenon—the worldwide rise of mass higher education—can be established by looking at the working-age population (25–64-year-olds) and the share of this group that has higher education. The numbers for 2020 are to be found in "Education at a Glance" (2021), the yearly data handbook published by the OECD (OECD, 2021). This handbook documents for 2020 an OECD average of 33% of this adult group that either has a bachelor's or master's or doctoral degree (European Union 2022 average 32%) (OECD, 2021, p. 48). To these, one can add 7% who have a short-cycle tertiary degree. Countries like the United Kingdom and United States show higher numbers (40% + 10% United Kingdom, 39% + 11% United States) compared to Germany and France (Germany 31% + 1%, France 25% + 15%). A simple prognosis on the basis of these data might lead to the conclusion that, regarding the relatively rich countries that are members in the OECD and the European Union, there is a trend toward half of the adult population acquiring degrees in higher education. In the United States it is already the case that half of the working hours of the whole population are contributed by persons who have a university degree (Autor, 2019).

Migration and the World University: Unification by Migration

The local situatedness of the individual university and the social inclusivity of the organization do not imply that students necessarily attend the university nearest to their home region. In medieval Europe, students were often not allowed to study in the university of the city their family lived in; students had to be migrants, and they were strangers in the cities where they studied—and the same was mostly true for teachers and professors. Being considered strangers allowed the university personnel to claim special rights and privileges and often a jurisdiction of their own, internal to the university (Stichweh, 1991c). The distances students travelled (mostly by foot) were often huge. Therefore, the medieval European universities were one big migration system, characterized by individual and group migrations. Groups of students from a specific city or region often moved to the same, in some cases far-distant university.

In the second half of the 18th century, there arose the idea of "national education" and, as a consequence, national university systems (Stichweh, 2004). Eighteenth-century mercantilism already institutionalized obligations to spend some time in the universities of the territorial state where one was born. Since then, one has to distinguish national and international migration of students. There is a steady growth of the absolute number of international students in the last 200 years. But this growth is mostly parallel to the enormous growth of student numbers in the world. Regarding the worldwide number of international students, one can point out a remarkable stability around 2%–3% of the worldwide student population that, at a specific point in time, studies at a foreign university.[10]

How to explain the stability of the share of international students in a university world in which all universities devise internationalization strategies? Since 1800 there are always some university systems that succeed to attract growing numbers of foreigners, and where, consequentially, foreigners are a growing part of the student population. At the same time, new national systems are built that become part of the global university system, offering national study options for those who had to go to a foreign university before. The interaction of these two countervailing forces probably explains the somehow astonishing stability of the international share of the global student population. The international migration of students and the integration of new universities and new university systems emerging in countries that had no such systems before are obviously two complementary features of the expansion and global integration of a world university system—one that is built by migration decisions just as by new national universities that substitute real local possibilities of serious academic study for the limited situation of finding such possibilities only in a foreign country.

The Intellectual Completeness and Multidisciplinarity of the University

The dominant medieval name for the university was "studium generale." This formulated both the social inclusiveness and universality of the university and its thematic universality (i.e., the inclusion of all learned and scientific knowledge systems into one organization), as it finally meant its global reach and the relevance, for all regions of the European world where universities emerged, of the knowledge produced and taught in these institutions. The thematic universality of the university may be seen as a surprise, as the rise of special schools for specific knowledge systems might have been seen as a more plausible development. In Europe there were early specialized medical schools in Salerno and Montpellier. But medical schools were, again and again, absorbed into or integrated into more general universities—and the reasons were obvious. Medical knowledge and its practitioners perceived the need for being connected to dominant knowledge systems, thought to be relevant for the learned and scientific reputation of medicine. These were, in the medieval situation, theology and later in early modern Europe and in modernity the scientific knowledge systems in the philosophical faculty.

It is once again the network character of knowledge that prevents the segregation of special schools and supports the university as a complete or universal knowledge system integrating all variants of scientific knowledge into one organization. An especially important case are the technical universities arising around 1850. After some decades nearly all of them added nontechnical disciplines, especially in the social sciences, more selectively in the humanities. Besides these technical universities, there are not many other types of special universities that count in the contemporary world. There are some universities specialized in the social sciences (LSE, Mannheim, New School), a significant number of liberal arts colleges and universities (Brown, Dartmouth) specializing in cultural sciences (social sciences and humanities), and universities with a focus on management (St. Gallen). In most of them, the universalizing impulse is weaker, probably for financial reasons.

The prominence and predominance of the "general university" ("studium generale") is one factor in the genesis of the university as a world organization. Universities become relatively big (300–500 professorships) and structurally similar, they are visible nodes in global knowledge networks, being, therefore, easily compared and ranked. Such global knowledge networks are, first, the cooperation and coauthorship networks of science and, second, the migration networks of scholars, scientists, and students.

THE FUNCTIONAL BIFOCALITY OF THE UNIVERSITY: THE RISE OF THE EDUCATION/ SCIENCE NEXUS AND THE INTEGRATION OF THE OTHER FUNCTION SYSTEMS OF SOCIETY

The university is, first of all, an organization (Luhmann, 1992b). As such, it decides on the inclusion of members (scholars, students, administration) and processes problems by taking decisions regarding problem solutions. As is the case for all organizations, it is an open question which kind of problems they consider as constitutive for the organization. In regard to modern universities, it can be said that they work on problems of (higher) education and at the same time on problems of examining, criticizing, and extending scientific knowledge. This is the historical synthesis of two sometimes diverging problem foci that brought about the modern university in the decades around 1800.

There are interesting tensions in the relation between the two primary problem foci of universities. Higher education is first of all a local business that defines the everyday activities of university members in the classes, seminars, and laboratories where they teach students the fundamentals of theories and methods in the sciences. As there are always obligations, dates, and deadlines connected to teaching, the localized activities of higher education normally can claim a priority on the agenda of university personnel. On the other hand, most of these university professionals probably have a value preference for research. Research activities are often localized, too, as far as one uses the localities provided by the university one works for. But research activities have no inherent connection to the locality of the university. The place where research operations are performed is often determined by the objects on which one does research. This means that the answer to the problem one tries to solve may have to be searched at far distant places in the world. And, furthermore, the public addressed by the communication of research results, in a sharp difference to teaching, is never a local public but always the world public of specialists working on or being interested in the respective problems. For the teacher the localized university is the place where the action is, for the researcher his or her university, even if it calls itself a research university "is not a place or a milieu but a pied-à-terre" (Rothblatt, 1997, p. 261). Not rarely, researchers practice a certain opportunism in either using the facilities provided by their university or making use of other facilities available elsewhere.

This tension of localized teaching and globalized research is constitutive for the functional bifocality of the modern university. Nonetheless, teaching and research are complementary. Science, even in its most recent and most advanced formulations, is the major and often only knowledge system university teaching is supposed to go back to. And as scientific knowledge, even of local circumstances and objects, is either world knowledge or no true knowledge at all, the strongly localized teaching invariably is part of a global knowledge system. And as the process of teaching science always demands a systematic organization of knowledge, there is in every teaching the possibility to discover knowledge deficits and to propose new ideas and unexplored possibilities. Therefore, good and systematic teaching can accidentally become research, even if the teacher had no intention to do research.

Although there are tensions and conflicts between higher education and science and between teaching and research, the structural coupling among the two functional complexes in the modern university is so close that all other societal functions are supplementary at best. One can combine a university with sports teams that represent the university in sports competitions or add religious services on certain occasions or earn money through economic/financial markets with patents or investment of endowment funds. All these activities do not become part of the core of the university as organization, which is primarily defined by the education/science nexus and its local and global realizations.

But there are two further ways to introduce the other function systems of society into the education/science nexus of the modern university. The dominant option is to claim that the function systems other than science have a knowledge base of their own that can be considered a type of scientific knowledge. This is postulated for law (considered as "science" in Germany, "jurisprudence" in the United Kingdom/United States, or part of the humanities elsewhere), medicine (which is integrated into science as "biomedicine"), theology (that still claims to be a kind of encyclopedia of the sciences in some Christian quarters or is mainly based on philology/history in more modern versions), education (that becomes "educational science" as part of the social sciences), sports (that can productively be studied from a multidisciplinary perspective), technologies (that as engineering sciences generate a new type of scientific disciplines after 1850), and finally for the economy (that is governed by managers who claim their knowledge base as management science). This idea of the knowledge bases of the other function systems being either traditional knowledge or new sciences of their own right allows for integration of teaching and research on these knowledge bases into the university. The only exception probably are the arts. It is not plausible for the system of arts (and it could even be considered degrading) to claim that the production of art is made possible by a kind of knowledge that is, at its core, a variant of scientific knowledge. Therefore, the arts mainly are not a part of the university. For them the education/science nexus is substituted by an education/arts nexus—and on this basis the arts generate higher educational institutions of their own, which are rarely integrated into the university.

The University as a Presence Institution: The Evolution of Interaction Systems

Two circumstances have been so far analyzed, which privilege or even demand the local presence of nearly all members of a university. The first regards the unilocality of the university, that is, the fact that most universities are strongly connected to one city (rarely to regions) and one campus within, or near to, the respective city (region) leading to a growth of the university mostly limited to this unitary place. The other circumstance is the localization of teaching.

From these circumstances arises a central dimension of nearly all universities. They are based on "interaction systems," that is, systems consisting of communicative exchanges among participants who share one physical space allowing reciprocal visual and auditory perception during these communicative exchanges. Such systems have been called "interaction systems" or the "interaction order" by Luhmann and Goffman (Goffman, 1983; Luhmann, 1975).

In its history the university invents ever-new types of interaction systems, which define this institution's "milieu interne." There is the "tutorial," a teaching institution consisting of a group of one teacher and one or several students advised by this teacher. First developed in Oxford and Cambridge (here called "supervision"), it spread in variants to many universities. Another type of interaction system is the "Seminar," introduced in Germany in 18th- and 19th-century universities. The Seminar consists of a small or medium number of students guided by a teacher, where a complex of scientific questions is systematically worked upon and furthered by discussions based on presupposed symmetries in knowledge processes.[11] A third, important type are "practical exercises," which mostly introduce students into scientific methods by exercising these methods in a setting where instruments or other resources necessary for these exercises are available. Finally, there is the most classical institution, the "Lecture," given by an academic teacher to a public that can be relatively small or can in other cases consist of hundreds of hearers. All these interaction systems exist in numerous variants and combinations in different universities and different university systems. Nowadays, there is a global space of types of interaction systems, the most advanced among them providing opportunities of transition from education to the participation in scientific research.

Besides these interaction systems belonging to higher education, further interaction systems that represent and realize scientific research arise in the "milieu interne" of the university. Among them is the "research colloquium," the scientific "workshop," and the academic "conference." This is not an exhaustive list. It is only meant as an illustration of this dense, interactive university milieu, where in teaching, research, and administration, ever-new forms of interaction are invented and institutionalized as claims on the available time of the members of the university.

THE UNIVERSITY AS A "HUMAN CAPITAL" INSTITUTION AND AS THE "CENTER" OF THE SYSTEM OF SCIENCE

There are two major production processes going on in the 20th- and 21st-century university. The first concerns the production of scientific truths as something that is not the exclusive domain of the university, as other organizations also participate in scientific research: the numerous research institutes established by national states and by charitable foundations based on private money; the industrial research laboratories, which in leading countries especially in Europe, Asia, and North America receive two-thirds of the total sum of research money spent on the search for truth and its applications; the traditional and new academies of science that, after dominating the 17th and 18th century, survived their 19th-century crisis for a comeback in the 20th century and often still have to find and define their specific function in the contemporary system of science, a function not yet fulfilled by competing organizations; the non-universitarian public intellectuals, some of whom do not only produce "definitions of the situation" (Parsons & Platt, 1974) but try to compete in the search for truth as part of a "third culture," transcending the division of the "two cultures" of science and humanities postulated by C. P. Snow (Snow, 1965; Stichweh, 2008). However, every single person who works in and publishes from one of these institutions has received the education enabling him or her to participate in the production of science at a university. In this respect the university has a monopoly in controlling the access to the production of science. On the basis of this double function—first, controlling the education of every contributor to scientific publications and, second, being the place where most of the significant scientific publications are written, read, commented, and criticized—the university can meaningfully be called the center of the system of science.

There is a second function the university fulfils in society. Over the centuries and decades, the names for this second function have changed. In Germany, around 1800, the most important word was *Bildung* ("self-cultivation" in the English 18th century) (Bruford, 1975). This means the individual that finds, through intellectual activity, a perspective on the world (*Weltbild*) and on this basis understands and then defines its role in society. The relation of university and society is furthermore changed by the ongoing disciplinary differentiation in universities and the occupational differentiation in society. Shortly after 1950, one could already speak about "the professionalization of everyone" (Wilensky, 1964) as a process that defined the centrality of the university in a "knowledge society." There is a complex knowledge system at the basis of any profession, which, at some point, has to be taught at the university. The third idea, in a way reverting to *Bildung*, is the idea that the university is the "Human Capital" institution. Again, this argues for the conception that highly generalized competences are instilled into individuals by the simple fact that they spend some years in institutions of higher education. These competences enable persons with a university education to fulfil social roles not precisely defined and limited by the subjects studied in the university.[12] People acquire general capabilities of dealing with texts and symbols that are later specified by the occupational roles they take.

University Rankings and the Constitution of One University World

National and international hierarchies among universities have always been postulated. These perceptions were based on the career paths of professors, the migration of students choosing certain universities, scientific discoveries and institutional innovations attributed to specific universities, and prizes received by university members, especially Nobel Prizes.

Such quality assessments were formalized in University and College rankings that came about in the early eighties. In 1983, *US News & World Report* published its first "Best Colleges Ranking." These national rankings identified hierarchies of teaching and research in relatively homogenized and well-known national spaces, with the primary intention of supporting prospective students in the selection of colleges and universities they wanted to apply to.

It was a surprise when in 2003, for the first time, a university in Shanghai published a global university ranking (the "Academic Ranking of World Universities"), making use of a methodology that identifies big universities with a very strong focus on a core of disciplines in the natural sciences. In 2004, a second ranking entered the market, the "Times Higher Education–QS World University Ranking" that was based on a cooperation between the biweekly "Times Higher Education Supplement" and the British education consultancy QS. These partners produced a ranking with a strong reputational focus (based on the communicated opinions of tens of thousands of academics and employers of academics). This reputational focus (50% of the evaluation) was coupled with bibliometric data and statistical data on academic personnel. Times Higher Education (THE) and QS separated as partners in 2009—and since then THE publishes its own "THE World University Rankings" that are based on 13 indicators: There is again a reputational component (separate for teaching and research) that amounts to 33%. The other 11 indicators are data on the internationality of personnel and students, on financial conditions (money from the state and industry), publication, citation and coauthorship data, and data on student/teacher ratios and graduate/undergraduate ratios. There are numerous other rankings. But until now these three rankings are clearly the most consulted and the most discussed from the family of rankings.

The introduction of rankings has some significant and transformative effects on the world landscape of universities. The first of these effects is that rankings constitute the system or demonstrate via systematic comparisons the existence of a world system of universities that they purport to describe. The second effect is that rankings "contribute to the worldwide transmission of educational and scientific ideas and ideals. If something is relevant for success in rankings . . . it is probable that it will diffuse through the world system of universities" (Pfeffer & Stichweh, 2015, p. 170). A third effect is that rankings are highly successful by being highly controversial. Rankings are criticized everywhere in Europe, North America, and Australia on the basis of their deficient methodologies. And they seem to be mostly accepted in Asia and Latin America as useful instruments for giving hints how to climb the ladder of academic excellence. These discussions will not go away and rankings will not go away. World rankings are only 15 years old. New, less controversial methodologies will surely be found as has always been the case in other domains of social science.

Rankings will be more useful and stay as successful as they are now if four conditions are fulfilled: They have to be research instruments that by new methods of comparison discover features of academic systems that one was not able to see before. Second, they will have to be informative for students in helping them to find exactly the university that is the right one for the plans they have and the competences they already possess.

Third, rankings will have to present exact and plausible data that will help politicians to have an understanding of their own when they try to shape higher education policies. Fourth, rankings as precise comparative descriptions of university worlds in a global perspective will help university administrators to find a niche and a strategy for one's own university that will ensure its productive survival.

SYSTEMS THEORY AND THE WORLD UNIVERSITY

This chapter has been written from the point of view of sociological systems theory. It is interesting to compare the two most influential authors in sociological systems theory—Niklas Luhmann and Talcott Parsons—in their sociological understanding of the university. To begin with Niklas Luhmann (1927–1988), the marginal place of the university in his sociological writings, especially in his contributions to the theory of society, is a surprise. There exists only one very small collection of sociological essays on the university (Luhmann, 1992a), all of which are occasional writings that do not demonstrate a theoretical interest in the university. Obviously, there are empirical and theoretical reasons for this disinterest.

On the empirical level, it is easy to see that Luhmann had been disappointed by the university to which he returned relatively late in his life (1968) after an interlude of nearly 20 years, in which public administration had been his primary field of professional activity, observation, and research. He perceived the university as only a small institution—and the university where he became a professor for 25 years (Bielefeld) did not fulfil the expectations he had invested in it. It had been planned as an "institution"—that is, as an "important societal unit" such as the family (Luhmann, 1992b, p. 90). But as an institution it had failed: "Aus der Institution ist nichts geworden."[13] It only became a normal organization.

Theoretically, Luhmann defined the university by the theory of functional differentiation, that is, the horizontal differentiation of function systems, among them "education" and "science." The university as organization participates in education and science. Luhmann preferred to study education as school education and science as a global communication system that is based in research organizations. There was no special place for the university: "Ich glaube nicht, dass es diese Zentralinstitutionen noch gibt, wo die gute Gesellschaft exemplarisch vorgeführt werden kann."[14]

In Talcott Parsons we find nearly exactly the opposite diagnosis. There is an unsuspected centrality of the university for modern society: "The university system constitutes the main institutionalized focus of trusteeship of this great development of secular knowledge and learning. It is perhaps the most important structural component of modern societies that had no direct counterpart in earlier types of society" (Parsons, 1961, p. 261). In Parsons there is a very long trajectory for this argument.

There is the central theoretical position of rationality, which is defined as solidarity between science and the everyday world in "The Structure of Social Action," his first book (Parsons, 1937b; Stichweh, 1980). Immediately after finishing this book, Parsons started his lifelong work on the sociology of the professions (Parsons, 1937a). He understood the professions as a central part of the structure of society. This centrality is based on strong links between traditions of learning, the university as the place of learning and of the education of professionals, and functional domains of social action (medicine, law, religion), in which the cognitive traditions of the university become institutionalized. This theorizing found its conclusion in Parson's last book on the American university (Parsons & Platt, 1974), which understands the university as a "fiduciary institution" that is the most important representative of "cognitive rationality" in the structure of society.

The present author started his work on the theory of the university with a reconstruction of the history of the early modern European university (Stichweh, 1988, 1991a) that combines perspectives from Niklas Luhmann and Talcott Parsons. The history of higher education as an autonomous system in society is interpreted in terms of the history of functional differentiation of society. Medieval higher education was still mostly a part of church organization and religious knowledge domains (although medieval Europe postulated a kind of European relevance and autonomy of the university system protected by the papacy and empire). In the early modern period the dominance of the expectations of the emerging territorial state is superimposed over this medieval level of structure formation. And then, in early 19th-century society, the fusion of the second scientific revolution (Brush, 1988) and the knowledge systems of the university adds a third functional contiguity (the science-education nexus) to the earlier structures. This book from 1991 and many writings since then (Stichweh, 2013, 2024) extended this view of the university system as a European and later world system of its own, being part of the functional differentiation of society and bringing about an institution that has become a big institution (no longer a small institution) with complex structural couplings to all the function systems of society and a phenomenal quantitative growth on the basis of processes of social inclusion in all regions of world society.

NOTES

1. Cf. for the first college in New England, today the most famous university in the world (Eliot, 1643).
2. In later centuries it additionally becomes a regional and a national institution.
3. There is the remarkable moment in 1795 when John Adams and Thomas Jefferson proposed to George Washington to transfer the whole faculty of the University of Geneva from Switzerland to the United States to establish a National University of the United States. But Washington did in no way favor this idea. He objected that one could not know if these professors were really Republicans, and this transplant of a whole university seems to have been perceived by him as an aristocratic move incompatible with the popular mind in America (Madsen, 1966, pp. 28–29).
4. See the case studies on Keele, Sussex, East Anglia, and Essex in Pellew and Taylor (2020).

5. It nearly disappeared in 2016/2017 but was finally saved by a much younger institution, the Italian state.
6. Article "Association of American Universities," https://en.wikipedia.org/wiki/Associati on_of_American_Universities.
7. Another indicator of stability is that only four institutions had to leave AAU (Clark, Catholic University, Nebraska-Lincoln, Syracuse). There were no closures or fusions.
8. This is the background to the idea of a "National University" (Madsen, 1966) that never came about.
9. The classical text is from Kant (1798).
10. From 1975 to 2013 the number of international students grew from 0.8 million to 4.1 million (UNESCO, 2015/2016, p. 44). In 2021, there are 4.8 million international students.
11. Cf. on the introduction of the seminar model in English reform universities in the 1960s, John Charmley (Charmley, 2020, p. 156), on Frank Thistlethwaite Vice Chancellor of the University of East Anglia (1961–1980): "influenced by positive American experience, Thistlethwaite insisted that the major vehicle of pedagogy would be the seminar—not only cheaper than the Oxford and Cambridge system of tutorials (or supervisions), but also facilitating group discussion in a way that the Oxbridge system did not."
12. Cf. (Goldin & Katz, 2008), esp. chapter 1, "The Human Capital Century," pp. 11–43.
13. "Nothing became of the institution" (p. 94).
14. "I do not believe that there are any longer these central institutions, where the good society could be demonstrated in an exemplary way" (Luhmann, 1992c, p. 123).

REFERENCES

Autor, D. H. (2019). Work of the past, work of the future. *AEA Papers and Proceedings, 109,* 1–32.

Branch, M. A. (2001). A more global Yale. *Yale Alumni Magazine, 65*(2), http://archives.yalealu mnimagazine.com/issues/01_11/global.html.

Brizzi, G. P. (1976). *La formazione della classe dirigente nel Sei-Settecento. I seminaria nobilium nell'Italia centro-settentrionale.* Il Mulino.

Bruford, W. H. (1975). *The German tradition of self-cultivation: "Bildung" from Humboldt to Thomas Mann.* Cambridge University Press.

Brush, S. G. (1988). *The history of modern science: A guide to the second Scientific Revolution, 1800–1950.* Iowa State Press.

Charmley, J. (2020). The University of East Anglia: From mandarins to neo-liberalism. In J. Pellew & M. Taylor (Eds.), *Utopian universities: A global history of the new campuses of the 1960s* (pp. 153–174). Bloomsbury.

Conrads, N. (1982). *Ritterakademien der frühen Neuzeit. Bildung als Standesprivileg im 16. und 17. Jahrhundert.* Vandenhoeck & Ruprecht.

Eliot, J. (1643). *New England's first fruits . . . First of the conversion of some of the Indians . . . Second of the progresse of learning, in the Colledge at Cambridge in Massachusetts Bay.* Henry Overton.

Goffman, E. (1983). The interaction order. *American Sociological Review, 48,* 1–17.

Goldin, C., & Katz, L. F. (2008). *The race between education and technology.* The Belknap Press of Harvard University Press.

Hansmann, H. (1990). Why do universities have endowments? *Journal of Legal Studies, 19,* 3–42.

Kant, I. (1798). Der Streit der Fakultäten. In W. Weischedel (Ed.), *Werke Bd. 9* (pp. 261–393). Wissenschaftliche Buchgesellschaft 1975.

Karabel, J. (2006). *The chosen: The hidden history of admission and exclusion at Harvard, Yale and Princeton.* Houghton Mifflin.

Kerr, C. (1994). *Higher education cannot escape history: Issues for the twenty-first century.* State University of New York Press.

Luhmann, N. (1975). Einfache Sozialsysteme. In N. Luhmann (Ed.), *Soziologische Aufklärung 2* (pp. 21–38). Westdeutscher Verlag.

Luhmann, N. (1992a). *Die Universität als Milieu. Kleine Schriften (hrsg. von André Kieserling).* Haux.

Luhmann, N. (1992b). Die Universität als organisierte Institution. In A. Kieserling (Ed.), *Niklas Luhmann, Die Universität als Milieu* (pp. 90–99). Haux.

Luhmann, N. (1992c). Erfahrungen mit Universitäten: Ein Interview. In A. Kieserling (Ed.), *Niklas Luhmann, Universität als Milieu* (pp. 100–125). Haux.

Madsen, D. (1966). *The national university: Enduring dream of the USA.* Detroit.

Meyer, J. W., & Schofer, E. (2007). The university in Europe and the world: Twentieth century expansion. In G. Krücken, A. Kosmützky, & M. Torka (Eds.), *Towards a multiversity? Universities between global trends and national traditions* (pp. 45–62). Transcript.

Moody, J. (2021). A guide to the changing number of U.S. universities. *US News & World Report*, April 27.

Müller-Benedict, V. (2015). Bildung und Wissenschaft. In T. Rahlf (Ed.), *Deutschland in Daten* (pp. 60–73). Bundeszentrale für politische Bildung.

OECD. (2021). *Education at a glance 2021: OECD indicators.* OECD.

Parsons, T. (1937a). Education and the professions. *International Journal of Ethics, 47*, 365–69.

Parsons, T. (1937b). *The structure of social action.* Free Press (of Glencoe).

Parsons, T. (1961). Introduction to Part Two "Differentiation and variation in social structures." In T. Parsons, E. Shils, K. D. Naegele, & J. R. Pitts (Eds.), *Theories of society* (pp. 239–264). The Free Press.

Parsons, T., & Platt, G. M. (1974). *The American university.* Harvard University Press.

Pellew, J., & Taylor, M. (Eds.). (2020). *Utopian universities: A global history of the new campuses of the 1960s.* Bloomsbury Academic.

Pfeffer, T., & Stichweh, R. (2015). Systems theoretical perspectives on higher education policy and governance. In J. Huisman et al. (Ed.), *The Palgrave international handbook of higher education policy and governance* (pp. 152–175). Palgrave Macmillan.

Rothblatt, S. (1997). The "place" of knowledge in the American academic profession. *Daedalus, 126*, 245–264.

Snow, C. P. (1965). *The two cultures: And a second look. An expanded version of the two cultures and the Scientific Revolution.* Cambridge University Press.

Stichweh, R. (1980). Rationalität bei Parsons. *Zeitschrift für Soziologie, 9*, 54–78.

Stichweh, R. (1988). System/Umwelt-Beziehungen europäischer Universitäten in historischer Perspektive. In *Wissenschaft, Universität, Professionen. Soziologische Analysen (2013)* (pp. 153–168). Transcript.

Stichweh, R. (1991a). *Der frühmoderne Staat und die europäische Universität. Zur Interaktion von Politik und Erziehungssystem im Prozeß ihrer Ausdifferenzierung (16.-18. Jahrhundert).* Suhrkamp.

Stichweh, R. (1991b). Die Bildung des europäischen Adels. In *Der frühmoderne Staat und die europäische Universität* (pp. 261–284). Suhrkamp.

Stichweh, R. (1991c). Universitätsmitglieder als Fremde in spätmittelalterlichen und frühmodernen europäischen Gesellschaften. In *Der Fremde. Studien zu Soziologie und Sozialgeschichte* (2010) (pp. 84–110). Suhrkamp.

Stichweh, R. (1992). Motive und Begründungsstrategien für Wissenschaftlichkeit in der deutschen Jurisprudenz des 19. Jahrhunderts. *Rechtshistorisches Journal, 11*, 330–351.

Stichweh, R. (2004). From the *Peregrinatio Academica* to contemporary international student flows: National culture and functional differentiation as emergent causes. In C. Charle, J. Schriewer, & P. Wagner (Eds.), *Transnational intellectual networks: Forms of academic knowledge and the search for cultural identities* (pp. 345–360). Campus.

Stichweh, R. (2008). Die zwei Kulturen? Gegenwärtige Beziehungen von Natur und Humanwissenschaften. *Luzerner Universitätsreden, 18*, 7–21.

Stichweh, R. (2013). *Wissenschaft, Universität, Professionen: Soziologische Analysen.* Transcript.

Stichweh, R. (2020). Der Beitrag der Religion zur Entstehung einer funktional differenzierten Gesellschaft. In M. Pohlig & D. Pollack (Eds.), *Die Verwandlung des Heiligen: Die Geburt der Moderne aus dem Geist der Religion* (pp. 173–187). Berlin University Press.

Stichweh, R. (2024). *Wissenschaft, Universität, Professionen*: Vol. 2. Transcript.

UNESCO. (2015/2016). *UNESCO Science Report: Towards 2030* (2nd. rev. ed. 2016). UNESCO.

Wilensky, H. L. (1964). The professionalization of everyone? *American Journal of Sociology, 70*, 137–158.

CHAPTER 21

SMALL WORLDS

Homeschooling and the Modern Family

ERIC MANGEZ AND ALICE TILMAN

INTRODUCTION

IT has become a truism to even mention it: The COVID-19 pandemic altered every single aspect of our lives globally—our work and leisure time, our rights and duties, our family lives, even our intimate relationships were impacted. One of the most noticeable perturbations has been the closing down of schools and the confinement of families inside their homes. A great many parents, those with young children most evidently, were suddenly assigned the task of organizing and supporting learning activities for their progeniture, while sometimes simultaneously working from home themselves. Unprepared, burdened with the new role forced onto them or disturbed by the virtual presence of teachers in their living room, many soon longed for the reopening of schools.

A small group chose instead to continue homeschooling their children even after the end of their confinements, thus contributing to raising the numbers of homeschoolers in many countries of the world. Though drastic in some cases, the increase resulting from the pandemic merely accelerated a preexisting, more profound and earlier trend. Beginning in the 1970s in the United States and eventually arising in most industrialized countries of the world, the homeschooling movement has been growing and extending its scope ever since its first appearance.

In an attempt to better understand the sociological dynamics underpinning this increasingly global phenomenon, we examine them through the lenses of systems theory. The chapter first discusses the turn to modernity, paying specific attention to the emergence of the modern family. We then reflect on complications arising from the functional differentiation of society and emphasize two potentially problematic dynamics—reductive and expansive—typical of modernity. Next, we examine how such dynamics play out in the specific case of the relationship between the family and school education. We then explore whether and why schooling may be perceived as a risk, and homeschooling as a solution, by some families. In the concluding section, we suggest understanding the homeschooling movement as a specific case within a broader range of social movements through which modernity reacts to its own self-made problems.

From Impersonal to Personal: The Modern Family

The very notion that children should be systematically educated, and that the two instances in charge of them, indeed monopolizing their existence, should be the family and the school, results from a not-so-distant evolution. Before the 17th and 18th centuries, for most of the population across Europe, schools played a marginal role. They were attended sporadically, if at all, and primarily dedicated to religious instruction. Were it to exist at all, one's school education was certainly not considered a key factor shaping one's destiny. The opposite could be said of one's family. The latter "did not penetrate very far into human sensibility" at the time, nor was it primarily concerned with education per se (Ariès, 1962, p. 411; see also Luhmann & Schorr, 2000, p. 62), but it played a central, indeed "multifunctional" role in society and was determinant in assigning its members to social subsystems (Luhmann, 1990). A person was given a place in society through membership of their family. The family, in other words, operated as the pivotal mechanism of social inclusion. To be part of a family was a public fact, not a private matter.

Over the long transition from premodern society to modernity, the old stratified order, in which a person's origin was deemed determinant for all aspects of their life, was then progressively replaced by a functionally differentiated order. Various types of social activity progressively released themselves from the moral, familial, and religious constraints that had constricted their development. Against sociological dogma, Luhmann famously described this emerging modern order as a loose, heterarchical ensemble of functionally differentiated systems (Mangez & Vanden Broeck, 2020, 2021). Art, law, science, education, politics, the economy, as well as other systems, became capable of developing themselves according to their own rules, so to speak. The turn to modernity thus required (premodern) families to hand over most of their traditional tasks to these emerging function systems and their specialized organizations (schools, companies, courts, States and administrations, etc.).

> Along with these structural changes of the primary type of differentiation, the family loses its function to regulate inclusion and exclusion. Families become private families, which, among other things, means that they no longer determine the lifestyle of their members and no longer operate under public supervision. (Luhmann, 2008, p. 41)

The family's loss of functions has been acknowledged by many scholars and gave rise to discussions about the function and specificity of the modern family. What remains of the family, historian Christopher Lasch thus asks, once "the school, the helping professions, and the peer group have taken over most of [its] functions," once "doctors, psychiatrists, teachers, child guidance experts, officers of the juvenile courts and other specialists began to supervise child-rearing, formerly the business of the family" (Lasch, 1977, p. xiv, xxi)? Praised by the outer fringes of both American conservatism and left-wing anti-authoritarianism, Lasch's answer asserts that the modern family has been stripped of all its prerogatives. Lasch places the blame on "capitalism" and the extension of its control over society "through the agency of management, bureaucracy, and professionalization" (Lasch, 1977).

Luhmann develops a different argument. On the one hand, he acknowledges that the turn to modernity deprived the family of many of its traditional roles: most crucially, it no longer has the function of a legitimate general instance of inclusion for society (Luhmann, 1990). However, in contrast to the controversial historian, Luhmann argues that the family as we know it today has only been able to acquire its own, modern, function as a result of such a loss. The argument runs as follows. Full inclusion through family membership, he explains, gave way to partial inclusion through function systems (Braeckman, 2006). The latter include individuals through the prism of their function: One is a (more or less successful) pupil in the educational system, a (more or less healthy) body in the medical system, a (more or less rich) participant in the economic system, and so on. Modern society, the argument continues, "differentiates and specifies modes of interaction within functional systems and their organizations to a previously inconceivable degree" (Luhmann, 2013, p. 139). Inclusion in society now demands that one live one's life as an individual career, navigating between impersonal function systems, facing an open and uncertain future.[1] At a loss, divided into different versions of oneself depending on functional divisions, the modern "in-dividual" (Nassehi, 2002, p. 128) can now hardly be fully included in society: "with the adoption of functional differentiation individual persons (. . .) must be regarded a priori as socially displaced" (Luhmann, 1986, p. 15). As a result of this evolution, Luhmann argues, the need for a specific space capable of recognizing the individual as a special person emerges and provides the closed, private, world of the family, or more broadly intimacy, with its function.

> with the loss of the family's political and productive functions and the increasing spread of schooling to the population as a whole, which opened up careers to children independently of their origins, the question of internal cohesion presented itself. In about 1800, the consequences were still felt by only a very small section of the population, but for them a substitute semantics was offered, which then gradually spread to larger sections of the population, namely, the notion of a personally, intimately grounded partnership based on a love match, and nevertheless enduring, in which the individual could find understanding and support for his specific individuality. (Luhmann, 2013, p. 240)

Its "loss of function" created a *difference* between the family and the rest of society: It made it possible for the family to become that space from which the impersonal becomes treated as personal. The semantics of the modern family, as a space for intimacy, could now "base itself on a factor which has never before influenced symbolic properties in this way, namely the *difference of impersonal and personal relationships*" (Luhmann, 1986, p. 152, emphasis in original). The function of the modern family emerges from, and thanks to, this (new) *difference* between the family and its increasingly complex environment. Whatever is experienced by family members in their daily lives outside the family (even the most impersonal experience of all) can reenter the private sphere and become thematized within the family as a personal matter. The difference between system (family) and environment (other systems, individual consciousness, bodies, etc.) reenters the system. This reentry turns the family into a space where the overall behavior and experience of its members "can be treated, made visible, monitored, cared for, supported" (Luhmann, 1990, p. 198). Viviana Zelizer (1985) noted that, as a result of the differentiation between the home and economic production in the 18th century, the valuation of children reversed radically: they became economically worthless and emotionally priceless, while the opposite had long been the case in medieval Europe (the finding is also echoed in Ariès, 1962). The family now operates as the specific function system where individuals can become included (communicatively) as persons. The "loss of function," then, does not imply a decrease in the social significance of the family, as feared by Lasch, but rather allows "a functional specification" of the family: Relieved of its traditional tasks, it could now intensify its orientation toward persons (Luhmann, 1990).

The generalization of school education results from the same process as does the modern family. Once the family no longer operated as the main instance of social inclusion, a new understanding of individual life courses could develop, which provided education with its raison d'être. Instead of being understood as the tightly coupled outcome of one's origin, as in medieval Europe, individual life courses came to be seen as changeable, malleable, and detachable from their past. Malleability was first considered a characteristic of the child (Ariès, 1962) and later extended to the entire life course (Luhmann, 2021). The now newly conceivable notion that one's life is open to various courses is the most fundamental condition for the emergence and systematization of modern education. Only then can the very intention to change people's life courses through instruction and the expectation of thus loosening the grip of their past on their future, emerge and serve as a foundation for the establishment of an education system.

The differentiation between school education and the family should not be interpreted as a transfer of functions that would give more importance to the former and less to the latter: As underlined by Philippe Ariès, the turning of the family into a site for upbringing and personal affection runs parallel to the progressive generalization of school education, "as if the modern family originated at the same time as the school, or at least as the general habit of educating children at school" (Ariès, 1962, p. 370). Both the school and the family became more specific and more important simultaneously (Tyrell & Vanderstraeten, 2007).

After Marx: The Problematic Consequences of Modernity

The differentiation between school education and the family raises the issue of their interrelations. Each system has acquired its own function: the family with its diffuse orientation toward persons, and school education with its more specific intention to change life courses through instruction. The problem of the relations between distinct functions can be considered highly typical of modernity. It can be raised not only for these two systems but also more broadly for all differentiated systems.

Talcott Parsons and Niklas Luhmann, the two key figures in the development of sociological systems theory, held different, even opposite, views on this problem. Writing mainly in the two first thirds of the 20th century, Parsons could still conceive of modernity as a series of normatively integrated national societies (with the United States as a paradigmatic case) capable of developing and coupling different subsystems (their economy, their education system, their polity, their family system, their religious system). Each system would help solve a specific problem and coordinate its operations with those of other systems by interchanging various services with them. Playing with a series of pattern variables—instrumental—expressive; neutral—affective; specific—diffuse; universal—particular—Parsons would for example differentiate between the family and the school and emphasize, inspired as he was by Emile Durkheim, the division of labor among them: Each would support the development of specific components of the structure of personality and complement the other (Parsons, 1959). Schools consider individuals as learners and treat them in a universalistic (vs. particularistic), neutral (vs. affective), and specific (vs. diffuse) fashion, while remaining in principle indifferent to their particular characteristics. The family, by contrast, is characterized by its particularistic, emotional, and diffuse relation to children. Through socialization in the family, individuals "internalize" values and then become available for schools, where, in turn, they learn to adjust to a specific universalistic-achievement system (Parsons, 1951), thanks to which they are eventually assigned a role in the economy and a status in society. Robert Dreeben (1968), adopting a typically Parsonian perspective, considered the type of expectations that schools project onto pupils and students to be representative of (thus adapted to, and preparing for) what is expected of individuals within a universalistic, affect-neutral, and performance-related modern society.

For Luhmann and Schorr (2000, p. 32), such a perspective "assumed too much harmony on the level of the societal system." Luhmann's view on modern society is in many ways more complex and more disillusioned than Parsons'. Instead of a world organized into national societies capable of coordinating their various functions, he defined modernity as a "world society" (Luhmann, 1971) differentiated into global function systems, each of which assumes the primacy of its own function over all others. He did not consider functional differentiation to be functional: There can be "no guarantee (. . .) that structural developments within function systems remain compatible with each other" (Luhmann, 1997, p. 76). He perceived and emphasized a "dark side" of functional differentiation (Teubner, 2021). The latter, he repeatedly explained, comes with a wide range of implications, including in particular "many problematic consequences": "functional systems of society burden themselves—and thus society—with problems produced by their own outdifferentiation, specialization, and focus on high performance" (Luhmann, 2013, p. 124).

Functional differentiation therefore cannot mean that each system can safely operate within its own reserved territory and offer its services to others. More chaotic and much less balanced situations are occurring. Building on Luhmann's work, Gunther Teubner (2011, p. 224) refers to these problems as "destructive dynamics" associated with "the one-sided rationality-maximization" of each function system. One can distinguish two dynamics through which functionally differentiated systems might create problems, which correspond to the two key attributes that characterize them: They offer a very specific (hence restricted) yet universal (and thus expandable) way of dealing with the world. On the one hand, systems operate indeed very specifically; they establish themselves by continuously cutting and severing the world. They come to be by excluding all that which they are not, most notably "what Pascal had called 'le coeur' and which is sometimes referred to today as the 'lifeworld'" (Luhmann, 2004b, p. 86). They tend to become obsessed with their own internal dynamics. Their very success, Luhmann explains, "depends upon neglect" (1997, p. 76). Functional differentiation thus incessantly leaves the world in a severed and mutilated condition. On the other hand, because each system relies on a universal function, it simultaneously tends to become invasive; it colonizes its surroundings, while simultaneously running the risk of itself becoming invaded by other logics. Systems are indeed inclined to turn ever more elements of their environment into their own logic, contributing thus to processes of potentially excessive marketization, politicization, juridification, scientification, medicalization, and indeed educationalization (see Luhmann, 2013, p. 95). And, Teubner remarks suggestively, "[e]xcessive juridification results in new injustices; (. . .) new pathologies arise from excessive medicalization" (Teubner, 2021, p. 513).

The perspective echoes ideas that had been developed much earlier. In a specific and still limited way, Marx had touched upon these problems—capitalism is dehumanizing the world, he famously argued—but, according to Luhmann, this critique remained too "restricted" (Luhmann, 1982, p. 342). For him, the dehumanizing process at work in the Marxist critique is not the curse solely of the economy. He therefore argued in favor of "the establishment of a non-Marxist Marx," one that would loosen its fixation with the economy and become sensitive to "parallel phenomena" at work "in different functional areas" (Luhmann, 1998, pp. 7, 9; see also Luhmann, 1982). It is certainly true that the economy cannot help but turn that which it observes into a commodity (thus colonizing and mutilating the world at the same time), but, Luhmann suggests, is that reductive-expansive dynamic not at work within other systems, too? Isn't it the case that the law, somehow similarly, can only apprehend the problems it deals with by alienating them from their full original breadth, so as to (re)construct them specifically into legal problems that it can then handle with its own means (Luhmann, 1969; Teubner, 1999)?

In Luhmann's perspective, reductive reconstructions of this kind are very characteristic of modern society. All function systems, not the economy alone, alienate. Education continuously expands its reach and simultaneously reduces individuals to pupils, students, or learners and ultimately retains nothing of them except for their academic performances (or failures). Such an indifference actually allows for the establishment of systems (see Vanden Broeck, Chapter 18, this volume).

It might be tempting to characterize modern society as an impersonal mass society and to leave it at that. As we have seen, however, such an assessment ignores the fact that modern society grew more impersonal and more personal at the very same time: In Luhmann's words (1986, p. 12), "it affords more opportunities both for impersonal and for more intensive personal relationships." With the functional differentiation of society, close and personal relationships, most notably in the context of the family, emerge and acquire a special, compensatory function. Like a *Haven in a Heartless World* (Lasch, 1977), they are expected to offer a familiar space, one that is "still understandable, intimate and close," a refuge to "cope with the unwholesomeness of the world" (Luhmann, 1986, p. 16, 153), "protection and support, as it were, against the dominant characteristics of modern society—against the economic necessity to work and exploit, against regulation by the state, against research that presses for technology" (Luhmann, 2013, p. 245). The refuge, however, is not necessarily safe; there can be no guarantee that the line drawn between the development of a private sphere of personal relationships (family, love, friendship) and other impersonal function systems will not be crossed.

AUTONOMY AND DEPENDENCE: THE SCHOOL, THE STATE, AND THE FAMILY

In his history of school education, Luhmann distinguishes three stages, each of which develops its own contingency formula and assumes a certain relationship between school education and the family. In the first, not yet fully modern stage, education is conceived of as the realization of one's natural perfection. Education then does not involve conveying knowledge but rather avoiding corruption, moralizing and, in this way, merely supporting every being in achieving "its perfection through transcending his state of being" (Luhmann & Schorr, 2000, p. 71). At this point in time, the hierarchical structure of society was still assumed to be self-evident; perfection was thus conceived of as adjusted to the stipulations of one's social status (kinship). Understandably then, the context of the family was considered just as valuable as, or even more valuable than that of school education. Sending children to schools was then still met with various forms of resistance on the part of families (Tyrell & Vanderstraeten, 2007). Because it had long conceived its offspring's life course as inscribed in the nature of their origin, the nobility in particular was not inclined to accept school education as a relevant resource. One only needed to let the good nature of the noble child flourish and protect it from the risk of corruption (Luhmann, 2013, p. 85). For the lower strata of society, resistance to schooling was due to more material motives: Children contributed to the maintenance of the household either directly as coworkers or indirectly as caregivers for their younger siblings and were therefore needed for work or at home. Excluding them from the world of work, Zelizer (1985, p. 12) explains, was "a difficult and controversial process." Their monopolization by the school was not welcome. School attendance was often not a priority for these families (Tyrell, 1987).

Initially, thus, the logic of the school was still subjected to, and dominated by, other logics. Resistances to schooling proved temporary. Little by little, school education and family education became admitted "as two equal possibilities; at first as alternatives and then, starting in the middle of the [18th] century, increasingly as successive phases in the education process" (Luhmann & Schorr, 2000, p. 76). The 19th century in Europe saw the emergence of a new contingency formula oriented toward "all-around educa-tion" (*Bildung*). While the perfection formula took for granted the existence of natural differences between human beings, and hence considered the family as a very suitable educational setting, the all-around formula moved some distance away from this as-sumption: Education came to be understood no longer as the realization of one's natural perfection but as gaining greater independence from one's origins through cognition. All-around education now involves instruction and determines what counts as know-ledge by relying on science and the university. "Science has the highest place in all-around education, and it is also its subject matter," while the family, for its part, becomes "marginalized as an overlapping domain" (Luhmann & Schorr, 2000, p. 91). The differ-ence between family upbringing and school education thus became sharper. All-around education is about making "subjects" capable of reflecting on their relation to the world thanks to instruction. So long as it relied on the all-around formula, education, however, could not yet be considered fully self-referential: The limits of what counted as know-ledge were still in the (external) hands of science.

In the second half of the 20th century, "learning to learn" became the dominant for-mula that organizes education in a different, autonomous way. With this new formula, science (or any other fundamental, normative ideal) no longer defines the limit of what is worth learning. Education achieves self-referentiality: Learning is at once in-dependent from its environment (it does not rely specifically on science or another ex-ternal instance) and capable of connecting with anything in its environment (it can be applied to anything, anyone, at any time). The sequence that goes from the first (human perfection) to the second (all-around education) and then to the third formula (learning to learn) has turned education into an increasingly self-referential domain: In the end, "the ability to learn formula barely includes any recognizable special relations to one of the environment domains" (Luhmann & Schorr, 2000, p. 70).

Before examining the implications of such a process for its familial environment, a remark must be made with regard to a specific problem in the differentiation of edu-cation. Education, Luhmann and Schorr argue, suffers from a technological deficit: It does not possess a symbolically generalized medium to support its operations (like money for the economy or truth for science, for example). As a social process, it lacks a medium to reach the learners' consciousness, its target. In order to compensate for this deficit, the main solution has consisted in relying on the State to ensure the organization of lengthy interactions between learners and teachers in the classroom (for a thorough development, see Vanden Broeck, 2020a, 2020b). Their co-presence is meant to compensate for the lack of a symbolically generalized medium. Education must rely on the state for, as a system, it does not have the means to ensure the actual organization of classroom interactions: It can teach, but it cannot make collectively binding decisions; it cannot force learners to attend school; and it cannot fund education or pay teachers. For all this, it has been dependent mainly upon the organizing ability of the state—but also on the support of families (Tyrell, 1987). The relationship among education, politics, and the family is, however, not a hierarchical or causal one. Education, one could tentatively argue, actually operates more like a sort of parasite: It uses these other systems' performances as a support for its own operations, which makes it dependent and autonomous at once. The COVID-19 pandemic has not proved that wrong; it has, in fact, rather revealed that with the relative retreat of the state, education could adapt, search, and become dependent upon other supports (platforms, families, technologies), which it somehow colonized as well in order to pursue its operations despite the (temporary) inability of states to organize schools and classrooms (see Vanden Broeck, 2021, and Chapter 18, in this volume). That many parents felt burdened by the situation is but a sign of this colonization.

Education's deficit thus turns it into a particularly demanding system, relying on both family support and the state; and actually requiring bringing together the entire population of young people, cut off from their families in classrooms, and having them spend a significant amount of their daily lives, for years, in the presence of their teachers and peers: "one can think of it as a concentration of people of the same age in a relatively big interaction system," "a system of immense size and incalculable complexity" (Luhmann & Schorr, 2000, p. 31, 19). No other function system has ever developed such requirements.

HOMESCHOOLING AS PROTEST

From the perspective of the family, the situation is not without risks. By attending school, one "is confronted for the first time and suddenly with a society that is no longer negotiated by the family" (Luhmann & Schorr, 2000, p. 31). The differentiation of education and its organization in classrooms allows for the creation of a peculiar social order, strictly distinct from its simultaneously operating and turbulent environment. What children learn from their teachers and the ways in which they might be affected by being socialized with their peers escape family control (Tyrell & Vanderstraeten, 2007). Luhmann's observation (2000, 2006) that the individual has no choice, if she wants to participate in modern society, but to place her trust in systems and organizations to which she has in fact "ceded control" thus proves all the more relevant for school education.

Luhmann and Schorr (1979/2000, p. 32) therefore raise the question: "how and with what repercussions and counter movements" can the family system "handle the socialization and education in schools"?[2] Reflecting on this question, one may think of the many ways in which families attempt to gain some control over the schooling of their children (the attention paid to selecting a given school, expectations with regard to staff training, etc.) or the ways in which family roles and everyday organization need to adjust to school education and its organization. When Luhmann and Schorr alluded to the "repercussions" and even the "counter movements" that schooling could produce on the part of families, it was not entirely clear what they had in mind precisely. They did not mention the homeschooling movement specifically. The latter had hardly begun at the time. It is, however, not difficult to interpret the homeschooling movement and the decisions that parents make to educate their children at home as counter-reactions to schooling.

Homeschooling is indeed typically practiced in these contexts with a highly developed educational system. The phenomenon first emerged in the United States, where it has been growing regularly since the 1970s, and later expanded in most developed countries across the world, notably in Europe, where it is now growing at a faster rate (Tilman & Mangez, 2021). Its expansion can therefore not be attributed to the lack of a formal system or to its underdevelopment. Instead, it must be put in relation to the development of schooling itself. It develops from, and expands together with, education systems.

All the historical accounts of the movement associate its emergence with two groups of homeschoolers.[3] The group within which the movement originated was made up of progressive parents inspired by John Holt. Permeated by a liberal ideology, they considered schools a too rigid environment for the differentiated needs of their children. Very critical of what they viewed as school education's reductive focus on the cognitive performances of their children, they were hoping to provide them with a richer, less one-dimensional, more personalized environment at home. Schools were criticized for being coercive bureaucratically organized environments. In the 1980s, another quite distinct group of homeschoolers, whose best-known leader at the time was Raymond Moore, emerged in the American landscape. Driven by the "conviction that educating their children is a God-given right and responsibility" (Kunzman, 2009, p. 6), these conservative Christians viewed public school education as too permissive and rose up against the secularization of society and its schooling system. Here again, it is easy to see the religious motivation underpinning this group of parents as reacting against the school system's one-sidedness.

In the two cases of orientation toward homeschooling by progressive parents and by conservative Christians in the United States, it can thus be argued that it is the increased self-referentiality of the educational system, that is, the very fact that education increasingly reduces the world to its own logic (Ball, 2000; Nóvoa & Yariv-Mashal, 2003) and develops a form of indifference to criteria that are not primarily scholastic, that leads one group (the expressive progressives) to consider the system inhuman and impersonal and the other (the religious conservatives) to deplore the absence of moral or religious limits within the system.

While these two orientations remain well represented among today's population of homeschoolers, the latter has grown more and more diversified. As noted by Gaither in his history of homeschooling in America, "[h]ome education is now being done by (. . .) many different kinds of people for (. . .) many different reasons" (Gaither, 2017, p. 282). Homeschooling families no longer belong solely to the fringes and now include the mainstream of American life. In many other countries of the world as well, an increasing number of "middle-grounders" (Collom & Mitchell 2005, p. 276), which identifies neither with right-wing religious groups nor with the libertarian Left, turn to home-schooling. They now form "a heterogeneous population with varying and overlapping motivations" (Collom, 2005, p. 331). New typologies have emerged in the literature to account for the increasing diversity of homeschoolers.[4]

The latest developments in research on homeschooling also show a tendency for the movement to become more and more organized. Most homeschooling families have actually never operated in isolation. From the early days of the movement, at a local level, parents from different families would coordinate themselves and organize some activities together or take turns to supervise a group of children. As time went by, self-organizing processes became more and more important, even professionalized (Kunzman, 2009; Stevens, 2003). In the United States, the practice is now underpinned by specialized communication (with many handbooks on "How to homeschool your children"), platforms and professionals offering their support, and private or even public institutions offering parents day-by-day assistance in their undertaking. Gaither speaks of hybrid forms of homeschooling where children actually combine a number of activities put in place by diverse organizations, some of which begin to look like schools.

According to Kunzman and Gaither (2013), homeschooling parents of all orientations share a common aspiration to take back "control" over their children's education and their family life. Murphy et al. (2017, p. 87) similarly consider "the control of their children and their education" to be the parents' "universal, prime motive for homeschooling." To make sense of the history of the movement and its most recent developments, Gaither speaks of a cycle where a first, long-lasting phase of delegation "to other institutions of functions that once lay very much within the realm of family responsibility" is now followed by a new, emerging and possibly "revolutionary," phase consisting of a "reversal of this longstanding pattern," and visible notably in the current development of homeschooling and other home-based practices: The "historic defer-ence to expertise" would be giving way to "a new spirit of self-reliance" (Gaither, 2017, pp. xii–xiii). Gaining back control seems to be a common denominator to all or most homeschooling families.

A close examination of the intersystemic relations between formal education and the private sphere of the modern family reveals the various ways through which school requirements increasingly penetrate family life and helps, in turn, to ex-plain the need that some families now feel to gain back control. Systems theorists find that the relationship between the school and the family has grown increasingly unbalanced. Schools tend to rely on families for a number of problems (Luhmann & Schorr, 1979, 2000) while the opposite is hardly the case: Family life as such cannot really count on school education to facilitate its own functioning (Tyrell, 1987; Tyrell & Vanderstraeten, 2007).

That school education tends to (re)shape family roles according to its own requirements becomes particularly visible when tensions develop in the family with regard to homework and school results: Even in their own families, children are increasingly regarded and valued, or devalued, for their performances as pupils (Tyrell & Vanderstraeten, 2007). Parents, for their part, are expected to become involved in solving a number of problems resulting from the differentiation of school education. Tyrell (1987, p. 108) draws attention to the significant "preparatory, accompanying and support services" which families make available to the school. He underlines distinct ways in which schooling colonizes families, thus turning them into a support system at its service: While homework evidently impacts family life and sometimes turns parents into unpaid school employees, the latter are also expected to ensure regular school attendance even when schooling itself fails to motivate their children and sometimes even triggers feelings of reluctance, anxiety, or school phobia. The very functioning of school education seems favorable to the creation of frustrations and disappointments, but, Tyrell further explains, in most cases, schooling merely leaves the task of processing these emotional states to families. The support that parents thus provide to their children with regard to school education should not be considered merely a family matter. It is, in fact, indicative of the simultaneously reductive and expansive force exerted by one system (the school) on another (the family).

The fact that the family has been turned into a support system for the school goes often unnoticed as such: It takes the appearance of solidarity and tensions between parents and their children, and thus seems internal to the family. From a system-theoretical perspective, however, these situations reveal school education's high level of dependence on family support. They merely show how the logic of school education may affect and intrude on family life.

CONCLUSION: MODERNITY'S COUNTER-REACTIONS

In this chapter, the differences between school education and the family have been reconstructed from the perspective of Niklas Luhmann's systems theory. In contrast with several other sociological traditions, systems theory does not attribute modernity's most central problems to the domination of a logic, class, narrative, or cultural orientation (against which alternatives could compete). What creates problems is rather the very form of (modern) society itself. And this means: not the predominance of a model, but rather the absence of such predominance, resulting in the tumultuous coexistence of different logics, each concerned with, and assuming the primacy of, its own function. Function systems tend to expand and impose their own specific logic over others.

In the context of this chapter, homeschooling has been discussed, not so much for its own sake but rather as a case of counter-reaction to functional differentiation. It illustrates how the exclusive and self-centered logics of modern society do indeed give rise to reactions in the form of social movements and protests, claiming and hoping to reorder modern society along lines that run against its functional differentiation: putting religion, love, the family, the nation, or whatever else, first as it were, or rather "above" other functions. Thus, the difference between schooling and homeschooling stems from the fact that at home, "the process of education [can remain] bound to the fulfillment—even to the primacy—of another function" (Luhmann & Schorr, 2000, p. 61).

Relying on systems theory makes it possible to identify the "form of the problem" (i.e., conflicting expansive-reductive systems) which is at work in these situations independently of its actual content (education and the family). In turn, it becomes possible to consider that the same form of problem or dynamic—Teubner (2011) calls it a dynamic of "regime-collisions"—might be at work with other systems and give rise to other social movements. To the extent that such movements react to highly advanced self-referential systems by ceasing to place their trust in their organizations (schools, hospitals, firms, courts, political parties, etc.), they will often take on the *appearance* of a retreat from modernity. Problems of trust "lead to feelings of alienation, and eventually to retreat into smaller worlds of purely local importance, to new forms of 'ethnogenesis', to a fashionable longing for an independent if modest living, to fundamentalist attitudes or other forms of retotalizing milieux and 'life-worlds'" (Luhmann, 2000, pp. 103–104). The rise of self-referential and conflicting systemic perspectives in the domain of education or in other domains (the economy, health, law, or politics, for example) tends to generate distrust of systems and their institutions and the emergence of particular "lifestyles" characterized by a form of withdrawal from the established systems.

The notions of retreat or withdrawal should not be taken as actual backward moves to nonmodern or premodern forms of existence. Such movements cannot be understood analytically as competing at the same "level" as functional differentiation itself. They are, in fact, an outcome of, and at the same time a reaction to, modernity. One must thus consider them as highly modern. They are processes through which modernity reacts to itself, to its own, self-made problems.

Notes

1. The process is analogous to what Habermas (1985, p. 325) calls the "colonization of the life-world by systemic imperatives."

2. The full quote reads as follows: "how and with what repercussions and counter movements the system of education's societal environment can handle the socialization and education in schools" (Luhmann & Schorr, 2000, p. 32). The notion of "the system of education's societal environment" refers to two "overlapping domains": the family and the economy.
3. For a history of the movement, see, for example, Collom & Mitchell, 2005; Gaither, 2017; Knowles et al., 1992; Murphy, 2013; Stevens, 2003; Van Galen, 1988.
4. Already in 1988, Mayberry suggested distinguishing four types of homeschoolers: "religious ideologues," "New Ager ideologues," "academic pedagogues," and "social-relational pedagogues." Pitman (1987) contrasted three types: "religious," "progressive," and "academic"; more recently, Gaither (2017) distinguished among "sectarian," "romantic," and "pragmatic." Other categorizations focus instead on the circumstances in which homeschooling decisions are made. Kostelecká (2010), for example, differentiates between "devoted" parent educators, who opt for homeschooling out of conviction, and parents who turn to it because of particular circumstances, while Lois (2013) differentiates between "first choicers" (mothers who see homeschooling as a logical extension of their commitment to stay at home with their young children) and "second choicers" (default choices in the face of what is considered to be unsatisfactory educational provision). As Bongrand and Glasman (2018) rightly note, homeschoolers include families whose parents are in fact "school seekers" but who, for various reasons, do not find school provision satisfactory to them.

References

Ariès, P. (1962). *Centuries of childhood: A social history of family life*. Knopf.

Ball, S. J. (2000). Performativities and fabrications in the education economy: Towards the performative society? *The Australian Educational Researcher, 27*(2), 1–23.

Bongrand, P., & Glasman, D. (2018). Instruction(s) en famille: Explorations sociologiques d'un phénomène émergent. *Revue française de pédagogie, 205*, 5–19.

Braeckman, A. (2006). Niklas Luhmann's systems theoretical redescription of the inclusion/exclusion debate. *Philosophy & Social Criticism, 32*(1), 65–88.

Collom, E. (2005). The ins and outs of homeschooling: The determinants of parental motivations and student achievement. *Education and Urban Society, 37*, 307–335.

Collom, E., & Mitchell, D. E. (2005). Home schooling as a social movement: Identifying the determinants of homeschoolers' perceptions. *Sociological Spectrum, 25*(3), 273–305.

Dreeben, R. (1968). *On what is learned in school*. Addison-Wesley.

Gaither, M. (2017). *Homeschool: An American history* (2nd ed., rev.). Palgrave Macmillan.

Habermas, J. (1985). *The theory of communicative action* (Vol. 2). Beacon.

Knowles, J. G., Marlow, S. E., & Muchmore, J. A. (1992). From pedagogy to ideology: Origins and phases of home education in the United States, 1970–1990. *American Journal of Education, 100*(2), 195–235.

Kostelecká, Y. (2010). Home education in the post-communist countries: Case study of the Czech Republic. *International Electronic Journal of Elementary Education, 3*(1), 29–44.

Kunzman, R. (2009). *Write these laws on your children: Inside the world of conservative Christian homeschooling*. Beacon Press.

Kunzman, R. (2017). Homeschooling and religious fundamentalism. *International Electronic Journal of Elementary Education, 3*(1), 17–28.

Kunzman, R., & Gaither, M. (2013). Homeschooling: A comprehensive survey of the research. *Other Education: The Journal of Educational Alternatives*, 2(1), 4–59.

Lasch, C. (1977). *Heaven in a heartless world*. Basic.

Lois, J. (2013). *Home is where the school is: The logic of homeschooling and the emotional labor of mothering*. New York University Press.

Luhmann, N. (1969). Normen in soziologischer Perspektive. *Soziale Welt*, 20(1), 28–48.

Luhmann, N. (1971). Die Weltgesellschaft. *Archiv für Rechts- und Sozialphilosophie*, 57, 1–35.

Luhmann, N. (1982). *The differentiation of society*. Columbia University Press.

Luhmann, N. (1986). *Love as passion: The codification of intimacy*. Harvard University Press.

Luhmann, N. (1990). Sozialsystem Familie. In *Soziologische Aufklärung 5* (pp. 196–217). VS Verlag für Sozialwissenschaften.

Luhmann, N. (1995). *Social systems*. Stanford University Press.

Luhmann, N. (1997). Globalization or world society: How to conceive of modern society? *International Review of Sociology*, 7(1), 67–79.

Luhmann, N. (1998). *Observations on modernity*. Stanford University Press.

Luhmann, N. (2000). Familiarity, confidence, trust: Problems and alternatives. *Trust: Making and Breaking Cooperative Relations*, 6, 94–107.

Luhmann, N. (2004a). Das Erziehungssystem und die Systeme seiner Umwelt. In D. Lenzen (Ed.), *Schriften zur Peadagogik* (pp. 209–244). Suhrkamp.

Luhmann, N. (2004b). Die Homogenisierung des Anfangs: Zur Ausdifferenzierung der Schulerziehung. In D. Lenzen (Ed.), *Schriften zur P€adagogik* (pp. 123–158). Suhrkamp.

Luhmann, N. (2006). *La confiance un mécanisme de réduction de la complexité sociale*, Economica.

Luhmann, N. (2008). Beyond barbarism. *Soziale Systeme*, 14(1), 38–46.

Luhmann, N. (2013). *Theory of society* (Vol. 2). (R. Barrett, Trans.). Stanford University Press.

Luhmann, N. (2021). Education: Forming the life course. *European Educational Research Journal*, 20(6), 719–728.

Luhmann, N., & Schorr, K. E. (2000). *Problems of reflection in the system of education* (R. A. Neuwirth, Trans.). Waxmann.

Mangez, E., & Vanden Broeck, P. (2020). The history of the future and the shifting forms of education. *Educational Philosophy and Theory*, 52(6), 676–687.

Mangez, E., & Vanden Broeck, P. (2021). Worlds apart? On Niklas Luhmann and the sociology of education. *European Educational Research Journal*, 20(6), 705–718.

Mayberry, M., (1988). Characteristics and attitudes of families who home school. *Education and Urban Society*, 21(1), 32–41.

Murphy, J. (2013). Riding history: The organizational development of homeschooling in the US. *American Educational History Journal*, 40(1/2), 335.

Murphy, J., Gaither, M., & Gleim, C. E. (2017). The calculus of departure. In The Wiley handbook of home education (pp. 86–120). Wiley.

Nassehi, A. (2002), Exclusion individuality or individualization by inclusion? *Soziale Systeme*, 8, Heft 1, S.124–135.

Nóvoa, A., & Yariv-Mashal, T. (2003). Comparative research in education: A mode of governance or a historical journey? *Comparative Education*, 39(4), 423–438.

Parsons, T. (1951). *The social system*. Free Press.

Parsons, T. (1959). The school class as a social system: Some of its functions in American society. *Harvard Educational Review*, 29, 297–318.

Pitman, M. A. (1987). Compulsory education and home schooling: Truancy or prophecy? *Education and Urban Society*, *19*(3), 280–289.

Stevens, M. L. (2003). The normalisation of homeschooling in the USA. *Evaluation & Research in Education*, *17*(2–3), 90–100.

Teubner, G. (2011). Constitutionalizing polycontexturality. *Social & Legal Studies*, *20*(2), 210–229.

Teubner, G. (1999). Drei persönliche Begegnungen. In Rudolf Stichweh (Hrsg.) *Niklas Luhmann—Wirkungen eines Theoretikers* (pp. 19–25). Transcript.

Teubner, G. (2021). The constitution of non-monetary surplus values. *Social & Legal Studies*, *30*(4), 501–521.

Tilman, A., & Mangez, E. (2021). L'instruction à domicile comme phénomène global. *Éducation et sociétés*, *45*, 123–141.

Tyrell, H. (1987). Die Anpassung der Familie an die Schule. In J. Oelkers & H.-E. Tenorth (Eds.), *Pädagogik, Erziehungswissenschaft und Systemtheorie* (pp. 102–124). Beltz.

Tyrell, H., & Vanderstraeten, R. (2007). Familie und Schule: Zwei Orte der Erziehung. In J. Aderhold & O. Kranz (Eds.), *Intention und funktion*. VS Verlag für Sozialwissenschaften.

Vanden Broeck, P. (2020a). Beyond school: Transnational differentiation and the shifting form of education in world society. *Journal of Education Policy*, *35*(6), 836–855.

Vanden Broeck, P. (2020b). The problem of the present: On simultaneity, synchronisation and transnational education projects. *Educational Philosophy and Theory*, *52*(6), 664–675.

Vanden Broeck, P. (2021). Education in world society: A matter of form. *European Educational Research Journal*, *20*(6), 791–805.

Van Galen, J. (1988). Ideology, curriculum, pedagogy in home education. *Education & Urban Society*, *21*, 52–86.

Zelizer, V. A. (1994). *Pricing the priceless child: The changing social value of children*. Princeton University Press.

PART II

POLICY CHALLENGES AND IMPLICATIONS OF GLOBAL PRESSURES ON NATIONAL EDUCATION SYSTEMS

INTRODUCTION TO PART II

PAOLA MATTEI AND JACQUELINE BEHREND

GLOBAL, NATIONAL, AND LOCAL SCALES OF GOVERNANCE IN EDUCATION POLICY

Education is a policy field dominated by political contestation and politically salient reforms at the global, national, and local levels of government. It is an area of state activities permeated by a constant struggle for public resources, and power among actors who hold different ideas and interests. These domestic conflicts shape the institutional framework within which globalized public policy reforms are then produced by international organizations and national institutions. We, therefore, need to simultaneously capture the national, local developments and global levels of education governance. This is why we do not depart a priori from a one-fits-all shared understanding of globalization, but we develop a pluralistic and transdisciplinary approach to the question of global policy reforms.

Moving on from the efforts of leading social theorists to conceptualize the process of globalization within a holistic framework that can be generalized to a wide population of cases globally, Part II of the Handbook analyzes the political and institutional factors that contribute to the substantive formulation and adoption of global policy reforms in education and their embeddedness at the national and local levels of governance in advanced and developing countries around the world. Thus, Part II is concerned with discussing complexities and variations across countries, in order to illuminate the persistence of political contestation and analyze the impact of global norms and ideas on local institutions and national education systems. The chapters engage with the complex processes of globalization and their different analytical dimensions by analyzing some of the most compelling political questions associated with key education reform agendas, emphasizing cross-national variations in a comparative perspective, and the active role of different political contexts, actors, and strategies which rarely converge in a one-fits-all concept of globalization. Some chapters will highlight the cultural dimensions of globalization, while others will focus on its economic ones. Globalization is used as a complex and multifaceted analytical tool that cannot be captured by one concept in isolation from the others.

Thus, this Part II of the Handbook explores the political implications of globalization on national and local education policy systems and subsystems and their institutional transformations, in order to substantiate the resilience of the nation state as an independent policy space characterized by specific policy advice systems, and governance tools. As such, the focus of Part II is cross-regional and seeks to highlight the importance of diverse political and historical contexts in the adoption and implementation of global education policy ideas. Some of the main research questions it seeks to address are as follows: To what extent has the adoption and implementation of global reform agendas resulted in homogeneous policies both across and within regions and countries? How do local education policy systems and institutions interact with the policies promoted by international organizations? What role do local actors such as teachers' unions play in mediating reforms in diverse contexts? How do different levels of governance interact in the education policy space, which includes reforms?

The chapters in Part II of this Handbook focus on public policy and governance issues, and they do so from diverse perspectives within the discipline of comparative politics and comparative public policy. Some chapters adopt a historical institutionalist approach, other chapters are concerned with the political economy of education policies and reforms, and another group of chapters focuses on the international relations dynamics behind education reforms advocated by international organizations. But all chapters in Part II pay due attention to the diverse political contexts, institutions, and actors that are central to understanding how education policy is implemented across regions, nation-states, and within countries. From a methodological standpoint, the chapters in Part II show methodological pluralism and adopt diverse tools as part of their research strategies. We have valued diversity and pluralism foremost over the intellectual ideology that globalization is an irreversible force shaping global convergence.

The authors in Part II of this Handbook use different entry points to analyze the interaction between globalization and education policy. Some chapters pay greater attention to economic globalization, while others concentrate mostly on political globalization. Both aspects of globalization are important in the case studies presented in the different sections and the diversity of the contributions aims to provide a broad and comprehensive analysis of the challenges that education policy faces in a globalized world.

Global education policies promoted by international actors and organizations are filtered through national and local institutions that mediate global processes within countries, and domestic structures and policy systems. Organization for Economic Cooperation and Development (OECD) countries continue to vary widely in the public resources they invest in education and the organization of educational systems (e.g., stratification, tracking systems). School systems, for instance, are among the most resilient and stable institutions over time. In addition, there are also important variations *within* countries, especially in federal states such as Argentina, Brazil, and the United States. In Latin America, the implications of globalization and integration into the world economy are varied, and there is great divergence among subnational regions that are more or less globalized.

The last section of Part II of the Handbook interrogates on the relationship among globalization, democratic governance, education policies, and investment in human capital in Latin America. The chapters adopt a multi-level perspective to assess the challenges offered by globalization to education policies and education spending in developing countries. A multi-level perspective means focusing both on initiatives undertaken by national states and by subnational or local governments, which are the administrative units in charge of education in many Latin American countries. Despite assertions that education policies are increasingly converging in a globalized world, Latin American countries vary widely in the resources they devote to education and the development of human capital. Some of the key research questions the chapters in this last section address are as follows: How do local power and globalization interact to produce different governance and policy outcomes? What determines local spending in education and the development of human capital? Do greater linkages to the globalized economy have effects on democratic governance, the development of human capital, and, specifically, education spending? What is the role of ideas and ideology in the implementation of subnational policies aimed at developing human capital? The chapters in this section attend to the relationship between the globalization of local economies and the development of human capital (with a specific focus on education spending), and address these research questions from a plurality of methodological perspectives. Paola Mattei has taken the editorial lead for Sections IV, V, VI, and VII of Part II, and Jacqueline Behrend has taken the lead on Section VIII.

Section IV: International Actors and Education Policy

Globalization is not a new concept in international and comparative education. Policy diffusion in the field of education promoted by international organizations such as UNESCO, the World Bank, the OECD, and others, hasve had a lasting impact on various dimensions of policy reforms around the world. The chapters in this section analyze the role of the OECD and international organizations in shaping global education policy, investigating the policy goals, and instruments used to shape education policy. Two major trends will emerge: the economistic-oriented actors added education as a field to their portfolio, and education-orientated international organizations with a regional focus flourished.

Martens, Niemann, and Krogmann (Chapter 22)'s contribution provides a mapping of how many and what types of international organizations work on education policy. They suggest that there has been an expansion of education competences within international organizations, drawing upon examples from the OECD and the World Bank, and others. Both organizations adopted the field of education to promote economic growth.

Ydesen and Enemark (Chapter 23) argue that for decades the Organisation for Economic Cooperation and Development (OECD) has played a pivotal role in shaping education worldwide; both in relation to member-states and non-member states. Research has amply demonstrated how nation states and domestic education institutions have transformed themselves in the image of global reforms, often orchestrated and facilitated by the OECD. Global governance processes have created key reference points for education worldwide in the shape of data, indicators, values, problem solutions, and even ideologies. Nevertheless, national education systems and local education practices remain diverse and complex. Therefore, research into the workings of global education requires analytical sensitivity to the interactions and intermeshing relations among local, national, and global agents, instruments, knowledge, data, and policies populating and constituting spaces.

Starting from this insight and drawing on archival sources from the OECD archive in Paris, the United States National Archive in Washington, DC, and the Brazilian National Archive in Brasilia, this chapter investigates the interactions and intermeshing relations in education between the OECD and two federal states—the United States, a member state, and Brazil, a non-member state—in a historical and comparative perspective. The United States was a key agent in the transition of the Organization for European Economic Cooperation (OEEC) to the OECD in 1961, whereas Brazil established close relations with the OECD in education in the late 1990s.

Looking across time and space creates a methodological opportunity of identifying recurring features and mechanisms in the trajectories of the very engine room of global education. Increasing knowledge about historical contingencies, a historical approach can create awareness of the historical constructs of today's education policies that otherwise seem to operate in a naturalized way according to an inherent logic.

Grek (Chapter 24) explores the transnational governance of education. Her contribution discusses the interactive visual rankings produced by the OECD, the World Bank, UNESCO, and the Gates Foundation as measurement tools. She argues that the increasing pressures for "decolonizing" education influence the visualization of data. The overall argument is that data visualization is a powerful tool of world-making.

Section V: The Responses of National Education Systems to Global Pressures

Education policies and reforms both at the global and local levels are embedded in institutional frameworks and political processes characterized by struggles among actors for power and resources to achieve competing goals. Policy making in the field of education remains politically contested and characterized by national policy subsystems. The nation state and domestic politics has been the predominant framework for analyzing education policy developments until recently. Does globalization really matter for national education systems? The chapters in this section focus on the contemporary challenges to the relationship between education and the state, and policy advice systems and national institutions. Central to the investigation is an analysis of how globalization has transformed, if at all, existing educational institutions and systems. The chapters in this section aim at developing an empirically based understanding of whether national systems are resilient and possibly globalization matters less than claimed by grand social theorists. Instead of taking a benign view of the relationship between the global and the national, the chapters will shed light on the complexity of the challenges posed to education by global scripts, ideologies, and the variations across countries.

The programmes led by the OECD, such as the Program in International Student Assessment (PISA), are used by national policy makers as a way to legitimize national reforms under the guise of promoting evidence-based decision-making. International policies can serve as policy-lever in national education reforms, and thus context shapes policies.

Volante (Chapter 25) shows that since the initial administration of the Program in International Student Assessment (PISA), governments have increasingly turned their attention to the policy implications stemming from this global benchmark measure. Educational jurisdictions such as Finland, South Korea, Hong Kong, Canada, and more recently Singapore, at various points in time, have been internationally lauded for their high achievement and touted as global reference societies by policymakers wishing to emulate their relative success. Yet, questions and concerns remain regarding the undue influence and policy recommendations promoted by the Organisation for Economic Cooperation and Development (OECD). This chapter explicates some of the dominant political narratives as well as sources of contestation attributed to PISA that have shaped global, transnational, and national education governance agendas. Overall, the chapter provides a critical analysis of the policy influence of PISA.

Many scholars and observers have assumed that globalization triggers convergence in many areas, including education policy and systems. Yet, while some change has happened, the central elements of countries' education systems have been relatively unaffected by globalization. The chapter by Garritzman and Garritzman (Chapter 26) explains this inertia, pointing at the politics of education. Taking a historical institutionalist perspective, the chapter shows that education systems created positive feedback effects generating path dependencies which make education systems increasingly resilient to change. A review and discussion of recent research underpins this reasoning, identifying three mechanisms, through public opinion, interest groups, and political elites, respectively.

Creating and diffusing knowledge about policies represents a challenge for both academics and practitioners. Galanti (Chapter 27) presents the state of the art on the topic. The literature has recently focused on this issue by proposing to view not the single advisor, but the policy advisory systems, intended as the systems of actors who deliver policy advice from within and from outside institutions in a given policy sector. These trends are also visible in the globalization of education policies, which creates pressures for policy diffusion, borrowing, or learning on local policy makers. This chapter aims at presenting the characteristics of policy advisory systems in education policies emerging in comparative perspective, with a particular focus on the OECD and the European countries, and at proposing a typology that considers how policy advice in education might be shaped as an interaction between domestic and international actors in a globalized world.

The chapter by Tolo (Chapter 28) illuminates the formation and development of the Norwegian National Quality Assessment System (NQAS) and how the actors have met this. The NQAS was established in 2004, in the wake of mediocre results from the PISA tests in 2001 and recommendations from the OECD. However, the analysis shows that the efforts to streamline the accountability system in line with OECD's advice have not shown to be successful in the Norwegian context due to culturally embedded factors that influence teachers and schools' work. These emphasize equality, trust in teachers, high participation in decision-making processes from different stakeholders, cross-party agreements, and decentralization. Instead, it seems that the need to professionalize the teaching profession is what is emphasized by strong stakeholders in the system and that these ideas are gaining ground.

SECTION VI: THE MASSIFICATION OF SECONDARY EDUCATION

One of the fundamental questions that the chapters in this section address is as follows: How are transnational norms and global policy programmes institutionalized by local and domestic policy makers? Can we argue that convergence in the conception of equality among secondary pupils, and more generally, of education policy globally eliminates national and local political contestation? The chapters investigate empirically these questions with original data, with a special focus on secondary schooling and the reforms of massification and extension of access to secondary pupils. It emerges that not one model of access to mass education existed and that education inequality remains a highly diversified and contested notion and policy across countries.

Besche-Truthe, Seitzer, and Windzio (Chapter 29) investigate the diffusion of the institution of mass education. They focus on the following research question: What effects do networks of cultural and colonial linkages have on the emergence of national mass education systems? The study applies social network analysis and network diffusion models in order to assess the impact of the expansion of mass education in 156 countries around the world from 1880 to 2010.

Gingrich, Giudici, and McArthur (Chapter 30) analyze original data from the European Value Survey to explore the patterns resulting from the policy choices of political parties and organized interests across advanced democracies in these three domains as well as the political determinants underlying these choices. In the postwar period, the focus of governments in advanced democracies generally shifted from generalizing basic education to staffing an increasing share of the population with more complex and specialized knowledge and skills through the expansion of secondary schooling. The demands of industrial development, heightened by the rise of the knowledge economy, meant policymakers across place and partisan divides have largely supported secondary expansion. However, despite these common trends lie ongoing differences across place in terms of the logic of the massification of secondary education, its ideal degree of differentiation among pupils and teachers, standardization of teaching and pedagogical practices, and the structure of control.

Recent surveys on adult competences (IALS, PIAAC) show that competences are positively correlated with schooling and parental background. However, the institutional differences across countries mediate the impact of these variables, thus leading to less/more egalitarian distributions of competences as well as to difference in the gradient of competences on employment probability and earnings. Cappellari, Checchi and Ovidi (Chapter 31) exploit existing data sets (among which the one proposed by Braga et al., 2013) to explore the varieties of educational systems, distinguishing them between *inclusive* and *selective* according to whether they are associated to less/more dispersed distribution of competences, once one controls for schooling and parental background. Typical reform indicators (that are time varying and can therefore be associated to different age cohorts) include duration of compulsory schooling, age of secondary school tracking, school autonomy, central examination, and student financial aid.

In the chapter by Ballarino and Panichella (Chapter 32), the authors propose that the Italian case illustrates the relations between expanding participation to education and educational inequality, on one side, and returns to education, on the other side. Theoretically, they rely on the OED triangle, the standard framework by which stratification research addresses issues of equality/inequality of opportunities, and refer to the debate counterposing modernization theory, according to which the expansion of education is part of a societal movement towards a more inclusive and just society, and reproduction theory, which to the contrary maintains that education, however expanded, is a key tool for the maintenance of opportunity hoarding and social closure. Empirically, they use a brand new data set deriving from the harmonization of a number of high-quality surveys, thus giving to the analyses more statistical power and thus better reliability, particularly concerning trends over time.

SECTION VII: GLOBALIZATION OF HIGHER EDUCATION AND SCIENCE

The globalization of higher education institutions and science has been a sustained and well-documented policy process, often taken to represent the irreversible influence of normative ideas, such as the use of world rankings, performance metrics, and other global governance instruments. It is often the case that scholarly accounts are about either/or logic of relations between the global context and national institutions. The nation state seems to be unravelling and destined to a marginal role in the global governance of education. Yet, science policy continues to be nationally funded and driven. There has been no fundamental destabilization of the nation-state, as a result of globalization of higher education and increased international mobility. Any binary dichotomy between the state and the globalized world has not helped the understanding of the relations among the global, national, and local scales. The chapters in this section look beyond the global versus national framework and contribute theoretically and empirically to a new definition of globalization, whereby globalization is not a zero-sum game. As argued by Kariya (Chapter 33), a perceived stage of modernity in any given society produced a cognitive framework to understand globalization. In order to understand different pathways to modernity, we have moved away from Eurocentric understandings.

The impact of globalization on education policy is related to the question of how each society understands modernity in a global political-economic context. Kariya argues that Japan is among a few non-Western countries to have experienced both "catch-up" (with the West) and what might be called a "post-catch-up modernization." The two phases of modernization, in a sense, represent and reflect how a society has responded to the globalizing world. Undergoing these two stages of distinct social transformation, Japanese society has encountered difficulties in making a smooth transition from catch-up to post-catch-up modernity in the "global era." This is particularly clear in the field of education. In this chapter, he places these Japanese experiences in a global context, and discusses what implications they have for sociological research on education as well as what theoretical contributions such a lens can contribute to recent debates on modernity and globalization.

To explicate this argument, Kariya focuses on policy discourses related to education reforms in Japan. Japan is a typical case of a "late" modernizing country, one which intended to design and establish a "modern" education system rapidly and extensively, where modernity has been understood and interpreted distinctively in the lately developed society, different from advanced "Western" modern nations. The Japanese experience undergoing the transition from the catch-up to the post-catch-up modernity is outstanding as a case of reflexive modernity in education in accommodating to rapid globalization. Discourse analyses of policy documents reveal that Japan's experiences indicate that reflections in modernity are influenced not only by their perceived past achievements but also by their perceptions of what is *sacrificed* underneath the achievements during a catching up modernization. Encountering the transitional stage to the post-catch-up modernity, political leaders began regarding the Japanese education as a constraint, one preventing the development of new competences and skills necessitated in the global era. This is because the education system and practices established under the catch-up are believed to sacrifice latent competences and skills to develop due to exam-driven and uniform education. To what extent have the reforms in this second stage effectively attained the policy goals? Have any side-effects of reforms emerged and how? The outcomes of reforms are dependent upon how accurately the diagnosis is made and how treatment is provided appropriately and sufficiently in the transition to post-catch-up development. Thus, in his chapter, he examines how goals of post-catch-up education reforms are socially constructed by leaders' (mis)cognitions of globalization, which he argues are influenced by their experiences in the two stages of modernization.

Along with communications, Marginson (Chapter 34) suggests that higher education and research are among the most globalized sectors and continued so in the decade after 2010 when there was a partial retreat from globalization of the political economy. In science the global system has arguably become primary in terms of knowledge formation, though the national scale remains highly determining in institutional higher education. The chapter discusses the main features of globalization in higher education and science (global systems, global connections, and global diffusion) and reviews the relationship between the global science system and the connected national science systems. It finishes with a discussion of scale and its materiality, and reflects on the potential contribution of plural scalar perspectives and Amartya Sen's transpositional analytical framework to understandings of higher education.

National science systems have become embedded in global science, and countries do everything they can to harness global knowledge to address national economic needs. However, Kwiek (Chapter 35) argues that accessing and using the riches of global knowledge can occur only through scientists. Consequently, the research power of nations relies on the research power of individual scientists. Their capacity to collaborate internationally and to tap into the global networked science is key. The constantly evolving, bottom-up, autonomous, self-regulating, and self-focused nature of global science requires deeper understanding; and the best way to understand its dynamics is to understand what drives academic scientists in their work. The author is particularly interested in the contrast between global science as a largely privately governed and normatively self-regulating institution and global science as a contributor to global collective public goods. The idea that science remains state-driven rather than curiosity-driven is difficult to sustain. In empirical terms, the chapter describes the globalization of science using selected publication, collaboration, and citation data from 2000 to 2020. The humanities increasingly diverge from social sciences in terms of the collaboration mix (with the share of single authorship exceeding 50% in the most advanced economies). Humanities emerge from the research as non-collaborative and non-internationally collaborative, with powerful implications for such metrics as output and citations at the micro-level of individual academics. The globalization of science implies also two different processes in two different system types: the growth of science in the Western world is almost entirely attributable to internationally co-authored publications; its growth in the developing world, in contrast, is driven by both internationally co-authored and domestic publications. Global network science opens incredible opportunities to new arrivals—countries as well as institutions and research teams. The global system is embedded in the rules created by scientists themselves and maintained as a self-organizing system, and nation-states have another major level to consider in their science policies: the global level. Kwiek suggests that globalization of science provides more agency, autonomy, collegiality, and self-regulation to scientists embedded in national science structures and involved in global networks.

China has invested significant public resources in the huge expansion of higher education which started in 1990. Higher education reforms have also embraced privatization, to a limited extent, and the internationalization of its higher education institutions. Tuition fees have been raised significantly in China, as shown by Mok Ka Ho, Ke, and Tien in their chapter (Chapter 36). With a strong conviction to transform the country and prepare its people to cope with the growing challenges of the globalizing market, the Chinese government has actively increased more opportunities for higher education. The higher education system in China has experienced the processes of massification and transnationalization, especially when the Chinese government has tried to diversify its higher education provision through non-state sector providers, including overseas partners setting up branch campuses. The chapter sets out against the broad political economy context to examine critically how the Chinese government has responded to the growing influences of globalization by internationalizsing and trasnationalizing its higher education. More specifically, this study examines the challenges and policy implications when higher education experiences internationalization and transnationalization in China. The key point is that globalization has intensified inequalities in China on the job market in an unexpected way. Massification has failed to provide equal access for the low socio-economic status students.

Tilak (Chapter 37) provides his insights into the most recent higher education reforms in India, focusing on the 2020 National Education Policy reform. He argues this is a path-breaking legislation given the path dependency of inertial approaches. After decades of neglect, higher education in India began receiving public attention. Apart from continuing problems relating to quantitative expansion, quality, and inequalities, the system also faces serious challenges with shortage of teachers, public funds, governance, and a rapidly growing commercially motivated private sector. The unforeseen crisis caused by COVID-19 added further problems to higher education. Reforming of higher education has been on the public agenda for quite some time: Some reforms have already been introduced, some are at the stage of discussions and deliberations; and the need for a search for new and innovative measures is also being realized. Tilak's chapter provides a critical review of some of the recent reforms introduced and the reforms that are being proposed in the most recent years. One of the main objectives is to increase the enrolment ratio to 50%. Currently it is 25%, and this is inadequate.

The chapter by Ollssen (Chapter 38) starts by considering 20th-century attacks on the idea of the public good from liberal quarters: from social choice theory, public choice theory, and from political liberalism, with reference to Kenneth Arrow, James Buchanan, Joseph Schumpeter, and John Rawls. Despite a prolonged attack against ideas of the good from liberal economists and political thinkers, spanning the period from the 1930s to the end of the 20twentieth century, the chapter argues that the concept of public good needs rehabilitating as a political concept. The concept of "self-interest" that guided the liberal economists, and the ontology of individualism that underpinned Rawls's writings, have not proved adequate to understanding politics and the logic of collective action in terms of which politics necessarily operates. The chapter argues that new models of science which gained ascendancy from the start of the 20twentieth century, as well as poststructuralist ideas, can assist in a reconceptualization of the idea of public good to guide politics, accommodate liberty and diversity, and overcome liberal objections.

Section VIII: Latin America: Local Power and Globalization

The idea of focusing on one world region in particular has the aim of zooming in on how the challenges mentioned in the chapters in the previous sections of Part II of this Handbook play out in developing countries that share some common historical and contextual factors but differ in how global policies are applied. Latin America is a vast and diverse region where, from a political perspective, globalization has involved pressures from international organizations for the adoption of global policies and from an economic perspective, globalization continues to signify the insertion of Latin American countries into the global economy through the export of commodities. These two perspectives raise different sets of questions and policy responses.

Globalization occurred in most Latin American countries alongside the process of democratization and, in some cases, decentralization. This section interrogates on the relation among globalization, democratic governance, and education policies and focuses on three main areas of inquiry: (a) a long-term perspective of education policies in the region as a whole; (b) education reforms and contestation; (c) education inequality, and variation in education spending and human capital investment within countries (i.e., at the subnational/regional level). By focusing on actors, processes, and contestation, the section highlights the challenges that education reforms face in different contexts. As noted earlier, policy convergence does not eliminate national and local contestation, and the case studies in this section show how similar policies interact with different sets of actors and processes both across countries and within countries, producing different outcomes. The chapters in this section include case studies of Argentina, Brazil, Chile, Colombia, Mexico, and Peru.

The first chapter by Laurence Whitehead (Chapter 39) lays the groundwork for an understanding of the long-term historical development of education systems in Latin America. Whitehead argues that three important characteristics of Latin American realities are heterogeneity, informality, and inequality. The chapter points out that formal education is regarded as one of the primary functions and achievements of the nation-state, and to the extent that many Latin Americans are still rather poorly served by public education, this can be seen as an indicator of state weakness or inadequacy. Some of the region's countries devote great efforts to education and deliver impressive results, but overall, performance is uneven. As the pandemic has shown, few schoolchildren in the region are being equipped to operate competitively in today's increasingly digitalized world. This is not to deny the long-term progress of Latin American educational provision, especially since the second half of the 20th century, but, at the same time, the chapter by Whitehead shows that educational results in the region have been patchy, inadequate, fragile, and subject to numerous setbacks.

Cuenca, García and Schneider et al. (Chapter 40) provide a paired comparison of reforms to teacher careers in Colombia and Peru. In the early 21st century, Colombia was one of the first countries in Latin America to devise a major, meritocratic reform to teacher careers. However, the reform applied only to new teachers, and their numbers grew slowly, reaching around half of teachers by 2020. Reforms in Peru started slowly in 2001. The two reforms were largely viewed as a success story, and the authors argue that critical to both reform successes was consistent policy implementation by a series of different technocratic ministers of education, combined with a muted union opposition.

The chapters by Behrend on Argentina (Chapter 41), and Batista and Dutt-Ross on Brazil (Chapter 42) scale down to the subnational level, which is the level of government that is mostly responsible for the implementation of education policy in both countries. Globalization in Latin America occurred alongside the dual processes of democratization and decentralization, which delegated authority and resources to subnational governments over key policies such as education and health. Decentralization gave rise to important variation in the quality of services offered to citizens of different localities, while democratization also spread unevenly across regions (Behrend and & Whitehead, 2016). The insertion of different subnational units into the global economy varies greatly across and within Latin American countries, and over the last decade it has to a great extent been linked to the commodity boom and primary exports. Many globalized industries are enclave economies or economies that do not rely on specialized local human capital (e.g., mining) or are not human capital intensive (soya production). Globalization has not had a homogeneous impact across the region and although the implementation of global education policies has been promoted by national governments, in federal countries, national policies are implemented by subnational governments. This can lead to selective implementation (Brinks, Levitsky & Murillo et al., 2019) in some cases or may show variations in the contestation surrounding national policies. The chapters on Argentina and Brazil show how education spending varies within these two countries despite national policies and legislation that specify the budget that each subnational unit is required to destine to education.

In Argentina, despite an education financing law that compelled all provinces to increase education spending, the chapter by Behrend (Chapter 41) shows that compliance with this norm has been heterogeneous. Although education spending increased from 2005, by 2018 it had stagnated or even decreased in many provinces. And, perhaps surprisingly, the richest district (the Autonomous City of Buenos Aires) is the district that has seen the greatest decline in investment in education. The uneven implementation and enforcement of education norms in Argentina shows that education remains a highly contested policy area.

The chapter by Batista and Dutt-Ross on Brazil (Chapter 42) also shows the significant variation in education spending that exists across states. Although the Brazilian Constitution stipulates relatively high minimum spending thresholds in education for all states, subnational variation exists. The authors highlight that, even in a globalized context, the socioeconomic characteristics of subnational units (states) play a role in determining the level of spending in education and, thus, in education policy more generally.

The chapter by Bleynat and Monroy-Gómez-Franco on Mexico (Chapter 43) addresses a fundamental question for developing countries: Does economic globalization reward education? Since the 1990s, Mexican governments have invested substantial resources and policy efforts in the education sector, and the result has been a significant increase in the level of education attainment at the aggregate level. However, the chapter shows that education coverage and quality remain highly uneven within Mexico, and there are major gaps that require urgent policy attention.

Moreover, despite greater investment in education, the authors show that globalizsation does not reward education, and it may even penalizse it in some cases. Mexico is now considered one of the most globalized economies in the world. Yet, remarkably, rising education levels have failed to raise wages across the board. Bleynat and Monroy-Gómez-Franco (Chapter 43) suggest that Mexico's insertion in global value chains has relied and continues to rely primordially on taking advantage of lower wages for any educational level. Today people with college degrees are paid less in real terms than they were 15 years ago. Over the same period, those with upper-secondary, lower-secondary, or primary education have seen their market incomes stagnate. Given how close wages are to subsistence level in Mexico, the authors argue, it is perhaps even more tragic from a welfare perspective. Despite the promise that education and globalization would reward the population with higher incomes, the authors find no evidence that either has improved living standards for Mexican workers.

The chapter by Mizala and Schneider (Chapter 44) highlights the highly politicized and contentious nature of education in Chile since the transition to democracy in 1990, which included waves of student protests after 2006 and the election of a former student protest leader as president in 2021. The education system set in place by the Pinochet dictatorship left the new democracy with a market, full-choice education system that was privatized, decentralized, largely unregulated, underfunded, and stratified. According to the authors, by the late 2010s, the market still existed but the education system was more regulated, centralized, better funded, and probably less stratified. In Chile, democracy increased pressure for quality as well as quantity in education. However, despite deep transformations in education policy, especially after 2014, education remains a contentious issue.

New Emerging Research Themes and Directions

We would like to suggest three main new themes emerging inductively from the chapters in Part II, though the richness of the theoretical debates and empirical findings cannot be entirely captured here. The authors themselves will offer their insights in each chapter about future developments and new research agendas without us wishing to impose them on the contributions in this part of the volume. The first theme is that the existing scholarly debates on globalization in the field of education, but not only, have emphasized the normative and ideational forces sustaining the policy diffusion of concepts and ideas that travel from one jurisdiction to another, from one educational system to a different one, overlooking the substantive and differentiated policy effects at local and subnational levels of governance. The global versus the nation-state dichotomy has analytical limitations, corroborated empirically by the chapters in Part II. This is no longer a fruitful framework because the global, national, and local scales of education policy are intertwined and interdependent in distinct ways. At the heart of the globalization literature there is the attempt to explain the increasing similarities of education policy outputs adopted around the globe, so-called convergence of global scripts (Mattei, 2014). We have learned that global world rankings and performance-based accountability in the higher education sector represent a good example of such policy convergence. Furthermore, the study of the massification of secondary schooling in Part II of this Handbook also indicates a convergence in the conceptions of equality among secondary pupils. The chapters in this part of the Handbook have presented original data and evidence that partly confirm the thesis of convergence of policy developments over time, especially in the early post-war period in developed countries. Globalization matters, indeed, in the policy domain of education, but there is a further need for tracing historically the policy changes to see how they become institutionalized in each specific context (Milner, Mattei and Ydesen 2021).

The second theme emerging from the chapters in this Part II of the Handbook is that convergence of transnational norms does not eliminate political contestation, at all levels of governance, be it international, national, or local. This is because global and transnational norms are institutionalized by local and domestic policy makers and stakeholders. The politics of education cannot be reduced to the top-down implementation of global policies designed by international organizations. From implementation studies, we learn that the process of transforming ideas into programmes is divisive, politically contested, and resourceful in terms of the discretion given to street-level bureaucrats (Hupe & Hill, 2021). A good example is the emergence of different models of pupilhood historically, as Gingrich, Giudici, and MacArthur argue in their contribution. This meant varying institutional developments of access to secondary education. What it means to be a secondary pupil, and what "equal status of pupil" means, remains highly contested, politically salient, and filtered through national and local institutions and political actors. The national scale of governance is inextricably intertwined with the global and local scales, not in a zero-sum game; the global itself is shaped by national actors and their political strategies and interests.

Therefore, global discourses of modernity through educational reforms cannot be taken to represent one model of development, and globalization cannot be reduced to a one-fits-all concept readily applicable across the world. The chapter by Kariya illuminates this point eloquently and develops a new conception of modernity and globalization from the study of Japan. Garritzman and Garritzmann also suggest that the key characteristics of countries' educational systems have hardly changed since the 1980s. In order to explain the resilience of educational institutions, they convincingly propose to focus on the policy feedback effects expected in education, which sustain the forces of path dependency (Pierson, 2014). The historical-institutionalist argument is also presented by Ydesen and Ereman's chapter on the ways in which OECD member countries use global reforms to legitimize domestic political agendas, as policy lever for domestic reform processes. Not only are global norms filtered through local institutions, but they can be influenced by local processes in unexpected ways. The comparative analysis between Brazil and the United States is indicative of such logics of relationships between the global and the local, which is far from being unidirectional. The chapters on Latin America also eloquently highlight such variation. Many Latin American countries adopted education reforms promoted by international organizations from the 1980s onwards and in the early 21st century, but the implementation of these reforms varied widely across countries. Even within countries education policy is applied unevenly and even selectively. Therefore, policy convergence does not necessarily imply convergence of outcomes.

The third overarching theme emerging from the contributions of Part II pertains to the observation and analysis of the unintended effects of the globalization of higher education, in particular for countries such as China and India. The massification of higher education in China, as argued by Mok Ka Ho et al, has failed to provide the expected equal access for the low-economic-status students. The mushrooming in China of transnational higher education institutions has not produced equal opportunities for all. On the contrary, Sino-foreign institutions charge very high tuition fees and produce inequalities in the transition to the labour market. In China, the gap between elite universities and the traditional ones has increased as a result of internationalization and globalization. Likewise, in India the internationalization of higher education institutions meant the entry of 385 new private universities in 2019. Many of these new providers are foreign universities setting up local campuses in India. The most recent 2020 National Education Plan, however, is path breaking in so far as it invites only a few universities from the top foreign ones to set up new campuses in India, in an attempt to limit the problem of rising inequalities. The Indian government has set a new ambitious objective for the enrolment rate to 50%. The cases of China and India show the pervasive and long-lasting effects of globalization agendas at the national levels and the new inequalities produced by that process.

All the chapters have been written during the first four waves of the COVID-19 global pandemic, and thus it was too early for authors to assess the long-lasting effects of the health care emergency on the global education field. Authors have decided not to engage in speculative writings about the future of society after COVID-19, and instead the majority of chapters takes a historical and long-term institutional perspective. However, the pandemic has left its mark on the education system in developing countries. School closures and, unequal access to technology and to the Internet have reinforced existing inequalities and have left part of the student population in developing countries out of the education system. As the chapter by Whitehead shows, according to UNICEF, by the end of 2020, 87% of the 160 million children in Latin America and the Caribbean had been out of the classroom for 8 months, and on average had lost 174 school days because of COVID-19, as compared to a world average of 40 days (UNICEF, 2020).[1] The long-term effect of COVID-19 on education systems poses challenges that will need to be addressed by governments and policy-makers.

NOTE

1. *Education on hold* (New York: UNICEF, November 2020).

References

Behrend, J., &and L. Whitehead, L. (2016). *Illiberal Practices: Territorial Variance within Large Federal Democracies.* (Baltimore: Johns Hopkins University Press).

Brinks, D., S. Levitsky, S., &and M. V. Murillo, M. V. (2019). *Understanding Institutional Weakness: Power and Design in Latin American Institutions.* (New York: Cambridge University Press).

Hupe, P., &and M. Hill, M. (2021). *Implementing Public Policy.* (London: Sage).

Mattei, P. (2014). *University Adaptation in Difficult Economic Times.* (New York: Oxford University Press). ISBN 9780199989393.

Milner, A., P. Mattei, P., & and C. Ydesen, C. (2021). "Governing education in times of crisis: State interventions and school accountabilities during the COVID-19 pandemic" *European Educational Research Journal, 20*(4), 520–539, ISSN: 1474-9041.

Pierson, P. (2014). *Politics in Time: History, Institutions, and Social Analysis* (Princeton and Oxford: Princeton University Press.

UNICEF. (2020, November). *Education on hold.* UNICEF.

.

SECTION IV

International Organizations and Education Policy

CHAPTER 22

THE EXPANSION OF EDUCATION IN AND ACROSS INTERNATIONAL ORGANIZATIONS

KERSTIN MARTENS, DENNIS NIEMANN, AND DAVID KROGMANN

INTRODUCTION

TODAY, international organizations (IOs) are significant actors in education policy. They analyze education policies, develop normative guidance, and provide financial support for education projects. Not only do IOs compile education data and make recommendations to their members, but they also distribute concepts and ideas that become a global standard. Simultaneously, education systems maintain national economic competitiveness in world markets to prepare their graduates for global competition in labor markets. Thus, national education systems need to respond to new challenges posed by globalization processes to keep up the pace in a constantly growing, knowledge-based economy that views education as the key to growth. Globalization understood as "the intensification of economic, political, social, and cultural relations across borders" (Holm & Sørensen, 1995, p. 1) has put IOs at the helm of international education policy. IOs, in this respect, are often viewed as a highly valued source for triggering and shaping national reform processes in education.

Beyond single or comparative case studies of few prominent IOs in the realm of education policy (e.g., Zapp, 2020), we know little about how many and what types of IOs work on education policy. Our knowledge on the population of education IOs

Funded by the Deutsche Forschungsgemeinschaft (DFG, German Research Foundation)–project number 374666841 – SFB 1342 remains limited. How many IOs deal with education, and how do they distribute across the globe? What is their main approach to education, and what views on education are they promoting? By applying an organizational ecology approach in this contribution, we examine how education as a policy field has spread across *and* within IOs over time.

In this chapter, we explore the population of education IOs to "map" the world of education IOs and to analyze its topography. We argue that the field has substantially expanded over time to 30 IOs that deal with education policy today. It is characterized by three types of education IOs: globally operating IOs that claim global validity of their education programs, regional IOs which are limited to a certain geographic area, and transregional IOs, where membership is bound by common cultural or religious characteristics. We explore how the distribution of education IOs developed over time. While education has always been a relevant issue for some IOs based on their mandate, others gradually adopted the topic and integrated it into their spectrum of activities. We find two trends that stand out: first, economistic IOs, particularly internationally operation development banks, have discovered education as a valuable field of activity, and secondly, education policy is a field where regionally operating IOs exist, often next to each other.

THE ORGANIZATIONAL ECOLOGY OF EDUCATION IOS—A THEORETICAL LENS

The analytical approach of organizational ecology can be applied as a heuristic framework for examining the population of IOs in education. Adapted to the social sciences most prominently by Hannan and Freeman (1977), the approach illuminates environmental and institutional factors that influence demographic changes in a population. Organizational ecology is marked by two complementary dimensions: organizational environment and intrinsic features (Abbott et al., 2016). The organizational environment dimension addresses how the institutional field is constituted and acknowledges externalities of the IOs' surroundings. The intrinsic features approach emphasizes endogenous factors of IOs to explain their capability of acting within a given institutional environment and explores factors which induce change or account for change. Hence, combining both could be seen as a promising analytical tool for developing a framework for examining developments and changes in the realm of (education) IOs. Thus, from the perspective of organizational ecology, one focuses on both the constitutive features of the organizational field and the characteristics of IOs within this field.

The concept of organizational environment is also related to the sociological concept of an "organizational field" and refers to what may be called topography. It comprises the underlying characteristics of the field, the density of relevant actors operating within it, and their relationship to each other. This concept illustrates the assortment of aggregated actors, which constitute an institutional environment. Thus, a population is marked by its degree of diversity. This means that in a highly diverse field, organizations can populate different niches within a community without interfering with each other. Also, the density of a population must be considered when analyzing an organizational field. IOs may also populate and cultivate a niche in policy issues and coexist without disturbing the vital interests of states or other IOs. If the field allows for specialization, more actors can find their niches and coexist without severe overlapping.

While the organizational environment approach focuses on the interaction between IOs and their environment, the concept of intrinsic features emphasizes the institutional design of IOs, which shapes their behavior and determines how autonomous IOs act in an organizational field. On the one hand, it draws from rational choice concepts, such as the principal-agent model (Hawkins et al., 2006; Nielson & Tierney, 2003), which implies the designers of IOs can actively influence the scope of possible actions of IOs. On the other hand, this approach is also congruent with approaches based on path dependency theories of historical institutionalism, which explains that the initial choices made by IOs may have long-term effects on the future of the organizational development (North, 1990; Pierson, 2004). One important issue in this regard concerns the scope of issues covered. Two notions are commonly distinguished, namely comprehensive and policy-specific concerns of IOs (Lenz et al., 2015). IOs with comprehensive scopes deal with more issue areas than those with specific policy concerns. Hence, comprehensive IOs could link issues of education policy with other topics in their portfolio, for instance economics or social security. Since IOs with comprehensive thematic scopes are designed with autonomous decision-making, they can easily expand to differing policy fields without an imposition from member states. This "mission-creep" is neither against the member states' interests nor does it violate their authority over the IO.

Taken together, the organizational environment and the intrinsic features have to be analyzed in tandem when assessing IO behavior within a given population. This means that exogenous developments enable some IOs which have specific intrinsic features to adapt more swiftly to a transformed environment. We note, for instance, that the leading economic paradigm shifted from Keynesianism to neoliberalism between the 1970s and early 1980s. This implies a different environment for education IOs since the development of education programs and their underlying ideas depends heavily on the disposition of the welfare state. Under Keynesianism, the regulatory input of states to their respective education system was prioritized over the controlling for the outcomes. With neoliberalism at the helm, investment in states' education systems lessened in importance. Accordingly, IOs that already favored a neoliberal view or were able to switch from Keynesianism to neoliberalism were also inclined to expand their influence and significance in education policy. In other words, the institutional adaptability of IOs yields survival in competitive organizational fields.

Identifying the Population of "Education IOs" and Analyzing Its Topography

Identifying and analyzing the population of active education IOs is neither an easy nor a straightforward task. What counts as an IO, and what counts as an education IO? For the purposes of setting boundaries, we look at "public" organizations, namely at IOs which are understood as intergovernmental organizations (IGOs), in which states are the prime members. Although some nongovernmental organizations (NGOs), such as the Gates Foundation, are financially strong and important players in the global education sphere, they were excluded from our analysis. Also, internationally operating think tanks, such as the Global Partnership for Education, are not part of our data set as states only function as donor countries and not as members. Similarly, intergovernmental organizations need to be distinguished from simple coalitions of states, such as the Education Reform Initiative of South Eastern Europe (ERISEE), which we also did not consider.

Instead, we examine IOs based on the Yearbook of International Organizations (YIO) as well as the Correlates of War (COW) data set. Every IO was individually examined as to whether it refers to education as a field of activity. In our search, we included all IOs in the education sector which relate to school education (primary and secondary level) and/or the tertiary education sector (higher education and vocational training). We define an IO as "education IO" if it maintains three complementary features regarding its policy programs, organizational structures, and desired scope. First, education must be mentioned in the IO's programmatic mission statement as a designated task of the IO (be it in the IO's preamble, founding treaty, amended treaties, or as one of its main aims as outlined in its current web presence). Second, it must have its own permanent organizational subdepartment, unit, or otherwise named structural component which specifically deals with issues of education or training. Third, the IO must address education *policy* issues. Hence, we exclude from our definition any IOs that deal with educational topics, such as teaching methods or coordinating scientific cooperation. For instance, the North Atlantic Treaty Organization (NATO) also has an educational focus, but its activities mainly address the training of its own staff with regards to security issues.

After reviewing the individual organizations, we identify a total of N = 30 organizations that form the population of active education IOs (Niemann & Martens, 2021), which we present in Figure 22.1. Education IOs differ regarding their geographical reach and their thematic scope. Both characteristics, however, are not mutually exclusive but overlap.

Geographically, we can distinguish among globally, regionally, and transregionally operating IOs. The World Bank and Organization for Economic Cooperation and Development (OECD), for example, are global education IOs. While the OECD is

THE EXPANSION OF EDUCATION   485

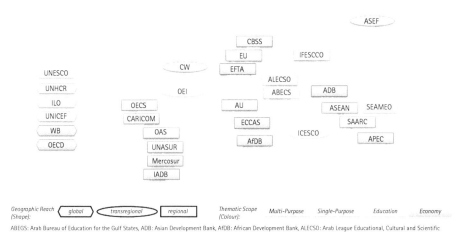

FIGURE 22.1 A world map of education international organizations.

clearly an IO with restricted membership criteria, that is, industrialized democracies, we classify it as a global education IO because its education activities are not exclusively provided to member countries, and the IO itself claims global validity in this field. Next to the United Nations Educational, Scientific, and Cultural Organization (UNESCO), other United Nations organizations, such as the United Nations High Commissioner for Refugees (UNHCR), the United Nations International Children's Emergency Fund (UNICEF), or the International Labour Organization (ILO), are active on a worldwide scale.

However, education is primarily dealt with by various regional IOs. Examples of such regional organizations include Caribbean Community (CARICOM), the Council of Baltic Sea States (CBSS), or the Economic Community of Central African States (ECCAS). In some regions, such as Southeast Asia or Latin America, several education IOs exist in parallel. As a third category of education IOs, transregional organizations are comprised of member states sharing traits other than geographical proximity. Notable transregional IOs include the Islamic World Educational, Scientific and Cultural Organization (ICESCO), in which membership is connected to Islam, and the Organization of Ibero-American States for Education, Science and Culture (OEI), which is made up only of "Iberophone" states.

Regarding the *thematic* scope of the 30 IOs in our sample, seven IOs reflect education as a primary activity through their mandate and name. These organizations have been installed with the intended purpose of focusing mainly on education policy as a major and, in some cases, solitary founding mission. This group includes the Southeast Asian Ministers of Education Organisation (SEAMEO), the Arab Bureau of Education for the Gulf States (ABEGS), the Arab League Educational, Cultural and Scientific Organisation (ALECSO), the Intergovernmental Foundation for Educational, Scientific and Cultural Cooperation (IFESCCO), the OEI, and ICESCO. Except for UNESCO, none of these education IOs are globally active but work through a regional, cultural, or religious defined purpose.

Most of the education IOs, however, cover several policy fields, with education being only one among many. This class comprises two subtypes. On the one hand, it is constituted by "multipurpose" IOs; that is, IOs that have a broader purpose, focusing on a wide scope of issue areas over a number of fields. Examples include the European Union (EU) and the South Asian Association for Regional Cooperation (SAARC), the African Union (AU), or the Union of South American Nations (UNASUR). In multipurpose IOs, the founding members did not intend to specifically address educational policy Although several of them included education topics from the very beginning, many of them moved into the policy field at times long after their inception, making education part of their programmatic mission *ex post*.

On the other hand, another group of education IOs are comprised of "specialized" or single-purpose IOs, which have a primary mission other than education, like the UNHCR or the ILO. These IOs first and foremost focus on refugee protection and labor rights respectively. The introduction of education transformed their mission to involve education issues within the realm of a primary mandate. For example, organizations like the OECD or the World Bank, which were set up with a specific mission in economic development, have gradually expanded their work into the education field.

Time-wise, we identify a number of general trends in the education IO population over the last 70 years. These trends differentiate according to geographical reach and thematic scope. Both dimensions reveal a continuous expansion of education IOs. In terms of the organizational ecology approach, the population became denser and more diverse over time. Overall, the number of IOs working in education policy increased from a mere two organizations in 1945, namely the ILO and UNESCO, to thirty organizations in 2018. The course of this expansion is rather steady. Over the decades, the population of education IOs expanded incrementally, with no sharp turn at any point in time. By the mid-1990s, the expansion slowed down and settled toward the end of the decade, with only two education IOs founded after 2005. This finding suggests that after a continuous growth and discovery of education as a significant field of IO activity over the last decades, the field is now saturated.

Economistic IOs—From a Niche to the Entire Education Field

Today, developments within the IO population regarding the thematic scope illustrate IOs with an original mandate in economic policy have become an important subgroup in the organizational field of education policy. As presented in Figure 22.2, almost one-third of today's entire education IO population has a primary focus on economic issues.

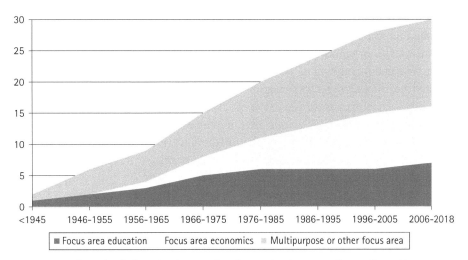

FIGURE 22.2 Growth of education international organizations over time—thematic scope.

Additionally, some of them are key players in international education policy. Most notably, several development banks now work on education. For instance, the World Bank views education as an intermediary means to fight poverty and to foster economic development. Similarly, for the OECD, education is decisive in generating human capital and in stimulating growth. Furthermore, both of these economically oriented IOs substantially contribute to the international education discourse and shape the framing of education: education as a means to drive economic development. Next to these two globally oriented economic IOs, several regional organizations and development banks are active players in the education field. Examples include the Asian Development Bank (ADB) and Mercosur, both of which focus on economic development and seek to maintain operations in the field of education.

It is especially noteworthy that economic IOs started including education policy in their programmatic missions more recently than other IOs, where their initial focus was not education. Figure 22.2 shows that multipurpose IOs and specialized IOs, which are not concerned with economic policy, started to address education policy earlier than economic IOs. Economic IOs were comparatively latecomers, addressing education policy around the late 1960s to mid-1970s. From 1956 to 1965, only one of five existing economic IOs in our sample engaged in education policy. By 1975, 50% of economic IOs dealt with education policy, and by 1996, all nine economic IOs included education in their portfolios.

Economic IOs started their activities in the field carrying a certain view on the purpose of education, particularly that an improvement in education will positively affect the development of a state. The established link among economic development, well-being, human capital generation, and education skills propels economic IOs to pursue education. Economic IOs recognize education improvements as an investment in a country's future capabilities to prosper economically. With their distinctive view on the purpose of education, most economic IOs were at odds with the views of other long-established education IOs, such as UNESCO or the ILO (Niemann, 2021). From the perspective of an organizational field, economic IOs increased the diversity of the education field in cultivating a niche for an economic approach in education. Since they populated a niche that reflects the nexus of education and economic development, they did not interfere with existing education IOs. However, over time several economic IOs expanded their educational activities, affecting the domains of other IOs. This increased the overall population density of education IOs and stimulated competition between IOs. The cases of the World Bank and the OECD illustrate the expansion of economic IOs in the realm of education.

World Bank

The World Bank transformed from a developmental aid agency to an active policy advisor in education that produces and disseminates knowledge. By doing so, it cultivated its own niche. While the Bank's concrete focus of developmental policies in education varied over time, the principal mission of the Bank, namely, to provide developmental aid to reduce poverty and foster human development, remained constant.

In education policy, we identify a steady expansion of ideas, issue areas, and bureaucratic structures in the Bank's programmatic activity over the years. From an earlier period to the late 1960s, the Bank entered the organizational field of education by conceptualizing education as beneficial for development. Moreover, education facilitated the on-site operation of direct developmental aid projects. Under Robert McNamara (in office 1968–1981), the Bank substantially broadened its education concepts and activities to include education and social policies for the economic development of states. Also, the IO altered its lending strategy and operational activities by improving the productive capacities of the poor (Mundy & Verger, 2015). In this phase, the Bank established the fundamental idea that improvements in education directly translate into economic well-being and overall societal improvements. In the 1970s and 1980s, the Bank established an organizational infrastructure to fund education projects focused on education research (Heyneman & Lee, 2016, p. 9). This illustrates the Bank's ability to populate additional domains (education research) previously occupied by other IOs (i.e., UNESCO).

By the early 1980s, the Bank implemented the predominant neoliberal architecture in its education program. The so-called Washington Consensus framed the Bank's education policy agenda in this era, where it reduced public sector expenditures, liberalized the markets, and privatized public enterprises (Mundy & Verger, 2015). The demise of neoliberal policies by the late 1980s to mid-1990s challenged the Bank's education program. Within the IO, a broader understanding of development emerged so that poverty acknowledged areas such as education and health (Vetterlein, 2012, p. 40). Hence, due to its intrinsic features, the Bank adapted to new environmental circumstances; under the presidency of James D. Wolfensohn (1995–2005), the World Bank introduced

THE EXPANSION OF EDUCATION   489

an evidence-based focus on policies and was redesigned as the "Knowledge Bank" to advise governments based on empirical findings. The IO sought to become a neutral policy advisor, so it could guide decision-making in education through knowledge production and identification of best practices. The reorientation of the Bank also created new opportunities for joint efforts with other IOs. For instance, the Global Knowledge Conference in 1997 brought together participants from all over the world and linked them to global communication (Zapp, 2017, p. 4). In the following years, the dialog with recipient states intensified, and the Bank introduced a holistic system approach. In addition, the IO took a closer look at the peculiarities of individual developing countries or regions and increasingly allowed for different approaches in developing education policies. Accordingly, the World Bank currently depicts itself as the "Solution Bank."

The principal aim of the Bank in education has been to "help developing countries reform and expand their educational systems in such a way that the latter may contribute more fully to economic development" (World Bank, 1974, p. i). The purpose of education in the Bank's discourse asserts an economistic leitmotif, which puts the utility of education to the fore. However, the notions have changed to a rather holistic and evidence-based understanding of education nowadays, which emphasizes the positive effects that high-quality education can have on economic *and* social developments. Alternative views on education are linked and subordinated to an economic reasoning, namely one that emphasizes a return on investment.

OECD

Like the World Bank, the OECD was created without a formal mandate in education. Over the course of its existence, however, the IO successively extended its thematic scope to issues of education. While the OECD is also an IO with a background in economic policies, it does not have the explicit developmental focus like the World Bank, but rather one that allocates a forum to enable policy cooperation and discourse among states (Wolfe, 2008, p. 208). Being an IO that exclusively relies on soft governance techniques, the OECD became an influential "knowledge broker" in education (Niemann & Martens, 2018), rather than providing financial support. In other words, the OECD started to cultivate a rather small niche in the organizational field of education and then continuously expanded its activities by providing a unique service to states. The history of the OECD's activities in education sheds analytical light on the evolution of this view.

From the early 1960s to the mid-1970s, the OECD addressed education in the context of scientific advancement when the Keynesianism paradigm was prevalent. The emphasis of the OECD's education perspective progressively shifted toward social equity objectives and became closely linked to issues related to the labor market (Papadopoulos, 1996). The Keynesianism principle shaped education, due to the assumption that firmer state intervention and centralization were beneficial for the overall outcome. With the establishment of the "Centre for Educational Research and Innovation" (CERI) in 1968 and the "Education Committee" in 1970, education policy was more formally institutionalized within the OECD, which underscored the relevancy of education topics for the IO (Martens & Wolf, 2006). In this period, the education perspective of the OECD was slightly decoupled from the overarching agenda of economic growth, and education developed into a more emancipated, self-contained issue within the IO.

In the mid-1970s, the OECD again turned its attention to education as an essential generator of economic growth (Rubenson, 2008). During the 1980s, this perspective strengthened, where neoliberal interpretations fueled the OECD's education initiatives, and the IO moved to a neoclassical supply-side orientation (Sellar & Lingard, 2014). Similarly, for other IOs and the OECD, the end of the Cold War heralded a decisive watershed moment (Woodward, 2008, p. 33). Due to the changing organizational environment, the OECD needed to redefine its mission and adapt its education activities. By referring to upcoming challenges due to globalization processes, the OECD emphasized the development of human resources to counteract emerging negative effects (Henry et al., 2001; OECD, 1996). The idea of preparing education systems for future challenges has become the keystone for the OECD's education work (OECD, 2010–2011). Additionally, the OECD produced empirical comparative data and scrutinized the member countries' education systems. Most prominently, the Programme for International Student Assessment (PISA) is a prominent example for this shift and contributed to the OECD's status as a leading IO in the field of education. The standardized large-scale assessment of education outcomes claims global validity and influences education reform processes in countries that did not participate in the study (Niemann & Martens, 2018). The data enabled policy actors to draw inferences on the returns of human capital produced through education. For instance, a strong positive correlation between economic effects and educational background was pointed out (OECD, 2009, p. 5).

The economic-focused education policy framework was settled mostly in the 1990s, when the aspect of equity was detached from issues of redistribution; instead, it was linked to the aspect of human capital in a globalized world. Education was increasingly heralded as "the policy key to the future prosperity of nations" (Henry et al., 2001, p. 30). Particularly, from the OECD perspective, education is a resource for innovation to manage economic challenges. After the establishment of the Directorate for Education in 2002 and the Global Forum on Education in 2005, it became clear that the OECD's work on education occupied a distinctive niche. The established bureaucratic structures enabled the OECD to become an increasingly independent producer and disseminator of knowledge in the education field (Morgan & Shahjahan, 2014, p. 198). Hence, the IO's intrinsic features allowed the OECD to expand its role in the organizational field of international education policy.

These findings regarding the development and expansion of economistic IOs that are active in the field of education today need to be contrasted with the position of long-established education IOs. IOs, like UNESCO, were already concerned with education policy for a long time before the economistic IOs entered the field. Within our theoretical framework, this next evolutionary step constituted a change in the population of education IOs and induced competition and adaptive pressure to existing IOs in the field. Different education IOs prioritized different ideas on education. Basically, a dualism between economic utilitarian views (World Bank and OECD) and idealistic humanistic (UNESCO) views can be identified. This dualism was embodied in the IO's education programs from the beginning and was translated into concrete actions and policy recommendations (Niemann, 2021). While both economistic IOs in our sample addressed education policy in the context of their economistic perspectives, UNESCO's view on education was traditionally different. The IO evaluated the purpose of education mostly from a humanistic angle and emphasized the positive effect of education on individual well-being and social integration processes and views educational development contributing to social justice and equality (Vaccari & Gardinier, 2019, p. 72).

Since latecomer IOs in education such as the World Bank and the OECD had more resources readily available and were backed by national governments, the well-established UNESCO perceived them as competitors within its niche. Contestation between both types of IOs was also amplified by fundamentally different leitmotifs regarding the purpose of education. Hence, the competition in the organizational education policy field was intensified by economistic IOs and the established IOs. In response, UNESCO was pressured to respond to the new developments to remain relevant. Therefore, the IO called for a new humanistic perspective that highlights both the economic and societal returns from an investment in education (UNESCO, 2014). While today the competition between the different types of education IOs eased (Niemann, 2021), there are still differences in how they evaluate the purpose of education. In sum, this constitutes a diversely characterized organizational field in education with various IOs occupying various but overlapping niches.

Regional and Transregional IOs— Tailored Toward Unique Needs

Parallel to these globally active IOs, a large and growing number of regional IOs has become ever-more relevant in international education policy. While the majority of global and transregional education IOs were established between 1945 and 1965, the population of regional IOs only experienced significant growth rates after 1965. However, as presented in Figure 22.3, the massive growth in the number of education IOs from the 1960s onward can be attributed almost solely to regional organizations. Hence, regional IOs significantly shape international education policy today, widening the organizational field. Since the mid-1960s, several regional IOs were founded with a focus on education; additionally, the existing IOs successively expanded to educational topics. Until 2018, the number of regional IOs grew from two in 1965 to twenty, as opposed to only six global and four transregional education IOs.

From a theoretical lens, regional education IOs found their niche in specific geographical contexts. Regional organizations that are primarily focused on education policy were often founded on the premise that successful education policy must be

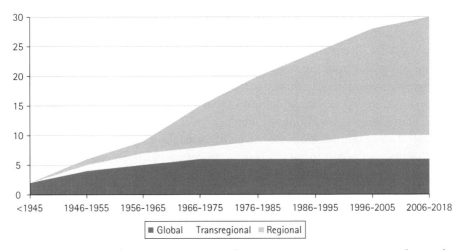

FIGURE 22.3 Growth of education international organizations over time—geographic reach.

mindful of region-specific factors such as religion, language, culture, and traditional norms and values. These organizations are uniquely situated within their respective regions (Krogmann, 2022a, 2022b). Due to their territorially limited focus, regional education IOs were able to better tailor their programs in education policy in order to meet the demands of certain groups of states. They represent connections between the *global* and the *local* and often engage in partnerships with globally oriented IOs like UNESCO or the World Bank for this purpose. Today, regional education IOs are present on all continents (except Antarctica).

The field of regional organizations is quite diverse in many ways. Some organizations, like the ABEGS, are small regarding their number of member states, budget, or scope. Others, like the Asia-Pacific Economic Cooperation (APEC), are substantial entities with a large number of member states and a wide range of objectives. In general, regional IOs have expanded their presence in education policy steadily since the 1940s, starting with the foundation of the Organization of American States (OAS) in 1948. By 1970, education IOs had been established in Southeast Asia (SEAMEO), the Gulf region (ABEGS), among Arab League states (ALECSO), and in the Caribbean (CARICOM). By 1985, even smaller entities covering only subregional membership, such as the Organisation of Eastern Caribbean States (OECS), joined the fray. Finally, in 2008, UNASUR became the youngest member of the community of regional IOs with a mandate in education policy.

Transregional education IOs are scarce compared to regional IOs, with the OEI and ICESCO being the only examples of transregional IOs that have a primary mandate and mission in education policy. Contrary to the field of regional IOs, the population of transregional IOs has not seen significant expansion. The only transregional IO in our sample founded since the early 1980s is the Asia-Europe Foundation (ASEF), established in 1997. To illustrate how regional and transregional IOs find and occupy their niches in the organizational field of education, ICESCO and SEAMEO will serve as examples in the following sections.

ICESCO

ICESCO[1] is a transregional education IO comprised of 54 member states with predominantly Muslim citizens spread over three continents. Established in 1981 as an official branch of the Organisation of Islamic Cooperation, ICESCO believes in education policy that is suitable for the international Muslim community, and its member states need to be mindful of and informed by Islam and Islamic values. The significance of religion for the organization's education policy is made clear from the first sentence of ICESCO's charter, which states that Islam is "a religion of peace and tolerance, represents a way of life and a spiritual, human, moral, cultural and civilizational force" (ISESCO, 2015, Preamble). Therefore, if ICESCO is to achieve its educational objectives, they have to be rooted "within the framework of the civilizational reference of the Islamic world and in the light of the human Islamic values and ideals" (ISESCO, 2015, Art 4 [a]). This idea competes with Western standards dominating in the global education field, which ICESCO views as incompatible with its traditional roots (Krogmann, 2022a). Looking to Western education systems as the singular source of inspiration for reforms in the Islamic world is counterproductive, according to ICESCO, because they are "alien to its cultural and civilizational references and incompatible with its socioeconomic context" (ISESCO, 2017b, p. 16).

There is significant overlap between ICESCO and other education IOs regarding its mission and member states, for example with the ABEGS and the ALECSO. All members of ABEGS are also members of ALECSO, while all member states of ALECSO are also member states of ICESCO. Both ABEGS and ALECSO have goals like ICESCO but pursue them on a smaller, region-based scale (Krogmann, 2022a). Although all three IOs primarily work in the same niche of the education policy field, interorganizational competition is limited. Rather, ICESCO, ALECSO, and ABEGS have been supportive of intensified cooperation with each other in the past. ICESCO officials have voiced the need to "increase synergy and enhance cooperation between ICESCO, ALECSO and ABEGS" (ISESCO, 2017a, p. 2). Reviewed through the organizational ecology lens, these three organizations can coexist and receive sufficient funding from their common members in parallel. It seems transregional and regional organizations can coexist in the same organizational field if they cooperate. Furthermore, if they share the same fundamental values and policy ideas, one niche in the organizational environment can be occupied by multiple organizations.

SEAMEO

In Southeast Asia, SEAMEO has become a major regional player in education policy. Founded in 1965, the organization facilitates cooperation in education, science, and culture among its member states. As such, education policy lies at the core of its mission. SEAMEO has championed a distinctly "holistic" set of education ideas since its inception, as it has attempted to balance the economic and social benefits of education policy (Krogmann, 2022b). According to SEAMEO, education should benefit individuals and society concerning both the economic and social needs. In recent years, SEAMEO has continuously supported this holistic view of education (SEAMEO, 2017a, p. iv), especially in the context of lifelong learning. For example, in its action agenda of 2017, SEAMEO proposed an association of lifelong learning to develop and implement "holistic and comprehensive lifelong learning approaches" (SEAMEO, 2017b, p. 36). The concept of quality of life, as defined by SEAMEO, aims to provide an all-around better "quality of life" for all citizens across its member states through education (SEAMEO, 2017a, p. xiii). Also, SEAMEO's education ideas have their own "flavor", where education policy is a tool in preserving the cultural roots of the region in both the individual and society (SEAMEO, 2013, 2017a, 2017b).

Similar to ICESCO, SEAMEO views itself as well-suited to tackle the challenges for education policy in the region by recognizing the cultural dimension of education. This dimension entails that education policy in Southeast Asia needs to be tailored toward its unique socioeconomic context to be successful (SEAMEO, 2017c). Therefore, located in a regional niche, SEAMEO pioneered international education policy. As the first education IO established for Southeast Asia, SEAMEO became the primary partner in policy implementation for both global education IOs and national governments aiming to set up projects in the region (Krogmann, 2022b). The relationship between SEAMEO and the Association of Southeast Asian Nations (ASEAN) illustrates the success SEAMEO has had in occupying its niche. When ASEAN was founded in 1970 by the same states that made up SEAMEO's members, its education department, although existent, was given very limited resources. Instead, SEAMEO became ASEAN's "strategic partner" in education, responsible for carrying out education policy following the "ASEAN core values" (Krogmann, 2022b). Today, SEAMEO's vast network of 26 regional centers employing more than 1,000 staff and personnel solidifies its status as the most relevant education IO in Southeast Asia. This decentralized structure reflects an intrinsic feature of the IO that enables it to adapt to upcoming exogenous challenges and, at the same time, allows SEAMEO to expand within the niche of regional education policy.

CONCLUSION

In brief, the world of education IOs has expanded gradually since World War II. Seen from an organizational ecology point of view, the population became denser and more diverse over time. Two observations stand out in this topography: first, economic IOs cultivate a distinct niche in education to fulfil their core mandate of enabling economic development (e.g., UNESCO or ILO). It has been shown that IOs with an economistic background, particularly the OECD and World Bank, expanded into the field of education and that they targeted education policy from an angle unlike established IOs, one which emphasizes the importance of skill formation through education for economic development. This interpretation of education challenged IOs with diverging views, like UNESCO, and stirred competition in the organizational field of international education policy. At the same time, the economistic IOs' ideas on education became universally transmitted and accepted by national stakeholders (Niemann et al., 2022). In consequence, the international education landscape significantly changed, and new ideas about the purpose of education shaped national reforms. Second, regional and transregional IOs occupy their particular niches within the realm of education IOs as relevant actors in their own right. The cases of ICESCO and SEAMEO illustrate how diverse this field has become. Incorporating cultural, religious, or regional values allows regional IOs to persist and thrive by producing adequate education policies for their respective member states.

NOTE

1. In 2020, the Islamic Educational, Scientific and Cultural Organization was renamed as Islamic World Educational, Scientific and Cultural Organization. As all documents referenced in this chapter have been published before 2020, they will be referenced using ICESCO's former denomination ISESCO.

REFERENCES

Abbott, K. W., Green, J. F., & Keohane, R. O. (2016). Organizational ecology and institutional change in global governance. *International Organization, 70*(2), 247–277.

Hannan, M. T., & Freeman, J. (1977). The population ecology of organizations. *American Journal of Sociology, 82*(5), 929–964.

Hawkins, D. G., Lake, D. A., Nielson, D., & Tierney, M. J. (Eds.) (2006). *Delegation and agency in international organizations*. Cambridge University Press.

Henry, M., Lingard, B., Rizvi, F., & Taylor, S. (Eds.) (2001). *The OECD, globalisation and education policy*. Pergamon.

Heyneman, S. P., & Lee, B. (2016). International organizations and the future of education assistance. *International Journal of Educational Development, 48*, 9–22.

Holm, H.-H., & Sørensen, G. (Eds.) (1995). *Whose world order? Uneven globalization and the end of the Cold War*. Routledge.

ISESCO. (2015). *Charter of ISESCO*. https://www.icesco.org/en/wp-content/uploads/sites/2/2020/01/charter-statutes.pdf

ISESCO. (2017a). *Address by Dr Abdulaziz Othman Altwaijri at the 4th Forum of International Organizations*. ISESCO.

ISESCO. (2017b). *Strategy for the development of education in the Islamic world*. ISESCO.

Krogmann, D. (2022a). International organizations and education in the Islamic world. In M. Windzio & K. Martens (Eds.), *The global development, diffusion, and transformation of education systems* (pp. 191–216). Palgrave Macmillan.

Krogmann, D. (2022b). Regional identities in international education organizations: The case of SEAMEO. In M. Windzio & K. Martens (Eds.), *The global development, diffusion, and transformation of education systems* (pp. 217–238). Palgrave Macmillan.

Lenz, T., Bezuijen, J., Hooghe, L., & Marks, G. (2015). Patterns of international organization: Task specific vs. general purpose. *Politische Vierteljahresschrift, 49*, 131–156.

Martens, K., & Wolf, K.-D. (2006). Paradoxien der Neuen Staatsräson. Die Internationalisierung der Bildungspolitik in der EU und der OECD. *Zeitschrift für Internationale Beziehungen, 13*(2), 145–176.

Morgan, C., & Shahjahan, R. A. (2014). The legitimation of OECD's global educational governance: Examining PISA and AHELO test production. *Comparative Education, 50*(2), 192–205.

Mundy, K., & Verger, A. (2015). The World Bank and the global governance of education in a changing world order. *International Journal of Educational Development, 40*(1), 9–18. doi:10.1016/j.ijedudev.2014.11.021

Nielson, D. L., & Tierney, M. J. (2003). Delegation to international organizations: Agency theory and World Bank reform. *International Organization, 57*(2), 241–276.

Niemann, D. (2022). International organizations in education: New takes on old paradigms. In M. Windzio & K. Martens (Eds.), *The global development, diffusion, and transformation of education systems* (pp. 127–161). Palgrave Macmillan.

Niemann, D., Krogmann, D., & Martens, K. (2022). Between economics and education—How IOs changed the view on education. In F. Nullmeier, D. González de Reufels, & H. Obinger (Eds.), *Impacts on social policy: Short histories in a global perspective* (pp. 189–200). Palgrave MacMillan.

Niemann, D., & Martens, K. (2018). Soft governance by hard fact? The OECD as a knowledge broker in education policy. *Global Social Policy, 18*(3), 267–283. doi:10.1177/1468018118794076

Niemann, D., & Martens, K. (2021). Global discourses, regional framings and individual showcasing: Analyzing the world of education IOs. In K. Martens, D. Niemann, & A. Kaasch (Eds.), *International organizations in global social policy* (pp. 163–186). Palgrave Macmillan.

North, D. C. (1990). *Institutions, institutional change and economic performance.* Cambridge University Press.

OECD. (1996). *Measuring what people know: Human capital accounting for the knowledge economy.* OECD.

OECD. (2009). *Bildung auf einen Blick 2009: OECD-Indikatoren. Zusammenfassung auf Deutsch.* OECD.

OECD. (2010–2011). *Work on education.* OECD.

Papadopoulos, G. (1996). *Die Entwicklung des Bildungswesens von 1960 bis 1990.* Peter Lang.

Pierson, P. (2004). *Politics in time: History, institutions, and social analysis.* Princeton University Press.

Rubenson, K. (2008). OECD education policies and world hegemony. In R. Mahon & S. McBride (Eds.), *The OECD and transnational governance* (pp. 242–259). UBC Press.

SEAMEO. (2013). *Strategic plan 2011–2020.* SEAMEO.

SEAMEO. (2017a). *SEAMEO basic education standards: Common core regional learning standards (CCRLS) in mathematics and science.* SEAMEO.

SEAMEO. (2017b). *Action agenda for the SEAMEO 7 priority areas.* SEAMEO.

SEAMEO. (2017c). *7 Priority areas—Implementation by SEAMEO member countries.* SEAMEO.

Sellar, S., & Lingard, B. (2014). The OECD and the expansion of PISA: New global modes of governance in education. *British Educational Research Journal, 40*(6), 917–936.

UNESCO. 2014. *UNESCO's medium-term strategy for 2014–2021.* 37 C/4. UNESCO.

Vaccari, V., & Gardinier, M. P. (2019). Toward one world or many? A comparative analysis of OECD and UNESCO global education policy documents. *International Journal of Development Education and Global Learning, 11*(1), 68–86.

Vetterlein, A. (2012). Seeing like the World Bank on poverty. *New Political Economy, 17*(1), 35–58.

Wolfe, R. (2008). From reconstructing Europe to constructing globalization: The OECD in historical perspective. In R. Mahon & S. McBride (Eds.), *The OECD and transnational governance* (pp. 25–42). UBC Press.

Woodward, R. (2008). Towards complex multilateralism? Civil society and the OECD. In R. Mahon & S. McBride (Eds.), *The OECD and transnational governance* (pp. 77–95). UBC Press.

World Bank. (1974). *Education sector working paper*. World Bank.

Zapp, M. (2017). The World Bank and education: Governing (through) knowledge. *International Journal of Educational Development*, 53(1), 1–11. doi:10.1016/j.ijedudev.2016.11.007

Zapp, M. (2020). The authority of science and the legitimacy of international organisations: OECD, UNESCO and World Bank in global education governance. *Compare*, 51(7), 1022–1041. doi:10.1080/03057925.2019.1702503

CHAPTER 23

THE OECD'S BOUNDARY WORK IN EDUCATION IN THE UNITED STATES AND BRAZIL

A Historical Comparative Analysis of Two Federal States

CHRISTIAN YDESEN AND
NANNA RAMSING ENEMARK

INTRODUCTION

FOR decades, the Organization for Economic Cooperation and Development (OECD) has played a pivotal role in shaping education worldwide, in relation to both member- and non-member states (Centeno, 2019). The literature amply demonstrates how nation states and domestic education institutions have transformed themselves in the image of global reforms, often orchestrated and facilitated by the OECD (Lawn & Grek, 2012; Niemann & Martens, 2018). Global governance processes have created key reference points for education worldwide in the form of data, indicators, values, problem solutions, and ideologies.

In terms of research, governance associated with globalization processes, including the role played by international organizations (IOs), has attracted widespread attention. The key debates in the field concern various versions of world culture theory, institutionalisms, and advocates of seeing policy processes as essentially heterogeneous (Mundy et al., 2016). Nevertheless, there appears to be wide recognition that national education systems and local education practices remain diverse and complex (Robertson, 2018). Therefore, research into the workings of global education requires analytical sensitivity to the interactions and intermeshing relations among local, national, and global agents, and instruments, knowledge, data, and policies populating and constituting complex spaces.

This complexity associated with understanding the shaping and workings of global governance processes becomes particularly relevant in national contexts that operate federal organizations with highly decentralized education systems. The relevance of this focus has gained momentum in the age of post–Cold War neoliberalism, where global competition and standards have become focal points for nation states and where the OECD espouses a distinct connection between education results and a nation's future competitive power.[1] Nation states have established numerous accountability mechanisms in an attempt to gain certainty and knowledge concerning delivery of education (UNESCO, 2017; Verger et al., 2019). Accountability and production of comparable data have become the criteria for membership in the global education architecture. Federally organized states face particular challenges in this respect.

The Western hemisphere's two most populous democracies, the United States and Brazil, are both characterized by highly decentralized education systems due to their federal organization (Crespo et al., 2000; Krejsler, 2018; Mcginn & Pereira, 1992). These two countries share the dilemma of establishing national accountability structures to ensure both quality in terms of delivering globally competitive (and comparative) outcomes and equality in terms of securing educational access, while preserving the remit of local governments. This federal dilemma has emerged not least because of the two countries' participation in the global education architecture in general and their engagement with the OECD in particular. While this dilemma became pronounced and discussed in the United States in the 1960s as a result of the emergent production of education data (Krejsler, 2020; McGuinn, 2006), Brazil encountered the dilemma beginning with its involvement as a non-member state of the OECD in the 1990s (OECD, 2011).

This chapter historically and comparatively explores the particular issues and dilemmas associated with federal states' involvement with the OECD using the United States, a member state, and Brazil, a non-member state, as its analytical focus. More specifically, we investigate boundary work—understood as negotiations and struggles about understandings, definitions, characteristics, and boundaries of normality and deviance (Eyal, 2012)—that takes place in the interactions between the OECD and the two case countries.

The chapter first covers the late 1960s with respect to the US case. In this period, the United States established a leading position in the organization after acting as the key agent in the transition of the Organization for European Economic Cooperation (OEEC) to the OECD in 1961 (Elfert & Ydesen, 2020). Moreover, the OECD Centre for Educational Research and Innovation (CERI) was established in 1968, signaling a clear organizational change reflecting education as a core OECD concern and area of analysis. The second period under consideration is the late 1990s, when Brazil pursued a strategy of internationalization and entered into formal relations with the OECD, culminating with participation in the first OECD Program for International Student Assessment (PISA) round in 2000. Silva (2019) sees this as a reform period in Brazilian public education, with adoption of results-based accountability instruments, often implemented in intentional and enthusiastic collaboration with IOs (Kauko et al., 2016, p. 561; Whitehead, Chapter 39, this volume). When in 1990 Brazil began its national assessments in basic education (SAEB), the country took inspiration from American national tests (Crespo et al., 2000). During this period, PISA was also designed and rolled out. PISA has since become a center of gravity in the development and shaping of global education architecture to the present (Lewis, 2020).

Looking across time and space creates a methodological opportunity to identify contrasting and recurring features and mechanisms at the very heart of global education governance. At the same time, a historical and comparative approach holds potential to create awareness and critical problematization of the constructs of today's education policies that otherwise seem to operate in a naturalized way according to an inherent logic. From the outset, this chapter raises the question: What explanatory power in terms of global education governance can be inferred from a historical comparative analysis of the OECD's boundary work with these two federal states?

ANALYTICAL LAYERS

Working with two case countries across time and space requires careful reflection on the analytical layers present and how these layers connect with issues discussed in contemporary research.

As noted, the United States and Brazil bear some apparent similarities because of their federal organization, but they remain distinctly different, not least because of their power positions. In this sense, this research inevitably involves attempts to understand the role and power positioning of the Global North and the Global South in the global education architecture (Edwards Jr. & Means, 2019). For instance, it has been argued that the United States has often sought to use IOs as vehicles to shape the world in its own image (Bürgi, 2019; Gilman, 2003). When the United States joined what essentially was their own invention, the OECD, in 1961, the federal government struggled with themes such as poverty, the Sputnik shock, and inequality—often related to racial segregation which may have legally ended in 1954 but that, in the 1960s, remained no less a factor in unequal access to educational opportunities.

Nevertheless, the United States saw education as a vehicle to export American culture to the rest of the world. In an internal US Government memo dated March 8, 1960, from O. J. Caldwell, Assistant Commissioner for International Education, to L. G. Derthick, Commissioner of Education, Caldwell argues that "Education must become the foundation of American foreign policy. This view is strongly supported by a growing sentiment among many economists, who teach that the development of human resources through education must be the first step toward economic and political advancement" (p. 1). Caldwell further argued that "education is the foundation of national power" and proposed "the establishment of a new Interdepartmental Committee to enable HEW

[Department of Health, Education, and Welfare], and the Office [of education], effectively to represent American education in the development of international educational policy" (p. 2).[2]

In contrast to the United States as a leading architect of the post–World War II global world order, Brazil found itself needing to implement reforms to fit into the global education architecture as defined by IOs. For instance, the OECD has functioned as a political "legitimizer" of internal reforms in Brazil (Silva, 2019). The inherently powerful position of the United States and the nature of the OECD as a "club of the rich" (Elfert & Ydesen, 2020) positioned Brazil as a recipient of US influence, exacerbated by a history of US–Brazil partnership programs across sectors (Kauko et al., 2016, p. 566). This is evident from a draft resolution for educational cooperation between the United States and Brazil which states that the National Institute for Educational Studies and Research in Brazil (INEP) was able to develop indicators allowing for cross-country comparisons due to "having received support from United States to adopt the methodology used by the Organization for Economic Cooperation and Development (OECD)."[3] This shows how the United States assisted in furthering agendas via the OECD in general and via its definitions and methodologies in particular.

In this sense, the dynamics between the OECD and each of the two case countries is very different. Nevertheless, this contrast serves as a privileged lens to gain insight into the shifting dynamics of global education governance and adds to our understanding of the role and agency of IOs (Elfert & Ydesen, 2023). Furthermore, the OECD itself struggled with determining its mandate and finding its identity in terms of education in the two periods covered for the United States and Brazil, the late 1960s and late 1990s, respectively. In this sense, this chapter sheds light on the struggles and negotiations over understandings, definitions, characteristics, and boundaries of normality and deviance in global education governance.

Theoretical Underpinnings, Empirical Data, and Methodology

Theoretical and methodological engagement with comparative research across time and space is complex and requires meticulous methodological considerations.

Focusing on the boundary work between the OECD and the two case countries draws on a Bourdieusian understanding of globalization processes as characterized by struggles and hierarchies orchestrated by officials, experts, and professionals strategizing to impose their classifications as legitimate (Ydesen, 2021). In this sense, a focus on the work of officials, professionals, and experts serves as an important prism to understand the workings of global education governance. This is where the boundary work—understood as negotiations and struggles about understandings, definitions, characteristics, and boundaries of normality and deviance—takes place (Eyal, 2012).

While this approach serves as an analytical lens, the comparative component between the two case countries calls for additional reflection. A key challenge in this respect is the role and significance of context. Drawing on Sobe and Kowalczyk (2013), we interpret context as "a set of historical discourses that interweave actors and objects and govern what it is possible to think" (p. 6). As pointed out in Bartlett and Vavrus (2018), "meaning is constantly remade; it cannot be predicted or determined in advance. And yet it is essential because it fundamentally shapes actions" (p. 190). From this perspective, each case country will be analyzed from different foci determined by the factors relevant to understanding the meanings produced (e.g., educational culture, education policies pursued and enacted, and organization of education authorities). Following Coleman and Collins (2006), Bartlett and Vavrus (2018) explain that "the research techniques and the delimitation of sites and people to include in a study must be emergent—scholars should follow the people, things, places, symbols, metaphors, objects and phenomenon of interest as we trace the 'contingency of the ethnographic object'" (p. 195). This accords well with what Sobe and Kowalczyk (2012) call a "study of assemblages" as a way of approaching and conceptualizing context. In their own interpretation, Bartlett and Vavrus (2018) draw on the Deleuze and Guattari (1987) understanding of assemblages as "temporary, unpredictable and evolving social entities composed of heterogeneous components" (p. 194).

In terms of comparative analysis, this chapter may be viewed as multisited research. This involves comparing how the boundary work unfolds "in different locations and at different scales, including transnationally" (Bartlett & Vavrus, 2018, p. 195). Here, we follow the three comparative axes proposed by Bartlett and Vavrus:

- The *vertical axis* urges comparison across micro, meso, and macro levels or scales.
- The *horizontal axis* encourages comparison of how similar policies and practices unfold across sites, often with distinctly different consequences.
- The *transversal axis*, which emphasizes change over time, urges scholars to situate historically the processes or relations under consideration.

This chapter draws on archival sources from the United States National Archive in Washington, DC, and the Brazilian National Archive in Brasilia, supplemented by sources from the OECD archive in Paris. Document selection follows an abductive approach of an initial inductive probe for thematic clusters followed by a systematic search for documents related to centralization, decentralization, federalism, and accountability. These documents are complemented by a number of previous studies into federalism and into the countries' relationship with the OECD. The contexts are continually reinterpreted throughout the selection process as the interweaving of actors and objects is uncovered (Sobe & Kowalczyk, 2013).

The vertical axis is followed across individual agents' roles and their collaboration with other actors, groups, and government branches. This means tracing policies from, for example, an individual administration official's memo to the political consequences at the ministerial level. Our notion of decentralization is not reduced to the respective states, but conceptually includes entities such as counties and municipalities, which in both Brazil[4] and the United States are influential in local education policy.

Context as a horizontal axis enables us to compare how policy issues (such as accountability of states) unfold differently across regional and national borders and how the perceived policy solutions and practices develop and are put into motion. The context, as a transversal axis (Bartlett & Vavrus, 2018, p. 195f.), considers the historically situated national education attainment crises of both countries. The United States experienced the "Sputnik shock" in 1957 following the successful Soviet launch of a satellite into space, and the political field immediately spilled into the educational arena (Buchardt & Plum, 2020; Krejsler, 2018). Brazil encountered "The Lost Decade" of economic stagnation in the 1980s (see also Whitehead, Chapter 39, this volume); the nation's entrance into the global market came to depend on mobilizing an increasingly educated workforce, politically allowing for extensive education reforms (Filho, 1993; Moraes Valença, 1998; OECD, 2011).

The chapter structure reflects these theoretical and methodological issues. The first two parts of the analysis are a contextual review of the boundary work in evidence in the two case countries. Then follows a comparative analysis using the three comparative axes as guiding principles. The concluding discussion sums up the main findings and engages with state-of-the-art research to critically reflect on the contributions of the chapter.

US Decentralization and the OECD

The end of the Marshall Plan rendered the OEEC an organization without a mission, and the OEEC evolved into the OECD, with the aim of enhancing international trade as a vehicle for growth and development while incorporating two non-European nations, the United States and Canada. Unable to exert direct control over the OECD, the United States developed a constructive relationship with an organization increasingly growing into its own. The new organizational setup demanded cooperation with government agencies, but the multitude of American agencies juggled intragovernmental murkiness of responsibility combined with a distinct emphasis on states' rights and on jurisdiction. This was exacerbated by the US Constitution not distinctly mentioning education (Krejsler, 2020), making it therefore subject to negotiation.

In the early days of the OECD, at the 1961 Washington Conference on education, US Secretary of State Dean Rusk made it clear that the United States had "great expectations about the possibilities of the OECD" (Papadopoulos, 1994, p. 40). These great expectations, however, were at times challenged by the unclear administrative and organizational relationship with the OECD on the part of the United States. As observed by Kjell Eide (1990)[5]:

> The attitude of the US to the educational collaboration in the OECD has always been marked by an internal struggle between the Department of State and the Department of Education, with the Department of Labour as a third intermittent actor. The different departments often disagree, and it seems somewhat unpredictable which of them will prove strongest in each case. (p. 28)

This description highlights the internal negotiations over which government agency was authorized and carried a mandate to enter into collaboration with IOs in education. The United States did ingeniously attempt to streamline agencies at the federal level, as evidenced by a 1962 letter to Commissioner McMurrin from Dr. Robert M. Rosenzweig, Assistant to the Commissioner. Rosenzweig urged the commissioner to become involved in the then vogue topic of the economics of education. Rosenzweig recommended handing over responsibility to the new Bureau of Research and Development.[6] It is no coincidence that the bureau was named "Research and Development," as the emphasis on state autonomy in the United States means that "central educational planning is constitutionally precluded" (Papadopoulos, 1994, p. 49). However, as evidenced by the United States holding great expectations for the work of the OECD, a loophole was found in that research and development was under federal authority, technically allowing for national policies. That research and development could serve as the federal access point into national legislation was seemingly never broadly communicated to the public in the following years. Harold Howe II, as Commissioner of Education, reassured the public that the federal government was not out to take control of educational matters.[7] Drawing a line between education on one side and research and development on the other can be construed as boundary work. Howe went on to describe special provisions included in the Elementary and Secondary Education Act of 1965 as "a final insurance against federal control"[8] and contended that, "[e]ducation can hardly claim exemption from a rule of nearly two centuries" as . . . "Assurances have been given on many occasions that the Office of Education has neither the authority nor the desire to interfere with the operation or management of local school affairs" (pp. 3–4). Nevertheless, within the agencies, it became increasingly clear that collaboration with IOs such as the OECD marked the need for intervention at the federal level. This, however, was successfully construed as different from interfering in local school affairs.

From the onset of the US–OECD relationship, unclear practices appeared commonplace due to a multitude of agencies and actors. In a memorandum dated March 20, 1962, Oliver J. Caldwell, Assistant Commissioner for International Education, wrote Dr. J. Boyer Jarvis, Special Assistant to the Commissioner, politely expressing frustration with being seemingly left out of a correspondence between the Commissioner of Education's office and Dr. Flynt of the National Science Foundation. Caldwell instructs Jarvis to direct matters involving IOs to the Division of International Education.[9] Caldwell points out that only in "this way can a unified approach be maintained, and our work coordinated with other agencies in the *international* field" (author's emphasis, p. 1), drawing a boundary between international and educational work. Half a year later, Caldwell was still working on streamlining internal collaboration between the OECD and US agencies. In a 1963 memorandum to the Commissioner of Education,[10] Francis Keppel, Caldwell describes how the "back-stopping for the US participation in these committees has been done by an array of federal agencies . . . the Office of Education has been only peripherally and spasmodically involved in the US participation bearing on these areas" (p. 1). Caldwell urged the various US agencies to extend national coordination regarding US collaboration with OECD, but his efforts suggest collaboration with OECD was not necessarily to be defined as membership in education agencies.

In a summary of the Seventh Meeting of the Education Investment Planning (EIP) Group of the Committee on Scientific and Technical Personnel (CSTP) held in Oslo, Norway, in 1965, Mary E. Robinson, acting director of the Program Planning Division, describes the highlights. Describing developments in the United States, Robinson writes about providing information about the current reorganization of the Office of Education as stemming partly from "education programs of the many federal agencies" (p. 3). In this context, it is noteworthy that Robinson's summary again confirms the image of a somewhat unclear organization of US authorities regarding engagement with the OECD.

Interestingly, Robinson also describes how the Secretariat of the OECD CSTP had formally requested a paper on the US education system and how this paper would "follow through the US Embassy, National Science Foundation (NSF) channel" (p. 3). This highlights how the Office of Education had multiple channels at its disposal, not specifically restricted to education.[11] When the paper, written by B. Hayward of the OECD secretariat, was presented, Bowen C. Dees, associate director at the American National Science Foundation, found that it gave a distorted picture of US education developments, because it failed to represent "[f]ederal education activities properly in the framework" of all the efforts taking place at the state level and in private education institutions (p. 3). In this sense, the reception given the Hayward paper is an indication of the negotiations taking place in terms of how the workings of the US education system were understood in international fora. From our theoretical angle, it seems that the United States was regarded as the odd one out regarding boundaries of normality and deviance.[12]

The multitude of channels in the US education system was also noted by examiners from the OECD in 1969 during their preparation for the "confrontation" regarding US research and development efforts.[13] The OECD examiners' comments and questions are a fruitful source for understanding the prevalent discourse on accountability and decentralization at the time.[14] They blend accountability and the organizational patterns of the US Government as follows: "Such fundamental issues as the ways in which the Presidency confers authority on, and requires accountability from, a multiplicity of agencies and the relations between the federal authorities and the States are the web and woof of our subject" (p. 7). It is clear that the examiners found the government structure intriguing, as they go on to state: "As far as possible we have resisted the temptation to follow these issues of fundamental structures too far from our remit" (p. 7). Nevertheless, they describe a country in crisis; President Nixon's task force on education is highlighted, alongside vivid accounts of "the world's richest and most powerful nation facing some of its deepest domestic crises" (p. 7). The comments and questions do not refrain from pointing out difficulties making sense of US government structure. Describing decision-making structures, they conclude: "In the U.S.A. administrative disjunctiveness is both rampant and deliberate" (p. 22). Nevertheless, the United States still received "special treatment" in that the examiners wanted to create a positive spin: "Its own submission shows that all is not well with the programme (the Research and Development programme, red.), but we believe that due credit to those responsible for the programme is not being given by the critics. Much of the criticism of them have been trivial and unfair" (p. 39). In later pages, the examiners "emphasise again that American practice in education has a massive effect upon educational practice throughout the world" (p. 46). This indicates that any comments toward US practice are implicitly related to a practice the OECD wants to enable, and thus there are no differences of opinion between the United States and the OECD concerning recommended practices. While the OECD hardly applauds the decentralized structure of the American system, it does warn that US practice "could carry over to a sort of 'educational imperialism,' "[15] as the US Commissioner of Education from 1966 to 1968, Harold Howe II, pointed out. This is the same commissioner who, in an interview given to FORUM, spins local decision autonomy as aiding diversity: "This is the tradition of local control which has made American education such a rich source of diversity."[16] Thus, while arguing internally that decentralization is a positive aspect of the US structure, there is a simultaneous scramble to intervene federally through a multitude of agencies following OECD recommendations. Thus, a pattern emerges in which referencing the OECD and/or international comparisons can serve as a powerful impulse to push boundaries in terms of federal authority and mandate; this relates to the era of federal activism that stretched from the mid-1950s through the 1970s (McGuinn, 2006; Ydesen & Dorn, 2022).

Brazilian Decentralization and the OECD

That IOs have taken issue with federal nation states is not exclusive to the OECD. During the 1970s and 1980s, Brazil cooperated with the World Bank, a common tendency for postdictatorial Latin American countries at the time (Kauko et al., 2016, p. 567).[17] A 1994 letter from the World Bank to an advisor to Brazilian President Cardoso substantially critiques the condition of the Brazilian education system.[18] Annual spending in 1993–1994 was estimated at US $250 per student, but poor states spent as little as US $30 on primary education per student annually. This variation "reflects, inter alia, the failure of the Ministry of Education to assist in the redistribution of education spending in such a way as to help municipalities and states of different income levels achieve minimum quality standards."[19] This argument suggests that Brazil needs assistance outside of normal government structures to improve equity, as these structures deviate from OECD countries' boundaries of normality. The need for outside policy advice also clearly places Brazil in a client position.

In a preliminary 1997 proposal on assessment as a government strategy to ensure education standards, the Ministry of Education was inspired by OECD education evaluation practices regarding the advantage of the comparable statistics needed "in order to improve education quality, in the context of integrating and making the hemisphere cooperation possible."[20] The Ministry of Education encourages multilateral research groups to further investigate how educational assessment standards can be achieved. Reference is made to US efforts in this area, pointing toward an initial probing for collaboration with the United States from the Brazilian Ministry of Education.

A US delegation subsequently visited Brazil in October 1997 and began working on a "Framework for a US-Brazil Partnership for Education."[21] The draft report consists of two opposing columns with different versions of the relevant document seemingly differentiating between suggestions from the US Department of Education and the Brazilian Ministry of Education and Sports, amply revealing the negotiations and boundary work involved.[22] The document describes how the Policy Dialogue on Standards between the two countries should include policymakers from both national and state levels, to "share experiences in the process of developing standards in a decentralized system" (p. 14). These efforts are linked explicitly to the International Educational Indicators (INES) program of the OECD, a project emphasized as being "heavily supported, both financially and intellectually, by the US National Centre for Education Statistics (NCES)" (p. 16), seemingly further justifying the partnership between the two parties. The draft agreement goes on to describe how Brazil can learn from US advances in teacher and school manager preparation programs through dialogue at all levels (local, state, and national) (p. 47). The US draft column describes how any "proposed action should have the potential to improve educational quality in one or both of the two countries" (p. 7). There is, however, no mention of how Brazil could assist the United States in bettering *its* quality of education; thus, this appears to be a one-sided improvement standard invoked from the Global North to the Global South. For example, both countries' version contains the phrasing "Brazil and United States work together to develop a world-class system of education statistics and indicators," but while the Brazilian draft version's sentence ends there, the American sentence goes on to include "in Brazil," alluding to the United States already believing that it has a world-class system (p. 16). This draft thereby positions the United States as a superior authority in helping Brazil gain access to the OECD club.

A document from the Ministry of Education and Sports and the Foreign Ministry (Itamaraty Palace), states:

> The United States agreed to maintain the technical support given to the INEP to promote its participation in the activities of the OCDE (OECD, red.), regarding indicators, as well as the technical support given by interface of the National Center for Educational Statistics (NCES).[23]

Once again, the United States acts as a negotiator for OECD in relation to indicators. Although Brazil by 1998 had developed a comprehensive national institute working with indicators (INEP) (Silva, 2019), it nonetheless accepted assistance from the US Education Department. This can be construed as the United States negotiating the boundaries of normality and defining the understandings Brazil needed to adopt to confer with OECD. Throughout these years of Brazilian collaboration with the United States, the OECD also developed PISA, which further consolidated collaboration between Brazil and OECD (and the United States). The first round of PISA coincided with Brazil's education reforms aimed at increasing equal access to and the quality of its education system (Schwartzman, 2013). In a 1999 speech, the federal Minister of Education, Paulo Renato Souza described how globalization and new technological advances require educational reforms in Brazil.[24] Education played a twofold role in the speech: It would develop the state but also enable upward social mobility for a Brazilian population plagued by high illiteracy rates. In an exchange of letters from September to November 2001 following the first round of PISA,[25] the federal Minister of Education, Paulo Renato Souza, writes the Minister of Foreign Affairs to inform him of the desire of INEP[26] to continue participating in PISA, as he believes participation "will promote indispensable tools to improve education quality in Brazil" (September 20, 2001). Recent research finds that Brazil is held as a valued non-member of the OECD, particularly as Brazil forms a bridge for the OECD to other Latin American countries and because of the country's high-level statistics organization (INEP) (Kauko et al., 2016; Silva, 2019). Thus, it seems that both the OECD and Brazil were satisfied with Brazil's participation in OECD activities in the 2000s.

Brazil's participation in the first round of the PISA test in 2000 was generally uncontested nationally (Bolívar, 2011). While the then newly established National Institute for Educational Research and Development (INEP), along with President Fernando Henrique Cardoso and Minister of Education Paulo Renato Souza, were aware of Brazil's high rate of grade repetition, and that illiteracy and poverty would most likely result in low PISA scores (as it did), the country eagerly participated in development and distribution of the test (Silva, 2019). The INEP president around the time of PISA's first round in 2000, Maria Helena Guimarães de Castro, for example, voiced support for different types of products for dissemination of PISA results due to "the complexity of our social and educational structure."[27] PISA was useful for Brazil to hold states accountable for state-school performance. This followed from the 1996 legislative change leading to increased decentralization combined with increased federal oversight (Silva, 2019, p. 112). Brazil therefore saw PISA as a potential instrument for implementing increased federal oversight. Throughout her time as president of the INEP, De Castro continued to advocate for the importance of comparable indicators (Castro, 2000). De Castro also shed light on another reason for Brazil's participation in PISA: the mobilization potential that President Cardoso had discovered, as "he also understood the value of coming last for mobilising the country to demand better education" (OECD, 2011, p. 183). Much as recent research has found for Mexico–OECD relations (Moreno-Salto & Robertson, 2021), comparison—and the "vertical vision" of ranking and competition—is a key operational modality mediating the power of PISA. This modality applies both internationally and within the organization of federal states.

Concluding Discussion: Comparative Patterns and the Role of Boundary Work

As the Western hemisphere's most populous democracies, participation by the federally based United States and Brazil in OECD programs encourages federal oversight over a unified education system with ideally little variation in content and quality. Therefore, even though the United States and Brazil hold different power positions, they nevertheless encounter the same dilemma in relation to the OECD: how to act as unified countries with nationwide comparable statistics when individual states have substantial influence over education policy. The United States has multiple agencies involved in collaboration with the OECD, leading to murky boundaries between the organization and government. This differs from Brazil, which instead delegates statistics work—including collaboration with the OECD—to its National Institute for Educational Research and Development (INEP). The OECD's focus on assessment and comparability in the 1990s ran concurrent with trends in Brazil's rapidly reforming education policy and served to legitimize the introduction of more accountability and assessment procedures as in other countries (Lingard, 2000, p. 46). In contrast, the United States had to circumvent federal organizational obstacles during the 1960s, when assessment trends were just emerging (Papadopoulos, 1994, p. 49).

In this sense, this chapter indicates and confirms the role of OECD as a legitimizer of education reforms found in other countries (Karseth et al., 2021; Ørskov, 2019; Papadopoulos, 1994). In terms of global education governance, this role should not be understood in an authoritarian sense, but more as the OECD serving as an international arena, reference point, and reservoir of arguments available for use by various agents engaged in policy reform. The style of reasoning permeating this reference point, though, is clearly a "vertical vision" of ranking and competition which, in a wider sense, hinges on human capital theory and the links between education and the economy. But the federal context does trigger important modifications to our understanding of educational governance in terms of complexity and boundary work.

Returning to our vertical and transversal axes, this chapter investigates federal issues in two historical contexts featuring countries with a great emphasis on educational decentralization. Both the United States and Brazil have faced the dilemma of creating centralized policies at the macro level in their nationally encouraged decentralized education systems. This dilemma can be considered an example of the enigmatic tendency of both the United States and Brazil to simultaneously pursue decentralization and centralization policies (Mcginn & Pereira, 1992).

While we began this chapter with a quote emphasizing the American understanding of education policy as foreign policy, the Brazilian Minister of Education between 1995 and 2002, Paulo Renato Souza, similarly viewed education policy as development policy.[28] Presidents of Brazil and the United States, in the 1990s and 1960s, respectively, were preoccupied with the role of education in national development. Lyndon Johnson (1963–1969) was, for example, the first American president to refer to himself as "education president" (Vinovskis, 2015), while Fernando Henrique Cardoso, in a letter to then President Bill Clinton, expressed his wish for education to become the key issue to discuss at the upcoming 1998 Santiago summit of the Americas.[29] The presidents' attention to education resulted in two extensive national policies in the form of the Elementary and Secondary Education Act (ESEA) of 1965 in the United States and the revised Education Act of 1996 (including the creation of FUNDEF) in Brazil (Verhine & Dantas, 2018). These policies reaffirm decentralized systems but include incentives for accountability measures that were previously state and municipal responsibilities, with the federal level concerned primarily with funding (OECD, 2011; Silva, 2019, pp. 115–118). The federal dilemma seems, for both the United States and Brazil, to entail balancing constitutional constraints of potential federal education policies in compulsory schooling systems while creating uniform policies allowing for comparable (intranational) statistics in coherent and organized federal agencies. In this sense, we find a connection with what Verger et al. (2019) describe as school autonomy with accountability (SAWA) reforms. This is a pattern of increasing federal authority in a top-down system of accountability which makes sense only when lower echelons are granted some level of autonomy. In the United States, the No Child Left Behind Act of 2001 epitomizes this development (Ydesen & Dorn, 2022).

On the horizontal axis, a picture emerges of the United States acting as "shaper" and Brazil as "taker" of policies due to the power relations in the time periods covered here. Brazil actively utilized national assessments to hold states accountable at a much faster pace than did the United States. PISA as an instrument served a multitude of purposes in Brazil, including easing federal oversight, becoming the basis for national educational reforms and—with the help of the United States—Brazil becoming part of the international "club." This enabled Brazil to compare itself with OECD countries. Even though this tends to pan out unfavorably for Brazil, it is still the OECD countries that Brazilian agencies rely on for comparison.[30] The contributions of this chapter perpetuate the notion of Brazil utilizing OECD indicators to increase accountability measures for states and as a legitimizer for rapid transformations in Brazilian education policy (Silva, 2019). The United States has in this regard served as a mediator—and a breaker of boundaries—for Brazil to join the OECD "club." In this sense, the Brazilian federal authorities exploited the Global North–Global South asymmetry to create leverage to more effectively govern the federal states. This indicates that Brazil subscribed to the OECD/US-led narrative about normality and deviance in education.

But while Brazil's organization tasked with carrying out assessment in the 1990s, INEP, was equipped to collaborate with OECD at the national level, the US agencies of the 1960s were challenged by an unclear distribution of roles. This murkiness in US organization may be due to states having much more power in the United States and because of a political culture characterized by marked skepticism of federal authority (Verhine & Dantas, 2018). While the United States took a leading role in shaping the OECD and its education programs, US national representatives engaging with OECD nevertheless sometimes felt a failure to understand the US education system and experienced the United States being categorized as the odd one out in the OECD arena. This has been a recurring feature in that the OECD—in its reports, recommendations, and reviews—has called for increased federal authority in their engagement with the United States.

An interesting finding is the boundary work that takes place in terms of how education should be construed. For the United States, education per se was positioned as something different from research and development in education, and a distinct line was drawn between national and international education work. This allowed federal agencies to marginalize state authority in these areas, allowing federal authorities to expand their mandate. For Brazil, the boundary work in the country's engagement with the OECD in general and American policy advisors in particular clearly positioned the country as a client in need of "normalization" according to Western standards. Engagement and interaction with OECD played an important role in both examples of the boundary work discussed here.

Notes

1. This connection is an essential feature of the Program for International Student Assessment. It has been argued particularly by Erik Hanushek, a senior fellow at the conservative Hoover institute, an often-used expert by the OECD (Auld & Morris, 2016; Ydesen & Bomholt, 2020). There is now a considerable literature criticizing this connection (e.g., Kamens, 2015; Komatsu & Rappleye, 2017; Ramirez et al., 2006; Stromquist, 2016).
2. O. J. Caldwell, Assistant Commissioner for International Education, to Commissioner of Education, L. G. Derthick; March 8, 1960; Office Files of Commissioner of Education; Entry No. A1122; Record Group 12; National Archives Building, Washington, DC.
3. Ministério da Educaçao e do Desporto (MEC) [Ministry of Education and Sports]; Minutes from the first meeting on the implementation of the BR-US agreement for education partnership; Archive of Paulo Renato Souza; February 16–18, 1998; Archival Reference: 01/0009208-001; Rio de Janeiro, National Archive of Brazil.
4. For more on the tripartite framework of municipalities, states, and government in Brazil, see Verhine and Dantas (2018).
5. Kjell Eide (1925–2011) was a Norwegian social economist. Between 1961 and 1964, Eide headed the OECD's work on education planning, and he served as the first board chair of the OECD Centre for Educational Research and Innovation (CERI) after its formal establishment in 1970. Eide's affiliation with the OECD education organization continued throughout the 1980s.

6. Dr. Robert M. Rosenzweig, assistant to the Commissioner of Education, to Commissioner of Education, Sterling M. McMurrin; March 29, 1962; Office Files of the Commissioner of Education; Entry No. A1122; Box 531; Record Group 12; National Archives Building, Washington, DC.

7. Harold Howe II, Commissioner of Education; Interview as printed in October–December 1966, Volume IX, Number 4 issue of *The General Electric FORUM*, published by General Electric, Schenectady, New York; Office Files of the Commissioner of Education, Entry No. A1122; Box 381; Record Group 12; National Archives Building, Washington, DC.

8. Harold Howe II, Commissioner of Education; Article and Remarks submitted on January 7, 1966, for publication in *The Nation's Schools*, published in Volume 77, No. 2, February 1966; Office Files of the Commissioner of Education, Entry No. A1122; Box 381; Record Group 12; National Archives Building, Washington, DC.

9. O. J. Caldwell, Assistant Commissioner for International Education, to Dr. J. Boyer Jarvis, Special Assistant to the Commissioner; March 20, 1962; Office Files of the Commissioner of Education, Entry No. A1122; Box 531; Record Group 12; National Archives Building, Washington, DC.

10. O. J. Caldwell, Assistant Commissioner for International Education, to Francis Keppel, Commissioner of Education; April 8, 1963; Office Files of the Commissioner of Education, Entry No. A1122; Box 531; Record Group 12; National Archives Building, Washington, DC.

11. Robert A. Kevan, Deputy Assistant, to Francis Keppel, Commissioner of Education, Summary of Seventh Meeting of the Education Investment Planning (EIP) Group; September 1965; Entry No. A1122; Box 322; Record Group 12; National Archives Building, Washington, DC, p. 3.

12. This point seems to have been a recurring feature of OECD policy recommendations to the United States. In 2011, the OECD explicitly called for clearer governance structures in the United States by emphasizing that "it is important to note that no unit of government at any level of the American education system seems to have the authority of a ministry of education in most of the countries portrayed here—not at the national level, not at the state level and not at the local level." (p. 251) ". . . finding ways to make all the parts work together is essential for producing the best results" (p. 253) (OECD, 2011).

13. OECD Archive in Paris, STP(69)9, Committee for Scientific and Technical Personnel, Educational Policy Reviews, Educational Research and Development in the United States: Examiners Report and Questions, Paris, November 12, 1969.

14. OECD Archive in Paris, STP(69)9, Committee for Scientific and Technical Personnel, Educational Policy Reviews, Educational Research and Development in the United States: Examiners Report and Questions, Paris, November 12, 1969.

15. Harold Howe II, Commissioner of Education; interview as printed in October–December 1966, Volume IX, Number 4 issue of *The General Electric FORUM*, published by General Electric, Schenectady, New York; Office Files of the Commissioner of Education, Entry No. A1122; Box 381; Record Group 12; National Archives Building, Washington, DC.

16. Harold Howe II, Commissioner of Education; interview as printed in October–December 1966, Volume IX, Number 4 issue of *The General Electric FORUM*, published by General Electric, Schenectady, New York; Office Files of the Commissioner of Education, Entry No. A1122; Box 381; Record Group 12; National Archives Building, Washington, DC.

17. Note that The World Bank encouraged and recommended decentralization during these years (Kauko et al., 2016).

18. Pedro Malan, president of the Central Bank of Brazil, to Paulo Renato De Souza, advisor to President-Elect Cardoso; Re: Notes on Economic and Sector Policies Prepared by World Bank Staff; Archive of Paulo Renato de Souza; November 14, 1994; Archival Reference: 01/0009408-015; Rio de Janeiro, National Archive of Brazil.

19. Pedro Malan, president of the Central Bank of Brazil, to Paulo Renato De Souza, advisor to President-Elect Cardoso; Re: Notes on Economic and Sector Policies Prepared by World Bank Staff; Archive of Paulo Renato de Souza; November 14, 1994; Archival Reference: 01/0009408-015; Rio de Janeiro, National Archive of Brazil.

20. Ministério da Educaçao e do Desporto (MEC) [Ministry of Education and Sports]; Proposal to Education Assessment in the context of American Hemisphere; Archive of Paulo Renato Souza; 1997; Archival Reference: 01/0009208-001; Rio de Janeiro, National Archive of Brazil.

21. Ministério da Educaçao e do Desporto (MEC) [Ministry of Education and Sports]; Draft Framework for a US-Brazil Partnership for Education; Archive of Paulo Renato Souza; October 1997; Archival Reference: 01-0009061-008; Rio de Janeiro, National Archive of Brazil.

22. Notably, the first page of the draft has a yellow highlight stating "With contributions from other USG Agencies" (presumably meaning other US government agencies). The United States is thus still utilizing a multitude of agencies on international matters.

23. Ministério da Educaçao e do Desporto (MEC) [Ministry of Education and Sports]; First meeting on the implementation of Brazil-US bilateral agreement; Archive of Paulo Renato Souza; February 1998; Archival Reference: 01/0009208-001; Rio de Janeiro, National Archive of Brazil.

24. Souza, Paulo Renato; Education and Development in Latin America: Rethinking Perceptions and Concepts, speech at BNDES Auditorium, Rio de Janeiro, International seminar of models and policies of development; June 22–23, 1998; Archival Reference: 01/0009092-001; Rio de Janeiro, National Archive of Brazil.

25. Letters exchanged between Paulo Renato Souza, Minister of Education, to Celso Lafer, Minister of Foreign Affairs, on the topic of PISA; September–November 2001; Archival Reference: Dossiê–219.2–Programa Internacional de Avaliação de Alunos (PISA)–Cx. 02; Rio de Janeiro, National Archive of Brazil.

26. The National Institute for Educational Studies and Research, an autonomous government organization responsible for education statistics, including PISA implementation in Brazil since the 1990s.

27. Ministério da Educaçao e do Desporto (MEC) [Ministry of Education and Sports], Maria Helena Guimarães Castro, director of National Institute for Educational Research and Development (INEP), to Andreas Schleicher, director of OECD's Indicators and Analysis Division; On BPC meeting; 2000; Archival Reference: Dossiê–219.2–Programa Internacional de Avaliação de Alunos (PISA)–Cx. 02 (Ano: 1999); Rio de Janeiro, National Archive of Brazil.

28. Souza, Paulo Renato; Education and Development in Latin America: Rethinking Perceptions and Concepts, speech at BNDES Auditorium, Rio de Janeiro, International seminar of models and policies of development; June 22–23, 1998; Archival Reference: 01/0009092-001; Rio de Janeiro, National Archive of Brazil.

29. Letter from Fernando Henrique Cardoso, president of Brazil, to William J. Clinton, president of the United States; Regarding the importance of basic education, Archive of Paulo

Renato Souza; May 1997; Archival Reference: 01-0009059-017; Rio de Janeiro, National Archive of Brazil.

30. Based on the Paulo Renato Souza Collection; 1995 to 1999 (presumed), Archive of Paulo Renato Souza; Archival Reference: 01/0009093; Rio de Janeiro, National Archive of Brazil.

REFERENCES

Auld, E., & Morris, P. (2016). PISA, policy and persuasion: Translating complex conditions into education "best practice." *Comparative Education, 52*(2), 202–229. https://doi.org/10.1080/03050068.2016.1143278

Bartlett, L., & Vavrus, F. (2018). Rethinking the concept of "context" in comparative research. In R. Gorur, S. Sellar, & G. Steiner-Khamsi (Eds.), *World yearbook of education 2019: Comparative methodology in the era of big data and global networks* (pp. 187–201). Routledge.

Bolívar, A. (2011). The dissatisfaction of the losers: PISA public discourse in Ibero-American countries. In M. A. Pereyra, H.-G. Kotthoff, & R. Cowen (Eds.), *PISA under examination: Changing knowledge, changing tests, and changing schools* (pp. 61–74). Sense.

Buchardt, M. (2020). Between "dannelse" and "real life". National Cultural Christianity in a Nordic Cold War education reform process. *IJHE. Bildungsgeschichte. International Journal for the Historiography of Education, 10*(2), 188–202. https://elibrary.utb.de/doi/abs/10.35468/IJHE-2020-02-05

Bürgi, R. (2019). Learning productivity: The European productivity agency—An educational enterprise. In C. Ydesen (Ed.), *The OECD's historical rise in education* (pp. 17–37). Springer. https://doi.org/10.1007/978-3-030-33799-5_2

Castro, M. H. G. (2000). *Brazil's participation in international comparative educational studies and assessments*. Personal Archive.

Centeno, V. G. (2019). The birth of the OECD's education policy area. In C. Ydesen (Ed.), *The OECD's historical rise in education: The formation of a global governing complex* (pp. 63–82). Springer. https://doi.org/10.1007/978-3-030-33799-5_4

Coleman, S., & Collins, P. (2006). *Locating the field space, place and context in anthropology*. Routledge.

Crespo, M., Soares, J. F., & De Mello e Souza, A. (2000). The Brazilian national evaluation system of basic education: Context, process, and impact. *Studies in Educational Evaluation, 26*(2), 105–125. https://doi.org/10.1016/S0191-491X(00)00011-0

Deleuze, G., & Guattari, F. (1987). *A thousand plateaus: Capitalism and schizophrenia*. Athlone.

Edwards Jr., D. B., & Means, A. (2019). Globalization, privatization, marginalization: Mapping and assessing connections and consequences in/through education. *Education Policy Analysis Archives, 27*, 123. https://doi.org/10.14507/epaa.27.5091

Eide, K. (1990). 30 years of educational collaboration in the OECD. International Congress "Planning and management of educational development," Mexico, March 26–30, 1990, 1990. http://unesdoc.unesco.org/images/0008/000857/085725eo.pdf

Elfert, M., & Ydesen, C. (2020). The rise of global governance in education: The OEEC and UNESCO, 1945–1960. In K. Gram-Skjoldager, H. A. Ikonomou, & T. Kahlert (Eds.), *Organizing the world—International organization and the emergence of international public administration 1920–1960* (pp. 73–89). Bloomsbury.

Elfert, M., & Ydesen, C. (2023). Global governance of education: The historical and contemporary entanglements of UNESCO, the OECD and the World Bank. *Educational Governance Research Series* (Series Eds. S. Carney & L. Moos). Springer.

Eyal, G. (2012). Spaces between fields. In P. S. Gorski (Ed.), *Bourdieu and historical analysis* (pp. 158–182). Duke University Press. https://doi.org/10.1215/9780822395430-002

Filho, J. C. D. S. (1993). The recent progress of decentralization and democratic management of education in Brazil. *International Review of Education–Internationale Zeitschrift Fiir Erziehungswissenschaft–Revue Internationale de Peadagogie, 39*(5), 391–403. https://link-springer-com.zorac.aub.aau.dk/content/pdf/10.1007/BF01261590.pdf

Gilman, N. (2003). *Mandarins of the future: Modernization theory in Cold War America*. Johns Hopkins Press.

Kamens, D. H. (2015). A maturing global testing regime meets the world economy: Test scores and economic growth, 1960–2012. *Comparative Education Review, 59*(3), 420–446. https://doi.org/10.1086/681989

Karseth, B., Sivesind, K., & Steiner-Khamsi, G. (Eds.) (2021). *Evidence and expertise in Nordic education policies: A comparative network analysis from the Nordic region*. Palgrave Macmillan.

Kauko, J., Centeno, V. G., Candido, H., Shiroma, E., & Klutas, A. (2016). The emergence of quality assessment in Brazilian basic education Contribution to the open call on "Effects of International Assessments in Education." *European Educational Research Journal, 15*(5), 558–579. https://doi.org/10.1177/1474904116662889

Komatsu, H., & Rappleye, J. (2017). A new global policy regime founded on invalid statistics? Hanushek, Woessmann, PISA, and economic growth. *Comparative Education, 53*, 166–191.

Krejsler, J. B. (2018). The "fear of falling behind regime" embraces school policy state vs federal policy struggles in California and Texas. *International Journal of Qualitative Studies in Education, 31*(5), 393–408. https://documentcloud.adobe.com/link/review?uri=urn:aaid:scds:US:25a39205-5b56-4c4c-8a81-62f2b4d0e011#pageNum=3

Krejsler, J. B. (2020). Imagining school as standards-driven and students as career-ready! A comparative genealogy of US federal and European transnational turns in education policy. In G. Fan & T. Popkewitz (Eds.), *Handbook of education policy studies: School/university, curriculum and assessment* (Vol. 2, pp. 351–383). Springer. https://documentcloud.adobe.com/link/review?uri=urn:aaid:scds:US:4952707a-b8c3-40dd-8cd0-10a856c9efee#pageNum=21

Lawn, M., & Grek, S. (2012). *Europeanizing education: Governing a new policy space*. Symposium Books.

Lewis, S. (2020). *PISA, policy and the OECD: Respatialising global educational governance through PISA for schools* (1st ed.). Springer. https://doi.org/10.1007/978-981-15-8285-1

Lingard, B. (2000). Federalism in schooling since the Karmel Report (1973). Schools in Australia: from modernist hope to postmodernist performativity. *The Australian Educational Researcher, 27*(2), 25–61. https://doi.org/10.1007/bf03219720

McGinn, N., & Pereira, L. (1992). Why states change the governance of education: An historical comparison of Brazil and the United States. *Comparative Education, 28*(2), 167–180. http://www.jstor.org/stable/3099429

McGuinn, P. (2006). *No Child Left Behind and the transformation of federal education policy 1965–2005*. University Press of Kansas.

Moraes Valença, M. (1998). The lost decade and the Brazilian government's response in the 1990s. *Source: The Journal of Developing Areas, 33*(1), 1–52.

Moreno-Salto, I., & Robertson, S. L. (2021). On the "life of numbers" in governing Mexico's education system: A multi-scalar account of the OECD's PISA. *Globalisation, Societies and Education*, 19(2), 1–15. https://doi.org/10.1080/14767724.2021.1880882

Mundy, K., Green, A., Lingard, B., & Verger, A. (2016). Introduction: The globalization of education policy—Key approaches and debates. In K. Mundy, A. Green, B. Lingard, & A. Verger (Eds.), *The handbook of global education policy* (pp. 1–20). John Wiley & Sons. https://doi.org/10.1002/9781118468005.ch0

Niemann, D., & Martens, K. (2018). Soft governance by hard fact? The OECD as a knowledge broker in education policy. *Global Social Policy*, 18(3), 267–283. https://doi.org/10.1177/14680 18118794076

OECD. (2011). Lessons from PISA for the United States, strong performers and successful reformers in education. OECD. https://documentcloud.adobe.com/link/review?uri= urn:aaid:scds:US:867548f9-b8ab-415b-825e-4cf4d10f70bf#pageNum=1

Ørskov, F. F. (2019). The OECD's historical rise in education. In C. Ydesen (Ed.), *The OECD's historical rise in education* (pp. 85–107). Springer. https://doi.org/10.1007/978-3-030-33799-5

Papadopoulos, G. S. (1994). *Education 1960–1990: The OECD perspective*. OECD historical series. Organisation for Economic Co-operation and Development.

Ramirez, F. O., Luo, X., Schofer, E., & Meyer, J. W. (2006). Student achievement and national economic growth. *American Journal of Education*, 113(1), 1–29. https://doi.org/10.1086/506492

Robertson, S. L. (2018). Researching global education policy: Angles in/on/out. In A. Verger, M. Novelli, & H. K. Altinyelken (Eds.), *Global education policy and international development: New agendas, issues and policies* (2nd ed.) (pp. 35–54). Bloomsbury.

Schwartzman, S. (2013). Uses and abuses of education assessment in Brazil. *Prospects*, 43, 269–288. https://doi.org/10.1007/s11125-013-9275-9

Silva, G. T. (2019). International cooperation from the perspective of INEP agents: The OECD and Brazilian public education, 1996–2006. In C. Ydesen (Ed.), *The OECD's historical rise in education: The formation of a global governing complex* (pp. 109–131). Springer. https://doi.org/10.1007/978-3-030-33799-5_6

Sobe, N., & Kowalczyk, J. (2012). The problem of context in comparative education research. *ECPS - Educational, Cultural and Psychological Studies*, 3(6), 55–74. https://doi.org/10.7358/ecps-2012-006-sobe

Sobe, N., & Kowalczyk, J. (2013). Exploding the cube: Revisioning "context" in the field of comparative education. *Current Issues in Comparative Education*, 16(1), 6–12.

Stromquist, N. P. (2016). Using regression analysis to predict countries' economic growth: Illusion and fact in education policy. *Real-World Economics Review*, 76, 65–74.

UNESCO. (2017). *Global education monitoring report: Accountability in education*. UNESCO.

Verger, A., Fontdevila, C., & Parcerisa, L. (2019). Constructing school autonomy with accountability as a global policy model: A focus on OECD's governance mechanisms. In C. Ydesen (Ed.), *The OECD's historical rise in education: The formation of a global governing complex* (pp. 219–243). Springer. https://doi.org/10.1007/978-3-030-33799-5_11

Verhine, R. E., & Dantas, L. M. V. (2018). Brazil: Problematics of the tripartite federal framework. In M. Carnoy, I. Froumin, O. Leshukov, & S. Marginson (Eds.), *Higher education in federal countries: A comparative study* (pp. 212–257). Sage. https://ebookcentral.proquest.com/lib/aalborguniv-ebooks/reader.action?docID=5494712

Vinovskis, M. A. (2015). *From a nation at risk to No Child Left Behind: National education goals and the creation of federal education policy*. Teachers College Press.

Ydesen, C. (2021). "Crafting globalization: A Bourdieusian historical approach to studying international organizations and global governance in education." In S. Robinson, J. Ernst, O. J. Thomasson, and K. Larsen (Eds.), *Societal change and transforming fields: Pierre Bourdieu in studies of organization* (pp. 134–154). Routledge.

Ydesen, C., & Bomholt, A. (2020). Accountability implications of the OECD's economistic approach to education: A historical case analysis. *Journal of Educational Change*, 21, 37–57. https://doi.org/10.1007/s10833-019-09355-1

Ydesen, C., & Dorn, S. (2022). The no child left behind act in the global architecture of educational accountability. *History of Education Quarterly*, 62(3), 268–290. doi:10.1017/heq.2022.11

CHAPTER 24

PLAYING GOD

*Education Data Visualizations and the
Art of World-Making*

SOTIRIA GREK

INTRODUCTION

INDICATORS have become ubiquitous devices for monitoring and assessing performance, as well as for supporting the implementation of social and environmental reforms around the world (e.g., the United Nations' 2030 Agenda for Sustainable Development). Most notably, the introduction of the Sustainable Development Goals (SDGs) in 2015 has consolidated the "data-driven" nature of contemporary approaches to grand challenges in the global public policy space (Merry, 2016). The aspirational and transformative policy agenda behind the SDGs is grounded on a complex interplay of infrastructures of measurement (Merry, 2019) that concerns a variety of monitoring and steering processes via a range of calculative governance tools. While the reliance on quantification has long been a defining feature of international development goals (Grek, 2020; Rottenburg, 2009; Shore & Wright, 2015), the SDGs unlike their predecessors—the Millennium Development Goals—introduced innovative qualities to the development and monitoring of cooperation in global governance. The SDGs seek (at least in theory) to promote participatory and consensus-driven processes that foreground the country-led nature of this agenda as opposed to the more top-down setup of their predecessors (Fukuda-Parr & McNeil, 2019).

As the global governance space is seen to become more participatory (Barry, 2012; Biermann et al., 2012), the role of indicators is evolving to not only assess the performance of countries but also encourage collective action to promote global solutions to global problems. The emerging paradigm of global governance declares the turn toward country "ownership" of how performance information is produced, communicated, and acted upon (Fukuda-Parr, 2016) and, crucially, reflects the increasing sensitivity toward issues of data "democratization" and the pressures to "decolonize" global governance (Quijano, 2007; Rottenburg, 2009). These critiques highlight how the historical, cultural, and sociological underpinnings of eminently Western technologies of quantification such as indicators can contribute to the "data colonization" of the Global North upon the Global South (Arora, 2016). In this chapter, I investigate how the discourse of participation embedded in the SDGs and the pressures to decolonize global performance measurement influences how data are visualized and communicated to heterogeneous global stakeholders. In so doing, I explore how performance data are visualized by key global actors to encourage country participation in transnational performance measurement initiatives.

Extant research has explored in depth the political work of numbers (Espeland & Sauder, 2007; Pollock et al., 2018; Sauder & Espeland, 2009; Slager & Gond, 2020) in different organizational contexts. However, the workings of rankings are particularly underinvestigated in settings where the very notions of "winners and losers" and the hierarchical ordering of performance are politically and ethically sensitive (Bandola-Gill, 2020; Bhuta et al., 2018). In this study, we detail how and why education data produced within the broader measurement infrastructure of the SDGs are visualized in interactive, indirect, and multivocal formats. The focus of the chapter is not on the production of the quantitative measures that constitute an indicator or how such indicators are used; rather, we investigate how performance data are visualized to communicate the political and rhetorical objectives of key actors involved in global performance measurement and monitoring initiatives.

This effort to unpack the criteria that inform the visualization of rankings in global public policy builds on current research conducted as part of the European Research Council Grant funded project "International Organisations and the Rise of a Global Metrological Field" (ERC-2016-StG, 2017–2022). A twofold methodological approach has been used; it seeks to capture the "best practices" and "standards" guiding the visualization experts as well as how these are translated into material practice. First, I contextualize the making of data visualizations by analyzing the rhetoric of the white papers and guideline documents produced by the American visualization software company Tableau. Tableau is a key player in the interactive data visualization IT landscape and is emerging as the "standard" to produce visualizations by key global players such as the World Bank, the Organization for Economic Cooperation and Development (OECD), and United Nations Educational, Scientific and Cultural Organization (UNESCO), to mention but a few. Contextualizing the analysis from the prism of Tableau's strategies and practices greatly assists in entering the rhetoric of contemporary approaches to information visualization. Secondly, I conduct a visual analysis of a data visualization "storyboard" that focuses on girls' education in Africa. This analysis shows that interactive and storytelling visual formats allow performance data to become more malleable, customizable, and—more importantly—"softer" in their messaging. Unlike static league tables, data storytelling leaves more room for users' interpretative predispositions; this may mitigate the crude reactivity pressures resulting from being seen as a bad performer; on the other hand, it increases trust in numbers and the broader acceptance of data production and monitoring in global challenges.

This chapter analyzes the ways that visual storytelling moves performance measurement away from league table formats toward a much more "inclusive" mode that intends to avoid disenfranchising countries of the Global South. The impellent pressures to decolonize global governance and the use of performance measures (Arora, 2016; Rottenburg, 2009) have profoundly affected how data are visualized in this setting and, thus, how they convey more ambiguous meanings that seek to balance the clarity of the message and its political acceptability. The "soft" governance via data in this context is linked to how their visual configuration is designed to increase participation and seek collective problem identification and action. Hence, the visualization of data has become a crucial rhetorical locus for international organizations—such as the OECD and the World Bank—to showcase the horizontal relationships between countries as equal participants in the global sustainability agendas they are seeking to promote.

Education Data Visualizations: Decolonizing Development While Monitoring Performance

In this chapter, I explore how data visualizations operate in the policy field of education. In public policy, the hierarchical ordering of performance is frequently concealed behind alluring visual artifacts in a variety of formats, such as interactive data maps, dashboards, and playful graphs (Lafortune et al., 2018). However, what is the reason for the increased use of such interactive visuals in, for example, several of the SDGs? What are the characteristics of these visualizations that make them more attractive to the experts and brokers of such large transnational governing agendas? Answers to these questions may be found in the move toward the "decolonization" of global governance and "data democratization" (Fukuda-Parr & McNeil, 2019).

Indeed, the increased sensitivity toward "decolonizing" development and global performance measurement emerged in response to critiques of the "coloniality" of knowledge-making (Quijano, 2007) that is implied in quantitative approaches to knowledge production. Such approaches are frequently criticized for being based on neoliberal ideals and on a Western understanding of rationality that enforces and glorifies competition among nations and institutions (Best, 2014). Recent research has condemned the "data colonization" of the Global North upon the Global South, which can be seen as combining "the predatory extractive practices of historical colonialism with the abstract quantification methods of computing" (Couldry & Mejias, 2019, p. 337); this is of particular concern for scholars of the expansion and commodification of big data in the Global South (Arora, 2016). As a result, initiatives aimed at systematizing the collection and use of country performance data could reinforce how the Global South remains at the "bottom of the data pyramid" (Arora, 2016).

In the case of large international learning assessments, country performance measurement has been shown to create the conditions for "southering," which suggests that "the presentation of the results as tables and world maps can result in exposing countries of the South to a pronounced deficit perspective" (Grotlüschen & Buddeberg, 2020, p. 1). These findings highlight how traditional, static rankings and league tables could systematically alienate the Global South, thereby exposing international organizations to the risk of being seen as new colonial powers. Recent studies have started to document how global actors are prone to sacrificing the robustness of their data validation practices to avoid disenfranchising specific countries (Grek, 2020) and that visualization practices are sensitive toward these pressures (Lafortune et al., 2018). However, this line of enquiry is still in its infancy and offers substantial potentialities for development for the study of data visualizations. In what follows, through the discourse and visual analysis of some of the rankings used in global poverty and the measurement of well-being, we investigate the visual and rhetorical strategies that influential global actors use to communicate the outcomes of performance measurement initiatives.

METHODOLOGICAL CONSIDERATIONS

A Visual and Discursive Analysis of Rankings

This chapter focuses on an analysis of how statistical data leverage on the visual semiotic mode to move beyond the crude reactivity mechanisms prompted by league tables and to convey meanings and opportunities for engagement to their users. A mode is "a socially shaped and culturally given semiotic resource for making meaning" (Kress, 2009, p. 79). The visual mode is in this case instantiated in the use of colors, shapes, lines, and a variety of interactive visual forms in rankings. As Meyer et al. (2018) argue, the visual mode has distinctive semiotic features (i.e., it enables particular forms of meaning construction), cognitive features (i.e., is processed differently than other modes, such as text) and reflects the cultural features of specific settings (i.e., the norms of a discourse community). The affordances of the visual mode not only make its perception more immediate than text or numbers but "the lack of a clear visual 'syntax' makes visual meaning fluid and indeterminate and strongly dependent on the viewers interpretative predispositions" (Meyer et al., 2018, p. 396). The visual mode can play a variety of argumentative functions: for example, it can offer clues for narrative building; it can construct fluid relationships between its constitutive elements and thus allow space for different interpretations; it can captivate the users and materialize complex ideas in a compelling manner (Greenwood et al., 2019; Meyer et al., 2018). In so doing, the visual mode can also play an implicit role in naturalizing and endowing value-laden ideas with matter-of-factual properties, thereby augmenting their rhetorical power and perceived authority.

The analysis of the interplay of different visual elements—such as colors, icons, headings, and graphics—allows us to unpack the rankings' rhetorical functions (see Quattrone, 2017). Some of the rhetorical functions connected to the use of visual items include their roles in guiding the user through an interface, illustrate relationships between elements, provide context and tone, focus attention, and increase the impact of specific messages (Greenwood et al., 2018). More specifically, visual analysis allows us to decode the rhetorical strategies deployed by the ranking makers and highlights how ranking visualizations are a form of expressive action that influences users' interpretations. While the commensuration and classificatory power of a ranking that relies on an orthodox league table format can be similar to that of a dynamic and interactive ranking visualization, this study foregrounds how the latter offers opportunities for engagement and interpretation that are not possible in grid-like, static formats.

From this perspective, visuals are value-laden materializations of specific visions of the world that make visible (or invisible) possible realities (Latour, 1986). Analyzing data visually and discursively foregrounds how visualization is not a soulless depiction but the outcome of a process of work:

> And it is the site for the construction of and depiction of social difference. To understand a visualization is thus to inquire into its provenance and the social work it does. It is to note its principles of exclusion and inclusion, to [. . .] decode the hierarchies and differences that it naturalises. And it is also to analyse the ways in which authorship is constructed or concealed and the sense of audience is realised. (Fyfe & Law, 1992, p. 1)

Data visualizations are an ideal site to explore these issues as they are largely made quantitatively and denote arithmetic values while relying systematically on visual codes (through shapes, colors, and lines) that connote social, moral, and political values. The visual and discursive analysis of data visualizations is an attempt to decode their constitutive elements in order to make sense of the ways visual elements work metaphorically and evocatively in the making of new ways of *seeing and knowing* the world. The underlying contention that inspires this approach is that "*social change is [. . .] a change in the regime of re-presentation*" (Fyfe & Law, 1992, p. 2, emphasis in original). The politically, ethically, and morally salient features of global performance measurement initiatives make this approach especially fitting to the study of data visualizations.

Data Sources and Analysis

To explore the formats and rhetoric of data visualizations, the chapter relies on two data sources: the critdiscourse analysis of guiding documents of an American data visualization company (Tableau) and the visual analysis of the gender inequalities in education in Africa. The case of Tableau is used in order to explore how visualization software and design companies understand and promote the work they do at the global stage.

Subsequently, the visual analysis of data explored this set of strategic principles in practice. The combination of these two methods allowed for an exploration of both the intentionality behind the data visualizations (i.e., the strategies employed by the data visualization experts) as well as the products of the work.

Tableau is a producer of interactive dashboards, the main purpose of which is to "help people see and understand data" (Tableau, 2020b). Tableau makes "analysing data fast and easy, beautiful and useful" (Tableau, 2020b). Although one among many data visualization companies that emerged and grew during the last couple of decades, Tableau appears as a leading producer not only of visuals but also "know-how" in this area, as they published over 100 "Whitepapers" (Tableau, 2020c). These publications fulfil a double function: first, they present Tableau's work in its different facets; and second, they market these solutions to organizations that seek expertise on data visualization. For this chapter, 50 of those "Whitepapers" were downloaded and examined. Critical discourse analysis (CDA) was applied to 16 selected Whitepapers based on their relevance to performance measurement and global governance. CDA is a particularly apt method for the analysis of data visualizations because it sees their discursive analysis as a key aspect of how certain understandings of the world are shaped and perpetuated (Fairclough, 1995; Wodak & Meyer, 2001). Hence, the analysis of the Tableau documents is useful for, on the one hand, showing what is technically possible, while on the other, explaining what the principles and perspectives of those designing the production of these visuals are. As such, it offers the necessary context for the analysis for the sources at the center of our study; that is, the analysis of ranking visualizations themselves.

ANALYSIS OF FINDINGS

In what follows, the section begins with a discourse analysis of the documents discussing the principles and guidelines employed by the experts that produce ranking visualizations for key actors in global policy. Specifically, I investigate the ethos that guides these visualization specialists and the values that inspire the work they perform for their clients in the global policy area. Second, we move to the visual analysis of data storytelling to explore its central quality as "soft" governing tool—namely, its objective to move beyond the identification of "winners and losers" in global performance assessments.

The Visualizers' Work: Interactive Data and Self-Service Analytics

Tableau describes its mission as delivering user-friendly data "for the people" (Tableau, 2020a), and this guiding principle is reflected in the values that inspire their design of interactive visualizations. According to Tableau's white papers, the central quality of visualizations should be their interactivity (Krensky, 2014). Interactivity is placed in stark opposition with the "old worldly" static presentation of authoritative data visualizations targeted solely at experts. Tableau proclaims the end of that era: "The age of 'look but don't touch' is over" (Krensky, 2014, p. 1). This principle is reflected in the interactive nature of data visualizations—whose benefits are "too manifest to ignore" (Krensky 2014, p. 7). Interactive data visualizations are assumed by Tableau to allow for more collaboration and dissemination. They are seen to prompt questions and reflection, improve understanding of complex datasets, and reduce the risk of "gut-level decision-making" that is dictated by the lack of understanding of data (Krensky, 2014). Furthermore, interactive visualization, according to Tableau, is the "panacea" for the information overload that individuals are experiencing in a data-driven society, as it

> Drives improvements in the analytical experience: [. . .] adopters are more likely than static visualizers to have improved their speed of decision and trust in underlying data [. . .] (it) fosters user development and engagement [. . .] Adopters of interactive data visualization have a more satisfied user base: Happy users are more productive and more likely to explore data and uncover new insights. (Krensky, 2014, pp. 7–8)

This evangelical perspective assumes that the ease of use will offer greater satisfaction, allow for more inquisitive approaches, and even increase one's intuition of possible new questions and solutions. At the same time, crucially, interactivity is also assumed to increase the *trust* in the data that sit behind the visual interfaces (Krensky, 2014).

The second key quality of interactive visualizations, according to Tableau, is their ostensible capacity to create new audiences that go beyond the traditional technocratic experts:

> There will always be a number of individuals who are power users. [. . .] For *most people*, however, that would be counterproductive. Instead, they *benefit from having data organised around specific topics*, with an emphasis on the most meaningful metrics. This approach is especially *critical when sharing data with the public, where little can be assumed about an end user's technical or subject matter expertise*. [. . .] The concept of data-driven decision making assumes that decision-makers have access to the right data, not to every available data set. (Tableau, 2020b, p. 4, emphasis added)

Perhaps the key term used in this document is the vision of creating "*self-service analytics*" (Tableau, 2020b, p. 6). According to Tableau, a key design principle is that little expertise is needed to interpret their interactive visualizations. To make information accessible to non-experts, an interface needs to offer cues that will provide an *intuitive* way to interact with the data. Tableau's interfaces aim to

> Enable stakeholders to perform basic analytical tasks, such as filtering views, adjusting parameters, quick calculations and drilling down to examine underlying data—all through an intuitive user interface that requires no special expertise. (Tableau, 2020b, p. 9)

However, the diversity of uses and features does not mean the possibilities are unlimited, as even the most interactive visualizations are grounded on the same baseline of a common dataset:

> Such discussions are much deeper and productive when everyone involved is looking at the same set of data—what is often called *a single source of truth*. (Tableau, 2020b, p. 9, emphasis added)

Hence, while the adaptable visual interface entices user involvement and encourages the manifestation of one's preferences in the construction of their view of the data, the ultimate "source of truth" is still the data *behind* the visual. As such, the personalization of data interfaces is not indefinite—visualizations are only as flexible as the software infrastructure and the underpinning data.

Finally, the emphasis is placed on the creation of one's own "data-worlds" through experimentation and enjoyment through interactive interfaces. This last point is key: A certain level of *edutainment* is necessary to engage users in what has traditionally been seen to be a prerogative of technocratic experts. According to a Tableau Senior Executive:

> We create a data culture that relies on language, is flexible and adaptive and is shared with others [. . .] we promote governance through empowerment that relies on learning and fun. (Jewett, 2019)

Such an explorative way of working with data implies that the interactive performance monitoring tools are trying to disguise their capacity to "name and shame" the entities they assess; as we saw in the quotation above, they aim to "empower," not to judge. They aim to be "flexible" and "adaptive," allowing a seemingly reflexive, developmental, and multivocal understanding of the data by all those involved. However, the "single source of truth"—and thus a hierarchical ordering of performance—still lurks beneath these playful interfaces. Hence, the affordances of interactive data visualizations also play an implicit naturalization work as, by prescribing specific set of interaction possibilities, they also divert attention away from the value-laden message that these artifacts seek to convey and the complex and messy reality they seek to connote visually and numerically.

What emerges from Tableau's documents is an effort to popularize the use of interactive visualizations. The users are encouraged to engage with the visualizations and explore the dimensions of data that are most compelling to them. As such, the visualizations become engines for production of multiple interpretations and lenses on data. In what follows, we analyze a series of ranking visualizations that were either produced with Tableau (e.g., in the case of the OECD) or were strongly inspired by its ethos, which is becoming the "standard" in the data visualization landscape.

Thus, the analysis of the design principles discussed earlier is central to understanding how data are visualized to operate as tools of global governance. The rankers translate these "industry standards" into classifications of countries and their performance in achieving societal goals—for example, eradicating poverty or improving gender equality. As I will show in the remaining section, the focus here is not on identifying "winners" and "losers," rather on balancing the clarity of message of the ranking and its political acceptability. In what follows, we explore the "soft" governance function of ranking visualizations by detailing how the design criteria of interactivity, discoverability, and personalization identified in Tableau's best practices are employed to moderate the political risk of ranking countries in league table format.

Visualization as Storytelling in Education

> Each of us walks around with a bunch of stories in our heads about the way the world works. And whatever we confront, whatever facts are presented to us, whatever data we run into, we filter through these stories. And if the data agrees with our stories, we'll let it in and if it doesn't, we'll reject it. So, if you are trying to give people new information that they don't have, they've got to have a story in their head that will let the data in. (Goodman, 2016)

This section will examine storytelling as an increasingly popular form of visualization in the education and development world. Storytelling in public policymaking has emerged in recent years as a powerful tool for policy makers and researchers to communicate complex messages in order to reach larger audiences. Either used as a knowledge brokering tool in negotiations among policy actors, or weaponized as an advocacy medium in activism, visual storytelling uses the essential elements of story-making across time and space: It is comprised by main characters, a setting, a plot, and a moral, in order to help make causal relationships apparent and to frame "facts" and data within particular narratives.

Crucially, the aim of visual storytelling, as we will see next, is less about communicating specific data fast. Rather, it relates to the making of larger frames of political values, where data, numbers, and performance monitoring via country rankings are only one of the building blocks of data "world-making." Instead of rational and objective, visual storytelling is wholly intepretivist in nature and function. Despite the appearance of an objective rationality purported by numbers, stories are meant to be used as tools of data translation. Their function is to construct the narrative frame within which a carefully selected data pool can offer objective comparative country and regional performance. At the same time, however, the comparison is carefully massaged and shaped in a way that a main problem is addressed, key challenges are discussed, and, usually, some solutions are offered.

Data storytelling is particularly interesting for the analysis of knowledge production for governing. Instead of concealing the in-built biases and assumptions that all objectivity-making requires, it does precisely the opposite. That is, it works with people's engrained worldviews and attempts to shape and reshape them by pressing toward the making of new political problems and political values. As the following analysis will show, although the basis of the *Left Behind* visual is the ranked comparison of African countries and world regions, data and the graphs are simply the setting of the story; the characters, the plot, and the moral message are the ones at center stage. This is not "facts versus values" evidence-making; the effect is, in fact, almost antithetical to the cold rationality of statistical numbers. Data storytelling uses facts *for* value-making and, in doing so, exploits the subjective and contingent nature of knowledge-making.

Left Behind focuses on girls' education in Africa.[1] It was produced for the UNESCO Institute for Statistics by Function, a data visualization studio based in Montreal. Its sources primarily draw upon administrative data from UIS. The visual focuses on the gender inequality problem and, in particular, the nonparticipation of African girls in education (see Figure 24.1).

The data visualization follows very closely the main features of a story; in fact, by using an introduction, as well as specific separate sections, the visual resembles closely the familiar feel and structure of a book. Its title page is very minimal; it offers a title and a subtitle with the background image of a girl reading, while sitting on the ground and leaning back on a wooden structure. More so than the actual image, the color palette used for the image immediately travels the audience to the dry, hot, dusty African plains. The image therefore follows a very common stylistic feature of art history; that is, it creates a sense of exoticism. In doing so, through the subtle connotations which align this one with numerous other stories about worlds distant from the West, the image has already served toward framing this story within well-known and classic art historical framings of picturing the "Other." These are not just any schools, any girls, or any countries: this is Africa (see Figure 24.2).

FIGURE 24.1 Front webpage of Left Behind visualization.

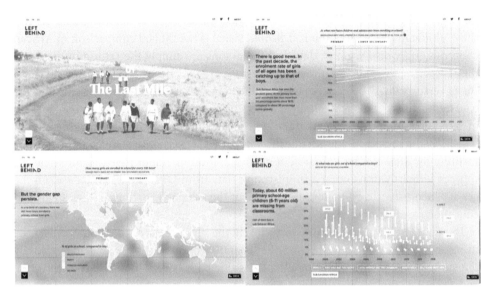

FIGURE 24.2 Snapshots of Left Behind visualization (1).

Against a slightly hazy background (a feature that continues in the whole visualization), the title fonts are simple, medium-sized, and white. There is a certain softness and stillness in the image, as we enter the world of the little girl reading. Despite the crisis in gender equity in education in Africa, the image travels us without any judgments or flashy messages. The title page offers the destination and the focus, while simultaneously creating the sensation of a slow, earthy, hot land where kids still play outside barefoot. The introductory section is structured in a very similar manner: questions ("What would your life be like if you only had 5 years of schooling?"), answers ("For some African girls, this is the most education they can expect, and they are the lucky ones"), and statements of crisis and hope ("Across the region, millions of girls are out of school and many will never set foot in a classroom"; "The world has renewed its promise to the millions of girls who have been left behind"). All the text is presented sentence by sentence as one scrolls through the visual, with the background images of girls in classrooms, in the same light creamy, dusky color hues.

The rest of the visualization is structured in the format of book chapters, always introduced with a title page (01. The Last Mile, 02. Barriers, 0.3 Persistence of Illiteracy among Women, 0.4 Poor school conditions, 05. More Teachers needed, especially women). Each "chapter" presents relevant data in maps or graph formats. The different pages and graphs are all interactive—they do comparisons of African countries or world regions over time or in ratios. The interactive graphs and maps can be manipulated by viewers through simple movements of the mouse over them. There is nothing extraordinary about these graphs; they follow the common characteristics of contemporary visualizations, following simple lines, laconic explanatory text, and modern design (see Figure 24.3).

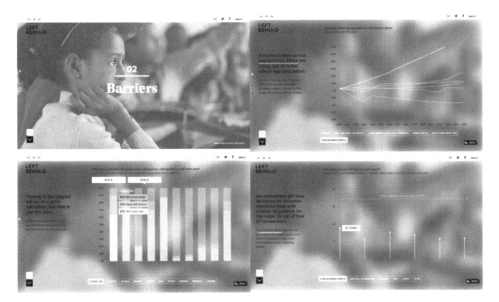

FIGURE 24.3 Snapshots of Left Behind visualization (2).

What is, however, much more interesting when one has a closer look is that all the data charts, maps, and graphs are very carefully chosen and put together: Some compare selected African countries (depending on the question, these countries are different every time but they are usually low in number). As a result, similar to the image, the data discussed are also fairly minimal, perhaps just a snapshot. Some graphs compare sub-Saharan Africa with other continents; and others just focus on simple ratios, between literate and illiterate women. Although all data can be accessed by clicking on the black rectangular box at the bottom right of the page, what is striking in every one of these graphs is the careful selection of comparative country or regional data. Although there is clear ranking of countries depending on how well or badly they perform in relation to gender equity, the ranking as a visual, quick, and blunt manifestation of best and worst performance is completely abandoned here. Although there are better and worse country cases (this is the function of any graph and therefore of these graphs, too), the comparison here only serves as an illustration of the wider political problem of gender inequity—this is further enhanced by the persistent alternating of country comparisons with world comparisons.

An analysis of those data visuals immediately reveals a range of differences and similarities: There is a balance of change and stability. Clarity is paramount. There is no alarmism, although negative performance is being reported, too. Although the main character remains the same (i.e., African girls, women, or teachers), the plot is very carefully crafted in order to move from setting the context (0.1 The Last Mile: "there are good news... but the gender gap persists"), to a discussion of all challenges (in "chapters" 2, 3, 4) to the relatively uplifting final section on the necessity to have a larger women teacher workforce. Finally, despite what otherwise would have been read as a major inequity crisis, the data visualization ends the story with nothing less than a "happy ending": "The good news is that the international community has not forgotten these girls." The intention here is for the visual not to paralyze but fill its viewers with optimism and positive resolve to tackle the problem; and although the text suggests that the SDGs have pledged to decrease inequality, it asks the viewer to also "have their say" (see Figure 24.4).

This is perhaps the first step in constructing actionable knowledge: enlist one's audience not only to read and understand, but to share their experience of the African girls' education story and mobilize others. Interestingly, the visual does not do any bullet-point language, like most traditional print reports do. While it offers a plethora of interactive information, allowing comparison of performances and progress over time, and although it digests data through some short statements in every page of the analysis, it finishes off with a simple question: "What do you think it will take to leave no girl behind?"

This question in many senses is at the crux of this paper's argument: rather than finish off with a definitive memorable statement, or a killer graph, apt for the severity of the issue, *Left Behind* ends with inviting the viewer to think for themselves; that is, to weigh the evidence offered and contextualize the issue within their own story-worlds and experiences. Needless to say, this does not mean that careful selection of data and arguments has not taken place here, and that all interpretations and questions are open: quite the contrary. It is precisely because of the meticulous orchestration of text, image, and data, as well as the precise crafting of the plot, that this kind of engagement can be invited. In reality, the question is primarily a rhetorical one: These are the multiple worlds that data visualizations fabricate, worlds into which specific and precise policy facts do not matter as much as the interpretive possibilities data (and especially an effective visual data story) can open up.

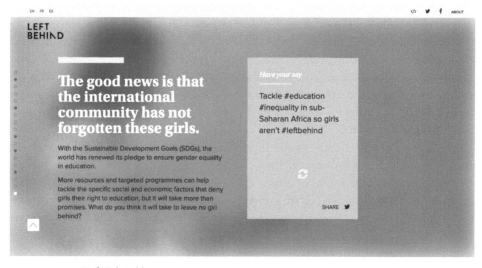

FIGURE 24.4 Left Behind last page.

DISCUSSION

Education performance data are generated in an institutional and political context that is shaped by ever-expanding infrastructures of measurement (Merry, 2019) and pressures to decolonize global governance (Rottenburg, 2009). This context is not only highly fragmented by the growing number of actors, but it is also participatory, as it requires constant mediation and brokerage (Bandola-Gill, 2020; Grek, 2020). The extant literature has privileged the analysis of rankings and performance league tables in the consumer economy (e.g., Jeacle & Carter, 2011; Pollock & D'Adderio, 2012; Pollock et al., 2018) or in commodified higher education domains such as business schools and law schools (e.g., Elsbach & Kramer, 1996; Espeland & Sauder, 2007; Free et al., 2009; Hazelkorn, 2011). However, in the context of global governance, rankings are aimed at producing different organizational and political effects. Focusing the "hearts and minds" of those who participate in global performance measurement initiatives requires intense transnational coordination. Furthermore, an increasingly pressing issue is the development of measurement approaches that avoid alienating low-performing countries by continuing to pressurize them to conform with "best practices" from elsewhere. International organizations and other key global players purport to design their measurement programs following equity paradigms, where all the countries—and especially the developing ones—are seen as leading on tackling the global challenges (Best, 2014).

Against this backdrop, the production of education performance data occupies a liminal space between the rigid assessment of a league table and participatory paradigms of global governance. It has to be produced in a way that navigates political pressures while communicating the urgency of the education problems as truly global—affecting the entire international community. A challenge is to leverage the power of current monitoring projects to entice participation in their measurement programs (Desrosières, 2015; Le Grand, 2003, 2007) while keeping at bay their documented capacity to trigger competitive behaviors that would be dysfunctional in the global policy space (e.g., a sense of zero-sum competition, gaming, cherry-picking, or the manipulation of data—see Espeland & Sauder, 2007; Merry 2016; Slager & Gond, 2020). Arguably, the global "need" for quantification and performance measurement has never been as perceivably legitimate as it is since the introduction of the SDGs framework. Simultaneously, there has never been as much attention paid to how global performance measurement may be a form of "southering" (Grotlüschen & Buddeberg, 2020) that presents developing countries as regions of persistent deficit, under the surveillance of Western institutions through different forms of quantification (Arora, 2016).

Performance measurements in this setting have to reflect multiple orders of worth that coexist, sometimes overlap, and potentially clash (Stark, 2009, 2020; see Ferraro et al., 2015). The "old" format of ranking countries—the league table—does not seem to be suitable to capture this multiplicity, as its main rhetorical focus is on the clarity of communication (at least at face value) of the ranking and in the immediate visibility of performance. The rankings' "new" visual formats seek to address this tension through their technical features and visual configuration in interactive dashboard templates. The qualities of interactivity, engagement, and trust are essential in heterarchical and polycentric settings such as the global governance space, where different "hierarchies and orderings intertwine and reproduce, none of which can claim to be dominant or even to be fixed" (Esposito & Stark, 2019, p. 15). Since no single order shared by all exists in such a space, the designers of rankings do not necessarily have to order performance hierarchically in an explicit manner anymore. Our findings highlighted how the maps of poverty or the interactive visuals of poverty over time indirectly rank performance and background specific countries from their visual representation. These visuals seek to achieve more "equitable" and politically acceptable messaging by "softening" the rankings' communicative power and appeal. Instead of ordering according to achievements, the visualizations increase the visibility of areas of concern and potential intervention without seeking to "shame" explicitly any country.

Through interactivity, the message of the data visual is not simply "fed" to the user; rather, although the messaging remains focused and clear, the user is also given the tools to engage with the digital interface. By "playing" with the interactive formats, the users can "play God": They can create their own views of the data via comparisons across time and space that they select.

This is, in many senses, a new form of "world-making": as argued by Latour (1986), visualizations stabilize specific versions of reality; they can make impossible things realistic and make possible objects more probable than others. In this chapter, discussing the *Left Behind* visualization, I explored how its interactivity not only allows for exploration of multiple aspects of the data but also enables their customization, by allowing the user to choose different value dimensions in accordance to their own preferences. They are conceived and designed (as evident in the discourse analysis of Tableau's white papers) to allow the user to create *their own data*. Consequently, they assess different versions of reality as shaped (as least to a degree) by the users. As such, interactive data visuals position the user in the role of the creator whose own version of the world is being assessed.

Further research in data visualizations needs to examine their qualities and effects in other policy arenas and contexts, explore the actors behind them (both those who produce them, but crucially those who commission and use them), and study their effects. Ultimately, if the governance of global, complex, and intertwined challenges—such as the current COVID-19 pandemic—unites us in needing to find common solutions, then more consensual approaches will have to be secured, approaches that go beyond divisions between North and South, or winners and losers. What is the future of the production of performance data and their visuals in this fluid, risky, and interdependent world? The events of the last couple of years suggest that any kind of forecasting is futile; only further research will tell.

Acknowledgments

This manuscript is part of a project that has received funding from the European Research Council (ERC) under the European Union's Horizon 2020 research and innovation program, under grant agreement no. 715125 METRO (ERC-2016-StG) ("International Organisations and the Rise of a Global Metrological Field," 2017–2022, PI: Sotiria Grek). Some of the theoretical and methodological discussion has been adapted from the author's previous article (with J. Bandola-Gill and M. Ronzani) (2021), "Beyond Winners and Losers: Ranking Visualizations as Alignment Devices in Global Public Policy*," In Ringel, L., Espeland, W., Sauder, M. and Werron, T. (Eds.) *Worlds of Rankings* (Research in the Sociology of Organizations, Vol. 74) (pp. 27–52). Emerald Publishing Limited, Bingley. https://doi.org/10.1108/S0733-558X20210000074027.

Note

1. http://uis.unesco.org/apps/visualisations/no-girl-left-behind/

References

Arora, P. (2016). The bottom of the data pyramid: Big data and the Global South. *International Journal of Communication, 10*, 1681–1699.

Bandola-Gill, J. (2020). The legitimacy of experts in policy: Navigating technocratic and political accountability in the case of global poverty governance. *Evidence and Policy*, article in press.

Barry, A. (2012). Political situations: Knowledge controversies in transnational governance. *Critical Policy Studies, 6*(3), 324–336.

Best, J. (2014). *Governing failure: Provisional expertise and the transformation of global development finance*. Cambridge University Press.

Bhuta, N., Malito, D. V., & Umbach, G. (2018). Introduction: Of numbers and narratives— Indicators in global governance and the rise of a reflexive indicator culture. In N. Bhuta, D. V. Malito, & G. Umbach (Eds.), *The Palgrave handbook of indicators in global governance*. Palgrave MacMillan.

Biermann, F., Abbott, K., Andresen, S., et al. (2012). Navigating the anthropocene: Improving Earth system governance. *Science, 335*(6074), 1306–1307.

Couldry, N., & Mejias, U. (2019). Data colonialism: Rethinking big data's relation to the contemporary subject. *Television and New Media, 20*(3), 336–349.

Desrosières, A. (2015). Retroaction: How indicators feed back onto quantified actors. In R. Rottenburg, S. E. Merry, S. Park, & J. Mugler (Eds.). *The world of indicators: The making of governmental knowledge through quantification* (pp. 329–353). Cambridge University Press.

Elsbach, K. D., & Kramer, R. (1996). Members' responses to organizational identity threats: Encountering and countering the Business Week rankings. *Administrative Science Quarterly*, 442–476.

Espeland, W. N., & Sauder, M. (2007). Rankings and reactivity: How public measures recreate social worlds. *American Journal of Sociology, 113*(1), 1–40.

Espeland, W. N., & Stevens, M. L. (2008). A sociology of quantification. *European Journal of Sociology, 49*(3), 401–436.

Esposito, E., & Stark, D. (2019). What's observed in a rating? Rankings as orientation in the face of uncertainty. *Theory, Culture & Society, 36*(4), 3–26.

Fairclough, N. (1995). *Critical discourse analysis: Theoretical study of language.* Longman.

Ferraro, F., Etzion, D., & Gehman, J. (2015). Tackling grand challenges pragmatically: Robust action revisited. *Organization Studies, 36*(3), 263–390.

Free, C., Salterio, S. E., & Shearer, T. (2009). The construction of auditability: MBA rankings and assurance in practice. *Accounting, Organizations and Society, 34*(1), 119–140.

Fukuda-Parr, S. (2016). From the Millennium Development Goals to the Sustainable Development Goals: Shifts in purpose, concept, and politics of global goal setting for development. *Gender and Development, 24*(1), 43–52.

Fukuda-Parr, S., & McNeil, D. (2019). Knowledge and politics in setting and measuring the SDGs: Introduction to Special Issue. *Global Policy, 10*(1), 5–15.

Fyfe, G., & Latour, B. (1992). Introduction: On the invisibility of the visual. In G. Fyfe & B. Latour (Eds.), *Picturing power: Visual depiction and social relations* (pp. 1–14). Routledge.

Goodman, A. (2016). If you're going to change the world, you better bring your stories: An interview with Andy Goodman. *Frank, 5,* http://frank.jou.ufl.edu/2016/09/change-stories/

Grek, S. (2020). Prophets, saviours and saints: Symbolic governance and the rise of a transnational metrological field. *International Review of Education, 66,* 139–166.

Greenwood, M., Jack, G., & Haylock, B. (2019). Toward a methodology for analyzing visual rhetoric in corporate reports. *Organizational Research Methods, 22*(3), 798–827. https://doi.org/10.1177/1094428118765942

Grotlüschen, A., & Buddeberg, K. (2020). PIAAC and the South—Is Southering the new Othering? Global expansion of dominant discourses on adult literacy. *European Journal for Research on the Education and Learning of Adults,* article in press.

Hazelkorn, E. (2011). *Rankings and the reshaping of higher education: The battle for worldwide excellence.* Palgrave.

Jeacle, I., & Carter, C. (2011). In TripAdvisor we trust: Rankings, calculative regimes and abstract systems. *Accounting, Organizations and Society, 36,* 293–309.

Jewett, M. (2019). *Tableau data day out.* http://www.tableau.com

Krensky, P. (2014). *Interactive data visualization: The IT perspective.* Aberdeen Group. http://www.sift-ag.com/wp-content/uploads/AR-Aberdeen-Interactive-Data-Visualization-EN.pdf

Kress, G. (2009). *Multimodality: Exploring contemporary methods of communication.* Routledge.

Lafortune, G., Gonzalez, S., & Lonti, Z. (2018). Government at a glance: A dashboard approach to indicators. In D. Malito, G. Umbach, & N. Bhuta (Eds.), *The Palgrave handbook of indicators in global governance* (pp. 207–238). Palgrave Macmillan.

Latour, B. (1986). Visualization and cognition. *Knowledge and Society, 6*(6), 1–40.

Le Grand, J. (2003). *Motivation, agency, and public policy: Of knights, knaves, pawns & queens.* Oxford University Press.

Le Grand, J. (2007). *The other invisible hand: Delivering public services through choice and competition.* Princeton University Press.

Merry, S. E. (2016). *The seductions of quantification: Measuring human rights, gender violence and sex trafficking.* University of Chicago Press.

Merry, S. E. (2019). The Sustainable Development Goals confront the infrastructure of measurement. *Global Policy, 10*, 146–148.

Meyer, R. E., Jancsary, D., Höllerer, M. A., & Boxenbaum, E. (2018). The role of verbal and visual text in the process of institutionalization. *Academy of Management Review, 43*(3), 489–555.

Pollock, N., & D'Adderio, L. (2012). Give me a two-by-two matrix and I will create the market: Rankings, graphic visualisations and sociomateriality. *Accounting, Organizations and Society, 37*(8), 565–586.

Pollock, N., D'Adderio, L., Williams, R., & Leforestier, L. (2018). Conforming or transforming? How organizations respond to multiple rankings. *Accounting, Organizations and Society, 64*, 55–68.

Quattrone, P. (2017). Embracing ambiguity in management controls and decision-making processes: On how to design data visualizations to prompt wise judgement. *Accounting and Business Research, 47*(5), 588–612.

Quijano, A. (2007). Coloniality and modernity/rationality. *Cultural Studies, 21*(2), 168–178.

Rottenburg, R. (2009). *Far-fetched facts: A parable of development aid*. The MIT Press.

Sauder, M., & Espeland, W. (2009). The discipline of rankings: Tight coupling and organizational change. *American Sociological Review, 74*(1), 63–82.

Shore, C., & Wright, S. (2015). Audit culture revisited: Rankings, ratings, and the reassembling of society. *Current Anthropology, 56*(3), 421–444.

Slager, R., & Gond, J-P. (2020). The politics of reactivity: Ambivalence in corporate responses to corporate social responsibility ratings. *Organization Studies*, article in press.

Stark, D. (2009). *The sense of dissonance: Accounts of worth in economic life*. Princeton University Press.

Stark, D. (2020). The performance complex. In D. Stark (Ed.), *The performance complex: Competition and competitions in social life* (pp. 1–28). Oxford University Press.

Tableau. (2020a). *Business intelligence and analytics software—Tableau*. https://www.tableau.com/en-gb

Tableau. (2020b). *About Tableau*. https://www.tableau.com/en-gb/about/mission

Tableau. (2020c). Whitepapers. https://www.tableau.com/learn/whitepapers

Wodak, R., & Meyer, M. (Eds.) (2001). *Methods of critical discourse analysis*. Sage.

SECTION V

The Responses of National Education Systems to Global Pressures

CHAPTER 25

THE PISA PENDULUM

Political Discourse and Education Reform in the Age of Global Reference Societies

LOUIS VOLANTE

INTRODUCTION

Since the initial administration of the Program in International Student Assessment (PISA) in 2000, governments around the world have increasingly turned their attention to the policy implications stemming from this triennial global benchmark measure. Educational jurisdictions such as Finland, South Korea, Hong Kong, Canada, and more recently Singapore, at various points in time, have been internationally lauded for their high achievement in reading, mathematics, and/or science literacy, and touted as global reference societies by policymakers wishing to emulate their relative success (Volante, 2018). Yet questions and concerns remain regarding the undue influence and policy recommendations promoted by the Organization for Economic Cooperation Development (OECD), which is responsible for the design and administration of this international achievement test of 15-year-olds. This chapter explicates some of the most notable policy discourses and central arguments that have accompanied PISA's role in shaping global, transnational, and national education governance agendas. Particular attention is devoted to the examination of highly reactive policy contexts that have used PISA to justify significant large-scale reforms. Brief case studies of the German, Japanese, English, and Canadian contexts are offered to illustrate how this international benchmark measure has been used to support and justify education reforms—some of which were under consideration prior to the release of PISA results. Overall, this chapter provides a critical analysis of the policy influence of PISA as well as the dominant rationales undergirding its use in policy spheres.

Genesis and Evolution of PISA as a Global Benchmark Measure

The OECD's interest in education began in 1964 when they provided the impetus for a new field of study known as the Economics of Education (Bank, 2012; Hanushek & Woessman, 2015; Ydesen, 2019). This new field suggested that economic growth may depend as much on increases in human capital (at that time measured by the number of years of education) as on the changes in physical capital (e.g., infrastructure, buildings, technology) (Svennilson et al., 1962). Over time, the concept of human capital evolved from a simplistic notion dependent on years of formal schooling to recognize the importance of the quality of school learning environments for both developed and developing nations. It is with respect to the quality of learning, that the education ministers of the OECD turned their attention in the 1990s, to the development of the PISA international survey to accurately measure student performance (OECD, 1997).

According to the OECD, PISA measures 15-year-olds' ability to use their reading, mathematics, and science knowledge and skills to meet real-life challenges. Touted as the world's most comprehensive and reliable indicator of students' capabilities, it is promoted as an effective measure to enable the "fine-tuning" of education policies. As noted by the OECD Director of the Directorate of Education and Skills, the international reports stemming from the triennial results provide the "state of education around the globe: to share evidence of the best policies and practices, and to offer our timely and targeted support to help countries provide the best education possible for all of their students" (Schleicher, 2019, p. 2).

Since the initial administration of PISA in 2000, which included 28 OECD countries and 4 partner countries, the list of participating countries and/or economies has steadily grown. The most recent administration of PISA in 2022 included over 80 nations (see https://www.oecd.org/pisa/aboutpisa/pisa-2022-participants.htm). Cross-national analyses of the policy reach of different international achievement measures have clearly suggested that PISA is the most prominent international survey used by governments around the world (Grek, 2009; Meyer & Benavot, 2013; Volante, 2018). Indeed, research suggests that many industrialized nations have focused almost exclusively on the policy implications stemming from PISA and have largely ignored the results of other prominent, and sometimes older measures, such as the International Association for the Evaluation of Educational Achievement (IEA), Trends in International and Mathematics Study (TIMSS), and/or the Progress in International Reading Literacy Study (PIRLS) (Volante, 2016).

It also worth noting that the focus of PISA testing and related OECD benchmark measures has also steadily expanded. In addition to reading, mathematics, and reading literacy domains, the OECD has gradually added assessments in areas such as financial literacy in 2012, collaborative problem-solving in 2015, and global competence in 2018. The OECD is also working on new tools to assess creativity and critical thinking in 2022 as well as the digital world assessment in 2025. Coupled with the PISA for Development (PISA-D), an assessment designed for low- and middle-income countries; Program for International Assessment of Adult Competencies (PIAAC), which assesses the literacy, numeracy, and problem-solving skills of adults aged 16–65; along with plans to introduce an International Early Learning and Child Well-Being Study (nicknamed "baby PISA"), which will assesses 5-year-olds, it is easy to understand how the OECD's extensive array of testing measures has made them the most widely recognized and important international organization in the transnational governance of education (Morgan & Volante, 2016).

PISA as a Soft Mode of Regulation

The tagline that accompanies every webpage of the OECD is "better policies for better lives" (see http://www.oecd.org/). Additionally, the leading statement on their education homepage (see http://www.oecd.org/education/) states "the OECD's work on education helps individuals and nations to identify and develop the knowledge and skills that drive better jobs and better lives, generate prosperity and promote social inclusion." Overall, the dominant narrative promoted by the OECD is that education serves important economic as well as social functions across societies and the policy recommendations stemming from their international surveys, such as PISA, are part of an evidence base that is meant to assist sovereign nations as they seek to "fine-tune" or revise policies aimed at promoting educational excellence. Collectively, the branding and messaging promoted are part of a larger global trend in education to move toward evidence-based decision-making in the field of education.

Although the OECD's policy recommendations are not based on binding legislative mandates requiring compliance such as those tied to national governments, a significant number of academics have asserted that the policy outreach and focus of this international organization unduly influence nations to focus on a narrow range of measurable skills (Andrews et al., 2014; Benavot, 2013; Goldstein, 2014; Lingard et al., 2016; Meyer & Zahedi, 2014; Volante et al., 2017). It has been argued that the collective efforts of the OECD via the publication of comparative data, along with country and thematic reviews, operate as a soft mode of regulation which skews the educational governance agendas of nation states around the world (Mahon & McBride, 2008). Additionally, some have noted that their expert advice amounts to a soft power and mechanism of transnational and global educational governance (Bieber & Martens, 2011; Neimann & Martens, 2018; Pereyra et al., 2011). Perhaps more noteworthy is the assertion that the OECD has demarcated normative governance practices that ultimately further liberal, market-friendly, economic policies which emphasize competition in the education sphere (Henry et al., 2001; Meyer, 2014; Rizvi & Lingard, 2010).

Although many of the latter criticisms are understandable, it should be noted that national standards-based accountability agendas that emphasize large-scale testing and student performance in select subject areas, such as reading and mathematics, existed in many industrialized countries well before the PISA program was officially launched (Volante, 2012). Moreover, the OECD is quick to point out that the PISA benchmark measure is under control of the OECD Governing Board, which includes representatives from each of the member states. From this perspective, it is ultimately participating nations that influence the direction, scope, and uptake of the OECD's education priorities (Volante et al., 2018).

Overall, the OECD's mandate in education has been viewed as a continuation of neoliberal globalization forces that seek to turn sectors of the education system into more efficiently run organizations, which are more accountable for student outcomes and the public expenditures they garner. The latter is a reasonable assertion, particularly when one considers the extensive range of reports and policy briefs such as "PISA in Focus" (see http://www.oecd.org/pisa/pisaproducts/pisa-in-focus-all-editions.htm) that accompany the release of the triennial results. These reports and briefs are widely disseminated on their open-access Web platform and provide snapshots of different countries that address topics such as school accountability, financing, performance-based pay incentives, and public funding of privately managed schools, to name a few.

Interestingly, Mahon's (2010) examination of policy discourses since the inception of PISA suggested that the OECD has increasingly moved away from traditional neoliberal prescriptions such as welfare cuts and structural adjustment to education in favor of greater public investment in child development programs. Similarly, their focus on equitable learning outcomes, particularly for at-risk student populations such as disadvantaged and immigrant students, has remained a critical component of their policy outlook and highlighted the importance of addressing achievement gaps (Volante et al., 2018, 2019); it appears the OECD's policy prescriptions may be more nuanced than encompassed by simple market-driven neoliberal solutions to reform. However, whether government policymakers make note of these subtle differences in their policy development processes is entirely another matter.

Political Discourse and Education Reform From Highly Reactive Policy Contexts

It is widely asserted that policymakers across various educational jurisdictions routinely turn to PISA to initiate "quick fixes" or even justify preexisting policy directions as part of their national reform agendas (Andrews et al., 2014; Chung, 2019; Pons, 2017; Volante et al., 2020). At the same time, OECD commissioned research suggests policy responses to PISA range from highly reactive to very modest or in some cases negligible (see Breakspear, 2012). Thus, from the OECD's perspective, the impact or influence they exert on education policy formation should not be exaggerated, since they contend many of their policy suggestions have not been implemented within participating nations (OECD, 2015). Despite these broad criticisms and counterpoints, it is also useful to more closely analyze the policy discourses and documented impact of this international measure within specific nations, since these types of select cases illustrate how PISA has actually been used as a policy lever. Brief snapshots representing Germany, Japan, England, and Canada are offered in the next section as a way to examine some of the heightened political discourse and educational reform initiatives that have accompanied the release of PISA results. Although these select nations are in no way representative of the 80 nations/economies that currently participate in PISA, they accentuate different aspects of policy borrowing tied to the notion of global reference societies.

Germany

The German context is the natural starting point for discussions related to heightened reactions to PISA results. Indeed, the lackluster German results during the initial administration of PISA in 2000 provoked "PISA shock"—a term that has now been widely used by popular media outlets around the world to describe national contexts which may be struggling with lackluster or declining results (see Adams, 2019; Aoki, 2017; Lewis, 2019). Collectively, the global rankings of 22nd (reading), 21st (mathematics), and 21st (science), along with high levels of performance variations related to socioeconomic backgrounds, precipitated the greatest shift in national education policies since the fall of the Soviet Union (Bank, 2012). The German education system was quickly reformed to emphasize national standards, centralized examinations and assessments, and education monitoring structures for evaluation purposes—essentially an evidence-based policymaking orientation that aligns with the OECD's mandate (Ertl, 2006; Grubera, 2006; Neumann et al., 2010). Rigorous quality control measures such as teacher professionalization, school inspections, self-evaluations, and centralized assessments were introduced in different combinations by the 16 federal states, or Lander, to provide oversight and school accountability (Grek, 2009). Eventually, German national assessments would also come to mirror the content and framework utilized by the PISA survey—a trend that would be replicated in other parts of the world such as in Canada and Ireland (Klinger et al., 2016; Morgan, 2016). Overall, the general consensus is that PISA served as the pivotal catalyst for Germany to embrace an output orientation to education reform and a culture of comparison in educational policymaking (Pons, 2011; Waldow, 2009).

It is worth noting that there was very little political resistance within Germany to the idea of replacing the traditional liberal arts view of education, which served to cultivate self-refinement and social cohesion, with a neoliberal emphasis on outputs (i.e., student achievement) for the purpose of economic prosperity (Knodel et al., 2013; Rotte & Rotte, 2007; Uljens, 2007). Indeed, the motivation to demonstrate strong leadership in response to public concern led to muted contestation for the significant reforms. Unsurprisingly, academic criticisms, based on research demonstrating unintended negative outcomes such as increased stress on students, parents, and teachers, as well as increased teacher attrition (Hartong, 2012; Munch, 2014; Rotte & Rotte, 2007), had little impact on German policymakers in the face of national improvements in both student achievement and equity since 2003 (Volante, 2015). Indeed, the German "success story" has even been touted as a model to be emulated in other parts of the world (Young, 2015). Overall, PISA provoked intense discourse between policymakers, researchers, and the general public, and put education on the map by making it a focus of public attention (Sälzer & Prenzel, 2014).

Japan

Although poor performance within Germany provoked shock in 2000, Japan's sharply declining performance in 2003—particularly with respect to reading literacy scores— reverberated with the general public and was highlighted in a litany of negative popular media news stories. Collectively, the slumping scores were instrumental in the justi-fication of a series of education reform proposals aimed at replicating Finland's initial PISA dominance (Takayama, 2009). Legislative bills such as the Program for Improving Reading Literacy (2005) were quickly introduced. Japan's Ministry of Education, Culture, Sports, Science and Technology (MEXT) also replaced the controversial *yutori* (low pres-sure) curriculum and introduced national achievement tests designed to emphasize skills directly referenced by PISA (Ninomiya & Urabe, 2011). Schools were also required to pub-licize their performance reviews and improvement plans on the basis of the data drawn from the national achievement test (Takayama, 2013). Collectively, the cadre of Japanese reforms associated with mediocre PISA results led to a more centralized model of school-related decision-making (Ho, 2006). These reforms were similar to those enacted within Germany, in that they aligned with a neoliberal political agenda that emphasized the im-portance of testing and national competitiveness (Volante, 2015).

Interestingly, slumping Japanese PISA scores, particularly in reading, during the last two administrations of PISA in 2015 and 2018 have recently led to a second wave of signif-icant policy reforms. New curriculum guidelines and vocabulary education programs are currently being developed by MEXT with the "aim to nurture student's ability to under-stand information and express their thoughts" (*The Japan Times*, 2019, para 15). However, while the first wave of reforms was tied to initial Finnish PISA dominance, more recent reforms within Japan are also being referenced against the backdrop of higher perfor-mance in neighboring Asian nations such as Singapore, Taiwan, Hong Kong, and Maccao (Tasaki, 2017). Nevertheless, systematic analyses of policy borrowing and media discourses within Japan still suggest Finland, despite a steady decline in performance over successive administrations of PISA, remains the most positively referenced nation that provides a "model educational culture" (Davis et al., 2018). Although some may con-sider this perplexing since other nations—including some outside of Asia (i.e., Estonia,

Canada)—have stronger PISA results than Finland, it does align with the favorable cultural status that Nordic countries have traditionally enjoyed across the globe.

England

England represents another educational context worthy of further consideration—particularly since Margaret Thatcher's government in the 1980s is largely credited with the close coupling of curriculum requirements with standardized testing that popularized the adoption of market logic to the realm of public institutions and schools (Volante, 2012). Interestingly, while England participated in PISA 2000 and 2003, the OECD's official position was that England's trends should only be reported from 2006 onward, due to the sampling problems in the first two administrations (Hutchison & Schagen, 2007). Despite these sampling issues and the significant achievement gaps found in students with disadvantaged socioeconomic backgrounds, the dominant narrative was that England's "success" may influence other international jurisdictions (Grek, 2009). From this perspective, England viewed itself as a reference society versus a receiver of best practices noted in other high-performing jurisdictions. Similarly, the relatively strong initial PISA results were also used to provide further support for the Educational Reform Act (1988), which introduced a national curriculum and centralized assessments of pupils.

With the release of mediocre PISA 2006 and onward, the English landscape quickly changed to emphasize high levels of blame on individual politicians (Dixon et al., 2013). Opposition parties effectively used PISA to support a narrative of declining standards and to legitimize the need for additional large-scale reforms. PISA's ascending status within national debates was used as an "informal baseline from which to measure the success of reforms currently being put in place" (Breakspear, 2012, p. 23). Declining results in successive PISA administrations prompted Michael Grove, the Secretary of State for Education, to announce a series of reforms which included more accountability, merit-based pay similar to the "world's best-performing" systems such as Shanghai, and a revised National Curriculum that would be more demanding, particularly in mathematics, and modeled on the approach of "high-performing" Asian nations such as Singapore (Thomas et al., 2016). Clearly, English politicians, unlike their German counterparts, were far more comfortable espousing neoliberal policies in response to successful Asian educational contexts.

Canada

Canada is the last nation to be profiled as it is one of the few countries around the world with no federal oversight of education—rather, education is solely under the jurisdiction of the ten provincial and three territorial governments. This decentralized system, when coupled with the reporting of disaggregated provincial PISA results, often makes for interesting, and sometimes, contentious debate on the merits of different education system structures and policies. Canadian policymakers not only look outward to other international contexts but also inward to other provinces, when referencing high-performing systems. This is particularly the case since the variation in provincial score differences has traditionally been quite significant. For example, in the most recent reported results for PISA 2018, average reading scaled scores ranged from 532 in Alberta, which was equivalent to third in the world, after China and Singapore, to 489 in New Brunswich, which was equivalent to 26th in world (Council of Ministers of Education Canada, 2019). These types of provincial differences now typically serve as the starting point for PISA-related policy discussions in Canada—not necessarily the infatuation with international jurisdictions such as Finland that captured the early attention of the Canadian educational establishment (Bennett, 2013). Thus, in many ways Canada has increasingly shifted its focus from international to domestic reference societies to support what is often characterized as "much needed" reforms.

In line with the previously noted discussed international jurisdictions, Canadian PISA results are also used to validate existing policies and justify planned reforms which typically underscore a neoliberal agenda (Brochu, 2014; Volante, 2008). Alberta, for example, traditionally has functioned as Canada's mini-Finland for referencing purposes and been lauded for its standardized testing and curriculum frameworks. Interestingly, recent declines in PISA rankings have been used to justify an expansion of testing within this province—not a reduction—which is supported by the available research (Wright-Maley, 2019). Similarly, Quebec and British Columbia, which also tend to score in the top of the provincial league tables, have also been praised for their school choice provisions and lower per pupil funding (see Hill & Clemens, 2019). Collectively, the popular media and government policymakers have tended to gravitate toward selective and instrumental uses of PISA results to advance unproven causal associations for the system structures they favor.

In addition to provincial comparisons, PISA has also been used in Canada to promote negative regional stereotypes (i.e., Atlantic provinces have weak education systems compared to Western and Central Canada). Although the latter has been observed in other countries such as Italy, where southern regions are considered weaker than those in the north (see Checchi & Verzillo, 2018), this does add another important layer of competition in a country where national unity has remained a salient issue since confederation. Overall, discourse analyses have indicated that the most senior policymakers—namely provincial education ministers—often make public statements related to PISA that are not contextualized or connected to the policies being enacted within their province (Stack, 2006). The latter suggest an arbitrary relationship between PISA results and the rationales provided for specific education reforms within Canada.

PISA, Human Capital, and the Legitimation of Policy Reforms

Human capital theory asserts that there are three large policy domains for which education is critical. First, a nation's skills are essential for economic growth in a highly competitive global environment. Second, the uneven distribution of human capital is a key determinant of income inequality. Third, the link between human capital and family background is a fundamental determinant of social mobility and the perpetuation of (dis)advantage (Burgess, 2016). To their credit, the OECD surveys have allowed researchers to conduct detailed studies, which suggests a range of social mobility exists across different nations in relation to how much education a person obtains (Volante & Jerrim, 2018). Although these findings may be embarrassing to some countries and strike at the heart of cherished notions of meritocracy, they do shed light on national differences, and policies, that have led to fairer education and economic systems. Nevertheless, as was previously suggested, how and under what circumstances one country is willing to "learn" from another in relation to international tests such as PISA is not a straightforward endeavor.

A closer examination of the "policy borrowing" phenomena often reveals a complex interplay of national and cultural issues that affect their expression in public debate and political discourses. For example, while jurisdictions such as Shanghai quickly gained prominence in the international rankings, they were viewed as a dystopian mirror image to Finland, which was seen as a "projection screen" for everything that was desirable in the German education policymaking debate (Waldow et al., 2014). When one considers that the German (and Japanese) reforms converged more closely with facets of high-performing Asian systems, which typically emphasize testing and performance, versus the Finnish model that promotes liberal, progressively inspired education system, it becomes apparent that discourses on this topic may serve more rhetorical versus substantive functions in some national contexts. Moreover, the unanimous rejection of Asian education across the German political spectrum suggests that important cultural biases may come to bear in the uptake and/or borrowing of policies.

In line with the OECD's position, the current discussion supports the idea that the role of global reference societies in steering evidence-based decisions should not be overstated. Indeed, discussions related to select policy measures, such as the introduction of educational standards and centralized instruments of assessment in Germany, predated the release of PISA results. The same can be said of the Japanese context where the *yutori* reform and the introduction of national achievement testing were under consideration by MEXT prior to the release of the 2003 PISA results (Takayama, 2008). From this perspective, it is evident that PISA can be used by politicians to legitimize policy decisions under the guise of promoting evidence-based decision-making (Waldow, 2009). Clearly, PISA is not a value-free scientific enterprise but can be politicized to justify preexisting educational reform objectives and/or sway sentiments tied to neoliberal reform agendas.

Conclusion

It is likely that the policy reach of the OECD in the education sphere will continue unabated for the foreseeable future—particularly given their plans to introduce new benchmark measures and tested domains across the life span. Collectively, the expanding cadre of OECD surveys may spur fundamental changes in how curricula and human capital are conceptualized and promoted across the globe. Knowledge in traditional domains such as reading, mathematics, and science may eventually be replaced by a focus on broader or more interdisciplinary foci such as creativity, collaborative problem-solving, and/or digital literacy. The OECD has even recently shifted some of its focus to capturing and reporting cross-national differences in student happiness, based on the surveys that accompany student achievement measures (Rappleye et al., 2019). No doubt, the latter areas will undoubtedly be fashioned in an image which aligns with the economic and social functions of schools, and as such, should be scrutinized and critiqued to avoid reductionist approaches to large-scale reform. International policymakers should also be wary of "simple lessons" to complex education problems that are often derived from cross-national comparisons of student achievement. Such simplistic solutions inevitably shrink the aims of education to those that are easily measurable (Kamens, 2013; Labaree, 2014; Zhao, 2020).

As the preceding discussion illustrated, what and from whom nations are willing to learn is not a neutral enterprise. Educational evidence stemming from PISA testing must inevitably find its way through a national (or regional) political prism which can accentuate, minimize, or even discount the validity of related scientific research. Indeed, why policymakers favor aspects of particular global reference societies over others in public discourses may be less about getting the evidence right as it is about avoiding getting the optics wrong. Both the previous German and Japanese cases underscored how the source of inspiration for educational reforms was not necessarily tied to the highest performing nations. Indeed, the reforms adopted in both nations moved them further away from more liberal child-centered approaches to education that is represented by the Finnish context they often reference. Conversely, the English context illustrated how declining PISA results could effectively be used to facilitate support for educational reforms that further emphasized neoliberal/market-based solutions. Lastly, the Canadian case illustrated how policymakers could also use domestic reference societies to justify planned reforms. Overall, policy borrowing primarily depends on the dominant perspectives within the context where the referencing is being done—not the context serving as the reference society (Steiner-Khamsi & Waldow, 2018).

Clearly PISA may serve more of a strategic function to justify select policies than an international scientific project to elevate and diffuse best practices across the globe. In many respects, the nature and scope of the use of PISA as a policy lever are akin to a pendulum—albeit a weighted one in favor of market-based neoliberal solutions—that bends in response to political predilections. The latter assertion converges with broader notions of policy development and implementation that underscore *situated cognition* in which the situation or context in which an agent (in this case policymakers) operates shapes sense-making, implementation, and the role of the policy (see Spillane et al., 2002). Thus, while many academics and educationalists may bemoan the expanding influence of the OECD in the field of education and the neoliberal globalization forces that are increasingly skewing the function of schooling, it is ultimately national governments that must be held accountable for the policy choices they have made *and* their skewed uses of global, and possibly regional, reference societies.

REFERENCES

Adams, P. (2019, December 8). Should Australia be in PISA shock? *The Sydney Morning Herald*. https://www.smh.com.au/education/should-australia-be-in-pisa-shock-20191203-p53gg5.html

Andrews, P., Atkinson, L., Ball, S., Barber, M., Beckett, L., et al. (2014, May 6). OECD and PISA tests are damaging education worldwide—academics. *The Guardian*. https://www.theguardian.com/education/2014/may/06/oecd-pisa-tests-damaging-education-academics

Aoki, M. (2017, August 28). Is Japan's annual student achievement test worth the cost? *The Japan Times*. https://www.japantimes.co.jp/news/2017/08/28/reference/japans-annual-student-achievement-test-worth-cost/

Bank, V. (2012). On OECD policies and the pitfalls in economy-driven education: The case of Germany. *Journal of Curriculum Studies, 44*(2), 193–210.

Benavot, A. (2013). Policies toward quality education and student learning: Constructing a critical perspective. *European Journal of Social Sciences, 25*(1), 67–77.

Bennett, P. W. (2013, December 13). How to reform education? Start with school choice. *The Globe and Mail*. https://www.theglobeandmail.com/news/national/education/how-to-reform-education-start-with-school-choice/article15955257/

Bieber, T., & Martens, K. (2011). The OECD PISA study as a soft power in education? Lessons from Switzerland and the US. *European Journal of Education, 46*(1), 101–116.

Breakspear, S. (2012). The policy impact of PISA: An exploration of the normative effects of international benchmarking in school system performance. *OECD Education Working Papers*, No. 71, OECD. https://doi.org/10.1787/5k9fdfqffr28-en.

Brochu, P. (2014). The influence of PISA on educational policy in Canada: Take a deep breath. *Solsko Polje, 25*(5/6), 73–86.

Burgess, S. (2016). *Human capital and education: The state of the art in the economics of Education*. IZA Discussion Paper No. 9885. https://ssrn.com/abstract=2769193

Checchi, D., & Verzillo, S. (2018). The role of PISA in regional and private/public debates in Italy. In L. Volante (Ed.), *The PISA effect on global educational governance* (pp. 127–148). Routledge.

Chung, J. (Ed.) (2019). *PISA and global education policy: Understanding Finland's success and influence*. Brill/Sense.

Council of Ministers of Education, Canada. (2019). *Measuring up: Canadian results of the OECD PISA 2018 Study—The performance of Canadian 15-year-olds in reading, mathematics, and science.* https://www.cmec.ca/Publications/Lists/Publications/Attachments/396/PISA2 018_PublicReport_EN.pdf

Davis, E. R., Wilson, R., & Dalton, B. (2018). Another slice of PISA: An interrogation of educational cross-national attraction in Australia, Finland, Japan and South Korea. *Compare: A Journal of Comparative & International Education, 50*(3), 309–331.

Dixon, R., Muller, M., Vakkuri, J., Engblom-Pelkkala, K., & Hood, C. (2013). A lever for improvement or a magnet for blame? Press and political responses to international education rankings in four countries. *Public Administration, 91*(2), 484–506.

Ertl, H. (2006). Educational standards and the changing discourse on education: The reception and consequences of the PISA study in Germany. *Oxford Review of Education, 32*(5), 619–634.

Goldstein, H. (2014). Responses to Andreas Schleicher's reply to open letter. *Policy Futures in Education, 12*(7), 880–882.

Grek, S. (2009). Governing by numbers: The PISA "effect" in Europe. *Journal of Education Policy, 24*(1), 23–37.

Grubera, K. H. (2006). The German "PISA-shock": Some aspects of the extraordinary impact of the OECD's PISA study on the German education system. *Oxford Studies in Comparative Education, 16*(1), 195–208.

Hanushek, E. A., & Woessman, L. (2015). *The knowledge capital of nations: Education and the economics of growth*. MIT Press.

Hartong, S. (2012). Overcoming resistance to change: PISA, school reform in Germany and the example of Lower Saxony. *Journal of Education Policy, 27*(6), 747–760.

Henry, M., Lingard, B., & Rizvi, F., & Taylor, S. (2001). *The OECD globalization and education policy*. Pergamon Press.

Hill, T., & Clemens, J. (2019, December 17). Ontario spends more on education while student test scores decline. *Toronto Sun.* https://torontosun.com/opinion/columnists/opinion-onta rio-spends-more-on-education-while-student-test-scores-decline

Ho, E. S-C. (2006). Educational decentralization in three Asian Societies: Japan, Korea, and Hong Kong. *Journal of Educational Administration, 44*(6), 590–603.

Hutchison, D., & Schagen, I. (2007). Comparisons between PISA and TIMSS: Are we the man with two watches? In T. Loveless (Ed.), *Lessons learned: What international assessments tell us about math achievement* (pp. 227–261). Brookings.

The Japan Times. (2019, December 4). *In international test, Japan sinks to lowest-ever rank for students' reading skills.* https://www.japantimes.co.jp/news/2019/12/04/national/japanese-students-drop-countrys-lowest-ever-rank-reading-international-test/

Kamens, D. (2013). Globalization and the emergence of an audit culture: PISA and the search for best practices and magic bullets. *Oxford Studies in Comparative Education, 23*(1), 117–139.

Klinger, D., DeLuca, C., & Merchant, S. (2016). Canada: The intersection of international achievement testing and educational policy development. In L. Volante (Ed.), *The intersection of international achievement testing and educational policy: Global perspectives on large-scale reform* (pp. 140–159). Routledge.

Knodel, P., Martens, K., & Niemann, D. (2013). PISA as an ideational roadmap for policy change: Exploring Germany and England in a comparative perspective. *Globalisation, Societies & Education, 11*(3), 421–441.

Labaree, D. (2014). Let's measure what no one teaches: PISA, NCLB, and the shrinking aims of education. *Teachers College Record, 116*(9), 1–14.

Lingard, B., Martino, W., Rezai-Rashti, G., & Sellar, S. (2016). *Globalizing educational accountabilities*. Routledge.

Lewis, B (2019, December 1). PISA tests boss: Wales education system has "lost its soul." *BBC News*. https://www.bbc.com/news/uk-wales-50592611

Mahon, R. (2010). After neo-liberalism? The OECD, the World Bank and the child. *Global Social Policy*, 10(2), 172–192.

Mahon, R., & McBride, S. (Eds.) (2008). *The OECD and transnational governance*. UBC Press.

Meyer, H. D. (2014). The OECD as a pivot of the emerging global educational accountability regime: How accountable are the accountants? *Teachers College Record*, 116(9), 1–20.

Meyer, H. D., & Benavot, A. (2013). *PISA power and policy: The emergence of global educational governance*. Symposium Books.

Meyer, H. D., & Zahedi, K. (2014). Open letter to Andreas Schleicher, OECD. *Policy Futures in Education*, 12(7), 872–877.

Morgan, C. (2016). Tracing the effect of the OECD PISA sub-nationally: Integration into Canada's decentralized educational system. *Global Social Policy*, 16(1), 47–67.

Morgan, C., & Volante, L. (2016). A review of the OECD's international education surveys: Governance, human capital discourses, and policy debates. *Policy Futures in Education*, 14(6), 775–792.

Munch, R. (2014). Education under the regime of PISA & Co.: Global standards and local traditions in conflict—the case of Germany. *Teachers College Record*, 116(9), 1–16.

Neimann, D., & Martens, K. (2018). Soft governance by hard fact? The OECD has a knowledge broker in education policy. *Global Social Policy*, 18(3), 267–283.

Neumann, K., Fischer, H. E., & Kauertz, A. (2010). From PISA to educational standards: The impact of large-scale assessments on science education in Germany. *International Journal of Science & Mathematics Education*, 8(3), 545–563.

Ninomiya, A., Urabe, M. & Urabe, M. (2011). Impact of PISA on education policy—The case of Japan. *Pacific Asian Education*, 23(1), 23–30.

Organisation for Economic Cooperation and Development. (1997). *Resolution of the council on a decentralized programme for the producing indicators on student achievement on a regular basis*. OECD. http://www.oecd.org/officialdocuments/publicdisplaydocumentpdf/?cote=C(97)176/FINAL&docLanguage=En

Organisation for Economic Cooperation and Development. (2015). *Education policy outlook 2015: Making reforms happen*. OECD. http://www.oecd.org/edu/education-policy-outlook-2015-9789264225442-en.htm

Pereyra, M. A., Kotthoff, H. G., & Cowen, R. (Eds.). (2011). *PISA under examination*. Sense.

Pons, X. (2011). What did we really learn from PISA? The sociology of its reception in three European Countries. *European Journal of Education*, 46(4), 540–548.

Pons, X. (2017). Fifteen years of research on PISA effects on education governance: A critical review. *European Journal of Education*, 52(2), 131–144.

Rappleye, J., Komatsu, H., Uchiba, Y., Krys, K., & Markus, H. (2019). "Better policies for better lives"?: Constructive critique of the OECD's (mis)measure of student well-being. *Journal of Education Policy*, 35(2), 258–282.

Rizvi, F., & Lingard, B. (2010). *Globalizing education policy*. Routledge.

Rotte, R. & Rotte, U. (2007). Recent education policy and school reform in Bavaria: A critical overview. *German Politics*, 16(2), 292–313.

Sälzer, C., & Prenzel, M. (2014). Looking back at five rounds of PISA: Impacts on teaching and learning in Germany. *Sosko Polje*, 25(5/6), 53–72.

Schleicher, A. (2019). *PISA 2018: Insights and interpretations*. OECD.

Spillane, J. P., Reiser, B. J., & Reimer, T. (2002). Policy implementation and cognition: Reframing and refocusing implementation research. *Review of Educational Research, 72*(3), 387–431.

Stack, M. (2006). Testing, testing, read all about it: Canadian press coverage of the PISA results. *Canadian Journal of Education, 29*(1), 49–69.

Steiner-Khamsi, G., & Waldow, F. (2018). PISA for scandalisation, PISA for projection: The use of international large-scale assessments in education policy making—An introduction. *Globalisation, Societies and Education, 16*(5), 557–565.

Svennilson, I., Harbison, F. H., Tinbergen, J., Bos, H. C., Poignant, R., Mober, S., & Lyons, R. F. (1962). *Policy conference on economic growth and investment in education*. OECD.

Takayama, K. (2008). The politics of international league tables: PISA in Japan's achievement crisis debate. *Comparative Education, 44*(4), 387–407.

Takayama, K. (2009). Politics of externalization in reflexive times: Reinventing Japanese education reform discourses through "Finnish PISA success." *Comparative Education Review, 54*(1), 51–75.

Takayama, K. (2013). OECD, "Key competencies" and the new challenges of educational inequality. *Journal of Curriculum Studies, 45*(1), 67–80.

Tasaki, N. (2017). The impact of OECD-PISA results on Japanese educational policy. *European Journal of Education, 52*(2), 145–153.

Thomas, S., Gana, Y., & Muñoz-Chereau, B. (2016). England: The intersection of international achievement testing and education policy development. In L. Volante (Ed.), *The intersection of international achievement testing and educational policy: Global perspectives on large-scale reform* (pp. 37–57). Routledge.

Uljens, M. (2007). The hidden curriculum of PISA: The promotion of neo-liberal policy by educational assessment. In S. T. Hopman, G. Brinek & M. Retzl (Eds.), *PISA zulfolge PISA—PISA according to PISA* (pp. 295–303). LIT Verlag.

Volante, L. (2008). The impact of international comparison testing in Canada. *Journal of the International Society for Teacher Education, 12*(2), 17–20.

Volante, L. (Ed.) (2012). *School leadership in the context of standards-based reform: International perspectives*. Springer. https://doi.org/10.1007/978-94-007-4095-2

Volante, L. (2015). The impact of PISA on education governance: Some insights from highly reactive policy contexts. *International Studies in Educational Administration, 43*(2), 103–117.

Volante, L. (Ed.) (2016). *The intersection of international achievement testing and educational policy: Global perspectives on large-scale reform*. Routledge. https://doi.org/10.4324/978131 5676777

Volante, L. (Ed.) (2018). *The PISA effect on global educational governance*. Routledge. https://doi.org/10.4324/9781315440521

Volante, L., DeLuca, C., Baker, E., Harju-Luukkainen, H., Heritage, M., Schneider, C., Stobart, G., & Wyatt-Smith, C. (2020). Synergy and tension between large-scale and classroom assessment: International trends. *Educational Measurement: Issues and Practice*. https://onlinelibrary.wiley.com/doi/abs/10.1111/emip.12382

Volante, L., Fazio, X., & Ritzen, J. (2017). The OECD and educational policy reform: International surveys, governance, and policy evidence. *Canadian Journal of Educational Administration and Policy, 184*, 34–48. https://journalhosting.ucalgary.ca/index.php/cjeap/article/view/16325

Volante, L., & Jerrim, J. (2018, November 19). Why a good education isn't always the key to social mobility. *World Economic Forum.* https://www.weforum.org/agenda/2018/11/educat ion-does-not-always-equal-social-mobility/

Volante, L., Klinger, D., & Bilgili, Ö. (Eds.) (2018). *Immigrant student achievement and education policy: Cross-cultural approaches.* Springer. https://doi.org/10.1007/978-3-319-74063-8

Volante, L., Schnepf, S., Jerrim, J., & Klinger, D. (Eds.) (2019). *Socioeconomic inequality and student outcomes: Cross-national trends, policies, and practices.* Springer. https://doi.org/ 10.1007/978-981-13-9863-6

Waldow, F. (2009). What PISA did and did not do: Germany after the "PISA-shock." *European Educational Research Journal, 8*(3), 476–483.

Waldow, F., Takayama, K., & Sung, Y-K. (2014). Rethinking the pattern of external policy referencing: Media discourses over the "Asian Tigers" PISA success in Australia, Germany and South Korea. *Comparative Education, 50*(3), 302–321.

Wright-Maley, C. (2019). Why Jason Kenney's "common sense" education platform gets it wrong. *The Conversation Canada.* https://theconversation.com/why-jason-kenneys-com mon-sense-education-platform-gets-it-wrong-119069

Ydesen, C. (Ed.) (2019). *The OECD's historical rise in education: The formation of a global governing complex.* Palgrave Macmillan.

Young, H. (2015, November 25). What can we learn from the great German school turnaround? *The Guardian.* https://www.theguardian.com/teacher-network/2015/nov/25/what-can-we-learn-from-the-great-german-school-turnaround

Zhao, Y. (2020). Two decades of havoc: A synthesis of criticism against PISA. *Journal of Educational Change, 21,* 245–266.

CHAPTER 26

WHY GLOBALIZATION HARDLY AFFECTS EDUCATION SYSTEMS

A Historical Institutionalist View

JULIAN L. GARRITZMANN AND SUSANNE GARRITZMANN

INTRODUCTION

GLOBALIZATION has become a crucial factor shaping our societies and economies and challenging policymakers around the globe (again).[1] The contributions in this handbook point out how and why globalization—in its many facets—affects education, education policy, and education systems. Our contribution applies a different perspective on the globalization-education nexus: Taking a historical institutionalist view (Hall & Taylor, 1996; Thelen, 1999), we argue and show that—despite common prophecies of doom—education systems are actually (surprisingly) resilient against the influence of globalization. Despite a reintensifying globalization trend (back to levels seen around 1880–1920) in terms of trade openness, capital openness, and migration, the key characteristics of countries' education systems have hardly changed since the 1980s and largely kept their respective institutional characteristics. Rather than seeing omnipresent globalization-induced change, we witness "path dependence" (Pierson 2000) and stability in the core elements of countries' education systems, particularly in terms of governance structures, the public–private relationship, the academic-versus-vocational orientation, and educational funding (see, e.g., Busemeyer, 2015; Garritzmann, 2016).[2]

Why? How can we explain this inertia? We argue—against the background of recent empirical scholarship in a historical institutionalist tradition—that institutional change is politically very difficult because preexisting (education) policies create so-called feedback effects (Mettler, 2002) that set incentives for policymakers to refrain from structural readjustments. We distinguish three types of such feedback effects: (1) on the level of individual citizens' attitudes and preferences (i.e., the mass politics of public opinion), (2) on the level of interest groups, and (3) on the level of political and administrative elites. We explain why these feedback effects have mitigated or moderated potential effects of globalization, resulting in a rather weak and indirect link between globalization and education system reform. We underpin these arguments with a systematic review of empirical scholarship on two of these levels: feedback effects on public opinion, on the one hand, and on interest groups, on the other hand.

Before developing our arguments, we hasten to mention two important caveats: Our arguments and analysis concentrate on the rich Organization for Economic Cooperation and Development (OECD) democracies. While our arguments travel to some degree also to other contexts (e.g., North East Asia and several Latin American countries), we acknowledge that entirely different dynamics are at play in autocracies as well as in less developed democracies (e.g., Ansell, 2008). This is so because the mechanisms we identify assume democratic accountability and a certain duration of established education systems (in order for policy feedback effects to develop). A second caveat is that while we bring forward arguments against a strong direct link of globalization on education systems, globalization might still matter in more diffuse indirect ways, for example by changing socioeconomic class compositions, party competition, or economic prosperity. Moreover, while not leading to change in the institutional characteristics, globalization might affect more minor or peripheral parts of the education systems. That is, far from claiming that globalization does not matter at all, we rather explain why the institutional characteristics of countries' education systems have remained unaffected by intensifying globalization.

We proceed as follows: In the next section, we start with a brief discussion of famous "pro-arguments" on the globalization-education nexus, that is, why many scientists and observers have believed that globalization does affect education systems, leading to an international convergence trend. Subsequently, we introduce our "counter-arguments," explaining how and why education systems have been quite resilient to change, rather than being characterized by institutional stability. We then underpin and illustrate these arguments by drawing on recent work on public opinion and interest groups. The final part concludes and points to some important questions for future work.

Why Globalization Might Affect Education

Globalization is a complex and multifaceted phenomenon, encompassing a political, an economic, and a sociocultural dimension (Mattei & Behrend, Part II Introduction, this volume). We focus here especially on the economic and the political dimensions of globalization. *Economic* globalization includes countries' (increasing) openness to the movement of goods (trade openness), money (financial openness), and people (migration openness). *Political* globalization includes the supra-nationalization of political authority and increasing political interdependence between national states. More often than not, however, the supranational influence takes the form of soft power, rather than hard power (see also Martens et al., Chapter 22, this volume). Note, however, that the arguments we make in the following do not depend on this definition and would also apply to sociocultural understandings of globalization.

The Globalization-Education Nexus in Education Science

We directly engage with two large bodies of work, one in education science, another in political science. First, in education science a larger literature has explored whether and how globalization affects education. Many studies (e.g., Ball et al., 2010; Carnoy, 1998; Jackson, 2016; Rizvi & Lingard, 2010; Spring, 2014) have claimed that globalization crucially affects education, contributing to trends of standardization and convergence (but see Marginson, Chapter 34, this volume). Yet, in our reading, this literature faces three challenges: First, it mostly concentrates on discourses, framings, and paradigms (and only sometimes policies), rather than analyzing effects on education systems, that is, really visible institutional change "on the ground." This leaves open the possibility that whereas discourses, framing, and paradigms (and maybe even policies) might respond to globalization, education institutions might still remain largely unaffected (see also McGinn, 1997).[3]

Second, this literature mostly focuses on curricula, educational contents, and educational skills and qualifications, rather than on the major institutional characteristics of countries' education systems (e.g., their type of education funding, the public–private relationship, their governance structures, or the degree of vocational versus academic orientation). It is more likely that such minor aspects of education provision are changed, whereas defining features of countries' education systems will remain stable. In more abstract terms and using the analytical language of public policy research, we would argue with Hall (1993) that "first-order change," that is, relatively minor change such as recalibrating policy instruments, is much more likely than "second-order" or "third-order change," the latter implying a change in the policy-guiding paradigms. Change is certainly happening, but at rather peripheral elements and in incremental ways, while the key institutional setups remain largely intact.

Third, most of this literature in education science does not offer research designs that would allow us to causally identify effects of globalization on education systems, thus leaving the evidence to be suggestive rather than conclusive. On the one hand, the causal mechanism(s) for how globalization might affect education systems are often undertheorized and empirically understudied. On the other hand, most existing empirical work only studies covariation (correlations), which obviously is prone to overlook potential reversed causality (i.e., endogeneity) and confounding, that is, the possibility that a third factor (e.g., deindustrialization, technological change, or societal change) drives both globalization and change in education. As long as these challenges of causal inference are not taken care of, the research designs cannot rule out that the possibility of a spurious relationship between globalization and education policy.

Overall, thus, this education science literature claims that discourses, framings, and paradigms have converged as globalization intensified, and that these "soft" powers relate to changes in teaching contents, curricula, and (sometimes) educational qualifications (e.g., Bieber, 2016; Fulge & Bieber, 2016; Spring, 2008). However, these changes in contents happen within—and without necessarily changing!—the defining institutional structures of education systems (e.g., the degree and kind of tracking in schools, the vocational vs. academic orientation, or the structure of educational funding and governance). Hence, we turn to a second literature.

The Globalization-Education Nexus in Political Science

In political science—more specifically in public policy, political economy, and welfare state research (where we also locate our arguments)—there are two main rival theories on the effects of globalization on public policies—social and education policy being prime examples. On the one hand, "compensation theorists" (Cameron, 1978; Katzenstein, 1985) argue that globalization threatens citizens in general and workers in particular (Scheve & Slaughter, 2004), who accordingly respond by demanding more social protection (Walter, 2010, 2017), resulting in larger welfare states (Garrett, 1998; Rodrik, 1997). In short, globalization should lead to higher welfare effort. Recent work has extended these arguments also to education policy. Ansell (2008, 2010), Boix (1998), and Dreher et al. (2008) found a positive association between countries' economic openness and their education spending; Busemeyer and Garritzmann (2017b, 2019) offer a potential mechanism by showing that globalization increases public support for education spending. Thus, compensation theorists would argue that globalization might—through various mechanisms—lead to education policy reform, in particular to educational expansion.

Efficiency theorists (Kurzer, 1991; Scharpf, 1991), on the other hand, expect the opposite relationship: Globalization makes it easier for companies (and wealthy individuals) to credibly threaten to leave a country, resulting in an international competition for capital, which eventually leads to a "race to the bottom" (Genschel, 2002), including lower taxation and accordingly lower public effort in social and education policy provision (Jahn, 2006; Marshall & Fisher, 2015). In short, globalization should put pressure on welfare states and education systems, contributing to fiscal austerity and necessary cutbacks (or privatizations).

Taken together, it has been discussed extensively in political science whether, how, and why globalization challenges policymakers. Most literature has focused on social policies and preferences toward redistribution, trade openness, and migration, but the arguments have recently also been extended to education policy. Current discussions focus on the question of under what conditions globalization leads to more public policy provision or challenges policymakers to cutbacks; but some prominent voices also question whether globalization matters at all—an approach we can label "globalization skeptics" (especially Iversen, 2001; Iversen & Cusack, 2000; Taylor-Gooby, 2002).

THE ARGUMENT: WHY GLOBALIZATION HARDLY AFFECTS EDUCATION SYSTEMS

How Policy Feedback and Path Dependence Affect Education

We neither deny that our world is increasingly globalized (again), nor that globalization can have important effects on societies and economies. Yet we do argue here that there is little reason to assume—and little evidence to empirically underpin—a direct and strong effect of globalization on substantial change in the key institutional characteristics of countries' education systems. We develop this argument in the following, applying a historical institutionalist perspective to the globalization-education nexus.

Our starting point is the observation that crucial elements of countries' education systems are hardly ever changed at all. In an impressive study, Thelen (2004) demonstrated that the design of today's vocational education and training systems can be traced back to the medieval time, whereas the postwar period is characterized mainly by institutional stability. Busemeyer (2015) and Garritzmann (2016) showed, in a similar vein, that countries' school and higher education systems were shaped in the early postwar decades (1940s–1970s), whereas substantial change in the institutional setup of countries' education systems has become increasingly unlikely since the 1980s (when the world began to reglobalize). How can we explain this puzzle?

Historical institutionalists (Hall & Taylor, 1996; Pierson, 2000; Skocpol, 1992; Thelen, 1999) argue that policymaking and political reforms never happen in a vacuum, but are largely shaped by preceding policy decisions. That is, policymakers at time t are constrained by policymaking at time $t-1$. The main argument for this reasoning is that policies can have so-called feedback effects (Gingrich & Ansell, 2012; Pierson, 1993), leading to "increasing returns" (Gingrich & Ansell, 2012; Pierson 2000), which result in "path dependence" (Thelen, 1999). In a famous dictum by Schattschneider (1935, p. 288): "new policies create a new politics."

A well-known example to visualize this logic stems from computer science: Analyses have shown that the letters on our standard typewriter, computer, or smartphone keyboards could be rearranged in such a way that typing could—in theory—be much more efficient (the so-called QWERTY keyboard should be changed) (David, 1985). Yet, as soon as we imagine that suddenly all letters were in a different place on our keyboards and our year- or decade-long training on the QWERTY keyboard was useless at best and misleading at worst, we would probably all want to keep our common keyboards—even if they are inefficient in theory. Having used a QWERTY keyboard has put us on a certain "path" that—even if inefficient—we would very much prefer to stay on. As this example illustrates, there are mechanisms (here: repeated behavior and learning) that can lead to path dependence, contributing to incentives not to divert from a certain path ("increasing returns").

These arguments have been transferred and applied convincingly to public policymaking (Mettler, 2002; Pierson, 2000; Skocpol, 1992; Soss & Schram, 2007; Thelen, 1999). Just like a keyboard, public policies can create feedback effects. For example, the way social policies are handed out can affect the public's support of these policies. A policy can thus over time create "its own constituency"; that is, the longer and the wider applied a (favorable) policy is, the more likely it is that policy beneficiaries will support this policy. As a result, it is—in democratic polities—increasingly difficult for policymakers to change these policies: Positive feedback effects lead to path dependence, contributing to policy stability. As an example, consider contribution-based pension systems: Once established, contribution-based pension systems are very hard to reform, because many workers have paid contributions for their entire working lives, contributing to strong positive feedback effects and path dependence.

Three Types of Policy Feedback Effects

In a landmark publication, Pierson (1993) distinguished policy feedback effects on three levels[4]: the level of (1) governmental elites, (2) interest groups, and (3) mass publics. First, policies might feed-back on governmental elites' preferences, perceptions, and behavior (channel 1), they might change the positions and/or power of certain interest groups (channel 2), and/or they might affect people's attitudes and preferences, thereby affecting the mass politics of public opinion (channel 3).

Since the initial publications in the 1990s, much empirical work has tested and further refined these arguments, discussing, for example, whether policy feedback is always self-reinforcing or whether it can also be self-undermining (Fernández & Jaime-Castillo, 2013; Jacobs & Weaver, 2015) and studying under what conditions policy feedback effects are more or less likely. While we here lack the space to discuss all of this work (for recent reviews, see Béland, 2010; Béland & Schlager, 2019; Campbell, 2012; Kumlin & Stadelmann-Steffen, 2014; Larsen, 2019), we simply highlight four core insights because we will derive the argument in the following that education is a policy area in which self-reinforcing feedback effects can be expected to (often) be particularly strong.

To start with, we know by now that the *size of the group* that is affected by a certain policy matters, as feedback effects and path dependencies are all the stronger the more people have been affected by a policy. Given that—in the advanced democracies—almost all citizens have spent a large part of their lives in education systems (often between 12 and 16 years) (Garritzmann et al., 2023), education is a policy that deeply affects people. Second, moreover, people participate in education during the so-called politically formative years or "impressionable years" (Dinas, 2010; Neundorf et al., 2013; Stoker & Jennings, 2008). People's perceptions and preferences at this age are particularly malleable, making it likely that they adopt their preferences to what they see and experience every day (S. Garritzmann, 2020). Third, and relatedly, policy feedback effects have been found to develop stronger when people have *direct and personal experience* with a policy (rather than only indirect contact). Again, this is very much the case for education policy, as (almost) all citizens have first-hand experience with education—additionally many people again are in close contact with education systems as parents, relatives, or grandparents. Finally, policy feedback effects are more likely to emerge in politically *salient and visible policy areas*, which again is very likely for the case of education, as kindergartens, schools, vocational education and training, and higher education are omnipresent in all our lives.

Consequently, we expect that strong policy feedback effects are very likely to develop in the area of education (we underpin this empirically in the next two sections). These feedback effects—on the level of governmental elites, interest groups, and mass publics—in turn make path dependence likely, as they increase the political costs of policymakers to fundamentally change existing education systems. As a result, we argue that education systems will be highly path dependent and accordingly hardly affected by globalization, especially given that globalization is a rather vague, diffuse, slowly evolving, and rather invisible process.

Just like globalization, education systems are complex phenomena. We can differentiate several educational sectors (from childcare via schools to postsecondary and further education) as well as several dimensions of education policy and education systems (e.g., enrollment levels, spending, or governance aspects). We argue that policy feedback effects are particularly strong for key institutional characteristics of countries' education systems such as the main type of education funding (public vs. private), the degree of privatization and public–private relationship (e.g., to what degree private educational providers play a role), the vocational versus academic orientation (to what degree and what kind of vocational education and training is offered in a country), and the type of governance (e.g., how educational institutions are steered internally and at what age educational tracking happens).

Path Dependence Prevails Over Globalization Pressures

In sum, we argue that there is no strong direct effect of globalization on change in the key characteristics of education systems because policy feedback effects—on three analytical levels—stabilize the status quo and contribute to path dependence. Put differently, policy feedback effects nullify or at least mitigate potential globalization effects on education reform. Consequently, while globalization might have become a dominant topic in sociopolitical discourse, it is likely to have at best rather minor effects on education policy and institutions—at least when it comes to the defining institutional characteristics of countries' education systems (such as their governance, the academic-vs.-vocational orientation, the public–private relationship, or the type of education funding).

There might be some indirect globalization effects or some effects "at the margins" of the education system (e.g., whether more students go abroad during their studies or what contents they learn in school), but the defining institutional setups will be rather unaffected by globalization. Put differently, we argue with Hall (1993) that policy change is much easier and much more likely when it comes to rather peripheral or detailed aspects of policies ("first-order change"), whereas change in the policy instruments ("second-order change") or changes in the policy-guiding paradigms and institutional settings ("third-order change") are much less likely. This is a well-known fact in public policy research, which—we argue—applies equally to the case of education policy. To break it down: despite increasing globalization, the Swedish education system is still very "Swedish," the German education system still shows a long "German" tradition, and the US-American system still has is very own characteristics.

In the following two sections we systematically review some recent empirical work to underpin these arguments. We focus on two analytical levels: the level of public opinion and the level of interest groups. The objective is to provide detailed insights into different kinds of policy feedback effects, to exemplify with detailed studies how legacies mitigate or moderate the globalization-education nexus. That is, rather than directly testing the globalization-education nexus[5] or the theorized moderation effects, we want to explain the institutional inertia by highlighting some of the *mechanisms* behind the path dependence. Our review thus concentrates on studies that have explored these feedback effects. We begin with the level of public opinion.

POLICY FEEDBACK ON PUBLIC OPINION TOWARD EDUCATION

The comparative study of attitudes and preferences toward education policy is a relatively new field, arguably at least partly due to a lack of good comparative survey data (for a recent review, see Busemeyer & Garritzmann, 2021). During the last decade, however, a number of publications have emerged, exploring determinants of attitudes and preferences toward education policy. Most importantly for the present purpose, several recent studies explicitly analyze feedback effects of education policy on public opinion toward education policy. We use this literature to underpin our theoretical argument. We focus on three exemplary areas: attitudes toward (a) education spending, (b) childcare, and (c) vocational education and training. We discuss these in turn.

Education Spending

The level and kind of education spending is a major element of education policy and education systems. Countries differ starkly in how much they spend on education, on the distribution, as well as the sources of this spending—most importantly the degree to which education funding stems from private sources (e.g., via tuition fees, companies, or donations) (see OECD, 2020, for a detailed descriptive overview). Recent empirical work has exploited this fact to analyze whether people's preferences and attitudes mirror these respective policy regimes. More concretely, Busemeyer et al. (2011) showed with fine-grained survey data from Switzerland that respondents favored exactly those kinds of education that they themselves had participated in. Respondents with vocational degrees favored higher spending on vocational areas, whereas respondents with academic backgrounds preferred extended spending on academic education. That is respondents' personal educational experiences affect their preferences, supporting policy feedback arguments on the micro-level. Moreover, the study shows that support for a focus on vocational education is higher in those Swiss cantons where vocational education is more common, lending support to a policy feedback story also on the macro-level.

Busemeyer and Garritzmann (2017a) extended and refined these analyses in a large public opinion survey in eight West European countries. Their analyses confirm the micro-level logic that respondents are particularly in favor of those parts of the education system that they themselves had participated in. Moreover, parents are found to support those sectors of the education system that their children are profiting from. Garritzmann et al. (2018) show that these arguments extend to social investment policies more generally, that is, policies that aim to create, preserve, or mobilize human skills and capabilities (Garritzmann et al., 2017). That is, public support for social investment policies is the highest among more educated people.

A methodological disadvantage of these studies is that they only rely on cross-sectional data and thus provide a rather weak test of policy feedback arguments. Garritzmann (2015, 2016), however, produces very similar results with repeated cross-sectional data. Using the case of higher education funding, his analysis shows that public opinion is much more in favor of financial student aid in those countries that already have generous support schemes—and that this support even increases further when the financial student support is further extended.

Finally, Busemeyer and Iversen (2014) illuminate "the other side of the coin" showing that public support for public education spending can be undermined with privatization. They argue and show that public support for public education spending is lower in countries with more privatized education system, claiming that privatization can "crowd out" public investments. Again, this supports the notion that countries' existing education systems feed-back on their citizens' preferences, thereby stabilizing the status quo.

Taken together, these studies show that the specific design of education policies has significant and substantive effects on public opinion toward these policies, providing a first empirical test of our arguments. Let's look at a second example.

Early Childhood Education and Care

Early childhood education and care (ECEC) is of utmost importance. Scholars and (many) policymakers agree by now that investments early in the life cycle can have substantial and consequential long-term effects on people's skills, development, and prosperity (e.g., Heckman, 2006). Consequently, a recent empirical literature has begun to analyze the politics of ECEC (e.g., Morgan, 2013; Neimanns, 2017). Most importantly for our purpose, recent research explored public opinion toward ECEC policy, often explicitly studying policy feedback effects.

Goerres and Tepe (2012), for example, explore attitudes toward ECEC in Germany and find support for a positive, self-reinforcing feedback story, as respondents raised in Eastern Germany (where public ECEC was much more common) are much more supportive of public ECEC than those in Western Germany. A similar finding occurs in vignette studies by Busemeyer and Goerres (2020) on attitudes toward childcare fees: Falsifying a pure self-interest story, Busemeyer and Goerres find that that respondents support those kinds of ECEC fees that are in place in their communities, in line with positive feedback arguments that reinforce the status quo. Neimanns and Busemeyer (2021) continue along these lines, demonstrating that the institutional structure of the existing ECEC systems shapes to what degree attitudes toward ECEC policies are conflicting between different classes.

Outlining an additional feedback effect of ECEC policy, Neimanns (2021a) argues that access to ECEC affects attitudes toward maternal employment. Where ECEC receives more public funding and access to ECEC is more equal, the public holds more supportive views on maternal employment. Working mothers, in turn, are strongly in favor of maintaining ECEC, which further contributes to preserving the status quo in ECEC policies. In another contribution, Neimanns (2021b) analyzes in more detail how public opinion results in status-quo-preserving policies. He shows that while preferences toward expanding ECEC are particularly strong among poorer individuals, these are basically irrelevant for those individuals' vote choices. That is, parties do not face incentives to change the ECEC policies if those who favor change do not voice their opinion or do not vote according to their opinion.

Taken together, several studies pointed at feedback effects that arguably could help to stabilize the existing systems against potential globalization-induced change.

Vocational Education and Training

Countries differ tremendously regarding how much emphasis they place on vocational education and training (VET) and what kind of VET they offer (i.e., school-based, firm-based, or dual apprenticeships, or only on-the-job training). By now it is widely recognized that the type of VET is a crucial determinant not only of countries' skill profiles but also of their patterns of youth unemployment (Müller & Gangl, 2003) and their type of capitalism (Hall & Soskice, 2001; Thelen, 2004). Countries' type of VET system is thus a defining part of their education system.

Recent research has analyzed public opinion toward VET policies. Busemeyer and Jensen (2012) found that—in line with self-reinforcing feedback effects—public support for VET is substantially higher in countries where a larger share of the population has attended VET programs. Di Stasio's (2017) fine-grained analysis continues along these lines, showing that the type of VET system affects how people think about the (vocational) education system. Respondents are particularly in favor of those types of VET that they themselves have experienced.

Moreover, analyses of Swiss survey data lend additional evidence to feedback arguments: Bolli et al. (2019) find that—despite intensifying globalization (and other megatrends like deindustrialization)—the perceived status of VET has remained constant between 2000 and 2012. That is, it is not the case that globalization pressure somehow has shifted Swiss attitudes toward this key element of their education system.

Going further, Abrassart et al. (2020) offer another interesting test of feedback arguments. Focusing on migrants, they analyze to what degree the preferences of first- and second-generation migrants resemble or differ from those of Swiss natives. They find an assimilation process over time, as second-generation migrants' education policy preferences are much closer to those of Swiss natives than those of first-generation immigrants. Again, this is fully in line with arguments about attitudes and preferences being shaped by existing institutional policy legacies.

In sum, the three examples illustrated evidence for policy feedback effects in several key elements of countries' education systems: preferences toward (a) the level and type of education spending, (b) ECEC, and (c) VET. Overall, these arguments underpin our claims about self-reinforcing policy feedback effects. This helps to explain, in our view, why countries' education systems are (surprisingly) stable, despite intensifying globalization (and other various socioeconomic and political challenges). Public opinion can be a powerful "signal" to policymakers when designing education reform—or opting for nonreforms (Busemeyer et al., 2020).

Extending the perspective beyond preferences toward education policy, there are also a range of studies on effects of education policy on other individual-level attitudes and behaviors. Mettler (2002) and Mettler and Soss (2004) argue that the design of education policy can shape patterns of political behavior, especially political turnout. S. Garritzmann (2020) extended these arguments, showing that the design of the respective education systems shapes political inequalities. Gingrich (2019) stretched the policy feedback arguments in yet another direction, studying whether education policies also affect political preferences more generally.

POLICY FEEDBACK ON INTEREST GROUPS

Interest groups play an important role in most education systems and can contribute to self-reinforcing feedback effects. In very general terms, interest groups aggregate the interests of their members and represent these in the political arena through, for example, lobbying, media campaigns, government consultation, or direct involvement in policymaking or implementation processes (Baumgartner & Leech, 1998; Klüver & Pickup, 2018). Interest groups that relate to a certain government institution, such as the education, pensions, or health system, have—and are called—vested interests: They are groups that benefit from the status quo of the system, that are interested in the further expansion of "their" institution, and that oppose reforms that threaten "their" institution (Moe & Wiborg, 2016).

A multitude of potentially influential interest groups can be identified in the education system, such as associations representing students, parents, or principals, labor unions, teachers' unions, private school associations, consultant groups like Bertelsmann, or bank associations. All of these interest groups have—at least partly—been shaped by the respective education systems and thus often have an interest in the preservation of the established education systems. Some of them are particularly powerful in the political arena and work to prevent institutional change (that might be driven by globalization). We here cover research that focuses on three powerful actors at three different levels of education: (1) teachers' unions in secondary education systems, (2) labor unions in vocational education and training (VET), and (3) banks in higher education. One could easily extend the illustration with additional actors and other educational sectors.

Teachers' Unions in Secondary Education Systems

From a comparative perspective, the crucial institutional differences between secondary education systems are their extent of stratification and standardization (Allmendinger, 1989). These institutional differences have emerged during the late 18th and early 19th centuries, when public education was expanded and education systems were established. Secondary education systems are challenged not only by economic globalization but also by political globalization, with the OECD's Program for International Student Assessment (PISA) being a major example in this regard. For the PISA study, the OECD regularly collects data on education outcomes—more concretely, mathematical and literacy skills—at the end of secondary education in a wide range of countries. Based on these data, the OECD rank-orders countries according to their education outcomes, highlights "best practice" examples, and formulates policy recommendations with regard to a range of aspects (e.g., Fulge et al., 2016; Niemann & Martens, 2018; Niemann et al., 2017; Martens et al., Chapter 22, this volume). Although none of the recommendations are binding, the PISA results attract a lot of attention among both politicians and publics across the globe, and this "soft power" is often assumed to have fostered globalization in secondary education.

However, despite the attention given to PISA both nationally and internationally, we do not see convergence toward a common type of education system that looks the same everywhere (e.g., Jakobi & Telteman, 2011; Niemann & Martens, 2018). Instead, core differences between education systems (such as the extent of tracking and stratification) have remained in place. One important reason for why we see so little globalization in secondary education systems is policy feedback—driven in particular by teachers' unions. Teachers' unions, as Moe and Wiborg (2016) describe from a comparative perspective, have emerged as vested interests in education systems across democracies and, in order to protect their jobs, salaries, and benefits, often have used their political power to prevent changes to the education system.

Germany, for example, often is cited as a country in which PISA triggered some education reforms—the so-called Pisa-shock. For example, policymakers shifted from an input- to an output-oriented perspective on the education system, established data-based educational monitoring, and expanded early childhood education in order to counter educational inequality (e.g., Busemeyer, 2015, chapter 5.1; Niemann & Martens, 2018; Niemann et al., 2017). However, the core element of the education system—its early and strict school tracking—has barely changed: Even though most *Länder* introduced a more comprehensive school type in the aftermath of the PISA results, only a minority of students attends the test and the highest academic track (*Gymnasium*) has remained untouched as has the early tracking after four years of primary school.

A main reason for this resilience is that in Germany different teachers' unions have formed around the different educational tracks and the politically powerful union of the *Gymnasium* teachers fiercely opposed the introduction of (truly) comprehensive schools—which would have threatened their occupational advantages (such as status, salaries, working with academically motivated students)—and successfully lobbied for the *Gymnasium* to remain untouched by reform initiatives (Busemeyer & Haastert, 2017; Nikolai et al., 2016). This illustrates how the establishment of early-tracking systems has created vested interests that subsequently limit policymakers' room for maneuver.

Further examples of policy feedback effects and the power of teachers' unions can also be found in other countries. For example, after France was criticized by the OECD for its strongly centralized education system and politicians aimed at reforming this, French teachers' unions mobilized for nation-wide strikes and successfully prevented the proposed decentralization reforms from being implemented (Dobbins, 2014, 2016). Yet teachers' unions are not only politically powerful actors at the national level. In Denmark, teachers' unions used their political power at the local level to preempt school choice policies that would negatively affect their professional advantages (Wiborg & Larsen, 2017).

Taken together, these examples illustrate that teachers' unions can be powerful political actors preventing institutional change in education systems at the national, subnational, or/and local level. This is fully in line with the feedback logic, and one important reason for why we observe so surprisingly little convergence in secondary education systems despite globalization (pressures).

Labor Unions in VET

As mentioned earlier, VET systems differ a lot in their institutional setup (e.g., Busemeyer & Trampusch, 2012; Hall & Soskice, 2001; Thelen, 2004; Graf, Chapter 3, this volume). Consequently, they are challenged by globalization to a different extent: While VET systems that provide more general skills might have an easier time adapting to a globalized world with increasingly complex skill profiles,[6] this might be more challenging and cumbersome in VET systems that provide more specific skills and are mostly governed in tripartite corporatism between employers, unions, and the state. Yet, even among countries with a strong focus on specific skills and corporatist governance structures, as Busemeyer and Vossiek (2016) show, there is neither a common reform trend nor convergence in VET systems.

Again, one important reason for the continuing existence of differences in VET systems is policy feedback: VET systems have generated vested constituencies—in particular, labor unions and employer associations—that have an interest in the maintenance of the established system and thus oppose reforms aiming at institutional change (Busemeyer & Vossiek, 2016). In line with this reasoning, Durazzi and Geyer (2020) highlight the important role of labor unions in shaping Germany's and Austria's political responses to the recent challenges of their dual VET systems. Similarly, Emmenegger, Graf, and Strebel (2020) suggest that change in the Swiss and German VET systems crucially depends on the historically established strength of labor unions in these countries, who will oppose reforms that limit their authority and power. And finally, Busemeyer (2015, chapter 5.1) describes how attempts of the European Union to harmonize VET have failed because labor unions (and partly employers' associations) in dual VET systems opposed the suggested reforms.

In sum, these contributions show evidence of strong feedback effects and path dependencies in VET systems that render (fast and structural) institutional change due to globalization less likely than one might have expected (see also Graf, Chapter 3, this volume).

Banks in Higher Education

While students in some countries, like Germany or Sweden, study free of charge, students in many other countries are charged tremendous tuition fees (see Garritzmann, 2016, for an overview, typology, and explanation of these differences). There have been numerous attempts in high-tuition countries to abolish or at least minimize tuition (see, e.g., the ongoing discussions in the United States and in Chile). So far, however, no country that had established a considerable level of tuition fees has abolished them. Why is that the case? The main reason is that once established, tuition fees create self-reinforcing feedback effects, which make them increasingly difficult to abolish. While some of these run via public opinion (Garritzmann, 2015, 2016) in line with the arguments made earlier, we focus here on another mechanism, running via banks.

In high-tuition countries (or generally in countries with financialized education systems), lending money to students is a huge business. In the United States, for example, student loans have not only been publicly subsidized but also state-guaranteed; that is, the government takes over debt in case of default. The 1998 Higher Education Act Reauthorization guaranteed banks a profit of 7.96% for all student loans (Mettler, 2009, p. 210). As a result, the main student lender, Sallie Mae (which was founded by the government in the 1970s but privatized in 1996), made a 2000% surplus over 10 years with these loans (Mettler, 2010, p. 806). It is not hard to imagine, then, why these banks might be opposed to changes in the funding of higher education. For them, it is simply a—state-guaranteed—billion-dollar business.

Detailed process-tracing analyses of the politics of higher education funding in the United States show that and how higher education policies have created reinforcing policy feedback effects by designing policies in a way that made banks extremely interested in maintaining the status quo (Hannah, 1996; Mettler, 2010; Skocpol, 1997). To illustrate: in the 1990s the banks founded a political action committee (PAC) to lobby for their interests, which by 2006 had become the "top donor within the entire finance and credit industry" (Mettler, 2010, p. 813). Accordingly, several reform efforts (under Presidents Bush and Clinton) failed—and even President Obama, despite holding a supermajority in Congress, was only barely able to change higher education policy and switch back to a "direct-lending system" where the government, rather than banks, loan money. This example illustrates why banks can be another powerful actor in the politics of education, contributing to path dependence.

CONCLUSION AND OUTLOOK

This chapter aimed to explain why—despite intensifying globalization—the main characteristics of education systems have remained unchanged. Taking a historical institutionalist view, we pointed at the role of self-reinforcing feedback effects, which contribute to path dependence, as they set incentives for policymakers to abstain from path-departing reforms. Following Pierson, we identified feedback effects of three levels and illustrated these arguments with an overview on recent empirical research on public opinion as well as on interest groups. We identified several mechanisms showing how and why feedback effects emerge and why they are so powerful.

More specifically, we illustrated with a systematic review of existing research how and why policy feedback effects emerge on the level of public opinion and on the level of interest groups, which in turn make policy and institutional change unlikely. Consequently, even socioeconomic megatrends like globalization (or deindustrialization and technological change) do not automatically exercise a strong direct effect on education policy and education systems, unlike many observers (including prominent voices in this handbook) prognosed. Rather, policy feedback effects work as an obstacle or hindrance to (rapid and transformative) change, stabilizing the status quo and contributing to path dependencies. As a result, while globalization might be omnipresent in political and social discourses, it hardly translates to policy and institutional change of education. As we argued herein, this is particularly true for the defining institutional characteristics of countries' education systems, such as the public–private relationship, the type of education funding, the governance structure (e.g., the degree and strength of educational tracking), and the interplay of academic and vocational education.

To reiterate, we neither deny that our world is increasingly globalized (again), nor that globalization can affect some aspects of education (e.g., student mobility, international orientation of science, teaching contents, or the emergence of global rankings). We do argue, however, that change in the key characteristics of countries' education systems is unlikely—just as historical institutionalists would predict.

Looking forward: While by now a number of studies exist and teach us a great deal about the politics of education reform and nonreform, many questions still remain open for future research. Here, we highlight five avenues for future research. To start with, despite recent advancements in the literature, we still have relatively little evidence for the effects and mechanisms of policy feedback in education policy. There are just a few studies on public opinion (mainly because comparative survey data on education are rare) and on interest groups; moreover, only very few studies have explored feedback effects on political and administrative elites. Much more could be done here.

Second, the literature remains largely focused on the rich developed democracies. This partly makes sense, as their education systems simply had more time to develop feedback effects; but it would still be crucial to understand much better how far these arguments travel to other country groups and what potential scope conditions of the arguments are (e.g., state capacity and programmatic rather than clientelistic party-voter linkages).

Third, methodologically speaking, the literature could benefit from embracing the recent advancements in causal inference more. To the best of our knowledge, all existing work on feedback effects on public opinion on education policy is correlational only, and strictly speaking, it does not allow for causal inference. The research on interest groups, in turn, is mostly qualitative using process-tracing or comparative case studies, which gets us closer to the causal mechanisms but raises questions about generalizability, causal effects, and effect sizes. New work making use of clever causal inference designs would thus be very welcome and would lend additional credibility to the literature, in particular vis-à-vis potential rival explanations and confounders.

Fourth, further theoretical advancements would be welcome. Policy feedback is a very complex phenomenon. Feedback effects can, for example, differ in their strength, their direction (self-reinforcing vs. self-undermining), their temporal duration (short term vs. long term), their target group (specific vs. broad), or their visibility. Here, we painted a rather simplified story to illustrate our arguments and theorized mechanisms. Future work could try to theoretically advance and empirically more fully test these claims in a unified framework.

Finally, our chapter explained why the main institutional characteristics of education systems are resilient to globalization pressure. However, as we also emphasized throughout, this does not imply that there is absolutely no effect of globalization on education. While we argued that the main institutional characteristics of education systems have hardly changed, there could be effects on other elements of education policy and education systems. Future research should explore more *which elements* of education policy and education systems are most likely to be affected by globalization and *under what conditions* globalization affects education policy and education systems (e.g., interacting with specific politico-economic actors, or during specific historical windows of opportunity). In sum, it could be studied more systematically which aspects of globalization (economic, social, or political) affect which elements of education systems and under what conditions. The goal of this present chapter was more modest in pointing at mechanisms why globalization effects have been much smaller than often expected.

Notes

1. More precisely: globalization has become an important force *again*, since the world used to be highly globalized around 100 years ago already (during a so-called first wave of globalization). Thus, we could speak about "reglobalization" nowadays, or about a "second wave" of globalization.
2. We thank Anna Kluge and Andrea Stork for helpful research assistance.
3. McGinn (1997, p. 41) concluded: "even after forty years of unceasing emphasis on economic integration, no national system of education is very different to what it was fifty years ago. The most recent wave of globalization appears to have had relatively little effect on the content of national education systems."
4. Pierson additionally introduced two mechanisms, one running through rational choice arguments, the other running through socialization, resulting in six types. We ignore this additional dimension here and focus on the three analytical levels.
5. See Busemeyer and Garritzmann (2017b) for a direct test of the hypothesis that globalization affects education spending.
6. These are, however, rather driven by deindustrialization and skill-biased technological change than by globalization.

References

Abrassart, A., Busemeyer, M. R., Cattaneo, M. A., & Wolter, Stefan C. (2020). Do adult foreign residents prefer academic to vocational education? Evidence from a survey of public opinion in Switzerland. *Journal of Ethnic and Migration Studies, 46*(15), 3314–3334.
Allmendinger, J. (1989). Educational systems and labor market outcomes. *European Sociological Review, 5*(3), 231–250.
Ansell, B. W. (2008). Traders, teachers, and tyrants: Democracy, globalization, and public investment in education. *International Organization, 62*(Spring), 289–322.
Ansell, B. W. (2010). *From the ballot to the blackboard: The redistributive political economy of education*. Cambridge University Press.
Ball, S. J., Dworkin, A. G., & Vryonides, M. (2010). Globalization and education: Introduction. *Current Sociology, 58*(4), 523–529.
Baumgartner, F. R., & Leech, B. L. (1998). *Basic interests: The importance of groups in politics and in political science*. Princeton University Press.
Béland, D. (2010). Reconsidering policy feedback: How policies affect politics. *Administration & Society, 42*(5), 568–590.
Béland, D., & Schlager, E. (2019). Varieties of policy feedback research: Looking backward, moving forward. *Policy Studies Journal, 47*(2), 184–205.

Bieber, T. (2016). *Soft governance, international organizations and education policy convergence: Comparing PISA and the Bologna and Copenhagen process.* Palgrave.

Boix, C. (1998). *Political parties, growth, and equality: Conservative and social democratic strategies in the world economy.* Cambridge University Press.

Bolli, T., Rageth, L., & Renold, U. (2019). The social status of vocational education and training in Switzerland. *KOF Working Papers* 451. https://www.research-collection.ethz.ch/handle/20.500.11850/323964.

Busemeyer, M. R. (2015). *Bildungspolitik im internationalen Vergleich.* UVK.

Busemeyer, M. R., Cattaneo, M. A., & Wolter, S. C. (2011). Individual policy preferences for vocational versus academic education: Microlevel evidence for the case of Switzerland. *Journal of European Social Policy, 21*(3), 253–273.

Busemeyer, M. R., & Garritzmann, J. L. (2017a). Academic, vocational or general? An analysis of public opinion towards education policies with evidence from a new comparative survey. *Journal of European Social Policy, 27*(4), 373–386.

Busemeyer, M. R., & Garritzmann, J. L. (2017b). The effect of economic globalization on compensatory and social investment policies compared: A multi-level analysis of OECD countries. *Danish Center for Welfare Studies (DaWS) Working Paper Series, 2*, 1–29.

Busemeyer, M. R., & Garritzmann. J. L. (2019). Compensation of social investment? Revisiting the link between globalization and popular demand for the welfare state. *Journal of Social Policy, 48*(3), 427–448.

Busemeyer, M. R., & Garritzmann. J. L. (2021). Public opinion on education policies: A multicountry perspective. In M. R. West & L. Woessmann (Eds.), *Public opinion and the political economy of education policy around the world* (pp. 17–53). MIT Press.

Busemeyer, M. R., Garritzmann, J. L., & Neimanns, E. (2020). *A loud, but noisy signal? Public opinion and the politics of education reform in Western Europe.* Cambridge University Press.

Busemeyer, M. R., & Goerres, A. (2020). Policy feedback in the local context: Analysing fairness perceptions of public childcare fees in a German town. *Journal of Public Policy, 40*(3), 513–533.

Busemeyer, M. R., & Haastert, S. (2017). Bildungspolitik: Nicht alles anders, aber manches. In F. Hörisch & S. Wurster (Eds.), *Das grün-rote Experiment in Baden-Württemberg* (pp. 69–96). Springer.

Busemeyer, M. R., & Iversen, T. (2014). The politics of opting out: Explaining educational financing and popular support for public spending. *Socio-Economic Review, 12*(2), 1–26.

Busemeyer, M. R., & Jensen, C. (2012). The impact of economic coordination and educational institutions on individual-level preferences for academic and vocational education. *Socio-Economic Review, 10*(3), 525–547.

Busemeyer, M. R., & Trampusch, C. (2012). The comparative political economy of collective skill formation. In M. R. Busemeyer & C. Trampusch (Eds.), *The political economy of collective skill formation* (pp. 3–38). Oxford University Press.

Busemeyer, M. R., & Vossiek, J. (2016). Global convergence or path dependency? Skill formation regimes in the globalized economy. In K. Mundy, A. Green, B. Lingard, & A. Verger (Eds.), *The handbook of global education policy* (pp. 145–161). John Wiley & Sons.

Cameron, D. R. (1978). The expansion of the public economy: A comparative analysis. *American Political Science Review, 72*(4), 1243–1261.

Campbell, A. L. (2012). Policy makes mass politics. *Annual Review of Political Science, 15*, 333–351.

Carnoy, M. (1998). Globalisation and educational restructuring. *Melbourne Studies in Education, 39*(2), 21–40.

David, P. A. (1985). Clio and the economics of QWERTY. *American Economic Review, 75*(2), 332–337.

Di Stasio, V. (2017). "Diversion or safety net?" Institutions and public opinion on vocational education and training. *Journal of European Social Policy, 27*(4), 360–372.

Dinas, E. (2010). The impressionable years: The formative role of family, vote and political events during early adulthood [PhD dissertation, European University Institute].

Dobbins, M. (2014). Explaining change and inertia in Swedish and French education: A tale of two corporatisms? *Policy Studies, 35*(3), 282–302.

Dobbins, M. (2016). Teacher unionism in France: Making fundamental reform an impossible quest? In T. M. Moe & S. Wilborg (Eds.), *The comparative politics of education: Teachers unions and education systems around the world* (pp. 87–113). Cambridge University Press.

Dreher, A., Gaston, N., & Martens. P. (2008). *Measuring globalisation—Gauging its consequences.* Springer.

Durazzi, N., & Geyer, L. (2020). Social inclusion in the knowledge economy: Unions' strategies and institutional change in the Austrian and German training systems. *Socio-Economic Review, 18*(1), 103–124.

Emmenegger, P., Graf, L., & Strebel, A. (2020). Social versus liberal collective skill formation systems? A comparative-historical analysis of the role of trade unions in German and Swiss VET. *European Journal of Industrial Relations, 26*(3), 263–278.

Fernández, J. J., & Jaime-Castillo, A. M. (2013). Positive or negative policy feedbacks? Explaining popular attitudes towards pragmatic pension policy reforms. *European Sociological Review, 29*(4), 803–815.

Fulge, T., Bieber, T., & Martens, K. (2016). Rational intentions and unintended consequences. In K. Mundy, A. Green, B. Lingard, & A. Verger (Eds.), *The handbook of global education policy* (pp. 453–469). John Wiley & Sons.

Garrett, G. (1998). *Partisan politics in the global economy.* Cambridge University Press.

Garritzmann, J. L. (2015). Attitudes towards student support. How positive feedback-effects prevent change in the four worlds of student finance. *Journal of European Social Policy, 25*(2), 139–158.

Garritzmann, J. L. (2016). *The political economy of higher education finance: The politics of tuition fees and subsidies in OECD countries, 1945–2015.* Palgrave Macmillan.

Garritzmann, J. L., Busemeyer, M. R., & Neimanns, E. (2018). Public demand for social investment: New supporting coalitions for welfare state reform in Western Europe? *Journal of European Public Policy, 25*(6), 844–861.

Garritzmann, J. L., Häusermann, S., Kurer, T., Palier, B., & Pinggera, M. (2023). The emergence of knowledge economies: Educational expansion, labor market changes, and the politics of social investment. In J. L. Garritzmann, S. Häusermann, & B. Palier (Eds.), *The world politics of social investment (Vol. I): Welfare states in the knowledge economy* (pp. 251–281). Oxford University Press.

Garritzmann, J. L., Häusermann, S., Palier, B., & Zollinger, C. (2017). WoPSI—The world politics of social investment: An international research project to explain variance in social investment agendas and social investment reforms across countries and world regions. *LIEPP Working Paper 64.* https://www.zora.uzh.ch/id/eprint/142576/

Garritzmann, S. (2020). Education systems and political inequality: How educational institutions shape turnout gaps [PhD dissertation, University of Konstanz].

Genschel, P. (2002). Globalization, tax competition, and the welfare state. *Politics & Society, 30*(2), 245–275.

Gingrich, J. (2019). Schools and attitudes toward economic equality. *Policy Studies Journal, 47*(2), 324–352.

Gingrich, J., & Ansell, B. (2012). Preferences in context: Micro preferences, macro contexts, and the demand for social policy. *Comparative Political Studies, 45*(12), 1624–1654.

Goerres, A., & Tepe, M. (2012). Doing it for the kids? The determinants of attitudes towards public childcare in unified Germany. *Journal of Social Policy, 41*(2), 349–372.

Hall, P. A. (1993). Policy paradigms, social learning, and the state: The case of economic policy-making in Britain. *Comparative Politics, 25*(3), 275–296.

Hall, P. A., & Soskice, D. (2001). *Varieties of capitalism: The institutional foundations of comparative advantage*. Oxford University Press.

Hall, P. A., & Taylor, R. C. R. (1996). Political science and the three new institutionalisms. *Political Studies, 44*(5), 936–957.

Hannah, S. B. (1996). The Higher Education Act of 1992: Skills, constraints, and the politics of higher education. *The Journal of Higher Education, 67*(5), 498–527.

Heckman, J. (2006). Skill formation and economics of investing in disadvantaged children. *Science, 312*, 1900–1902.

Iversen, T. (2001). The dynamics of welfare state expansion: Trade openness, deindustrialization and partisan politics. In *The new politics of the welfare state*, edited by Paul Pierson, 45–79. Oxford University Press.

Iversen, T., & Cusack, T. R. (2000). The causes of welfare state expansion: Deindustrialization or globalization? *World Politics, 52*(3), 313–349.

Jackson, L. (2016). Globalization and education. *Oxford Research Encyclopedia of Education*. https://oxfordre.com/education/view/10.1093/acrefore/9780190264093.001.0001/acrefore-9780190264093-e-52

Jacobs, A. M., & Weaver, K. (2015). When policies undo themselves: Selfundermining feedback as a source of policy change. *Governance, 28*(4), 441–457.

Jahn, D. (2006). Globalization as "Galton's problem": The missing link in the analysis of diffusion patterns in welfare state development. *International Organization, 60*(2), 401–431.

Jakobi, A. P., & Teltemann, J. (2011). Convergence in education policy? A quantitative analysis of policy change and stability in OECD countries. *Compare: A Journal of Comparative and International Education, 41*(5), 579–595.

Katzenstein, P. J. (1985). *Small states in world markets: Industrial policy in Europe*. Cornell University Press.

Klüver, H., & Pickup, M. (2018). Are they listening? Public opinion, interest groups and government responsiveness. *West European Politics, 42*(1), 91–112.

Kumlin, S., & Stadelmann-Steffen, I. (2014). *How welfare states shape the democratic public: Policy feedback, participation, voting, and attitudes*. Edward Elgar.

Kurzer, P. (1991). Unemployment in open economies: The impact of trade, finance, and European integration. *Comparative Political Studies, 24*(1), 3–30.

Larsen, E. G. (2019). Policy feedback effects on mass publics: A quantitative review. *Policy Studies Journal, 47*(2), 372–394.

Marshall, J., & Fisher, S. D. (2015). Compensation or constraint? How different dynamics of economic globalization affect government spending and electoral turnout. *British Journal of Political Science, 45*(2), 353–389.

McGinn, N. F. (1997). The impact of globalization on national education systems. *Prospects*, *27*(1), 41–54.

Mettler, S. (2002). Bringing the state back in to civic engagement: Policy feedback effects of the G.I. Bill for World War II veterans. *The American Political Science Review, 96*(2), 351–365.

Mettler, S. (2009). Promoting inequality. The politics of higher education policy in an era of conservative governance. In L. Jacobs & D. King (Eds.), *The unsustainable American state* (pp. 197–222). Oxford University Press.

Mettler, S. (2010). Reconstituting the submerged state: The challenges of social policy reform in the Obama era. *Perspectives on Politics, 8*(3), 803–824.

Mettler, S., & Soss, J. (2004). The consequences of public policy for democratic citizenship: Bridging policy studies and mass politics. *Perspectives on Politics, 2*(1), 55–73.

Moe, T. M., & Wiborg, S. (2016). *The comparative politics of education: Teachers unions and education systems around the world*. Cambridge University Press.

Morgan, K. J. (2013). Path shifting of the welfare state: Electoral competition and the expansion of work-family policies in Western Europe. *World Politics, 65*(1), 73–115.

Müller, W., & Gangl, M. (2003). *Transitions from education to work in Europe: The integration of youth into EU labour markets*. Oxford University Press.

Neimanns, E. (2017). Public opinion and social investment: How political-institutional context shapes support and opposition towards expanding childcare. *GSDS Working Paper, 2017–13*. Konstanz. https://nbn-resolving.org/urn:nbn:de:0168-ssoar-61273-9

Neimanns, E. (2021). Unequal benefits—Diverging attitudes? Analysing the effects of an unequal expansion of childcare provision on attitudes towards maternal employment across 18 European countries. *Journal of Public Policy, 41*, 251–276.

Neimanns, E. (2021b). Preferences, vote choice, and the politics of social investment: Addressing the puzzle of unequal benefits of childcare provision. *Journal of Social Policy, 51*(4), 945–965.

Neimanns, E., & Busemeyer, M. R. (2021). Class politics in the sandbox? An analysis of the socio-economic determinants of preferences towards public spending and parental fees for childcare. *Social Policy & Administration, 55*(1), 226–241.

Neundorf, A., Smets, K., & García-Albacete, G. M. (2013). Homemade citizens: The development of political interest during adolescence and young adulthood. *Acta Politica, 48*, 92–116.

Niemann, D., & Martens, K. (2018). Soft governance by hard fact? The OECD as a knowledge broker in education policy. *Global Social Policy, 18*(3), 267–283.

Niemann, D., Martens, K., & Teltemann, J. (2017). PISA and its consequences: Shaping education policies through international comparisons. *European Journal of Education, 52*(2), 175–183.

Nikolai, R., Briken, K., & Niemann, D. (2016). Teacher unionism in Germany: Fragmented competitors. In T. M. Moe & S. Wilborg (Eds.), *The comparative politics of education: Teachers unions and education systems around the world* (pp. 114–143). Cambridge University Press.

OECD. (2020). *Education at a glance 2020: OECD indicators*. OECD. https://doi.org/10.1787/69096873-en.

Pierson, P. (1993). When effect becomes cause: Policy feedback and political change. *World Politics, 45*(4), 595–628.

Pierson, P. (2000). Increasing returns, path dependence, and the study of politics. *American Political Science Review, 94*(2), 251–267.

Rizvi, F., & Lingard, B. (2010). *Globalizing education policy*. Routledge.

Rodrik, D. (1997). *Has globalization gone too far?* Institute for International Economics.

Scharpf, F. W. (1991). *Crisis and choice in European social democracy*. Cornell University Press.

Schattschneider, E. E. (1935). Politics, pressures and the tariff. https://agris.fao.org/agris-search/search.do?recordID=US201300714530

Scheve, K. F., & Slaughter, M. J. (2004). Economic insecurity and the globalization of production. *American Journal of Political Science, 48*(4), 662–74.

Skocpol, T. (1992). State formation and social policy in the United States. *American Behavioral Scientist, 35*(4–5), 559–584.

Skocpol, T. (1997). The Tocqueville problem: Civic engagement in American democracy. *Social Science History, 21*(4), 455–479.

Soss, J., & Schram, S. F. (2007). A public transformed? Welfare reform as policy feedback. *The American Political Science Review, 101*(1), 111–127.

Spring, J. (2008). Research on globalization and education. *Review of Educational Research, 78*(2), 330–363.

Spring, J. (2014). *Globalization of education: An introduction*. Routledge.

Stoker, L., & Jennings, M. K. (2008). Of time and the development of partisan polarization. *American Journal of Political Science, 52*(3), 619–635. doi:10.1111/j.1540-5907.2008.00333.x

Taylor-Gooby, P. (2002). The silver age of the welfare state: Perspectives on resilience. *Journal of Social Policy, 31*(4), 597–621.

Thelen, K. (1999). Historical institutionalism in comparative politics. *Annual Review of Political Science, 2*(1), 369–404.

Thelen, K. (2004). *How institutions evolve: The political economy of skills in Germany, Britain, the United States, and Japan*. Cambridge University Press.

Walter, S. (2010). Globalization and the welfare state: Testing the microfoundations of the compensation hypothesis. *International Studies Quarterly, 54*(2), 403–426.

Walter, S. (2017). Globalization and the demand-side of politics: How globalisation shapes labor market risk perceptions and policy preferences. *Political Science Research and Methods, 5*(1), 55–80.

Wilborg, S., & Larsen, K. R. (2017). Why school choice reforms in Denmark fail: The blocking power of the teacher union. *European Journal of Education, 52*(1), 92–103.

CHAPTER 27

....

POLICY ADVICE AND POLICY ADVISORY SYSTEMS IN EDUCATION

....

MARIA TULLIA GALANTI

INTRODUCTION

THE complexity of public policies poses serious challenges for both experts and policymakers. On the one hand, the wicked nature of the policy problems increases the demand of knowledge as a means to inform decisions; on the other, decisions depend on aspects other than pure knowledge, such as values and ultimately politics, making the actual use of knowledge a controversial issue (Weiss, 1979). Public policy scholars increasingly focus on a specific aspect of knowledge production in the policymaking, that is, the dynamics of policy advice. More specifically, policy advice can be described as an activity that includes "research, data analysis, proposal development, consultation with stakeholders, formulation of advice for decision makers, guiding policy through governmental and parliamentary processes, and the subsequent evaluation of the outcomes of the policy" (Gregory & Lonti, 2008, p. 838).

In particular, the study of the policy advisory systems and the interactions inside the policy subsystems offers a structural perspective on the capacity of the policy advice to influence the policymaking process. In other words, the study of the policy advisory systems acknowledges that influence of the advisors comes not only from scientific evidence and technical knowledge (Craft & Howlett, 2012) but also from representativeness and legitimacy (Hustedt & Veit, 2017), being the result of the contingent matching of the supply of technical solutions by internal and external advisors with a multifaceted demand by local policymakers (Halligan, 1995).

By focusing on policy advice and policy advisory systems, this chapter aims to offer a different perspective on the role of the international actors in shaping education reforms at the domestic level, taking seriously their role as policy advisors and their interaction with local policymakers. While the literature on global education policies emphasizes the growing importance of the international organizations in reform processes (also considering ideas and discourses) at the domestic level, it also acknowledges that the varied influence of these actors is mediated by local policymakers, by their need for legitimacy, and by the political and administrative architecture of a country (Mundy et al., 2016). In this chapter, the concepts of policy advice and policy advisory systems are presented to discuss how the configurations of a set of advisors in one country affect the borrowing of policy ideas and discourse on global education policies (Rizvi & Lingard, 2010; Steiner-Khamsi, 2004). It does so by focusing on relevant actors and logics emerged in the study of the policy advisory systems and of global education in the European countries.

Policy Advice: From the Anecdotal to a Systemic View

Taking on a structural approach to the study of policy advice, scholars in public policy described the institutionalization of advisory practices in different countries to understand the influence of policy advice in policymaking (Halligan, 1995). The influence of the advisor can be conceived in terms of the adoption of the policy solutions by the proximate policymakers, as a matching between a political demand and a technical offer of policy advice that is strongly contingent upon situations (Craft & Howlett, 2012). Therefore, also global actors in education policies can play a key role in this relationship, and particularly so as suppliers of ideas, discourses, but also evidence and knowledge, in the globalized education world (Ball, 2013). Nonetheless, they compete for influence with several other internal and external advisors who address a multifaceted political demand.

Therefore, it is important to shift the analytical focus from the individual—the single expert or the single advisor—to the system—the set of different advisors and their relations. A policy advisory system is defined as "the interlocking set of actors, with unique configurations in each sector and jurisdiction, who provide information, knowledge and recommendation for action to policy-makers" (Halligan, 1995, as referred to in Craft & Howlett, 2012, p. 80). In other words, this scholarship proposed that the number and type of actors involved in policy advice can make a difference in shaping policy decisions.

In this line of reasoning, the influence of advice over the policymaking derives from the proximity of the policy advisors to the decision-makers, and from the control that the government can exert on the content of their advice, thus emphasizing a strong cleavage between advisors belonging to the public service, advisors being internal to government, and advisors being external to the public sector (from academia to interest groups, from think tanks to international organizations) (Halligan, 1995).

The systemic view of policy advice suggests the dominant actors in policy advice depend both on the politico-administrative traditions (Craft & Halligan, 2017) and on the specific features of the policy sector (Craft & Wilder, 2017).

As for the number and type of dominant advisors at the national level, most of the evidence about the policy advisory systems has been collected on the Westminster countries, where policy advice is a formalized role, and the civil service is traditionally the first knowledge producer for the government. Other studies attempted a description of the advisory system in countries with other politico-administrative systems. In Continental countries such as Germany, the Netherlands, or Denmark, key actors in policy advice are both the bureaucracies and the advisory bodies representing the different interests in the neo-corporatist policymaking (Hustedt & Veit, 2017). In Napoleonic countries, while the civil servants are less involved in policy advisory activities (Aubin & Brans, 2020), a central role in policy advice is traditionally played by the ministerial cabinets, namely a staff of personal advisers, who are hired when a minister takes office on a temporary basis and who assist the minister in identifying and formulating problems, in outlining policy, and in everyday decision-making (Hustedt et al., 2017). In Napoleonic countries, the role of the public administration in policy advice is conditioned by the type of relations between the politicians and the bureaucrats (Peters, 2008) and the overall policy capacity (including the analytical one) of civil servants. In fact, the administrative system of the Napoleonic countries is politicized at the top in most countries (e.g., in France, in Spain, in Italy, in Belgium), but the tone of the relationship between the politicians and the bureaucrats can be very different, ranging from collaboration or competition in countries where the policy capacity is high (as in France or in Spain), to conflict or isolation in countries with scarce policy capacities (as in Italy).

Another important feature that shapes the number and type of the advisors in these countries is the type of policymaking (Hustedt & Veit, 2017). In fact, in countries with neo-corporatist and more coordinative policymaking, the accessibility of the policy advisory system to external actors is higher. On the contrary, in pluralist systems the access to the policymaking and thus to the system of advice is more competitive and conflictual, with less coordination among internal and external actors.

Therefore, the literature on the policy advisory systems suggests that, at the national level, the set of actors composing the national advisory systems is depending on the type of the politico-administrative system (neutral or politicized civil service), on the one hand, and on the prevalent style of policymaking (pluralist or neo-corporatist), on the other. In Westminster countries, the main policy advisors are the civil servants in a neutral civil service, and the access of the external advisors is competitive and scarcely institutionalized, so that external knowledge is contracted by competition among a number of highly active think tanks and diverse organizations. In the Continental countries, the professional bureaucracies still play a key role in policy advice, often with an anticipatory policy style, but the advisory system is open to external actors that act as coordinate advisors into institutionalized advisory boards and councils (Hustedt & Veit, 2017, p. 45). In Central European countries, the main actors in policy advice are the ministerial cabinets, while the politicized civil service may still play a crucial role as incidental advisors (Aubin & Brans, 2020), and the advisory system is open to a number of coordinated policy advisors institutionalized in councils and boards (Fobé et al., 2013). In Southern European countries, where the policy advisory system has not been studied in detail, one might expect that, given the Napoleonic administrative tradition and a rather politicized public administration, the ministerial cabinets and the (capable) bureaucracies in the public administration play a crucial role in advice. At the same time, the access to the advisory system to other external actors would be more fragmented and competitive, depending also on the dynamics of social concentration in the different policy sectors. Table 27.1 presents the main advisors in the different systems.

Another aspect of interest in the literature on the policy advisory systems relates to the dynamics of change of those systems, which again have been empirically studied mostly in the Westminster countries (Craft & Halligan, 2017; Hustedt, 2019). A general trend of deinstitutionalization of traditional advisory practices is discernible in all countries, from the Westminster (Craft & Halligan, 2017) to the Napoleonic (with the evidence of an ongoing decabinetization; Brans et al., 2017, p. 58). In a nutshell, the deinstitutionalization of the policy advisory systems relates to the impact of a number of macro phenomena—such as the globalization of the economy, the governance shift in politics, or the administrative reforms with the downsizing of public administration—that brought to the end the monopoly of knowledge by a few domestic actors (Craft & Howlett, 2012), while opening the way to the pluralization of the advisors, on the one hand, and the differentiation of the content of their policy advice, on the other (Blum & Brans, 2017; Pattyn et al., 2022; Veit et al., 2017; Galanti & Lippi, 2022).

As for the pluralization of actors, trends toward the externalization (or conversely, the internalization) of the policy advisory system (PAS) have been described in different countries. The externalization of the PAS can be defined as the relocation of advisory

Table 27.1 Configurations of Policy Advisory Systems According to the Politico-Administrative System and Prevailing Policymaking Style: A Structural Perspective on Policy Advice

	Pluralist Policymaking (or Social Concertation)	Neo-Corporatist Policymaking
Neutrality in politico-administrative relations	PAS in Westminster countries—bureaucratic advice and competition for external advice (United Kingdom, Canada, Australia)	PAS in Continental Europe——bureaucratic advice and coordination of external advice (Germany, Netherlands, Denmark)
Politicization in politico-administrative relations	PAS in Southern Europe—cabinet advice and competition for external advice (Italy, Spain, Greece)	PAS in Central Europe—cabinet advice and coordination of external advisors (Belgium)

PAS, policy advisory system.

activities previously performed inside government organizations to places outside of government (Vesély, 2013, p. 200). More broadly, it signals the growth of external advice from an array of actors, from academics to think tanks, from interest groups to policy consultants, from civic society to international organizations. Externalization is considered as a consequence of changes in both the supply and the demand for policy advice (Craft & Howlett, 2013, p. 190). As for the supply, externalization may be caused by both the decrease of internal capacities and the expansion of a competitive marketplace for advice. As for the demand, the externalization of advice is seen as a consequence of the wicked nature of the policy problems (requiring more expertise and specialization) or as a consequence of political factors (such as the attempts to exert more political control and responsiveness over administration or the adherence to the ideological orientations) (Vesély, 2013, p. 206).

At for the differentiation of the content of the advice, the literature pointed to the increasing politicization of policy advice, intended as the provision of nontechnical or nonsubstantive advice to decision-makers, ranging from personal opinion and experience about public opinion and key stakeholders' views, to partisan electoral advice (Craft & Howlett, 2013, p. 191). The trend toward politicization signals that the relevant content of policy advice is not only substantive and technical but also procedural and political (Craft & Howlett, 2012). This echoes the idea of the move from one idealized model of policy advice, the rational and positivist "speaking truth to power model" of advice legitimized by knowledge, toward a post-positivist "sharing truth with multiple actors" model of advice, where the legitimacy of the advice comes not only from its scientific rigor but also from its representativeness of the demands of the relevant actors in the society (Prince, 2007).

Therefore, this scholarship highlights that the monopoly of traditional advisors is eroding in all countries, and that both the technical and the political content of the advice matter for the influence. This aspect emerges with clarity if we focus on the specific configurations of policy advice inside the different policy subsystems (Craft & Wilder, 2017; Halligan, 1995, p. 42). The so-called second wave of studies emphasizes that it is not only the proximity to policymakers but also the interactions and the cohesiveness of a policy subsystem that determines the features of the advisory networks, and thus the dynamics of advisory influence in the system. How systems of advisors coalesce in networks depends on the access of policy advisors to the policy subsystem, and on their ideational compatibility with the policy subsystem (Craft & Wilder, 2017).

In other words, the features of the policy subsystem shape the dynamics of the sectoral advisory networks. For example, when both the ideational compatibility and the accessibility of external actors to the advice is high, the policy advisory network will be collaborative; when the ideational compatibility is low but the accessibility is high, the policy advisory network will be contested; when the access for alternative forms of advice is low and the ideational compatibility is high, the advisory network will be hegemonic; finally, when no access or ideational compatibility is present, the advisory network will be closed and isolated (Craft & Wilder, 2017).

As both the features of the policy subsystems and the configurations of the sectoral advisory networks as subsets of the national policy advisory system are a matter of empirical investigation, the following paragraph draws on the scholarship on policy advice in globalized education to highlight what type of advisors may prove crucial for education reforms in the European countries.

Policy Advice in Education in a Globalized World: Competition Between Internal and External Advisors

Given the importance of the ideational compatibility and of the policy subsystem cohesiveness, focusing on policy advice in education policies is significant and challenging at the same time. It is significant, because the globalization of education opens the way to a number of international organizations into domestic policymaking (Ball, 2012; Carney & Klerides, 2020); and it is challenging, because few studies address explicitly the role of policy advice and of the policy advisory systems in shaping policymaking in education. This paragraph discusses the evidence over policy advice in education around two main issues: the policy advisors in education policymaking in a globalized world, and the influence these advisors have on policymaking in education, in terms of shaping reform design and adoption.

As for who the advisors are, traditional internal advisors still play an important role in education policies in the different countries. While the civil service remains crucial in Westminster systems (Ball, 2012), not only the cabinets and the Ministerial bureaucracies but also the education advisory councils seem to play a pivotal role in Central and Southern European countries (Van Damme et al., 2011). These advisory bodies have a double function: a problem-solving function, as they contribute to offering knowledge for effective policy decisions; and a legitimacy function, as they contribute to democracy by strengthening the input side of the advisory process. As they act in a competitive environment for advice, these advisory councils work as boundary organizations that have to respond to multiple principals such as the state, the society, and the world of science (Van Damme et al., 2011, p. 142). At the same time, other external domestic advisors such as think tanks and private foundations have been studied as key actors in inspiring major reforms in different European countries, with a strategic use of both ideas and scientific evidence (Ball, 2012; Olmedo & Grau, 2013).

Despite the relevance of domestic actors for policy advice in education, the most interesting developments pertain to the growing importance of the international organizations as actors in global education (Carney & Klerides, 2020; Mundy et al., 2016). With particular reference to the European context, the literature emphasized the role of the Organization for Economic Cooperation and Development (OECD) and of the European Union (EU) in shaping education reforms in several countries (Ozga et al., 2011). Though the global mechanisms for influence range from the hard power of imposition to softer forms of dissemination and interdependence (Dale, 1999), the main themes that emerge in the European context are the process of harmonization of policies at the European level, and the use of the standardized and comparative evaluations (such as the OECD's Program for International Student Assessment [PISA]) on the performance of the students, which can be used in very different ways by domestic government.

Therefore, the literature on the role of the international organizations shows that their influence in domestic education policies is debatable. While it is acknowledged that the advice of the international organizations is not the only factor that drives education reforms (Rautalin et al., 2019), its impact can vary significantly, depending on the content of the advice and on the interaction with the local contexts, in a similar vein to the phenomena of policy borrowing (Steiner-Khamsi, 2004). On the one hand, the comparative and standardized data and the information provided by the international organizations can be used to respatialize governing relations and to push for evidence-based policymaking in education (Ozga et al., 2011); on the other hand, studies have shown that the same data and information can be used by local policy actors as a form of domestic policy legitimation (Grek, 2009).

As a matter of fact, the advice of the OECD and of the EU is nowadays delivered through a number of vehicles—from knowledge and information with the PISA, to regulatory instruments such as the Open Method of Coordination and the recommendations of the European Commission and of the OECD through the country thematic reports. These different types of advice are juridically nonmandatory; still, they are able to activate different pressures for domestic policy reforms, including social learning (Grek, 2017). At the same time, the same type of advice can bring very different consequences in the different countries, according to the context and the historical traditions of education (Michel, 2017). A very well-known example is the reception of the first round of the OECD's PISA results in the early 2000s, leading to different policy outcomes in Germany and in England. While the (negative) PISA results were able to ignite a debate in Germany, ultimately bringing an ideational turn in education and the introduction of evidence-based policymaking in education, the same (negative) data did not activate meaningful reforms in England in the short run, for apparently practical reasons (Knodel, et al., 2013, pp. 426–430). England was already attuned with the competitive education framework promoted by the PISA, and it was equipped with a domestic evaluation system, so that the awareness of the importance of international comparisons grew progressively. Therefore, what makes the international organizations become influential advisors in domestic education systems ultimately relates also to how local policymakers receive and use their advice.

Following this line of reasoning, it seems plausible that the influence of the international organizations as advisors in domestic policymaking depends both on the access of their advice to the education system and on the ideational compatibility of the content of their advice.

As for the access, the literature on globalized education describes different ways for the international advisors to enter the domestic advisory networks. The usual and most frequent way is through the public debate over education reforms, sometimes limited to the discursive level (Grek et al., 2009). For example, the PISA result can be reported by the media—though with varied depth—as a justification to intervene in education (Pons, 2011; Rautalin et al., 2019). At the same time, the advice of the international actors may have direct access to policymakers in the supranational contexts, such as the expert groups at the European level, offering a neutral arena for debate among the member states (Elken, 2018). Finally, the international advisors can play a boundary spanner role in connecting the different actors of the education system in a country, providing both information and tailored policy solutions to national demands (Grek, 2020).

In all these cases, it seems plausible that what makes the difference is also the ideational compatibility of the content, the goals and the instruments proposed by the advice, along with the perception of the legitimacy of the advisors. For example, the international organizations are influential when there is a match between their objectives and the overarching policy goals of the domestic actors (Grek et al., 2013; Elken, 2018, p. 346). In some other cases, their influence derives from their capacity to assemble effective data and policy mix, thus offering policy solutions that are acceptable and appropriate in the national education system (Auld & Morris, 2016; Grek, 2020; Michel, 2017; Takala et al., 2018); finally, the influence of the advice of the international organizations does not depend on hierarchical relations, but on the horizontal interactions at the local level with domestic actors: While acting as boundary spanners, they are able not only to deliver knowledge and advice but also to build educational consensus (Grek, 2020).

POLICY ADVISORY SYSTEMS IN EDUCATION: FROM CONFIGURATIONS TO IMPACT

As the review on the literature on policy advice in education has shown, both the composition and the dynamics of the policy advisory systems in education are a matter of empirical investigation in the different countries. Advisory networks in education can be considered as a subset of a wider national policy advisory system where the capable bureaucracies play a key role, while the number and type of external actors delivering policy advice may be variable, as the degree of representation and coordination among advisors. At the same time, the dynamics in the sectoral advisory network depend on the features of the education subsystems in each country. Ideational and coalition cohesiveness in the subsystem may vary from one country to the other, and in time, also considering the level of centralization or decentralization of the decision-making and the level of school autonomy.

The review of the literature on policy advice in education suggests some relevant points in this regard. First, the composition of the advisory network in education depends on the features of the school system and its policy legacies in terms of diffused beliefs and policy instruments, but it is also shaped by contingent political factors. In other words, the demand side of policy advice in education matters for the number and type of advisors that ultimately play a role in reforms. Policymakers may thus purposefully expand the network of the advisors internal to the public services—which remain the key advisors, especially in systems with higher policy capacities—to different external advisors (Goyal & Saguin, 2019).

Second, the content of the advice in education remains a controversial issue. On the one hand, in many national contexts what works as evidence in the field of education and, more specifically, what type of evidence is legitimate are still debatable (Auld & Morris, 2016). While the collection of complete and comparable data may prove difficult in most countries (Pons, 2011), the importance of ideas in defining expected outcomes and performance in schools makes expert advice difficult to handle, so that evidence-based policies as a result of policy advice often represent the exception, rather than the norm. Therefore, it is also how policy advisors assemble evidence and solutions, and therefore the supply side of policy advice, that shape the impact of policy advice in education reforms (Rautalin et al., 2019).

Taking on the perspective of what matters for the demand and the supply of advice in education, one can reason about the conditions that shape the composition and the dynamics of education advisory networks, on the one hand, and about what makes policy advice in education effective, on the other.

Structures of Advisory Networks in Education

As said, the literature on policy advisors in education suggests that the political demand plays an important role in defining the main advisors, and thus the structures of the advisory network at the subsystem level. Policymakers control the access to the policy advisory networks in education. As a matter of fact, the accessibility of the education subsystem determines the number of influential internal or external advisors. In a traditionally closed education subsystem, the expectation is that the traditional internal actors to the school system (such as the civil servants but also the unions and other representative associations) will be key actors in the education advisory network at the domestic level; at the same time traditionally decentralized school systems will be more open to the advice of a number of external advisors, ranging from education advisory boards to pedagogists and, eventually, the international organizations.

Nonetheless, the actual composition of the advisory network in education may also strongly depend on the political orientation of the government and its reform strategy.

Studies on the role of the OECD and the EU in advising education revealed that the presence of these advisors in the public debate and, most importantly, the actual use of their advice are more likely when the ideas of the advisors match with the preferences of local policymakers (Grek, 2020; Steiner-Khamsi, 2004). In other words, it seems plausible that the actual externalization of policy advice in education also depends on the strategies of the government in promoting (or in stopping) education reforms. If the policymakers seek to legitimize their action from within the school system, thus adopting internal legitimacy strategies, external actors are less relevant, while internal and bureaucratic actors will maintain a crucial role. Instead, if the policymakers pursue a legitimation that is external to the school system, the appeal to the knowledge offered by external actors, such as the academics, the think tanks, and the international organizations, will be much more relevant (Capano & Lippi, 2018). In particular, these external advisors may become crucial not only as suppliers of evidence and recommendations but also as intermediaries for policy advice, as demonstrated by the ability of the OECD to play as a boundary spanner in fragmented contexts (Grek, 2020).

Not only do the political demand but also the cohesiveness of the education subsystem matters to the structure of the advisory networks. It is plausible that the ideational compatibility between the policy subsystem and the advisors (in the content, in the purpose, in the issues, in the relations of the advice) will pave the way to collaborative relationships within the advisory network, or even to competition between internal and external advisors (Craft & Wilder, 2017). Instead, the lack of ideational compatibility between the subsystem and the advisors will lead to an isolated advisory network, where traditional internal actors dominate advice, or to a contested advisory network, with the presence of external advisors who challenge the ideas in the subsystem.

This type of reasoning can be summarized in a typology that shows how the political demand and the subsystem characteristics shape the composition and the dynamics of advisory networks in education (see Table 27.2).

A coordinated advisory network is more likely to result when the policymakers pursue internal legitimation strategies, and the ideational compatibility is high. Here we expect an advisory network involving traditional advisors and boards, where internal advisors such as the ministerial bureaucracies, institutional advisors, and key stakeholders such as the trade unions play a key role in shaping reforms (Van Damme et al., 2011). This type of network shaped the education reforms under the center-left

Table 27.2 The Configuration of Advisory Networks in Education

	High Ideational Compatibility	Low Ideational Compatibility
Internal legitimacy	Coordinated advisory network in education	Isolated advisory network in education
External legitimacy	Competitive advisory network in education	Contested policy network in education

government and the Minister Berlinguer in 1997 in Italy. The minister aimed at realizing a paradigmatic change in the education system toward school autonomy, and he worked to build internal legitimacy to reassure the internal stakeholders and allow coordination with the bureaucracies, the unions, and the schools (Capano & Lippi, 2018).

When the policymakers pursue internal legitimacy and the ideational compatibility between the subsystem and the advisors is low, we might expect a close and isolated advisory network, where bureaucratic actors deliver advice in a close and cohesive network. This type of network could emerge when reform is triggered by situations of deep crisis and uncertainty, such as during the first months of the COVID-19 pandemic. Education policies in Italy could be again a case in point. The need to urgently activate the distance teaching in all the country after March 2020 pushed the government to build a closed and isolated network of internal advisors, with the ministerial bureaucracies and the education research institute INDIRE, to quickly learn from the very few and experimental experiences of online teaching. A special commission of experts was also appointed by the Minister, but the advisory report by the commission was never released by the Ministry and did not enter in the public debate, thus signaling its limited influence. At the same time, internal stakeholders such as the unions and a percentage of the teachers initially resisted to the development of other solutions, remaining peripheral to both advice and decisions during the first months of the pandemic (Pavolini et al., 2021).

Instead, if the legitimacy for reform is sought also outside the policy subsystem, we expect an advisory network that is open to external advisors who may also become key advisors if they share ideational compatibility with the actors in the education subsystem, with a competition between internal and external actors over advice. A case in point is the reforms in Italy by the center-right government with Minister Moratti between 2001 and 2006, when the policymakers sought for external legitimacy from both the society and the international institutions, creating a competitive environment between internal and external advisors. Another example is the reform triggered by the 2000 PISA results in Germany and England. While the German government needed the legitimation coming also from external and international actors to allow for a paradigmatic shift in the school system, important internal actors such as the state governments and other domestic advisors ultimately played a role in defining the instruments to push the school system toward a more competitive arrangement (Grek, 2009; Knodel et al., 2013).

Finally, when external legitimacy is pursued but the ideational compatibility between the advisors and the subsystem is rather low, a contested network of advice will include external actors who may challenge internal actors and advisors in the subsystem, such as in the case of the Minister Gelmini under the center-right government in Italy between 2008 and 2011. The minister sought external legitimacy from the EU in a period where Italian public spending was highly constrained by austerity and fiscal rigor. International advisors may eventually play a role of intermediation and brokerage, acting as boundary spanners to articulate and diffuse advice to the other actors in the subsystem in order to overcome resistances to change. This seems to be the role that the OECD has played in several countries where its recommendations were welcomed because of the capacity of this international organization to work with local stakeholders (Grek, 2020).

ADVISORY CONTENT AND POSSIBLE IMPACTS ON REFORMS

Another relevant question for the impact of policy advice relates to its content, and to how it is perceived and used by the policymakers. As the literature on policy advice in education has shown, the possibility for different types of advisors to influence reforms depend also on the compatibility of the contents, the purposes and the instruments proposed by the advisors with both the political goals of policymakers and the ideas and practices rooted in the education system. The latter aspect suggests that the characteristics of the advice, and not just the configuration of the advisory network, matters for education reform. The studies on the role of the international organizations in shaping reforms highlighted that the same evidence and recommendations were received quite differently in the different contexts (Grek, 2009; Knodel et al., 2013; Michel, 2017), not only because of the goal acceptability, but also because of the type of policy instruments proposed as solutions (Capano & Lippi, 2018).

A conceptualization of the impact of policy advice in education—in terms of the use of the advice and of the related knowledge—can be useful in this respect. The public policy literature usually distinguishes different uses of knowledge, ranging from an instrumental use (oriented to problem-solving) to a symbolic use (oriented to legitimacy). Weiss (1979) described different models of research utilization that can be used to derive different uses of policy advice as knowledge utilization: an enlightenment (or instrumental) use, a political use, and a tactical use. While the instrumental use is linked to a rational problem-solving logic, the political use of advice occurs when policymakers use advice and knowledge ex post, to justify decisions taken according to other criteria (partisan, ideological), thus signaling their need for legitimacy. A third possibility is that policymakers use advice in a tactical way, by emphasizing the collaboration with the advisors but without using the related evidence or advice in their decisions, ultimately referring to the experts for a legitimizing function.

Following this line of reasoning, one can see that the use of advice in education policy ranges from the instrumental, to the political, to the tactic, or to the nonuse. The argument is that the use of advice in education is determined by the characteristics of the supply side of the advice relationship, and in particular by the content of the advice articulated as policy goals and as policy instruments.

On the one hand, the acceptability of the overarching goals of education policies between the advisor and the policymaker is crucial in determining the use of advice. Sharing the same views about education and the same ideas about the expected outcomes of education policies strongly favors the positive reception of the advice, while paving the way to effective policy change. Instead, where the goals of the advisors and of the policymakers are different, the lack of goal acceptability may bring to a tactical or even mimetic use of advice, or even to its nonuse, ultimately reinforcing the status quo.

On the other hand, the availability and coherence of the policy instruments proposed as solutions by the advisors can make the difference on the overall response of policymakers to the advice. As a matter of fact, reforms are a battle of ideas as much as of instruments, as the brightest ideas without the policy capacities to implement them may bring huge failures, also in terms of political consent (Wu et al., 2015). To be effective, policy advice has to propose solutions in terms of policy instruments that are available and sustainable for actors in the domestic education subsystem. While the coherence between the policy goals and the policy instruments proposed by the advisors matters for the quality of the overall design of the reform (a coherent package of goals and instruments logically favors higher effectiveness), the availability of solutions that can be implemented easily and without great resistances from the actors in the subsystem proved to be quite appealing for policymakers. On the contrary, recommending instruments that require a redistribution of resources in the subsystem and that ultimately can be perceived as nonacceptable could make the advice less appealing for policymakers.

Therefore, Table 27.3 interprets the impact of policy advice (in terms of its use by the policymakers) on the basis of the acceptability of the policy goals and of the availability of the policy instruments offered by the advisors.

When the policy goals are acceptable and the instruments are available, the use of the advice will be instrumental and finalized to problem-solving, possibly bringing radical or nonincremental change in education policies. This seems to have been the case of the reform of the German education system after the first release of the PISA data in the early 2000s (Grek, 2009). The evidence provided by the OECD was used to both reform the purpose of the education system toward a lifelong learning model and to set a system for students' evaluation that was not available at the time.

If the policy goals of the advice are acceptable, but the instruments are not available, the use of the policy advice is more likely to be political: Policymakers will refer to the experts' advice ex post, in order to legitimize decisions taken for political reasons. In this case, the advice is likely to be used to legitimize either stability or incremental change.

Table 27.3 The Use of Policy Advice in Education Based on Goal Acceptability and Instruments Availability

	Policy Instruments Available	Policy Instruments Unavailable
Policy goals acceptable	Instrumental use of advice—transformative impact	Political use of advice—incremental impact
Policy goals unacceptable	Tactical use of advice—incremental or no impact	Nonuse of advice—no impact

This seems to have been the case in the reception of the PISA results in the United Kingdom in early 2000: While the model of education promoted by the OECD was coherent with the reform of education implemented 20 years before, the PISA data were not considered at first as a legitimate instrument, given the availability of domestic data on the performance of students (Knodel et al., 2013).

When there is unacceptability of goals, but the recommended policy instruments are available, the use of advice is likely be tactical: Policymakers will refer in the public debate to the knowledge and expertise of reputed experts to legitimize their actions, but they will not use it in the actual design of the solutions, leading to incremental change or stability, because they basically pursue alternative goals. In these cases, the reference to the advice of the international organizations may be confined to discourse (Schlaufer, 2016). This might be the case of education reforms driven by austerity measures that adopted spending review mechanisms and the downsizing of teachers' recruitment as instruments to realize the containment of the public expenditure, while leaving the overarching goals of the school system unvaried. The case of the Gelmini reforms on teachers' recruitment in Italy could be one case in point.

Finally, when the content of the advice combines both unacceptable goals and unavailability of instruments, it is likely that policymakers will not use the advice, with no impact on education reform. This is basically due to the cost (in terms of political consent) of promoting evidence-based policies that go against the existing beliefs and the rooted practices in the school system. Again, the Italian reforms since 1997 show the difficulties in making the advice of the expert relevant on key issues such as the introduction of a merit-based system and the evaluation of teachers in the closed Italian education subsystem.

CONCLUSIONS

Policy advice and the policy advisory systems are increasingly considered as a key variable to understand the role of knowledge and expertise in policymaking. As a matter of fact, how advisors can be influential on policy reforms depends also on the matching between the demand and the offer of advice by an increasing number of actors.

To investigate these issues, this chapter draws on the literature on policy advice and the policy advisory system to reflect on the influence of advice over policymaking in education. This literature highlights that both the configuration of advisors at the national and sectoral levels and the dynamics inside the education subsystem matter for influence. More specifically, it is not only the proximity to the policymakers that matters but also their strategies for legitimation, the ideational compatibility between the advisors and the other actors in the subsystem, and the acceptability of the advice in terms of both the goals and the instrument recommended. The idea is that it is the matching between the demand and the supply that becomes crucial to determine both the externalization and the impact of the advice.

The importance of the role of policy advisors in shaping education policy reform emerged clearly from the reading of the (limited) literature that explicitly addresses policy advice as a practice and experts as advisors in education in the European context. While the globalization of education represents a window of opportunity for new entrants in the domestic advisory systems, the literature on policy advice in education suggests that the impact of the external advisors on education policies does not depend only on the reputation of the advisor, nor on the quality of the research provided, but on the political will of the policymakers and on the interactions of experts and advisors with both traditional internal advisors and local policymakers. The actual composition of the advisory system in education and the interactions of the advisors with the school system remain matters of empirical investigation in each country. Similarly, the scope and intensity of evidence-based policymaking have not yet been investigated systematically in the area of education, where what counts as evidence is still debated, both in the political and in the academic debate. Therefore, this chapter is an attempt to conceptualize the advisory relationships in the sector of education by focusing on both the structure of the advisory network and on the content of the policy advice in terms of goal and instruments. In so doing, the chapter uses the existing literature on reform processes in education to propose two typologies as conceptual instruments to understand the role that the policy advisory system and the content of the advice have in shaping domestic reforms. Overall, the typologies on the configuration of advisors and on the use of advice in education are intended to offer tools to investigate the role of political demand and of legitimacy in shaping the dynamics in education policies, and they will need to be tested against more systematic empirical and comparative research.

References

Aubin, D., & Brans, M. (2020). Policy advisory styles in the Francophone Belgian civil service. *International Review of Administrative Sciences*, 86(3), 463–478.

Auld, E., & Morris, P. (2016). PISA, policy and persuasion: Translating complex conditions into education "best practice." *Comparative Education*, 52(2), 202–229.

Ball, S. J. (1990/2012). *Politics and policy making in education: Explorations in sociology.*

Ball, S. J. (2013). *The education debate* (2nd ed.). Policy Press.

Blum, S., & Brans, M. (2017). Academic policy analysis and research utilization for policymaking. In M. Brans, I. Geva-May, & M. Howlett (Eds.), *Routledge handbook of comparative policy analysis* (pp. 341–359). Routledge.

Brans, M., de Visscher, C., Gouglas, A., & Jaspers, S. (2017). Political control and bureaucratic expertise: Policy analysis by ministerial cabinet members. In M. Brans & D. Aubin (Eds.), *Policy analysis in Belgium* (pp. 57–58). Policy Press.

Capano, G., & Lippi, A. (2018). How decision-makers make the "right choice"? Instrument selection between legitimacy and instrumentality: Evidence from education policy in Italy (1996–2016). *Rivista Italiana di Politiche Pubbliche*, 13(2), 219–254.

Carney, S., & Klerides, E. (2020). Governance and the evolving global education order. *European Education*, 52(2), 81–86. doi:10.1080/10564934.2020.1769308

Connaughton, B. (2010). "Glorified gofers, policy experts or good generalists": A classification of the roles of the Irish ministerial adviser. *Irish Political Studies*, *25*(3), 347–369.

Craft, J. (2015). Conceptualizing the policy work of partisan advisers. *Policy Sciences*, *48*(2), 135–158.

Craft, J., & Halligan, J. (2017). Assessing 30 years of Westminster policy advisory system experience. *Policy Sciences*, *50*(1), 47–62.

Craft, J., & Howlett, M. (2012). Policy formulation, governance shifts and policy influence: Location and content in policy advisory systems. *Journal of Public Policy*, *32*(2), 79–98.

Craft, J., & Howlett, M. (2013). The dual dynamics of policy advisory systems: The impact of externalization and politicization on policy advice. *Policy and Society*, *32*(3), 187–197.

Craft, J., & Wilder, M. (2017). Catching a second wave: Context and compatibility in advisory system dynamics. *Policy Studies Journal*, *45*(1), 215–239.

Dale, R. (1999). Specifying globalization effects on national policy: Focus on the mechanisms. *Journal of Education Policy*, *14*(1), 427–448.

Eichbaum, C., & Shaw, R. (2008). Revisiting politicization: Political advisers and public servants in Westminster systems. *Governance*, *21*(3), 337–363.

Elken, M. (2018). Expert group institutionalization and task expansion in European education policy-making. *European Educational Research Journal*, *17*(3), 335–348. https://doi.org/10.1177/1474904117720406

Fobé, E., Brans, M., Vancoppenolle, D., & Van Damme, J. (2013). Institutionalized advisory systems: An analysis of member satisfaction of advice production and use across nine strategic advisory councils in Flanders (Belgium). *Policy and Society*, *32*(3), 225–240.

Galanti, M. T., & Lippi, A. (2022). Government research institutes in the Italian policy advisory system. *International Review of Administrative Sciences*. https://doi.org/10.1177/0020852321 1070510

Goyal, N., & Saguin, K. (2019). Capacity, control, and content: The supply of think tank policy advice in India. *Policy Studies*, *40*(3–4), 337–352.

Gregory, R., & Lonti, Z. (2008). Chasing shadows? Performance measurement of policy advice in New Zealand government departments. *Public Administration*, *86*(3), 837–856.

Grek, S. (2009). Governing by numbers: The PISA "effect" in Europe. *Journal of Education Policy*, *24*(1), 23–37.

Grek, S. (2017). Socialisation, learning and the OECD's reviews of national policies for education: The case of Sweden. *Critical Studies in Education*, *58*(3), 295–310.

Grek, S. (2020). Facing "a tipping point"? The role of the OECD as a boundary organisation in governing education in Sweden. *Education Inquiry*, *11*(3), 175–195.

Grek, S., Lawn, M., Lingard, B., Ozga, J., Rinne, R., Segerholm, C., & Simola, H. (2009). National policy brokering and the construction of the European education space in England, Sweden, Finland and Scotland. *Comparative Education*, *45*(1), 5–21.

Grek, S., Lawn, M., Ozga, J., & Segerholm, C. (2013). Governing by inspection? European inspectorates and the creation of a European education policy space. *Comparative Education*, *49*(4), 486–502.

Halligan, J, (1995). Policy advice and the public service. In B. G. Peters & D. J. Savoie (Eds.), *Governance in a changing environment* (pp. 138–172). McGill/Queens University Press.

Howlett, M. (2019). Comparing policy advisory systems beyond the OECD: Models, dynamics and the second-generation research agenda. *Policy Studies*, *40*(3–4), 241–259. doi:10.1080/01442872.2018.1557626

Hustedt, T. (2019). Studying policy advisory systems: Beyond the Westminster-bias? *Policy Studies, 40*(3–4), 260–269.

Hustedt, T., Kolltveit, K., & Salomonsen, H. H. (2017). Ministerial advisers in executive government: Out from the dark and into the limelight. *Public Administration, 95*(2), 299–311.

Hustedt, T., & Veit, S. (2017). Policy advisory systems: Change dynamics and sources of variation. *Policy Sciences, 50*(1), 41–46.

Knodel, P., Martens, K., & Niemann, D. (2013). PISA as an ideational roadmap for policy change: Exploring Germany and England in a comparative perspective. *Globalisation, Societies and Education, 11*(3), 421–441.

Maley, M. (2015). The policy work of Australian political staff. *International Journal of Public Administration, 38*(1), 46–55.

Michel, A. (2017). The contribution of PISA to the convergence of education policies in Europe. *European Journal of Education, 52*(2), 206–216.

Mundy, K., Green, A., Lingard, B., & Verger, A. (2016). Introduction: The globalisation of education policy. In *The handbook of global education policies* (1st ed., pp. 1–20). John Wiley & Sons.

Olmedo, A., & Grau, E. S. C. (2013). Neoliberalism, policy advocacy networks and think tanks in the Spanish educational arena: The case of FAES. *Education Inquiry, 4*(3), 22618.

Ozga, J., Dahler-Larsen, P., Segerholm, C., & Simola, H. (2011). *Fabricating quality in Europe: data and education governance*. Routledge.

Pattyn, V., Blum, S., Fobé, E., Pekar-Milicevic, M., & Brans, M. (2022). Academic policy advice in consensus-seeking countries: The cases of Belgium and Germany. *International Review of Administrative Sciences, 88*(1), 26–42. https://doi.org/10.1177/0020852319878780

Pavolini, E., Argentin, G., Falzetti, P., Galanti, M. T., Campodifiori, E., & Le Rose, G. (2021). Tutti a casa. Il sistema di istruzione italiano alla prova del Covid-19. *Social Policies, 8*(2), 255–280.

Peters, B. G. (2008). The Napoleonic tradition. *International Journal of Public Sector Management, 21*(2), 118–132.

Pons, X. (2011). What do we really learn from PISA? The sociology of its reception in three European countries (2001–2008). *European Journal of Education, 46*(4), 540–548.

Prince, M. J. (2007). Soft craft, hard choices, altered context: Reflections on 25 years of policy advice in Canada. In L. Dobuzinskis, M. Howlett, & D. Laycock, *Policy analysis in Canada: The state of the art* (pp. 95–106). University of Toronto Press.

Rautalin, M., Alasuutari, P., & Vento, E. (2019). Globalisation of education policies: Does PISA have an effect? *Journal of Education Policy, 34*(4), 500–522.

Rizvi, F., & Lingard, B. (2010). *Globalizing education policy*. Routledge.

Schlaufer, C. (2016). Global evidence in local debates: The Programme for International Student Assessment (PISA) in Swiss direct-democratic debates on school policy. *Policy & Politics, 44*(4), 547–561.

Steiner-Khamsi, G. (2004). *The global politics of educational borrowing and lending*. Teachers' College Press.

Takala, T., Kallo, J., Kauko, J., & Rinne, R. (2018). One size for all? Policy advice of the world Bank and the OECD on quality assurance and evaluation of school education in Russia, Brazil, and China. In A. W. Wiseman & P. M. Davidson (Eds.), *Cross-nationally comparative, evidence-based educational policymaking and reform* (International Perspectives on Education and Society, Vol. 35) (pp. 301–319). Emerald. http://dx.doi.org/10.1108/S1479-367 920180000035009

Van Damme, J., Brans, M., & Fobé, E. (2011). Balancing expertise, societal input and political control in the production of policy advice: A comparative study of education councils in Europe. *Halduskultuur—Administrative Culture, 12*(2), 126–145.

Veit, S., Hustedt, T., & Bach, T. (2017). Dynamics of change in internal policy advisory systems: the hybridization of advisory capacities in Germany. *Policy Sciences, 50*(1), 85–103.

Veselý, A. (2013). Externalization of policy advice: Theory, methodology and evidence. *Policy and Society, 32*(3), 199–209.

Weiss, C. H. (1979). The many meanings of research utilization. *Public Administration Review, 39*(5), 426–431.

Wu, X., Ramesh, M., & Howlett, M. (2015). Policy capacity: A conceptual framework for understanding policy competences and capabilities. *Policy and Society, 34*(3–4), 165–171.

CHAPTER 28

THE FORMATION AND DEVELOPMENT OF A NORWEGIAN ACCOUNTABILITY SYSTEM

ASTRID TOLO

INTRODUCTION

In the last 40 years, neoliberal ideas have influenced the global trend in educational accountability. These ideas have been underpinned by Tyler's rationale (1949) about the interconnection between curriculum, instruction, and evaluation at the school level, which gradually developed into ideas of Management by Objectives (MbO) at a global level (Black & William, 2018; Kridel, 2010). In line with this, governing bodies defining *economic growth* as the foremost goal for education have implemented performance standards as the primary measure of success. Since the 1980s, the establishment of coherent and transparent systems of accountability based on MbO has been on the agenda of The World Bank, UNESCO, and the Organization for Economic Cooperation and Development (OECD) (Spring, 2015) but also in many countries such as Chile, the United States, and England (Ball, 1990; Gysling, 2016). When the OECD's Program for International Student Assessment (PISA) was conducted for the first time in 2000, this trend accelerated, and today the OECD is considered the most powerful actor in the global picture (Spring, 2015). A common term for the OECD approach is *managerial accountability* (Mattei, 2009). In short, this is the process where targets are set from afar (O'Neill, 2004) as global standards (Landri, 2018), and the achievements are measured by metrics (Baird et al., 2017).

How different countries have embraced this trend varies (Eurydice, 2005; Grek, 2020; Mattei, 2009) and what is at stake in, for example, the central European countries is not the same as in Britain. In central Europe and Norway, the main consequences of the new managerialism are to be found in the redefinition of the profession's roles and the organization. Based on a study of the new managerialism in Germany, Italy, and Britain, Mattei (2009) describes how the new way of governing schools affects the different actors' roles, for example, to school leaders being given the main change agent's role.

Researchers who are critical of neoliberalism's influence point out that accountability systems based on performance standards set from afar force schools to work in certain ways that intervene with the profession's desire to make their own choices (Baird et al., 2017; Baird & Elliott, 2018; Hopfenbeck et al., 2015; Mausethagen et al., 2018; O'Neill, 2013; Ranson, 2003; Tolo et al., 2020; Ydesen & Bomholt, 2020). Professional choices are based on the professional knowledge base, ethics, and development of internal control systems (Grimen, 2008a, 2008b). When the profession's core values are under pressure from neoliberal accountability systems, they need to identify what is considered problematic and work to influence the development in a direction they find more favorable. The critique leads to an argument to strengthen the teaching profession from being a semi-profession (Etzioni, 1969) to a full profession.

SCOPE AND METHOD

In this chapter, I will illuminate how Norway has implemented a system of accountability called the Norwegian National Quality Assessment System (NQAS) to respond to the OECD's advice. The research question is: *Why did Norway establish a national quality assessment system, how did it develop, and what consequences have NQAS had for teachers, school leaders, and school bureaucrats?* The motivation to conduct this examination of the NQAS is to understand the history and ideas underpinning the Norwegian system and understand why and how it evolved and how the teaching profession relates to it. A historical institutionalist (HI) approach is suited to do this. Following Steinmo's (2008) interpretation of what a HI approach implies, I will focus on the intricate interplay among institutions, fundamental ideas, and actors' roles and behaviors. More specifically, I will look at how NQAS was initiated, how the teachers and schools have received it, what has been difficult, and how actors in the system have found solutions for it that are balancing different interests. The analyses draw on empirical research and experiences from Norway, studies and projects I have been involved in myself,[1] and other empirical studies.

Institutions like the NQAS form behaviors through formal rules and informal norms. Therefore, I include information about the formal mechanisms in the accountability system and research illuminating the informal norms of accountability and how they have evolved through history and been formed by global and national ideas, values, and beliefs. This provides a lens to see how actors have played and play an active role. Several research reports and articles about the NQAS are used to analyze the case from multiple empirical angles. I will especially emphasize the significance of teachers' normative engagement because of their direct responsibility to the students (Leicht & Fennel, 2008), thus the importance of the expert knowledge they administer.

Norway may serve as an interesting example of how an accountability system has emerged for several reasons. Norwegian policymakers have developed a system that addresses both answerabilities to specific standards and broad responsibility as described in the national mission statement in the Education Act (Ministry of Education and Research, 2020). Trying to safeguard these two considerations simultaneously seems to have hindered the establishment of a coherent accountability system (Hatch, 2013) based on neoliberal ideas alone and opened for a continuous discussion about quality in education based on perspectives from the teaching profession.

Perspectives on Accountability and Trust

All over the world, teachers, parents, governments, nongovernmental organizations, politicians, and others are held to account to offer the best education possible for children and youth. The core of educational accountability is to define the *rights* to education and the corresponding *duties*. It must be clarified "who is required to do what for whom, and why they are required to do it" (O'Neill, 2002, p. 28) but also for whose benefit are they doing it, by which means, and with which consequences (Burk, 2005; Ydesen & Andreasen, 2014).

Accountability mechanisms in education are most often meant to enhance learning (Bovens et al., 2014). This implies that schools and teachers are expected to work systematically and investigative to improve practice (Tolo et al., 2020). Different stakeholders can carry out accountability in many ways, and a blend of different approaches is evident in most countries. In the Global Education Monitoring (GEM) Report from 2017, UNESCO identifies electoral, legal or regulatory, market and performance, professional, and social approaches to accountability. Managerial accountability is a blend of legal or regulatory and market- and performance-based accountability. I will briefly outline the managerial approach, which seems to be dominant in the world today. I will do this by adopting perspectives from the British philosopher Onora O'Neill's works on accountability (O'Neill, 2002, 2004).

Following professional ways of working, the professional knowledge base, the ethical standards, and egalitarian values are used in internal accountability procedures (Grimen, 2009). The intention is to show different external stakeholders how the obligations are met and what is difficult to achieve and why, so that the external stakeholders can judge the professional work's trustworthiness (O'Neill, 2002). As mentioned before, teachers have been considered a semi-profession (Ezioni, 1969) and not as strong as, for example, the medical profession. One can therefore discuss to what degree internal accountability procedures are evident in the occupation of teaching.

Managerial accountability works differently than professional accountability. During the 1980s, teachers were suspected of serving their own interests—and not the interests of the society and economy in many countries. In England, for example, Thatcher claimed teachers function more like radical and ideological interest groups than knowledge providers (Ball, 1990). By this, she weakened the idea that professionals should hold each other accountable and clean up their own ranks. Strong economic stakeholders developed neoliberal forms of accountability and discharged the professional ideal of "self-government." Neoliberalism was often dressed in a socialist-like language that made it easier for larger parts of the population to accept it (Bockman, 2019), and the ideas gained ground in several countries and sectors where one could imagine it would have met great resistance. Transparency was an important feature of this new way of thinking, and showing clear results became crucial. Therefore, the new systems were based on "objective" measurements made public so that different stakeholders could judge whether the institution fulfilled its obligations. The main driver for these approaches today is the OECD (Lingard et al., 2017; Spring, 2015; Ydesen & Bomholt, 2020).

Policymakers developed the new systems of accountability because trusting professionals were seen as naïve—and building quality assessment systems based on facts and numbers could reduce the reliance on trust (O'Neill, 2002). But exchanging trust with accountability systems has shown to be problematic for several reasons. In a managerial accountability system, performance is judged by setting targets, measuring whether targets are achieved, judging the outcome, and sanctioning when needed. Stakeholders in power set targets from afar (O'Neill, 2004, p. 270), and they are not negotiable. However, targets might be contested and represent a limited view of the organization's mission. Also, targets might be unrealistic to achieve, and professionals can be accused of doing a bad job when the targets have failed. But all kinds of accountability presuppose some trust, so establishing systems that erode trust in any of the actors involved is not wise. Thus, to make a system work at all, O'Neill claims, people must trust the system and the ones that operate it (O'Neill, 2002).

The Norwegian Backdrop

Describing the NQAS as one institution (Steinmo, 2008) is somewhat challenging because it is not a coherent institution but rather a blend of formal rules and norms that influence each other (Hatch, 2013). It is also characterized by the fact that different stakeholders hold each other to account in different ways (UNESCO, 2017). However, there is a reporting line that goes upward toward state authorities. The reason for this relatively informal structure is to be found both in history and in the very basic national ideas about how to govern education. Norway has a long history of considering the local school as one common ground for all children in the community, emphasizing students' progress and achievement. The high level of participation and trust in the society, including trust in teachers and trust in the cross-party cooperation between politicians and between politicians and the unions, is a key to understand why, as we shall see, the process has been slow. When everybody has a say in the process, it takes time. Even though global ideas about how to govern education gained a foothold in the 1980s, it took 15 years from the OECD's advice in 1987–1988 (OECD, 1989) to the establishment of the NQAS in 2004. To explain how the different actors have received the NQAS and how the process has gone on after 2004, it seems crucial to understand these fundamental values and conditions within the Norwegian education system.

Egalitarian values and trust-based relations characterize the Norwegian education system. Although Norway does not succeed in all areas, it makes an effort to offer inclusive education for all students based on a common prescriptive curriculum so they can learn to work and live together (Welle-Strand & Tjeldvoll, 2002). Standardized teacher education and regulatory legislation (Helgøy & Homme, 2016) have been high on the political agenda as well as in the teaching profession for almost 150 years. Until post–World War II, Norway was the only European country with a unitary school system implemented as compulsory education for all (Lauglo, 1989). The unified, compulsory, and comprehensive school system as we know it today is built on the Basic Education Act from 1969.

There have been persistent conflicts over student assessment within this system, which escalated in the early 1970s with discussions about when grades should be introduced (Tveit, 2009). In 1972, it was decided that students in primary school should not receive grades, which is still the case. The argument against grading has been that it is unnecessary to grade students' work until grades have a function for selection. It is not before being admitted to upper secondary school that grades have a sorting function. Arguments about grading as a motivational factor have been neglected by those who do not advocate for grades. Also, there has been a weak tradition for assessments based on criteria and a strong tradition for assessments based on norms focusing on progress and achievement. This implies that trust in teachers' professional judgment is institutionalized and regulated (Hopfenbeck et al., 2015). On the other hand, this is also why students' legal security is considered weak when it comes to grades (Tveit, 2009). Thus, grades (or numbers) as sources of information that can be aggregated and tell something about teaching and schools' quality is an alien thought.

THE ESTABLISHMENT OF THE NQAS AND WHAT IT INCLUDES

The OECD's first recommendation about establishing a coherent accountability system in Norway was formulated in a report from 1989, based on an expert evaluation in 1987–1988 (OECD, 1989). In this report, the Norwegian focus on equality, the extensive cooperation between the stakeholders, the decentralized school system, and local autonomy were emphasized. The report also points to a lack of information about the relationship between resources and results and a lack of control and assessment mechanisms. Besides, they identified skepticism among teachers toward researchers and research-based knowledge. The recommendations that followed emphasized the need to implement a quality assessment system with tests that gave the government information on students' knowledge in schools. More specifically, they recommended a careful practice where it was not possible to trace results back to single schools or students. The OECD's recommendations were followed up in a white paper (Meld. St. 37 [1990–1991]) about governance in education which stated that the educational sector should implement management by objectives and emphasized the need for measuring a broad spectrum of the schools' activities, broader than what could be drawn from exam results, which was then the only measurement in schools (Lillejord et al., 2020, 2021).

The first political discussions leading to the NQAS took place during the 1990s. A large reform that extended the length of obligatory school from 9 to 10 years and gave a right to 13 years of education for all students was introduced in 1997. This reform intended to prepare the Norwegian society to transition to the "knowledge society" (Helsvig, 2017; Tolo, 2017). This reform was also an administrative reform. Before the reform, education policy had been implemented through instructions from the ministry. The instructions were developed by a range of powerful expert committees consisting of representatives from schools and great loyalty toward schools. The situation was characterized by stability and a high level of trust between stakeholders (Helgøy & Homme, 2016). At the end of the 1980s, a huge shift started to weaken the expert committees' power and replace this with external stakeholders' external control mechanisms and influence. Instead of getting instructions about what to do from "their own," the sector was increasingly confronted with targets set from a distance and held accountable for achieving these (Helsvig, 2017). Under these conditions, the Confederation of Norwegian Enterprise propounded the recommendations from the OECD. One of the powerful figures in the ministry, Kjell Eide, who had followed the OECD's work closely since the beginning in the 1960s also pushed for support to the recommendations (Helsvig, 2017). It led to a cross-party agreement about establishing a new accountability system, but some disagreement about what it should consist of and the degree of transparency and control (Fevolden & Lillejord, 2005; Lillejord et al., 2020).

The next reform's triggering factor was the PISA results in 2001, shaking Norway as one among several countries (Lundgren, 2011). Then, the work to establish a test-based school accountability system accelerated. The minister of education in 2001, Kristin Clemet, repeated the more than 10-year-old message from the OECD (1989) that the Norwegian government had no information of the students' level of performance. Besides, she criticized the sector for the severe lack of assessment competence (Hopfenbeck et al., 2013). The Norwegian Directorate for Education and Training (DET) was established in 2004 and the NQAS. DET's mandate is to follow up political decisions; thus, they became responsible for the NQAS. The most central instrument in the NQAS was national tests. However, the curriculum from the 1990s was no longer fit for this purpose, and in 2006 a new curriculum customized to fit the management by objectives system and the developing accountability system was implemented.

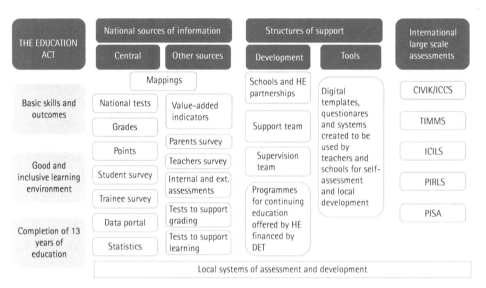

FIGURE 28.1 Overview of the National Quality Assessment System (NQAS). A translated and adjusted version of a figure first presented by the expert group on value-added assessment in schools (Lillejord et al., 2020, p. 20).

The NQAS in 2021

Before unraveling what happened next, I will present an overview of the main structure of the NQAS as it appears today (see Figure 28.1). The NQAS is based on the Education Act and includes national and international sources of information and structures for supporting development.

The system is based on the Education Act, which is shown in the first column. The assessments are focused on basic skills and outcomes, including learning environment and completion of 13 years of education for all.

The second column gives an overview of the sources of formal information. Some of the sources are centrally defined and obligatory. Others are offered by the DET but can also be developed locally. All schools must participate in national tests and surveys. The national tests are in reading, numeracy, and English and are conducted at the beginning of years 5, 8, and 9. Grades are implemented from year 8 and exams from year 10. Student surveys and trainee surveys are being conducted every year. All data and templates for development are presented in a national Web portal accessible for municipalities and school leaders.

The third column shows the DET's kind of support, which consists of development support from inspectors engaged by the county governor/DET, and tools that local actors can use. It also shows programs and initiatives financed through the DET but carried out by the higher education (HE) institutions or in partnership between schools and HE institutions. The structures of support can be viewed in different ways. They can be considered as "soft accountability" where the intention is to implement change by using national tests as the most central tool (Hall, 2017), which means narrowing and clarifying standards of education based on a neoliberal ideological fundament (Landri, 2018). On the other hand, they can also be considered spaces for deliberate discussions about the quality of education and how to enhance different kinds of qualities based on schools' broad mission as stated in the Education Act. Given the decentralized system of control by county governors and the municipals' autonomy, we observe variations throughout the country in this respect.

The fourth column shows the international large-scale assessments (ILSAs) Norway is involved in. The results from these tests are frequently mentioned in policy documents and used in public debates to legitimate political choices, as is documented in the general literature concerning the use of ILSAs (Baird et al., 2017).

School leaders are locally responsible for self-assessment in their own schools. Schools are expected to learn from the assessment information (data) and develop as learning organizations. Municipal bureaucrats (for primary and lower secondary) and county bureaucrats (for upper secondary) are responsible for overseeing that the quality assessment work is done locally, and they offer support where needed. The extent to which they get involved in the schools' quality work varies from municipality to municipality (or county). The county governor has a control function, but there are no sanctions connected to the accountability system per se, only support for development. DET manages the national structure and the support functions that are not covered by the local authorities.

Research Illuminating How the NQAS Works

Along with the implementation of the NQAS research has been conducted to illuminate several aspects of how it works. Some researchers have, for example, described and investigated the most central instruments in the NQAS, the national tests, the mapping tests, and the student survey (Blömeke & Olsen, 2018). Others have studied the instruments' use, for example, the interpretation and use of national tests for development (Gunnulfsen, 2017; Mausethagen et al., 2018, 2019). Studies have also been conducted focusing on how external assessment in inspections is carried out (Hall, 2017; Hall & Sivesind, 2015), and for the program Assessment for Learning (Hopfenbeck et al., 2013, 2015), which has had a major influence in Norway. In the following, I will present some of what the research has shown.

Blömeke and Olsen (2018) find the *instruments* to have good quality. However, they call for (1) a clearer purpose of the tests, (2) possibilities to link the different tests and surveys in the system to make a better picture of what is going on, (3) inclusion of a broader set of competencies in the measurements, (4) implementation of indicators to describe contexts, (5) implementation of systematic assessment of the instruments which are used, and (6) better ways of reporting and communicating the test results (Blömeke & Olsen, 2018).

National tests are mandatory for all schools and are conducted in grades 5 and 8 in reading, counting, and English, and in grade 9 in reading and counting. The tests measure basic skills as they are described in the curriculum. The purpose of the tests is somewhat contradictory. On one side, they are said to give system information, which means aggregated information about the school and municipality's performance. On the other side, the information is detailed down to student level and used for formative purposes. The first version of the national tests developed in 2004 was assessed and found to have deficient qualities (Lie et al., 2005; Blömeke & Olsen, 2018). Also, there were loud protests, especially from the student organization (Tveit, 2009). Therefore, new versions of the test were developed and introduced in 2007. In addition to improving the test quality, the time for conducting the test was also changed from spring to early autumn, so teachers more immediately could use the results formatively in their work with single students.

However, the way schools are competent to use national tests for school improvement varies (Gunnulfsen, 2017; Mausethagen et al., 2018, 2019). When discussing national test results in schools, the actors take on roles characterized as not very productive as they all seem to have their own agendas (Gunnulfsen, 2017). The school leader's role is considered decisive concerning follow-up and further development, but not all school leaders can take this lead. School leaders are downplaying their own authority (Mausethagen et al., 2019) and act as narrators and enthusiasts (Gunnulfsen, 2017). Middle leaders act like messengers and enforce when teachers show resistance (Gunnulfsen, 2017). Teachers are using the national test result meetings to focus on improving test scores in the next round and not on how to develop professional practice in a broad sense (Mausethagen et al., 2018). This shows that even though the test instruments themselves are good, it is demanding to use these to ensure good education and develop practice. It confirms that the school leaders are given new roles as agents for a new managerial model of governance (Mattei, 2009) and how difficult this role might be.

School inspections have a long tradition in Norway and have been conducted in many different ways throughout history. Since 2006 they became a part of the NQAS, and the tests and surveys mentioned earlier work as a foundation for the school organization's assessments. The directorate has delegated the responsibility for inspections to the County Governor's Offices (Hall & Sivesind, 2015), while the directorate has developed a handbook to be used as a framework. According to the directorate for education and training, the current practice is that schools are selected for inspection based on risk assessment and includes guidance. From 2006 until today, the inspections' political intentions have gradually shifted focus from control toward learning (Hall, 2017). From 2014 to 2017 the inspections focused on students' legal rights, including how schools work with learning outcomes, school-based self-assessment, and management. From 2018, management is not explicitly mentioned, but special education and school environment are included among the themes involved. According to the directorate, the inspections have led to competence development at all levels. The school owners have changed their routines and offer follow-up for more schools than those selected for inspections (Utdanningsdirektoratet, 2018b). However, research finds that the inspections are mostly focused on legal and pragmatic issues and narrowed by the templates used for the inspections (Hall, 2017). Municipals' follow-up by bureaucrats varies somewhat randomly between a control-oriented and a development-oriented approach (Prøitz et al., 2021). This indicates that using the inspections for school development and learning is not a straightforward task, thus challenging the capacity of the County Governors' inspectors, municipality bureaucrats' work, and the school leaders' internal work with their staff.

One of the programs for continuing education for school leaders and teachers offered from 2010 to 2018 is the national program Assessment for Learning (AfL). Norway officially uses the term and program AfL, which is equivalent to "formative assessment," focusing on students' progress and how teaching can be improved to meet students' needs (Stobart, 2008). The program was introduced due to the perceived lack of assessment competence among teachers, school leaders, and school bureaucrats and the need for such competence to handle the NQAS and the new curriculum in 2006. In 2009, AfL was stated in the regulations to the Education Act, and in 2010 a national training program was established.

The initiative to implement AfL was taken by a group of bureaucrats in the DET, whom researchers from England and Scotland inspired. The Minister of Education from 2005 to 2007, Øystein Djupedal from the Socialist Party, was hesitant to implement such a program because he feared resistance from teachers who were tired of reforms. However, a pilot was implemented in 2007, called "Better Assessment Practices." After this pilot, the Minister of Education from 2009, Kristin Halvorsen, also from the Socialist Party, was confident that the ideas of AfL were a positive strategy forward for the Norwegian school. She gave the go-ahead to the directorate to establish a national implementation program from 2010, and it was running until 2018, with a total budget of 148 MNOK (Hopfenbeck et al., 2013; Utdanningsdirektoratet, 2018a). Norwegian teachers have generally embraced this initiative, as the formative assessment is seen as a meaningful focus concerning students', teachers', and schools' learning (Hopfenbek et al., 2015). It is also important to note that AfL requires both trust in teachers and a soft accountability system that has no sanctions tied to it (Heitink et al., 2016), and therefore AfL is well suited for the Norwegian conditions. However, AfL is a demanding form of assessment, and good practice requires high competence from teachers and the school organization. Although the emphasis on AfL seems successful, it is also evident that it takes many years and hard effort to implement it as the school leaders and teachers search for sensible ways of practicing this kind of assessment in their schools, classrooms, and subjects (Hopfenbeck et al., 2015). Even if AfL is not usually emphasized as a part of the NQAS, it is highly relevant because the kind of assessment competence gained through this program is a prerequisite to making the formative aspects of the NQAS work.

FOLLOW-UP FROM THE OECD AND RESPONSES FROM NORWAY

Seven years after the establishment of NQAS, the extensive report with the title OECD Reviews of evaluation and assessment in education NORWAY (Nusche et al., 2011) propounds OECD's recommendations for further development. The report (Nusche et al., 2011) assesses what is positive and negative about the Norwegian system, seen from the OECD's perspective. The strong political will to establish, develop, and support the NQAS is highlighted. The main informants for the report, the DET, who also administer the NQAS, are referred to as promoting the quality agenda positively (p. 27). Demands placed on school owners (that means counties and municipalities) to monitor quality and the establishment of external accountability through school inspections (p. 27) are also highlighted as positive. Other perceived positive developments are that regulations regarding assessment are made clearer, a range of self-assessment tools to be used by schools are developed, and there has been a substantial effort to build collective responsibility at the local level. The negative sides, according to the OECD, are summarized in three main recommendations and carefully outlined as challenges.

The negative findings and recommendations for further development are that Norway should "(1) refine and expand national competence goals and provide clearer guidance concerning expected learning progressions and criteria for assessment in different subjects, (2) develop an evidence-based statement or profile of what teachers are expected to know and be able to do, as a reference framework to guide teacher appraisal, professional development and career progression, and (3) establish an agreed framework of process quality indicators for school evaluation that can help schools review and improve core elements of their practice such as teaching and learning, curriculum management, assessment approaches, and management and leadership" (Nusche et al., 2011, pp. 9–10).

One response to this has been an extensive overhaul of the curriculum to clarify the content and priorities. An extensive process has been going on for several years, and the curriculum was ready for implementation in 2020–2021. A recent report evaluating this process concludes that the government has succeeded in including different stakeholders in their work. However, there are disagreements over how much clearer the curriculum has become (Karseth et al., 2020).

Another response has been to try to establish a system for teacher assessment (Lillejord et al., 2018). A first step was made in 2013. To avoid known pitfalls, the Ministry of Education pointed out two working groups to establish a broad knowledge fundament. One group of researchers went through the research literature (Lillejord et al., 2014) and another group presented the schools' and teachers' views and interests. The second step was to outline a design to be piloted and tested, and the third step was small-scale implementation followed by research. However, the whole thing ended with a slowdown of the process, no clear results from the small-scale trial, and no teacher assessment system.[2] Why it ended this way is not obvious, but Lillejord et al. (2018), who were all involved in the trial in different ways, label teacher evaluation as a major problem characterized by ambiguity and uncertainty, conceptual difficulties, and practical challenges. The main problem here was too many and conflicting goals at stake (Lillejord et al., 2018).

A third response has been to establish a system of process quality indicators. Value-added indicators (Coleman et al., 1966; Hanushek, 1971, 1992) have been introduced in the Norwegian education system from 2017/2018. Value-added indicators consider that students' background has more impact on students' results than the schools' teaching. By modeling this, it should be possible to identify the schools' contribution to students' learning and further point out what successful schools do to succeed. The Norwegian model balances national test results (primary and lower secondary school) and exams (upper secondary school) with earlier results and the students' socioeconomic background. To identify success factors, this means identifying what a school that adds value to the students learning does; the results from the modeling are seen in the light of characteristics of the schools. The development of the value-added indicators has been going on in Norway since 2004 through many projects. However, an expert group established by the government in 2020 to evaluate the use of the value-added indicators finds, in line with international research, that it is not easy to single out significant common traits that characterize successful schools (Lillejord et al., 2020). The key to understanding how schools can add value to students' learning is to understand how schools work. Therefore, the expert group concludes in their first report that the added value indicator is not suited to identify single factors about how schools work to promote learning (Lillejord et al., 2020). In other words, the indicators do not produce information that schools can use formatively.

Although Norway has tried to follow the OECD's recommendations from 2011, this work has not led to any obvious improvement in the areas that were emphasized. On the productive side, there has been a broad engagement in the sector at times (Karseth et al., 2020), which can be interpreted as a sign of success in the sense that teachers, school leaders, and municipal, county, and national administrators as well as HI institutions and politicians take responsibility for the development of the Norwegian school together. This implies the following: The processes are slow, and the suggested recommendations have not been successful, which may first express that the various mechanisms in NQAS must give meaning to the actors before they accept them. Second, all actors need time to learn and develop the expert knowledge they need to put the system into practice. Third, if the system does not work satisfactorily for the actors involved, they are left to figure out what to accept, what to emphasize, and what to change and how. In this sense, the process could be characterized as democratic based on professional ways of working, not streamlined, which characterizes neoliberal processes.

The Demand for Professionalization

We have now illuminated why and how Norway established a national quality assessment system and how the actors have met this. The examination has shown that there has not been a "top-down" implementation process implementing a fixed system. Instead, it has been trials and errors over many years where the actors have been involved in the development. It has been a difficult and demanding process trying to balance different interests (Hatch, 2013), and the results are ambiguous. The neoliberal ideas of management by objectives (Kridel, 2010) have shown to collide with ideas of professional sensemaking and trusting relations (O'Neill, 2002). The government's use of standards and intentions of profit and efficiency (Leicht & Fennel, 2008) has been met by professionals who emphasize local knowledge gained from teaching and teachers' relationships with the students. Thus, working out clearer competence goals, teacher assessment system, and "objective" quality indicators as were the OECD recommendations for Norway (Nucshe et al., 2011) have shown not to be efficient approaches in Norway.

One of the important things that have come out of this process is that the professional perspective has been increasingly emphasized. For example, in the New National Strategy for Teacher Education 2025 (Ministry of Education and Research, 2017), it is stated:

> It is the government's ambition to permanently strengthen the Norwegian teaching professions. The investments being made now are important in order to prepare for a future in which knowledge and competencies will become increasingly important. The aim is for kindergartens and schools to draw on the teaching professions' own professional strengths to enhance quality. (p. 5)

By this statement, the government signals that the profession's authority should be integral to the accountability system. However, this must be prepared for by strengthening the profession.

The discussions about professions and professional practice have changed from the 1960s and 1970s to the present as the focus has shifted from traits that characterize professions and professional organizations toward organizational and institutional claims regarding what professionals should be able to do (Leicht & Fennel, 2008). Handling accountability is one of these things. The Norwegian case analysis shows that to make the accountability system work in terms of organizational learning (Bovens et al., 2014), there is a need for a teaching profession that can use assessment data and research-based knowledge as a basis for their work. Ezioni (1969) named teachers a semi-profession because this group of workers is similar to a profession but separates from professions because they do not produce their own knowledge. The power of the full professions lies in the fact that they control their own knowledge domain.

We need to ask if and how the new policy for teacher education (Ministry of Education and Research, 2017) expects teachers, school leaders, and bureaucrats to be involved in knowledge production systematically? This policy indicates that teachers will be involved in defining, producing, discussing, and distributing their own assessment data and feed this into the pool of professional expert knowledge. Further, it indicates that teachers will be treated as influential actors in the system, which means valuing how they make sense of things and how they maneuver in a daily uncertain practice based on what Friedson (1967) formulates as personal, "systematically biased, experience" (p. 134). It further acknowledges that teachers' competence constitutes fine-grained expert knowledge (Flyvbjerg, 2011), which is important to understand and develop to move forward. The local actors' engagement represents a shift from an objective and standard-based focus to a normative and discretionary focus in the assessment. Instead of seeing standards as the key, standards become one of the tools.

Norway has a strong local self-government tradition where municipalities invest in educational policies and informal trust-based assessments where teachers' professional judgments are central (Hopfenbeck et al., 2015; Skedsmo & Mausethagen, 2017). The Educational Act from 1997 states that municipalities are responsible for securing the necessary level of teacher competence. This stems from a long tradition where municipalities, parents, teachers, and students have been stable actors in education's local governance since 1837 (Homme, 2008). Teacher organizations are still strong and united, and the student union has shown a strong commitment, especially about the development and use of national tests and issues concerning student assessment (Tveit, 2009).

What we have learned is that establishing an accountability system in Norway has not been a straightforward task. The assessment instruments themselves and how they work together in a system and over time need to be adjusted and improved (Blömeke & Olsen, 2018). But we have also learned that establishing such a system engages teachers, school leaders, and bureaucrats in such a way that they in turn hold politicians and the OECD to account. The Norwegian case adds to the knowledge we have about securing the quality of education by showing how development of assessment competence and accountability systems demand effort at all education system levels. In the global picture, the Norwegian case may stand out as an example of resistance toward neoliberal influence.

Notes

1. The main source is described in Hopfenbeck et al. (2013). The study was founded by the Norwegian Ministry of Education.

   I have also been heading partnership cooperation between the University of Bergen and Bergen municipality (2017–2020) on action research involving 15 schools and municipality bureaucrats. The County Governor founded the project with support from the DET under the program Decentralized Competence Development, one of the development support programs involved in the NQAS.

2. On the DET's webpage there is a guide for how teachers and students together can assess teaching. This guide is voluntary to use and is presented as a help for practicing

school-based assessment. It is developed by the student organization, the teachers' union, the central association of municipalities, and the DET. The webpage says the guide is not new, but still relevant, and especially because it was decided in 2017 that the students should be involved in school-based evaluations (https://www.udir.no/kvalitet-og-kompetanse/kvalitetsarbeid-i-opplaringen/undervisningsvurdering-rettleiar/).

REFERENCES

Baird, J. A., Andrich, D., Hopfenbeck, T. N., & Stobart, G. (2017). Assessment and learning: Fields apart? *Assessment in Education: Principles, Policy & Practice, 24*(3), 317–350.

Baird, J. A., & Elliott, V. (2018). Metrics in education—Control and corruption. *Oxford Review of Education, 44*(5), 533–544.

Ball, S. J. (1990). *Politics and policy making in education: Explorations in policy sociology.* Routledge.

Black, P. J. & William, D. (2018). Classroom assessment and pedagogy. *Assessment in Education: Principles, Policy & Practice, 25*(6), 551–575.

Blömeke, S., & Olsen, R. V. (2018). På vei mot et sammenhengende nasjonalt kvalitetsvurderingssystem. *Acta Didactica Norge, 12*(4), 1–21.

Bockman, J. (2019). Democratic socialism in Chile and Peru: Revisiting the "Chicago boys" as the origin of neoliberalism. *Comparative Studies in Society and History, 61*(3), 654–679. http://dx.doi.org.pva.uib.no/10.1017/S0010417519000239

Bovens, M., Goodin, R. E., & Schillemans, T. (Eds.). (2014). *The Oxford handbook of public accountability.* Oxford University Press.

Bovens, M., Schillermans, T., & Goodin, R. (2014). Public accountability. In M. Bovens, R. E. Goodin, & T. Schillemans (Eds.), *The Oxford handbook of public accountability* (pp. 1–20). Oxford University Press.

Burke, J. C. (2005). The many faces of accountability. In *Achieving accountability in higher education: Balancing public, academic, and market demands* (pp. 1–24). Jossey-Bass.

Coleman, J. S., Campbell, E. Q., Hobson, C. J., McPartland, J., Mood, A. M., Weinfield, F. D., & York, R. L. (1966). Equality of educational opportunity. U.S. Government Printing Office.

Etzioni, A. (1969). *The semi-professions and their organization: Teachers, nurses, social workers.* Free Press.

Eurydice. (2005). *Key data on education in Europe 2005.* European Communities.

Fevolden, T., & Lillejord, S. (2005). *Kvalitetsarbeid i skolen.* Universitetsforl.

Flyvbjerg, B. (2011). Case study. In N. Denzin & Y. S. Linkoln (Eds.), *The Sage handbook of qualitative research 4* (pp. 301–316). Sage.

Freidson, E. (1967). The professional mind. *CA: A Cancer Journal for Clinicians, 17*(3), 130–136.

Grek, S. (2020). Facing "a tipping point"? The role of the OECD as a boundary organisation in governing education in Sweden. *Education Inquiry, 11*(3), 175–195.

Grimen, H. (2008a). Profesjon og kunnskap. In A. Molander & L. I. Terum (Eds.), *Profesjonsstudier* (pp. 71–86). Universitetsforlaget.

Grimen, H. (2008b). *Profesjon og profesjonsmoral.* In A. Molander & L. I. Terum (Eds.), *Profesjonsstudier* (pp. 144–160). Universitetsforlaget.

Grimen, H. (2009). *Hva er tillit?* Universitetsforlaget.

Gunnulfsen, A. E. (2017). School leaders' and teachers' work with national test results: Lost in translation? *Journal of Educational Change, 18*(4), 495–519.

Gysling, J. (2016). The historical development of educational assessment in Chile: 1810–2014. *Assessment in Education: Principles, Policy & Practice, 23*(1), 8–25.

Hall, J. B., & Sivesind, K. (2015). State school inspection policy in Norway and Sweden (2002–2012): A reconfiguration of governing modes? *Journal of Education Policy, 30*(3), 429–458.

Hall, J. B. (2017). Examining school inspectors and education directors within the organisation of school inspection policy: Perceptions and views. *Scandinavian Journal of Educational Research, 61*(1), 112–126.

Hanushek, E. (1971). Teacher characteristics and gains in student achievement: Estimation using micro data. *The American Economic Review, 61*(2), 280–288.

Hanushek, E. (1992). The trade-off between child quantity and quality. *Journal of Political Economy, 100*(1), 84–117.

Hatch, T. (2013). Beneath the surface of accountability: Answerability, responsibility and capacity-building in recent education reforms in Norway. *Journal of Educational Change, 14*(2), 113–138.

Heitink, M. C., Van der Kleij, F. M., Veldkamp, B. P., Schildkamp, K., & Kippers, W. B. (2016). A systematic review of prerequisites for implementing assessment for learning in classroom practice. *Educational Research Review, 17*, 50–62.

Helgøy, I., & Homme, A. (2006). Policy tools and institutional change comparing education policies in Norway, Sweden and England. *Journal of Public Policy, 26*(2), 141–165.

Helgøy, I., & Homme, A. (2016). Educational reforms and marketization in Norway—A challenge to the tradition of the social democratic, inclusive school? *Research in Comparative and International Education, 11*(1), 52–68.

Helsvig, K. (2017). *Reform og rutine. Kunnskapsdepartementets historie*. Pax Forlag.

Homme, A. D. (2008). *Den kommunale skolen. Det lokale skolefeltet i historisk perspektiv*. Universitetet Bergen.

Hopfenbeck, T., Tolo, A., Florez, T., & El Masri, Y. (2013). *Balancing trust and accountability. The assessment for learning programme in Norway: A governing complex education systems case study*. OECD.

Hopfenbeck, T. N., Petour, M. T. F., & Tolo, A. (2015). Balancing tensions in educational policy reforms: Large-scale implementation of Assessment for Learning in Norway. *Assessment in Education: Principles, Policy & Practice, 22*(1), 44–60.

Karseth, B., Kvamme, O. A., & Ottesen, E. (2020). Evaluering av fagfornyelsen—politiske intensjoner, arbeidsprosesser og innhold. Universitetet i Oslo.

Kridel, C. (Ed.). (2010). *Encyclopedia of curriculum studies* (Vol. 1). Sage.

Landri, P. (2018). *Digital governance of education: Technology, standards and Europeanization of education*. Bloomsbury.

Lauglo, J. (1989). *Folkestyrt skole i internasjonalt perspektiv*. I. K. Jordheim (red.) Skolen 1739–1989. Norsk grunnsiole 250 år. NKS-Forlaget.

Leicht, K. T., & Fennel, M. L. (2008). Institutionalism and the professions. In R. Greenwood, C. Oliver, K. Sahlin, & R. Suddaby, *The Sage handbook of organizational institutionalism* (pp. 431–448). Sage.

Lie, S., Hopfenbeck, T. N., Ibsen, E., & Turmo, A. (2005). Nasjonale prøver på ny prøve. *Rapport fra en utvalgsundersøkelse for å analysere og vurdere kvaliteten på oppgaver og resultater til nasjonale prøver våren*. Institutt for lærerutdanning og skoleforskning.

Lillejord, S., Bolstad, A. K., Fjeld, S., Isaksen, L. S., Lund, T., Myhr, L. A., & Ohm, H. M. (2020). *Ekspertgruppen for skolebidrag. Kunnskapsgrunnlaget. Del 1 av oppdrag fra Kunnskapsdepartementet*. Ministry of Education and Research.

Lillejord, S., Bolstad, A. K., Fjeld, S., Isaksen, L. S., Lund, T., Myhr, L. A., & Ohm, H. M. (2021). *Ekspertgruppen for skolebidrag. En skole for vår tid. Sluttrapport*. Ministry of Education and Research.

Lillejord, S., Børte, K., Ruud, E., Hauge, T. E., Hopfenbeck, T. N., Tolo, A., Fischer-Griffiths, P., Smeby, J. (2014). *Former for lærervurdering som kan ha positiv innvirkning på skolens kvalitet: En systematisk kunnskapsoversikt*. Kunnskapssenter for utdanning.

Lillejord, S., Elstad, E., & Kavli, H. (2018). Teacher evaluation as a wicked policy problem. *Assessment in Education: Principles, Policy & Practice, 25*(3), 291–309.

Lingard, B., Sellar, S., & Lewis, S. (2017). Accountabilities in schools and school systems. In *Oxford research encyclopedia of education*. Retrieved 1 May. 2023, from https://oxfordre.com/education/view/10.1093/acrefore/9780190264093.001.0001/acrefore-9780190264093-e-74

Lundgren, U. P. (2011). PISA as a political instrument. In M. A. Pereyra, H. G. Kotthoff, & R. Cowen (Eds.), *PISA under examination: Changing knowledge, changing tests, and changing schools* (pp. 17–30). Sense.

Mattei, P. (2009). *Restructuring welfare organizations in Europe: From democracy to good management?* Palgrave Macmillan.

Mausethagen, S., Prøitz, T., & Skedsmo, G. (2018). Teachers' use of knowledge sources in "result meetings": Thin data and thick data use. *Teachers and Teaching, 24*(1), 37–49.

Mausethagen, S., Prøitz, T. S., & Skedsmo, G. (2019). School leadership in data use practices: Collegial and consensus-oriented. *Educational Research, 61*(1), 70–86.

Meld. St. nr. 37. (1990–1991). *Om organisering og styring i Utdanningssektoren*. Kirke-, utdannings- og forskningsdepartementet.

Ministry of Education and Research. (2017). Teacher education 2025. National Strategy for Quality and Cooperation in Teacher Education. https://www.regjeringen.no/contentassets/doc1da83bce94e2da21d5f631bbae817/kd_teacher-education-2025_uu.pdf

Ministry of Education and Research. (2020). Act relating to primary and secondary education and Training (the Education Act). https://lovdata.no/dokument/NLE/lov/1998-07-17-61/KAPITTEL_1#KAPITTEL_1

Nusche, D., Earl, L., Maxwell, W., & Shewbridge, C. (2011). *OECD reviews of evaluation and assessment in education*. OECD.

OECD. (1989). *OECD-vurdering av norsk utdanningspolitikk. Norsk rapport til OECD: ekspertvurdering fra OECD*. Aschehoug.

O'Neill, O. (2002). *A question of trust: The BBC Reith Lectures 2002*. Cambridge University Press.

O'Neill, O. (2004). Accountability, trust and informed consent in medical practice and research. *Clinical Medicine, 4*(3), 269–276.

O'Neill, O. (2013). Intelligent accountability in education. *Oxford Review of Education, 39*(1), 4–16.

Prøitz, T. S., Mausethagen, S., & Skedsmo, G. (2021). District administrators' governing styles in the enactment of data-use practices. *International Journal of Leadership in Education, 24*(2), 244–265.

Ranson, S. (2003). Public accountability in the age of neoliberal governance. *Journal of Education Policy, 18*(5), 459–480.

Skedsmo, G., & Mausethagen, S. (2017). Nye styringsformer i utdanningssektoren-spenninger mellom resultatstyring og faglig-profesjonelt ansvar. *Norsk pedagogisk tidsskrift, 101*(2), 169–179.

Spring, J. (2015). *Globalization of education. An introduction*. Routledge.

Steinmo, S. (2008). Historical institutionalism. In D. Porta & N. Keating (Eds.), *Approaches and methodologies in the social sciences: A pluralist perspective* (pp. 118–138). Cambridge University Press.

Stobart, G. (2008). *Testing times: The uses and abuses of assessment.* Routledge.

Tolo, A. (2017). *Kompetanse og lærerprofesjonalitet.* Fagbokforlaget.

Tolo, A., Lillejord, S., Petour, M. T. F., & Hopfenbeck, T. N. (2020). Intelligent accountability in schools: A study of how school leaders work with the implementation of assessment for learning. *Journal of Educational Change, 21*(1), 59–82.

Tveit, S. (2009). Educational assessment in Norway—A time of change. In *Educational assessment in the 21st century* (pp. 227–243). Springer.

Tyler, R. W. (1949). *Basic principles of curriculum and instruction.* University of Chicago Press.

Utdanningsdirektoratet. (2018a). Erfaringer fra nasjonal satsing på vurdering for læring. https://www.udir.no/tall-og-forskning/finn-forskning/rapporter/erfaringer-fra-nasjonal-satsing-pa-vurdering-for-laring-2010-2018/1.innledning/

Utdanningsdirektoratet. (2018b). Rapport, Felles nasjonalt tilsyn på opplæringsområdet 2014–2017. http://www.udir.no/regelverk-og-tilsyn/tilsyn/felles-nasjonalt-tilsyn/felles-nasjonalt-tilsyn-2014-2017

UNESCO. (2017). Global Education Monitoring Report 2017/18: Accountability in education. https://unesdoc.unesco.org/ark:/48223/pf0000259338

Welle-Strand, A., & Tjeldvoll, A. (2002). The Norwegian unified school—A paradise lost? *Journal of Education Policy, 17*(6), 673–686.

Ydesen, C., & Andreasen, K. E. (2014). Accountability practices in the history of Danish primary public education from the 1660s to the present. Education Policy Analysis Archives, 22, 120.

Ydesen, C., & Bomholt, A. (2020). Accountability implications of the OECD's economistic approach to education: A historical case analysis. *Journal of Educational Change, 21*(1), 37–57.

SECTION VI

The Massification of Secondary Education

CHAPTER 29

DIFFUSION OF MASS EDUCATION

Pathways to Isomorphism

FABIAN BESCHE-TRUTHE, HELEN SEITZER, AND MICHAEL WINDZIO

INTRODUCTION

In the 1880s, only a handful of Western countries had large enrolment rates in state-organized schooling. At that time, universal mass primary education was nonexistent in most parts of the world. Over the course of just a few decades, however, the picture has changed dramatically, and enrolment figures have risen at an accelerating speed. International organizations (IOs) fostered this trend by declaring "universal primary education" as a raison d'état through commitments like the Millennium Development Goals and the Education for All initiative.

In this chapter, we are investigating the diffusion of the institution of mass education systems through the observation of enrolment trends. We define the establishment of a "mass education system" in a country as an exceedance of the threshold of an overall enrolment of 40% in primary education for boys and girls combined. In contrast to other studies (Griffiths & Imre, 2013; Meyer et al., 1992; Ramirez, 2013), our approach focuses on countries' interdependencies to explain the institutional development of mass education. In doing this, we apply social network analysis to estimate the effects of contagion on the emergence of mass education in 156 countries around the world from 1880 to 2010. Previous scholarship has either stressed national factors which contributed to the evolution of state-led mass education (Lindert, 2004a, 2004b; Paglayan, 2020) or focused on global discourses that might have had universal power and influence in shaping education policies (Boli et al., 1985; Craig, 1981). In contrast, our study highlights the influence of different cultural predispositions and the hierarchical influence of Western countries through colonialism on the diffusion of mass education. We argue that policy diffusion does not occur in a vacuum and policy implementation is not free from external influences. Diffusion in its narrow sense is a "process where prior adoption of a trait or practice in a population alters the probability of adoption for the remaining non-adopters" (Strang, 1991, p. 325). Valente (1999) argued that the connection of subjects in networks is a necessary condition for these processes to happen. Ties in networks facilitate communication and therefore diffusion. Valente introduced the dynamics of social networks into the concept and analysis of diffusion. Accordingly, we ask the question: What effects do networks of cultural and colonial linkages have on the emergence of national mass education systems?

Research on the emergence and global development of systems of mass education have surged in the social sciences since the late 1970s (Busemeyer & Trampusch, 2011; Gift & Wibbels, 2014; Jakobi & Martens, 2010). In this context, studies extended their scope to the diffusion of similar syllabi (Benavot & Riddle, 1988; Meyer, 1977) and expenditure on public as well as private education (Wolf & Zohlnhöfer, 2009). However, international dependencies that might foster or hinder worldwide diffusion, such as cultural linkages or colonialism, have not yet received much attention (except, e.g., Brock & Alexiadou, 2013). Inspired by the neoinstitutionalist thesis of the diffusion of rational state goals and modern state structures, a tendency toward isomorphism in bureaucratic institutions such as education has been detected (Jakobi & Teltemann, 2011; Meyer & Ramirez, 2005).

However, since the pathways to this isomorphism have been comprehensively analyzed (e.g., Meyer and Ramirez, 2005), different explanations have emerged. We refer to *functionalist* and *neoinstitutionalist* theories to explain the diffusion of mass education. Furthermore, we introduce our own theoretical assumption that a country's membership in different "cultural spheres" shapes the establishment of state-led mass education. In addition, we include networks of colonial relations, which are the prime example of hegemonic power imbalances in countries' relationships with one another. Enhancing the research of Meyer et al. (1992), we focus on the effects of these networks on the diffusion of mass education by using the more recent methodological framework of network diffusion analysis.

FUNCTIONALIST AND NEOINSTITUTIONALIST VIEWS

In general, mass education closely relates to a society's transition into modernity (Pinker, 2018, ch. 16). A crucial characteristic of modernity is the differentiation of society into distinct institutionalized subsystems that tend to focus on their own criteria of rationality (Turner, 1998, p. 53), such as capitalist economies, law and bureaucracy, education, and science. However, at the same time they are interdependent in that each subsystem provides resources to other subsystems. The emerging nation states in the 18th century increasingly centralized power and responded to the challenge of integrating their multicultural populations by providing literacy to the masses (Weymann, 2014, pp. 41–42). In combination, economic growth and mass education laid the foundation of democratic institutions (Lipset, 1957). Facilitated by standardized public education, modern individuals disengaged themselves from collectivism and identification with local kin groups. They learned to play multiple roles, but to identify with them less, and at the same time developed higher cognitive capacities, thereby breaking new ground for modern science and technology (Chase-Dunn & Lerro, 2013, p. 294). However, Max Weber (1920, pp. 203–204) was already aware of the ambivalent relationship between modernization, education, and personal freedom. If institutionalization expands into all areas of society, there is barely any existence outside of institutions and their specific criteria of rationality. This results in the "iron cage." In contrast to the early puritans who *wanted to* be a "person of vocation" (*Berufsmensch*), we *have to* be (Weber, 1920, p. 203). In this regard, functionalism means that modern capitalism and bureaucracies evolved into dynamically operating systems that produce the specific kind of well-adapted individuals they need (Münch, 1992, p. 623). In a worst-case scenario, modern education creates "specialists without spirit" (Weber, 1920, p. 204), who are focused entirely on their respective field but have lost touch with the deeper meaning of what they do. Weber's early analysis of modernization and institutionalization strongly inspired the neoinstitutionalist approach developed by John W. Meyer (1977) and colleagues from the 1970s onward (see later discussion).

Another functionalist argument highlights the role of the state and global economic competition. Mass education results from an ever-deeper integration of nation states into the global economy. Mass education gives countries a competitive advantage (Griffiths & Imre, 2013, p. 51). The surge of human capital theory, which follows a logic of linear development, made it necessary for countries to educate their workers (Griffiths & Arnove, 2015). With the acceleration of industrial work processes and later the massive expansion of the service sector, an educated labor force became an indispensable necessity for national economies.

A similar argument is made in the world systems approach formalized by Immanuel Wallerstein: If the state is the prime locus of wealth accumulation, then a weak state cannot accumulate as much wealth as a strong state would (Wallerstein, 2007, p. 53). To keep a strong state, political leaders in the 19th century needed to address the increasing demands of their population and to integrate their *citizens* both politically and socially. Education is supposed to help prevent conflicts over societal participation from escalating into revolutions. Thus, everyone—workers, women, migrants, and so on— was integrated into the political system to pacify any arising conflicts, and this was to be accompanied by an integration into mass education systems. These lines of research bring forth an impressive theoretical strand to explain specific country-level variations in education systems (Meyer et al., 1992).

The neoinstitutionalist theory generally regards the emergence of mass education as the result of an ideology of universalistic individualism. The argument is that education "expands where institutional forms emphasizing the individual dominate" (Boli et al., 1985, p. 150). In this view, and in line with Max Weber's idea on the effect of modern institutions on wider society, mass education systems followed a "modern" developmental path of social "rationalization" and were formed in unison with institutions. Modern institutions emphasize the individual, the nation state, and above all the important role of individuals for the progress of the nation state (Ramirez, 2013). Given the tendency toward the "iron cage," however, individuals' influence on the nation state is just a taken-for-granted "myth." Such "myths" constitute the ideological framework on which state institutions are built, and education serves to transform individuals into members of these new institutions (Boli et al., 1985, p. 156). These "myths" of individualism, statehood, and social institutions are the very glue that holds our modern world together.

Interestingly, in earlier works, the neoinstitutionalist group of sociologists that introduced world society theory and which was headed by John W. Meyer acknowledged differences in the paths taken toward mass education systems (Boli et al., 1985). Only in later publications do they morph into just one all-encompassing argument (Meyer et al. 1992, 1997). We agree that universalistic individualism was a driving force behind the development of society that originated in the Western world during the Middle Ages and the Reformation, culminating with the enlightenment (Pinker, 2018). Indeed, Protestant thought and its propagation have immensely accelerated the spread of capitalistic orientation and institutions (Weber, 1920) as well as of universalistic education, as all individuals needed to be literate in order to read the scriptures (Boli et al., 1985, p. 158). The nation state acts rationally in the interest of development and progress (Boli et al., 1985, p. 159). This rather top-down emergence of mass education can be seen in a majority of European countries in which state regulations on compulsory education preceded mass enrolment. This holds true, for example, in corporatist Denmark as well as in Catholic Austria and Spain. Yet Catholic-dominated countries might be slower than Protestant-dominated ones to achieve high enrolments (Lindert, 2004b, p. 35). For instance, the South American Catholic Church showed resistance toward secular mass education for fear of losing its religious monopoly (Frankema, 2009, p. 361). However, Catholic polities also embraced an individualistic turn in the 19th century and increasingly fostered education for the majority of their subjects. Both paths yielded the same result of mass education operationalized by large enrolment rates.

In later publications, neoinstitutionalists' initial ideas of various ways to establish mass education systems seem to be of less importance. Meyer et al. (1992) mainly focused on "classic" world cultural arguments, in which the convergence toward a similar education system and therefore the introduction of mass education is independent of local cultural predispositions.

Bringing Culture Back In

Just a few decades before most European and Western countries introduced compulsory education laws, Tocqueville (1835) cautioned in his book *Democracy in America* against simply copying the American political institutions if they did not fit to the morally binding norms, values, customs, and practices of a country's citizens. In Tocqueville's view, the Protestant culture that the British colonizers transferred to the United States, Canada, Australia, and New Zealand is very special and considerably different to, for instance, South American and Northern African values and customs (Basáñez & Inglehart, 2016, p. 33). Taking these considerations into account, Eisenstadt (1986) argued that different global cultures emerged in the wake of ancient civilizations during the Axial Age between 800 and 200 BCE, starting with early Israel and Greece, early Imperial China, the Christian Roman Empire and Medieval Europe, Hinduism, Buddhism, and, later, Islam. All these cultural groups would follow a different path into modernity. Culture and identity are still important issues in political science research (Fukuyama, 2018), although Huntington (1996) has been harshly criticized for his idea of "fault lines," whereby international conflict is likely to increase due to "civilizational" differences.

Cultural differences have sparked scientific interest and motivated huge data collections, for example, in the famous study of Hofstede and Bond (1984) or the World Values Survey (Norris & Inglehart, 2011); they have shown that Western people tend more toward individualism and independence and less toward obedience and conformity (among others Basáñez & Inglehart, 2016). From a global and comparative perspective, Westerners with their culture of achievement are WEIRD people (Western, educated, industrialized, resourceful, democratic) and seem to be the exception rather than the rule (Schulz et al., 2019). This has direct consequences on a theoretical model of the expansion and emergence of mass education systems.

Neoinstitutionalism values the idea that humans live within, and strongly depend on institutionalized norms that guide individual behavior (Meyer, 2010, p. 5). In an ever more globalized world society, individuals and especially organizations are interested in common standards when navigating through the contingencies of the world. Due to the activities of IOs, Western models tend to spread around the globe.

Meyer et al. (1997, p. 146) illustrate their argument with this famous example: If a deserted island were to be discovered, it would not take long for it to have democratic institutions, welfare systems, and indeed even education programmes similar to most of those found in other countries; this is also because IOs exert normative pressure. Nevertheless, there are still remarkable cultural differences between societies with respect to significant aspects such as gender roles, religious identities, individualism, autonomy, hierarchy, and collectivism (Schulz et al., 2019). If the preservation of culture and identity did indeed become more important over the recent decades, as argued by Fukuyama (2018), Huntington (1996), Knöbl (2007), and Chua (2018), we would expect that different cultural configurations determine the emergence and expansion of mass education and thereby accelerate or delay the materialization of the universal picture of mass education that we see today.

Neoinstitutionalists acknowledge that cultural differences might have had an influence on the ways in which public education systems were initially introduced (Boli et al., 1985). While they see this effect as diminishing over time, we theorize in contrast that cultural affiliation always had a determining effect of some sort. Consequently, a crucial question is how to define and measure different global cultures. Inspired by existing cultural typologies, we rely on a set of countries' cultural characteristics such as indicators of political liberties, rule of law, gender roles, dominant religion, language group, government ideology, classification of civilization, and similar colonial past (Seitzer et al., 2021; see Windzio & Martens, 2021 for detailed information) and apply a two-mode network analysis to generate a fuzzy set typology of what we call "cultural spheres" (see later).

THE EFFECTS OF COLONIALISM

The influence of foreign actors' hegemonic power relations, such as colonialism, is often already exercised in the initial institutionalization of state education systems, even if more complex interdependencies between colonial powers and colonized countries are possible. Indeed, most non-Western civilizations had some sort of schooling before colonization began (Craig, 1981, pp. 191–192). The objectives were similar around the globe: among others, to train religious leaders, bureaucrats, and doctors as well as to spread literacy and numeracy throughout the elite in order to uphold social power structures. On the other hand, education in its non- or informal form is ingrained in every human society and the reason for the advancement of *Homo sapiens* as an entire species. When regarding the transition into a Western-style mass education, it is clear that "[h]ow contact with the West affected these patterns depended both on the character and strength of the indigenous traditions and on the policies pursued by the West and its agents" (Craig, 1981, p. 192).

In many African countries, the influence of Islam on national education systems is evident. Especially in remote rural regions, the Koran schools ("maktabs") provided the only accessible primary education, while in other regions they competed with state primary schools (Brock & Alexiadou, 2013, p. 137). While the "maktabs" are religious educational establishments rather than state schools, the substitutive role they played in certain contexts could have counteracted the adoption and spread of Western mass primary education. In contrast, early missionary schools, which constitute the widest spread of Western education, might have had an accelerating effect on the transition from an informal schooling system to one that was standardized according to the Western way of education (Craig, 1981, pp. 192–193). Additionally, the huge economic inequalities left by colonialism, which includes among other things the strong political influence of a land-owning elite, possibly had a negative influence on the accessibility of the education system to the masses (Lindert, 2004a). In South America, the specific colonial legacy of huge economic inequality is regarded as one factor in explaining the late transition toward mass enrolment (Frankema, 2009, p. 370).

Researching the history of mass education means to acknowledge specific interdependencies in their changing strength. A thorough analysis must consider diffusion "under the conditions of colonialism" and "under conditions of continuing post-colonial ties" (Kuhlmann et al., 2020, p. 81). Thus, we decided to introduce colonial linkages into our estimations of the diffusion of mass education.

Data and Methods

In the empirical part of this chapter, we put the assumptions regarding the influence of different cultural spheres and international horizontal influences due to colonialism to the test. We operationalize mass education more conservatively than Meyer et al. (1992) and extend the time frame of inquiry. For our dependent variable we chose an enrolment threshold of 40% and assessed primary school enrolment rates of N = 156 countries from 1880 to 2010.

We define enrolment as the share of children enrolled in the respective age group for primary education as defined by each nation state. The data set combines previously collected data from Lee and Lee (2016), Benavot and Riddle (1988), and several enrolment ratios from the UNESCO Institute for Statistics (http://data.uis.unesco.org/). These data were interpolated for missing data points, and a principal component analysis (PCA) was performed as a method to combine information from different sources (Seitzer & Windzio, 2021). The resulting enrolment trend allows us to distinguish the point in time at which the enrolment ratio in a given country reached the critical value of our 40% threshold, that is, the inception of a mass state education system.

Figure 29.1 shows the overall development of primary education for boys and girls combined for our developed model between 1880 and 2010, divided by cultural clusters in 1950 on the left (see also Figure 29.2), and divided by world regions from the Maddison project on the right.[1] Both graphs show the different slopes and the timing of each slope meeting the 40% threshold; it is therefore a good indicator to gauge when the goal of mass education—defined as 40% enrolment in primary education, instead of 10% in Meyer et al. (1992, p. 137)—has been reached around the globe. Overall, the global trend shows a steep increase in enrolment after 1920 until 2010. Both depictions of different groupings of countries show that particularly Western and Anglo-American countries had already reached a higher level of enrolment in 1880 and thus met the threshold of mass education earlier. This depiction also shows the striking differences in enrolment trends between geographical regions, but also that these differences can be found in the clustering of countries by cultural characteristics as well. While the cultural and geographical regions are somewhat similar, we do believe, that geography on its own is not a

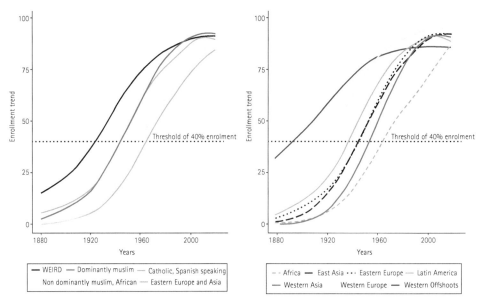

FIGURE 29.1 Average enrolment in primary education distinguished by cultural spheres from 1950 and Maddison regional clusters.

sufficient indicator for the spread of mass education, but rather a catch-all-indicator, as cultural practice has been and still is highly dependent on one's location. This graphical result supports what previous research has discussed: Formal education in its current form has been established first by Western countries and later spread around the globe. It also foreshadows the results of our analysis: Culture functions as a mediator for the establishment of mass education, ultimately leading to different pathways to modernity.

We created a comprehensive data set on cultural characteristics, including indicators of political liberties, rule of law, gender roles, dominant religion, language group, government ideology, classification of civilization, and colonial past (Besche-Truthe et al., 2020). The data constitute a valued and time-variant two-mode network in which countries are connected to cultural characteristics if they share them. In case of continuous measurements, for example, an index of gender equality, we generated quartiles in which countries are either members or not. A projection of the two-mode network on the vertex-set of countries results in a valued network of countries connected by their proximity in terms of cultural characteristics. Countries can have multiple connections to one another: When they share the language group "Atlantic-Kongo" in addition to the same dominant religion, they have a connection with a weight of 2. The higher the cultural proximity between two countries, the higher the number of ties—that is, the stronger the weight of the connection between them. We expect that with increasing tie strength, which is the "pipe structure" behind the diffusion process, the likelihood of "contagion" of mass education should increase, given that the threshold level of 40% enrolment has not yet been reached.

DIFFUSION OF MASS EDUCATION   623

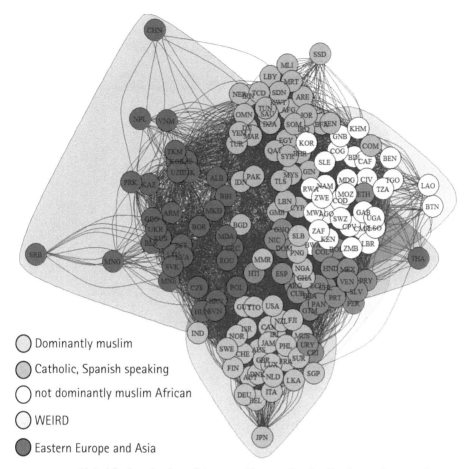

FIGURE 29.2 Global "cultural spheres" in 1950. (Source: Besche-Truthe et al., 2020; Seitzer et al. 2021)

Figures 29.2 and 29.3 show the "cultural spheres" networks for the years 1950 and 2010. For both years, we applied the *Louvain* algorithm as a network clustering method. The figure shows a (weighted) tie if countries share at least three cultural characteristics as defined by our data set. The colors indicate a country's affiliation with a cultural sphere as a result of the clustering. Although this algorithm results in distinct clusters, the visualizations clearly show the fuzzy set character of cultural spheres as well as the overlapping boundaries between them. Moreover, the decidedly nonessentialist character of our typology of cultures becomes apparent, in that cultural spheres change over time. While of course acknowledging that some countries do not fit precisely to the respective label, we found a solution with five clusters for the year 1950 that can be roughly described as 1. WEIRD, 2. dominantly Muslim, 3. catholic, Spanish speaking, 4. not dominantly Muslim African, and 5. Eastern Europe and Asia. In contrast, we discovered a three-cluster solution in the year 2010: We find Western countries on the right of the

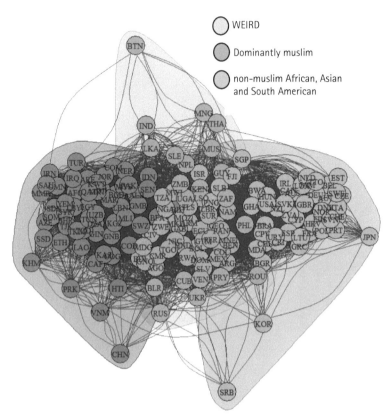

FIGURE 29.3 Global "cultural spheres" in 2010. (Source: Besche-Truthe et al., 2020; Seitzer et al., 2021)

network, predominantly Muslim countries on the left, and non-Muslim African, Asian, and South American countries that show more traditional gender-role orientations in between.

Furthermore, we created a network consisting of colonial ties between countries. We base the network on time-variant data spanning as far back as the 16th century. The recently published "COLDAT" data set by Bastian Becker (2019), which depicts colonial ties for European colonizers, serves as a base. Together with data from CEPII and our own data collection based on multiple sources, we added more colonial relationships, for example, "colonizations" by the Persian and Russian Empires. We follow the same definition of colonization as CEPII: A colonial relationship should involve long-term civilian administration that includes significant settlement (Mayer et al., 2008). Short-term military occupation does not fit the criteria.

We value connections of countries as 1 if they have a colonial relation in that year. From the end of colonization onwards the values are decreasing using a decay parameter. This parameter is calculated via an exponential function ($\exp(-t/40)$) which has a rather steady and slow decay of the value, with, for example, 0.97 one year after colonization, 0.77 ten years after colonization, and 0.08 hundred years after colonization.

We predict adoption rates by using a *discrete-time logistic hazard model*. Our dependent variable is the absorbing destination state of having an enrolment rate larger than or equal to 40% (enrolment smaller than 40% = 0, and enrolment larger than and equal to 40% = 1). Once a country has crossed this threshold of mass education, it drops out of the risk set.

We take our "cultural spheres" and "colonial ties" networks as the underlying structures for calculating exposure to countries which have already achieved mass education. We apply the R package *netdiffuseR* (Yon & Valente, 2020) and calculate exposure by taking the ratio of weighted connections with countries that have adopted compulsory schooling and those that have not. If a country is only connected to those that have adopted a mass education system, that is, more than 40% enrolment, exposure is 1; if none have adopted, exposure is 0. As potential confounders, we control for GDP per capita (Inklaar et al., 2018), levels of democratization (0 to 9 scale) (Lührmann et al., 2018), and time dependence by estimating piecewise constant baseline rates.

Lastly, we face a problem with nonindependent observations: There are historical time periods in which several countries did not exist because they were part of a larger unit. An ideal-typical example of this is the case of the former Yugoslavia, which was made up of various countries, including among others Serbia and Croatia. Our approach to address this problem is to regard Serbia and Croatia as "spatial patches" that were *at risk* of establishing a mass education system *before*, *during*, and *after* Yugoslavia existed. Yugoslavia will not be regarded as a subject in our data set, but Serbia, Croatia, and all other countries which formerly belonged to Yugoslavia are indeed distinct subjects. These subjects are, however, not statistically independent from one another. We account for the statistical nonindependence of observations when they were part of an overarching cluster by using the corrected standard error (Huber-White correction) (Zeileis et al., 2020), but it does not impose any standard error correction in the hazard model for country-years *not* belonging to the respective cluster or to any other cluster.

Figure 29.4 shows different groups of countries classified by their difference to the mean adoption time (see Rogers, 2003, p. 281). The majority of early adopters (until

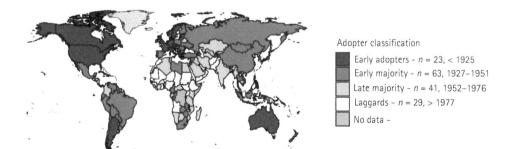

FIGURE 29.4 Classification of adopters of mass education.

1951) are located in Europe and other Western countries, such as the United States and Australia. The introduction of state-organized mass education therefore seems to have a Western origin. It diffused mainly to South American, South Asian, and Central as well as Eastern European states. The majority of late adopters (last introduction in 1976) and laggards (introductions only starting from 1977) are located on the African continent as well as in the Middle East. Descriptively, the global picture supports our hypothesis of a cultural component accelerating or slowing the introduction of state-led mass education.

RESULTS

Table 29.1 shows the result of our network diffusion analysis. As stated before, the dependent variable, namely the hazard rate of introducing mass education, is a country's exceedance of the 40% enrolment threshold in primary education. We transformed coefficients into hazard ratios.

The dependent variable has a median of M = 1949, meaning half of all countries included in the sample reached the 40% enrolment threshold until that year. These results

Table 29.1 Diffusion of Mass Education (1880–2010), Discrete-Time Logistic Hazard Model, N = 156 Countries, Hazard Ratios

	Dependent Variable	
	Enrolment Threshold of 40%	
	(1)	(2)
Rate t(0–24)	0.001^{***}	0.001^{***}
Rate t(25–49)	0.002^{***}	0.002^{***}
Rate t(50–74)	0.004^{***}	0.004^{***}
Rate t(75–99)	0.001^{***}	0.001^{***}
Rate t(100–130)	0.001^{***}	0.001^{***}
GDP per capita/10,000 USD	3.465^{***}	3.550^{***}
Democratization	1.225^{***}	1.229^{***}
Cultural spheres net.: w. exposure (lag 1 year)	67.922^{***}	68.465^{***}
Colonies net.: w. exposure (lag 1 year)	–	1.074
Observations	10288	10288
Log likelihood	−627.285	−627.209
Akaike inf. crit.	1270.569	1272.418
Bayesian inf. crit.	1328.479	1337.567

$+ p < 0.1; {}^{*} p < 0.05; {}^{**} p < 0.01; {}^{***} p < 0.001.$

Source: WeSIS database, own computation.

show a considerably late introduction of mass education despite early efforts to implement compulsory education. The earliest observed crossings of the 40% enrolment threshold were reached by New Zealand in 1880, in 1897 by Czechia, and 1898 by Sweden. Countries that only recently reached the sufficient level of enrolment include Djibouti (2006), Afghanistan (2004), and South Sudan (2004).

Model 1 shows a significant positive effect for GDP per capita, indicating that countries with a higher GDP are at greater "risk" of reaching the 40% enrolment threshold. In our model, democratization also shows a significant positive effect, though to a lesser extent than GDP per capita. Since our dependent variable is the exceedance of an enrolment threshold, our finding does not contradict Paglayan's (2020) assessment of there being no relationship between further expansions of primary enrolment rates. The most interesting result, however, is the positive and significant effect of exposure in the "cultural spheres" network. Countries exposed to culturally similar countries that have already established mass education are at increased risk of adopting mass education as well. The effect is very large, hinting at a diffusion process that is very strong inside of cultural spheres. In other words, if a large number of culturally similar countries have developed mass education systems in which at least 40% of primary school-age children are enrolled, the pressure gets so high for the countries within this cultural sphere that have not done so, that it is very unlikely they would not also eventually attain mass education. Even when controlling for domestic factors like economic development and democracy scores, this effect holds.

Colonial legacies seem to have no effect on the outcome or on the effects or model fit. Accordingly, this predictor does not explain any additional variance in our model.

Ultimately, we can prove three things with this innovative estimation method: First, the global diffusion of state-led mass education follows a path that is determined by the cultural similarity of countries showing fuzzy boundaries as opposed to hard "fault lines." Second, colonial interdependencies neither significantly hinder nor accelerate the global diffusion process. Lastly, domestic factors do play a role in the speed of achieving a 40% primary enrolment rate, but, despite functionalist claims, they are not the sole explanatory indicators.

CONCLUSION

In this chapter we analyzed the introduction of mass education, approximated by an enrolment threshold of 40% for a total of 156 countries between 1880 and 2010. We focused on the effect of countries' similarity in cultural spheres and horizontal interdependencies through colonialism on the diffusion of state-led mass education systems.

The motivation of our analysis was to enhance functionalist and neoinstitutionalist arguments with a nonessentialist concept of culture. While functionalism highlights the specific contributions of education to modern societies and their differentiated institutional subsystems, world system theory points to human capital formation and competition in the global economy. Neoinstitutionalism, in contrast, focuses on the structuring effects of institutions and institutionalized expectations. Inspired by Max Weber's comparative analysis of rationalization in different cultures, neoinstitutionalism predicts a diffusion of modern Western institutions all over the world, also in the field of education. Today, it is a taken-for-granted expectation that nation states should provide education for major parts of their populations. In our view, however, neoinstitutionalism abandoned its early considerations of culture and of different global cultures in the world. In our study, we tried to bring culture back into the analysis of global education. By measuring a country's culture through various indicators and by describing the distance or proximity of two countries with respect to culture using a time-varying two-mode network approach, we operationalized our concept of (time-varying) "cultural spheres" in a way that allows for a fuzzy set topology and overlapping boundaries, and thereby avoided an essentialist view of global cultures.

First, exposure to adopters of mass education through cultural similarity ties showed huge and significant results. Culture seems to be a facilitator of communication as well as a driver of assimilation of organizational structures, leading to the diffusion of institutions like mass education. We could not show, however, that colonial legacies had a significant effect on the introduction of mass education systems. This result further confirms our assumption that local culture has a strong influence on the introduction of a Western-style mass education system. Even though colonial hegemony is predictive of many international relations such as trade flows or political alliances, it is not predictive of the introduction of Western-style mass education. This could indicate that there is local resistance to the introduction of an education system systematically socializing children in "the Western way."

Furthermore, we found a significantly positive effect of GDP per capita, which supports existing theories, as well as a positive effect of democratization. According to our results, increasing democratization contributed to rising educational standards.

We conclude that culture does indeed determine the introduction of mass education. The nonsignificant result of colonial relations as well as the significant effect of democratization can both be traced back to being a result of culture as well. We therefore recommend the inclusion of culture in further analyses on the spread of welfare policies to further distinguish between the different pathways into modernity.

Future research should also consider the content of education. According to the functionalist argument, the curriculum is important for a country's differentiation into institutionalized subsystems. For instance, Spain was a laggard in economic development despite the fact that major parts of the population had access to basic education. However, education was controlled by the Catholic Church for a long time—meaning that first and foremost, children were mainly taught basic manual skills and catechism (Pinker, 2018, p. 234). We therefore expect that the curricula in terms of moral philosophy, ethics, and religion fall in line with the respective cultural sphere a country belongs to.

APPENDIX

List of Countries Included in the Analysis

Afghanistan, Angola, Albania, United Arab Emirates, Argentina, Armenia, Australia, Austria, Azerbaijan, Burundi, Belgium, Benin, Burkina Faso, Bangladesh, Bulgaria, Bahrain, Belarus, Bolivia, Brazil, Bhutan, Botswana, Central African Republic, Canada, Switzerland, Chile, China, Côte d'Ivoire, Cameroon, Congo–Brazzaville, Colombia, Comoros, Cape Verde, Costa Rica, Cuba, Cyprus, Czechia, Germany, Djibouti, Denmark, Dominican Republic, Algeria, Ecuador, Egypt, Spain, Estonia, Ethiopia, Finland, Fiji, France, United Kingdom, Georgia, Ghana, Guinea, Gambia, Guinea-Bissau, Greece, Guatemala, Guyana, Honduras, Croatia, Haiti, Hungary, Indonesia, India, Ireland, Iran, Iraq, Israel, Italy, Jamaica, Jordan, Japan, Kazakhstan, Kenya, Kyrgyzstan, Cambodia, South Korea, Kuwait, Laos, Liberia, Libya, Sri Lanka, Lesotho, Lithuania, Luxembourg, Latvia, Morocco, Moldova, Madagascar, Mexico, North Macedonia, Mali, Myanmar, Montenegro, Mongolia, Mozambique, Mauritania, Mauritius, Malawi, Malaysia, Namibia, Niger, Nigeria, Nicaragua, Netherlands, Norway, Nepal, New Zealand, Oman, Pakistan, Panama, Peru, Philippines, Papua New Guinea, Poland, Portugal, Paraguay, Qatar, Romania, Russia, Rwanda, Saudi Arabia, Sudan, Senegal, Singapore, Solomon Islands, Sierra Leone, El Salvador, Serbia, South Sudan, Suriname, Slovakia, Slovenia, Sweden, Eswatini, Syria, Chad, Togo, Thailand, Tajikistan, Timor-Leste, Trinidad & Tobago, Tunisia, Turkey, Tanzania, Uganda, Ukraine, Uruguay, United States, Uzbekistan, Venezuela, Vietnam, Yemen, South Africa, Zambia, Zimbabwe.

NOTE

1. Maddison Historical Statistics | Groningen Growth and Development Centre | University of Groningen (rug.nl).

REFERENCES

Basáñez, M. E., & Inglehart, R. (2016). *A world of three cultures: Honor, achievement and joy.* Oxford University Press.

Becker, B. (2019). Colonial dates dataset (COLDAT). doi:10.7910/DVN/T9SDEW.

Benavot, A., & Riddle, P. (1988). The expansion of primary education, 1870–1940: Trends and issues. *Sociology of Education, 61*(3), 191–2010.

Besche-Truthe, F., Seitzer, H., & Windzio, M. (2020). *Cultural spheres—Creating a dyadic dataset of cultural proximity.* SFB 1342 Technical Paper Series/5/2020. SFB 1342.

Boli, J., Ramirez, F. O., & Meyer, J. W. (1985). Explaining the origins and expansion of mass education. *Comparative Education Review, 29*(2), 145–170. https://www.jstor.org/stable/1188401

Brock, C., & Alexiadou, N. (2013). *Education around the world: A comparative introduction.* Education around the world series. Bloomsbury.

Busemeyer, M. R., & Trampusch, C. (2011). Review article: Comparative political science and the study of education. *British Journal of Political Science, 41*(2), 413–443. doi:10.1017/S0007123410000517

Chase-Dunn, C. K., & Lerro, B. (2013). *Social change: Globalization from the Stone Age to the present.* Taylor & Francis Group. https://ebookcentral.proquest.com/lib/gbv/detail.action?docID=4332804

Chua, A. (2018). *Political tribes: Group instinct and the fate of nations.* Bloomsbury.

Craig, J. E. (1981). Chapter 4: The expansion of education. *Review of Research in Education, 9*(1), 151–213. doi:10.3102/0091732X009001151

Eisenstadt, S. (1986). *The origin and diversity of Axial Age civilizations* [ACLS Humanities E-Book edition]. SUNY series in Near Eastern studies. State University of New York Press. http://site.ebrary.com/lib/alltitles/docDetail.action?docID=10588725

Frankema, E. (2009). The expansion of mass education in twentieth century Latin America: A global comparative perspective. *RHE / JILAEH, 27*(3), 359–396. doi:10.1017/S0212610900000811

Fukuyama, F. (2018). *Identity: The demand for dignity and the politics of resentment* (1st ed.). Farrar Straus and Giroux.

Gift, T., & Wibbels, E. (2014). Reading, writing, and the regrettable status of education research in comparative politics. *Annual Review of Political Science, 17*(1), 291–312. doi:10.1146/annurev-polisci-080911-131426

Griffiths, T. G., & Arnove, R. F. (2015). World culture in the capitalist world-system in transition. *Globalisation, Societies and Education, 13*(1), 88–108. doi:10.1080/14767724.2014.967488

Griffiths, T. G., & Imre, R. (2013). *Mass education, global capital, and the world: The theoretical lenses of István Mészáros and Immanuel Wallerstein.* Palgrave Macmillan.

Hofstede, G., & Bond, M. H. (1984). Hofstede's culture dimensions. *Journal of Cross-Cultural Psychology, 15*(4), 417–433. doi:10.1177/0022002184015004003

Huntington, S. P. (1996). *The clash of civilizations and the remaking of world order.* Free Press.

Inklaar, R., de Jong, H., Bolt, J., & van Zanden, J. (2018). Rebasing "Maddison": New income comparisons and the shape of long-run economic development. *GDC Research Memorandum* GD-174. https://ideas.repec.org/p/gro/rugggd/gd-174.html.

Jakobi, A. P., & Martens, K. (2010). *Mechanisms of OECD governance: International incentives for national policy-making?* Oxford University Press.

Jakobi, A. P., & Teltemann, J. (2011). Convergence in education policy? A quantitative analysis of policy change and stability in OECD countries. *Compare: A Journal of Comparative and International Education, 41*(5), 579–595. doi:10.1080/03057925.2011.566442

Knöbl, W. (2007). *Die Kontingenz der Moderne: Wege in Europa, Asien und Amerika.* Theorie und Gesellschaft 61. Campus-Verlag.

Kuhlmann, J., González de Reufels, D., Schlichte, K., & Nullmeier, F. (2020). How social policy travels: A refined model of diffusion. *Global Social Policy, 20*(1), 80–96.

Lee, J.-W., & Lee, H. (2016). Human capital in the long run. *Journal of Development Economics, 122*, 147–169. doi:10.1016/j.jdeveco.2016.05.006

Lindert, P. H. (2004a). *Growing public: Social spending and economic growth since the eighteenth century: Volume 1: The story.* Cambridge University Press.

Lindert, P. H. (2004b). *Growing public: Social spending and economic growth since the eighteenth century: Volume 2: Further evidence.* Cambridge University Press.

Lipset, S. M. (1957). *Political man: The social bases of politics.* Doubleday & Company.

Lührmann, A., Tannenberg, M., & Lindberg, S. I. (2018). Regimes of the world (RoW): Opening new avenues for the comparative study of political regimes. *PaG, 6*(1), 60–77. doi:10.17645/pag.v6i1.1214

Mayer, T., Head, K., & Ries, J. (2008). The erosion of colonial trade linkages after independence. *CEPII Working Paper* (2008-27). http://www.cepii.fr/PDF_PUB/wp/2008/wp2008-27.pdf

Meyer, J W. (1977). The effects of education as an institution. *American Journal of Sociology, 83*(1), 55–77.

Meyer, J. W. (2010). World society, institutional theories, and the actor. *Annual Review of Sociology, 36*(1), 1–20. doi:10.1146/annurev.soc.012809.102506

Meyer, J. W., Boli, J., Thomas, G. M., & Ramirez, F. O. (1997). World society and the nation-state. *American Journal of Sociology, 103*(1), 144–181. doi:10.1086/231174

Meyer, J. W., & Ramirez, F. O. (2005). Die globale Institutionalisierung der Bildung. In J. W. Meyer, G. Krücken, & B. Kuchler (Eds.), *Weltkultur: Wie die westlichen Prinzipien die Welt durchdringen.* Dt. Erstausg., 1. Aufl. (pp. 212–234). Edition zweite Moderne. Suhrkamp.

Meyer, J. W., Ramirez, F. O., & Soysal, Y. N. (1992). World expansion of mass education, 1870–1980. *Sociology of Education, 65*(2), 128. doi:10.2307/2112679

Münch, R. (1992). *Die Struktur der Moderne: Grundmuster und differentielle Gestaltung des institutionellen Aufbaus der modernen Gesellschaften.* 1. Aufl. Suhrkamp-Taschenbuch Wissenschaft 978. Suhrkamp.

Norris, P., & Inglehart, R. (2011). *Sacred and secular: Religion and politics worldwide* (2nd ed.). Cambridge studies in social theory, religion, and politics. Cambridge University Press.

Paglayan, A. S. (2020). The non-democratic roots of mass education: Evidence from 200 years. *American Political Science Review,* 1–20. doi:10.1017/S0003055420000647

Pinker, S. (2018). *Enlightenment now: The case for reason, science, humanism, and progress.* Viking.

Ramirez, F. O. (2013). Reconstituting children: Extension of personhood and citizenship. In D. I. Kertzer & K. W. Schaie (Eds.), *Age structuring in comparative perspective* (pp. 143–166). Social Structure and Aging series. Taylor and Francis.

Rogers, E. M. (2003). *Diffusion of innovations* (5th ed.). Free Press. http://www.loc.gov/catdir/bios/simon052/2003049022.html

Schulz, J. F., Bahrami-Rad, D., Beauchamp, J. P., & Henrich, J. (2019). The church, intensive kinship, and global psychological variation. *Science (New York, N.Y.), 366*(p. eaau5141). doi:10.1126/science.aau5141

Seitzer, H., Besche-Truthe, F., & Windzio, M. (2021). The introduction of compulsory schooling around the world: Global diffusion between isomorphism and "cultural spheres." In M. Windzio & K. Martens (Eds.), *Global pathways to education: Cultural spheres, networks, and international organizations* (pp. 37–64). Palgrave McMillan.

Seitzer, H., & Windzio, M. (2021). *Development of historical enrolment trends.* SFB 1342 Technical Paper Series/6/2021. SFB 1342.

Strang, D. (1991). Adding social structure to diffusion models. *Sociological Methods & Research, 19*(3), 324–353. doi:10.1177/0049124191019003003

Tocqueville, A. de (1835). *Democracy in America.* Liberty Fund.

Turner, J. H. (1998). *The structure of sociological theory.* Thompson.

Valente, T. W. (1999). *Network models of the diffusion of innovations.* Quantitative methods in communication. Hampton Press.

Wallerstein, I. M. (2007). *World-systems analysis: An introduction.* Duke University Press.

Weber, M. (1920). *Gesammelte Aufsätze zur Religionssoziologie*. Mohr.

Weymann, A. (2014). *States, markets and education: The rise and limits of the education state*. Transformations of the state. Palgrave Macmillan. http://gbv.eblib.com/patron/FullRecord. aspx?p=1609140.

Windzio, M., & Martens, K. (2021). The global development, diffusion, and transformation of education systems: Transnational isomorphism and "cultural spheres." In M. Windzio & K. Martens (Eds.), *Global pathways to education: Cultural spheres, networks, and international organizations* (pp. 1–35). Palgrave Macmillan.

Wolf, F., & Zohlnhöfer, R. (2009). Investing in human capital? The determinants of private education expenditure in 26 OECD countries. *Journal of European Social Policy* 19(3): 230–244. doi:10.1177/0958928709104738

Yon, G. V., & Valente, T. W. (2020). *NetdiffuseR: Analysis of diffusion and contagion processes on networks*. Zenodo.

Zeileis, A., Köll, S., & Graham, N. (2020). Various versatile variances: An object-oriented implementation of clustered covariances in R. *Journal of Statistical Software*, 95, 1–36. https://doi.org/10.18637/jss.v095.i01.

CHAPTER 30

THE POLITICS OF EQUALITY IN SECONDARY EDUCATION ACROSS WEALTHY POSTWAR DEMOCRACIES

JANE R. GINGRICH, ANJA GIUDICI,
AND DANIEL MCARTHUR

INTRODUCTION

WHILE the expansion of primary education in Europe, North America, and the Antipodes occurred largely in the mid- to late 19th century, the rise of mass secondary education was a postwar phenomenon (Ansell & Lindvall, 2013, 2020; Green, 1990; Paglayan, 2021). In the pre–World War II period, only in a handful of countries did more than a third of youth enroll in secondary education. Today, the vast majority of children in wealthy democracies complete upper-secondary education (Barro & Lee, 2013).

On the face of it, the postwar period was one of convergence on a particular kind of equality in education—the equality of access to the status of being a secondary pupil. However, by focusing on shifts at the critical lower-secondary stage (Wiborg, 2009), this chapter shows that even as wealthy democracies converged on the norm that all youths should have equal status as pupils, this equality rested on different conceptions of what it means to be a pupil. Policymakers fought over how to stratify categories of pupils and the degree to which their educational experiences should be standardized, defining equality in different ways.

The chapter then turns to the European Social Survey to investigate patterns of intergenerational educational mobility across birth cohorts in long-standing European democracies. This section examines how the global expansion of the norm of secondary attainment intersected with national variation in lower-secondary education to shape opportunities. Institutional variation early in the postwar period is associated with different patterns of intergenerational mobility. While these institutional effects weaken over time, the massification of secondary education did not eliminate all differences between countries. The conclusion examines this pattern in more depth, showing how the massification of secondary education raised new institutional questions about equality. Collectively, this chapter provides a broad overview of both convergence in norms of equality in access to education and the ongoing divergence in the translation of these norms into institutions and experiences.

Conceptualizing Institutional Equity in Educational Expansion

Modern education systems were built on the idea that (almost) everyone can and has a right to learn. At the same time, however, they also act as "sorting machines" that classify students into categories and allocate opportunities (Kerckhoff, 1995). Education systems are, then, both central institutions for structuring equality and for reproducing inequality (Domina et al., 2017).

The literature on postwar educational politics tends to emphasize one or the other of these dynamics. Scholars adopting bird's-eye perspectives examine the common trend toward expansion and the associated reduction in educational inequalities. Based on comparative analysis of nearly all countries, work following the "World Polity" tradition argues that common expansions in educational enrolment (Meyer et al., 1992), standardized curricula (Benavot et al., 1991), and more equal structures (Furuta, 2020) are evidence of global processes of homogenization. These processes result from national elites aligning local education systems with the global norms at the heart of modern statehood. Other studies focus less on the diffusion of norms than on shared economic pressures. Accordingly, national policymakers pursue similar educational expansion in order to equip their populations with knowledge and skills in the face of technological change (Goldin & Katz, 2008). Both normative and economic pressures push policymakers to recognize children as *equal in their status as secondary pupils*.

However, transnational norms need to be enacted by policymakers with varied distributive preferences and institutional capacity to act. Work on specific reform processes depicts how competing parties and educational stakeholders, far from orienting themselves toward common equalizing norms, took widely differing positions on how to institutionalize them. As a result, postwar democracies selected different paths depending on local political majorities (e.g., Ansell, 2010; Busemeyer, 2015; Gingrich, 2011; Österman, 2018), parties' and stakeholders' beliefs (Baldi, 2012; Wiborg, 2009), and electoral institutions (Iversen & Stephens, 2008). Democratic contestation produced different definitions of *equality among secondary pupils*.

Without wanting to definitively discriminate between these two approaches, this chapter adds to the debate by showing how the diffusion of the expansion of pupilhood at the secondary level rested on ongoing conflict over the nature of pupilhood.

To do so, we develop a novel inventory and systematization of lower-secondary educational reforms since 1945 in 18 countries.[1] Because the literature on educational reform argues that different rationales may drive decision-making in democratic and nondemocratic contexts (Ansell, 2010; Paglayan, 2021; Stasavage, 2005) and in those at different levels of economic development, we choose to focus on a large sample of advanced democracies.

To evaluate convergence in conceptions of the equal *status* of being a pupil, we code reforms extending the compulsory education period, removing fees, and eliminating educational "dead ends" that did not grant access to further formal education. To systematically assess the extent to which policymakers defined pupilhood in equalizing ways, we draw on Allmendinger's (1989) well-known conceptualization of stratification and standardization of secondary education. We first code the extent of stratification by identifying changes in the age of streaming, number of streams, and opportunities to move from one stream to another. Streaming is defined as the formal division of pupils into a track that leads to a varying qualification, or that provides access to a selective school. We then code efforts to standardize pupil experiences through the upgrading and equalization of provision, curricula, and teacher training across territories, with the aim of creating more uniform onward opportunities within a given stream. We focus on these variables, rather than financial standardization, as they are more directly comparable across countries; however, we recognize that differences of equality in funding remain important. We measure these reforms using international reports, official policy documents, and historical and contemporary case-based literature from the analyzed countries. Tables 30.1 and 30.2 outline the core variables.

The chapter shows first that a common trend toward equality in status does indeed emerge. However, postwar secondary expansion also shows significant cross-sectional and temporal variation in terms of underlying definitions of pupilhood.

Stratified Secondary Institutions and Definitions of Pupilhood: The Early Postwar Years

While 19th-century reforms equalized primary provision in industrial countries, at the secondary level, in the early postwar years, the equal status of children as secondary pupils was *not* universally accepted. A child's class, ethnicity, gender, or place of residence dramatically shaped their likelihood of remaining a pupil in the postprimary period.

Table 30.1 Development of Secondary Access, Stratification, and Standardization in 17 Advanced Economies, 1950–2020

| Country | Access | | | | | | Stratification | | | | | | Standardization | | | |
| | Minimum Leaving Age | | Dead Ends | | Fees | | Age of First Streaming | | Number of Streams | | Bridges | | Common Certificate | | Common Curriculum | |
	1950	2020	1950	2020	1950	2020	1950	2020	1950	2020	1950	2020	1950	2020	1950	2020
Australia NSW	15	17	No	No	No	No	11	16	2	1	No	Yes	No	Yes	No	Yes
Austria	14	18	No	No	Yes	No	10	10	4	2	No	Yes	No	No	No	No
Belgium	14	18	Yes	No	Yes	No	12	12	4	4	No	Yes	No	Yes	No	Partial
Canada Ontario	14	18	No	No	No	No	14	18	2	1	Partial	Yes	Partial	Partial	Partial	Partial
Denmark	11	16	Yes	No	No	No	14	16	3	1	No	Yes	No	Yes	No	Yes
Finland	13	18	Partial	No	Partial	No	11	16	2	1	Partial	Yes	No	Yes	No	Yes
France	14	18	Yes	No	Partial	No	11	15	2	1	No	Yes	No	Yes	No	Yes
Germany Bavaria	14	18	No	No	Yes	No	10	10	2	3	No	Yes	No	No	No	No
Ireland	14	16	No	No	Yes	No	12	15	3	1	No	Yes	No	Yes	No	Yes
Italy	11	18	Yes	No	Yes	No	11	14	2	1	No	Yes	No	Yes	No	Yes
Japan	12	15	No	No	No	No	15	15	1	1	Yes	Yes	Yes	Yes	Yes	Yes
The Netherlands	13	18	No	No	Partial	No	12	12	5	3	Partial	Yes	No		No	Partial
Norway	14	16	Yes	No	Yes	No	12	16	2	1	No	Yes	No	Yes	No	Yes
New Zealand	15	16	Yes	No			18	16								
Sweden	15	16	No	No	No	No	11	16	2	1	Yes	Yes	No	Yes	No	Yes
Switzerland Zurich	14	16	No	No	Yes	No	12	12	3	4	No	Yes	No	No	No	No
UK England	15	18	No	No	No	No	11	16	2	1	Partial	Yes	Yes	Yes	No	Yes

Table 30.2 Standardization and Level of Lower-Secondary School Teacher Training

	Standardization of Training Length and Requirements Across Tracks			Minimum Teaching Training Level for Nonacademic and Comprehensive Lower Secondary
	1950	1980	2020	
Australia - NSW	No	Partly	Yes	1945: postsecondary college 1973: tertiary training college 1988: university
Austria	No	No	Yes	1945: upper secondary 1962: tertiary pedagogic academy 2013: university and academy cooperation
Canada Ontario	No	Yes	Yes	1945: university
Denmark	No	Yes	Yes	1945: postsecondary 1966: tertiary training college 2000: university
Finland	No	Yes	Yes	1945: upper or postsecondary 1971: university or college of education 1970s: university
France	No	No	Yes	1945: postsecondary 1978: university 1989: autonomous university institute 2005: university
Germany Bavaria	No	No	Length of degrees differs	1945: upper or postsecondary 1958: tertiary pedagogic academy 1970: university
Germany Nordrhein-Westphalia	No	No	Yes	1945: tertiary pedagogic academy 1998: university
Greece	No	No	Yes	1945: postsecondary 1982: university
Ireland	No	Partly	Yes	1945: postsecondary 1970s: university and university associated college
Italy	No	Yes	Yes	1945: postsecondary 1962: university
Japan	No	Yes	Yes	1945: postsecondary 1949: college and university
The Netherlands	No	Partly	Two different degrees exist	1945: postsecondary 1970: tertiary college or university
Norway	No	Yes	Yes	1945: postsecondary 1969: autonomous tertiary college 1996: university
Portugal	No	Yes	Yes	1945: lower- or postsecondary 1979: university

(continued)

Table 30.2 Continued

	Standardization of Training Length and Requirements Across Tracks			Minimum Teaching Training Level for Nonacademic and Comprehensive Lower Secondary
	1950	1980	2020	
Spain	No	Partly	Yes	1945: upper secondary 1970: university school (except vocational school teachers) 1990: university
Sweden	No	Yes	Yes	1945: postsecondary 1950: tertiary school for education 1984: university
Switzerland Zurich	No	No	Length of degrees differs	1945: postsecondary 1978: tertiary autonomous college 2000: tertiary university of teacher education (autonomous)
England and Wales	No	Partly	Different routes and degrees exist	1946: nongraduate tertiary college 1972: elimination of nongraduate route but different degrees remain in place

Many children could legally leave school between the ages of 11 and 14—before the age of completion of lower-secondary education (see Table 30.1). In countries where the compulsory age extended into the secondary level, many systems still allowed children to complete their compulsory education in some form of upper-primary schooling, such as the "quatrième degré" in Belgium, the nonexam middle school of Denmark, or upper-primary schools in France. These schools were often academic dead ends. Even where upward progression might have been possible in theory—that is, through an exam offering onward access—the lack of curricular standardization rendered this path difficult in practice. For instance, in predemocratic Portugal, students had to pass a French exam to access upper-secondary schooling; however, French was not part of the upper-primary curriculum (Mendonça, 2011).

It was not just that pupils could leave school before the end of lower-secondary education, but in many cases, secondary education was not accessible to the masses. Parents often had to pay for access to more demanding courses. For instance, fees were required to access an Austrian Gymnasium (until 1962), a Norwegian Realskole (until 1959), or an Italian Scuola Media (until 1962), the exclusive ladders into higher education in these countries at the time. While (limited) scholarships often existed for talented pupils lacking financial means, they only covered fees for a minority of students. Moreover, in countries such as Ireland or Australia, the great majority of secondary institutions were private schools with autonomy over selection, limiting access for many pupils (Campbell & Sherington, 2006; Taighde ar Oideachas, 1965).

Barro and Lee (2013) show that in 1955, in only half of the countries studied here, did more than a third of the 20- to 24-year-old cohort (pupils in the late 1940s) possess *some* secondary education, and only in Japan, Australia, and the United States had more than a third of this cohort completed secondary education. A 1965 study by the Council of Europe provides more detailed data on enrolment, demonstrating that even in the early 1960s gaps remained; over 96% of 15-year-olds in Germany were in school, compared to only 42.3% of 15-year-olds in England and 53.4% in France.

Prewar education structures nearly universally (the United States is a partial exception) institutionalized substantial differentiation in the definition of secondary pupilhood. After spending 4 to 6 years in free and comprehensive primary schools, children were largely streamed into academic and nonacademic programs.

From this point onward, children's educational experiences differed. Pupils who had been selected into academically oriented schools were usually instructed by graduate teachers and would study a curriculum mirroring the structure of academic disciplines (Cha, 1991). In contrast, postprimary curricula generally combined more holistic pedagogical approaches with, often gendered, prevocational skills. For instance, according to the 1963 Austrian curriculum regulations, girls enrolled in postprimary schools were supposed to spend 4–5 lessons out of 29 practicing needlework and housekeeping, while boys received 2 hours of woodwork instruction out of 27 (Austria, 1963). For their peers in the academic-secondary gymnasium, only 1 needlework or woodwork lesson was compulsory (out of 31.5). And while the postprimary pupils received instruction in broad and skill-centered subjects such as "lessons in general knowledge" (Austria, 1963), gymnasium pupils were schooled in mathematics, physics, and history and social studies (Austria, 1964). In all countries but the United States and Japan, the teachers who delivered postprimary curricula had not graduated in a subject, but rather had acquired a general pedagogic education in a post- or upper-secondary training institution (see Table 30.2).

These differences in formal stratification combined with a lack of standardization in provision. As outlined earlier, the quality of teaching and curricular control varied across types of schools and areas. In some countries, these differences were institutional. Rural schools in Norway, Denmark, Sweden, and parts of Canada, for instance, faced different legal requirements in terms of annual hours of instruction or the length of compulsory schooling.

Even where there were no formal inequalities across rural and urban areas, the costs of secondary education were considerably higher for pupils living in rural communities. The 1958 "International Conference on Education" (UNESCO & IBE, 1958) examined rural provision, with most countries reporting few legal disparities, but substantial practical differences, in class sizes, access to secondary schools, and qualified teachers across areas. For instance, in the 1959–1960 school year, 69% of Italian communes did not dispose over a secondary school (ISTAT, 1962). Similarly, the 1965 Irish *Investment in Education* report found that while pupils living in urban and more affluent areas normally only had to walk short distances to access a secondary school, up to 15% of pupils in Ulster had to travel more than 10 miles to receive secondary education (Taighde ar

Oideachas, 1965, p. 268). Combined with weak transportation infrastructure and a lack of boarding schools, situations like these strongly limited educational opportunities in rural regions.

Institutional Equity in the Period of Massification (1950–1980)

The early postwar period saw three decades of extensive attention to education reforms that looked to alter these triple inequalities—extending *access* to the status of secondary pupil to all children, creating more uniform definitions of pupilhood by reducing *stratification* and increasing *standardization*. However, while the former moves were nearly universally successful, the latter two met a more varied fate.

By the mid- to late 1960s, there was little political debate over whether to expand secondary access to all children (with similar developments later in Portugal, Spain, and Greece following their democratic transitions). Policymakers debated the extent of funding, the length of compulsory schooling, and other features—but there was widespread consensus that the state was a guarantor of mass secondary education (Meyer et al., 1992). The conservative parties that had resisted expansion in the early part of the 20th century (Ansell & Lindvall, 2013), by the 1960s, neither rhetorically nor policywise fundamentally questioned the idea that young people should be *able* to stay in school. For instance, while the 1953 manifesto of the Austrian Christian-democratic ÖVP still expressed skepticism toward expanding secondary education, announcing that it wanted to "draw young people's attention to the high value of manual work, particularly in our time of reconstruction, and warn them of overestimating desk jobs and the impending danger of an ever dissatisfied academic proletariat accumulating" (ÖVP, 1953, p. 5), by 1970, this same party argued that "everyone should be able to attend and graduate from a school appropriate to their talents and achievements" (ÖVP, 1970, p. 13).

The most visible policy behind this new consensus, as shown in Table 30.1, involved reforms expanding the length of compulsory schooling to the end of lower-secondary (14–16), and in some cases even to the end of upper-secondary (18), reducing the possibilities for early exit.

Next to the expansion of the compulsory period of schooling, early reforms eliminated academic dead ends, with a wave of reforms through the 1950s and 1960s integrating postprimary schools into comprehensive or multipurpose secondary schools, or converting them into new secondary schools. These moves occurred even in the countries that maintained early streaming, creating both educational ladders into upper-secondary and higher vocational education. These reforms increasingly aligned lower-secondary curricula, either by eliminating tracking entirely or through reforms that equalized the time dedicated to relevant subjects across tracks. From the 1960s, not only subjects such as history and sciences, but also foreign languages, the traditional mechanism of selection into elite education, became a standard across secondary education (Cha, 1991). The weakening of prevocational elements also decreased structural and curriculum differentiation linked to ascriptive criteria such as gender or ethnicity. By the mid-1960s, almost all children had a path to remain a pupil through their teen years.

The school building projects of the 1960s further spread new secondary schools to rural regions, and combined with improved transportation and increased child allowances, the costs for rural children to stay in school fell. Policymakers across Europe and beyond eliminated fees—with major shifts in Austria (1962), Finland (1968), and Zurich, Switzerland (1960). In many countries, reforms also reduced fees in confessional schools, with Belgium (1958), France (1959), and the Canadian province of Ontario (1984) extending funding on terms largely equal to non-confessional schools. Although the politics of these moves often followed accommodation with the Church, they also effectively extended access to pupils that depended on these schools. By the time Minister of Education O'Mailley surprised his cabinet in announcing Ireland would abandon secondary school fees in 1967 (Fleming & Hartford, 2014), secondary education was largely free to all children in wealthy democracies.

These shifts, combined with a growth in the size of baby boom cohorts, produced a dramatic increase in educational spending. Tanzi and Schuknecht (2000), looking at historical education spending in wealthy democracies for which there is long-run data, find that education spending increased by an average of 0.7% of GDP between 1937 and 1960, but by 2.4% of GDP between 1960 and 1980.[2]

However, this general move toward accepting the equal status of children as pupils rested on a more contentious renegotiation of what it meant to *be* a pupil. In nearly all countries, as policymakers extended access to secondary schooling to a broader group, they had to address the question of what kind of education to extend. In so doing, two debates opened up about the nature of equality among pupils—whether to reduce formal stratification and whether to standardize the experiences of pupils within streams.

In most countries, proposals to eliminate early tracking and create a more uniform category of lower-secondary pupil entered the political agenda between 1950 and 1970. The extent to which policymakers actually restricted academic elite streams or delayed selection into them, however, varied (Brunello & Checchi, 2007; Österman, 2018). Table 30.1 shows the variable move toward reduced streaming across countries. While many did destratify, the moves were not universal—some countries retained early selection and multiple streams.

At the same time, through the 1960s and 1970s, policymakers invested substantial time debating how far to standardize quality across secondary schools. The educational literature identifies this period as the start of an era in which policymakers began relying more heavily on scientific advice provided by universities, international organizations, and newly institutionalized research divisions (Mundy et al., 2016). The integration of postprimary schools into the secondary level, with its more regularized diploma, curricula, and examination systems, further centralized educational authority.

Curriculum regulations, from primary to teacher training, became longer and increasingly detailed, in an attempt to standardize teaching based on scientific criteria. In federal countries such as the United States and Switzerland, standardization efforts also meant that the federal governments acquired new competencies in education financing or certificate regulation, although they did not become centralized states.

In tracked systems, policymakers debated whether to create more commonality across tracks, particularly to increase the attractiveness of the nonacademic tracks for parents and employers (Giudici et al., 2023). In detracked systems, politicians and experts disagreed on whether the new comprehensive schools should offer pupils a homogeneous curriculum and certification, or whether they should internally sort pupils into different paths, levels, electives, or courses.

In Table 30.2 we present two indicators of these shifts, focusing on the teaching profession: whether lower-secondary-age children in different types of schools are educated by teachers with the same level and length of training, and the level of training for teachers employed at this stage. As outlined earlier, in the early postwar period, pupils in academic tracks would receive their education from graduate, often upper-class, teachers who had themselves climbed to the top of the educational ladder, whereas upper-primary pupils were taught by teachers trained in pedagogy-focused upper-secondary institutions. Table 30.2 shows that, over time, all countries tertiarized teacher training, transferring it either to universities or tertiary institutes. In countries that detracked their education systems, the standardization and elevation of teacher requirements normally accompanied structural reforms. In countries that maintained formal tracking or destandardized curricula, separate reforms equalized the level of training required to teach secondary pupils.

Despite these general shifts, as with stratification, standardization processes varied. The extent of student choice and selection varied across countries with regard to the curriculum—affecting the standardization of skills across a student cohort—and schools themselves—shaping the sorting of the student population.

While the Nordic countries moved to regulate within school streaming, many other countries kept substantial curricular diversity, allowing selective pathways or electives (e.g., Latin or classical languages) that created differing onward opportunities. These differences meant that pupils often continued to experience teachers with different academic credentials as well as depth of pedagogical training or specialization, depending on their track or path.

Differences across schools also existed. In some countries, the state was able to overcome opposition from educational stakeholders and implement de facto comprehensive structures; in others, parents and schools maintained much autonomy over resources or school structures that allowed sorting and variation on the ground. The debates around zoning restrictions for high schools in 1950s New South Wales (Campbell & Sherington, 2006), the busing policies in the United States, as well as their less well-known counterparts in the United Kingdom (Esteves, 2019), all provide examples.

Nearly half of industrial democracies, such as France, Ireland, the Netherlands, Belgium, and parts of Australia and Canada, also chose to engage in the expansion of secondary schooling in cooperation with private (usually religious) schools. This process involved linking the increased state funding of private schools, especially in underserviced areas, to stricter rules on curricula, admissions, and quality (see Ansell & Lindvall, 2020, for a discussion of these dynamics in primary schools). The institutionalization of state–private relations provided financial and regulatory stability for private providers but also institutionalized a more diverse set of providers in these countries.

These varying paths, when taken together, entrenched three quite different models of pupilhood. The first, emerging in the Nordic countries, rested on a uniform definition of pupils—both destratifying and standardizing experiences. The social-democratic governments of the Nordic countries radically detracked secondary education through the 1960s by introducing 9-year comprehensives aimed at tackling both class and territorial inequality (Wiborg, 2009). From that point onward, with the exception of some limited internal differentiation, secondary school pupils, regardless of their grades and ability, all sat in the same classrooms, and received the same instruction, delivered by teachers with an equal training, and with a curriculum merging academic and more concrete content (Carlgren & Kallos, 1997; Wiborg, 2009).

A second model emphasized uniform opportunities but not experiences, advocating destratification but not standardization. France (1975) and Italy (1962) postponed streaming to age 14/16, as did democratizing southern European countries such as Spain (1970, 1990), Portugal (1975, 1986), and Greece (1976, 2000). However, their comprehensive schools looked quite different from the standardized Scandinavian model. While policymakers in these countries also wanted to expand access to lower classes and rural regions, they opted for curricula that largely mirrored the academic tradition allowing ongoing elite pathways. Combined with stricter grading and examination practices, these systems produced less homogenous certifications or higher failure rates (Ambrosoli, 1982; Bolívar, 2015).

The Anglo countries (with some local exceptions) followed a similar logic. These countries moved toward comprehensive structures, reducing or eliminating academically selective schools and establishing common curricula, but continued to allow pupils to select a wide range of prevocational and academic electives, creating differentiated pathways. For instance, the 1989 Irish Junior Certificate Programme, which introduced a common certification and curriculum structure for all lower-secondary pupils, allowed them to choose among 22 subjects of examination with 2 or 3 levels each, ranging from Latin to Classical Studies to Home Economics and Typewriting (Ireland, 1989). In sum, this model emphasized institutional equality in structures, but not uniformity in pupil experiences.

Finally, a third model emphasized differentiation among pupils in terms of opportunities, while focusing on regulating quality within each stream. A number of countries maintained early academic streaming: Austria (age 10), Belgium (age 12), Germany (age 10), the Netherlands (age 12), and parts of Switzerland (ages 11–13). Proponents of more radical structural reforms (usually on the political left) in these countries were defeated by coalitions of secondary teachers' unions, conservative parties, and parents' organizations (Greveling et al., 2015; Henkens, 2004; Pultar, 2021; Rieger, 2001; Wiborg, 2009).

However, it is not the case that these education systems remained unreformed. These countries opened access to upper-secondary education by building new schools in underserviced regions, creating upward ladders into higher vocational sectors, aligning the curriculum across tracks to facilitate transfers, and homogenizing the qualifications of secondary teachers. Here the goal was to create different paths that provided a clear signal to employers and future educational providers about pupils' skills.

National policymakers, then, defined the nature of secondary pupils in highly varying ways. The Nordic countries emphasized a single model of pupilhood as a route to equity, while the Continental countries entrenched a highly stratified model in which pupils entered different streams at a young age but had common experiences within them. France, the Anglo countries, and Southern European countries emphasized a degree of institutional equality in status, while allowing pupils to follow highly variable paths.

Thus collectively, the institutions of compulsory secondary education systems became more homogeneous in how they understood equality in access across industrialized democracies between 1950 and 1980, but not in the definition of pupilhood. Why? The literature here is broad, and our discussion can only be cursory, but a number of perspectives emerge.

Case studies and the comparative literature largely agree that both economic and political imperatives in the early postwar period created a broad consensus on the need to expand access to secondary education. Changes in the economic structure increased the demand for skilled labor. These shifts meant that many employer organizations—who often had strong links to center-right parties—began to call for educational expansion. For instance, in 1959 Zurich, mechanical engineers founded an employer committee to lobby politicians for secondary expansion (Rieger, 2001). Similar initiatives emerged elsewhere. As labor demand shifted from independent (often inherited) positions (e.g., as shop owners) to the provision of services, the value of educational certificates as routes to middle-class employment also increased for parents and pupils. In the face of these changes, voters demanded more educational opportunities, further giving parties on the left and the right strong incentives to expand.

These common developments, however, did not eliminate political contestation. On the nature of such contestation, the literature is divided.

One line of work emphasizes varying ideological traditions across countries. For instance, several studies comparing non-detracking in Germany to other contexts argue that German universities during the Nazi dictatorship hindered the scientific innovations that, in other countries, produced increasing evidence on the role of tracking in the reproduction of inequality (Baldi, 2012; Heidenheimer, 1974). These studies have the benefit of highlighting the importance of knowledge for (partisan) policymaking. Indeed, other authors have remarked how, the left was especially long divided about whether tracked or comprehensive systems provided better opportunities for talented working-class pupils (Paulston, 1968; Wiborg, 2009). However, this line of argument has difficulties explaining why countries which experienced weaker forms of "Gleichschaltung" (e.g., the Netherlands or Belgium) or which were not occupied at all (e.g., most Swiss cantons) also maintained tracking, while for instance Italy, Greece, or Spain, which experienced long periods of (academic) oppression, did introduce comprehensive structures.

A second line of studies focuses on partisan ideology and electoral competition as key drivers of reform (Östermann, 2018; Wiborg, 2009). From this perspective, left-wing parties, whose ideology emphasizes the need for institutions to foster societal equality, were generally more supportive of detracking than the right, for whom equality is no core concern. As emphasized by Wiborg (2009), where left-wing parties were dominant or capable of forging coalitions with other interested parties, they were able to implement comprehensive reforms.

This literature provides a crucial theorization of parties' distributive goals when deliberating on equality expanding reforms. However, the emphasis on parties alone cannot explain why center-right parties in a number of countries, from Australia (New South Wales) to France, Spain, or Belgium, actually pushed for comprehensive reforms, and sometimes were even behind their implementation.

A third argument emphasizes not just ideological and electoral imperatives, but economic ones. Busemeyer (2015), for instance, links the party literature to the "Varieties of Capitalism" tradition, examining the relationship between vocational and higher education in producing different patterns of support for stratification. According to Busemeyer, party families not only hold different views on distribution but also on the broader economic model. In countries with less developed specific skill provision, parties on the right were less vested in the education system. However, in the Continental European countries, the Christian Democrats emerged to protect stratification due to their strong links to both employers and employee organizations vested in the vocational model. Only in the Scandinavian countries, with a strong ideological left, did full detracking occur.

This work makes an important contribution, but historically, the link between vocational systems and tracking and standardization remains contested. Many actors vested in systems of vocational skilling were not opposed to destratifying reforms, for example, the main union federations in Germany (Sass, 2022).

More research is therefore needed to understand how parties navigated the politics of postwar educational structures. Case studies suggest the central role of coalitions including educational stakeholders, such as teachers and (religious) educational providers, in shaping these reforms. For instance, in Germany, organizations of academic secondary teachers, who stood to lose status and employment opportunities from comprehensive reforms, allied with parents' organizations and the church to oppose detracking, both on the streets and through the Christian-Democratic party (Helbig & Nikolai, 2015). Right-wing parties dominating governments in countries such as the United Kingdom or France did not have the same relationship to teacher unions and were therefore freer to implement reforms that lowered the status of academic secondary tracks (Giudici et al., 2023).

While this brief chapter cannot settle these debates, the key point that emerges is that contestation among political actors vested in differing notions of pupilhood through varying institutions, and that these institutions have proven to be quite stable over time (Table 30.1).

CONVERGING PUPIL EXPERIENCES?

Did the simultaneous expansion of access, but variation in the definition of pupilhood, matter for the way equity *actually* emerged across time and place? How did these trajectories matter collectively? To answer these questions, we link the aforementioned institutional variation over time and place to educational mobility across generations using data from the European Social Survey.

There is a large literature in sociology, education, and economics that examines the ways in which the degree of stratification and standardization of education systems shapes inequalities based on family background. There is much evidence that school systems with earlier tracking show greater family background inequalities in test performance and skills (Hanushek & Wößmann, 2006; Heisig & Solga, 2015; Van de Werfhorst & Mijs, 2010). Several studies examining postwar cohorts show that reforms raising the tracking and minimum school leaving ages weakened the influence of parental background on educational attainment (Braga et al., 2013; Brunello & Checchi, 2007; Meghir & Palme, 2005; van de Werfhorst, 2019). The implications for long-term occupational and income mobility are less clear (Checchi & van de Werfhorst, 2018; Jerrim & Macmillan, 2015; Meghir & Palme, 2005) perhaps because of the importance of other labor market institutions (Österman, 2018) or family behaviors (Pöyliö et al., 2018).

In this section we use data for 16 countries or regions in Western Europe[3] from nine waves of the European Social Survey (ESS) conducted between 2002 and 2018 to examine how changes in the three types of equality outlined earlier—access, stratification, and standardization—mattered for pupils' mobility experiences. Because these institutions were experienced collectively, our interest is in how they matter collectively; thus, we combine the eight variables set out in Table 30.1 into an *index of educational opportunity*. The index involves rescaling all variables to vary between 0 and 1, and reversing the items associated with greater stratification or lower standardization. We measure each variable at 5-year intervals, linking them to native-born individuals aged 25 + who were born between 1936 and 1990. The resulting sample size is around 141,000.

We expect that educational expansion in the early postwar period led to dramatic increases in lower-secondary attainment across Europe, especially among the children of low-educated parents. As a result, there should be a convergence across countries in terms of educational attainment, given the expansion of access. However, given the aforementioned literature, we further expect that the association between educational opportunity and attainment should be weaker where more unequal definitions of pupilhood (greater stratification or less standardization) remained in place.

Figures 30.1 and 30.2 plot trends in the probability of completing lower- and upper-secondary education by country and year of birth from 1936 to 1990. Trends are disaggregated by whether at least one of the cohort members' parents had themselves completed that level of education. Among those born in the 1930s and 1940s, there are large differences between countries in the impact of parental education on the

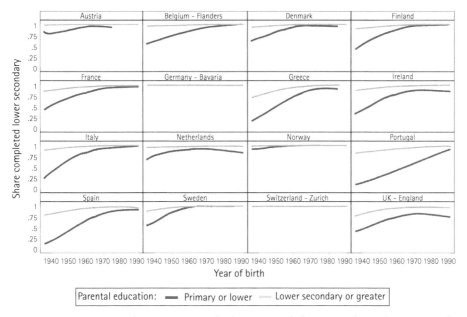

FIGURE 30.1 Association between parental education and share completing lower-secondary school by country/region and birth cohort. In some regions/years, all parents have completed lower-secondary education. Smoothed lines estimated using lowess.

(Data from European Social Survey 2002–2018, N = 141,209)

share completing lower-secondary education. At this point, lower-secondary completion rates were already high in countries such as Germany (Bavaria) and Switzerland (Zurich). By contrast, in southern European countries such as Italy, Spain, and Portugal, the children of those who did not complete lower-secondary school were as many as 50 percentage points less likely to complete it than the children of highly educated parents. This situation changed dramatically across the postwar period. Increases in attainment were overwhelmingly concentrated among the children of less educated parents, thus reducing (and in some cases eliminating) family background differences in attainment. These increases primarily took place in birth cohorts born prior to 1970, leading to a pronounced cross-national convergence.

Figure 30.2 shows that the substantive story for upper-secondary education is similar. In most countries, attainment rose for the children of high-educated parents, but less than for children of low-educated parents, once again leading to reduced inequalities in attainment by family background. Attainment gaps are almost eliminated in France, Bavaria, and Scandinavia in post-1970 cohorts. While attainment gaps remain in southern European countries, they are substantially smaller than among the cohorts born in the 1930s–1940s. By contrast, England has seen little decline in attainment gaps.

To what extent are decreases in the attainment gap associated with educational institutions? To address this question, we estimate educational attainment by parental education, birth cohort, and country. Estimates are derived from a multilevel linear

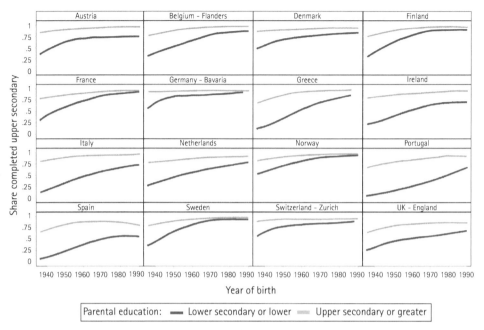

FIGURE 30.2 Association between parental education and share completing upper-secondary school by country/region and birth cohort. Smoothed lines estimated using lowess.

(Data from European Social Survey 2002–2018, N = 141,088)

regression model with a binary measure of completion of upper secondary as the outcome and a binary measure of parental completion of upper secondary as a predictor. Individuals are nested within country cohorts and countries, and random slopes on parental education allow the association between parent and child education to vary both within and between countries. This strategy takes account of the well-known "partial pooling" property of multilevel models to produce robust estimates even in those birth cohorts with small sample sizes (Gelman & Hill, 2007).

Figure 30.3 plots upper-secondary completion rates by country or subnational region and 5-year birth cohort against the index of educational opportunity. Among cohorts born between 1936 and 1965, there is a strong association between educational opportunity and the probability of completing upper-secondary education. Higher opportunity institutions have only a moderate association with attainment among the children of highly educated parents, but a large one among children of less educated parents. Moving from low-opportunity institutions to high-opportunity institutions is associated with a substantial decline in the attainment gap. This association is, of course, not necessarily causal, although other studies do provide some evidence that these reforms caused weakening attainment gaps (Braga et al., 2013). By contrast, in cohorts born after 1966, there is no association between institutional opportunity and attainment. This finding may partially reflect a ceiling effect, given that countries had converged on generally higher opportunity institutions by the time these cohorts were in education. The

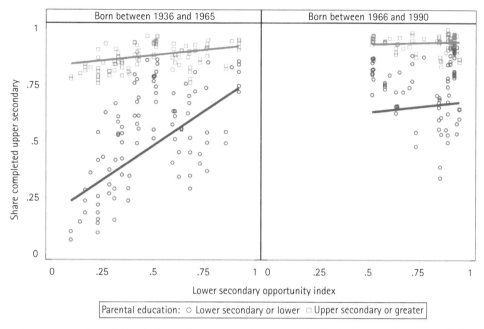

FIGURE 30.3 Association between lower-secondary opportunity index and share completing upper-secondary education. Estimates of attainment by parental education, country/region, and 5-year birth cohort. N = 352.

(Data from European Social Survey 2002–2018)

decreased predictive power of formal institutions may also reflect the shifting institutional terrain around equity in education, something we return to later.

Table 30.3 confirms these conclusions using ordinary least squares regression models fit separately to pre- and post-1966 birth cohorts. Completion of upper-secondary education is the response variable. Explanatory variables are parental education, the opportunity index, and an interaction between them. All models control for age and gender and cluster standard errors by country cohort, and use the ESS poststratification weight. Baseline models in column (1) are modified by controlling for confounding variables in a variety of ways, including country and cohort fixed effects (column 2); country-specific time trends and trends in the association between family background and educational attainment (column 3); country-specific associations between family background and educational attainment and country-specific time trends (column 4).

In most models the coefficient on the opportunity index is positive (though not always significant), suggesting that in contexts with more equal institutions the children of the low educated are more likely to complete upper-secondary education. The interaction between parental education and educational opportunity is negative in all models, suggesting that the association between parental background and child attainment is weaker in contexts with greater educational opportunity. However, the interaction effect is larger in absolute size in cohorts born before 1966, and not always

Table 30.3 Association Among Parental Education, Educational Opportunity, and Completion of Upper Secondary

	(1)	(2)	(3)	(4)
			Country Trends and	Country Trends and
		Country and Cohort	Parental Education	Parental Education
	Baseline	Fixed Effects	Trends	Interactions
Cohorts Born Before 1966				
Educational opportunity	0.531***	0.107**	0.070	0.097***
	(0.073)	(0.040)	(0.038)	(0.028)
Parent completed upper secondary	0.662***	0.525***	0.417***	0.443***
	(0.033)	(0.028)	(0.059)	(0.031)
Educational opportunity X Parent completed upper secondary	−0.532***	−0.389***	−0.280***	−0.353***
	(0.063)	(0.046)	(0.065)	(0.036)
N	86,826	86,826	86,826	86,826
Cohorts Born After 1966				
Educational opportunity	−0.069	0.113	0.246**	0.298**
	(0.134)	(0.088)	(0.089)	(0.097)
Parent completed upper secondary	0.264**	0.359***	0.340***	0.412***
	(0.096)	(0.058)	(0.059)	(0.052)
Educational opportunity X Parent completed upper secondary	0.038	−0.179*	−0.152	−0.242**
	(0.132)	(0.078)	(0.087)	(0.089)
N	54,383	54,383	54,383	54,383

OLS models. Data from 2002–2018 ESS. All models control for gender and age (with quadratic term). Standard errors in parentheses. $^*p < 0.05$, $^{**}p < 0.01$, $^{***}p < 0.001$.

significant for cohorts born after 1966 suggesting that these institutions matter less for educational outcomes among younger generations. Of course, even before 1966 there is a great deal of heterogeneity among country cohorts, suggesting that institutions are only one of many factors in shaping educational outcomes.

Conclusion: Equity of Pupilhood in Massified Systems?

The third section argued that the global diffusion of the norm of equal status of pupils did not necessarily lead to equal definitions of pupilhood. The fourth section showed that different understandings of equal pupilhood led to profoundly different opportunities for early postwar cohorts. However, the massification of secondary education meant a weakening impact of these varied structures. Does that imply a more homogenous understanding of pupilhood ultimately triumphed?

The analysis of European Social Survey data suggests that the answer is likely no. It shows ongoing differences in social mobility persist across countries, even as the major disparities in postwar institutions weakened. Work on social mobility suggests that even where access is not based on prior academic achievement, disparities in resources and differences in the socioeconomic composition of school intakes based on residential segregation by race or income can shape opportunities (Chetty & Hendren, 2018; Mayer, 2002). Against this backdrop many scholars believe that trends toward increased school autonomy and parental choice are likely to exacerbate rather than reduce family background differences in educational attainment in the future (Ball, 1993). In this concluding section we argue that these claims signify a shift in the terrain for debates about equal pupilhood.

By the 1980s, the massification of secondary education combined with smaller birth cohorts put both cost and quality on the agenda. Thus, a new phase of secondary reform emerged, one where the terms of debate shifted from formal stratification to operational differentiation, and from bureaucratic standardization to school accountability. Quality— not institutional equality—was increasingly at the heart of reform rhetoric (Ball, 2008; Gingrich, 2011). This resulted in new questions about what equal pupilhood entails.

First, policymakers in the 1980s moved away from debating the extent of formal stratification across schools to new forms of *differentiation*. From an organizational perspective, the 1980s heralded three major types of reforms: decentralization to local governments, increasing formal school autonomy, and marketization-oriented reforms linking funding to pupil choices (Gingrich, 2011). Proponents of these reforms argued that increasing differences in the delivery of education across schools in the short run— often via competitive mechanisms—would increase overall performance in the long run (Chubb & Moe, 1990). Critics argued that the gains of greater differentiation could be captured by more elite groups, reducing equity (Ball, 1993). In other words, old debates about whether pupilhood should entail formal equality within institutions or a more differentiated character emerged in new guises.

Again, we see substantial variation across countries in how policymakers actually reshaped institutions. In the 1980s, countries such as France, Denmark, and Sweden all engaged in substantial decentralization of school funding and human resources to the local level. These moves effectively took apart aspects of the educational bureaucracies that developed through the 1960s and 1970s, in Sweden even dismantling the powerful National Board of Education.

At the same time, in a diverse range of countries—from the United States to Sweden and New Zealand—both left- and right-wing governments increased schools' autonomy over budgets, personnel, and curricula, at the expense of central or local government. From 1980 to 2000, reforms sanctioning school autonomy emerged in Spain and France (1985); England and Wales (1988); Sweden (1991); Austria, United Kingdom, Scotland (1993); Norway (1994); and Italy (1998).

Alongside these decentralizing reforms, in countries as different as Ireland, Flemish speaking Belgium, or New South Wales in Australia, the 1980s saw a revival of private (often state-funded or subsidized) secondary education, and especially of schools which had not aligned their curricula and selection procedures to the comprehensive model (Campbell & Sherington, 2006; Clarke, 2010). Some countries, such as the United States (charter schools), England ("free schools" and academies), and Sweden ("free schools"), further expanded the possibilities for new private providers. The result has been the emergence of quite varied amounts of school autonomy, local control, and private competition across countries—with the Anglo and Scandinavian countries moving further in this direction than Southern European countries. These shifts were and continue to be almost universally contentious. Debates about decentralization and privatization remain relevant, with countries like Sweden reconsidering some of the earlier marketizing reforms (Åstrand, 2016).

Second, policymakers also turned to new forms of standardization—moving away from regulating inputs but toward increased *accountability* mechanisms through monitoring and inspection of performance. States traditionally monitored the quality of education systems by drafting budget and curriculum regulations, controlling the use of textbooks, and outlining criteria for teacher certification. Inspectorates monitored the implementation of these rules, and testing mainly served to regulate student progression and streaming. During the 1970s and 1980s, in response to student protests and changes in pedagogy, some countries moved toward more "child-centered" approaches, reducing testing and grading. These shifts began to soften some of these input regulations, while maintaining substantial bureaucratic control.

By the 1980s, this approach was under pressure. On the one hand, across advanced economies, controversies emerged around topics such as sex education (Zimmerman, 2015), new maths (Moon, 1986), or multilingual education (Schmidt, 2000)—putting more substantial reform on the agenda. As John Major stated in 1993, innovative pedagogical methods were "Fashionable, but wrong. [. . .] Our children must be taught what they need to know. That's why we need a national curriculum. It's why we need national testing."[4]

The institutionalization of international standardized testing through the Program for International Student Assessment (PISA) furthered this movement, drawing attention to uneven performance. The aforementioned decentralizing shifts, combined with a backlash against the kind of continuous curriculum innovation and equalization that had characterized the 1960s and 1970s, produced new demands for testing and accountability policies.

In response, from the 1980s, some countries moved to a tightening of curriculum regulations and stricter, outcome-based monitoring. These shifts involved the introduction of monitoring tests intended to assess students' progress. As with marketizing reforms, however, these shifts varied in their structure and application. In some countries, like Australia or England, monitoring tests are highly public and used to assess schools; in others, such as primary school tests in Ireland, the results are confidential and not disseminated publicly. These moves, like previous ones, have been contested. Teachers and experts denounced limits on professional autonomy, as well as expressed fears that the educational pressure to "teach to test" limited the time to be dedicated to students' individual interests and inclinations (Milner, 2013).

Thus, if the period from 1950 to 1980 was defined by institutional debates over equality among pupils in terms of standardization and stratification, debates from the 1980s onwards have been characterized by questions of whether to drive quality through differentiating and accountability reforms. As in the earlier period, while these shifts arose across many contexts, there is no single model that has emerged. This trajectory suggests that even in the era of mass pupilhood, the question of what it means to be a (secondary) pupil remains fundamentally contested. Whether the deep disruption of COVID-19, and the rise of new online learning platforms, signify a new phase of contestation remains to be seen.

Notes

1. Australia, Austria, Belgium, Canada, Denmark, Finland, France, Germany, Greece, Ireland, Italy, the Netherlands, Norway, Portugal, Spain, Sweden, Switzerland, and the United Kingdom. See the SCHOOLPOL project (ERC 759188, https://schoolpol.web.ox.ac.uk).
2. Australia, Austria, Belgium, Canada, France, Germany, Ireland, Italy, Japan, Netherlands, New Zealand, Norway, Sweden, Switzerland, and the United Kingdom.
3. In federal countries where subnational states have substantial responsibility for education, we focus on one or more of the most populous states.
4. http://www.johnmajorarchive.org.uk/1990-1997/mr-majors-speech-to-1993-conservative-party-conference-8-october-1993/

References

Allmendinger, J. (1989). Educational systems and labor market outcomes. *European Sociological Review*, 5(3), 231–250.

Ambrosoli, L. (1982). *La scuola in Italia dal Dopoguerra ad oggi*. Il Mulino.

Ansell, B. W. (2010). *From the ballot to the blackboard: The redistributive political economy of education*. Cambridge University Press.

Ansell, B. W, & Lindvall, J. (2013). The political origins of primary education systems: Ideology, institutions, and interdenominational conflict in an era of nation-building. *American Political Science Review, 107*(3), 505–522.

Ansell, B. W, & Lindvall, J. (2020). *Inward conquest: The political origins of modern public services*. Cambridge University Press.

Åstrand, B. (2016). From citizens into consumers: The transformation of democratic ideals into school markets in Sweden. In F. Adamson, B. Åstrand, & L. Darling-Hammond (Eds.), *Education reform: How privatization and public investment influence education* (pp. 73–109). Routledge.

Austria. (1963). Verordnung: Lehrpläne der Volks-, Haupt- und Sonderschulen, *Bundesgesetzblatt für die Republik Österreich, 1963*(134), 691–834.

Austria. (1964). Verordnung: Erlassung von Lehrplänen für die Unterstufe des Gymnasiums, *Bundesgesetzblatt für die Republik Österreich, 1964*(163), 967–1059.

Baldi, G. (2012). Schools with a difference: Policy discourses on education reform in Britain and Germany. *West European Politics, 35*(5), 999–1023.

Ball, S. J. (1993). Education markets, choice and social class: The market as a class strategy in the UK and the USA. *British Journal of Sociology of Education, S14*(1), 3–19.

Ball, S. J. (2008). *The education debate*. Policy Press.

Barro, R., & Lee, J. W. (2013). A new data set of educational attainment in the world, 1950–2010. *Journal of Development Economics, 104*, 184–198.

Benavot, A., Cha, Y.-K., Kamens, D., Meyer, J. W., & Wong, S.-Y. (1991). Knowledge for the masses: World models and national curricula, 1920–1986. *American Sociological Review, 56*(1), 85–100.

Bolívar, A. (2015). The comprehensive school in Spain: A review of its development cycles and crises. *European Education Research Journal, 14*(3–4), 347–363.

Braga, M., Checchi, D., & Meschi, E. (2013). Educational policies in a long-run perspective. *Economic Policy, 28*(73), 45–100.

Brunello, G., & Checchi, D. (2007). Does school tracking affect equality of opportunity? New international evidence. *Economic Policy, 22*(52), 782–861.

Busemeyer, M. R. (2015). *Skills and inequality: Partisan politics and the political economy of education reforms in Western welfare states*. Cambridge University Press.

Campbell, C., & Sherington, G. (2006). *The comprehensive public high school: Historical perspectives*. Palgrave Macmillan.

Carlgren, I., & Kallos. D. (1997). Lessons from a comprehensive school system for curriculum theory and research: Sweden revisited after twenty years. *Journal of Curriculum Studies, 29*(4), 407–430.

Cha, Y.-K. (1991). Effects of the global system on language instruction, 1850–1986. *Sociology of Education, 64*(1), 19–32.

Checchi, D., & van de Werfhorst, H. G. (2018). Policies, skills and earnings: How educational inequality affects earnings inequality. *Socio-Economic Review, 16*(1), 137–160.

Chetty, R., & Hendren, N. (2018). The impacts of neighborhoods on intergenerational mobility II: County-level estimates. *The Quarterly Journal of Economics, 133*(3), 1163–1228.

Chubb, J. E., & Moe, T. M. (1990). *Politics, markets, and America's schools*. Brookings Institution.

Council of Europe. (1965). *School systems, a guide*. CoE.

Clarke, M. (2010). Educational reform in the 1960s: The introduction of comprehensive schools in the Republic of Ireland. *History of Education, 39*(3), 383–399.

Domina, T., Penner, A., & Penner, E. (2017). Categorical inequality: Schools as sorting machines. *Annual Review of Sociology, 43*, 311–330.

Esteves, O. (2019). *The "desegregation" of English schools: Bussing, race and urban space, 1960s–1980s*. Manchester University Press.

Fleming, B., & Harford, J. (2014). Irish educational policy in the 1960s: A decade of transformation. *History of Education, 43*(5), 635–656.

Furuta, J. (2020). Liberal individualism and the globalization of education as a human right: The worldwide decline of early tracking, 1960–2010. *Sociology of Education, 93*(1), 1–19.

Gelman, A., & Hill, J. (2007). *Data analysis using regression and multilevel/hierarchical models*. Cambridge University Press.

Gingrich, J. (2011). *Making markets in the welfare state*. Cambridge University Press.

Giudici, A., Gingrich, J., Chevalier, T., & Haslberger, M. (2023). Center-right parties and post-war secondary education. *Comparative Politics, 55*(2), 193–218.

Goldin, C., & Katz, L. F. (2008). *The race between education and technology*. Cambridge University Press.

Green, A. (1990). *Education and state formation*. St. Martin's Press.

Greveling, L., Amsing, H. T., & Dekker, J. H. (2015). Rise and fall of the comprehensive school idea in the Netherlands. *European Educational Research Journal, 14*(3–4), 269–292.

Hanushek, E. A., & Wößmann, L. (2006). Does educational tracking affect performance and inequality? Differences-in-differences evidence across countries. *Economic Journal, 116*(510), 63–76.

Heidenheimer, A. J. (1974). The politics of educational reform. *Comparative Education Review, 1*(3), 388–410.

Heisig, J. P., & Solga, H. (2015). Secondary education systems and the general skills of less- and intermediate-educated adults: A comparison of 18 countries. *Sociology of Education, 88*(3), 202–225.

Helbig, M., & Nikolai, R. (2015). *Die Unvergleichbaren. Der Wandel der Schulsysteme in den Deutschen Bundesländern seit 1949*. Klinkhardt.

Henkens, B. (2004). The rise and decline of comprehensive education. *Paedagogica Historica, 40*(1–2), 193–209.

Ireland. (1989). Junior certificate programme. https://www.education.ie/en/Circulars-and-Forms/Active-Circulars/M16_89.pdf

ISTAT (1962). *Annuario Statistico Italiano*. Tip. Elzeviriana.

Iversen, T., & Stephens, J. D. (2008). Partisan politics, the welfare state, and three worlds of human capital formation. *Comparative Political Studies, 41*(4–5), 600–637.

Jerrim, J., & Macmillan, L. (2015). Income inequality, intergenerational mobility, and the Great Gatsby curve: Is education the key? *Social Forces, 94*(2), 505–533.

Kerckhoff, A. C. (1995). Institutional arrangements and stratification processes in industrial societies. *Annual Review of Sociology, 21*, 323–347.

Mayer, S. E. (2002). How economic segregation affects children's educational attainment. *Social Forces, 81*(1), 153–176.

Meghir, C., & Palme, M. (2005). Educational reform, ability, and family background. *American Economic Review, 95*(1), 414–424.

Mendonça, A. (2011). *Evolução da política educativa em Portugal*. http://www3.uma.pt/alicem endonca/conteudo/investigacao/evolucaodapoliticaeducativaemPortugal.pdf

Meyer, J, W., Ramirez, F. O., & Soysal, Y. N. (1992). World expansion of mass education, 1870–1980. *Sociology of Education*, 65(2), 128–149.

Milner, R. H. (2013). *Policy reforms and de-professionalization of teaching*. National Education Policy Center.

Moon, B. (1986). *The "new maths" curriculum controversy*. Falmer Press.

Mundy, K., Green, A., Lingard, B., & Verger, A. (2016). The globalization of education policy—Key approaches and debates. In K. Mundy, A. Green, B. Lingard, & A. Verger (Eds.), *The handbook of global education policy* (pp. 1–20). Blackwell.

Österman, M. (2018). Varieties of education and inequality: How the institutions of education and political economy condition inequality. *Socio-Economic Review*, 16(1), 113–135.

ÖVP. (1953). *Alles für Österreich. Programmatischen Leitsätze*. Österreichische Volkspartei.

ÖVP. (1970). *Fortschritt und Sicherheit*. Österreichische Volkspartei.

Paglayan, A. S. (2021). The non-democratic roots of mass education: Evidence from 200 years. *American Political Science Review* 115(1): 179–198.

Paulston, R. G. (1968). *Educational change in Sweden: Planning and accepting the comprehensive school reforms*. Teachers College Press.

Pöyliö, H., Erola, J., & Kilpi-Jakonen, E. (2018). Institutional change and parental compensation in intergenerational attainment. *British Journal of Sociology*, 69(3), 601–625.

Pultar, A. (2021). The elusiveness of the common school in Austria. *Comparative Education*, 57(3), 341–359.

Rieger, A. (2001). Bildungsexpansion und ungleiche Bildungspartizipation am Beispiel der Mittelschulen im Kanton Zürich. *Swiss Journal of Educational Research*, 23(1), 41–71.

Sass, K. (2022). *The politics of comprehensive school reforms*. Cambridge University Press.

Schmidt, R. (2000). *Language policy and identity politics in the United States*. Temple University Press.

Stasavage, D. (2005). Democracy and education spending in Africa. *American Journal of Political Science*, 49(2), 343–358.

Taighde ar Oideachas. (1965). *Investment in education*. Stationery Office.

Tanzi, V., & Schuknecht, L. (2000). *Public spending in the 20th century: A global perspective*. Cambridge University Press.

UNESCO and International Bureau of Education. (1958). *Facilities for education in rural areas*. UNESCO.

van de Werfhorst, H. G. (2019). Early tracking and social inequality in educational attainment: Educational reforms in 21 European countries. *American Journal of Education*, 126(1), 65–99.

van de Werfhorst, H. G., & Mijs, J. B. (2010). Achievement inequality and the institutional structure of educational systems: A comparative perspective. *Annual Review of Sociology*, 36(1), 407–428.

Wiborg, S. (2009). *Education and social integration*. Palgrave Macmillan.

Zimmerman, J. (2015). *Too hot to handle: A global history of sex education*. Princeton University Press.

CHAPTER 31

EXAMINING THE IMPACT OF EDUCATIONAL REFORMS ON SCHOOLING AND COMPETENCES IN PIAAC

LORENZO CAPPELLARI, DANIELE CHECCHI, AND MARCO OVIDI

INTRODUCTION

RECENT surveys on cognitive skills show that competences are positively correlated with schooling and parental background. However, the institutional differences across countries mediate the relationship between these variables, thus affecting the degree of inequality in the distribution of competences as well as the gradient of competences on employment probability and earnings. We intend to exploit existing data sets to explore the association between alternative measures of human capital and the institutional framework characterizing different countries. Our main finding is that institutional changes that induce more schooling in the population are associated with a higher level of cognitive competences (namely literacy and numeracy), even taking into account their demographic and social origins. Besides effects on educational inequalities among the cohorts affected, educational reforms may also exert intergenerational effects and change the educational distribution among future generations. Jerrim and MacMillan (2015), using cross-country data, argue that educational attainment of the parents is among the main factors of intergenerational mobility and that income inequality plays an important role for the transmission of advantage from parents to children. However, research exploiting the staggered rollout of educational reforms within countries finds little intergenerational impact of reform-induced increases of parental education (Black et al., 2005; Oreopolous et al., 2006). In our setting we cannot explore intergenerational issues because the intergenerational educational process is only measured with respect to schooling and does not report information on competences in the parent generation.

Two main caveats are in order before presenting our results. The first one is the choice of the outcome variables. While there is a large literature on the effect of institutions on schooling, either measured by years of schooling or by the share of population attaining a specific degree, there is more limited evidence on their effect on competences, mainly obtained by student surveys (Hanushek & Woessman, 2011). Very little is known about whether reforms are correlated to competences in the adult population. Hanushek et al. (2015) show that adult competences are a better measure of human capital, being correlated to individual earning and providing a larger explanatory power than schooling. Cappellari et al. (2017) discuss the potential endogeneity of both schooling and competences: When using reforms as instruments, they show that schooling affects wages via numerical skills.

The second caveat is the definition and measurement of what is generally classified as educational reform. The Organization for Economic Cooperation and Development (OECD, 2019) provides a comprehensive analysis of the recent policy discourse in the educational debate, which is mostly focused on responsibility division among institutional layers.[1] More generally, it is quite difficult to determine the boundaries of what the term "educational reform" includes. Some reforms are easy to define (e.g., raising the years of compulsory schooling) and easy to measure in their impact (e.g., measuring the fraction of compliant students). Other reforms are more difficult to define (e.g., raising the qualification requirement of teachers) and even harder to measure (e.g., measuring the fraction of compliant teachers), especially when the final outcome is unspecified by the policymakers, who often use vague terms such as "improving the quality of education."

In this chapter, we try to address both issues, providing evidence on the association between reforming activities of governments and educational outcomes in the adult population. The reforming activities of governments is captured by collecting information on institutional changes, as already done in Braga et al. (2013, 2020). The next section discusses the advantages and limits of such an approach. The educational attainment in the adult population is obtained from the survey microdata of the Program for the International Assessment of Adult Competencies (PIAAC; OECD, 2013) and is measured by two alternative indicators: years of schooling (for most countries derived from the highest educational attainment) and numeracy (measured by the scores of survey respondents in cognitive tests). The third section describes our outcome variables and discusses the matching of individual data with the reform timing. The fourth section discusses the association between reforms and outcomes, and the fifth section concludes.

Educational Reforms

As a measure of educational reforms, we exploit the data set created by Braga et al (2013). The data set is built by identifying all policy interventions that occurred in Europe over the last century (1929–2000). The reforms affect various dimensions of education, covering preprimary education, expansion of compulsory education and comprehensiveness, teachers' qualification, school autonomy and accountability, university autonomy and selectivity, and students' funding. While it is generally possible to identify the "sign" of the reform (whether it is inclusive or exclusive, i.e., augmenting or reducing school participation), it is impossible to assess the impact of each reform, since the size and/or the coverage are often unknown in the original source (mostly various issues of the Eurydice annual report). By counting the number and the orientation of reforming activity, one can infer the goals of the policymaker, without being able to identify his or her effectiveness. We take the degree of activism in policymaking as indicative of the orientation of governments, a sort of revealed preference approach.[2] In addition, we can also consider the sign, because the original database classifies inclusive policies with a positive sign and policies that restricted the access to schooling with a negative sign.

In Braga et al. (2013), these reform indicators were matched to various waves of different data sets in order to increase the precision of estimated impact on the distribution of years of schooling.[3] On the contrary, in the present chapter we match the indicators

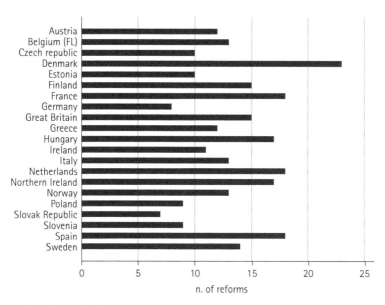

FIGURE 31.1 Number of reforms per country.
Note: only "expansionary" reforms (i.e., in a positive direction) matched to PIAAC cohorts.

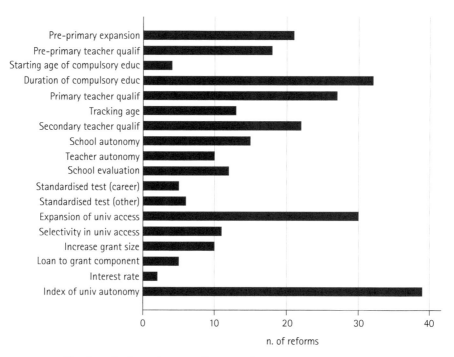

FIGURE 31.2 Number of reforms by area of intervention.

to a unique cross-section collected in 2012, interpreted as a pseudo-panel. In Figure 31.1, we plot the countries available in PIAAC for which we have information on reforming activity in education. The graph shows that some countries (like Denmark) were more active than others (notably Germany and Slovakia) in repeatedly modifying their educational systems. More illuminating is Figure 31.2, showing the interventions by domain of action, where we can observe that the two most impacted areas are the duration of compulsory education and the regulation of university autonomy, even though the latter regulation waves typically occurred later in time. Teachers' qualification is also a frequent domain of intervention, while student financing at the tertiary level remains in the background (not surprisingly, since in the European context most universities are public and almost free). Finally, in Figure 31.3, we group reforms by stages of education, separating compulsory (primary and secondary plus preprimary, which is compulsory in few cases) from noncompulsory (tertiary education). This graph confirms that more active countries in reforming their educational systems (notably the Nordic countries and the Netherlands) were such in all domains.

The timing of the reforms varies over the last century, as can be grasped from Panel A of Figure 31.4. We can identify two clear waves of educational reformism: One occurred under the pressure of student protest at the end of the 1960s, and a second one occurred under the pressure of budget cuts and/or transition to market economies occurred during the 1990s. However, the timing of the reform does not necessarily coincide with the distribution of the affected birth cohorts. Once again following Braga et al. (2013), we

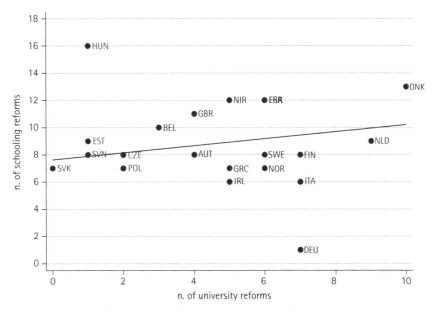

FIGURE 31.3 Activism of countries in the main areas of education.

Note: linear fit excludes outliers (Hungary and Germany).

assume that each reform hit the cohort born n years earlier, where n=3 for preprimary, n=6 for primary, n= 10 for secondary, and n = 15 for tertiary (in order to account for anticipation and expectation effects).[4] This is our main identification assumption for understanding the impact of reforms on outcomes, consisting in the idea that two adjacent birth cohorts experience almost identical environments and only differ in their exposure to a specific reform; in fact, cohorts born in country i in year t are confronted with cohorts born in the same country in year t+1, and not with cohorts born in country j in year t.

The distribution of the relevant populations by birth cohorts and number of reforms experienced is given by Panel B of Figure 31.4. It shows that earlier cohorts experienced a rather stable institutional environment up to the end of the baby-boom generation, after which reforming the educational systems became widespread. The generation born one decade later (1979–1980) was the most affected by government activism.

Individual Educational Outcomes

The PIAAC survey rounds we consider were conducted between 2011 (1st round) and 2017 (3rd round) in 39 countries (34 OECD member countries and 5 partner countries). The survey measures adults' proficiency in key information-processing skill—literacy, numeracy, and problem-solving—and gathers information on their family background and educational careers. In what follows, we focus our attention on numeracy; evidence

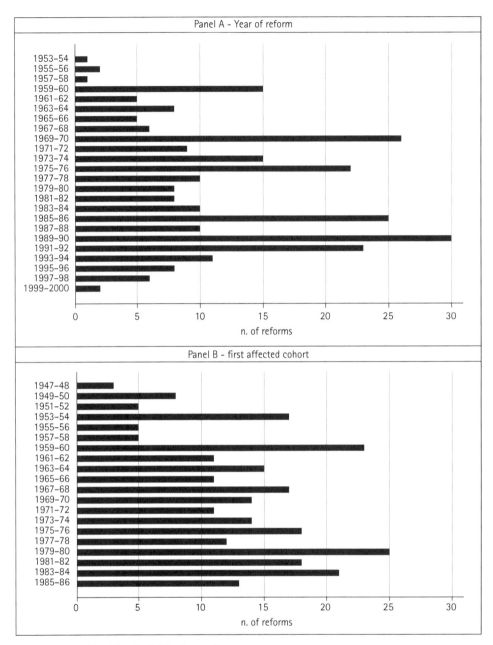

FIGURE 31.4 Matching individuals to reforms.

on other dimensions of cognitive ability, such as literacy, goes in the same direction as the one discussed next.

We are interested in assessing whether and which of these reforms were effective in (a) raising individual schooling and (b) improving cognitive competences, since these two variables capture different dimensions of individual human capital. There are other dimensions (e.g., technological abilities, problem-solving, or noncognitive skills) that could be investigated, but unfortunately information on these dimensions is scattered and not available for all countries. By matching existing survey data with our measures of educational reforms, we identify 21 countries (those reported in Figure 31.1) for which we select the population aged between 25 and 65.

There are some problems when using raw values of these variables that need to be accounted for. The first issue is that years of schooling are a time invariant measure, while cognitive skills decline with age. As a consequence, when using a single cross-section, one should control for the effect of individual age on skills.[5] In addition, years of schooling and cognitive skills are positively correlated, but causation may go in both directions: More educated individuals possess a higher level of competences, but smarter (and more competent) individuals may also stay in schools longer.[6]

We look at the relationship between the human capital variables in Figure 31.5. The idea behind this exercise is that there exists a "structural" relationship between education and numeracy, such as education increases (in a causal sense) the numerical competences in the population. The structural mechanisms stem from the fact that by staying longer at school individuals learn more and improve their skills. There are two alternative (and noncausal) interpretations that may well account for a positive gradient of numeracy with schooling. First, individuals may be characterized by a heterogeneous degree of intrinsic ability, which co-determines education and competences. The positive gradient would then just be a reflection of intrinsic ability. Second, younger individuals could be characterized by higher education (due to upward secular trends in education) and higher numeracy (due to age-related decay in numeracy).

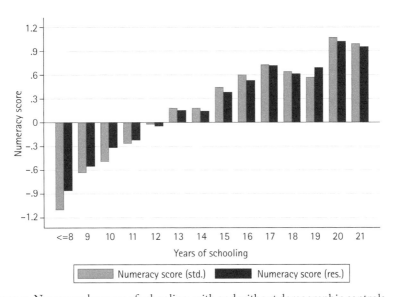

FIGURE 31.5 Numeracy by years of schooling, with and without demographic controls.

In this event, the positive gradient would just be an age effect. Disentangling between causal and noncausal interpretations is beyond the scope of this chapter. Still, it is interesting to verify how strong the association between the two variables is. Indeed, the graph indicates the existence of a strong association between the two variables. Also, the gradient is virtually unaffected by considering numeracy after correcting it for age effects,[7] which suggests that the uncovered correlation is not just an artifact of differences in human capital between age groups. Finally, it is worth noting how the gradient is not constant along the educational distribution, but there is a jump in numerical competences among individuals who have attained a PhD, corresponding to 20 years of schooling or more.

Eventually, schooling is permanent but increases over birth cohorts, as a consequence of increasing scholarization in the population, and this may introduce spurious correlation between reforming activity and education. In Figure 31.6, we consider the historical evolution of educational reforms and the trends in human capital accumulation. To achieve this, we plot 5-year moving averages of both reform indicators (grouped by domain of intervention) and human capital indicators by birth cohorts. The left axis measures cumulated reform intensity on a 0–1 scale, while the right axis reports human capital variables (years of schooling and numeracy) measured in standard deviation units.[8] Looking first at the human capital variables, we can appreciate the remarkable increase that has occurred throughout the post–World War II era. This evolution takes on a logistic shape, with a slow increase in the first 10 years, an acceleration in the baby-boomer cohorts, and a final slowdown phase for the cohorts born after the

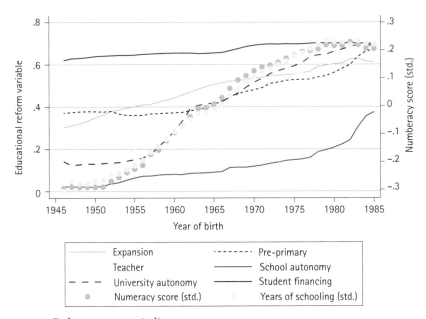

FIGURE 31.6 Reform summary indices.

Note: all series plotted are 5-year moving averages.

mid-1970s. Interestingly, the pattern is very similar across the two human capital variables considered. However, while for years of education the pattern can be clearly interpreted as an upper trend in attainment, for numeracy an interpretation based on a (negative) logistic decay with age may well account for the evidence. Upward trends over birth cohorts also characterize the reform indices in general, but the slope is not as steep as for the human capital variables, which suggests that reforms alone cannot explain the increase in average attainment over the period. Behavioral factors such as peer effects and intergenerational spillovers may have reinforced and amplified the institutional impulse.

THE EFFECTS OF EDUCATIONAL REFORMS

The evidence depicted in Figure 31.6 suggests the existence of a positive association between reforming activity of government and educational attainment in the population. Before investigating this association in greater detail, we would like to make clear that we cannot claim pure causation going from reform to education, since reforms could have been introduced as a policy response to behavior already observed in the relevant population. Consider, for example, an increase in the years of compulsory education. This typically occurred under the pressure of teachers and opinion leaders, in a situation where a fraction of students was already compliant (and therefore unaffected by the reform), while the treated would be the students that would have not continued to stay in school had not it been made compulsory. However, such a clear-cut situation does not always exist, and the beneficiaries of the reforms are not always easy to identify. In the absence of (clearly detectable) exogenous variations in the policy stance of governments, and without the possibility to restrict the set of potentially treated students, we limit ourselves to claim the existence of an association between reforms and educational attainment, both at the mean of the distribution as well as in its dispersion. Our presumption is that a reform raising the mean and reducing the dispersion in the outcome variables is effective in including more individuals in the social and economic dimensions of life.

We begin our discussion of the results in Figure 31.7A, which represents our main findings. We plot years of schooling and numeracy against an index of intensity of educational reforms. The index is obtained by progressively cumulating the reform indices described in earlier over birth cohorts within countries. Within a country, different birth cohorts are matched to different values of the index depending on how intense the reform activity of that country has been up to the year in which a cohort can be potentially affected by the reform. Over time, reform activity typically assumes the form of educational expansions, which we record as an increase of the reform index. In some cases, reforms had the opposite direction and implied a limitation of educational supply or access, which we record as a decumulation of the reform index. The index obtained by accumulating or decumulating the reform indicator is then grouped in quintiles. The outcome variables on the vertical axis of the graph

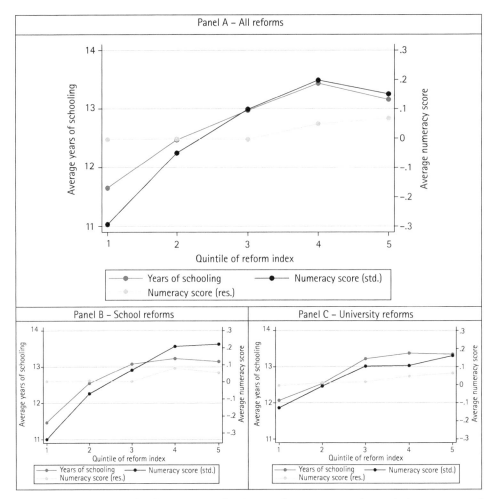

FIGURE 31.7 Impact of reforms onto schooling and competences (means), by intensity of reforming activity.

Note: observations are grouped by "cumulative" reform variables. Cumulative reform variables are computed by adding 1 each time there is a reform and by subtracting 1 each time there is a "negative" reform (very few, <10% of reforms). Residuals are computed after a regression of standardized numeracy score on quadratic age polynomial and country fixed effects. All PIAAC observations are used to compute residuals (also those younger than 25) in order to capture the age profile of skills.

are the average of the outcomes by quintiles, averages being calculated over countries and birth cohorts. We consider two outcomes, namely years of schooling and the standardized numeracy score.[9]

Panel A of Figure 31.7 considers all the reforms recorded in our data in conjunction without distinguishing between the educational levels at which each reform takes place. The graph shows a clear gradient between the intensity of educational reforms and human capital accumulation. In comparing cohorts in the lowest quintile of educational reforms with those in the highest, average educational attainment increases by 2 years. Also, the same comparison indicates a sizeable increase of numerical competences, of about 40% of a standard deviation. Thus, the countries that have exerted a more intense reforming activity (see Figures 31.1 and 31.3, which identify the group of Nordic countries and the Netherlands) are also characterized by more educated and competent populations. Notice that such a claim is based on within-country variation, due to matching birth cohorts to the year when a reform takes place.

In each case we can observe a tendency toward concavity of the relationship, indicating that the marginal effectiveness of educational reforms decreases with the level of human capital. Looking at the competences-reforms profile after removing age effects reveals a flatter relationship, that is, higher competences in the bottom quintiles (mostly populated by older cohorts) and lower proficiency in the top quintiles (mostly populated by younger cohorts), consistently with the idea that competences are subject to decay with age.

In Panels B and C of Figure 31.7, we distinguish educational reforms according to the educational level in which they impact, namely schooling reforms (Panel B) versus university reforms (Panel C). Regardless of the level of education impacted, the figure shows that years of schooling and numeracy are similarly increasing in the intensity of reforms, even when controlling for the effects of age.

The differential impact of reform activities by type of reform is further investigated by breaking down the reform indicator into six categories: four categories refer to reforms of the schooling system (preprimary education, educational expansions, teachers' management, and school autonomy), while two categories attain to university education (university autonomy and students' financing). These six categories are built up by aggregating the 18 policy areas previously discussed in the second section. Without reporting additional graphs for ease of exposition,[10] we find that the greatest impact on educational attainment seems to be exerted by reforms that expanded access to education (including tertiary enrolment), reflecting the greater scope that these may have in increasing years of completed education in comparison with educational expansions at lower levels of the educational system. In turn, schooling reforms appear more effective than teachers' reforms in affecting years of education. Also, all reforms correlate positively with numeracy skills, but the correlation weakens considerably once skills are purged from age effects.

* * *

When we consider the variance of outcomes in the same population cohort as an indicator of policy ineffectiveness, we find that the more active countries obtain a less dispersed distribution of schooling but not of competences. In fact, the evidence discussed so far demonstrates the existence of a relationship between the intensity of educational reforms and the average level of human capital in the population. However, changes in the average attainment may miss the different patterns that this relationship may follow along the educational distribution. To gain a fuller understanding of

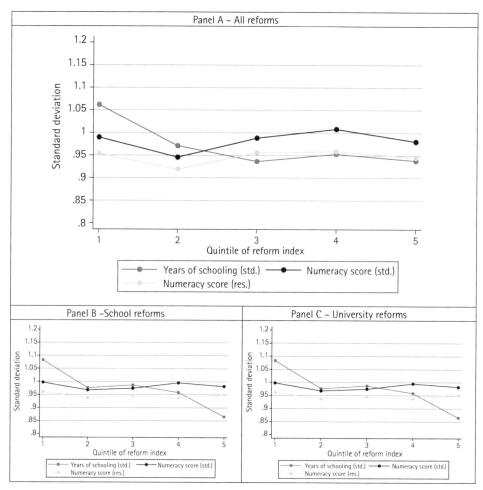

FIGURE 31.8 Impact of reforms onto schooling and competences (variance), by intensity of reforming activity.

the impacts of educational reforms, we therefore turn our attention to their relationship with the dispersion of human capital, depicted in Figure 31.8. Human capital dispersion is measured by the standard deviation of years of education or numeracy within country-by-cohort cells. The graph shows a clear negative relationship between the intensity of reform activity and educational dispersion. This is a mechanical effect due to the fact that the maximum level of education that someone can possibly attain did not change much over time, being stable at about 18 years of education for a full educational cycle from primary school to university completion. Because of this fixed upper limit, educational reforms designed to increase the average attainment are also bound to reduce the dispersion of attainment. Different is instead the case of numeracy dispersion, for which we cannot detect any negative gradient in relationship to educational reforms. If anything, the pattern is weakly increasing, which suggests that the increase in average education induced by the reforms may have implied heterogeneous choices in terms of the field of additional studies, with only some individuals impacted by the reform within each cohort country opting for numeracy-enhancing fields. Moreover, even within numeracy-enhancing fields, there may be heterogeneity in numerical proficiency for any given level of educational attainment, further contributing to the (weakly) increasing pattern depicted in the graph. Overall, the graph accords with the idea that the benefits (returns) of education are heterogeneous in the population. It is also worth noting that there is not much difference between raw and age-conditioned numeracy, which suggests that age does not account for much of numeracy dispersion.

Concluding Remarks

In this chapter we have shown that educational reforms undertaken in the last century in a large subset of European countries have been effective in raising the quantity and quality of human capital in the current adult population. Both years of schooling and cognitive skills are positively associated with the intensity of the reforming activity of governments, which is interpreted as an indicator of political priorities. While the effect on the means of the distribution is easy to identify, less clear is the association with their variances. The dispersion in years of schooling declines with reforms, whereas we do not register identical pattern for cognitive skills.

Given the limited sample sizes of the PIAAC survey, our results can only be taken as suggestive, and a more careful identification of a specific reform and a group of treated people would be required in case of causal statement. However, we believe that our contribution highlights the main methodological problems occurring when aiming to measure the effects of reforms in education.

The first one is that reforms come in swarms, and it is quite difficult to disentangle one from the other. If a government increases the years of compulsory education, it is also likely to ease the transition to subsequent stages of education; similarly, if a government aims to raise the qualification of the teaching profession, it is also likely to give more teaching autonomy to the same teachers. As a consequence, in this chapter we have adopted a shortcut of simply counting the number of reforms. One would have liked to weight them by their impact, but the latter is exactly the unknown variable that we tried to uncover in this chapter.

The second methodological contribution is that one should not rely on a single outcome variable, typically the (average) years of schooling in the population. We have shown that two correlated dimensions of individual human capital (namely schooling and competences) do react in different ways to the same reforms. Disentangling the two is extremely difficult, unless one can rely on a steady benchmark. Therefore, discussing the results on one, while neglecting the other, is conceptually weak.

The third contribution is the identification of the potential effects of reforms using within-country variations associated with (adjacent) birth cohorts. As long as reforms hit individuals based on their age, we can always distinguish between a group of treated (those born after the enactment of the reform) and a group of controls (those born before the introduction of the reform). More robust identifications would exploit also geographical differentiation, but in a cross-country comparative analysis these details are impossible to capture.

NOTES

1. OECD (2019) collects education policy priorities by official document reading and by interviewing relevant actors. From the evidence collected in the report, three priorities appear more prevalent among the review of OECD countries: (1) tackling unclear or unbalanced division of responsibility between national and local authorities and schools (indicated in 32 national education system reviews); (2) improving teacher qualifications, skills, and training (31 national education system reviews); and (3) defining national education priorities and goals (27 education systems).
2. An alternative (and opposite) interpretation could consider the fragmentation of policy action, due to government instability. However, these indices are built over a large sample of countries and years, thus making this hypothesis less reliable.
3. Braga et al. (2013) include the European Social Survey (ESS), European Union Statistics on Income and Living Conditions (EUSILC), the International Adult Literacy Survey (IALS), and International Social Survey Program (ISSP).
4. In other words, a reform fostering the university enrolment introduced in 1968 is assumed to affect all cohorts born after 1953, and so on.
5. The simplest way to "clean" the effect on age on cognitive skills is to regress individual competences on age and age square, and take the residual of such a regression.
6. Using the same data set, Cappellari et al (2017) claim the existence of a recursive structure, where reforms affect schooling, which raises cognitive skills, which in turn lead to higher earnings.
7. The light grey bar reports the standardized values of numeracy (i.e., after subtracting its mean and dividing by the standard deviation, in order to have a new variable with zero mean and unitary standard deviation), while the dark grey bar exhibits the residuals from a regression over age, age squared, and country fixed effects.
8. In this exercise, we do not consider the residualized indicator of numeracy because it does not covary with the birth year by construction, as the year of birth is part of the control variables deployed in the regression model used for generating the residuals.
9. In doing so, it is important to take into account that while years of schooling are presumably not subject to life cycle changes for the adult population, the same does not apply to numeracy scores due to the decay of competences with age, implying that the competences of older cohorts will be underestimated due to the decay. Since older cohorts will typically be observed at the early stages of educational expansions, the decay of competences with age will lower any positive association between educational expansions and competences. To account for this possibility, we also show average numeracy by reform quintiles after filtering out the effect of age through regression analysis.
10. Available upon request from the authors.

References

Black, S. E., Devereux, P. J., & Salvanes, K. G. (2005). Why the apple doesn't fall far: Understanding intergenerational transmission of human capital. *American Economic Review*, 95(1), 437–449.

Braga, M., Checchi, D., & Meschi, E. (2013). Institutional reforms and educational attainment in Europe: A long run perspective. *Economic Policy*, 73, 45–100.

Braga, M., Checchi, D., Scervini, F., & Garrouste, C. (2020). Selecting or rewarding teachers? International evidence from primary schools. *Economics of Education Review*, 76(C).

Cappellari, L., Castelnovo, P., Checchi, D., & Leonardi, M. (2017). Skilled or educated? Educational reforms, human capital and earnings. *Research in Labor Economics*, 45, 173–197.

Hanushek, E., Schwerdt, G., Wiederhold, S., & Woessmann, L. (2015). Returns to skills around the world: Evidence from PIAAC. *European Economic Review*, 73(C), 103–130.

Hanushek, E., & Woessman, L. (2011). The economics of international differences in educational achievement. In E. A. Hanushek, S. Machin, & L. Woessmann (Eds.), *Economics of education* (Vol. 3, pp. 89–200). North-Holland.

Jerrim, J., & Macmillan, L. (2015). Income inequality, intergenerational mobility, and the Great Gatsby curve: Is education the key? *Social Forces*, 94(2), 505–533.

OECD. (2013). *The survey of adult skills: Reader's companion*. OECD.

OECD. (2019). *Education policy outlook 2019: Working together to help students achieve their potential*. OECD. https://doi.org/10.1787/2b8ad56e-en.

Oreopoulos, P., Page, M. E., & Huff Stevens, A. (2006). The intergenerational effects of compulsory schooling. *Journal of Labor Economics*, 24(4), 729–760.

CHAPTER 32

EDUCATIONAL EXPANSION AND INEQUALITY

School in Italy in the Second Part of the 20th Century

GABRIELE BALLARINO AND NAZARENO PANICHELLA

INTRODUCTION

IN this chapter we look at the Italian case in order to shed light on the relation between expanding participation to education and socioeconomic inequality. As it has been convincingly demonstrated, the expansion of educational participation is a global process (Schofer & Meyer, 2005), but modern mass school systems were created and designed at the national level (Ramirez-Boli, 1987). This process unfolded differently over countries, because of the different institutional legacies from the past and the different position of each country in the international division of labor. Italy is then an interesting case in point, since after World War II its socioeconomic structure underwent a relatively rapid and profound process of change, by which the country went from a mostly agricultural and economically backward one to being one of the leading economies in the world (Toniolo, 2013). The rapidity by which Italy changed its structural socioeconomic parameters, in the space of a generation, allows for observation, in a relatively short period, of changes that elsewhere took much more time.

To analyze the association between educational expansion and social stratification, we rely on the standard framework by which stratification research addresses issues of equality of opportunities, the OED triangle (Blau & Duncan, 1967). We also refer to the debate counterposing modernization theory, according to which the expansion of education is part of a societal movement toward a more inclusive and fair society, and reproduction theory, which to the contrary maintains that education, however expanded, is above all a key tool for the maintenance of opportunity hoarding and social closure.

Empirically, we use a new data set deriving from the harmonization of a number of high-quality surveys, thus giving to the analyses higher statistical power and reliability, particularly concerning trends over time.

The chapter is divided into three parts. In the first, we review the main theoretical arguments provided by stratification research concerning the relations between education and socioeconomic inequality and their trends over time, counterposing modernization theory and reproduction theory. In the second, we describe Italian school policies after World War II, as well as the pattern of educational participation over time for each school level. In the third part, finally, we analyze the changes over time of the relation between education and inequality, as influenced by increasing school participation.

EQUALIZATION OR REPRODUCTION?

According to modernization theory, the key feature of social stratification in modern societies is that individuals are allocated to their occupational position on the basis of achievement—that is, on what they have done and/or are able to do. To the contrary, in premodern societies, individuals are allocated to their occupation by ascription, namely on the basis of their characteristics at birth, particularly their family and group belonging (Lipset & Bendix, 1959; Treiman, 1970). The birth of mass schooling is a key step in this process, since modern school is based on an inclusive idea of citizenship: In principle, all students are equal, regardless of their family of origin, gender, and skin color. During the early history of mass schooling, citizenship was conceived in the frame of the national state, while after the disasters of two world wars fought in the name of nationalism, in many countries its definition came closer to a supranational concept of "humanity" (Meyer et al., 2007).

According to the liberal theory of modernization, however, the transition from an occupational allocation based on ascription to one based on achievement does not depend on cultural and political factors, but mostly on economic mechanisms, above all the process of industrialization and the associated growth of market competition. Competition forces firms to select among job candidates according to their skills, in order to increase productivity, decrease costs, and sell their products or services more cheaply than their competitors, who, to the contrary, select their workers on the basis of their belonging to some social group. This mechanism, called "competence principle" (Weber, 1922) or "increased merit selection" (Whelan & Layte, 2002), increases the weight of school degrees in the labor market, weakens the intergenerational transmission of occupations within the family, and stimulates school participation. Given schools are governed by universalistic mechanisms, the process of modernization is then characterized by the substitution of the latter to ascription and social belonging. The internal boundaries of social stratification, defined by belonging, become less rigid and the probability increases for individuals to be socially mobile, that is, to be found in a social stratum different from the one of their parents.

This process also has a political side, namely the development of liberal democracy, based on the rule of law and on the citizens being equal with respect to it. Economic historians, indeed, have developed an ideal-typical distinction between "inclusive institutions," open to all individuals, such as those of political systems based on free elections and an open market, and "extractive institutions," who work differently for different social groups, for instance an authoritarian political system or an economy dominated by monopolies protected by the politiical system (Acemoglu & Robinson, 2012). While the former allows and promotes a peaceful competition based on skills and effort, the latter establish hierarchies based on social belonging, and typically are associated to the rule by a well-organized minority.

Liberal theories of modernization, then, provide an optimistic view of the secular trends of social stratification and inequality. Inequality decreases as a result of the structural changes of the economy and the polity, among which the diffusion of the competence principle as the key mechanism for the occupational allocation of individuals, in turn related to the expansion of schooling (Kuznets, 1955; Lenski, 1966). Correspondingly, the role of ascriptive belonging on occupational outcomes gradually disappears. School plays a key role in this process, as it provides individuals with the skills required by the labor market on the basis of their effort and merit as students. With mass schooling, the heritage principle, on which the division of labor and the allocation of social position is based in premodern societies, gives way to what is called "meritocracy" (Bell, 1973; Goldthorpe & Jackson, 2006).

The outlook of social reproduction theory is completely different. According to this perspective, the function of modern school systems is the maintenance of social stratification, as part of a web of power relations defining the dominance of some social groups and the subordination of others. This theory was developed slightly later than modernization theory, under the influence of the student movement of the 1960s and 1970s. It derives from Marxism, although Marx and Engels, themselves well-schooled intellectuals born in wealthy families, did not pay much attention to schooling in their writings, probably because mass schooling was still in its beginning during their times. While the better-known versions of reproduction theory were crafted by French theorists (Althusser, 1972; Bourdieu & Passeron, 1972), the analytical version proposed by American Marxist economists Bowles and Gintis (1976) is more convincing from the standpoint of empirical social science.

According to Bowles and Gintis, the modern school system is geared more to the socialization of individuals to social power relations than to the teaching and learning of literacy or numeracy. School selection is not related to the disciplinary knowledge of pupils, but on their compliance to authority. The key concept of the theory is indeed the "correspondence principle" between the organization of the modern school systems and the workings of capitalism. This idea is not unlike the core propositions of modernization theory, but turned upside down. First, schooling is a socialization to authority, as already stated. Second, rewards to schooling are external to its activities, in the same way the wage is external to the worker's activity. As workingmen and clerks do not work because of the pleasure they get from their job, but because they need the wage to survive, students do not find any pleasure in school activities, which they do because they have to achieve the title. Third, school learning and teaching are fragmented into a number of disciplines, as society is fragmented into a number of social groups because of the division of labor. Fourth, school tracking is neither a way to improve learning nor a way to specialize students' skills in view of their future jobs, but it educates students to different social positions. The lower school levels and secondary vocational tracks educate workers, and correspondingly mostly require passive reception and compliance, while secondary academic schools and colleges educate managers, professionals, and entrepreneurs and then, to the contrary, require autonomy, creativity, and the active elaboration on what is learned. In brief, teaching and learning vary as a function of the position in the social hierarchy students are waiting to be allocated to.

Keeping in mind this theoretical counter-position between modernization and reproduction theory, we move now to a description of the Italian educational system and of its recent history.

SCHOOL DESIGN, REFORMS, AND EXPANSION IN ITALY FROM THE 1950S TO THE 2010S

Comparative research on school systems sees standardization, stratification, and vocational specificity as three major dimensions of analysis (Allmendinger, 1989; Bol & van de Werfhorst, 2013). Standardization indicates how much teaching and learning are the same for all students enrolled in the same grade, all over the system. It is positively associated to the level of organizational and administrative centralization of the system, while school autonomy is negatively related to it. The second dimension, stratification, relates to differences in the study paths available to students. Normally, vertical and horizontal stratification is distinguished. The former refers to the length of studies. Horizontal stratification, or tracking, refers to the extent to which students follow different study paths, for instance academic or vocational secondary schools. Finally, vocational specificity refers to the way schools are related to the labor market. It is high in so-called dual systems, where vocational tracks include a strong component of firm-based training, while it is low when high schools are "comprehensive," that is, without occupationally relevant curricula and titles. The crucial factor defining the level of vocational specificity is the role of firms in vocational schools: The more they are involved, the more the system is vocationally specific (Busemeyer & Trampusch, 2012).

Based on these dimensions, let us now sketch a brief historical picture of the Italian educational system and of its expansion (Ballarino, 2015a, 2015b; Ballarino & Panichella, 2021; Bertola & Sestito, 2013; Ventura, 1998). After World War II, the Italian school system was highly standardized and stratified, and low on vocational specificity. It had been shaped in this way by the previous fascist regime through a wide school reform introduced in 1923. In fact, the system was already centralized, since it had been designed according to the French model after the country's unification (1861). School autonomy was very low and even the ancient universities had lost most of their previous autonomy to the national ministry of education. The fascist reform increased the degree of stratification of the system, which had been relatively low under the previous liberal governments, creating a selective system with a strong hierarchy among the tracks students were divided into after elementary school. At the top of the hierarchy was the *liceo classico*, with limited places as the only secondary track allowing access to all university faculties, while at the bottom were a number of dead-end tracks, including some vocational ones and a *liceo femminile* for future wealthy housewives. The reform also centralized vocational-technical education to the ministry of education, while it had been previously governed by the ministry of the economy with substantial autonomy of schools. In this way, most of the links between schools and firms were severed, further decreasing the vocational specificity of the system.

During the postwar decades, school systems all over the world became gradually less stratified and elitist, under the push of a more inclusive concept of citizenship (Meyer et al., 2007). Italy was among the early European countries to de-stratify the first layer of secondary education, as soon as in 1962 (Barbagli, 1982). The reform created a comprehensive lower secondary school (*scuola media unica*), and to this day it is still considered among the major progressive policies enacted by post–World War II Italian governments. Other minor reforms followed in the same decade, gradually weakening the hierarchy among secondary tracks and opening enrollment to all university faculties to secondary graduates.***

A second wave of structural school reforms took place in the 1990s, aiming at decentralizing the system by allowing more autonomy to both schools and universities, and at further de-stratifying upper secondary school. Differently from the previous one, this reform only partially succeeded: School and university autonomy was indeed introduced as a principle, but the system remained substantially centralized. The de-stratification of upper secondary school could not be enacted because of strong opposition in the polity and from both teachers and public opinion. However, in the same period a substantial academization of technical schools took place gradually, thereby further decreasing the links between schools and firms.

In the following decade, a third wave of reforms took place. While the branching point of secondary education was kept at age 14, the hierarchy among tracks was substantially relaxed and a number of vocational dead-end tracks were eliminated, to be substituted by short vocational courses run by the regions. A substantial reform of university curricula was also enacted, in the frame of the Europe-wide Bologna Process, of which Italy was among the starters, together with France and Germany. The reform substituted the previous 4- to 6-year degrees with a two-level (bachelor's and master's) system, aiming at increasing university graduates by reducing the length of studies and improving the occupational orientation of courses (Ballarino & Perotti, 2012).

It is interesting to note that all three waves of reforms, despite having been enacted by very different political coalitions,[1] were to a good extent bipartisan, as government and opposition parties shared a number of concerns, most notably the opportunity of increasing school participation. Even in the 2000s, when a newly introduced majoritarian electoral system created two rival coalitions with quite different school policy agendas (Ballarino, 2015a), a bipartisan continuity in the process of school policymaking could be often observed (D'Amico, 2010).

With this in mind, let us now look at the secular pattern of expansion of participation to primary and secondary school in Italy, presented in Figure 32.1. It appears that while primary education was already universal for the cohorts born in the late 1930s, the actual postwar school boom took place at the secondary level, where participation increased with a very steep slope, starting with the cohorts born in the 1950s. The attainment of a lower secondary degree (after 8 grades), which up to the 1990s was the compulsory level of education, was universal with the cohorts born in the 1970s, while the attainment of upper secondary (after 13 grades) reached 90% for people born in the 1990s and then remained at this level. The expansion of participation to secondary school was seminal, in that it provided skilled workers and cadres for the country's industrial development taking place in the 1950s and 1960s, particularly in the northern regions (Ballarino et al., 2014).

Interestingly, the pattern of the expansion does not seem to be related to the timing of the reforms. In particular, the cohorts born in the early 1950s, when the curve of the

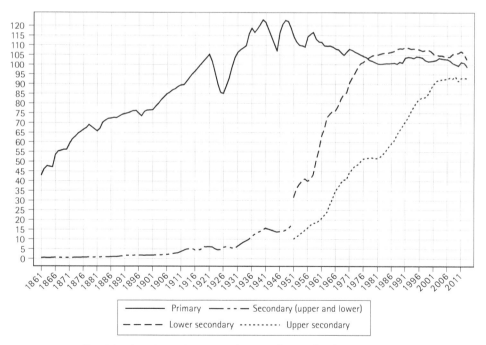

FIGURE 32.1 Participation in primary and secondary school, 1861–2014: percentage of individuals reaching each title, by year of birth.

(*Source*: Author's own elaboration on ISTAT historical series)

expansion becomes steeper, were schooled more than a half-decade before the comprehensive lower secondary school was created (from the 1962/1963 school year). Similarly, the expansion of upper secondary does not appear to be related to the de-stratification of the 2000s.[2] This means that political reforms supported a process of increasing participation which was already under way as a bottom-up process, according to the "contagion" model proposed by both the sociology and the economics of education (Galor, 2006; Meyer et al., 1979, 1992).

According to the contagion model, schooling is diffused by imitation. Once a school system is established, families observe its occupational and status benefits, and then choose to school their children. Then, the pattern over time of the schooled proportion of the population follows the logistic curve typical of contagion processes, including three stages. At the start, the process is slow, as it depends on the number of people already "infected," schooled in our case. Then as the number of infected (schooled) people increases, the speed of the process increases exponentially, in a second stage of "explosive" growth. Finally, when all the nonimmune population is infected, in our case when all the available population is schooled, the process slows down in a third stage of saturation.

The three stages of expansion are clearly to be seen in Figure 32.1, concerning secondary education. For primary education, we just see the final part of the stage of explosive growth and then the following stage of saturation, while for both lower and upper secondary education the shape of the logistic curve is easily seen.

Figure 32.2 extends the picture to tertiary education and allows a comparative outlook. The figure shows the substantial variation of the expansion of educational participation over countries and school levels. For instance, Germany shows the highest levels of secondary school achievement, together with the United States, but ranks relatively low for what university graduations are concerned. Italy shows relatively low levels of school expansion with respect to other countries included in the figure, with the exception of Spain and China. Participation appears particularly low concerning tertiary education, where, however, a substantial expansion with the cohort born in the 1970s is to be seen.

School and Social Stratification in Italy

The OED Triangle

To study the processes of social mobility and the role of education therein, stratification research uses the analytical frame known as "OED triangle," introduced by Blau and Duncan (1967), and represented in Figure 32.3. It allows for analyzing the intergenerational reproduction of social inequality, and it might then be used to gauge the

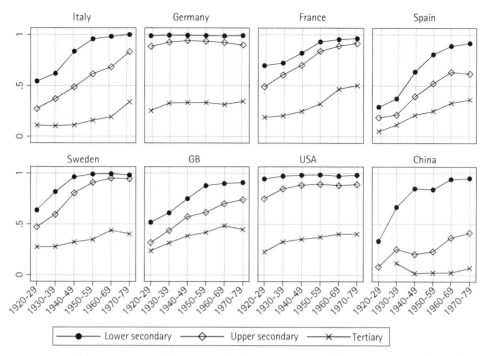

FIGURE 32.2 The expansion of school participation in eight countries: percentage getting at least a lower-secondary, upper-secondary, and tertiary degree, by cohort of birth.
(*Source*: Author's elaboration on European Social Survey data for European countries, General Social Survey for the United States; International Social Survey Program for China)

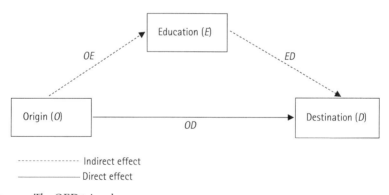

FIGURE 32.3 The OED triangle.

(*Source*: Blau & Duncan, 1967)

merits of the theories of modernization and of reproduction. The triangle represents the processes underlying the intergenerational transmission of social position by its three vertices, where O is the social status of the family of origin, D the social status achieved by individuals, and E is their education.

In the triangle, the intergenerational association between the status of the family of origin (O) and the destination status achieved (D) is decomposed in three processes corresponding to its three sides. The OE side represents the association between status of origin (O) and achieved education (E), that is, the processes creating inequality of educational achievement by family background. The ED side indicates the association between achieved education (E) and the status of destination (D), that is, the processes by which education gets rewarded on the labor market. Finally, the OD side indicates the "direct" effect of status of origin (O) on destination (D) over and above education. The product of the OE and ED sides is indeed known as the "indirect" effect of O on D. The OD side refers, then, to those processes, related to the status of origin, providing occupational advantage or disadvantage to individuals with the same educational level.

The triangle allows for decomposing the processes by which the sons and daughters of entrepreneurs, professionals, and managers are more likely to achieve an upper-class position than their schoolmates born in a working-class family. In particular, the mediating role of the school takes place through two different selection processes: OE and ED. In a meritocratic society, where all individuals are provided with equal opportunity to reach the more rewarding and prestigious social positions, the two processes should be based on opposite principles (Goldthorpe, 2007; Kivinen et al., 2007). The first process, OE, should select individuals on the basis of an inclusive, merit-based logic, providing all individuals with the same opportunity of school achievement, whichever their status of origin. The second process, ED, should, to the contrary, work according to a discriminatory logic of selection, since it aims at allocating the occupational positions to those who are more suited because of their education, according to the competence principle.

Before introducing our analysis, it is useful to spend a few words on our definition of social position, for both O and D, in terms of social class. There are many possible different definitions of social position, and many definitions of social class, referring to different sociological traditions (Wright, 2005). Here we use the neo-Weberian approach, pioneered by John Goldthorpe and his coauthors (Breen, 2005; Goldthorpe, 2007), nowadays the most frequently used in international comparative research. According to the neo-Weberian approach, a social class includes a set of relatively similar occupations, which similarly influence the life opportunities of their incumbents. This definition does not refer either to exploitation or to social classes as a focus of political action, two ideas associated with the Marxist theory of class and often found in the current public discourse concerning inequality (Jackson & Grusky, 2018; Wright, 2005).

The neo-Weberian class scheme we use is the Italian version of the so-called EGP scheme (Cobalti & Schizzerotto, 1994; Goldthorpe, 2007).[3] It includes six social classes, namely, the service class (bourgeoisie), including entrepreneurs of medium and large firms, professionals and managers; nonmanual workers of intermediate qualification, clerks or white collar; independent workers and owners of small businesses, the urban petty bourgeoisie; farmers and small agricultural entrepreneurs, the agricultural petty bourgeoisie; dependent manual workers in manufacturing and services, the urban working class; dependent manual workers in farming, the agricultural working class. Other neo-Weberian schemes are available, who better reflect the postindustrial changes of the economy (Güveli et al., 2007; Oesch, 2013), but the one we chose is better suited to describe the long-run changes of social stratification in a country like Italy, where occupation in agriculture was still relevant up to the 1950s.

Inequality of Educational Opportunities

We start our analysis from the OE side of the triangle, indicating to what extent achieved education is associated with the social class of origin. A situation where no association exists is just an analytical abstraction, since it is well-known that school ability is associated with the family of origin, particularly with parental education. The basis of this association lies in genetic potential (Freese, 2018), as well as in the familiar transmission of ability, taking place during the daily life together (Ermisch et al., 2012). Sons and daughters of educated people are stimulated by activities which are conducive to better school results in a number of ways, from seeing their parents spending time with books, to being enrolled in non-school afternoon classes in arts, sports, and other activities (Lareau, 2011).

What is relevant to the OE association is then its trend over time. A decrease over time of the association might be taken as an indicator of increasing meritocracy, while its stability, or even an increase, would suggest a persistence over time of the school advantage associated with having been born in an upper- or middle-class family. Such an analysis over time has long been one of the key empirical endeavors of stratification research, and there is a huge literature on both the outcomes and the detailed mechanisms by which they might be explained (Breen & Jonsson, 2005; Erikson, 1996).[4]

Figure 32.2 reports the trend of the OE association over cohort of birth, as estimated by a cumulative logit model where O is measured by the parental highest social class, and including controls for gender, geographical area of residence, and for the interaction between paternal and maternal education.[5] The cumulative logit model estimates, for each cohort and class of origin, the logarithm of the ratio (log-odds) between the percentage of individuals who did not achieve a tertiary title and the percentage who did achieve it, by means of a set of parameters (gamma) that provide a general measure of the association. A second set or parameters (delta, not reported for sake of brevity) constrain the estimate to the same ratio calculated for the lower titles.[6] In the graph, the gamma parameters are expressed as differences with respect to the service class, set to 0 as the reference category.

Figure 32.4 clearly shows how the differences between the service class and the remaining classes decrease over time, indicating a reduction of inequality of educational opportunities. The decrease is particularly strong for the cohorts born in the first half of the 20th century, while in the more recent decades the trend of convergence has slowed down, according to a pattern found in most countries for the same period (Breen et al., 2009; Breen & Müller, 2020). Convergence was stronger for the agricultural classes, who were more at disadvantage, but is also to be seen for the urban classes such as the

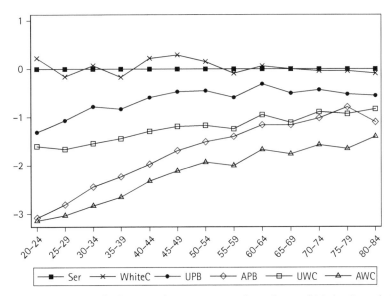

FIGURE 32.4 Inequality of educational opportunities by cohort of birth. Cumulative logit model: log-odds distance in the probability not to achieve a tertiary title with respect to the service class (set to 0).

(*Source*: Author's elaboration on data from Istat Multiscopo [1998–2003–2009]; ILFI [1997–2005]; National Survey on Social Mobility [1985], European Social Survey [2002–2018], EU-Silc [2005–2011], and Sharelife [2008–2009])

petty bourgeoisie and the working class. In the case of the former, the key mechanisms explaining the catch-up are the building of rural roads and the development of public transport it enabled, which made it possible for pupils living in remote areas to get to school, and the mechanization of agriculture, which increased returns to schooling to agricultural workers. In the case of the latter, schooling was mostly favored by the economic security of families, in turn related to increasing employment security and to the welfare state guarantees, and also by decreasing school selection (Ballarino et al., 2009).

An analysis by school levels, not reported for lack of space, provides additional detail (Ballarino & Panichella, 2021; Ballarino & Schadee, 2010). A substantial convergence among classes took place at the lower school levels, where participation reached the saturation level, as seen in Figure 32.1. Concerning upper secondary, there was a convergence between bourgeoisie and clerks, while for the other classes some difference still persists. Finally, at the tertiary level, the distances between classes remained the same over time. Then, the decrease of inequality estimated by the cumulative model depends mostly on the expansion of participation to primary and lower secondary school, where a ceiling effect takes place: once all children of the upper class have achieved the title, inequality can only decrease. At the higher levels inequality of educational opportunities persists, but for the offspring of the white-collar class. However, the equalization at the lower levels involved more people than the persistence of inequality at the higher levels, so the result is a decrease of inequality. Among the two theories outlined earlier, modernization theory appears to be closer to reality, although the persistence of inequality at the higher educational levels might be taken as partially supporting reproduction theory.

Returns to Education

Let us come, now, to the ED side of the triangle, the association between education and occupational outcomes. Also in this case, we focus on the trend over time. We cannot describe, for lack of space, the details of the debate concerning the mechanisms underlying this association, where human capital theory and credentialing theory are the main opposing hypotheses, respectively related to modernization and reproduction theory (Bills, 2003). According to both theories, however, with the expansion of educational participation returns to school titles should decrease over time. As the number of holders of a given degree increases, its signaling value on the labor market decreases, with a process similar to monetary inflation called "inflation of educational credentials" (IEC; Collins, 1979).

However, recent research in economics has shown in many countries a widening wage gap between the holders of a college degree and the remaining workers, explained by the so-called skill-biased technological change (SBTC) hypothesis (Acemoglu, 2002). According to this argument, the evolution of technology, driven by global market competition, enables firms to substitute by machines the jobs of low-qualified and low-educated workers, raising productivity but worsening these workers' market situation. The same process gives more value to the skills of college-educated workers, whose jobs become more important to manage the development of technology and its application to production, in a global competitive economy. Similar effects are associated to the off-shoring or manufacturing and services, another economic trend related to the global expansion of markets.

It has to be noted that the IEC and SBTC arguments are not necessarily opposed, since they look differently at returns to education. IEC theory is interested in the trend over time of the occupational destinations associated to a given school degree, while SBTC looks at the trend over time of the difference between returns to different titles, in particular between college and high school. The former looks at the absolute returns to a given school title, the latter at its relative returns, with respect to other titles. In line of principle, it is then not excluded that both phenomena might happen at the same time (Bernardi & Ballarino, 2016).

Figure 32.5 shows the trend over cohorts of the ED association, where E is measured by the four main school titles and D is measured in two ways: in the left-hand panel, as the probability to enter the bourgeoisie; in the right-hand panel, as the probability to avoid the working class. The occupational condition is measured with reference to the first job, in order to have the same measure for people of different age and avoid biases related to career effects. The graphs report estimates from linear probability models,

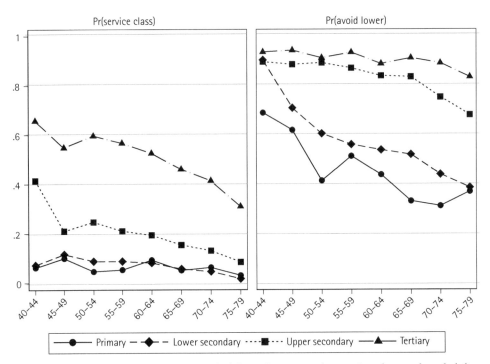

FIGURE 32.5 Returns to education: probability of entering the service class and probability of avoiding the working class, by school level and cohorts. Linear probability models: average predictions.

(*Source:* Author's elaboration on ISTAT-Multiscopo [2003–2009] data)

by education and cohort of birth, including controls for parental class, and the interaction among paternal and maternal education, gender, and geographical area of residence.

For both outcomes, it appears that college graduates are advantaged with respect to the holders of lower titles, as expected. However, their occupational condition definitely worsens over time. The likelihood of college graduates entering the service class was nearly 70% among those born in the early 1940s. However, this probability has decreased by more than half over time, reaching 35% in the most recent cohorts. An even stronger trend concerns upper secondary graduates, whose probability went from 40% to about 10%. Lower secondary and primary graduates show, as expected, negligible probabilities to access the top occupations.

Concerning the probability to avoid the working class, by achieving at least a middle-class job, the condition of college graduates did not change much over time. Going from the first to the last cohort we observe their probability decrease from slightly more than 90% to about 80%. To the contrary, the condition of secondary graduates, whose number increased much more, as we have seen in Figures 32.1 and 32.2, gets dramatically worse over time. In the cohort born in the early 1940s, both upper and lower secondary graduates had around a 90% probability to get a middle-class job, only slightly lower than college graduates. By the cohort born in the late 1970s, the probability had reduced to 70% and 40%, respectively.

Both IEC and SBTC theories are then supported by these results. As hypothesized by the former, the expansion of education is associated to decreasing occupational returns to titles, and the decrease is stronger for secondary titles, where expansion was stronger. Then, the college occupational premium with respect to secondary degrees became stronger, particularly concerning the probability to access at least a middle-class job. A college degree is no longer a ticket to the top occupations, but it remains a good safety net against low-qualified jobs.

The Direct Effect of Origin on Destination

We come now to the third side of the triangle, namely the direct OD association, also known as DESO (direct effect of social origin). In this way, we study whether there is an association between origin and destination even among individuals with the same level of education. If it is so, this means families are able to provide their offspring with a further occupational advantage, besides the one related to education (Bernardi & Ballarino, 2016; Erola & Kilpi-Jakonen, 2017). The mechanisms underlying this advantage include both investments and endowments. The former include many types of actions purposively enacted by parents in order to improve the occupational outcomes of their sons and daughters. A nonexhaustive list of these actions would include involving them in a family business; anticipating their inheritance; exploiting familiar networks in order to provide them with useful information, as well as with trust or even favoritism on the part of employers; and many other ones. Endowments include a number of skills and personality traits that make individuals more productive and/or more likely to be hired, for instance consciousness or extroversion. Such skills are transmitted during daily family life, without purpose, similarly to the case of school-related ability that was mentioned earlier among the mechanisms favoring educational inequality.

Figure 32.6 shows our estimates of the trend over time of the OD association, measured as the difference in the probability of reaching the service class (left-hand panel) and to avoid the working class (right-hand panel) between the service class, again set to 0 as the reference category, and the remaining classes. As in the previous models, besides own and parental education, the estimates also control for gender and geographical area of origin.

First, the graph shows that the direct effect of social origin is much weaker than the effect of education on occupational destination, as seen in Figure 32.5. In general, in Italy as elsewhere, the former is measured at between one-fourth and one-third of the latter (Bernardi & Ballarino, 2016; Blau & Duncan, 1967). This would give support to modernization theory, according to which the weight of the family in occupational attainment is much lower than that of school. However, according to our estimates, the direct effect is not waning over time, as predicted by modernization theory. It actually increased somehow for what concerns the probability to access the service class, but it decreased

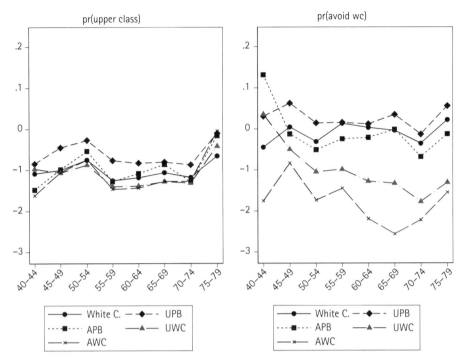

FIGURE 32.6 Direct effect of social origin on the probability of entering the service class (upper panel) and avoiding the working class (lower panel) by education and cohort of birth. Linear probability models: beta coefficients with robust standard errors.

(*Source*: Author's elaboration on ISTAT-Multiscopo [2003–2009] data)

for the probability to avoid the working class. Quite interestingly, comparative evidence shows the DESO to be higher in Southern Europe, and particularly in Italy, than elsewhere (Ballarino & Bernardi, 2016). This might depend, among other things, on the weight of small businesses in the country's economy.

As suggested, the existence of the DESO and its stability over time might be taken as evidence again the claims of the modernization theory, according to which the expansion of education has the effect of equalizing the occupational opportunities of individuals born in different social classes. However, previous research for the United States has found the OD association to be quite lower for the college educated (Hout, 1988; Torche, 2011). If education is not the great equalizer assumed by modernization theory, college education might then come close to it. We check this argument for the Italian case by the models reported in Table 32.1, where the OD association is estimated separately for holders of different school titles. The results of this exercise give only partial support to the "college as the great equalizer" argument. In the case of access to the service class, the direct OD effect is stronger for the upper secondary and the tertiary educated, opposed to what was predicted by the argument, while in the case of avoiding the working class the OD effect for the tertiary educated is indeed quite small, and nonsignificant for most classes.

Table 32.1 Direct Effect of Social Origin on the Probability of Entering the Service Class (Upper Panel) and Avoiding the Working Class (Lower Panel), by Education

	Pr(service)							
	Primary		Lower Secondary		Upper Secondary		Tertiary	
	β	σ	β	σ	β	σ	β	σ
Ref: Service								
White-collar	−0.07*	(0.04)	−0.06***	(0.01)	−0.12***	(0.01)	−0.11***	(0.02)
UPB	−0.05	(0.04)	−0.02	(0.01)	−0.07***	(0.01)	−0.07***	(0.03)
APB	−0.05	(0.04)	−0.04***	(0.01)	−0.11***	(0.02)	−0.12***	(0.04)
UWC	−0.05	(0.04)	−0.06***	(0.01)	−0.13***	(0.01)	−0.18***	(0.03)
AWC	−0.06*	(0.04)	−0.06***	(0.01)	−0.14***	(0.02)	−0.11**	(0.05)
Constant	0.16***		0.17***		0.45***		0.52***	
	(0.05)		(0.05)		(0.09)		(0.11)	
Observations	2,128		11,458		11,047		4,270	
R-squared	0.04		0.03		0.09		0.15	
	Pr(avoid lower)							
	Primary		Lower Secondary		Upper Secondary		Tertiary	
	β	σ	β	σ	β	σ	β	σ
Ref: Service								
White-collar	−0.07	(0.09)	−0.04	(0.03)	0.01	(0.01)	0.01	(0.01)
UPB	0.10	(0.08)	0.03	(0.03)	−0.01	(0.01)	0.00	(0.01)
APB	0.08	(0.08)	−0.08***	(0.03)	−0.05***	(0.02)	0.01	(0.02)
UWC	−0.07	(0.08)	−0.20***	(0.02)	−0.09***	(0.01)	−0.03**	(0.01)
AWC	−0.14*	(0.08)	−0.26***	(0.03)	−0.15***	(0.02)	−0.05**	(0.02)
Constant	0.59***		1.03***	0.59***	1.06***		0.96***	
	(0.10)		(0.10)	(0.10)	(0.10)		(0.05)	
Observations	2,128		11,458		11,047		4,270	
R-squared	0.10		0.08		0.08		0.05	

Linear probability models: beta coefficients and robust standard errors.

Source: Author's elaboration on ISTAT-Multiscopo (2003–2009) data.

It is also possible to estimate the total, or gross, OD association, including both the direct and the indirect effect, which includes the effect of education. According to recent research evidence, the gross OD association has been decreasing over time, in Italy as elsewhere, thereby increasing the so-called social fluidity, that is, the independence between origin and destination (Barone & Guetto, 2020; Breen & Müller, 2020). This pattern is explained by two phenomena we have already met, namely the decreasing OE association and the increasing proportion of college graduates, for whom the OD association is lower.

Conclusions

It is now possible to recap our results concerning social stratification in Italy, guided by the OED triangle. First, all three associations included in the triangle are different from 0, and positive. Those who come from a higher class have a higher probability to get a high school title (OE); those who have higher school titles have higher chances to get a good job (ED); those who come from a higher class have a higher probability to get a good job with respect to their counterparts with the same education but from a less advantaged family background (OD). The direct effect of the family of origin on occupational destination, however, is much weaker than the indirect effect, mediated by education.

Second, both the OE and the ED associations are decreasing over cohorts. Both patterns are related to the expansion of school participation. As school expands, children from the disadvantaged classes are enabled to get a primary or lower secondary title, and many of them also an upper secondary one, thereby reducing their disadvantage with respect to their counterparts coming from the upper class. However, this very process increases the number of degree holders in the labor market, decreasing the occupational value of their titles, with a pattern of inflation of educational credentials that, in our observational window, is at its strongest for secondary school titles, where the expansion was stronger.

Third, the OD association net of education, the so-called DESO, is substantially stable over time, pointing to the persistence of the possibility, for parents, to influence the occupational careers of their offspring, even with respect to their competitors with similar level of education.

These patterns are not substantially different from the ones observed for other affluent countries. In comparative perspective, however, it is interesting to add that Italy shows relatively persistent educational inequality (Breen et al., 2009), relatively low returns to education (Bernardi & Ballarino, 2014), and a relatively high direct effect of social origin on destination (Ballarino & Bernardi, 2016).

The general picture suggests, then, a strong impact of schooling on social stratification and inequality, as assumed by modernization theory. Mass schooling enabled individuals from the lower classes to improve their qualifications, thereby decreasing inequality and favoring the occupational upgrading observed, in Italy as elsewhere, during the second half of the previous century (Ballarino & Panichella, 2021; Cobalti & Schizzerotto, 1994). However, as we have seen, after World War II the expansion of schooling has mainly been a bottom-up process, without a clearly recognizable effect on the part of educational policies, despite the latter's orientation toward inclusion. Once a school system is created, and the socioeconomic benefits of schooling are recognized by the population, the expansion of education and its impact on social stratification do not appear to depend much on school policies. Moreover, a disequalizing effect of family background persists over time, giving some support to reproduction theories.

Notes

1. The 1960s reforms were designed by a government including the Christian Democrats and the Socialists, but they were voted in by the opposition Communist Party as well. The 1990s reforms were enacted by a series of center-left governments who in the second half of the decade also included the former communists, while the reforms of the 2000s were enacted by a center-right government.
2. See Schizzerotto et al. (2018) for a different point of view on this issue.
3. A very similar scheme is the ESeC, adopted for administrative statistics (Rose & Harrison, 2014).
4. See Triventi (2014) for a review concerning the Italian case.
5. This interaction allows for a more precise measure of family background. We have recently shown that including both parents in the measurement of social origins changes the estimation of the trend of educational inequalities over time (Ballarino et al., 2021).
6. See Ballarino et al. (2009) for details.

References

Acemoglu, D. (2002). Technical change, inequality, and the labor market. *Journal of Economic Literature*, 40(1), 7–72.

Acemoglu, D., & Robinson, J. A. (2012). *Why nations fail: The origins of power, prosperity and poverty*. Crown.

Allmendinger, J. (1989). Educational systems and labor market outcomes. *European Sociological Review*, 5(3), 231–250.

Althusser, L. (1972). Ideology and ideological state apparatuses. In L. Althusser, *"Lenin and Philosophy" and Other Essays* (pp. 85–126). Monthly Review Press.

Ballarino, G. (2015a). School in contemporary Italy: Structural features and current policies. In U. Ascoli and E. Pavolini (Eds.), *The Italian welfare state in a European perspective: A comparative analysis* (pp. 181–208). Polity Press.

Ballarino, G. (2015b). Higher education, between conservatism and permanent reform. In U. Ascoli and E. Pavolini (Eds.), *The Italian welfare state in a European perspective: A comparative analysis* (pp. 209–236). Polity Press.

Ballarino, G., & Bernardi, F. (2016). The intergenerational transmission of education and inequality in fourteen countries: A comparison. In F. Bernardi & G. Ballarino, *Education, occupation and social origin: A comparative analysis of the transmission of socio-economic inequalities* (pp. 255–282). E. Elgar.

Ballarino, G., Bernardi, F., Requena, M., & Schadee, H. (2009). Persistent inequalities? Expansion of education and class inequality in Italy and Spain. *European Sociological Review, 25*(1), 123–138.

Ballarino, G., Meraviglia, C., & Panichella, N. (2021). Both parents matter: Family-based educational inequality in Italy over the second half of the 20th century. *Research in Social Stratification and Mobility, 73,* 100597. doi:https://doi.org/10.1016/j.rssm.2021.100597.

Ballarino, G., & Panichella, N. (2021). *Sociologia dell'istruzione.* Il Mulino.

Ballarino, G., Panichella, N., & Triventi, M. (2014). School expansion and uneven modernization: Comparing educational inequality in Northern and Southern Italy. *Research in Social Stratification and Mobility, 36,* 69–86.

Ballarino, G., & Perotti, L. (2012). The Bologna process in Italy. *European Journal of Education, 47*(3), 348–363.

Ballarino, G., & Schadee, H. (2010). Allocation and distribution: A discussion of the educational transition model, with reference to the Italian case. *Research in Social Stratification and Mobility, 28,* 45–58.

Barbagli, M. (1982). *Educating for unemployment: Politics, labor markets, and the school system. Italy, 1859–1973.* Columbia University Press.

Barone, C., & Guetto, R. (2020). Education and social fluidity in contemporary Italy: An analysis of cohort trends. In R. Breen & W. Müller (Eds.), *Education and intergenerational mobility in Europe and the United States* (pp. 196–223). Stanford University Press.

Bell, D. (1973). *The coming of post-industrial society.* Basic Books.

Bernardi, F., & Ballarino, G. (2014). Participation, equality of opportunity and returns to tertiary education in contemporary Europe. *European Societies, 16*(3), 422–442.

Bernardi, F., & Ballarino, G. (Eds.) (2016). *Education, occupations and social stratification: A comparative analysis of the transmission of socio-economic inequalities.* Elgar.

Bertola, G., & Sestito, P. (2013). Human capital. In G. Toniolo (Ed.), *The Oxford handbook of the Italian economy since unification* (pp. 249–270). Oxford University Press.

Bills, D. B. (2003). Credentials, signals and screens: Explaining the relationship between schooling and job assignment. *Review of Educational Research, 73*(4), 441–469.

Blau, P. M., & Duncan, O. D. (1967). *The American occupational structure.* Free Press.

Bol, T., & Van de Werfhorst, H. G. (2013). Educational systems and the trade-off between labor market allocation and equality of educational opportunity. *Comparative Education Review, 57*(2), 285–308.

Bourdieu, P., & Passeron, J.-C. (1972). *Reproduction in education, society and culture.* Sage.

Bowles, S., & Gintis, H. (1976). *Schooling in capitalist America: Educational reform and the contradictions of economic life.* Basic Books.

Breen, R. (2005). Foundations of a neo-Weberian class analysis. In E. O. Wright (Ed.), *Approaches to class analysis* (pp. 31–50). Cambridge University Press.

Breen, R., & Jonsson, J. (2005). Inequality of opportunity in comparative perspective: Recent research on educational attainment and social mobility. *Annual Review of Sociology, 31,* 223–243.

Breen, R., Luijkx, R., Müller, W., & Pollak, R. (2009). Non-persistent inequality in educational attainment: Evidence from eight European countries. *American Journal of Sociology, 114,* 1475–1521.

Breen, R., & Müller, W. (Eds.) (2020). *Education and intergenerational mobility in Europe and the United States.* Stanford University Press.

Busemeyer, M. R., & Trampusch C. (2012). The comparative political economy of collective skill formation. In M. R. Busemeyer & C. Trampusch (Eds.), *The political economy of collective skill formation* (pp. 3–38). Oxford University Press.

Cobalti, A., & Schizzerotto, A. (1994). *La mobilità sociale in Italia*. Il Mulino.

Collins, R. (1979). *The credential society: An historical sociology of education and stratification*. Academic Press.

D'Amico, N. (2010). *Storia e storie della scuola italiana. Dalle origini ai giorni nostri*. Zanichelli.

Erikson, R. (1996). Explaining change in educational inequality—Economic security and school reforms. In R. Erikson & J. O. Jonsson (Eds.), *Can education be equalized? The Swedish case in comparative perspective* (pp. 95–112). Westview.

Erikson, R., & Jonsson, J. O. (1996). Explaining class inequality in education: The Swedish test case. In R. Erikson & J. O. Jonsson (Eds.), *Can education be equalized? The Swedish case in comparative perspective* (pp. 1–63). Westview Press.

Ermisch, J., Jäntti, M., & Smeeding, T. M. (Eds.) (2012). *From parents to children: The intergenerational transmission of advantage*. Russell Sage.

Erola, J., & Kilpi-Jakonen, E. (2017, Eds.). *Social inequality across the generations: The role of compensation and multiplication in resource accumulation*. Elgar.

Freese, J. (2018). The arrival of social science genomics. *Contemporary Sociology, 47*(5), 525–536.

Galor, O. (2006). From stagnation to growth: unified growth theory. In P. Aghion & S. Durlauf (Eds.), *Handbook of economic growth* (pp. 171–293). North-Holland.

Goldthorpe, J., & Jackson, M. (2006). Education-based meritocracy: The barriers to its realization. In A. Lareau & D. Conley (Eds.), *Social class: How does it work?* (pp. 93–116). Russell Sage.

Goldthorpe, J. H. (2007). *On sociology* (2nd ed.). Stanford University Press.

Güveli, A., Need, A., & de Graaf, N. D. (2007). The rise of "new" social classes within the service class in the Netherlands: Political orientation of social and cultural specialists and technocrats between 1970 and 2003. *Acta Sociologica, 50*, 129–146.

Hout, M. (1988). More universalism, less structural mobility: The American occupational structure in the 1980s. *American Journal of Sociology, 93*(6), 1358–1400.

Jackson, M., & Grusky, D. (2018). A post-liberal theory of stratification. *British Journal of Sociology, 69*, 1096–1133.

Kivinen, O., Hedman, J., & Kaipainen, P. (2007). From elite university to mass higher education: Educational expansion, equality of opportunity and returns to university education. *Acta Sociologica, 50*, 231–247.

Kuznets, S. (1955). Economic growth and income inequality. *American Economic Review, 45*, 1–28.

Lareau, A. (2011). *Unequal childhoods: Class, race and family life*. University of California Press.

Lenski, G. (1966). *Power and privilege: A theory of stratification*. McGraw-Hill.

Lipset, S. M., & Bendix, R. (1959). *Social mobility in industrial society*. University of California Press.

Meyer, J. W., Ramirez, F. O., Frank, D. J., & Schofer, E. (2007). Higher education as an institution. In P. J. Gumport (Ed.), *Sociology of higher education. Contributions and their contexts* (pp. 187–221). Johns Hopkins University Press.

Meyer, J. W., Ramirez, F. O., & Soysal, J. N. (1992). World expansion of mass education. *Sociology of Education, 65*(2), 128–149.

Meyer, J. W., Tyack, D., Nagel, J., & Gordon, A. (1979). Public education as nation-building in America: Enrollments and bureaucratization in the American states, 1870–1930. *American Journal of Sociology, 85*(3), 591–613.

Oesch, D. (2013). *Occupational change in Europe: How technology and education transform the job structure*. Oxford University Press.

Ramirez, F. O., & Boli, J. (1987). The political construction of mass schooling: European origins and worldwide institutionalization. *Sociology of Education, 60*, 2–17.

Rose, D., & Harrison, E. (Eds.) (2014). *Social class in Europe: An introduction to the European socio-economic classification*. Routledge.

Schizzerotto, A., Abbiati, G., & Vergolini, L. (2018). Espansioni e contrazioni della partecipazione scolastica in Italia dall'inizio del XX secolo ad oggi. Il ruolo delle riforme scolastiche e delle vicende economiche. *Annali di Statistica, 147*(13), 95–118.

Schofer, E., Meyer, J. W. (2005). The worldwide expansion of higher education in the twentieth century. *American Sociological Review, 70*, 898–920.

Toniolo, G. (2013). An overview of Italy's economic growth, In G. Toniolo (Ed.), *The Oxford handbook of the Italian economy since unification* (pp. 3–36). Oxford University Press.

Torche, F. (2011). Is a college degree still the great equalizer? Intergenerational mobility across levels of schooling in the United States. *American Journal of Sociology, 117*(3), 763–807.

Treiman, D. J. (1970). Industrialization and social stratification. In E. O. Laumann (Ed.), *Social stratification: Research and theory for the 1970s* (pp. 207–234). Bobbs-Merril.

Triventi, M. (2014). Le disuguaglianze di istruzione secondo l'origine sociale: Una rassegna della letteratura sul caso italiano. *Scuola democratica, 2*, 321–341.

Ventura, S. (1998). *La politica scolastica*. Il Mulino.

Weber, M. (1922/1978). *Economy and society*. English translation. University of California Press.

Whelan, C. T., & Layte, R. (2002). Late industrialization and the increased merit selection hypothesis: Ireland as a test case. *European Sociological Review, 18*(1), 35–50.

Wright, E. O. (2005). Foundation of a neo-Marxist class analysis. In E. O. Wright (Ed.), *Approaches to class analysis* (pp. 4–30). Cambridge: Cambridge University Press.

SECTION VII

Globalization of Higher Education and Science

CHAPTER 33

CAN NON-WESTERN COUNTRIES ESCAPE FROM CATCH-UP MODERNITY?

The Troubling Case of Japan's Education Reforms in a Global Era

TAKEHIKO KARIYA

INTRODUCTION

ANALYSES of the relationships between globalization and education in a given society require, theoretically and empirically, investigation into how the society understands and interprets the phenomenon called globalization as it is applied to education policymaking. Since the term *globalization* has multiple, often vague, meanings (Ritzer & Dean, 2015), the ways in which globalization is understood and interpreted in different societies as well as different periods are also varied. So are the impacts of globalization on education and education policy across different societies. For some countries, education for immigrants' children is the main policy issue, while in other countries climbing up the global league table ranking or increasing study abroad enrollments, either incoming and/or outgoing, may matter most. Global competition in economy and in science and technology are also related to education policymaking in many countries. Despite the multiplicity of meanings and impacts of globalization on education and education policy, we argue that ways of understandings and interpretations of globalization should contribute to creation of the knowledge basis on which policymaking is cognitively framed. But what kind of knowledge has become a basis for understanding globalization? How and what problems in education are identified and conceptualized based on such knowledge by political and intellectual leaders as well as the public in each country? In answering these questions, this chapter delves into the relationship between globalization and education policymaking.

In this regard, Japanese experiences provide both sociological and policy implications for other (specifically non-Western) societies to consider the relationship between globalization and education policymaking. To elucidate the significance of Japan's experiences in answering the aforementioned questions, we argue that Japan is among a few non-Western countries to have experienced both "catch-up" (with the West) and what might be called a "post-catch-up" modernization. The importance of the concept of "post-catch-up" modernity, a phrase coined by the author (Kariya, 2018, 2019, 2021), lies in its difference from the concepts of "postmodernity." In more carefully taking account of different pathways to reach modernity, particularly among non-Western societies, a theory of post-catch-up modernity pays attention to how the shapes of "post-modernity" are conceived and socially constructed in each society in considering the different pathways to reach modernity, thus inevitably influencing the conception and the shapes of "postmodernity" in the society.

The two phases of modernization, as discussed in this chapter, represent and reflect how a given society has responded to a globalizing world and global era. Undergoing these two stages of distinct social transformation, the society has encountered and identified difficulties in tackling problems allegedly in accommodating to globalization over the period that the society thrived to make a smooth transition from catch-up to post-catch-up modernity. This story is particularly evident when the focus is placed on education and education policy.

To answer the aforementioned questions, this chapter will focus on policy discourses related to education reforms in Japan in the 1980s. We will intentionally choose and analyze the education policy discourse in the 1980s, rather than more recent years, because the impact of understanding of modernity and globalization among Japanese leaders can be captured in the clearest form in that period, which will provide a clear starting point for the educational reform agendas that have continued to the present.

How did Japanese political and intellectual leaders understand Japan's experiences of the two staged modernizations in relation to globalization? What cognitive frameworks have been developed based on such understanding of Japan's modernity in the global historic context? How have educational reforms been guided by those cognitive frameworks in relation to globalization? In answering these questions through the lens of sociology of knowledge (Kariya & Rappleye, 2020), this chapter attempts to contribute to a better understanding of the relationship between globalization and education (including educational policy) in the form of a new theoretical framework we call "post-catch-up" modernity.[1]

In the following sections, first, we briefly describe how Japan's experiences were commonly perceived as "catch-up" modernization by the majority of political and intellectual leaders in Japan. Secondly, we will examine how a transitional period toward "post-catch-up" modernity was conceived. Discourse analyses of policy-related documents during the 1980s will reveal how the "post-catch-up" modernity framework was established over the 1980s, and how the framework contributed to problematization in education.

Thirdly, we will analyze what ideology linked with a conception of globalization came to play a pivotal role in constructing problems in Japan's education, which led logically to the education reforms that followed. In reasoning for education reforms, we will find that there was a political debate spanning most of the 1980s, which was conceptually framed within the post-catch-up modernity, one that explicitly sought to avoid failure in Western welfare states. This failure was actually coined the "British disease" by Japanese politicians and influential intellectual leaders who committed to education policymaking.

Based on the result of discourse analysis in these sections, in the Conclusion we will argue what theoretical and policy implications the case of Japan's experiences in modernization and globalization can provide. We will also trace what has happened in Japanese society and education since the 1980s, focusing on the ideological influences of the policy discourse in that time which have led to unexpected, even ironic, social changes in Japan.

"Catch-up" Modernization and Education

In Japan of the 1980s, there were numerous policy debates over how to reform various policy areas for the 21st century. Education reform was no exception. In the course of these policy debates, a common perception of Japan's modern history up until the time among political and intellectual leaders was that Japan's modernization experience up through the 1980s was a "catch-up" model (Kariya, 2019, 2021; Rappleye & Kariya, 2011). Based on the perception of Japan's historic momentum that the catch-up modernization had ended by that point, problems in education were conceptually framed and problematized. Education policy debates, therefore, argued that this historic momentum should have been the starting point from which to envision the future prospects of the nation and the policies to realize them.

One of the most evident and straightforward statements which demonstrates this perception can be found in a report published by a high-profile blue-ribbon council composed of famous scholars and social critics under then Prime Minister Ōhira Masayoshi over the late 1970s to early 1980s. The Council was named "Ōhira Policy Study Group" (Ōhira Seisaku Kenkyūkai). One of the volumes of the report states:

> In order to "catch up" as speedily as possible with the advanced nations of the West, Japan has proactively pushed forward with modernization, industrialization and westernization since the Meiji Restoration. As a result, Japan succeeded in reaching

the stage of a mature, highly industrial society, and everyone has come to enjoy freedom and equality, progress and prosperity, economic wealth and the convenience of modern life, high education and high welfare standards, as well as advanced scientific technology. These are all qualities we can be proud of in the world. (Age of Culture Research Group, 1980, p. 2)[2]

To the Council members, the alleged end of catch-up meant the end of "Westernization" of Japan, as a variant of globalization (Ritzer & Dean, 2015), which was framed in the global historical politico-economic context. Based on this conception of Japan's modernization, the obvious question for the Council was "What should come next?" The report continued:

Japan's modernization (industrialization and westernization) and its maturation into a highly industrial society implies the end of any models involving the need to align to, or to "catch up with." From now on, *we need to find our own path to follow.* (Age of Culture Economic Management Group (ACEMG), 1980, p. 14; the emphasis is by the author)

As analyzed in greater detail in my other writings (Kariya, 2018, 2019, 2021), the knowledge base of "catch-up modernization" and the end of it was shared with a policymaking advisory board for education as well. To this end, the Ad Hoc Council on Education Reforms (AHCER) was the main actor. AHCER was organized by Prime Minister Nakasone Yasuhiro in the mid-1980s and became the most powerful and influential education policymaking body (Schoppa, 1991), producing proposals that have continued to greatly impact education reforms priorities since the 1980s (Ichikawa, 1995). Importantly, the policy proposals of AHCER were, in principle, guided by the views shared with the Ōhira Council. Guided by the knowledge of the end of "catch-up modernization," AHCER emphasized the importance of transforming Japan's education in accordance with the conception of post-catch-up era toward the 21st century. Accordingly, the policy proposals viewed Japanese education as locked in a catch-up mode of education. It thus sought to shift education into a means whereby the next generations would be taught "creativity" and "individuality." A typical statement reflecting the conception of catch-up modernization is, for example, found in the following statement from the final report of AHCER:

(I)t is undeniable that Japan's traditional education has mostly rested upon the tendency of cramming knowledge by rote memorization. The society of the future will require us not merely to acquire knowledge and information, but to further develop the ability to express, create, think with our heads, and to make appropriate use of that knowledge and information. Creativity is closely connected to individuality, and only when individuality is fostered can creativity be nourished. (AHCER, 1988, p. 278)

This statement clearly addresses an articulation of the idea that Japan had "no model to borrow" and thus needed to "find our own path to follow" (ACEMG, 1980). AHCER also pointed out several other defects of Japanese education over the period of catch-up:

> We imported and adopted from Western advanced industrial countries such things as their advanced sciences and technology as well as social institutions, and we emphasized efficiency in order to swiftly promote their dissemination. From a broader perspective, in terms of both content in teaching and pedagogy, as a result of these, a rigidly uniform education system was pre-ordained. (AHCER, 1988, p. 9)

> We need to recognize here that the "negative side-effects" of Japan's modern-industrial-civilization, its "catch-up model" of modernization, and/or its rapid economic growth in the post-war period, is seen as leading to the deterioration of children's inner self and contributing to a society built upon foundations that damaged the physical and mental health conditions of human beings, tainted interactions among people, and had negative influences on culture and education. (AHCER, 1988, p. 50)

As shown here, AHCER diagnosed that Japan's problems were a uniform education system, cramming knowledge by rote memorization, and deterioration of children's sense of healthy inner self, all of which were considered "negative side effects" of Japan's catch-up modernization. In declaring that Japan had completed its catch-up, those policymakers alleged that the post-catch-up age should have necessitated Japan's education solving these problems through the reforms they were proposing. As analyzed in greater detail elsewhere (Kariya, 2018, 2019, 2021; Rappleye & Kariya, 2011), the underling premises of AHCER's diagnoses on Japan's education, which were founded on the conception of "post-catch-up" modernity, have continued influencing education policies in Japan right up to the present.

Post-Catch-Up Modernity and Globalization

To understand impacts of globalization on those conceptions, in the next step we will analyze how such perceptions of Japan's modernity can be placed in the global politico-economic context. How and what problems allegedly associated with globalization were socially constructed under the understanding of "catch-up" model of modernization? How were the impacts of globalization on Japanese society perceived and interpreted through the cognitive framework of targeted "post-catch-up" modernity? We will analyze these relationships in this section. In doing so, we pay attention to one of the most influential figures in AHCER, Prof. Kenichi Kōyama, then at Gakushūin University. Kōyama was not only a central member of the Council but also a powerful spokesperson on behalf of AHCER by publishing popular journal articles and books on the reforms proposed by AHCER.

Ōtake (1994), an eminent political scientist, positions Kōyama as a leading ideologue for AHCER. According to him, Kōyama was one of the central policy advisors for the Ōhira and the Nakasone administrations. Ōtake also describes Kōyama as an assertive advocate and contributor to the incorporation of neoliberalism, the ideological pillar of the turn of the 1980s, into Japan's education policy.

To become an influential ideologue of neoliberalism for Japan's education policy, Kōyama was intellectually and politically affected not only by the neoliberal ideology as the most globally dominant socioeconomic theory at the time, but he was also under the influence of perceived global "real" situations at that time. Put differently, his perception of Japan's post-catch-up modernity is closely linked with Japan's future position in the global politico-economic context. In exploring this relationship, we focus on a discourse that appeared in his book entitled *The Lesson of the British Disease* (Kōyama, 1978) in order to examine his understanding of modernity and the impact of globalization on his thoughts, which later became incorporated into the premises underpinning the AHCER policies.

Although the following analysis pays attention to the discourse of one single leading intellectual, Kōyama, we contend that his views on Japan's modernity and positionality in the global context represented those of his contemporary political and business leaders in Japan.[3] While some critiques saw Koyama's views leaning toward too nationalistic and/or neoliberal ideologies (e.g., Horio, 1993), those critical voices had very limited influences on the mainstream arguments on policymaking processes, as discussed later.

As the title of the book suggests, over the latter half of the 1970s, the long-term decline of British economy was regarded by Japanese intellectuals, politicians, and business leaders as a visible and undeniable failure of Western welfare states, which was, in the views of Japanese leaders, represented by the decline of Great Britain, which was thus coined the "British disease." Britain was intentionally selected by the Japanese leaders because it was representative of the once world-leading Western civilized and industrialized nations, which had previously provided an idealistic model for Japan. In this book, Kōyama identifies four symptoms of the British disease: (a) economic stagnation, loss of the spirit of ingenuity; (b) financial collapse, denial of the principle of competition and state intervention in economic activities; (c) chronic strikes; and (d) political instability. He then hones in on the problem of the welfare state, invented by Western modernity, as the purported cause of these symptoms:

> In the early days of the welfare state, it was an ideal that there should be no such thing as people living in poverty because of their disadvantages in society, and that we should extend a hand of love to them. . . . However, in the midst of this idealistic and dream-fulfilling movement, unexpected and serious side effects have arisen and expanded, with very ironic results. (Kōyama, 1978, p. 24)

Kōyama calls this "the paradox of [Western] civilization" (Kōyama, 1978, p. 24) and goes on to say:

> First, it is the decline of the free and creative vitality of society; second, it is the weakening of the spirit of self-reliance and the increasing dependence on the state, the collapse of the principle of free competition and the enlargement of the state; third, it is the expansion of the ego in individuals and the decline of morals; and fourth, it is the decline in the decision-making capacity of national societies. (Kōyama, 1978, p. 38)

Kōyama, drawing on Huizinga, considers these diseases of the developed nations, represented by the British disease, as "negative side effects of industrial civilization. In other words, it is a paradox that Western modernity is facing." Here we find how Kōyama positions "modernity" in this paradox. Under this assumption, how did this view impact his view of globalization? According to him,

> Industrial civilization has continuously expanded the scope of public services based on the premise that the creation of a prosperous, convenient, and very caring nation state is in line with human nature. From education, healthcare, and pensions to housing and other services, modern society has constantly expanded the scope of those public services. However, in direct relation to the problem of public finances, the problem of financial collapse has emerged, as the tendency to increase public finances cannot be sustained, and at the same time, the problems of various negative sociological and psychological side effects have become more serious. In other words, the developed countries have had to learn through bitter experience that, in the long run, this will lead to a vicious circle that will eventually debilitate the spirit of self-reliance and the vitality of society through complex circuits within society. (Kōyama, 1978, p. 178)

Although the sentence begins with "industrial civilization," the reference is to, without a doubt, (Western) modern society. In other words, in his understanding, Western modernity was deemed to be established based on the principle of "the premise that the creation of a prosperous, convenient, and very caring state is in accord with human nature." While the welfare state is superimposed on modernity, the paradox is that this debilitates the "spirit of self-reliance," another principle of modernity, and robs society of its vitality. Based on this understanding of modernity, the following conclusion is drawn:

> A liberal society must be run on the principles of self-reliance, self-help, and free competition, and the state must not intervene and overprotect citizens' lives and business activities more than necessary. (Kōyama, 1978, p. 179)

> This means, secondly, that Japan must not imitate the social security and welfare system represented by the Western and Northern European welfare states. (Kōyama, 1978, p. 180)

This conception of British disease played a pivotal role here in addressing a clear warning to Japanese leaders that Japan must not follow the same pathway in advancing its modernity. Given the concrete images of the failure in Western welfare states represented by Great Britain, Japanese leaders were cautioned that their "post-catch-up" stage of development should not imitate the western welfare states. Importantly, the image creation of British disease was possible and meaningful to the Japanese leaders at that stage only when Britain was placed in the global politico-economic context at that time. Kōyama's understanding of modernity and globalization as presented here is exactly what we would call the neoliberalism. Yet what is more important for our analysis is that his understanding was based on the very striking and easily understandable impasse of the welfare states among the advanced Western European countries of his time, such as the British disease vis-à-vis the future challenge for Japan's post-catch-up modernity. By understanding modernity from the image of the "reality" of the Western societies of their time, rather than positively idealizing and dreaming of advanced Western civilization, they translated the limitations of "Western" welfare-state-cum-modernity into global politico-economic terms.

In contrast to this stalemate of mature Western modernity, Japan's modernization was seen as a catch-up model, and it was recognized that it had been already complete. As Kōyama puts it:

> In retrospect, we can say that for about 100 years since the Meiji Restoration, Japan has been running the country in accordance with the long-term national goal of catching up with and overtaking the advanced nations of Western Europe. And it is thought that the nation's 100-year plan, which was set at the time of the Meiji Restoration, was achieved around 1970, or to put it very strictly, in 1968, exactly 100 years after the Meiji Restoration. However, since that time, Japan has been in a kind of goal-less state. There have been various expressions such as an age without a map, a voyage without a chart, and an age of lost goals, but this state of affairs gradually expanded after about 1970. It seems that this confusion is still spreading in the political, economic, social, and cultural spheres today. (Kōyama, 1978, p. 176)

This understanding of modernization, that Japan is in a state of "goal loss," was a common feature of the discourse of other catch-up modernization theorists, who predict that Japan's long-term national goal of catching up with and overtaking the advanced nations of Western Europe was completed, and that the loss of this goal must have occurred after the goal was achieved (Kariya, 2019). This is the same logic that the Ōhira Policy Study Group problematized the loss of a clear model as the task "to find our own path to follow."

If Japanese leaders understood modernization as a catch-up model, a form of "Westernization," then the goal was thought to be achieved when Japan caught up. As long as a society has experienced social transformation based on the accepted and adopted values and institutional framework of modernity, such as "nation-states," "democracy," "capitalist economy," "progress," "freedom and equality," "human rights," and so on, modernity, in theory, never ends. Nonetheless, in the Japanese historical context over the 1970s and 1980s, we saw the end of modernity and modernization conceived by the mainstream political and intellectual leaders (Kariya, 2019). Thus, the issue of "what comes after" of Japanese modernization, which is witnessing the impasse of Western modernity, is connected as follows:

> For the past 100 years, Japan has been industrializing and modernizing, making use of the advantages of its traditional culture, but basically imitating the models of the developed countries of the West. . . . However, after catching up at a rapid pace, Japan eventually became a member of the OECD, a club of developed countries in 1964, and reached a position where it could run with the rest of the group of developed countries. Nonetheless, at that time, the developed countries were actually becoming confused and sick in many ways. Namely, the developed countries were in a state of confusion and disease in many ways. Therefore, if Japan were to follow the developed countries with the same attitude as before, the diseases of the developed countries, such as the British disease and the Scandinavian disease, would be imitated at a very fast pace, in the same way that the tempo of economic growth was very fast. We have entered such a phase. (Kōyama, 1978, p. 176)

By exemplifying the British disease as an acute and actual case, these statements succeeded in giving credibility to the impression, even without substantial evidence. In such a way, the new phase of post-catch-up was conceived by connecting the impasse of modernity itself (regarded as something *universal* in the global historical context, thus *universality*) with the loss of goals brought about by the end of Japan's catch-up modernization (something *specific* to Japan as a non-western modernity, thus *particularity*), and by overlaying this with the image of an "age without a model" that both Japan and the advanced nations of Western Europe were allegedly facing. In this regard, Koyama's argument represents a form of "post-Westernization," a counterargument toward the "West," but in a different form from postcolonialism (Ritzer & Dean, 2015).

AGENDA SETTING FOR AHCER POLICY PROPOSALS

Kōyama's understanding of Japan's modernity permeated the AHCER policy proposals. To analyze how his understanding reflected on the proposals, we will delve into discourse in another popular book of Kōyama, entitled *Educational Reform for Freedom* (Kōyama, 1987), which is a collection of already published essays appearing in popular magazines while he was a member of the Council.

In this book, Kōyama pointed out problems of Japanese education in the mid-1980s as follows:

> To overcome the three problems of Japanese school education: (1) uniformity, (2) closedness, and (3) non-internationalism, it is necessary to recognize the root causes of these problems. In summary, these three evils are all concentrated in the evils of

the "catch-up" modernization era of education in Japan since the Meiji era. First, in the process of rapid modernization, industrialization, and westernization of Japan after the Meiji era, the modern school system imported from Europe and the U.S. was essentially one of state control and uniformity, with modern rationalism and industrialism at its core. . . . Such a modern school system has been a great success in today's industrially advanced countries, including our own, but its success has already brought it to the end of its useful life as a system and it has become obsolete, manifesting various pathological symptoms of the disease of advanced countries in the midst of the end of modernity and the transition from an industrial society to a post-industrial society. (Kōyama, 1987, pp. 24–25)

This statement elucidates his understanding of modernity as a disease of the industrialized countries, and the problems that Japanese education has come to face through the era of catch-up modernization. The modern school system, which was created as a catch-up, is constructed by overlapping the recognition of problems specific to Japan, conceived as *particularity*, such as the "inherently strong character of state control and uniformity," and the setting of issues facing modern society during the historical transition of the end of modernity, conceived as *universality* at the alleged global standard.

In this way, the historical background of the end of catch-up modernization enabled Japan to think realistically about "education aiming at the creation of a universal yet unique culture" (Kōyama, 1987, pp. 49–50) from a broad comparative, global, cultural perspective and from a broader historical perspective that goes beyond modernity. More importantly, this shift was also superimposed on the turning point of Western modernity. According to Kōyama, "the end of the era of catch-up modernization in Japan coincided with the end of the era of industrial civilization since the Industrial Revolution in the industrially advanced countries of Europe and the United States" (Kōyama, 1987, p. 232). This is an overlap between the universal period of Western modernity and the period of modernization specific to Japan. Therefore, in his views, the time for reform should be NOW. The maturation of Japanese society (i.e., the end of catch-up), according to his argument, has given us the intellectual foundation to think realistically about "education that aims to create a universal yet unique culture" from a broader historical perspective that should go beyond (Western, universal) modernity. Here, too, the perspective of the integration of the particular and the universal, which had troubled intellectuals before Kōyama, such as Maruyama Masao among others, was pushed forward against the backdrop of Japan's seemingly successful experience of catch-up modernization.

Kōyama's statement evidently overlapped with the report of AHCER quoted earlier in this chapter as follows:

At the same time, the world and humankind have entered a turning point in the history of civilization, from the modern industrial society to the advanced information society of the 21st century. The era of imitation, materialization, and uniformity is over; the new era demands creativity, quality, and individuality. Education must respond to these demands. We must recognize that the devastation of education, as seen in the excessive consciousness of the credentialism, the competition for entrance exams with a focus on the standardized test score, school violence, and juvenile delinquency, is a pathological phenomenon brought about by uniformity and rigidity in Japan's education, and we must break through the uniformity, closedness, and non-internationalism of the past and promote fundamental reforms to realise diversity, openness, and internationalism. (Kōyama, 1987, p. 75)

The points made here are based on the neoliberal ideology and are related to the administrative and fiscal reforms being promoted in other developed countries. Kōyama, however, also emphasizes, "it is not just about fiscal problems or tinkering with administrative systems," but should be "based on deep reflection on the diseases of the developed countries that have led to the collapse of human relationships, the decline of religious, moral and emotional values, and the loss of the spirit of self-reliance and self-help" (Kōyama, 1987, p. 118). Therefore, it was justified as an issue that is not limited to Japan but "beyond modernity" as stated here:

> In this respect, I believe that the current educational reform (the report of AHCER) is a step forward in the history of civilization, after a hundred years of catch-up modernization, and after several hundred years of global modernization and industrialization since the Industrial Revolution. I have been arguing that the reform must include a fundamental overhaul of the compulsory education, the public education, thus the whole school system, all of which were embedded in the modern nation-state. (Kōyama, 1987, p. 103)

> After the end of the modern era, we are now entering an era beyond the modernity, and a comprehensive review of compulsory education must mean re-examining the merits and demerits in the state-monopolised education and reconsidering the limit of state coercion. On the basis of the high cultural and educational standards that Japan has now achieved, it must make a complete break with the vestiges of the evil state-controlled education, which subordinated culture and education to the central government. (Kōyama, 1987, p. 106)

The prescription for this is a return to self-reliance, self-help, and self-responsibility. It is important to note that the "evil state-controlled education" is compatible with the image of a state-led modernization under the "developmental state" (Johnson, 1982). The challenge of breaking away from the developmental state, which should lead to deregulation and "liberalization of education"—a challenge common to late-modernizing societies—can be discussed in the context of universality in the global context rather than particularity specified solely in Japan to dismantle subordination to government.

According to Kōyama, Japanese could no longer look to the developed countries for models. Poor imitation would only lead to the disease of advanced nations. Thus, a unique path for Japan was set as the task of the development of Japanese people capable of self-reliance and self-help, but not imitating Western individualism because Kōyama thought it was a main reason for their decline. This was a return to the Japanese value of self-reliance and self-help (*Jijo-jiritsu* in Japanese), which was linked to premises of neoliberalism, but not to Western liberalism since Kōyama also regarded it as an ideology closely linked to the Western individualism. The value of self-reliance and self-help was thus placed in Japan's own tradition, or more correctly, the invented tradition of modernizing Japan (Kariya, 2019).

Although his neoliberalist argument was brought up to the table at AHCER, neoliberal reforms were not fully accepted at the end. Instead, in the report ideas of neoliberalism were reinterpreted, modified, and moderated *pedagogically* as a policy statement that the future Japanese education should respect individuality and creativity. The "spirit of self-reliance and self-help" was partly encompassed as the phrase of respecting individuality, but the neoliberal ideology, whose main goal was to deconstruct the state-controlled education system, was much diluted. Since then, pedagogical slogans of respecting and nurturing individuality and promoting individualization in learning in classrooms have repeatedly appeared as the main goals in education reforms in Japan to date (Kariya, 2021), while the state-controlled education has remained with only limited changes (Kariya & Rappleye, 2020).

Conclusion

In this chapter, I have intentionally chosen and analyzed the education policy discourse in the 1980s, rather than more recent policy documents. The reason for this is, first, that it provided a clear starting point for the educational reform agendas and goals that have continued right up to the present. The individualization of learning and the creation of an education that respects each child's individuality have come to be the consistent goals of the various educational reform proposals that have followed. It can be said that the educational reform debates and proposals at AHCER over the 1980s have underpinned the principal premises for the reforms in the subsequent three decades (Terawaki, 2019). The second reason is, more importantly, that the perceptions of Japan's leaders on the transition to post-catch-up modernity over the 1980s influenced so evidently the agenda setting for education policy that the impact of understanding of modernity and globalization can be captured in the clearest form in this period.

As discussed in this chapter, non-Western countries that commenced modernization late undertook a form of deliberate modernization by following other developed (Western) nations as their models (Gilman, 2003). This can be characterized as catch-up modernization, as so aptly illustrated in the case of Japanese experiences. At some point in the process, however, societies may stop playing catch-up, give up, switch to other methods, or, as in Japan's experiences, come to the realization that it is complete. As such, standing on a theory of post-catch-up modernity, we can pose the following questions: How will the issues and problems of education be recognized and problematized in such a transition period of catch-up modernization toward post-catch-up? How will each society then position itself in the global politico-economic context? How does such positioning affect the formulation of educational policies? How has that society's understanding of modernity vis-à-vis globalization come to be embedded therein? Answering theoretically and empirically these questions through the lens of a variety of modernization experiences across (non-Western) societies can, we believe, shed new light on our understanding of modernity and the impacts of globalization.

The impact of globalization on education and education policy is, as this chapter depicted, closely related to the question of how each society understands and positions its own modernity in a global politico-economic context. In order to move away from Eurocentric understandings of modernity (i.e., any forms of post-Westernization) and reconsider the impact of globalization on education and educational policy, it is necessary to incorporate such a diversity of modernizations and the diverse pathways to modernity into the debate. This is because we believe that the knowledge constructed over the period of modernizations provides an important cognitive framework for understanding the impact of the phenomenon called globalization. Put differently, a perceived stage of modernization/modernity produced a cognitive framework to understand the globalizing world. To demonstrate such an evident example of this, this chapter has ventured to analyze the education policy discourse of Japan in the 1980s.

One may argue that Japan's experiences as such are so unique to Japan that they are not applicable to other non-Western countries, many of which experienced colonization unlike the case of Japan. The ways of "post-Westernization" must take different forms from those of Japan. The differences must reflect on the discourse and perceptions around Western influences and their own modernizations. Nevertheless, at least in the realm of education, more accurately, "modernized education," the conception of "catch-up" with advanced countries is deemed to be shared among "modernizing elites" (Bhambra 2014) in those countries as well. Their conceptions of catch-up may vary dependent on the country's positionality in the global politico-economic context as well as its self-understanding of "development" (Bhambra, 2014). As long as any forms of conception of catch-up are shared among those "modernizing elites," however, a theoretical consideration of "post-catch-up" is useful to understand the issues of "what comes after" the catch-up among those elites. The analysis of the discourse among them, therefore, will contribute to enhance our comprehension of the relationships among education policymaking, modernity, and globalization, as discussed in this chapter. In this regard, it is important to study the relationships under the framework of "post-catch-up" in other East Asian countries such as South Korea, Taiwan, and China. These countries have developed their economy and science and technology, as well as democratized their polity, except for China. In this regard, these East Asian countries shared a form of "catch-up," but they may have different views on "post-catch-up" because of their timings and stages of the completion of catch-up (happened later than Japan). Although it is an attractive comparative study on "post-catch-up" modernity, it is beyond the scope of this chapter. To further undergird the theory of "post-catch-up" modernity, it is also necessary to locate the concept in broader theoretical contexts of modernity, modernization, and globalization (Bhambra, 2014), which also admittedly requires further research.

Lastly, over these historical trajectories, we may then ask whether Kōyama's dream of an education based on the principles of self-reliance and self-help has come true. Education reforms following the AHCER proposals have constantly and repeatedly set goals in education as emphasizing the importance of individualization of learning and the creation of an education that respects each child's individuality. Repetition and succession of almost the same slogans for reforms as such, in a sense, evidence that the reforms commenced since the late 1980s have not been regarded successful enough to achieve the goals by policymakers. The same goal setting has also incorporated the policy to accommodate globalization more directly. Japanese government has implemented policy to foster "global human resources," who should not only be fluent in English but also should be active and independent individuals (Kariya, 2018) to maintain Japan's competitiveness in the global economic competition. In reality, however, since then Japan's competitiveness has rather been declining (International Institute for Management Development, 2020).

Was Japan then able to avoid the British disease through the education reforms as Kōyama advocated? The frank answer is "No." Japan's experiences since the 1980s indirectly prove that the reforms have failed in that term. It is admittedly true that Japan was able to cut the social welfare budget and maintain a "small government" to some degree. However, since the collapse of the so-called asset bubble economy in the early 1990s, Japan has faced long-lasting economic stagnation, which continues to date. And that is not all. Associated with the long economic slump, the increased loss of stable employment has placed Japanese young adults in more difficult family situations (Ochiai, 2014). With the limited welfare support to them from the "small" government, the birth rate continued to fall for a long time. Stubborn gender inequality has also accelerated this trend (Schoppa, 2006). On the other hand, the growing elderly population has given rise to the most advanced aging society in the world. At the end, the cost of social welfare for the elderly has constantly increased while the decreasing revenue to the government due to the long-lasting economic stagnation and the demographic changes, the symptoms of which are now called "Japanese disease," which ironically resulted by escaping from the British disease. Note that those social changes were, along with the "second demographic transformation" (Lesthaeghe, 2014) as a universal trend, accelerated primarily by the impacts of Japan's economic, employment, and social policies rather than those of education policies.

If this is the case, what impact have the education reforms had on Japanese society? It is often argued that neoliberal deregulation reforms in employment were behind the scenes of those social changes. In this regard, the education reforms since the AHCER proposals have, despite their failures in mitigating the state-controlled education system, succeeded in propagating the ideology of neoliberalism by emphasizing the importance of individuals' independence and individuality through individualization of learning. In this regard, Kōyama's dream of cultivating the spirit of self-reliance and self-help for next generations left its legacy to individualization in risk-taking (Beck, 1992; Beck & Grande, 2010), which may increase personal risks in their life chances (Suzuki et al., 2010) such as in employment and in education (Kariya, 2018, 2021). Under such a normative basis of individualization, if you fail academically in school, it is you who should be blamed for your failure, which in your later career may result in a lower socioeconomic status, which is also purported as your own individual failing. The emphasis on individuals' independence and individuality through individualization of learning thus is well compatible with the neoliberalism ideology. In this sense, Kōyama's dream has partly come true, but it has ironically been captured in the Japanese disease. The transition to post-catch-up is still in a muddle. This may be the reason for the repetition and succession of the goal of nurturing active and independent individuals in Japan's education reforms.

NOTES

1. As discussed later, this chapter focuses on a socially constructed and shared understanding of "modernity," particularly among "modernizing elites" (Bhambra, 2014) in a society, rather than arguing for substantial aspects of modernity.
2. Japanese materials are translated by the author.
3. Koyama's view on "British disease" was deemed to have great impact on Toshio Dokō, one of the most influential business leaders in that time, who was appointed by Prime Minister Nakasone as the chairperson of Provisional Council on Administrative and Fiscal Reform. The Council proposed ample and influential policies led by the neoliberal ideology. The conception of "British disease" was also incorporated in the government social welfare policies entitled "Japanese style welfare society," which avoided a Western model of welfare states (Kariya, 2019).

REFERENCES

Beck, U. (1992). *Risk society: Towards a new modernity*. Sage.
Beck, U., & Grande, E. (2010). Varieties of second modernity: The cosmopolitan turn in social and political theory and research. *British Journal of Sociology, 61*(3), 409–443.
Bhambra, G. K. (2014). *Connected sociologies*. Bloomsbury Academic.
Bunka no jidai kenkyū gurūpu (Age of Culture Research Group). (1980). *Ōhira sōri no seisaku kenkyūkai hōkokusho 1 bunka no jidai (PM Ōhira's Policy Study Groups Report No.1 The Age of Culture)*. Cabinet Councilor's Office (Ed.). Ministry of Finance Printing Bureau.
Bunka no jidai no keizai keiei kenkyū gurūpu (Age of Culture Economic Management Group) (ACEMG)). (1980). *Ōhira sōri no seisaku kenkyūkai hōkokusho 7 bunka no jidai no keizai keiei (Report No.7 Economic Administration in an Age of Culture)*. Cabinet Councilor's Office (Ed.). Ministry of Finance Printing Bureau.
Gilman, N. (2003). *Mandarins of the future: Modernization theory in Cold War America*. Johns Hopkins University Press.
Horio, T. (1993). *Taiwashū: Kyōiku wo sasaeru Shisō (Collected dialogues on ideas behind education)*. Iwanamishoten.
Ichikawa, S. (1995). *Rinkyōshin go no Kyōiku Seisaku (Education policy in the post AHCER age)*. Kyōikukaihatsukenkyūjo.

International Institute for Management Development. (2020). *IMD World Competitiveness Ranking 2020*. https://www.imd.org/wcc/world-competitiveness-center-rankings/world-competitiveness-ranking-2020/

Johnson, C. (1982). *MITI and the Japanese miracle: The growth of industrial policy, 1925–1975*. Stanford University Press.

Kariya, T. (2018). Meritocracy, modernity, and the completion of catch-up: Problems and paradoxes. In A. Yonezawa, Y. Kitamura, B. Yamamoto, & T. Tokunaga (Eds.), *Japanese education in a global age—Sociological reflections and future directors* (pp. 287–306). Springer.

Kariya, T. (2019). *Oitsuita Kindai, Kieta Kindai* (*Who killed Japan's Modernity? What comes after catch-up?*). Iwanamishoten.

Kariya, T. (2021). Japan's post catch-up modernity: Educational transformation and its unintended consequences. In H. Takeda & M. Williams (Eds.), *Routledge handbook of contemporary Japan* (pp. 304–317). Routledge.

Kariya, T., & Rappleye, J. (2020). *Education, equality, and meritocracy in a global age: The Japanese approach*. Teachers College Press, Columbia University.

Kōyama, K. (1978). *Eikokubyō no Kyōkun* (*The lesson of the British disease*). PHP Shuppan.

Kōyama, K. (1987). *Jiyū no tameno Kyōiku Kaikaku* (*Educational reform for freedom*). PHP Shuppan.

Lesthaeghe, R. (2014). The second demographic transition: A concise overview of its development. *Proceedings of the National Academy of Sciences*, December 23, 2014, *111*(51), 18112–18115.

Ochiai, E. (2014). Leaving the West, rejoining the East? Gender and family in Japan's semi-compressed modernity. *International Sociology*, *29*(3), 209–228.

Ōtake, H. (1994). *Jiyūshugiteki kaikaku no jidai (Reforms in the neo-liberal era)*. Chūōkōronsha.

Rappleye, J., & Kariya, T. (2011). Reimagining self/other: Catch-up across Japan's three great education reforms. In D. Willis & J. Rappleye, *Reimagining Japanese education* (pp. 51–83). Symposium Books.

Rinji kyōiku shingi kai. (Ad Hoc Council on Education Reforms) (AHCER). (1988). *Kyōiku kai- kaku ni kan suru tōshin – Rinji kyōiku shingi kai dai 1–4 (saishū) tōshin (The first to forth reports)*. Ōkurashō insatsukyoku.

Ritzer, G., & Dean, P. (2015). *Globalization a basic text*. Wiley Blackwell.

Schoppa, L. (1991). *Education reform in Japan: A case of immobilist politics*. Routledge.

Schoppa, L. J. (2006). *Race for the exits: The unravelling of Japan's system of social protection*. Cornell University Press.

Suzuki, M., Ito, M., Ishida, M., Nihei, N., & Maruyama, M. (2010). Individualizing Japan: Searching for its origin in first modernity. *British Journal of Sociology*, *61*(3), 513–538.

Terawaki, K. (2019). Heisei no Kyōiku Kaikaku no Kiten Rinkyōshin (AHCER as the origin of education reforms over the three decades). https://www.kyobun.co.jp/management/m2019 0307_02/

CHAPTER 34

THE GLOBAL SCALE IN HIGHER EDUCATION AND RESEARCH

SIMON MARGINSON

INTRODUCTION

IF globalization means intensified convergence and integration at the global scale (Conrad, 2016; Held et al., 1999), higher education, especially research and science in the sector, are notable in the extent to which they have become globalized. Yet action at the local and national scales is often determining. This chapter reviews trajectories of globalization in all sectors and higher education since the early 1990s and explores the intersection between global and national science. This draws attention to the explanatory value of scale, and the chapter closes with remarks about scale as materiality, perspective, and understanding.

PARTIAL GLOBALIZATION AND HIGHER EDUCATION

Anglo-American Globalization in the 1990s

The advent of communicative globalization in the 1990s was a fundamental historical change, akin to the generalization of printing in late medieval Europe and the widespread diffusion of transport driven by fossil fuels in the 19th century. It transformed and continues to transform the conditions of possibility of higher education, scholarship, research, and science. The networked world would have been a fundamental change in any era, and in any era its meanings were bound to be articulated by the particular historical context, itself continually moving and changing. So it has been in the 1990s and after.

The proportion of the world's population connected through the Internet grew from 0.05% in 1990, many in early-adopting US universities, to 6.53% in 2000 and 15.67% in 2005 (World Bank, 2021). The rollout of the communications network coincided with the triumph of American global policy following the dissolution of the Soviet Union in 1991, and the spread of neoliberal deregulation in trade and finance, facilitated by country adjustment to the templates of the World Trade Organization (Rodrik, 2018). Taken together, geopolitics, the high capitalist neoliberal ascendancy, communications, financial flows, the offshoring of production, trade liberalization, worldwide consumption, and iconic brands suggested an outcome combined, singular, and hegemonic: Anglo-American economic, cultural, and technological globalization seemed on the brink of remaking the world as an Americanized world order.

Social theory saw it somewhat differently, varying in the extent to which it welcomed American-ness, but universally celebrating the more porous political and cultural borders and the potentials of an emerging cosmopolitan super-space. Arjun Appadurai (1996) stated that "I have come to be convinced that the nation-state, as a complex modern political form, is on its last legs" (p. 19). This was good: The nation state system "seems plagued by endemic disease" (p. 20). Ulrich Beck (2005) declared that the "national era" was passing and the "cosmopolitan era" had begun (p. 2). Saskia Sassen (2002) talked of the "partial unbundling or at least weakening of the nation as a spatial unit." The architecture of cross-border flows, in which global cities were central, "increasingly diverges from that of the interstate system" (p. 1). In *Globalization and Organization* (2006), Gili Drori, John Meyer, and Hokyu Hwang found that the locus of activity had moved above the state, to Americanized world society, where common templates "construct the world as an integrated collectivity," and downward below the state to the real players, the "autonomous organizations" (p. 19). This resonated with the global/local dual ("glolocal") referenced in public commentary on globalization.

In retrospect, the degree of agreement is very striking. So is the degree of error. What distinguished all these arguments was the either/or logic of relations between the global and national scales—the assumption that "globalization" necessarily meant a reduction in the role or potency of the nation. In the 1990s, the possibility that both global and national structure/agency could advance simultaneously was less considered. Yet historically, the evolving nation state had always been joined at the hip to global developments. The rise of the modern form of the state in the 19th century was stimulated by global convergence, comparison, and competition among Britain, Prussia, and France, and later the United States, Japan, and others (Bayly, 2004). This suggested that notwithstanding the anti-statist and "submerged state" ideology in the politics of deregulation, the accelerated globalization of the 1990s meant not the withering of the nation state, but a change in its conditions of operation and of its activities, while all units of the world order became more engaged and interdependent. Not everyone saw the state as finished or even diminished. In their magisterial overview of globalization, with its detailed review across multiple fields, Held and colleagues (1999) carefully kept the question open.

Higher Education and Neoliberal Globalization

In higher education, the second half of the 1990s launched a long wave of globalization in student and academic mobility, research collaboration, offshore campuses, the diffusion of common systemic and institutional templates, the global rankings that began in Shanghai in 2003 (ARWU, 2021), and evolving national and local policies on fostering cross-border passage, international collaboration in science, and global university missions. In higher education policy, much rhetorical emphasis was placed on the abstract imperatives of the "global knowledge economy." This was somewhat misleading. While some Anglophone systems (United Kingdom, Australia, and New Zealand) commercialized international education, this was not the majority approach. Across the world, the fecund globalization in universities and science derived primarily from communicative and cultural globalization, in association with the cheapening of travel, rather than from economic globalization and neoliberal markets—though as with globalization in general, for a time all of the drivers in higher education seemed to coincide, albeit on specifically Anglo-American terms. While the default position in universities everywhere was the need to respond to global changes, one school of thought reasserted "internationalization," grounded in cooperation within a multilateral order, foreign aid and cultural relations, in opposition to the business approach to cross-border education and the advocacy of neoliberal economic globalization (Knight & de Wit, 1995).

The 1990s in higher education were also associated with continuous processes of corporate and quasi-market reform, beginning in the neoliberal Anglo-American countries at the end of the 1980s and spreading across the world into the 2000s. These reforms, which were nuanced by country with varying mixes of changes in governance and economics, were orchestrated by national governments. In this there was no apparent reduction in the policy potency of governments, though their roles were changing. Marketization enabled states to devolve part of the responsibility for funding and outcomes downward. They used the game settings of more competitive systems (Marginson & Considine, 2000) to determine the nature, outcomes, and cost of the work less through direct administrative fiat and more through programmed self-regulation, "governmentality" (Burchell et al., 1991) and "responsibilization" (Rose, 1999) in Foucault's sense. The discourse of neoliberal globalization became blended with discourses about university marketization (Olsson & Peters, 2005), for example in the commercial market in international education where it was practiced, and the positioning of institutional science as the platform for industrial innovation. Nevertheless, even in the case of the global student market which brought to practitioner universities corporate freedom and revenue, the activity in higher education was platformed and regulated by the Anglo nation states. For neoliberal governments, higher education was a new way to generate revenue from the export of services, but science policy as such continued to be nationally driven and funded.

In higher education studies, the "glonacal" paper by Marginson and Rhoades (2002) criticized the claims in social theory, popular discussion, and higher education itself that a global/local dialectic was displacing the role of the nation state. The paper was grounded in observation of the multiscalar strategies pursued by university executives. Marginson and Rhoades argued that, on one hand, the global scale had become more significant in higher education and research; while, on the other hand, increased global integration and activity did not necessarily constitute a decline in the role of national government. Higher education was irreducibly global, national, and local at the same time, and agency was exercised in each scale. Scales were not mutually exclusive, and relations between scales were an open question. It was important to understand what was happening in each scale, the potential of simultaneous multiple actions in different scales, and the strategic intersections between scales. For example, when governments applied funding parcels to develop new world-class universities (Salmi, 2009) as science powerhouses, this combined national and local-institutional agency in fostering agency and activity at the global scale, in the process transforming local-institutional agency into also becoming global-institutional agency.

The glonacal argument also left open the possibility that spatiality in higher education and elsewhere was heterogeneous—that the scales were not ascending structural replicas of each other in the manner of scale invariance, but were diverse and fundamentally different, heterogeneous, in their materiality, agency, and relations. Further, rather than higher education being holistically globalized, different aspects or subsectors, not to mention different institutions or localities, could be variously implicated in scales. Friedman's (2018) study of elite universities in the United States and United Kingdom finds that despite the stated commitment of university leaders to their global mission, "everyday nationalism" was often more fundamental in determining their actions. Likewise, international student mobility constitutes a large part of the student body in many Western universities without substantially changing the curriculum (Marginson et al., 2010). However, science is different from higher education in this regard. Global networking in science is often primary in the formation of knowledge, and in all countries, even the United States, the bulk of published knowledge originates from elsewhere. The national and global scales are more equally weighted in science than in education, where mission, students, curriculum, and pedagogy are primarily shaped by national-local factors. Further, where global influences have the most weight in universities, for example in the normative power of global rankings and in the role of research performativity in mediating university prestige, there global science is integral.

Unevenness and Sectorality: Post-1990s Globalization

Two decades after the highpoint of Anglo-American globalization, it is instructive to compare the 1990s/2000s forecasts to the outcomes, in general and in higher education and science.

There has been no fundamental destabilization of the nation state form. The contrary is the case. Supported by a modernization of government partly stimulated by global integration, in East Asia and parts of Southeast Asia, South Asia, Africa, the Middle East, and Latin America, nation-building has proceeded at a faster pace than prior to 1990, facilitating and fostering both the spread of high-participation higher education systems (Cantwell et al., 2018) and national science systems (Marginson, 2020). The uplift of states has not happened everywhere. However, it has been sufficiently broad and grounded to lay to rest both the claims of world system theorists that the "periphery" is trapped in permanent dependency in a Euro-American world and cannot lift itself (Smith, 1979; Wallerstein, 1974), and the globalist assumptions that modernization is secured by global networks, markets, or "world society" operating independently of states. The conflictual geopolitics after 9/11 in 2001, the stabilization of economies after the 2008–2010 shock, and the diverse governance of the 2020–2021 pandemic all indicate the continuing central role of nation states in human affairs. This does not mean that 1990s globalization has been unilaterally reversed. The outcome has been mixed and complex, uneven by social sector, demonstrating that spatial transformations are not necessarily universalizing. The apparent simultaneity of sectoral tendencies in the 1990s, as with the coupling of globalization with Anglo-American neoliberalism which for a time seemed to provide a unifying framework for the emerging spatiality, has proven to be episodic rather than permanent.

Comparing globalization in five domains demonstrates that the process has been partial and uneven. First, the communicative network has continued to expand outward: By 2018, 50.76% of the world's population accessed the Internet in some way (World Bank, 2021). Second, and associated with this, the process of cultural convergence has continued. This does not mean that a single world culture has formed, and the global communicative space is unstable: The rise of China suggests that Sinic-specific cultures will be more strongly asserted in the future (Jacques, 2012); and the fractured US–China relations after 2016 foreshadow a world of technological conflict and possibly the evolution of a bipolar communications system (Inkster, 2020), with potential for cultural deconvergence.

Already, third, Anglo-American globalization in political economy and political culture has given way to a more multipolar order. It is now clear that there are several civilizational blocs in which agents see the world in distinctive ways (Macaes, 2018). Each bloc is too large and robust to be reduced wholly to domination by another: the United States, still the strongest, Western Europe, China, Japan, and Russia; and emerging India, Iran, Brazil, and Latin America, and perhaps Indonesia. With the rise of East Asia, and nation-building and development in Southeast Asia, Africa, and Latin America, "East–South" relations are now as important as "North–South" relations. In volume terms the China-India nexus in trade will become the world's largest in the future (Pieterse, 2018). The combination of intensified global convergence and more empowered difference is creating a new kind of world. "Due to the onset of global interdependence," the present period is "the first time that such a diverse set of orders intensely and continuously interact with each other" (Macaes, 2018, p. 2).

Fourth, consistent with partial decline in the neoimperial Anglo-American hegemony, and in contrast with the continuing spread of global communications, there has been a slowing and possibly a reversal in the 1990s formation of world economic markets. In the decade after the 2008 recession, multinational profits declined by 25%, partly because of competition from modernized local firms; the share of exports accounted for by cross-border supply chains stopped growing, and foreign direct investment declined sharply (*The Economist*, 2017). There were few efficiency gains from the further lowering of trade barriers, the number of losers generated by trade liberalization, like American workers displaced by offshoring, grew (Rodrik, 2018, pp. 5–7, 27), and after 2015, in association with fractious politics between the major blocs, competitive protectionism returned.

Fifth, however, the global trajectory of higher education, and more so that of science, has more closely resembled that of global communications than that of global economics. When economic globalization faltered after 2008, the globalization of higher education and science continued. There have been low barriers to the mobility of ideas and data, and, prior to the 2020 pandemic, to faculty and student travel across borders. Opportunities to work and study in other countries are uneven by country and subject to periodic tensions in which the regulative potentials of the nation state are reasserted. For example, the United States has been notable in providing a relatively open door to foreign scientists, and as the largest science system in the wealthiest economy has been a magnet for talent. But between 2017 and 2021, the nation imposed bans affecting travel from some Middle Eastern countries (Chinchilla-Rodriguez et al., 2018), and from 2018 it began to "decouple" its scientific connections with China (Sharma, 2020), inhibiting the mobility of students and researchers (Lee & Haupt, 2020). Nevertheless, until the 2020 onslaught of the COVID-19 pandemic, aggregated global student mobility rose each year, from 1.95 million in 1998 to 5.57 million in 2018, an annual increase of 5.39% (UNESCO, 2021), much faster than the annual growth of 3.58% in combined world GDP PPP (World Bank, 2021).

This decoupling of sector trajectories—the continuing globalization of higher education and research while the economy became more nation-bound—suggests that the dynamics of global integration and convergence in universities and science are more cultural than economic, and lays to rest the lingering idea that the economy drives everything else. It also highlights the paradoxical importance of national political economy, which houses and resources scientific institutions and personnel, in sustaining global scientific activity that ranges beyond the writ of the nation state itself. Universities are central players in science, especially the basic science that constitutes new knowledge. Almost nine published papers in ten have at least one university author (Powell et al., 2017, pp. 2, 8–9). Yet universities, especially the public or national universities that dominate research in most countries, are not created from above by global science. They have local histories and in the modern era they are emphatically platformed by nation states. Though the national economy is not the engine of science in terms of its cognitive evolution, the nation provides conditions for science. Most importantly, it is the main provider of the cash flows that are the indispensable fuel of science. Global science and nation states are necessary for the output of science in particular locations, while neither on its own is sufficient. The ongoing conjunction between (a) cultural and interagential globality and (b) national political economic conditions, a conjunction that varies from nation to nation, and can be partly (though only partly) steered at a national level, is central in the evolution of science.

As will be discussed next, there has been a remarkable growth of the networked global system of science, which did not really exist prior to 1990. Yet no withdrawal of the nation state is evident, from either science or the universities housing science, and the aggregated national investment in university science has grown as a proportion of GDP in most nations (OECD, 2021). "The growth of the global network in science does not mean we are witnessing the death of the nation-state or even a reduction in its influence in scientific investments," as Leydesdorff and Wagner remark (2008, p. 324). Nationally coauthored papers have expanded mightily alongside internationally coauthored papers (NSB, 2020). The worldwide network of scientists has emerged alongside national science systems, separate from them and overlapping with them. These developments negate the idea of globalization as zero-sum with nation states and suggest the need to inquire more closely into the ongoing relations between global and national science (Marginson, 2021).

GLOBAL RESEARCH AND SCIENCE

In the last three decades, global science—that is, the published science included in the main bibliometric collections, Web of Science (WoS) and Scopus—has been extraordinarily dynamic. This definition of science excludes all gray literature in the form of reports, working papers, and non-peer-reviewed materials; nearly all work in languages other than English; diverse work in national and local social sciences; nearly all works in the humanities and the arts; and all endogenous knowledges (Marginson & Xu, 2021). Despite these exclusions, codified global science has grown at scale. Journal papers and other publications in Scopus rose from less than one million in 1996 to over two and a half million in 2018. Between 2000 and 2018 papers grew by 5% per year while world GDP grew by 3.5% per year. Scientific output grew in almost every country, especially emerging nations like China, India, Brazil, and Iran. There has also been a great growth of internationally collaborative projects, fruits of the expansion of networks and indicating a tendency to the globalization (integration) of knowledge at the world level. Between 1996 and 2018, the proportion of papers coauthored in more than one research organization, mostly universities, grew from 47.4% to 77.5%. Papers with national collaborations rose from 35.1% to 44. 4%, and internationally coauthored papers rose from 12.4% to 22.5% (NSB, 2020, S5A-32). The last proportion compares with just 1.9% of articles in Web of Science (WoS) in 1970 (Olechnicka et al., 2019, p. 78), indicating the extent of scientific globalization. The international share of papers rose markedly in most, though not all, science countries, and all leading science universities. The international share of citations also jumped, again indicating the tendency to the globalization of knowledge in the science-based disciplines (Leiden University, 2020; NSB 2020, Table S5A-32).

The growth in volume and networked activity has been attended by the spread of scientific capacity across the world, and signs of an emerging multipolarity in relations of power in science, paralleling the similar pattern in the political economy. Science is no longer confined as it was before 1980 to Europe, North America, the European settler states, Japan, and Russia. The group of science-producing countries has become much larger and more diverse. In the 30 years after 1987, the number of countries with 90% of bibliometric output rose from 20 to 32. Twice this number had an endogenous science system in which some doctoral researchers were homegrown. Half of the countries showing an especially rapid growth in papers, above the world annual rate, were countries with national per capita incomes below the world average. Viable national science systems have spread from the wealthy countries to many middle-income countries and some poorer countries. China and India are now first and third in the world in the volume of science papers produced, and China is rapidly increasing its high-citation papers, especially in the physical sciences, engineering, and related disciplines such as computing and mathematics (Grossetti, 2013, p. 2225; NSB, 2020, Table S5A-2; World Bank, 2021). The advent of a large, robust, rapidly expanding global science system is a development of the greatest historical importance, foreshadowing other potential human association on the global plane.

"Scientific knowledge is produced in almost every country across the globe. Scientists are organised in global epistemic communities that codify their knowledge in peer-reviewed articles published in specialist international journals" (Wuestman et al., 2019, p. 1772). The core components of the global science system are fourfold: (1) codified scientific knowledge, (2) scientists who communicate and collaborate with each other, (3) the processes of networked communications and publications, and (4) the conventions and protocols regulating the work. Global science is constituted by self-regulation—by the norms, rules, languages, conventions, protocols, behavioral codes, and standard operating procedures that govern collaborative work, production, recognition, and publication and are necessary to scientific activity and the institutions in which it is housed (King, 2011). The norms and protocols of self-regulation extend beyond data handling, peer review, and author attribution to include the use of English as the sole language of global science. While most of these norms and protocols can be traced to origins in specific national systems, especially science in the United States and the United Kingdom, they have become widely adopted in global science despite, or because of, their national-cultural specificity. However, these norms and protocols are not enforced directly by neoimperial political dominance but by scientists themselves, concentrated in hegemonic Euro-American universities.

Global and National Science

At the same time, the core components of global science, scientists engaged in networked cognitive labor on a worldwide basis who share the results of their work in papers, are possible only under specific outer conditions, including funding, organizations, governance, and rules. These conditions are largely constituted nationally and in local institutions, rather than, like networked communications, on a global basis. Partly for that reason the outer conditions, and the associated incentives, effects, and distributions, absorb most attention when science is discussed: Policy and politics are largely national rather than global in scale. In the national scale, the systems of governance, policy, regulation, and management not only enable but sometimes impede science, including global science. State agencies—and, to an extent, universities—have formal power to order resource configurations and events.

As indicated, funding power is crucial, both in absolute terms and when decision-makers prioritize specific fields; and states also regulate cross-border people mobility in science. Some states, notably China, also influence information flow by controlling the Internet. Further, national and institutional policies, rules, and performance management can speed or retard cross-border association and scientific output. On the whole, states have encouraged the growth of global science, though this is not guaranteed.

Science is most usefully understood as a combination of the global system, with the respective national systems. Table 34.1 summarizes the distinctions by type of system. The crucial points about the relation between global and national science are that global science is a distinctive system in its own right, which can be distinguished from national science systems—or more precisely, global-local science has different and specific dynamics in relation to national-local science—and that global science is both separate from national science and interactive with it. The global scale in social life is distinctive and has causal potential. Unless these factors are acknowledged, the dynamics of scientific knowledge are inexplicable.

While the dominant strand of scientometrics models global science as an outcome of national science and readily breaks it down quantitatively into constituent national systems, as if global relationships can be arbitrarily assigned in pieces between zero-sum national categories, other work focuses on primarily on cross-border dynamics in science (Marginson, 2021). Leydesdorff and Wagner (2008) and Wagner et al. (2015) identify the global system both empirically and theoretically. Leydesdorff and Wagner (2008) state that "international collaboration in science can be considered as a communications network that is different from national systems and has its own internal dynamics" (p. 317). They emphasize the dynamic growth of global science, and the autonomy and openness of the network, the way in which it is open to new national systems and research groups, and does not always reflect the configuration of geopolitical power (Wagner et al., 2015). "The global network has a culture, pathways, and norms of communication specific to its structure, and diverging from national, regional, or disciplinary norms" (Wagner et al., 2017, p. 1646). The fastest growing networked relations in global science are those between scientists in different emerging systems, which are not necessarily mediated by the leading players (Choi, 2012). Global science is an emergent self-forming and self-regulating organization created through the structures, processes, and contents of scientific collaboration, rather than through conscious design.

Table 34.1 Global Science System and National Science System in Basic Science

	Global Science System	National Science System
Core components	Knowledge, people, networked communications, norms, and practices	Nation state ordered and resourced institutional structure of science activity
Enabling conditions	Resources, institutions, and (often national) agencies/policies/rules	Political and economic stability and policy commitment to science activity
Main functions	Production and circulation of new knowledge via networked activity	Legal, political, financial conditions of science. Some knowledge, applications
Boundary	World society	Nation state
Normative center	No normative center	Nation state
Knowledge contents	Papers published in journals admitted by WoS and Scopus	Most contents of global journals plus further nationally circulated materials
Social relational contents	Collegial groups of scientists operating in networks	Government agencies, research organizations, networked scientists
Collective loyalty	Diffuse: disciplinary community as persons and as shared knowledge	Concentrated: national and institutional authorities
Incentives	Cognitive discovery and accumulation, individual status	Applications of science; revenues; individual cognitive, career and status
Regulation	Local self-regulation on the basis of global collegial scientific norms	National law, official regulation, policy, financing systems, cultural norms
Resourcing	Mostly from national systems. Limited international sources	Primarily national government. Other public and private sources
How this system affects the other system	Knowledge potential of global science stimulates state funding	National resources, institutions and personnel underpin global science

The relation between national and global science is symbiotic. While national science platforms and resources global science, global science in turn provides motivation and momentum for the accelerated development of national science, by constituting a common pool of knowledge from which ongoing technological innovations are sourced. Nations secure benefits not by cornering and monopolizing a segment of global science but by sourcing the shared global resource, in the manner of the medieval commons. All nations need to access that emerging global science. Despite the fact that not all the science discoveries directly benefit the economy of the nation in which they occur, it seems that states are impelled to continually improve scientific infrastructure and invest in projects (*The Economist*, 2021). For governments, national scientific capacity is an end in itself, a means of managing uncertainty and perhaps, they hope, of controlling the future.

Importantly, however, the two systems of science are not identical, and there is a fault line between them. The global system has no normative center. In that respect it is very different from national science systems that are normed and ordered by nation states. Hence, the global-national synergy is not always-already automatic. It cannot be taken for granted and requires conscious effort. Globally inclined scientists must work their way through and around national structures and cultures in order to do the work they want to do; and national policymakers try, partly successfully, to direct or at least to influence the work of global scientists according to nationally determined criteria, like herding cats.

Under some circumstances, there is global/national conflict. Lee and Haupt (2020) review the then emerging US-China conflict in science and technology, finding that this had a normative form in competing notions of science. They describe an opposition between "scientific globalism," grounded in a prima facie commitment to cross-border scientific collaboration as a global common good, and "scientific nationalism," or "technological nationalism," grounded in the belief that "nation states support, and seek to control, science and technology not to spur innovation for economic and social benefit itself, but for the state to harness the power of science to national advantage . . . in order to become relatively more powerful than rival nations" (Cantwell, 2021, p. 104). Scientific globalism and scientific nationalism are incompatible and have very different implications for national policy. Arguably, multiscalar science is associated with both sets of practices and effects (King, 2011). The many-sided efforts of US authorities in 2018–2021 to decouple US and Chinese science—shortening or cancelling the visas of Chinese researchers and students, discouraging collaborative schemes, blocking joint appointments, collecting intelligence on students who are in the Communist Party of China, energizing think tank reports on Confucius Institutes and planting the media stories, stigmatizing scientists with plural associations in Chinese and US systems, strenuously implicating Chinese science in a discourse about human rights in Xinjiang and selling that to embassies across the world—show that strong nations can weaken global connections in science and diminish the potentials of combined discovery.

In this way the relation between global and national scales in science can be rendered more or less zero-sum, though with difficulty. Sustaining the "imagined community" of the nation (Anderson, 2006) by dividing what has been mutually generated is herculean work. However, for most of the time, states assert their role not by seeking to control (and, if necessary, prohibit) global linkages and flows but by using their funding power to connect to the global pool of knowledge and to channel the activity of national scientists within it. While this entails a lesser level of direct control, when compared with the administered national science systems prior to 1990, the global pool is a gift that cannot be refused.

Will this largely constructive division of labor between global and national science persist? Relations in global science can be modified by national government direction of scientists, even though governments are scarcely able to substitute for cognitive judgment. It is conceivable that the US-China imbroglio may lead to a part-fracturing of the global science network, the excision of strategically sensitive domains of knowledge from global sharing, even a weakening of cross-border disciplinary community as the mode of cognitive organization. However, the early signs are that US-China scientific cooperation will prove more robust than some in the US government might want. In the first year of the COVID-19 pandemic in 2020, there was impressive collaboration in biomedicine (Lee & Haupt, 2021). This is not to say that the evolution of national policy and funding is irrelevant to the global system. Major changes, such as Brexit, the cessation of UK membership of the European Union at the end of 2020, affect patterns of partnership and output. The United Kingdom may again become a party to Horizon Europe, the European Union's main granting program, but as a non-member country unable to secure full funding on the basis of merit, and this is likely to result in an overall reduction in the number of joint projects and publications within Europe. UK science is strongly networked in global science, and it is likely that in the longer term its researchers will conduct more partnerships in the Anglosphere, and East Asia, than would have been the case if it had stayed in Europe. The UK national science system may see a reduction in the flow of incoming talent, which had been facilitated by European Union free movement. However, if mobile science talent flows to the national systems of Germany, the United States, or Italy rather than the United Kingdom, this is unlikely to modify the overall growth trajectory of global science.

Concluding Thoughts: Scale in Higher Education and Science

The history of globalization since 1990 shows that for the most part it has evolved not as a subtraction from the role of nation states, but as a change to that role, and sometimes an augmentation of it. The 1990s theorists who predicted the decline of the nation state, as if the existential framework was one of zero-sum trade-off, global versus national, turned out to be grossly incorrect. Science is a good example of this. In science the nation state is always centrally involved, for example in funding and regulation, and it never ceases in the attempt to leverage autonomous global science to its advantage. The evolution of the global science system provides national science systems with a larger pool of cognitive resources and a strong motivation to build their own national capacity in order to engage successfully. At the same time, it is possible that in the future, particular states may attempt to control science to the point of disrupting the autonomous global network. The developing US–China tensions, which are partly manifest in technology policy, will test this possibility.

The global dimension and its formation through globalization have three primary spatialities (Conrad, 2016; Held et al., 1999; Marginson, 2011). First, interdependent systems at the world level, such as climate in the natural world, or the integrated communications networks, or the global science system, that condition the actions of national and local agents. Second, there are cross-border connections and relations, for example in trade, and people mobility in the form of migration, whether permanent or temporary, for example for the purposes of education for periods of a year or more, or for purposes of scientific collaboration. Unlike global systems, global connections do not trigger an initial change in national structures, but when they are "regular and sustained," they can be "embedded in processes of structural transformation" (Conrad, 2016, p. 64) and "shape societies in profound ways" (p. 9). Held et al. (1999) refer to this as "institutionalization," meaning the "regularisation of patterns of interaction and consequently, their reproduction across space and time" (p. 19). Cross-border connections can have locally confined impacts, and they may leave some places untouched, but as the world becomes increasingly integrated, the transformative potential of regular global connections is advanced, affecting people not directly engaged in cross-border activities. In higher education and science, there is a difference between inter-national relations, dealings across borders that leave the character of nationally based science unchanged, and global relations which are ontologically distinct from nations and have the potential to change practices at the national and local levels. Third, there is the worldwide diffusion of ideas, models, and behaviors, which is again transformative at scales below that of the global and may lead to a growing synchrony of events and sensibilities, and paralleling developments, in different parts of the world. One example in higher education and science is the worldwide spread of the comprehensive research-intensive university form, which began in 19th-century Germany before becoming adapted in the United States as the large comprehensive "multiversity" (Kerr, 2001) and then spreading across the world in the 20th century and into the 21st.

It is immediately apparent that higher education and science are implicated in all three modes of globalization. Publication constitutes a worldwide system of codified knowledge in English, and there are many international organizations servicing universities and science. There is much cross-border data transfer and people mobility. Scientific knowledge and higher education practices are highly visible and subject to rapid and dynamic diffusion; and the process of diffusion in turn provides favorable conditions for the growth of global system such as science, and regulatory global comparisons such as university rankings (Hazelkorn, 2015). However, it is vital to recognize the global scale is not simply an extension of the national scale, or a replication of it, as if all scale—local, regional, national, meta-national, regional, and global—is "scale-invariant," and the global is patterned in a replica of the lower planes, like ferns or florets (Katz & Ronda-Pupo, 2019); or the national is simply inserted in a determining global, and the local is inserted in a determining national, in the deductive sequence of the *matryoshka*, the Russian dolls. As the comparison of global science and national science shows, scales are different in kind, heterogeneous, and their fecund intersections are by no means automatic or free of tension. In higher education and science, lines of determination are changing, eclectic, and flowing between all scales, bottom up as well as top down. No single scale is ultimately causal in one or every context.

Scales are part of the conditions of the world, and they are also choices that human agents make. Herod (2008) remarks that in the study of human geography "scale" is seen in two ways: as a material domain or as a mode of perception and understanding. Arguably, scale in both of these respects can be causal. Perspectives governed by scale have material consequences, conditioning the imaginings that are possible, and the actions necessary or desired. "By changing the unit of analysis of operation at the reflexive level one obtains a different perspective on the system under study" (Etzkowitz & Leydesdorff, 2000, p. 114). Conrad (2016) makes a similar point: "The choice of scale always has normative implications" (p. 156).

Different understandings of scale expand the mind or diminish what can be seen and imagined. The enemy of understanding is single-scalar essentialism. The normative globalism of the 1990s was premised on the assumption that the national scale and its causal weight were shrinking—an assumption with had little empirical basis. This is "methodological globalism." The more prevalent limitation in the study of higher education and science, and many other social phenomena, is that the national scale is rendered so powerful in governing thought that it is hard to see a separated global scale at all. "'Methodological nationalism' is grounded in the belief that the nation/state/society is the natural social and political form of the modern world" (Beck, 2005, pp. 43–50; Shahjahan & Kezar, 2013; Wimmer & Schiller, 2002, p. 301). Through the methodological nationalist lens, global phenomena can be only understood as functions of the nation and observed within the national scale. Associated with methodological nationalism is what Conrad (2016) calls the "internalist" fallacy, in which national societies are seen to entirely determine their own affairs, generating "explanations that slight or even completely disregard external influences and factors" (p. 88), such as cross-border connections, and world-level science systems. Such explanations are common. Not all social science understands that the reality that it confronts draws from and reifies in turn is multiple in form.

How then to reconcile the perspectives that multiple scales can offer? Sen (1999) emphasizes the irreducible multiplicity of phenomena. Higher education can be understood from different disciplinary perspectives, different national-cultural viewpoints, and also in terms of different scales. Sen (2002) has developed a "trans-positional" method of integrating the perspectives obtained from different perspectives (Sen, 2002, p. 467), thereby bringing additional phenomena into view and broadening understanding of the relational terrain. Though transpositionality is never a comprehensive or final process, each extension of vision, and each act of reconciliation, constitutes a methodological gain.

References

Anderson, B. (2006). *Imagined communities: Reflections on the origins and spread of nationalism* (Rev. ed.). Verso.

Appadurai, A. (1996). *Modernity at large: Cultural dimensions of globalization.* University of Minnesota Press.

ARWU (Academic Ranking of World Universities). (2021). http://www.shanghairanking.com/index.html

Bayly, C. (2004). *The birth of the modern World 1780–1914: Global connections and comparisons.* Blackwell.

Beck, U. (2005). *Power in the Global Age: A new global political economy* (K. Cross, Trans.). Polity.

Burchell, G., Gordon, C., & Miller, P. (Eds.) (1991). *The Foucault effect: Studies in governmentality.* University of Chicago Press.

Cantwell, B. (2021). Concepts for understanding the geopolitics of graduate student and postdoc mobility. In J. Lee (Ed.), *US power in international higher education* (pp. 94–112). Rutgers University Press.

Cantwell, B., Marginson, S., & Smolentseva, A. (2018). *High participation systems of higher education.* Oxford University Press.

Chinchilla-Rodríguez, Z., Bu, Y., Robinson-García, N., Costas, R., & Sugimoto, C. (2018). Travel bans and scientific mobility: Utility of asymmetry and affinity Indexes to inform science policy. *Scientometrics, 116*(1), 569–590. https://doi.org/10.1007/s11192-018-2738-2

Choi, S. (2012). Core-periphery, new clusters, or rising stars?: International scientific collaboration among "advanced" countries in the era of globalization. *Scientometrics, 90*(1), 25–41. https://doi.org/10.1007/s11192-011-0509-4

Conrad, S. (2016). *What is global history?* Princeton University Press.

Drori, G., Meyer, J., & Hwang, H. (Eds.) (2006). *Globalization and organization: World society and organizational change.* Oxford University Press.

The Economist. (2017, January 28). The retreat of the global company.

The Economist. (2021, January 16). The case for more state spending on R&D.

Etzkowitz, H., & Leydesdorff, L. (2000). The dynamics of innovation: From national systems and 'Mode 2' to a triple helix of university-industry-government relations. *Research Policy, 29*(2), 109–123. https://doi.org/10.1016/S0048-7333(99)00055-4

Friedman, J. (2018). Everyday nationalism and elite research universities in the USA and England. *Higher Education, 76,* 247–261.

Grossetti, M., Eckert, D., Gingras, Y., Jégou, L., Larivière, V., & Milard. B. (2013). Cities and the geographical deconcentration of scientific activity: A multilevel analysis of publications (1987–2007). *Urban Studies, 51*(10), 2219–2234. https://doi.org/10.1177/0042098013506047

Hazelkorn, E. (2015). *Rankings and the reshaping of higher education: The battle for world-class excellence* (2nd ed.). Palgrave.

Held, D., McLew, A., Goldblatt, D., & Perraton, J. (1999), *Global transformations: Politics, economics and culture.* Stanford University Press.

Herod, A. (2008). Scale: The local and the global. In S. Holloway, S. Rice, G. Valentine, & N. Clifford (Eds.), *Key concepts in geography* (2nd ed., pp. 217–235). Sage.

Inkster, N. (2020). *The great decoupling: China, America and the struggle for technological supremacy.* Hurst and Company.

Jacques, M. (2012). *When China rules the world: The end of the Western world and the birth of a new global order.* Penguin.

Katz, J., & Ronda-Pupo, G. (2019). Cooperation, scale-invariance and complex innovation systems: A generalization. *Scientometrics, 121*(2), 1045–1065. https://doi.org/10.1007/s11192-019-03215-8

Kerr, C. (2001). *The uses of the university* (5th ed.). Harvard University Press.

King, R. (2011). Power and networks in worldwide knowledge coordination: The case of global science. *Higher Education Policy*, 24(3), 359–376. https://doi.org/10.1057/hep.2011.9

Knight, J., & de Wit, H. (1995). Strategies for internationalisation of higher education: Historical and conceptual perspectives. In EAIE (European Association for International Education), *Strategies for internationalisation of higher education: A comparative study of Australia, Canada, Europe and the United States of America* (pp. 5–32). EAIE.

Lee, J., & Haupt, J. (2020). Winners and losers in US-China scientific research collaborations. *Higher Education*, 80(1), 57–74. https://doi.org/10.1007/s10734-019-00464-7

Lee, J., & Haupt, J. (2021). Scientific collaboration on COVID-19 amidst geopolitical tensions between the US and China. *Journal of Higher Education*, 92(2), 303–329. https://doi.org/10.1080/00221546.2020.1827924

Leiden University. (2020). *CWTS Leiden ranking*. https://www.leidenranking.com/ranking/2020/list

Leydesdorff, L., & Wagner, C. (2008). International collaboration in science and the formation of a core group. *Journal of Informetrics*, 2(4), 317–325. https://doi.org/10.1016/j.joi.2008.07.003

Macaes, B. (2018). *The dawn of Eurasia: On the trail of the new world order*. Penguin.

Marginson, S. (2011). Imagining the global. In R. King, S. Marginson, & R. Naidoo (Eds.), *Handbook of higher education and globalization* (pp. 10–39). Edward Elgar.

Marginson, S. (2020). Public and common goods: Key concepts in mapping the contributions of higher education. In C. Callender, W. Locke, & S. Marginson (Eds.), *Changing higher education for a changing world* (pp. 249–264). Bloomsbury.

Marginson, S. (2021). Heterogeneous systems and common objects: The relation between global and national science. Centre for Global Higher Education Special Report, April. ESRC/OFSRE Centre for Global Higher Education.

Marginson, S., & Considine, M. (2000). *The enterprise university: Power, governance and reinvention in Australia*. Cambridge University Press.

Marginson, S., Nyland, C., Sawir, E., & Forbes-Mewett, H. (2010). *International student security*. Cambridge University Press.

Marginson, S., & Rhoades, G. (2002). Beyond national states, markets, and systems of higher education: A glonacal agency heuristic. *Higher Education*, 43(3), 281–309.

Marginson, S., & Xu, X. (2021). Moving beyond centre-periphery in science: Towards an ecology of knowledge. *CGHE Working Paper* 63. ESRC/OFSRE Centre for Global Higher Education. https://www.researchcghe.org/perch/resources/publications/working-paper-63.pdf

NSB (National Science Board). (2020). *Science and engineering indicators*. https://ncses.nsf.gov/pubs/nsb20201

OECD (Organization for Economic Cooperation and Development) (2021). *Main science and technology indicators*. https://stats.oecd.org/Index.aspx?DataSetCode=MSTI_PUB

Olechnicka, A., Ploszaj, A., & Celinska-Janowicz, D. (2019). *The geography of scientific collaboration*. Routledge.

Olssen, M., & Peters, M. (2005). Neoliberalism, higher education and the knowledge economy: From the free market to knowledge capitalism. *Journal of Education Policy*, 20(3), 313–345. https://doi.org/10.1080/02680930500108718

Pieterse, J. (2018). *Multipolar globalization: Emerging economies and development*. Routledge.

Powell, J. W., Baker, D. P., & Fernandez, F. (Eds.) (2017). *The century of science: The global triumph of the research university*. Vol. 33. International Perspectives on Education and Society. Emerald. https://doi.org/10.1108/S1479-3679201733

Rodrik, D. (2018). Populism and the economics of globalization. *Journal of International Business Policy*. https://drodrik.scholar.harvard.edu/files/dani-rodrik/files/populism_and_the_economics_of_globalization.pdf

Rose, N. (1999). *Powers of freedom: Reframing political thought*. Cambridge University Press.

Salmi, J. (2009). *The challenge of establishing world-class universities*. World Bank. https://openknowledge.worldbank.org/bitstream/handle/10986/2600/476100PUB0Univ101Officialo Use0Only1.pdf?sequence=1&isAllowed=y

Sassen, S. (Ed.) (2002). *Global networks, linked cities*. Routledge.

Sen, A. (1999). Global justice: Beyond international equity. In I. Kaul, I. Grunberg, & M. Stern (Eds.), *Global public goods: International cooperation in the 21st century* (pp. 116–125). Oxford University Press.

Sen, A. (2002). *Rationality and freedom*. Harvard University Press.

Shahjahan, R., & Kezar, A. (2013). Beyond the "national container": Addressing methodological nationalism in higher education research. *Educational Researcher*, *42*(1), 20–29. https://doi.org/10.3102/0013189X12463050

Sharma, Y. (2020, December 12). US targets Chine talent in drive to "decouple" science. *University World News*.

Smith, T. (1979). The underdevelopment of development literature: The case of dependency theory. *World Politics*, *31*(2), 247–288.

UNESCO (United Nations Educational, Social and Cultural Organization). (2021). Institute of Statistics. http://data.uis.unesco.org

Wagner, C., Park, L., & Leydesdorff, L. (2015). The continuing growth of global cooperation networks in research: A conundrum for national governments (W. Glanzel, Ed.). *PLOS ONE*, *10*(7), e0131816. https://doi.org/10.1371/journal.pone.0131816

Wagner, C., Whetsell, T., & Leydesdorff, L. (2017). Growth of international collaboration in science: Revisiting six specialties. *Scientometrics*, *110*(3), 1633–1652. https://doi.org/10.1007/s11192-016-2230-9

Wallerstein, I. (1974). The rise and future demise of the world capitalist system: Concepts for comparative analysis. *Comparative Studies in Society and History*, *16*(4), 387–415.

Wimmer, A., & Schiller, N. (2003). Methodological nationalism and beyond: State building, migration and the social sciences. *Global Networks*, *2*(4), 301–334.

World Bank. (2021). *Indicators*. https://data.worldbank.org/indicator

Wuestman, M., Hoekman, J., & Frenken, K. (2019). The geography of scientific citations. *Research Policy*, *48*, 1771–1780. https://doi.org/10.1016/j.respol.2019.04.004

CHAPTER 35

THE GLOBALIZATION OF SCIENCE

The Increasing Power of Individual Scientists

MAREK KWIEK

INTRODUCTION: THE EMERGENT GLOBAL SCIENCE

AT the country level, science consists of two distinctive and heterogeneous systems: the global science and national science systems (Marginson & Xu, 2021). National science systems have become embedded in global science and countries, albeit for different reasons, but mostly to increase their economic competitiveness and to do everything they can to harness global knowledge to national economic needs. However, accessing and using the riches of global knowledge can occur only through scientists. Consequently, the research power of nations, among other factors, relies on the research power of individual scientists—their capacity to collaborate internationally and to tap into the global networked science is key. Being beyond global science networks and working on purely local research agendas, the academic community risks marginalization, thereby causing a loss of the interest among their national research-subsidizing patrons as well as losing the opportunity to influence the development of science.

Global networked science can be analyzed through a variety of methodologies; however, quantitative science studies are probably best equipped to explore the extent of the globalization of science in spatial and temporal, individual and collective, national and cross-national dimensions using global publication and citation data. The global changes in how science is conducted are fundamental, and the accounts of these transformations abound (Adams, 2013; Gui et al., 2019; Wagner, 2008; Wang & Barabàsi, 2021). The general picture is well-known: for example, as Dong et al. (2017) show in their study of science in the past 100 years, the size of a publication's author list tripled and the rate of international collaborations increased 25 times; moreover, over 90% of the world-leading innovations (as measured by the top 1% most-cited papers) generated by teams in the 2000s was four times higher than that in the 1900s. The number of scholars and the number of publications grew at an exponential rate, doubling every 11 and 12 years, respectively. Finally, the share of single-authored publications shrank from 80% to 15%, with science shifting from individual work to collaborative effort.

Further, the global map of science has changed in the past 100 years, with the increasing global diversification of scientific efforts—from the absolute dominance of the northeastern United States, the United Kingdom, and Germany in the 1900s to the leadership of both US coasts and Continental Europe in the second half of the 20th century to the rapid rise of research in Asia and other continents in the 21st century (Dong et al., 2017, p. 1444). The global science system currently indicates a larger, more competitive multicentric core. In terms of social network analysis, a bipolar world of science led by Anglo-Saxon countries is gradually being replaced by a tripolar world, which includes Europe, North America, and Asia-Pacific.

Consequently, what has emerged in the past three decades is "a truly global scientific system" (Melkers & Kiopa, 2010, p. 389) or "a multipolar science world" (Veugelers, 2010) in which the scientific workforce is differently located, new trends in international collaboration have emerged, and the distribution of publication impact between traditional science powerhouses and the new entrants differs from decade to decade. Science is increasingly becoming a global system that comprises both advanced and less developed countries, with the global connectedness in science becoming important for both (Barnard et al., 2015). The depth and breadth of global science intensify, and the size of the global science network increases. The globalization of science implies a growing number of countries participating in international research collaboration and the ties between countries being much closer than before, thereby leading to decentralization (Gui et al., 2019) or pluralization (Marginson, 2018) of science. Collaboration remains dominated by science superpowers such as the United States, the United Kingdom, Germany, and several European countries, but countries where science is still emerging—such as China, followed by Brazil and South Korea—are ever more influential in the global network of science. The traditional Anglo-American academic hegemony is being challenged by new entrants (Marginson & Xu, 2021) in an increasing number of academic fields.

Collaboration processes in science occur within different geographical units and, therefore, can be classified as regionalization, nationalization, and globalization; however, publication and citation data indicate that we are moving toward "a truly interconnected global science system" (Waltman et al., 2011, p. 574) in which globalization intensifies more than the other two processes. Using distance-based measurements of globalization, Waltman et al. (2011) reveal an evolution from a loosely connected 20th-century nation state science system to a 21st-century interconnected and internationally networked global science system, characterized by increasingly large distances among research partners. Science is globalizing at a steady rate; the authors have calculated what they termed the mean geographical collaboration distance for science as a whole, showing that between 1980 and 2009, the distance increased from 334 km to 1,553 km. The increase in collaboration distances occurred at different speeds: for example, the proportion of rather long partnerships (publications with the geographical collaboration distance of more than 5,000 km) has increased almost fivefold (Waltman et al. 2011, p. 576).

The emergent picture of global science differs substantially from the traditional perspectives of how science works and which basic layers it consists of; specifically, the global networked science that challenges the traditional accounts of relationships between science and nation states (Kwiek, 2005) and welfare states (see Mattei, 2009). We have studied the changing relationships between the university and the state under globalization pressures; however, our main focus was on the impact of globalization on public sector services, welfare state architectures and funding, viewing higher education as an important claimant to public financing and analyzing higher education as directly competing with other segments of the welfare state (Kwiek, 2005, 2015) rather than on the globalization of science itself.

From a global perspective, the most important factor in the gradual development of studies on the globalization of science was probably the increasing availability of digital data on scholarly inputs and outputs—the data on research funding, productivity, and collaboration, paper citations, and academic mobility—that offer unprecedented opportunities to explore the structure and evolution of science (Fortunato et al., 2018). Without access to global data, it would have been impossible to study the global networks of scientists, institutions, and ideas, novelty in science, academic career dynamics, the role of team science, or the citation dynamics from a global perspective. The globalization of science is currently explored under different conceptual labels and research agendas: the science of science (Clauset et al., 2017; Fortunato et al., 2018; Wang & Barabàsi, 2021; Zeng et al. 2017), meta-research or research on research (Ioannidis, 2018), computational social science (Edelman et al., 2020), quantitative science studies and studies of science and technology and its indicators (Glänzel et al., 2020), and others. In the previous decade, there has been an influx of natural, computational, and social scientists who together "have developed big data-based capabilities for empirical analysis and generative modeling that capture the unfolding of science, its institutions, and its workforce" (Fortunato et al. 2018, p. 1). For example, the science of science complements contributions from related fields such as scientometrics, informetrics, economics of science, and sociology of science. Social science is believed to be entering a golden age, with a rise in interdisciplinary teams working together that are leveraging the explosive growth of available data and computational power, as part of the big data revolution (Buyalskaya et al., 2021). In other words, the globalization-driven big data revolution in science is utilized to study the globalization of science itself.

GLOBAL SCIENCE AND NATION STATES

Generally, in the past 400 years, science has been affected by two major currents: nationalization and denationalization, with the latter often referred to as "globalization"

(Crawford et al., 1993). At various levels, one or the other trend dominated in science. The primary reason why the nationalization trend is powerful despite globalizing pressures is that higher education, labor markets, science career paths, knowledge-producing institutions, and research funding are overwhelmingly national. Consequently, global science has a strong national relevance and all national science systems have at least some global relevance. There is no global science without a national funding base for research and training: Global science requires national funding to keep research infrastructure running and personnel costs covered. There are no global salaries in academic science yet (although the idea can refer to the corporate science originating from multinationals, as in the case of global pharmaceutical or computing industries and their publications). Simultaneously, as Freeman (2010, p. 393) argues, the globalization of scientific and engineering knowledge is "the most potent aspect of modern globalization."

The relationship between science and the nation state has traditionally been strong, as nation states were the main patrons and sponsors of research. However, Caroline Wagner et al. suggest that the shift in science toward the global actually challenges the relationship between science and the state (Wagner et al., 2015, pp. 11–12). Since the end of the Cold War, the relationship between science funding and national identities as embodied in nation states has shifted considerably: The growth of international collaboration is decoupling science from the goals of national science policies (Wagner et al., 2015).

Thus, the globalization of science theme captures the tension between global science and national sovereignty and can be viewed from the perspective of the sociology of science, particularly in the Mertonian tradition. Sociologists of science described four norms under which the scientific community works: universalism, disinterestedness, communalism, and organized skepticism (Merton, 1973). As portrayed in the historical sociology of science (Mallard & Paradeise, 2008), actual scientists were supposed to be intrinsically cosmopolitan figures: Mertonian norms were meant to present an accurate picture of the manner in which "science really works." Unlike politics, science was portrayed as disinterested and objective, and unlike religion, it was portrayed as skeptical. However, as the authors strongly emphasize, Robert Merton developed his ideas in the context of the Cold War in which the science practiced in the United States fundamentally differed from the science practiced in Soviet Russia and his ideas were first developed during World War II. Thus, it is worth remembering that the Mertonian tradition in the sociology of science, with its vision of ideal science and ideal scientists working in ideal meritocracy-based social environments and clear rules at the foundation of social stratification in science, is heavily embedded in a particular historical context (Kwiek, 2019a).

In Merton's somehow ideal account, science is described as a curiosity-driven and disinterested systematic investigation, and its ultimate goal is to find truth without regard to political, social, or cultural interests (Cantwell & Grimm, 2018, p. 130). However, as the economics of science indicates, scientists and universities respond to incentives and even such shop-floor level characteristics of the science system as relative salaries in the sector—or entry academic salaries compared with entry salaries of other professionals—have an impact on who does science and who does not (Stephan, 2012, p. 5). Self-selection into science determines its future, as cross-sectoral mobility is rare and undervalued in most higher education systems.

Recognition and reputation are key in science both as ends in themselves and as the means for acquiring the resources to continue doing science. Scientists are not rewarded for their efforts, like the time spent on research, but for their achievements—discoveries reported in publications, preferably with high impact in the scientific community and beyond. Stephan (2012) describes the nature of science not as a winner-take-all contest (in which there are no rewards for being second or third) but as a tournament arrangement (in which the losers obtain certain rewards as well which keeps individuals in the game of science despite not winning) (Stephan, 2012, p. 29). However, in terms of salaries, the top performers in research are clearly overrepresented among the academic top earners, at least in the 10 European systems studied (Kwiek, 2018a).

Certain analysts emphasize the critical role of the global dimension in science, while others indicate that the national dimension—under changing national politics—may fight back. From the perspective of what Cantwell and Grimm term "the geopolitics of academic science," there are two prominent lines of competition between states: the competition for internationally mobile researchers and the competition to develop the strongest research universities. The world-class university project leads to the concentration of resources in selected elite universities and within certain disciplines, thereby possibly leading to the deprivation of public funds for other universities and other disciplines and possibly leading to the bifurcation of higher education systems between a small set of world-class elite institutions and a large set of demand-absorbing rest, thereby increasing vertical stratification in higher education and academic science (Cantwell & Marginson, 2018; Marginson, 2016). Academic science is reported, on the one hand, to be a global and cooperative enterprise and, on the other hand, to be a "nationalist endeavor designed to bolster state power relative to rivals" (Cantwell & Grimm, 2018, p. 144) with emergent tensions. In their account, we may now be entering a period of "cultural-economic nationalism, coupled with a technological-information globalism," with a constant tension "to reap the gains of global technology development for national purposes" (Cantwell & Grimm, 2018, p. 145).

National geopolitics of higher education may go hand in hand with nationalism in academic science in which national interests and national purposes are of significance in the context of the arms race propelled by global university rankings. Scientific globalism has finally come to meet scientific nationalism today, but the two logics have coexisted for a long time, being rooted in the very idea of modern science—with the root metaphor of the former being the "republic of science" and for the latter being the "national innovation system." The rationale for support of science has been the addressing of grand scientific challenges and fostering international collaboration, on the one hand, and supporting global competitiveness and social and economic relevance, on the other (Sà & Sabzalieva, 2018, p. 153).

In an influential paper on the emerging global model of the research university, Mohrman et al. (2008) argued that nation states have less influence over their universities than they did in the past. Global research universities have special missions which transcend the boundaries of the nation state, educate from a global perspective, and advance the frontiers of knowledge worldwide. Their special emphasis is on international interaction among universities across national boundaries. As the authors argue, these global research universities "operate beyond the control of the nation-state, leading to new policy dilemmas for national governments" (Mohrman et al., 2008, p. 15). Under the pressures of globalization, of which the globalization of science is a part, nation states are less able than before to control their destinies—they are more dependent upon universities for their knowledge production and their human capital, including doctoral students and doctorates in strategic research fields, both of which are essential for national, economic, and social development.

Simon Marginson draws a useful distinction between "nation-centered" globalization (with an endless race between nations) and "world-system" globalization (which has a dynamic independence from nations and across all of them). The latter encourages not merely global convergence, but integration into a single system whose ultimate logic is the dissolution of the nation state. In science, the integration into a single system has already happened: Global science in practice "can no longer be wholly contained within a single country or blocked at the border. . . . States and WCUs [world-class universities] have to position themselves to advantage within these global systems that they can neither evade nor completely control" (Marginson, 2018, p. 73). World-class universities are among the most globalized social institutions today—while the national research environment and funding are of considerable significance. The tension is evident because research capacity is global but national funding for research and development (R&D) plays a key role in sustaining it. Therefore, higher education institutions, Marginson argues, are best understood as semi-dependent institutions that are irretrievably tied to the state; in contrast, world-class institutions are best understood as semi-independent institutions that are irretrievably tied to both the state and global science. Consequently, top institutions clearly have double allegiance: to nation states hosting (and still mostly funding) them and to global science with its strict rules and ranking-oriented definitions of success at institutional levels.

How Do Global Networks in Science Operate?

The development of a global science system has its own dynamics of network formation. Research and scholarly inquiry are structured by rules, conventions, and intellectual property rights as well as by publishers' business agendas, on the one hand, and collegial academic gatekeeping, on the other (Marginson, 2018). Both national and global science are structured by the university hierarchy, and the knowledge produced in universities with prestige and resources has higher visibility and status than the knowledge produced elsewhere. There are also at least three other dimensions of inequalities: by country, by language, and by disciplines (Marginson, 2018, p. 36). Consequently, while global science is produced in most institutions, countries, languages, and disciplines, its highest impact is reserved for publications originating from world-class universities that are located mostly in Anglo-Saxon countries and published in English in science, technology, engineering, mathematics, and medicine (STEMM) disciplines.

As Wagner et al. (2015) argue, "the active and robust global network is proof of its own usefulness. Researchers gain enough benefit from it that they are willing to extend the extra time and effort to maintain long-distance communications" (p. 12). The network is considered a new organization of science on the world stage: It adds to and complements national systems. The researchers examined a global network of science and have indicated that it has grown denser but not more clustered: There are a large number of additional connections, but they are "not grouping into exclusive 'cliques'" (Wagner et al., 2015, p. 1).

The networks operate by clear rules. "They grow from the bottom up rather than from the top down. Networks become complex as they grow and evolve. Their organization is driven by the forces and structures—preferential attachment and cumulative advantage, trust and social capital creation, and the incentive system that leads scientists to share data and exchange information" (Wagner, 2008, p. 105). Perhaps what is most important for the future is that policymakers across the globe must first understand the dynamics of changes in order to be able to govern national science systems; it is only then that they will be able to devise incentives for scientists and integrate them skillfully within national recognition and reward systems in science. There is a long way to go from understanding global dynamics to incentivizing individual scientists within national systems so that what they do in science reflects at least a few national science policy priorities.

The major issue is how to link academic knowledge production in one place with benefits resulting from this production to the same place as "the connection between supporting research and reaping its benefits can be quite tenuous" (Wagner, 2008, p. 107). The constantly evolving, bottom-up, autonomous, self-regulating, and self-focused nature of global science requires deep understanding and skillful support for certain directions of its development, for instance, toward more local applications, as compared to other directions. The reason for this is simple: Networks in science "cannot be controlled; they can only be guided." These networks evolve continuously according to the needs of scientists and the incentives made available to them. However, importantly, these needs and incentives most often "revolve around the desire for recognition in its broadest sense" (Wagner, 2008, p. 118). The best way to understand the dynamics of global science is to understand what drives academic scientists in their work, with the comprehension of mechanisms of academic recognition in the forefront. It is important to note that recognition in science is a rather fragile social and professional mechanism.

In this chapter, we are particularly interested in the fundamental contrast between two opposing views: global science as a largely privately governed, networked, and normatively self-regulating institution (as in King, 2011) and global science as an emergent contributor to global collective public goods (as in Marginson, 2018). There is a discernible tension between the input side, or what motivates scientists to do science, and the output side, or what the results and outcomes of doing science are. As global science is increasingly outside the gaze of governments (King, 2011, p. 359), it may be moving to a more private sphere—"one of sociability rather than sovereignty, and the one that is characterized by loose ties and curiosity-driven scientific ambitions" (King, 2011, p. 359). The primary driver of global science is individual scientists who wish to collaborate with the best of their peers (Royal Society, 2011). Collaboration in research is curiosity-driven and reflects "the ambitions of individual scientists for reputation and recognition, not least as a means of pursuing their own research agendas," and new communication technologies facilitate the growing importance of "largely private" forms of global collaboration (King, 2011, p. 360). In other words, scientists may be increasingly collaborating as they wish, if they wish, and in the areas they wish, which, at a massive scale, is new from a historical perspective.

Linking global science to national military and economic competitiveness, national economic policies, and science priorities is becoming increasingly difficult in the academic setting in which global science implies radically increasing individual freedom regarding the modalities and intensities of collaboration. The idea that science remains a powerfully state-driven and state-dependent rather than predominantly curiosity-driven and scientist-dependent is rather difficult to sustain. Global science is moving from scientific nationalism toward science as a public good, while simultaneously serving personal scientific ambitions of thousands of scientists and scholars.

In King's account (King, 2011, pp. 362–367), self-regulatory and collaborative processes of science are conceptualized as networks that are beyond the supervision of governments. Global science is a constantly emergent system in the sense that it is the outcome of the numerous interdependent, individual, and decentralized normative decisions of individual scientists and scholars. Science is comprised of "interacting individuals and networks reproducing norms and standards"; these norms are principles for what is allowed and what is not, and the rules show which directions and procedures are desirable and which are not: "scientists form a moral community with an agreed outlook as to appropriate behavior" (King, 2011, p. 365). Clearly, governing this heterogeneous community and steering its academic behaviors, including collaboration and publishing behavior, is a tricky issue; however, with a thoughtful set of incentives, it is not impossible for national governments.

What emerges through an accumulation of numerous decentralized and individual choices of scientists is convergence on the global research standards. King emphasizes that what is new in global science is that it occurs "largely behind the back of the nation-state, despite powerful political rhetoric espousing the competitive economic necessity of scientific nationalism in the knowledge economy" (King, 2011, p. 367). Understanding new dynamics in global science systems requires understanding the role of individual motivations for reputation and esteem in science: "science as a social institution always requires the energy and innovation that comes from ambitious and career-enhancing researchers" (King, 2011, p. 367).

Collaboration in science often involves costs—that is, the time and the resources required as investments. Collaboration cannot be disentangled from reward systems in science, from how they operate, and what their major incentives are. In systems with powerful incentives to collaborate, collaboration grows faster; in systems with limited incentives to collaborate, collaboration grows at a slower pace (and new EU member states in Europe are a perfect example of systems of slow growths related to limited incentives in reward systems; see the EU-15/EU-13 comparison in Kwiek, 2020). Additional collaboration in science must be reflected in either the ways in which scientific reputation can be built up or in the ways in which competitive resources for research are nationally distributed, based on competing research proposals (Engels & Ruschenburg, 2008).

Scientists—particularly those in the elite layers of affluent systems—appear to increasingly act as free agents, carefully selecting research collaborators in what Wagner terms the general shift from "national systems" to "networked science" and moving freely within a global network (Wagner, 2008, p. 25). According to Wagner, "national prestige is not the factor that motivates scientists as they work in their laboratory benches and computers. . . . within social networks, scientists seek recognition for their work and their ideas" (Wagner, 2008, p. 59). Precisely, emergent global science systems increasingly rely on King's "career-enhancing researchers" who seek recognition for what they do in science. If they cannot obtain such recognition in their national systems, they might choose to migrate to other systems or to quit academic science.

The mechanisms of "cumulative inequality" in global science imply that the rich (in terms of reputation, citations, research funds, and personnel) get richer (King, 2011, p. 368); moreover, vertical stratification of the academic profession in global science creates a divide between the "haves" and "have-nots" (Wagner, 2008, p. 1; see my monograph on inequalities and the role of social stratification in science, Kwiek, 2019a). These new inequalities are compounded by the value ascribed to knowledge produced in different countries, disciplines, and in different languages, which are reflected in dominating citation patterns.

As national ties in science weaken, the role of individual scientists and individual motivation appears to increase (Kato & Ando, 2016), and individual scientists compete intensely within an "economy of reputation," involving "battles over resources and priorities" (Whitley, 2000, p. 26). The growth of global science, among other factors, is an outcome of the rational choices of individual scientists seeking to maximize their own research output and impact (Hennemann & Liefner, 2015, p. 345). The phenomenon of preferential attachment—that is, "seeking to connect to someone already connected" (Wagner, 2018, p. 76)—guides scientists' collaboration behavior across systems and institutions. A scientist's rising reputation (and associated access to critical resources such as data, equipment, and funding) implies that "other researchers are increasingly likely to want to form a link with her" (Wagner, 2008, p. 61). Highly productive scientists attract similar individuals from elsewhere (King, 2011, p. 368) and international networks are created around these key people in global science, as they are highly attractive because they offer knowledge, resources, or both (Wagner, 2018, p. 70), while bearing in mind major gender difference: Male scientists are reported to be more internationally collaborative (and less collaborative in general) than female scientists (Kwiek & Roszka, 2020).

What Global Data Tell Us About the Globalization of Science

In this section, we briefly describe the globalization of science using selected publication, collaboration, and citation data applied to several dimensions of globalization processes. The timeframe used is 2000–2020, unless otherwise stated, and the data come from Scopus (2021) and its SciVal (2021) functionality; the 25 countries (Top 25) analyzed are the largest global knowledge producers as of 2020 (articles only) and the 25 universities are top national knowledge producers (articles only) in the top 25 countries. The data were collected in the period of March 15–17, 2021.

The Globalization of Science Versus Institutions, Sectors, and Individuals

Each scientist involved in academic knowledge production leaves traces of his/her activities in his/her printed publications; our knowledge regarding the globalization of science is generally based on numerous heterogeneous data sources (biographical, administrative, financial, publications, citations, collaboration etc.) produced at different levels (from the micro-level of individual scientists to the mezo-level of institutions to the macro-level of countries and regions) with different methodologies (from interviews to surveys to analyses of bibliometric data sets). However, the globalization of science can be traced using temporal, topical, geographical, and network analyses or traced over the years, countries, and institutions, research teams, and individual scientists, as well as academic disciplines by the expanding databases of globally indexed publications, with all commonly discussed limitations.

The traces left by scientists in the form of globally indexed publications reveal the concentration of research at all levels, from individuals to institutions to countries. Among approximately 20,000 institutions active in the world (Scopus, 2021), there is no more than 1,000 involved in competitive, global academic knowledge production. The SciVal platform of the Scopus database (SciVal, 2021) indicates that in 2015–2020, the total number of academic institutions involved in global academic publishing was not higher than 9,000 (8,633). These were accompanied by institutions from corporate (6,130), government (2,523), medical (1,859), and other (797) sectors. In the period of analysis, the largest share of global knowledge production comes from the academic sector, followed by the government and corporate sectors. The top knowledge producer in the corporate sector is IBM, with Samsung, Microsoft, GlaxoSmithKline, and AstraZeneca in the top 10; the top 50 corporate institutions involved in global academic publishing include multinationals such as Pfizer, Intel, Merck, Siemens, Novartis, Johnson & Johnson, Airbus Group, Bayer, ABB Group, and Sanofi-Aventis. In the government sector, the top producer is the Chinese Academy of Sciences, with CNRS in France, Russian Academy of Sciences, National Research Council of Italy, and National Institutes of Health in the United States in the top 10; in the medical sector, the top producer is Mayo Clinic in Rochester, Minnesota, with Dana-Farber Cancer Institute in Boston, Massachusetts, in the top 10. Overall, from a global perspective, the academic sector is the key knowledge producing sector and a key participant in the globalization of science.

If a threshold of 5,000 publications within the decade of 2010–2019 is used, then the number of all institutions above the threshold shrinks to 1,590, and these could be called world-class universities. There are 934 institutions with at least 10,000 publications, 153 with at least 50,000, and 24 with at least 100,000 publications of all types, globally. Harvard University is by far the largest global knowledge producer, with more publications than almost all countries (except for 22; for example, in Europe, Harvard has more publications than Denmark, Austria, Portugal, or Norway, as well as Mexico, Israel, or Malaysia globally).

If we examine the research-focused rankings, the Leiden ranking 2020 lists 1,176 universities with at least 800 publications in the 2015–2018 period and the ARWU World University Ranking 2020 lists 1,000 universities. Specifically, in more regional terms, 41% of universities in the top 100 of the ARWU ranking are located in the United States; 66% of universities are located in one of the following five countries: the United States, the United Kingdom, France, Switzerland, and Australia; and the upper 10 countries constitute 83% of the locations.

As globalization of research progresses, the concentration of research intensifies at the level of individual scientists and scholars with respect to both output and impact or publication and citation numbers. Four in ten of 6,167 Clarivate's highly cited researchers in 2020 originate from US universities (41.5%), seven in ten originate from the top five countries (71.8%), and 84.2% from the top ten countries. Only approximately 1% of globally publishing scientists (of approximately 15 million in the period 1996–2011) constitute the "continuously publishing core" of the academic profession, with at least a single paper published every year within the 16 years studied. However, they are responsible for 41.7% of all papers published in the same period (Ioannidis et al., 2014, p.

1). Moreover, approximately 1% of the most cited scientists in 118 scientific disciplines in 2015 received 21% of all citations, a sharp increase from 14% in 2000 (Nielsen & Andersen, 2021, p. 5). The upper 10% of scientists and scholars in terms of research productivity are responsible for approximately half of all academic knowledge production in 11 European systems across 7 major clusters of disciplines (and are often termed "research top performers") (see Kwiek, 2016, 2018b).

The Globalization of Science Versus Global Innovations

While it is useful to focus on the overall potential of a country as viewed via its total number of publications, it is more revealing to trace global transformations through high-quality publications only. Specifically, in this section, we focus on the top 1% of highly cited publications (used as a proxy of high quality, with all limitations; see Tahamtan & Bornmann, 2019) and publications published in the top 1% of highly ranked journals. We assume that the top 1% of articles in terms of impact, as indicated through the citations attracted, are global innovations—or at least innovations globally recognized by other scientists—in academic science, and the publications in the upper 1% of journals are on average at least good candidates to become global innovations in the future.

Table 35.1 presents the distribution of top publications in top knowledge-producing countries (as of 2020) in the two decades in the period 2000–2020 (country codes are provided in Table 35.4). The left panel indicates the changes in the percentages and the right panel in the numbers of publications over time. European systems—such as Switzerland, Belgium, and the Netherlands—from a global perspective, produce relatively high percentages and relatively small number of top publications. In terms of numbers, China already produces more top publications than the United States, and both are followed by the United Kingdom, Germany, Italy, and Australia. China continued to improve in terms of high-quality publications every year; in 2010, China had five times less of such publications than the United States; in 2015, it had only half of such publications compared with the United States; and in 2020, the difference increased substantially (with China overtaking the United States, with approximately 11,000 compared with approximately 8,000). All selected countries performed above expectations in their top publications, the expectation being the production of 1% of such publications; however, a few countries increased their numbers substantially: Apart from China, the highest increase in top publications in the past 5 years was noted in Italy (by 58%) in Europe as well as in Iran (by 348%) and India (by 174%) globally. Simultaneously, the number of top publications originating from the United States in 2020 and 2010 was similar, and a 17% decline was noted for the 2015–2020 period (Table 35.1, right panel); the numbers for other countries were only slightly declining or increasing.

Table 35.1 High-Impact Publications: Proportion (%) of Publications in the Top 1% of Publications by Citations

Country	Average 2000–2020	2000	2010	2015	2020	Country	Total 2000–2020	2000	2010	2015	2020
CHE	2.9	2.1	3	3.5	2.4	CHN	67,497	107	1,561	4,550	10,900
BEL	2.3	1.2	2.3	2.8	2.3	USA	167,559	5,944	8,233	9,536	8,064
AUS	2.0	1.2	1.9	2.1	2.2	GBR	48,174	1,250	2,214	3,091	3,343
NLD	2.7	1.8	2.8	3	2.2	DEU	36,889	832	1,845	2,476	2,179
GBR	2.1	1.6	2.2	2.4	2.1	ITA	19,659	327	874	1,278	2,014
ITA	1.6	0.9	1.6	1.8	2.0	AUS	20,650	291	827	1,420	1,972
SWE	2.2	1.3	2.3	2.5	2.0	CAN	24,465	551	1,193	1,547	1,668
CAN	2.0	1.6	2.1	2.2	1.9	IND	9,000	62	266	559	1,529
CHN	1.2	0.2	0.7	1.2	1.8	FRA	23,919	565	1,151	1,535	1,511
IRN	0.8	0.1	0.4	0.6	1.8	ESP	15,373	194	715	1,068	1,311
FRA	1.7	1.1	1.7	1.9	1.7	NLD	18,538	358	923	1,231	1,128
DEU	1.8	1.2	2	2.1	1.6	IRN	4,655	2	78	246	1,101
USA	2.1	2.1	2.3	2.2	1.6	KOR	10,618	82	412	762	1,070
ESP	1.4	0.8	1.4	1.6	1.5	JPN	17,669	548	761	998	1,069
TWN	0.9	0.5	0.7	1	1.4	CHE	15,148	301	681	1,105	924

Note: Output in top 1% citation percentiles by country and publication year, 2000–2020, all publication types included, all fields of research and development combined, in descending order for 2020, top 15 countries in each panel only, in percent (left panel, world average = 1) and publication number (right panel).

Publishing in top journals (Kwiek 2021) leads (on average) to higher field-normalized citation rates due to the very construction of journal percentile ranks in Scopus based on citations received in the previous 4 years. In Europe, the share of publications in high-impact journals that exceeds expectations is noted for Switzerland, the Netherlands, the United Kingdom, Belgium and Sweden, as well as for Australia, Canada, and the United States globally (all with over 4% of their publications in this category in 2020; see Table 35.2). Among East Asian countries, China, Korea, and Taiwan fare much worse. However, with regard to the number of publications in top journals, China is globally unbeatable in terms of increase in publication numbers, with 2,700 publications in 2010, 7,100 in 2015, and as many as 17,600 in 2020, which amounts to an increase of 149% in the 2015–2020 period, with very high probability of overtaking the United States in the next few years as it did in the case of high-impact publications. In certain fields of research, China in 2020 is already publishing a higher (in agricultural sciences and engineering and technologies) or equal (in natural sciences) number of articles in the top 1% of journals than the United

THE GLOBALIZATION OF SCIENCE   741

Table 35.2 Publications in High-Impact Journals, Proportion (%) of Publications in the Top 1% of Journals

Country	Average 2000–2020	2000	2010	2015	2020	Country	Total 2000–2020	2000	2010	2015	2020
CHE	5.1	4.5	5.4	5.4	5.1	USA	339,080	1,1441	16,337	18,199	21,343
NLD	5.3	5.1	5.6	5.8	4.9	CHN	110,039	363	2,676	7,095	17,646
AUS	3.8	3.5	3.6	3.9	4.3	GBR	95,466	2,945	4,405	5,599	6,954
CAN	4.1	4.2	4.1	4.1	4.3	DEU	70,781	1,853	3,421	4,213	4,810
GBR	4.4	4.2	4.5	4.6	4.3	CAN	48,851	1,313	2,275	2,821	3,816
USA	4.5	4.6	4.7	4.4	4.3	AUS	38,068	725	1,502	2,545	3,730
BEL	4.4	4.0	4.8	4.7	4.2	FRA	47,307	1,343	2,400	2,813	2,874
SWE	4.3	3.4	4.2	4.9	4.2	ITA	35,611	965	1,666	2,152	2,515
DEU	3.6	3.0	3.9	3.7	3.6	NLD	35,891	920	1,748	2,318	2,482
FRA	3.5	3.2	3.7	3.6	3.2	ESP	31,612	531	1,549	2,090	2,385
CHN	2.0	0.9	1.2	1.9	2.9	KOR	24,742	245	1,001	1,892	2,301
KOR	2.7	1.8	2.4	2.9	2.9	JPN	38,464	1,792	1,712	1,856	1,981
ESP	3.0	2.4	3.2	3.3	2.7	CHE	25,368	563	1,189	1,632	1,961
ITA	3.0	3.2	3.2	3.1	2.6	SWE	20,362	492	861	1,380	1,497
TWN	2.7	2.5	2.8	2.9	2.3	BEL	16,297	371	800	1,065	1,172

Note: Publications in top 1% journal percentiles (by Scopus CiteScore percentile) by country and publication year, 2000–2020, all publication types included, all fields of research and development combined, in descending order for 2020, top 15 countries in each panel only, in percent (left panel, world average = 1) and publication number (right panel).

States. The largest remaining gap in article production in these journals by the two academic superpowers is in the medical sciences, as well as in humanities and social sciences, which are traditionally underrepresented in large data sets of the Scopus and Web of Science genre.

The Globalization of Science Versus Publishing Patterns in Academic Disciplines

In general, research literature (usually focused on the STEMM fields) reveals that international collaboration has been on the rise across countries, institutions, and academic disciplines as well as among scientists and scholars. Social sciences and humanities are usually omitted from analyses, following arguments that neither Scopus nor Web of Science databases adequately reflect knowledge production in these fields. However, it is useful to show the changing distribution of the various collaboration types over time across all major fields of research and development, notwithstanding limitations. It is suffice to say that among 41,462 journals listed in Scopus, there are 5,002 journals allocated to arts and humanities and 10,199 allocated to the social sciences. Further, international research collaboration (and consequently global publishing patterns) can be analyzed in the context of three other collaboration types: institutional, national, and single authorship (or no collaboration). The four collaboration types are complementary, and the globalization of science can be analyzed through the changing intensity of international collaboration over time. The six fields of research and development used here, following the OECD, are agricultural sciences, engineering and technologies, humanities, natural sciences, medical sciences, and social sciences.

Perhaps the most surprising effect of such a global disaggregated approach to academic publishing and collaboration patterns is the powerful and increasing gap between social sciences and the humanities. In the last two decades, while social sciences clearly follow the patterns characteristic of natural sciences, the humanities increasingly diverge from social sciences, moving in a fundamentally different direction in terms of the collaboration mix.

Let us consider the collaboration mix for all fields of research and development combined (Figure 35.1) and compare this general picture with the picture of ongoing changes in collaboration in natural sciences, social sciences, and humanities over the period of two decades (2000–2020; Figures 35.2, 35.3 and 35.4). In our approach, the changing collaboration patterns studied through percentages at the country and institutional levels reflect the changing publishing patterns at the level of individual scientists and scholars affiliated with institutions in these countries. Thousands of individual-level publishing decisions are reflected in aggregated pictures of collaboration at higher levels of analysis.

The collaboration patterns in natural sciences (Figure 35.2) follow the patterns of global science in general (or of all fields combined): in all countries, international collaboration has been on the rise in the last two decades. Increasing international collaboration has occurred at the expense of institutional collaboration and no collaboration (or single-authored) research, both of which have been declining in percentage terms; while institutional collaboration and solo research have been reducing, national collaboration has been stable or, in numerous cases, increasing in percentage terms. In particular, the stability of national collaboration both from a global perspective and in natural sciences indicates the importance of the national embeddedness of science. International collaboration does not appear to crowd-out national collaboration in any of the countries; at the global level (see World in Figures 35.1 and 35.2), national collaboration has increased substantially—from 26% in 2000 to 35% in 2010 and 42% in 2020.

The striking feature of the changing collaboration mix by academic fields is that the role of international collaboration in the humanities is marginal, and in most countries it increases very slowly. In contrast, in the social sciences, the most important trend is the increase in international collaboration, predominantly at the expense of single-authored research—single-authored publications tend to dominate in the humanities;

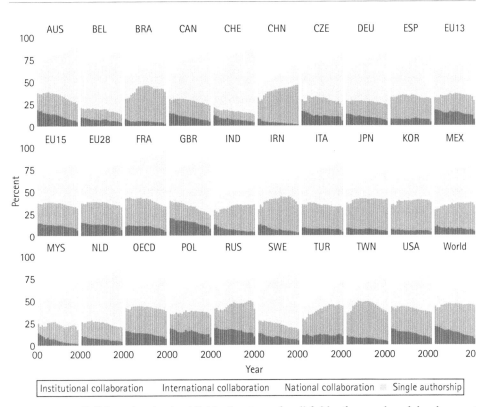

FIGURE 35.1 Collaboration (and publishing) patterns for all fields of research and development combined: powerful and increasing international collaboration at the expense of institutional collaboration, with stable national collaboration: top 25 global knowledge producers in 2020 (plus EU-28, EU-15, EU-13, OECD, and the world), articles only, SciVal data, 2000–2020 (%).

while in social sciences, the decrease in solo research is substantial (which is evident at the global level in the World box in Figure 35.3), the share of solo research in the humanities in almost all countries still exceeds 50%. Figures 35.3 and 35.4 graphically depict the powerful divergence, which appears to be increasing over time, between social sciences and humanities and has not been emphasized in current literature on the globalization of science.

With regard to the powerful global social sciences/humanities divide, while the global percentage of single-authored articles declined from approximately half to approximately one-fourth (from 49% to 23% between 2000 and 2020) in the former, in the latter, there was only a slight decline from 67% to 56% at the global level (see World in Figure 35.4). In the social sciences, all 25 countries and 5 agglomerates of countries studied noted significant declines in shares of single-authored articles and, in most cases, significant increases in shares of internationally collaborative articles, with stable shares of national collaboration over time. International collaboration in the humanities has been relatively insignificant in most countries, except for several European systems. The share of solo articles in 2020 exceeded 40% of all academic knowledge production in the

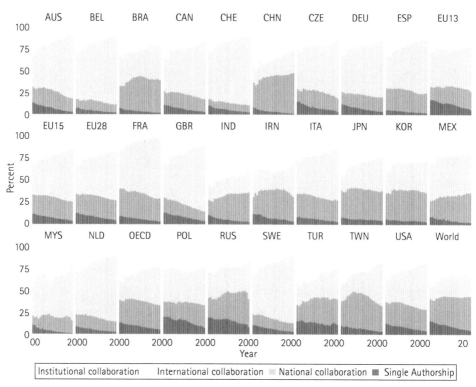

FIGURE 35.2 Collaboration (and publishing) patterns in the natural sciences: powerful and increasing international collaboration at the expense of institutional collaboration, with stable national collaboration: top 25 global knowledge producers in 2020 (plus EU-28, EU-15, EU-13, OECD, and the world), articles only, SciVal data, 2000–2020 (%).

humanities in all countries and agglomerates studied, except for three European countries (Belgium, the Netherlands, and Switzerland) and four newcomers to the global top knowledge producers (China, Indonesia, Iran, and Malaysia). Further, single authorship is the dominating mode of publishing in the humanities and its share exceeds 50% in the most advanced economies: The percentage of solo articles in 2020 was 55% for EU-28, 55% for the OECD, and 51% for the United States.

The changing publishing patterns have their implications for funding at the individual level and beyond. While in most national funding agencies and national excellence initiatives across the globe, social sciences and humanities are grouped together, it must be clear to the academic community, policymakers, and grant makers that the divergence in publishing patterns between the two academic fields has been widening in the last two decades.

Humanities are clearly non-collaborative, and clearly non-internationally collaborative, with powerful implications for metrics such as average output levels and average citation levels at the micro level of individual academics. Individual productivity in all fields except for the humanities is increasing mostly due to the full counting of

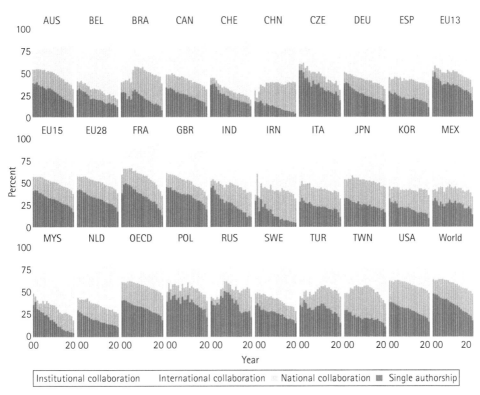

FIGURE 35.3 The collaboration (and publishing) patterns in the social sciences: increasing international collaboration with radically declining single authorship (no collaboration) and stable national collaboration: top 25 global knowledge producers in 2020 (plus EU-28, EU-15, EU-13, OECD, and the world), articles only, SciVal data, 2000–2020 (%).

publications written in teams; when the fractional counting method is applied, productivity is seen to be relatively stable over time. However, in the special case of the humanities, with single authorship as a dominating publishing pattern, individual output without using fractional counting methods, may appear small by comparison; moreover, as literature shows, citations to single-authored articles are lower than those to collaborative articles. The social sciences/humanities divide has its practical implications, disadvantaging humanists whenever they are in a head-on competition for research grants and awards with social scientists, and clearly promoting social scientists wherever the emphasis on publication and citation metrics dominates in the assessment of grant proposals. The traditional expression "social sciences and humanities" in the globalizing science and scholarship loses its traditional sense and can lead to unfair results in competitions among individuals, departments, and institutions.

The changing international collaboration rate by discipline and country is presented in Figure 35.5: The top 25 countries can be clustered into low internationalization systems (such as Poland, Russia, Turkey, and India) and high internationalization systems (such as Switzerland, Sweden, Belgium, the United Kingdom in Europe, or Australia

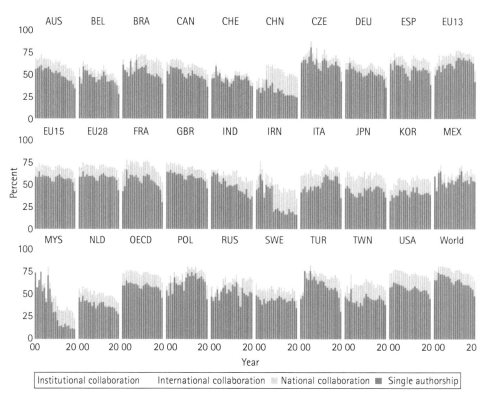

FIGURE 35.4 Collaboration (and publishing) patterns in the humanities: powerfully dominating single-authorship (no collaboration), with a marginal role of slowly increasing international collaboration and stable national and institutional collaboration: top 25 global knowledge producers in 2020 (plus EU-28, EU-15, EU-13, OECD, and the world), articles only, SciVal data, 2000–2020 (%).

globally), with China in humanities and social sciences and the United States in agricultural sciences and natural sciences slowly increasing their international collaboration.

The differences in the international collaboration rate in the top 25 countries are reflected only to a certain extent in the differences between the 25 largest knowledge producing universities (articles only) located within these countries (see Figure 35.6). For example, Harvard is more highly internationalized in terms of research than the United States, and Paris-Saclay University is more highly internationalized than France; the most highly internationalized among the selected national universities are the Swiss Federal Institute of Technology Zurich, Karolinska Institute, and KU Leuven, with rates of approximately 70% in 2020; the least internationalized are Anna University in India and Islamic Azad University in Iran (approximately 14% and 28% in 2020, respectively); in Central and Eastern Europe, both Lomonosov Moscow State University and Jagiellonian University in Cracow, with low and stable internationalization levels in 2000–2020 (approximately 30% and about 40% in the two decades), can be contrasted

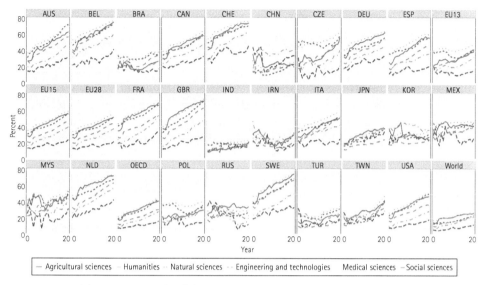

FIGURE 35.5 The international collaboration rate (percentage of internationally collaborative publications) by field of research and development, top 25 global knowledge producers in 2020 (plus EU-28, EU-15, EU-13, OECD, and the world), articles only, SciVal data, 2000–2020 (%).

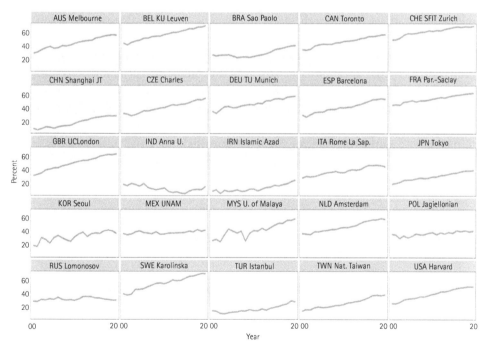

FIGURE 35.6 The international collaboration rate (percentage of internationally collaborative publications), all fields of research and development combined, 25 biggest knowledge-producing universities in the top 25 global knowledge-producing countries (as of 2020), articles only, SciVal data, 2000–2020 (%).

with Charles University in Prague, with the rate reaching approximately 55% in 2020 and increasing over time.

Apart from changing percentages over time, the internationalization of science is also reflected in publication numbers changing over time. National output can be divided into two categories: articles involving international collaboration and all others—that is, domestic articles, including both single-authored and national and institutional collaborations (see Adams, 2013, p. 558). From this perspective, a major finding is that the increase in annual output in the period 2000–2020 in major European systems such as the United Kingdom, France, the Netherlands, Switzerland, Finland, Belgium, Sweden, and Germany and in non-European systems such as the United States, Australia, Canada, and Japan is almost entirely accounted for by international collaborations (see Figure 35.7). In contrast, in catching-up systems (such as India, Brazil, Iran, Mexico, Turkey, Russia, Poland, or Malaysia), there is an increase in national collaboration output. The most illustrative contrast is between the two global powerhouses: While the United States noted no increases in national publications, China noted a huge increase in the previous two decades (compare the two green areas for both countries in Figure 35.7). While domestic output in the former cluster of countries remained almost flat during the study period, the number of internationally coauthored articles increased steadily. The dark blue areas in Figure 35.7 indicate the growth in numbers of international collaborative publications, while the red line indicates the declining share of domestic publications; however, the declining share in a country does not have to imply declining numbers.

The current power of research in the widely understood Western world resides in the growth of internationalization as seen through the volume of internationally coauthored output; the number of domestic publications has not changed in the past two decades. The globalization of science implies two different processes in two different system types: the growth of science in the Western world is almost entirely attributable to internationally coauthored publications, and its growth in the developing world is driven by both internationally coauthored and domestic publications, with different mixes in different systems.

The Globalization of Science Versus System Size, Citation Impact, and Preferred Collaboration Partner Countries

The international collaboration rate across the 25 top countries is not generally correlated with national research output (defined as the total number of articles in 2000–2020). Plotting the percentage of internationally coauthored articles against system size in terms of article numbers (Figure 35.8) indicates that correlation is negligible (R^2 = 0.03). Bubble sizes confirm that systems with low international collaboration rates have low field-weighted citation impact (FWCI), as defined by Scopus, as in the case of Iran, Turkey, and India (as well as China, with the second-largest number

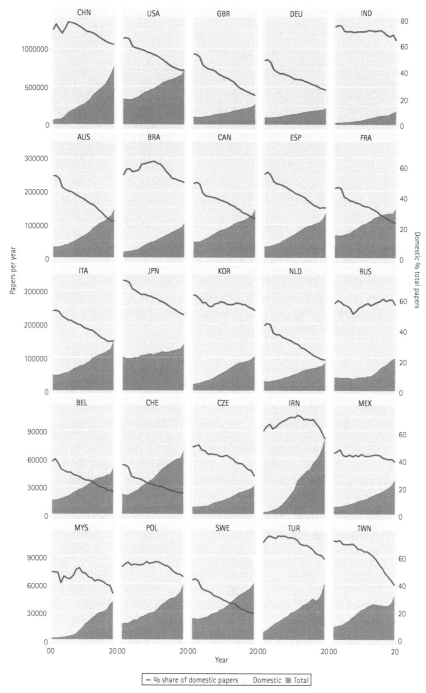

FIGURE 35.7 Total (dark blue), domestic (green), internationally collaborative publications (left axis) and the percentage of domestic publications (right axis) for the top 25 global knowledge producers (2000–2020).

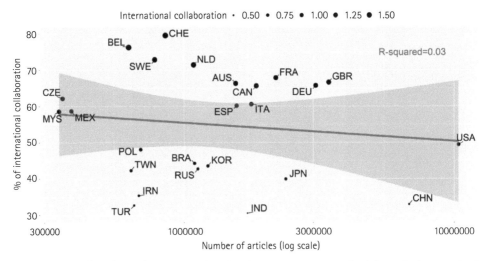

FIGURE 35.8 Correlation between total national output 2000–2020 (articles only; log number) and percentage share of articles published in international collaboration, averaged for the period 2000–2020 (articles only); 95% confidence interval in gray; bubble size reflects average field-weighted citation impact (FWCI) for internationally coauthored articles for the period. All fields of research and development are combined.

of collaborative articles, which is a clear outlier in Figure 35.8, along with the United States).

In Figure 35.9, the citation impact (the FWCI) of publications written in international collaboration is plotted against the citation impact of those written in national collaboration. Field normalization of scientometric indicators avoids distortions caused by different fields (Waltman & van Eck, 2019, p. 282). As measured in Scopus, the FWCI is the ratio of citations actually received to the expected world average (which equals 1) for the subject field, publication type, and publication year. Nationally coauthored publications are cited less often than expected in almost all European countries (i.e., countries to the left of the vertical line in Figure 35.9), with Brazil, Taiwan, Russia, China, and the United States slightly above the global average. Further, papers involving national collaboration had a higher citation impact on global science than international collaborations in the majority of countries (those below the red dashed line) for different reasons: the global superpowers China and the United States; Poland, France, and Iran, where both nationally and internationally coauthored papers had a high citation impact (cross-disciplinary differences are not discussed here because of word count constraints). At the aggregated level of all fields combined, the citation impact of internationally coauthored publications was above the expected field-weighted global average in the vast majority of European systems, but not global systems, analyzed. National collaboration produced globally impactful papers only in

THE GLOBALIZATION OF SCIENCE 751

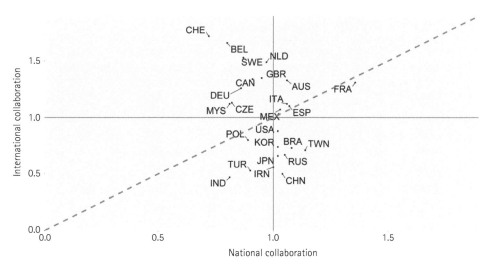

FIGURE 35.9 Field-weighted citation impact (FWCI) by publication type (internationally coauthored, nationally coauthored), articles only, self-citations included, average for the period 2000–2020, all fields of research and development combined.

Spain, Italy, France, and Australia (quadrant 2) as well as in the United States and China (quadrant 4).

Finally, global science is characterized by different thickness of research pairings between countries and institutions: Certain pairings emerge as clearly preferred, following preferential attachment mechanisms in international collaboration. Preferred research pairings differ significantly in terms of their global visibility (as operationalized by the citation impact of internationally coauthored publications).

We studied 25 thickest research pairings among our 25 top countries for the period 2015–2020, combined (Table 35.3, left panel). For all the countries involved, except the Netherlands, irrespective of the size of their science systems, the single most frequently collaborating partner is the United States. Other strong preferred collaboration links are intra-European or with China (in the case of the United Kingdom and Canada). The European integration in research, powerfully supported by European funding, enables the treatment of European countries as a single entity: In this case, among the globally thickest collaboration pairs, there would only be the United States (with Canada), China (with East Asian and Pacific systems of Japan, Korea, and Australia), and Europe. China and the United States form the most powerful global link, followed by the links between the United States and the United Kingdom, Germany, and Canada. Further, collaboration patterns for 28 European systems (Kwiek, 2020) indicate that geographical, linguistic, and historical ties still matter; for example, Spain is the top collaboration partner for Portugal, Finland for Estonia, Germany for Austria and the Czech Republic, France for Romania, and the Czech Republic for Slovakia. The United States remains the number-one collaborating partner for most European countries, including the

Table 35.3 Top 25 Collaboration Partnerships

Rank	Partner Country 1	Partner Country 2	Publications 2015–2020	FWCI	Rank	Partner Country 1	Partner Country 2	Publications 2015–2020	FWCI
1	USA	CHN	344,409	1.93	1	GBR	NLD	63,171	3.25
2	USA	GBR	205,699	2.74	2	USA	NLD	71,185	3.22
3	USA	DEU	161,699	2.64	3	USA	CHE	65,749	3.12
4	USA	CAN	159,744	2.51	4	GBR	FRA	76,171	3.05
5	GBR	DEU	107,731	2.85	5	ITA	DEU	66,662	3.01
6	USA	FRA	106,311	2.85	6	GBR	ESP	60,658	3.01
7	USA	AUS	100,188	2.90	7	GBR	AUS	74,803	3.00
8	USA	ITA	99,589	2.83	8	USA	ESP	72,830	2.95
9	GBR	CHN	93,151	2.28	9	GBR	ITA	79,438	2.93
10	CHN	AUS	80,656	2.40	10	DEU	FRA	72,956	2.91
11	GBR	ITA	79,438	2.93	11	ITA	FRA	62,089	2.91
12	USA	JPN	78,246	2.40	12	USA	AUS	100,188	2.90
13	GBR	FRA	76,171	3.05	13	GBR	DEU	107,731	2.85
14	GBR	AUS	74,803	3.00	14	USA	FRA	106,311	2.85
15	DEU	FRA	72,956	2.91	15	USA	ITA	99,589	2.83
16	USA	ESP	72,830	2.95	16	USA	GBR	205,699	2.74
17	USA	NLD	71,185	3.22	17	CHE	DEU	62,336	2.68
18	USA	KOR	68,723	2.08	18	USA	DEU	161,699	2.64
19	ITA	DEU	66,662	3.01	19	USA	CAN	159,744	2.51
20	USA	CHE	65,749	3.12	20	CHN	AUS	80,656	2.40
21	GBR	NLD	63,171	3.25	21	USA	JPN	78,246	2.40
22	CHE	DEU	62,336	2.68	22	GBR	CHN	93,151	2.28
23	ITA	FRA	62,089	2.91	23	CHN	CAN	59,148	2.27
24	GBR	ESP	60,658	3.01	24	USA	KOR	68,723	2.08
25	CHN	CAN	59,148	2.27	25	USA	CHN	344,409	1.93

Note: Most prolific pairs 2015–2020, sorted by number of coauthored publications (left) and field-weighted citation impact (FWCI) of coauthored publications (right).

largest knowledge producers (the United Kingdom, Germany, France, Italy, and Spain). However, in the top five ranks, the citation impact is highest for intra-European pairings of systems and European-American pairings; citation impact is lowest for joint US-Chinese publications. Within these top five pairs, internationally coauthored papers are cited 3.01–3.25 times more than the world average for similar publications. The networks formed by the thickest collaboration links within the 25 top countries are depicted in Figure 35.10, based on frequency and citation impact.

THE TENSIONS OF GLOBAL SCIENCE

The rise of new scientific powers as seen in the earlier empirical sections—in terms of collaborations, impact, and the role of highly innovative/highly cited papers—breaks the traditional global balance of science (Adams, 2013). The picture of the globalization of science as presented earlier is clearly linked to tensions in collaboration between the developed and developing (and richer/poorer in terms of gross domestic product [GDP] and higher education expenditure on research and development [HERD]) countries. Global network science opens incredible opportunities to new arrivals—countries as well as institutions and research teams. The advantages and disadvantages for the producers of traditional Euro-American top knowledge versus new entrants to global science collaborations differ, with possibly diversified implications for knowledge-producing personnel in developed/developing science systems. Globalization provides a context in which international collaboration in research provides channels through which developing countries can access the knowledge of developed countries more easily than ever before in the history of science. While, on the one hand, predominantly win-win collaboration types are certainly dominant (Wagner, 2008), free-riding behavior in knowledge production in developing economies is also possible, with possibly negative consequences for the global balance in the labor market for academic scientists (Freeman, 2010).

What is also at stake in the emergent tensions between the two clusters of countries (developed and developing) is public funding for academic research and the role of the public in the distribution of tax-based funding in the future. The core policy issue is why

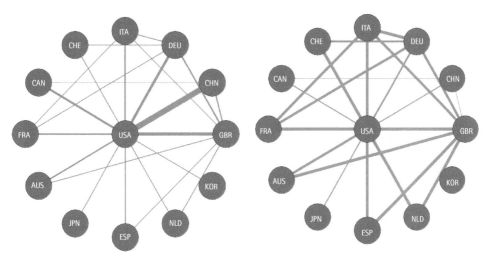

FIGURE 35.10 The network of internationally coauthored articles (in 2015–2020 combined), with only 25 most prolific pairs globally. Consequently, only edges with 59,148 (China-Canada) or more co-publications are displayed. The thickness of edges based on frequency of collaboration (left) and impact of collaboration as viewed through FWCI (right).

Table 35.4 Countries in This Chapter and Their ISO 3-Character Country Codes

AUS	Australia	ITA	Italy
BEL	Belgium	JPN	Japan
BRA	Brazil	KOR	South Korea
CAN	Canada	MEX	Mexico
CHN	China	MYS	Malaysia
CHE	Switzerland	NLD	Netherlands
CZE	Czech Republic	POL	Poland
DEU	Germany	RUS	Russia
ESP	Spain	SWE	Sweden
FRA	France	TUR	Turkey
GBR	United Kingdom	TWN	Taiwan
IND	India	USA	United States
IRN	Iran		

states fund academic research in general and fund highly internationally collaborative academic research as conducted in world-class universities in particular. The rationale presented by national governments may not fit the new reality of globally interconnected network science as conducted by highly internationalized scientists. Thus, national governments are indeed in a delicate position in which they seek national benefits and local applications in internationally produced and collaborative cutting-edge research, perhaps not being fully aware of the increasingly globalized and networked nature of science in which there appears to be no easy means to connect national funding to local benefits and applications. Policymakers and national funders of research may be immersed in the traditional vision of national science in contrast with individual scientists who are increasingly reaping the benefits of global science.

The nature of the new global science fits perfectly into the always-present, more-private-than-public nature of implementing science for individual, career-enhancing purposes, with individual scientists and their motivations to conduct science at the very center of academic enterprise. Under the dominance of the Mertonian norms in the traditional imaginary of the academic profession, the role of this private nature has been systematically undervalued. However, we can trace the theme of the critical role of individual academic prestige and recognition in science in a long line of research from Hagstrom (1965) to Wagner (2018).

The simple fact is that global science is funded by national governments; there is no global funding for research available on a large scale (except for philanthropy funding made available for selected grand challenges in research from global players such as the Bill & Melinda Gates Foundation, with total grant payments since inception totaling 54.8 billion USD in 135 countries). The national/global tension is much stronger in highly developed economies, with powerful academic science systems supported by strong public funding, than in less developed economies, with weak and publicly underfunded science systems. However, global science cannot be stopped, but the distribution of long-term gains and losses among collaborating partners in the global economy is far from clear, except for a general assumption that international research collaboration is good for global science and beneficial for societies at a global level, particularly from the perspective of science as a global collective good. However, in order to understand and apply knowledge and continue to function as full partners in global science, nations require their own science infrastructure and trained personnel, particularly doctoral students and young doctorates, even in difficult economic times (see Mattei, 2014). Consequently, as Chinchilla-Rodriguez et al. (2019, p. 6) argue, national scientific independence relies on government investment in research.

There is a variety of forms of control in research collaboration, from loose to strict controls at various levels; in informal collaboration, typically, both governmental and institutional control are limited. However, governments, institutions, and funding agencies also have limited control over collaboration in the case of formalized and funded collaboration: the control over who collaborates with whom and who is doing what in science once funding is granted to national principal investigators with their international research teams is limited. The notions of international research collaboration as assumed by the funders, the grantees in national funding schemes, and their international collaborators may differ substantially. As Wagner (2006, p. 171) explained, "the question for developing countries is not how to get into collaboration with Germany, the United Kingdom or the United States, but how to take applicable knowledge from the network (no matter where it is located), make it relevant to local needs and problems, and tie it down." From the perspective of developing countries, the crucial aspect is to bring the results of collaboration back to the country, thereby enabling the meeting of local needs.

The globalization of science does not imply that the global science system is created or planned by a single entity (the most natural candidate being the global science powerhouse, the United States); the global system is embedded in the rules created by scientists themselves and maintained as a self-organizing system. The implication of this is that nation states have another major level to consider in their science policies: the global level that accompanies, rather than replaces, the regional, national, and local levels. While public funding is key to the development of global science, innovations can occur anywhere and only scientists are able to identify and locate them and find ways to make them locally applicable. "It may become increasingly difficult to track spending outputs and outcomes, which has been the model for much of public accountability for science in the past" (Leydesdorff & Wagner, 2008, p. 324).

GLOBAL SCIENCE AND THE POWER OF INDIVIDUAL SCIENTISTS

One thread continues across all previous sections and requires a summary: the rise of global science as closely related to transformations that occur at the shop-floor level of science and at the micro-level of individual scientists. Their motivation is important because collaboration choices at the micro-level of individual scientists determine international collaboration at the macro level of countries (Kato & Ando, 2017).

There is substantial support in the literature regarding international research collaboration for the argument that the extent of such collaboration ultimately depends on the scientists themselves (Kato & Ando, 2016; King, 2011; Melin, 2000; Royal Society, 2011; Ulnicane, 2021; Wagner, 2008, 2018; Wagner & Leydesdorff, 2005). Faculty internationalization is considered to be shaped more by deeply ingrained individual values and predilections than by institutions and academic disciplines (Finkelstein et al., 2013) or, particularly, by governments and their agencies (Wagner, 2018).

In their study on the role of global connectedness in the development of science in middle-income countries, Barnard et al. (2015) emphasized the increasing role of individual scientists. The global and national science systems are connected not so much through formal institutional collaborative ties but through individual scientists and their work: "it is the individual person which spans the local and the global worlds." In other words, at the level of the individual researcher, there is no trade-off between local connectedness and global connectedness in research and they should be considered as "complements" but rather as "substitutes." Consequently, the scientific connections between more and less advanced countries are created through individual scientists (Barnard et al., 2015, pp. 400–401).

Perhaps, most importantly from the perspective of this chapter, the shift from a nationally centered scientific system to a global science system implies that it is increasingly the researchers, rather than national authorities, who set the rules of implementing science. The networked model of science is an open system, with opportunities open to new entrants, particularly new countries. However, it is individual scientists and their decisions that make the difference and change the course of science at the global level. Collaborative networks emerge from the choices of hundreds of scientists who shape the growth and evolution of networks "seeking to maximize their own welfare" (Wagner, 2008, p. 10).

For decades, extant research literature has been dealing with the question of why academic scientists collaborate with other academic scientists. Perhaps the best answer is the simplest one: "scientists collaborate because they benefit from doing so" (Olechnicka et al., 2019, p. 45). From this perspective, scientists as "calculating individuals" are increasingly engaging in international collaborations because they are benefiting more from such collaboration—in terms of promotion, tenure, prestige, or access to research funding—rather than from any other type of collaboration (national, institutional). Scientists indicate "a pragmatic attitude to collaboration—when there is something to gain, then that particular collaboration will occur, otherwise it will not" (Melin, 2000, p. 39).

Perhaps the most notable feature of science today is the presence of self-organizing networks, spanning the globe. These networks consist of researchers "who collaborate not because they are told to but because they want to . . . Scientific curiosity and ambition are the principal forces at work in the new invisible college" (Wagner, 2008, p. 2).

Scientists work within networks and the networks are constituted of the connections among these scientists. Scientists tend to collaborate across national borders because they "seek excellence" and want to work with the most outstanding scientists in their field (Royal Society, 2011, p. 57); they seek "resources and reputation" (Wagner & Leydesdorff, 2005, p. 1616); academic reward structures incentivize them to exploit collaboration and internationally coauthored publications to their own advantage (Glänzel, 2001). To this extent, collaboration is driven by an "intrinsic motivation to succeed" and "the motivation for better achievement" (Kato & Ando, 2016, p. 2). As such, it is largely curiosity-driven and reflects "the ambitions of individual scientists for reputation and recognition" (King, 2011, p. 24). The traditional postwar "governmental nationalism" in science coexists with this global science, as scientists believe that their curiosity-driven (rather than state-driven) approach "best serves their personal scientific ambitions" (King, 2011, p. 361).

Wagner and Leydesdorff (2005, pp. 1610–1611) tested the hypothesis that global science is an emergent, self-organizing system where the selection of a research partner and research themes relies upon choices made by the scientists themselves. They tested whether international research collaboration could be shown to arise "from the self-interest of researchers to link together rewards, reputation, and the resources offered by a collaborative network," referring to the concept of self-organization (see Melin, 2000; Ulnicane, 2021) and examining bibliometric data using network analysis. In addition, they studied the mechanism of preferential attachment at the field level and concluded that individual choices of scientists to collaborate internationally may be motivated by reward structures within science and influenced by the global abundance of collaborators and the weak ties among them: Weak ties are relatively easy to create and sever because people are not working side by side, and the social obligations that may arise from such collaboration within the same institutions are weaker.

The relationship among major collaboration types—international, national, institutional, and solo research or no collaboration—are complex and depend on numerous factors that are internal or external to national science systems. The development of global networked science may be best viewed through preferential attachment mechanisms. Preferential attachment mechanisms employed to explain the individual behavior of scientists seeking collaboration imply that scientists wish to form links with other scientists of higher reputation or gain access to critical resources or funding: "preferential attachment clearly operates to the advantage of those at the top of the system, whether we think of them as individual scientists or as entire countries" (Wagner, 2008, p. 62). As Marginson comments, "researchers in the same or related disciplines want to work with each other. They fulfill their individual and collective agency by creating knowledge. . . . Knowledge flows freely, and science and its connections continue to grow and spread in all directions" (Marginson, 2020, p. 50). Therefore, the emergence of global science is indicative of the power wielded by individuals in science: "scientists and engineers are free to follow their own interests and careers wherever those may lead. . . . Most scientists will seek to enhance their reputations or gain access to resources, regardless of the interest of their nation of origin, and perhaps even at its expense" (Marginson, 2020, p. 64).

Global science, regulated by intraprofessional interactions, provides agency to "autonomous researchers" (Marginson & Xu, 2021). Scientists rely on their "individual and collective goals, cognitive cultures, knowledge, imagination, associations, beliefs and habits" and global research agendas depend on global autonomous collegial networks (Marginson & Xu, 2021, p. 33). Marginson and Xu's notion of agency in collegial global science resonates well with the notion of free agents in global networked science in Wagner (2008) and the notion of autonomy in King (2011).

As King (2011) emphasizes, the emergent global science enhances the opportunities for researchers to undertake collaborative projects across territorial boundaries that are beyond the direct control of national governments. Global networks in science are viewed as exceeding the power of governmental scientific nationalism, as they are privately governed and self-regulatory in nature. Scientists collaborate across the globe because the collaborative high-quality science satisfies their "individual curiosity and the career desire for esteem, reputation, and scientific autonomy" (King, 2011, pp. 370–371). Global science is controlled by researchers themselves, with key standardizing features being "stronger notions of autonomy, objectivity, testability, and peer judgment" (King, 2011, p. 372). The invisible college of global science is driven by the needs of the knowledge-creating community (Wagner, 2008, p. 32).

In other words, global science provides more agency, autonomy, collegiality, and self-regulation to scientists embedded in national science structures and involved in global networks of science—unequal and highly stratified (Kwiek, 2019a, 2019b) but nevertheless open. The future of global science is in the hands of millions of scientists across the globe, who make individual decisions on whether or not to collaborate, and if collaborate—with whom, be they institutional, national, or international partners in research. Individual motivations drive scientists to collaborate in research and shape global science. It is safe to say that the role of individual scientists in the globalization of science (as well as the power of micro-level analysis in which individual scientists rather than institutions or countries are the unit of analysis) is underestimated and deserves much more scholarly attention.

ACKNOWLEDGMENTS

I gratefully acknowledge the research assistance provided by Dr. Wojciech Roszka. I also acknowledge the support of the Ministry of Science and Higher Education through its Dialogue grant 0022/DLG/2019/10 (Research Universities).

REFERENCES

Adams, J. (2013). The fourth age of research. *Nature, 497*, 557–560.
Barnard, H., Cowan, R., Fernandez de Arroyabe Arranz, M., & Muller, M. (2015). The role of global connectedness in the development of indigenous science in middle income countries.

In Daniele Archibugi & Andrea Filippetti (Eds.), *The handbook of global science, technology, and innovation* (pp. 386–410). Wiley-Blackwell.

Buyalskaya, A., Gallo, M., & Camerer, C. F. (2021). The golden age of social science. *PNAS*, *118*(5), e2002923118.

Cantwell, B., & Grimm, A. (2018). The geopolitics of academic science. In B. Cantwell, H. Coates, & R. King (Eds.), *Handbook on the politics of higher education* (pp. 130–148). Edward Elgar.

Cantwell, B., & Marginson, S. (2018). Vertical stratification. In B. Cantwell, S. Marginson, and A. Smoletseva (Eds.), *High participation systems of higher education* (pp. 125–150). Oxford University Press.

Chinchilla-Rodriguez, Z., Sugimoto, C., & Larivière, V. (2019). Follow the leader: On the relationship between leadership and scholarly impact in international collaborations. *PLoS One*, *14*(96), Article e0218309.

Clauset, A., Larremore, D. B., & Sinatra, R. (2017). Data-driven predictions in the science of science. *Science*, *355*(6324).

Cole, J. R., & Cole, S. (1973). *Social stratification in science*. University of Chicago Press.

Crawford E., Shinn T., & Sörlin S. (1993). The nationalization and denationalization of the sciences: An introductory essay. In E. Crawford, T. Shinn, & D. Sörlin (Eds.), *Denationalizing science: Sociology of the sciences: A yearbook* (vol. 16). Springer.

Dong, Y., Shen, Z., Ma, H., & Wang, K. (2017). A century of science: Globalization of scientific collaborations, citations, and innovations. *KDD 2017 Applied Data Science*, 1437–1446.

Edelmann, A., Wolff, T., Montagne, D., & Bail, C. A. (2020). Computational social science and sociology. *Annual Review of Sociology*, *46*(1), 61–81.

Engels, A., & Ruschenburg, T. (2008). The uneven spread of global science: Patterns of international collaboration in global environmental change research. *Science and Public Policy*, *35*(5), 347–360. doi:10.3152/030234208x317160

Finkelstein, M., & Sethi, W. (2014). Patterns of faculty internationalization: A predictive model. In F. Huang, M. Finkelstein, & M. Rostan (Eds.), *The internationalization of the Academy: Changes, realities and prospects* (pp. 237–258). Springer.

Finkelstein, M. J., Walker, E., & Chen, R. (2013). The American faculty in an age of globalization: Predictors of internationalization of research content and professional networks. *Higher Education*, *66*(3), 325–340.

Fortunato, S. et al. (2018). Science of science. *Science*, *359*(6379), eaao0185.

Freeman, R. B. (2010). Globalization of scientific and engineering talent: International mobility of students, workers, and ideas and the world economy. *Economics of Innovation and New Technology*, *19*(5), 393–406. doi:10.1080/10438590903432871

Glänzel, H. F., Moed, U., Schmoch, & Thelwall, M. (Eds.) (2020). *Springer handbook of science and technology indicators*. Springer.

Glänzel, W. (2001). National characteristics in international scientific co-authorship relations. *Scientometrics*, *51*(1), 69–115.

Gui, Q., Liu, C., & Du, D. (2019). Globalization of science and international scientific collaboration: A network perspective. *Geoforum*, *105*, 1–12. doi:10.1016/j.geoforum.2019.06.017

Hagstrom, W. O. (1965). *The scientific community*. Basic Books.

Hennemann, S., & Liefner, I. (2015). Global science collaboration. In D. Archibugi & A. Filippetti (Eds.), *The handbook of global science, technology, and innovation*. Wiley.

Ioannidis, J. P., Boyack, K. W., & Klavans, R. (2014). Estimates of the continuously *Publishing Core* in the scientific workforce. *PLoS One*, *9*(7), e101698.

Kato, M., & Ando, A. (2016). National ties of international scientific collaboration and researcher mobility found in nature and science. *Scientometrics*, *110*(2), 673–694. doi:10.1007/s11192-016-2183-z

King, R. (2011). Power and networks in worldwide knowledge coordination: The case of global science. *Higher Education Policy*, *24*(3), 359–376.

Kwiek, M. (2005). *The university and the state: A study into global transformations*. Peter Lang.

Kwiek, M. (2015). Reforming European universities: The welfare state as a missing context. In P. Zgaga, U. Teichler, H. G. Schuetze, & A. Wolter (Eds.), *Higher education reform: Looking back—Looking forwards* (pp. 101–128). Peter Lang.

Kwiek, M. (2016). The European research elite: A cross-national study of highly productive academics across 11 European systems. *Higher Education*, *71*(3), 379–397.

Kwiek, M. (2018a). Academic top earners: Research productivity, prestige generation and salary patterns in European universities. *Science and Public Policy*, *45*(1), 1–13.

Kwiek, M. (2018b). High research productivity in vertically undifferentiated higher education systems: Who are the top performers? *Scientometrics*, *115*(1), 415–462.

Kwiek, M. (2019a). *Changing European academics: A comparative study of social stratification, work patterns and research productivity*. Routledge.

Kwiek, M. (2019b). Social stratification in higher education: What it means at the micro-level of the individual academic scientist. *Higher Education Quarterly*, *73*(4), 419–444.

Kwiek, M. (2020). What large-scale publication and citation data tell us about international research collaboration in Europe: Changing national patterns in global contexts. *Studies in Higher Education*, *81*, 493–519.

Kwiek, M. (2021). The prestige economy of higher education journals: A quantitative approach. *Higher Education*, *81*, 493–519.

Kwiek, M., & Roszka, W. (2020). Gender disparities in international research collaboration: A large-scale bibliometric study of 25,000 university professors. *Journal of Economic Surveys*. https://doi.org/10.1111/joes.12395

Leydesdorff, L., & Wagner, C. S. (2008). International collaboration in science and the formation of a core group. *Journal of Informetrics*, *2*(4), 317–325.

Mallard, G., & Paradeise, C. (2008). Global science and national sovereignty: A new terrain for the historical sociology of science. In G. Mallard, C. Paradeise, & A. Peerbaye (Eds.), *Global science and national sovereign* (pp. 1–39). Routledge.

Marginson, S. (2016). Global stratification in higher education. In S. Slaughter & B. J. Taylor (Eds.), *Higher education, stratification, and workforce development* (pp. 13–24). Springer.

Marginson, S. (2018). *The new geo-politics of higher education*. CGHE Working Paper no. 34.

Marginson, S. (2020). The world research system: Expansion, diversification, network and hierarchy. In C. Callender, W. Locke, & S. Marginson (Eds.), *Changing higher education for a changing world* (pp. 35–51). Bloomsbury.

Marginson, S., & Xu, X. (2021). Moving beyond centre-periphery science: Towards an ecology of knowledge. CGHE Working Paper no. 63, April 2021.

Mattei, P. (2009). *Restructuring welfare organizations in Europe: From democracy to good government*. Palgrave.

Mattei, P. (Ed.) (2014). *University adaptation in difficult economic times*. Oxford University Press.

Melin, G. (2000). Pragmatism and self-organization: Research collaboration on the individual level. *Research Policy*, *29*, 31–34.

Melkers, J., & Kiopa, A. (2010). The social capital of global ties in science: The added value of international collaboration. *Review of Policy Research*, *27*(4), 389–414.

Merton, R. K. (1973). *The sociology of science: Theoretical and empirical investigations*. University of Chicago Press.

Mohrman, K., Ma, W., & Baker, D. (2008). The research university in transition: The emerging global model. *Higher Education Policy*, *21*(1), 5–27. doi:10.1057/palgrave.hep.8300175

Nielsen, M. W., & Andersen, J. P. (2021). Global citation inequality is on the rise. *Proceedings of the National Academy of Sciences*, *118*(7), e2012208118.

Olechnicka, A., Ploszaj, A., & Celinska-Janowicz, D. (2019). *The geography of scientific collaboration*. Routledge.

Royal Society. (2011). *Knowledge, networks, and nations. Global scientific collaboration in the 21st century*. The Royal Society.

Sá, C., & Sabzalieva, E. (2018). Scientific nationalism in a globalizing world. In B. Cantwell, H. Coates, & R. King (Eds.), *Handbook on the politics of higher education* (pp. 130–148). Edward Elgar.

SciVal (2021). The global dataset. http://www.scival.com (restricted access).

Scopus (2021). The global dataset. http://www.scopus.com (restricted access).

Stephan, P. (2012). *How economics shapes science*. Harvard University Press.

Tahamtan, I., & Bornmann, L. (2019). What do citation counts measure? An updated review of studies on citations in scientific documents published between 2006 and 2018. *Scientometrics*, *121*, 1635–1684.

Ulnicane, I. (2021). Self-organisation and steering in international research collaborations. In K. Kastenhofer & S. Molyneux-Hodgson (Eds.), *Community and identity in contemporary technosciences* (pp. 107–125). Springer.

Veugelers, R. (2010). Towards a multipolar science world: Trends and impact. *Scientometrics*, *82*, 439–456. https://doi.org/10.1007/s11192-009-0045-7

Wagner, C. S. (2006). International collaboration in science and technology: Promises and pitfalls. In L. Box & R. Engelhard (Eds.), *Science and technology policy for development, dialogues at the interface* (pp. 165–176). Anthem Press.

Wagner, C. S. (2008). *The new invisible college: Science for development*. Brookings Institution Press.

Wagner, C. S. (2018). *The collaborative era in science: Governing the network*. Palgrave Macmillan.

Wagner, C. S., & Leydesdorff, L. (2005). Network structure, self-organization, and the growth of international collaboration in science. *Research Policy*, *34*(10), 1608–1618.

Wagner, C. S., Park, H. W., & Leydesdorff, L. (2015). The continuing growth of global cooperation networks in research: A conundrum for national governments. *PLoS ONE*, *10*(7), 1–15.

Waltman, L., Tijssen, R. J. W., & van Eck, N. J. (2011). Globalisation of science in kilometres. *Journal of Informetrics*, *5*(4), 574–582. doi:10.1016/j.joi.2011.05.003

Waltman, L., & van Eck, N. J. (2019). Field normalization of scientometric indicators. In W. Glänzel, H. F. Moed, U. Schmoch, & M. Thelwall (Eds.), *Springer handbook of science and technology indicators* (pp. 281–300). Springer.

Wang, D., & Barabási, A.-L. (2021). *The science of science*. Cambridge University Press.

Whitley, R. (2000). *The intellectual and social organization of the sciences*. Oxford University Press.

Zeng, A., Shen, Z., Zhou, J., Wu, J., Fan, Y., Wang, Y., & Stanley, E. (2017). The science of science: From the perspective of complex systems. *Physics Reports*, *714–715*, 1–73.

CHAPTER 36

CHINA'S RESPONSES TO GLOBALIZATION AND HIGHER EDUCATION REFORMS

Challenges and Policy Implications

KA HO MOK, GUO GUO KE, AND ZHEN TIAN

INTRODUCTION

SINCE the late 1970s, China started economic reforms to transform the economic sphere and other dimensions of development. During the Cultural Revolution in 1966–1976, higher education had stopped development. The post-Mao leadership realized the strategic importance of higher education for supporting the development of the country; thus, higher education was resumed. In the last few decades, higher education in China has experienced significant transformations (Gao, 2018). In particular, the call for higher education and the quest for world-class university status that began in the late 1990s significantly transformed China's higher education, making it competitive in the region and even globally and revealing its steady but significant rise in various global university leagues (Mok & Kang, 2021; Mok & Marginson, 2021). Recognizing the strategic role of higher education not only in transforming the research and knowledge community but also in supporting the country's economic restructuring, the Chinese government has continually invested in higher education research with strong incentives injected for promoting innovation and entrepreneurship (Ekrem & Tugcu, 2021; Mok et al., 2020; Xie et al., 2014).

Similar to her counterparts in the Asia-Pacific region, the Chinese government has made serious attempts to address the growing influences of the globalizing trends of higher education development, which could be succinctly featured by the massification, privatization, internationalization, and transnationalization of higher education (Mok & Han, 2017; Mok & Yu, 2014). The serious effort put together by the Chinese government to internationalize and transnationalize higher education offerings has also diversified student learning and university programs, impacting on graduate employment (Mok et al., 2018; Xiong & Mok, 2020). The rise of international scientific research producing impactful research, together with the success in internationalizing its higher education, has undoubtedly positioned China as an emerging global power (Kennedy, 2019; Marginson, 2011; Wu, 2015). This study sets out against the broader political economic context to examine critically how the Chinese government has responded to the growing influences of globalization by internationalizing and trasnationalizing its higher education. This study also examines the challenges and policy implications when higher education experiences internationalization and transnationalization in China. The first part of the chapter discusses the major trends in higher education development in response to globalization. The second part focuses on examining the social consequences of internationalization/transnationalization of higher education, specifically examining the intensified transgenerational inequality in education during the processes of internationalization and transnationalization of higher education. Finally, the chapter discusses major challenges and policy implications when China's higher education has gone through such significant transformations.

China's Responses to Globalization and Higher Education Reforms

Massification of Higher Education

Recognizing the importance of higher education expansion under the knowledge-based economy, together with responding to the globalizing trends driving for internationalization/transnationalization of higher education, many countries, particularly in East Asia and the Pacific, have made serious attempts to transform their higher education systems through higher education expansion, internationalizing student learning experiences and quests for world-class status through strategic investments in selected universities to rank high in global university leagues (Mok & Jiang, 2017a; Mok & Kang, 2021). The growth of higher education in East Asia, specifically in South Korea, Japan, Taiwan, and Hong Kong, is incredibly extraordinary (Mok & Jiang, 2018; Neubauer et al., 2017). Similar to her counterparts in the region, China has experienced a significant expansion in higher education through public and private provisions, as well as engaging overseas partners to offer transnational education experiences to meet the pressing education needs of the citizens (Jiang, 2017; Mok, 2016; Mok & Han, 2017).

China is a latecomer in the massification of higher education relative to other Western nations (Mok & Jiang, 2018). Nevertheless, the higher education market has

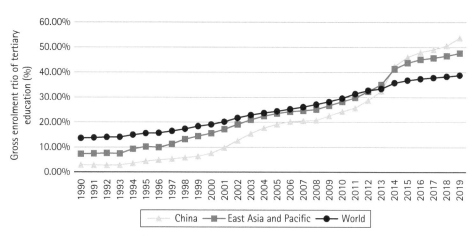

FIGURE 36.1 Expansion of higher education in China, East Asia, and Pacific and the world (1990–2019). (*Source*: World Bank. https://data.worldbank.org/indicator/SE.TER.ENRR)

grown rapidly since 1999, and the gap is steadily diminishing following such an expansion. After 2014, China's gross enrolment rate increased even higher than the world average. According to World Bank statistics (Figure 36.1), the enrolment rate grew slowly from 2.97% to 5.86% from 1990 to 1998; China expanded the higher education sector in 1999, raising the enrolment rate raised dramatically from 6.39% in 1999 to 22.44% in 2009. By 2019, the ratio reached 53.76% when China's higher education development transformed from the elite stage to the mass stage (up to 50%) in recent decades (Trow, 1974).

Privatization and Marketization of Higher Education

With higher education dramatic expanding, the Chinese government began to face the shortages of funding in educational development (Mok, 2002). Furthermore, with the changes in the economy and the modernization construction (Yang, 2002), centralized management is no longer appropriated in the higher education sector. Therefore, to solve the difficulties of single national funding and scarce resources, the Chinese central government has carried out marketization and decentralization to encourage the non-state sector to establish private higher institutions using each expansion policy and improving the autonomous right (Mok, 2000, 2005).

According to Mok and Lo (2007), the marketization of higher education has three primary manifestations, namely, reducing the proportion of government investment in higher education, increasing non-state (including the market, individuals, and families) investment in higher education, strengthening the relationship between higher education and the private sector, and developing the relationship between universities and industries. To enhance the role of private higher education institutions, the role of the government also switches from a sole provider to the regulator for establishing the quasi-market and emphasizing the efficiency, flexibility, and effectiveness to adopt corporate managerialism on the higher education sector (Braun & Merrien, 1999; Mok & Lee, 2003; Mok & Lo, 2001). Under the context, the privatization of higher education thus rapidly developed and significantly increased the number of private higher education institutions. The diversification of higher education offers more selection to respond to social demand actively.

Internationalization and Transnationalization of Higher Education

Driven by economic globalization and the rapid development of service trade, higher education is considered as one of the service industries and has been included in the General Agreement on Trade in Service by the World Trade Organization (WTO). After China joined the WTO, it gradually became involved in the global economic environment (Yang, 2010). It not only participates in economic competition but also in the talent's competition. The Chinese government began to amend relevant legislation to be consistent with WTO rules by enabling foreign education institutions to introduce high-quality foreign educational resources to China. In 2003, the regulation of the People's Republic of China on Chinese-Foreign Cooperation in Running Schools was introduced and implemented, aiming to co-promote effectively the teaching and scientific research level and improve the comprehensive educational capacity (Mok, 2007).

It is against this policy context that the number of transnational higher education projects and institutions later continuously extended the scale. In 1995, only two cooperative programs could grant a foreign degree, but the number had reached 2,342, including 1,090 undergraduate projects and institutions, by the end of June 2018 (Huang, 2010; Sharma, 2018). However, a detailed study of the destination areas of these transnational projects shows that most of them are concentrated in the eastern coastal areas, which are the most prosperous in China, and families of students need to have the economic capacity to afford such cooperative programs because of expensive tuition fees (Mok, 2007). In other words, higher education expansion is partly financed by continuously increasing the proportion of tuition (Marginson, 2011). Such an increase is sustained by family investment in education that is grounded in Confucian values (Zha, 2011).

Against the changing of the higher education context, this chapter aims to examine how the massification and transnationalization of higher education have challenged the graduate employment and intensified the transgenerational inequality in China.

SOCIAL CONSEQUENCES OF THE MASSIFICATION AND TRANSNATIONALIZATION OF HIGHER EDUCATION

Higher Education and Transgenerational Inequality

A few major studies have demonstrated that economic inequality primarily arises from unequal opportunity, which is mainly caused by the factors beyond personal control, including family background, race, gender, parental education level, parental occupation, and place of birth (Roemer, 1993, 1998). Further studies on the inequality caused by unequal educational opportunity have attracted wide attention (Becker & Tomes, 1986). Family foundation affects posterity to access educational opportunities (Li, 2006; Mok & Jiang, 2017a). In China, parents believe education is the primary channel for the intergenerational transmission of socioeconomic status. It improves the socioeconomic status of the educator (Blanden et al., 2007) and influences the human capital and socioeconomic status of offspring through intergenerational transmission. From the same perspective on the Great Gatsby curve, the transmission of wealth and human capital from parents to children is an essential determinant of employment and ability for earnings (Jerrim & Macmillan, 2015). Simultaneously, human capital theory supports parents' investment behavior. Education is a primary instrument to obtain the higher economic return, wherein the higher the education level, the greater the economic returns (Gillies, 2017).

Chan and Ngok (2011) stated that, against the regional economic disparities, as well as the impact of marketization and internationalization of higher education, the consequences of transferring educational obligation and responsibility from the central government to the local government caused educational inequality and further exacerbated and forced parents and students to carry the burden of higher tuition fees. The reason is that the institutions raised tuition fees to sustain their own financial needs, whereas the government reduced the number of institutions under its direct management. The investment differentiation between elites' universities and regular universities has intensified, increasing the gap (Carnoy, 2011). Similar to Luo et al. (2018), Mok and Jiang (2017b) argued that the massification of higher education fails to provide equal access for the low socioeconomic status students, making entering elite universities and acquiring a decent job in the labor market difficult.

Therefore, family background plays a vital role for students accessing elite or transnational universities that require families to have a financial foundation to afford their children. According to earlier research by Blau et al. (1967), inequality in the education system makes high-quality educational resources easier to obtain by the dominant class and considers family background as the precondition. Mok and Jiang (2017) further demonstrated this argument that higher education expansion brings more admission inequality because of family background. In particular, the emergence of transnational higher education may reinforce social inequality because students who studied in transnational higher institutions are from advantaged family backgrounds (Mok et al., 2017).

The diversification of higher education reflects the stratification of different classes in real society. Some scholars used reproduction concepts to describe the relationship between education and social stratification (Collins, 2019). As Li (2006) mentioned, cultural reproduction affects access to education. The cultural reproduction model refers to "parents with higher cultural and educational backgrounds have an advantage in terms of educational opportunities for their children." In this model, parents' educational expectations, cultural capital, and human capital are internalized into their children's learning motivation and performance and indirectly transformed into educational opportunities. The parents' cultural education level can be inherited and continued by the offspring, thus completing the cultural reproduction process of the family. The same perspective from earlier studies (Bourdieu, 1973; Bowles & Gintis, 1975; Mare, 1981) argues that a crucial transgenerational transmission phenomenon is observed in educational reproduction; that is, the higher the education level of the parents, the higher the education level of their children. The difference in parental education level reflects the difference in family educational expectations and concepts (Bourdieu, 1973).

Transgenerational and Graduate Employment

The inequality of higher education has further derived many studies on the graduates' employment inequality. The competitiveness of educational opportunities increases employment competitiveness, especially under the human capital theory, highlighting higher education return (Becker & Lewis, 1993; Psacharopoulos, 1985). In other words, university graduates have more opportunities for upward society and employment (Mok & Wu, 2016). However, more studies point out that university students obtain their first job through their family connection. Support provided by the family is not limited to education but also the position in the labor market and strengthens their competitiveness in social mobility (Brown et al., 2011; Dale, 2015). Macmillan et al. (2015) found a similar observation that 40% of students from private schools achieved higher status careers than 28% of students from public school backgrounds. For graduates to obtain a more high-status occupation, their parents have socioeconomic advantages. Peking University's research team (Wen, 2005) researched higher education and graduate employment. They found that family background heavily influences graduates' employment. Students from a wealthy family will have more chances of getting a job and starting with a high salary. Furthermore, from the investigation by Mok et al. (2017), the disparities are more visible, the salary level and job nature of transnational higher education graduates are competitive, and the time spent on getting their first job is relatively short.

Transnational higher education offers more choices to meet the pressing demand for an individual to access higher education, but accessibility is not evenly distributed. The threshold of admission and employment after graduation also involves family background support. However, we must ask a critical question: Who can enjoy such choices? The answer is obvious that individuals and families with sufficient financial abilities and other resources can enjoy such learning experiences. The following discussion will further analyze whether the phenomenon resulted in transgenerational inequality; the transmission is including not only the intergenerational transfer of assets and resources (not necessarily in monetary terms) but also other resources (nonmonetary support such as social capital and cultural capital). The question of whether such transfers would have affected young peoples' job opportunities and eventually upward social mobility will be discussed (Green & Mok, 2013; Lauder, 2014; Mok & Wu, 2016).

Research Method and Data

Data Sets

This study drew on transnational cooperative education and regular higher education data collected from two rounds of the online questionnaire survey. The data cover most provincial-level divisions in mainland China, except for Hainan province. The analysis sample is based on respondents who graduated in 2020. The sample of graduate employment included 543 respondents. The transnational higher education data are mainly based on pooled nationally representative Sino-foreign cooperative institutions and projects. We also extracted regular higher education data as a reference for comparison. To ensure a balanced representation, we used stratified and cluster sampling in stages one and two, respectively. In the first stage, stratified sampling was used to select Sino-foreign universities. In the next stage, cluster sampling was used to distribute the questionnaire to college students at the selected universities. Meanwhile, we collected regular higher education data through online snowball sampling. These sampling strategies should have provided a good representation of the target population despite the moderated response rate and the gender ratio.

Variables

We focused on the analysis in graduate employment under different education programs. The main dependent variable is the higher education graduate employment situation, which we separated into three aspects, namely, first job performance, employment service assistance, and career development expectation.

The main independent variable is binary in the social level that indicates whether a respondent attended transnational higher education (0 = regular higher education, 1 = transnational education). Given that the family education variable usually reflects a family's social capital and economic resources (Israel 2001), we considered the influence of family background on employment inequality and added a second independent variable at the individual level related to family educational background. Parents' education was defined as years of schooling (6 = primary, 9 = lower secondary, 12 = upper secondary, 15 = junior college, 16 = four-year college, 19 = graduate school). This study also included gender (0 = male, 1 = female), political identity (0 = not communist party member, 1 = Communist Party member) as control variables. The analysis of graduate employment is based on descriptive analyses. We will explain the corresponding measures in the major finding section.

Statistic Model

The statistical analysis of this study is mainly based on a stepwise linger regression model. Given that we want to examine the graduate employment trend of inequality in the massification and transnationalization of higher education, our focus is the interaction effects between the education program and family educational background (mainly measured by parents' education) on graduate employment. The analyses are mainly implemented with SPSS 26. Robust standard errors are reported.

Major Finding: Increasing Inequality in Youth Employment

Graduates' Employment Trends

The graduates' employment trends are measured by the first job performance of graduates from different educational programs, which is reflected in the employee organization, monthly salary, and the time spent to find the first job. Table 36.1 indicates that more than 90% of respondents in both types of educational programs were able to find their first job within 6 months after graduation. However, in terms of the nature of the work organizations and the monthly salary level, graduates from the two educational programs showed different characteristics. More than half of the respondents who graduated from Sino-foreign cooperative programs were employed by private companies and foreign companies, whose monthly salary levels fall in the 4,000–12,000 RMB range. The top two employers of respondents who graduated from regular higher education universities are domestic private companies and state-owned enterprises. Approximately 85% of them had a monthly salary of less than 8,000 RMB for the first job.

Table 36.1 Major Findings of Higher Education Graduates' First Job Performance in China

Time Taken to Find the First Job After Graduation	Sino-Foreign Cooperative Education	National Regular Higher Education
Within 3 months	55.7%	64.9%
3 to 6 months	35.2%	27.0%
6 months to 1 year	6.7%	6.0%
1 year and above	2.4%	2.1%
Company Nature of First Job Employment	Sino-Foreign Cooperative Education	National Regular Higher Education
State-owned enterprise	18.1%	20.1%
Private enterprise	29.5%	45.6%
Foreign companies	16.2%	4.5%
Government agencies	6.2%	6.6%
Nonprofit organizations	0.5%	0.6%
Self-employed	1.0%	1.2%
Salary Level for First Job Employment	Sino-Foreign Cooperative Education	National Regular Higher Education
Less than 4,000 RMB	14.3%	39.3%
4,000–8,000 RMB	43.8%	45.0%
8,000–12,000 RMB	24.8%	11.4%
12,000–15,000 RMB	11.0%	3.0%
15,000–20,000 RMB	3.3%	0.9%
More than 20,000 RMB	1.0%	0.3%

Employment Services and Assistance

The foregoing discussions have shown how China, being an affluent country in Asia, has encountered disparity and inequality in higher education. In our survey, we tried to explore whether the employment assistance and services obtained by the graduates are helpful for their employment. We divided employment assistance and service into two dimensions, provided by higher educational institutions and personal social networks. Table 36.2 shows that respondents attending Sino-foreign cooperative programs may seek university employment services more frequently compared with respondents attending regular higher education. For graduates of both educational institutions, external help for employment comes more from personal social network and family. The specific help that the two groups of respondents received from external social networks is mainly reflected in job information.

Table 36.2 Major Findings of Employment Services and Assistance for Higher Education Graduates in China

The Frequency of Seeking Employment Services and Information From the University Before Graduating	Sino-Foreign Cooperative Education	National Regular Higher Education
Often	44.3%	22.8%
Occasionally	38.1%	50.8%
Only when needed	16.7%	24.0%
Never	1.0%	2.4%
Views About the Most Helpful Employment Services Provided by the University	Sino-Foreign Cooperative Education	National Regular Higher Education
Local internship opportunities	71.9%	55.6%
Off-campus internship opportunities	50.0%	30.9%
Employment skills training	61.4%	43.8%
Curriculum vitae revision	47.6%	21.9%
Alumni mutual network	60.5%	38.1%
School-enterprise cooperation	69.0%	52.6%
Views About What Kinds of Activities During Studies in the University Are Helpful for Employment	Sino-Foreign Cooperative Education	National Regular Higher Education
Professional courses study	73.3%	65.5%
Societies activities	37.6%	30.0%
Extracurricular communication with teachers	44.8%	30.3%
Internship and social practice	80.0%	81.7%
Network social activities	57.1%	59.5%
The Greatest Source of Help in Finding the First Job After Graduation	Sino-Foreign Cooperative Education	National Regular Higher Education
Family or relatives	17.6%	28.5%
Networks developed before university	18.1%	14.7%
Networks developed in the university	45.7%	41.4%
University employment office	15.2%	7.8%
Others	2.9%	6.0%
Extra Employment Assistance Provided for the First Employment	Sino-Foreign Cooperative Education	National Regular Higher Education
Provide corresponding work information	69.0%	63.4%
Help prepare job application materials	11.9%	12.9%
Help submit job application materials	9.0%	6.3%
Arrange the job interview	5.2%	7.5%
Provide services to target employers	1.9%	4.2%
Others	2.4%	3.6%

Table 36.3 Major Findings of Higher Education Graduates' Career Development Expectation in China

Views About Whether Academic Experience Is Helpful for Career Development	Sino-Foreign Cooperative Education	National Regular Higher Education
Extremely helpful	27.6%	21.9%
Helpful	68.6%	68.8%
Not sure	2.9%	6.6%
Unhelpful	1.0%	2.4%
Not helpful at all	—	0.3%
Views About Whether Academic Experience Is Helpful for First Employment	**Sino-Foreign Cooperative Education**	**National Regular Higher Education**
Extremely helpful	25.7%	16.2%
Helpful	65,7%	68,8%
Not sure	5.2%	9.3%
Unhelpful	2.9%	5.1%
Not helpful at all	0.5%	0.6%
Views About the Main Concerns of First-Time Employment	**Sino-Foreign Cooperative Education**	**National Regular Higher Education**
Wage and income	21.0%	21.9%
Career development	62.4%	44.1%
Family issue	4.8%	5.7%
Employment time costs	11.9%	28.2%
Views About Socioeconomic Status 3 Years After Graduating	**Sino-Foreign Cooperative Education**	**National Regular Higher Education**
Raised dramatically	9.5%	3.3%
Improve	81.9%	76.0%
Stay the same	7.1%	19.8%
Decline	1.0%	0.9%
Dramatically drop	0.5%	—

Graduates' Attitudes Toward Employment and Career

In addition to the aforementioned objective factors, we also investigated the attitudes of graduates. More than 90% of the respondents believe that their academic experience is helpful to their graduate employment and future career development (Table 36.3). However, talking to the main concerns for the first job, respondents from different educational programs showed different preferences. Graduates from Sino-foreign cooperative programs pay more attention to sustainable career development, whereas respondents from regular higher education focus more on successful

Table 36.4 Descriptive Statistics for Graduate Employment Linear Regression Model

Variable	Mean (SD)
Dependent Variable	
Monthly salary	2.06 (1.042)
Independent Variables	
Graduate institutions	.37 (.484)
Employment units	.88 (.681)
Employment considerations	1.30 (1.060)
Family education background	5.10 (1.687)
External employment assistance	2.50 (1.212)
Demographic Variables	
Gender	.46 (.499)
Political identity	.32 (.466)

employment in a short term. Regarding their expectations of personal socioeconomic status in the next 3 years, graduates of Sino-foreign cooperative programs have shown more positive attitudes compared with respondents from regular higher education universities.

Inequality in Higher Education Graduate Employment

The aforementioned data show that graduates from distinct educational programs have distinct characteristics in terms of employee performance and career expectations. The analysis then starts with a linear regression analysis model (Table 36.4). The inequality of graduate employment is measured by the level of first job monthly salary (1 = less than 4,000 RMB, 2 = 4,000–8,000 RMB, 3 = 8,000–12,000 RMB, 4 = 12,000–15,000 RMB, 5 = 15,000–20,000 RMB, 6 = more than 20,000 RMB). The independent variables include graduate programs (0 = regular higher education, 1 = transnational cooperative education), family educational background (1 = no formal education, 2 = primary, 3 = lower secondary, 4 = upper secondary, 5 = technical secondary school, 6 = junior college, 7 = four-year college, 8 = graduate school), external employment assistance (1 = family or relatives, 2 = social networks developed before university, 3 = social networks developed during university, 4 = university employment office, 5 = others), employment institution (0 = government agencies and state-owned enterprises, 1 = domestic private companies, 2 = foreign and joint enterprises, 3 = nonprofit organizations), and employment considerations (0 = wage and income, 1 = career development, 2 = family concern, 3 = employment time costs). Table 36.5 presents a linear regression model by taking

Table 36.5 Linear Regression Models of Graduate Employment Inequality (B value and T value)

	Model (1)	Model (2)	Model (3)
Employment Status Variables			
Employment considerations	−.062	−.046	−.038
	(−1.454)	(−1.110)	(−0.911)
Employment units	−.066	−.072	−.077
	(−1.562)	(−1.753)	(−1.864)
Employment Assistance			
Graduate institutions	.723***	.641***	.615***
	(7.968)	(7.125)	(6.839)
External employment assistance	.095*	.107**	.092**
	(2.248)	(2.594)	(2.594)
Family educational background	.215***	.133***	.136***
	(5.147)	(5.147)	(5.310)
Control Variables			
Gender	.040	.036	.039
	(0.937)	(0.872)	(0.957)
Political identity	.092*	.070	.063
	(2.178)	(1.702)	(1.527)
_cons	1.790***	1.144***	.905***
	(0.055)	(0.137)	(0.164)
N	543	543	543
R square	.113	.157	.169

Notes: $*p < 0.05$, $**p < 0.01$, $p*** < 0.001$.

gender (0 = female, 1 = male) and political identification (0 = non-communist, 1 = communist) as control variables.

Model 1 indicates that transnational cooperative education strongly predicts respondents' employment performance. Respondents who graduated from transnational cooperative education universities or programs, have a more educated family, and have abundant external employment assistance are more likely to earn a higher monthly salary in their first employment. They are also more optimistic in the 3 years about their future socioeconomic status. Furthermore, the political identity variable is positively significant at the 0.05 significance level, suggesting that the overall increase in employment opportunities for transnational higher education graduates does not mean that the new advantages would be equally distributed.

Models 2 and 3 examine the family educational background and external employment assistance effects on graduate employment trends, respectively. The results show that family educational background and external employment assistance have a significant impact on the monthly salary of graduates' first employment. This result is highly consistent with previous studies (Ge, 2015; ILO, 2012; Mok, 2016). Furthermore, the value of R square indicates that three variables, namely, graduate institution, family educational background, and external employment assistance in Model 3, have a stronger explanatory power compared with the other two models. Our interpretation suggests that education inequality is further expanded under the transnationalization of higher education. Moreover, the inequality of family social capacities has further aggravated the employment inequality caused by the expansion of transnational cooperative education.

Globalization of Higher Education in China: Challenges and Policy Implications

Putting the data and analysis together, the massification and transnationalization of higher education have intensified inequality in education in China. Human capital theory predicts that, all other things being equal, raising participation in higher education will initially increase inequality as the rates of return rise and will then decrease inequality as expansion reaches mass levels and rates of return decline (Mok & Jiang, 2017a). However, our study indicated a different scenario emerging when higher education has been affected by the strong tide of transnationalization and marketization, where individuals and families must take up the significant financial responsibility in gaining higher education opportunities. This study has shown that transnational cooperation of higher education may increase employment inequality, particularly when transgenerational support, such as economic investment and social capital transformation, affected people's higher education admissions, prospective job opportunities, and career development considerations. In this light, the transnationalization of higher education has indeed made educational inequality even worse because it further widens the employment gap between the graduates with transnational learning experiences and those without. Similar findings are reported by recent research conducted by Liu (2021) and Xiong and Mok (2020).

However, our data do not include the differences in the teaching methods, course design, and curriculum settings of the two distinct educational programs in the analysis. In this study, the respondents who graduated from two kinds of educational programs showed a slight difference in views of ability enhancement through higher education programs (Table 36.6). Graduates of Sino-foreign cooperative education programs have more positive views on ability improvement during university experience, which may

Table 36.6 Views About Ability Enhancement During Higher Education Experience

Views About Which Abilities Have Significantly Improved Through Higher Education Experience	Sino-Foreign Cooperative Education	National Regular Higher Education
Tolerance	73.80%	61.30%
Curiosity	64.80%	42.90%
Self-confidence	77.60%	62.10%
Determination	69.00%	55.20%
Self-awareness	58.60%	51.30%
Problem-solving	77.70%	69.30%
International perspective	68.40%	46.80%
Language skills	70.90%	62.10%
Communication skills	78.10%	66.30%
Creativity	59.50%	45.00%
Critical thinking	71.40%	58.80%

also have a certain degree of impact on graduate employment trends. The reason behind this inequality trend in graduate employment requires further research.

Our analysis presented the major strategies that the Chinese government has adopted to address the growing impact of globalization through transforming higher education. The various "zations" featured by the massification, privatization, internationalization, and transnationalization processes have significantly transformed higher education in China. Through such transformations, China is now becoming an increasingly important country contributing to higher education learning and research, innovation, and knowledge transfer activities. Nonetheless, the success behind these reform processes is not without costs and risks. The present study has highlighted the negative social consequences, particularly when transgenerational inequality is intensified after transnationalizing higher education. Although more Chinese students do enjoy more learning opportunities after the massification of higher education in China, our analysis has demonstrated the widening gap between individuals with sufficient family support and those without. The intergenerational transfer of resources, more specifically, the social and cultural capitals with strong network resources that individuals coming from families with higher socioeconomic status enjoy would further intensify social and educational inequalities, as presented herein. The present study provides rich empirical evidence to support the theoretical debates regarding varied capitals that individuals process, which would significantly impact their educational experiences and the subsequent employment, as outlined in the earlier part of this chapter. If the Chinese government at different levels has failed to manage the widening gap and diverse expectations of citizens, the intensified educational inequality could be easily turned into social and even political problems. The perceived unequal treatments in education, if not managed well, could easily become a social problem requiring careful management and appropriate governance. Indeed, China confronted the outcry for the better management of the high costs resulting from the privatization and marketization of education, health, and housing in the 1990s, and social harmony and social cohesion was adversely affected (Mok & Kang, 2020). Given the negative impact of the growing social/educational inequalities, the Chinese government should adopt public/social policies appropriate for managing the transgenerational inequality.

Our discussions on China's responses to globalization through internationalizing/transnationalizing higher education have also raised questions regarding the value of international/transnational education. In the last decade, people have begun to question the value of internationalization of higher education, especially when some major concerns are being raised about who would benefit from international/transnational higher education. Our present study suggested the intensified inequality resulting from the internationalization/transnationalization of higher education, and similar concerns have been raised in other parts of the world. Some critics even question international higher education only favoring the elites and those coming from rich families and not disadvantaged students from less competitive classes/families (Mok & Wang, 2020). Connecting the present case of China to the broader debates of internationalization of higher education, we would appreciate the complexity of the issues, which deal not only with higher education but also other social and public policies related to youth transition from education and work. The internationalization/transnationalization of higher education issues would become even more complex when higher education systems across the globe experience different degrees of impact after the COVID-19 pandemic. In the post-COVID-19 era, which higher education systems could afford to continue transnational/international learning? The social and economic impact of the COVID-19 pandemic would suggest that the world will become even more divided. The gap between the rich and the poor, the gap between the Global North and Global South, and the gap between those who can and cannot enjoy international/transnational learning would bring diverse social, economic, cultural, and political consequences (Altbach & de Wits, 2020; Mok & Marginson, 2021).

Drawing comparative and international perspectives from higher education reforms in other Asian countries in terms of massification, privatization, internationalization, and transnationalization of higher education, we observed similar social consequences resulted from such transformations. A recent special issue provided a critical examination of how the massified and internationalized master education has affected student learning and graduate employment in Taiwan, South Korea, Chain, and Japan (Jung, 2020a, 2020b; Yang & Chan, 2020; Yang & Shen, 2020). Many countries and regions are confronting the severe challenges of youth transition from education to work (Brown et al., 2020; Green & Henseke, 2020; Mok & Jiang, 2018). Graduate employment has indeed become an increasingly complex given educational, social, economic, and political issues (Boden & Nedeva, 2010; Clarke, 2018; Goldin & Katz, 2009). Countries with better financial capacity could invest more strategically for enhancing students' international/

transnational learning to empower them in the "war of talent." However, individuals entering the position war would find unequal treatments and diverse experiences with different forms/levels of support either from their governments or families.

CONCLUSION

Critical reflections of the Chinese case upon the broader globalization and higher education issues show that the higher education transformation experiences in China are not unique, although the Chinese case demonstrates significant higher education changes within a relatively short period. In conclusion, the Chinese case presented in this study reinforces the theoretical debates, highlighting the significant impact of accessing social and cultural capitals; network resources would shape university graduates' position when participating in the position war (Brown, 2003; Brown et al., 2020; Mok, 2016). The intensified inequality contributed by the internationalization/ transnationalization of education has become a growing trend in Asia and other parts of the world. Responding to such a global trend, governments in general and educational institutions must adopt appropriate measures and policies in managing the challenges of globalization with higher education reforms resolving the dilemmas highlighted in this study.

REFERENCES

Altbach, P. G., & Hans, D.-W. (2020). Postpandemic outlook for higher education is bleakest for the poorest. *International Higher Education, 102,* 3–5.

Becker, W. E., & Lewis, D. R. (Eds.). (1993). *Higher education and economic growth.* Kluwer academic publishers.

Becker, G. S., & Tomes, N. (1986). Human capital and the rise and fall of families. *Journal of Labor Economics, 4*(3), Part 2, S1–S39.

Blanden, J., Gregg, P., & Macmillan, L. (2007). Accounting for intergenerational income persistence: Noncognitive skills, ability and education. *The Economic Journal, 117*(519), C43–C60.

Blau, P. M., Ducan, O. D., & Tyree, A. (1967). *Measuring the status of occupations.* Tavistock.

Boden, R., & Nedeva, M. (2010). Employing discourse: Universities and graduate "employability." *Journal of Education Policy, 25*(1), 37–54.

Bourdieu, P. (1973). *Cultural reproduction and social reproduction.* Tavistock.

Bowles, S., & Gintis, H. (1975). The problem with human capital theory—A Marxian critique. *The American Economic Review, 65*(2), 74–82.

Braun, D., & Merrien, F.-X. (1999). Governance of universities and modernisation of the state: Analytical aspects. In D. Braun & F.-X. Merrien (Eds.), *Towards a new model of governance for universities? A comparative view* (pp. 9–33). Jessica Kingsley.

Brown, P. (2003). The opportunity trap: Education and employment in a global economy. *European Educational Research Journal, 2*(1), 141–179.

Brown, P., Lauder, H., & Ashton, D. (2011). *The global auction: The broken promises of education, jobs, and incomes.* Oxford University Press.

Brown, P., Lauder, H., & Cheung, S.-Y. (2020). *The death of human capital?: Its failed promise and how to renew it in an age of disruption.* Oxford University Press.

Carnoy, M. (2011). As higher education expands, is it contributing to greater inequality? *National Institute Economic Review, 215*(1), R34–R47.

Chan, W.-K., & Kinglun, N. (2011). Accumulating human capital while increasing educational inequality: A study on higher education policy in China. *Asia Pacific Journal of Education, 31*(3), 293–310.

Clarke, M. (2018). Rethinking graduate employability: The role of capital, individual attributes and context. *Studies in Higher Education, 43*(11), 1923–1937.

Collins, R. (2019). *The credential society: An historical sociology of education and stratification.* Columbia University Press.

Dale, R. (2015). Employability and mobility in valorization of higher education qualifications. In *International symposium on globalization, changing labour market and social mobility: Challenges for education and urban governance.* The Education University of Hong Kong.

Erdem, E., & Tugcum, C. T. (2012). Higher education and unemployment: A cointegration and causality analysis of the case of Turkey. *European Journal of Education, 47*(2), 299–309.

Gao, Y. (2018). Massifaication of higher education in China: Problems and solutions. In A. Wu & J. Hawkins (Eds.), *Massification of higher education in Asia* (pp. 9–19). Springer.

Ge, C., Kankanhalli, A., & Huang, K.-W. (2015). Investigating the determinants of starting salary of IT graduates. *ACM SIGMIS Database: The DATABASE for Advances in Information Systems, 46*(4), 9–25.

Gillies, D. (2017). Human capital theory in education. *Encyclopedia of Educational Philosophy and Theory,* 1–5. https://doi.org/10.1007/978-981-287-532-7_254-1

Goldin, C., & Katz, L. F. (2009). *The race between education and technology.* Harvard University Press.

Green, A., & Mok, K.-H. (2013). Expansion of higher education, graduate employment and social mobility: An Asia and Europe dialogue. In *Hong Kong Educational Research Association Annual Conference.* Hong Kong Institute of Education.

Green, F., & Golo, H. (2016). The changing graduate labour market: Analysis using a new indicator of graduate jobs. *IZA Journal of Labour Policy, 5*(1), 14.

Huang, F. (2010). Transnational higher education in Japan and China: A comparative study. In D. W. Chapman, W. K. Cummings, & G. A. Postiglione (Eds.), *Crossing borders in East Asian higher education* (pp. 265–282). Springer.

Ilo, I. (2012, June 1). *Global estimate of forced labour: Results and methodology.* International Labour Organization, 13. https://www.ilo.org/global/topics/forced-labour/publications/WCMS_182004/lang--en/index.htm

Jerrim, J., & Macmillan, L. (2015). Income inequality, intergenerational mobility, and the Great Gatsby curve: Is education the key? *Social Forces, 94*(2), 505–533.

Jiang, J. (2017). Higher education in China. In G. W. Noblit (Ed.), *Oxford research encyclopedia: Education.* Oxford University Press. https://doi.org/10.1093/acrefore/9780190264 093.013.207

Jung, J. (2020a). Master's education in massified, internationalized, and marketized East Asian higher education systems. *Higher Education Policy, 33*(4), 613–618.

Jung, J. (2020b). Master's education in Hong Kong: Access and programme diversity. *Higher Education Policy,* 33/4, 711–733.

Kennedy, A. (2019). China's rise as a science power: Rapid progress, emerging reforms, and the challenge of illiberal innovation. *Asian Survey, 59*(6), 1022–1043.

Lauder, H. (2014). Jobs or skills? The role of education in the 21st century. In *Keynote speech presented at the 2014 APERA–HKERA Annual Conference.* Hong Kong Institute of Education.

Li, C. (2006). Sociopolitical change and inequality in educational opportunity: Impact of family background and institutional factors on educational attainment (1940–2001). *Chinese Sociology & Anthropology, 38*(4), 6–36.

Liu, D. (2021). Habitus, campus experience, and graduate employment: Personal advancement of middleclass students in China. *Journal of Education and Work, 34*(3), 344–355.

Luo, Y., Guo, F., & Shi, J. (2018). Expansion and inequality of higher education in China: How likely would Chinese poor students get to success? *Higher Education Research & Development, 37*(5), 1015–1034.

Macmillan, L., Tyler, C., & Vignoles, A. (2015). Who gets the top jobs? The role of family background and networks in recent graduates' access to high-status professions. *Journal of Social Policy, 44*(3), 487–515.

Mare, R. D. (1981). Change and stability in educational stratification. *American Sociological Review,* 72–87.

Marginson, S. (2011). Higher education in East Asia and Singapore: Rise of the Confucian model. *Higher Education, 61*(5), 587–611.

Mok, K-.H. (2002). Policy of decentralization and changing governance of higher education in post-Mao China. *Public Administration and Development, 22*(3), 261–273.

Mok, K.-H. (2005). Globalization and educational restructuring: University merging and changing governance in China. *Higher Education, 50*(1), 57–88.

Mok, K.-H. (2007). Questing for internationalization of universities in Asia: Critical reflections. *Journal of Studies in International Education, 11*(3–4), 433–454.

Mok, K.-H. (2016). Massification of higher education, graduate employment and social mobility in the greater China region. *British Journal of Sociology of Education, 37*(1), 51–71.

Mok, K.-H. (2020). Marketizing higher education in post-Mao China. *International Journal of Educational Development, 20*(2), 109–126.

Mok, K.-H., & Han, X. (2017). Internationalization and transnationalization of higher education: A review of the Asia Pacific region. In K.-H. Mok (Ed.), *Managing international connectivity, diversity of learning and changing labour markets* (pp. 47–72). Springer.

Mok, K.-H., Han, X., Jiang, J., & Zhang, X. (2017). International and transnational learning in higher education: A study of students' career development in China. *Centre for Global Higher Education Working Paper Series, 21,* 1–23.

Mok, K.-H., Han, X., Jiang, J., & Zhang, X. (2018). International and transnational education for whose interests? A study on the career development of Chinese students. *Higher Education Quarterly, 72*(3), 208–223.

Mok, K.-H., & Jiang, J. (2017a). Questing for entrepreneurial university in Hong Kong and Shenzhen: The promotion of industry-university collaboration and entrepreneurship. In D. E. Neubauer, K.-H. Mok, J. Jiang (Eds.), *The sustainability of higher education in an era of post-massification* (pp. 155–133). Routledge.

Mok, K.-H., & Jiang, J. (2017b). Massification of higher education: Challenges for admissions and graduate employment in China. In K.-H. Mok (Ed.), *Managing international connectivity, diversity of learning and changing labour* markets (pp. 219–244). Springer.

Mok, K.-H., & Jiang, J. (2018). Massification of higher education and challenges for graduate employment and social mobility: East Asian experiences and sociological reflections. *International Journal of Educational Development, 63*, 44–51.

Mok, K.-H., & Kang, Y. (2020). Social cohesion and welfare reforms—the Chinese approach. In A. Croissant & P. Walkenborst (Eds.), *Social cohesion in Asia: Historical origins, contemporary shapes and future dynamics* (pp. 26–49). Routledge.

Mok, K.-H., & Kang, Y. (2021). A critical review of the history, achievements and impacts of China's quest for world-class university status. In E. Hazelkorn (Ed.), *Research handbook on university rankings: History, methodology, influence and impact* (pp. 366–381). Edward Elgar.

Mok, K.-H., & Lee, M. (2003). Globalization or glocalization? Higher education reforms in Singapore. *Asia Pacific Journal of Education, 23*(1), 15–42.

Mok, K.-H., & Lo, H.-C. (2001). Marketization and the changing governance in higher education: A comparative studies of Hong Kong and Taiwan. In *International Conference on Marketization and Higher Education in East Asia, 7–8.*

Mok, K.-H., & Lo, Y.-W. (2007). The impacts of neo-liberalism on China's higher education. *Journal for Critical Education Policy Studies, 5*(1), 316–348.

Mok, K.-H., & Marginson, S. (2021). Massification, diversification and internalisation of higher education in China: Critical reflections of developments in the last two decades. *International Journal of Educational Development, 84*, 102405.

Mok, K.-H., Wang, Z., & Neubauer, D. (2020). Contesting globalisation and implications for higher education in the Asia–Pacific region: Challenges and prospects. *Higher Education Policy, 33*(3), 397–411.

Mok, K.-H., Welch, A., & Kang, Y. (2020). Government innovation policy and higher education: The case of Shenzhen, China. *Journal of Higher Education Policy and Management, 42*(2), 194–212.

Mok, K.-H., & Wu, A. M. (2016). Higher education, changing labour market and social mobility in the era of massification in China. *Journal of Education and Work, 29*(1), 77–97.

Mok, K.-H., & Yu, K.-M. (2014). Introduction: The quest for regional hub status and transnationalization of higher education: Challenges for managing human capital in East Asia. In K.-H. Mok & K.-M. Yu (Eds.), *Internationalization of higher education in East Asia: Trends of student mobility and impact on education governance* (pp. 1–26). Routledge.

Neubauer, D. E., Mok, K.-H., & Jiang, J. (Eds.) (2017). *The sustainability of higher education in an era of post-massification*. Routledge.

Psacharopoulos, G. (1985). Returns to education: A further international update and implications. *Journal of Human Resources*, 583–604.

Roemer, J. E. (1993). A pragmatic theory of responsibility for the egalitarian planner. *Philosophy & Public Affairs*, 146–166.

Roemer, J. E. (1998). *Equality of opportunity*. Harvard University Press.

Sharma, Y. (2018). Ministry ends hundreds of Sino-foreign HE partnerships. *University World News, 513.* https://www.universityworldnews.com/post.php?story=20180706154106269

Trow, M. (1974). Problems in the transition from elite to mass higher education. In *Policies for Higher Education* (pp. 51–101). OECD.

Wen, D. (2005). The impacts of SES on higher education opportunity and graduate employment in China. *Peking University Education Review, 3*(3), 58–63.

Wu, X. (2015). *Empires of coal: Fueling China's entry into the modern world order, 1860–1920.* Stanford University Press.

Xie, Y., Zhang, C., & Lai, Q. (2014). China's rise as a major contributor to science and technology. *Proceedings of the National Academy of Sciences, 111*(26), 9437–9442.

Xiong, W., & Mok, K.-H. (2020). Critical reflections on mainland China and Taiwan overseas returnees' job searches and career development experiences in the rising trend of anti-globalisation. *Higher Education Policy, 33*(3), 413–436.

Yang, C.-C., & Chan, S.-J. (2020). Massified master's education in Taiwan: A credential game? *Higher Education Policy, 33*(4), 619–635.

Yang, J., & Shen, W. (2020). Master's education in STEM fields in China: Does gender matter? *Higher Education Policy, 33*(4), 667–688.

Yang, R. (2002). *Third delight: The internationalization of higher education in China*. Psychology Press.

Yang, R. (2010). International organizations, changing governance and China's policy making in higher education: An analysis of the World Bank and the World Trade Organization. *Asia Pacific Journal of Education, 30*(4), 419–431.

Zha, Q. (2011). China's move to mass higher education in a comparative perspective. *Compare: A Journal of Comparative and International Education, 41*(6), 751–768.

CHAPTER 37

REFORMING HIGHER EDUCATION IN INDIA IN PURSUIT OF EXCELLENCE, EXPANSION, AND EQUITY

JANDHYALA B. G. TILAK

GLOBAL CONTEXT

GLOBALLY higher education is expanding very fast. Student numbers are exploding, and the number of universities and other institutions of higher education is rising at exponential growth. Student composition is undergoing rapid changes as well. Young people from middle and lower socioeconomic backgrounds are increasingly found on university campuses, and they enter universities with different kinds and levels of aspirations; the aspirations of the parents are also varying, exerting heavy influence on student behavior. Governments and societies at large also have changing expectations from the universities, demanding tangible, visible, significant, quantifiable, and measurable outcomes. Not only the composition of students but also the composition of teachers is undergoing drastic changes, as they also enter the academic profession with varying quality, abilities, knowledge, and commitment, and with different kinds of aspirations and aptitudes for teaching and research. Furthermore, this is the era when knowledge is exploding with the frontiers of knowledge changing quickly and the disciplinary boundaries disappearing, the latter leading to emergence of multidisciplinary, interdisciplinary, and transdisciplinary areas of knowledge. Some specific emerging areas of knowledge include artificial intelligence, data analytics, machine learning, big data, cognitive computing, financial technology, robotics, and so on, which are entering into the university curricula. The phenomenon of change is also entering the pedagogy of teaching and research. The blackboard-chalk-and-talk method of teaching and brick-and-mortar universities are being replaced by online, distance methods of teaching, blended teaching, personalized learning, smart and flipped classrooms, and virtual universities. Thus, every aspect of higher education—students, teachers, universities, pedagogy, and so on—is characterised by a high and new version of diversity. The nature, definition, and mission of universities are also subject to varied interpretations. Public and private, national and international, academic and vocational (technical), research and teaching, for-profit and not-for profit, entrepreneurial and knowledge-concentrated universities, small and large, and various other kinds and forms of universities are emerging and growing. Globalization further necessitates that universities serve national as well as global development; produce locally relevant and globally competitive knowledge; and produce citizens with national values but also global citizens for rapidly changing national as well as global markets. The system of higher education is becoming increasingly complex and volatile. All these factors place heavy pressures on universities to perform—to perform better and differently from the past.

The onset of the era of globalization and the associated developments have necessitated reforms in higher education in many countries of the world. Ideological imperatives of globalization have impacted higher education systems everywhere. As the welfare state policies are compelled to go into oblivion, the market ethos invaded higher education systems, and narrow financial considerations began to dominate the policy discourses. State–university relationships are redefined; rationale for public subsidies for higher education is questioned; cost recovery measures have been introduced; the idea of a university as a creator, repository, and disseminator of knowledge gave in to the idea of the university as a marketplace, and higher education as a commodity; students as consumers/customers and teachers as suppliers; the academic profession has been drawn away from its traditional values, weakening the idea of the university. The private sector took the center stage, displacing the public sector in higher education. The pursuit of excellence has replaced concerns about equitable access to higher education. On the whole, the landscape of higher education has taken altogether new forms and colors. The whole world is grappling with these changes, and higher education in India is no exception.

As the trajectory of development has undergone a significant change with the introduction of economic reform policies at the beginning of the 1990s in India and around the same period in many other countries, it is widely held that major reforms need to be introduced in higher education. The reforms introduced in many countries cover issues relating to governance, finance, expansion, and quality—all pro-market. Simultaneously some (e.g., Marginson, 2011; Singh, 2013; Tilak, 2008, 2010a; UNESCO, 2015) began arguing for the resurrection of the role of the state, and the noble character of the university as a public good, lest the university as a noble institution becomes an endangered species. It is in this context that one has to critically review the attempts being made to reform higher education.

The saga of higher education reforms in independent India is a long story of great excitement and disappointment. During the post-independence period, India witnessed a spectacular expansion of its higher education. The expansion that took place after 1990 has been most impressive. But the exponential growth seems to have taken place at the cost of quality and equity. Pursuit of excellence has been an important objective of higher education reforms. But given the distinct character of the Indian society, riddled with socioeconomic and structural inequalities, historical legacies, and democratic political structure, equity in higher education has also necessarily been an important objective. Added to all these is the need to meet global needs while simultaneously fulfilling national considerations. Balancing these diverse considerations, reforming higher education has not been an easy task. The task has indeed been complicated by the low enrollments in higher education, relatively low levels of economic development, low economic levels of living of the population, severe underfunding of higher education, shortage of quality faculty, highly overregulated but poorly governed systems, rise in managerialism, erosion in university autonomy and accountability, low levels of quality and standards in higher education in general, and above all, dominance of private players with vested interests. This chapter critically reviews independent India's earnest endeavors toward reforming its higher education, focusing on the major attempts being initiated since 2020 to prepare higher education to face the emerging national and global challenges of the 21st century. However, as it is not possible to be exhaustive in its coverage of issues in higher education, it concentrates on a few select major issues.

HIGHER EDUCATION IN INDIA

Ancient India had one of the finest education systems in the world, with famous centers of higher learning and a highly educated society. But external invasions and colonial rule have transformed India into an illiterate society (Basu, 1974; Dharmpal, 1983). At the time of independence in 1947, the literacy rate was a mere 12%; there were barely 20 universities and 500 colleges with about 200,000 students (Raza, 1991). After independence, India made impressive strides in developing the second largest system of higher education in the world—with 1,113 universities and 43,796 colleges, 93% of which are necessarily affiliated with one or more public universities, and 1.6 million teachers and 41.3 million students (in 2020–2021). The system produces about 10 million graduates every year. It has moved over a long period from a slow-growth system to a rapid-growth one.

While quantitatively the growth is impressive, the higher education system is plagued with a multitude of problems, including issues concerning access, equity, quality, and governance. The gross enrolment ratio is only 27.3% in 2020–2021, which is considered inadequate to meet the development goals of the nation. The quantitative growth itself has not only been too small, but it has also not been smooth. The growth which was slow and steady during the first three decades has been rapid after 1990; the fast growth experienced during the post-1990 period has been induced by the private sector, which in turn caused widening of inequalities in access to higher education between the rich and the poor, and the fall in overall quality and standards in education, and gave scope for several unfair practices to enter into the system. High-quality institutions are too few to meet the demand. Among the 1,000 or so universities, only a few figure in global university rankings; there are no world-class universities. Higher education is predominantly dominated by undergraduate education; postgraduate education and research have not progressed much. Graduate unemployment has become an important issue; the skill component in higher education is found to be infinitely small. Erosion in autonomy and inadequate public funding, along with a critical shortage of qualified and committed teachers, are considered the most important reasons for the poor performance of higher education. Only a minority of institutions—around 14% of colleges and 35% of universities—have been accredited by government bodies by 2020. Several efforts have been made in independent India to address some of the critical problems, but major curricular, organizational, and structural reforms are still due. Earlier attempts to reform higher education put a high premium on continuity. But the social contexts within which universities are located have dramatically changed in most countries, including India. As a result, as Gornitzka et al. (2005) observed, most systems have experienced and have had to come to terms with the turbulence associated with enormous increases in their scale and a great widening of the student community, together with major changes in modes of governance and even in the objectives of higher education. All this requires new approaches to higher education.

This chapter provides a short history of a large number of commissions and committees set up in India to suggest reforms in higher education beginning with the pre-independence era; it briefly presents a critical appraisal of the strengths and weaknesses of each policy proposal and then goes on to discuss a few major aspects of the National Education Policy of 2020, which is the latest effort at offering a large package of reforms for higher education, in addition to school education. Looking at the entire education as a continuum, the policy also proposes radical reforms in school education. However, this chapter concentrates on higher education, which is undergoing a major transition.

PUBLIC POLICIES AND APPROACHES TO REFORM HIGHER EDUCATION IN INDIA

Even before independence, India identified some of the major education challenges that it faced and the needed reforms, as there were only a small number of universities and colleges, and the graduates produced were not adequate in number and in skills and knowledge to run departments of the colonial administration. The main intent of the colonial administration was to produce graduates to run the British administration in India (Woodrow, 1862), who would maintain a high degree of "attachment and loyalty to British rule" (Naoroji, 1901, p. 233). However, measures proposed by several committees and official resolutions of the British Raj, for example, in the Government of India Resolution of 1913 that accepted removal of illiteracy as an objective, but not the provision of compulsory education, or by the Sadler Commission (1919) that was to look into the conditions and prospects of the University of Calcutta, but in reality looked at higher education in the country as a whole, and the Hartog Committee (1929), which advocated consolidation of schools rather than expansion, and restricted admissions in higher education with an objective to safeguard quality, have not been effective in the development of higher education in British India in terms of numbers or quality of graduates. They helped neither the British rule nor the Indian society. Access to higher education was extremely restrictive to the higher echelons of society. To the vast Indian society, it was irrelevant education.

The independent India rightly recognized educating its children and youth as one of the most important challenges to set the newly independent nation on the path of progress and prosperity. Faced with the challenging task of conceiving and developing a national system of education, particularly at a time when the problems of economic recovery and the rehabilitation of those displaced by partition of the country were daunting, immediately after independence, the government of India appointed the University Education Commission, popularly known as the Radhakrishnan Commission in 1948 (Government of India, 1951) (known after the name of its chairman, a distinguished scholar, philosopher, and former vice- chancellor of Banaras University, who later became the president of India) to look into the needed measures to reform and develop a national higher education system in the country that would be based on Indian philosophy of life—liberal and humanitarian, and serving national interests and fulfilling development needs of the newly independent nation. Even though efforts were made to implement some reforms proposed by the Commission, recommendations such as those relating to examinations and curriculum remained unattended and, as a result, the colonial legacy of universities as mainly examination-based focused institutions that were job-oriented remained intact. In fact, not only in the case of examinations but also the very "Europeanized" model of development of higher education institutions took firm roots and continues to dictate the approach in independent India. As Basu (1989, p. 167) observed, while such dependency is probably inevitable given the long colonial rule and technological and economic superiority of the West, "it makes Indian academics imitative and dampens originality." Recommendations of the Radhakrishnan Commission to restructure higher education to enable students to understand the aims of life and social philosophy in the larger background of Indian philosophy, to introduce religious education, and so on, did not receive any attention from the educational administrators. The University Grants Commission (UGC) was set up in 1952, which was also a recommendation of the Radhakrishnan Commission, with a larger mandate of reforming higher education in curricular, academic, regulatory, governance, and financing areas. Subsequently a good number of universities and institutions of higher education were established. Public initiatives played a dominant role during this phase. Most of the universities and colleges were public institutions. Even private institutions enjoyed large-scale financial support in the form of grants from the public exchequer; they are known as government-aided private institutions. Private funds as well as individuals played key roles in the cause of higher education

(UGC, 2003). With rapid growth in higher education during the first three Five-Year Plan periods (1950–1951 to 1965–1966), quite a few serious problems began to surface. Prominent among them were educational inflation, graduate unemployment, lowering of standards in higher education, and devaluation of degrees. The trade-offs among quality, quantity, and equity became visible, with growing graduate unemployment and widening inequalities. The Education Commission (1966) (chaired by D. S. Kothari, an eminent educationist and then chairman of the UGC) had suggested consolidation of higher education, rather than its further expansion. The Education Commission (1966), which was comprehensive in scope and covered the entire education system, recognizing the relationship between education and national development, proposed a large set of sweeping reforms in education. The first National Policy on Education in 1968 (Government of India, 1968), which was based on the report of the Education Commission, did initiate a few major reforms in higher education. The 1968 policy was followed by some rather unsuccessful efforts toward consolidation of higher education, though some major initiatives were made such as strengthening of centers of advanced study to promote research in universities. But in general, many policy recommendations could not be taken up or fully implemented for various sociopolitical and structural reasons; as Naik (1982) remarked, many of the recommendations were yet to be implemented and those that were taken up were poorly implemented. The trajectory of higher education was pulled by populist pressures in the direction of quantity at the cost of quality. The political and economic problems caused by the Indo-Pakistan War in 1965, the nationwide drought, and spiraling inflation were partially responsible for the inability of the government to take many of the policy recommendations made by the Education Commission. The 1986 policy (Government of India, 1986) and the revised policy (Government of India, 1992) resulted in some reforms in higher education such as establishment of academic staff colleges in the universities for providing faculty development opportunities, state councils of higher education for better planning and coordination of higher education in the states, and rural universities in a few places on the lines of Mahatma Gandhi's thinking on transformation of rural areas. But in general, of the several important policy recommendations, many could not be taken up or fully implemented for various sociopolitical and structural reasons. As Altbach and Chitnis (1993, p. 11) observed, while change has characterized Indian higher education, deliberate efforts to implement reforms have not been successful.

However, reforming higher education has been on the public agenda all the time. Several committees and commissions were regularly constituted, which proposed a series of reforms, including in the areas of governance and public funding. The nature of reforms suggested and/or introduced in the neoliberal framework in the post-1986 period, or more clearly after 1990, is much different. In the light of increasing trends of liberalization, privatization, globalization, internationalization of higher education, the emergence of global ranking mechanisms of universities, the idea of world-class universities, global competition for talent and skills, and changing world policies in higher education, new packages of reforms have been suggested by several expert committees, some of which became known as neoliberal reforms. "Many of the recent initiatives in policy reforms mark a transition in the history of higher education in independent India—from a system embedded in welfare statism to a system partially based on quasi-market principles and finally to a system based on a neo-liberal market philosophy" (Tilak, 2012a, p. 36). Higher education in India, like in many other countries, is compelled to embrace the corporate ethos and new managerialism which is profit-driven. However, an impressive feature of this period has been a very high rate of growth in higher education, but the nature of growth itself is characterized by several weaknesses. In the post-1986 period, or more appropriately known as the post-"adjustment" period (structural adjustment policies were adopted in the early 1990s), several committees and commissions were constituted such as the Birla-Ambani Committee (Government of India, 2000), C. N. R. Rao Committee (Government of India, 2005), National Knowledge Commission (2007, 2009), Justice Verma Commission on teacher education (Government of India, 2012), and the Yashpal Committee (Government of India, 1999). In addition, several committees constituted by the UGC, the All India Council for Technical Education (AICTE), and the Central Advisory Board of Education have proposed a series of reforms. Both the Ambani-Birla Committee and the National Knowledge Commission were chaired by top industrialists, the latter by Sam Pitroda. The Yashpal Committee was chaired by an educationist—Yashpal himself. Despite noting the critical importance of the role of the state in development of higher education in several developed countries of the world, the Ambani-Birla Committee strongly suggested that government should leave higher education altogether to the private sector, and that it should confine itself to school education. Further, it pleaded for legislation of the private university bill, which was pending since 1995 (Government of India, 1995) and also suggested that the user pay principle be strictly enforced in higher education. The National Knowledge Commission also made similar recommendations. It further favored opening the Indian higher education sector to foreign universities and allowing Indian universities to go abroad, and simply to facilitate trade in higher education. The Yashpal Committee has argued more for rejuvenation of higher education, defragmentation of knowledge, and care in relying on private university systems and even internationalization. It also favored less regulation of the universities by the government, stating that universities should be self-regulating institutions. The C. N. R. Rao (an eminent scientist and chairperson of the Scientific Advisory Council to the Prime Minister of India) Committee has advised cautious internationalization—that is, opening of higher education in India for the entry of only the best institutions in the world and erecting safeguards against entry of greedy and cheap foreign institutions looking for quick monetary returns who might invade the Indian higher education system and create chaos.

Though there was no formal education policy per se during the period of 1986–2020, quite a few initiatives were taken toward reforming higher education, partly responding to the recommendations of the committees and commissions, and partly as a part of initiatives planned in the framework of the 5-year plans. After the introduction of economic reform policies in early 1990s, the approach to higher education changed, and it began to be viewed more as a private good, the responsibility of which lies with the individual; privatization of higher education was given a big boost. Many big corporations have begun to look at higher education as an attractive area for high-yield investment. The "traditional" private higher education system that was philanthropy-based and/or supported by state funds gave in to the "new" mode of the private sector in higher education. As a result, compared to almost zero private universities in the 1980s, the number increased to 446 universities (in addition to 10 government-aided private institutions deemed to be universities) by 2020–2021 (AIHES, 2020). Between 2010–2011 and 2020–2021, that is, in about 10 years, the number of private universities (excluding deemed institutions) quadrupled from 87 to 365, while public universities increased hardly by 1.4 times. At the college level, two-thirds of the colleges are in the fee-dependent private sector (compared to less than 60% a decade ago), and 14% are under the government-aided private sector; hardly one-fifth of the colleges are government colleges. On the whole, more than two-thirds of the higher education system is in the private hands. Thus, expansion in public universities and colleges has been very little, while the growth in private institutions has been phenomenal. Interestingly, private colleges that constitute two-thirds of all colleges account for only 44% of total enrolment, and government colleges constituting only one-fifth of all account for 55% of total enrolment. More importantly, these private institutions are almost exclusively student fee-dependent, and many tend to be commercially oriented and profit-motivated, treating higher education as a private profit-making machine. They receive no direct funding from government and are run on a "self-financing" basis, a euphemism for full cost-recovering (or in practice, profit-making) institutions. They do, however, receive indirect funding. In addition to tax incentives in setting up educational institutions, students are eligible for public scholarships, fee reimbursements/waivers, and public subsidies in education loans; staff are eligible to compete for research funds from public sources; and the institutions might occasionally get special development grants from the government. Private players have entered higher education "for personal gain introducing unscrupulous practices that seem to exploit the students and the community" (Mathur, 2022, p. 73). With aggressive marketing campaigns through online platforms, television, radio, and print, they often mislead the gullible students, the parents, and even the employers in the labor market. As Altbach (2012, pp. 131–132) sums up, "Most of the growing private sector has little semblance of academic culture . . . most institutions are for-profit, offering vocationally popular qualifications with no aspirations to conduct research. Most of the teachers are part-time and, few, if any, have long-term or permanent employment arrangements. There is no shared governance; top managers control all aspects of the institutions." A long absence of public policy in higher education (Tilak, 2004) has enabled unregulated, unplanned, and chaotic rapid growth of private higher education in the country.

In the eleventh 5-year plan period, a massive expansion of higher education was taken up and the numbers of central universities (funded by union government), Indian Institutes of Technology (IITs), and many other technical and professional institutions were doubled or more than doubled. The phase of expansion has continued, and in all, these numbers were tripled over a short period: from 19 central universities, 7 IITs, and

6 Indian Institutes of Management (IIMs) at the beginning of the eleventh 5-year plan (i.e., in 2007), to 54 central universities, 23 IITs and 20 IIMs (by 2022). Though in the respective categories these figures mean big increases, in the massive higher education system, these numbers relating to central public institutions are small. Some of these central institutions, particularly the old ones, are, however, of reasonably high quality and some figure in the global rankings of universities.

Governments in many states also responded to popular democratic pressures and allowed expansion in universities and colleges under the jurisdiction of the state governments, but given the resource constraints, more in the private sector. The consequence is mushrooming of private institutions everywhere in large numbers. While the union government thus focused on quality in higher education, state governments have adopted a different approach and allowed massive expansion under the private sector and deliberately sacrificed quality (Carnoy & Dossani, 2012). It seems that the union government concentrates on quality in its minuscule number of institutions; state universities and government colleges which are few in number serve the equity purpose; and the overwhelmingly large number of private universities and colleges, which constitute respectively one-third and two-thirds of all, tend to facilitate increase in access to some extent. The 16 open universities and distance education programs in 112 dual-mode universities help in the massification of higher education. In the process, the three core dimensions—access, quality, and equity—seem to get delinked from each other.

As adequate resources could not be provided from public exchequer to the new and even the old institutions, realizing the need to mobilize additional resources for higher education and following global trends, cost recovery measures were introduced in India in the early 1990s as an important step toward easing the financial burden on the public exchequer. A drastically restructured national education loan program to be operated by commercial banks was launched with partial state subsidies on interest rates for disadvantaged sections of the population (Tilak, 2009). Along with this, following the recommendation of a committees constituted by the UGC (1993) and the ACITE (1994), almost all higher educational institutions were required to mobilize about 20% of the recurring budgets of the universities through student fees and other nonstate sources. Accordingly, many public institutions have steeply raised the tuition and introduced user charges on several items in university administration.The availability of educational loans has lent further justification for these measures, which include a reduction in the number of scholarships and the total budget allocations to scholarships in higher education. Other tendencies of privatization have also penetrated deeply into public higher education. Resource mobilization, generation of internal revenues, efficiency in the use of resources, reduction in costs, and so on have become common parlance in the university administration, even sidelining core education goals; and goals of financial administration have begun to figure at the top of the agenda not only in private but also in public universities. The infiltration of private features in public universities has drastically changed the very nature of public universities (Tilak, 2012b).

As most universities began making efforts to generate resources through fees and other sources, state subsidies began to gradually shrink (Tilak, 1998). Universities that have not made intense efforts of raising resources through fees and other sources allowed a decline in per-student expenditure and thereby in the quality of education. Such a trend of reduction in state subsidies was also supported by a policy discussion document of the Government of India (1997) that defined, for the first time, higher education as a "non-merit good," indicating that government subsidies for higher education would need to be reduced drastically, though subsequently higher education was reclassified as a "merit good of type II," meaning that it need not necessarily be subsidized at the same level as "merit goods of type I" like elementary education and primary healthcare.

With a view to improve higher education in India, a few more measures were also introduced, withdrawn, and reintroduced. Examples of such instances of the recent past include scrapping and reintroduction of the National Eligibility Test for recruitment of teachers in higher education, introduction and withdrawal of academic performance indicators for evaluation of teachers' performance, introduction and scrapping of a 4-year degree program (in the University of Delhi), which in a modified form has been taken up following the National Education Policy of 2020, moves and announcements regarding common entrance tests, frequent changes in the methods of national assessment and accreditation, status of academic programs of open universities, including recognition, derecognition, rerecognition of degrees offered through open and distance education mode, announcements on the validity of MPhil and PhD courses in these institutions, questions on the status of teachers in open universities, status of deemed universities, and so on. Each one was a rush job, necessitating amending, reamending, and even superseding the previous ones. The frequent u- (and inverted u) turns reflecting a situation of policy dilemmas on the part of the state add a lot of confusion to every one—to the students, the parents, the teachers, the administrators, the employers, and the entire society. The twists and turns can be attributed to the absence of a clear coherent long-term policy and vision on higher education and long-term planning. The system is managed by executive orders and quick-fix solutions, and they are not seriously thought over from the vantage point of a long-term vision and a holistic perspective. The lack of a clear and coherent policy approach also gave scope for judicial intervention and not less frequently to contradictory judgments by the judiciary, whether it relates to private institutions, minority status, fees, admissions, reservations, or validity of degrees offered by the open universities or others on distance mode, and so on (Tilak, 2020). All of these can be attributed primarily to the absence of clear, coherent, long-term planning, policy, governance, and vision on higher education (Tilak, 2004).

On the lines of national missions in elementary education and secondary education, which, along with teacher education, were integrated in 2018 into one mission, a national higher education mission (*Rashtriya Ucchatara Shiksha Abhiyan*)—a holistic scheme of development for higher education—was launched in 2013–2014, as an umbrella scheme of the union government under mission mode with a view to revive the character and quality of state institutions, to correct regional imbalances in the growth of higher education institutions, and to improve equity. This, subsuming all existing central schemes in the sector, such as support for the creation of new "model" degree colleges, new professional colleges, infrastructural support to universities and colleges, faculty recruitment, faculty improvement programs, and programs of leadership development of educational administrators, was conceived as an overarching scheme for funding the state universities and colleges by the union government in order to achieve the aims of equity, access, and excellence. Accordingly, there were some modifications in the funding mechanisms and the flow of funds as well. This seemed to have helped in upgradation of infrastructure, establishing new universities and colleges, and launching of new teaching and research programs. Yet another institution created in higher education in India in the recent years was the Higher Education Financing Agency (HEFA), a joint venture of the Ministry of Education, Government of India, and Canara Bank (a public-sector commercial bank) for financing on a loan basis the creation of capital assets in premier educational institutions and to enable them to excel and reach the top in global rankings, by financing the building of world-class infrastructure, including research and development. The HEFA launched in 2016–2017 provides loans at competitive interest rates for capital assets creation. It is planned to mobilize resources from the market by way of equity from individuals/corporations and by issue of bonds to finance the requirements. An important feature of the HEFA that results in a shift in the policies on public funding higher education is a shift from grants to loans, though for limited purposes. In addition to encouraging, rather necessitating, better internal resource generation through incentives, it allows universities to make substantial investments through market borrowings that can be repaid over a longer period. In case of public institutions, interest is paid by the government. All this marks a new phase in policies of funding higher education in India.

Quite a few of the recommendations made by the numerous commissions and committees were taken up, but one of the main problems has been the gap between promise and practice. There have also been some serious unsuccessful efforts toward reforming higher education in the recent past. Reforms were planned to be introduced through a series of legislative measures. In 1995 the Government of India introduced a bill in the Parliament for the establishment of private universities (Government of India, 1995). The objective was to properly regulate the growth of private universities in the country. When the bill could not go through successfully, state governments, taking advantage of education being in the "concurrent" list in the Constitution of India, took the initiative of making state-level legislations for the establishment of private universities (Tilak, 2004). In a short period, many states have made such an act and facilitated rapid, rather uncontrolled growth of private universities. Alas, the union government did not feel the need to do anything. In 2010, the Government of India proposed as many as nine major bills relating to reforming higher education, but none of them could successfully go through the Parliamentary process, owing to "stiff resistance from the votaries of both public and private sectors" (Mathur, 2022, p. 74) and conflicting interests of political parties. The several bills referred to subjects such as regulation of entry of foreign educational institutions, prohibition of unfair practices in higher education, setting up of educational tribunals, setting up a national-level accreditation and regulatory authority for higher education, setting up of universities for innovation, setting up a national commission for higher education and research to replace all the then existing regulatory bodies, and to forge public–private partnership in education (Tilak, 2010). Some of these proposals resulted from the recommendations made by the National Knowledge Commission (2009). Some of the proposals aim at promoting private interests and further privatization of education, while some aim at checking corrupt practices, particularly in private medical education institutions. Even though the proposals were associated with a few major weaknesses, they would have set a big reform process in higher education, obviously not contentious-free as many of them are neoliberal in their very nature.

The poor governance system of higher education is widely commented upon as inefficient, ineffective, and outdated (Chandra, 2017b; Mathur, 2020; Qamar, 2020). There may be several factors that can explain the poor performance and even the failures in reforming higher education in India. Prominent among them are the dominance of the commercially motivated private sector in higher education that has grown at an alarming rate, even threatening to altogether displace the public sector; the unholy but strong nexus among political actors, administrators, and private investors in education; inadequate regulatory structures and mechanisms; insufficient public funding; critical shortage of manpower; corruption; other structural factors; and, above all, the lack of a strong national commitment to reform higher education, reflected inter alia in poor policy orientation and poor public funding to reform higher education. The highly inadequate resource allocations and their wavering flow to higher education (Tilak, 2016) indeed betray the stated intent of reforms, as all reforms require huge additional funding, in addition to a consistent flow of funds for the sustenance of the system. Explaining why reforming higher education is so hard, many noted that all political parties are internally split, and the status quo has a large number of adherents across all players (bureaucracy, managements, regulating bodies which themselves are not autonomous in their functioning, faculty, students, parents, and business houses), who profit greatly though variedly, from the current inertia; furthermore, a direct line of continuity traverses between politicians, industry-scale coaching centers, private universities and colleges, and the university classroom itself (see, e.g., Chandra, 2017a). For example, when the questionable practices of private institutions, such as charging exorbitant fees, were widely known, the then government proposed in the twelfth 5-year plan to remove the clause that necessitates private institutions to operate on the principle of not-for-profit and to openly allow entry of profit-seeking players into the education sector to flourish. However, this did not find favor within the government, though many continue to strongly favor such a move (e.g., McCowan, 2004; Tooley, 1999; see also Bhargava, 2020).

Thus, even though there is no policy per se, many policy initiatives were taken under executive orders, during a long period of "policy vacuum," some of which were implemented and some of which failed. All this suggests that the system is characterized by the absence of a "culture of change" (Fullan, 2001). At the same time, it also stresses the urgent need for a package of coherent, well-thought-out, and carefully formulated reforms taking a long-term view of national progress and global developments, and plans for their effective implementation. The need for a radical shift in public policy on education to supplement developmental efforts is widely highlighted (Drèze & Sen, 2013).

REFORMS PROPOSED IN THE NATIONAL EDUCATION POLICY OF 2020

With this background, it will be interesting to critically examine the reforms proposed by the National Education Policy of 2020 (Government of India, 2020), which can be seen as filling the long-felt policy vacuum. The policy was based on the "draft" policy prepared by a committee chaired by a renowned space scientist and former head of the Indian Space Research Organization, Dr. K. Kasturirangan (Government of India, 2019). So it may be necessary to consider both the documents, hereafter referred to as the draft and the policy, in this context. It is also important to note that this is the first major policy document per se on education that the Government of India released after the change in development trajectory in the 1990s initiated with structural adjustment reforms, a period also associated with the recognition of a huge demographic dividend and an extraordinary revolution in information and communications technology, in addition to several national and global developments.

Though higher education has expanded to become the second largest system in the world, after China, this is considered highly inadequate for a country to realize its aspirations to become economically advanced. Accordingly, the 2020 policy aims at further expansion of higher education so as to reach a gross enrolment ratio of 50% by 2035 from around 25% in 2018–2019, adding 34 million additional students by 2035, implying that the march toward massification of higher education will be fast. Enrollments have to be doubled, growing at a rate of growth of 4.7% per year, while the actual rate growth has been around 2% in the recent years. A high gross enrolment ratio itself will not result in higher economic growth and development; nevertheless, a high enrolment ratio of this kind that ensures an abundant supply of skilled and higher educated manpower is conceived to be necessary for fast and sustained economic growth of the nation. This is also needed as a response to demographic changes and democratic pressures for expansion of higher education and thereby to fulfill the growing aspirations of new generations of youth in a democratic society.

Beyond this quantitative target, the policy makes a few path-breaking proposals for reforming the higher education system in such a way that it evolves into a new ecosystem of integrated and holistic higher education with large, well-resourced, and vibrant multidisciplinary institutions. The policy, aiming to be comprehensive, covers a large gamut of issues, including curriculum, administration, governance, privatization, and internationalization. Recognizing education as a public good, the policy aims at providing inclusive, equitable and high-quality education while increasing access to educational opportunities universally.

Restructuring the University System

Multidisciplinary Institutions

Presently, nearly half the universities in India are single-faculty universities: 188 universities for technical education, 63 universities of agriculture and allied subjects, 71 medical universities, 26 law universities, 27 language (19 Sanskrit and 8 other language) universities, and 121 universities, each offering programs in one of the other subjects such as defense, petroleum, forensic sciences, education, and economics (in 2020–2021). Of the 1,113 universities, only 615 are "general" universities, which can be regarded as comprehensive universities, and of the nearly 44,000 colleges, 36% (of which 82% are private) offer only a single program. Such mono (single)-faculty-based universities are based on a truncated and fragmented understanding of the very concept of university and its development, and they do not contribute to knowledge development, as the Yashpal Committee (Government of India, 1999) has argued strongly, as much as comprehensive universities do, which provide opportunities for interactions among students and faculty from different disciplines and offer abundant scope for cross-pollination of ideas. Universities that focus on engineering and technology or management, or such single disciplines, tend to refuse to recognize the loss of not having humanities and social sciences, liberal arts, and so on, in producing well-rounded personalities so important for the development of a humane society, as Martha Nussbaum (1998) stated. Such a severely fragmented system of higher education is found to be contributing to further fragmentation of knowledge and cubicle-ization of learning, wrecking the higher education edifice. The single-discipline-based universities (particularly "institutions deemed to be universities"—a unique type of university in India that is established by bypassing the normal procedures of going through the national Parliament or state legislatures, but enjoying a high degree of autonomy, which are in large numbers) cannot be regarded as universities per se, going by the very basic definition of a university. Except for a few institutions such as the Indian Institute of Sciences, Bengaluru, and the Indian Agricultural Research Institute, Delhi, established in the 1950s, and a few other public institutions established during the 1960s, 1970s, and 1980s, a vast majority of the post-1980s institutions are private, fee-based ones. That such institutions are harmful to the development of higher education has been stated earlier by many, and they also recommended doing away with such institutions. For example, André Beteillé (2004) and Amrik Singh (2004) observed that such institutions have caused grave injury to the very concept of a university, as they do not qualify to be universities in the proper spirit of the term; and that they need to be discontinued. The Yashpal Committee (Government of India, 1999) has clearly argued for conversion of all mono-field institutions, including the IITs, into multidisciplinary institutions for better knowledge creation and development.

Recognizing this and the "long tradition of holistic and multidisciplinary learning, from universities such as Takshashila and Nalanda" in ancient India, which had thousands of students from India and the world studying in vibrant multidisciplinary environments, and which amply demonstrated the type of great success that large multidisciplinary research and teaching universities could bring in, and the modern universities that were set up in India until the early 1970s, which were comprehensive in nature and scope, and that many of the best and highest-ranking universities in the world have been comprehensive, the 2020 policy promises to develop a nationwide ecosystem of vibrant multidisciplinary world-class universities and colleges, breaking disciplinary boundaries in knowledge development and dissemination. Accordingly, it says that all institutions of higher education will be transformed into multidisciplinary higher education institutions, each offering a bouquet of disciplines—professional education, vocational education, and all areas of higher education to be an integral part of higher education, eliminating the hard distinction among general, professional, technical, and vocational subjects. All single-stream higher education institutions, including colleges, will be gradually phased out. All this, in addition to immensely raising the employability of graduates, as the Yashpal Committee argued would help in better production of knowledge and its dissemination, as students and faculty from different disciplines mingle with each other, interact formally and informally, inducing them to think beyond disciplinary boundaries, giving a scope for cross-pollination of ideas and helping in evolving of multidisciplinary and even interdisciplinary perspectives on issues and also at the same time facilitating mutual learning of various types of skills and values from peers that the employers and the larger society look for. This can contribute significantly to the enrichment of higher education and research and its contribution to development of the society.

In fact, the approach of the policy is to develop not simply multidisciplinary institutions, but liberal education-based multidisciplinary institutions and interdisciplinary programs. The liberal arts–based multidisciplinary approach may enable students to develop inquisitive minds and to gain an arsenal of skills such as creative and critical thinking; imagination; complex problem-solving; communication; teamwork; coordination; management of people, time, and work; analytical skills; writing skills; research and investigative approaches; cognitive flexibility; and many more skills that are easily transferable across different work environments, as it provides "a combination of transferable and uniquely human skills, to help them adapt and continuously learn to work in [a] challenging environment" (Kasturirangan & Kumar, 2022, p. 11). Such multidisciplinary institutions can contribute significantly to the enrichment of several disciplines and higher education and research as a whole, which in turn contributes immensely to the development of society (Stember, 1991). The policy strongly advocates that students in science and technology disciplines would benefit immensely from taking additionally liberal arts courses, as liberal arts make engineers, scientists, technologists, doctors, and other professionals more humane. On the whole, development of multidisciplinary institutions and sustainable interdisciplinary curriculum will indeed be a major challenge.

The multidisciplinary institutions also offer a high degree of flexibility and convenience to students to choose in their degree programs subjects across different discipline streams, such as liberal arts and humanities, along with science, technology, engineering, or medicine. The policy adopts a broad scope of liberal arts, as inclusive of "all branches of creative human endeavour, including mathematics, science, vocational subjects, professional subjects, and soft skills" (p. 36). The current inflexible system restricts students to a specific discipline of study and a specific career or line of work for the rest of their working life. In fact, at the school level itself, "a rigid separation of disciplines, with early specialization and streaming of students into narrow areas of study" (p. 33) takes place. As UGC (2003, p. 27) stated, educational opportunities and traditions that Indian universities have built up since independence have been able to produce graduates, capable only of pursuing limited careers, but, in the new globally competitive environment that is emerging in the country, the Indian student is now required to develop a multi-faceted personality to cope up with the rapid changes in the world at large. Accordingly, the intention of the policy behind its proposal of a multidisciplinary approach is not just to prepare graduates "for one's first job," as stated in the draft policy, "but also for one's second job, third job and beyond. With the coming fourth industrial revolution and the rapidly changing employment landscape, a liberal arts education is more important and useful for one's employment than ever before" (pp. 224–225). This may enable students to adopt an interdisciplinary and eventually transdisciplinary approach that not only "integrates several discipline-specific approaches but also extends these approaches to generate fundamentally new conceptual frameworks, hypotheses, theories, models and methodological applications that transcend their disciplinary origins" (Kasturirangan & Kumar, 2022, p. 9). The goal is for transdisciplinarity to become the norm by 2047.

Some may have be apprehensive about the transition of specialized institutions like IITs and IIMs into comprehensive institutions, as it may result in a loss in relative advantage they have in terms of specialization and in producing competent and specialized technical graduate manpower; it is feared that "depth" in a specific discipline might get sacrificed in favor of "breadth" across a range of disciplines. But it has to be noted that interdisciplinarity requires a priori a firm grounding on solid disciplinary platforms. Hence, careful design of the programs is necessary. It requires teachers of high caliber— "a team of scientists and social scientists at the frontiers of their disciplines" (Raina, 2021, p. 107)—university teachers spending time and researching on the form and content of undergraduate and graduate programs. As of now, interdisciplinarity is lacking in theoretical perspectives and broader conceptual frameworks; a philosophical engagement with varied and variegated interdisciplinary studies is essential for a better understanding of the nature, method, and criteria of interdisciplinarity (Choudhary, 2018). The development of multidisciplinary universities also requires redistribution of power and structures within universities which poses a serious systemic constraint (Straus, 1973). Sustenance of such multidisciplinary institutions also requires assured sustained funding; otherwise, they may regress to the traditional type of institutions (Mosey et al., 2012). On the whole, development of multidisciplinary institutions and sustainable interdisciplinary curriculum will indeed be a major challenge.

While efforts are being made to implement the policy of developing multidisciplinary institutions, as some institutions like the IITs began offering interdisciplinary programs, at the same time, single faculty universities, such as forensic university, rail and transport university, aviation university, defence university, police university, digital university, teachers' university, and forestry university, are also being set up or are being proposed to be set up. "Skill universities" are also coming up in good numbers. It may be expected that from the beginning they will be comprehensive institutions.

Reclassification of Universities

Recognizing that some of the world-class universities are research universities, that research university is a key institution in social and economic progress in the emerging knowledge society, that the research university is "the mother of knowledge society" (Patel, 2016, p. 239), and that India has none, the policy advocates the development of research universities in the country. It categorizes institutions of higher education into research (or research-intensive) universities (Type I universities), teaching (or teaching-intensive) universities (Type II universities), and teaching colleges (Type III institutions). This categorization is hoped to help each university to have a clear focus and in the process to develop itself into a world-class university, some as high-quality research universities and some as high-quality teaching universities, which may eventually figure in the global rankings. After all, global rankings have become a policy concern worldwide to underpin and quicken the process of reforms in higher education (Hazelkorn, 2008, p. 193). There is already a national scheme of Institutions of Eminence, launched in 2017, with the objective of identifying 20 universities (public and private) to develop world-class standards in teaching and research. The scheme's potential to promote eminence is doubted by some, mainly because "the policy planners, administrators and regulators have their own compulsion which does not necessarily help them [make] the best decision" (Qamar, 2022, p. 95). Further, the new categorization in the policy may be contrasted with the classification recommended by the Federation of Indian Chambers of Commerce and Industry (FICCI, 2015), which is differently focused: (a) research-focused universities, which will be centers of excellence with state-of-the-art research ecosystems; (b) career-focused universities that will provide industry-aligned dynamic curricula and pedagogy, focusing on job-oriented skills; and (c) foundation institutions of higher education that offer a wide variety of programs, focusing on broad-based and holistic education to improve access across all social classes. Though there are some similarities between the two classifications, the proposal of the policy seems to be better conceived. According to the FICCI's proposal, some universities will be exclusively employment-oriented, some research-focused, and some focused on the development of character and values among students, as if they are mututally exclusive objectives. The policy visualizes all institutions of higher education to be conducting research and teaching programs, though in varying proportions, as teaching and research are indispensable functions of every university; and all focus on developing broad-based and holistic education along with imparting skills required for dynamic labor markets; they also perform the third mission of universities: the social responsibility, which is otherwise forgotten (Tilak, 2022).

Though many scholars favor such a categorization, differentiating various types of universities (e.g., Jalote, 2021), some critiques feel that such a categorization of universities in the policy into research universities and teaching universities does not recognize the interlinkages between teaching and research, and they are apprehensive of a likely grave danger of harming both and the neglect of the twin core functions of a university. Further, it is felt that research is already not a high-priority area in many universities and the deficiency of research culture is very high in India (Patel, 2016); and now many teaching universities may get the message that they can ignore research altogether, and research-intensive universities may pay less attention to teaching programs and their quality. Thus, there is a danger of both research and teaching suffering with low priority. It is also likely that the government funding may get concentrated on Type I universities—the research universities. The hierarchy of universities it proposed—that Type III institutions can aspire over the years to become Type II universities and Type II universities to gradually become Type I universities—would lead to discriminatory treatment by the state in its funding; that is, Type II and Type III institutions may get relatively neglected. As Robinson (2019, p. 30) feared, the new labeling which is "both impractical and invidious" may lead to "stratification and further lack of access to funding and inequalities of resources for those in 'teaching' universities who are currently engaged or wish to pursue research. It will quite possibly kill research in many universities, instead of building their capacities for research." The policy, however, states that all institutions of higher education will be engaged in research. While the critical importance of research in universities can be least contested, it may have to be recognized that teaching and research are inseparable entities of a university; a "researcher-teacher" may be able to nurture students with practical, experience-driven perspectives, and a "teacher-researcher" will be able to provide strong theoretical foundations. Both will arouse curiosity among the students and create hunger for knowledge development and assimilation. Hence, a proper balance is to be maintained between teaching and research in every university.

Integrated Higher Education Institutions

While most universities in India offer postgraduate (master's and research) programs, a vast majority of colleges offer only undergraduate study (bachelor's degree) programs. Though colleges and all universities are expected to be involved in both teaching and research, because of this disjointed system, research is getting confined to mostly a few universities, master's study programs to all the universities, and undergraduate teaching to colleges. Only 2.9% of colleges are found to be running a PhD program, and only 55% of the colleges are found to be running postgraduate teaching programs (2020–2021). Such a system is also found to be responsible for low student transition rates from undergraduate to postgraduate studies and research programs and for a skewed distribution of enrollments between undergraduate and postgraduate studies. For instance, more than 85% of the students in higher education in India are enrolled in undergraduate studies;

and less than 15% in postgraduate and 0.5% in research studies. In universities like the University of Tokyo, the numbers are roughly evenly divided between undergraduate and graduate students. Though the distribution favors undergraduate students in many universities, the distribution is not as skewed as in India. So the need to integrate the system was recognized for quite some time, in such a way that teaching and research, on the one hand, and undergraduate and postgraduate studies, on the other, are integrated and both are given more or less equal priority. The Yashpal Committee has suggested that every institution of higher education should offer undergraduate, postgraduate, and research programs. The present policy also proposes the same: All institutions of higher education will offer undergraduate and graduate (postgraduate and doctoral research) programs.

Large Universities

"Small may be beautiful" in the case of highly specialized research organizations, but not in the case of universities and colleges, and not at all in the case of multidisciplinary universities and colleges. In India, 17% of the colleges have an enrolment below 100; 65% have enrolment below 500 in 2020–2021; and in only 4% of the colleges the enrolments were above 3,000. On the whole, the average size of a higher education institution is about 646 students; the corresponding figure is 465 in private colleges, 1,057 in government-aided colleges, and 1,097 in government colleges. In contrast, in China, the corresponding figure is about 16,000 (Ravi et al., 2019). That many universities and colleges in India have an unviable enrolment size is widely known. Quite a few universities have an enrollment below 4,000. The Education Commission (Government of India, 1966) highlighted this point and suggested optimal sizes that needed to be ensured. But underoptimized institutions in terms of size continued to grow in number.

Noting that there are too many small-sized universities and colleges, the policy underlines the need to make every institution big in enrolments, so that they become pedagogically, economically, and managerially viable, and corresponding economies of scale could be reaped. The economies of scale are not just economic; they are also academic. The draft proposes that universities should have a minimum on-campus student enrollment of 5,000 and a target of 25,000 or more, and colleges should have a minimum enrollment of 2,000 and a target of 5,000 or higher, each with residential facilities. Equally important is the size of the faculty: 70% of the top 200 universities in the world rankings have a faculty size of above 1,000, while only 2% of the universities in India have such a faculty size (Jalote, 2021, p. 33). This means a large-scale program of mergers and closures needs to be attempted by looking at the size of enrollments and faculty. Though lower and even upper limits of enrolments cited earlier are still very low, and the minimum levels should be much higher, as targets for a short-term period, it is a welcome proposal for reform. It may be desirable to aim at a size of about 25,000–50,000 in the case of universities and to about 5,000–10,000 in the case of colleges. If India really plans for large university campuses with 50,000–80,000 students, like quite a few public universities in the United States and other countries, or as a few countries like China are planning to do, or even with smaller size as suggested by the draft, there may not be any requirement of so many universities. So considering a variety of relevant parameters, a well-planned program of consolidation and mergers has to be taken up. Apart from economic benefits of such a consolidation of higher education institutions in the form of fall in cost per student, it will also help more importantly in strengthening the institutions with a big critical mass of students in each institution for academic rejuvenation. Large universities also provide scope for students and faculty to come together from various social, cultural, economic, and regional—including beyond national borders— backgrounds, providing a vibrant environment of learning of different cultures and how to live with, and to learn from, people of different religions and cultures (Tilak, 2018a). Simply put, such universities ensure a high degree of diversity, which is an essential feature of a good university, promoting personal growth and a healthy society (Teichler, 2004; UNESCO, 2003). This also contributes to strengthening one of the four important "pillars of higher learning," viz., "learn to live" with others (International Commission on Education for the Twenty-First Century, 1996). Thus, this proposed reform can be expected to produce a huge set of externalities.

Too Many Universities? Norms and Consolidation

The policy promises an education system consisting of "large, multidisciplinary universities and colleges, with at least one in or near every district" (p. 34). There are already, on average, nearly 3 universities for every 2 districts and 67 colleges per district in the country. The National Knowledge Commission (2007) suggested, with no clear basis, however, having something like 1,500 universities in the country. India seemed to be going in this direction. The number of universities and colleges is growing fast. Between 2014–2015 and 2020–2021, 343 new universities were set up, albeit a majority in the private sector; that is, the number increased by 57 per year on average! Similarly, 2 new colleges came up per day during the same period.

Will the policy result in setting up more universities and colleges? If the policy is strictly implemented, going by simple calculations, based on the numbers and norms given in the draft policy (one research university for every 5 million population, one teaching university for every 500,000 population, and one teaching college for every 200,000 population, and in addition to these norms, every district to have at least one of each category), by 2030 there may be approximately 3,800 universities (766 research universities and 3,000 teaching universities) and 8,000–10,000 colleges. It means that on average there will be 5 universities and 10–13 colleges per district. So while consolidation aims at reducing the number of educational institutions, these norms may indeed result in a larger number, particularly in the case of universities, while the number of colleges may come down. Obviously closure of an educational institution is more difficult than opening new institutions in democratic societies like India. In fact, experience shows that the latter is much easier and more plausible, given the influence of strong democratic forces for the expansion of higher education facilities. After all, they also serve as vote banks (Rudolph & Rudolph, 1972). So unless strong measures are initiated, and efficient norms are adopted, more and more universities and colleges will be set up. As already noted, the number of universities and colleges is not sustainable, with small enrolments and inadequate human, physical, and financial resources. Moreover, availability of a university within every district means less mobility of people from state to state and even within the state from district to district for higher education, reducing diversity in student population in the universities. Thus, there is a bigger danger of losing the nature and the contribution of universities, if there are too many, say one in every district. If universities are located in every district, students do not feel the need to go outside the district for higher education; every university will have students drawn from within the district population. Not only students but also, given the policies of some of the states to ensure large shares of employment to the natives of the given state, teachers and administrators are recruited from within the district or state. Note that there are no transfers among teachers (or nonteaching staff) between several universities even within a state, while only teachers in government colleges are transferable within the given state. The policy also does not propose any such mobility; in fact, the draft proposes the contrary: recruitment of teachers (even in government colleges) at the institutional level, intending to promote institutional commitment. As a result, universities become more and more local and localized institutions and even parochial in nature, losing diversity, a necessary feature of a good university. "Universe" in such universities will be the district, and the horizons of knowledge will be confined to district boundaries. This may cause the biggest damage to the very concept of a university, going against what the National Policy on Education of 1986 clearly asserted: "the universal character of universities and other institutions of higher education has to be underscored" (p. 5). This is already happening with rapid proliferation of colleges and universities in every nook and corner of the country. University planning need not necessarily adopt the same criteria that school planning is based on, such as demographic parameters (population), geographical units (villages/towns/districts), and physical distance. What is needed is, as argued in the draft policy, not exactly in a different context, "a thoughtful consolidation of existing HEIs into a fewer number of HEIs, considering issues of access, distribution, and the quality of existing and future outcomes" (p. 217). Implementation of this may indeed pose a grave challenge, in addition to the challenge of huge resource requirements. Plans of consolidation or mergers should also include plans for ensuring an upscaling of academic programs in number as well as quality, infrastructure—classrooms, libraries, laboratories, playgrounds, hostels, and so on—number of teachers, and other conditions, so that every student and teacher is better off than before the merger. Otherwise, consolidation has no meaning. One may note that in the 1970s, when some consolidation was attempted, it resulted in a decline in enrollments and a decline in public expenditure.

Critics may argue that such a proposal would be at the cost of democratic ideals of realizing social mobility aspirations through higher education among the economically and socially disadvantaged groups, as household costs would increase for students to travel to reach colleges or universities or to stay in a place away from home. But it may be noted that the proliferation of universities everywhere may meet the social aspirations of the economically and socially marginalized strata, by improving their access to higher education and helping increase in overall enrollments; and instead closures and mergers of institutions might increase household costs of acquiring higher education. The question that one may have to examine is, What is the use of providing higher levels of access to poor-quality higher education that only raises enrollments in ill-equipped institutions and poor-quality teachers, and helps in the production of degrees but not high-quality graduates well-suited for jobs in the dynamic labor markets or graduates with well-rounded personalities for creating a humane society? The half-baked graduates might add to the social and economic problems the nation faces. The "demographic dividend" may eventually turn out to be a demographic disaster. It is necessary that, along with mergers and closures, student support mechanisms, including affordable hostels, safe transport, and financial support to the disadvantaged strata, are scaled up.

Reforms for Better Regulation and Improved Governance

Recognizing that the present system of governance is characterized by laxity, sluggishness, and lack of autonomy, the policy recommends a major restructuring the architecture of the regulatory system of higher education. The importance of regulation of higher education in India was recognized from the beginning. It is widely noted that higher education needs to be regulated to ensure planned and coordinated development, quality of education, equity, and social justice, and to prevent unfair practices (Ayyar, 2015). Access, equity, accountability, and quality formed the four guiding principles of regulation. Starting with the UGC and ACITE, over the years, the number of regulating bodies has increased to as high as 16, but governance has not improved; in fact, it has deteriorated. As Qamar (2017) observed, India moved from no regulator regime (until 1925) to a loose coordinator (1926–1956) when the Inter-University Board was involved in loose coordination of the universities until 1952, when the UGC was established, to the sole regulator (1957–1992), during which period the UGC was the only main regulating body, and finally to a regime of multiple regulators (post-1993) with many parallel bodies working simultaneously without much coordination, but with overlapping and even conflicting roles and responsibilities. This was also due to blurring boundaries of responsibilities between them. As Ghosh (2019, p. 27) also sums up, from "a loosely regulated transitory phase from British India to independent India" and "a phase of strong regulation by the state in and post-independence India," India experiences "a dispersed yet still not so easily discernable phase of regulation post-1986 till date." Recognizing that the system is "overregulated and least governed by multiple bodies," the National Knowledge Commission (2009) and also the Yashpal Committee (2009) have suggested, though for different reasons, to develop one regulating body in place of all the then-existing bodies in higher education—the National Knowledge Commission favoring it as a single-window system to facilitate easy business in education—in opening new institutions, introducing new programs, easy entry and exit into and from the educational market, and so on, and the Yashpal Committee favoring such a body to defragmentize knowledge development and to promote a holistic and integrated higher education system.

Now the draft policy originally proposed setting up a National Education Commission as the apex body in education to be headed by the Prime Minister/Education Minister. But eventually the policy did not favor this and instead resolved to set up a Higher Education Commission of India (HECI) as the apex body of higher education, to be supported by four vertical institutions, viz., National Higher Education Regulatory Council (NHERC) as a single regulating body for regulation of all higher education institutions (both public and private, and technical and nontechnical—possibly excluding medical and legal education), National Accreditation Council (NAC), as an apex-level meta accrediting agency, responsible for assessment and accreditation that will be carried on by diverse and multiple public and private accreditation institutions and agencies, Higher Education Grants Council (HEGC) to oversee the disbursement of grants to institutions, and General Education Council (GEC) to frame graduate attributes (expected learning outcomes) from higher education institutions, with the help of National Higher Education Qualification Framework (NHEQF) and National Skills Qualifications Framework (NSQF). In addition, the GEC will be concerned with issues such as credit transfers and the equivalence of degrees. The NHERC will be responsible for framing rules and procedures for setting up new higher education institutions. The HEGC will exclusively focus on funding aspects. The policy thus proposes separate institutes with nonoverlapping roles and responsibilities. The HEGC will replace the UGC; the existing National Accreditation and Assessment Council (NAAC) will transform itself into NAC as a meta-accrediting body, and the assessment and accreditation will be carried on by diverse and multiple public and private accreditation institutions and agencies. Bodies such as the Indian Council for Agricultural Research (ICAR), Veterinary Council of India (VCI), National Council for Teacher Education (NCTE), Council of Architecture (CoA), and the National Council for Vocational Education and Training (NCVET) will be professional standard-setting bodies. In the draft it was proposed that all the regulating bodies, including the UGC and All-India Council for Technical Education, were to be replaced by the Higher Education Commission, in line with the recommendation made earlier by the Yashpal Committee and the National Knowledge Commission. But the policy does not say so. Perhaps the UGC and AICTE will continue to function while performing modified roles. A draft bill to set up HECI and repeal the UGC Act of 1956 is yet to go to the Parliament. Plans to set up and reorganize other structures have been initiated.

Some of the recent attempts to reform the governance structure in higher education with an aim to improve accountability and transparency have led to the centralization of administration, reduced role of the professoriate, erosion in the autonomy of institutions, increase in government control, and an overall decline in the quality of leadership, innovation, and creativity at the institutional level. Mechanisms of governance have also impacted assessment and accreditation, funding, and balance in the development of various disciplines, and the pattern of growth of private and public institutions. The now proposed governance structure aims at addressing some of these issues, and it is yet to be seen how effective will be the details, which are yet to be worked out. The effectiveness of the restructured governance system also depends upon how efficiently the HECI coordinates the functioning of the several bodies, though their functions are defined to be nonoverlapping, and how universities and colleges respond to various initiatives. The proposals requiring the institutions to have a body of governors and to prepare institutional development plans covering issues relating to faculty recruitment, upgrading of physical infrastructure, improvement in teaching and learning, and setting their own benchmarks for progress on various fronts have the potential to strengthen the autonomous functioning of the institutions and reach higher levels of quality and excellence.

A closely related issue is the autonomy of the states in making education policies. Particularly since the 42nd amendment to the Constitution in 1976 shifting education from the "state list" to the "concurrent list," the role of the union government has been on the rise (Tilak, 2018b). Citing the new architecture of the regulatory system, along with measures such as national eligibility and entrance examinations for admission in higher education—undergraduate and postgraduate studies, proposals for common standards-setting bodies, and so on—critics argue that the present policy further restricts the role of the state governments in education, in favor of the union government. It is widely felt that the role of the states to make their own educational policies is being overlooked. However, except in the case of a few specific issues, such as introducing a fee reimbursement scheme, most states have not made any distinct policies of their own in higher education, and they have been largely implementers of the national policies and the guidelines received from the UGC.

Curricular and Other Academic Reforms

Four-Year Bachelor's-Degree Program

In an era when technical knowledge and skills carry high premium in the labor markets, there are only a few who strongly highlight the importance of arts and humanities in human development, and this is being slowly and even widely understood. Given this, it will be heartening to note that the policy strongly favors liberal arts–based education and recommends provision of 4-year liberal undergraduate programs with multiple exit options, which provides the full range of liberal education with a choice of common core and specializations, including specifically majors and minors. It is hoped that a certain proportion of the curriculum—at the course level or the program level—is reserved for "dialogue" among multiple disciplines and their respective methodologies; "in the spirit of a true dialogue, the purpose must not be to overtly challenge multiple viewpoints and chose a 'correct' one, but to help students recognise the promise and the value in considering more than one viewpoint" (Kasturirangan & Kumar, 2022, p. 12). The policy offers flexibility to the students in three areas, namely, in choosing a combination of subjects, duration of the study, time schedule (to exit and enter later at a time convenient to the students), and institutions and their mix.

With multiple exit options, the 4-year program offers a certificate for those who complete the first year in a discipline or field, including vocational and professional areas, and exit, or a diploma after 2 years of study, or a bachelor's degree after a 3-year program. The 4-year degree program that offers an honors degree to those who complete all 4 years of study is, of course, the preferred option that will also include building research capacities allowing the graduates to go for further higher education and/or a PhD program. This is similar to, but not exactly the same as, the one that was introduced in the University of Delhi in 2012–2013, and which was rolled back in 2014, much before at least one full cycle of the experiment could be completed, as it turned controversial because of its sudden introduction, lack of proper planning, and absence of required support. According to the policy, this will be not only in general education but also in teacher education (BEd degrees) and in other areas of professional and technical education—in fact, in all higher education. The policy favors gradually moving all bachelor's-degree programs toward a 4-year degree program, taking a more comprehensive liberal education approach. Further, the policy, by providing for instituting Academic Bank of Credit (ABC), gives freedom for the students to design their own study program and shift between several universities and colleges across the country and also distribute the education program for a longer period of time.

The proposed 4-year degree program has many laudable objectives. This can also be seen as an important opportunity to address several maladies of the existing bachelor's-degree program in India, highlighted by many (e.g., Mohanty, 2019), and to thoroughly overhaul it. Hence, it may be welcome, but a couple of questions may arise: Will this, with provision for multiple exit options result in production of half-baked graduates? While the provision for multiple exits takes away the derogatory term—"the dropouts"—and names them as certificate or diploma holders, it is doubtful that these credentials will bring significant benefits for them. As Deshpande (2020) observes, "earlier, the indivisibility of the degree provided an incentive for students and families to try hard to complete their degrees. Meaningless short-term credentials will encourage families to withdraw their wards from education." The multiple exit options should not result in more dropouts or in the production of incomplete graduates. It is also feared that it may lead to a chaotic situation, creating a hierarchy of bachelor's degrees.

The 4-year degree program is indeed an ambitious idea, as it provides for multiple entry and exit options. The needed curricular reforms may pose a serious challenge to the universities, as they really require highly "imaginative and flexible curricular structures [that] will enable creative combinations of disciplines for study" (p. 37) in such a way that it provides simultaneously (1) skills that can provide decent employment for those who exit after the first or second year with a diploma/certificate; (2) skills and knowledge good for employment and/or further higher education for those who exit after 3 years with a degree; and (3) skills, knowledge, and research capacities suitable for employment, for admission in further higher (master's-level) education, and for admission in doctoral research programs for those who complete the 4-year program. All this is in addition to developing "intellectual, aesthetic, social, physical, emotional, and moral [capacities of students] in an integrated manner" (p. 36). The transformation of undergraduate programs to be able to make students research-oriented is feared to be a cumbersome process, and there is a danger of producing ill-prepared students for research studies, severely impacting the quality of doctoral studies, while the idea is to catch students young, when their creativity and energy are at their peak. It is also difficult to visualize that such a course structure will necessarily raise employability of graduates, and that it will not further accentuate graduate unemployment. That one can go for research studies without pursuing a master's-degree program may affect the already shrinking numbers going for postgraduate studies. Further, this requires teachers with extraordinary skills and knowledge when there is a real dearth of quality teachers. The provision for mobility of students across different institutions during a given course of study also requires effective coordination between the institutions. The institutions will have a tough job of preparing plans for such coordination. Further, this along with some recent measures of introducing vocational education/training courses at the undergraduate level that involve simultaneous provision of skills and education, though primarily aims at addressing the problem of graduate unemployment, reflects a big change in our approach to understanding the purpose of higher education. For a long time the goal of higher education is considered as knowledge creation and dissemination (production of "general human capital"); and the objective of training programs is to inculcate skills (creation of "specific human capital") (Becker, 1962, 1975). Now its purpose is being redefined to include skill inculcation, in addition to knowledge development, as skilling is brought into every domain of education. Traditional theories make a sharp distinction between the two, education and training; but the policy tends to gloss over this distinction. The distinction is increasingly considered wasteful and irrelevant, as education is also a kind of training of the mind in reason and judgment and it is meant to develop certain "skills"; and education must recreate such training (Muller, 1974). However, care has to be taken to ensure that the heavy focus on skills will not eventually turn universities into skill factories, though as per the policy, skill is a much broader concept than is usually understood. In short, development of the 4-year undergraduate degree program may indeed pose the biggest challenge to educational planners.

Value Education

Recognizing that while being global, the curriculum in higher education needs to have an Indian core that serves India first, the policy makes it clear the need to lay special emphasis not only on liberal arts but also, drawing from rich ancient Indian heritage, on human values, respect, and ethics, including ethics of social engagement and service, scientific temperament, constitutional values of democracy, equality and justice, Indian and foreign languages, India-centric values, ancient knowledge, and a wide variety of generic and specific skills, including soft skills for the holistic development of the youth. This will contribute to the production of a new generation of youth of special character with virtues for the global society, who will take pride in the rich Indian culture, values, heritage, and languages. The policy aims at restructuring the entire higher education system, bringing India back to its cultural and epistemic roots. Human values should permeate and form part of all the activities in universities. This is one of the major proposals made in the policy covering all levels of education from pre-primary to higher education and is envisaged as an important instrument of nation-building.

Such a focus of the policy on Indian culture, languages, ancient knowledge and values and corresponding curricular and pedagogic reforms, and initiatives to change the medium of instruction (from English to local languages, for example, Hindi) in higher education, including in engineering and technology, is hailed by many and at the same time is condemned by some as attempts to "saffronize" Indian education and to further the Hindu nationalist agenda by the party in power (Athreya & van Haaften, 2020) and the move to shift to the Hindi medium in higher education as one marking a retrograde paradigm shift in education (Patnaik, 2019). Shift of the medium to Hindi in higher education is also argued to discourage internationalization of higher education, as foreign universities may not be interested in it (Altbach, 2022), as graduates in English language, and those who studied in the English medium are considered to have better communication skills and exposure to diverse cultures, which the modern industry and service sectors value (Srivastava, 2022).

Funding Education and Research

While the policy recognizes that public funding is critical for the development of education, it does not offer any new initiatives relating to the financing of higher education, or education as a whole, except stating that (a) the long-cherished goal of allocating 6% of GDP to education, as recommended by the Kothari Commission in 1966 and resolved in the National Policy on Education (Government of India 1966, 1968), will be pursued, (b) public-spirited philanthropic private resources will be mobilized, and (c) the scope for enhancing cost recovery will be examined. These and other methods suggested for mobilizing additional resources for higher education are not altogether new. Recent efforts relating to these measures have not yielded much. The draft has made an important recommendation on public expenditure on education—to double the government spending as a proportion of government total spending on all sectors in a 10-year period. But this proposal does not figure in the policy. In fact, along with this, it could have been suggested to raise the proportion of GDP allocated to education by 0.25% or so every year, so as to reach the goal of 6% of GDP in 8–10 years. Had such proposals been made in the policy, it would have assured a steady flow of funds to education and ease financial constraints to a great extent. Though the policy recognizes that public funding is "extremely critical for achieving the high-quality and equitable public education system that is truly needed for India's future economic, social, culture, intellectual progress and growth" (p. 61), in the absence of any major policy initiative on public financing of education, one may fear that the higher education sector may continue to be crippled by limited public funding.

However, the special emphasis the policy lays on research and support for research is worth mentioning. Focusing on development of high-quality research, it recommends setting up a National Research Foundation (NRF), through an Act of Parliament, with an annual grant of Rs. 200,000 million (0.1% of GDP), which will be an autonomous body for funding, mentoring, and building the capacity for quality research in India in sciences, technology, social sciences, and arts and humanities. It will "aim to seed, grow and facilitate research" in all disciplines through a competitive and peer-review-based process and build research capacity at academic institutions across the country (p. 209). Its funds will be accessible to both public and private institutions. The draft rightly notes that India invests an "exceedingly small proportion of GDP" in research and innovation, while many countries invest at least three times higher (p. 266). The draft also notes that the low level of spending (about 0.6%–0.7% of GDP) is reflected naturally in the extremely small research-output numbers. In the union budget (2020–2021) an amount of Rs. 5,000 million has been allocated as an initial 5-year grant to the NRF. The funding by the NRF is expected to be additional to the funding of research by exiting research funding bodies.

Other Reforms

Private Education

The draft policy makes a special mention of growth of commercial interests in education. Particularly in the case of teacher education, it has been observed: "heartbreakingly, the teacher education has been beleaguered with mediocrity as well as rampant corruption due to commercialisation" (p. 283) and argues for checks on growth of commercial interests in education and even immediate shutdown of these institutions, as argued by Justice Verma Commission in the recent past. While the draft proposes to close down all commercially oriented private institutions in not only teacher education, but also in all areas of education, the policy, recognizing the difficulties in closing down these institutions, resolves that "multiple mechanisms with checks and balances [will be developed that] will combat and stop the commercialisation of higher education. This will be a key priority of the regulatory system" (p. 48). The policy proposes to depend upon accreditation mechanism and the regulatory powers of the National Higher Education Regulatory Council in this regard. Many doubt how far these will be able to combat rampant commercialization in higher education. In fact, proposals to ensure that the private institutions are on equal footing with public institutions, granting the same level of autonomy as public institutions in matters relating to finances, admissions, recruitment, assessment, and accreditation, and so on, besides "light" but tight regulation, "progressive fee determination," and so on can be seen as the pro-private stand that the policy takes. Many view the policy as promoting more and more monetization, privatization, and commercialization of education in the country (see Priya, 2020). The existing clause of philanthropy cannot be expected to deter the forces of commercialization of higher education, as the experience shows. The system actually requires drastic measures to check the growth of undesirable forms of private higher education.

Higher Education of Socioeconomically Disadvantaged Groups

Realizing that unless the quality and standards of higher education are enhanced zealously and sustained at a high level through various measures, the system will not serve national development, the policy places heavy emphasis on improving quality and standards in higher education so that Indian universities reach world-class levels. According to critiques, while doing so, the policy does not pay adequate attention to issues relating to inequalities in higher education. The policy does acknowledge the lack of educational access and equality in the case of the marginalized groups and stresses making "appreciable improvements" to aid disadvantaged sections of the society. It further states,

> [the] policy must provide to all students, irrespective of their place of residence, a quality education system, with particular focus on historically marginalized, disadvantaged, and underrepresented groups. Education is a great leveller and is the best tool for achieving economic and social mobility, inclusion, and equality. Initiatives must be in place to ensure that all students from such groups, despite inherent obstacles, are provided various targeted opportunities to enter and excel in the educational system. (p. 4)

Critics also doubt the wisdom of policymakers in the grouping of all disadvantaged and marginalized groups like scheduled castes, scheduled tribes, minorities, and other socioeconomically backward sections into one category of socioeconomically disadvantaged group (SEDG) or underrepresented group, as if the several groups are homogenous, while each subcategory itself is not homogenous, requiring specific policy attention. The policy is also silent on the issue of reservations in academic institutions, which became an issue of contention in the recent past, and as states compete with each other in adding more and more castes to the category of reservations, increasing the quotas to account for far beyond 50% norm that the Supreme Court of India has set as an upper limit in 1992; there is no mention of caste at all in the policy (Roy, 2020). The policy recognizes that education is the single most important tool for achieving social equity and justice, but it does not pay adequate attention to effectively translating it into action. But the policy in fact does not offer much, except promising strengthening of scholarships schemes, provision of fee waivers, and so on to the disadvantaged sections.

The government of India developed an act in 2019 that provides for 10% additional reservations in education and employment to "economically weaker sections" that do not come under any caste/community-based reservation, as an additional category of disadvantaged sections. This is actually not a recommendation of the policy, but is considered highly progressive.

Internationalization of Higher Education

Internationalization of higher education includes five major components, viz., international students, international faculty, international curriculum, international teaching and research programs, and foreign universities or their campuses. Many universities tend to focus primarily on the first and the last aspects, that is, international students, and setting up campuses abroad, though others are not totally ignored. Universities also follow different practices, such as running twinning programs, offering dual or joint degrees, and so on. While internationalization is not a new phenomenon, it is viewed nowadays as almost necessary, as it receives a high weightage in the global rankings of universities, and international research publications and projects have high research impact.

On the entry of foreign universities, the policy adopted the same approach that was recommended by the CNR Rao Committee in its report on entry of foreign universities into India (Government of India, 2005), to identify and invite a few from among the top 200 universities in the world to come to India and set up universities or campuses and to take necessary measures so as not to allow entry of fly-by-night operators and greedy entrepreneurs. The selective approach recommended in the policy is admirable. The policy states clearly, "high performing Indian universities will be encouraged to set up campuses in other countries, and similarly, selected universities e.g., those from among the top 100 universities in the world will be facilitated to operate in India" (p. 39). Indian policy planners have already identified some 250 universities from 60 countries to set up their campuses in India and/or to offer programs under twinning arrangements. This is in contrast to the proposals in the form of draft bills relating to entry and regulation of foreign universities prepared in the recent past, which facilitate opening Indian higher education to outsiders on a licensing pattern to any eligible party, considering higher education as a commodity for international trade, almost on the lines of the General Agreement on Trade in Services (GATS) (Tilak, 2011). Also contrary to what was suggested by some in the recent past, the present policy made it clear that such universities will have to follow all the regulatory, governance, and content norms applicable to Indian universities. Given all this, the selective approach recommended in the policy is admirable.

India's interests in allowing foreign institutions, are, in part, to provide access to students to global quality education and to save scarce outward remittances of forging exchange on account of studies going abroad, which was as high as US$5,165 million in 2021–2022, though it is well known that students primarily go abroad not just for higher studies but also for subsequent immigration and job opportunities. More than 200,000 Indian students chose the United States as their higher education destination in 2021–2022, marking a 19% increase over the previous year. The total loss of revenue due to students moving abroad is estimated to be US$17 billion per annum (FICCI, 2022). Among the Indian students aspiring to go abroad, there are some who can pay high levels of fees and incur heavy expenditures, some who can afford taking loans and go abroad, and some who cannot afford loans nor have the ability to incur high levels of expenditures; the last category of students, though they strongly wish to go abroad, may not go abroad at all. The intention of the government is to meet the aspirations of the third category of students and to arrest at least partially the staggering numbers of students among the second category going abroad, and save foreign exchange and at the same time to attract foreign direct investments in education. Entry of foreign universities and twinning arrangements aim at addressing these issues only partially.

The policy has already stimulated global interest among foreign players to enter India, as the highly regulated higher education system is found to be opening up. Global players view the Indian policy as allowing commercial interests to set up institutions and do business. Generation of profits is still a major priority for many of them. Hence, it is necessary to see that the entry regulations are carefully formulated and are strictly enforced, lest all kinds of foreign institutions come into India, poach faculty from

Indian institutions, induce unhealthy competition, and pose many more problems to higher education that may threaten the very survival of the Indian universities. After all, there are many foreign universities which are aggressively planning to capture higher education markets in developing countries and make profits. Hence, guidelines need to be carefully prepared for developing twinning and other similar arrangements. A draft central legislation has been made recently, namely International Financial Services Centres Authority (Setting up and Operation of International Branch Campuses and Offshore Education Centres) of 2022 (https://ifsca.gov.in/PublicConsultation), that allows top 500 universities and "other" foreign institutions to establish campuses and offer programs in the state of Gujarat in India in areas of financial management, FinTech, science, technology, engineering, and mathematics. Comprehensive guidelines that would be applied all over India are being prepared by the UGC, which promises to give freedom to the institutions, inter alia, to decide admission criteria and fee structure. The draft regulations prepared by the UGC (Setting up and Operation of Campuses of Foreign Higher Educational Institutions in India Regulations 2023) that provide a special dispensation regarding regulatory, governance, and content norms, which mean practically a high degree of autonomy to the foreign institutions, are perceived by some as harming the growth of Indian higher education, besides being not exactly in line with the intention of the national policy. The policy also, however, allows greater freedom to the foreign universities, as it says that "such universities will be given special dispensation regarding regulatory, governance, and content norms on par with other autonomous institutions of India" (p. 39). Experts (e.g., Altbach, 2022), however, caution foreign institutions from jumping into higher education activities in India, given the existing regulatory mechanisms. Foreign institutions seem to be more interested in making twinning arrangements than setting up their campuses. Given the experience of other developing countries, it is likely that few high ranking universities will be interested in setting up their own campuses in India, that too without huge public subsidies.

Another important dimension of internationalization of higher education is attracting foreign students to India, apart from setting up campuses abroad by Indian institutions. The policy resolves, "India will be promoted as a global study destination providing premium education at affordable costs thereby helping to restore its role as a *Vishwa Guru*" (p. 39). This is a gigantic task and significant efforts are needed in this direction. While about 500,000 Indian students go abroad for studies every year, hardly 50,000 foreign students are enrolled in Indian institutions, and a majority of them are from neighboring countries and Africa, whose education in India is also subsidized by the government of India. Apart from suggesting setting up an international students office at each institution of higher education to coordinate all matters relating to foreign students arriving from abroad, as suggested in the policy, many innovative plans have to be chalked out. The "Study in India" program, a flagship project introduced by the government of India to develop India as a prime education hub for international students in higher education, is yet to take major initiatives. India faces tough challenges in this, as it has to face global competition.

DISCUSSION

To sum up, the reforms proposed in the National Education Policy of 2020 cover several areas of higher education. Some of the proposals are path-breaking, many deserve applause, some are unacceptable, and quite a few require rethinking. Some recommendations are similar to those made by earlier committees like the National Knowledge Commission, the Yashpal Committee, and the Justice Verma Commission. In the literature, some of these and other proposals have been critically discussed earlier (e.g., Tilak, 2019). Some have already been introduced; initiatives for the implementation of some more are being made, and many others are at various stages. On the whole, there are many positives and some negatives. Some are too damaging to the system, some do not recognize our and others' contemporary and historical experiences, and many require serious deliberations. While the overall approach is praiseworthy, some of the underlying assumptions are unrealistic and questionable. For example, the policy assumes "light but tight" regulation will work in India. It aims at developing an ecosystem of higher education institutions which are self-regulated. The policy proposes that every university will be mainly governed by an independent board of governors. Through this, it seems to presume that higher education institutions will self-regulate themselves. With the existing elaborate regulatory structure, the government's ability to effectively regulate and ensure that all, particularly the private institutions, adhere to the norms, stipulations, directions, and terms prescribed by the state, has been found to be rather poor. Indeed, there is a need for more effective measures of regulation. Second, the policy also assumes that the private sector in education in India will be benevolent and honest and work with integrity; the private institutions will fix fair fee levels, and they will be fair in admission, recruitment, and so on. This is not supported by experience. The policy further assumes that philanthropic contributions will flow in a big way to meet the needs of the education sector. This is also an untenable assumption, given the poor record in the past. As Lawrence Summers (2006) observed, private higher education in Asian countries like India is far different from philanthropy-based private higher education in the United States. One has to recognize this. Third, the policy assumes that commercialization can be curbed easily. Despite executive and judicial interventions, this has been proved impossible, in a sociodemocratic setup with players of dubious interests. Fourth, the policy lays special emphasis on the use of digital technology for improvement in quality as well as the spread of higher education. Using digital infrastructure already a variety of higher education programs are offered through an initiative called SWAYAM (Study Webs of Active-Learning for Young Aspiring Minds)—India's massive open online course through DTH channels—launched in 2017. The policy proposes creating a National Educational Technology Forum (NETF), "to provide a platform for the free exchange of ideas on the use of technology to enhance learning, assessment, planning, administration, and so on, both for school and higher education" (p. 56). NETF has already been set up, and this is expected with a mandate to provide independent evidence-based advice to government agencies on technology-based interventions; to build intellectual and institutional capacities in education technology; to envision strategic thrust areas in this domain; and to identify technological interventions for the purpose of improving teaching-learning and evaluation process, supporting teacher preparation and professional development, enhancing educational access, and so on. Educationists agree with the potential benefits of using technology in classrooms, but they are also apprehensive of extensive reliance on technology for either improvement of quality or for widening access (Kumar, 2023). For example, Kearsley (1998, p. 47) argues that technology is "primarily, if ironically, a distraction (on a grand scale) from what matters most—effective learning and good teaching." It is also feared that indiscrete use of digital technology leads to the commodification of education, eroding the ideals of universities and creating a quasi-market of higher education (Chattopadhyay, 2020).

Lastly, the policy described by many as "a very ambitious policy" (e.g., Varma et al., 2021) requires a huge quantum of resources. Many policies could not be taken up in the past essentially due to a severe paucity of funds. Hence, special efforts are needed to raise public resources substantially, besides making efforts to generate from philanthropic sources. Dependence on student fees or private-sector contributions may not be a feasible or desirable approach. But the policy does not offer any innovative measures for raising resources. Any major infusion of funds into higher education is not yet promised.

Above all, the most significant point is the policy underlines that the system requires major overhaul, comprehensive reforms need to be attempted, and piecemeal/quick fix solutions will not work. After all, educational policy is always and everywhere a political issue, and today the higher education system "exists in a highly toxic political and societal environment—as is the case in many countries" (Altbach, 2022), with several positive and weak features. An important message that comes very loudly from the draft and the policy is as follows: The education sector urgently requires drastic major reforms, and the system cannot wait any longer. Unless major reforms are attempted now, national development goals will be at risk.

The success of any public policy lies in its implementation. In a federal system it is essential that states and union government work together in building the new educational edifice. Education in India is a "concurrent" subject—the states and the union government have responsibility for it. Both have to commit to the policy in letter and spirit; but some states (e.g., Kerala, Tamil Nadu, and West Bengal) have already rejected the policy, posing a hard roadblock for nationwide implementation. Both have to raise their allocations to higher education considerably. An effective coordination between union government and the states is needed; they should share a common long-term vision for the development of education and for the implementation of each component of the educational policy. Since education is a long-term activity with serious long-term implications for the future of the nation, a long-term vision, and not short-term compulsions, should guide the educational planners. Educational policies failed or were successful in India in the past and in many other countries because of political commitment. A strong and sustained national commitment is an essential prerequisite for the successful implementation of any public policy.

It is widely noted that higher education is a public good that produces a variety of externalities, which are not just economic in terms of productivity and wages. There are social, economic, political, cultural, dynamic, and technological externalities. They are also not confined to the boundaries of nations; hence, as Joseph Stiglitz (1999) and also the UNESCO (2015) observed, higher education and research are global public goods. The National Education Policy recognizes education as a public good. This is important, as no other public policy document said so in independent India. If the educational reforms in education are grounded on this philosophical approach, many of the problems India faces can be avoided in the future.

CONCLUDING OBSERVATIONS

India is currently the fastest growing large economy in the world. Its higher education system also experiences the fastest growth. Theoretically, it transitioned from an elite system to a mass system, as the gross enrolment ratio rose much above 15%—the minimum level defined to enter the phase of massification, and now it aims at transitioning into a universal system with a goal of 50% plus enrollment ratio (Trow, 1973, 2000). But at the same time it is plagued with innumerable problems, including quality, expansion, and equity. As Pankaj Chandra (2020) describes:

> the higher education ecosystem operates in two distinct worlds with very insignificant crossover. It reflects the ethos of the larger society. There is one world where institutions could be rural as well as urban, both government or private but where the quality of preparation of students and teachers is low, domain knowledge is low, commitment to the purposes of education and the institution [is] low, motivation to improve the learning environment is low, professionalism is low, financial resources are low, motivation of founders and trustees to engage with the institution is low but the control is high, infrastructure is poor, [the] work environment is uninspiring and where desire and ability to bridge deficits in students is also low. . . . And then there is the other world that is aspirational as it is difficult to get in because it is easy to fly out, where the so-called "best" converge, where a semblance of merit exists, where all conversations are over information and facts, where insights don't count, and where access to the world is the aspiration. (pp. 7–8)

All attempts to reform higher education systems around the world are to bridge the gap between the two worlds and to make a quick move from the first to the other world. Presently higher education systems worldwide are subject to sweeping reforms. Many countries began focusing on rejuvenating and even restructuring their higher education systems. In the increasingly globalized and competitive world, the critical importance of graduate manpower in national and global development is being widely recognized. Partly following the initiatives made by the World Bank in developing higher education systems (World Bank, 2002, 2009, 2011) and international developments such as the emergence of global university ranking systems (Tilak, 2016a), and the idea of world-class universities, most developing countries also began paying attention to their higher education systems and pursuing excellence in higher education. National plans are being drawn to reform their higher education systems, improve their relative position in global rankings, develop or set up world-class universities, build knowledge societies, and thereby raise their rates of economic growth. Developing countries intend to use their higher education systems to break the developing country syndrome and emerge at least as middle-income countries in the classification of the World Bank. The availability of quality graduate manpower produced in developing countries at a relatively low cost is also seen by advanced countries as an advantage for them.

Reforming higher education has become an important item of the development agenda of many countries. But the process of reforms is not an easy task. Most resource-poor countries face a myriad of challenges in this regard. As a result, the increased role of the private sector in higher education, resort to cost recovery measures, reliance on relatively inexpensive methods (like the use of technology for teaching), and so on have become inevitable. Education markets have emerged at national and global levels. Access, quality, and equity, modified respectively as expansion, excellence, and equity, continue to be the daunting trio of concerns in higher education. The saga of educational policy in India is one of a few impressive achievements, a few disappointments, and a few conspicuous failures. There have been quite a few attempts at reforming higher education during the post-independence period. They have produced varying outcomes. After all, as widely recognized, reforms provoke new power games and reconfigure power relations (Musselin & Teixeira, 2014). This chapter has presented a short critical account of independent India's endeavors toward reforming its higher education, including specifically the latest education policy.

Many policy initiatives made earlier could not be taken to their logical end in implementation. A part of the explanation lies in the socioeconomic conditions the country was to face. The first National Policy on Education in 1968 became a victim to the post-Indo-Pakistani War effects, inflation, nation-wide drought, and so on, which derailed the planning of all sectors, including education, and the plan holiday was to be declared. The 1968 Educational Policy went into the background. The National Education Policy of 1986, the second policy in independent India, was followed by the downfall and return of the ruling party in government, which led to partly revising the policy in 1992. The period was also associated with severe economic crisis and the reluctant embrace of structural adjustment polices that initially had a very serious adverse effect on education sector but, more importantly, changed drastically the color and nature of the development path (Tilak, 1992, 1996). Soon the 1986/1992 policy became redundant, and there was a policy vacuum for nearly three decades, during which period the system was managed more by executive orders and kneejerk reactions to the problems, and the development of higher education lacked focus. There has been a policy vacuum for a long period, and the vacuity has been filled by the 2020 National Educational Policy that aims at ushering in a series of transformative reforms. But it was taken in the midst of the global health crisis caused by COVID-19, when the entire education system and even the country were under lockdown, though the draft policy came out a few months earlier. The pandemic inflicted serious immediate damaging effects on all sectors, including education, specifically higher education (Tilak, 2021a; Tilak & Kumar, 2022).

The effects of the pandemic are yet to be fully gauged. These are important, but only partially responsible factors. The political economy factors matter a lot in a democratic society in successfully rejuvenating its education systems (Tilak & Panchamukhi, 2023). The success of the policy reforms in higher education depends upon unwavering will and strong social commitment or a national obsession to the cause of higher education, which has been unfortunately missing so far in India. However, the NITI Ayog (2022) confidently conjectures, "when India turns 75 on August 15, 2022, it will mark a moment that comes, but rarely in history, when we step out from the old to the new." This chapter, which has presented a short critical account of the policy initiatives of reforming higher education in independent India, concludes with a hope that "the era of a New India will be heralded; an era where India begins its journey to become a global leader in thought and action" and reemerge as *Viswa Guru* in higher education.

REFERENCES

AICTE (All-India Council for Technical Education). (1994). *Report of the High-Power Committee for Mobilisation of Additional Resources for Technical Education.* All India Council for Technical Education in India, New Delhi (Chairman: Dr. D. Swaminadhan).

Altbach, P. G. (2012). The prospects for the BRICs: The new academic superpowers? *Economic and Political Weekly, 47*(43) (Oct. 27), 127–137.

Altbach, P. G. (2019). *A half-century of Indian higher education.* Sage.

Altbach, P. G. (2022). India's higher education is opening up. But is it ready? *University World News,* November 5. https://www.universityworldnews.com/post.php?story=2022110209 3858736

Altbach, P. G., & Chitnis, S. (Eds.). (1993). *Higher education reform in India.* Sage.

Athreya, A., & Van Haaften, L. (2020). Modi's new education policy: A next step in the saffronisation of India? *Mondiaal Nieuws,* August 26. https://www.mo.be/en/analysis/modi-s-new-education-policy-next-step-saffronisation-india

Ayyar, R. V. V. (2015). *Unfashionable thoughts: An ex-policymaker's perspective on regulation in education.* Centre for Policy Studies, Gayatri Vidya Parishad.

Basu, A. (1974). *The growth of education and political development in India, 1898–1920.* Oxford University Press.

Basu, A. (1989). Indian higher education: Colonialism and beyond. In P. G. Altbach & V. Selvaratnam (Eds.), *From dependence to autonomy* (pp. 167–186). Springer. https://doi.org/10.1007/978-94-009-2563-2_7

Becker, G. S. (1962). Investment in human capital: A theoretical analysis. *Journal of Political Economy, 70*(5), 9–49.

Becker, G. S. (1975). *Human capital: A theoretical and empirical analysis with special reference to education* (2nd ed.). National Bureau of Economic Research.

Bhargava, A. (2020). Declare education "for profit": Educationists, private schools urge govt. *Business Standard,* January 28. https://www.business-standard.com/article/education/decl are-education-for-profit-educationists-private-schools-urge-govt-120012801670_1.html

Carnoy, M., & Dossani, R. (2013). Goals and governance of higher education in India. *Higher Education, 65*(5) (May), 595–612.

Chandra, P. (2017a). Governance in higher education: A contested space (Making the university work). In D. Kapur & P. B. Mehta (Eds.), *Navigating the labyrinth: Perspectives on India's higher education* (pp. 253–264). Orient & BlackSwan.

Chandra, P. (2017b). *Building universities that matter: Where are Indian institutions going wrong?* Orient & BlackSwan.

Chandra, P. J. (2020). Governing academic: Within and without. *Journal of Educational Planning and Administration, 34*(1) (Jan.), 5–20.

Chattopadhyay, S. (2020). National education policy, 2020: An uncertain future for Indian higher education. *Economic and Political Weekly, 55*(46) (Nov. 21), 23–27.

Choudhary, R. K. S. (2018). Towards a philosophy of interdisciplinarity. *Journal of Educational Planning and Administration, 32*(3) (July), 173–182.

Deshpande, S. (2022). As students gear up for university, the devil is in the NEP's details. *Indian Express*, July 6.

Dharmpal. (1983). *The beautiful tree* (1st ed.). Biblia Impex.

Drèze, J., & Sen, A. (1996). *India: Economic development and social opportunity*. Oxford University Press.

FICCI (Federation of Indian Chambers of Commerce and Industry). (2015). *State-focused roadmap to India's "vision 2030."* New Delhi.

FICCI. (2022). *Higher education in India: Vision 2047*. New Delhi.

Fullan, M. (2001). *Leading in a culture of change*. Jossey-Bass.

Ghosh, S. (2019). Regulation and higher education: The imperative. *Educational Quest: An International Journal of Education and Applied Social Science, 10*(1) (April), 27–36.

Gornitzka, Å., Kogan, M., & Amaral, A. (Eds.) (2005). *Reform and change in higher education: Analysing policy implementation*. Springer Nature.

Government of India. (1951). *Report of the University Education Commission (1949–1951)*. (Chairman: Sarvepalli Radhakrishnan). Government of India.

Government of India. (1966/1971). *Education and national development: Report of the Education Commission (1964–1966)*. (Chairman: Dr. D. S. Kothari). NCERT.

Government of India. (1968). *National policy on education*. Ministry of Education.

Government of India. (1986). *National policy on education*. Ministry of Education.

Government of India. (1995). The Private Universities (Establishment and Regulation) Bill, 1995. [Reproduced in *New Frontiers in Education, 25*(3), 290–308.]

Government of India. (1997). *Government subsidies in India*. Department of Economic Affairs, Ministry of Finance.

Government of India. (2000). *A policy framework for reforms in education*. A report submitted by special subject group on Policy Framework for Private Investment in Education, Health and Rural Development. Prime Minister's Council on Trade and Industry, Government of India (Mukesh Ambani-Kumaramanglalam Birla Report). http://www.nic.in/pmcouncils/ reports/education [Executive summary in *Journal of Indian School of Political Economy, 15*(4) (2003), 840–845.]

Government of India. (2005). *Report of the Committee on Entry of Foreign Universities in India*. https://prayatna.typepad.com/education/2005/09/cnr_rao_committ.html

Government of India. (2009). *Report of the Committee to Advise on Renovation in and Renovation and Rejuvenation of Higher Education* (Chairperson: Yashpal). Ministry of Human Resource Development. https://mhrd.gov.in/sites/upload_files/mhrd/files/docum ent-reports/YPC-Report_0.pdf

Government of India. (2012). *Vision of teacher education in India: Quality and regulatory perspective vision of teacher education in India quality and regulatory perspective—Report of the high-powered commission on teacher education constituted by the Hon'ble Supreme Court of India* (Justice J. S. Verma Commission). Ministry of Human Resource Development. https://mhrd.gov.in/sites/upload_files/mhrd/files/document-reports/JVC%20Vol%201.pdf

Government of India. (2019). *Draft national education policy 2019* (Dr Kasturirangan Committee Report). Ministry of Human Resource Development, Government of India. https://mhrd.gov.in/sites/upload_files/mhrd/files/Draft_NEP_2019_EN_Revised.pdf

Government Resolution on Education Policy. (1913). *Indian education policy 1913: Being a resolution issued by the Governor General in Council on the 21st February 1913.* Superintendent Government Printing, India.

Hartog Committee. (1929). *Report of the Auxiliary Committee of the Indian Statutory Commission (Hartog Committee).* Government of India.

Hazelkorn, E. (2008). Learning to live with League tables and ranking: The experience of institutional leaders. *Higher Education Policy, 21,* 193–215.

International Commission on Education for the Twenty-First Century. (1996). *Learning: The treasure within; report to UNESCO of the International Commission on Education for the Twenty-First Century.* UNESCO.

Jalote, P. (2021). *Building research universities in India.* Sage.

Kasturirangan, K., & Kumar, V. (2022). Liberal education: A 21st century imperative. *Journal of Educational Planning and Administration, 36*(1) (Jan.), 5–13.

Kearsley, G. (1998). Educational technology: A critique. *Educational Technology 98*(38), 47–51.

Kumar, K. (2023). Technology and education today. *Social Change, 52*(4), 467–477.

Marginson, S. (2011). Higher education and public good. *Higher Education Quarterly, 65*(4) (Oct.), 411–433.

Marginson, S. et al. (Eds.) (2022). *Changing higher education in India.* Bloomsbury.

Mathur, K. (2020). State, market and governance of higher education. In N. V. Varghese & G. Malik, *Governance and management of higher education in India* (pp. 25–43). Sage.

Mathur, K. (2022). Changing perspectives: Neo-liberal policy reform in education and health in India. In K. B. Saxena (Ed.), *Private sector participation in public services* (pp. 66–81). Aakar.

McCowan, T. (2004). Tooley's seven virtues and the profit incentive in higher education. *Journal for Critical Education Policy Studies, 2*(2), 1–15.

MOE (Ministry of Education). (2022). *All-India Survey on Higher Education 2020–21.* Government of India. https://www.education.gov.in/sites/upload_files/mhrd/files/statistics-new/AISHE%20Report%202020-21.pdf

Mohanty, M. (2019). The poor B.A. student: Crisis of undergraduate education in India. *Journal of Educational Planning and Administration, 33*(1) (Jan.), 5–17.

Mosey, S. Wright, M., & Clarysse, B. (2012). Transforming traditional university structures for the knowledge economy through multidisciplinary institutes. *Cambridge Journal of Economics, 36*(3), 587–607.

Muller, S. (1974). Higher education or higher skilling? *Daedalus, 103*(4), 148–158.

Musselin, C., & Teixeira, P. N. (Eds.) (2014). *Reforming higher education public policy design and implementation.* Springer Nature.

Naik, J. P. (1982). *Education Commission and after.* APH.

Naoroji, D. (1901). *Poverty and un-British rule in India.* Swan Sonnenschein & Co.

National Knowledge Commission. (2007). *Report to the nation 2006* (Chairperson: Sam Pitroda). Government of India.

National Knowledge Commission. (2009). *Report to the nation 2007* (Chairperson: Sam Pitroda). Government of India. http://kshec.ac.in/perspectives/NKC%20Report%20to%20the%20Nation%202006.pdf

NITI Ayog. (2022). Vision for new India @75. National Institution for Transforming India, Government of India. https://www.niti.gov.in/index.php/vision-new-india75

Nussbaum, M. C. (1998). *Cultivating humanity: A classical defence of reform in liberal education*. Harvard University Press.

Patel, P. J. (2016). Research culture in Indian universities. *Social Change, 46*(2), 238–259. [Reprinted in Tilak, J. B. G. (Ed.) (2022). *Education in India: Policy and practice* (pp. 220–248). Sage.]

Patnaik, P. (2019). On the draft national policy on education. *Social Scientist, 47*(9/10) (Sept.–Oct.), 556–557.

Priya, L (2020). How does the national education policy accelerate the privatisation of higher education? *EPW engage: Economic and Political Weekly, 55*(30) (July 25). https://www.epw.in/engage/article/education-policy-2020-privatisation-higher-education

Qamar, F. (2019). Essentials for excellence in higher education. *Journal of Educational Planning and Administration, 33*(2) (April), 85–103.

Qamar, F. (2020). Regulation of higher education in India. In N. V. Varghese & G. Malik (Eds.), *Governance and management of higher education in India* (pp. 44–70). Sage.

Raina, D. (2021). The future of higher education: Through the lens of the history and philosophy of science. *Journal of Educational Planning and Administration, 35*(1) (April), 97–108.

Rao, C. N. R. Committee. (2005). *Entry of foreign universities in India*. Government of India.

Ravi, S., Gupta, N., & Nagaraj, P. (2019). *Reviving higher education in India*, Research Paper No. 112019-01. Brookings Institution India Centre. https://www.brookings.edu/research/reviving-higher-education-in-india/

Raza, M. (Ed.) (1991). *Higher education in India: Retrospect and prospect*. Association of Indian Universities.

Robinson, R. (2019). An academic's response: Draft national education policy, 2019. *Economic and Political Weekly, 54*(30) (July 27): 28–32.

Roy, K. (2020). National education policy needs close scrutiny for what it says, what it doesn't. *Indian Express*, July 31.

Rudolph, S., & Rudolph, L. (Eds.) (1972). *Education and politics in India*. Harvard University Press.

Sadler Commission (Calcutta University Commission) (1919). *Report of the Calcutta University Commission 1919*. Calcutta.

Sengupta, A. (2020). Rapid growth of private universities. *Economic and Political Weekly, 55*(22) (May 30), 45–52.

Singh, A. (2004). *The challenge of education*. ICFAI University Press.

Singh, M. (2013). Re-inserting the "public good" into higher education transformation. In R. King, S. Marginson, & R. Naidoo (Eds.), *The globalisation of higher education* (pp. 562–577). Elgar.

Srivastava, S. (2022). Why tech companies are hiring English graduates. *Education Times*, December 5. https://www.educationtimes.com/article/job-trends-market-mantra/95991430/why-tech-companies-are-hiring-english-graduates

Stember, M. (1991). Advancing the social sciences through interdisciplinary enterprise. *Social Science Journal, 28*(1), 1–14.

Stiglitz, J. (1999). Knowledge as a global public good. *Global Public Goods, 1*(9), 308–326.

Straus, R. (1973). Departments and disciplines: Stasis and change: Significant multidisciplinary activity requires a redistribution of power within universities, *Science, 182*(4115), 895–898.

Summers, L. (2006). Private higher education: Opportunities and challenges. *Span 47*(3) (May–June). US Embassy in India.

Teichler, U. (2004). Changing structures of the higher education systems: The increasing complexity of underlying forces, UNESCO Forum Occasional Forum Series, Paper No. 6—"Diversification of Higher Education and the Changing Role of Knowledge and Research," 2–15.

Tilak, J. B. G. (1992). Education and structural adjustment. *Prospects, 22*(4), 407–422.

Tilak, J. B. G. (1996). Higher education under structural adjustment. *Journal of Indian School of Political Economy, 8*(2) (April–June), 266–293.

Tilak, J. B. G. (1998). Changing patterns of financing education. *Journal of Indian School of Political Economy, 10*(2), 225–240. [Reprinted in Tilak, J. B. G. 2018. *Dilemmas in reforming higher education in India* (pp. 306–335).Orient BlackSwan.]

Tilak, J. B. G. (2004). Absence of policy and perspective in higher education. *Economic and Political Weekly, 39*(21), 2159–2164.

Tilak, J. B. G. (2008). Higher education: A public good or a commodity for trade? *Commitment to Higher Education or Commitment of Higher Education to Trade, Prospects (UNESCO), 38*(4), 449–466. [Reprinted in Tilak, J. B. G. 2018. *Higher education, public good and markets* (pp. 10–34). Routledge.]

Tilak, J. B. G. (2009). Student loans and financing of higher education in India. In *Student loan schemes: Experiences of New Zealand, Australia, India and Thailand and way forward for Malaysia* (pp. 64–94). IPPTN and Penerbit Universiti Sains Malaysia Press. [Reprinted in Tilak, J. B. G. 2018. *Dilemmas in reforming higher education in India* (pp. 236–271). Orient BlackSwan.]

Tilak, Jandhyala B. G. (2010a). Universities: An endangered species? *Journal of the World Universities Forum, 3*(2), 109–127.

Tilak, J. B. G. (2010b). Policy crisis in higher education: Reform or deform? *Social Scientist, 38*(9–12), 61–90.

Tilak, J. B. G. (2011).*Trade in higher education. The role of the general agreement of trade in services (GATS)*. UNESCO International Institute for Educational Planning.

Tilak, J. B. G. (2012a). Higher education policy in India in transition. *Economic and Political Weekly, 4*(13), 36–40.

Tilak, J. B. G. (2012b). Financing of higher education: Traditional *versus* modern approaches. *Yükseköğretim Dergisi / Journal of Higher Education* (Istanbul, Turkey), 2(1) (April), 28–37. [Reprinted in Tilak, J. B. G. 2018. *Higher education, public good and markets* (pp. 100–118). Routledge.]

Tilak, J. B. G. (Ed.) (2013). *Higher education in India: In search of equality, quality and quantity. Readings on the economy, polity and society* (Essays from Economic and Political Weekly). Orient BlackSwan.

Tilak, J. B. G. (2016a). Global rankings, world-class universities and dilemma in higher education policy in India. *Higher Education for the Future, 3*(2) (July): 1–18. [Reprinted in Tilak, J. B. G. 2018. *Dilemmas in reforming higher education in India* (pp. 472–497). Orient BlackSwan.]

Tilak, J. B. G. (2016b). A decade of ups and downs in public expenditure on higher education. In N. V. Varghese & G. Malik (Eds.), *India: Higher education report* (pp. 307–332). Routledge.

Tilak, J. B. G. (2018a). On planning university development: Shibboleths versus stylized facts, *Social Change, 48*(1), 131–152. [Reprinted in Tilak, J. B. G. 2018. *Education and development in India: Critical issues in public policy* (pp. 553–580). Palgrave Macmillan.]

Tilak, J. B. G. (2018b). India: The unfulfilled need for cooperative federalism. In M. Carnoy, I. Froumin, O. Leshukov, & S. Marginson (Eds.), *Higher education in federal countries: A comparative study* (pp. 258–305). Sage.

Tilak, J. B. G. (2019). Perennial problems and promising but perplexing solutions: A critique of the draft national education policy 2019 (A.N. Sinha Memorial Lecture 2019). *Social Change, 49*(4), 686–712.

Tilak, J. B. G. (2021a). The COVID-19 and education in India: A new education crisis in the making, *Social Change, 51*(4) (Dec.), 493–513.

Tilak, J. B. G. (Ed.) (2021b). *Education in India: Policy and practice.* Sage.

Tilak, J. B. G. (2022). Social responsibility of higher education [8th Diplai Sinha Memorial lecture]. *Social Change, 52*(4) (Dec.), 478–490.

Tilak, J. B. G., & Kumar, A. (2022). Policy changes in global higher education: What lessons do we learn from the COVID-19 pandemic? *Higher Education Policy, 35*(3) (Sept.), 610–628.

Tilak, J. B. G., & Panchamukhi, P. (2023). Globalisation and political economy of education development in South Asia. In R. Tierney, F. Rizvi, & K. Ercikan (Eds.), *International encyclopedia of education* (4th ed., pp. 425–446). Elsevier. https://doi.org/10.1016/B978-0-12-818 630-5.01050-2

Tooley, J. (1999). Should the private sector profit from education? The seven virtues of highly effective markets, *Educational Notes* no. 31. Libertarian Alliance.

Trow, M. (1973). *Problems in the transition from elite to mass higher education.* Carnegie Commission on Higher Education.

Trow, M. (2000). From mass higher education to universal access: The American advantage. *Minerva, 37* (Spring), 1–26.

UGC (University Grants Commission). (1993). *UGC funding of institutions of higher education, Report of Justice Dr. K. Punnayya Committee, 1992–92.* University Grants Commission, New Delhi.

UGC. (2003). *Higher education in India: Issues, concerns and new directions.* New Delhi.

UGC. (2008). *Higher education in India: Issues related to expansion, inclusiveness, quality and finance.* New Delhi.

UNESCO. (2015). *Rethinking education: Towards a global common good?* UNESCO.

Varghese, N. V., & Malik, G. (Eds.). (2016). *India higher education report 2015.* Routledge.

Varma, A., Patel, P., Prikshat, V., Hota, D., & Pereira, V. (2021). India's new education policy: A case of indigenous ingenuity contributing to the global knowledge economy? *Journal of Knowledge Management, 25*(10), 2385–2395.

Woodrow, H. (1862). Macaulay's minutes on education in India [written in the years 1835, 1836, and 1837 and now first collected from records of the Department of Public Instruction]. C. B. Lewis at the Baptist Mission Press.

World Bank. (2002). *Constructing knowledge societies: New challenges for tertiary education.*Washington, DC.

World Bank. (2009). *The challenge of establishing world-class universities.* Washington, DC.

World Bank. (2011). *The road to academic excellence: The making of world-class research universities.* Washington, DC.

CHAPTER 38

THE REHABILITATION OF THE CONCEPT OF PUBLIC GOOD

Reappraising the Attacks From Liberalism and Neoliberalism From a Poststructuralist Perspective

MARK OLSSEN[*]

INTRODUCTION

I argue in this chapter that the concept of public good needs rehabilitating as a normative value necessary to guide politics in a global age. While many would pay lip service to such a thesis today, to argue the case means to argue against the mainstay of liberal economics and political theory during most of the 20th century. I will show why perspectives that deny the existence or possibility of a public good are mistaken. The good, I will claim, represents shared interests and concerns between people, that is, interests held in common, and as such can inform a theoretical understanding of politics, education, and ethics. Given such an approach, I will argue, the dangers and problems with the idea of the good can be reconceptualized in a way that can accommodate variability or difference, not trample on individual rights, avoid the dangers with collective politics associated with Marx and Hegel, and thus overcome classical liberal objections.

---

[*] This work was originally published in *Review of Contemporary Philosophy*, *20*(2021), 7–52. I thank the publishers for allowing its reproduction in this book.

ATTACKS AGAINST THE IDEA OF GOOD

The attack on the idea of a public interest, or public good, can be seen developing in America since the 1930s in the work of writers such as Henry Calvert Simons, father of the Chicago School of economics,[1] and Kenneth Arrow, who became associated with social choice theory, and was to become a major influence on writers such as James Buchanan and other writers associated with the "new right." A major effect of Arrow's work was to severely restrict the legitimate role of the state. As Amartya Sen (2002, p. 330) reports, Arrow had been asked by Olaf Helmer, a logician at the Rand Corporation, "In what sense could collectivities be said to have utility functions?" Arrow determined that no satisfactory method for aggregating a multiplicity of orderings into one single ordering existed. Hence, there was "a difficulty in the concept of social welfare" (Arrow, 1950, the title of the article). The outcome was a PhD that formulated the General Possibility Theorem, which was a modification of the old paradox of voting. As Sen (2002, p. 262) notes, this theorem was "an oddly optimistic name for what is more commonly—and more revealingly—called Arrow's 'impossibility theorem,'" in that it describes "that it is impossible to devise an integrated social preference for diverse individual preferences." Arrow's claim, essentially, was that a unified coherent social welfare function, expressing a single value, such as a public interest, could not be expressed from the disaggregated preferences of individuals, without dictatorially discounting some at the expense of others. As Arrow (1951, p. 24) states it:

> If we exclude the possibility of interpersonal comparisons of utility, then the only method of passing from individual tastes to social preferences which will be satisfactory, and which will be defined for a wide range of sets of individual orderings, are either imposed or dictatorial. (Emphasis in original)

In Sen's account, Arrow's work was central to developments in welfare economics and "fits solidly into a program of making the analysis of social aggregation more systematic" (Sen, 2002, p. 343). Such work has relevance, says Sen (343), "in the context of political thought in which aggregative notions are used, such as the 'general will' or the 'common good' or the 'social imperative.'"

Arrow's work was also to influence James Buchanan, the father of public choice theory. Two of Buchanan's articles published in the *Journal of Political Economy* reveal the major influence of Arrow's work in his own conception of the public interest.[2] As aggregating or "summing" of individual interests to get a "public good" was not deemed logically possible, Buchanan and Tullock proposed a "unanimity rule" as the only feasible decision-rule that could guide government, but then immediately agreed that "it seems highly likely that agreement would normally be almost impossible" (Buchanan & Tullock, 1962, p. 69).

Lying behind such an analysis is a strong normative commitment to free-market individualism which for Buchanan provides a common rationality linking the economic and political worlds. This libertarian quality of Buchanan's work is reflected also in his deeply individualist approach to public affairs. As far as political prospects were concerned, only those that resulted from the subjective choices of individuals were acceptable. Collective entities such as a "society" or "the public interest" were held not to exist because they were reducible to individual experiences. This "methodological individualism" was fundamental to Buchanan's reduction of collective entities such as the public good to the dispositions and motivations of individuals. As he acknowledged in *The Calculus of Consent*, "the whole calculus has meaning only if methodological individualism is accepted" (Buchanan & Tullock, 1962, p. 265).

It is on this basis that public choice theory attacks as "myth" the idea that government or public service is able to serve the public good. Influenced by William Niskanen on "bureaucratic growth"; Anthony Downs on "political parties" and "democracy"; Mancur Olson on "interest groups"; and Gordon Tullock on "rent-seeking" behavior,[3] it asserts the view that the notion of the public good is a fiction which cloaks the opportunistic behavior of bureaucrats and politicians as they seek to expand their bureaus, increase their expenditures, and maximize their personal advantages. In *An Economic Theory of Democracy*, Anthony Downs (1957) applied public choice axioms of "self-interest" to politics. In *The Limits of Liberty* (1975), Buchanan maintains that a coincidence of interests between the civil servant's private interests and their conception of the public interest ensues, such that "within the constraints that he faces the bureaucrat tends to maximise his own utility" (Buchanan, 1975, p. 161). By such an approach, as Brian Barry argues in *Political Argument* (1990), Buchanan and Tullock "aim to destroy a whole tradition of political theorizing" (p. 256). Essentially, "the public has no place in their world." This is the tradition that recognizes the existence and "promotion of widely shared common interests—public interests—the most important reason for the existence of public authorities" (p. 256).

An attack on the good can be seen also in political economists such as Joseph Schumpeter, whose book *Capitalism, Socialism and Democracy* (1943/1976) expressed the classical episteme of science as it had rejected medieval frames of thought, linking the concept of good to the classical doctrine of democracy. Schumpeter identified the pre-Enlightenment philosophy of democracy as "that institutional arrangement for arriving at political decisions which realize the common good by making the people decide issues through the election of individuals who are to assemble in order to carry out its will" (1976, p. 250). The common good functioned as "the obvious beacon light of policy which is always simple to define and which every normal person can be made to see by means of rational argument" (p. 250). Schumpeter opposed the idea. First, he denied any notion of "a uniquely determined common good that all people could agree on or be made to agree on through the force of rational argument." Second, he appealed to the fact that "some people may want things other than the common good" as well as "to the much more fundamental fact that to different individuals and groups the common good is bound to mean different things" (p. 251). Third, even if a general good, such as the utilitarian good of maximizing pleasure, could be agreed upon, essential conflicts (such as whether "socialism" or "capitalism" should prevail, or over the limits and nature of "health," for instance) would be left unresolved, thus conflict would remain (pp. 251–252). Schumpeter's criticisms represented a condemnation of the two major senses of public interest or good that were present when he wrote: first, against aggregative conceptions, such as utilitarianism, which claimed that the good represented the "sum" of individual interests; second, against normative conceptions, derived philosophically rather than empirically, associated with Plato, Marx or Hegel.

Attacks on the idea of the good were also to receive support from mainstream political liberalism from the second half of the 20th century, as developed by the likes of John Rawls (1971), Robert Nozick (1974), Bruce Ackerman (1980), Ronald Dworkin (1978), and Karl Popper (1962). The approach was in terms of deontology versus consequentialism, science versus teleology, or neutrality versus perfectionism.[4] Arguments were anti-teleological, claiming that no general good, or *summon bonum*, exists that can furnish a nondespotic conception. Popper can be seen expressing this view in a nutshell: "most of the modern totalitarians are quite unaware that their ideas can be traced back to Plato. But many know of their indebtedness to Hegel . . . They have been taught to worship the state, history, and the nation" (Popper, 1962, p. 11). In Popper's view, Hegel takes Plato to new heights with his "insistence upon the absolute moral authority of the state, which overrides all personal morality" (1962, p. 31).

In common with Schumpeter, 20th-century liberals opposed conceptions of the public good on the grounds that the idea represents a danger to liberty. Throughout the 20th century, it was generally true that the conception of the good as a criterion of morality and value became superseded by the idea of rightness where the individual's duties were taken as the locus of value. For classical liberals, the argument was represented in terms of a preference for "state neutrality" and against what they called "state perfectionism," the latter which defined ends in relation to pre-established values. The case against perfectionism was developed also by Rawls in *A Theory of Justice* (1971, pp. 291–292), where he explicitly rejects perfectionist public policies such as "subsidizing universities," or "opera," or "theatre," on the grounds that these institutions are "intrinsically valuable." For state action on perfectionist grounds could only be justified based on "unanimity," and unanimity, as Rawls had learned from James Buchanan and Gordon Tullock, was almost impossible to achieve. For Rawls, perfectionism entailed that the state favored unitary moral ideals, such as expressed in the idea of a public good, and could not be neutral in the sense they represented all actors. Liberal theory should favor "neutrality" which flows from the social contract which enables individuals to pursue "their own good in their own way," free from "coercive" notions such as public good. Thus, the foundation for political authority for Rawls is not the common good, but the free contract of rational individuals.

For Rawls, any theory which prioritizes the good over the right means that individual values and ends are sacrificed, or compromised, for collective ends. Although utilitarianism proposed a more empirical model seeing the good as the aggregation of individual interests, thus avoiding commitment to positing good as an independent normative value, it was criticized by Rawls because it promotes the priority of maximizing aggregate utility or happiness, and then defines right conduct as what maximizes good. As such, it ignores the "separateness of individuals," says Rawls, because it relies on a "trade-off" across lives (1971, p. 27). As Kymlicka expresses the point, "it generalizes from what is rational in the one-person case to what is rational in the many-person cases" (1991, p. 23). Consequently, a single individual must sacrifice her own benefit for someone else, or on the altar of some conception of collective happiness.

Given these views, it is not entirely surprising that in the second half of the 20th century some social scientists rejected the concept of the public interest out of hand. In his book, *The Public Interest* (1960), Glendon Schubert labeled the concept as a "childish myth" (p. 348) and concluded that "the concept is best discarded altogether" (pp. 223–224).[5] Political scientists Robert Dahl and Charles Lindblom concluded that "a precise examination would show that [the term public interest] can mean nothing more than whatever happens to be the speaker's own view as to a desirable public policy" (1963, p. 501). In a similar way, Frank Sorauf argued that the concept should be "expunged from vocabularies" (1957, p. 638). Clearly such a concept was not in favor, after being represented throughout much of the century as being incompatible with the dictates of science. One must at least entertain the proposition that fashion rather than reason accounted for their arguments. As Lewin expresses the point, "[d]uring the 1950s and 1960s the scientific approach adopted in the natural sciences became the ideal among trend-setting social scientists" (1991, p. 2).

Arguing for the Public Good

It will be my argument in this chapter that abolishing the idea of the public good is mistaken. I am not alone in advocating such a thesis. Without intending to provide a comprehensive list, those advocating for some use of the concept of the public interest include Woodrow Wilson (1887), John Dewey (1927), and Walter Lippmann (1927, 1955), as well as a varied assortment of more recent academics.[6] We could add to this list any number of major political philosophers, including Jeremy Bentham, Karl Marx, G. W. F. Hegel, J. J. Rousseau, T. H. Green, F. H. Bradley and Bernard Bosanquet, Karl Polanyi, Karl Mannheim, Harold Laski, R. H. Tawney, R. G. Collingwood, and Hannah Arendt, to name but a few. Rather than seek to summarize individual academics, however, I will simply focus on the two major pivots of focus in broad terms. These can be categorized as (a) utilitarianism and (b) normative approaches.

Utilitarianism, championed by Bentham, advanced aggregative approaches, which is to say that the public good represented simply the aggregation or summing of individual self-interests or preferences. It has been influential as a basis for welfare economics, and as intended by Bentham at least, constituted a movement of social reform which sought to "maximize" the good, defined in terms of the principle of utility, that is, "the greatest happiness of the greatest number." In its classical form it was premised upon the assumption of individual preferences calculated on the basis of the pleasure or pain experienced by each individual. It is the concept of interests that constitutes my major objection to the theory. Value is defined in terms of pleasure or happiness in purely subjective terms. The lack of any "external," or "objective" criteria for determining value, and its failure to adequately theorize the interpersonal dimension of selfhood in order to provide an objective criterion of human needs is a major weakness. My view owes some debt to Thomas Scanlon, who also rejects subjective preferences as the basis for the valuation of outcomes, arguing for "an objective criterion of the relative importance of various benefits and burdens" (1978, p. 95).[7] Such a view is important, given that people can have inconsistent desires, mental health problems, varying levels of incapacity, where their own subjective interests become a poor basis for enacting policy. Frequently people are unclear as to what their self-interest is or how to obtain it.[8] In addition, the interests and preferences of people frequently conflict.

Although I have taken utilitarianism into account, my argument employs a normative model of the good. While this recognizes subjective interests, shared interests, objective interests, and needs, it theorizes these in relation to institutional processes of democracy. I will argue that the concept of "self-interest" that guided the liberal economists has not proved adequate to understanding politics and the logic of collective action in terms of which politics operates. The collective dimension of individuals lives cannot be articulated or represented through aggregating interests. It is not simply that individuals may be mistaken as to their own interests, or that they experience vulnerabilities and dependencies where they frequently require assistance, but the method of aggregation employed fails to articulate a method or process whereby individual interests can be represented collectively in an appropriate way.

The liberals tried to represent anything but the direct aggregation of the preferences of individuals as suspiciously dictatorial. Claims to define the objective, that is, real interests or needs of individuals, require a dictatorial intervention in their view. Yet what they failed to focus upon was the institutional processes by which individuals are represented at the level of the collective, that is, the mechanisms and processes of procedure by which individual interests can be collectively expressed and acted upon. As democracy is the institution through which individual aspirations and considered convictions are translated into collective action, through the intermediary processes of government and democratic institutions, and under the watchful eye of the media, these democratic processes constitute a more effective and more reliable mechanism for representation of "interests" than any "sleight of hand" of claiming to focus on "preferences" directly. The democratic process is the mechanism through which the real interests of individuals are articulated as a public good. For it is the democratic process that ensures that individuals concerns are debated, deliberated, adapted, and refined, where the method of "reflective equilibrium" becomes institutionalized to ensure effective ongoing, self-correcting representation and action. The democratic process constitutes the most effective mechanism through which the interests of individuals can be represented, and their integrity and rights respected.[9]

It is this attention to process and procedure that the liberal economists failed adequately to articulate. Their grounds for making preferences ontologically primary were tied to their social contract assumptions. In Buchanan and Tullock, the contractarian assumptions were those of self-interested maximizers and a laissez-faire market. As Jules Coleman maintains, "[t]he contractarian approach to collective choice is to ask which voting rule rational persons would choose" (1989, p. 210). In advocating a "unanimity rule" Buchanan and Tullock have given rise to an industry of analysis and criticism which I am not intending to survey in detail here.[10] Suffice it to note that the demand for unanimity as a decision-rule romanticizes the market as the bedrock for politics, falsely claims to emulate science, and relies on a model of laissez-faire and competitive economics that is not realistic.[11] A voting rule to be fair must be normatively meaningful.[12] The unanimity rule proposed as the optimal decision-rule for politics constitutes, as many have observed, a conservative defence of the status quo.[13] Paradoxically, if adopted as a universal rule, it denies that different decision-rules may be relevant at different times; it enables the minority to tyrannize the majority and prevent change; it ignores the costs associated with engineering unanimous consensus and the sheer inertia that would result from a government's inability to carry out change (including its electoral pledges); and it fails to explain why other decision-rules (e.g., majority rule, two-thirds majority) are not satisfactory. Indeed, in a frequently cited article, Douglas Rae (1975) put forward a contractarian defence of majority rule maintaining that consensual decision-making as put forward by Buchanan and Tullock (a) doesn't lead to greater efficiency, and (b) that it is simple majority rule that in fact maximizes the convergence between public choice and individual preference.[14]

My own approach has also been influenced by poststructuralist political theory. This can offer a reinterpretation of politics and knowledge in the light of the new science of complexity that seeks to offer a normative justification of the common or public good in nonteleological, nondialectical, and nonreligious terms, and subject to democratic constraint. It also takes power relationships into account as an integral component of normative theory and helps to understand liberal approaches in a new light. The individualism that grounds the ontology of 20th-century liberals, whether economists or political theorists, can no longer receive support from the physical sciences in the way most thought to be the case. Many explicitly harked back to eminent Enlightenment philosophers such as Condorcet, Hobbes, Locke, Descartes, or Kant, who in turn developed their own writings homologous with Newton and in conformity to the classical synthesis. That the defeat of the classical model of science and rise of complexity approaches from the start of the 20th century, including quantum and postquantum approaches,[15] the seminal contributions of Henri Poincaré[16] and Albert Einstein,[17] has constituted a revolution in science characterized by a change from individualism to systems theory; and from reductionism to nonreductionism. The implications of this are far more profound than liberal philosophers have acknowledged. Instead of seeking to theorize the collective out of existence, it is necessary to articulate and consider both the collective and individual dimensions of politics. In a systems approach, while the living are morally foundational, it is no solution to deny the efficacy of the collective or political levels of existence. Science is something quite different to what it was held to be in Newton's day. Science can now theorize holistic entities, interconnectedness, collective politics and ideas of the common good in thoroughly scientific, materialist, or naturalist terms. Largely unaware of the implications of the shift from ontological individualism to a systems approach, most economists and political theorists in the 20th century have continued to be guided by the axioms and spirit of the classical model, and have been unsympathetic to ideas of the public or common good, to holistic analyses, or to notions of the collective as integral dimensions of selfhood and politics.

Although poststructuralist and postmodernist philosophy has been slow to develop normative theories, notwithstanding work by Badiou (2001),[18] Levinas (1969, 1985, 1998), and Derrida (1978, 1995, 1999, 2001), I offer a model of what I term "continuance ethics" or the "ethics of life continuance" as a contribution to this area. Although influenced by poststructuralism, as well as Anglophone utilitarianism, the difference with the latter are sufficiently great to warrant a different term. In brief, continuance offers an objective rather than subjective theory of value and is concerned with (1) survival as a collective and individual project, and (2) well-being, where well-being is satisfied if (a) basic needs are provided for, and (b) opportunities, benefits, and burdens are distributed justly. Normatively, it specifies an ethic of equal consideration for all where such an ethic can be justified both instrumentally and probabilistically as constituting the best (i.e., most likely) policy to ensure life continuance for all. To effect this, it adopts "Bentham's dictum," as expressed by Mill, the maxim that "everybody to count for one, nobody for more than one" (Mill, 1910, p. 58). Policies, values, actions, principles, and ways of life deemed to be valuable for traversing the future are claimed to constitute an objective basis for establishing a conception of good. Unlike utilitarianism, the aim is not to make the majority better off, but to ensure the survival and well-being of all as the best policy for assuring the survival and well-being of each.

Continuance ethics as set out in previous work (Olssen, 2009, 2010, 2015a, 2015b; Olssen & Mace, 2021) is premised upon a constructivist historical ontology that asserts the irreducibility of the normative,[19] paired with an anti-foundationalism that is disjunctive with other ethical systems on offer, viz. Kantian, Aristotlelian, Hegelian, Marxist, Utilitarian, Social Contract, Levinasian, or, conceptualized in terms of familiar themes: "ethics of identity," the "ethics of difference," "multiculturalism," "dialogical ethics," "liberal ethics," "alterity," and so on. In contrast to approaches in postmodernist ethics, informed by Levinas or Derrida, continuance ethics aims to consistently represent, develop out of, and express the postructuralism of Foucault. While the theoretical depth of this analysis is further articulated in other work, in this chapter I aim to demonstrate how the concept of life continuance can lend normative support to a political ethics that can aid democracy and constrain the ship of state.[20]

The reductionist views of the liberal philosophers mentioned earlier must in this sense be seen today as incongruent with emerging new paradigms of science. Consequently, they failed to represent individuals sufficiently as social and historical subjects who are interconnected and interdependent with each other and to the structures of social and political support. Writing as they do from a flawed conception of the subject, guided by the ontological individualism that characterizes their philosophical worldview, it is not surprising that they have difficulty theorizing how both the collective and individual dimensions of policymaking are not just important but essential to politics.

We can also appreciate here, as many of their critics did, that common sense derived from ordinary lived experience did expose flaws in the liberals' arguments, even on their own terms. The fact is that governments, as well as social organisations, like schools, *do* make and enact policies; if not in the public interest, in whose interests do they act? Under what conditions can a government take collective action? Politicians and media frequently invoke the public good to describe what they do (see Held, 1970, pp. 9–11). Most people would find it perfectly acceptable if we say that a high standard of nutrition for citizens is *in* the public interest. Similarly, most would find it acceptable if we say that clean air is a public good. While there is lots of analytic scope for balancing the public interest against special interests, or seeking to ascertain which interests are common to all members of the public, or splitting hairs over border-line cases, the orientating conception adopted in this chapter is that certain policies, goods, and benefits are in the interests of all members of the community, that is, for *anyone*.[21] In Britain, the National Health Service fits this conception, in that it is in everyone's interest, especially as no one can precisely predict their own needs in this respect. The state's regulation in respect to land or property development is also typically deemed to be for the public good.[22]

I will argue in this chapter that a conception of public good is required, not just for politics, but for education, economics, and ethics and morality as well. I will argue further that such a proposition can today be justified as congruent with the major onto-epistemological postulates of science, as it has been reconfigured from the start of the 20th century. Importantly, here, the systems perspective I will employ dictates that meaning is both public as well as individual. I will argue that even moral labels of right and wrong are not definable unless a meta-conception of value, that is, a good, is presupposed; and further, that liberal ideas of freedom are indistinguishable from licence unless a prior public conception of value is assumed. In this sense, I argue that all values are social in the same way that the subject is socially and historically constituted. It is because norms of continuance are public that they constitute the sources of our ethical and moral beliefs. Liberals have failed to understand the true sources of values and normativity, just as they have failed to understand that from the start of the 20th century, science no longer grounds their individualist ontology.

Not all the Anglo-American philosophers shared the individualism over onto-epistemological axioms that I am charging the liberal economists and political theorists mentioned earlier. One who was ahead of his time was G. H. von Wright (1963a), who was aware of the central importance of the social and cultural basis of value. Von Wright suggests that a metaethic is presupposed even in the definition of our ordinary moral labels:

> That good is better than bad obviously is a *logical* truth. But it is not a truth of "ordinary" logic. Someone may wish to say that it is a truth "by definition." But what *are*

the definitions of "good," "bad," and "better," which would show that good is better than bad? It is not at all obvious how this question should be answered. (von Wright, 1963a, p. 42)

In this sense, I will argue that a conception of good far from being inimical to liberty is required for it. While individuals' actions will be situationally specific and require technical, judgmental, and strategic skills, the ontological source of their ethical categories and definitions is public. It will be shown further that institutional development, including public education, presupposes a conception of good as an effective precondition for individuals' development, including agency and liberty. In this sense, I will claim that the public good establishes norms of moral action which obligate members of society to act in certain ways. I will further claim that such a conception of good is indeed "comprehensive," in the way Rawls opposed, and can act fairly in its treatment of different citizens through democratic processes. Although it may not always be strictly "neutral" with respect to all the different ends of private actors, such a conception can be *fair* in the context of a deeper commitment to the future well-being and survival of humanity in general.

THOMAS HILL GREEN AND THE DEMOCRATIC JUSTIFICATION FOR PUBLIC GOOD

To get a firm grip on my stated aim to develop a normative conception of good, I will initially return to Thomas Hill Green's (1941) idea of the "common good." Green clearly thought that this was an important idea. While Green's conception is unsatisfactory on several grounds, I will suggest that any such weaknesses within Green's theory can be offset by a dose of poststructuralism, that is, a rethinking of the issues utilizing insights drawn from poststructural social and political philosophy, including complexity science as it has developed from the start of the 20th century.

In enunciating the "principles of political obligation," Green defines citizens' obligations to the state as dependent upon the state's pursuit of justice and the common good.[23] Green's conception can be criticized in that it is too state-centric, and insufficiently adapted to the global age. In addition, Green's attachment to the philosophy of Hegel constitutes a serious obstacle because it invokes medieval notions of purposes and motives in nature, teleological ideas of dialectical progression in history, ideas of Perfectionism and divine providence, and generally contradicts the postulates of modernist science. While Green's Hegelianism is therefore problematic, many of his social democratic insights can be reformulated in nonidealist terms; terms quite compatible with newly emergent conceptions of science from the start of the 20th century.

It is in this sense that Green's specific arguments for a common good appear both sensible and plausible independently of his metaphysical beliefs. For Green, it is based on the state acting in its role as trustee that the obedience of citizens can be secured. The state for Green is necessary to secure the tasks that citizens are unable to complete as individuals. The state must perform these tasks on practical grounds, for there are some collective matters which individuals are not able to do for themselves. As the state's capacity is greater than the individual's capacity to co-ordinate and acquire knowledge on a vast array of issues (e.g., natural disaster, health, nutrition, education, planning, the establishment of opportunities, etc.), then within national and global territories, the state is best equipped to act for the public good. "Obligation arises," says Green, "from the lack of sufficiency of each individual acting alone" (1941, §54). By such a statement, Green opposes the doctrines of exclusive egoism and self-dependence as characterized the mainstay of the liberal tradition.

Green also enables a conceptualization of the common good in conformity to representative models of democracy, thus avoiding problems associated with Rousseau's location of sovereignty in the general will.[24] Although Rousseau no doubt intended to salvage a genuine sovereignty of the citizenry, the ambiguity created through the transference of sovereignty to the general will makes Rousseau formulation unsuitable to ground a theoretical argument for the public good.[25] "Is there any truth in speaking of sovereignty *de jure* founded upon the *volonté générale*?" asks Green (1941, §95). No, he responds, because sovereignty must reside in a determinate relation between leaders and led. In this, Green agrees with liberal writers influenced by Austin who recognized sovereignty as only legitimately residing in "a determinate person or persons" (Green, 1941, §83). "The *volonté générale*, on the other hand, it would seem, cannot be identified with the will of any determinate person or persons; it can indeed, according to Rousseau, only be expressed by a vote of the whole body of subject citizens" (§83). Green concludes that given "the term sovereign having acquired [Austin's meaning], Rousseau was misleading his readers when he ascribed sovereignty to the general will" (§85).

For Green, then, it is ultimately the democratic process that safeguards individuals and communities against the public good. As he notes, "there is an ultimate sovereignty of the people" (1941, §59); "the power placed in the state constitutes a fiduciary trust placed in [it]" (§151); for there can be no "right divine to govern wrong" (§63). He continues, "if [the state] ceases to serve this function, it loses the claim on our obedience" (§62). Green's collectivism is thus democratically safeguarded, and individual rights are not occluded by a conception of good. State legitimacy, in turn, requires and depends, not an act of consent, but some standard or rule of right, indirectly derived from the good, but not reducible to it (§115). Such a "standard of right" should be "recognised as equally valid for and by the person making the demand and others who form a society with him" (§115). "Such a recognised standard in turn implies institutions for the regulation of men's dealing with each other" (§115). It is this "rule of right . . . to which the law ought to conform" (§137).

Green is thus sensitive to potential conflicts between individuals and collective power. If an individual should disagree with the public good, "he should do all he can by legal methods to get the command cancelled but till it is cancelled he should conform to it. . . . It is the social duty of the individual to conform and he can have no right

THE REHABILITATION OF THE CONCEPT OF PUBLIC GOOD   835

. . . that is against his social duty" (§100). Green sees personal goods as only able to be sacrificed to the common good when such a good can be demonstrated as not necessary to all persons' well-being, or when it is not crucial for personal flourishing and the development of each. Clearly the inequality of power between the state and the citizen constitutes a potential source of injustice which Green's theory of democratic government is intended to protect. What is required is a robust conception of democracy (including rights) which offers genuine protection of citizen/individuals against the state and within civil society. Difficulties that might develop in this relationship between citizens and the state must be dealt with by further "deepening" democracy.

Green's writing is frequently seen as informed by idealism on the grounds that he postulates an inner unity between individual conscious reason and its collective societal development. As Green's student and friend R. L. Nettleship tells us in his *Memoir of T. H. Green* (1906), "Green argues for the most utilitarian of political schools on idealist principles" (p. 17). Following "Wordsworth, Carlyle, Maurice, and probably Fichte" (p. 25), Green "found [in them] the congenial idea of a divine life or spirit pervading the world, making nature intelligible, giving unity to history, embodying itself in states and churches, and inspiring individual men of genius" (pp. 25–26). For Green, says Nettleship, "human intelligence is God realizing himself in the particularities of nature and man's moral life" (p. 51). Mind is thus "the self-development of an eternal spirit" (p. 25). Rather than posit a distinction "between consciousness and its unknown opposite," Green posits a distinction "between a less and a more complete consciousness" (p. 112). As Green expresses it, the belief in an ideal reality is "not the admission of an ideal world of guess and aspiration alongside of the empirical, but the recognition of the empirical itself as ideal." This in turn, "transmits, not to an analysis of what is beyond experience, but to analysis of what is within it" (Green, 1885, pp. 179 and 449).

Notwithstanding Green's commitment to many of the tenets of British Idealism,[26] I maintain that the public good can be represented in nonidealistic terms. In this sense, it need not draw on support from teleology, divine providence, or Perfectionism, but can draw its justification from the new dictums of complexity science, as well as from a postmodernist conception of normativity that befits the new models of science, which I have elaborated in previous work (see Olssen, 2008, 2009, 2010, 2015a, 2015b; Olssen & Mace, 2021). To say that there is an objective metanormative standard by which good and bad can be distinguished in discourse is not in itself necessarily idealist. It may derive from a social or political standard of surviving which escapes perfection in the classical (Greek) sense, implies no inner necessity or determinism, posits no determinate end toward which nature tends, and contains no theory of intelligent design, or of purposes, which seek to explain the origins of things. At the same time, it relies upon no metaphysical criterion beyond the world as it exists for us. One can posit an end, I will argue, based simply on a normativity immanent in life itself; that portrays development proceeding in an open context of indefinite possibilities with no specific telos; but relates only to the practical ends of living beings in relation to the continuance of life itself. In that this posits life continuance as a good which can guide ethics and morality, it can thus be represented as part of a broadly "realistic" vision of life and politics. While such a view is facilitated by the quantumizing social philosophy of poststructuralism, similar views can still be found expressed by some in earlier times. At the start of the 20th century, for instance, Reginald Rogers observed: "An ethical system which asserts that the Perfect is attainable may be called 'idealistic.' One which denies that we have sufficient evidence on this point, while recognising that a relative good is attainable, may be termed 'realistic'" (1911, p. 15).

The Complexity Turn: Quantumizing the Social Sciences

Rehabilitating the idea of the good is assisted to some degree in that it is more in accord with the spirit of science today. At the start of the 21st century, developments in science radically reconstructed our ways of understanding the world.[27] The first crack in the classical Newtonian synthesis came at the very start of the century with Rayleigh and Jeans study of black body radiation, followed in quick succession by the research of Max Plank,[28] Henri Poincaré,[29] Albert Einstein,[30] and the quantum theorists Niels Bohr,[31] Werner Heisenberg,[32] and Erwin Schrödinger,[33] and Paul Dirac.[34] The old certainties of the classical paradigm were not just revised, but substantially reconceptualized. At the microscopic level, the laws of quantum mechanics superseded those of classical mechanics; at the level of the universe, Newtonian physics has been surpassed by relativistic physics. Although classical mechanics remains valid, it has undergone substantial revision in terms of its major concepts.[35] In terms of complexity formulations that subsequently influenced poststructuralism, Poincaré's research was pivotal. Poincaré advanced the field of "topology" and "systems thinking" in mathematics, opposed logicism in favor of an historical approach, and his work on the stability of the solar system (the three-body problem), dynamical systems theory, and recurrence established the foundations of chaos theory.[36]

Poincaré was to influence the work later in the century of the Belgium physicist/chemist Ilya Prigogine. In a range of publications from 1980s to 2004, Prigogine developed a complexity formulation relevant to both the physical and social sciences. In works such as *Order Out of Chaos* (1984), written with Irene Stengers, and *Exploring Complexity* (1989), written with Grégoire Nicolis, it is claimed that complexity theory offers a bold new and more accurate conception of science and the universe. Incorporating insights from quantum mechanics and relativity theory, this new conceptualization built on developments from the beginning of the 20th century which superceded standard models as "corrections to classical mechanics" (Nicolis & Prigogine, 1989, p. 5). Prigogine criticizes Newtonian mechanics and quantum theory which represented time as reversible, meaning that it was irrelevant to the adequacy of laws.[37] Complexity theory builds on and intensifies the "temporal turn" introduced by this "correction." Prigogine places central importance on time as real and irreversible.

With Newton, say Prigogine and Stengers (1984), the universe is represented as closed and predictable. Its fundamental laws are deterministic and reversible. Temporality is held to be irrelevant to truth and the operation of laws.

The "complexity turn" (Urry, 2005) enables us to reframe idealist insights and understand liberal objection to theories of the good in a new light. Complexity theory reinstates a holism of *reciprocal interactions of system and parts* which replaces the priority in idealist philosophy of the *whole determining the parts*, and the consequent overemphasis upon uniformity. The thesis that the properties of wholes cannot be accounted for in any simple additive sense as an aggregation of its component parts constitutes an ontological principle as relevant to the social sciences as to physics and chemistry. New properties arise through the interactions of parts through the process of *emergence*. Emergents are defined as "the simple effects of combined actions" (Morin, 2008, p. 100). In an open system, possibilities are endless. Such processes operate within open systems where parts and wholes are linked in a dynamic, precarious, and unstable tension. Systems comprise "polyrelational circuits" made up of "elements," "interrelations," "organization," and "whole." As such, the system is "a totality of polycentric dispersion" where small perturbations can derail and effect the whole (2008, p. 104). Society can be viewed in such a model as a complex dynamical system. In such a conception, "the notion of emergence is at the very heart of the theory of the system" (2008, p. 105).

As such, "[t]he system . . . is neither 'form,' nor 'content,' nor elements conceived in isolation, nor the whole itself, but all of these linked in and through the organization that transforms them" (2008, p. 107). Within any system, both the macro-structure and micro-structure of parts interact, mutually affecting each other, and permitting indefinite recombination, thus ensuring new entities and structures can emerge. Language, the brain, consciousness, and life can be seen as emergent phenomena. It is through interactions at different magnitudes, which push a system beyond a threshold, that ontological emergence takes place, and it is this that defeats the possibilities of reductionism. Emergence, says Morin, "implies a rootedness in what is non-reducible and non-deducible, in what in physical perception, resists our understanding and our rationalization" (Morin, 2008, p. 105). Because relations and occurrences are contextual and contingent, it is not possible to predict macro properties from a knowledge of the micro and vice versa. It also defeats the possibilities of universal laws as constituting a sufficient explanation for events—context is all. In this systems paradigm, the dynamic and nonlinear assert themselves alongside the static and linear, and nonequilibrium and equilibrium operate as both temporary and intermittent. Additive and linear models are now supplemented by nonadditive, dynamic, and nonlinear ones. The ontological idea of a closed universe, an idea which came out of the Middle Ages, and which still characterized Hegel's thought, became replaced, as Alexander Koyré (1965, 1968) notes, by the conception of an open universe characterized by infinite possibilities, uncertainty, and chance.

One implication of complexity is that priority is placed on political regulation as a positive state mechanism for the management and coordination of matters of urgency, economic failure, as well as for the provision of structures of services and opportunities for citizens. This reflects the complexity postulates of interconnectedness, interdependency, vulnerability, and insufficiency of the parts in relation to the whole. Such interdependencies and vulnerabilities would prima facie appear to lend support to the idea of a more active state where independent political coordination at the level of the system or collective is required. This contrasts with the liberal idea of a minimal state which might appear justified in terms of a notion of individual autonomy. Although Green appealed to idealism on matters of mind and truth, writers like Foucault theorized the rise of positive state power, not as liberals do, as an errant political choice, but unavoidably, as the result of materially instantiated changes in the structures and processes of the early modern period. For Foucault, positive state power, or "bio-power," represented a new material modality of power consequent upon the emergence of the state system and the necessity of state regulation. States pursued positive public purposes because they couldn't do anything else.[38] The public good becomes more significant, then, as societies change, manifesting increased real shared concerns and interests. Collective politics becomes *necessary*, it can be argued, consequent upon the onset of crises, increases in population, conflicts over state boundaries, the increasing importance of health, natural calamities, and so on. And as the collective becomes more necessary, so, too, does the domain of the good.

Complexity theory also enables a resolution of another core criticism of idealist philosophy by classical liberals. This concerns the overemphasis on unity, as expressed in the "doctrine of harmony" between the state and the citizen. This was a consequence of the fact that, in Hegelian philosophy, the whole determined the character of the parts, thus resulting in uniformity. Liberals criticized the idealists for positing man as citizen who existed only as a public being within the shadow of the state (Government + Civil Society = State) and "imprisoned by its own creation" (Seth, 1897, p. 291). Both German and Oxford Idealism posited an essential unity between the individual and society. As James Seth explains it:

> So perfect was the harmony between the individual and the State, that any dissociation of the one from the other contradicted the individuals' conception of ethical completeness. It is to this sense of perfect harmony, this deep and satisfying conviction that the State is the true and sufficient ethical environment of the individual, that we owe the Greek conception of the ethical conception of the State. (1897, p. 282)

The innovation of complexity dynamics, through its emphasis on the reciprocal interaction of part(s) and whole, introduces a new nominalist conception of iteration where the future doesn't simply repeat the past and where repetition or reproduction of structures and identities over time both reproduce the past in the future and also simultaneously individuates or differentiates its different elements in relation to the whole. In this way harmony or uniformity is theorized in terms whereby uniqueness and difference are simultaneously enacted. Repetition is characterized by difference, and the future is marked by uncertainty and rupture. While every action in time bares the character of what went before, each also necessarily differentiates itself within the whole. There is an irreducible dependence of the individual on the social and the general, yet also an infinite individuation and differentiation of each element within the whole. Another consequence explains how the individual subject can be both historically and socially constituted, yet unique. While each subject lacks an essence or substance (*ousia*), in Aristotle's sense, ontological uniqueness is constituted in terms of differential effects of environment in relation to the different locations in space/time and through the differential affects exacted as a consequence of time irreversibility.

Complexity theory also enables a theorization of contingency in history in terms of which the scope or expansiveness of what we mean by the good, concerning the domain of core values like liberty, could undergo alteration. Nothing could be more evident than at the start of the 21st century with the emergence of new global issues around climate change, overpopulation, nuclear power, terrorism, or viral pandemics, that the state's role is once again necessarily being altered. Contingent changes are altering the calculus of individual versus group interests in terms of which state actions and global agencies act. In this sense, climate change and uncontrolled population growth constitute veritable "tragedies of the commons," as Garrett Hardin (1968) claims, indicating the interconnectedness between the collective and the individual. For Hardin, because of the rational pursuit of self-interest, both nations and individuals are led to overexploit and therefore abuse the commons, with the result that "the freedom of the commons brings ruin to all" (1968, p. 1243). Yet this would entail that the greater the problems of security facing communities, or humanity, the greater the level of *shared* relative to *individual* interests, and the greater the shadow of the future over contemporary events. It would suggest that in relation to issues such as climate change or terrorism, the emergence of new shared concerns or strengthening of existing ones. For, as danger in the outside world increases, the calculus of what constitutes self-interest (for an individual or group) and what constitutes the "common interest" (of a group or nation, or humanity) also changes.

For the intertwined nature of these global issues means—increasingly—that the conditions for the development of *each* presupposes the maintenance of adequate conditions for development for *all*. The dual theorization of macro- and micro-levels, or system and part(s), as well as the principle of nonreductionism from one to the other, necessitates an understanding of structural supports to individual development, as well as minimizing the disaffections of subunits within the whole, as a necessary requirement for the development of each. Continuance is thus both individual and systemic and necessitates a conception of both shared as well as private ends, with appropriate normative values for each level. In a nutshell, because complexity highlights uncertainty, unpredictability, entropy and accident, and increasing inequality, it would seem reasonable to infer that state and global structures are necessary to regulate and coordinate to ensure shared interests and needs are safeguarded or provided for.

Complexity also explains how systems generate new patterns of activity through dynamic interactions over time, thus facilitating a readier appreciation of the *constructed* nature of the good, and of its periodic reformulation and change in history.[39] By eschewing essentialism, the good is not seen teleologically as a destiny of nature, or in terms of static ahistorical foundations—whether *Forms*, *Cogito*, or *Nature*—but rather as a contingently ordered constellation that expresses human interests and concerns in history. After the linguistic turn, the constructed good is subject to indefinite change and reformulation, as contingent developments in history will force new elements to be differentially weighted or balanced according to actual changes in the real conditions of existence. This is the sort of conception that Michel Foucault advances in his interview with Michael Bess in 1980:

> What is good is something that comes through innovation. The Good does not exist . . . in an a-temporal sky, with people who would be like Astrologers of the Good, whose job it is to determine what is the favorable nature of the stars. The good is defined by us, it is practiced, it is invented. And this is a collective work. (Foucault, 2014, p. 9)

In this model, human actions in history are normative and goal-orientated, but not subject to intelligent design, "purposeful," or determined by nature or God.

One implication of complexity in nature and society is that priority is placed on political regulation as a positive state mechanism for the management and coordination of matters of urgency and economic failure, as well as for the provision of structures, services, and opportunities for upcoming generations of citizens. Because systems have their own problems of steering independently of the parts, independent political coordination at the level of the system or collective is *required*. Old ideas based upon economic "self-regulation," "equilibrium," or "laissez-faire" sit uncomfortably with complexity's emphasis on uncertainty, disequilibrium, indeterminism, unpredictability, and random independent systems dysfunctions. By emphasizing system imperatives in relation to sensitive dependence on context, bifurcation, unforeseen developments, and unintended consequences, an emphasis is placed on the *necessity of coordination* at both the state and global levels to manage the shared concerns of citizens. The corollary of this is the need for a *constructed ethic of the good* which guides both collective politics and individual ethics.

By reintroducing a conception of the good, we can also resolve a major antimony of liberal theorizing on the issue of freedom. For unless freedom and choice are structured by a theory of value, that is, of public good, through which the shared choices of individuals are normatively anchored and given direction, then a purely negative conception of freedom, which is indistinguishable from *licence*, will result. If freedom is defined purely according to the subjective preferences of individuals, then the liberal must celebrate and tolerate *any* choices, including any individual who might define their life mission trivially, by counting blades of grass on the village lawn, or by playing push-pin, or exercising some similar trivial preference, as Jeremy Bentham endorsed.[40] For classical liberals, lacking any theory of the public character of meaning, have no standard by which choices can be evaluated and ranked, or given meaning independent of an individual's preferences. In *Utilitarianism*, John Stuart

Mill (1910, pp. 7–9) seriously called his own liberal credentials into question when he criticized Bentham by distinguishing "higher" from "lower" pleasures.[41] Green picked up on Mill's lead and defined a robust conception of good as necessary to freedom. Only if freedom is seen, as Green (1888, pp. 371–372) argued, as the ability of an individual to choose between different *worthwhile* ends can a meaningful conception of freedom as a public good be salvaged.[42] And if only worthwhile freedoms are encouraged, then what is worthwhile must be determined according to good, that is, to a metaconception of value which is irreducibly normative and which promotes or inhibits life continuance for each and all.

On this basis, it can be argued that liberals like Rawls, who claim to be consistent antiperfectionists, fail to sustain their conceptions without themselves assuming a general conception of what a good life is. As Martha Nussbaum argues, Rawls cannot develop an account of important life resources like education and health as "primary goods" without himself relying upon a comprehensive moral conception of good which takes "some stand about what functions are constitutive of human good living" (1988, p. 152). Such a good is "comprehensive" in the sense that the state cannot be entirely neutral between all social groups or values.[43] It would need to emphasize certain values and skills as important, values such as tolerance, trust, respect for diversity, and civic institutions, and reorder the importance and priority of particular values (stability *vs.* liberty) at different times relative to the circumstances that pertain.

In *Capitalism, Socialism, and Democracy*, Schumpeter (1976) says that while we must reject the classical conception of good of old, as a particular representation of the will of the people, in that it reads purposes and ends into nature, there is nothing to "debar us from trying to build up another and more realistic one" (pp. 252–253). Despite his antagonism toward the classical doctrines of good, Schumpeter sees nothing amiss with representing shared human interests in history as common interests, by which he means "not a genuine, but a manufactured will. And often this artifact is all that in reality corresponds to the *volonté générale* of the classical doctrine" (p. 263). Schumpeter continues, "[s]o far as this is so, the will of the people is the product and not the motive power of the political process" (p. 263). Here, Schumpeter is accepting what an adequate conception today in fact requires: The good represents not a mysterious soul, or spiritual or motivating force within nature, but is rather the necessary product of historical social process as individuals and groups seek to actualize the collective agency that is necessary to the realization of their *shared* interests qua individuals and groups. As Gerhard Colm argues:

> One might say that an essential condition for the existence of a democracy is some degree of common conviction that certain achievements serve the variety of ultimate values. In other words, the public interest is the life hypothesis of a pluralistic society—enabling people with different religions, different philosophical convictions, or different subconscious value systems to have a common ground for promoting their various ultimate values. Without this common ground, representing

more than an accidental coincidence of individual interests, a pluralistic democracy could not exist. (1960, p. 300)

In the language of complexity science, influenced as they were by quantum theories, it is quite conceivable that such a good can be articulated as a set of probabilities. Although liberalism demonized the concept of the collective throughout the 20th century, seeing anything but a negative conception of the state's role as invariably leading to totalitarianism, it is vital today to resurrect *a legitimate conception of the concept of collective, and articulate an adequate and necessary sense of its use* (see Morss, 2016). Again, Colm has a perspective:

> It is a misunderstanding . . . to contend that the concept of the public interest presupposes a totalitarian philosophy. Totalitarianism refers to the manner in which decisions are made in a society. What is to be regarded as the public interest can be determined in a dictatorial manner, or it can result from democratic processes. (1960, p. 301)

It is this more "worldly" conception of the good life, not as a metaphysical destiny or telos, nor as part of the world of objective and eternal Forms, but as a general but objective set of developmental values concerned with human good living, incorporating both survival and well-being of all, that a new complexity-based conception of the good with its undergirding values of interconnectedness, entanglement, and insufficiency supports. The good thus takes on a distinctly sociological character concerned with articulating the politically necessary values and practices that ensure the continuation of the project of life into the future.[44]

Such a good, also, is not contradicted by a postulate of self-interest, contra Schumpeter, Buchanan, and the neoliberals, when they maintained that the public good functioned solely as a "cloak" to disguise the self-interested opportunism of bureaucrats. While many would argue that Buchanan importantly drew attention to the need for systems of monitoring and accountability, the fact that individuals will act opportunistically does not logically displace or exclude the idea of the public good.[45] This is to say, the two concepts are not in fact mutually exclusive. Indeed, it is the good that regulates and moderates individual and group self-interest and behavior both in terms of law and ethics. This was David Hume's view. In his *Political Writings*, while recognizing the significance of self-interest, unlike Buchanan, he sees it not as disqualifying the idea of public good, but rather as quite compatible with it. As he says: "[b]y this interest we must govern him, and, by means of it, make him, notwithstanding his insatiable avarice and ambition, co-operate to public good" (Hume, 1994, p. 113).

Complexity theories of science and poststructuralism put the good firmly back on the agenda. They do this, first, through adherence to a social and historical constructionist conception of the subject, and of meaning, by which the sources of all values are public and social; and, second, by placing a greater emphasis upon systems, connectedness, interactions, interdependencies, insufficiencies, and vulnerabilities.

DEONTOLOGY AND TELEOLOGY

If I am to truly rehabilitate the idea of the public good, several other issues need to be addressed, of which I can only briefly and schematically allude to here. In a recent book, *Can Virtue Make Us Happy? The Art of Living and Morality*, Otfried Höffe maintains not only that the good must be reinstated alongside the right, but that "teleological and deontological ethics don't have to exclude each other" (2010, p. 270). Höffe continues:

> [A] primarily deontological ethics allows only for action-internal reflection, whereas a far-reaching teleological ethic also allows for action-external reflection over consequences . . . ethics is more meaningfully, even necessarily, deontological in its foundation; and in contrast, ethics is teleological with respect to the "application" of principles to certain regions of life and concrete situations. (Höffe, 2010, p. 270)

Höffe's statement invites the question: In what senses can teleology be reconciled not simply with Kantian deontology but also with the forms of explanation that characterize science? Aristotelian teleology is a theory of final causes which sees all matter and life as having inherent natural ends and purposes. This in turn developed in the Middle Ages to entail a theory of origins through intelligent design. This conception of teleology was rejected in the Enlightenment where science sought to explain nature mechanically (in terms of basic postulates such as size, matter, shape, motion) without appeal to inherent ends or purposes. After Aristotle, some of the scholastics sought to restrict teleology to intentional agents, humans or God (see Johnson, 2005, ch. 1).

While Aristotle's conception of teleology as a theory of final causes based on essentialist naturalism was deemed incompatible with science, whether there is a minimal or "weaker" sense in which a form of teleology can be utilized in regrounding a conception of good constitutes a meaningful question. For if any sense of teleology is to serve today in rehabilitating a concept of the good on the basis of an immanent normativity in life, it clearly needs to avoid positing occult or religious categories, entelechies or vital spirits, appeals to intelligent design or innate purposes, to perfection, or of being incompatible with science. If the concept of life continuance is open to criticism as marking a retreat to an unacceptable conception of already discredited teleological thinking, as some liberals claim, then, by extension, any attempt to rehabilitate a conception of the public good on that basis will also founder.

In her book *The Virtue Ethics of Hume and Nietzsche*, Christine Swanton notes that Friedrich Nietzsche avoided commitment to what she calls "strong teleology" of the Aristotelian sort (2015, p. 196). She records that for Nietzsche, there is "no telos proper to human beings qua human—rather we create ourselves in an ongoing process" (p. 196). Nietzsche is an inspiration for the conception of life continuance utilized here to reinstate a conception of the good, as I have previously documented (Olssen, 2009, ch. 2; 2021, ch. 4). Swanton cites Simon May, who says, "for Nietzsche, unlike Aristotle, the perfect and final actualization of a clear and fixed potential is neither possible nor knowable nor should be sought" (May, 1999, p. 109, cited in Swanton, 2015, p. 197). She also cites Alexander Nehemas (2001, p. 261, cited in Swanton, 2015, p. 197), who asserts much the same thesis, saying that "becoming does not aim at a final state."

It is not possible in the space allowable to do full justice to such an issue. What I can say is that a minimal sense of teleology is quite possible which eschews conceptions of "purposes," "natural essences," "inner forces," "ideals of perfection," and that allows for a conception of goals as an open-ended and unending process that applies only to living beings and that is wholly compatible with science. As Alexander Koyré (1950/1965) notes, while the doctrine of teleology described a universe that was finite and hierarchically ordered, the change in conception to a universe that is open, indefinite, and infinite alters the equation concerning how teleology ought to be configured. With the Enlightenment, such a shift implied a rejection, says Koyré, of all elements from science based on:

> value, perfection, harmony, meaning, and aim, because these concepts, from now on *merely subjective*, cannot have a place in the new ontology. . . . Or to put it in different words: all formal and final causes as modes of explanation disappear from—or are rejected by—the new science and are replaced by efficient and even material ones. Only the latter have the right of way and are admitted to existence in the new universe of hypostatized geometry. (Koyré, 1950/1965, pp. 7–8)

While major figures such as Bacon (1561–1626), Descartes (1596–1650), and Spinoza (1632–1677) embraced the rejection of final causes, as Monte Ransome Johnson (2005, p. 25) points out, they did not reject such a doctrine "without qualification."[46] In addition, says Johnson, "later prominent scientific revolutionaries, such as Gassendi (1592–1655), Boyle (1627–1691), Newton (1642–1727), and Leibniz (1646–1716) actively countenanced final causes, even in the context of natural science" (Johnson, 2005, p. 25). Many of these figures felt that the early modernists had been too radical and that it was not easily possible to reject final causes, or at least conform in all respects to mechanical method with respect to intentional agency, even if it was possible to conform to mechanism where nature and nonintentional agency was involved. Complexity science has moderated the importance of mechanism, supplementing it with emergentist holist types of analysis characteristic of nonequilibrium physics, implying a shift as Ilya Prigogine puts it, "from being to becoming" as a consequence of the effects of time irreversibility on the dynamics of large systems, as well as of thermodynamic systems and fields (2003, p. 39). The inclusion of "irreversibility" profoundly changes our views of nature, says Prigogine—"the future is no longer given. Our world is a world of continuous 'construction' ruled by probabilistic laws and no longer a kind of automation. We are led from a world of 'being' to a world of 'becoming'" (Prigogine, 2003, p. 39).

It is my view that the Enlightenment "threw out the baby with the bathwater."[47] Today, it is necessary to reincorporate a minimal and revised sense of teleology back into science in order to explain social life and ethics. Schematically, such a proposal would require the arguments and conclusions as follows:

THE REHABILITATION OF THE CONCEPT OF PUBLIC GOOD   845

- In that life continuance posits a normativity immanent to life it is fully compatible with a materialistic, scientific forms of explanation of the origins of life. As such, continuance implies no extra-materialistic residue, entelechy, or vital spirit, beyond what can be accounted for by a thesis of scientific materialism.[48]
- Continuance posits no final "end state," no "specific goals," no "terminus," but only "an end without an end," a process, which is life itself.[49]
- Continuance rejects the concept of "purposes," which Kant termed *Naturzweck* ("natural purpose" or "natural end").[50]
- Continuance also posits no standard of perfection; no true self or state of the world which we must aim at.[51]
- Continuance implies no process of design, and no designer. It does not theorize about origins.[52]

Furthermore, an ethics can be constructed which does not read goals into nature:

- There are better and worse ways to continue life. This accounts for law, politics, education, ethics, and morality.[53]
- Continuance frames ethics in relation to only three things: (1) one must attend to oneself, (2) avoid harming oneself, others, the world, and (3) facilitate and assist ongoing continuance of life as best one can within the life situation one finds oneself in. This goes beyond social contract ethics in that it recognizes responsibilities to animals, environment, and supererogation.[54]
- Continuance also frames morality: actions which intentionally impede the continuance of each and all are represented as immoral; what facilitates or actively assists continuance norms are represented as moral.[55]
- As a normativity immanent in life, which manifests and expresses itself in each instance of life, and in relation to the common environment which life inhabits, continuance necessarily entails *shared interests, benefits, and concerns*. These constitute the basis for a conception of the common good without denying divergent interests or a democratically agreed framework where liberty can be enacted.[56]

A soft sense of teleology can incorporate a conception of ends and goals as *constructed* and which allows for diversity compatible with continuance:

- Continuance posits only ends and goals which are those of life itself and which can realize themselves variously in an open field of possibilities. These are the ends associated with survival and prospering and are themselves contingent upon a drive to survive and prosper. This notion of teleology is also adopted by Theodore R. Schatzki when he says: "By 'teleological' I mean orientated towards ends: the teleological character of activity consists in people performing actions for ends" (2010, p. xiii).[57] These goals and ends are constructed rather than natural.
- In philosophical terms, such a good is not "unitary" in the sense that Popper saw Plato, Marx, and Hegel. While the good acknowledges shared, that is, common

interests, it also acknowledges divergent ones, which among a global polis are likely to be innumerable.[58]

- Continuance norms operate in all living beings, individually and collectively. These do not only refer to intentional agency, as many nonintentional actions impact upon continuance, as do the unintended effects of intentional actions.[59]
- As the state represents the collective or shared dimensions of personhood, in the quest for life continuance, its legitimacy is linked to how well it carries out these functions.[60]
- The more dangerous or insecure life is, the greater the significance the collective dimension becomes vis-à-vis individual capacity or autonomy. Issues such as climate change or viral pandemics provide empirical confirmation of such a hypothesis.
- As life continuance is premised upon the social and historical nature of the self, normative value is social, and must logically be articulated in a conception of good.
- The tasks required by continuance are experimental, problem-centered, and critical. One must overcome obstacles and clear away illusions and mystifications, hence an important role for critical education as essential for democracy.[61]

All of these propositions could be argued for further if time and space permitted. In short, the good can be resurrected because science no longer forbids it, and one is no longer dependent on Hegelian idealism—the dialectical progression of history; the teleological conception of the good; the equation of the real with the rational; or Hegel's religious eschatology.

THE GOOD OF CONTINUANCE

As it is assumed that all people will support that the project of humanity should be continued, that is, that life is worthwhile, this postulation of an imminent normativity meets the conditions of the unanimity rule. It may be the only postulation that can be unanimously agreed upon by all, but indeed, it is enough, as all other matters can in theory be resolved via a political process.[62] As it would quickly be decided that democracy offered the best chances of success at continuance, being the only method that would prevent "a war of all against all," all others matters would be resolved via democratic processes. This would include the shape and character of the democratic process itself.

Such a good can also be justified as self-evident by philosophical analysis through reasoned argument, however. As von Wright tells us in *Norm and Action*, "[o]ne sense in which a norm can be said to be valid is that it *exists*" (1963b, p. 195). The norm of life continuance can be validated empirically through reflection for humans and for all living beings. From tying one's shoelaces, to "grasping" and "sucking" reflexes that new infants manifest, beyond saying that it constitutes the background habitus to our lives far more than we ordinarily acknowledge or possibly are aware of, it is also too obviously true on serious reflection as to warrant further argument for such a thesis here.

Once objectified as a principle, however, life continuance enables us to understand the bases to our ethical and moral actions, not as emanation from an objectively existing external world of Forms, but, like the proverbial donkey who pursues a carrot dangling in front of her eyes but attached to a wire around her neck, as immanent within life itself. It generates irreducible normative truths. The mathematical problem in this sense could be constructed as something similar to a rational choice game: a certain number of living beings occupying a finite territory with finite resources and inhabiting an environment with a certain capacity to support them. Under such circumstances, with enough information, the good can be "calculated." What such calculations will show, I am confident, is that among the surest policies to continue life will include the following goods: clean air, clean water, a form of sustenance that is secure, a cultural ethos of trust, a public education system, and a disputes resolution process that is democratic (to minimize resentment and inhibit a "war of all against all"). These would offer the *best* chances for survival. While such a good is not derived directly through aggregative individual interests, preferences, or wants, it does meet the terms of unanimity on the one crucial issue, as stated earlier, and taking that issue at its word, it gives everything else over to the democratic process. What the good of life continuance really does is simply codify or articulate the implicit reasoning behind individual and collective politics as we carry it out in the world on a daily basis.

Unlike Kant's principle of universalization, continuance formulates ethical actions from the contingency of the present. It asks, What needs to be done? and in doing so, it can formulate a political agenda of pressing tasks as defined in the context of both time and location. Criteria such as urgency are also considered. While some tasks will reflect the universal conditions of existence, such tasks will be discursively modulated and practically overlaid according to the contextual exigencies of time and space. In the present conjuncture both viral pandemics and climate change will significantly affect the discourses and dynamics of the good in terms of what one ought to do, what is fair and just, what is more prudent, more sensible, more appropriate, and more beneficial. All these normative aspects derive from the mechanics of continuance conceived as a problem of how humanity can successfully traverse the future. Although this constitutes a nonmoral criterion for ethics, morality, and normativity, the issues of survival pose practical and normative imperatives which require definite tasks. The future stretches before us as a goal to be achieved and surpassed, which paradoxically articulates itself as a series of moral obligations as well as appropriate and prudent normative actions; this is to say, *that the future translates as an imperative for specific actions and specific conducts.* The existence of viral pandemics and climate change elevate the importance of the collective dimensions of personhood and signal a whole new orientation to politics, to personal and group comportment, to the central importance of knowledge and expertise, as well as to the constructions of subjectivity, of space, of time, of social distance, and the normative basis of both individual and collective interactions and conduct. The new norms of appropriateness themselves will define a new basis for both ethics and morality.

If we act on the provision that rights operate as important protections for individuals against the collective, and that duties or obligations cannot simply or easily be traded for the sake of supposed better consequences in the future, or some conception of the greater good, then we must reject theoretically the emphasis that utilitarianism has traditionally placed upon "maximization." Neither "maximization" nor "the majority principle" is adequate to ground normative theory. Majority preferences are not relevant to defending minority religious rights, or any other minority group rights, for instance. To articulate the good in terms of what is necessary to survival and well-being is not something that one seeks to "maximize" on behalf of the "greatest number." Rules of right are themselves sacrosanct for all because they ensure orderly conduct and fair play, that is, justice, without which the goods of stability and security, plus much else, would collapse. They cannot be traded in any easy sense.[63]

Compared to Bentham's "felicific calculus," set out in his *Introduction to the Principles of Morals and Legislation* (1960), the means of calculating the value of an action for continuance ethics is not the oversimplified method of Bentham's model of utility. Partly, the value of an action will be contingently related to time and place. In times of urgency, such as the present time of a global viral pandemic, when life continuance itself is threatened, the collective dimensions of selfhood will assume greater importance, and individual freedom will be constrained. In that the continuance calculus avoids the "maximizing" strategy, it also avoids the "averaging" character of utilitarianism. Proof-bearing propositions and strategies, following complexity science, are those that are most probable to achieve success. This is to say, a society where people are treated justly is most likely to succeed. Agendas which respect the mutual dependence of "each and all" are more likely to succeed, at least in public policy terms. As regards the calculus of continuance, no actions or rules are prohibited unless they impede or are detrimental for continuance itself. Actions and rules which harm others, or harm oneself, or harm social structures, are prohibited or discouraged. Ultimately, the value of each action, or rule, must be judged according to the contingent circumstances of time and place. Continuance is thus a political ethic and form of public morality and thus gives a greater weight to outcomes and consequences than would be the case in respect of purely private moral matters. Its locus is in an important sense institutional. Continuance is in this sense consequentialist but not utilitarian. It values welfare, security, liberty and individuality, and nondomination, as well as reasonable equality, as constituting the conditions most likely to succeed for moving forward.[64] Except in times of crisis or urgency, rather than being concerned to promote the *best* policy, it seeks to establish limits and set boundaries. As opposed to utilitarianism, as Nagel says, "[where] the method of combination is basically majoritarian," and policy is enacted "from a general point of view that combines those of *all* individuals," for the ethic of continuance "something is acceptable from a schematic point of view that represents in essentials the standpoint of each individual" (Nagel, 1978, p. 86). Thus, the specific standpoint of each individual or group from the contingency of their present situation where continuance is assessed in terms of difference and specificity rather than uniformity constitutes a major departure from the universalizing tendencies of both utilitarianism and Kantianism.

THE GOOD AND THE RIGHT

Behind liberals' suspicions of the priority of good one may see two related concerns as remaining: (a) that the individual will be sacrificed on the altar of the collective, often expressed in terms that there is no basis for imposing values that run contrary to individual preferences; and/or (b) that the means will be sacrificed in order to justify the ends (consequentialism). These objections are often presented against utilitarianism but can also be directed against Marx or Hegel. Such arguments are maintained, for instance, by Popper, in *The Open Society and Its Enemies* (1962), and by Rawls in *A Theory of Justice* (1971), as noted earlier. Bernard Williams (1973, Sec. 5) argues similarly that in maintaining an almost complete attachment to the collective goal of aggregate happiness, "[utilitarianism] fails to acknowledge the central importance of liberty for each individual and the ways and means that they define their lives and give them meaning" (see Dworkin, 2011, p. 383, for a similar view). Scanlon considers Williams's view as "pure self-indulgence. . . . Simply to demand freedom from moral requirements in the name of freedom to pursue one's own individual projects is unconvincing" (1978, p. 97).

Simply seeking to attack or abolish the good in order to resolve contradictions is not only unconvincing; it is also not a *plausible* option. Regarding the relation between the right and the good, there is a strong argument to suggest that the right presupposes the good if one is not to fall into contradiction. In an ontological sense, this is required if meanings and values are social and historical. It was in order to resolve conundrums that arise within deontological ethics that J. C. Ewing thought that "Kant's deontological rule requires supplementation [by a conception of good]" (1953, p. 63).[65] This is because right and wrong presuppose a theory of good which defines what is right and what is wrong in order to establish their content. It will enable us, also, said Ewing, to know how to resolve ethical conflicts when ethical principles of duty conflict.

An earlier attempt at reconciling teleological and deontological ethics can be seen in David Ross's book, *The Right and the Good* (1930). Ross sought to find a compromise between the deontology and consequentialism by stressing the importance of consequences as determining the rightness of an action, while rejecting an exclusive emphasis on them. Further, he defended moral duties but rejected the absolute character of them as holding in all times and places. To this end, he introduced the idea of "prima facie duty" to "signify an obligation that only holds subject to not being overridden by a superior obligation" (Ewing, 1953, p. 78). Prima facie duties covered situations where there may be a conflict of duties, or where the "context" or "situation" rendered what might normally be regarded as a duty, as perverse. An example might be telling a lie in order to protect the whereabouts of a Jew being hunted by the Nazis. By acknowledging this, and "relativizing" the notion of a duty in this way, Ross is, contra Kant, acknowledging the ultimate link between the right and the good or, in other words, the ultimate dependence of the right on the good. Ross's notion of prima facie duties can be incorporated, and understood, in the light of continuance ethics, for again, it is continuance that here serves as a metaethic to "regulate" the applicability of principles to actions, resulting in either the abandonment or uptake of the duty concerned.

Although reinstating the good in moral terms reintroduces concerns regarding consequentialism, Ewing would argue that it is no solution to this antimony of liberalism to argue a reductionist case. One face of this concern might postulate a situation where one breaks a promise to achieve some greater good at the time. Deontologists criticized utilitarians on similar grounds for prioritizing the outcomes of each action as being what counts; hence, they could break a promise if they held that a subsequent action led to a greater good in overall terms. Despite the importance of consequences, rights are not ignored. Scanlon argues for what he calls a "two-tier" approach "that gives an important role to consequences in the justification and interpretation of rights, but which takes rights seriously as placing limits on consequentialist reasoning at the level of casuistry" (1978, p. 94). My own view of Scanlon's point here is that such a general principle would require appraisal and judgment in relation to application in each situation. My response in terms of continuance ethics is that while continuance places importance on outcomes and consequences, the value given to rights, actions, and rules does not disappear. At the same time, within a systems perspective, a general theory of rights offers protections and entitlements to each in relation to others and to the whole. Approaching the issues in terms of continuance also assists with establishing what consequences are to be considered important. Each situation will require judgment, reflection, and deliberation. If the good represents the shared values of life continuance as a process without closure, the same continuance norms also specify the sanctity of the right with its obligations to tell the truth, not to lie, or steal, as set rules except where a prima facie reason can be justified to do otherwise. Rather than such rules being universal, pace Kant, continuance norms regulate actions to grant exceptions in specific situations depending upon contingent circumstances of time and place. Hence, to reuse the example from earlier, if the Nazi SS guards arrive at your door and ask the whereabouts of the Jew you are harboring, you can lie to them; indeed, morally, *you ought to lie to them*.

A second response here is that where conflicts exist between the good and the right, they cannot be resolved as liberals have tried to do by abolishing the idea of the good. A great deal of liberal objections to the good are simply a method for establishing the exclusive legitimacy of a deontological moral framework. If the right presupposes the good, tensions and conflicts between them can only be resolvable through legal, political, and institutional processes, including norms of public scrutiny, transparency, and accountability. In political terms, conflicts between the right and the good, like the dangers of collective power, are resolvable when we recall that relations between the right and the good are *political relations*. This is to say that individual rights are ultimately protected through *legal machinery* and through *democratic mechanisms*. Conflicts resulting from a domination by collective power must be resolvable at the political level in terms of dispute resolution mechanisms. Where there are conflicts between individual rights and collective ends, or between duties and consequences, these must be adjudicated through a publicly mandated institutional procedure in terms of public norms of transparency and accountability. In cases of personal morality, where one—say—breaks a promise to achieve a "greater" good, this may be resolved by "giving an account of oneself." In a complex society, structured by contingently varying conflicting situations, the possible types of conflict between rights and duties, on the one hand, and consequences and ends, on the other, will be infinite—not just in terms of content but also in terms of the possible application of principles. In this context, the good and the right must be justified in each situation. In cases of conflict, depending upon the situation, one should be able to "give an account of oneself," demonstrate veracity and sincerity, apologize, file a grievance, or take legal action. This is why a democratic culture is so important, because democracy ensures that both individual and collective rights and entitlements can coexist, that one is not sacrificed on the altar of the other.[66]

Importantly, in this sense, practical policy formulation proceeds according to the good, but nevertheless we can agree that individual actions must accord with those duties and obligations defined as right. This is because the right represents the rules of engagement which codify the way in which a good life is represented and operationalized for a multiplicity of projects that partake of it at a particular time. There is then a relation between the good and the right, but it is not helpful to attribute any categorical normative priority to one over the other. Rules of right represent the way the good life is operationalized and rendered available for all. In this sense, they regulate *process* which establishes rules of engagement and action. It is in the public spheres of politics, law, and morality, where the good and the right are accommodated, one to the other. Where individuals decide that the "law is an ass" or "morality is an ass," as may well happen in a complicated world,[67] should they choose to disregard the right, they should be prepared to publicly demonstrate the legitimacy of their decision (i.e., they should keep the receipts!). It is through collective publicly accountable authority, via democratic processes, law, and personal integrity, which regulates the relation of right to the good, and ultimately saves us from the dangers that some see in "aggregative," "collective," or "consequential" theorizing.

Education as a Global Public Good

So far, I have suggested that liberalism cannot abolish the good without falling into contradiction. The good, I have suggested, is necessary to both ethics and politics in a global age. The norms of continuance generate a unitary scheme of moral concepts and actions which ought to guide every individual in different times and places. Although unitary, such a scheme permits a multiplicity of different ways of life and is quite compatible with pluralism within limits.[68] Values such as trust and respect for norms of civility endlessly differentiate within discourse and yet retain a common core within definite limits. Trust, like clean air, is in the interests of all and facilitates continuance. Trust presupposes a social context of civility and involves counting on, and being counted on, by others. To seek to abolish the good results in a dangerous individualism which stands opposed to, or fails to recognize that individuals have both solitary and shared dimensions to their development and identities, a shared dimension which necessitates both institutional and collective politics, which in turn requires increasing regulation and positive political (state and global) action in an increasingly dangerous and uncertain world. To put it starkly, without recognition of this collective dimension of personhood, individuals themselves will perish. While democracy presupposes a conception of individual liberty, liberty in turn presupposes and can be guaranteed by effective economic and political action.

In representing the good in terms of what is necessary for the survival of life, policy will not be formulated in relation to "idealistic utopias," or the "perfectibility of man,"[69] but rather based on *sustainability* and sensible forward planning. Such a nonmetaphysical good shows affinity with Brian Barry's conception of the public interest, as well as with Hannah Arendt's conception of public life. Barry (1990) considers a public good as constituting something that benefits all members of a community in an abstract or general sense in their capacity *as citizens*. A public interest is defined as "those interests which people have in common *qua* members of the public" (p. 190). He cites George Cornewall Lewis, from his book *Political Terms*, who defines public as opposed to private interests as "that which has no immediate relation to any specified person or persons, *but may directly concern any member or members of the community, without distinction*" (cited in Barry, 1990, p. 190) (emphasis added). Barry then cites Jeremy Bentham who in "Principles of the Penal Code" defines "public offences" as:

> Those which produce some common dangers to all members of the state, or to an *indefinite number of non-assignable individuals* although it does not appear that they are in particular more likely to suffer than any other. (Bentham, 1931, p. 240, cited in Barry, 1990, p. 190; emphasis added)

On this definition the public good affects everyone equally, not necessarily in any actual situation, but *potentially*. These constitute shared interests, which Barry defines as "interests in common to all members of a community" (p. 207). In Barry's view, the public interest can be promoted in two senses. The first is negative by prohibiting things such as the erection of "flashing neon lights in the Cotswolds" (p. 208). The second is positive, such as the "erection of parks and benches, roads, etc. such as might be constructed by a local community" (p. 208). What is clear here is that the public good includes all those values—security, stability, liberty, contentment—for the project of humanity and life itself to continue onward into the future.

The appeal to complexity theory stated here, influenced as it is by systems theory and poststructuralism, sees the interests of individuals and society as entwined "through and through" and, in this sense, sees individuals as public beings "through and through." As Hannah Arendt (2000) says, the public realm represents a "common world" which "gathers us together and yet prevents our falling over each other" (p. 201). The word *public*, she says, signifies the world itself insofar as it is common to all of us and distinguished from the "privately owned place in it" (p. 201). The public realm, then, constitutes "a transcendence into a potential earthly immortality" whereby without it, "no politics, strictly speaking, no common world and no public realm, is possible" (p. 202). As for Kant, then, for Arendt, the objective foundation of the shared public interest, which constitutes the foundation for denoting its normative, political, ethical, and moral imperatives, operates under the rubric of a "good" (i.e., *the Public Good*), which arises "by virtue of the right of common possession of the surface of the earth" (Kant, 1795/1994, AK 8, p. 358), constitutive of a world with *finite and limited resources which are shared together*. For, "under the condition of a common world . . . everybody is always concerned with the same object" (Arendt, 2000, p. 205). Ultimately, then, it is the indisputable materiality of this shared common concern that grounds the argument for the reinstatement of good.

Education constitutes such a public good par excellence, as education is an interest shared by all. Education also influences the ability of both individuals and societies to continue life and achieve well-being. Knowledge in this sense is a shared public good, which is to say that it is indispensable for democracy. Only public action can guarantee the development of the knowledge necessary to overcoming obstacles, providing security and expertise for the future. Education should be publicly provided, as well as secular, compulsory, and free. In an increasingly unstable, crowded, and dangerous world, it is especially important that major institutions serve the global common good and are not primarily vehicles to promote individual or class status and/or wealth aspirations. Knowledge socialism, where education and training, skills and knowledge, are all freely accessible and transparent, constitutes an essential prerequisite for the pooling of resources and the tackling of global problems that today constitute our shared destiny.

Conclusion

The reinstatement of the good is justified on the basis of shared interests and public benefits, thereby circumventing the traditional criticisms of the classical liberals against ideas of the good. Those who defend the concept of the public good now also find that their arguments can more easily be justified according to the precepts and axioms of science as reconceptualized after the turn of the 20th century. This is because the new science constituted not just a revision of the classical synthesis, but a revolution. Instead of being individualist and reductionist, the new science stressed interconnectedness, systems, and nonreductionism, effectively reconfiguring the relations between the one and the many to emphasize both the collective as well as individual dimensions of life. Because complexity approaches to science also stress concepts such as insufficiency, uncertainty, nonpredictability, the unintended consequences of actions, as well as random and chance events, the importance of state agency and collective power in the service of citizens is emphasized. Contemporary models of science today fully justify that selfhood has a collective dimension which requires collective action proportionate to the dangers in the environment, and constrainable by democratic means. Once the

854   MARK OLSSEN

collective dimension of selfhood is acknowledged, liberal attacks of the idea of the good become obsolete.

NOTES

1. See Simons (1948).
2. See Buchanan (1954a, 1954b) and Arrow (1950, 1951).
3. See Niskanen (1971); Downs (1957, 1962, 1967); Olson (1965); and Tullock (1965).
4. Deontology derives from the Greek word *déon*, which translates as obligation or duty, or in terms of "what is binding," or "proper." In reference to the study of normative ethics, it referred for Kant to the fact that moral actions should be based on strict rules (never lie, never steal, etc.) rather than consequences. Although the other terms used here will be explained further later, good-based theories, such as Aristotle's posit, an end or telos (happiness or *eudaimonia*) to which all action aspires. Such an end is "teleological" by definition and also "perfectionist" in that it posits certain standards to be achieved.
5. Schubert says that "there is no public-interest theory worthy of the name," and he rejects that there ought to be such a theory (1960, pp. 223–224).
6. Cassinelli (1958), Benn and Peters (1959), Musgrave (1959), Benn (1960), Colm (1960), Hart (1961), Cohen (1962), Friedrich (1962), Rees (1964), Flathman (1966), Held (1970), Benditt (1973), Cochran (1974), Barry (1964, 1990), Pitkin (1981), Lewin (1991), Bobbio (2000), Campbell and Marshall (2002), Bozeman (2007), Meyerson (2007), and Johnson (2017), to name just some.
7. Although influenced by poststructuralism, I have read across both Continental as well as the Anglo-American philosophy. Scanlon is one who has influenced me from the latter, in terms of interests and consequences, and in relation to the irreducibility of normative truths, but not his contractualism, conception of rationality, or the subject.
8. See Sen (1982) and Weale (1983). Philosophers such as Thomas Scanlon (1978), John Harsanyi (1976), and H. L. A. Hart (1963, pp. 25–34; 1966, pp. 58–63) have also distinguished the need to consider "objective" as well as "subjective" preferences, thus supporting forms of paternalism.
9. Although I do not defend paternalism in this chapter, given my resolution to the classical utilitarian focus on preferences, a soft form of paternalism could be defended. In this sense, H. L. A. Hart's statement that "paternalism—the protection of people against themselves—is a perfectly coherent policy" (1966, p. 61) adds yet a further reason that builds toward a socially responsible democratic policy that enables the state to act for and on behalf of individuals in times of need.
10. See Rae (1975), Coleman (1989), Barry (1990), Shapiro (1990, pp. 79–125), Nelson (2010), and Weale (2020, ch. 6). All of these authors raise serious criticisms of the unanimity principle.
11. In *The Calculus of Consent*, Buchanan and Tullock note the likelihood that the unanimity rule may not actually apply for any real-world decisions, and they also acknowledge that unanimity may be costly and difficult to achieve (1962, p. 69).
12. While it claims to be merely aggregational, and non-normative, as Shapiro (1990) says, the model actually "'distorts' preferences" (p. 94) and "rests on a misleading theory of action" (p. 92) in that it unjustifiably privileges actions that mimic what the market would produce.

13. Buchanan and Tullock justify it on the grounds that (a) it is the decision-rule that would be chosen by self-interested subjects acting rationally; (b) it is by definition acceptable to all; (c) that such a rule ensures the inviolability of the person; (d) that it is fully inclusive of all individuals. It also (e) mimics consumer preferences in the market and is sensitive to property rights distribution. Hence, they say, "only if a specific constitutional change can be shown to be in the interests of all parties shall we judge such a change to be an improvement" (1962, p. 14). *Constitutional* is defined by them in broad terms, including economic, taxation, welfare, and property rights issues.

14. Buchanan and Tullock can also be accused of being ambivalent; hence, they say: "were decision-making costless, rational voters would choose a unanimity rule. Because decision-making is not costless, simple majority is the second-best solution" (1962, p. 215). The issue concerning ambivalence is a fairly standard criticism of Buchanan and Tullock. William Nelson notes, for instance, that, in chapter 8 of *The Calculus of Consent*, they proceed to argue "that something closer to majority rule might be preferable all things considered given the costs of reaching a consensus" (2010, p. 83). See also Coleman (1989, passim).

15. Quantum mechanics displays the same themes of other complexity approaches, viz. connectedness, systems analysis, indeterminism, but has had less influence on my own thought for various reasons. One is the differences existing between different accounts of quantum theory, between the early developers of the theory, as well as between interpreters of the theory. It is not clear, for instance, whether the thesis of "uncertainty," proposed by Heisenberg, is an epistemological, methodological, or ontological thesis; that is, whether it is a thesis concerning "ignorance," or one of "radical indeterminacy." Secondly, on one interpretation, as a form of "mechanics," quantum theory must still be seen as "deterministic" in ways that Poincaré's work, and Prigogine's work later in the century, surpassed. Thirdly, I tend to agree with much of Einstein's criticisms of quantum theory, in his initial debate with Niels Bohr, and later in the mid-thirties in his famous paper with Podolsky and Rosen, concerning the "incompleteness" of quantum theory (Einstein et al., 1935). For these reasons, quantum theory, although a background influence in that the main drift of its perspective fits the complexity model, has less direct influence on my own representation of complexity, which draws most directly on Poincaré and Prigogine, both in terms of science and philosophy of science. Poincaré's conventionalism also fits very closely with poststructural philosophy, especially as regards his opposition to logicism (set theory) and to metaphysical realism, his prioritization of a "relational" historical ontology, as well as in his conception of system or structure as not existing independently of its parts (see Poincaré, 1902, p. 25; 2011, passim; 1913, pp. 209, 484; 2017, pp. 2–5) (on quantum mechanics, see Gribbon, 1998; Polkinghorne, 1984).

16. Poincaré's resolution of the "three body problem" established him as the father of chaos theory in that it defeated arguments for linear determinism, certainty, predictability, and closure in science. Also, of importance, Poincaré's introduction of the topological model for physics and mathematics indirectly re-establishes the centrality of holism and systems thinking in ontology for both the physical and nonphysical sciences. (See Poincaré, 1890, 1891, 1902, 1908, 1911, 1913, 2017; Duplantier et al. 2010, Pomian, 1990; Rae, 2004; Skiadas, 2018; Worrall, 1989.)

17. Einstein's four seminal papers of 1905 in the German scientific journal *Annalen der Physik* can be seen as marking the death nell of the Classical paradigm that would forever change

physics and the elementary forces that constitute it: electromagnetism, space/time, and their interrelations.

18. Badiou's slim volume on ethics, written in the summer of 1993, while in the countryside in France, in the space of two weeks, is intended by him, as he says, "as no more than a preliminary sketch" (2001, p. lvi). Further discussion of his work and its parallels to my own postmodern ethics of continuance, which I developed before coming across his volume, is taken up in greater scope in my forthcoming book (Olssen, 2021).

19. Anglo-American philosophy and poststructuralism utilize a similar conception of constructivism, due to its common ancestry in Kant. It includes a sense of normative discourse as constructed in history and operating under certain specified conditions, from which can be derived justifiable principles of practice. Wedgwood (2007) argues that all action governed by rational beliefs is normative and orientated to an end or goal (see especially, ch. 7: "The Normativity of the Intentional"). Also see Ginsborg (2015, passim), Scanlon (2014), and Weale (2020, ch. 3). Scanlon argues "that a constructivist account of the normative domain is appealing because it seems to offer a way of explaining how normative judgments can have determinate truth values that are independent of us while also providing a basis for our epistemological access to these truths and an explanation of their practical significance for us" (2014, p. 91).

20. See my books (Olssen, 2009, 2021) for a more detailed treatment of these issues.

21. For discussions of the various analytic uses of the concepts of "interests" (special interests, group interests) versus "good" (public good, common good), see Barry (1964, 1990), Benditt (1973), Lewin (1991), and Campbell and Marshall (2002).

22. The concepts of public good and public interest are treated as equivalent in this chapter. The two main approaches are the "aggregational" approach of the utilitarian philosophers, where the good is nothing more than the sum of its members, and "normative" approaches, which include all the rest, both benign and dangerous. It is a normative democratic conception that I will argue for in this chapter.

23. Green's views were made in his *Lectures on the Principles of Political Obligation* (1941), first delivered at Oxford University in 1879–1880.

24. Rousseau had distinguished the "General Will" as distinct from and as transcending the "will of all" which gave it a metaphysical quality and made its link with popular sovereignty problematic.

25. Many writers have claimed this, but see Polin (1969, pp. 9–10), who says that Rousseau's supposition that sovereignty was in constant exercise because "when an individual has once given himself to the whole, he gives himself through the whole to himself" offered support for a collective sovereignty that legitimated authoritarian rule.

26. Idealism, whether German or British, was influenced by Hegel, and posited the central role of the ideal or the spiritual in the interpretation of experience.

27. See Prigogine and Stengers (1984), Nicolis and Prigogine (1989), Kaufmann (1995), Capra (1996), and Mitchell (2009).

28. Plank's "constant" was an important influence upon Einstein.

29. See note 2.

30. See note 3.

31. See Bohr (1958).

32. See Heisenberg (1959).

33. See Schrödinger (1995).

34. Dirac invented quantum field theory in 1928, providing a unified account of the wave/particle duality without paradox (see Polkinghorne, 1984, p. 2; Dirac, 1982).
35. This has included concepts to do with the meaning of "trajectories" and "initial conditions."
36. See Poincaré (1890, 1891, 1902, 1908, 1911, 1913, 2017). Also see Duplantier et al. (2010), Skiadas (2018), and Rae (2004, pp. 108–114, 122) for an overview and pertinent comments concerning Poincaré's contribution. Also see note 15.
37. If a film can represent motion running backward in the same way as running forward, then it is said in physics that time is reversible. The rotation of the hands of a clock is reversible, whereas tearing a piece of paper is irreversible. Prigogine does not deny that time reversibility has relevance but wishes to add that in many areas, including life itself, time is irreversible.
38. This was also Karl Polanyi's thesis in *The Great Transformation* (1957) when he argues that far from ideologies or ideas being important in the growth of state power in the 19th century, it was really a matter of practical necessity.
39. See note 19.
40. Bentham had famously said: "prejudice apart, the game of push-pin is of equal value with the arts and sciences, of music and poetry. If the game of push-pin furnishes more pleasure, it is more valuable than either" (Bentham, 1830, p. 206). As Alan Ryan says regarding Bentham's position that individual preferences must remain the sole criteria for exercising freedom: "This is, in Bentham, a necessary truth." Cited from Vergara (2011, p. 9). See Ryan's lecture, "Moving on from Bentham: Quantity and Quality," Utilitarianism, Third Lecture. http://users.ox.ac.uk/~ajryan/lectures/Utilitarianism/Mill%20Lecture%203.pdf
41. Mill was defending the thesis that poetry, music, and theater were more worthy pursuits than a trivial game. Because the criteria for making such a judgment must come from outside the individual, Mill is presupposing a conception of external, objective value, that is, a good.
42. See Green (1888, pp. 371–372).
43. School policies concerning language, the observance of holidays on days of national importance, or religious observances are not "neutral," for instance.
44. In saying that the good must take on a sociological character, I do not intend that it is merely "conventional," for it can meaningfully be asked whether any policy, accepted by social convention, really is *best* for life continuance itself.
45. See my article (Olssen, 2018) where I also maintain the thesis concerning the mutual compatibility of selfish individual interests and the public good.
46. These mainly concerned the applicability of teleology to intentional or living beings (see Johnson, ch. 1).
47. I have previously maintained this thesis with respect to psychology. See Olssen (1993, 2014).
48. For a discussion of materialist theories for the origin of life, see Simon Conway Morris (1998) and Stephen C. Meyer (2010, ch. 2). For a discussion of the issue of vitalism, see Georges Canguilhem (1994, ch. 13). Chapter 13 is titled "Knowledge and the Living." The first section of the chapter is titled "The Vitalist Imperative."
49. See Swanton (2015, ch. 10) for a discussion of these matters in Nietzsche.
50. See Kant, *Critique of Judgement* (1914, §§64–65) for a discussion of "natural purposes." See Ginsborg's discussion of Kant's thesis (2015, pp. 317–318).

51. See Swanton (2015, pp. 196–199) for Nietzsche's views in reference to teleology.
52. For a discussion of the issues surrounding the design thesis with reference to Kant, see Ginsborg (2015, pp. 229–237, 250–253, 337–339, 231–232, 237–243, 254– 262, 274–278, 321–339, 342–345. For Kant's discussion, see *Critique of Judgement* (1914, §§75, 78, 414).
53. While this generates an objectivist criterion, judging from the present, as in complexity science, is inexact and experimental.
54. Duties thus go beyond "what we owe to each other" (Scanlon, 1998). Also see Olssen (2021) for a fuller discussion of these issues.
55. This insight is Nietzschean. See Swanton (2015) and Olssen (2009).
56. Not all interests are common; besides shared interests can be realized or pursued differently (as in nutrition).
57. See Ginsborg (2015). In relation to Aristotle, see Johnson (2005).
58. Mancur Olson (1965, p. 36) says: "The larger the group, the less it will further its common interests." In many cases, divergent and common interests will be co-present, and express each other simultaneously at different levels of generality. Thus, while there is a common need for sustenance, individuals and groups diverge on how it is achieved.
59. See Schatzki (2010, p. 117) for a discussion of intentionality with reference to Donald Davidson's writings on the topic (1980, pp. 3–20).
60. The collective or shared aspects of personhood are centrally what liberal philosophy has omitted to emphasize, radically affecting their ontology of the world.
61. "Problematizations," for Foucault, orientate an approach to the present and operate as a central concept of his research (see Foucault, 1988, p. 257). Foucault was indebted to Nietzsche for his activist ontology. Swanton says (2015, p. 198) that "overcoming" as an "active engagement with the world" is also Nietzsche's central thesis. Bernard Reginster says that "overcoming" is what is central to Nietzsche's concept of the "Will to Power" (Reginster, 2006, pp. 130–132).
62. I claim here that as respects life continuance, unanimity, or very near unanimity, would be possible to infer even if articulated in different ways.
63. In that such rights are not absolute, however, where there is a conflict between right and good, resolution frequently proceeds at the institutional level, in parliament or the courts.
64. Reasonable equality is quite compatible with a mixed economy which recognizes wealth and income disparities, rewards for motivation, initiative, effort, dessert, and merit. The application of specific policies, such as progressive taxation, may be useful at certain times.
65. Bhikhu Parekh (2005, p. 22) also undermines the ability of Kant's universalization rule to stand on its own when he notes that "it is possible to universalize and consistently will the principle that one should always tell the truth irrespective of its consequences. It is equally possible to will consistently that one should tell the truth unless it causes harm to others. Since the Kantian test is met by both, it does not tell us which one to opt for."
66. It is for this reason that amongst other things, the state provision of legal aid is essential to liberty and the expression of rights. The curtailment of legal aid under austerity in the United Kingdom and other Western nations over the last two decades has significantly disadvantaged individual citizens who, except for the wealthy few, lack the resources to effectively redress rights grievances.
67. Wherever duties conflict, some rule in relation to good will need to be appealed to in order to hierarchically rank one over the other. It is also the case that rules of right are not absolute for they derive from the good of continuance. Where a rule becomes nonsensical, direct appeal to life continuance usurps the grounds.

THE REHABILITATION OF THE CONCEPT OF PUBLIC GOOD   859

68. Isaiah Berlin believes that "the ends of men are many . . . [and] that the belief that some single formula can in principle be found whereby all the diverse ends of men can be harmoniously realized is demonstrably false" (1958, p. 71). My counterargument to Berlin is that pluralism, to be intelligible, must presuppose limits, so that unacceptable views can be excluded (see Olssen, 2010, ch. 4).

69. I take this phrase from the title of a book by John Passmore (1972).

REFERENCES

Ackerman, B. (1980). *Social justice in the liberal state.* Yale University Press.

Arendt, H. (2000). The public and the private realm: Part IV, The Vita Activa. In P. Baehr (Ed.), *The portable Hannah Arendt* (pp. 182–230). Penguin.

Arneson, R. J. (2000). Perfectionism and politics. *Ethics, 111*(1), 37–63.

Arrow, K. (1950). A difficulty in the concept of social welfare. *The Journal of Political Economy, 58*(4), 328–346.

Arrow, K. (1951). *Social choice and individual values.* Wiley.

Badiou, A. (1993/2001). *Ethics: An essay on the understanding of evil* (P. Hallward, Trans.). Verso.

Barry, B. (1964). The public interest. *Proceedings of the Aristotelian Society, 38*(S), 1–18.

Barry, B. (1967/1990). *Political argument: A reissue with a new introduction.* Harvestor/Wheatsheaf.

Benditt, T. M. (1973). The public interest. *Philosophy & Public Affairs, 2*(3), 291–311.

Benn, S. I. (1960). "Interests" in politics. *Proceedings of the Aristotelian Society, 60,* 123–140.

Benn, S. I., & Peters, R. S. (1959). *Social principles and the democratic state.* Allen & Unwin.

Bentham, J. (1823/1960). *An introduction to the principles of morals and legislation* (W. Harrison, Ed.). Oxford University Press.

Bentham, J. (1830). *The rationale of reward.* Robert Heward.

Berlin, I. (1958). *Two concepts of liberty.* Clarendon Press.

Blaumol, W. J. (1961). *Economic theory and operations analysis.* Prentice-Hall.

Bobbio, N. (2000). *In praise of meekness: Essays on ethics and politics.* Polity Press.

Bohr, N. (1958). *Atomic physics and human knowledge.* John Wiley.

Bozeman, B. (2007). *Public values and public interest: Counterbalancing economic individualism.* Georgetown University Press.

Buchanan, J. M. (1954a). Social choice, democracy, and free markets. *Journal of Political Economy, 62*(2), 114–123.

Buchanan, J. M. (1954b). Individual choice in voting and the market. *Journal of Political Economy, 62*(3), 334–343.

Buchanan, J. M. (1975). *The limits of liberty: Between anarchy and leviathan.* University of Chicago Press.

Buchanan, J. M., & Tullock, G. (1962). *The calculus of consent: Logical foundations of constitutional democracy.* University of Michigan Press.

Campbell, H., & Marshall, R. (2002). "Utilitarianism's bad breath": A re-evaluation of the public interest justification for planning. *Planning Theory, 1*(2), 163–187.

Canguilhem, G. (1994). *A vital rationalist: Selected writings from Georges Canguilhem* (F. Delaporte, Ed.). Zone Books.

Capra, F. (1996). *The web of life: A new synthesis of mind and matter.* Flamingo/HarperCollins.

Cassinelli, C. W. (1958). Some reflections on the concept of the public interest. *Ethics, 69*(1), 48–61.

Cochran, C. E. (1974). Political science and "the public interest." *The Journal of Politics, 36*(2), 327–355.

Coleman, J. (1989). Rationality and the justification of democracy. In G. Brennan & L. E. Lomasky (Eds.), *Politics and process: New essays in democratic thought* (pp. 194–220). Cambridge University Press.

Cohen, J. (1962). A lawman's view of the public interest. In C. J. Friedrich (Ed.), *Nomos V: The Public Interest*. Atherton.

Colm, G. (1960). In defense of the public interest. *Social Research, 27*(3), 295–307.

Dahl, R., & Lindblom, C. (1963). *Politics, economics, and welfare*. Harper Torchbook.

Davidson, D. (1980). Actions, reasons, causes. In D. Davidson (Ed.), *Essays on actions and events* (pp. 3–20). Oxford University Press.

Davies, P. (1989). *The cosmic blueprint: New discourses in nature's creative ability to order the universe*. Simon and Schuster.

DeLanda, M. (2006). *A new philosophy of society: Assemblage theory and social complexity*. Continuum.

Deleuze, G. (1987). *A thousand plateaus: Capitalism and schizophrenia* (B. Massumi, Trans.). Continuum.

Deleuze, G. (1994). *Difference and repetition* (P. Patton, Trans.). Columbia University Press.

Derrida, J. (1978). Violence and metaphysics in the thought of Emmanuel Levinas. In *Writing and difference* (pp. 79–153). Routledge & Kegan Paul.

Derrida, J. (1995). *The gift of death* (D. Will, Trans.). Chicago University Press.

Derrida, J. (1997/2001). *On cosmopolitanism and forgiveness*. Routledge.

Derrida, J. (1999). *Adieu to Emmanuel Levinas* (P.-A. Braut & M. Naas, Trans.). Stanford University Press.

Dewey, J. (1927). *The public and its problems*. H. Holt & Co.

Dirac, P. A. M. (1982). *The principles of quantum mechanics* (4th ed.). Oxford University Press.

Downs, A. (1957). *An economic theory of democracy*. Harper.

Downs, A. (1962). The public interest: Its meaning in a democracy. *Social Research, 29*(1), 1–36.

Downs, A. (1967). *Inside bureaucracy*. Little, Brown & Co.

Duplantier, B., Nonnenmacher, S., & Rivasseau, V. (Eds.) (2010). *Chaos: Poincaré Seminar 2010*. Birkhäuser.

Dworkin, R. (1977). *Taking rights seriously*. Harvard University Press.

Dworkin, R. (1978). Liberalism. In S. Hampshire. (Ed.), *Public and private morality* (pp. 113–143). Cambridge University Press.

Dworkin, R. (2011). *Justice for hedgehogs*. Oxford University Press.

Einstein, A., Podolsky, B., &Rosen, N. (1935). Can quantum-mechanical description of physical reality be considered complete? *Physical Review, 47*, 777–780.

Ewing, A. C. (1953). *Ethics*. English Universities Press.

Flathman, R. (1966). *The public interest*. John Wiley & Sons.

Foucault, M. (1972). *The archaeology of knowledge*. Tavistock.

Foucault, M. (1980/2014). Power, moral values and the intellectual. Interview by Michael Bess on 3rd November 1980 in San Francisco, republished by Eugene Wolters, 6th January 2014, as "In a sense I am a moralist." http://www.critical-theory.com/read-me-foucault-interview-in-a-senseI-am-a-moralist/

Foucault, M. (1988). The concern for truth. Interview with Francois Ewald, in L. D. Kritzman (Ed.) and A. Sheridan (Trans.), *Politics, philosophy, culture: Interviews and other writings, 1977–1984*. Routledge.

THE REHABILITATION OF THE CONCEPT OF PUBLIC GOOD   861

Foucault, M. (2003). Lecture at the College de France 17th March 1976. In M. Bertani & A. Fontana (Eds.), A. I. Davidson (English Series Ed.), D. Macey (Trans.), *Society must be defended: Course lectures, 1976*. Allen Lane.

Foucault, M. (2007). Security, territory, population. In M. Senellart (ed.), A. I. Davidson (English ed.), & G. Burchell (Trans.), *Lectures at the College de France 1977–1978*. Palgrave Macmillan.

Foucault, M. (2008). *The birth of biopolitics: Lectures at the College de France 1978–1979* (M. Senellart, Ed. & A. I. Davidson, English ed., G. Burchell, Trans.). Palgrave Macmillan.

Friedrich, C. J. (1962). *The public interest*. Atherton Press.

Ginsborg, H. (2015). *The normativity of nature: Essays on Kant's Critique of Judgement*. Oxford University Press.

Green, T. H. (1885). *The works of Thomas Hill Green, Vol. 1* (R. L. Nettleship, Ed.). Longman, Green & Co.

Green, T. H. (1888). *The works of Thomas Hill Green, Vol. 3*. (R. L. Nettleship, Ed.). Longman, Green & Co.

Green, T. H. (1941). *Lectures on the principles of political obligation*. Longman, Green & Co.

Gribbin, J. (1998). *Q is for quantum: Particle physics from A–Z*. Weidenfeld & Nicholson.

Halewood, M. (2005). On Whitehead and Deleuze: The process of materiality. *Configurations*, 13(1), 57–76.

Hallowell, J. H. (1963). Plato and the moral foundation of democracy. In T. L. Thorson (Ed.), *Plato: Totalitarian or Democrat?* Prentice-Hall.

Hardin, G. (1968). The tragedy of the commons. *Science, 162*, 1243–1248.

Harsanyi, J. C. (1976). *Essays on ethics, social behaviour, and scientific explanation*. Reidel.

Hart, H. L. A. (1961). *The concept of law*. Oxford University Press.

Hart, H. L. A. (1963). *Law, liberty and morality*. Stanford University Press.

Hart, H. L. A. (1966). Paternalism and the enforcement of morality. In P. Radcliff (Ed.), *Limits of liberty: Studies of Mill's on liberty* (pp. 58–63). Wadsworth.

Heisenberg, W. (1959). *Physics and philosophy*. Allen and Unwin.

Held, V. (1968). On the meaning of trust. *Ethics, 78*, 156–158.

Held, V. (1970). *The public interest and individual interest*. Basic Books.

Höffe, O. (2010). *Can virtue make us happy? The art of living and morality*. Northwestern University Press.

Hume, D. (1994). *Political writings*. Hackett.

Johnston, J. (2017). The public interest: A new way of thinking for public relations. *Public Relations Inquiry, 6*(1), 5–22.

Johnson, M. R. (2005). *Aristotle on teleology*. Oxford University Press.

Kant, I. (1914). *Critique of judgment* (J. H. Bernard, Trans.). MacMillan.

Kant, I. (1785/1948). *Groundwork of the metaphysic of morals* (H. J. Paton, Trans.). Hutchinson University Library.

Kant, I. (1970). *Political writings*. Cambridge University Press.

Kant, I. (1795/1994). Towards perpetual peace: A philosophical sketch. In I. Kant, *Political writings* (H. B. Nisbet, Trans., & H. Reiss, Ed., 2nd ed.). Cambridge University Press.

Kaufmann, S. (1995). *At home in the universe: The search for laws of complexity*. Viking/Penguin.

Koyré, A. (1950/1965). The significance of the Newtonian synthesis. *Archives Internationales d'Histoire des Sciences, 3*, 291–311. [Reprinted in *Newtonian Studies*, London, 1965, pp. 3–24].

Koyré, A. (1968). *From the closed world to the infinite universe*. Johns Hopkins University Press.

Kymlicka, W. (1991). *Liberalism, community, culture*. Clarendon.

Levinas, E. (1969). *Totality and infinity: An essay on exteriority* (A. Lingus, Trans.). Duquesne University Press.

Levinas, E. (1985). *Ethics and infinity: Conversations with Philippe Nemo* (R. A. Cohen, Ed.). Duquesne University Press.

Levinas, E. (1998). *Entre Nous: On thinking-of-the-other* (M. B. Smith & B. Harshav, Trans.). Columbia University Press.

Lewin, L. (1991). *Self-interest and public interest in Western politics* (D. Lavery, Trans.). Oxford University Press.

Lippmann, W. (1927). *The phantom public.* Harcourt, Brace & Co.

Lippmann, W. (1955). *Essays in the public philosophy.* Little Brown.

May, S. (1999). *Nietzsche's ethics and his war on "morality."* Clarendon Press.

Meyer, S. C. (2010). *The signature in the cell: DNA and the evidence for intelligent design.* HarperOne.

Meyerson, D. (2007). Why courts should not balance rights against the public interest. *Melbourne University Law Review, 31*(3), 873–903.

Mill, J. S. (1910). Utilitarianism. In *John Stuart Mill: Utilitarianism, on liberty, and representative government* (pp. 1–60). J.M. Dent & Sons.

Mitchell, M. (2009). *Complexity: A guided tour.* Oxford University Press.

Moore, G. E. (1922). The refutation of idealism. In *Philosophical studies* (pp. 1–30). Routledge & Kegan Paul.

Morin, E. (2008). *On complexity* (R. Postel, Trans.) Hampton Press.

Morris, S. C. (1998). *The crucible of creation: The burgess shale and the rise of animals.* Oxford University Press.

Morss, J. (2016). *International law and the law of collectives.* Routledge.

Musgrave, R. A. (1959). *The theory of public finance.* McGraw-Hill.

Nagel, T. (1978). Ruthlessness in public life. In S. Hampshire (Ed.), *Public and private morality* (pp. 75–92). Cambridge University Press.

Nehemas, A. (2001). How one becomes what one is? In J. Richardson & B. Leiter (Eds.), *Nietzsche* (pp. 255–280). Oxford University Press.

Nelson, W. (2010). *On justifying democracy.* Routledge.

Nettleship, R. L. (1906). *Thomas Hill Green: A memoir.* Longmans, Green, and Co.

Nicholson, P. P. (1990). *The political philosophy of the British idealists: Selected studies.* Cambridge University Press.

Nicolis, G., & Prigogine, I. (1989). *Exploring complexity.* Freeman.

Niskanen, W. A. (1971). *Bureaucracy and representative government.* Aldine-Atherton.

Nozick, R. (1974). *Anarchy, state, utopia.* Blackwell.

Nussbaum, M. (1988). Nature, function, capability: Aristotle on political distribution. *Oxford Studies in Ancient Philosophy, 1*(S), 145–184.

Olson, M. (1965). *The logic of collective action.* Harvard University Press.

Olssen, M. (1993). Science and individualism in educational psychology: Problems for practice and points of departure. *Educational Psychology: An International Journal of Experimental Educational Psychology, 13*(2), 155–172.

Olssen, M. (2008). Foucault as complexity theorist: Overcoming the problems of classical philosophical analysis. *Educational Philosophy and Theory, 40*(1), 96–117.

Olssen, M. (2009). *Towards a global thin community: Nietzsche, Foucault and the cosmopolitan commitment.* Paradigm.

THE REHABILITATION OF THE CONCEPT OF PUBLIC GOOD   863

Olssen, M. (2010). *Liberalism, neoliberalism, social democracy: Thin communitarian perspectives on political philosophy and education*. Routledge.

Olssen, M. (2014). Framing and analysing education research: A recent history of transactions from a Foucauldian perspective. In A. D. Reid, E. P. Hart, & M. A. Peters (Eds.), *A companion to research in education* (pp. 215–228). Springer.

Olssen, M. (2015a). Ascertaining the normative implications of complexity for politics: Beyond agent-based modelling. In E. Kavalski (Ed.), *World politics at the edge of chaos: Reflections on complexity and global life* (pp. 139–168). SUNY Press.

Olssen, M. (2015b). Discourse, complexity, normativity: Tracing the elaboration of Foucault's materialist concept of discourse. *Open Review of Educational Research*, 1(1), 28–55.

Olssen, M. (2018). Neoliberalism and democracy: A Foucauldian perspective on public choice theory, ordo liberalism and the concept of the public good. In D. Cahill, M. Konings, M. Cooper, & D. Primrose (Eds.), *Sage handbook on neoliberalism* (pp. 384–396). Sage.

Olssen, M. (2021). *Constructing Foucault's ethics: A poststructuralist moral theory for the 21st century*. Manchester University Press.

Olssen, M., & Mace, W. (2021). British idealism, complexity theory and society: The political usefulness of T. H. Green in a revised conception of social democracy. *Linguistic and Philosophical Investigations*, 20, 7–34.

Parekh, B. (2005). Principles of a global ethic. In J. Eade & D. O'Byrne (Eds.), *Ethics and global politics* (pp. 15–34). Ashgate.

Passmore, J. (1972). *The perfectibility of man*. Duckworth.

Pitkin, H. F. (1981). Justice: On relating private and public. *Political Theory*, 9(3), 327–352.

Poincaré, H. (1890). Sur le problème des trois corps et les équations de la dynamique. *Acta Mathematica*, 13(1/2), 1–270.

Poincaré, H. (1891). Le problème des trois corps. *Revue générale des sciences pures et appliquées*, 2, 1–5.

Poincaré, H. (1902). *La science et l'hypothèse*. Flammarion.

Poincaré, H. (1908/1920). *Science et methode*. Flammarion.

Poincaré, H. (1911). *La valeur de la science*. Flammarion.

Poincaré, H. (1913/1982). *The foundations of science: Science and hypothesis, the value of science, science and method* (Translations of Poincaré 1902, 1911, 2008). University Press of America.

Poincaré, H. (2017). *Science and hypothesis: The complete text* (Translation of Poincaré 1902; M. Frappier, A. Smith, & D. J. Stump, Trans.). Bloomsbury.

Polanyi, K. (1944/1957). *The great transformation*. Beacon Press.

Polin, R. (1969). John Locke's conception of freedom. In J. W. Yolton (Ed.), *John Locke—Problems and perspectives* (pp. 1–18). Cambridge University Press.

Polkinghorne, J. C. (1984). *The quantum world*. Penguin Books.

Pomian, K. (Ed.) (1990). *La querelle du determinisme. Philosophie de la science aujourd'hui*. Gallimard/Le Debat.

Popper, K. (1962). *The open society and its enemies*. Harper Torchbooks.

Prigogine, I. (2003). *Is future given?* World Scientific.

Prigogine, I., & Stengers, I. (1984). *Order out of chaos*. Bantam.

Protevi, J. (2006). Deleuze, Guattari and emergence. *Paragraph*, 29(2), 19–39.

Rae, A. (2004). *Quantum physics: Illusion or reality?* (2nd ed.) Cambridge University Press.

Rae, D. W. (1975). The limits of consensual decision. *The American Political Science Review*, 69(4), 1270–1294.

Rawls, J. (1971). *A theory of justice*. Harvard University Press.

Rees, W. J. (1964). The public interest. *Proceedings of the Aristotelian Society, 38*(S1), 1–38.

Reginster, B. (2006). *The affirmation of life: Nietzsche on overcoming nihilism*. Harvard University Press.

Ritchie, D. G. (1998). *Collected works, Vol. 1*. Thoemmes Press.

Rogers, R. A. P. (1911). *A short history of ethics*. Macmillan.

Ross, D. (1930/2002). *The right and the good* (P. Stratton-Lake, Ed.). Oxford University Press.

Scanlon, T. M. (1978). Rights, goals, and fairness. In S. Hampshire (Ed.), *Public and private morality* (pp. 93–113). Cambridge University Press.

Scanlon, T. M. (1998). *What we owe to each other*. Belknap Press.

Scanlon, T. M. (2014). *Being realistic about reasons*. Oxford University Press.

Schatzki, T. R. (2010). *The timespace of human activity: On performance, society, and history as indeterminate teleological events*. Lexington Books.

Schrödinger, E. (1995). *The interpretation of quantum mechanics*. Ox Bow Press.

Schubert, G. (1960). *The public interest*. The Free Press.

Schumpeter, J. (1943/1976). *Capitalism, socialism, democracy*. Routledge.

Sen, A. (1982) (Ed.). *Choice, welfare and measurement*. Basil Blackwell.

Sen, A. (2002). *Rationality and freedom*. The Belknap Press/Harvard University Press.

Seth, J. (1897). *A study of ethical principles* (8th rev. ed.). William Blackwood & Sons.

Shapiro, I. (1990). Three fallacies concerning majorities, minorities, and democratic politics. In J. W. Chapman & A. Wertheimer (Eds.), *Majorities and minorities* (pp. 79–125). New York University Press.

Simons, H. C. (1948) *Economic policy for a free society*. The University of Chicago Press.

Singer, P. (1993). *Practical ethics*. Cambridge University Press.

Skiadas, C. (Ed.) (2018). *The foundations of chaos revisited: From Poincaré to recent advancements*. Springer.

Smolin, L. (2013). *Time reborn: From the crisis in physics to the future of the universe*. Houghton Mifflin Harcourt.

Sorauf, F. J. (1957). The public interest reconsidered. *The Journal of Politics, 19*(4), 616–639.

Swanton, C. (2015). *The virtue ethics of Hume and Nietzsche*. Wiley/Blackwell.

Tullock, G. (1965). *The politics of bureaucracy*. Public Affairs Press.

Urry, J. (2005). The complexity turn. *Theory, Culture, Society, 22*(5), 1–14.

Vergara, F. (2011). Bentham and Mill on the "quality" of pleasures. Revue d'études Benthamiennes. doi:10.4000/etudes-benthamiennes.422

Weale, A. (1983). *Political theory and social policy*. Macmillan.

Weale, A. (2020). *Modern social contract theory*. Oxford University Press.

Wedgewood, R. (2007). *The nature of normativity*. Clarendon Press.

Wempe, B. (2004). *T. H. Green's theory of positive freedom: From metaphysics to political theory*. Imprint Academic.

Wheeler, C. (2006). The public interest: We know it's important, but do we know what it means?. In R. Creyke & A. Mantel (Eds.), *AIAL Forum 48* (Australian Institute of Administrative Law) (pp. 12–26).

Williams, B. (1973). A critique of utilitarianism. In J. J. C. Smart & B. Williams (Eds.), *Utilitarianism: For and against*. Cambridge University Press.

Wilson, J. (1887). The study of administration. *Political Science Quarterly, 2*(2), 197–222.

Worrall, J. (1989). Structural realism: The best of both worlds. *Dialectica*, 43(1/2), 99–124.

Wotton, B. (1945). *Freedom under planning*. Allen & Unwin.

Wright, G. H. von (1963a). *The logic of preference*. Edinburgh University Press.

Wright, G. H. von (1963b). *Norm and action*. Humanities Press.

Young, I. M. (2007). *Global challenges: War, self-determination and responsibility for justice*. Polity Press.

SECTION VIII

Latin America

CHAPTER 39

EDUCATIONAL CHALLENGES IN LATIN AMERICA

An Outline From Conquest to COVID-19

LAURENCE WHITEHEAD

INTRODUCTION

THE 20 republics of contemporary Latin America share many common attributes, including five centuries of asymmetrical exchange with powerful external hegemons, and a markedly "centrifugal" distribution of populations and lines of communication. These are features that are often listed to differentiate the subcontinent from other parts of the world include heterogeneity, informality, and inequality. They are, of course, huge approximations, but they serve as a necessary starting point for any attempt to characterize the overall realities of the region's educational experiences, and this remains so even in the early 21st century.

The pandemic of 2020/2021 throws this systemic configuration of features into sharp relief, and threatens to further aggravate preexisting obstacles to regional well-being and developmental potential. For example, Latin America's mostly poor and in some cases dreadful Program for International Student Assessment (PISA) scores now seem sure to degenerate further. According to a UNICEF report at the end of 2021, fifth-grade students in the state of São Paulo had fallen back to the level of performance achieved 14 years earlier in terms of their basic mathematics, and by 10 years in language skills (UNICEF, 2022). Meanwhile the UN Economic Commission for Latin America (2022) reported that the LAC region had recorded the longest school closures in the world (on average 40 weeks with no in-person classes, or long periods of interruption affecting in-person learning for 167 million students at all educational levels). The probability of completing secondary education in 18 Latin American countries is estimated to have fallen from 56% to 42%, with the largest fall (almost 20%) for families with a low level of education. Since less than 50% of the population has a broadband Internet connection and only 9.9% have high quality fiber-optic connections at home, the majority of students can only access digital instruction via weak mobile phone connectivity (if that), and inevitably dropout rates have soared among the less well-off. The ECLAC report searches for a positive side to this situation, pointing to the scope for informal educational offsets from family support and innovative teacher instruction but, for a substantial proportion of this cohort of students, damaging lifetime effects are likely to linger. The most vulnerable to such setbacks are those from the most insecure homes, younger students, minorities, and girls.

Students of comparative education can learn much by including Latin America within their purview, not least because in many important respects the region presents in the starkest of forms the problems existing (often in a less visible form) in much of the rest of the world. But before focusing on specific examples of these educational features, it is important to set the stage with some comments on the overall setting in which they are embedded.

To start with, some reflection is required on what "education" refers to in such a heterogeneous and unequal social context, where the "formal" structures of official teaching and learning penetrate most unevenly. In the modern world, formal education is regarded as one of the primary functions and achievements of the nation state, and to the extent that many Latin Americans are still rather poorly served by public education, this can be seen as an indicator of state weakness or inadequacy. In fact, some LAC countries not only devote great efforts to the educational function, but actually deliver impressive results worthy of international respect. Overall, however, performance is patchy and leaves huge gaps—for example, far too few of the current generation of schoolchildren in the region are being equipped to operate competitively in today's increasingly digitalized world. Even the efforts of the best performing states are precarious and may be subject to serious slippages due to periodic setbacks and resource constraints, as dramatized by the current pandemic. Educational inequalities and heterogeneous coverage are also major features of formal instruction in most other parts of the world, but when reinforced by such temporal instabilities, they are particularly damaging in this large region. Widespread informality can compound these difficulties, although it can also generate some offsetting compensations—Latin America's vibrant popular culture reflects the vitality of informal education outside the range of official instruction.

HISTORICAL BACKGROUND

Such unevenness and instability in the provision of formal education is nothing new for the region. Indeed, there were some impressive episodes of high performance even before the arrival of the Europeans. Thus, all Aztec children were supposed to participate in an elaborate system of formal education, directed mainly to training for the hardships of war. Teaching was based on Náhuatl history collective memory and cosmovision, and included instruction concerning their spectacular architecture and advanced techniques of water management and plant cultivation (Infante, 1998). In 2012, an elite Aztec school was excavated in the heart of Tenochtitlán. Similarly, the Mayans provided their elites with formal schooling in astronomy and related specialisms. In Cuzco, the Inca elite were required to attend 4 years of tutoring, between the ages of 12 and 16. In the absence of writing, Inca educators placed great emphasis on memorizing, and year three was devoted to mastery of the *quipu* system of accounting and record keeping, which also helped students memorize poetry and epic history. The elite of both sexes received the same length of instruction, although the syllabus for girls was more domestic. There were annual examinations, and at graduation from the full 4-year course the sovereign pierced the ear of these "children of the sun." Beyond this charmed circle, instruction in Quechua and the *quipu* system was also more widely disseminated throughout the Empire. In fact, the entire population was required to have fluency in Quechua. But both these systems were utterly shattered after the Conquest (Morales, 1967).

There were also major educational experiments by the Catholic Church during colonial times—the Jesuit *Reducciones* provide the most famous—and abruptly terminated—of examples,[1] among a variety of important clerical endeavors. A succession of universities was founded either by papal bull or royal privilege, mostly modeled on the charter of the University of Salamanca. The underlying objective of colonial education was to promote the Catholic faith, the Spanish (or Portuguese) language, and to consolidate European rule.

During the 19th century, both the church and the state made periodic and fitfully effective efforts to promote formal education among the limited sectors of the population most subject to their sway. In all these cases, however, public instruction at best reached a fraction of the total population of the region, and although there were some substantial advances, these were followed by major reversals. In particular, the wars of independence caused lasting damage. It was not generally until the 20th century that constitutional promises to create an educated citizenry turned into broader and more durable public education drives. These, in turn, have waxed and waned according to such economic exigencies as commodity booms and currency crises, and the vagaries of sociopolitical instabilities. So the heterogeneous and unequal features of contemporary public education have a deep history. This is what Latin Americans have learned to expect from formal education, not the smooth expansion of quality and quantity imagined (and perhaps in fortunate cases even achieved) elsewhere.

For this reason, this chapter cannot limit its conception of "education" narrowly to the formal protocols of public provision. If school buildings are subject to recurrent electricity cuts, if teachers can be expected to spend substantial periods of their career on strike (or even manning barricades), if extortionists are liable to threaten the drivers of school buses, such "informal" experiences are also highly educational and so require consideration here. Moreover, beyond state provision other sources of organized instruction (notably private religious schools and international sources of education) can have powerful effects on the whole system. This is so even outside Latin America. Within the region the patchy and erratic coverage of the public system left space for a wide range of less official alternatives—currently including bible schools, sports clubs, sambadromes, digital and television classes, business in-house training schemes, and online as well as direct private tuition. Over the past century a medley of political parties, *sindicatos,* feminists, and *indigenistas,* as well as promoters of various forms of traditionalism—from *capoeira* to Latin mass—have also intermittently offered educational opportunities.

Nowadays, instruction in English rather than Spanish and Portuguese can carry added prestige (whereas French was often ascendant in the 19th century, and before that Latin).[2] In the 1970s, Cuba encouraged Russian, while Japanese came into fashion in 1980s Brazil, and Chinese has acquired a recent cachet. Such international fluency is especially valued by those thinking of emigrating or dependent on remittances, and foreign qualifications can offer a passport to elite employment. This, too, has deep historical roots (for three centuries of colonial rule the best positions were reserved for those educated on the Iberian Peninsula—notably among the clergy—and even today foreign educated priests occupy strategic positions in the Catholic hierarchy). In a subcontinent where the labor market has always been extremely heterogeneous and stratified, it follows that the provision of education will be fragmented and unbalanced.

Such introductory points are inescapably schematic. What follows is a highly condensed survey of the subcontinent's vast and patchily studied educational panorama. The choice of a long-run historical and comparative perspective is intended to set the stage for contemporary debates about education in Latin America, including brief consideration of some foundational issues.

The Expansion of State Educational Provision

Colonial Education

During the colonial period, the imperial authorities were under no legal obligation to provide education to anyone, and the major source of instruction was the church, which not only supported some schools for the children of the faithful in favored (essentially small urban) centers but also endowed and supervised a series of high-profile universities in the cathedral cities of Spanish America (there was no university in Brazil until after Independence).[3] As noted earlier, the Jesuits also provided considerable education to a large sector of the *guaraní* population, until Pombal introduced *iluminista* state education in Portugal and in 1758 ousted the Order, not only in Europe but also in Brazil. Spain followed suit in Paraguay in 1767, leaving the "indios" with no substitute source of protection and instruction. The generation-long upheaval of the Independence Wars further disrupted such schooling as had reached the colonies, while stimulating the more improvised and crisis-driven forms of informal instruction required to equip soldiers and their followers with the rudiments for survival in wartime.

The New Republics in the 19th Century

The new republics founded in the early 19th century drew much of their constitutional ideas either from France (where the Revolution dethroned the universities and secularized education according to Enlightenment principles, and Napoleon adopted the policy of state educational provision), or from the protestant United States, where nondenominational instruction was a foundational issue. But, of course, throughout the Western Hemisphere slaves and indigenous peoples were excluded, as were nearly all women and most manual laborers. In theory, these new states came to assume direct responsibility for educating the nation, although this principle was long contested in many places by both the church and those elite interests (e.g., many large landowners) that might lose out from the emergence of a secularized and educated citizenry. Early enthusiasm for educational experiments understood as part of the "emancipation" agenda of the new Republics soon faltered in the post-independence turmoil, but never completely disappeared.[4] Even where the principle was agreed, the practice was often very slow to follow, in particular because of the budgetary implications. However, a few republics were ahead of the rest—notably Argentina, Chile, Costa Rica, and Uruguay.

In Chile, the break with Spain disrupted the limited pre-existing elite educational provision, and the new republic only assumed responsibility for the *Liceo*. Primary education was left to local initiatives. There were only 664 children receiving basic education in the seven primary schools of Santiago in 1812, and almost no teachers. To address this, in 1821, the Santiago *cabildo* adopted the "monitorial" system of schooling favored by British Benthamites, whereby each row of children was instructed by an older child, with one teacher overseeing the delegated instruction. The founder of this system was the London Quaker Joseph Lancaster. In 1824, Simon Bolivar invited Lancaster to Caracas to establish monitorialism there as well (Baeza Ruz, 2022).

Engerman, Mariscal, and Sokoloff have highlighted the precocity of educational expansion in Canada and the United States in contrast to 19th-century Latin America: "even the most progressive Latin American countries, such as Argentina and Uruguay, were more than 75 years behind the United States and Canada in providing wide access to primary schooling and attaining high levels of literacy. Most of Latin America was unable to achieve these standards until well into the twentieth century, if then." This is broadly correct, although it is colorblind and unreflective about the nature of education, and the discriminatory treatment of First Nation peoples and Francophones across North America, and the segregated provision in the United States. They argue that both lower per capita income and higher inequalities in the distribution of power provide partial explanations for the lag in educational provision in Latin America, although they note that other factors also require subsequent investigation given the differences within the Hispanic world (Engerman et al., 2002).[5] Engerman and Sokoloff have also argued that, in general, the rise of literacy in the Western Hemisphere *preceded* suffrage expansion, and therefore could not have been caused by it (Engerman & Sokoloff, 2001). Similarly Agustina Palgayan asserts that public provision of primary schools generally *preceded* democratization and so again the latter cannot have caused the former (Palgayan, 2020).[6] Both these studies rely on comparative databases that assign specific dates to the variables under investigation in each country. They thereby reduce extended and interacting historical sequences to precise events that can be assigned one-way causal connections. In addition to the doubtful methodology of this procedure, the national event dating of these studies is imperfect and merits closer historical scrutiny.

Soifer's study of Chile places the process in the context of precocious state-building and looks beyond the variables of centralization, elite cohesion, and resource mobilization (e.g., under President Manuel Montt in the 1850s) to add the important role played by regional administrations. These not only implemented instructions from Santiago, but went further to extend and deepen their implementation (Soifer, 2009). Jens Hentschke (2016) further elaborates on the state-building explanation for Uruguay, where he stresses the positivist ideational input of some key reformers, and provides comparisons with Argentina and Chile. Nineteenth-century Costa Rica also diverged from the rest of Central America, with far-reaching developmental consequences when, in 1869, it established free and mandatory education for all citizens. Molina and Palmer have identified a strong demand for the acquisition of literacy from below (peasants, urban workers, and rural migrants) well before the launch of a systematic campaign for mass literacy by the central state. They also highlight the linkage between rising literacy and popular democracy (between 1917 and 1919 a short-lived dictatorship attempted to switch spending from schools to the military, but that provoked a successful popular backlash) (Molina & Palmer, 2004). During the guano age, the Peruvian state made weaker efforts to spur local authorities into making minimal educational provision, but it was not until 1895 that Lima managed to insert the central state into local education policy in a significant way (Soifer, 2013).

Government-promoted primary education was minimal in Imperial Brazil, although given its elitist focus higher education fared somewhat better (Schwartzman, 2003). Under the Empire, the only rudiments of public primary education were in the capital. The first public secondary school (the Colegio Pedro Segundo) opened in Rio in 1838. Higher education began the previous decade, first with a military school in Rio, and two law schools (in São Paulo and Recife), and two medical schools (in Rio and Bahia). The remote residential Caraca School in Minas Gerais soon followed. Gilberto Freyre provides an evocative portrait of education at the Pedro Segundo Academy (which became the National Gymnasium under the Republic) and observes that the imperial system tended "to unify the regional cultural centers: Rio de Janeiro, Bahia, São Paulo, Olinda, and Recife. This encouraged high standards instead of spreading education thin and substituting quantity for excellence" (Freyre, 1986, p. 114).

It took the establishment of the Republic (in 1889), and the arrival of significant streams of immigrants in Rio and São Paulo in the following decade, to kick-start educational development—and much of the early school provision was in German,

Italian, and Japanese (Freyre, 1986).[7] Recent research suggests that those São Paulo municipalities starting early on public education achieved developmental gains that can still be detected a century later, in contrast to other locations that lagged behind (Filho & Coliteste, 2010).[8] Beyond São Paulo state, according to Aldo Musacchio, local funding for primary education varied not only according to the distribution of commodity revenues between Brazilian states, but also because some elites who could afford it chose not to invest in it. Low education spending was also traceable to two historical antecedents—a high dependence on slave labor before abolition and/or the prevalence of cotton production (Musacchio, 2014). Musacchio's contribution to a cross-national study of educational history in the four BRICS nations, which attributes some of their persisting economic weaknesses to the delayed provision of basic education, notes that around 1910 only 15% of Brazilian school-age children were enrolled in primary education, as compared to over 80% in Germany and the United Kingdom (Chaudhry et al., 2011).

Ewout Frankema has provided a more granular comparative analysis for the 20th century that highlights Latin America's emphasis on enrolment rather than completion as a key indicator of the educational performance. In her view, high repetition and dropout rates held back regional development, and the focus on tertiary education was attained at the cost of neglecting the *quality* of the underfunded primary education sector (Frankema, 2009).

The Language of Instruction

Language of instruction was also a delicate issue, and it reduced educational advances in various parts of the Caribbean, Central America, and the Andes, with apparently adverse consequences for long-term development potential. For example, following the US seizure of Puerto Rico in 1898, the occupiers tried unsuccessfully to establish English as the medium of instruction in all the island's schools—at all levels between 1904 and 1916, and from fifth grade upward between 1917 and 1934. After three destructive decades, the failure of this insensitive policy led to it being restricted to high school level from 1935 until the eventual restoration of Spanish in 1949 (Cebollero, 1945).[9] English was also imposed in Panama for a while, and the US model of community-elected school boards was briefly introduced there, although as in Puerto Rico, this decentralization was soon abandoned. The most durable example of linguistic inflexibility as a source of educational handicap, and probably the most developmentally harmful, is provided by Haiti, where French is still imposed on public education despite the social prevalence of the Creole language (ostensibly recognized as of equal standing) (Avalos & Augustin, 2017).[10] After 1932, Brazil also promoted instruction in Portuguese at the expense of the various immigrant-supported schools that had been teaching in Italian, German, and Japanese. Likewise in Argentina, where although some instruction persisted in immigrant languages (mostly Italian, but also Polish, Hebrew, and even Welsh), it was progressively marginalized by the expansion of state education in Spanish. But by far the most widespread example of successful language imposition in disregard of student culture and competence was where Spanish was forced upon indigenous peoples in Mexico, Central America, and the Andes, and local language use curtailed or outright banned.[11] In Peru, for example, books in Quechua were prohibited from 1920 onward. Only Paraguay failed in its drive to obliterate Guaraní. This insistence on creating a monolingual nation was part and parcel of the Comtean "positivist" outlook imported from 19th-century France, which informed the *Estado Docente* (the Teaching State) upsurge of the first half of the 20th century.

The "Estado Docente" (1900–1950)

Before 1900 there were some scattered and fitful efforts to widen the provision of primary education (e.g., by Sarmiento in Argentina and Eugenio María de Hostos in Chile and the Dominican Republic). But in broad terms, and referring to the region as a whole, it was during the first half of the 20th century that public provision of compulsory primary education became almost universal (Newland, 1994), while in the second half of the century the expansion of publicly supported secondary and higher education dominated the public policy agenda. Carlos Newland underscores the fiscal logic that impelled top-down educational activism, especially between 1900 and the 1930s Depression. His focus is primary schooling in Spanish America—the Brazilian process was delayed until a federal Education Ministry was created in 1932. As national tax revenues rose with the rise of export economies, ministries of education gained resources that allowed for the expansion of the provision of state primary education, while local and municipal sources of financial support languished. Rising international trade, investment, and immigration also spurred the growth of urban centers, and basic schooling was accordingly tailored to the resulting demand for enhanced labor skills. Positivist ideas also contributed. State education was supposed to promote hygiene, national pride, and patriotic obedience, as well as worker productivity. In some countries (Chile and Guatemala), military instruction was particularly prized.[12]

For Latin America as a whole, Newland estimates that whereas 5.2% of the total population were in school in 1900 (out of a school age total of 18%), 50 years later 10.7% were enrolled, out of a smaller potential total of 15.1%. As a consequence, nominal literacy rose from 28% of the adult population in 1900 to 48% in 1925, and 64% in 1950 (although he considers that *functional* literacy was significantly lower) (Newland, 1994, pp. 450–452). By the 1920s, educational reformers were challenging the imposed uniformity and deadening content of the state syllabus. Gabriela Mistral in Chile was a particularly prominent advocate of cultural pluralism and the encouragement of diverse local educational initiatives—including for Catholics and Jews, and by the 1930s John Dewey's opposition to educational utilitarianism, rote learning, and corporal punishment gained a wider hearing. But as the *Estado Docente* expanded, the logic of bureaucracy tended to outweigh the advice of such reformers, especially because massified teacher training (*escuelas normales*) required a standardized pedagogy. In the Bolivian *altiplano*, for example, indigenous communities had been eager to develop schools under their own control and founded a celebrated *escuela-ayllu* at Warisata in 1931 to disseminate their ideas of education. But within a decade the state had appropriated it from its founders and imposed a top-down alternative model (Brienen, 2002).[13] Moreover, since parents and local communities were excluded from school governance, while education ministry supervision was remote, teachers often became a self-referring corporation, sometimes strongly dissident (Newland, 1994, pp. 459–461).

Although state provision of primary education dominated the field, it was accompanied by some modest expansion of private education, again under centralized supervision. For Latin America as a whole, Newland estimates that 12% of primary schooling was privately supplied (with 30% in Chile and 20% in Ecuador). Private schools were not necessarily confined to an urban elite, but they were more likely to provide instruction in foreign languages—especially English, but also some French, German, Italian, Japanese, and even Yiddish. By then, 40% of *Escuela Normal* teaching was privately provided (Newland, 1994, pp. 464–466).[14]

Higher education developed according to a different logic—as signaled by the University Reform Movement that spread rapidly from Córdoba to the rest of Argentina, and into Peru, Chile, and Mexico between 1918 and 1921, and beyond thereafter. The agenda of the Reform Movement promoted free higher education in politically autonomous universities, for authorities to be elected by students as well as faculty, and for education programs relevant to the needs of the community (Blanquer & Trindade, 2000, p. 21).

State Education and Religion

After three centuries of colonial rule, the Catholic Church was deeply embedded in society throughout what became known as Latin America, and although the new republics proclaimed a separate sphere of public citizenship and socialization, the advance of secular state authority was slow, highly contested, and subject to pushbacks.

It was not until 1880 that religious instruction was removed from the public curriculum in Mexico, with Argentina following suit in 1884, but in 1886 Colombia reinstated the subject (where it became permanent feature). In Chile, Costa Rica, the Dominican Republic, and later in Panama, religion was taught in state schools, although as the *Estado Docente* and the *Escuelas Normales* expanded, the tug-of-war between clerical and secular instruction reappeared in new settings. Only in Mexico (with the 1917 Constitution) was the teaching of the catechism actually persecuted, but radical anticlericalism provoked a major rebellion (the "Cristero" war of 1926–1929), and although "socialist" education was promoted in the 1930s (Vaughan, 1997)[15] and prescribed textbooks maintained a rigid secular posture supported by the powerful teachers union, for some 70 years, Mexican society remained heavily devout.

In Brazil the termination of the Monarchy was followed by a brief burst of curbs on Catholic privileges, but this soon faded. In fact, the shift soon proved bracing: "It is evident that Catholic schools gained a new vigor with the presence of academically trained foreign priests and nuns in the country after the founding of the Republic . . . [they] . . . did much to improve methods of primary and secondary education in Brazil, including such items as supervised sports and recreation. These activities had been introduced in the Anglo-American schools of the time, possibly with the intention of competing with Catholic educators in influencing the youth of Brazil. Competition furnished by the American schools in turn stimulated the Catholics to greater efforts to develop a predominantly Latin culture in tropical America" (Freyre, 1986, pp. 313–316).

The religious beliefs of most Latin Americans have drawn strength from informal sources of instruction that have proved capable of outlasting or at least counterbalancing the secularizing thrust of most state education. It may also be suggested that this extra-official outlook was so strongly entrenched that state educators charged with overcoming it were sometimes driven to the embrace of equally encompassing counter-ideologies—initially masonic, subsequently often Marxist. But neither the Mexican—nor even the Cuban—Revolution succeeded in actually deploying state power to eradicate popular faith. This is obviously a very schematic framework, and in practice in each country and each historical period the interaction between secularizing and religious positions was much more complex, and multistranded. However, the broader point is what matters here, for it demonstrates (*pace* Durkheim) that the impact of "formal" education and "official" teaching is strongly mediated by other socially embedded forms of instruction, socialization, and collective guidance.

These religious/secular tussles over education evolved and mutated as the 20th century progressed. During the 1930s and 1940s, Catholic intransigence was not infrequently stiffened from Europe, as clerical-fascist dictatorships imposed their counter-reformation agendas in Spain and Portugal, and Soviet communism presented an extreme ideological alternative. During the first two decades of the postwar era, Christian Democratic initiatives repositioned parts of the church in favor of inclusive reformism (reinforced by the new teachings of the Second Vatican Council) with an assertive educational agenda. In some arenas—such as Northeast Brazil—it was the need to head off the example of the Cuban Revolution's mass literacy campaign that most spurred the church into activism. But as "national security" dictatorships took over in the 1960s and 1970s, the church became torn between those tempted toward the theology of liberation (notably in Central America) and those aligned with "patria, familia, y tradición." Eventually the theme of human rights provided a new source of reconciliation which also served to at least partially bridge the divide with most secularists. This fast-changing and turbulent ideological background provides the context within which rival educational projects were developed.[16] The institutional setting also underwent an upheaval as the achievement of more or less universal primary education provided the foundation for an explosive growth in public provision of both secondary and higher education—until the "sudden stop" imposed by the continent wide debt crisis of 1982.

The Massification of Secondary and Higher Education, 1950–1982

As access to primary education became universal, the foundations were laid for the massive expansion of secondary and higher education that followed. Even countries with inadequate primary infrastructure, mostly producing barely literate and almost innumerate teenagers, recorded very rapid increases in secondary enrolment.[17] But note that dramatic increases in overall student numbers concealed large regional and social divergences that, if anything, increased over time.[18] For example, the number of university students registered in Brazil rose from 44,000 in 1950 to 430,000 in 1970 and 1,345,000 in 1982. In Mexico the increase was from 118,000 in 1970 to 785,000 in 1982. (The rate of increase was lower in Argentina and Chile because the starting level was higher, but there, too, in absolute numbers growth was explosive; Blanquer & Trindade, 2000, pp. 23–24). However, this massification was accompanied by a dramatic increase in dropout rates, underscoring the severity of underlying deficiencies in basic provision. It was during this period of explosive growth in student numbers that universities became the main nodal point for anti-government protests, initially nonviolent but eventually spawning guerrilla movements and precipitating full-scale confrontations and military retaliations.[19]

Among the various explanations that have been offered for the region's acute and persisting problems of education coverage and quality, macro-economic factors have been invoked (primary exporting required limited human capital), as well as cultural arguments (the reproduction of dominant conservative cultural models and ideologies). Perhaps most interesting has been Jonathan Di John's invocation of Albert Hirschman's exit-voice framework (Di John, 2007). This proposes that the combination of low direct taxes and high levels of private primary enrolment provides exit options for the wealthy and reduces their incentive to exercise their "voice," in the face of poor education performance. Communist regimes such as Cuba suppress the option of parental exit (other than full departure from the island) and thus achieve otherwise unattainable levels of school coverage and educational throughput. In capitalist Latin America, surveys consulted by Judith Tendler found business elites generally unsupportive of initiatives to improve education.[20] No single explanation is likely to encompass the wide diversity of experiences observable, and in unequal and inflation-prone societies, it is also important to consider differentiated teacher attitudes toward different parental strata. But whatever the dynamics, this fiscally funded massification of the whole education system ran up against almost state insolvency in 1982.

THE 1982 DEBT CRISIS AND THE UPSURGE IN MARKETIZED EDUCATION

State spending on education was already under stress before the suspension of sovereign debt servicing that spread throughout Latin America in 1982, and the pressures became much more severe during the ensuing "lost decade" (Ornelas, 2019). The underlying expansion of educational enrollment could not be durably curbed—let alone reversed—but alternative sources of finance were more urgently needed, and the whole structure of the sector was accordingly reshaped. Secondary school enrollments continued to rise to the point where in many countries 4 years of post-primary instruction has become the norm, although the fees for good schools are inaccessible, and students at inferior schools often show patchy levels of attendance (perhaps due to part-time employment). Massification continues unabated at many universities.[21] Student enrollment numbers at the University of Buenos Aires (UBA) exceeds 300,000, and in the National Autonomous University of Mexico (UNAM), it has approached the half-million mark, while the number of accredited institutions (often just degree factories) has also exploded to above 5,000. A rising proportion of GDP is devoted to this sector, and within that total the "private" component has expanded particularly fast. After 2000, student enrollment in private establishments surpassed that of public institutions, with tuition fees an increasing proportion of total funding there as well.

This post-1982 progression has taken different courses in different countries and subregions, but the underlying pattern can be summarized under the rubric of "marketization." The immediate aftermath of the debt crisis involved a period of social turmoil, with devaluations, emergency budget cuts, teacher strikes and student protests, and heightened instability. Over time, promises of free and universal public education were abandoned, and state shrinking paved the way for a more diversified, uncoordinated, and fragmented pattern, with much increased private (fee-paying) provision. Education policy reforms reduced direct central controls, with more delegated authority and indirect government supervision (e.g., more emphasis on teacher training and evaluation rather than ministerial command and control). Unions remained important, but they came under pressure to adapt, with less emphasis on contests over annual pay rounds (as inflation subsided) and more engagement with indirect benefits (e.g., pensions), and the reform agenda.

In her comparison of teacher organization reactions to education reform in Argentina, Brazil, and Mexico in the 1990s, Aurora Loyo pays due attention to the contrasts between the three cases, but notes the poor results overall. In "Argentina and Brazil, the idea that trade unions were the biggest obstacle to reformist success obscures the fact that the very formulation of the policies included in education reform—upon being implemented in very problematic economic and political contexts—suffered from formulation errors and lack of modesty. To sum up, teachers unions cannot and should not carry the blame for the limited results . . . in their most important objective, often forgotten, which is that the systems must provide more and better education for their populations" (Loyo, 2019, p. 291).[22]

Private schools and universities (already prevalent in Brazil and Colombia) spread more widely, increased their share of the market, and thereby increased competitive pressure on established state providers. In some settings, parents and students-as-consumers gained leverage. Pinochet's dictatorship was in the vanguard on such matters, but the diffusion effects of what came to be known as "neoliberalism" increased after the return to civilian and democratic government in Chile stabilized and deepened these shifts, rather than reversing them, and as World Bank–inspired international conditionality locked a new educational orthodoxy into place. Two key elements were the state accreditation of private educational establishments and teacher evaluations. (Chapter 40 by Cuenca et al., this volume, reviews the relatively successful cases of Colombia and Peru.) The injustices and bad outcomes that many associate with this neoliberal educational philosophy have recently inspired society-wide repudiations—notably, but by no means only—in the case of Chile in 2019, as discussed here and in Chapter 44 by Mizala and Schneider.

A broadly market-related approach has operated in a variety of different guises across the subcontinent, with more success in some countries and regions than in others. For example, in Uruguay, Ricardo Ehrlich and the Frente Amplio have promoted a strategy of educational diversification that contrasts with Chilean marketization, which has received more social acceptance and generated better outcomes. There was always fitful resistance and pushback, but for some two decades the momentum remained with advocates of educational reform and the "rollback" of state direction. It was not until the early 21st century, with a recovery in export earnings and the displacement of the Washington Consensus funders by a rising China, that "pink tide" governments came to office and undertook stronger measures to curb the growing privatization of the education sector.

This very general overview of the past four decades glosses over major variations in the trajectories and outcomes of the 20 diverse republics of Latin America. Among the new factors capable of disrupting large swathes of organized educational provision, three deserve particular consideration—the digital revolution; the rise of evangelical radicalism; and the enhanced presence at local level of drug trafficking networks. Such information sources of socialization are capable of disrupting large swathes of organized educational provision. In consequence, almost all these marketizing public policy experiments are unfolding in a patchy and inconsistent manner. As with earlier policy cycles, these, too, meet diverse sources of informal resistance, and may be confronted by major and frontal challenges to their core tenets.

Most of the vast contemporary literature on education in present-day Latin America (produced by scholars, governments, and international institutions) concerns formal sector reform and upgrading. It is aspirational, top-down, and "modernizing" in outlook. This includes the work of the international financial institutions, the Organization for Economic Cooperation and Development (OECD) and UNESCO, and even United Nations Sustainable Development Goal 4 (a commitment to "ensure inclusive and equitable quality education and promote lifelong learning opportunities for all" by 2030). However, for all the valuable evidence assembled by such sources, this official discourse always seemed overly optimistic—and all more so in the wake of the 2020–2022 COVID-19 pandemic (see, in particular, Busso & Messina, 2021, ch. 7).

An alternative and more skeptical perspective deserves a hearing. The chapters by Batista and Dutt-Ross on Brazil (Chapter 42) and Bleynat and Monroy-Gómez-Franco (Chapter 43) on Mexico in this volume find little empirical support for the idea that market opening could be counted on to stimulate improved educational performance. This chapter focuses on fragmentation, underperformance, and the multiple informal obstacles to the declared intentions of educational public policymaking. These are mostly long-standing and deeply embedded, although additional difficulties arise from digitalization. On the basis of past experience and present performance, it seems unlikely that currently planned educational agendas can be relied on to overcome the acute inequalities and performance deficits that have persisted for so long. In terms of school segregation by socioeconomic status, the top five nations participating in PISA are all in this region (Chile, Costa Rica, Mexico, Panama, and Peru). And more than 40% of the region's secondary enrollments are in private schools, as compared to about 10% in the OECD as a whole (Busso & Messina, 2021).

Whereas the academic study of education systems tends to isolate formal education, and to assess its development as an autonomous subsystem under the direction of supportive government, on a broader view, officially sanctioned teaching is only one among a competing array of educational influences acting on successive generations of young adults. And alternative sources of organization—including television companies, advertisers, digital gaming designers, evangelical churches, and even drug traffickers and subversive indoctrinators—may also bid to instruct them. When public educational provision is rolled back or decapitalized, other forces in society stand ready to expand into the resulting "ungoverned spaces."

There is certainly much diversity within this overall context of poor formal educational outcomes. Some sectors (such as urban digital hubs), some subregions (such as parts of São Paulo), and even some countries (Chile, Uruguay) do relatively well. Thus, for example, 10 Latin American countries participated in the OECD's sixth PISA evaluation for 2018. Of these, 15-year-olds from Chile and Uruguay scored best. On average, Chilean students perform 3 years ahead of the Dominican Republic, the worst of the 10. However, despite huge international acclaim for Chile's supposedly superior performance compared to its neighbors,[23] the nation's student population has become ever more vehement in its repudiation of the "neoliberal" essence of its educational provision, to such an extent that following the massive *estallido* of October 2019, the citizenry as a whole demanded a constitutional change with a full-scale overhaul of education voiced as a leading priority.

As the PISA results confirm, the inequalities of outcome are still vast in even the best performing Latin American nations. Whereas the top 2% of students from Uruguay and Brazil performed at the same level as the best 9% of students in all countries studied, *within* each of these two, students from the most disadvantaged backgrounds were on average 4 years behind students from better-off backgrounds. Considering the Latin American set as a whole, the average student was 3 years behind the OECD average. One in two did not reach the basic level of proficiency in reading that would enable them to identify the main idea in a text, and so would not be equipped to continue learning (compared to one in five in the OECD countries). In one or two countries—especially Peru—there had been significant improvements in student performance over time, albeit from a low base. Colombia was alone in not defaulting in 1982, and its recent educational initiatives show it continuing to perform as an outlier (although internal violence and huge population displacements, and now the influx of Venezuelan refugees undermine the best of plans). But in most of the major nations—Argentina, Brazil, and Mexico—not much change was recorded over PISA's two decades of assessment. Costa Rica and the Dominican Republic both displayed declining literacy scores (Di Gropella et al., 2019), but the greatest educational disaster must surely be that of Venezuela (not included in the PISA measurements). But all across the Caribbean and Central America the retreat or absence of effective state support and the shrinkage/disappearance of employment opportunities causes the current generation of young adults to turn to emigration, or perhaps extra-legal activities, and to try to acquire the skills for success in those areas. Parts of the Amazon and the Andes regions that have only recently begun to experience modern education are also at risk of dropping away.

The year 2020 will greatly intensified these negative trends. In Puerto Rico, for example, many schools were damaged by the January 2020 earthquake, and the entire school system was then closed from March onward. The pandemic struck unevenly across most of the subcontinent (perhaps worst in Ecuador), but by the second half of the year almost the entire student population of Latin America was deprived of direct schooling, and more partial closures lingered into 2022. Colombia and Uruguay may have done well to provide free simple laptops to many students, but for the great majority virtual education was not an option. Formal instruction simply ceased, and for most students about a full year of formal education seems to have been entirely lost. Subsequent recovery may allow a fortunate minority of students to catch-up, and new opportunities should emerge in healthcare and digital services. But for most, the pandemic is more likely to prove an irrecoverable setback, and for many even the most basic restoration of formal education will be delayed by fiscal restraints. In many sectors disrupted by the COVID-19 shock (hospitality, tourism, local retail), the impact will be to speed up the erosion of opportunities, rather than to force constructive adjustment. As the informal and extra-legal parts of Latin American society expand, so, too, will the associated influence of informal instructional processes.

Conclusion: An Underlying Pattern of Fitful and Lopsided Advances, Subject to Reversals

This panoramic survey could only touch on a limited set of highlights from the vast, diverse, and variable experiments in educational development that have been attempted over two centuries of Latin America's postcolonial existence. The choice was therefore to emphasize not the internal rationale for these experiments but rather the external restraints on their fulfillment.

Throughout a long history, the subcontinent has experienced many successive waves of top-down educational ambition, often followed by massive reversals. This is not a story of timeless ignorance belatedly overcome through the arrival of modern enlightenment. Without great educational achievements in such subjects as astronomy, engineering, and architecture, neither the Aztec nor the Inca Empire could have achieved its splendor. Nor would the Jesuit Missions have bequeathed such legacies. Great colonial universities also stand testimony to a pre-independence knowledge base of considerable force. All these faced abrupt liquidation, and although the last two centuries have displayed more continuity and cumulative advance, there, too, we can identify many false starts, sharp setbacks, and violent course changes. Among the educational projects that first surged and then faltered, we might mention positivism, anarchism, revolutionary nationalism, ultramontane traditionalism, liberation theology, universal literacy campaigns, the Summer Institute of Linguistics (SIL), the importation of business schools, neoliberal restructuring, standardized teacher evaluations, decolonial instruction, and the mass expansion of opportunities for study abroad. To some extent such initiatives may have coexisted and even enriched each other, but overall, they were competitive, partial, and unstable. Their collective legacy, two decades into the 21st century, is a fragmented, incoherent, and profoundly inequitable provision of formal educational opportunities, much more a reflection of Latin American social realities[24] than an engine of transformation.

Many informal constraints and negative feedback loops have contributed to this unsatisfactory and potentially dangerous outcome. Ethnic and linguistic pushback surely blocked some initiatives; the failure to secure parental and community support was often a weakness; ideological divisions (on religion, national identity, and also partisan politics) led to the dismantling of useful advances; periodic financial crises punctuated reform drives; and international influences were by no means always constructive. At certain stages, the rise of teacher and student unions spurred progress, but in other periods they became obstacles to sound educational provision. The central difficulty has been the absence of a solid and consensual view of what education is for, and how it should be conducted.[25] Mexico under the López Obrador administration provides a vivid contemporary illustration of the pattern. Substantial efforts had been made over the previous two decades to bring Mexican education into closer conformity with what international experts regarded as "best practice."[26]

Most of the obstacles listed herein are also issues that to some degree beset the delivery of modern educational services everywhere. However, in Latin America they are more visible, and may produce more seriously flawed outcomes, than in many other parts of the world. One explanation for this could be path dependency—given the recurrence of unsatisfactory cycles, all participants may adjust their conduct in ways that reproduce past patterns. In addition, there are also underlying disagreements about the purposes and content of education—with employers having one agenda, teachers another, parents a third, and the region's fragmented communities of faith, locality, identity, and political allegiance adding to the conflict. Successive governmental and international orthodoxies can further destabilize the educational agenda, especially since they can also be swayed by various veto groups who may prefer to block unwelcome endeavors rather than to coexist with educational projects they consider hostile to their interests (better an uneducated population than one indoctrinated by a rival power group?).

For all that, there is unequivocal evidence of the long-term progress of Latin American educational provision, especially since the second half of the 20th century. This survey chapter in no way seeks to deny or obscure such achievements. Among recent remarkable advances one might cite the provision of free laptops to all Uruguayan primary school children (which greatly eased the impact of pandemic school closures); impressive subnational results achieved through decentralized educational reforms in Ceará in Brazil; the latent demand for intercultural initiatives currently in contemporary Mexico (Pollmann, 2017); and diverse programs aimed at academics returning from study abroad and at promoting new forms of international research and teaching collaboration. Such scattered advances can support "islands of promise in turbulent waters," but the region's heterogeneity, informality, and acute inequalities limit their impact. This largely explains the patchy, inadequate, and fragile results. Compared to other large global regions, such obstacles to the diffusion of good practices are particularly visible in Latin America.

Better overall educational outcomes require frank assessment of the nature and scale of these structural impediments. This summary overview points toward the kind broadly framed and long-term diagnosis that is needed.

Acknowledgments

With grateful acknowledgments to Jacqueline Behrend, Jean-Michel Blanquer, Andrés Malamud, Luis Roniger, Diego Sánchez Ancochea, Simon Schwarzman, and my lifelong inspiration, the late A. H. Halsey.

NOTES

1. Between 1604 and their expulsion in 1767, the Jesuit Order created some 50 *Reducciones* spread across a vast area that includes the whole of today's Paraguay and also large territories in the interior of Bolivia and Brazil. In these highly organized centers, they taught religion and morals but also music, dance, sculpture, church architecture, agriculture, and arithmetic to the large *guaraní* populations under their control. Since they failed to propagate the Spanish language, instruction was in *guaraní*. The educational syllabus was provided to all males up to 15 years of age, and all females up to 13. Their musical achievements were particularly outstanding (Areco, 2019).

2. Another early contender in Northeast Brazil and parts of the Caribbean, as well as Manhattan, was Dutch; it was eclipsed, however, by the 18th century (except in Curaçao and Suriname).

3. Santo Domingo housed the first university in the Americas, founded a century before Harvard, in 1538. The University of San Marcos, Lima (1551), is the oldest Western Hemisphere university in continuous operation. In contrast with the medieval inspiration of the first dozen universities, the Napoleonic model shaped Cartagena (1824), Buenos Aires (1826), Venezuela (1827), Uruguay (1833), and Chile (1847). These were supposed to promote education at all levels, to train professionals (notably for public service) and to stimulate academic disciplines (Blanquer & Trindade, 2000, pp. 16–17). Brazil only created its first officially designated "university" in Rio in 1920, although strong law, medicine, and military schools had a much longer pedigree.

4. Miller (2000) covers the long 19th century, with Argentina, Chile, and Peru as the main cases.

5. Observers who are not colorblind can see that the United States imposed unrelenting educational segregation for a full century after the Civil War, with social and human capital effects that continue up to the present day. In Latin America, discriminations of various kinds were also rife, but in general ethnic gradients were less absolute, so when schooling eventually arrived it (sometimes) provided more scope for upward mobility.

6. The contrast in educational provision separating communist Cuba from democratic Guatemala should suffice to confound naïve regime type explanations of superior performance.

7. São Paulo made special efforts to promote primary education in the 1890s, with major long term developmental effects. In 1906 the federal government belatedly tried to modernize national education. But it was not until 1932 that a national Ministry of Education was established, after which teaching in Portuguese became mandatory.

8. Inertia is not the full explanation here: An additional consideration is that the State Constitution of São Paulo reserved a specific proportion of the sales tax to educational spending.

9. Spanish was only made the sole official language of the island in 1991.

10. French Guyana is subject to EU rules about the provision of education in locally spoken languages.

11. The Summer Institute of Linguistics (SIL) initiated a small, but revealing, countermovement. Founded by a US evangelical pastor, W. C. Townsend, in Guatemala in the 1930s, it aimed to translate the Bible into every indigenous language to bring God's truth to the heathen. President Cardenas authorized the SIL into Mexico to teach them literacy, and it arrived in Peru, Ecuador, and Bolivia in the 1950s. Then in 1973 the Colombian

government rescinded an 80-year Concordat that had reserved religious instruction in the *territories nacionales* to the Catholic Church, and also allowed in the SIL.

12. Carlos Escudé's (1988) study of the Argentine school curriculum highlighted its authoritarian and nationalistic contents.

13. The original model stressed "unscientific" education in arts, poetry, music, and service to the local community. The memory of this Warisata lived on, however, and was invoked in 2008 by the MAS government when it revived indigenous knowledge as part of its ambitious popular education agenda, which included a legal requirement for teachers and bureaucrats to speak the indigenous language of their region.

14. In Argentina, the first Jewish school was set up in 1891, and by the 1960s there were over 100 kindergartens, 60 elementary schools in Buenos Aires and 50 in the provinces, together with 15 high schools, although receiving only between 12% and 20% of school-age Jewish children. Likewise in Brazil, Jewish schools attracted less than 20% of the catchment, although in Chile the figure was closer to 60%. In Bolivia and Ecuador, Jewish children mainly studied at the German schools (Glikson & Ketko, 1967, p. 63).

15. Vaughan focuses on state provision of "socialist" education in the rural schools of Puebla and Sonora, and traces the conflictual two-way processes of negotiation between state and local communities that shaped the content and cultural impact of educational expansion.

16. One of the most celebrated and radical of pushbacks against centralized state education came from the Austrian philosopher and theologian Ivan Illich, whose anti-authoritarian tract *Deschooling Society* (1973) attracted great attention in Latin America during the era of military domination.

17. "At secondary level, expansion has been considerable, even in countries with an inadequate primary infrastructure. A growing dichotomy is evident as schools continue to perpetuate classical values and forms while failing to establish links with the labour market. The effect is seen in growing pressure on higher education, where rapid expansion has led to fragmentation of institutions and depreciation of standards" (Rama & Tedesco, 1979). Well-rated secondary schools granted entrance by examination. Many also gave preference to students from associated primary schools. The concept of equal opportunity of access ran counter to deep-seated beliefs about social differentiation.

18. For example, Plank (1987) uses diffusion hypotheses to explain the persistence of wide regional disparities in enrollment rates across states and regions up to 1980.

19. The October 1968 "Massacre of Tlatlelolco" in the center of Mexico City was perhaps the most spectacular episode (spurred partly by *Les Évènements* in Paris and anti-Vietnam outbursts in the United States), but in reality it was only one flashpoint in a greater storm.

20. Judith Tendler cited by Di John (2007, footnote 35).

21. In 2014, the total enrollment at the National Autonomous University of Mexico (UNAM) was 342,542, compared to 166,738 at the next largest—the National Polytechnic Institute—and 116,424 at the University of Guadalajara.

22. The associated chapter on educational inclusion in Argentina under the Kirchners recognizes that more resources were provided but notes that this was accompanied by the rise of private education, especially in the big urban centers. Jason Beech concludes: "The process of privatization contributes to widening inequalities, fragmentation and segregation. Furthermore, since most private schools that cater for the lowest socioeconomic groups belong to the Catholic church and receive subsidies from the state, those movements contribute to the erosion of the laicity of some provincial educational systems" (p. 39).

23. In fact, in 2018 Chile ranked 42nd out of the 79 countries PISA assessed.
24. As portrayed, for example, in Whitehead (2009).
25. The central issue raised by Paulo Freire in his ground-breaking *Pedagogy of the Oppressed* (1973), where he contrasts "education for a bank" with "education for a community." His prior advocacy of "conscientização" involved not only reading the word but also the world. Taken up as a rural literacy campaign in Northeast Brazil (his region), it inspired great enthusiasm but also helped elicit the 1964 US-backed military coup. He was exiled for 15 years, while his approach to education was suppressed.
26. Carlos Ornelas has chronicled the achievements of the Mexican reform process up to the end of 2018, but his last comment is that "it is now on the verge of vanishing because the President elected in July 2018 threatens to dismantle it completely" (2019, p. 13). Indeed, in the ensuing two years major reversals have taken place already, and a radically different approach is being pursued.

References

Areco, S. (2019). The genesis of Paraguay education: The Jesuit contribution. UFMGS. *Cadernos de História da Educação, 18*(3), 878–896.

Avalos, M., & Augustin, J. (2017). Haiti's language-in-education policy: Conflicting discourses at the local level. In N. Rudolf & A. Fuad (Eds.), *Conceptual shifts and contextualized practices in education for glocal interactions* (pp. 37–54). Springer.

Baeza Ruz, A. (March 2, 2022). The birth of the primary school in Chile: The role of the Hispanic Anglosphere. Lecture delivered at the Latin American Centre, Oxford University.

Blanquer, J.-M., & Trindade, H. (Eds.) (2000). *Les défis de l'éducation en Amérique Latine.* IHEAL.

Brienen, M. (2002). The clamor for schools: Rural education and the development of state-community contact in highland Bolivia, 1930–52. *Revista de Indias, 62*(226), 615–650.

Busso, M., & Messina, J. (2021). *The inequalities crisis: Latin America and the Caribbean at the crossroads.* IDB.

Cebollero, P. A. (1945). *A school language policy for Puerto Rico.* Baldrich.

Chaudhry, L., Musacchio, A., Nafziger, S., & Yan, S. (2011). Big BRICS, weak foundations: The beginning of public elementary education in Brazil, Russia, India and China. June 24, 2011. http://williams.edu

Di Gropella, E., Vargas, M. J., & Yanez-Pagans, M. (2019). What are the main lessons from the latest results from PISA 2018 for Latin America? *World Bank Blogs*, December 6, 2019.

Di John, J. (2007). Albert Hirschman's exit-voice framework and its relevance to problems of public education performance in Latin America. *Oxford Development Studies, 35*(3), 295–327.

Engerman, S., & Sokoloff, K. (2001). The evolution of suffrage institutions in the New World. NBER Working Paper 8512. October 2001.

Engerman, S., and Sokoloff, K. (2002). The evolution of schooling institutions in the Americas. www.laisumedu.org/fonteras/Mariscal.Then

Escudé, C. (1988). Contenido nacionalista de la ensenanza de la geografia en la Republica Argentina 1879–1986. In A. Borón & J. Faundez (Eds.), *Malvinas Hoy: Herencia de un Conflicto* (pp. 3–43). Puntosur.

Filiho, I. C., & Coliteste, R. P. (2010). Educational performance: Was it all determined 100 years ago? Evidence from São Paulo, Brazil. Munich Personal Research Archive.

Frankema, E. (2009). The expansion of mass education in twentieth century Latin America: A global comparative perspective. *Journal of Iberian and Latin American Economic History*, *27*(3), 359–396.

Freire, P. (1973). *Pedagogy of the oppressed*. Continuum.

Freyre, G. (1986). *Order and progress: Brazil from monarchy to republic*. California University Press.

Glikson, P., & Ketko, S. (Eds.) (1967). *Jewish communal services*. The International Conference of Jewish Communal Service.

Hentschke, J. (2016). *Philosophical polemics, school reform, and nation-building in Uruguay, 1868–1915: Reforma Vareliana and Battlismo from a Transnational Perspective*. Bloomsbury-Nomos.

Illich, I. (1973). *Deschooling society*. Penguin.

Infante, F. D. (1998). *La Educación de los Aztecas*. Panorama.

Loyo, A. (2019). Teacher unions and educational reforms. In C. Ornelas (Ed.), *Politics of education in Latin America: Reforms, resistance, and persistence* (pp. 272–292). Brill.

Miller, N. (2000). Education for citizenship; Beyond morality and patriotism. In *Republics of knowledge* (ch. 10). Princeton University Press.

Molina, I., & Palmer, S. (2004). Popular literacy in a tropical democracy: Costa Rica 1850–1950. *Past and Present*, *184*(1), 169–207.

Morales, R. C. (1967). *Protohistoria Andina:propedéutica*. Universidad Técnica.

Musacchio, A. (2014). Colonial institutions, trade shocks, and the diffusion of elementary education in Brazil, 1889–1930. *Journal of Economic History*, *74*(3), 730–766.

Newland, C. (1994). The Estado Docente and its expansion: Spanish American elementary education, 1900–50. *Journal of Latin American Studies*, *26*(2), 449–467.

Ornelas, C. (Ed.) (2019). *The politics of education in Latin America: Reforms, resistance, and persistence*. Brill.

Palgayan, A. (2020). The non-democratic roots of mass education: Evidence from 200 years. *American Political Science Review*, *115*(1), 179–198.

Plank, D. N. (1987). The expansion of education: A Brazilian case study. *Comparative Education Review*, *31*(3), 361–376.

Pöllmann, A. (2017). Intercultural education and the realization of intercultural capital in Mexico. *Interdisciplinary Mexico*, *6*(12), 79–93.

Rama, G. W., & Tedesco, C. (1979). Education and development in Latin America (1950–75). *International Review of Education*, *25*(2/3), 187–211.

Schwartzman, S. (2003). The challenges of education in Brazil. *Oxford Studies in Comparative Education*, *13*(2).

Soifer, H. D. (2009). The sources of infrastructural power: Evidence from nineteenth century Chilean education. *Latin American Research Review*, *44*(2), 158–180.

Soifer, H. D. (2013). Elite preferences, administrative institutions, and educational development during Peru's aristocratic republic. In M. A. Centeno & A. E. Ferraro (Eds.), *State and nation-making in Latin America and Spain: Republics of the possible* (pp. 247–270).

UN Economic Commission for Latin America. *Challenges and opportunities for secondary education in Latin America and the Caribbean during and after the pandemic*. http://www.cepal.

org/en/insights/challenges-and-opportunities-secondary-education-latin-america-and-caribbean

UNICEF. (2022). *The state of the global education crisis.* January 2022, p. 16. https://www.unicef.org/media/111621/file/

Vaughan, M. K. (1997). *Cultural politics in revolution: Teachers, peasants, and schools in Mexico 1930–40.* University of Arizona Press.

Whitehead, L. (2009). *Latin America: A new interpretation.* Palgrave.

CHAPTER 40

TECHNOCRATS AND UNIONS IN THE POLITICS OF REFORMING TEACHER CAREERS IN COLOMBIA AND PERU

RICARDO CUENCA, SANDRA GARCÍA,
AND BEN ROSS SCHNEIDER

INTRODUCTION

COLOMBIA and Peru are part of an Andean wave of major reforms to teacher careers since 2000 (Cuenca, 2015; Elacqua et al., 2018). Colombia led the wave in 2002 followed by Peru in 2007. Ecuador embarked on major reforms in 2009, and Chile revamped careers in 2016. Common to all these reforms (as well as similar measures in Mexico 2013–2019) was a shift to meritocratic means for hiring teachers (by examination and public competition [*concurso*] rather than by educational degree and political meddling) and for promoting teachers to higher salary scales (by regular evaluation rather than seniority and advanced degrees).[1]

Education systems in Colombia and Peru show many overall similarities in enrollment expansion, low average performance on Program for International Student Assessment (PISA), recent improvement in PISA scores, and success in consolidating reforms and reducing politics in hiring. Colombia and Peru were the countries in Latin America that improved most on PISA assessments from 2000 to 2015. They were also among the five countries that advanced furthest on the Serce (2006) and Terce (2013) UNESCO assessments (Elacqua et al., 2018, pp. 10–11) (details in the second section).

The macro context in both countries was propitious with functioning democracies (though turbulent in Peru in the late 2010s) and steady economic growth, especially during the commodity boom of the 2000s. Among general theories of education politics, many posit a link from electoral politics to education spending and outcomes (Brown & Hunter, 2004). Democracy may have given a boost to government spending on education and the expansion to nearly full enrollment. However, democracy has, in theory (Bruns et al., 2019), in other cross-national research (Dahlum & Knutsen, 2017), and in our two cases, had less direct impact on education quality. In part, education was rarely a top voter concern. Across Latin America, when asked about a country's biggest problems, respondents rarely say education, and since 2006, respondents in Peru and Colombia have been below the regional average of survey respondents citing education (Schneider, 2024).

Other theories expect civil society to play a large role, but in both countries civil society organizations, especially of business and parents, had little effect (Table 40.1). Even though they should be the most intensely interested in education outcomes, parents are dispersed and numerous and hence rarely able to overcome obstacles to collective action. Business lack of interest is more surprising, since business in principle is the main "consumer" of the output of education systems, and the levels of skills affects the costs of producing and strategies of investment. And yet business showed little active engagement with education reform.[2]

In civil society, teachers' unions are usually the strongest organizations as well as the mostly likely to oppose education reform. This opposition is well documented in earlier studies of Latin America (Bruns & Luque, 2015; Grindle, 2004). In comparative terms, Fecode (*Federación Colombiana de Educadores*) and Sutep (*Sindicato Único de Trabajadores de la Educación del Perú*) were not as implacably opposed as unions in Mexico and Ecuador but not as amenable to negotiated settlements as in Chile (Schneider, 2022). While both Fecode and Sutep went on disruptive strikes during the reform period, they ultimately acquiesced though without a ringing endorsement of the reforms. In surveys, teachers generally support the main features of career reform: hiring by merit and later performance evaluations.

Table 40.1 Main Actors in Education Politics in Peru and Colombia

	Peru	Colombia
Technocracy	Active	Active
Political parties	Absent	Absent
Teachers' unions	Initial opposition and then acquiescence	Late negotiation
Business	Absent	Absent
Parents	Absent	Absent

Ultimately, in both cases, technocrats in government were crucial in initiating and maintaining career reforms. Effective reform in education takes time (Bruns et al., 2019), and hence requires analysis of what factors kept reforms going. In both Peru and Colombia, ministers of education and their teams were consistently technocratic and pro-reform, even through the political turmoil in Peru in the late 2010s. Peru and Colombia stand out generally in Latin America for the prominence of their technocracies, especially in finance and healthcare (Dargent, 2015).

A remarkable political aspect of education reform in Peru is that reforms survived after 2007 across four different presidents, from across the political spectrum, and their seven education ministers (see Appendix). The first surprise was that Ollanta Humala (2011–2016) (who campaigned on center-left) continued reforms of his predecessor Alan Garcia (center), then Pedro Pablo Kuczynski (known as PPK, 2016–2018, center right) continued Humala's reforms. Finally, the caretaker Vizcarra government (2018–2020) let reform implementation proceed. After almost two decades, the reforms were mostly consolidated (at least until the election of Pedro Castillo in Peru in 2021 (considered further in the conclusion). By 2018, 73% of teachers were in agreement or totally in agreement with periodic evaluations (Minedu, 2018, p. 21).[3]

How did the reforms survive the turnover in presidents and ministers? It was clearly not due to presidential reelection as in Ecuador, nor to party continuity as in Chile, nor to lasting support in civil society and a strong policy network, as sometimes in Brazil (Schneider, 2024). Continuity resulted from ephemeral parties, unobstructive teachers' unions, and in consequence politically unencumbered technocracies (Muñoz & Baraybar, 2021). Noninstitutionalized political parties and the related high levels of turnover among legislators reduced pressure on the education system for clientelist resources. Parties in both Peru and Colombia are among the least institutionalized in the region (see third section).

The reform to teacher careers in Colombia came at the end of the Pastrana government in 2002 in the midst of a fiscal crisis. An emergency law gave the president extraordinary decree powers for 6 months to enact a legal statute for teaching careers. Statute 1278 created a new meritocratic career with examinations to enter and evaluations for promotions, but significantly only for new hires. So, after 2002, the teacher corps split in two with those hired before covered by the old statute, and new hires by the new. By 2017, 58% of secondary school teachers and 48% of primary teachers had been hired under the new statute (Bonilla-Mejía et al., 2018).

The main subsequent change to the 2002 statute was to the evaluations for promotions. Through 2015, the evaluation was a written test on teachers' disciplinary and pedagogical knowledge. In 2015, Fecode and the ministry negotiated a new evaluation, Diagnostic and Educational Evaluation (*Evaluación con Carácter Diagnóstico Formativa* [ECDF]), focused on teacher practices in the classroom using multiple instruments like a classroom video evaluated by peers, student evaluations, school director assessments, and a self-evaluation. Under the new system (similar to Chile's), teachers receive qualitative feedback on the results of the evaluation. Teachers who do not pass have to take courses designed to improve shortcomings found in the evaluation (and thus get the corresponding salary raise).[4]

At first glance the reform processes can look quite different with a bypass reform in Colombia versus cascading reforms in Peru with successive reforms covering all teachers. Yet the main protagonists—unions, parties (by their absence), and technocrats—were quite similar. Analyzing both reform processes reveals the common factors that helped technocrats prevail over unions and parties. The main difference in reform trajectories was the union-government negotiation over new evaluations in Colombia in 2015 which—though recent—may contribute to greater acceptance of reforms among teachers.

The main protagonists were domestic. However, the reforms fit an emerging discourse among major multilateral agencies. Although there is no consensus on the beginning of the transition from a bureaucratic to a meritocratic approach to teaching careers, there were two major sources of international influence. On the one hand, the construction of a discourse led by the Organization for Economic Cooperation and Development (OECD) (and later joined by the World Bank and the Inter-American Development Bank) at the beginning of the 21st century postulated the need to redesign teaching careers in order to strengthen the profession (OECD, 2004). On the other hand, the disappointing results of the evaluations of the education reforms of the 1990s in Latin America led to the conclusion that teacher training, one of the fundamental pillars of these reforms, was insufficient to improve the quality of teachers' work and its impact on student learning. This discourse was led by UNESCO and especially by its Regional Bureau for Latin America (OREALC-UNESCO, 2007).

The second section provides a brief background on the two education systems. The third section examines the main actors in the reform stories. The fourth and fifth sections trace the progress of reforms over time.

BACKGROUND: RISING SPENDING, ENROLLMENT, AND LEARNING

In the last two decades, both Peru and Colombia maintained primary enrollment over 90% (see Figure 40.A1 in the Appendix). At the secondary level, enrollment rose from about two-thirds to three-quarters by the 2010s. Enrollment rates stagnated there in Colombia but continued to climb slowly in Peru. Colombia has spent around 3% of GDP on primary and secondary education (see Figure 40.A2 in the Appendix). Spending rose sharply from 2.5% of GDP in 2007 to 3.5% in 2009, but it sank back to 3.2% in 2018. The consistent difference in total government spending in Peru (around 1% of GDP less) may be due in part to the larger private sector in Peru which employs 36% of teachers (Cuenca, 2017, p. 15). Spending per pupil in Peru in primary school rose sixfold to $932

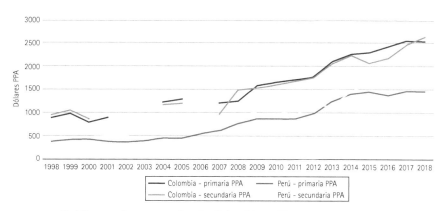

FIGURE 40.1 Public spending per student in Colombia and Peru, 1998–2018.

from 2000 to 2015 and fivefold in secondary school to US $1,056 (Cuenca & Vargas, 2018, p. 14). In Colombia, from 2000 to 2015, spending per student in primary school rose 2.9 times and in secondary school 2.4 times (to US$ 2,081) (Figure 40.1).

In 2017, Colombia had 319,000 teachers in the public sector (6% of whom were teacher directors) (Bonilla-Mejía et al., 2018). By 2019, Peru had a total of 576,000 teachers (Chiroque Chunga, 2020, pp. 1, 3). Of these, 383,000 worked in public schools, and the rest (over a third) in the private sector. Of public school teachers in Peru, 146,000 or 38% were temporary, contracted teachers (compared to 30% in Colombia; Bertoni et al., 2018, p. 27).[5] So, only 243,000 (or 42% of all teachers) were subject to the new career rules in Peru and only 9% of them were hired under the new merit procedures in place since 2014 (Puch & Salas, 2020, p. 79). Of permanent teachers (*nombrados*), 79% were still in the first three of eight levels in the new career ladder (Chiroque Chunga, 2020, p. 3). Average gross hourly wages (including benefits) were US $16 in Colombia and $9 in Peru (Bertoni et al., 2018, p. 27). Salaries in Peru are among the lowest in Latin America.

As noted earlier, Peru and Colombia scored the largest gains in Latin America on PISA assessments (Figure 40.2). Of course, many factors went into these gains, but evidence from Colombia (where it is easier to compare teachers on old and new career tracks) suggests the career reforms contributed.

In sum, Peru and Colombia came into the 21st century with rising school enrollment but with low-quality and poor—though improving—learning results. Successive governments since 2000 dramatically boosted per-student spending.

Main Protagonists in Reform Politics

As signaled by our title, the two most important protagonists were teachers' unions and technocrats in ministries of education. The reforms started in both cases and mostly unfolded without becoming salient electoral or party issues (as they did in Chile and

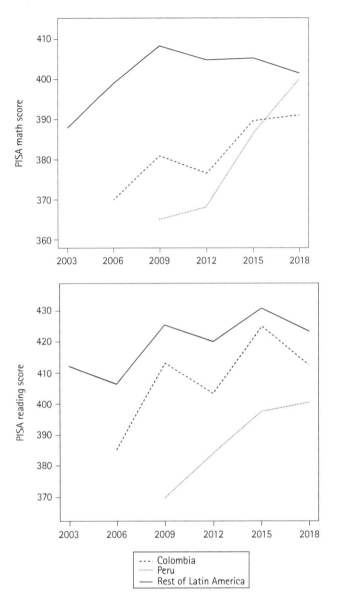

FIGURE 40.2 PISA scores for Colombia, Peru, and Latin America, 2003–2018.
(*Source*: OECD). Rest of Latin America includes other countries that participated in Pisa: Chile, Uruguay, Mexico, Argentina, Brazil, and Costa Rica (though no scores for Chile in 2003, Costa Rica in 2003 and 2006, and Argentina in 2003 and 2015). The Dominican Republic is excluded because it participated only in 2015 and 2018.

Ecuador). Groups in civil society were mostly absent, especially, and surprisingly, business and parents.

Teachers' Unions

To understand the weakness of Sutep requires a deeper dive into internal union politics (Schneider, 2022). A first issue was low union density; more than half of teachers did not belong (Bruns & Luque, 2015, p. 301). Estimates vary, but most sources put Sutep density at less than half (compared to a regional median of 77% and density of 87% for Fecode; Schneider, 2022) and falling in the 2000s in part because of the rapid expansion of temporary hires—who were less likely to join a union—to over 40% by the late 2010s. A second debilitating issue, discussed later, is internal, often regional, dissident opposition movements which grew after 2000.

The last main political weakness is the lack of capacity to deliver votes in national elections, due largely to radical leadership in Sutep and the lack of stable parties in the political system overall. The lack of heft in national elections derives in part from the dominance by a tiny splinter party, Patria Roja, as shown by the distribution of teacher votes in the first round election in 2006.[6] Only 2.4% of teachers voted Patria Roja compared to .24% national voting for the Left (Chiroque Chunga, 2008, p. 63). However, the rest of the teachers split their votes across the ideological spectrum: 24% for Humala (campaigned center left), 21% for Paniagua (center), 20% Garcia (center), and 15% for Flores (right). After 2006, Sutep endorsed—with the strategy of "mal menor" (lesser evil)—whichever candidate was running against the right-wing Fujimoristas, first Humala on the left, then Pedro Pablo Kuczynski (PPK) on the right (interview with Hamer Vallena, November 14, 2019). In Peru's fluid, no-party electoral context, Sutep was unable to find a stable, viable party that could channel its participation in elections.

Organizational fracturing further debilitated Sutep (interview with Juan Pablo Silva, March 18, 2016). Conare was the first and main dissident faction, followed later by dissident subfactions of Conare and regional affiliates that demanded internal union democracy. Conare was reportedly connected to Sendero Luminoso and split then along lines within the rump Sendero (armed struggle or not). In 2021, with the election of Conare leader Pedro Castillo as president, these dissident factions regrouped as a separate union, *Federación Nacional de Trabajadores del Perú* (*Fenate Perú*).

In Colombia, Fecode, the teacher union, was founded in 1958 (for history, see Pulido, 2008) and comprises 33 regional unions. According to their official numbers, in 2016 Fecode had 270,000 affiliated teachers (87% of public schools teachers).[7] The organization is led by the Executive Committee with 15 members elected by direct vote by union members for 4-year terms. Currently, the Executive Committee has 11 men and 4 women (relative progress, since previously they were all men).

Fecode was not riven by break-away factions as in Sutep, but it had greater internal political diversity in the Executive Committee, and as in Peru, lacked close stable ties to political parties. Committee members came from a variety of left parties and factions (as is common in other unions with direct elections, like Chile; Schneider, 2022). As in Peru, the lack of institutionalized parties deprived Fecode of a lasting ally, so Fecode has endorsed a range of candidates like Manuel Santos in 2014 (center) and Gustavo Petro in 2018 (left).

Civil society and policy networks were supportive but did not have much influence on career reforms. In Peru, relatively few education nongovernmental organizations (NGOs) had emerged by the 2000s. GRADE (Grupo de Análisis para el Desarrollo) and IEP (*Instituto de Estudios Peruanos*) were important think tanks and research institutes but covered all policy areas, not just education. One of the reasons parents were not more involved, beyond the usual problems of collective action in large dispersed groups, is because so many children in Peru had migrated to private schools: about a third nationally, up from a quarter in 2011, and close to half in Lima (Chiroque Chunga, 2015, p. 4).

Business in Peru officially backed the reforms, but one leader in Confiep (*Confederación Nacional de Instituciones Empresariales Privadas*), the multisectoral peak association, said it was "cheap talk" (*de boca para fuera*) not backed up with more active support (interview with María Isabel León, January 19, 2016). Some businesses were involved in the *Foro Educativo* (a small NGO with a handful of staff), but that was more corporate social responsibility than policy support (interview with Juan Pablo Silva, March 18, 2016). Foro Educativo, however, was still the largest civil society platform in Peru, and in 2007 closely accompanied the discussion on the teaching career. Where Foro Educativo, think tanks and academics, and international organizations like IDB had more influence was in engaging policymakers on substantive and technical issues in implementing career reforms.

Peru's Consejo Nacional de Educación (CNE, National Council of Education) is a government body made up of 25 specialist members (including academics and former ministers). It is a "hinge" between the state and civil society. In CNE's elaboration of the National Education Projects (in 2006 and 2020), the Council contributed to the debate on the teaching career and had a leading role in 2011 in the elaboration of the *Marco de Buen Desempeño Docente* (Benchmark for Good Teacher Performance).[8] One former minister who met with CNE regularly characterized it as less of a policy protagonist and more of a "good sounding board" (interview with Jaime Saavedra, March 5, 2021).

Similar to Peru, civil society and policy networks in Colombia did not have much influence on career reforms, particularly in the early 2000s. While some members of NGOs participated in the commission in 2002 that advised on the teachers statute (for instance, the director of Fundación Corona, an NGO that at that time was involved in education), there was little participation of organizations as a whole. In the 2010s, some NGOs and social movements focused on education emerged. In particular, the movement "Todos por la Educación," promoted by a group of youth, led to the signing of an "education agreement" (*pacto por la educación*) asking future governments to commit to education as a national priority (but not centered on teacher reform per se).

Fundación Compartir played an important role in the 2010s advocating for investments in education quality, particularly on teachers. Fundacion Compartir is an NGO that had focused on education and housing since the 1990s. One of its most visible activities has been to give national teacher awards. The Foundation also funded a study (García et al., 2014) published in 2014 and launched in a public event where the founder of Fundación Compartir gave the report to President Juan Manuel Santos. The president committed to incorporate the study recommendations, many related to career reform (particularly, improvements in teachers training, evaluation, and salaries).

Political Parties

Levels of party system institutionalization are correlated with absolute PISA scores, with Uruguay and Chile regional leaders in both categories (Schneider, 2024). However, the relationship is inverted in the case of recent change in PISA scores with leaders Peru and Colombia having the feeblest party systems among large countries in Latin America (Schneider, 2024).[9] By another ranking of party institutionalization across 18 countries of Latin America, Colombia ranked 12th and Peru 17th (Mainwaring, 2018, p. 58).

By the early 2000s, previously vibrant party systems in Peru and Colombia had collapsed (Muñoz & Dargent, 2016; Seawright, 2012). One new party, *Fuerza Popular* (*fujimorista*), seemed to be growing into a more institutionalized party until it too almost collapsed in the late 2010s. Among eight unicameral legislatures in Latin America, Peru had the third highest level of turnover with just over 20% on average reelected (1995–2008). Reelection is even less common in the upper house in Colombia, just 12% (1999–2008) (second lowest of eight countries in Latin America). However, reelection to the lower house is more common at 52%, around the median for eight countries in Latin America (Estrada, 2016, pp. 15–16). Effective use of education resources for clientelism takes time, which was rare for parties and politicians in Peru and Colombia. Thus, the positive impact of weak parties on education came indirectly by giving freer rein to technocrats.

Technocracy

As mentioned earlier, technocrats from the Ministry of Education and other public agencies played major roles in implementing career reforms. Across six countries of Latin America, Colombia (76%) and Peru (67%) had the highest share of technocrat ministers of education from 2000 to 2020.[10] The comparable share in Brazil was 65% technocrats, in Ecuador 60%, in Mexico 48%, and in Chile 32% (Schneider, 2024).

In Colombia, for example, early in 2002 the commission created to design the teacher statute was mainly composed by technocrats (people from academia and people with previous experience in the education sector either as education vice ministers, education secretaries or directors of NGOs working on education). Also, not only were most education ministers during the implementation reform technocrats but also their vice-ministers and other appointed staff.

For many, the power of technocrats derives from their expertise and backing from powerful groups like business (Dargent, 2015; Schneider, 1998). This may be truer for economic ministries, but less so for education ministers where expertise is not as crucial (interview with Jaime Saavedra, March 5, 2021), and backing by business less relevant. Thus, the main reason for technocratic longevity is the absence of challenges from other stakeholders, especially political parties (Muñoz & Baraybar, 2021).

In sum, among the core protagonists, technocrats were strong and unions relatively weak. Fecode had higher density and fewer internal divisions than Sutep, but, as discussed in the next section, was sidelined during initial reforms. Given its organizational and political problems, Sutep was rarely able to affect policy, though it could and did impose high political costs by striking. Among factors that did not have much impact in either country were several of the usual suspects—business, parents, and political parties. NGOs, think tanks, academics, and international organizations were sometimes active participants, but their influence was mostly on technical issues in design and implementation rather than propelling reforms along.

THE EVOLUTION OF REFORM POLICY AND POLITICS IN COLOMBIA

The politics of career reform and implementation have lasted two decades in both countries. This section focuses on two key moments of change in Colombia: in 2002 when the new statute was first adopted and 2015 when the ministry negotiated with Fecode an overhaul of the evaluation system. Both moments revealed the power and influence of unions and technocrats. The years in between belonged mostly to technocrats.

In Colombia in the early 2000s, the government introduced a structural reform to the teaching career that split the profession in two. Before 2002, teachers were subject to decree 2277 (the "old statute") that regulated initial hiring based on educational degrees or prior experience and determined promotions and salaries according to seniority and further degrees or training. In 2002, after failing to pass similar legislation in Congress, the government issued decree 1278 (the "new statute"), which sets meritocratic rules for teacher careers. Under the 1278 statute, teachers were hired through a public competition (*concurso*), continued tenure depended on performance, and evaluations determined promotions.

Emergency legislation in 2002 on redistributing resources in education gave the president 6 months to create a new teacher statute by decree. The government first appointed a commission with members from Fecode, the Ministry of Education, and a group of experts from universities, business, and foundations working on education. In addition, several technocrats from the Ministry of Planning and the National Department for Planning (*Departamento Nacional de Planeación*) participated in drafting the new statute (Garcia et al., 2020). Even though Fecode was formally on the commission, union leaders did not participate in drawing up the final text of the reform. Fecode complained that the reform was decided unilaterally by the government (Niño, 2012). However, that government officials opted to apply the new career statute to new teachers only showed their fear that covering all teachers would provoke too much opposition and thus implicitly acknowledged Fecode's power.

Initial implementation of the 2002 reform was the responsibility of Minister Cecilia Vélez (previously secretary of Education for Bogotá). This was a time when Fecode was in some disarray and divided after intense disputes with the Pastrana government, including a strike of 37 days. In fact, between 2002 and 2003 protest actions by Fecode declined (Pinilla, 2010). These conditions, added to the ample political capital of president Álvaro Uribe at the beginning of his term, gave the government space to maneuver to implement the new statute. The implementation of the new teacher statute was gradual and conducted largely by technocrats. The first 8 years were all under the same minister Velez and a technical team (technocrat vice-ministers) who managed the rollout of meritocratic hiring procedures (*concursos*) and the system of evaluations for promotion.

These were years of little dialogue between Fecode and the government (Pulido, 2008) but not conflict-free. One point of contention was the new hiring process (*concurso*). In 2005, Fecode called for mobilizations to boycott a call for hiring (Pulido, 2008). Despite the union's opposition, the government held rounds of hiring from 2004 to 2009 and hired 97,640 teachers out of a total of 750,838 candidates who applied (Figueroa et al., 2018).

From the beginning, another controversial sticking point was evaluations. Fecode also rejected evaluation as a means for promotion considering it a "punitive" or "extortionate" policy (Pulido, 2008). Moreover, Fecode claimed that the government was using evaluations as a means to block promotions and thus control total payroll and "subordinate teachers to fiscal adjustment policies" (Ávila, 2012). Since 2004, Fecode has demanded, unsuccessfully, a single statute (*estatuto único*) to replace both 2277 and 1278 statutes. Fecode's proposal for a new single statute looked a lot like the old 2277 with emphasis on teacher education and publications, tenure, and no evaluations (eliminate "the trap of competence evaluations"; Niño, 2012).

The main inflection point came in 2015 with the revised system of evaluation. President Juan Manuel Santos had been elected to a second term in 2014, with support from Fecode, and education, along with peace and equality, was one of the pillars of Santos's National Development Plan (*Plan Nacional de Desarrollo*). In the months leading up to 2015, several organizations of civil society, including Fundación Compartir and academics, participated actively in debates on education quality and especially salaries and evaluations for teachers. Then, in early 2015, during a strike by teachers, the government and Fecode reached agreement on a new scheme for teacher evaluations.

The government gave up little on negotiated evaluations and refused the longstanding Fecode demand to create a new, single teacher statute (Garcia et al., 2020). Teacher representation in these negotiations was skewed in that most Fecode members were old-statute teachers and few new-statute teachers belonged to the union. As part of the agreements to end the strike, in addition to the new "diagnostic, learning evaluation" (*evaluacion diagnostica y formativa*), the government and Fecode agreed to a 12% salary increase for all teachers and a bonus of 14% for teachers in the highest level of the old statute 2277. New statute teachers were not happy with these agreements and claimed that Fecode "negotiated in favor of the 'oldest' teachers to the detriment of the new" (Suárez, 2015).

The evaluation system negotiated in 2015 continues, though suffering from numerous logistical problems.[11] Fecode complained also about poor information given to teachers on the results of the evaluations and on the offer of remedial courses for teachers who fail the evaluation. Fecode argued that the lack of promotions had undermined the formative/learning character of the evaluation, and continued to rail against the "application of a neoliberal policy of fiscal adjustment" (Fecode, 2020).

The merit reforms survived due largely to gradual implementation and technocratic continuity in government, as well as negotiations in 2015 with Fecode to revamp teacher evaluations. The weakness of political parties noted earlier facilitated technocratic continuity. A high cost of the bypass strategy (making the reform only for new hires) was a long process of implementation. Even 20 years later, almost half of all teachers were hired under the old 1979 statute (in part because the system for teacher pensions discourages retirement) and therefore not subject to evaluations.[12] This can also explain in part the endurance of the reforms, since the union is divided and does not necessarily represent the teachers affected by the "new" statute.

Overall, the teacher career reform seems, despite some union reservations, consolidated. At least the meritocratic spirit of the new career has survived. The reform has had positive effects on several dimensions. First, the hiring process has recruited more competent candidates (Brutti & Sánchez, 2017). Second, teachers under the new statute have lowered dropout rates (Ome, 2013) and improved student performance on standardized tests (Brutti & Sánchez, 2017).

The Evolution of Reform Policy and Politics in Peru

In Peru, the reform process, and ultimate success of the career reforms, was mostly a story of technocratic continuity, little union opposition, and ephemeral political parties. Coming into the 21st century, Peru had one of the lowest performing education systems in Latin America in both coverage and quality. From this low base, successive governments (unrelated to one another) bumped up spending dramatically, expanded access, and retooled teacher careers. Peruvian reformers also advanced in piecemeal fashion, though in a different incremental path than in Colombia. The Toledo government started the first reforms in 2001 with teacher evaluations, though without revamping teacher careers. The Garcia government in 2007 enacted the first comprehensive teacher reform. However, like the 1278 statute in 2002 in Colombia, it applied only to new hires and teachers who voluntarily switched. And advancing up the career ladder was voluntary. The Humala government then made it mandatory for all teachers in 2012. Teacher hiring was by *concurso* and advancing up the eight levels of the career ladder was by evaluation.

Discussions and first attempts at reforming teacher careers began in the government of Alejandro Toledo (2001–2006) (who had a PhD in education from Stanford University). The Toledo government sponsored a broad public debate with civil society organizations, including Sutep, on priorities for education. Out of these discussions, the government drafted a plan with six priorities, one of which was reforming teacher careers (interview Patricia Andrade, former vice-minister of education, November 14, 2019). In 2002, the government instituted teacher evaluations and public *concursos* for hiring (Cuenca, 2020).

Beginning with the administration of Alan Garcia (2006–2011), successive governments designed and implemented a complete transformation of teacher careers: training, hiring, promotion (scaling eight career levels), and pay. Teacher reform in 2007 got off to a rocky start. Despite discussions during the Toledo government, education was not a major campaign issue in 2006 nor did it feature in Garcia's inauguration speech.[13] Before the 2007 law, the Garcia government set the tone of reform politics with an examination required for all teachers in late 2006. Initially, the minister of education, Chang, and the general secretary of Sutep, Caridad Montes, reached an agreement, and Sutep publicly recommended that teachers take the exam.

However, this comity unraveled as Sutep leadership came under fire from the left dissident wing, Conare, fueled in part by incendiary comments by Garcia. The exam and the broader reform then proceeded without negotiation with the union. Sutep still notes on its website that it was not consulted on the 2007 law. In fact, the government went on the offensive against Sutep, most significantly by slashing in early 2007 the number of paid union organizers (*licencia sindical*) from 303 to 30 (Chiroque Chunga, 2008, p. 69).

Over time, steady and substantial salary raises likely lessened union and teacher opposition to the career reforms. During the presidency of Ollanta Humala (2011–2016), average teacher salaries rose by 40% (Chiroque Chunga, 2015, p. 2). In 2015, average monthly salaries for career-track teachers (*nombrados*) was $680. Teacher salaries, however, were still among the lowest in Latin America (Cuenca & Vargas, 2018, pp. 21–22).

Continuity has also characterized economic and other policy areas. Efforts to explain this continuity in education have usually relied on technocracy and identified a range of technically trained officials who move around the bureaucracy but stay in it. The transition in 2011 to President Ollanta Humala was a critical turning point for the teacher reform. Sutep supported Humala's election and felt betrayed when he appointed two technocrats, first Patricia Salas (2001–2013) and then Jaime Saavedra (2013–2016). Minister Salas took the previous government's teacher reform and made it compulsory and got it (*Ley de Reforma Magisterial*) passed by congress by late 2012.[14]

When Salas left in 2013, Humala appointed Jaime Saavedra, an economist by training who had worked in the World Bank and other multilateral agencies as well as GRADE (a major think tank in Lima) and other government positions in Peru. Saavedra then went ahead in implementing the new teacher career, staffing top ministry positions with a group of young economists (interview with Juan Pablo Silva, March 23, 2016). Saavedra ended up as Humala's most popular minister, more popular than the president himself, so it was less of a surprise when the next president, Pedro Pablo Kuczynski, appointed Saavedra to stay on as minister. However, Saavedra soon after ran into problems with an opposition-controlled congress that ultimately forced him out over allegations of corruption. Saavedra returned to the World Bank, but his technocratic successors continued reform implementation, despite successive presidential resignations and impeachments.

Public opinion gave additional encouragement to technocrats. In 2007, among the 63% of respondents who knew about the new 2007 law, 53% approved of it. By a similar margin, 60% of respondents disapproved of Sutep's strike (and disapproved of the strike more than four other contemporary protests in other sectors) (Ipsos, 2007). In 2012, opinions were more divided. On the Sutep strike then, 54% disapproved. However, only 45% though the government should proceed with the new career law of 2012, and 42% thought the president should not keep his education minister, Patricia Salas (who in fact did not last much longer in the government) (Ipsos, 2012). Later, a 2017 survey did not ask about the career law overall, but it did find that 84% of respondents though teachers should pass exams to enter teaching and to be promoted.[15] Overall, though, the impact of public opinion was modest, both because respondents were often divided and because they did not have parties to represent these views beyond the surveys.

In sum, despite initial opposition from the teachers' union, the teacher reform in Peru has been largely implemented.[16] From 2014 to 2018, the ministry conducted 17 evaluations "with relative success and low levels of contention" for a total of 1.2 million evaluations (more than two per teacher) (Cuenca, 2020, p. 20).

COMPARISONS AND CONCLUSIONS

What potential lessons could be drawn from these two cases? First, reforming teacher careers is easier when unions are organizationally and electorally weaker. Union density in Sutep was lower than the regional average. Fecode had higher density overall, but lower for new-statute teachers, the only segment that was growing. Moreover, in both countries, significant numbers of teachers were on temporary contracts and thus less likely to join unions. Sutep additionally suffered internal fractures by dissident regional unions. In elections, both unions endorsed both left and mainstream candidates, but they could not use leverage over members to ensure large blocks of voters (the way political machine unions in Ecuador and Mexico could; Schneider, 2022).

Second, consulting and negotiating with unions can smooth the path to teacher acceptance and reform consolidation. Sutep and Fecode did call politically costly strikes and could have done more to sabotage implementation (as the unions in Mexico did). Instead, unions and teachers came to accept the reforms in part probably because unions participated in setting the terms of evaluation—in the specifics of "buen desempeño" in Peru in the early 2010s and in reforming evaluations in Colombia in 2015.

Third, reforms endured in both countries, despite lacking major support through elections, political parties, or civil society. This success without social or political coalitions might give some cheer to isolated would-be reformers elsewhere. However, even orphaned reforms require some backing within the government to sustain them. Thus, fourth, the general technocratic tradition (Dargent, 2015) in both countries encouraged presidents (from across the political spectrum in Peru) to appoint strings of technocrats to the ministries of education who worked to keep the reforms going. Technocrats in both countries (and especially Saavedra in Peru) gained some performance legitimacy in elite and public opinion as standardized test scores rose, and rose more than neighbors in Latin America. Technocratic leadership helped build a discourse on the need for greater social valuation of teachers, as well as the importance of meritocracy in teacher career development. However, fifth, another factor bolstering technocracy is weakly institutionalized parties, severely so in Peru.

Enduring technocratic support was crucial because, sixth, career reforms take a long time, several decades at least. Unlike career reforms in Mexico and Ecuador, and more like the series of reforms in Chile, both Peru and Colombia rolled out partial reforms initially—in Colombia by applying new careers only to new hires and in Peru because the evaluation in early 2000s got wrapped into voluntary career reforms in 2007 and later into mandatory careers in 2012. And both reforms will take longer into the future to get all teachers into new careers through meritocratic hiring procedures.

Although it is still too early (as of September 2021) to tell exactly what they mean, developments in 2021 in both countries portended possibly profound shifts in education politics. In Colombia, starting in 2019, diverse social groups, including students, indigenous groups, and several unions—Fecode among them—took to the streets in massive demonstrations against the center-right government. In early 2020, the pandemic suspended these protests, but in 2021 demonstrations broke out again, further fueled by the economic shock caused by pandemic restrictions. Fecode actively participated in these protests and was even a member of the strike committee (*Comité del Paro*), an organization of the main civil society associations engaged in the mobilization. This engagement gave Fecode greater visibility and political traction heading into the presidential elections of 2022.

At the same time, COVID-19 led to school closures for more than a year. One of the reasons Fecode had joined the protests was to demand that schools remain shuttered. Later, after several months of negotiation, the government reached an agreement with Fecode to open schools. This agreement, in addition to settling salary and working conditions, raised again the terms of the teacher career. The government promised to create a tripartite commission with representatives from Fecode, the Ministry of Education, and Congress to come to a consensus on a new teacher statute, opening the door to a possible single statute covering all teachers (that Fecode has demanded for years).

In Peru, in July 2021, Pedro Castillo, a former primary school teacher and the union leader responsible for the last large-scale national teachers' strike (2017), took office as president. President Castillo had led a dissident faction, Conare, opposed to SUTEP. Shortly after taking office, the labor ministry gave this faction, now called Fenate-Peru, official recognition, recognition long denied by previous governments. Teachers are now split for the first time since Sutep was founded in 1972. The immediate consequence is to further weaken Sutep, but longer-term impacts are still open questions.

APPENDIX

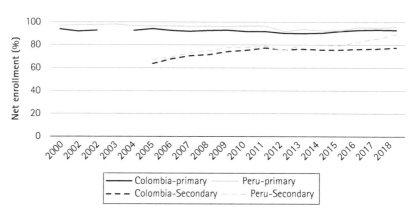

FIGURE 40.A1 Net enrollment in Colombia and Peru, 2000–2018.

(*Source*: World Bank Data Bank)

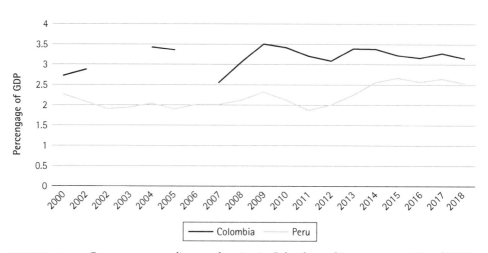

FIGURE 40.A2 Government spending on education in Colombia and Peru, 2000–2018 (% of GDP).

(*Source*: World Bank Data Bank)

Ministers of Education, 2000–2020

Colombia

Minister Name	Type	Dates in Office	Total Months Served
Francisco José Lloreda	Politician	July 2000–Aug. 2002	25
Cecilia María Vélez	Technocrat	Aug. 2002–Aug. 2010	96
María Fernanda Campo	Technocrat	Aug. 2010–Aug. 2014	48
Gina Parody	Politician	Aug. 2014–Nov. 2016	27
Yaneth Giha Tovar	Technocrat	Nov. 2016–Aug. 2018	21
María Victoria Angulo	Technocrat	Aug. 2018– Dec. 2020	29

Peru

Minister Name	Type	Dates in Office	Total Months Served
Nicolás Lynch	Politician	July 2001–July 2002	12
Javier Sota Nadal	Technocrat	Feb. 2004–July 2006	29
José Antonio Chang	Politician	July 2006–March 2011	56
Patricia Salas	Technocrat	July 2011–Oct. 2013	27
Jaime Saavedra	Technocrat	Oct. 2013–Dec. 2016	38

From 2017 to 2020, there was a rapid succession of ministers, all technocrats, none of whom remained in office for a full year.

ACKNOWLEDGMENTS

We are grateful to BreAnne Fleer, Lucas Marín, and Madai Urteaga for research assistance and to Eduardo Dargent and Paula Muñoz for comments on earlier drafts. Schneider thanks JWEL for support. Ricardo Cuenca has been a member of the CNE, president of Foro Educativo (the most important NGO in education), and minister of education (2021). In the text, we cite evidence from this personal experience as an interview with him.

NOTES

1. There is no simple translation for *concurso*. In hiring, *concurso* means a public call for applications, usually an examination, and a public ranking of applicants. Overall, governments enact *concursos* to replace nontransparent, usually clientelist hiring practices.
2. On reasons for this disengagement, see Schneider (2013, 2021a).
3. Some teachers though still mistrusted evaluations, in part due to government bungling of evaluations in the 2010s (Cuenca & Vargas, 2018, p. 24). Some strikes in late 2010s, led by dissident regional unions, demanded major changes to the evaluation system.

4. After 2018, this opportunity for promotion through coursework was limited to only the top 12% of those who failed the evaluation.
5. The numbers of contracted teachers rose markedly in the 2010s in part because so few candidates passed entry exams and so remained on yearly contracts (Guadalupe et al., 2017, p. 25).
6. For an analysis of how Patria Roja maintained dominance in Sutep leadership, see Schneider (2022).
7. https://fecode.edu.co/index.php/quienes-somos/historia.html
8. Some lament that the PEN does not have more impact on policymaking (Guadalupe et al., 2017, p. 241). Until the mid-2010s, CNE lacked staff. By 2021, CNE had 22 professional staff (cne.gob.pe). This staff would help it get beyond a "basically ritual function" (Guadalupe et al., 2017, fn 241).
9. At some stages, parties were major obstacles to reform, especially in Peru where Congress forced out minister Jaime Saavedra and later presidents (and their ministers) Kuczynski and Viscarra.
10. The percentage is the share of months from 2000 to 2020 the minister position was held by technocrats. In Peru, a number of politician ministers—Lloredo, Chang, and Lynch—were borderline technocrats and had limited engagement in political careers. See Appendix.
11. The government nominated an implementation committee for the new evaluation with representatives from Fecode, the Ministry of Education, and ICFES (*Instituto Colombiano para la Evaluación de la Educación*). In this process, academics and experts on the subject of teacher evaluations had a preponderant role in consultations on various tools for such evaluations (including academics from Harvard University and the Bill and Melinda Gates Foundation, the IDB), and experts from Chile (who had worked with similar evaluations there).
12. Old statute teachers had a unique arrangement whereby teachers could start collecting a pension at age 50, and a double pension at 55, and continue teaching and receiving their regular salary (Azuero, 2020).
13. Chiroque Chunga (2008) provides a detailed analysis of the first two years of the Garcia government.
14. Only 50,000 of 280,000 teachers had opted for the new career track (interview with Juan Pablo Silva, former vice minister of education, March 23, 2016).
15. *La Republica*, "El 85% de peruanos respalda la evaluación a maestros, según GfK," August 26, 2017. https://larepublica.pe/politica/1079004-el-85-de-peruanos-respalda-la-evaluac ion-a-maestros-segun-gfk/?ref=lre
16. Interview with Ricardo Cuenca. However, one issue limiting the impact of the teacher reform was the high number of contracted, temporary teachers (43% in 2020; Encuesta Nacional Docente, Ministerio de Educación).

References

Ávila, J. (2012). Despedagogización y desprofesionalización de la profesión docente en Colombia: el Decreto 1278 de 2002. *Educación y Cultura, 95*, 19–28.

Azuero, F. (2020). El Sistema de Pensiones En Colombia: Institucionalidad, Gasto Público y Sostenibilidad Financiera. *Macroeconomía del Desarrollo, 206*.

Bertoni, E., Elacqua, G., Jaimovich, A., Rodríguez, J., & Santos, H. (2018). *Teacher policies, incentives, and labor markets in Chile, Colombia, and Perú: Implications for equality*. Inter-American Development Bank.

Bonilla-Mejía, L., Cardona-Sosa, L., Londoño-Ortega, E., & Trujillo-Escalante, L. (2018). *Quiénes Son Los Docentes En Colombia? Características Generales y Brechas Regionales*. Amsafe Rosario.

Brown, D., & Hunter, W. (2004). Democracy and human capital formation education spending in Latin America, 1980 to 1997. *Comparative Political Studies, 37*(7), 842–864.

Bruns, B., & Luque, J. (2015). *Great teachers: How to raise student learning in Latin America and the Caribbean*. World Bank.

Bruns, B., Macdonald, I., & Schneider, B. R. (2019). The politics of quality reforms and the challenges for SDGs in education. *World Development, 118*, 27–38.

Brutti, Z., & Sánchez, F. (2017). Meritocracy for public teachers: Evidence of success from Colombia. *SSRN Electronic Journal*.

Chiroque Chunga, S. (2008). Sindicalismo docente peruano durante el gobierno Aprista. In J. Gindin (Ed.), *Sindicalismo Docente en América Latina* (pp. 46–103). Amsafe Rosario.

Chiroque Chunga, S. (2015). Reforma Educativa en Marcha? *Ideele Revista, 253*.

Chiroque Chunga, S. (2020). *Situación Laboral del Docent Peruano del Sector Público*. Lima.

Cuenca, R. (2015). *Las Carreras Docentes en América Latina: La Acción Meritocrática para el Desarrollo Profesional*. Lima.

Cuenca, R. (2017). *Moving toward professional development: The teacher reform in Peru (2012–2016)*. Lima.

Cuenca, R. (2020). *La Evaluación Docente en el Perú*. Lima.

Cuenca, R., & Vargas, J. (2018). *Perú: El Estado de Políticas Públicas Docentes*. Lima.

Dahlum, S., & Knutsen, C. H. (2017). Do democracies provide better education? Revisiting the democracy–human capital link. *World Development, 94*, 186–199.

Dargent, E. (2015). *Technocracy and democracy in Latin America: The experts running government*. Cambridge University Press.

Elacqua, G., Hincapié, D., Vegas, E., & Alfonso, M. (2018). *Profesión: Profesor en América Latina ¿Por Qué Se Perdió El Prestigio Docente y Cómo Recuperarlo?* Inter-American Development Bank.

Estrada, H. (2016). *Reelección de Autoridades Elegidas por Votación Popular en Países de América Latina, Estados Unidos y Francia*. Lima.

Fecode. (2020). Informe de la Delegación de Fecode ante la Comisión de Implementación – CDI. Federación Colombiana de Trabajadores de la Educación (Fecode). https://fecode.edu.co/images/ecdf/tercera%20cohorte/Informe_CDI_20_de_enero_de_2020.pdf

Figueroa, M., García, S., Malonado, D., Rodríguez, C., Saavedra, A. M., & Vargas, G. (2018). *La Profesión Docente en Colombia: Normatividad, Formación, Selección y Evaluación*. Fundación Compartir.

García, S., Maldonado, D., Perry, G., Rodríguez, C., & Saavedra, J. E. (2014). *Tras la Excelencia Docente: Cómo Mejorar la Calidad de la Educación para Todos los Colombianos*. Fundación Compartir.

Garcia, S., Maldonado, D., & Muñoz-Cadena, S. (2020). Policy analysis in education policy in Colombia. In P. Sanabria-Pulido & N. Rubaii (Eds.), *Policy analysis in Colombia* (pp. 153–167). Policy Press.

Grindle, M. (2004). *Despite the odds: The contentious politics of education reform*. Princeton University Press.

Guadalupe, C., León, J., Rodríguez, J., & Vargas, S. (2017). *Estado de la Educación en el Perú: Análisis y Perspectivas de La Educación Básica*. Grade.

Ipsos. (2007). Opinion Data Resumen de Encuestas a la Opinion Publica. *Ipsos APOPO, 7*(90).

Ipsos. (2012). Opinion Data Resumen de Encuestas a la Opinion Publica. *Ipsos APOYO, 12*(56).

Mainwaring, S. (2018). *Party systems in Latin America: Institutionalization, decay, and collapse.*

Minedu. (2018). *Encuesta Nacional a Docentes de Instituciones Educativas Públicas y Privadas 2018.* Lima.

Muñoz, P., & Baraybar, V. (2021). Patronage appointments and technocratic power in Peru. In F. Panizza, B. G. Peters, & C. Ramos (Eds.), *Patronage in transition in Latin America.* University of Pittsburgh Press.

Muñoz, P., & Dargent, E. (2016). Patronage, subnational linkages, and party-building: The cases of Colombia and Peru. In S. Levitsky, J. Loxton, & B. Van Dyck (Eds.), *Challenges of party-building in Latin America* (pp. 187–216). Cambridge University Press.

Niño, S. (2012). El Estatuto Docente: Un Asunto Estratégico Para La Educación y Los Maestros. *Educación y Cultura, 95,* 40–44.

OECD. (2004). *Teachers matter: Attracting, developing and retaining effective teachers.* OECD.

Ome, A. (2013). El Estatuto de Profesionalización Docente: Una Primera Evaluación. *Cuadernos Fedesarrollo, 43.*

OREALC-UNESCO. (2007). *Educación de Calidad Para Todos: Un Asunto de Derechos Humanos.* Santiago, Chile.

Pinilla, A. (2010). El Magisterio y la Movilización Social en el Contexto Educativo a Principios del Siglo XXI. *Historia y sociedad,* (18), 107–128.

Puch, M. A., & Salas, A. C. (2020). *¿Llegamos a La Meta de La Carrera? Una Evaluación de Impacto de La Carrera Pública Magisterial Sobre El Rendimiento Académico y Las Competencias Socioemocionales de Los Estudiantes En El Perú.* Lima.

Pulido, O. (2008). La Federación Colombiana de Educadores (FECODE) y la Lucha por el Derecho a la Educación: el Estatuto Docente. *Laboratorio de Políticas Públicas - Serie Ensayos & Investigaciones, 31,* 5–54.

Schneider, B. R. (1998). The material bases of technocracy: Investor confidence and neoliberalism in Latin America. In M. Centeno & P. Silva (Eds.), *The politics of expertise in Latin America* (pp. 77–95). Palgrave Macmillan UK.

Schneider, B. R. (2013). *Hierarchical capitalism in Latin America—Business, labor, and the challenges of equitable development.* Cambridge University Press.

Schneider, B. R. (2024). *Routes to reform: Education politics in Latin America.* Oxford University Press.

Schneider, B. R. (2022). Teacher unions, political machines, and the thorny politics of education reform in Latin America. *Politics and Society, 50*(1), 84–116.

Seawright, J. (2012). *Party-system collapse: The roots of crisis in Peru and Venezuela.* Stanford University Press.

Suárez, H. (2015). El Paro de Maestros y Sus Agridulces Resultados Un Éxito Como Movilización Social: Un Fracaso a Los Ojos de Los Maestros. *Las 2 Orillas.* https://www.las2orillas.co/el-paro-de-maestros-sus-agridulces-resultados/

CHAPTER 41

SUBNATIONAL VARIATIONS IN EDUCATION AND POLICY INNOVATION IN ARGENTINA

JACQUELINE BEHREND

INTRODUCTION

IN federal systems like Argentina, education is often shaped to a considerable extent by subnational politics. This provides a comparative basis for evaluation and learning within a nation state and not just between states. This chapter focuses on Argentina to show how public policies that are developed by national governments, but implemented at the subnational level, can lead to important variations within countries. This variation is increasingly relevant in Latin American nations, which are often unequal and have territorially uneven patterns of development. But, at the same time, highly decentralized countries offer the opportunity for subnational jurisdictions to innovate with public policies or build on national policies to improve the quality of services they offer their citizens. Territorial conflicts and uneven patterns of implementation of national policies evidence the ideological differences that exist between political elites at different levels of government (Eaton, 2017).

How does the implementation of national education policies vary at the subnational level and what factors can potentially explain this variation? At the same time, what scope is there for subnational jurisdictions to innovate and develop pioneering education policies or, on the contrary, to lag behind? Federalism and decentralization can give rise to important variation and unevenness, but they can potentially also enable innovation by subnational jurisdictions. Although the latter is less frequent than the former, these initiatives merit attention. As Tarrow (1978) argued many years ago, it is through the territorial units they live in that men and women organize their relations with the state, and these relations are mediated by local factors, including local actors, structures and processes (e.g., a more or less diversified economic structure, different institutions, local political elites, subnational veto players like the Church and civil society organizations, partisan alignments, ideology, etc.). These all play an important role in how public policies and institutions are implemented and enforced throughout a country.

The effects of globalization and integration into the world economy in developing countries are varied, not only between countries, but also within them. Globalization first came to Argentina in the 1870s, with its insertion into the world economy as an exporter of commodities. The recent wave of globalization in Latin America occurred alongside the dual processes of democratization and decentralization, which delegated authority and resources to subnational governments over key policy areas such as education and health. Democratization spread unevenly within countries, while decentralization gave rise to important variation in the quality of services offered to citizens of different localities (Behrend, 2011; Behrend & Whitehead, 2016; Gibson, 2005; Giraudy et al., 2019; Niedzwiecki, 2018). This shift to multilevel governance, even in countries that already had subnational autonomy due to their federal design, gave rise to territorial conflicts between levels of government and to policy challenges of increasing relevance (Eaton, 2017).

Although globalization imposed an agenda of education reforms on Latin American countries, the implementation of these reforms interacted with local conditions and territorial interests. Even within a single country, the implementation of education reforms varied across the national territory. Argentina is an example of how the local reformulates the global: Local institutional and political cultures affect the proposals put forward by international agencies (Gvirtz & Beech, 2007). As scholars have highlighted, educational systems can be resistant to global influences even if on the outside they appear to be adopting these influences.[1] Similarly, subnational education systems can also develop resistances to the adoption of global education policies by national governments. But, in some cases, they can build on global policies and develop their own initiatives. Federal countries add a layer of complexity to governance and the implementation of public policies. In federal countries, rule writers are often unable to constrain the authorities that are required to enforce the law, even if the norm stipulates control mechanisms (Brinks et al., 2019). Provincial governments have an important margin of freedom in the implementation of laws and policies, and this can lead to implementation gaps or weak implementation. Subnational governments can also obstruct the implementation of national policies.[2] But the potential also exists for overimplementation, policy innovation, and policy challenges.

Like many Latin American countries, Argentina has a center and a periphery, and large-scale processes, such as democratization, education financing and reform, and health provision, play out differently in these varied settings. Argentina is a geographically extensive, diverse, and uneven country and provides interesting variation in education spending and education policies within its borders. This chapter scales down to the subnational level, which is the level of government that is responsible for the implementation of education policies in Argentina, to investigate this variation. Scaling down to the subnational level is important for several reasons. As Snyder (2001) argues, comparativists often rely on national means and aggregate data when studying countries that have high levels of internal heterogeneity. This leads to important fallacies because aggregate national data do not allow us to see whether policy results are uniform across the national territory or whether subnational variation exists. This has important consequences for policymaking in general and education policy in particular. Illiteracy, school attendance, Internet connectivity, and education spending show important subnational variation, as will be shown in this chapter. Focusing on subnational variations allows both scholars and policymakers to understand and handle the spatially uneven nature of many political processes (Snyder, 2001).

This chapter draws on the literature on federalism, historical institutionalism, subnational democratic variation, and decentralization to develop the argument that global processes are not only reconfigured by national political processes but also by local politics. The different levels of governance affect how global policies are adopted, contested, and implemented. As we scale down to the subnational level, we can observe how different political actors and institutions interact and produce divergent policy outcomes.

Territorial variations, and subnational policy challenges and innovations that are anchored in subnational autonomy, are therefore the object of this chapter. To this end, the chapter focuses specifically on two policy areas: the 2005 Education Financing Law and its uneven implementation and enforcement across different territorial units; and the initiatives developed by some subnational units to provide digital education to primary school students. The chapter proceeds as follows. In the first section, the chapter provides the historical background of the development of state education in Argentina and briefly focuses on the internationalization of education policies. It then turns to the process of decentralization of education that took place in Argentina over a period of two decades. The chapter then builds on this to show the heterogeneity that can be found when we look at education indicators through the lens of subnational variation. The chapter then turns to the analysis of a specific public policy—the 2005 Education Financing Law—and shows how levels of implementation and compliance varied across subnational jurisdictions. The following section looks at how the subnational variations outlined in the previous sections affected the transition to online education during the COVID-19 pandemic in 2020–2021. Then, the chapter zooms in on three subnational initiatives of digital education. The final section concludes and uses the case of Argentina to develop some arguments of general interest to the literature on education policy, decentralization, and subnational governance.

Globalization, International Influences, and the Development of a State Education System

Education systems in Latin America were modeled on different international influences since the origins of state education in the 19th century. Argentine former president

Domingo Faustino Sarmiento, who is widely seen as the father of state education in the country, traveled to the United States in the mid-19th century, was fascinated by the schools and pedagogy developed there, and adopted many of those ideas in the development of a national education system in Argentina. As the chapter by Whitehead (Chapter 39, this volume) shows, international influences were important in the early development of state education in most Latin American countries, and the first schools were set up early on by the Jesuits.

Argentina achieved massive education and literacy early in the 20th century—albeit with subnational variations—and with greater success than other countries in the region. UNESCO's most recent literacy data (2018) places literacy at 99% of the population over the age of 15 in Argentina and makes it more comparable to Southern European nations than to its fellow Latin American countries with regard to literacy.[3] In the UNESCO dataset, Uruguay's literacy rate is also 99% of the population over 15, while neighboring Chile's is 96%, and Brazil and Mexico, the two other large Latin American federations, have literacy rates of 93% and 95%, respectively.[4] However, when it comes to student performance in reading, science, and mathematics, Argentine students perform well below Organization for Economic Cooperation and Development (OECD) countries.[5]

In the 19th century, Argentina developed a state-centered education system that was very successful in attracting the school-aged population to primary schools and in promoting a national identity (Beech & Barrenechea, 2011). According to Beech and Barrenechea (2011), as early as 1930, 95% of the population of the city of Buenos Aires was literate. Of course, the situation was not the same in all districts, but public education spread throughout Argentina and was fundamental in promoting social mobility and giving the middle class access to political power. Public education was also strongly promoted in the early 20th century by the Radical Party, which represented the middle class's ascent to political power. Thus, education had a major role in the construction of the Argentine nation and state, and in enabling first the middle class and then the working class to reach political power. For this reason, the notion of public education has a very strong symbolic power in Argentina that has persisted over the years (Beech & Barrenechea, 2011).

Public (state) universities were also an important source of social mobility in Argentina. In 1918, the *Reforma Universitaria* (University Reform) student protests began at the subnational level in Córdoba in demand of social reform and democratization. The movement then extended to all national universities in Argentina. These reforms, approved under the Radical Party government of Hipólito Yrigoyen, sanctioned university autonomy, tripartite government (faculty, students and non-faculty workers), and open access. In 1947, the government of Juan Domingo Perón made all public universities free of charge. These characteristics of state universities remain in place to the present day.

In the 1960s and 1970s, pro-market discourses began to have influence in Latin America, and Argentina was not an exception. However, pro-market reforms in education were not introduced in Argentina until the 1990s. While in the 19th century education reforms were imported from individual countries (France, the United States), in the late 20th century education reform was influenced more by international agencies. Institutions such as the OECD, UNESCO, and the World Bank began to exert important influence in the dissemination of education proposals. In the 1980s and 1990s, there was a new wave of education reforms in Latin America. These were global reforms that aimed at adapting education systems for the 21st century (Gvirtz & Beech, 2007). However, Gvirtz and Beech (2007) argue that although the internationalization of education policy intensified in Latin America in the 1980s and 1990s, education policy across countries became more similar only at the level of official rhetoric. The way these policies were adopted in each country showed marked differences. Pushing this argument further and scaling down to the subnational level, the Argentine case shows that, even within a single country, the way national education policies are implemented con be contested at the subnational level.

Some authors argue that globalization has led to a decline in the role of nation-states and even refer to globalization as "deterritorialization". Yet, as Scholte argues, "globalization is not antithetical to territoriality" (Scholte, 2002, p. 90). Globalization interacts with local processes in various ways, and local practices, cultures, and institutions can shape the way national and global policies are implemented. The shift in the spatial reach of social relations does not mean that the global displaces or takes precedence over the local, or even over national processes and influences (Held & McGrew, 2002). Despite the influence of international agencies in the development of public policies, the local level remains fundamentally important and needs to be scrutinized in order to take stock of important variations in how education policies are implemented and play out across territory.

Decentralization and Education Reform

In the late 1980s and 1990s, many countries throughout the world embraced decentralization policies. Decentralization was seen as a solution to political and economic problems. In a context of democratization, one set of theories argued that decentralization would improve democracy by bringing decision-making closer to the peoples. Another set of theories argued that in a context of debt crisis and reduction of government expenditure, decentralization would provide a more efficient allocation of resources (Falleti, 2010). In Argentina, what drove the decentralization of education reform was the central government's intention to pass on responsibilities to subnational governments out of a need to cut central expenditures. State spending on education was already under stress before the 1982 debt crisis and pressures increased in the ensuing decade.

Decentralization of education involved the transfer of responsibilities and authority from the national level to subnational (provincial) levels of government and began in Argentina in the late 1970s, under authoritarian military rule. In 1978, the administration and management of primary schools was transferred to the provinces. Initially, the transfer of responsibilities was unfunded, and schools were transferred to the provinces without an increase in the automatic transfers to provinces.[6] The decentralization process was completed in 1991–1992, under the democratic presidency of Carlos Menem, with the transfer of secondary schools to the provinces. Over 2,000 schools and 700,000 students were transferred to provincial jurisdictions. At the same time, 72,000 teachers became provincial state employees (Falleti, 2010).[7] This second transfer was also unfunded and led to important variation in teachers' salaries across the nation, a problem that persists to date. The government's argument was that provinces would be able to afford absorbing secondary schools because there was an increase in tax collection and, therefore, in the amount of revenue provincial governments received from the federal government (Falleti, 2010). In practice, decentralization reinforced the disparities that are often observed in the implementation of public policy in federal countries.

The unevenness of the Argentine education system is evidenced across different levels. On the one hand, resources are unequally distributed between schools in poor and middle-class districts, which tend to have better buildings and other resources provided by the education community (Beech & Barrenechea, 2011).[8] Better qualified teachers often prefer these schools and select them deliberately because there are fewer social conflicts, they are often located in more accessible neighborhoods, and they have better infrastructure. As Beech and Barrenechea (2011) observe, school performance is strongly correlated with socioeconomic status and Argentina evidences high dispersion in results in international assessment tests such as the Program for International Student Assessment (PISA). At the same time, there are important differences across provinces. Illiteracy rates and school attendance vary across provinces; public investment in education also varies; and, since teachers are provincial employees, teacher salaries also vary.

The transfer of responsibilities and the subnational disparities in teacher salaries was contentious in the 1980s and 1990s and led to conflicts with teachers' unions. The Federal Education Law (1993) had established that public investment in education should be doubled in 5 years starting in 1993. However, the law was not properly enforced and low investment in education and disparities in teachers' salaries across the country gave rise to intense mobilizations. The most salient of these conflicts was the 2-year campout and protest organized by the national umbrella teachers' union CTERA (Confederación de Trabajadores de la Educación) between 1997 and 1999. Teachers from throughout the country set up a tent in front of Congress in 1997 to demand an education financing law (Behrend, 2000). The protest, which lasted 2 years, ended with the approval of a fund to provide an "incentive" (bonus) for teachers. However, this solution was partial and patchy and did not address the fundamental problem of subnational unevenness and heterogeneity.

In 2005, under the presidency of Néstor Kirchner, Congress sanctioned an Education Financing Law (Law No. 26,075 of 2005) that aimed at increasing investment in education, science, and technology progressively from 2006 to 2010, with the objective of reaching 6% of GDP in 2010.[9] The law established minimum spending thresholds for all subnational jurisdictions and a contribution from the national government to reduce heterogeneity across provinces. One of the law's aims was to eradicate illiteracy across the country.

A few months after the Education Financing Law was sanctioned, a new National Education Law (Law No. 26,206) was enacted in 2006, which derogated the Federal Education Law of 1993. According to Beech and Barrenechea (2011), this law aimed at reinstating the values of public education. It stipulated a tangible increase in teachers' salaries and investment in education and science, as well as reestablishing technical schools.[10] The law states that responsibility for education is shared by the national state, provinces, and the Autonomous City of Buenos Aires (which, for all purposes, is equal to a province).[11] Article 5 also says that the function of the national state is to establish education policy and enforce its compliance, "respecting provincial and local specificities."[12] With regard to the funding of state education, the law established a minimum spending threshold on education of 6% of GDP, which included the education spending of the provinces (including the City of Buenos Aires) and the national government.[13] Another important point established in this law was that the national state was banned from signing bilateral or multilateral free trade agreements that "imply conceiving education as a for-profit service or that encourage any form of mercantilization of public education."[14]

WHAT KIND OF SUBNATIONAL VARIATION IN EDUCATION?

Argentina is a diverse and uneven country, but performance is not uneven in all areas. With a long history of state schooling, Argentina achieved high levels of literacy and school attendance across provinces in aggregate terms. Argentina's literacy, at 99% in the population over the age of 15 by 2018, is well above the regional average of 94%.[15] In the discussion that follows, I use data from the 2010 census, which is the last national census, because it is the most recent data that are disaggregated by province. In 2010, the aggregate illiteracy rate in Argentina among the population over the age of 10 was 1.9%.[16] However, as Figure 41.1 shows, there are provinces that underperform, while many others are closer or above the national average. If we consider underperforming provinces to be those that exhibit an illiteracy rate above the national average (1.9%), there are 15 provinces that have higher than average illiteracy rates. Of this set, seven provinces have illiteracy rates that are above 3%. These are the northern provinces of Chaco, Corrientes, Formosa, Jujuy, Misiones, Salta, and Santiago del Estero. These seven provinces are among the provinces that score lowest on the UNDP's Human Development Index (HDI) for 2016, as Table 41.1 shows.[17] The province of Chaco has the worst

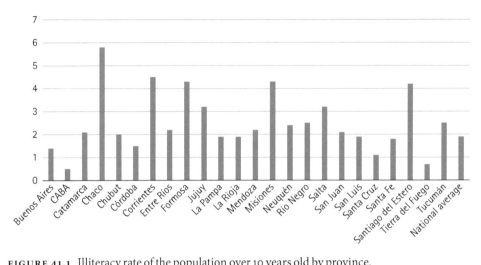

FIGURE 41.1 Illiteracy rate of the population over 10 years old by province.
(*Source*: Author's elaboration on data from the 2010 National Census, INDEC)

Table 41.1 UNDP Human Development Index for Provinces With the Highest Illiteracy Rates

National average	0.848
Chaco	0.816
Corrientes	0.825
Formosa	0.822
Jujuy	0.834
Misiones	0.829
Salta	0.830
Santiago del Estero	0.818

Source: Author's elaboration on data from the UNDP Human Development Index 2016. UNDP (2017). Cited in Argentine Education Ministry, Pan-American Health Organization and World Health Organization (2020), *Indicadores básticos Argentina 2020.*

illiteracy rates in the country, with 5.8% of the population over 10 years old that cannot read and write. This makes Chaco more similar to Andean countries like Ecuador or Peru than to the highest ranking provinces. Of this group of underperforming provinces, Chaco also has the lowest score on the HDI (0.816). The best performing districts are the autonomous city of Buenos Aires (CABA) and the province of Tierra del Fuego,

SUBNATIONAL VARIATIONS IN EDUCATION 919

with illiteracy rates of 0.5% and 0.7%, respectively. The Patagonian province of Santa Cruz, Buenos Aires province, and the province of Córdoba follow suit with the lowest illiteracy rates. The city of Buenos Aires is the largest city in the country and has a population of over three million. Although it is a city and is geographically smaller than the remaining districts, which are provinces, its population is comparable to the provinces of Córdoba or Santa Fe.[18] It has the second highest score on the HDI (0.885), well above the national average of 0.848. It is also the most urbanized district in the country. The province of Tierra del Fuego is the least populated district in the country and is located in the southernmost part of Argentina. It has the highest score on the HDI (0.887).

The aggregate school attendance rate for Argentina is 93.7%, but if we scale down to the subnational level, there is also some variation, as Figure 41.2 shows. Nine provinces are below the national average in school attendance, but the dispersion is low. There are only two provinces—Santiago del Estero and Misiones—that have an attendance rate below 90%. Santiago del Estero's attendance rate is 88.8%, while that of Misiones is 89.8%. Again, the highest attendance rate is that of the small province of Tierra del Fuego (98.2%) followed by the city of Buenos Aires (96.7%).

What explains this variation in illiteracy rates and school attendance? Structural factors are very likely part of the explanation. As Table 41.1 shows, provinces that underperform in these two education indicators (illiteracy and school attendance) are provinces that score comparatively lower on the Human Development Index. In geographical terms, these provinces are located in the North of Argentina, which is the poorest, less diversified, and more peripheral region of the country. The economy of these provinces is largely agricultural. In some cases, like the provinces of Corrientes, Formosa, and Santiago del Estero, the local economy has low levels of diversification and specialization, while in others, there are enclave economies. But another preponderant factor is the urban-rural divide. The city of Buenos Aires is 100% urban, but in the province of Santiago del Estero, almost 32% of the school population is rural and

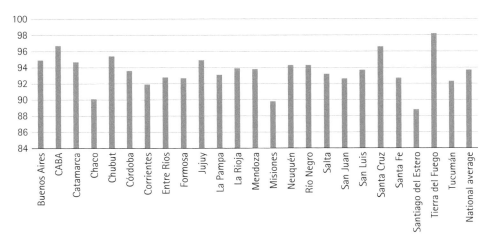

FIGURE 41.2 School attendance by province.

(*Source*: Author's elaboration on data from the 2010 National Census, INDEC)

schools are usually smaller, combine different age groups and grades in a single class-room, and may have a single teacher for all levels. In Formosa, 20.5% of the school population lives in rural regions, while in Misiones, 19%.

Institutional variation also exists. For example, there is variation in the structure of primary and secondary education across provinces. Half the provinces have 7 years of primary education and 5 years of secondary education, while the remaining half has 6 years of primary education and 6 years of secondary education.[19] This institutional variation is related to how education reforms were implemented in each province.

THE EDUCATION FINANCING LAW AND UNEVEN IMPLEMENTATION

In this context of subnational variation and unevenness, the Education Financing Law (2005) was enacted to guarantee an increase in public spending on education, science, and technology, with the aim of guaranteeing "equal opportunities of learning" (Article 1, *Ley de Financiamiento Educativo* No. 26,075, 2005, my translation) and ensuring that the population of all provinces had similar access to quality education. The law stipulated the gradual increase in education spending in order to reach 6% of GDP by 2010 and this was to be achieved through a joint effort by the national government and the 24 subnational jurisdictions. Article 12 of the law further specified that provinces could not spend less on education as a percentage of total public expenditure, and per student, than what they had spent in 2005. The year 2005 was therefore used as a baseline against which to measure the gradual increase of education spending across the country. One of the central aims of this law was to eradicate illiteracy in all provinces and ensure the enrollment of 100% of the population of 5-year-olds in schools. To this end, the increase in education spending was to be destined mainly to improve teacher salaries, hire new teachers to attend to the increase in the student population, and improve teacher training to guarantee quality education (Article 5, *Ley de Financiamiento Educativo* 2 No. 26,075, 2005). Article 7 of the law established the creation of a specific allocation of funds in the national budget to contribute to the provinces' education spending effort. These funds were to be distributed among provinces with the aim of achieving equitable conditions among provinces, according to specific criteria. The amount allocated to each province was to be calculated on the basis of the school population in each district, the incidence of rural schooling in each jurisdiction, and school attendance rates.[20] Article 14 added further criteria related to each jurisdiction's financial capacity and its efforts to increase education spending.[21] The law also established sanctions for provinces that failed to increase their public spending on education from 2005 onward, which involved the withdrawal of the specific funds allocated to those provinces.[22]

Higher spending on education obviously does not automatically or even necessarily translate into better performance of the education system. But ensuring that the public education system is well-funded is a reasonable starting point. Although most provinces gradually increased education spending each year to comply with the law, compliance was disparate across provinces and provinces varied in the budget they allocated to education. Some increased their education spending immediately following the approval of the law, while others did so in a more erratic way or, in a few cases, even decreased their education expenditure. The analysis of how provinces complied with this law provides an interesting lens to understand subnational variation in education policies, even if it focuses on only one aspect: education financing. It shows how federalism and local politics interact with national education policies and how, despite attempts to make education more homogeneous across provinces, in practice, enforcement of this law proved to be difficult.

Problems of weak or uneven enforcement are not new in Argentina or Latin America. Latin America has a long tradition of designing and "borrowing" institutions to enhance the quality of democracy and address the problems caused by pervasive social inequalities (Brinks et al., 2019). Yet these institutional changes have often resulted in norms that exist on paper, but are implemented weakly or unevenly across the national territory. As a result, they fail to generate the outcomes that policymakers had hoped for. One of the reasons that these authors identify for these implementation gaps is that multiple levels of government may hinder the enforcement of laws that national governments seek to enforce.

Brinks et al. (2019) highlight that there are two types of institutional weakness: noncompliance and instability. Noncompliance may be associated with limited enforcement efforts, either by national or subnational authorities. A second source of weak enforcement may occur when those who write the rules (e.g., lawmakers) cannot constrain those who are in charge of enforcing the norm. In Argentina, laws are designed by national authorities, but subnational authorities have autonomy over education, and the subnational authorities in charge of implementing education laws may lack interest in the norm and implement it half-heartedly. Different coalitions that support or are against the norm may exist at different levels of government, or there may be greater societal resistance to a norm in some provinces. In order to ensure a relatively homogeneous application of norms, national authorities need to have the willingness and capacity to monitor their enforcement.

National authorities' monitoring role may vary over time depending on the political party that governs at the national level, international pressure, changing priorities, or, as has often occurred in Latin America, as a result of economic shocks. This is what Brinks, et al. (2019) refer to as instability, which is also an important source of institutional weakness. Economic shocks can lead to institutional change, but they can also slow down the enforcement of some norms, especially those that involve greater disbursements for specific policy areas. Nondiversified economies or economies that depend on the export of natural resources are especially vulnerable to such shocks. Institutional instability is also caused by unstable coalitions, when those who design the rules are no longer in office to ensure enforcement. Frequent alternation in office may also be a source of instability.

The Education Financing Law is an interesting case to analyze the implementation and enforcement problems mentioned by Brinks et al. (2019). Table 41.2 shows the evolution

Table 41.2 Evolution of Subnational Education Spending in Argentina, 2005–2018

Province	2005	2006	2007	2008	2009	2010	2011	2012	2013	2014	2016	2016	2017	2018
Buenos Aires	34.7%	36.2%	36.5%	38.9%	37.9%	31.1%	37.6%	38.2%	38.4%	35.7%	36.1%	32.3%	31.8%	31.40%
Catamarca	23.8%	24.1%	22.8%	26.0%	27.5%	26.1%	25.6%	24.4%	23.4%	23.3%	24.3%	26.5%	26.3%	25.80%
Chaco	27.4%	31.8%	32.6%	30.5%	32.2%	28.6%	32.3%	31.8%	30.9%	28.4%	28.3%	28.1%	30.5%	28.10%
CABA	24.5%	25.6%	26.2%	25.7%	26.2%	27.2%	26.2%	25.5%	21.7%	22.9%	22.4%	19.7%	18.1%	17.10%
Chubut	24.6%	24.8%	26.7%	26.0%	27.4%	24.3%	29.0%	30.0%	30.8%	29.1%	31.1%	30.8%	29.9%	28.2%
Cordoba	25.7%	26.3%	26.7%	29.2%	28.9%	21.8%	27.5%	29.8%	30.1%	29.6%	28.1%	27.1%	24.6%	21.10%
Corrientes	29.1%	30.5%	31.1%	33.6%	34.5%	29.0%	34.5%	33.7%	33.8%	32.9%	32.6%	34.3%	30.9%	29.60%
Entre Ríos	25.2%	25.6%	26.6%	27.7%	27.9%	24.1%	28.9%	27.3%	27.8%	26.6%	28.4%	27.9%	26.7%	26.50%
Formosa	21.1%	25.5%	27.7%	27.1%	30.4%	22.6%	24.4%	23.3%	22.8%	22.3%	23.2%	24.0%	22.8%	23.40%
Jujuy	29.6%	32.3%	34.0%	34.5%	31.9%	31.4%	32.1%	30.1%	29.5%	26.7%	28.2%	27.0%	23.3%	21.60%
La Pampa	23.3%	24.2%	25.6%	27.8%	30.1%	23.0%	29.5%	31.6%	31.0%	30.6%	32.8%	31.8%	27.2%	27.00%
La Rioja	18.3%	20.5%	23.3%	24.9%	25.9%	25.3%	25.8%	25.4%	25.5%	23.2%	24.9%	25.1%	20.9%	21.10%
Mendoza	28.5%	27.8%	29.2%	30.4%	31.2%	29.1%	31.7%	30.7%	30.3%	29.0%	30%	28%	25.7%	23.60%
Misiones	22.6%	24.7%	27.5%	28.5%	29.1%	28.2%	31.6%	30.8%	28.6%	28.2%	27%	32%	30.0%	26.30%
Neuquén	23.3%	24.9%	25.3%	27.5%	27.7%	24.5%	29.5%	28.8%	28.3%	27.3%	29.0%	28.7%	28.7%	26.10%
Rio Negro	27.8%	29.6%	30.1%	31.4%	31.3%	30.6%	33.2%	33.5%	34.9%	33.0%	33.2%	31.6%	30.6%	27.80%
Salta	23.6%	25.0%	24.0%	25.8%	25.3%	24.9%	26.7%	25.8%	25.0%	28.0%	29.3%	29.6%	28.9%	28.60%
San Juan	24.5%	23.6%	25.0%	24.9%	27.9%	28.7%	30.5%	28.8%	25.6%	26.3%	26.1%	25.5%	22.9%	21.30%
San Luis	19.9%	21.2%	21.4%	20.7%	16.9%	17.4%	18.5%	21.9%	26.3%	28.8%	31.6%	30.4%	29.3%	23.50%
Santa Cruz	12.8%	11.6%	14.3%	19.1%	20.1%	18.6%	20.8%	23.6%	24.2%	28.0%	26.6%	28.9%	27.1%	25.00%
Santa Fe	29.2%	30.9%	33.5%	35.8%	37.3%	30.4%	35.7%	37.1%	36.2%	33.9%	32.1%	30.8%	28.4%	27.30%
Santiago del Estero	23.7%	22.5%	22.8%	22.0%	27.4%	24.3%	24.0%	25.1%	22.5%	21.0%	20.1%	22.3%	23.1%	21.70%
Tierra del Fuego	22.4%	23.6%	25.6%	29.1%	28.0%	24.2%	28.1%	27.6%	28.8%	29.8%	29.2%	28.1%	25.0%	21.60%
Tucuman	22.5%	23.0%	25.3%	25.7%	28.3%	27.3%	26.9%	28.1%	29.1%	25.6%	26.3%	26.5%	24.0%	23.00%
Country total (%)	27.5%	28.6%	29.4%	31.0%	31.5%	27.4%	31.3%	31.5%	30.8%	29.7%	30.0%	28.6%	27.3%	25.70%

Source: Author's elaboration on data from the Dirección Nacional de Planeamiento de Políticas Educativas, Ministerio de Educación de la Nación.

of subnational education spending in the 24 jurisdictions since the approval of the law in 2005 until 2018. Note that the law stipulated an increase in education spending until 2010, but the validity of the law was extended by decree in subsequent years. Provinces' baselines in 2005 were very heterogeneous. The distance between the province that most spent on education and the one that spent the least was huge. The province of Buenos Aires destined 34.7% of its total government expenditure to education in 2005, while the province of Santa Cruz destined slightly less than 13% of its public expenditure to education.

At an aggregate level, average public expenditure on education in Argentine provinces in 2005 was 27.5% of total public expenditure, as Table 41.2 shows. By 2011, aggregate education expenditure had increased two percentage points, with some variation from year to year, and the spending pattern of some districts had improved, in line with the requirements of the Education Financing Law. By 2015, education expenditure had increased to 30% of all public expenditure at an aggregate level and all subnational districts had complied with the law. Some provinces, particularly those that started with a lower baseline in 2005, showed a significant increase in the percentage of public spending destined to education and, in general, the initial heterogeneity in public spending on education became less pronounced. However, the increase in education spending was not linear and tended to oscillate in some years. For example, in 2010 practically all provinces decreased their education expenditure, but increased it again in the following year. The trend began to decline significantly after 2016, as will be shown later.

Buenos Aires and Santa Cruz were at the highest and lowest end of public spending on education when the law was approved. With an estimated population of 17,196,396, Buenos Aires province is home to over one third of the population of Argentina and 36.8% of the school population.[23] It and has the greatest number of schools, teachers, and students in the country. It has one of the lowest illiteracy rates (1.4%), and school attendance is also above the national average, at almost 95%. But it is a large and diverse province that is home to most of Argentina's urban poor. Following the approval of the Education Financing Law, the province of Buenos Aires increased its education spending every year, reaching 38.9% of public expenditure in 2008 and declining slightly in 2009. In 2011, 2012 and 2013 the province of Buenos Aires was back on track and public spending on education reached 38.4% of total public expenditure in 2013. A sharp drop in public spending on education in the province of Buenos Aires occurred in 2016, after the election of a new governor from the center-right political coalition Cambiemos. María Eugenia Vidal was elected governor of the province of Buenos Aires at the end of 2015. She belonged to the conservative party Propuesta Republicana (Pro), which was the leading member of the Cambiemos coalition, and during her term in office confrontation with teachers' unions was very high. Despite the decline in education spending after 2016, Buenos Aires province was still the district that spent the most on education in 2018, when education spending in Buenos Aires province was 31.4% of total public spending.

The province of Santa Cruz, which spent the least on education when the Education Financing Law was approved in 2005, evidenced the greatest increase in education spending. Santa Cruz, which is located in the Patagonian region of southern Argentina, has a population of 347,593. Although its education spending at the start of the period was the lowest, illiteracy and school attendance indicators were well above the national average. Only 1.1% of the population was illiterate and school attendance was 96.6%, as Figures 41.1 and 41.2 show. By 2011, Santa Cruz had caught up with other provinces and continued to increase its spending on education until 2016. In 2016, education spending in Santa Cruz was almost 29%, slightly above the national average.

The autonomous city of Buenos Aires shows the importance of ideological differences in the implementation of national laws. This district, which is the richest and most cosmopolitan in the country, openly challenged the premises on which the National Education Law was based and, after 2011, was the only district that evidenced an opposite trend in education spending. Its illiteracy rate is 0.5%, the lowest in the country, while school attendance is 96.7%, the second highest after Tierra del Fuego. When the Education Financing Law was approved in 2005, the city of Buenos Aires was already three percentage points below the national average in public spending on education (24.5% compared to 27.5%), as Table 41.2 shows. From 2005 until 2010, the city of Buenos Aires increased its public spending on education yearly until it reached 27.2% in 2010, but in 2011 education spending began to drop until it reached 17.1% in 2018, by far the lowest in the country and with a national average of 25.7% that year.

What explains the low levels of education spending in the richest and most cosmopolitan district of Argentina? The explanation is both partisan and ideological. Pro-market discourses on education appealed to a broader audience in the city of Buenos Aires. In 2007, the conservative party Propuesta Republicana (Pro) was elected for the first time to subnational executive office, and Mauricio Macri became mayor of the city of Buenos Aires. Until 2010, the date stipulated by the Education Financing Law, the new city government complied with the law. But after 2010, the district began to reduce its education spending. While it reduced spending on public schools, the district increased subsidies for private schools. The city of Buenos Aires has the greatest percentage of students that attend private as opposed to public schools in Argentina. Figure 41.3 shows the distribution of the student population between public and private schools in each province. In

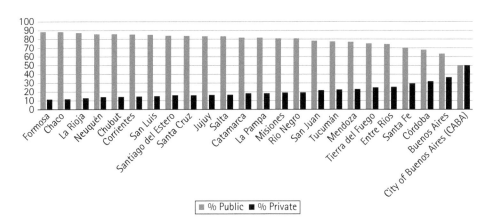

FIGURE 41.3 Percentage of students enrolled in public and private schools by province.

(*Source*: Author's elaboration on data from the Secretaría de Innovación y Calidad Educativa, 2015)

most provinces, over 80% of students attend public (state) schools. In Formosa, Chaco, and La Rioja, over 87% of students attend public schools. In the city of Buenos Aires, 49.9% of students attend public schools, while more than half of the school population (50.1%) is enrolled in private schools.[24] This has important consequences for education policy and education spending at the local level because if the majority of its electorate chooses private over public schools, the local government has fewer incentives to invest in public education.

Why do families opt out of the public education system in the city of Buenos Aires? One reason may be the deterioration of public education provision, but this explanation begs the question of why, in the face of declining state education, families opt out of the system instead of demanding better quality education. Di John (2007) argues that in many Latin American countries there is a higher supply of private schools than in other regions of the world. This provides an "exit" option for upper income groups who have the possibility of sending their children to private schools and therefore fail to exercise their "voice" and demand better public schools in the district. Di John (2007) argues that political parties in Latin America have also largely failed to aggregate demands for better education, so there are no strong demands for quality education either from families or political parties.[25] The growth of private education in the face of declining public investment in education in the city of Buenos Aires shows that the wealthy have the option to exit the public education system and therefore have fewer incentives to exercise their voice. The city of Buenos Aires also allocates an important part of its education budget to private schools. In 2006, the city of Buenos Aires destined 17% of its education budget to subsidizing private schools.[26] This trend continued in the following years.[27] Therefore, while it reduced public spending on education, the city of Buenos Aires increased state subsidies for private schools. Two other provinces destined more than the city of Buenos Aires to subsidizing private schools: Córdoba (24%) and Santa Fe (20%). However, in Córdoba 68% of the school population attends state schools and in Santa Fe, 70.5%. In contrast, the provinces of Chubut and Formosa destined only 3% of their education expenditure to subsidizing private schools,[28] and in those provinces, over 88% of the school population attends state schools.[29]

How did education spending evolve in the provinces with the highest illiteracy rates after the approval of the Education Financing Law? As Figure 41.1 shows, the provinces of Chaco, Corrientes, Formosa, Jujuy, Misiones, Salta, and Santiago del Estero had the highest illiteracy rates in Argentina in the 2010 census, which ranged from 5.8% in Chaco to 4.2% in Santiago del Estero. Chaco's education spending was at the national average in 2005, and after the approval of the law it increased gradually until it reached 32.3% in 2011. Although, following the national trend, it decreased after 2016, it did not revert to the same level of 2005 and in 2018 was above the national average. A similar trend was observed in the provinces of Corrientes, Misiones, and Salta. In the provinces of Formosa, Jujuy, and Santiago del Estero, however, the Education Financing Law proved insufficient to ensure an increase in education spending in the long term. Formosa and Santiago del Estero were below the spending average in 2005 and, although public education spending increased during the period, by 2018 it was well below the national average. In Santiago del Estero, public spending on education in 2018 was even below the 2005 baseline. In Jujuy, the province was above the national spending average in 2005 and increased its education spending after the approval of the law, but the decline in its education spending was more pronounced after 2016, to the point that by 2018 it was not only four percentage points below the national average, but it was also spending eight percentage points less on education than in 2005. In Jujuy, a governor from the center-right Cambiemos coalition had also been elected in late 2015.

In 2015, public expenditure on education reached 5.78% of GDP and was close to complying with the aim established in the Education Financing Law (2005) and the National Education Law (2006). But after 2016, it declined to 4.8% of GDP in 2019.[30] Why did implementation and enforcement of the law become weaker? At the end of 2015, Mauricio Macri, from the center-right Cambiemos coalition was elected president of Argentina and a new government took office at the national level. At this point, policy instability ensued: those who had designed the rules at the national level were no longer in office, and public funding for education became more unstable and weakly enforced. Although Article 7 of the Education Financing Law (2005), which established the funds that the federal government was required to transfer to provinces, was extended by decree in the following years, in practice, the percentage of GDP that was spent on education declined with the change in national authorities. As head of government of the city of Buenos Aires, Macri had decreased public spending on education in his second mandate, and this same policy was implemented at the national level after his election as president.

Economic Globalization and Education Spending in the Argentine Provinces

Economic globalization, understood as the integration of local economies to the world economy, can also hypothetically affect the implementation of education policies in highly decentralized countries. It is not just nation states that become more interrelated, but also regions and local jurisdictions within nation states. More globalized local economies presumably have greater links to the outside world, and this could be an incentive to invest more on education and human capital in order to prepare their citizens for the complexities and demands of the 21st century. However, the type of export that predominates and the way that subnational units integrate their economies to the world economy are important to understand the incentives that subnational governments have to invest additional resources in education. In the international division of labor, some countries and, within them, specific regions, base their economies on the export of commodities. Since independence, Argentina's economic links to the rest of the world were through the export of beef and grains, first to Europe and, more recently, to Russia and China. In the last three decades, the expansion of soya and mining increased this type of insertion into the world economy. But Argentina is a diverse and heterogeneous country, and this is particularly visible in the diverse economic structures that are found across the country. Different types of economic structure provide varying incentives for state–society relations, which have effects on the types of policies that are implemented (Behrend & Bianchi, 2017).

Do a province's economic structure and its insertion into the global economy have effects on education policies and, in particular, on how much each subnational jurisdiction invests in education? Although compliance with the Education Financing Law was high, particularly because the federal transfers stipulated by the law were conditional on increased public spending in education by each jurisdiction, some provinces made a more consistent effort to increase their education spending and to maintain higher levels of investment over time, even after the coalition that had promoted the reform was no longer in office at the national level.

One way of measuring the globalization of a local economy is to focus on the weight of exports as a percentage of provincial GDP. The provinces whose economies are more linked to external markets in Argentina are exporters of commodities (soya and other grains, beef, and minerals.). Primary exports require limited human capital, and the subnational districts that are most exposed to global markets have few incentives to invest more than the required minimum in education and human capital.

Figure 41.4 shows the weight of exports in the local economy of each subnational unit in Argentina and the percentage of education spending over total public spending. The provinces of San Juan and Catamarca stand out as those where exports are a major proportion of provincial GDP. In San Juan, exports account for 80% of GDP, while in Catamarca exports account for 66% of provincial GDP. These are provinces with a highly

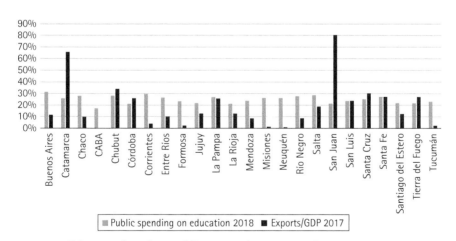

FIGURE 41.4 Education Spending and Exports in the Argentine Provinces

(*Source*: Author's elaboration on data from the Argentine Chamber of Commerce and Services, *Perfiles Exportadores Provinciales 2018* and the Dirección Nacional de Planeamiento de Políticas Educativas, Ministerio de Educación de la Nación)

concentrated economy based on gold and copper mining that is very specialized, but not very diversified (Behrend & Bianchi, 2017). Although San Juan is also a producer of wine, olives, and olive oil, mining outweighs all other economic sectors. Catamarca has a similar production profile. Mining in these two provinces is not labor intensive and generates very few jobs. In Catamarca, for example, the public sector is the most important employer (Behrend & Bianchi, 2017). Therefore, although mining is a highly specialized sector, it is dominated by foreign firms, employs very few workers, and the highly skilled workers that are required by those industries are usually hired outside the province or country. There are few incentives to invest in human capital. As Table 41.2 shows, San Juan's public spending on education was below the national average in 2018 and throughout most of the period of analysis. Catamarca was also below the national average in education spending from 2005 to 2017 and was at the national level in 2018, when the national average of public spending on education dropped to an all-time low in the period (25.7%). Although in terms of exports these two provinces are the most globalized, this type of globalization, based on the export of commodities with a low demand for skilled labor, did not have positive effects on education spending. Provinces receive royalties for mining in their jurisdictions, so, in theory, they have an additional pool of resources that they can destine to the policy areas they wish to strengthen. But the decision to invest more on education hinges on political elites' ideological preferences or the existence of a policy coalition that supports investment on education.

After San Juan and Catamarca, the provinces of Chubut, Santa Cruz, Tierra del Fuego, Santa Fe, and Córdoba are the ones that evidence the highest exports as a percentage of GDP, although their exports are significantly lower. Exports represented 34% of Chubut's GDP in 2017, 30% of Santa Cruz's GDP, almost 27% in Tierra del Fuego, 27% in Santa Fe, and 26% in Córdoba, as Figure 41.4 shows. Chubut's exports are mostly primary products, especially seafood and aluminum, while the province of Santa Cruz mostly exports minerals and seafood.[31] Tierra del Fuego exports mostly fish, gas, and industrial products. Santa Fe and Córdoba have similar export profiles that concentrate mostly on soya bean and oil, products derived from soya bean, corn, and, to a lesser extent, car parts and cars.[32] Of this set of provinces, Chubut was below the average spending on education in 2005, but by 2018 it was well above the average spending on education and destined 28% of its public expenditure to education. Santa Cruz started out with the lowest education spending in Argentina, gradually increased in the period under analysis, but was slightly below average in 2018. Tierra del Fuego was below the national spending average on education throughout the period. Santa Fe was consistently above the national spending average throughout the period, while Córdoba, with a similar economic structure, was below the spending average throughout the period. A greater insertion into the global economy therefore does not appear to have an impact on public investment in education in the Argentine provinces, mainly because the insertion of the most globalized provinces into the world economy in this period was through the export of primary products which do not require skilled labor and, therefore, do not provide incentives for the development of policy coalitions that seek to promote greater investment in education and human capital.

The COVID-19 Pandemic and Education in Argentina: Uneven Local Contexts

The COVID-19 pandemic spread across the world in early 2020, and school closures were a frequent response in many countries. From one day to the next, students and teachers at all levels of education migrated to online learning. How well prepared was the school population for this sudden transition to online education? In developing countries, where there are gross inequalities in access to the basic technology needed for online education, including limited Internet connectivity for many, the pandemic reinforced existing inequalities in access to education. These inequalities existed between students of different social backgrounds in the same district, between subnational jurisdictions, and between urban and rural settings. The experience of students who had good broadband connection and access to computers at home was radically different to those who did not and—with any luck—had to download school contents from their parents' mobile phones.

How did the subnational variations outlined in the previous sections affect the school population in Argentina? It is still too early to have a full picture of the consequences of school closures in different subnational jurisdictions, but, on the basis of the previous discussion, some preliminary ideas can be advanced.

In the city of Buenos Aires, Internet access is widely available, and most homes have at least one connection to the Internet, as Figure 41.5 shows. But in the province of Formosa, in 2019, 1 year before the COVID-19 pandemic broke out, only 30% of homes had Internet access. In Mendoza and San Juan, Internet access was only slightly higher,

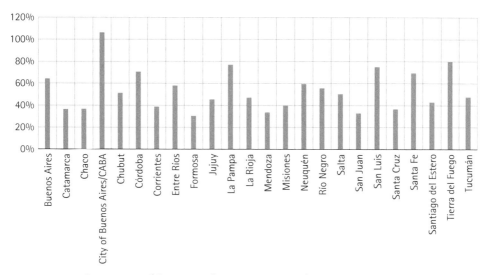

FIGURE 41.5 Percentage of homes with internet access by province, 2019. Note: In some jurisdictions internet access is over 100% because there is more than one point of access per home.

(*Source*: Author's elaboration on data from the Observatorio Argentinos por la Educación)

and the situation was quite similar in the provinces of Catamarca, Chaco, and Santa Cruz. Indeed, in half the provinces, less than 50% of homes had access to the Internet. If we focus on the provinces that have the highest levels of illiteracy (Chaco, Corrientes, Formosa, Jujuy, Misiones, Salta, and Santiago del Estero) and lowest levels of school attendance (Santiago del Estero, Misiones, and Chaco), lack of Internet access is cause for concern. Outside the city of Buenos Aires, few provinces had the minimum Internet requirements to guarantee equitable online education. And even in the city of Buenos Aires access to the Internet was disparate across different social backgrounds: While some homes had more than one point of access, many homes in poor neighborhoods had no access to the Internet.

Aside from Internet access, students needed to have some sort of device that could connect to the Internet and, at a minimum, download homework, or, ideally, connect to online platforms or videoconferences with their teachers in order to continue their education during the pandemic. This was also an important source of variation across different social sectors and between different subnational units. According to a recent survey carried out in poor neighborhoods throughout the country, 80% of students surveyed used a mobile phone to do their schoolwork.[33] In contrast, 45% of students who attended private schools said they used computers or notebooks to do their schoolwork. In poor neighborhoods only 11% of students had their own device, while the remaining 89% shared the device they used to do their schoolwork with their parents and siblings.[34]

In the years prior to the COVID-19 pandemic, national and subnational jurisdictions undertook several initiatives to bridge the technology gap and provide students with access to information technology. In 2010, the national government launched a novel "digital inclusion" program called *Conectar Igualdad*. The aim of this program was to equip teachers and students with computers and develop digital and technological skills. To this end, the program contemplated the distribution of laptops to teachers and students of secondary public schools, special education schools (for students with disabilities), and teacher training institutes.[35] By 2014, the program had distributed 4,553,631 laptops to teachers and students of all provinces.[36] Like the Education Financing Law, the implementation of this program suffered after the election of the new national government in late 2015. In 2018, the Macri government cancelled *Conectar Igualdad* and put an end to the distribution of laptops to students and teachers. When the COVID-19 pandemic spread throughout the world in 2020, students and teachers in Argentina were no longer equipped with the minimum technological requirements needed to make the transition to online education.

Three Cases of Subnational Policy Innovation

In federal countries, elected subnational authorities can use their authority, resources, and legitimacy to design and implement education policies that diverge or innovate on national policies. Territorial units can be fertile ground for policy experimentation and innovation. In Argentina, the first initiatives in digital education took place at the subnational level. The province of Río Negro and the province of San Luis launched digital education initiatives in 2005 and 2007, respectively.[37] These policies were prior to the national government's *Conectar Igualdad* program. In Río Negro, the initiative involved equipping schools with "mobile digital classrooms," which consisted of sets of portable computers and equipment that could be moved from one classroom to another. In San Luis, *Todos los Chicos en la Red* was based on the one-laptop-per-child model in primary schools. La Rioja, Córdoba, the city of Buenos Aires, and the province of Buenos Aires also implemented one-to-one digital education programs, and the province of Misiones combined the mobile classroom with the one-to-one approach.[38]

These subnational digital education programs were similar to *Conectar Igualdad* in some respects, but mostly focused on primary schools, a level of education not covered by the national government's program. In what follows, I briefly describe three such programs implemented by the autonomous city of Buenos Aires, the province of San Luis, and the province of La Rioja and focus on the policy innovations that subnational districts can undertake in federal countries. These three provinces are very different from each other. The city of Buenos Aires is the capital of Argentina, economically the most developed district and the most cosmopolitan city in the country. San Luis and La Rioja are located in the Cuyo region, close to the border with Chile. La Rioja has a less developed economic structure, and less than 50% of homes in the province have Internet access, but it is at the national average in illiteracy rates and school attendance. San Luis is a small province that in the 1980s underwent a state-led industrialization process and, politically, has always sought to maintain autonomy from the federal government (Behrend, 2011). School attendance and illiteracy in San Luis are also at the national average. These three subnational jurisdictions implemented programs that aimed at increasing access to technology and digital education for students and teachers in public schools.

San Luis was a pioneer in digital education and implemented a provincial program in 2007 called *Todos los Chicos en la Red*. The program contemplated the distribution of netbooks for all children from first to sixth grade and a notebook for each teacher in public schools and was part of a broader public policy aimed at increasing connectivity in the province, providing equipment for schools, and training students and teachers in information technology (IT) skills. Its implementation started in the smallest districts of the province and then moved to the two largest cities, Villa Mercedes and San Luis. The program not only included IT training for teachers and students but also for parents.[39] Shortly after the creation of *Todos los Chicos en la Red*, in 2009, a provincial law established the installation of free Wi-Fi throughout the province. This was an innovative public policy that had no parallel in any other subnational district in Argentina. At the same time, the government launched a plan to stimulate the purchase of home computers, which included fiscal credits worth 50% of the price paid for the computer. By 2009, 70% of homes had computers.[40] In 2019, a few months before the COVID-19 pandemic began and forced school closures throughout the country, San Luis was one of the provinces with greatest connectivity: 75% of homes had Internet access. Although it is still early to see how school closures affected education in each province, San Luis was in a better position to face the transition to online education than most other provinces in Argentina. According to a recent study, only 13% of students in the last year of primary school in San Luis had no Internet access at home during the pandemic. This placed San Luis in the first quartile of Internet access in the country.[41]

In 2009, the province of La Rioja launched a digital education program that was based on the one-laptop-per-child model and aimed at providing students in primary schools (urban and rural) and special schools, with their own laptop computers.[42] The Joaquín V. González program, as it was called, also involved setting up Internet connections in all schools. To that end, the provincial government had to install optic fiber wiring throughout the province. Between 2010 and 2011, the program distributed 96,363 portable computers. Of these, 45,636 netbooks went to primary school students and 3,974 laptops to primary school teachers.[43] The program also expanded to secondary schools and worked in tandem with *Conectar Igualdad*, providing 20,000 netbooks to students and 2,000 laptops to teachers, 4,600 netbooks to students in teacher training institutes, and 1,032 laptops to professors in teacher training institutes. As in San Luis, the distribution of laptops was accompanied by training in digital education.[44] Despite these efforts, when the COVID-19 pandemic forced the closure of schools in 2020, 23.6% of students in La Rioja still did not have access to the Internet at home.[45] La Rioja fared better than many other provinces in Argentina, but, in comparison, in San Luis, the decision to install free Wi-Fi across the province, combined with the distribution of laptop computers, placed the province in a better position to face migration to online education.

In 2011, the city of Buenos Aires implemented the *Plan Sarmiento*, a digital education program that distributed netbooks to primary school students and teachers. Between 2011 and 2016, 302,532 netbooks were distributed to students and 26,381 notebooks to teachers.[46] Although the city of Buenos Aires decreased its education expenditure in this period, it nonetheless launched this program that followed a similar logic to *Conectar Igualdad*, with the difference that the *Plan Sarmiento* targeted primary school students and *Conectar Igualdad* secondary school students. As in La Rioja, the *Plan Sarmiento* complemented *Conectar Igualdad*. Students used the netbooks in the classroom and at home. But in 2017, in line with the national government's dismantlement of *Conectar Igualdad*, the city of Buenos Aires changed the focus of the *Plan Sarmiento* from the one-to-one model to a mobile digital classroom model that provided equipment for schools, but no longer distributed individual computers to students.[47] This was an unfortunate policy change, because when the COVID-19 pandemic forced schools to shut down, few primary school students in the city of Buenos Aires had their own computer to follow online classes. Public school students were ill-equipped to connect to online classes, download material, or complete their coursework.

These three cases show the importance of subnational levels of government for policy innovation in federal contexts or in countries with a decentralized education system. National public policies are fundamental for developing more inclusive education systems, but subnational governments can also play a major role in policy innovation or in developing what Eaton (2017) calls "policy regimes." The cases of San Luis and La

Rioja are particularly notable and show the importance of agency in the design of innovative public policies. In contrast to the city of Buenos Aires, San Luis and La Rioja are not among the most developed in the country, yet they were pioneers in implementing subnational digital education programs, and San Luis stands out in its innovative policies.

Concluding Remarks

What new insights does scaling down to the subnational level bring to the analysis of education policy in federal or highly decentralized countries? This chapter shows that a focus on subnational levels of government can provide a more adequate approximation to how public policy is implemented throughout a single country and can show the different governance challenges that are faced *within* countries. Many years ago, Stein Rokkan (1970) alerted that the whole-nation bias can provide an inadequate approximation to our understanding of how politics and governance unfold. This chapter builds on this insight and on the research carried out by subnational scholars in the last two decades to show how subnational variations matter.

Aggregate data on illiteracy, school attendance, and policy implementation can obscure important variations that need to be taken into account if we want to ensure that education policy is evenly implemented throughout a country. As this chapter shows, although illiteracy tended to be higher in provinces that are economically less developed, education spending followed a different pattern than we might expect. And, contrary to what one intuitively might imagine, innovative education policies were not designed only in the most developed districts. Ideology and partisan alignments are central to understanding the policies political elites implement with greater or lesser enthusiasm. In Argentina, subnational jurisdictions that lag behind in terms of economic development have designed and implemented innovative policies to promote digital education in their territory. Focusing on multilevel governance allows us to observe the contested nature of policymaking across territory and how subnational political elites can lag behind in the implementation of national policies, but they can also be pioneers in designing and implementing policies that are later adopted at the national level.

This chapter began by arguing that federalism and decentralization can be a source of unevenness between subnational units and can lead to important implementation gaps, as in the Education Financing Law. But they can also be an opportunity to experiment and develop innovative public policies. San Luis's digital education program is a vivid example of this. As Tarrow (1978) argued many years ago, peripheries can be enclaves of diversity in which social (or policy) experimentation can be carried out. They can also mount challenges to national government policies and contest models of development (Eaton, 2017). The ideological and territorial interests of governors and presidents don't always align, and this can give rise to contestation (Eaton, 2017), but also to innovation, as this chapter has shown. Understanding the relations between different levels of government is fundamental to see how major policy issues are fought out across territory

934 JACQUELINE BEHREND

(Tarrow, 1978). The challenge that both comparativists and policymakers face is to take stock of the diverse interactions among actors, structures, and processes at different levels of government that produce divergent outcomes.

Notes

1. See, for example, Beech and Barrenechea (2011).
2. Niedzwiecki (2018) shows how subnational elites in Argentina and Brazil obstructed the implementation of social assistance programs launched by national governments.
3. According to the UNESCO Institute for Statistics, in 2018, literacy in Argentina was 99% of the population over 15, the same as in Italy and Spain and one point higher than Greece. Data available at https://data.worldbank.org/indicator/SE.ADT.LITR.ZS
4. UNESCO Institute for Statistics.
5. See PISA test results for Argentina: chrome-extension://efaidnbmnnnibpcajpcglcle findmkaj/viewer.html?pdfurl = https%3A%2F%2Fwww.oecd.org%2Fpisa%2Fpubli cations%2FPISA2018_CN_ARG.pdf&clen=1280798&chunk=true. The analysis of subnational variations in education does not take into account PISA test results because the available data does not discriminate by province.
6. Automatic transfers from the national to the provincial level are governed by a federal revenue-sharing law (Ley de Coparticipación Federal Law 23,548 of 1988), which was subsequently modified by different fiscal pacts.
7. Municipal governments' role in education provision is very minor, mostly at the level of kindergarten. Whereas in Brazil municipalities have a greater responsibility in the provision of primary education, in Argentina, primary schools are the responsibility of provincial governments (Falleti, 2010).
8. Argentine state schools have *cooperadoras*, which are parent associations that raise funds and organize voluntary work to improve school infrastructure.
9. Article 1, *Ley de Financiamiento Educativo* (2005). https://www.argentina.gob.ar/normat iva/nacional/ley-26075-112976/texto
10. See *Ley de Educación Nacional*, No. 26,206 (2006). chrome-extension://efaidnbmnnnibp cajpcglclefindmkaj/viewer.html?pdfurl = https%3A%2F%2Fwww.argentina.gob.ar%2Fsi tes%2Fdefault%2Ffiles%2Fley-de-educ-nac-58ac89392ea4c.pdf&clen=114322&chunk=true
11. Article 4, *Ley de Educación Nacional*, No. 26,206 (2006). chrome-extension://efaidnb mnnnibpcajpcglclefindmkaj/viewer.html?pdfurl = https%3A%2F%2Fwww.argentina. gob.ar%2Fsites%2Fdefault%2Ffiles%2Fley-de-educ-nac-58ac89392ea4c.pdf&clen=114 322&chunk=true
12. Article 5, *Ley de Educación Nacional*, No. 26,206 (2006).
13. Article 9. *Ley de Educación Nacional*, No. 26,206 (2006).
14. Article 10, *Ley de Educación Nacional*, No. 26,206 (2006). Author's translation.
15. Data from UNESCO cited by the World Bank in https://data.worldbank.org/indicator/ SE.ADT.LITR.ZS?locations=ZJ
16. See https://www.indec.gob.ar/indec/web/Nivel3-Tema-4-33. The next census is scheduled for April 2022.
17. The province of La Rioja also scores low on the HDI, with a score of 0.833, but it performs better than the rest in literacy rates.
18. The city of Buenos Aires had an estimated population of 3,068,043 in 2018 according to projections based on the 2010 national census, while Córdoba's population was 3,683,937 and Santa Fe's population was estimated at 3,481,514. See Argentine Education Ministry,

Pan-American Health Organization and World Health Organization (2020), *Indicadores básicos Argentina 2020*, chrome-extension://efaidnbmnnnibpcajpcglclefindmkaj/viewer. html?pdfurl = https%3A%2F%2Fwww.argentina.gob.ar%2Fsites%2Fdefault%2Ffiles%2Fi ndicadores_basicos_2020.pdf&clen=629386&chunk=true

19. See Argentine Education Ministry. Anuario Estadístico 2018. https://www.argentina.gob. ar/sites/default/files/anuario-estadistico-datos-2018-web.pdf

20. Article 8, *Ley de Financiamiento Educativo* No. 26075 (2005). https://www.argentina.gob. ar/normativa/nacional/ley-26075-112976/texto

21. Article 14, *Ley de Financiamiento Educativo* No. 26075 (2005). https://www.argentina.gob. ar/normativa/nacional/ley-26075-112976/texto

22. See Article 17, *Ley de Financiamiento Educativo* No. 26075 (2005). https://www.argentina. gob.ar/normativa/nacional/ley-26075-112976/texto

23. School population data are from 2003 and were included in Annex I of the Education Financing Law. See *Ley de Financiamiento Educativo No. 26,075, Anexo I* (2005). https:// www.argentina.gob.ar/normativa/nacional/ley-26075-112976/texto

24. See Secretaría de Innovación y Calidad Educativa. 2015. *Sistema Educativo Nacional: Informe Estadístico 2015.*

25. The student protests in Chile are an exception (see Mizala and Schneider, Chapter 44, this volume).

26. See Mezzadra et al. (2010). Aportes estatales a la educación de gestión privada en la provincia de Buenos Aires. Documento de trabajo No. 51. CIPPEC. https://www.cippec. org/wp-content/uploads/2017/03/2525.pdf

27. See Asociación Civil por la Igualdad y la Justicia. 2011. *Subsidios Estatales a Escuelas de Gestión Privada en la Ciudad de Buenos Aires: falta de transparencia y profundización de las desigualdades.* https://acij.org.ar/wp-content/uploads/2011/11/Subsidio-a-privadas-web.pdf\

28. See Mezzadra and Rivas (2010).

29. See Secretaría de Innovación y Calidad Educativa. 2015. *Sistema Educativo Nacional: Informe Estadístico 2015.*

30. Aggregate data on public spending on education as a percentage of GDP is taken from the World Bank: https://datos.bancomundial.org/indicador/SE.XPD.TOTL.GD.ZS?locati ons=AR&most_recent_year_desc=true

31. World Bank: https://datos.bancomundial.org/indicador/SE.XPD.TOTL.GD.ZS?locati ons=AR&most_recent_year_desc=true

32. World Bank: https://datos.bancomundial.org/indicador/SE.XPD.TOTL.GD.ZS?locati ons=AR&most_recent_year_desc=true

33. See Tiramonti, G., Volman, V., & Braga, F. (2021). *Conectividad y dispositivos: actividades escolares de los alumnos de barrios populares durante la interrupción de clases presenciales.* Observatorio Argentinos por la Educación. chrome-extension://efaidnbmnnnibpcajpcglcle findmkaj/viewer.html?pdfurl = https%3A%2F%2Fcms.argentinosporlaeducacion.org%2Fme dia%2Freports%2Finforme-conectividad-y-dispositivos.pdf&clen=846342&chunk=true

34. See Tiramonti et al. (2021).

35. See Decree 459/2010. http://servicios.infoleg.gob.ar/infolegInternet/anexos/165000-169 999/165807/norma.htm

36. See Fundación Lúminis: https://www.fundacionluminis.org.ar/datos-abiertos-educac ion/netbooks-entregadas-por-localidad-y-provincia-hasta-el-2014

37. See Tedesco, J. C., Steinberg, C., & Tófalo, A. (2015). Programa TIC y Educación Básica: Informe General". UNICEF. chrome-extension://efaidnbmnnnibpcajpcglclefindmkaj/viewer. html?pdfurl = https%3A%2F%2Fwww.unicef.org%2Fargentina%2Fmedia%2F546%2Ff ile%2FInforme%2520general.pdf&clen=2396695&chunk=true

38. See Tedesco et al. (2015).
39. See Odicino, M. C. (2009). Implementación y resultados de la incorporación de las TIC en el proceso de enseñanza-aprendizaje. Oral presentation at the Congreso de Educación Enseñando en Entornos Digitales. chrome-extension://efaidnbmnnnibpcajpcglclefindm kaj/viewer.html?pdfurl = https%3A%2F%2Fwww.buenosaires.gob.ar%2Fareas%2Feducac ion%2Fed%2Fpdf%2Fmcodicino.pdf&clen=114017&chunk=true
40. See Odicino (2009).
41. See Artopoulos, A. (2021). *¿Cuántos estudiantes tienen acceso a internet en su hogar en Argentina?* Report published by Observatorio Argentinos por la Educación. chrome-extension://efaidnbmnnnibpcajpcglclefindmkaj/viewer.html?pdfurl   = https%3A%2F%2Fcms.argentinosporlaeducacion.org%2Fmedia%2Freports%2FArgxEd u_Conectividad_Coronavirus_.pdf&clen=868687&chunk=true
42. In contrast to the other national and subnational one-to-one programs, the one implemented in La Rioja provided laptop computers to students in both public and private schools. See Ministerio de Educación, Ciencia y Tecnología de la Provincia de La Rioja, "Plan de Inclusión Digital."
43. See Ministerio de Educación, Ciencia y Tecnología de la Provincia de La Rioja, "Plan de Inclusión Digital."
44. See Ministerio de Educación, Ciencia y Tecnología de la Provincia de La Rioja, "Plan de Inclusión Digital."
45. See Artopoulos (2021).
46. See Gobierno de la Ciudad de Buenos Aires, *Plan Sarmiento Buenos Aires. Informe de Monitoreo 2017.* https://www.buenosaires.gob.ar/sites/gcaba/files/ueicee2018_seguimi ento_plan_sarmiento.pdf
47. At this point, the city of Buenos Aires was governed by Horacio Rodríguez Larreta, also from the center-right Propuesta Republicana.

References

Ardanaz, M., Leiras, M., & Tommasi, M. (2014). The politics of federalism in Argentina and its implications for governance and accountability. *World Development, 53,* 26–45.

Artopoulos, A. (2021). ¿Cuántos estudiantes tienen acceso a internet en su hogar en Argentina?" Report published by Observatorio Argentinos por la Educación. chrome-extension:// efaidnbmnnnibpcajpcglclefindmkaj/viewer.html?pdfurl=https%3A%2F%2Fcms.argen tinosporlaeducacion.org%2Fmedia%2Freports%2FArgxEdu_Conectividad_Coronavir us_.pdf&clen=868687&chunk=true

Beech, J., & Barrenechea, I. (2011). Pro-market educational governance: Is Argentina a black swan? *Critical Studies in Education, 52,* 279–293.

Behrend, J. (2000). The *carpa blanca*—Civil society and democratic process: A study of teachers' protests and political response in Argentina, 1997–1999 [MPhil thesis in Latin American Studies, University of Oxford].

Behrend, J. (2011). The unevenness of democracy at the subnational level: Provincial closed games in Argentina. *Latin American Research Review, 46,* 150–176.

Behrend, J., & Bianchi, M. (2017). Estructura económica y política subnacional en Argentina. *Caderno CRH, 30,* 217–235.

Behrend, J., & Whitehead, L. (2016). *Illiberal practices: Territorial variance within large federal democracies.* Johns Hopkins University Press.

Brinks, D., Levitsky, S., & Murillo, M. V. (2019). *Understanding institutional weakness: Power and design in Latin American institutions*. Cambridge University Press.

Di John, J. (2007). Albert Hirschman's exit-voice framework and its relevance to problems of public education performance in Latin America. *Oxford Development Studies, 35*, 295–327.

Eaton, K. (2017). *Territory and ideology in Latin America: Policy conflicts between national and subnational governments*. Oxford University Press.

Falleti, T. (2010). *Decentralization and subnational politics in Latin America*. Cambridge University Press.

Gibson, E. L. (2005). Boundary control: Subnational authoritarianism in democratic countries. *World Politics, 58*, 101–132.

Giraudy, A., Moncada, E., & Snyder, R. (2019). *Inside countries: Subnational research in comparative politics*. Cambridge University Press.

Gvirtz, S., & Beech, J. (2007). The internationalization of education policy in Latin America. In M. Hayden, J. Levy, & J. Thompson (Eds.), *The SAGE handbook of research in international education* (1st ed., pp. 462–475). Sage. https://doi.org/10.4135/9781848607866.n39

Held, D., & McGrew, A. (2002). The great globalization debate: An introduction. In D. Held & A. McGrew (Eds.), *The global transformations reader: An introduction to the globalization debate* (pp. 1–79). Polity Press.

Mezzadra, F., & Rivas, A. (2010). Aportes estatales a la educación de gestión privada en la provincia de Buenos Aires. Working Document No. 51. CIPPEC. https://www.cippec.org/wp-content/uploads/2017/03/2525.pdf

Niedzwiecki, S. (2018). *Uneven social policies: The politics of subnational variation in Latin America*. Cambridge University Press.

Odicino, M. C. (2009). Implementación y resultados de la incorporación de las TIC en el proceso de enseñanza-aprendizaje. Oral presentation at the Congreso de Educación Enseñando en Entornos Digitales. chrome-extension://efaidnbmnnnibpcajpcglclefindmkaj/viewer.html?pdfurl=https%3A%2F%2Fwww.buenosaires.gob.ar%2Fareas%2Feducacion%2Fed%2Fpdf%2Fmcodicino.pdf&clen=114017&chunk=true

Rokkan, S. (1970). *Citizens, elections, parties: Approaches to the comparative study of the processes of development*. David McKay Company.

Scholte, J. A. (2002). What is global about globalization? In D. Held & A. McGrew (Eds.), *The global transformations reader: An introduction to the globalization debate* (pp. 84–91). Polity Press.

Snyder, R. (2001). Scaling down: The subnational comparative method. *Studies in Comparative International Development, 36*, 93–110.

Tarrow, S. (1978). Introduction. In S. Tarrow, P. J. Katzenstein, & L. Graziano (Eds.), *Territorial politics in industrial nations* (pp. 1–27). Praeger.

Tedesco, J. C., Steinberg, C., & Tófalo, A. (2015). Programa TIC y Educación Básica: Informe General. Report published by UNICEF. chrome-extension://efaidnbmnnnibpcajpcglclefindmkaj/viewer.html?pdfurl=https%3A%2F%2Fwww.unicef.org%2Fargentina%2Fmedia%2F546%2Ffile%2FInforme%2520general.pdf&clen=2396695&chunk=true

Tiramonti, G., Volman, V., & Braga, F. (2021). Conectividad y dispositivos: actividades escolares de los alumnos de barrios populares durante la interrupción de clases presenciales. Report published by Observatorio Argentinos por la Educación. chrome-extension://efaidnbmnnnibpcajpcglclefindmkaj/viewer.html?pdfurl=https%3A%2F%2Fcms.argentinosporlaeducacion.org%2Fmedia%2Freports%2Finforme-conectividad-y-dispositivos.pdf&clen=846342&chunk=true

CHAPTER 42

ECONOMIC GLOBALIZATION AND EVOLUTION OF EDUCATION SPENDING IN THE BRAZILIAN FEDERATION, 2013–2019

CRISTIANE BATISTA AND STEVEN DUTT-ROSS

INTRODUCTION

THE financial crisis undergone by Latin America in the 1970s, coupled with the explosive foreign debt crisis of the subsequent decade, gave rise to a model that started being applied to countries in the region since the mid-1980s prescribed by the World Bank, the International Monetary Fund, and the US government, the so-called Washington Consensus. The model advanced a structural adjustment to be applied through privatization and market-oriented liberal policies, focused on the deregulation of the economy, commercial and financial opening, the privatization of the public sector, and the reduction of state intervention in the supply of goods and services of a social nature. In the short term, the objective was to diminish the fiscal deficit through the reduction of public spending.

In practice, countries that did not rely on a structured and professionalized welfare state, with consistent universal social policies, began adopting adjustment policies with the aim of opening commerce and achieving fiscal equilibrium in detriment of social policies. In order to compensate for the lack of a consolidated social safety net, these countries were left with no option but to implement emergency social policies, whose focus was no longer universal, characterizing them as assistance states, or as public benefactors, and not as states built upon a foundation of universalism, equality, and gratuity of services.[1] In turn, countries that already relied on universal social policies (social pension, basic education, and healthcare) witnessed the further deterioration of their already precarious social conditions due to the dismantling of such policies.

In sum, this was the context of the advent of globalization in Latin America which spurred the academic debate concerning the impact of commercial liberalization on the production of domestic public policy. The goal of part of these works was to discover whether the intense process of internationalization of markets, productive systems, and the trend toward monetary unification, to which countries in the American continent subscribed, resulted in the loss of sovereignty. One of the main questions asked by these academic studies was whether the crises of the 1970s and 1980s—which led to consequences in terms of macroeconomic, financial, and productive imbalances—also affected the internal economic and political decisions of developing countries to the extent they homogenized patterns of production and consumption, thus imposing at the international level the implementation of neoliberal policy.[2]

There is no consensus within the literature investigating the impact of globalization on domestic public policies in countries affected by commercial liberalization. One strand of investigation, applied to the countries belonging to the Organization for Economic Cooperation and Development (OECD), favors the theory of "compensation" according to which globalization stimulates investment in human capital with the goal of protecting the population against the damage caused by exposure to the international market.[3] Another strand in the literature contends that, for the case of Latin American countries, the most adequate one is the "efficiency" theory according to which greater exposure to international competition results in, contrary to the first strand, diminished social spending as a form of containing public spending.[4] However, some studies on the region go beyond and seek to prove that greater or lesser impact of globalization on public policy varies according to the indicator of commercial liberalization utilized and how data were treated, whether in aggregate or nonaggregate form.[5]

A part of the comparative analyses typically focuses on the national political context, making comparisons between countries, and in general does not consider the subnational context in federative political systems. This is especially the case in studies looking at the effect of globalization on domestic policies. This procedure can be explained considering the fact that economics is a subject that is in principle international and national in scope and is thus less vulnerable to local influence. However, we would like to argue that globalization is not a phenomenon that occurs beyond the boundaries of the national state and its institutions, especially when there are federalist political systems. The regional dynamic among nations is conceived and organized by each country, by negotiations and policies that, although global, must deal with national or even subnational political systems and scenarios.[6]

One must take into additional account that in the Brazilian case the advent of globalization brought along proposals of fiscal, administrative, and social decentralization. In terms of social policy specifically, with the exception of the welfare system, many actions were carried out gradually, transferring federal attributions to the state and local levels of government. In education in particular, the 1988 Federal Constitution and its posterior amendments determined that states and municipalities earmarked at least 25%

of their budget toward the maintenance and development of teaching. Although the Constitution stipulates a binding level of spending, a first glance at data allows us to observe a variation among states and at different times. This leads us to question whether, despite the supposed rigidness of this expense and in the context of globalization, this variation can be attributed to the systematic effects of other political, socioeconomic, and/or sociodemographic variables.

Building upon a critical evaluation of studies on the effect of commercial opening on local public policies, this investigation focuses on some of the factors that impinge upon the expenditure executed by states in a decentralized policy area like education that has constitutionally mandated minimum spending thresholds, in the period spanning from 2013 to 2019. One of the independent variables we will be observing is the degree to which these subnational units open up to the international market, which will be measured as a function of net exports.

Very often in this literature we observe the use of the most extensive possible temporal series, as for example, the period covering the entirety of the period of redemocratization, that is, since the new Constitution came into being. However, considering the expense indicators in education concerns as to the consistency of data requires some caveats, such as attention to the uniformity in the criteria used to group these expenses. Methodological changes adopted by the National Treasury (*Secretaria do Tesouro Nacional*) in 2015, the body responsible for the consolidation of accounting data of all subunits of the Brazilian federation, including those pertaining to education, made it possible to obtain consistent data specifically for this period.[7]

This chapter is organized in three sections (in addition to this introduction and the final remarks). The first one briefly recounts the process of decentralization of educational policy in Brazil. The second one presents a synthesis of the studies on the impact of globalization on domestic public policies and the main theories in this regard. It also synthesizes literature on the diversification of economies and the results of policies. Lastly, the third section presents our methodology in addition to the main findings of this exploratory analysis.

The Decentralization of Education in Brazil

The 1980s marks the period of redemocratization in Brazil and the emergence of the project of state reform, whose main goal consisted of reducing the participation of the Union and increasing the role of subnational units in the decision-making process and administration of public policy.[8] This process made way for political, fiscal, and administrative decentralization and the "restoration" of federalization as the main hope for the improvement of public services and the promotion of income distribution.[9] The main issue decentralization was expected to solve was ensuring that services followed the same format but also catered to regional and local needs and specificities. The reforms carried out the following decades through common legislation, constitutional amendments, or ministry-level norms reshaped the coordination of each area of public policy and reinforced the commitment of subnational units in social policy.

The pattern of state intervention in the realm of social policy had been characterized until then by fragmented policies that were often interrupted and often dependent upon charity institutions. Education, in particular, was crippled by technological and curricular lags, an insufficient and unequal coverage of the educational network, and student retention due to the low quality of services offered.[10] In 1983, still under the aegis of the 1967 Federal Constitution, Amendment number 24, known as the Calmon Amendment, marked the return of educational policy to the national agenda as it stipulated that the Union had the obligation of annually investing no less than 15% of the income from taxes in the maintenance and development of education, whereas states, the Federal District, and municipalities were to reserve at least 25%. Later, the 1988 Federal Constitution ratified education as a citizen right and established it as a duty of the state, expected to find solutions as public policy and not as the result of voluntary collaboration of citizens. In addition, it increased the minimum mandatory percentage to be followed by the Union to 18% and maintained state spending at 25%.[11] The Constitution thus enacted education as a state responsibility and as a political right, moving beyond the practice of educational programs that were either emergency-driven, directed at certain groups, or dependent upon charity.

Although these constitutional mechanisms defined the minimum percentages of investment in each subnational unit in the realm of education, there was a gap in terms of the definition of individual responsibilities. In order to correct this distortion, Constitutional Amendment number 14 was sanctioned in 1996, determining that the three levels of government ought to act in collaboration and in tandem through the division of responsibilities according to the level of education. Thus municipalities were entrusted with child and basic education, the states and the Federal District were made responsible for basic and intermediate education, and the Union for higher education. In addition to these attributions, Amendment 14 enacted the Fund for the Maintenance and Development of Elementary Education and Strengthening of Teacher Training (*Fundo de Manutenção e Desenvolvimento do Ensino Fundamental e de Valorização do Magistério* [FUNDEF]), comprising funds from states and municipalities.[12] The distribution of FUNDEF (later renamed FUNDEB) resources varies according to the proportion of the number of schools enrolled in state and municipal elementary education network and earmarks 60% of its resources toward teachers' salaries. The remaining 40% goes toward the development and maintenance of elementary education.[13]

As discussed, even though the decentralization of education in Brazil is prior to redemocratization, the new configuration of the state brought about the need to restructure social policy in general and educational policy in particular, according to the new roles of states and municipalities, in addition to acknowledging the need to improve its quality considering international standards in an increasingly globalized and competitive scenario. The 1988 Federal Constitution was a legal watershed of this new model of organization of the state and social policy in Brazil and greatly impacts the current reality of spending.

Today, studies on the effect of globalization in domestic policy seem to have lost ground in the specialized literature especially in comparison to the academic output in the 1980s and 1990s. This, however, does not seem to be the result of the weakening of its effect but rather reflects an accommodation to a new reality in which frontiers, especially economic ones, have been breached. With this in mind, our main goal in this chapter is to analyze the behavior of spending in a specific social policy—education—in a still globalized context.[14] In other words, we set out to identify some of the factors that affect net spending in each state in a more recent period, spanning from 2013 to 2019. One of these factors is the degree to which these subnational units open up their economies to the international market, which will be measured in terms of exports.

In this section we have seen that spending in education became strongly regulated after the 1988 Federal Constitution and later amendments came into effect, entailing a reduction of discretion of local political actors in terms of the decision-making process of the policies. On the other hand, our decision to use educational spending as a dependent variable, with a relatively high minimum spending threshold that is constitutionally mandated, is decisive, given its rigidity. The fact that this spending is rigidly defined leads us to assume that there will be no significant variation attributed to the systematic effects of political, socioeconomic, and/or sociodemographic variables. This is what we shall see.

It is important to point out that our goal in this chapter is outright descriptive rather than explanatory. We build upon the hypothesis that commercial opening/liberalization impacted social spending in OECD countries (Garret, 1998) and also in Latin America (Stokes, 1997). In this sense, we are not putting forward a hypothesis to test, nor advancing a new explanation of the impact of globalization on social spending. We believe, however, that an exploratory analysis of the available information provides rich material for future analyses, employing more rigorous and "scientific" contours.

GLOBALIZATION, SOCIOECONOMIC STRUCTURE, AND PUBLIC POLICY

Garret (1998), in a study focusing on OECD countries, verifies that globalization limited the capacity of governments to stimulate the economy, adopting the classical Keynesian recipe of loose monetary policy and public debt. It argues that for left-leaning governments globalization increases the political incentives for the redistribution of wealth, in addition to actions aimed at preventing the poor and workers from the insecurity caused by greater exposure to market competition, as a form of "compensation." These actions, in turn, would be rendered viable through the significant increase of taxes and social public spending.

Analyses regarding the Latin American context argue that "efficiency" theory is the most adequate theory for the region. According to Stokes (1997), greater exposure of national economies to international competition leads to the uniform adoption of economic policies that favor the market and diminishes the role of the state in social life. According to the author, there is an intense conflict among electors and markets concerning the economic policy to be adopted. On one hand, electors push politicians toward social security policies aiming at social well-being in an incremental campaign until elections, while markets push politicians toward public policies whose goal is efficiency and implementing reforms that did not undergo the referendum of elections. In sum, Stokes's argument eliminates in the context of commercial liberalization any causal component originating from domestic institutions and points to the fact that Latin American countries are more vulnerable to market pressure and thus can be more adequately explained by the theory of "efficiency" than the theory of "compensation," as Garret proposes for OECD countries.[15]

In another study based on Latin America, Takahashi (2001) finds that in a globalized world, the increase of social spending is explained by the political desire of politicians of simultaneously achieving economic growth and social equality. More specifically, economic liberalization of countries in the region would have been responsible for greater fragmentation of the labor market and consequently the gap between the formal and informal sectors, including in terms of each one's preferences regarding social spending priorities. In this sense, formal sector workers would have a more favorable view of social security spending because, theoretically, they already have this protection ensured by law. On the other hand, informal sector workers would prefer more investment in health and education, since access to these services would not be legally ensured. Therefore, the author's main hypothesis is that the greater the size of the informal sector—a growth caused by globalization—the greater the demand for spending in healthcare and education.[16] According to Takahashi, political institutions and the government's ideology have minimal influence on the variation of social spending, which, in Latin America, would be a product of the economy rather than politics.

Takahashi's work (2004) is inspired by Kaufman and Segura-Ubiego (2001), who in their study also on Latin America, came to the conclusion that the effects of political variables on aggregate social spending are weak and inconsistent, but that globalization and domestic policies have a far more complex impact when social spending is treated in a disaggregated way.[17] In the first analysis of the data (aggregate social spending), the authors find that, in the short term, commercial liberalization has a negative impact on social spending. However, once data are disaggregated into spending with pension, on one hand, and healthcare and education—so-called human capital—on the other, there is evidence that commercial expansion reduces investment in social security, even if its impacts on investment in healthcare and education remain unclear. Kaufman and Ubiego's main conclusion is that each one of the three categories of social spending—aggregate, social security, and human capital—undergoes influence of different sets of political and economic factors. In sum, if on one side the restriction globalization imposes upon aggregate social spending, specifically social security, does not apply to spending in human capital, on the other side an improvement of health and education indicators cannot be observed either.[18]

Following the same line of reasoning, also concerning the Latin American context, Avelino et al. (2005) conclude that different indicators of commercial liberalization lead to radically distinct results. Measured in relation to current GDP, commercial liberalization negatively impacts aggregate social spending; however, if the measurement is made using purchase power parity (PPP), the impact is positive albeit nonsignificant. Yet, when disaggregating data on social spending on healthcare, education, and social security, a positive and significant association with spending on education and social security can be observed.

Although part of the literature questions the autonomy of domestic policy in a globalized context, especially in developing nations, our gambit in this study is based on two central premises: the premise of the structuring nature of economic development and its impact on the production of public policy; and the premise of the relative autonomy of states in shaping local economic and social policies. There is a literature that analyzes the relationship between voter preferences and the local structural environment. Although this literature makes reference to electoral behavior and not public policy results, its findings encourage an analysis based on these premises.[19] Allow us to make our case.

In terms of the first premise, the research conducted by Santos et al. (2018) can serve as an example. The authors set out to advance a unified theory of state politics in Brazil in which the degree of economic development of states as well as the ideology of state governments and their alignment to the federal government plays a determinant role in the variation of spending on healthcare and education. The tests carried out for the period of 2012–2013 indicated that, in the comparative analysis of theories derived from political sociology and political science, both showed relevant results. With regard to the political sociology perspective, a positive relation was found between education spending and level of urbanization of the Brazilian states, and states with higher levels of urbanization displayed greater spending on education.[20] With regard to the political science perspective, the econometric tests showed that states governed by left-wing parties who had a legislative majority spent more on healthcare, although these results do not occur with the same consistency in the area of education spending.

For a broader context, a study conducted by Batista (2008) shows a variation in terms of social spending in Latin American countries during the 1980s and 1990s, indicating the commercial liberalization did not undermine the autonomy of these nations in terms of the ability to determine public policy. The tests developed by the author show that the factor with the greatest effects on healthcare and education spending is linked to domestic characteristics, such as the ideology of the head of the executive and the level of legislative support.

Regarding the premise of economic structure and its impact on public policy, one important reason to consider socioeconomic variables can be found in the studies authored by Desposato (2001). According to the author, voters in states with lower indicators of economic development would be more vulnerable to the clientelistic style of political exchange, given the material immediate needs of these localities that are lacking in goods and services. In other words, politicians and parties who are more capable of providing short-term benefits for voters have a greater shot at achieving success in the ballot box. Otherwise, voters in states with higher indexes of educational levels prioritize agendas in which goods and services are considered public policy issues, even if long-term ones, and thus prefer candidates who display a more ideological or program-based platform.

Following a similar line of reasoning, a recent study by Barberia et al. (2018) considers the variation of productive structures in states in order to verify greater or lesser incidence of economic vote, estimated based on the probability of re-election of incumbent office holders. In other words, in political units endowed with greater industrial development and an advanced services sector and that are less fiscally dependent, agendas that prioritize the local economy would lead to compensation. In practical terms, voters in more industrialized regions who prioritize the economic agenda create jobs and thus preserve jobs, an effect conditioned by the fiscal autonomy of the state vis-à-vis government transfers. Otherwise, in states in which the agricultural sector is the main productive activity, electors did not decide their vote for state governor based on the economic conditions of the state.[21] In this sense, according to the authors, the alternation or continuation of parties in control of state governments, via economic results linked to public policies, would depend on the degree of industrialization and labor organization of that geographic locality and the fiscal autonomy of the incumbents.

For the purposes of our argument, an important change must be pointed out: the economic diversification of states previously considered underdeveloped and whose economies were based on agriculture, and that have now also become major exporters of raw materials. Brazil's rural economy has undergone a profound transformation with the injection of capital, high increases of productivity, and a structure geared toward the production of commodities. Geographically, production is concentrated in the South and Midwest regions of the country, and no longer in the Northeast.[22] This last region has become basically urban and focused on industry and services. Once fertile ground for *coronelismo* (Nunes Leal, 1946) and *governismo* (Zucco, 2008), the Northeast is more pluralistic economically and politically. Thus, in the decades after redemocratization, the economy's profile has changed, with more diversity in areas once characterized by large rural properties.

The question here therefore is to unveil how these changes impacted social policy in states. Our argument considers that the variable to be observed is the expenditure effectively executed in each state in the period from 2013 to 2019. The objective is to identify some intervening factors that can account for these expenditures, such as the export economies of subnational units of the Brazilian federation (specifically the net value of exports), which is used here as a proxy for globalization, especially in regions with a commodity-based economy.

Methodology and Results

Exploratory analysis can be defined as a set of techniques capable of extracting and summarizing an investigated phenomenon. It allows researchers to identify any type of trend or behavioral pattern and employ them in the construction of inferences when there is little previous knowledge concerning the structure of relationships that involve the phenomena being investigated. The information contained in a data set can be summarized through adequate numerical measurements, named summary statistics, or descriptive statistics through their central and noncentral values, their dispersion, or form of distribution of values around the average (Favero & Belfiore, 2017).

In this sense, this exploratory study was carried out considering the relationship between the variables *resources paid on education* and *net total exports* (*Free on Board*) by state and by year—2013 to 2019. The collection and analysis of data were carried out using the R statistical programming language (R Core Team, 2020). Data concerning spending in education were collected through the System of Accounting and Fiscal Information of the Brazilian Public Sector.[23] This indicator represents the second stage of execution of spending by the government; it is preceded by earmarking and followed by the effective payment. Meanwhile, the data on exports were extracted from *ComexStat*, a consultation system for the extraction of data on Brazilian exports,[24] which compiles on a month-by-month basis database information on exports and imports from the Foreign Trade System (*Sistemas de Comércio Exterior*—SISCOMEX).[25]

After concentrating this base into a single data set, the procedure was to transform both the resources paid on education and the net export values, which are provided in nominal values, in year-adjusted real values for 2019. In other words, the effect of inflation was discounted for the period analyzed using the Consumer Price Index (*Preços ao Consumidor Amplo*—IPCA) as the measure of inflation.[26] Next, both variables were calculated per capita, dividing their initial values by the population. The goal was to standardize the information and thus allow for variable crossing and also to avoid distortions in the comparison of states of different population sizes.[27] Lastly, for the intersection of variables, we used the Spearman correlation coefficient, a nonparametric variable used to measure the association between two quantitative/ordinary variables.[28]

The results of the Spearman correlation tests for the period ranging from 2013 to 2019 are shown in Table 42.1 and indicate a negative association between spending in education and exports. For an exploratory analysis, this means that the higher total net exports of a state, the lower spending in education tends to be.

The dispersion diagrams illustrated in Figure 42.1 translate graphically the correlation between educational spending and net exports.

As the correlation coefficients have already shown, the dispersion diagram reveals a negative association between spending in education and the net total value of exports. Regarding education, most states are plotted close to the spending line of

Table 42.1 Correlation Coefficient Between Education and Exports, per Capita 2013–2019

Year	Correlation
2013	−0.12
2014	−0.04
2015	−0.04
2016	−0.12
2017	−0.14
2018	−0.08
2019	−0.12

1,000 *reais* per inhabitant, with the exception of a few states in the North region and the Federal District.[29] As stated earlier, the decision to transform the resources paid on education in a per capita indicator was made considering the need to standardize the information and allow a comparison between Brazilian states with differing population sizes. The result of this, for example, is that the state of Bahia, ranked sixth in resources paid on education and the fourth most populous state, is among the states with the lowest levels of spending per capita. On the other hand, Roraima, one of the states with the lowest spending and population, is among those with the highest per capita levels.

Regarding exports, during the period being investigated, the state of Mato Grosso stands out as the lead exporter and ranks at a relatively intermediate level in terms of educational spending, although still above states whose economies are based on services such as those located in the Northeast region. This point deserves to be highlighted. The state of Mato Grosso, along with the state of Goiás and Mato Grosso do Sul, belongs to the Midwest region of the country. The economies in this region have become geared toward the production of commodities, with intense capital investment and enhancement of productivity. Among the main exports of Mato Grosso are agricultural commodities such as soy, corn, and cotton. On the other hand, the dispersion diagrams show states of the Northeast regions, whose economies are largely dependent on services, with lower levels of export.

Table 42.2 synthesizes the five main export items according to region in 2019.

Figure 42.2 allows us to visualize the distribution of educational spending and exports in the Brazilian territory. As already revealed by the dispersion diagrams, the maps suggest that the states in the North are those that most invest in education per capita, and that the state of Mato Grosso is the lead exporter. It is important to mention that the gray-colored areas of the map indicate the lack of available information for the states of Pará and Rio Grande do Norte in 2014 and the state of Alagoas in 2016 and 2017.

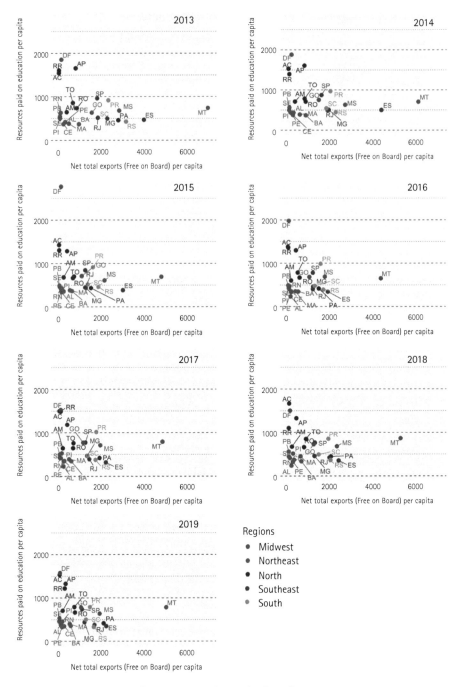

FIGURE 42.1 Resources paid on education, by total value of exports per capita 2013–2019.
(*Source*: Based on data from the National Treasury and COMEXSTAT)

Table 42.2 Five Main Export Items, by Geographical Region in 2019

	Midwest	Northeast	North	Southeast	South
1	Soybeans, including crush, excluding seeds	Soybeans, including crush, not for seeding	Iron ore and its concentrates, except for pyrites (pyrite ashes), nonagglomerated	Crude oil	Soybeans, including crush, not for seeding
2	Corn grain, excluding seeds	Wood chemical pastes, soda or sulphate based, except for dissolution pastes, semi-whitewashed or whitewashed, from nonconifers	Other copper minerals and their concentrates	Iron ore and its concentrates, except for pyrites (pyrite ashes), nonagglomerated	Edible poultry parts and offal, frozen
3	Deboned beef, frozen	Calcinated aluminum	Soybeans, including crush, excluding seeds	Raw coffee beans, non-decaffeinated	Non manufactured tobacco, totally or partially stemmed, Virginia grade flue cured leaves
4	Mash and other solid residues from soybean oil extraction	Combustible oil	Calcinated aluminium	Other cane sugars	Wood chemical pastes, soda or sulphate based, except for dissolution pastes, semi-whitewashed or whitewashed, from nonconifers
5	Wood chemical pastes, soda or sulphate based, except for dissolution pastes, semi-whitewashed or whitewashed, from nonconifers	Other semi-manufactured iron or nonalloyed steel products, with rectangular cross-sections, composed by less of 0.25% carbon in weight	Deboned beef, frozen	Other airplanes and air vehicles, unloaded, weighing more than 15 tons	Mash and other solid residues from soybean oil extraction

Source: Based on COMEXSTAT data.

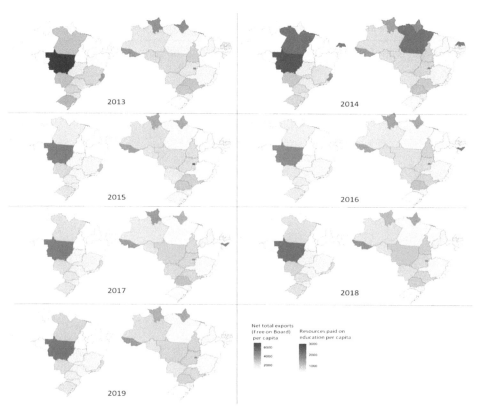

FIGURE 42.2 Distribution of exports and spending on education per capita in Brazil, 2013–2019.
(*Source*: Based on data from the National Treasury and the COMEXSTAT)

The result of the exploratory analyses, employing Spearman correlation, reveals an inversely proportional association between spending in education and exports (the proxy used here for globalization). However, the maps and dispersion diagrams show that the state of Mato Grosso, located in the Midwest region, stands out in terms of exports. This is associated with an intermediate level, comparatively speaking, of spending on education, yet above most Brazilian states. On the other hand, we observe that states whose economics are based on services, such as those in the Northeast, display lower levels of per capita spending on education. What do these results suggest?

As stated earlier, our objective in this chapter is first and foremost descriptive in nature, and not explanatory. Our aim is not to conduct statistical models, hypothesis tests, nor advance explanations about the effect of globalization on educational spending. Rather, our intent is to develop an exploratory analysis of the available data and thus lay out material for future investigations. With this aim in mind, we were able to observe that, based on the correlation coefficients, and on the dispersion diagrams and maps, a systemic negative correlation in the course of time, that is, for all years at the macro-level, between executed expenditure in education and net export values. However, when taking a closer look at the results for each state and region, we noticed that the state with the highest net exports is the state of Mato Grosso, whose economy is largely based on the export of agricultural commodities. Nevertheless, this state shows an intermediate level of educational spending per capita, higher than states whose economies are based on services and industry.

FINAL REMARKS

This chapter sought to identify the main factors that determined educational spending by the Brazilian states between 2013 and 2019. Our intent was to identify in particular whether the new pattern of commercial insertion of the Brazilian economy in the global market, based on the demand for agricultural and primary products, affects the educational spending of subnational units. We argued that in some Brazilian states the intensification of exports, based on commodities, has an impact on the decision-making capacity related to social spending compared to states that are more dependent upon services and domestic industry.

The achieved results based on the Spearman correlation coefficient, dispersion diagrams, and maps indicated that, at a macro-level, there is a negative association, albeit a weak one, consistent throughout the whole period under analysis. In other words, in the aggregated data, we could see that, in our case, greater exposure to international competition reduces investment in social areas with the aim of containing public spending, as defended by the theory of efficiency. However, the analysis disaggregated by state reveals a positive association between exports and spending on education in the state of Mato Grosso, currently the largest exporter of commodities in Brazil.

In turn, the state of Bahia, located in the Northeast of the country, and whose economy is based on services, commerce, and industry, is ranked sixth in executed expenditure in education, and fourth in population, and appears among those with the lowest level of per capita spending in this category. Meanwhile, some states in the North region, such as Acre, Amapá, Roraima, and Tocantins, are among those that display a higher level of educational spending[30] It is important to remember that this result is affected by our decision to homogenize information converting all data relative to educational spending to per capita terms, dividing total sums by population. The North region has 8% of the Brazilian population and is one of the least densely populated regions, while the Northeast is the second in population and home to one third of the Brazilian population.

As stated in the previous section, the choice to use educational spending as a dependent variable, with relatively high minimum spending thresholds that are stipulated by the Constitution, is decisive for our purposes since, in principle, it could lead us to suppose that there will be no variation that can be attributed to the effect of other variables, whether political, socioeconomic, and/or sociodemographic. This is not the case, however. In fact, greater clarity in terms of the impact of these variables on a policy that is rigidly fixed by the Constitution would require another type of analysis, one that would involve the variation of educational spending in Brazilian states beyond the constitutional minimum.

This study, however, proposed an exploratory investigation. The aim was to identity some determining factor in net executed expenditure according to state, and the choice to use this indicator was sufficient to observe some impact of factors that are not necessarily constitutional. Our aim, as stated earlier, was not to carry out statistical inferences through the testing of hypotheses, given the insufficiency of information and methodological restrictions. However, what we are able to extract from the available data suggests the relevance of further investigations to be carried out with greater depth focusing on the effects of globalization on social spending that is regulated in subunits of federal systems. An example would be verifying the hypothesis that states whose economies are based on dynamic and capital-intensive agriculture have more resources available to invest in social policy beyond the minimum constitutional threshold, in the sense of protecting the population from the fluctuations of the international economy and thus contributing toward the reduction of social inequality and poverty.

The principles of universalism, equality, and gratuity of education stipulated by the 1988 Federal Constitution must be upheld and ensured by public policies that are consistent with the expansion of investment, and not its reduction or stagnation. The trend in Brazil is to bind social budgets to expenses, and not investment. In times of economic and political upheaval, the first cuts in spending tend to be in the areas of education and healthcare, as in 2016 during the government of Michel Temer, who ascended to the presidency following the impeachment of Dilma Rousseff. At the time, a Constitutional Amendment was approved—the so-called Public Spending Limit Constitutional Amendment—which thwarted the expansion of social spending for the next 20 years.

The 1988 Federal Constitution was the legal watershed of a new model of Organization of the Brazilian state, attributing federal subunits with responsibilities, including in terms of spending, in relation to social policy. The study in this chapter indicates that, even in a globalized context, the socioeconomic characteristics of states play a role in determining the level of spending in education and thus, even if only in the long run, in public policy in the area. This prompts reflections concerning a new agenda of investigation.

NOTES

1. Soares (2001).
2. See Avelino et al. (2005); Garret (1998); Kaufman & Ubiego (2001); and Stokes (1997).
3. Garret (1998).
4. Kaufman & Ubiego (2001); Stokes (1997).
5. Avelino et al. (2005) verified that commercial liberalization, measured in relation to the gross domestic product (GDP), has a negative impact on aggregate social spending. However, if the utilized measurement is party purchase power (PPP), the impact is positive of nonaggregate social spending on education and social security.
6. See Loureiro (2017).

7. In 2015, the System of Accounting and Fiscal Information in the Brazilian Public Sector (*Sistema de Informações Contábeis e Fiscais do Setor Público Brasileiro*) was created, substituting the System of Accounting Data Collection (*Sistema de Coleta de Dados Contábeis* [SISTN]).
8. This section was inspired by Batista, C. (2018). A Educação no Brasil pós-Constituição de 1988. In P. Cerdeira, F. Vasconcello, R. Sganzerla, *Três Décadas de Reforma Constitucional. Onde e como o Congresso Nacional procurou modificar a Constituição de 1988* (pp. 389–398). FGV Direito Rio.
9. Arretche (2004).
10. Gómez (1999).
11. Federal Constitution, article 212.
12. To learn more about the impact of FUNDEF on the education financing process in Brazil, see Vazquez (2003).
13. The FUNDEB is a special fund comprising resources from the taxation and transfers from states, Federal District, and municipalities that must be bound to education. Its creation substituted the FUNDEF after Constitutional Amendment no. 53/2006 and was regulated by Law no. 11.494/2007 and Decree no. 6.253/2007 as a permanent instrument of public education funding. It is currently regulated by Law no. 14.113, de 25 (FNDE, 2017).
14. The areas that comprise social spending are social welfare, servant benefits, healthcare, education, social assistance, food and nutrition, housing, basic sanitation, labor, agrarian development and culture, labor, and income (Castro et al., 2012).
15. It is important to point out that the study carried out by Garret (1998) applies to European countries with parliamentary political systems, while Stokes's studies (1997) focus on the Latin American context of presidentialism.
16. Takahashi (2004) employs the sum of public spending on education and healthcare as one of the indicators—as percentage of GDP, public spending of the central government and per capita expenditure in US dollars in 1995—described as spending on human capital.
17. See also Avelino et al. (2005).
18. One of the author's interpretations of this result is that the healthcare and education sectors follow a distinct political logic compared to social security, for example, which tend to be more vulnerable to the dynamics of electoral competition and political participation.
19. Examples of these analyses can be found in Desposato (2001); Borges (2011); and Zucco and Power (2013).
20. Regarding spending on healthcare, the results point in the opposite direction of what is expected.
21. Ebeid and Rodden (2006) argue that policies geared toward economic development are favored in urban areas, while the economy in rural areas is more dependent on climate factors and less on political action.
22. The North region comprises the following: Acre, Amapá, Amazona, Pará, Rondônia, Roraima and Tocantins. Northeast: Alagoas, Bahia, Ceará, Maranhão, Paraíba, Pernambuco, Piauí, Rio Grande do Norte, and Sergipe. Midwest: Goiás, Mato Grosso, and Mato Grosso do Sul. Southeast: Espírito Santo, Minas Gerais, Rio de Janeiro, and São Paulo. South: Paraná, Rio Grande do Sul, and Santa Catarina. Federal District: Brasília.
23. https://siconfi.tesouro.gov.br. The data download was performed through the R library *rsiconfi* (BARBALHO, 2020).
24. http://www.mdic.gov.br/balanca/bd/comexstat-bd/ncm/EXP_2013.csv and http://www.mdic.gov.br/balanca/bd/comexstat-bd/ncm/EXP_2019.csv

25. https://portalunico.siscomex.gov.br/portal/
26. Conversion made using the Central Bank API and deflateBR package (Meireles, 2018).
27. Data on size of population in each state were extracted from the website of the *Instituto Brasileiro de Geografia e Estatística* (IBGE): https://www.ibge.gov.br/estatisticas/sociais/populacao/9103-estimativas-de-populacao.html?=&t=resultados
28. The Spearman coefficient is used as an alternative to the Pearson correlation coefficient in cases where there is no bivariate normal distribution and no presence of outliers or ordinal variables.
29. It is worthwhile to point out that, as the capital of the federation, the Federal District is atypical as its spending obligations are the same as of municipalities.
30. The economy of the North region is based on mining, tourism, agriculture, and livestock.

References

Arretche, M. (2004). Federalismo e Políticas Sociais no Brasil: Problemas de Coordenação e Autonomia. *Revista São Paulo em Perspectiva, 18*(2), 111–141.

Avelino, G., Brown, D. S., & Hunter, W. (2005). The effect of capital mobility, trade openness, and democracy on social spending. *American Journal of Political Science, 49*, 625–641.

Barbalho, F.. (2020). rsiconfi: Accounting Data of Brazilian Public Sector. R package version 0.0.0.9000.

Barberia, L., Avelino, G., & Zanlorenssi, G. (2018). Economic voting in Brazil's gubernatorial elections, 1994–2014. *Publius: The Journal of Federalism, 49*(2), 221–249.

Batista, C. (2008). Partidos Políticos, Ideologia e Política Social na América Latina: 1980–1999. *DADOS - Revista de Ciências Sociais, Rio de Janeiro, 51*(3), 633–672.

Batista, C. (2018). A Educação no Brasil pós-Constituição de 1988. In P. Cerdeira, F. Vasconcello, & R. Sganzerla, *Três Décadas de Reforma Constitucional. Onde e como o Congresso Nacional procurou modificar a Constituição de 1988* (pp. 389–398). Direito Rio.

Borges, A. (2011). The political consequences of centre-led redistribution in Brazilian federalism. *Latin American Research Review, 46*(3), 21–45.

Brasil. Decreto n. 660/92. *Aprova o Sistema Integrado de Comércio Exterior—SISCOMEX e sua obrigatoriedade às operações de importações e exportações*. Diário Oficial da República Federativa do Brasil, Brasília.

Desposato, S. (2001). *Institutional theories, societal realities and party politics in Brazil* [PhD dissertation, University of California, Berkeley]. http://swd.ucsd.edu/abstract.pdf

Ebeid, M., & Rodden, J. (2006). Economic geography and economic voting: Evidence from the US states. *British Journal of Political Science, 36*, 527–547.

Favero, L. P., & Belfiore, P. (2017). *Manual de Análise de Dados—Estatística e Modelagem Multivariada com Excel®, SPSS® e Stata®*. GEN LTC, p. 1216.

Garrett, G. (1998). *Partisan politics in the global economy*. Cambridge University Press.

IBGE. (2020). *Estimativas da população residente para os municípios e para as unidades da federação brasileiros com data de referência em 1° de julho de 2020* [notas metodológicas]. IBGE.

Kaufman, R., & Ubiergo, A. S. (2001). Globalization, domestic politics and social spending in Latin America: A, Time-series cross-section analysis, 1973–1997. *World Politics, 53*(July), 553–587.

Loureiro, M. R. (2017). Democracia e Globalização: Políticas de Previdência Social na Argentina, Brasil e Chile. *Lua Nova, 100,* 187–223. https://doi.org/10.1590/0102-187223/100

Meireles, F. (2018). deflateBR: Deflate nominal Brazilian Reais. R package version 1.1.2., 2. https://CRAN.R-project.org/package=deflateBR

Nunes Leal, V. (1975). *Coronelismo, enxada e voto: o município e o regime representativo no Brasil.* Alfa-Ômega.

Portal Siscomex. *Programa Portal Único de Comércio Exterior.* http://portal.siscomex.gov.br/

R Core Team. (2020). R: *A language and environment for statistical computing.* R Foundation for Statistical Computing. https://www.R-project.org/

Santos, F., Batista, C., & Dutt-Ross, S. (2018). Ideologia versus Sociologia na Política Estadual Brasileira. *Revista de Economia Política, 38,* no. 4 (153): 670–689.

Soares, L. T. R. (2001). *Ajuste Neoliberal e Desajuste Social na América Latina.* Vozes.

Stokes, S. (1997). Are parties what's wrong with democracy in Latin America? Trabalho apresentado no 20º Congresso da Latin American Studies Association (LASA), Guadalajara.

Takahashi, Y. (2004). Determinants of social spending in Latin America: Globalization, political institutions, and labor market. Trabalho apresentado no Encontro Annual da American Political Science Association, Setembro 2–5.

Vazquez, D. A. (2003). *Educação, Descentralização e Desequilíbrios Regionais: Os Impactos do FUNDEF* [Dissertação (Mestrado em Economia), Instituto de Economia da Unicamp, Campinas, SP]. http://repositorio.unicamp.br/jspui/handle/REPOSIP/286217

Zucco, C. (2008). The president's "new" constituency: Lula and the pragmatic vote in Brazil's 2006 presidential elections. *Journal of Latin American Studies, 40,* 29–49.

Zucco, C., & Power, T. (2013). Bolsa Família and the shifts in Lula's electoral base; 2002–2006: A reply to Bohn. *Latin American Research Review, 48,* 3–24.

CHAPTER 43

DOES GLOBALIZATION REWARD EDUCATION?

Evidence for Mexico

INGRID BLEYNAT AND LUIS MONROY-GÓMEZ-FRANCO

INTRODUCTION

GLOBALIZATION and education are among the most debated topics within the field of economic development. In a best-case scenario, integration into international markets can allow low- and middle-income countries to diversify their export baskets to encompass the products of sectors that generate higher value-added (Cadot et al., 2011; Hausmann et al., 2007). These sectors, usually in manufacturing industries of different types, are expected to adopt more efficient production techniques and undergo technological upgrading, requiring them to employ a more educated labor force and pay higher wages (Hartmann et al., 2017; Santos-Paulino, 2017). As a result, the accumulation of human capital becomes a condition for outward-looking growth.

Within Latin America, Mexico stands out as being highly integrated into global markets. Over recent decades the country has signed multiple free trade agreements, and it is often described as one of the most open economies in the world. In 2020 foreign trade (the sum of exports and imports) amounted to 78% of GDP, with manufactures representing 17% of the total, compared to the region's respective averages of 46% and 13%.[1] In addition, Mexico has seen a significant improvement in the educational attainment of its population. Starting in the 1990s, Mexico drastically expanded education coverage, leading to a reduction of the gap in years of schooling between rich and poor. In this context, the country saw a substantial reduction of its educational Gini coefficient, which has been identified as a key driver in the fall in income inequality during the 2000s (López-Calva & Lustig, 2010). More recently, Mexico has seen a further increase in the proportion of people with complete upper secondary degrees, which grew from 21% to 25% of the total from 2005 to 2019, while those with college degrees or higher went from 11% to 18% over the same period. This chapter looks at the interplay between these trends in Mexico to assess whether employment in globalized sectors rewards human capital accumulation, as implied by the optimistic narrative given earlier. While we limit our focus to the impact of education on wages, we hope our analysis may contribute to a broader discussion of how contemporary capitalism, including its educational and cultural manifestations, shapes the material well-being of Mexicans.

The chapter proceeds as follows. The first section describes the country's education system and tracks the improvement in the educational attainment of the labor force since 2005, highlighting the gains made by female workers over this period. The second section introduces our two data sources, the National Survey on Occupation and Employment (*Encuesta Nacional de Ocupación y Empleo*, or ENOE) and the 2013 National Input-Output Matrix, and explains how we use them. The third section identifies globalized and nonglobalized economic sectors, classified according to the North American Industry Classification System (NAICS). It also maps the regional and sex patterns of employment in highly globalized industries. The fourth section presents the interaction between the degree of globalization and the educational level of the labor force in different economic sectors. The fifth section then analyzes whether globalization rewards education by using a modified Mincer approach to estimate the evolution of the educational premium by trade exposure of the employment sector. The final section concludes.

RECENT TRENDS IN EDUCATIONAL ATTAINMENT IN MEXICO

As we are interested in analyzing the effects of globalization on the returns to educational investments by workers, a first necessary step is to look at the changes in the educational attainment of the Mexican labor force at the aggregate level, and the educational system within which these took place.

The Mexican educational system comprises three levels. The first segment is basic education, subdivided into initial education (for children 4–6 years old) and primary education (7–12 years old). Secondary education is divided into lower (12–15 years old) and upper secondary education (15–18 years old). Upper secondary comprises high schools and technical schools that grant either a certificate comparable to a high school degree, or a technical degree, which since 2013 is recognized as a final degree. Finally, the third level comprises undergraduate and postgraduate studies. For the 2019–2020 school year, out of 100 students who began primary education, 27 completed college-level studies and only 1 graduated with a technical degree. During the same academic year, 36.5 million students were enrolled in the system, of which 69.2% were in primary education

(SEP, 2020). The vast majority of Mexican students attend public-sector institutions (86% of all students), which are mostly free at point of access. The educational level with the highest private-sector participation is college education, where 30% of students are enrolled in private institutions (SEP, 2020).

The country's current large and complex educational system is the product of a series of reforms implemented starting in the early 1990s (Arnaut & Giorguli, 2010). The first two major changes pertained to primary and lower secondary education and led to a significant expansion of schooling among Mexican children. First, the combination of a political agreement among the federal government, state governments, and the National Teachers Union in 1992 and the General Law of Education of 1993 (Ley General de Educación) decentralized educational policy at the primary and lower secondary levels and made 12 years schooling mandatory for all. State governments became responsible for the management and operation of local educational centers and the training of new teachers. At the same time, under this new law, the federal government retained responsibility for regulating and planning the national curriculum and for the unity and cohesiveness of the national education system. The second major change that took place in this decade was the consolidation of a nationwide system of teacher training, evaluation, and promotion. This included a series of teacher evaluations (which were subsequently extended to administrative personnel) that linked wage increases to teachers' performance. The goal was to promote the continuous training of teachers within the system and to guarantee a general improvement in education quality at the primary and lower secondary levels (Santibañez & Martínez, 2010).

Arnaut and Giorguli (2010) identify some of the achievements and shortcomings of these reforms. On the one hand, the decentralization of educational administration and delivery enabled adjustments of teaching processes to specific regional and state conditions, particularly up to 2007, when federal expenditures were allocated following progressive criteria and thus favored some of the most disadvantaged groups in the country. An example of this is the production of textbooks and official school materials in indigenous languages and the design of school programs aimed at closing the educational gap between rural indigenous populations and the rest of the country (Salmerón Castro & Porras Delgado, 2010). On the other hand, education funding—90% of which pays for teachers and other school personnel—remains limited and unequal, especially in terms of stark asymmetries in the expenditures made by specific states out of their own budgets. This reinforces disparities as poorer, more rural states with geographically scattered populations also face higher education delivery costs than do more affluent, urban ones. Given the relatively small size of the contributions made by some of the poorest state governments, breaking this specific vector of inequality and improving education quality across the country requires a stronger commitment of financial resources and redistributive effort by federal bodies (Mancera Corcuera, 2010).

Despite these and other shortcomings affecting the quality of the education available, especially to the most disadvantaged pupils in the country, it is clear that years of schooling went up considerably at both the national and state levels. This was in part a result of government efforts to guarantee access to educational settings across the territory and in part a result of the conditionalities attached to social programs such as Progresa (first rolled out in 1997 and later renamed Oportunidades and Prospera) (Araujo & Macours, 2021). The proportion of Mexican children aged 5 to 14 that did not attend either primary or lower secondary school declined from 16.5% in 1990 to 10.2% in 2000 and 5.8% in 2015. At the same time, the standard deviation between states went down from 2.2 to 1.6 and to 0.7 in the same years. That is, the pattern of improvement was replicated at the subnational level, with all states showing similar trends. Even the worst-performing states in 2015, Oaxaca and Puebla, achieved a level below 7% (Mancera Corcuera, 2010).

A third major set of changes to the Mexican educational system between 1990 and 2010 involved the expansion of upper secondary and both public and private college-level education opportunities. In terms of upper secondary education, Lorenza Villar Lever (2010) describes a process of quantitative democratization, thanks to higher investment by the federal and state governments, but also highlights a range of persistent qualitative inequalities that continue to plague the system. In 1990, 2.1 million students enrolled in upper secondary education, but 60% of 15- to 18-year-olds did not attend school at this level. By 2000, this had grown to 3 million students, and the nonattendance rate had fallen to 48%. This trend continued, and by the academic year of 2006–2007, only 40% of the relevant age cohort was not enrolled. Progress, however, was not geographically even. While in Mexico City (formerly the Federal District) 92% of 15–18 year olds attended, in Michoacán, only 46% did. Moreover, completion rates remained problematic and present geographical diversity. The national average dropout rate was 15.5% in 2006–2007, but in Puebla and Nuevo León, for example, they were 11.7% and 22.2%, respectively. Pupils from rural, indigenous, or marginal urban households enroll at substantially lower rates than those from more urban, affluent ones. They also have significantly higher dropout rates, and those who graduate obtain qualifications that are of lower actual or perceived quality (Villa Lever, 2007). To address these issues in 2008, the federal government began attempts to overhaul upper secondary education. This led to a revision of the heterogeneous curricula on offer to focus on shared general competencies and enhanced and systematized evaluation and certification processes (Székely Pardo, 2010).

In terms of college-level education and above, Tuirán and Muñoz analyze the evolution of the system. The number of enrolled students had grown significantly in the 1970s, before the austerity that followed the debt crisis of 1982 put the public system under impossible strain. In this context, poorly regulated private institutions picked up some of the demand, diversifying their offering. By 1989, there were 129 public sector institutions (among federal, state, and technological institutes) compared with 341 private ones. By the early 1990s, the system could only cover 14% of the population between 19 and 23 years, the same level as over a decade earlier. Starting then, and in order to respond to a growing demand for places, the federal government supported and financed an expansion in public provision of higher education opportunities (Mendoza Rojas, 2010). In particular, the period saw the creation and expansion of technological and polytechnic universities throughout the country. Specifically, between 1990 and 2008, 61 technological universities opened their doors, while from 2000 to 2008, 23 new polytechnic universities were built. These universities offer 2-year college degrees in specific technical areas, in order to allow their students an easy entrance to the labor market. However, the lion's share of expansion of higher education opportunities took place among private universities. Private universities more than quadrupled, numbering 1,476 institutions by 2008. This growth in the number of public and private institutions offering higher education degrees, combined with the funding of more places in public ones, led to an increase in the gross coverage rate for the population between 19 and 23 years old, from 12% in 1990 to 27% in 2008. As a result, in the academic year 2008–2009, there were 2.1 million students enrolled in 2,539 institutions. Of these, 34% attended 1677 private universities, while the remaining 66% were spread between 843 public ones. Among those in the public sector, 44% of students attended federal and state public universities, while 16% attended public technological institutions. The rest of those enrolled in public institutions attended teacher training institutions (Tuirán & Muñoz, 2010). While there has been significant progress in creating systems of evaluation and accreditation of degrees, there remains a high level of heterogeneity of the quality of degrees issued. What is more, the greater socioeconomic diversity of the student bodies requires stronger public policy interventions to enhance equality of access. In 2008, only 5 out of 100 young people from the bottom income decile had access to higher education. Barriers of entry affect not just the very poor. In deciles 2 to 7, less than 20 out of 100 people of the relevant age have access, compared with 60 out of 100 in the top decile. Federal authorities have tried to intervene by expanding the offer of technical degrees across the country and by designing scholarship programs (Tuirán & Muñoz, 2010).

The effect of these transformations can be seen in the changes to the composition of the labor force by educational attainment in recent years. Figure 43.1 plots

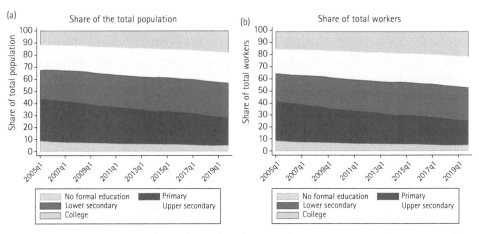

FIGURE 43.1 Composition of population by educational attainment. Note: Lower-secondary school corresponds to the *secundarias* in the Mexican educational system, while upper-secondary school corresponds to *bachillerato* and technical degrees.

(*Source*: ENOE, multiple years)

the evolution of the educational composition of the Mexican population and labor force from 2004 to 2019 based on data from the National Survey on Occupation and Employment (ENOE). One of the most salient trends of the period is the increase in the share of people, and in particular workers, with secondary education (either complete lower secondary or complete upper secondary, which, as we mentioned earlier, includes optional technical orientations). People with complete lower secondary education represented 25% of the total population and 23% of those employed in 2005, both rising to about 29% in 2019. Those with complete upper secondary education represented 20% of the total population and 21% of the working population in 2005, both rising to 25% in 2019. The share of people with a college education also increased over the period. However, at this level of educational attainment, the difference between workers and the wider population is even more marked. The share of workers with college education grew from 17% to 21%; for the population as a whole, it went from 11% to 18%. The over-representation of the college-educated in the labor force suggests a positive selection process in which a college degree incentivizes the participation of the holder in the labor market.

Mexican women have made significant gains in terms of the accumulation of human capital in recent years. Figure 43.2 portrays the evolution of educational attainment of employed workers by sex during the same period. Although both sexes experienced an increase in their average educational attainment, the process was more pronounced for women. The share of female workers with a college education went from 15% in 2005 to 25% by 2019. In contrast, men with the same level of qualification went from 14% to 19% of all employed men. For upper secondary education, the pattern inverts. The share of women with this level of education grew from 24% to 26%, while for men it increased from 17% to 24%.

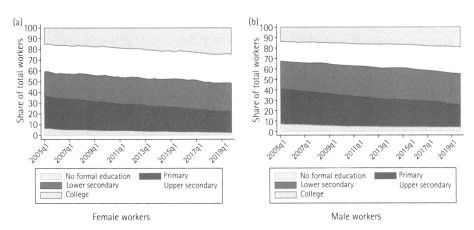

FIGURE 43.2 Composition of the employed population by educational attainment and sex. Note: Lower-secondary school corresponds to *secundaria* in the Mexican educational system, while upper-secondary school corresponds to both *bachillerato* and technical degrees.

(*Source*: ENOE, multiple years)

While the share of men (employed or not) with a college education is the same as the share of male workers, female workers are substantially more likely to have a college degree than nonworking women: To be more precise, 25% of working women had a college education in 2019 compared with 17% of all women. This is a sign of positive selection into work by these women, meaning that women with a college degree are more likely to work than their peers with lower qualifications (López-Acevedo et al., 2020).

DATA

To estimate the educational premium in Mexico, nationally and subnationally, we use the National Survey on Occupation and Employment (*Encuesta Nacional de Ocupación y Empleo*, or ENOE). The ENOE is the official Mexican labor force household survey carried out by the National Institute of Statistics and Geography (*Instituto Nacional de Estadística y Geografía*, or INEGI), and it is representative of the population aged 15 years or over at country and state levels. The survey is collected quarterly and captures a large set of sociodemographic indicators, including respondents' educational attainment, while also providing information on their labor income and their sector of occupation.

The information on the labor income of the interviewee is obtained through two questions. The first one asks directly for the income received by the worker during the month before the interview. If the respondent refuses to answer, the interviewer asks her to indicate the range, in multiples of minimum wages, where her labor income is located. Recent literature shows that the number of people that decline to answer the first question has increased over time. This literature also finds that the nonresponse pattern is nonrandom. Workers with higher levels of education tend to avoid answering the first question more frequently than those with lower levels of education (Campos-Vázquez, 2013; Rodríguez-Oreggia & Videla, 2015). This nonrandomness in the nonresponse produces a bias in the raw data concerning the wage distribution. To reduce the effect of this bias, we follow Campos-Vázquez (2013)'s proposal to employ imputation methods to assign an observed value on earnings to workers who do not provide a specific amount. Specifically, we use the hot-deck technique, which groups individuals according to a predetermined set of sociodemographic variables, imputing a value for earnings to those individuals that lack this information.

Our second data source is the national-level Input-Output Matrix for the Mexican economy in 2013, also from INEGI. This is the most recent year for which this is available. In order to make it consistent with the information generated by the ENOE, we employ this source at a three-digit level, classifying economic sectors according to the North American Industry Classification System (NAICS). This generates 76 economic sectors after discarding those corresponding to the public administration and the central bank. From the Input-Output Matrix, we also obtain the data on imported inputs and exports of final goods at the economic sector level, alongside the value-added in the sector. We use this information to calculate our measure of a sector's exposure to globalization.

IDENTIFYING GLOBALIZED SECTORS

Mexico's current insertion pattern in the international economy can be traced back to the aftermath of the debt crisis when the country was compelled to liberalize trade and capital flows as part of a broader set of neoliberal structural reforms. Maximum tariffs were reduced from 100% in 1982 to 25% in 1985 (Kose et al., 2004). That year foreign trade stood at 26% of GDP. As a continuation of this trend, Mexico joined the General Agreement on Tariffs and Trade (GATT) in 1986, committing to further reductions in tariffs and quotas. By 1990, foreign trade had risen to 39% of GDP.[2] The next and most significant milestone came with the signing of the North American Free Trade Agreement (NAFTA), which went into effect in 1994. Over the following two decades and a half, trade continued to grow faster than GDP, reaching a historical high of 81% of GDP in 2018.[3] Particularly salient was the increase in the share of manufactures, which went from 11.9% to 73% of all merchandise exports between 1980 and 1994. By 2019, manufactures represented 80% of total merchandise exports.[4]

The growth of maquiladoras, assembly plants benefiting from duty- and tariff-free access to imported materials and machinery, was central to this change in Mexico's export profile. Maquiladoras employ relatively cheap, predominantly female workers to transform imported inputs into final products to be exported mostly to the US market. While they originated in the mid-1960s, their heyday began in the 1980s, when they became a major source of much-needed foreign currency (Sklair, 2011). Their linkage to the United States was cemented with the passing of NAFTA, which gave Mexico-based firms preferential access to that market and thus further incentivized the inflow of foreign direct investment into the sector (Castillo & de Vries, 2018). However, China's entry into the World Trade Organization in 2001, and thus the US market, curtailed the sector's growth in the early years of the 21st century. Several studies identify a displacement of Mexican exports by Chinese competition, leading to a contraction of production and employment in the Mexican manufacturing sector, particularly in maquiladoras (Dussel-Peters & Gallagher, 2013; Gallagher et al., 2008; Lin, 2015; Sargent & Matthews, 2009; Utar & Torres-Ruíz, 2013). Although there is evidence that this displacement of Mexican exports to the United States has halted since 2010 (Lin, 2015), the sector has not managed to recover its earlier dynamism.

In an effort to reach other export markets, Mexico has also signed multiple free trade agreements with other countries and economic blocks, becoming one of the most open economies in the world.[5] However, this has not significantly changed the degree of concentration of the destination of exports. In 1990, Mexico sold 70% of its exports to the United States. This share increased to 88% in 2000 before going down to a still dominant 76% in 2017. On the other hand, the concentration of imports has diminished during the

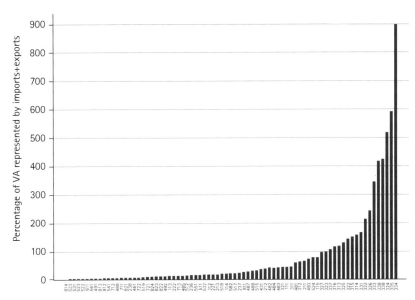

FIGURE 43.3 Economic sectors by degree of globalization. Note: See the NAICS code guide for the correspondence between each code and subsector.

(*Source*: 2013 Mexican Input-Output table, INEGI)

same period. Imports from the United States shifted from representing 67.5% of the total in 1990 to 71.7% in 2000 and 46.4% in 2017. In contrast, imports from China went from 0.79% in 1990 to 17.64% of total imports in 2018.[6]

We now proceed to describe the level of globalization of the Mexican productive structure. To identify the exposure to globalization of a given sector, we use the value of its exports and imported inputs. We measure the exposure of a sector to globalization through the ratio of the sum of imported inputs and exports to total value added in the sector. Notice that the value of this ratio can exceed 1, and a larger value implies a larger exposure to globalization. We define sectors at the top quintile of the distribution of this variable as being heavily exposed, while those in the bottom quintile are considered unexposed to globalization.

Figure 43.3 plots the degree of exposure to globalization of each sector in the Mexican economy. The graph shows significant heterogeneity in terms of exposure. While some sectors are highly integrated into foreign markets, others have virtually null exposure to them. Out of 76 sectors in the economy, only 24 have an exposure level above 50%, with only 16 of them showing an exposure above 100%. At the bottom end of this distribution, 23 sectors have an exposure level below 10% of their value-added. As the average degree of exposure of a sector in the Mexican economy is 79%, it is clear that even in a heavily globalized economy like Mexico's, participation in international markets is highly uneven throughout the productive structure.

Figure 43.4 compares the sectors at the top and the bottom quintile of the distribution of the degree of globalization. All the sectors that compose the top quintile belong to the manufacturing industry, with an average exposure of 294%. It is worthwhile noting that

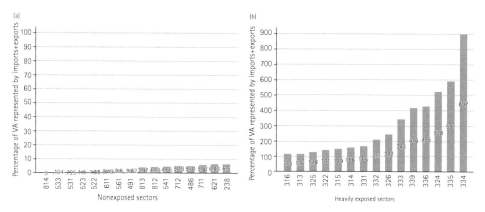

FIGURE 43.4 Sectors in the bottom and top quintiles of exposure. Note: (a) shows the sectors in the bottom quintile of our exposure measure, while (b) shows those in the top quintile. For *nonexposed* sectors, the NAICS codes correspond to the following industries: 238 Specialty Trade Contractors; 486 Pipeline Transportation; 491 Postal Services; 522 Credit Intermediation and Related Activities; 523 Securities, Commodity Contracts, and Other Financial Investments and Related Activities; 531 Real Estate services; 533 Lessors of Nonfinancial Intangible Assets (except Copyrighted Works); 541 Professional, Scientific, and Technical Services; 561 Administrative and Support Services; 611 Educational services; 621 Ambulatory Health Care Services; 711 Performing Arts, Spectator Sports, and Related Industries; 712 Museums, Historical Sites, and Similar Institutions; 812 Personal and Laundry Services; 813 Religious, Grantmaking, Civic, Professional, and Similar Organizations; 814 Paid domestic work. For *heavily-exposed* sectors, the NAICS codes are as follows: 313 Textile Mills; 314 Textile Product Mills; 315 Apparel Manufacturing; 316 Leather and Allied Product Manufacturing; 324 Petroleum and Coal Products Manufacturing; 325 Chemical Manufacturing; 326 Plastics and Rubber Products Manufacturing; 331 Primary Metal Manufacturing; 332 Fabricated Metal Product Manufacturing; 333 Machinery Manufacturing; 334 Computer and Electronic Product Manufacturing; 335 Electrical Equipment, Appliance, and Component Manufacturing; 336 Transportation Equipment Manufacturing; 339 Miscellaneous Manufacturing.

(*Source*: 2013 Mexican Input-Output table, INEGI)

even among this subset of sectors, there is substantial variation. The least exposed sector in the top quintile, furniture production,[7] has an exposure of 104%, while the most exposed sector in the economy, computer and electronic equipment,[8] has an exposure of 900%. In contrast, the least exposed sectors are a mixture of different types of services with an exposure of 2% on average. The least exposed sector in the whole economy is domestic service work, with null exposure. The most exposed sector among the bottom quintile of our measure is "services provided by speciality contractors," with an exposure of 5%. This includes marketing and outsourced office support services, among others.

The strong participation of Mexico's manufacturing sector in global value chains has been widely discussed in the international trade literature (see, among others, Contreras et al., 2012; Crossa & Ebner, 2020; Dussel-Peters, 2018; de Gortari, 2019). This literature provides information on the type and average size of the firms participating in such chains. Due to specific technological requirements, firms tend to be medium to large, which varies from sector to sector. For example, most globalized productive units are medium-sized (10–50 workers) in light-manufacturing industries, whereas large units (with more than 100 workers) are the norm among heavy manufacturers. An exception to this pattern, documented by Contreras et al. (2012), is computation and electronic equipment, where small businesses have managed to insert themselves at the upstream segments of their value chains.

A less discussed feature is the range of sectors whose productive structure is not substantially linked to the global markets.[9] As Figure 43.4 shows, nonexposed sectors are composed of nontradable services (including personal services, real estate, cultural, educational, and healthcare services) and financial and professional services. The presence of financial services (NAIC codes 522 and 523) among these sectors is somewhat surprising, particularly considering that foreign banks dominate the Mexican financial sector (Etchemendy & Puente, 2017; Haber & Mussachio, 2013). This result implies that globalization in terms of firm ownership does not necessarily lead to the globalization of the productive structure. It also highlights that by focusing on the globalization of the productive structure, we can directly observe the relationship between trade integration and labor markets, which tends to be obscured when the focus is on capital flows.

What are the key geographical characteristics of heavily exposed sectors? Globalization in Mexico presents a marked subnational dimension. Figure 43.5 maps the current geographical distribution of employment in heavily globalized industries

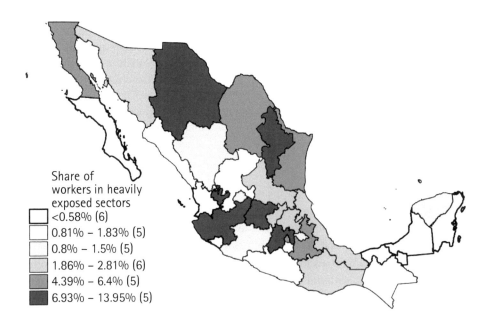

FIGURE 43.5 The geographical location of heavily globalized sectors in terms of employment (share of total jobs in each state). Note: The map shows the distribution of the population employed in heavily globalized sectors. We identify these sectors as those belonging to the fifth quintile of the distribution of the exposure variable.

(*Source*: Authors' calculations using data from ENOE)

regarding the share they represent of total jobs available in each state. As can be seen, these industries have a larger share of total employment in states in the north, the west, and the center of the country. The concentration of this type of employment in these regions is in line with the historical location of manufacturing industries. It also highlights the relative and sustained disconnection of the country's south from the global economy (Hanson, 1998a, 1998b; Moreno-Brid & Ros, 2009).

In the last two decades, the geographical dispersion of employment in globalized sectors has somewhat increased, away from the center of the country. In particular, Table 43.1 shows that although Estado de México remains the state with the largest concentration of jobs in globalized sectors, other states such as Guanajuato, Coahuila, and Aguascalientes have increased their participation in global value chains. This is linked to the growth of the car industry in those states (Cedillo-Campos et al., 2007; Lampón et al., 2018). In contrast, in Mexico City, workers' participation in globalized sectors has diminished, primarily due to the deindustrialization process (Parnreiter, 2010). It is also possible to observe the consistently low rates of globalized employment in the states in the south of the country (Oaxaca, Chiapas, and Guerrero), where less than 2% of total globalized employment is located.

Table 43.1 Distribution of Globalized Employment Across Mexican States, 2005Q1 to 2019Q4 (Share of Total Employment in the Globalized Sectors)

State	2005:I	2010:I	2019:IV	State	2005:I	2010:I	2019:IV
Estado de México	16.98	16.69	13.95	Hidalgo	1.97	1.74	1.95
Mexico City	8.36	7.21	4.87	Oaxaca	1.90	1.91	1.86
Jalisco	7.55	7.95	6.98	Tlaxcala	1.72	1.52	1.84
Guanajuato	6.71	8.83	9.61	Aguascalientes	1.30	1.43	1.76
Nuevo León	6.47	6.90	7.25	Guerrero	1.29	1.55	1.15
Puebla	6.18	5.50	4.39	Durango	1.13	1.03	1.51
Chihuahua	6.14	5.38	6.93	Sinaloa	1.08	0.91	0.91
Baja California	4.83	3.90	5.27	Chiapas	1.07	1.21	1.02
Coahuila	4.30	4.20	6.44	Morelos	0.92	0.93	0.89
Tamaulipas	4.07	4.28	4.62	Tabasco	0.59	0.55	0.58
Veracruz	2.80	2.95	2.27	Zacatecas	0.48	0.58	0.82
Yucatán	2.36	2.32	1.83	Campeche	0.46	0.46	0.44
Michoacán	2.29	2.28	1.63	Quintana Roo	0.34	0.37	0.42
Querétaro	2.09	2.42	2.53	Nayarit	0.23	0.28	0.28
Sonora	2.04	2.39	2.76	Colima	0.21	0.18	0.22
San Luis Potosí	2.01	1.97	2.81	Baja California Sur	0.11	0.15	0.18

Source: ENOE, various years.

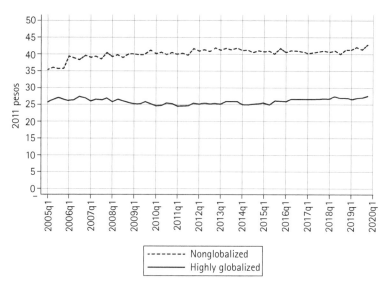

FIGURE 43.6 Female participation in the workforce of highly globalized and nonglobalized sectors. Note: The highly globalized sectors are those in the fifth quintile of the exposure distribution, whereas the nonglobalized ones are those in the bottom quintile.

(*Source*: ENOE, multiple years)

Regarding the sex composition of the labor force, highly globalized sectors did not experience significant change over the period studied. Moreover, Figure 43.6 shows that nonexposed sectors have a consistent higher share of female workers than the most exposed sectors. This results from the presence of highly feminized sectors among those with almost null exposure to global markets, such as personal services and domestic paid housework. Importantly, Figure 43.6 also indicates that the percentage of female workers in the nonexposed sectors increased by almost 10 percentage points from 2005 to 2019. In contrast, the proportion of female workers in the most exposed sectors of the economy increased only slightly over the same period. Finally, it is notable that female participation in globalized sectors (28% of total workers) remained well below the level of female labor participation in the overall Mexican economy (50%) in 2019.

Education Levels, Wages, and Degree of Globalization

We are now in a position to start interacting our variables of interest. Figure 43.7 plots the degree of globalization of each economic sector in 2013 against the share of its workers with complete lower-secondary education or more. The vertical red line represents the share of workers with lower secondary education or more in the total workforce. The

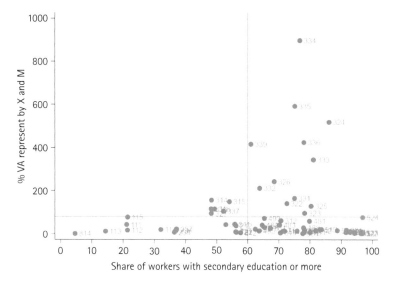

FIGURE 43.7 Economic sectors by the level of education of their workers and degree of globalization. Note: For each economic sector, the vertical axis shows the degree of globalization while the horizontal axis shows the share of its workers with complete lower-secondary education or more. The horizontal and vertical lines show the averages for the whole economy. Thus sectors in the bottom right quadrant have above-average levels of education and below the average degree of globalization. See the appendix (Table 43.A1) for a list of the sectors in each quadrant.

(*Sources*: 2013 Mexican Input-Output table [INEGI] and ENOE)

horizontal line represents the average degree of exposure to foreign markets of a sector in the economy.

The first noticeable element in the figure is that most of the Mexican economy lies in the bottom-right quadrant. This means that most sectors are less exposed to globalization and have a more educated workforce than the national average. This would suggest that a relatively highly qualified labor force is not sufficient for a sector to participate in global markets—more educated workers are found at all levels of globalization. However, it is also clear that sectors with a labor force with lower than average education (to the left of the vertical line) are less likely to be heavily exposed. This is the case of most agricultural sectors (SCIAN codes 111, 112, 113, 114, 115) and paid domestic work (SCIAN code 834).

The other end of the figure, the top-right quadrant, shows the 12 heavily exposed sectors with more than the average share of highly qualified workers. As Figure 43.4b pointed out, these sectors belong to the manufacturing sector and are linked to traditional heavy industries (chemical, machinery production, electrical and electronic components, and computer equipment). In contrast, the six sectors with above-average exposure and a lower-than-average share of qualified workers (top-left quadrant) are in the textiles and wood industries. That is, they belong to what has traditionally been considered light manufactures.

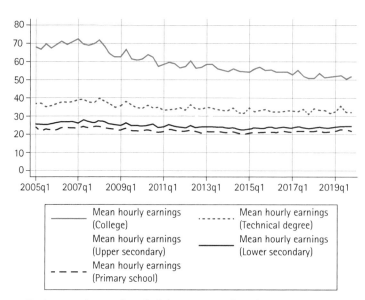

FIGURE 43.8 Evolution of mean hourly labor incomes by educational level (at constant 2011 prices).

(*Source*: ENOE, multiple years)

Before directly exploring the effects of globalization on the returns associated with different levels of educational attainment as measured by completed degrees, we present the overall evolution of mean labor incomes in the Mexican economy. As Bleynat et al. (2021) show, labor incomes have suffered in Mexico since the 1980s. Moreover, the minimum wage has been particularly low, though it has recently begun to recover (Martínez-González, 2020; Moreno-Brid et al., 2014). In this context, Figure 43.8 displays the evolution of the mean labor income since 2005 by workers' educational attainment in constant pesos at 2011 prices. While the incomes of workers with primary or lower secondary education have remained stagnant during the period under study, incomes have gone down for workers with upper-secondary or college degrees.

The contraction has been particularly stark among the most educated. Figure 43.8 evinces a secular decline in the incomes of workers with a college degree in the economy as a whole. In 2005, their mean hourly income in real terms was 69 Mexican pesos (8.84 dollars PPP), whereas, by 2019, it was close to 52 pesos (6.66 dollars PPP), representing an accumulated loss of 25% over 15 years.

If we compare workers in highly globalized and nonglobalized industries, we find the same decline for both samples. Figure 43.9 indicates a similar pattern of income loss for workers in the most exposed and the nonexposed sectors of the economy. Both show a fall in college-educated workers' wages of the same magnitude: 23% between 2005 and 2019. This trend has been linked to the increase in the supply of college-educated workers in an economy that was growing very slowly.[10] As different authors point out,

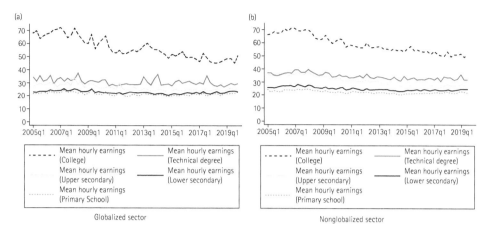

FIGURE 43.9 Mean hourly labor income by educational level in highly globalized and nonglobalized sectors (at constant 2011 prices). Note: The globalized part of the economy refers to the fifth quintile in the distribution of the exposure variable. The nonglobalized part comprises the industries in the first quintile of the same distribution.

(*Source*: ENOE, various years)

the combination of these facts has generated misallocation problems in the labor market (Levy & López-Calva, 2020; Ros, 2015).

Does Globalization Reward Education in Mexico?

In the previous section, we described the evolution of wages in Mexico at different educational levels. We now turn to an analysis of wages that breaks down the characteristic of workers in more detail, following the classical Mincerian approach (Mincer, 1974), in which earnings are a function of job experience and years of education. Formally, this is

$$\ln W_i = \beta_0 + \beta_1 s_i + \beta_2 e_i + \beta_3 e_i^2 + u_i \qquad (1)$$

in which W_i is the hourly labor income of individual i, s_i corresponds to her years of education, and e_i corresponds to her years of work experience, either measured directly or age $-6-s$. The coefficient of interest is β_1, which indicates the returns to an additional year of education. However, this estimation technique assumes that the returns are linear and constant to all years of education and that there are no discontinuities. Previous research by López-Calva and Macías (2010) demonstrates that this assumption does not correspond to the Mexican case, in which returns vary by educational level completed, not by years of schooling. Taking into account this fact, Morales-Ramos (2011) proposes the following modified version of the classical Mincerian equation:

$$\ln W_i = \beta_0 + \sum_{j=1}^{k} \beta_j D_{ij} + \beta_{k+1} e_i^2 + u_i \tag{2}$$

In this version D_{ij} is a dummy variable that takes a value of one for educational level j, attained by individual i, out of k total educational levels. β_j (for $j = 1$ to k) is then an estimate of the return associated with education level j. For our specific case, we consider five education levels: without primary education, completed primary education, completed lower secondary education, completed upper secondary education (excluding technical degrees), a technical degree, and a completed college degree. In this section, we opted to separate the technical degree from the upper secondary to investigate if the former type of degree, supposedly more linked to the needs of the industrial labor market, receives a higher premium than traditional upper secondary education. The omitted category in the regression is completed primary education.

RESULTS

The results in Figure 43.10 indicate that the returns to all four levels of education above complete primary have declined since 2005. For high school education, the downward trend accelerated from 2012 onward. That year, Congress modified Articles 3 and 31 of the Mexican Constitution, making upper secondary schooling mandatory for all Mexicans. Congress also recognized a technical degree as an end-of-educational-trajectory degree. Up to that point, a technical degree gave a near-identical return to a high school degree; afterward, a technical degree entailed a higher premium.

It is worth discussing the case of the returns to a college education, as they have suffered the largest drop during the period under analysis. Over the 15 years under examination, the wage premium associated with a college degree relative to a person with complete primary school fell from 225% to 130%. This is consistent with the contraction of the average wage for college-educated workers reported in Figure 43.8 and existing literature on the dynamics of inequality in Mexico (Campos-Vázquez & Lustig, 2019; Campos-Vázquez & Vélez-Grajales, 2015).

The literature has proposed two complementary explanations for this trend. The first one links it to the expansion of the supply of potential workers with a college degree or postgraduate qualification (Campos-Vázquez & Vélez-Grajales, 2015), which we documented in Figure 43.1. The second explores an interacting factor that the same literature has identified: the process of obsolescence of the skills of older cohorts. According to the evidence presented by Campos-Vázquez et al. (2016), this process has had a more substantial effect on earnings of workers who hold a college degree than on

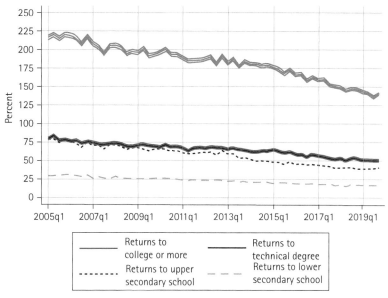

FIGURE 43.10 Evolution of the educational premium with respect to complete primary education.

(*Source*: ENOE, multiple years)

those of people the same ages with lower levels of educational attainment.[11] Moreover, their results suggest that workers in high-paying occupations have faced a decline in the returns they receive for each level of education, but the decline has been sharper among older workers in administrative positions. In particular, these authors find that a reduction in the demand for managers and directors has disproportionally hurt the older cohorts.

We then modify equation 2 to include an interaction between sex and educational attainment to identify differences in the returns to education by sex. The resulting equation is the following:

$$\ln W_i = \beta_0 + sex_i + \sum_{j=1}^{k} \beta_j D_{ij} + \sum_{j=1}^{k} \gamma_j \left(D_{ij} \times sex_i\right) + \beta_{k+1} e_i + \beta_{k+3} e_i^2 + \sum_{r=1}^{4} \tau_r I_{r,i} + u_i \quad (3)$$

in which sex is a dummy variable that takes a value of 1 for observations corresponding to women and 0 otherwise. The returns to education for female workers with educational attainment j will be given by $\beta_j + \gamma_j$, while for men they are given b β_j y. We also include a series of dummy variables that control for regional variation, $I_{r,i}$. We show the resulting values for each quarter in Figure 43.11.

Two findings are notable. The first one is that the returns to college education and high school for female workers were higher than for male workers throughout most of the period under analysis (and throughout the whole period for the case of college).

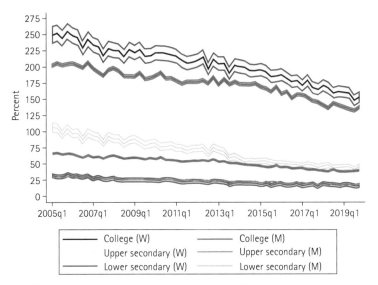

FIGURE 43.11 Evolution of the educational premium with respect to complete primary education by sex. Notes: In all cases, the returns are with respect to having a complete primary education. W refers to the returns for female workers and M for the returns for male workers. US corresponds to upper secondary (not including technical degrees), and LS corresponds to lower secondary.

(*Source*: ENOE, multiple years)

The second is the steeper fall in the returns to a college education experienced by women than the one experienced by men. The same occurs in the case of the returns to upper secondary education. Both patterns are consistent with the lower levels of female labor force participation and the changes in the educational composition of the female and male Mexican populations. We saw earlier that the growth in college-educated workers has been faster for women than for men, which may explain the more rapid decline in the college premium for women. This is also consistent with the evidence on vertical segregation of women within occupations, meaning that women are found less frequently in the higher positions of each occupation (Orraca et al., 2016), and on the effects of sex-based discrimination in the northern states of Mexico (Ochoa-Adame et al., 2021).

With this general framework in mind, we can zoom in to analyze the effects of globalization on Mexican workers' labor income by estimating the following regression. The sample is composed of only the workers of both the highly globalized and the nonglobalized sectors as defined in the third section, and we now add an interaction term between educational level and a dummy for whether the sector is highly globalized or not globalized:

$$\ln W_i = \beta_0 + G_i + \sum_{j=1}^{k} \beta_j D_{ij} + \sum_{j=1}^{k} \phi_i \left(D_{ij} \times G_i \right) + \beta_{k+1} e_i + \beta_{k+3} e_i^2 + sex_i + \sum_{r=1}^{4} \tau_r I_{r,i} + u_i$$

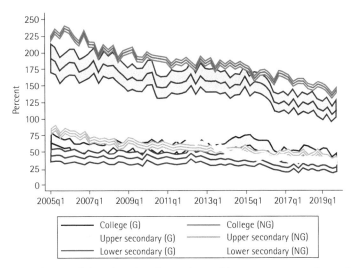

FIGURE 43.12 Evolution of the educational premium with respect to complete primary education by level of exposure of their sector of employment. Note: The highly globalized part of the economy refers to the fifth quintile in the distribution of the exposure variable. The nonglobalized part comprises the industries in the first quintile of the same distribution. In all cases, the returns are with respect to having a complete primary education. G refers to highly globalized sectors and NG to nonglobalized.

(*Source*: ENOE, various years)

in which G_i is a dummy variable that takes a value of 1 if worker i works in one of the heavily exposed sectors and 0 if they work in one of the nonexposed sectors. As control variables, we include experience, squared experience, sex of the worker, and a series of dummy variables to account for the regional differences (I). For the workers in the heavily exposed sectors, the returns to educational level j are given by $\beta_j + \phi_j$ and for the workers in nonglobalized sectors, they are given b β_j y. In Figure 43.12, we plot the results of this estimation.

Our results indicate that the returns to college education are marginally higher in the nonglobalized sectors than in the heavily globalized one: ϕ is negative for college education. That is, globalization does not reward education—it may even penalize it. This suggests that Mexico's insertion in global value chains has relied and continues to rely primordially on taking advantage of lower wages for any educational level. What is more, in both sets of sectors, those returns have decreased secularly since 2005. In addition, in the nonglobalized sectors, we also observe a fall in the returns to upper secondary education, which accelerated after 2013.

Is there a sex pattern to this penalization of education in globalized sectors? In Figure 43.11 we displayed the differences in the returns to education between male and female workers in the Mexican economy, indicating a higher return for the latter. To analyze how these differences interact with exposure to globalization, we estimate the returns for the globalized and the nonglobalized sectors for two separate samples: one composed of

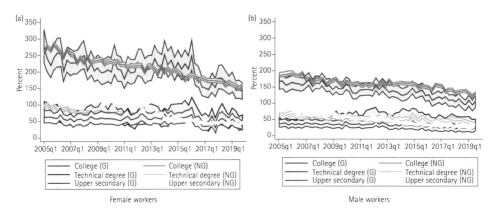

FIGURE 43.13 Evolution of the educational premium with respect to complete primary education by level of exposure of their sector of employment and sex. Note: The globalized part of the economy refers to the fifth quintile in the distribution of the exposure variable. The nonglobalized part comprises the industries in the first quintile of the same distribution. In all cases, the returns are with respect to having a complete primary education. G refers to the globalized sectors and NG to the nonglobalized.

(*Source*: ENOE, various years)

only employed men, and the other composed only of employed women. Figure 43.13 presents our final set of results.

We find that both sexes have faced a declining trend in the returns to college education independently of how integrated to international markets the sectors they work in are. For female workers, however, it is worth noting that whereas in nonglobalized sectors the decline in the premium was a secular process unfolding throughout the first two decades of the 21st century, in globalized sectors we see a sharp drop at the beginning of 2016. Before that year, the point estimate of the returns remained practically constant. This drop coincides with the election of Donald Trump as president of the United States, which triggered considerable uncertainty about the future of NAFTA and consequently hurt the performance of the globalized sector. At the same time, the government shifted wage policy toward increasing the real value of the minimum wage, which compressed wages across educational levels. The combination of the high level of education of female workers and the discrimination women experienced in maquiladoras in the northern states might be behind it (Ochoa-Adame et al., 2021). In the case of male workers, the returns in both types of sectors fell secularly during the whole period. The fall for men was more significant in the most globalized sectors than in the nonglobalized ones.

A priori, we expected higher returns to college education in the heavily exposed sectors. Research suggests that exposure to global markets fosters technology adoption by firms (Syeda Tamken, 2017). If these technologies complement higher qualifications, they should result in a higher return for college education in the exposed sectors than in the nonexposed. This, however, is not the case in Mexico. In an analysis of the country's manufacturing sector, Iavocone and Pereira-López (2018) suggest that adopting new

Table 43.A1 Sectors by Their Degree of Globalization and Concentration of Workers With Complete Lower Secondary Education

High Globalization and Low Concentration of Workers With Lower Secondary Education or More		High Globalization and High Concentration of Workers With Lower Secondary Education or More	
Sector Code	Sector Name	Sector Code	Sector Name
313	Textile mills	322	Paper manufacturing
314	Textile product mills	323	Printing and related support activities
315	Apparel manufacturing	324	Petroleum and coal products manufacturing
316	Leather and allied product manufacturing	325	Chemical manufacturing
327	Nonmetallic mineral product manufacturing	326	Plastics and rubber products manufacturing
337	Furniture and related product manufacturing	331	Primary metal manufacturing
		332	Fabricated metal product manufacturing
		333	Machinery manufacturing
		334	Computer and electronic product manufacturing
		335	Electric equipment, appliance, and component manufacturing
		336	Transportation equipment manufacturing
		339	Miscellaneous manufacturing industries

Low Globalization and Low Concentration of Workers With Secondary Education or More		Low Globalization and High Concentration of Workers With Secondary Education or More	
Sector Code	Sector Name	Sector Code	Sector Name
111	Crop production	211	Oil and gas extraction
112	Animal production and aquaculture	221	Utilities
113	Forestry and logging	312	Beverage and tobacco product manufacturing
114	Fishing, hunting, and trapping	430	Wholesale commerce
115	Support activities for agriculture and forestry	481	Air transportation
212	Mining (except oil and gas)	482	Rail transportation
236	Construction of buildings	483	Water transportation
237	Heavy and civil engineering construction	484	Truck transportation

(continued)

Table 43.A1 Continued

Low Globalization and Low Concentration of Workers With Secondary Education or More		Low Globalization and High Concentration of Workers With Secondary Education or More	
Sector Code	Sector Name	Sector Code	Sector Name
238	Specialty trade contractors	485	Transit and ground passenger transportation
311	Food manufacturing	488	Support activities for transportation
321	Wood product manufacturing	491	Postal service
721	Accommodation	493	Warehousing and storage
722	Food services and drinking places	511	Publishing industries, except Internet
812	Personal and laundry services	512	Motion picture and sound recording industries
814	Paid domestic workers	515	Broadcasting, except Internet
		517	Telecommunications
		522	Credit intermediation and related activities
		523	Securities, commodity contracts, and other financial investments and related activities
		524	Insurance carriers and related activities
		531	Real estate
		532	Rental and leasing services
		533	Lessors of nonfinancial intangible assets
		541	Professional, scientific, and technical services
		561	Administrative and support services
		611	Educational services
		621	Ambulatory healthcare services
		622	Hospitals
		623	Nursing and residential care facilities
		624	Social assistance
		711	Performing arts, spectator sports, and related industries
		712	Museums, historical sites, and similar institutions
		713	Amusement, gambling, and recreation industries
		811	Repair and maintenance
		813	Religious, grantmaking, civic, professional, and similar organizations

technologies implies more significant benefits for those in technical tasks than those in clerical ones. As technical tasks require less formal qualifications, this means a complementarity between new technologies and secondary education. In contrast, college-educated workers are more frequently employed in clerical tasks, which prevents them from benefiting from technological adoption. In the case of commercial activities, the introduction of new technologies hurts the wages of clerical workers while not affecting the wages of manual workers. This produces the same pattern observed in manufacturing in decreasing the wage gap between clerical and technical workers but through a different mechanism. In this case, the new technologies substitute clerical tasks, reducing the clerical workers' wages. While this might explain the failure of globalization to favor college education, it does not explain that the return to technical degrees has also declined over the period.

In contrast, in sectors such as finance, administrative and support services, real estate, and professional services, new technologies are usually complementary to higher formal qualifications associated with nonroutine tasks (Philippon & Reshef, 2012; Sebastian & Biagi, 2018). This would help to explain why, even when the supply of college-educated workers increases substantially in the 15 years under analysis, the drop in the returns to this degree was smaller in the nonexposed sectors.

Conclusion

Mexican governments since the 1990s have invested substantial resources and policy efforts in the education sector, and the result has been a significant increase in the level of educational attainment at the aggregate level. However, as we have discussed in this chapter, coverage and quality remain highly uneven. As Miranda-Lopez (2018) documents, there are major gaps across the country that require urgent attention. Data from the most recent census of school infrastructure finds that in 2014, while 100% of private primary schools had fully functional toilets for students, less than 70% of schools in rural and indigenous communities had them. Moreover, less than 60% of public schools have a working computer and less than 40% have access to the Internet. At the same time, policy continues to push to raise enrollment in higher education. The administration of Andres Manuel López Obrador has implemented a program named Universidades Benito Juárez to increase the number of public universities in the country and to further decentralize them out of Mexico City. By June 2020, 100 new campuses had been built and were ready to start operations, providing 44,000 new places for students at the college level (Expansión, 2020). In the private sector, expansion also continues unabated, but many programs still lack external evaluation or accreditation and may not be providing students with the competences and skills they need for the labor market (OECD, 2019). While progress has been undeniable, the system needs more planning, resources, and regulation to address these issues.

Concurrent with its educational expansion, Mexico has become increasingly open to foreign trade and investment through NAFTA and other such agreements, and it is now considered one of the most globalized economies in the world. In both of these policy areas, then, Mexico has been an excellent student of the Washington Consensus, which advocated economic opening, decentralization, and increased expenditures on education. Yet the effect of these reforms has not been all that Mexican policymakers and Washington-based policy advisors would have hoped for. From an economic perspective the purpose of both opening and education must be to raise real incomes. But while globalization has successfully increased trade and reshaped Mexico's export profile, it has not raise wages, regardless of workers' characteristics, the sectors in which they are employed, or where in the country their jobs are located. Even more remarkably, improved education levels have failed to raise wages across the board. Today people with college degrees or upper-secondary education are paid less in real terms than they were 15 years ago. Over the same period, those with lower secondary or primary education have seen their market incomes stagnate which, given how close they are to subsistence level, is perhaps even more problematic from a welfare perspective. Despite their promise, we find no evidence that either globalization or education has improved living standards for Mexican workers.

ACKNOWLEDGMENTS

The authors would like to thank Jacqueline Behrend, Eduardo Ortíz-Juárez, and Paul Segal for their comments.

NOTES

1. Data from the World Development Indicators, World Bank.
2. World Bank, DataBank.
3. World Bank, DataBank.
4. World Bank, DataBank.
5. Among others, with the European Union, Japan, Israel, and 10 Latin American countries.
6. World Bank, World Integrated Trade Solution.
7. SCIAN code 337.
8. SCIAN code 334.
9. It is important to note that our measure of exposure does not fully overlap with the distinction between tradable and nontradable goods and services. As we consider the role of imported inputs, nontradable activities that use them show a strictly positive degree of exposure, when only focusing in the tradeability of the goods or services produced would imply a zero exposure value.
10. For a review of the different explanations of the stagnation of the Mexican economy in the past 40 years, see Ros (2013).
11. Ferreira et al. (2021) identify a similar process taking place in Brazil.

References

Araujo, M. C., & Mancours, K. (2021). Education, income, and mobility: Experimental impacts of childhood exposure to Progresa after 20 years. *IDB Working Paper Series* 1288.

Arnaut, A., & Giorguli, S. (2010). Introducción general. In A. Arnaut & S. Giorguli (Eds.), *Los Grandes Problemas de México. Educación* (pp. 233–268). Colegio de Mexico.

Bleynat, I., Challú, A., & Segal, P. (2021). Inequality, living standards, and growth: Two centuries of economic development in Mexico. *Economic History Review, 74*(3), 584–610.

Bustos, A., & Leyva, G. (2017). Towards a more realistic estimate of the income distribution in Mexico. *Latin American Policy, 8*(1), 114–126.

Cadot, O., Carrère, C., & Strauss-Kahn, V. (2011). Export diversification: What's behind the hump? *The Review of Economics and Statistics, 93*(2), 590–605.

Campos-Vázquez, R. (2013). Efectos de los ingresos no reportados en el nivel y tendencia de la pobreza laboral en México. *Ensayos Revista de Economíia, 32*(2), 23–54.

Campos-Vázquez, R., Chávez. E., & Esquivel, G. (2018). Estimating top income shares without tax return data: Mexico since 1990s. *Latin American Policy, 9*(1), 139–163.

Campos-Vázquez, R., López-Calva, L. F., & Lustig, N. (2016). Declining wages for college-educated workers in Mexico: Are younger or older cohorts hurt the most? *Revista de Economía Mundial, 43*, 93–111.

Campos-Vázquez, R., & Lustig, N. (2019). Labour income inequality in Mexico: Puzzles solved and unsolved. *Journal of Economic and Social Measurement, 44*(4), 203–219.

Campos-Vázquez, R., & Vélez-Grajales, R. (2015). Movilidad de corto plazo en ingresos laborales: El caso mexicano. In R. Vélez-Grajales et al. (Eds.), *México: ¿El motor inmóvil?* (pp. 623–657). Centro de Estudios Espinosa Yglesias.

Castillo, J. C., & de Vries, G. (2018). The domestic content of Mexico's maquiladora exports: A long-run perspective. *The Journal of International Trade and Economic Development, 27*(2), 200–219.

Castillo-Negrete-Rovira, M. (2017). Income inequality in Mexico 2004–2014. *Latin American Policy, 8*(1), 93–113.

Cedillo-Campos, M., Sánchez-Garza, J., & Sánchez-Ramírez, C. (2007). The new relational schemas of inter-firms cooperation: The case of the Coahuila automobile cluster in Mexico. *International Journal of Automotive Technology and Management, 6*(4), 405–418.

Contreras, O., Carrillo, J., & Alonso, J. (2012). Local entrepreneurship within global value chains: A case study in the Mexican automotive industry. *World Development, 40*(5), 1013–1023.

Crossa, M., & Ebner, N. (2020). Automotive global value chains in Mexico: A mirage of development? *Third World Quarterly, 41*(2), 1–22.

De Gortari, A. (2019). Disentangling global value chains. *NBER Working Paper* 25868.

Dussel-Peters, E. (2018). *Cadenas Globales de Valor. Metodología, teoría y debates*. Facultad de Economía, Universidad Nacional Autónoma de México.

Dussel-Peters, E., & Gallagher, K. (2013). NAFTA's uninvited guest: China and the disintegration of North American Trade. *CEPAL Review, 110*, 83–108.

Etchemendy, S., & Puente, I. (2017). Power and crisis: Explaining varieties of commercial banking systems in Argentina, Brazil and Mexico. *Journal of Politics in Latin America, 9*(1), 3–31.

Expansión Política. (2020, June 20). El gobierno de AMLO va por 40 nuevas universidades Benito Juárez.

Ferreira, F., Firpo, S., & Messina, J. (2021). Labor market experience and falling earnings inequality in Brazil: 1995–2012. *The World Bank Economic Review*.

Gallagher, K., Moreno-Brid, J. C., & Porzecanski, R. (2008). The dynamism of Mexican exports: Lost in (Chinese) translation. *World Development*, 36(8), 1365–1380.

Haber, S., & Mussachio, A. (2013). These are the good old days: Foreign entry and the Mexican banking system. *NBER Working Papers* 18713.

Hanson, G. (1998a). North American economic integration and industry location. *Oxford Review of Economic Policy*, 14(2), 30–44.

Hanson, G. (1998b). Regional adjustment to trade liberalisation. *Regional Science and Urban Economics*, 28(4), 419–444.

Hartmann, D., Guevara, M., Jara-Figueroa, C., Aristarán, M., & Hidalgo, C. (2017). Linking economic complexity, institutions and income inequality. *World Development*, 93, 75–93.

Hausmann, R., Hwang, J., & Rodrik, D. (2007). What you export matters. *Journal of Economic Growth*, 12, 1–25.

Iacovone, L., & Pereira-Lopez, M. (2018). ICT adoption and wage inequality: Evidence from Mexican firms. *World Bank Policy Research Working Paper* 8298.

Kose, A., Meredith, G., & Towe, C. (2004). How has NAFTA affected the Mexican economy? Review and evidence. *IMF Working Paper* 04/59.

Lampón, J. F., Cabanelas, P., & Delgado-Guzmán, J. (2018). Claves en la evolución de México dentro de la cadena de valor global de la industria de autopartes. El caso del Bajío. *El Trimestre Económico*, 85(339), 483–514.

Levy, S., & López-Calva, L. F. (2020). Persistent misallocation and the returns to education in Mexico. *The World Bank Economic Review*, 34(2), 284–311.

Lin, Y. (2015). Is China relinquishing manufacturing competitiveness to Mexico in US markets? *China and the World Economy*, 23(4), 104–124.

López-Acevedo, G., Freije-Rodríguez, S., Bahena, M. A. V., & Medeiros, D. C. (2020). Changes in female employment in Mexico: Demographics, economics, and policies. Institute of Labour Economics, *IZA Discussion Paper* 13404.

López-Calva, L. F., & Macías, A. (2010). ¿Estudias o trabajas? Deserción escolar, trabajo temprano y movilidad en México. In J. Serrano Espinosa & F. Torche (Eds.), *Movilidad Social en México. Población, desarrollo y crecimiento* (pp. 165–188). Centro de Estudios Espinosa Yglesias.

López-Calva, L. F., & Nora Lustig (Eds.). (2010). *Declining inequality in Latin America: A decade of progress?* Brookings Institution Press.

Mancera Corcuera, C. (2010). Financiamiento de la educación básica. In A. Arnaut & S. Giorguli (Eds.), *Los Grandes Problemas de México. Educación* (pp. 159–184). Colegio de Mexico.

Martínez-González, G. (2020). Efectos sobre el empleo del salario mínimo en México. *Análisis Económico*, 35(89), 9–35.

Mendoza Rojas, J. (2010). Tres décadas de financiamiento de la educación superior. In A. Arnaut & S. Giorguli (Eds.), *Los Grandes Problemas de México. Educación* (pp. 391–418). Colegio de Mexico.

Mincer, J. (1974). *Schooling, experience and earnings*. Columbia University Press.

Miranda-López, F. (2018). Infraestructura escolar en México: Brechas traslapadas, esfuerzos y límites de la política pública. *Perfiles Educativos*, 40(161), 32–52.

Morales-Ramos, E. (2011). Los Rendimientos de la Educación en México. Banco de México, *Working Papers Series* 2011-07.

Moreno-Brid, J. C., & Ros, J. (2009). *Development and growth in the Mexican economy: An historical perspective.* Oxford University Press.

Moreno-Brid, J. C., Garry, S., & Monroy-Gómez-Franco, L. A. (2014). El "Salario mínimo en México. *EconomíaUNAM, 11*(33), 78–93.

Ochoa Adame, G., García, A. T., & García Cruz, M. B. (2021). Discriminación salarial y calificación por género en los estados de la frontera norte de México: un análisis por sector de actividad. In A. Vazquez & J. Martínez (Eds.), *Mercado de trabajo y Crecimiento: Análisis teóricos y aplicados para el caso de México* (pp. 19–37). Universidad Autónoma de Chihuahua.

OECD. (2018). The future of Mexican higher education promoting quality and equity. *Reviews of National Policies for Education.*

Orraca, P., Cabrera, F.-J., & Iriarte, G. (2016). The gender wage gap and occupational segregation in the Mexican labour market. *EconoQuantum, 13*(1), 51–72.

Parnreiter, C. (2010). Global cities in global commodity chains: Exploring the role of Mexico City in the geography of global economic governance. *Global Networks, 10*(1), 35–53.

Philippon, T., & Reshef, A. (2012). Wages and human capital in the US finance industry: 1909–2006. *The Quarterly Journal of Economics, 127*(4), 1551–1609.

Rodríguez-Oreggia, E., & López Videla, B. (2015). Imputación de ingresos laborales. Una aplicación con encuestas de empleo en México. *El Trimestre Económico, 82*(32), 117–146.

Ros, J. (2013). *Algunas tesis equivocadas sobre el estancamiento económico de México.* Colegio de Méexico / UNAM.

Ros, J. (2015). *¿Cómo salir de la trampa del lento crecimiento y alta desigualdad?* El Colegio de México / UNAM.

Salmerón Castro, F., & Delgado, R. P. (2010). La educación indígena: fundamentos teóricos y propuestas de política pública. In A. Arnaut & S. Giorguli (Eds.), *Los Grandes Problemas de México. Educación* (pp. 509–546). Colegio de México.

Santibáñez, L., & Martínez, J. F. (2010). Políticas de incentivos para maestros: carrera magisterial y opciones de reforma. In A. Arnaut & S. Giorguli (Eds.), *Los Grandes Problemas de México. Educación* (pp. 125–158). Colegio de México.

Santos-Paulino, A. U. (2017). Estimating the impact of trade specialisation and trade policy on poverty in developing countries. *The Journal of International Trade and Economic Development, 26*(6), 693–711.

Sargent, J., & Matthews, L. (2009). China versus Mexico in the global EPZ industry: Maquiladoras, FDI quality and plant mortality. *World Development, 37*(6), 1069–1082.

Sebastian, R., & Biagi, F. (2018). The routine biased technical change hypothesis: A critical review. Publications Office of the European Union.

Secretaría de Educación Pública (SEP). (2020). *Principales cifras del sistema educativo nacional. 2019–2020.* Secretaría de Educación Pública, Dirección General de Planeación, Programación y Estadística Educativa.

Székely Pardo, M. (2010). Avances y transformaciones en la educación superior. In A. Arnaut & S. Giorguli (Eds.), *Los Grandes Problemas de México. Educación* (pp. 313–336). Colegio de México.

Sklair, L. (2011). *Assembling for development: The Maquila industry in Mexico and the United States.* Routledge.

Syeda Tamkeen, F. (2017). Globalisation and technology adoption: Evidence from emerging economies. *The Journal of International Trade and Economic Development, 26*(6), 724–758.

Tuirán, R., & Muñoz, C. (2010). La política de educación superior: Trayectoria reciente y escenarios futuros. In A. Arnaut & S. Giorguli (Eds.), *Los Grandes Problemas de México. Educación* (pp. 359–390). Colegio de México.

Utar, H., & Torres-Ruiz, L. (2013). International competition and industrial evolution: Evidence from the impact of Chinese on Mexican maquiladoras. *Journal of Development Economics*, *105*, 267–287.

Villa Lever, L. (2007). La educación media superior: ¿igualdad de oportunidades? *Revista de la Educación Superior*, XXXVI (1), 93–110.

Villar Lever, L. (2010). La educación media superior: su construcción social desde el México independiente hasta nuestros días. In A. Arnaut & S. Giorguli (Eds.), *Los Grandes Problemas de México. Educación* (pp. 271–312). Colegio de México.

CHAPTER 44

FACTIOUS EDUCATION POLITICS IN CHILE, 1981–2021

Enduring Contention Over Privatization, Inequality, and Quality

ALEJANDRA MIZALA AND BEN ROSS SCHNEIDER

INTRODUCTION: AN EDUCATION FIXATION

IN the beginning, there was Milton Friedman. In 1955, Friedman published a short article proposing a market remedy for underperforming education systems. Part of its attraction was its simplicity—give families a voucher worth the average cost of a child's education and, by their uncoordinated decisions on which schools to choose, the new market would reward good schools and punish (and ultimately close) the laggards. Nonetheless, Friedman's proposal had few takers in the real world until 1981 when Chile implemented a full national voucher system. The architects of this reform were directly inspired by Friedman's theory.[1]

Importantly for later policy debates, this voucher reform was one of an expansive basket of neoliberal policies enacted during the Pinochet dictatorship by the "Chicago boys" (so-called in Spanish due to their years of study at the University of Chicago). These included policies to free up markets through trade liberalization, ending price controls and other types of state intervention, and privatizing state-owned enterprises. The neoliberal package in Chile also included longer-term policies to privatize pensions and education. In the decades after the 1980s, politics polarized with strong defenders of the full neoliberal model on the right and vocal critics of the whole package—including markets in education—on the left.

Although critical of many aspects and excesses, the center-left coalition, *Concertación de Partidos por la Democracia* (Concertación), that took over in 1990 with the transition to democracy, maintained the basics of the neoliberal model of free trade, free markets, limited government intervention, and vouchers in education. However, decades of Concertación governments after 1990 made many adjustments to the neoliberal model they inherited, and most of these adjustments, including especially in education, went in the direction of greater government regulation (Mizala & Schneider 2014a, 2020).

Education politics in Chile have been exceptionally intense, especially since student demonstrations began in 2006 (Figure 44.1). In opinion surveys, Chile is one of the only countries in Latin America where respondents often rank education among the top problems facing the country (Schneider, 2021). These and other surveys bear witness to how far and wide education debates have permeated Chilean society and polity. Education is a regular item of debate: on television, in other news media, among academics (the scholarly literature is greater on Chile than elsewhere in Latin America, especially adjusted for population), and, of course, on the streets in hundreds of demonstrations over the past 15 years.

Unlike much of the rest of Latin America, education politics also came to infuse electoral and party politics, and most cleavages on the thematic issues followed left-right partisan politics. The initial reforms in the 1980s came with explicit neoliberal ideology from a right-wing dictatorship, and, after the transition to democracy in 1990, right-wing parties staunchly defended the market-oriented voucher system. The center-left Concertación accepted the voucher system, but consistently worked to regulate it, with gradual but increasing success.

To understand the evolution of education policy since democratization in 1990 requires attention to several core features of Chilean politics: (1) political institutions that overrepresented the right and gave it effective veto power through much of the post 1990 period, (2) a raucous student movement that challenged that overrepresentation and helped develop a stronger electoral base on the left with keen interest in education

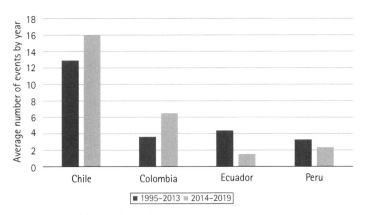

FIGURE 44.1 Protests and demands in education.

(*Source*: Integrated Crisis Early Warning System [ICEWS] Dataverse; https://dataverse.harvard.edu/dataverse/icews)

reform, and (3) well-developed academic research and an associated policy network that provided evidence to back up political demands for change and shaped technical aspects of reforms. These factors were evident in a series of post-1990s reforms, especially in the most important systemic reforms of the second government of Michelle Bachelet (2014–2018).

The general theories that best frame the analysis of education politics in Chile focus on (1) ideas and ideologies; (2) distributional conflict and power resource theory (PRT); and (3) policy networks. Unlike politics in most of Latin America (and elsewhere), debates in Chilean politics—generally and on education—reflected fairly coherent ideologies of neoliberalism versus social democracy (Blyth, 2002; Hall, 1993). At the same time, policy shifts in education clearly reveal distributional struggles, and the power of the left and allies (in protests and elections) to prevail in some of these struggles (PRT) (Ansell, 2010; Huber & Stephens, 2012). Lastly, the specific design of policy shifts depended on the evolving consensus in the education policy network comprised of several dozen top ministry officials and advisors, academics, and experts from civil society in education (think tanks, foundations, and nongovernmental organizations) (Mizala & Schneider, 2020; Rhodes, 2012).

The general context in Chile over the past three decades has been one of stable politics (post-2019 turbulence notwithstanding) and steady economic growth that raised Chile from middle-income to high-income status according to the World Bank. Education spending grew in absolute and relative terms and more than doubled as a percent of GDP (Figure 44.2).

This chapter is organized around the main thematic issues that have been at the center of political debate and contention: state versus market (second section), profit versus nonprofit (third section), stratification and inequality (fourth section), and quality upgrading and teacher careers (fifth section). In each policy area, governments have

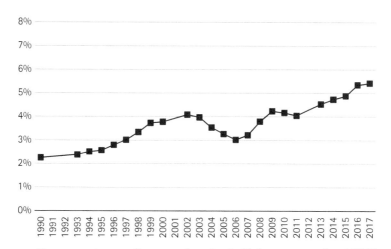

FIGURE 44.2 Government expenditure on education in Chile 1990–2017 (% of GDP).

(*Source*: UNESCO Institute for Statistics)

undertaken reforms with different intensity and timing over the last four decades, with the most sweeping reforms coming in the second Bachelet government (2014–2018). The following sections give some background on each thematic issue and then focus more selectively on major points of inflection.

State Versus Market: Privatization and Vouchers

State versus market is the master narrative that runs through all the other issues in education. The Pinochet regime pushed a neoliberal agenda of market liberalization and privatization earlier and further than any other country in Latin America. And the military government pushed privatization further in education than all but a few countries in the world (Cummings et al., 2021).

In 1981, the government implemented a country-wide voucher system and decentralized public schools to municipalities. In this system, the government granted a per-student subsidy to all public and private-voucher schools, and all families were allowed to take their voucher to the school of their choice. Before 1981, some private schools, mostly religious, already received public funds. For them, public support continued with vouchers, and this segment, private-voucher schools, then grew well beyond their religious origins. By 1990, public school enrollment had dropped from almost 80% to 60% and those attending private-voucher schools had increased to more than one third (Figure 44.3). By the late 2010s, roughly 55% of children were enrolled in private-voucher schools, 35% in public schools, and 10% attended private-paid schools.

By the 1990s, four institutional features of the education system stood out. First, from the beginning, the voucher was flat and did not vary with family income. Second, private-voucher schools (but not public schools) were allowed to select and reject students. Third, though initially proscribed, a 1993 law allowed primary and secondary private-voucher schools (but only secondary public schools) to charge additional fees to families (under a withdrawal schedule that reduced the government subsidy as parental fees rose). This system—known as "shared financing" (*financiamiento compartido*) or copayments—expanded rapidly from 16% of the voucher enrollments in 1993 to about 80% in 1998, stabilizing thereafter (Mizala & Torche, 2017). Fourth, in 1991 a special Teacher Statute for municipal schools centralized collective bargaining and gave teachers a set of associated protections and benefits. Teachers in private-voucher schools came under the same Labor Code as other private-sector workers (Mizala & Schneider, 2014a).

The center-left Concertación coalition, in power from 1990 until 2010, increased the real value of the voucher, targeted assistance to schools serving the most deprived populations, and made the Teacher Statute less rigid. However, the central features of the voucher system remained basically unchanged until 2015. Studies on the outcomes

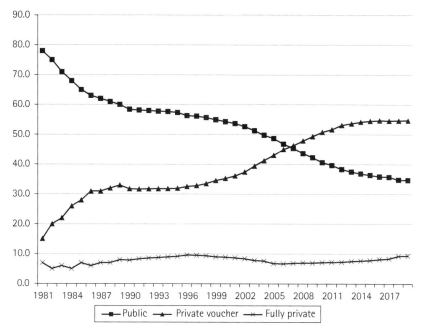

FIGURE 44.3 Enrolment in public, private voucher, and private schools, 1981–2019.

(*Source*: Unidad de Estadísticas, Ministerio de Educación)

of the Chilean voucher system agree that it helped attain universal coverage, but it did not noticeably improve quality or equality.[2] Over these and other issues, tensions flared up often between those defending the equal right to high-quality education through regulation against others arguing for freedom of education. Freedom in this instance meant largely the right of the private sector to create and manage schools as they saw fit, and the freedom of parents to choose schools.

For market competition among schools to result in improvements in the quality of education, parent choices must depend on school quality and ability to promote learning. However, if parents see school choice as a means of obtaining better peer groups, regardless of achievement, there will be no competitive pressure to improve quality (Hsieh & Urquiola, 2006; Mizala & Urquiola, 2013). Moreover, interpreting information about school effectiveness is not easy for many parents, and there is scant evidence of students switching to more effective schools (Mizala & Urquiola, 2013).

Concertación governments changed the basic voucher model little, but they sought a variety of ways to regulate it and shift incentives. A new General Education Law approved in 2009 included measures to regulate the effects of marketization and privatization. The government also created two oversight bodies in 2011: a Quality Assurance Agency to oversee academic performance and a Superintendency of Education to monitor public spending. These institutions set minimum quality standards and increased the government capacity to monitor and assess the quality of school provision, both public and private. To promote greater equity, the government created a means-tested, preferential voucher in 2008 that increased the value of the voucher for children from poor families (more details in the fourth section).

The major inflection point, and victory of left critics of marketization, came after 2013 and Michele Bachelet's decisive re-election. The Inclusion Law of 2015 ended copayments, established a centralized school admission system, and forbade for-profit voucher schools. The aim of the Inclusion Law was to avoid the adverse effects of stratification and inequality in educational opportunities generated by the school-choice system. In terms of quality, a law on a National Teacher Policy in 2016 created a new teacher career (details in fifth section). Finally, since 2017, the administration of public schools has been gradually transferred from the municipal governments to 70 new local public education services.

Much of street protest in Chile has been against this basic market and voucher model, and many protesters would like to scrap the voucher system altogether. However, left alliances in Congress always preferred regulation to abolition, and the powerful right wing has fervently defended the market model.

Profit Versus Nonprofit: From Protests to Prohibition

The issue of profit-making by schools and universities has always exercised student protesters. Profit-making in education is, of course, related to the overarching debate on public versus private education. However, ending profits in schools and universities became an issue in its own right because students were so adamant in their opposition. From the early 2006, demonstrations by high school students (called the "pingüinos/ penguin" protests because of the student uniforms) showed that opposition to profits was a core issue (Donoso, 2013; Kubal & Fisher, 2016). University students continued protests against profits in waves of protests after 2011. By then, in public opinion polls, fully 80% of respondents opposed profits in education (CEP, 2011). On the other side, for school owners this was a major concern of self-interest, and a lot of owners shared these concerns because around two thirds of private-voucher schools were for profit by the 2010s (Elacqua, 2012, p. 448).[3]

What made the issue additionally fraught was the devious ways that owners took their profits out. Had owners added up revenues, subtracted expenses, and taken part of any remaining surplus, the debate could have been different. Such an approach would have been legal for private-voucher schools (but not universities). However, instead, profits at both university and school levels were usually siphoned off surreptitiously through rent or service contracts. That is, owners created separate companies that in turn rented buildings to schools or supplied them with other consulting services. For university owners, where profits were not legal, the incentives for taking profits out via rent were clear, but less so for school owners.

These underhanded practices had at least three likely impacts on the dispute on profits. First, for students and other opponents, the fact that profits flowed illegally out of education reduced faith in government ability to regulate profits and increased suspicions that the government did not want to offend school owners. Second, the fact that owners could find ways around regulations bolstered arguments that stopping profits could only be done by ending private property in education. And third, new policies to thwart profit taking would have to be more sophisticated than just outlawing profits, which ultimately inspired government regulations obliging schools to buy their buildings.

For many students and left-wing parties, making profits in basic functions of the state was simply unethical. In contrast, right and center groups had no problem with public funding for for-profit schools and argued that for-profit schools expand the range of educational options for families. For these groups, proper regulation to ensure quality and equity was more important than issues of ownership and profit. Along these lines, the Presidential Advisory Council for the Quality of Education in 2006 during President Bachelet's first administration did not reach an agreement to ban for-profit schools, but instead created the Superintendency of Education to monitor the use of public resources by the schools.

Nonetheless, when she announced her candidacy in April 2013, Bachelet declared her first commitment was to end profits in education (Tome, 2015, p. 194). The second Bachelet administration (2014–2018) passed the Inclusion Law of 2015 that prohibited for-profit schools.[4] Schools had to be legally nonprofit and also the owners of their buildings had to block taking profits through rent payments. The debate in Congress over the proposed law evolved along three axes. First, the center-left parties argued that when there are profits in education, economic interests prevail over educational ones to the detriment of education quality. The right-wing parties considered that profits and good education are not incompatible, but that it was necessary to regulate earnings to ensure the quality of the education provided.

Second, the center-left parties believed that eliminating profits and students' selection by schools would improve social integration at the school level and provide a more inclusive education. The right-wing parties argued that what is relevant for the quality of education is the teacher–student relationship within the classroom and prohibiting profits does not improve this relationship. Third, on the issue of the purchase of buildings by schools, the center-left parties argued that it was better to pay a mortgage than to pay a rent, since at the end schools would own the property. The right-wing parties argued that the banks would profit from mortgages to the schools and that the schools would divert voucher money to pay for the mortgage instead of improving the quality of education (Holz & Medel, 2017). At first, in the Law approved in 2015 schools were given 12 years to buy the buildings where they operated. Later, in 2017, the Bachelet government allowed regulated rents for voucher schools.

In sum, from 2006 when the Pingüinos put profits at the core of their demands, it took nearly a decade of further street protests, growing support in public opinion, and a decisive electoral victory in 2013 to get to legislation outlawing profits.

STRATIFICATION, INEQUALITY, AND REDISTRIBUTION BY VOUCHER

Chile has long been a highly unequal country in income, wealth, and other dimensions, education included (PNUD, 2017). Education was first stratified across the 20th century with a tenth or so of enrollments in fully private, tuition-charging schools for the economic and political elite. Then two features built into the voucher system worked to produce a stark social stratification across schools: copayment fees and student selection by the schools. However, a decade of bottom-up pressure—protests and elections—brought major redistributive changes in 2015.

In 1993, surprisingly, the new center-left government granted schools the right to charge copayments on top of the voucher. At this time, the Concertación government wanted badly to raise taxes to fund other social programs. However, the right-wing opposition would only agree to tax increases (and the right had veto power) in exchange for allowing copays, an unambiguous indication of how important these fees were to the right (Cummings et al., 2021). Such fees alone created a system where parents choose schools according to their willingness and capacity to pay. By 2015, copayments totaled 16% of spending in private-voucher schools.[5] In addition to fees, private-voucher schools were also granted the right to select students which they could use to insure middle-class homogeneity. This homogeneity in turn attracted many parents who selected schools primarily for the peers their children would have (Canales et al., 2016).

By 2010s, the voucher system had very effectively sorted students by class (Hsieh & Urquiola, 2006; Mizala & Torche, 2012). By a government measure of socioeconomic segregation in 2013, 80% of students from the bottom two income quintiles attended public municipal schools, while 90% of students from the fourth, upper income quintile went to private-voucher schools. Of the richest quintile, 80% attended fully private schools (Inzunza et al., 2019, p. 500).[6] On various indices of school segregation, Chile ranked among the most segregated in Latin America on data from PISA 2015 (Krüger, 2019) though ranked somewhat lower with data from TERCE 2013 (Murillo & Martínez-Garrido, 2017). Moreover, the flat voucher did not take into account the international evidence that it is costlier to educate students living in poverty, in single-parent households, or with poorly educated parents (Duncombe & Yinger, 2005). Thus, schools had incentives to select students from rich families and exclude poorer students.

Student demonstrations after 2006 decried this inequality and segregation (Bellei & Cabalin, 2013; Donoso, 2013; Kubal & Fisher, 2016). In response to these and other criticisms, President Bachelet established the Presidential Advisory Council on the Quality of Education in 2006. For the first time, all major stakeholders in education (around 80 members) were in the same forum to debate their continuing large differences of opinion. However, the council could not come to a unanimous position on reforms. The members of the so-called social block—students, teachers, and representatives of parent associations—rejected the Council's final report because it lacked more radical reforms. This group demanded, among other things, the prohibition of student selection by schools, banning for-profit schools, more funding for public schools than private ones, and the de-municipalization of public schools (Cummings et al., 2021; Mizala & Schneider, 2014b). These issues returned to the reform agenda in Bachelet's second government (2014–2018).

The first Bachelet government also pushed legislation for the Preferential School Voucher (Subvención Escolar Preferencial) (first proposed by the Lagos government in 2005). Approved in 2008, the law transformed the flat voucher system into a means-tested one. It established an additional per-student subsidy for poorer students and an extra subsidy for schools with a high proportion of disadvantaged students. By 2020, the preferential voucher added between 65% (primary) and 37% (secondary) to the standard voucher. In schools with high concentrations of poor students, the preferential voucher (SEP, Subvención Escolar Preferencial) added 74% in primary schools and 42% in secondary schools (Mineduc data) (Figure 44.4).

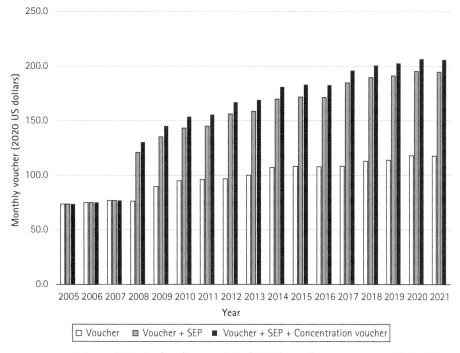

FIGURE 44.4 Values of standard and means tested (SEP) vouchers, 2005–2021. Note: Value of the regular per-student voucher shown in light gray, value of the regular voucher plus the SEP means-tested voucher at a SEP school (Voucher + SEP) shown in dark gray, and value of the regular voucher plus means-tested voucher plus the maximum poverty concentration subsidy (60% or more priority students at the school) (Voucher + SEP + Concentration Voucher) shown in black. Values are for students in fourth grade in schools with full school shifts. US$ December 2020 (exchange rate Ch$709.75 per dollar).

(*Source*: Ministry of Education)

For schools, opting into the preferential-voucher program was voluntary, and it came with strings attached in terms of conditions and provision of a medium-term learning plan.[7] In 2008, the first year of the reform, 93% (99% by 2011) of primary municipal schools—where poorer students were concentrated—enrolled in the program. In contrast, only 52% of primary private-voucher schools enrolled in the first year, rising by 2014 to 72% (Mizala & Torche, 2017). Research to date has shown positive effects of SEP on student test scores (Correa et al., 2014; Navarro-Palau, 2017). SEP also helped poorer students improve scores more, and the reform had increasingly favorable impacts over the medium run (5–6 years) (Mizala & Torche, 2017, p. 180).

In 2013, Bachelet returned to run again for president. Her electoral campaign and support coalition were put together in the wake of over 2 years of frequent student demonstrations and street protests.[8] Consequently, education reform was high on the campaign agenda. Bachelet's electoral platform headlined three core areas of fundamental reform, starting with education, followed by tax and constitutional reform. The education reform included proposals on (1) new regulations for preschool education, (2) prohibition of student selection by schools, elimination of parental copayments, and prohibition of profit-making in education, (3) a national teaching career to improve teaching quality (covered in the next section); and (4) de-municipalization of public education as well as reforms to higher education. The second fundamental reform was in taxation, largely designed to finance the costly education reforms.

Reforms of item (2)—no selection, no copay, and no profit—were the heart of the most controversial reform, the Inclusion Law of 2015 (Cummings et al., 2021). The law ended copayments (replaced by extending the Preferential School Voucher to middle-class students), granted a per-student bonus to free-of-charge schools, and increased per-student subsidies. By 2018, 93% of students already attended a free-of-charge school. The new law also established a new centralized school admission system and prohibited student selection by schools.[9] Also, for-profit private-voucher schools must convert themselves into nonprofit corporations or foundations, and the rents they pay for their buildings are now regulated according to the law.

Passage of the 2015 Inclusion Law was one of the most radical changes to the voucher system since its inception. But it did not by any means end debates on regulating schools to achieve greater equality. In 2019, President Sebastián Piñera's administration proposed to Congress a new project to allow some leeway for schools to select students and to reverse the centralized admission system created by the Inclusion Law. This "Just Admission Project" addressed one of the issues that generated the strongest opposition to the Inclusion Law from parents and the Catholic Church. The Piñera government was unable to get this bill and others changing the Inclusion Law through Congress, but the initiative clearly signaled that the right does not consider the Inclusion Law as settled business.

In sum, inequality and segregation have long been divisive issues. The right vigorously supported student selection, copayments, and profits. Student protests, in long waves after 2006, put these issues on the top of the electoral agenda. And Bachelet's decisive victory in 2013, powered by poorer voters, opened the way for the Inclusion Law of 2015 that drastically transformed private-voucher schools and the education system overall. Together the 2008 law on preferential vouchers and the Inclusion Law added up to a major redistribution of resources to poorer students.

QUALITY UPGRADING BY REVAMPING TEACHER CAREERS

In the Friedman model, the market was supposed to take care of quality. Families would move their children from bad schools to good schools. The latter would expand, the former close, and the government could watch from the sidelines. In practice, Chile's experience provided little evidence of Friedman's vision. In general, critics of school choice would not be surprised (Fiske & Ladd, 2001). They claim that the likely effect in the practice of school choice is segregation and inequality in educational outcomes (Epple & Romano, 1998). In Chile, governments after 1990 intervened in the education system to improve quality by implementing school improvement and pedagogical renewal programs (as well as support programs focused on the poorest schools), extending the school day, and strengthening the teaching profession, the most complex reform.

In principle, a decentralized, market system leaves issues of hiring, salaries, and working conditions of teachers up to markets and school directors as was mostly the case in private-voucher schools in Chile. In public municipal schools, the fraught politics of the transition to democracy in 1990 produced legislation that recentralized labor relations. More specifically, in 1990, the Colegio de Profesores pressed the newly elected center-left Concertación government to reverse the decentralized system created during the Pinochet dictatorship and return teachers to their prior civil service status.

The Concertación government did not reverse decentralization of public schools or the voucher system, but it did try to accommodate other demands through a new Teacher Statute that granted public school teachers tenure and centralized wage negotiations. This episode is a good example of how political mobilization by powerful stakeholders can introduce complications into purer Friedmanite models, in this case centralized labor relations in a decentralized voucher system. Once the Statute was enacted, however, successive governments pursued reforms to make it less rigid and to introduce incentives that were more market compatible and connected to education quality.

Subsequent Concertación governments introduced first collective and then individual evaluations and bonuses. The first collective incentive was the National System of School Performance Evaluation (*Sistema Nacional de Evaluación del Desempeño de los Establecimientos Educacionales* [SNED]) created in 1996. The goal was to reward and incentivize good performance of teachers in public and private-voucher schools. Every 2 years schools with excellent results receive a collective bonus (Mizala & Romaguera, 2004). In the 2000s, governments introduced additional individual incentives that further differentiated salaries with individual incentives (Pedagogical Excellence Award [Asignación de Excelencia Pedagógica, AEP], Red Maestro de Maestros [Master Teacher Network]).[10]

These incentives linking pay to performance were part of regular salary negotiations between the Colegio de Profesores and the Ministry of Education. As is common elsewhere, the teacher association in Chile opposed the performance incentives initially. Two key factors facilitated the introduction of incentive pay despite Colegio opposition. First, from the early 1990s both sides entered negotiations expecting final compromise and agreement in part because the high costs of lengthy strikes, and over time because of the precedent of previous negotiations. Second, salaries grew rapidly throughout this period, so union leaders could get both substantial gains in base salaries and accede to government pressure to add on incentive payments on top (Mizala & Schneider, 2014a).

The second Bachelet government passed a National Teacher Policy in 2016 (Mizala & Schneider, 2020). This was a systemic policy covering teachers in both municipal and private-voucher schools: (1) higher entrance requirements and accreditation for teacher preparation programs; (2) early career mentoring for incoming teachers; and (3) professional development system for long-term career advancement. This career ladder had five levels and provided for increased salaries and professional opportunities at each level. The ladder had three required steps (Beginning, Early, and Advanced) and two further voluntary steps (Expert I and Expert II).

To climb through the career levels, teachers have to demonstrate pedagogical skills measured through a portfolio of teacher evaluations and disciplinary and pedagogical knowledge (through written tests). If assessments detect shortcomings, then schools can offer in-service professional development programs (with central financing). The law also set maximum time limits for teachers to progress through the first three obligatory steps. Teachers who do not pass in the maximum time can no longer teach in publicly funded schools. The National Teacher Policy boosted starting salaries by a third, and after 16 years teachers at the highest level can earn more than 50% over the previous maximum salary.[11]

Already by 2018, teacher buy-in was substantial. Although disagreeing with some components of the new law, 69% of teachers in voucher schools, public and private, thought there should be a national evaluation system, and 66% thought that teachers should go through evaluations to move up the career ladder (Elige-Educar, 2018, p. 1). Once in full operation, this new career system will cost US$2.3 billion per year: a huge increase in new spending equivalent to 0.9% of GDP and 3.8% of total public spending (Mizala & Schneider, 2020, p. 7). Thus, center-left governments after 1990 adopted a long series of reforms to professionalize the teacher corps and to link economic rewards to superior teaching performance. Overall, salaries rose significantly and steadily, and more talented students (as measured by university entrance exams) started entering the teaching career.[12]

However, these career reforms have not ended debates over education quality, because student scores on PISA and SIMCE (the national standardized achievement test) still do not show substantial improvements (Figure 44.5 and Figure 44.6). From 2006

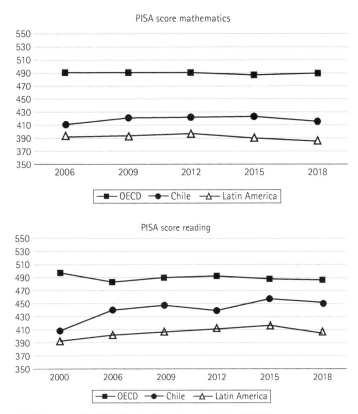

FIGURE 44.5 PISA scores in Chile, Latin America, and the OECD, 2000–2018.

to 2018, the bright spot was reading scores that improved by around 40 points, a major gain as the OECD calculates that 30 points is roughly equivalent to a year of instruction. In this gain, Chile moved away from the average for Latin America (a difference of 45 points) and closer to the OECD (lagging by 35 points in 2018). In math, Chile's scores have been flat (though pulling away from Latin America as its average falls). In SIMCE tests, although there has been some progress (except in 12th-grade language test), in recent years the rate of improvement has tended to stagnate. Several factors could explain this plateau, especially since 2009. Ironically, frequent student protests (and teacher strikes) demanding better education disrupted school calendars and left less time for instruction. And the career reform will not have much effect until years hence when teachers trained under the new higher standards graduate and when most teachers have been hired under the new career law.

In sum, teacher career went through a series of reforms through 2016 that added in successive performance incentives, first collective and then individual. The 2016 teacher career is a systemic and integral policy that includes selection and initial teacher preparation, novel teachers' induction, and a professional development system that includes teachers in private-voucher schools.

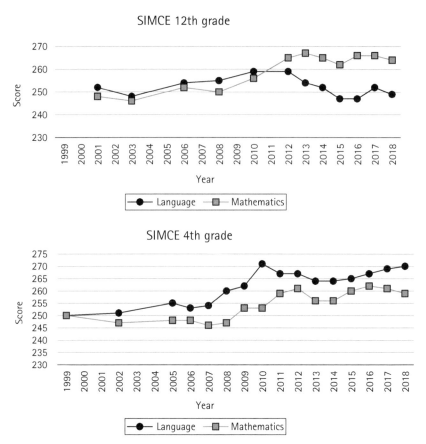

FIGURE 44.6 SIMCE scores 1999–2018.

Conclusions

In 1990, the Pinochet dictatorship bequeathed to the new democracy a market, full-choice education system that was privatized, decentralized, largely unregulated, underfunded, and stratified (with no extra help for poor students). By the late 2010s, the market still existed but the education system was much more regulated, centralized (on some dimensions), much better funded (with extensive additional resources for poor students), and probably less stratified. One of the few constants over the past three decades has been change (see Appendix).

Chile is one of only a handful of countries with national systems of school choice.[13] The others can be arrayed along a continuum with New Zealand on the unregulated, free market end, the Netherlands on the more regulated end, and Sweden and Denmark in between. The 2015 Inclusion Law moved Chile from the New Zealand end to the more regulated Dutch end. The oldest systems, over a century old, in Denmark and the Netherlands are consolidated and not contested, though aspects like inequality can become controversial. In the more recent, late 20th-century systems in Chile, New Zealand, and Sweden, openly neoliberal governments pushed school choice, and opponents on the left continue to oppose them.

This neoliberal versus anti-neoliberal divide still animates Chilean politics and provides one reason to think that reform and contention in education politics will continue. While education was less prevalent in the 2019 social eruption (*estallido social*) than it had been in earlier rounds of protests, the impact of the *estallido* is likely to reverberate through education policies for years to come. On the right, the efforts (mostly stillborn) of the Piñera government to rescind policies of the Bachelet government suggest that the right will continue to make counter-reform a high priority. And education as a social right versus market visions will likely animate debates in the assembly to draft a new constitution.

How do these dynamics of education policy and politics fit with major theories of the political economy of education? Micro-level theories focused narrowly on reform champions (Grindle, 2004), policy entrepreneurs (Rhodes, 2012), or technocrats (Cuenca et al.,) are rendered less useful by the mass politics that drove change in Chile. The dozens of experts in Chile's policy network influenced the design of specific reforms, but only after mass protests and electoral campaigns put education reform on the national agenda. This dynamic is especially evident in policies that significantly redistribute resources as was especially the case with the Inclusion Law (Cummings et al., 2021). Here, right-wing elite opposition blocked redistribution for years until student street protests and left mobilization of poorer voters in the 2013 elections tipped the balance in favor of sweeping reforms. This dynamic is more attuned to regime characteristics (democracy) and power resource theory (PRT), though with modifications. In Chile, democracy ultimately increased pressure for quality as well as quantity (Dahlum & Knutsen, 2017) and the left lacked the organized backing from labor (as in social democracies), but still triumphed.

APPENDIX

Chronology of Major Policy Changes in Chilean Education

- 1981—Decentralization of public education to the municipal level. Implementation of a country-wide school choice (voucher) system
- 1991—Teacher Statute (Estatuto Docente)
- 1996—National System of School Performance Evaluation (SNED)
- 2000–2003—Teachers' Performance Evaluation and Individual Incentives
- 2008—Preferential School Voucher granted larger subsidies for poorer students.

- 2009 General Education Law
- 2011—Superintendency of Education
- 2011—Education Quality Agency
- 2015—Inclusion Law prohibited profits, copays, and student selection
- 2016—National Teacher Policy

ACKNOWLEDGMENTS

Mizala thanks ANID/PIA/Basal Funds for Centers of Excellence FB0003 for research support. Schneider thanks J-WEL (Abdul Latif Jameel World Education Lab) at MIT for funding support and Peter Cummings, BreAnne Fleer, and Emilia Simison for research assistance. Parts of this chapter draw on Mizala and Schneider (2014b).

NOTES

1. In Chile the references to Friedman, who was alive through 2007, were clearly acknowledged. Friedman visited Chile in 1975 and 1981.
2. Many studies on the relative performance of private-voucher compared to municipal schools in standardized tests arrived at divergent conclusions. However, using new data and a better methodology, Lara et al. (2011) found positive but very small or insignificant differences between both school types.
3. Of the four other national systems of school choice, only Sweden and New Zealand allow for-profit schools, and their private sectors account for less than 15% of enrollments. The Netherlands and Denmark, along with Chile post 2015, prohibit profits (Cummings et al., 2021).
4. For more details on the Inclusion Law, see Bellei (2016), Cummings et al. (2021), Holz and Medel (2017), and Zancajo (2020).
5. Municipal schools also got additional funding (8%) but from municipal governments, not directly from parents (Bertoni et al., 2018, p. 5).
6. Stratification was less for fourth graders in 2002, with around three-fourths of municipal school students coming from the bottom three income quintiles and three-fourths of private-voucher students coming from the top three quintiles (Mizala & Torche, 2012, p. 135).
7. Schools had to sign an agreement committing them to enrolling all students who applied, not charging copayments to poor students, retaining poor students regardless of their academic performance, and achieving improvements in student learning, especially for poor students.
8. In 2011, students' demands centered on free public education, quality education across all tiers of the system, an end to loopholes that allow "nonprofit" universities to turn a profit, and a more affordable and accessible university system as a whole.
9. When a school is oversubscribed, slots are allocated by a random admission procedure. The system is similar to those in New Orleans, Boston, and New York public schools, as well as in Amsterdam and Belgium.
10. In 2004, a new law modified the SNED to increase the total award, to raise incrementally the proportion of schools awarded bonuses, and to establish a graduated scale

among winning schools. Also, in 2008 education assistants have been incorporated as beneficiaries of the SNED.

11. The policy also improves teaching conditions through the increase of nonteaching, preparation time from 25% to 35% of the work week.

12. Requiring higher test scores of students entering pedagogy programs and closing nonaccredited programs has greatly reduced the number of students preparing to be teachers—down 39% since 2011—raising concerns about potential shortages.

13. For further comparison, see Cummings et al. (2021).

References

Ansell, B. (2010). *From the ballot to the blackboard: The redistributive political economy of education.* Cambridge University Press.

Bellei, C. (2016). Dificultades y Resistencias de Una Reforma Para Des-Mercantilizar La Educación. *Revista de la Asociación de Sociología de la Educación (RASE), 9*(2), 232–247. https://dialnet.unirioja.es/servlet/articulo?codigo=5663945

Bellei, C., & Cabalin, C. (2013). Chilean student movements: Sustained struggle to transform a market-oriented educational system. *Current Issues in Comparative Education, 15*(2), 108–123. https://eric.ed.gov/?id=EJ1016193

Bertoni, E., Elacqua, G., Jaimovich, A., Rodríguez, J., Santos, H. (2018). *Teacher policies, incentives, and labor markets in Chile, Colombia, and Perú: Implications for equality.* https://publications.iadb.org/en/teacher-policies-incentives-and-labor-markets-chile-colombia-and-peru-implications-equality

Blyth, M. (2002). *Great transformations: Economic ideas and institutional change in the twentieth century.* Cambridge University Press.

Canales, M., Bellei, C., & Orellana, V. (2016). ¿Por Qué Elegir Una Escuela Privada Subvencionada? Sectores Medios Emergentes y Elección de Escuela En Un Sistema de Mercado. *Estudios pedagógicos (Valdivia), 42*(3), 89–109. https://scielo.conicyt.cl/scielo.php?pid=S0718-07052016000400005&script=sci_arttext

CEP. (2011). *Estudio Nacional de Opinión Pública N°64, Junio-Julio 2011.* Santiago, Chile.

Correa, J., Parro, F., & Reyes, L. (2014). The effects of vouchers on school results: Evidence from Chile's targeted voucher program. *Journal of Human Capital, 8*(4), 351–98. https://www.journals.uchicago.edu/doi/10.1086/679282

Cummings, P., Mizala, A., & Schneider, B. R. (2021). Chile's inclusion law in education: Student protests and the drive to reregulate an unequal system.

Dahlum, S., & Knutsen, C. H. (2017). Do democracies provide better education? Revisiting the democracy–human capital link. *World Development, 94*, 186–h99.

Donoso, S. (2013). Dynamics of change in Chile: Explaining the emergence of the 2006 Pingüino movement. *Journal of Latin American Studies, 45*(1), 1–29. http://journals.cambridge.org/abstract_S0022216X12001228

Duncombe, W., & Yinger, J. (2005). How much more does a disadvantaged student cost? *Economics of Education Review, 24*(5), 513–532. https://www.sciencedirect.com/science/article/pii/S0272775704001207?casa_token=_QmpoEGnshkAAAAA:mVgRkfEBvWiVsIqSNIjUeCBvc903O9CMXQk69V9tcZOcMiUZ7_tGFuTkg6uzi8j3RxaezbeNLQ

Elacqua, G. (2012). The impact of school choice and public policy on segregation: Evidence from Chile. International Journal of Educational Development, 32(3), 444–453.

Elige-Educar. (2018). *Voces Docentes: Tercera Versión de La Encuesta Nacional a Profesores y Profesoras de Aula*. Santiago, Chile.

Epple, D., & Romano, R. E. (1998). Competition between private and public schools, vouchers, and peer-group effects. *American Economic Review, 88*(1), 33–62. https://www.jstor.org/stable/116817?casa_token=bMlUflosiBcAAAAA:PH8ccQukYfXdw-FSI8CPkCEguQ2j2m6rFMYbfNzvrYfYPuHODXCjrBphi3k8QcjL7CTKqsiw0fErBX9-brVcUbhcPn8Zp2nVrGvMNQFiN4qYoKKzMHw

Fiske, E., & Ladd, H. (2001). *When schools compete: A cautionary tale*. Brookings Institution.

Grindle, M. (2004). *Despite the odds: The contentious politics of education reform*. Princeton University Press.

Hall, P. (1993). Policy paradigms, social learning, and the state: The case of economic policymaking in Britain. *Comparative Politics, 25*(3), 275. https://www.jstor.org/stable/422246?casa_token=SgRbZRnODHsAAAAA:1GyDa2e7URXYp7M_S_GSdW_SlBUsjHC5LlnorNfyNDoY1FUEQmdg1KS_j4vygiJAU1MPmX1DdHv2jiUhmKAVxzJEjOTctdVz_SFBYEj7HUylTX79DJs

Holz, M., & Medel, C. (2017). El Debate Parlamentario y de Los Actores Sociales En Sede Legislativa. In *El Primer Gran Debate de La Reforma Educacional* (pp. 1–216). Ministerio de Educación de Chile.

Hsieh, C. T., & Urquiola, M. (2006). The effects of generalized school choice on achievement and stratification: Evidence from Chile's voucher program. *Journal of Public Economics, 90*(8–9), 1477–1503. https://www.sciencedirect.com/science/article/pii/S0047272705001672?casa_token=aaPYDnFeCNcAAAAA:agxxjY99wYkpxXRsAXucmCMY3GqvuJX57lPntFy8n7bzOxdwydPolAG948BFVtJSEPrHTNouKg

Huber, E., & Stephens, J. D. (2012). *Democracy and the left: Social policy and inequality in Latin America*. University of Chicago Press.

Inzunza, J., Assael, J., Cornejo, R., & Redondo, J. (2019). Public education and student movements: The Chilean rebellion under a neoliberal experiment. *British Journal of Sociology of Education, 40*(4), 490–506. https://www.tandfonline.com/doi/full/10.1080/01425692.2019.1590179

Krüger, N. (2019). Socioeconomic school segregation as a dimension of educational exclusion: Fifteen years of evolution in Latin America. *Education Policy Analysis Archives, 27*, 8. https://epaa.asu.edu/ojs/article/view/3577

Kubal, M. R., & Fisher, E. (2016). The politics of student protest and education reform in Chile: Challenging the neoliberal state. *The Latin Americanist, 60*(2), 217–242. http://doi.wiley.com/10.1111/tla.12075

Lara, B., Mizala, A., & Repetto, A. (2011). The effectiveness of private voucher education: Evidence from structural school switches. *Educational Evaluation and Policy Analysis, 33*(2), 119–137. https://journals.sagepub.com/doi/abs/10.3102/0162373711402990

Mizala, A., & Romaguera, P. (2004). School and teacher performance incentives: The Latin American experience. *International Journal of Educational Development, 24*(6), 739–754. https://www.sciencedirect.com/science/article/pii/S0738059304000574

Mizala, A., & Schneider, B. R. (2014a). Negotiating education reform: Teacher evaluations and incentives in Chile (1990–2010). *Governance, 27*(1), 87–109.

Mizala, A., & Schneider, B. R. (2014b). The political economy of regulating the private provision of education in Chile. In M. Cammett & L. Maclean (Eds.), *The politics of non-state social welfare in the global south* (pp. 195–215). Cornell University Press.

Mizala, A., & Schneider, B. R. (2020). Promoting quality education in Chile: The politics of reforming teacher careers. *Journal of Education Policy*, *35*(1), 132–144. https://www.tandfonl ine.com/doi/full/10.1080/02680939.2019.1585577

Mizala, A., & Torche, F. (2012). Bringing the schools back in: The stratification of educational achievement in the Chilean voucher system. *International Journal of Educational Development*, *32*(1), 132–144.

Mizala, A., & Torche, F. (2017). Means-tested school vouchers and educational achievement: Evidence from Chile's universal voucher system. *The ANNALS of the American Academy of Political and Social Science*, *674*(1), 163–183. http://journals.sagepub.com/doi/10.1177/00027 16217732033

Mizala, A., & Urquiola, M. (2013). School markets: The impact of information approximating schools' effectiveness. *Journal of Development Economics*, *103*(1), 313–335. https://www. sciencedirect.com/science/article/pii/S0304387813000333?casa_token=tSQ8u7DSsrQAA AAA:rYPFJp5Pst9CfW3mkRort9M9VfjYt8BroSgXfiA13BODb-_D7wnqRzdjeh5qElvjT_5 F6J_bEA

Murillo, F. J., & Martínez-Garrido, C. (2017). Estimación de La Magnitud de La Segregación Escolar En América Latina. *Magis*, *9*(19), 1–30. http://revistas.javeriana.edu.co/index.php/ MAGIS/article/view/18608

Navarro-Palau, P. (2017). Effects of differentiated school vouchers: Evidence from a policy change and date of birth cutoffs. *Economics of Education Review*, *58*, 86–107. https://www. sciencedirect.com/science/article/pii/S0272775716303235?casa_token=wgj5ozfqyaIAA AAA:j_ysKEIkYkmRVHdgud9gtdhlf2OcU_zlJa4dphvCoxXo7QyyiUU205_xitQA3hS N1zP7HhnRcw

PNUD. (2017). *Desiguales: Orígenes, Cambios y Desafíos de La Brecha Social En Chile*. PNUD.

Rhodes, J. (2012). *An education in politics: The origins and evolution of No Child Left Behind*. Cornell University Press.

Schneider, B. R. (2024). *Routes to reform: Education politics in Latin America*. Oxford University Press.

Tome, Christopher. 2015. ¡No lucro! . . . from protest catch cry to presidential policy: Is this the beginning of the end of the Chilean neoliberal model of education? *Journal of Educational Administration and History*, *47*(2), 193–208.

Zancajo, A. (2020). Schools in the marketplace: Analysis of school supply responses in the Chilean education market. *Educational Policy*, *34*(1), 43–64.

INDEX

For the benefit of digital users, indexed terms that span two pages (e.g., 52–53) may, on occasion, appear on only one of those pages.

ABB Group, 737–38
ability to learn
  contingency formula, 416
  early childhood education, 418
academic capitalism, 161
academic disciplines, publishing patterns
  in, 741–48
academic drift, 203–4
  concept of, 199
Academic Ranking of World Universities
  (ARWU), 132
academic revolution, 198
academic science, 732
accessibility, higher education, 38–42
accountability
  education, 596–97
  organizational learning, 606
  secondary education, 93
acculturation, 18–19
Ackerman, Bruce, 827
action, local, 55
actionable knowledge, 216–17
activism, countries and education reforms,
  661f, 661
actor(s)
  curricula, 106
  institutional logics, 174–75
  mediation mechanisms and
    instruments, 155–57
actor-network theory, 161
actor-structure theory, 161
actorhood, 122, 153
  claims of, 164n.1
  myth of, 10–11, 23n.6

Ad hoc Council on Education Reforms
  (AHCER), 698–99, 708
  agenda setting for policy proposals, 703–6
Adams, John, 439n.3
adaptive education process
  global guidelines for, 418–19
  monitoring tools, 419
  person categories in early childhood
    education, 419–20
Addey, Camilla, 61–62
African Union (AU), 486
agency, globalization, 195–96
agents of institutional change
  teachers as, 171–75
  See also teacher(s)
age of nation-states, 29
AGIL (Adaptation, Goal attainment,
  Integration, Latency), system needs,
  353, 356–57
Airbus Group, 737–38
algorithmic governmentality, 41
algorithmic management, 41
all-around education (*Bildung*), 407–8, 450
All India Council of Technical Education
  (AICTE), 788–90
Alliance for Initial and Further Education and
  Training, 87–88
Allianz für Aus- und Weiterbildung (AfAW),
  85, 87–88
Altbach, Philip G., 15–16
alterity, 831
American advantage, 34
American Sociological Review (journal), 104
American universities, 53–54

American University, The (monograph), 354
American University of Dubai (AUD), 339–40
American University of Sharjah, 339–40
Amnesty International, 134–35
analytical realism, Parsons on, 353
Andersen, Niels Åkerstrøm, 401n.4
Anderson, Benedict, 183–84
Anna University, 746–48
anthropology, 4
  action as local, 55
  globalization seen from, 53–55
  remaking policies locally, 62–64
  travel means translation, 55
Anthropology & Education Quarterly
  (journal), 61
anthropology of education, 52–53
anti-authoritarianism, left-wing, 445
Appadurai, Arjun, 164, 712
apparatus
  notion of, 16–17
  term, 30
  See also learning apparatus
Apple, 105
Arab Bureau of Education for the Gulf States
  (ABEGS), 485–86, 493
Arab League Educational, Cultural and
  Scientific Organisation (ALECSO),
  485–86, 492, 493
Arendt, Hannah, 828, 852–53
Argentina
  cases of subnational policy
    innovation, 930–33
  Conectar Igualdad, 930–31, 932
  COVID-19 pandemic and education
    in, 929–30
  decentralization and education reform,
    911–12, 915–17, 933–34
  development of state education
    system, 913–15
  economic globalization in
    provinces, 926–28
  Education Financing Law, 913, 917, 920–26,
    927
  education policies in, 912–13, 915–17
  education spending and exports in
    provinces, 927f
  education spending in, 926–28

evolution of subnational education
    spending in, 922t
  globalization in, 912, 913–15
  illiteracy, school attendance and policy
    implementation, 933
  illiteracy rate of population by
    province, 918f
  percentage of homes with internet access by
    province, 929f
  percentage of students enrolled in public and
    private schools by province, 924–25, 924f
  Plan Sarmiento, 932
  school attendance by province, 919f
  subnational variation in education, 911–
    12, 917–20
  Todos los Chicos en la Red, 930–32
  UNDP Human Development Index by
    province, 918t
Ariès, Philippe, 446
Aristotle, 838–39, 843
Arrow, Kenneth, 825
Article 26, United Nations Charter, 32–33
ARWU World University Ranking, 738
Asia-Europe Foundation (ASEF), 492
Asia-Pacific Economic Cooperation
  (APEC), 492
Asian countries, mobility of international
  students, 334–36
Asian Development Bank (ADB), 486–87
assessment, reforms, 376
Assessment for Learning (AfL), 601, 603–4
Association of American University (AAU), 53
Association of Southeast Asian Nations
  (ASEAN), 494
associations of private charity, 412
Astiz, Fernanda, 147
AstraZeneca, 737–38
Australia
  inequalities, 215
  secondary education, 81–82
Austria
  Christian-democratic OEVP, 84–85
  curriculum regulations, 83
  Gymnasium, 81
  labor unions, 567
autonomy
  concept of, 253–54

concepts of vertical and horizontal, 257–58
education system, 411
horizontal, 257
school education, 393, 449–51
avant la lettre, 192, 202–4
Axial Age, 619
Aydarova, Elena, 61–62

Bachelet, Michele, Chile, 990, 991, 992–93, 994–95
Baker, David, 147
Banca Monte dei Paschi di Siena, 53, 426
banks in higher education, policy effects on, 567–68
Barry, Brian, 826, 852
Basic Education Act (1969), 598
Bateson, Gregory, 361–62
Bayer, 737–38
Beck, Ulrich, 195–96, 712
Becker, Bastian, 624
Beech, Jason, 887n.22
Bentham, Jeremy, 828–29, 840–41, 848, 852
Bergen municipality, 607n.1
Berlin, Isaiah, 859n.68
Bernstein, Basil, 316
Bertelsmann, 259–60
Bess, Michael, 839–40
"Better Assessment Practices" pilot, 603–4
bifocality, functional, universities, 432–34
Bildung, 59, 407–8
Bill & Melinda Gates Foundation, 754–55, 908n.11
biomedicine, 57–58
Birla-Amabani Committee, India, 788–89
Bismarck, Otto von, 413–14
Bloom, Benjamin, 416
Böhme, Gernot, 396
Bohr, Niels, 836, 855n.15
Bollywood, 332–33
Bologna Accord, 219
Bologna Process, 109–10, 195–96, 676
Bolsonaro, Jair, Brazil, 108
Bonds, Eric, 221
Bosanquet, Bernard, 828
Bourdieu, Pierre, 248, 395
education in making transnational class, 306
field of colonialism, 258–59

field theory, 248–51
French fields of (higher) education, 260–61
social differentiation, 260–61
Bourdieu's field theory, 200
Bradley, F. H., 828
branching pathways, 81–82
Bratton, Benjamin, 397–98
Brazil
advent of globalization, 939–40
Bolsonaro, 108
correlation coefficient between education and exports, 946, 947t
cosmopolitan education across, 308
decentralization and OECD, 506–9
decentralized education system, 499, 940–42
distribution of exports, 947, 950f
education spending, 951–52
Federal Constitution, 939–40, 941–42, 952
globalization, 942–45
"The Lost Decade", 503
main export items by geographical region (2019), 947, 949t
methodology and results, 946–51
OECD and, 511
public policy, 942–45
Public Spending Limit Constitutional Amendment, 952
purchase power parity (PPP), 944, 952n.5
reforms, 98
resources paid on education (2013-2019), 946, 948f
socioeconomic structure, 942–45
spending on education per capita (2013-2019), 947, 950f
Brazilian National Archive, Brasilia, 502
Bretton Woods system, 415–16
Brexit, 721–22
BRIC countries, 10–11
bricolage
institutional logics, 184–85
power to mobilize and communicate, 184–85
term, 184
British disease, 703
Japan avoiding, 708
Koyama's view on, 709n.3
symptoms of, 700
term, 700

INDEX

British Idealism, 856n.26
"Britishness" self-promotion tools, 314
Brown vs. Board of Education, 180–81
bubbles of privilege, 307
Buchanan, James, 825–26, 827
Bucher, Tiana, 41
Buddhism, 619
Buddhist monastic systems, 176

Calculus of Consent, The (Buchanan and
    Tullock), 826, 854n.11, 855n.14
Caldwell, Oliver J., 500–1, 504–5, 511n.2,
    512nn.9–10
Campbell, John, 156, 160–61
Canada, 158
    education reform and political
        discourse, 545–46
    for-profit and nonprofit organizational
        actors in textbooks, 134, 134*f*
    international governmental and
        nongovernmental organizational actors
        in textbooks, 134–36, 135*f*
    open employment system, 299
Canadian Pacific Railway, 134
Can Virtue Make Us Happy? (Höffe), 843
capability approach (CA), 273–74
    conditions of capabilities
        deployment, 279–80
    deployment of real freedom, 280
    evaluating educational justice, 279
    modern social grammar, 281
    open basis for evaluation, 279
    semantics of, 282
    Sen and Nussbaum, 278
    specific temporality of education, 279
capacitating justice, education and,
    268, 278–80
capitalism, 4, 6–7, 11–12, 22, 176, 202, 445, 674–75
    Foucault on, 30
    Marx, 23n.3
    world-level, 16
Capitalism, Socialism, and Democracy
    (Schumpeter), 826–27, 841
capitalist society, 361–62
capitalization of learning, 34
Cardoso, Fernando Henrique, 506–7,
    513–14n.29

care paradigm, vulnerability, 272
Caribbean Community (CARICOM), 485
Castells, Manuel, 195–96
Castillo, Pedro, 98, 101, 111
catch-up modernization, 706–7
Catholic Church, 53, 871, 887n.22
    Chile, 994
    education by, 628
    Latin America, 877, 878
    South American, 618
Central Advisory Board of Education,
    India, 788–89
Charles University, 746–48
Charmley, John, 440n.11
Chicago School, economics, 825
childcare, 418
    early childhood education and, 79
childhood education, 77
Chile
    Bachelet administration, 990, 991, 992–93,
        994–95
    chronology of major education reform,
        999–1000
    Concertación coalition, 988–90, 995–96
    education politics in, 986–87
    enrolment in public, private voucher, and
        private schools (1981-2019), 989*f*
    fixation on education, 985–88
    government expenditure on education
        (1990-2017), 987*f*
    Inclusion Law of 2015, 990, 991, 994–95,
        998–99
    National System of School Performance
        Evaluation (SNED), 995–96, 999,
        1000–01n.10
    National Teacher Policy, 996
    Pinochet regime, 988, 998
    PISA scores, 997*f*
    power resource theory (PRT), 987, 999
    Preferential School Voucher, 994
    Presidential Advisory Council for the
        Quality of Education (2006), 991, 992–93
    privatization and vouchers, 988–90
    protests and demands in education, 986*f*
    reforms, 98
    SEP (Subvención Escolar Preferencial)
        preferential voucher, 993, 993*f*, 994

shared financing, 988
SIMCE (national standardization achievement test), 996–97, 998f
state *vs* market, 988–90
teacher careers and upgrading education, 995–97
China, 42–43
Cultural Revolution, 762
data sets, 768
descriptive statistics for graduate employment linear regression model, 773t
economic reforms, 762
employment services and assistance, 770, 772t
expansion of higher education, 764f
globalization of higher education in, 762–63, 775–78
global science, 718
graduate employment trends, 769
graduates' attitudes toward employment and career, 772–73
graduates' first job performance in, 770t
higher education and transgenerational inequality, 766–67
higher education graduates' career development expectations, 773t
inequality in youth employment, 769–75
internalization and transnationalization of higher education, 765
linear regression models of graduate employment inequality, 774t
mass schooling and higher education, 42–43
massification of higher education, 763–64
mobility of international students, 334–36
One Belt, One Road (BRI) initiative, 335–36, 342
privatization and marketization of higher education, 764–65
research method and data, 768–69
responses to globalization and higher education reforms, 763–65
rise of, 715
social consequences of massification and transnationalization of higher education, 766–68

statistic model, 769
transgenerational and graduate employment, 767–68
variables, 768–69
Western forms of schooling, 57
Chinese Academy of Sciences, 737–38
Christian Church, 54
Christian Democrats, 92, 689n.1
Christian Roman Empire, 619
Christianity
reform message, 368
religion, 54
Western European, 176
church, religion and, 54
citation impact, globalization of science, 748–52, 751f
citizens, 852
city, university and the, 425–26
civic military model, schooling in Brazil, 108
civil society organizations (CSOs), 126–27
Civil War, 312–13
Clarivate Analytics, 132, 738–39
CNRS in France, 737–38
coercion, 51, 154
Cold War, 98, 120, 121, 490, 731
Cole, W., 158–59
Coleman, Jules, 830
collaboration
global governance, 215–16
globalization of science, 748–52
partnerships of countries, 752t
See also global science
collective sense-making, 179
collectivisms, 98
Collingwood, R. G., 828
Colm, Gerhard, 841–42
Colombia
comparison with Peru, 904–6
democracy in, 96–97
education reforms, 98–99
education systems in, 96
evolution of reform policy and politics, 900–2
government spending on education (2000-2018), 99–100, 906f
main actors in education politics in, 97, 892t
ministers of education (2000–2020), 907

Colombia (*cont.*)
  net enrollment in (2000–2018), 906*f*
  PISA scores for, 100, 896*f*
  political parties, 899
  protests and demands in education, 986*f*
  public spending per student (1998–2018),
    99–100, 895*f*
  spending, enrollment and learning in,
    894–95
  teachers' unions, 97–98, 896–98
  technocracy, 899–900
colonial education, Latin America, 872–73
colonialism, mass education and, 620–21
ComexStat, Brazil, 946
common good
  democratic justification for public
    good, 833–36
  idea of, 833
communication, 17–18
  cultural logics, 178–79
  hybridization, 184–85
  power of, 178–79
communism, 96
Communist Manifesto, The, 222
Communist Party, 689n.1, 721
compensation theorists, 557
competence principle, mechanism of, 673
competency management, notion of, 34
competition, market principle, 219
complexity theory, 838
complexity turn, 837
compulsory power, 54
computer science, path dependence, 558–59
Conare, 111
conceptual isolationism, 254–55, 256, 261n.1
Concertación (*Conceración de Partidos por la
  Democracia*), Chile, 988–90, 995–96
Conectar Igualdad, digital inclusion program,
  930–31, 932
Confederation of Norwegian Enterprise, 599
Confucius Institutes, 721
consciousness, 17–18
Consejo Nacional de Educación (CNE),
  Peru, 101
conservatism, American, 445
conservative Christians, homeschooling,
  452–53

constitution, 381n.12, 436–38
constitutional, 855n.13
constrained innovation, 81–82
constructed ethic of the good, 840
Consumer Price Index, Brazil, 946
contagion model, education reform, 677–78
contesting knowledge, elites influence, 221
context
  school education and, 389–96
  transnational education and, 396–400
Continental countries, policy advisory
  systems, 578–79
contingency formulas, 18, 406–7
continuance, good of, 846–48
continuance ethics, 831
conversion, 82*t*
  institutional change, 81–83
Correlates of War (COW) data set, 484
correspondence principle, concept of, 674–75
Coser, Lewis, 360
cosmology of contingency, 12–13
cosmopolitan capital, 309–10
cosmopolitan education, 305–11
  elite schools' global outreach, 311–18
  habitus becoming cosmopolitan
    capital, 309–10
  new neoliberal type of elite
    cosmopolitanism, 306–7
  socially stratified, practices, 306–10
  views and practices across social
    groups, 307–9
  See also elite education
cosmopolitanism
  globalization and, 312
  new international tracks and schools, 319
  new neoliberal type of elite, 306–7
  term, 306
Council of Architecture (CoA), 805
Council of Baltic Sea States (CBSS), 485
Council of Europe, 81–82
countries, educational reforms by, 659–60, 659*f*
COVID-19 pandemic, 215–16
  altering lives globally, 443
  disruption of, 93
  education and, 450–51
  education in Argentina, 929–30
  education policy in Italy, 586

Fecode, 110–11
    global health crisis by, 817
    global student mobility, 716
    governance challenges, 532
    higher education in China, 777
    impact on globalized economy, 222–24
    Latin America, 881–82, 883
    online education during, 913
    San Francisco Unified School District
        (SFUSD), 139
    US-China scientific cooperation, 721–22
Creativity Action Service (CAS), 316–17
"Credential Society, The" (Collins), 104
critical discourse analysis (CDA), 523
Croatia, mass education system, 625
Cross-Border Education Research Team
    (C-BERT), 339, 340–41
Crouch, Colin, 11–12
C. R. Rao committee, India, 788–89, 812
CTERA (*Confederación de Trabajadores de la
    Educación*), Argentina, 916
Cuban, Larry, 394
Cuban Revolution, 878–79
cultural change
    institutional change, 175–77
    teachers, 174–75
cultural clusters
    average enrollment in primary
        education, 622f
    colonial ties networks, 625
    cultural spheres, 625
    global cultural spheres (1950), 623f
    global cultural spheres (2010), 624f
    primary education, 621–22
cultural differentiation, 55
cultural logics, 170–71
    institutional change and, 175–79
    institutional logics and, 176
    national differences as variation in, 172–73
cultural nationalism, school textbooks, 107–8
cultural rationalization, 18–19
    principle of, 10–11
Cultural Revolution, China, 762
culture(s)
    concept of, 52
    global higher education and popular, 332–33
    national, of teaching, 173–74

otherness and, 271–72
    term, 171
cumulative inequality, mechanisms of, 736
curricula
    education, 106–8
    emphases on organizations, 133–37
    knowledge in textbooks, 35–38
    Norwegian education, 604
    theory, 161
    tightening regulations, 93

Dahl, Robert, 828
Dale, Roger, 148
Dana-Farber Cancer Institute, 737–38
dangerous classes, 15
Darwin, evolution, 380
data colonization, 518–19
    Global North upon Global South, 520–21
    See also data visualization
data storytelling, *Left Behind* visual, 526–30,
    527f, 528f, 529f, 530f, 532
data visualizations
    analysis of, 519–20
    analysis of findings, 523–30
    data sources and analysis, 522–23
    education, 520–21, 526–30
    interactive data and self-service
        analytics, 523–26
    Left Behind visual, 526–30, 527f, 528f, 529f, 530f
    methodological considerations, 521–23
    storyboard, 519–20
    as storytelling in education, 526–30
    visual and discursive analysis of
        rankings, 521–22
    work of visualizers, 523–26
datafication, transmission of
    information, 219–20
Davidson, Donald, 858n.59
debt crisis (1982), Latin America, 880–83
de Castro, Maria Helena Guimarães, 508–9,
    513n.27
decentralization, Argentina, 915–17
Dees, Bowen C., 505
democracy, 11–12, 829
    common good and, 834
    global levels of, 96–97
    pre-Enlightenment philosophy of, 826–27

Democracy in America (Tocqueville), 619
democratic mechanisms, 850–51
Democratic Revolution, 354
democratic society, 361–62
Denmark, 139
    Globalife project, 299–300
    inequalities, 215
    teachers' unions, 566
deontology, 843–46, 854n.4
Derrida, Jacques, 399–400
Derthick, L. G., 500–1
Deschooling Society (Illich), 887n.16
DESO (direct effect of social origin), 685–86, 686t, 688
deterritorialization, Argentina, 915
Deutsche Forschungsgemeinschaft (DFG), 420
DeVos, Betsy, 102
Dewey, John, 828
Diagnostic and Educational Evaluation, 99
dialogical ethics, 831
Diesterweg, Adolf, 410
differentiation
    education system, 362–63
    modern society, 356–58
    professionalism and, 358–60
    secondary education, 93
digital data, modeling of education, 220
digital learning apparatus, 239–42
digital revolution, 881
digital technology, global
    platformization, 397–98
digitization, transmission of
    information, 219–20
Di John, Jonathan, 879
"Diploma Disease, The" (Dore), 104
Dirac, Paul, 836
discrete-time logistic hazard model, 625
displacement, 82t
    institutional change, 81–82
dispositif, term, 30
distributive equality, 281–82
divergent pedagogies, schooling, 58–59
divine eternity, 368
Djupedal, Øystein, 603–4
Dobbins, Michael, 155–56
Dokó, Toshio, 709n.3

Downs, Anthony, 826
Dreeben, Robert, 363n.2, 447
drift, 82t
    institutional change, 81–83
Drori, Gili, 712
Duke of Edinburgh Award, 314
Durkheim, Emile, 352–53, 391–92, 447
duties, education, 596
Dworkin, Ronald, 827
dynamics, globalization, 195–96

early childhood education (ECE)
    adaptive educational process, 417–18
    education leading to general human
        formation, 413
    education leading to moral
        perfection, 412–13
    family childhood for all, 413–15
    global, as learning process, 420
    global guidelines for adaptive education
        process, 418–19
    global program of, 404
    institutionalised, 412–15
    learning ability of educational processes
        of, 418–20
    person categories of adaptive educational
        interaction in, 419–20
    reconfiguration of, 416–18
    school and kindergarten in 19th century,
        412–13
    school-oriented educational program, 418
    state's lack of interest in, 412
early childhood education and care (ECEC),
    policy feedback, 562–63
early childhood education and childcare, 79
East Africa Higher Education Area, 334
East Asia and Pacific, expansion of higher
    education, 764f
East Asia's CAMPUS initiative, 334
East China Normal University, 340
Eastern Europe, 155–56
ECE. *See* early childhood education (ECE)
Economic Community of Central African
    States (ECCAS), 485
economic globalization, 287–88, 290, 555–56
Economic Theory of Democracy, An
    (Downs), 826

Economics of Education, 540
economy, 16
Economy and Society (journal), 353–54
Ecuador
   protests and demands in education, 986*f*
   reforms, 98
Ed Tech movement, India, 160
education
   anthropologies of, 52–53
   "catch-up" modernization and, 696–99
   as central in social stratification, 104–6
   conceptions of globalization in, 147
   configuration of advisory networks in, 585*t*
   COVID-19 pandemic and, 222–24
   curricula, 106–8
   decline in liberal hegemony, 100, 110
   decline in liberal models of society, 100–1,
      110
   differentiation and inclusion, 356–58
   enrollments, 101–2
   expansion, 101–4
   expansion of organizational actors
      in, 124–32
   globalization of, 3, 4, 5
   as global public good, 851–53
   in global terms, 213
   historical new institutionalism (HI)
      in, 78–80
   impact on, 100–11
   knowledge-based economy, 16
   Mexico, 957–62
   modern expansion, 96–97
   modern forms and beyond, 14–18
   nongovernmental organizations in United
      States, 125*f*
   organization, 109–11
   organizational expansion, 130–31
   pedagogy, 108–9
   policy advisory systems in, 583–84
   policy and, 18–21
   political party platforms and expenditures
      on, 103*f*
   political support, 102
   postwar liberal expansion of, 102–3
   post-World War II democratization of, 268
   relationship among world culture,
      organization, and, 123*f*

religious systems of, 176
rise of emphases on organization in
   content, 132–38
school, and its context, 389–96
structure, 101–4
systems theory, 17–18
term, 100
understanding, 51
universalized regime, 109–11
visualization as storytelling in, 526–30
world map of countries with,
   organization, 111*f*
See also globalization and education;
   inclusive education
Education Act, Norway, 596, 600–1, 607
Education Act of 1996, 510
education associations, domestic, by country,
   126, 127*f*
Education Commission (1966), 786–87
Education Financing Law, Argentina, 913,
   916–17, 920–26, 927
"Education for All"
   celebration of, 32
   conferences, 37–38
   global norms and practices, 98
   initiative, 615
   national development, 42
   resistance to agenda, 33
education of the educator, 405–6
education organization, 119, 128–29, 128*f*
education over life course, globalization and,
   297–300
education policy. *See* international
   organizations (IOs); policy advice
education reform
   Argentina, 915–17
   Canada, 545–46
   central importance of organizations, 371–74
   communication, 372
   England, 545
   evolution, 376–79
   Germany, 543–44
   ideals and values, 374
   Japan, 544–45
   open questions, 379–80
   political discourse and, 542–46
   See also reform(s)

Education Reform Initiative of South Eastern Europe (ERISEE), 484
education science
    globalization-education nexus in, 556–57
    university, 57–58, 432–34
education spending
    Argentina, 922*t*, 923, 926–28
    Brazil, 951–52
    globalization and, 561–62
    public opinion, 561–62
education system
    autonomy, 411
    differentiation of, 362–63
    pedagogical goals of, 406–7
    See also state performances for the education system
educational certification, 44
educational credentialism, 105–6
educational institutions, globalization and, 293–97
educational organization, adaptive, 417–18
educational reform(s), 657–61, 669–70
    impact on schooling and competences, 666*f*, 668*f*
    individual educational outcomes, 661–65
    number of reforms by area of intervention, 660*f*
    number of reforms per country, 659*f*
    outcome of, 665–69
    quantity and quality of human capital, 669
    reforms by stages of education, 661*f*
    school, 666*f*, 667, 668*f*
    summary indices, 664*f*, 664–65
    term, 658
    timing of reforms, 662*f*
    university, 666*f*, 667, 668*f*
    See also Program for the International Assessment of Adult Competencies (PIAAC)
Educational Reform Act (1988), 545
Educational Reform for Freedom (Kōyama), 703
educational revolution, 34–35, 354
educational systems
    organizational space, 293–94
    qualificational space, 293–94
educationalization, 12–13
educators, training of, 79

edutainment, 525
efficiency theorists, 557
EGP scheme, 680–81
Ehrlich, Ricardo, 881
Eide, Kjell, 503, 511n.5
eigenvalues, 357, 364n.4
Einstein, Albert, 830–31, 836, 855n.15, 855–56n.17
elaboration, institutional logics, 182–83
Elementary and Secondary Education Act (ESEA), 510
elite education, 304–5, 320n.1
    colonial heritage, 312–14
    creating close-knit global elite, 315–16
    emergence of new model of international education, 316–17
    global outreach and cosmopolitan identities, 311–18
    international education appealing for national elites, 317–18
    international tracks as competitive assets in school markets, 318
    new international curricula and schools, 316–18
    schools for girls, 307
    strategies of internationalization and international elite schools, 314–15
    See also cosmopolitan education
elites, expertise and, 220–22
embeddedness, 179
emergence, process of, 837
employability, 34
    learning, 34
    term, 270
empowerment, 272, 279
England, education reform, 545, 586
"Englishness" children's education, 315
Enlightenment, 214, 830–31, 844
Enlightenment principles, 873
ENOE. *See* National Survey on Occupation and Employment (ENOE)
entertainment, 121
entrepreneurs, institutional change, 183
entrepreneurship, learning, 36–38
environment
    education, 387
    rationality, 387–88

epistemic governance, experts, international organizations, and, 216–18
epistemic nationalism, 248–49, 258
equal opportunities
  legal, 275
  normative principle of, 268
  principle of equality of resources, 275
  principle of meritocratic, 275
  reformulations of principle of, 274–76
equality
  education, 77
  reform value, 371, 375
  secondary pupils, 78
Erdogan, Recep, 103
Escudé, Carlos, 887n.12
escuelas normales, 876–77
Espeland, Wendy, 132
Esposito, Elena, 386
estado docente, Latin America, 875–77
ethics of difference, 831
ethics of identity, 831
ethnographie, 52
Ethnography and Education (journal), 61
ethos, 305–6
European Alliance for Apprenticeship (EAfA), 85, 88–89
European Commission, 65, 88, 195–96
  integrated flexicurity approach, 38
  Making the European Area of Lifelong Learning a Reality, 32–33
  reforms in education, 397
  Teaching and Learning: Towards the Learning Society, 32
European Community, 63–64
European countries, expansion of school participation, 678, 679f
European governance platforms, 85
European Higher Education Area, 79
European Institute for Family Education, 110–11
European Qualifications Framework (EQF), 34–35
European Research Council (ERC), 533
European Research Council Grant, 519–20
European Social Survey, 77, 92, 670n.3
European society, stratum, 54–55
European Union (EU), 17–18, 29, 40, 42, 61–62, 78–79, 109–10, 216–17, 249–50, 259–60, 397, 486

Brexit, 721–22
  governmentalization of, 30–31
  national school system, 398
  OECD and, 581–82
  projectification of education, 385–86
  transnationalization on fields of education, 250–51
European Union Statistics on Income and Living Conditions (EUSILC), 670n.3
European universities, 53–54
Europeanization, globalization and, 16–17
everyday nationalism, 714
evil state-controlled education, 705
evolution
  reforms, 376–79
  structural change in, 378–79
Ewing, J. C., 849, 850
examination, textbooks, 38
excessive inequalities, 9–10
expansion, 9–10
expertise, elites and, 220–22
experts
  authority of, 43
  international organizations, 216–18
  network of, 216–17
Exploring Complexity (Prigogine), 836–37
externalization, policy advice, 213
extractive institutions, 674

family, school, the state, and, 449–51
Fecode, Colombia, 101, 105–7, 908n.11
Federal Constitution, Brazil, 939–40, 941–42, 952
Federal Education Law (1993), Argentina, 917
Federal Institute of Technology Zurich, 746–48
feedback effects
  early childhood education and care (ECEC), 562–63
  education policies, 554–55
  types of policy, 559–60
  vocational education and training (VET), 563–64
  See also policy feedback
field, term, 194
field approach, higher education, 196–97
field concept, globalization and, 200

1016 INDEX

field theory
innovations in postnational analysis, 255–59
open questions for postnational analysis, 259–61
postnational field analysis, 251–55
relational approach, 249
research program, 248–51
See also postnational field analysis
Fields Medals, 132
financial crisis, Latin America in 1970s, 938
first choicers, homeschoolers, 456n.4
First Nation peoples, 873–74
flexibility, higher education, 38–42
flexicurity, learning, 36–37, 38
Fliedner, Georg Heinrich Theodor, 412–13
Florida State University, 340–41
Foreign Trade System, Brazil, 946
formal education, Latin America, 870–72
formal institutions, 171
formalizations, education system, 397
forme scolaire, 400
Foro Educativo, Peru, 101
Foucault, Michel, 16–17, 29, 30, 132, 831, 839–40
France, 156–57
colonial policy, 313
elite schools, 314–15
European classes, 318
international tracks and schools, 319
schooling of girls, 34
Francophones, 873–74
Frankema, Ewout, 875
freelance, learning, 36–37, 38
Freire, Paulo, 888n.25
French Revolution, 8
Frente Amplio , 881
Freyre, Gilberto, 874
Friedman, Jonathan, 23n.5
Friedman, Milton, 985, 995
Froebel, Friedrich, 413
function systems, 12–13
functional bifocality, university, 432–34
functional literacy, 876–77
functionalist argument, mass education, 616–17, 627–28
functionally differentiated society
all-around education (*Bildung*), 407–8

conversion of educational setting to self-reference, 405–6
differentiation and inclusion, 356–58
differentiation and professionalism, 358–60
education in, 351, 362–63
education system of, 405–8
pedagogical goals of education system, 406–7
pedagogy diverging from social aims, 407–8
schooling of, 360–62
system and loose coupling, 355–56
system and structure, 352–55
See also state performances for the education system
functions, education, 363
Fundación Compartir, Colombia, 102, 106
Fundación Corona, Colombia, 101–2
Fund for Maintenance and Development of Elementary Education and Strengthening of Teacher Training (FUNDEF), Brazil, 941
futurity
term, 330
Whiteness as, 330–31
futurization of the future, 12–13

Gakushūin University, 699–700
Gale Group, Associations Unlimited database, 126
Gandhi, Mahatma, 786–87
Garcia, Alan, Peru, 98, 108
Gates Foundation, 484
Gellner, Ernst, 394
GEMS Education, 315
General Agreement on Tariffs and Trade (GATT), 963
General Agreement on Trade in Service, 765
General Education Council (GEC), India, 804
general good, 827
General Land Law for the Prussian States (1794), 412
General Law of Education, Mexico, 958
General Possibility Theorem, 825
general university, prominence and predominance of, 56–57

Geneva International School, 316
geopolitics of academic science, 732
Georg Eckert Institute for International
    Textbooks, 35–36
German Democratic Republic, 414–15
German Empire, 410–11, 413–14
German Idealism, 838, 856n.26
German Twelfth Report on Children and
    Youth, 419
German universities, Nazi dictatorship, 92
Germany
    Alliance for Initial and Further Education
        and Training, 85
    banks in higher education, 567
    closed employment system, 299
    early childhood education and care
        (ECEC), 563
    education reform, 565, 586
    education reform and political discourse,
        543–44
    Georg Eckert Institute for International
        Textbooks, 35–36
    Globalife project, 298
    inequalities, 215
    KMK Reform of 2009, 87
    labor unions, 567
    national state, 249–50
    rise in mass higher education, 55
    tracking inequality, 92
    universities, 55
"getting it right"
    legitimate nation state, 35
    nation state identity, 30
    state responsibility, 30–31
Giddens, Anthony, 195–96
GlaxoSmithKline, 737–38
global
    label, 60
    term, 55
global academization, studies of vocational
    education and training (VET), 86–89
Global Campaign for Education, 32
global citizen education (GCE), 305
global citizens, 307, 310–11
Global Citizenship Foundation, 317
global communications, 715–16
global economics, 716

global economy, 4
global education, 305
    See also cosmopolitan education
global educational elites, definition, 304
Global Education Monitoring (GEM)
        Report, 596
Global Education Reform, 60
Global Forum on Education, 490
global governance
    collaboration, 215–16
    decolonization of, 520
    education performance data, 531–32
    emerging paradigm of, 518–19
global higher education (HE), 328–29, 341–42
    international branch campuses (IBCs),
        338, 339–40
    literature, 328
    media, 331–32, 333
    mobility of imaginaries, 331–33
    mobility of people, 333–38
    mobility of resources, 338–41
    popular culture, 332–33
    race and racism, 341–42
    racialized politics of, 329
    "Whiteness" and, 329–30, 333
global isomorphism, 81–82
global justice, 22
Global Knowledge Conference, 488–89
global leaders, 307
global liberal order, postwar period, 96–97
global liberal society, culture of, 98
Global North, 258–59, 518–19
    elite schools in, 309–10
    global education architecture, 500
    global higher education, 332–33
    mobility of international students, 334–38
global outreach, elite schools, 311–18
Global Partnership for Education, 54, 484
global platformization, transnational
        education, 397–98
global reforms, schooling, 59–61, 60*t*, 65–66
global research, science and, 717–22
global resonance, concept of, 177
global science, 717–22
    basic science, 720*t*
    collaboration partnerships (top 25), 751–52,
        752*t*

1018   INDEX

global science (*cont.*)
collaboration patterns in humanities,
742–43, 746f
collaboration patterns in natural sciences,
742, 744f
collaboration patterns in research and
development, 742, 743f
collaboration patterns in social sciences,
742–43, 745f
countries and ISO country code, 754t
emergent, 728–30, 758
field-weighted citation impact (FWCI) of
publications, 748–51, 750f, 751f
future of, 758
global data informing, 737–52
global innovations and, 739–41
high-impact publications, 740t, 741t
institutions, sectors, and individuals,
737–39
international coauthored articles, 748–50,
750f
international collaboration, 745–46, 747f
international collaborative publications,
748, 749f
internationalization of science, 748, 749f
national science systems and, 728
nation states and, 730–33
network of internationally coauthored
articles, 751–52, 753f
operation of networks, 733–37
power of individual scientists, 755–58
publishing patterns in academic
disciplines, 741–48
system size, citation impact and preferred
partner countries, 748–52
tensions of, 753–55
global society
changes in, 99–100
system-ness of, 112
Global South, 518–19, 520
elite schools in, 309–10
global education architecture, 500
global higher education, 331–32
mobility of international students, 334–36,
337–38
teachers in, 175–76
textbook distribution in, 56

global trends, legitimating models of, in
textbooks, 36–37, 36f
Globalife project, 288, 290, 292, 301
aim of, 297
countries studied in, 288
countries with labor market, 295–97
country-specific educational institutions
and returns to education, 293–97
life course hypothesis, 295
qualification-employment-relationship
hypothesis, 295–96
research design, 297
role of education over life course, 297–300
skill polarization hypothesis, 296
uncertainty and globalization, 297–300
globalization, 3–5
Anglo-American, in 1990s, 711–12
anthropological research on schooling
and, 64–65
case studies, 86–89
centrality and dual status of, in world
culture theory, 150–52
concept of, 21
COVID-19 pandemic and, 222–24
creating uncertainty, 289f, 291–92
cultural analyses of, 23n.1
digital learning apparatus, 239–42
education, 3, 4, 5
education in Mexico and, 971–72
education spending in Argentina, 926–28
elites and expertise, 220–22
Europeanization and, 16–17
fields and, 200
four structural shifts of, 288–90
higher education, 195–96
higher education and science, 723
impacting life course transitions, 289f
institutional construction of new forms
of, 159–62
institutional filters and, 289f, 292
logics of institutional mediation of, 155–57
meaning of, 53
Mexico and degree of, 968–71
modernity and, 22–23
national educational developments
and, 32–35
nation state and, 30–32

neoinstitutionalism (NI), 157
neoliberal, 213–14, 215
notion of, 21–22
post-1990s, 714–17
post-catch-up modernity and, 699–703
problematic consequences of, 9–14
research strands, 163t
second wave of, 570n.1
seen from anthropology, 53–55
term, 40, 328–29, 695–96
vocational education and training
    (VET), 77–78
globalization and education, 554–55, 568–70
    argument on affects, 558–61
    banks in higher education, 567–68
    early childhood education and care
        (ECEC), 562–63
    education spending, 561–62
    globalization-education nexus in education
        science, 556–57
    globalization-education nexus in political
        science, 557–58
    labor unions in VET, 566–67
    path dependence prevails over globalization
        pressures, 560–61
    policy feedback and path
        dependence, 558–59
    policy feedback on interest groups, 564–68
    policy feedback on public opinion, 561–64
    teachers' unions in secondary education
        systems, 565–66
    three types of policy feedback effects,
        559–60
    vocational education and training (VET),
        563–64
Globalization and Organization (Drori, Meyer,
    and Hwang), 712
globalization-education nexus, 554, 561, 570n.5
    in education science, 556–57
    in political science, 557–58
    See also globalization and education
globalization pressures, gradual institutional
    change and, 83–84
globalization theories, theories of (modern)
    society, 5–9
globalization trend, empirical examination
    of, 290–91

globalized reflexive societies
    culture, otherness, and construction of
        identities, 271–72
    inclusion and new grammar of, 270–73
    inequalities and domination, 272–73
    from integration to social cohesion, 273
    relationship to space and time, 270–71
    vulnerability and empowerment, 272
glonacal argument, higher education, 713–14
Goethe, Johann Wolfgang, 399–400
Goldthorpe, John, 680
good
    attacks against the idea of, 825–28
    See also public good
good society, 42
    legitimating models of, in textbooks, 36f
Google, 105
Government of India Resolution
    (1913), 786–87
government of men, 30, 31
governmentality, 713
governmentalization of learning
    digitalization and onlinization, 41
    technologies, 41
graduate employment
    attitudes toward employment and
        career, 772–73
    descriptive statistics for linear regression
        model, 773t
    inequality in higher education, 773–75
    linear regression models of inequality, 774t
    services and assistance, 770, 772t
    transnational higher education and, 767–68
    trends of, in China, 769
    See also China
grammar school (*Gymnasium*), 409
    all-around education in, 410–11
Grandes Ecoles, 260–61
Great Britain, 53, 158
Green, T, H., 828
Green, Thomas Hill, 833–36
    common good, 833
grit, importance of, 34
gross enrollment ratio (GER), 44–45n.1
Grove, Michael, 545
growth mindsets, 34
Guatemalan Mayan children, schooling, 57–58

Gymnasium
  all-around education in, 410–11
  grammar school, 409
  teachers' unions, 566

Habermas, Jürgen, 385
habitus, 253–54, 306–7
Halvorsen, Kristin, 603–4
Hanushek, Erik, 511n.1
Hardin, Garrett, 839
Harsanyi, John, 854n.8
Hart, H. L. A., 854n.8, 854n.9
Hartog Committee, India, 786–87
Harvard University, 33, 53–54, 112, 355,
  746–48
Haven in a Heartless World (Lasch), 449
Hegel, G. W. F., 826–27, 828, 845–46
Hegelian idealism, 846
Heisenberg, Werner, 836, 855n.15
Helmer, Olaf, 825
Hentschke, Jens, 874
heterarchy, 352
HI. *See* historical new institutionism (HI)
higher education, 29
  academic drift concept, 199
  accessibility and flexibility, 38–42
  Anglo-American globalization in 1990s,
    711–12
  childhood education to, 77–78
  China, 42–43
  expansion for women across regions,
    39–40, 39f
  fields and globalization, 200
  field-theoretical research, 249–50
  globalization, 195–96
  glonacal argument, 713–14
  iinternationalization and
    transnationalization of, in China, 765
  institutional logics and markets, 202–3
  isomorphism in, 197–200
  legitimacy of, 44
  manpower planning and, 34
  massification of, in China, 763–64
  massification of, in Latin America, 879
  national geopolitics of, 732
  national policy, 43
  neoliberal globalization and, 713–14

nongovernmental organizations in United
  States, 126f
organizational theory, 191–92
partial globalization and, 711–17
policy effects on banks in, 567–68
populations, 200–1
prevalence for a system approach, 194–95
privatization and marketization of, in
  China, 764–65
reconfiguration of relationship between
  VET and, 84–85
scholars, 204
scholarship, 193–94
science and, 722–24
standardization and routinization, 41
from system to field, 196–97
transgenerational inequality and, 766–67
unevenness and sectorality, 714–17
universities, 34–35
views about ability enhancement
  during, 776t
worldwide rise of mass, 55
See also global higher education (HE);
  massification of higher education
Higher Education Act Reauthorization
  (1998), 567–68
higher education as a system, 201
Higher Education Cannot Escape History
  (Kerr), 53
Higher Education Financing Agency (HEFA),
  India, 792–93
Higher Education Grants Council (HEGC),
  India, 804
higher education institutions (HEIs), 311–12
  private and public, 129, 130f
higher education literature, 206n.1
Hinduism, 619
Hirschman, Albert, 879
historical institutionalism, 23n.4, 483
historical materialism, 23n.3
historical new institutionalism (HI)
  case selection, methods, and data, 84–85
  globalization pressures and gradual
    institutional change, 83–84
  modes of change in relation to
    characteristics of political context and
    targeted institution, 82t

path dependency and modes of gradual change, 80–83
review in education, 78–80
historical new institutionism (HI), 76–77
Höffe, Otfried, 843
Holt, John, 452
homeschooling, 15
advocates of, 110
COVID-19 pandemic and, 443–44
first choicers and second choicers, 456n.4
from impersonal to personal, 444–46
latest developments in research on, 453
phenomenon of, 452
as protest, 451–54
taking back control of children's education, 453
types of homeschoolers, 456n.4
homogenization, education, 394–95
Hong Kong, "study mothers" and "parachute kids", 311
Honneth, Axel, 276
Horizon Europe, 721–22
horizontal autonomy, 257
concepts of vertical and horizontal, 257–58
Howe, Harold, II, 504, 505–6, 512nn.7–8, 512nn.15–16
Humala, Ollanta, Peru, 98, 108–9
human capital
educational reform, 658, 669
relationship between variables, 663–64, 663f
Human Capital institution, university, 59
human capital theory, 547
human nature, moral completion of, 407
humanities, collaboration patterns in, 742–43, 746f
humanity, concept of, 673
Hume, David, 842
Hungary, 103, 107
Hwang, Hokyu, 712
hybrid organizations, education expansion, 130–31
hybrid programs, relationship of vocational education and training (VET) to higher education (HE), 86–87
hypermodernity, 13–14
hypostatization, 389–90

IB (international curriculum), 316, 317
IBM, 105
Iceland, 53
ICTs. *See* information and communication technologies (ICTs)
identities, construction of, 271–72
illiberalism, 9–10
Illich, Ivan, 887n.16
imagined community, 30, 721
impossibility theorem, Arrow's, 825
inclusion, modern society, 356–58
Inclusion Law of 2015, Chile, 990, 991, 994–95, 998–99
inclusive education
capacitating justice, 268, 278–80
culture, otherness, and construction of identities, 271–72
global framework for education, 269–70
grammar of globalized reflexive societies, 270–73
inequalities and domination, 272–73
from integration to social cohesion, 273
recognitive justice, 268, 276–78
redistributive justice, 268, 274–76
relationship to space and time, 270–71
theories of justice, 273–80
vulnerability and employment, 272
inclusive institutions, 674
Independence Wars, 872–73
index of educational opportunity, 92
India, 108
Committee for teacher education, 810
Ed Tech movement, 160
education challenges, 786–87
elementary education, 792–93
global science, 718
Internationalization at Home policy, 340
internationalization of higher education, 812
National Education Policy, 338–39, 804, 817
policy for education system, 802
policy for research and development, 809–10
policy vacuum, 794–95
proposed 4 year degree programs, 807
public policy, 815–16

India (*cont.*)
  reforming higher education, 788–92, 793–95
  restructuring architecture of regulatory system, 804
  secondary education, 792–93
  single-faculty universities, 796
  small-sized universities and colleges, 801–2
  technical knowledge and skills, 806–7
  universities with undergraduate study programs, 800–1
Indian Council for Agricultural Research (ICAR), 805
INDIRE, education research institute, 586
industrial civilisation, 701
industrial democracy, 11–12
Industrial Revolution, 121, 354, 704
INEGI. *See* National Institute of Statistics and Geography (INEGI)
inflation of educational credentials (IEC), 683–85
informal institutions, 171
information, transmission of, 219–20
information and communication technologies (ICTs), 183–84, 287–88, 290, 291–92
information suppression, elites influence, 221
informational globalization, 287–88, 290
innovation(s), 367
  term, 369
  word, 368–69
institution, term, 171
institutional change
  cultural change, 175–77
  cultural logics and, 175–79
  entrepreneurs and mechanisms of, 160–61
  globalization pressures and gradual, 83–84
  modes of gradual, 81–82
  policies and, 159–60
  power to communicate and define, 178–79
  resonance, 177–78
  role of discourses and ideas, 159–60
  teachers as agents of, 171–75
institutional homogenization, 198
institutional interstitiality, theory of, 177–78
institutionalizations, politics of situated, 158–59
institutionalized liberal order, 96–97
institutional logics
  actors, levels and, 174–75

cultural logics and, 176
depth of institutionalization, 181–82
elaboration of, 182–83
global diffusion of, 179–83
legitimacy and "taken for granted", 181–82
markets and, 202–3
micro-processes across levels, 179–81
term, 202–3
institutional power, 54
institutional theory, 81
institutions, sectors, and individuals, globalization of science, 737–39
instructional change
  entrepreneurs and mechanism of, 160–61
  policies and, 159–60
instruction language, Latin America, 875–76
instruments, mediation mechanisms, actors and, 155–57
Intel, 737–38
interaction systems, evolution of, 434–35
interactive data, data visualization, 523–26
Inter-American Development Bank, 99
interest groups
  banks in higher education, 567–68
  labor unions in VET, 566–67
  policy feedback on, 564–68
  teachers' unions in secondary education systems, 565–66
Intergovernmental Foundation for Educational, Scientific and Cultural Cooperation (IFESCCO), 485–86
intergovernmental organizations (IGOs), 484
Internal Revenue Service, 125–26
International Adult Literary Survey (IALS), 670n.3
International Association for the Evaluation of Educational Achievement (IEA), 131–32, 540
International Association for the Evaluation of Educational Development, 109
International Association of Science, Ethics, and Integrated Education, 110–11
International Baccalaureate Diploma Program (IBDP), 316–18
international branch campuses (IBCs), global higher education, 338, 339–40

"International Conference on Education"
(1958), 83–84
International Council for Evangelical
Theological Education, 110–11
international education, 305
appealing for national elites, 317–18
competitive assets in school markets, 318
emergence of new model of, 316–17
International Educational Indicators (INES)
program, 507
international elite schools,
internationalization and, 314–15
International Federation for Parents
Education, 110–11
international governmental organizations
(IGOs), 151–52
in Canadian and US textbooks, 134–36, 135f
in cross-national textbooks, 135–36, 136f
internationalization, 713
term, 328–29
International Labour Organization (ILO),
484–85, 486
international large-scale assessments (ILSAs),
Norway, 601
International Monetary Fund, 31, 938
international nongovernmental organizations
(INGOs), 122–23, 128, 151–52
in Canadian and US textbooks, 134–36, 135f
in cross-national textbooks, 135–36, 136f
international organizations (IOs), 215, 615
actors in education policy, 481–82
characteristics, 215
economistic, 486–91
education policy, 494–95
epistemic governance and experts, 216–18
from Keynesianism to neoliberalism, 483
geographic, 484–85
geographic reach of education growth,
491, 492f
identifying the population of education
IOs, 484–86
Islamic World Education, Science and
Culture Organization (ICESCO),
485, 493
multipurpose, 486
neoliberal globalization, 215
OECD, 489–91, 498–99

organizational ecology of education, 482–83
regional and transregional, 491–94
Southeast Asian Ministers of Education
Organisation (SEAMEO), 485–86,
492, 493–94
thematic scope of, 485–86, 487f
time-wise, 486
World Bank, 488–89
world map of education, 485f
International Social Survey Program
(ISSP), 670n.3
international standards, 15–16
intervention(s), educational reforms by,
659–60, 660f
*Introduction to the Principles of Morals and
Legislation* (Bentham), 848
Investment in Education (Irish report), 83–84
IOs. *See* international organizations (IOs)
Irish *Investment in Education* report, 83–84
iron cage, 616–18
Iron Curtain, fall of, 287–88, 290, 415–16
Islam, 619
Islamic Azad University, 746–48
Islamic Educational, Scientific and Cultural
Organization, 495n.1
Islamic World Education, Science and
Culture Organization (ICESCO),
485–86, 493, 495n.1
Isle of Man, 53
isomorphism, 6, 14–15, 150, 177, 203–4
concept of structural, 198
higher education, 197–200
Israel, inequalities, 215
Italian *imbarazzo*, 400
Italian Scuola Media, 638
Italy
closed employment system, 299
contagion model, 677–78
direct effect of origin on destination, 685–88,
686f
education and socioeconomic
inequality, 672
education reform, 565–66, 585–87
Globalife project, 298
inequality of educational opportunities,
681–83, 682f
OED triangle, 678–81

1024 INDEX

Italy (*cont.*)
    participation in primary and secondary
        school, 677*f*
    returns to education, 683–85, 684*f*
    school and social stratification in, 678–88
    school design, reforms, and expansion
        (1950s to 2010s), 675–78
    school policies, 673

Jagiellonian University, 746–48
Japan
    Ad Hoc Council on Education Reforms
        (AHCER), 698–99
    agenda setting for AHCER policy
        proposals, 703–6
    "catch-up" modernization, 697–99
    education reform and political
        discourse, 544–45
    individual identity, 173
    inequalities, 215
    logics of mass schooling, 172–73, 181–82
    mobility of international students, 334
    modernity, 696
    national educational ministry, 178–79
    post-catch-up modernity and globalization,
        699–703
    rationalized myths, 177
    secondary education, 81–82
    teacher's status, 172
    Top Global University Project, 338–39
    Western forms of schooling, 57
Jarvis, J. Boyer, 504–5
Jefferson, Thomas, 439n.1
Jesuit Order, *Reducciones*, 871, 886n.1
Joaquín V. González program, 932
Johnson & Johnson, 737–38
Johnson, Boris, radical plan for vocational
    education, 103
Johnson, Monte Ransome, 844
Jones, Peter, 61–62
Journal of Political Economy (journal), 825
journals
    publications in high-impact, 740–41, 741*t*
    publishing patterns in academic
        disciplines, 741–48
jurisprudence, 57–58
justice, 267

capacitating, 268, 278–80
conceptions of social, 268
recognitive, 268, 276–78
redistributive approach to, 268, 274–76, 282
See also social justice
Justice Verma Commission, India, 810

Kamens, David, 23n.7
Kant, Immanuel, 847
Kantianism, 848
Karolinska Institute, 746–48
Kasturirangan, K., India, 795
Kenway, Jane, 312–13
Keppel, Francis, 504–5
Kevan, Robert A., 512n.11
Keynesianism
    principle, 489–90
    shift from, to neoliberalism, 483
Khudsen, Hanne, 401n.4
kindergarten, Froebel's concept, 413
Kirby, Kenton, 63
Kirchner, Néstor, Argentina, 916–17
KMK (Standing Conference of the Ministers
        of Education and Cultural Affairs of the
        Länder), 84–85
    reform of 2009, 87
knowledge, good society model, 42
knowledge actors, 216–17
knowledge administration, elites
    influence, 221
knowledge broker, OECD, 489
knowledge economy, 34, 361
    agenda, 214–15
    case studies, 86–89
knowledge production
    elites influence, 221
    politicization of, 213
knowledge society, 34, 361–62, 599
    construction of, 104
    global, in education, 96
    neoliberal culture, 98–99
knowledge workers, 16, 295
KOF Globalization Index, 290–91, 291*f*
Koran schools (maktabs), 620–21
Koyama, Jill, 62–63
Kōyama, Kenichi, 699–703, 708
Koyré, Alexander, 837, 844

Krishnamurti Foundation, 63–64
Kuczynski, Pedro Pablo, 98, 101, 109
KU Leuven, 746–48

labor unions, vocational education and training (VET), 566–67
laissez-faire, 840
language of instruction, Latin America, 875–76
Lasch, Christopher, 445
Lascoumes, Pierre, 156–57
Laski, Harold, 828
late bloomers, 34
Latin America, 869–70
    advances and reversals, 884–85
    colonial education, 872–73
    debt crisis (1982) and marketized education, 880–83
    elite schools, 313–14
    the *estado docente* (1900-1950), 876–77
    expansion of state educational provision, 872–79
    globalization in, 939
    historical background of education, 870–72
    language of instruction, 875–76
    massification of secondary and higher education (1950-1982), 879
    new republics in 19th century, 873–75
    PISA scores for, 100, 869–70, 896*f*, 997*f*
    state education and religion, 877–79
Law and Justice Party, Poland, 107–8
layering, 81–82, 82*t*
Lazzarato, Maurizio, 29–30
learners' psychic systems, consciousness, 17–18
learnification of governing, 41
learning
    governmentalization of, 34, 36–37
    managementalizaiton of, 34
    notion of, 18
    term, 34
learning apparatus, 16–17, 242–44
    assemblage of, 232–39
    digital, in action, 239–42
    forms of problematization, 232–33
    material inscriptions, 233–36
    personalization, 41, 42
    profiling ideal, 41

strategic response, 236–39
    time and space, 39
    world of, 42
learning question, from social question to, 230–32
learning to learn, 450
learning to learn formula, 18
Lecture, interaction system, 59
Left Behind visual
    data visualizations, 526–30
    front webpage of, 527*f*
    last page of, 530*f*
    snapshots of, 528*f*, 529*f*
Le Galès, Patrick, 156–57
legal machinery, 850–51
legitimacy
    concept of, 171
    institutionalization, 181–82
legitimate nation state, 30–31, 35
Lesson of the British Disease, The (Kōyama), 700
Levin, Rick, 32–33
Lewis, George Cornewall, 852
liberal arts colleges and universities, 56
liberal democracy, 674
liberal ethics, 831
liberalization of education, 705
life course, 418
life course transitions, impact of globalization on, 289*f*
lifelong learning, 29
    concept of, 415–16
    notion of, 34
lifeworld, 448
Limits of Liberty, The (Buchanan), 826
Lindblom, Charles, 828
Lingard, Bob, 164
Lippmann, Walter, 828
Lisbon Process, 219
listening to the science, 44
local
    remaking policies, 62–64
    term, 55
Lomonosov Moscow State University, 746–48
Lopez Obrador administration, Mexico, 884–85, 979
loss of function, family, and society, 446
lost decade, 880

Loyo, Aurora, 880–81
Luhmann, Niklas, 61–63, 112, 351, 352, 355, 362,
    364n.5, 386–88, 405, 447
  catastrophe, 395–96
  climax, 393–94
  exposition, 391–92
  fall, 394–95
  functional differentiation, 12
  global world society, 9
  rise, 392–93
  systems theory, 4–5, 13–14, 22, 23n.1, 454–55
  writing and stages as classical drama,
    391–96
Luther's Reformation, 368–69
Lycées français à l'étranger, France's colonial
    policy, 313

McMurrin, Commissioner, 504
McNamara, Robert, 488
Macri, Mauricio, 924–25, 926, 936n.47
Madrassah, 176
Major, John, 93
*Making the European Area of Lifelong Learning
    a Reality* (European Commission), 32–33
Malan, Pedro, 513nn.18–19
Malaysia
  global education hubs, 340–41
  mobility of international students, 334
malleability, child characteristic, 446
managementalization of learning, 34
Management by Objectives at a global level
    (MbO), 594
managerial accountability
  OECD, 594
  society and economy, 597
Mangez, Eric, 397, 401n.4
Manifesto Project, 102
Mannheim, Karl, 828
market-based reform ideology, 60
marketization, 713
marketized education, Latin America, 880–83
Marshall Plan, 503
Marx, Karl, 4, 448–49, 826–27, 828, 845–46
  capitalism, 23n.3
Marxism, 12, 674
Masao, Maruyama, 704
Masayoshi, Ōhira, 697

"Massacre of Tlatlelolco" (October 1968),
    887n.19
mass education
  adopters, 628
  bringing culture back in, 619–20
  classification of adopters of, 625–26, 625*f*
  cultural characteristics, 621–24
  cultural clusters (1950), 623*f*
  cultural clusters (2010), 624*f*
  data and methods, 621–26
  development of primary, for boys and girls,
    621–22, 622*f*
  diffusion analysis, 626–27
  diffusion of, 615–16, 626*t*
  discrete-time logistic hazard model, 625
  effects of colonialism, 620–21
  emergence and global development of
    systems, 616
  functionalist, 627–28
  functionalist view, 616–17
  list of countries in analysis, 629
  neoinstitutionalist, 627–28
  neoinstitutionalist view, 616, 617–18, 619–20
  See also secondary education
mass education system, 615–16
massification of higher education
  China, 763–64
  Latin America, 879
mass schooling, 29
  China, 42–43
  commitment to, 32–33
  higher education and, 35, 44
  teachers and nation state, 172
  world culture, 151
Masters of Business Administration (MBA)
    programs, 136
material inscriptions, learning, 233–36
matryoshka, Russian dolls, 723
May, Simon, 843–44
Mayo Clinic, 737–38
media, educational technology, 398–99
medical schools, 56
medicine, 57–58
Medieval Europe, 619
medium of education, life course, 418
mega-platforms, 397–98
Meiji Restoration, Japan, 702

Melters, Benedikt, 401n.6
Memoir of T. H. Green (Nettleship), 835
Menem, Carlos, Argentina, 916
Merck, 737–38
Mercosur, 486–87
Merton, Robert, 731–32
methodological globalism, 724
methodological nationalism, 4, 724
Mexican Revolution, 878
Mexico
  composition of employed population by
    educational attainment and sex, 961, 961f
  composition of population by educational
    attainment, 960–61, 960f
  Constitution, 972
  data, 962–63
  distribution of globalized employment
    across states, 967, 967t
  economic sectors by degree of globalization,
    964, 964f
  economic sectors by level of education of
    workers and degree of globalization,
    968–69, 969f
  education levels, wages, and degree of
    globalization, 968–71
  evolution of educational premium and
    complete primary education, 972, 973f
  evolution of educational premium and
    complete primary education by level of
    exposure of employment sector, 975, 975f
  evolution of educational premium and
    complete primary education by level of
    exposure of employment sector and sex,
    975–76, 976f
  evolution of educational premium and
    complete primary education by sex,
    973, 974f
  evolution of mean hourly labor incomes by
    educational level, 970f, 970
  female participation in workforce, 968f, 968
  geographical distribution of employment,
    966f, 966–67
  globalization and education, 956–57, 971–72
  identifying globalized sectors, 963–68
  Lopez Obrador administration, 979
  mean hourly labor income by educational
    level, 970–71, 971f

NAFTA, 963, 976, 979–80
  results, 972–79
  sectors by degree of globalization and
    concentration of workers with complete
    secondary education, 977t
  sectors in bottom and top quintiles of
    exposure, 964–65, 965f, 966
  trends in educational attainment in, 957–62
Meyer, John, 147, 150, 616–17, 618, 712
Microsoft, 737–38
migration, world university and, 430–31
milieu interne, 59
Mill, John Stuart, 840–41
Millennium Development Goals, 518, 615
Ministry of Education, Culture, Sports,
    Science and Technology (MEXT),
    Japan, 544
Mistral, Gabriela, 876–77
MIT, 33
mobility practices, transnational
    education, 310–11
model educational culture, Japan, 544–45
modern education, 14–18
modern family, from impersonal to
    personal, 444–46
modern society, 4
  globalization theories of, 5–9
  role of education in global, 15
modernity, 12–14, 21
  cultural rules of, 23n.6
  Eurocentric understandings, 707
  globalization and, 22–23
  post-catch-up, and globalization, 699–703
  problematic consequences of, 447–49
  ration action as hallmark of, 385
  social grammar, 268
  Western, 702–3
modernization, 673
  "catch-up", 696–99
  development and, 367
  liberal theory of, 673–74
  phases of, 696
  "post-catch-up", 696
  reproduction theory and, 673
  social reproduction theory and, 674–76
Montt, Manuel, 874
Moore, Raymond, 452

moral vocabulary, 222
morphogenesis of education
   education, rationality, and its other
      side, 385–89
   school education and its context, 389–96
   transnational education and its context,
      396–400
movement
   of ideas, forms of schooling, 57–59
   of ideas for reforming schooling, 59–64
   of people, 56–57
   term, 53
   of things, 56
   things, ideas, and people, 53
   wide-spread diffusion, 55
multiculturalism, 831
multiple levels
   frames of experience, 179–81
   global diffusion of institutional
      logics, 179–83
multipolar science world, 729
Musacchio, Aldo, 874–75

NAICS. *See* North American Industry
   Classification System (NAICS)
Napoleon, 873
Napoleonic countries, policy advisory
   systems, 578–79
nation, 21
National Accreditation and Assessment
   Council (NAAC), India, 805
National Accreditation Council (NAC),
   India, 805
National Autonomous University of Mexico,
   887n.21
National Center for Charitable Statistics
   (NCCS), 125–26
National Council for Teacher Education
   (NCTE), 805
National Council for Vocational Education
   and Training (NCVET), India, 805
national cultural models,
   hybridization, 184–85
national culture, 173
   teaching, 173–74
National Curriculum, England, 545
national education

globalization and, 32–35
  idea of, 56
National Education Commission, India, 804
National Education Law, Argentina, 917
National Education Policy, 338–39, 795, 817
National Eligibility Test, India, 792
National Health Service, 832
National Higher Education Qualification
   Framework (NHEQF), India, 805
National Higher Education Regulatory
   Council (NHERC), India, 805
National Institute for Educational Research
   and Development (INEP), 509
National Institute for Educational Studies
   and Research in Brazil (INEP), 501,
   513n.26
National Institute of Statistics and Geography
   (INEGI), 962–63
National Institutes of Health, 737–38
nationalism, economic forms of, 99
National Knowledge Commission, India, 788–89,
   802, 804, 810
National Policy on Education (1968), India,
   786–87, 802, 815–16
National Polytechnic Institute, 887n.21
National Research Council of Italy, 737–38
National Research Foundation, India, 809–10
national science
   basic science, 720*t*
   global and, 718–22
National Science Foundation (NSF), 504–5
national science systems, 728
   global science and, 728
   See also global science
National Skills Qualifications Framework
   (NSQF), India, 805
National Socialism, 55
National Socialist, 414–15
National Survey on Occupation and
   Employment (ENOE), Mexico, 957,
   960–61, 962
National System of School Performance
   Evaluation (SNED), Chile, 995–96, 999,
   1000–01n.10
National Teachers Union, Mexico, 958
National Treasury, Brazilian federation, 940
National University, idea of, 438n.8

National University of Singapore, 338–39, 340
National University of the United States, 440n.8
"Nation at Risk, A" report, 33
nation state, 21, 22
  education and training systems, 214
  globalization and, 30–32
nation state model, Westphalian roots (17th-century), 30
natural sciences, collaboration patterns in, 742, 744f
Nazarbayev University (NU), 338–39
NCLB. *See* No Child Left Behind (NCLB)
necessity of coordination, 840
Nehemas, Alexander, 843–44
Nelson, William, 855n.14
neocolonialism, 15–16
neoinstitutional theories, 96, 175–76
  liberal world society, 112
  success of, 111
neoinstitutionalism (NI), 17, 147, 148–49
  educational research, 148
  mass education, 627–28
  mediation mechanisms, actors, and instruments, 155–57
  mediation of educational globalization, 155–59
  methodology, 149–50
  political dimension and, 152–54
  politics of situated institutionalizations, 158–59
  surrounding globalization, 157
  tools of, 157
neoinstitutionalist, label, 162–64
neoinstitutionalist parochialism, 148
neoinstitutionalist view, mass education, 616, 617–18, 619–20
neoliberal globalization
  higher education and, 713–14
  nation states, 215
neoliberalism, 881
  accountability, 597
  education, 19–20
  Japan, 700
  market competition, 60
  policy, 61
  post-Cold War, 499
  shift from Keynesianism to, 483

Netherlands, 63–64
  cosmopolitan education across, 308
  international tracks and schools, 319
Nettleship, R. L., 835
network clustering method, *Louvain* algorithm, 623–24
network globalization, 287–88, 290
networked society, information, and communication technologies (ICT), 183–84
networks, global science, 733–37
new institutionalism (NI)
  concepts of, 198
  research strands, 163t
  tools of, 164
Newland, Carlos, 876–77
New Public Management, 157, 268
new republics in 19th century, Latin America, 873–75
New York Times (newspaper), 105
Nicolis, Grégoire, 836–37
Nietzsche, Friedrich, 843–44
Niskanen, William, 826
N'Krumah, advocacy network, 32
Nobel Prizes, 132
No Child Left Behind (NCLB), US policy, 62–63
nongovernmental civil society organizations, 99
nongovernmental organizations (NGOs), 484
nonprofit management education (NME), growth by program type in United States, 137t
Nord Anglia, 315
Norm and Action (von Wright), 846
North American Free Trade Agreement (NAFTA), 963, 976, 980
North American Industry Classification System (NAICS), 957, 962–63
North Atlantic Treaty Organization (NATO), 484
North Korea, 37
Norway
  Educational Act (1997), 607
  follow-up from OECD, 604–5
Norwegian Directorate for Education and Training (DET), 599, 600–1, 607–8n.2
Norwegian Ministry of Education, 607n.1

Norwegian National Quality Assessment System (NQAS)
  Assessment for Learning (AfL), 601, 603–4
  demand for professionalization, 606–7
  establishment and what it includes, 598–99
  follow-up from OECD and responses from Norway, 604–5
  historical institutionalist (HI) approach, 595
  instruments, 601–2
  national tests, 602
  Norwegian backdrop, 597–98
  overview of, 600f
  research illuminating of, 601–4
  school inspection, 602–3
  scope and method, 595–96
  status in 2021, 600–1
Norwegian Realskole, 81
not-for-profit organizations, universities, 34
Novartis, 737–38
Nozick, Robert, 827
NQAS. See Norwegian National Quality Assessment System (NQAS)
Nussbaum, Martha, 278, 796, 841
Nyere's Education for Self-Reliance, 63–64
NYU Abu Dubai, 339–40
NYU Shanghai, 340

OED (origin, education, destination) triangle, 678–81, 679f, 688
Ohira Policy Study Group (Ōhira Seisaku Kenkyūkai), 697, 698, 702
Olson, Mancur, 826, 858n.58
one-class primary school (Volksschule), 409
  diligence and piety through, 409–10
O'Neill, Onora, 596
"One Laptop per Child" program, 63
online databases, 149
On What Is Learned in School (Dreeben), 363n.2
Open Method of Coordination (OMC), 219
Open Society and Its Enemies, The (Popper), 849
Orban, Viktor, 103
Order Out of Chaos (Prigogine), 836–37
Organisation of Eastern Caribbean States (OECS), 492
Organisation of Islamic Cooperation, 493
organization(s)
  boundaries of interaction, 371–72

central importance in reforms, 371–74
curricular emphases on, 133–37
education, 109–11
educational communication, 372
evolution of society, 380
participation in organizational society, 133, 137–38
population ecology, 382n.19
reform, 382n.18
relationship among world culture, education, and, 123f
rise of emphases on, in education, 132–38
structures of, 372–73
systems theory, 371, 373
See also international organizations (IOs)
organizational actors
  expansion in education, 124–32
  increased actorhood, 124–25, 131–32
  increased numbers, 124, 125–31
organizational environment
  approach, 483
  concept of, 482–83
organizational field, concept of, 482–83
organizational revolution, education, 119–21
organizational society, 139
organizational theory, higher education and, 191–92
organizational transformation
  education, 120–21
  schooling and society, 14–15
Organization and Decision (Luhmann), 20–21, 376–77
Organization for Economic Cooperation and Development (OECD), 54–55, 59–60, 63, 65, 77–78, 99, 131–32, 151–52, 201, 216–17, 259–60, 267–68, 415–16, 501, 519–20, 539, 594, 881–82
  accountability system in Norway, 598–99
  analytical layers, 500–1
  Argentina, 914–15
  Asian students in higher education, 334
  Brazilian decentralization and, 506–9
  Center for Educational Research and Innovation (CERI), 416, 489–90, 499–500
  collecting education policy, 670n.1
  comparable patterns and role of boundary work, 509–11

Confederation of Norwegian Enterprise, 599
countries, 102
COVID-19 pandemic, 223
Economic Surveys, 217
educational policy recommendations, 416–17
educational reform, 658
European Union (EU) and, 581–82, 584–85
global education, 484–85, 489–91
global governance, 498
inclusive education, 270
interest in education, 540–41
managerial accountability, 594
policy feedback effects, 555
Program for International Student Assessment (PISA), 218, 250–51, 490, 499–500, 565–66, 581–82, 583, 997f
recurrent education, 416–17
responses from Norway, 604–5
theoretical underpinnings, empirical data, and methodology, 501–3
theory of compensation, 939
US decentralization and, 503–6
Organization for European Economic Cooperation (OEEC), 499–500
Organization of American States (OAS), 492
Organization of Ibero-American States for Education, Science and Culture (OEI), 485–86
Ornelas, Carlos, 888n.26
Orthodox Church, 107–8
otherness, culture and, 271–72
Outschool, Californian *ed tech* start-up, 398–99
overeducation, 35
Oxford Idealism, 838
Ozga, Jenny, 11–12

Palgayan, Agustina, 873–74
Panama Canal Zone, 340–41
Panama's City of Knowledge, 340–41
pandemic of 2020/2021, Latin America during, 869–70
Papua New Guinea, 63
"parachute kids" transnational education, 311
Parekh, Bhikhu, 858n.65
parent-teacher associations (PTAs), 139
Paris-Saclay University, 746–48

Parks, T., 158–59
Parsons, Talcott, 12, 61–63, 352–53, 385, 391–92, 447
partial globalization, higher education and, 711–17
particularity, 703, 704
path dependence, 554
   basic idea of, 80–81
   globalization pressures, 560–61
   policy feedback and, 558–59
Patria Roja, 897, 908n.6
pedagogy
   diverging from social aims, 407–8
   education, 108–9, 394
   education system, 411
   goals of education system, 406–7
   school education, 393
Pedagogy of the Oppressed (Freire), 888n.25
Peking University, 767
people, movement of, 56–57
People's Republic of China
   Chinese-Foreign Cooperation in Running Schools, 765
   See also China
perfectionism, 833
Perón, Joan Domingo, Argentina, 914
personalization, 41, 42
Peru
   comparison with Colombia, 904–6
   democracy in, 96–97
   education reforms, 98, 99
   education systems in, 96
   evolution of reform policy and politics, 902–4
   government spending on education (2000-2018), 99–100, 906f
   main actors in education politics in, 97, 892t
   ministers of education (2000-2020), 907
   net enrollment in (2000-2018), 894–95, 906f
   PISA scores for, 100, 896f
   political parties, 899
   protests and demands in education, 986f
   public spending per student (1998-2018), 99–100, 895f
   spending, enrollment and learning in, 894–95
   teachers' unions, 97–98, 896–98
   technocracy, 899–900

1032   INDEX

Pestalozzi, Johann Heinrich, 414
Pfizer, 737–38
PIAAC. *See* Program for the International
    Assessment of Adult Competencies
    (PIAAC)
Piaget, Jean, 416
Pierson, Paul, 155–56
Piñera, Sebastín, 994, 999
PISA. *See* Program for International Student
    Assessment (PISA)
Plank, Max, 836
Plan Sarmiento, digital education
    program, 932
platformization, global, 397–98
Plato, 826–27, 845–46
Poincaré, Henri, 830–31, 836, 855n.16
Poland, Law and Justice Party, 107–8
Polanyi, Karl, 828, 857n.38
policy
    making authorized, 61–62
    as practice of power, 61
    remaking, locally, 62–64
policy advice
    advisory content and possible impacts of
        reforms, 587–89
    advisory systems in education, 583–84,
        589–90
    education in globalized world, 581–83
    from anecdotal to systemic view, 577–81
    goal acceptability, 564, 588t
    impact of, on education, 587–89
    instrument availability, 564, 588t
    politicization of, 580
    policy advisory systems and, 576–77, 589
    policymaking and, 577–79
    policy subsystems, 580–81
    possible structures of advisory networks in
        education, 584–87
    role of policy advisors, 590
    structural perspective on, 579t
policy advisory systems
    configuration of advisory networks, 585t
    configurations of, 579t
    definition, 577
    in education, 583–84
    evidence on Westminster countries, 578
    externalization of, 579–80

policy advice and, 583–84, 589–90
    structures of advisory networks in
        education, 584–87
policy borrowing, phenomena, 547
policy feedback
    early childhood education and care
        (ECEC), 562–63
    education spending, 561–62
    interest groups, 564–68
    path dependence and, 558–59
    public opinion toward education, 561–64
    types of effects, 559–60
    vocational education and training
        (VET), 563–64
policy reforms, PISA, human capital
    and, 547–48
policymaking, configurations of policy
    advisory systems, 579t
political action committee (PAC), 568
Political Argument (Barry), 826
political context, targeted institution and,
    82–83, 82t
political globalization, 287–88, 290, 555–56
political imperative, education for rapidly
    changing society, 415–16
political parties, Colombia, and Peru, 899
political party platforms, state expenditures in
    education, 103f
political relations, 850–51
political science, globalization-education
    nexus in, 557–58
political sociology, polities by, 153–54
political support, education, 102
Political Terms (Lewis), 852
Political Writings (Hume), 842
politicization, knowledge production, 213
politics, 153–54
polity, concept of, 153–54
Polizey, modern policies of building social
    order, 54–55
Popper, Karl, 827, 845–46
population, higher education, 200–1
population ecology, organizations, 382n.19
populism, 9–10, 42, 96–97
"post-catch-up" modernity
    concept of, 696
    Japan, 707

postliberal reactions, 10–11
postliberalism, 99–100
postnational field analysis
    concept of autonomy, 253–54, 257–58
    concept of capital, 253
    conceptual isolationism, 254–55
    education and higher education, 257
    field of, 251–55
    geospatial scales, 252–53, 258, 260
    global field of power, 258
    label, 251
    methodological design, 254, 256
    qualitative methods, 254
    study of education and higher
        education, 254–55
    theory, 251–55
    treating scale of fields as variable
        property, 256–57
poststructuralism, 854n.7, 856n.19
poverty, 54
power
    active exercise of, 153–54
    compulsory, 54
    forms of, 54
    global schooling, 53–55
    institutional, 54
    policy as practice of, 61
    productive, 54
    structural, 54
power to communicate and define, cultural
        logics, 178–79
presence institution, university as, 434–35
Prigogine, Ilya, 836–37, 844
primary education, Italian school system,
        677, 677f
Princeton, 53–54
Princeton Review, 138
principle component analysis (PCA), 621
private institutions, universities, 34
private schools
    global average enrollments by schooling
        level, 129, 129f
    higher education institutions (HEIs),
        129, 130f
privatization, education, 14–15
problematization, learning apparatus, 232–33
productive power, 54

professionalism, world society, 358–60
professionalization
    definition, 358–59
    Norwegian quality assessment system, 606–7
profiling ideal, 41
Program for Improving Reading Literacy,
        Japan, 544
Program for International Student Assessment
        (PISA), 32–33, 54, 93, 109, 216–17, 218,
        250–51, 490, 499–500, 511n.1, 594
    Argentina, 916
    Canada, 545–46
    Colombia and Peru, 96
    England, 545
    genesis and evolution of, as global
        benchmark measure, 540–41
    Germany, 543–44
    human capital and legitimation of policy
        reforms, 547–48
    initial administration of, 539
    international tests, 131–32
    Japan, 544–45
    Latin America, 869–70, 882
    making authorized policy, 62
    PISA for Development (PISA-D), 61–62,
        540–41
    political discourse and education
        reform, 542–46
    secondary education systems, 565–66
    shock, 543
    as soft mode of regulation, 541–42
    test, 594
    transnational education policy, 251–52
    use as policy lever, 548–49
Program for the International Assessment of
        Adult Competencies (PIAAC), 540–41
    individual educational outcomes, 661–65
    number of reforms by area of
        intervention, 660f
    number of reforms per country,
        659f, 659–60
    survey microdata of, 658, 669
    See also educational reform(s)
progress, term, 369
Progress in International Reading Literacy
        Study (PIRLS), 540
progressive parents, homeschooling, 452–53

projectification
  education, 385–86
  transnational, 397
protest, homeschooling as, 451–54
public administration
  reform, 381–82n.13
  shift from government to governance, 139
public choice theory, 825
public good, 825
  arguing for the, 828–33
  concept of, 824, 832, 856n.22
  democratic justification for, 833–36
  education as a global, 851–53
  the good and the right, 849–51
public institutions, universities, 34
public interest
  conception of, 825
  concept of, 856n.22
Public Interest, The (Schubert), 828
public offences, 852
public opinion of education, policy
    feedback, 561–64
public schools, higher education institutions
    (HEIs), 129, 130f
Public Spending Limit Constitutional
    Amendment, Brazil, 952
publishing, high-impact publications, 740–41,
    740t, 741t
purchase power parity (PPP), Brazil,
    944, 952n.5
purposes, concept of, 845

Qatar, global education hubs, 340–41
quality, reform value, 371, 375
quality assessment. *See* Norwegian National
    Quality Assessment System (NQAS)
quality indicators, Norwegian education, 605
quantification, transmission of information,
    219–20
quantum mechanics, 830–31, 855n.15
Quebec, management policy in schools, 160–61
Quranic schools, 58

racism
  global higher education (HE) and, 341–42
  race and, 341–42
  See also Whiteness

Radhakrishnan Commission (1948), 786–87
Radical Party, Argentina, 914
Rae, Douglas, 830
Rand Corporation, 825
rankings, university, 436–38
rational action, hallmark of modernity, 385
rationality
  conception of, 385–86
  education, 396–97
  Luhmann's redefinition of, 386–88
  notion of, 386
  other side of, 388
  study of, 385
  system and environment, 387–88
rationalization, 6, 18–19
  double logic of, 153
rationalized myths, 151, 170–71, 183
  resonance, 177, 178
Rawls, John, 274, 276, 827, 841
recognitive justice
  education and, 268, 276–78
  modern social grammar, 281
recurrent education, 416–17
  concept of, 416
  young child in context of, 416–17
redistribution of income, 381n.11
redistributive justice, education and,
    268, 274–76
Reducciones, Jesuit Order, 871, 886n.1
reflexive perception, 392–93
reflexivity, adaptive educational
    process, 417–18
reform(s), 367
  in ancient tradition, 368–69
  assessment of, 376
  central importance of organizations, 371–74
  contradictions in purpose, 374–75
  education, 370
  equality, 371, 375
  evolution, 376–79
  as generalized global phenomenon, 369–71
  guiding principle of, 370
  Italy's school design, and expansion (1950s
      to 2010s), 675–78
  movements, 368
  organizations, 369–70
  process of, 370–71

quality, 371, 375
term, 369
word, 368–69
See also education reform
reformatio, deformatio and, 368
Reformation, 618
Reforma Universitaria (University Reform), Argentina, 914
regime-collisions, dynamic of, 455
reglobalization, 570n.1
Reich Law on Youth Welfare (1922), 414
Reich School Conference (1921), 414
religion
    Christianity, 54
    church and, 54
    Latin America, 877–79
Renaissance, 4–5
reproduction theory
    modernization and, 673
    outlook of social, 674
Republic of Panama, global education hubs, 340–41
research activities, universities, 57
research and development
    collaboration patterns in, 742, 743f
    international collaboration rate, 745–48, 747f
    national funding for, 733
resonance, cultural logics, 177–78
responsibilization, 713
retreat, notions of, 455
returns to education, Italy, 683–85, 684f
revolution, term, 369
Right and the Good, The (Ross), 849–50
rights, education, 596
Robinson, Mary E., 505
Rockwell, Elsie, 58–59
Rodriguez Larreta, Horacio, 936n.47
Rogers, Reginald, 837
Rosenzweig, Robert M., 504, 512n.6
Ross, David, 849–50
Round Square, 314
Rousseau, J. J., 828
Rousseff, Dilma, 952
Rusk, Dean, 503
Russian Academy of Sciences, 737–38
Ryan, Alan, 857n.40

Saavedra, Jaime, 108, 908n.9
Sadler Commission, India, 786–87
Sahlberg, Pasi, 60–61
Salas, Patricia, 108–9
Samsung, 737–38
San Francisco Unified School District (SFUSD), 139
Sanofi-Aventis, 737–38
Santos, Juan Manuel, 102, 106
Sarmiento, Domingo Faustino, 913–14
Sassen, Saskia, 712
Sauder, Michael, 132
Saxe, Geoffrey, 63
Scanlon, Thomas, 828–29, 850, 854n.8
scapegoating, public education, 19–20
Schatzki, Theodore R., 845
Schmidt, Vivien, 148
scholarship, higher education, 193–94
school autonomy with accountability (SAWA) reforms, 510
school choice, 105
school education
    autonomy and dependence, 449–51
    catastrophe, 395–96
    climax, 393–94
    context and, 389–96
    exposition, 391–92
    fall, 394–95
    family and, 446
    generalization of, 446
    as greedy institutions, 360
    Luhmann's writing and stages as classical drama, 391–96
    reforms, 666f, 667, 668f
    rise, 392–93
schooled society
    functionally differentiated, 360–62
    idea of, 14
"Schooled Society, The", 32
schooling
    definition, 52
    divergent pedagogies, 58–59
    forms of, 57–59
    global average in private enrollments, 129f, 129
    global reforms, 59–61, 60t
    implications, 65–66

schooling (*cont.*)
  making authorized policy, 61–62
  movement of ideas for reforming, 59–64
  new universal, 57–58
  ongoing differentiation, 64–65
  policy as practice of power, 61
  power, 65
  remaking policies locally, 62–64
  states, 65
  understanding, 51
  Western-style, 57–58
schooling the family, 358
Schorr, Karl-Eberhard, 405
Schrader-Breymann, Henriette, 414
Schrodinger, Erwin, 836
Schubert, Glendon, 828
Schumpeter, Joseph, 826–27
science
  all-around education, 450
  collaboration processes in, 729–30
  global and national, 718–22
  global and national systems, 720t
  global map of, 729
  global networking in, 714
  global research and, 717–22
  globalization of, 730
  scale in higher education and, 722–24
  US-China conflict, 721
  See also global science
science, technology, engineering, and
    mathematics (STEM), 31, 296–97
  percentage of female STEM majors, 40f
  women's share graduates, 40
  women's share of enrollments, 39–40
science, technology, engineering,
    mathematics, and medicine (STEMM)
    disciplines, 733–34, 741–42
Science Citation Index-Expanded, 132
scientific globalism, 721
scientific knowledge, learning apparatus, 38
scientific management, Taylor's conceptions
    of, 131
scientific nationalism, 721, 735–36
scientific rationalization
  definition of, 121–22
  individual empowerment and, 122
  rise of, 123

scientists, global science, and power of, 755–58
SciVal, 737–38
Scopus, 717, 737–38, 741–42
Scott, Richard, 147
Scottish government (TSG), 218
Scottish National Party (SNP), 218
secondary education, 79
  academic streaming, 92
  accountability mechanisms, 93
  Anglo countries, 91
  association of parental education,
      educational opportunity and
      completion of upper-, 92, 650t
  baby boom cohorts, 86
  building projects of 1960s, 85
  competition of lower-, 80–81, 636t
  converging pupil experiences, 646–51
  destratification, 90–91
  differentiation, 93
  early reforms of, 85
  equal status of pupils, 86–87
  equality among pupils, 78
  equity of pupilhood, 651–53
  Germany, 92
  index of educational opportunity, 92
  India, 792–93
  industrial democracies, 90
  institutional equity in expansion, 634–35
  institutional equity in period of
      massification (1950-1980), 635–40
  Italian school system, 676–77, 677f
  key drivers of reform, 92
  massification of, 651–53
  massification of, in Latin America, 879
  Nordic countries and, 88–89, 90, 92
  policymakers, 87–88
  probability of completing lower- and
      upper- by country and year of birth, 92,
      647f, 648f
  reforms, 93
  rise of mass, 76–77
  standardization, 83, 84, 87, 88, 90–91, 93
  standardization and level of lower-, teacher
      training, 83, 637t
  stratification, 83, 84, 88, 93
  teachers' unions in, 565–66
  teaching profession, 88, 637t

upper-, completion rates by country, 92, 649f
second choicers, homeschoolers, 456n.4
Second Vatican Council, 878–79
secular society, 361–62
self-government, professional ideal of, 597
self-guided learning, 405–6, 407–8, 416–17
self-interest, concept of, 829
self-reference, conversion of educational setting to, 405–6
self-reliance and self-help, 705–6
self-service analytics, data visualization, 523–26
Seminar, interaction system, 59
Sen, Amartya, 278, 825
sensemaking
  educational technology, 160
  institutional change, 184
Serbia, mass education system, 625
Serres, Michel, 395–96, 401n.6
Seth, James, 838
Shanghai Ranking, universities, 60–61, 131–32
Siemens, 737–38
Silva, Juan Pablo, 101, 109
Simmel, Georg, 389
Simons, Henry Calvert, 825
Simons, Maarten, 16–17, 20
Singapore
  inequalities, 215
  mobility of international students, 334
situated cognition, 548–49
situated institutionalizations, politics of, 158–59
skill-biased technological change (SBTC) hypothesis, 683, 685
skills, term, 270
Smelser, Neil, 363n.3
snakelike procession
  metaphor of, 198
  modeling of colleges, 198
Snow, C. P., 59
social apparatus, 16–17, 30–31
social cohesion
  human development and, 273
  inclusive education, 273
  notion of, 280
social grammar, modernity, 268
social groups, cosmopolitan education across, 307–9

social justice
  approaches to, 282
  capacitating, 268, 278–80
  conceptions of, 268
  questions of, 281
  recognitive, 268, 276–78
  redistributive, 268, 274–76
social media, 42
social production theory, modernization and, 674–76
social question, 31
social science(s), 730
  collaboration patterns in, 742–43, 745f
  university specialty, 56
Social Sciences Citation Index, 132
social stratification, education as central in, 104–6
social system, education as, 17–18
Social System, The (Parsons), 353
Social Systems (Luhmann), 355
socialisation, 401n.2
Socialist Party, Norway, 603–4
Socialists, 689n.1
socialization
  definition, 391–92
  education in schools, 456n.2
  school education, 392
society
  education for rapidly changing, 415–16
  integration of function systems of, 432–34
socioeconomic status, 104
sociological institutionalism, 91n.3
sociology, 4
socio-sciences, 105
soft accountability, 600–1
soft Europeanization, 79
soft power, 51, 54, 61, 65
solutionism, 224
Sorauf, Frank, 828
sorting machines, 77–78
South Asian Association for Regional Cooperation (SAARC), 486
South Korea, 38, 139
  educational expansion in, 34
  global education hubs, 340–41
  mobility of international students, 334
  student socialization preparation, 337

Southeast Asian Ministers of Education Organisation (SEAMEO), 485–86, 493–94
Souza, Paulo Renato, 508–9, 510, 513nn.20–21, 513nn.23–25, 513n.28, 514n.30
Soviet Union
  collapse of, 37, 120, 121
  dissolution of, 712
Spain
  closed employment system, 299
  Globalife project, 298
Spearman coefficient, 946, 951, 954n.28
spirit of self-reliance, 701, 706
Sriprakash, Arathi, 63–64
standardization, 60, 60t, 84, 675
Stanford School, 206n.2
Stanford University, 137
Starting Strong policy, ISCED, 418–19
state, evolving role of the, 22
state education
  Argentina, 913–15
  Latin America, 877–79
state-mandated educational goals, 408
state neutrality, 827
state perfectionism, 827
state performances for the education system, 408–11
  all-around education in grammar school education, 410–11
  diligence and piety through one-class primary school education, 409–10
  organizational formation and full inclusion, 408–9
  relevance of educational goals to society, 409–11
  system autonomy, 411
state planning, 30
STEM. *See* science, technology, engineering, and mathematics (STEM)
Stengers, Irene, 836–37
Stiglitz, Joseph, 815–16
storytelling in education, visualization as, 526–30
strategic action fields (SAFs), 200
stratification, 84
  education in Chile, 992–95
  Italian school system, 675

strong state, notion of, 7
structural power, 54
structured agenda, 216–17
  education, 216–17, 222, 224
studium generale
  general university, 56–57
  medieval name for university, 56
"study mothers", transnational education, 311
Summer Institute of Linguistics, 884, 886–87n.11
summon bonum, 827
Sundberg, Daniel, 160
sustainability, 852
Sustainable Development Goals (SDGs), 54, 518
Sutep, 101, 109
Swanton, Christine, 843–44
Sweden
  banks in higher education, 567
  Globalife project, 299–300
  inequalities, 215
Switzerland
  elite schools, 315
  international schools, 315–16
  vocational education and training, 564
system
  education, 387
  rationality, 387–88
  term, 194–95
system approach, higher education, 194–95
system autonomy, education system, 411
system concept, higher education, 196–97
system needs
  AGIL (Adaptation, Goal attainment, Integration, Latency), 353, 356–57
  Parsons's analyses of, 362
system references, 406
systemness, 355–56
systems theory
  concept, 373
  education as global system, 17–18
  evolution, 378–79
  Luhmann's, 4–5, 390, 454–55
  mobilizations of individualism, 112
  paradigms of, 355
  world university, 438–39
systems thinking, 836

Tableau, 519–20, 523
  interactive visualization, 523–24, 525
  white papers, 532
taken-for-granted
  institutionalization, 181–82
  institutions, 176
  legitimacy and, 181
  rationales of schooling, 172
taken-for-granted myth, 617–18
taken-for-grantedness, concept of, 171
targeted institution, political context and,
    82–83, 82t
Tawney, R. H., 828
Taylor, Frederick, 131
teacher(s)
  actors, levels, and institutional logics, 174–75
  agents of institutional change or stability,
    171–75
  collective sense-making, 179
  frames of experience, 179–81
  mass education and nation state, 172
  national cultures of teaching, 173–74
  national differences as variation in cultural
    logics, 172–73
  Norwegian education, 604–5
  role of, 170–71
  training of, 79
teachers' unions
  Colombia and Peru, 896–98
  secondary education systems, 565–66
Teaching and Learning: Towards the Learning
    Society (European Commission), 32
teach to test, 653
technical universities, 56
technocracy, Colombia, and Peru, 899–900
technological nationalism, 721
teleology, 843–46
  conception of, 843
Temer, Michel, 952
Tendler, Judith, 879, 887n.20
terrorism, 9–10
Teubner, Gunther, 448
textbooks
  curricular emphases on organizations, 133–37
  expansion of curricula in, 35–38
  for-profit and nonprofit organizational
    actors in Canadian and US, 134, 134f

international governmental and
    nongovernmental organizational
    actors, 135–36, 136f
international governmental and
    nongovernmental organizational actors
    in Canadian and US, 134–36, 135f
  models of "good society" in, 36f
  rural schools in Global South, 56
  sense of agency and empowerment, 37–38
Thatcher, Margaret, 545, 597
Thelen, Kathleen, 155–56
Theory of Justice, A (Rawls), 274, 827, 849
Theory of Society (Luhmann), 355–56
things, movement of, 56
Tilman, Alice, 401n.4
Times Higher Education (THE), 60, 109,
    259–60
TIMSS, 109, 173
Tobin, Joseph, 59
Todos los Chicos en la Red, digital education
    program, 930–32
Toledo, Alejandro, Peru, 107–8
Top Global University Project, 338–39
topology, 836
totalitarianism, 842
Townsend, W. C., 886–87n.11
training of teachers and educators, 79
transformative competencies, term, 271
transgenerational inequality, higher education
    and, in China, 766–67
translation, travel meaning, 55
transnational education
  context and, 396–400
  from travel to long-lasting mobility
    practices, 310–11
  graduate employment and, 767–68
  mobility practices, 310–11
  "study mothers" and "parachute kids", 311
transnational projectification, 397
transnationalism, term, 306
transparency, accountability, 597
Treaty of Westphalia (1648), 30–31
Trends in International and Mathematics
    Study (TIMSS), 540
triangle of coordination, 202–3
Trump, Donald, 976
trust, education, 596–97

1040   INDEX

Tsing, Anna, 53
Tullock, Gordon, 827
Turkey, 103, 107
Tyack, David, 394

unanimity rule, 825, 830
uncertainty
  globalization and increasing, 291–92
  impact of globalization on, 289*f*
UNESCO. *See* United Nations Educational,
  Scientific, and Cultural Organization
  (UNESCO)
Union of South American Nations
  (UNASUR), 486
United Arab Emirates (UAE), 339–40
  global education hubs, 340–41
United Kingdom, 63–64
  COVID-19 death rates, 222
  education reform, 565
  fields of education, 257
  international tracks and schools, 319
  Johnson in, 103
  open employment system, 299
United Nations (UN), 30–31, 55, 77–78
  Article 26 of Charter, 32–33
  Convention on the Rights of Persons with
    Disabilities, 79
  Economic Commission for Latin
    America, 869–70
  High Commissioner for Refugees
    (UNHCR), 484–85, 486
  Human Development Index (HDI),
    Argentina, 917–20, 918*t*
  International Children's Emergency Fund
    (UNICEF), 63–64, 484–85
  International School, 316
  Sustainable Development Goals, 881–82
United Nations Educational, Scientific, and
  Cultural Organization (UNESCO),
    59–60, 68, 99, 109–10, 151–52, 222,
    267–68, 269–70, 484–85, 486, 519–20,
    881–82, 914
  Argentina, 914–15
  Institute for Lifelong Learning, 415–16
  Institute for Statistics, 129, 621
  International Standard Classification of
    Education (ISCED), 418–19

United States
  banks in higher education, 567–68
  cosmopolitan education across, 308
  decentralization and OECD, 503–6
  decentralized education system, 499
  decline of liberal, 10–11
  education nongovernmental
    organizations, 125*f*
  for-profit and nonprofit organizational
    actors in textbooks, 134, 134*f*
  Globalife project, 298–99
  growth of nonprofit management education
    (NME) by program type, 137*t*
  higher education nongovernmental
    organizations in, 126*f*
  inequalities, 215
  international governmental and
    nongovernmental organizational actors
    in textbooks, 134–36, 135*f*
  international tracks and schools, 319
  OECD and, 510
  open employment system, 299
  prewar education, 82–83
  secondary education, 81–82
  Sputnik shock, 503
United States National Archive, Washington,
  DC, 502
universal, new, schooling, 57–58
universality, 703, 704
  principle of, 16
universalization, Kant's principle of, 847
universalized education regime, 109–11
universals, 57
Universidad de San Marcos, 886n.3
university, 34–35
  city and, 425–26
  educational reforms, 666*f*, 667, 668*f*
  functional bifocality of, 432–34
  growth of nonprofit management education
    (NME) by program type, 137*t*
  as human capital institution, 435–36
  inclusion into, 428–30
  intellectual completeness and
    multidisciplinarity of, 431–32
  localization of, 425–26
  persistence of, 426–28
  rankings, 436–38

Shanghai Ranking, 131–32
transformation into organizational actors, 131
as world organization, 51
See also world university
University Education Commission, India, 786–87
university governance, ideal types of, 155–56
University Grants Commission (UGC), India, 788–90, 804
University of Bergen, 607n.1
University of Bonn, 420
University of California campuses, 53
University of Chicago, 985
University of Delhi, 806–7
University of Salamanca, 871
University of Wisconsin-Madison, 338–39
University of Wollongong, 339–40
University Reform Movement, 877
Urban Institute, 125–26
Uribe, Álvaro, Colombia, 105
USAID, 109–10
US-Brazil Partnership for Education, 507
US-China relations, 715
US-China tensions, 722
US National Centre for Education Statistics (NCES), 507
US News & World Report (magazine), 60, 131–32
US Policy, No Child Left Behind (NCLB), 62–63
utilitarianism, 828–29, 848
Utilitarianism (Mill), 840–41

value
    definition of, 828–29
    meta-competition of, 832
Vanden Broeck, Pieter, 17–18
"Varieties of Capitalism" tradition, 92
Vélez, Cecilia, Colombia, 105
Veterinary Council of India (VCI), 805
Vidal, María Eugenia, 923
video-cued ethnography, 59
Villar Lever, Lorenza, 959
Vincent, Guy, 400
virtual communities, 44
Virtue Ethics of Hume and Nietzsche, The (Swanton), 843–44
visualization, storytelling in education, 526–30

vocational education and training (VET), 77–78, 79–80
    Alliance for Initial and Further Education and Training (AfAW), 87–88
    European Alliance for Apprenticeships (EAfA), 88–89
    governance reforms in, 87–89
    gradual institutional change to, 89–91
    higher education (HE) and, 89–90
    hybrid study programs, 86–87
    KMK reform of 2009, 87
    labor unions in, 566–67
    policy feedback, 563–64
    reconfiguration of relationship to higher education (HE), 84–85, 86–87
vocational specificity, Italian school system, 675–76
Volkskindergarten, 414
Volksschule (one-class primary school), 409
    diligence and piety through, 409–10
von Wright, G. H., 832, 846
voting rule, 830
voucher system, Chile, 992–95
vulnerability, 272

Wagner, Caroline, 731
Wahlström, Ninni, 160
Wallerstein, Immanuel, 617
Washington, George, 439n.3
Washington Consensus, 488–89, 938
Watters, Audrey, 398–99
WCT. *See* world culture theory (WCT)
wealth distribution, polarization of, 11–12
Web of Science (WoS), 717, 741–42
Weber, Max, 153, 352–53, 385, 400–1n.1, 616–18
Weick, Karl E., 359
Weimar Republic, 414–15
WEIRD people (Western, educated, industrialized, resourceful, democratic), 619
Weltbild, perspective on the world, 59
Western Education, 620–21
Westernization, catch-up model, 702–3
Western-style schooling, 57–58
    ongoing differentiation, 64–65
    power, 65
    states, 65

Westminster countries, policy advisory systems, 578–79
Whiteness
as futurity, 329, 330–31, 342–43n.3
mobility of imaginaries, 331–33
mobility of people, 333–38
mobility of resources, 338–41
perception, 329–30
phenomenon, 329
See also global higher education (HE)
Whitepapers, Tableau, 523–24
Wilderspin, Samuel, 412
Williams, Bernard, 849
Wilson, Woodrow, 828
Wiseman, Alexander, 147
Wolfensohn, James D., 488–89
women
ascendency in higher education, 40–41, 40*f*
expansion of higher education access, 39–40, 39*f*
working-class education, 363n.3
world, expansion of higher education, 764*f*
World Bank, 54–55, 59–60, 63–64, 99, 109–10, 129, 486, 491, 519–20, 763–64, 881
Argentina, 914–15
Chile, 987
global education, 484–85, 488–89
Latin America, 938
world-class universities (WCUs), 733
World Congress of Families, 110
world culture, 5, 9, 154, 173
definition of liberal, 120
expansion organizational actors in education, 124–32
organizational revolution, 119–21
relationship among education, organization and, 123*f*
rise and globalization of liberal and neoliberal, 121–22
rise of emphases on organization in education, 132–38
theory of, 150
world polity and, 150–54
world culture theory (WCT), 5, 6, 9, 147
centrality and dual status of globalization in, 150–52

cultural analyses of globalization, 23n.1
educational globalization, 152
education and policy, 18–21
globalization in, 10
liberal order, 13–14
modern education, 14
political dimension, 152–54
principle of cultural rationalization, 10–11
World Development Indicators, 101
world educational revolution, 29, 32
world-level culture, 4–5
world-making
form of, 532
See also data visualizations
world map
domestic education associations by country, 126, 127*f*
World Congress of Families, 111*f*
world market, 4
world order, 150–51
world organization
modern university as, 55
university as, 51
world polity, 18–19, 151–52, 154
concepts of, 152
political dimension, 152–54
structuration of, 91n.3
tradition, 78
world society, 5, 6, 9, 154, 714–15
building blocks, 29
concept of, 152, 179
Luhmann's systems theory, 9–10
Luhmann's theory of global, 7–8
modernity as, 447–48
neoinstitutional theories of education, 111
See also functionally differentiated world society
world system, 5, 9
globalization, 733
modern forms of education, 14–18
Wallerstein's, 6, 23n.1
World Trade Organization (WTO), 215, 712, 765, 963
World University
concept of, 32–33
migration and, 430–31
World Values Survey, 619

World War II, 30–31, 32, 42, 55, 97–98, 120, 134–35, 151, 171–72, 184–85, 352–53, 414–16, 731
Wu, Jinting, 62

Yale, 32–33, 53–54
Yale University, 340
Yashpal Committee, India, 788–89, 796, 804, 814
Yasuhiro, Nakasone, 698, 709n.3

Yearbook of International Organizations (YBIO), 127–28
Year of International Organizations (YIO), 484
Yeshiva, 176
Yrigoyen, Hipólito, Argentina, 914
Yugoslavia, mass education system, 625

Zelizer, Viviana, 446